THE OXFORD HANDBOOK OF
GABRIEL GARCÍA MÁRQUEZ

THE OXFORD HANDBOOK OF
GABRIEL GARCÍA MÁRQUEZ

Edited by
GENE H. BELL-VILLADA
and
IGNACIO LÓPEZ-CALVO

OXFORD
UNIVERSITY PRESS

Oxford University Press is a department of the University of Oxford. It furthers the University's objective of excellence in research, scholarship, and education by publishing worldwide. Oxford is a registered trade mark of Oxford University Press in the UK and certain other countries.

Published in the United States of America by Oxford University Press
198 Madison Avenue, New York, NY 10016, United States of America.

© Oxford University Press 2022

All rights reserved. No part of this publication may be reproduced, stored in a retrieval system, or transmitted, in any form or by any means, without the prior permission in writing of Oxford University Press, or as expressly permitted by law, by license, or under terms agreed with the appropriate reproduction rights organization. Inquiries concerning reproduction outside the scope of the above should be sent to the Rights Department, Oxford University Press, at the address above.

You must not circulate this work in any other form
and you must impose this same condition on any acquirer.

Library of Congress Cataloging-in-Publication Data
Names: Bell-Villada, Gene H., 1941- editor. | López-Calvo, Ignacio, editor.
Title: The Oxford handbook of Gabriel García Márquez /
Gene H. Bell-Villada & Ignacio López-Calvo.
Description: New York, NY : Oxford University Press, [2022] |
Includes bibliographical references and index. |
Identifiers: LCCN 2021027783 | ISBN 9780190067168 (hardback) |
ISBN 9780190067175 | ISBN 9780190067182 (epub) |
ISBN 9780190067199
Subjects: LCSH: García Márquez, Gabriel, 1927-2014—Criticism and interpretation. |
García Márquez, Gabriel, 1927-2014—Influence. |
Colombian literature—20th century—History and criticism. |
Authors, Colombian—20th century—Biography.
Classification: LCC PQ8180.17.A73 Z816 2022 | DDC 863/.64—dc23
LC record available at https://lccn.loc.gov/2021027783

DOI: 10.1093/oxfordhb/9780190067168.001.0001

3 5 7 9 8 6 4 2

Printed in Canada by Marquis Book Printing

In memoriam Audrey Dobek-Bell (1945–2013),
loving spouse

In memoriam Dr. David William Foster (1940–2020),
a great mentor and friend

Contents

Acknowledgments — xi
About the Editors — xiii
Contributors — xv

Introduction to Gabriel García Márquez — 1
   Gene H. Bell-Villada and Ignacio López-Calvo

PART I SOCIOHISTORICAL AND LITERARY BACKGROUNDS

1. Scripting Gabriel García Márquez's Life — 15
   Stephen M. Hart

2. García Márquez and Magical Realism — 31
   Wendy B. Faris

3. García Márquez and the Global South — 50
   Magalí Armillas-Tiseyra

4. Modernization and Culture in García Márquez's Caribbean — 77
   Marcela Velasco

5. Gabriel García Márquez and the Remaking of the World Canon — 96
   Juan E. De Castro

6. García Márquez and His Precursors — 110
   Lois Parkinson Zamora

7. Fictions of Difficult Love in García Márquez — 126
   Aníbal González

PART II RACE, ETHNICITY, AND GENDER

8. Imagining the Afro-Caribbean in García Márquez's Fiction — 145
   Adelaida López-Mejía

9. Amerindian Wayúu Legacy and Garciamarquezian Literary Fable — 169
   Juan Moreno Blanco

10. The Power of Women in Gabriel García Márquez's World — 187
    Nadia Celis-Salgado

PART III WORLDWIDE INFLUENCES AND LEGACY

11. García Márquez in Africa — 209
    Regina Janes

12. The Arabs and Gabriel García Márquez — 232
    Heba El Attar

13. García Márquez in China — 246
    Wei Teng

14. South Asian Readings of Gabriel García Márquez — 264
    Sonya Surabhi Gupta and Shad Naved

15. *One Hundred Years of Solitude* and Its Influence in Japan — 277
    Gonzalo Robledo

16. Spain in the Making and Reception of García Márquez's Works — 292
    Álvaro Santana-Acuña

PART IV KEY THEMES AND LEITMOTIFS

17. Myth and Poetry in Macondo — 323
    Mercedes López-Baralt

18. Style and Surprise in García Márquez — 341
    Michael Wood

19. García Márquez's Global Travel Writing beyond the Iron Curtain, 1955–1959   354
MARIANO SISKIND

20. Dark Ecology in *One Hundred Years of Solitude* and *Love in the Time of Cholera*   373
WILLIAM FLORES

21. Repetition and Alchemy in *One Hundred Years of Solitude*   391
RENÉ PRIETO

22. Music as Formal and Signifying Feature in García Márquez's Mature Fiction   413
GENE H. BELL-VILLADA AND MARCO KATZ MONTIEL

23. Coloniality and Solitude in García Márquez's Public Speeches and Newspaper Articles   439
IGNACIO LÓPEZ-CALVO

PART V KEY WORKS

24. Writing and Politics in García Márquez's Early Works   457
MARÍA HELENA RUEDA

25. The Protean Viewpoint in *One Hundred Years of Solitude*   473
ERIK CAMAYD-FREIXAS

26. Monstrous Innocence and Its Expression in García Márquez's Tales   492
MARY LUSKY FRIEDMAN

27. Fate and Free Will in *Chronicle of a Death Foretold*   512
PHILIP SWANSON

28. Pathology, Power, and Patriarchy in *The Autumn of the Patriarch* and *The General in His Labyrinth*   524
HELENE C. WELDT-BASSON

29. Modernity and Its Ruins in *Of Love and Other Demons*   538
NEREIDA SEGURA-RICO

30. The Later Work of Gabriel García Márquez 558
    Nicholas Birns

31. The Threefold Selves in García Márquez's Writing 574
    Robert Sims

32. The Filmic Literary Works of Gabriel García Márquez 596
    Alessandro Rocco

Index 613

Acknowledgments

Our sincerest thanks go out, first of all, to Elda Granata, editor at Oxford University Press, who initially approached Gene Bell-Villada to suggest that he put together and craft this *Handbook*. Great is our gratitude!

In addition, Bell-Villada sincerely acknowledges a mini-sabbatical from Williams College that enabled him to labor full time on this volume in the spring of 2020. He further extends friendly thanks to Ignacio López-Calvo for coming aboard during the early stages as coeditor of this project, the latter's numerous other professional duties notwithstanding.

Finally, to our thirty-some fellow contributors to this volume, we are deeply grateful for their original, provocative, and revealing insights into Gabriel García Márquez: a master author, fabulist, and public intellectual whose artistic range and worldwide resonance never cease to amaze us (and whose works have served us as refuge during a period of uncertainty and anxiety). Our warmest thanks to all!

GB-V
IL-C
October 2020

About the Editors

Gene H. Bell-Villada is the Harry C. Payne Professor of Romance Languages at Williams College. His publications relevant to this project include *García Márquez: The Man and His Work* (1990; winner of the New England Council of Latin American Studies Best Book Prize, 1991; second edition, revised and expanded, 2010, translated into Spanish and Turkish) and three edited collections focused on the Colombian author: *Gabriel García Márquez's "One Hundred Years of Solitude": A Casebook* (2001); a book of interviews, *Conversations with Gabriel García Márquez* (2006, translated into Dutch and Turkish); and *Gabriel García Márquez in Retrospect: A Collection* (Lexington Books, 2016). In addition, he is the author of *Borges and His Fiction: A Guide to His Mind and Art* (1981; second edition, revised and expanded, 2000); a history of the ideology and issue of "Art for Art's Sake" (1996; finalist, National Book Critics Circle Award; translated into Serbian and Chinese); a memoir, *Overseas American: Growing up Gringo in the Tropics* (2005); and two volumes of fiction. In his scholarly work, Bell-Villada has consistently striven to reach an audience beyond the strictly academic. (Incidentally, when *One Hundred Years of Solitude* was a selected title for Oprah's Book Club in 2004, Bell-Villada served as a consultant for readers and appeared briefly on the TV program.) His latest authored work is *On Nabokov, Ayn Rand and the Libertarian Mind: What the Russian-American Odd Pair Can Tell Us about Some Values, Myths and Manias Widely Held Most Dear* (2013).

Ignacio López-Calvo is University of California, Merced Presidential Endowed Chair in the Humanities and professor of Latin American literature. He is the author of more than ninety articles and book chapters, as well as eight books on Latin American and US Latino literature and culture: *Saudades of Japan and Brazil: Contested Modernities in Lusophone Nikkei Cultural Production* (2019); *Dragons in the Land of the Condor: Tusán Literature and Knowledge in Peru* (2014); *The Affinity of the Eye: Writing Nikkei in Peru* (2013); *Latino Los Angeles in Film and Fiction: The Cultural Production of Social Anxiety* (2011); *Imaging the Chinese in Cuban Literature and Culture* (2007); *"God and Trujillo": Literary and Cultural Representations of the Dominican Dictator* (2005); *Religión y militarismo en la obra de Marcos Aguinis 1963–2000* (2002); *Written in Exile: Chilean Fiction from 1973–Present* (2001). He has also edited the books *Hydrohumanities: Transforming Currents for Uncertain Futures* (coedited with Kim De Wolff and Rina Faletti, forthcoming); *The Oxford Handbook of the Latin American Novel* (coedited by Juan E. De Castro, forthcoming); *The Cambridge History of Chilean Literature* (forthcoming); *The Humanities in the Age of Information and Post-Truth* (coedited with Christina Lux, 2018); *Latinx*

Writing Los Angeles: Nonfiction Dispatches from a Decolonial Rebellion (coedited with Victor Valle, 2018); *The Humanities in a World Upside Down* (2017); *Contemporary Latin American Fiction* (2017); *Critical Insights: Roberto Bolaño* (2015); *Roberto Bolaño, a Less Distant Star: Critical Essays* (2015), *Magical Realism (Critical Insights)* (2014); *Peripheral Transmodernities: South-to-South Dialogues between the Luso-Hispanic World and "the Orient"* (2012); *One World Periphery Reads the Other: Knowing the "Oriental" in the Americas and the Iberian Peninsula* (2009); *Alternative Orientalisms in Latin America and Beyond* (2007); and *Caminos para la paz: Literatura israelí y árabe en castellano* (coedited with Cristián H. Ricci, 2008). He is the cofounder and coexecutive director of the academic journal *Transmodernity: Journal of Peripheral Cultural Production of the Luso-Hispanic World*, as well as the coexecutive director of Palgrave Macmillan book series Historical and Cultural Interconnections between Latin America and Asia and the Anthem Press book series Anthem Studies in Latin American Literature and Culture Series.

Contributors

Magalí Armillas-Tiseyra is an associate professor in the Department of Comparative Literature at the Pennsylvania State University. She is the author of *The Dictator Novel: Writers and Politics in the Global South* (2019), a comparative study of novels about dictators in Latin American and African literatures. Other work has appeared in venues such as *Research in African Literatures*, the *Cambridge Journal of Postcolonial Literary Inquiry*, *The Global South, Studies in the Novel*, and *PMLA*, as well as the edited collections *Unmasking the African Dictator: Essays on Postcolonial African Fiction* (2014) and *The Global South Atlantic* (2018). She was a founding member of the forum on the Global South at the Modern Language Association and codirector of the digital project *Global South Studies*.

Nicholas Birns is the author of *Theory after Theory: An Intellectual History of Literary Theory from 1950 to the Early 21st Century* (2010). He is coeditor, with Juan E. De Castro, of *Vargas Llosa and Latin American Politics* (2010). His other books include *Barbarian Memory: The Legacy of Early Medieval History in Early Modern Literature* (2013); *Contemporary Australian Literature: A World Not Yet Dead* (2015); and *The Hyperlocal in Eighteenth- and Nineteenth-Century Literary Space* (2019). He has contributed to *The New York Times Book Review, The Hollins Critic, Exemplaria, Transmodernity, MLQ*, and *Partial Answers*. Birns teaches literature courses at NYUSPS in the Center for Applied Liberal Arts.

Juan Moreno Blanco is a teacher-researcher at the School of Literary Studies of the Universidad del Valle, Cali, Colombia. He received a PhD in Iberian and Latin American studies from the Université Bordeaux 3-Michel de Montaigne. He specializes in Colombian literature, cartographies of interculturality and literary hermeneutics. His latest publications in the Editorial Program of the Universidad del Valle are *Transculturación narrativa: La clave wayúu en Gabriel García Márquez* and *Novela histórica colombiana e historiografía teleológica a finales del siglo XX* (2015); editor and coauthor of *Gabriel García Márquez: Literatura y memoria* (2016); editor and coauthor of *Cien años de soledad 50 años después* (2017); editor and coauthor of *El ejercicio del más alto talento: Gabriel García Márquez cuentista* (2019); editor and coauthor of *Gabriel García Márquez: Nuevas lecturas* (2020); editor and coauthor of *Literatura y cultura en los cuentos de Gabriel García Márquez* (2021) and author of *El relato del Uno y el Otro en Henao y Arrubla, Nicolás Gómez Dávila y Gabriel García Márquez* (forthcoming). He translated William Marx's *La haine de la littérature* (2017) and (with J.S. Rojas) Camille

Dumoulié's *Littérature et philosophie. Le gai savoir de la littérature* (2021) from French to Spanish.

Erik Camayd-Freixas is professor of Hispanic studies at Florida International University. He has lectured internationally on linguistic, literary, and cultural studies; immigration; ethics; and social theory. The recipient of numerous academic and human rights awards, he has published *Realismo mágico y primitivismo* (1998), *Primitivism and Identity in Latin America* (2000), *Etnografía imaginaria* (2012), *Orientalism and Identity in Latin America* (2013), and *U.S. Immigration Reform and Its Global Impact* (2013), as well as numerous articles and chapters on discourse analysis, literary theory, and historiography in a transatlantic and transpacific context.

Nadia Celis-Salgado is an associate professor at Bowdoin College (US), where she teaches Latin American, Caribbean and US-Latinos' literature and culture. A graduate of the Universidad de Cartagena, Colombia, Prof. Celis received her PhD from Rutgers University, where she also specialized in gender and women's studies. Her research explores embodiment, subjectivity, and intimate relations in Hispanic Caribbean literature and popular culture, as a means to understand gender, power, and violence in Caribbean and Latin American societies. Celis-Salgado's scholarly articles include works on Colombian Caribbean authors Marvel Moreno, Fanny Buitrago, and Gabriel García Márquez, as well as essays on dance and performance. Celis coedited the critical collection *Mayra Santos-Febres y el Caribe contemporáneo* (2011). Her book *La rebelión de las niñas: El Caribe y la "conciencia corporal"* (2015) was awarded the Nicolás Guillén Award by the Caribbean Philosophical Association, an Honorable Mention of the Premio Iberoamericano Award by the Latin American Studies Association (LASA). Her current book project studies Gabriel García Márquez's deployment of love and the relation of both intimate and public violence to social power. This project was awarded a residential fellowship by the Harry Ransom Center (UT Austin).

Juan E. De Castro is an associate professor in Literary Studies at Eugene Lang College of Liberal Arts at the New School. Among his publications are *The Spaces of Latin American Literature: Tradition, Globalization and Cultural Production* (2008); *Mario Vargas Llosa: Public Intellectual in Neoliberal Latin America* (2011); *Writing Revolution in Latin America: From Martí to García Márquez to Bolaño* (2019); and *Bread and Beauty: The Cultural Politics of José Carlos Mariátegui* (2020).

Heba El Attar is professor of Spanish at the Department of World Languages, Literatures, and Cultures at Cleveland State University. She has degrees in Spanish language, simultaneous interpretation, and peninsular and Latin American literatures from the universities of Ain Shams (Cairo), Complutense (Madrid), and Wisconsin (Milwaukee). Her scholarship includes articles and book chapters on the novel, poetry, press, and films by Chileans of Palestinian descent. Among her published translations and co-translations are novels and books by Carlos Fuentes and García Márquez. Her creative work includes two documentaries on Chileans of Palestinian descent, one of which, *Christian Palestine in Chile*, was screened at six international film festivals.

Wendy B. Faris recently retired as distinguished research professor in and former chair of the English Department at the University of Texas at Arlington. She is the author of *Carlos Fuentes* (1983); *Labyrinths of Language: Symbolic Landscape and Narrative Design in Modern Fiction* (1988); and *Ordinary Enchantments: Magical Realism and the Remystification of Narrative* (2004). She coedited (with Lois Parkinson Zamora) *Magical Realism: Theory, History, Community* (1995). She has just published an article on Ben Okri's *Dangerous Love*, another one forthcoming on Haruki Murakami's *1Q84*, and is currently working on the relations between modernist painting and literature.

William Flores is associate professor of Spanish and coordinator of the Spanish for the Professions Program at Southern Connecticut State University. He has nineteen years of experience as full-time faculty. His recent work includes peer-reviewed publications in various academic journals and scholarly works such as *Ecocrítica poscolonial y literatura moderna latinoamericana* (2015) and "Satire, Ecocentrism, and Luddite Discourse in *One Hundred Years of Solitude*: Regional Approaches for a Global Environmental Crisis," in *Gabriel García Márquez in Retrospect* (2016). His scholarly research focuses on twentieth- and twenty-first-century Hispanic literature; theory of satire; narratology; and postcolonial theory, particularly ecocritical approaches to the study of modern Latin American narratives.

Mary Lusky Friedman is professor of Spanish at Wake Forest University in Winston-Salem, North Carolina. She is the author of *The Self in the Narratives of José Donoso (Chile 1924–1996)* (2004) and *The Emperor´s Kites: A Morphology of Borges' Tales* (1987).

Aníbal González is professor of modern Latin American literature in the Department of Spanish and Portuguese at Yale University. A Guggenheim fellow, he is the author of seven books of literary criticism and scholarship. His recent publications include *Love and Politics in the Contemporary Spanish American Novel* (2010) and *In Search of the Sacred Book: Religion and the Contemporary Latin American Novel* (2018).

Sonya Surabhi Gupta is professor of Latin American studies at Jamia Millia Islamia, New Delhi, India. Her research interests center on literary and cultural studies in a comparative context of India and Latin America, as well as translation studies. She has translated important works from Spanish to Hindi, including Gabriel García Márquez's *Cien años de soledad* (*Ekant ke Sau Varsh*, 2003), Camilo José Cela's *La familia de Pascual Duarte* (*Pascual Duarte ka Parivaar*, 1991), and Rodolfo Walsh's *Operación masacre* (*Operation Qatle-Aam*, 2021), as well as an anthology of stories by Indian women writers in Spanish translation titled *Lihaf: Cuentos de mujeres de la India* (Madrid, 2001). She is also the editor of *Subalternities in India and Latin America: Dalit Autobiographies and the Testimonio* (2021).

Stephen M. Hart is professor of Latin American film, literature, and culture and pro-vice-provost (Latin America) at University College London. He is a corresponding member of the Academia Peruana de la Lengua Peruana and has been awarded an honorary doctorate by the University of San Marcos, as well as two Orders of Merit, one by the Peruvian government and the other by the National University of Trujillo. He has published a literary biography of Gabriel García Márquez (2010), which has been translated into Chinese (2014) and Spanish (2016). He has also published a new biography of the first saint of the Americas, Santa Rosa de Lima (2017), as well as a critical edition of her apostolic process, published in the same year, funded by a senior research fellowship held at the Leverhulme Trust.

Regina Janes, emeritus professor of English, Skidmore College, is the author of *Inventing Afterlives: The Stories We Tell Ourselves about Life after Death* (2018); *Losing Our Heads: Beheadings in Literature and Culture* (2005); *Edmund Burke and Irish Affairs* (2002); *"One Hundred Years of Solitude": Modes of Reading* (1991); and *Gabriel García Márquez: Revolutions in Wonderland* (1981), the second book in English about García Márquez. A Clifford Prize recipient and frequent contributor to *Salmagundi* and *Scriblerian,* she has published recently on García Márquez "Revisiting García Márquez among the Bananas" (Modern Language Quarterly, 2010); "Gabriel García Márquez: Politics and Death across His Life of Writing," in *Gabriel García Márquez in Retrospect: A Collection,* edited by Gene H. Bell-Villada (2016); and "African Writers Reading García Márquez," translated into Korean by Woo Suk-kyun (*Global World Literature,* 2021).

Mercedes López-Baralt is a member of the Puerto Rican Academy of Spanish Language and the Academy of the Spanish Language. She has a PhD in anthropology from Cornell University as well as an honorary PhD from the University of Puerto Rico, where she worked as a professor in the Department of Hispanic Studies for forty years. She has been distinguished also by the University of San Marcos in Lima, Peru, with the title of Honorary Professor and is recipient of two awards in Cuzco for her works on Peruvian literature: a medal from the city and a medal from the Andean University of Cuzco. López-Baralt has authored twenty-three books, among them *El mito taíno*; *La gestación de Fortunata y Jacinta: Galdós y la novela como reescritura*; *Icono y conquista: Guaman Poma de Ayala* (first prize from the Institute of Puerto Rican Literature); *Guaman Poma, autor y artista*; *El retorno del Inca rey: Mito y profecía en el mundo andino*; *La poesía de Luis Palés Matos* (critical edition) (second prize from the Institute of Puerto Rican Literature); *Orfeo mulato: Palés ante el umbral de lo sagrado* (Honorable Mention from the Puerto Rico Pen Club); *Para decir al Otro: Literatura y antropología en nuestra América*; *Llévame alguna vez por entre flores* (Honorific Mention from the Puerto Rico Pen Club); *El Inca Garcilaso, traductor de culturas*; *Una visita a Macondo: Manual para leer un mito*; *Miguel Hernández, poeta plural* (first prize in the essay genre from the Puerto Rico Pen Club); and, in collaboration with her sister Luce López-Baralt, *La carne muere y el verso vuela: La poesía metafísica de Pedro Salinas y Luis Palés Matos.* She has also authored an anthology of Puerto Rican literature, an edition (in collaboration with John V. Murra) of José María Arguedas's letters, and an annotated edition of two works by Inca Garcilaso de la Vega (*Comentarios reales* and *La Florida del Inca*). She is a member of the advisory committee of the reviews *Colonial Latin American Review, América sin nombre, Semiosfera,* and *Mitologías hoy,* and also of the advisory committee in the University of Alicante's Mario Benedettti Center. Other awards: the Institute of Puerto Rican Culture's Medal, the Ricardo Alegría medal, la Medalla Ricardo Alegría, and the distinction of Humanist for the year 2001 from the Foundation of the Humanities. She currently has a book in progress: *Sólo el misterio nos hace vivir: Lorca y la poética del enigma*.

Adelaida López-Mejía is professor emerita of Spanish, Occidental College, Los Angeles. She has published articles on Gabriel García Márquez in prestigious venues such as *Bulletin of Hispanic Studies, Revista de Estudios Hispánicos, Revista Hispánica Moderna*, and *MLN (Modern Language Notes)*. Her early articles approached the work of García Márquez from a psychoanalytic perspective, whereas her more recent articles analyze the NobelPrize-winning author's fiction in the context of its representation of race.

Marco Katz Montiel played trombone with Paquito D'Rivera and Jimmy Owens on "Tubby the Tuba Meets a Jazz Band" (Koch), composed the musical settings for Pablo Neruda's *Las piedras del cielo* (Centaur), and wrote *Music and Identity in Twentieth-Century Music from Our America—Noteworthy Protagonists* (2014). A *salsero* who received a nomination from *Latin NY Magazine* for his trombone playing on Charlie Palmieri's *The Heavyweight* (Alegre), Marco now teaches writing and literature in the Department of English at The King's University in Canada.

Shad Naved is currently assistant professor in comparative literature and translation studies at Ambedkar University Delhi, India. He holds a PhD in comparative literature from UCLA, a master's in women's studies from the University of Oxford and a master's in cultural studies from the English and Foreign Languages University, Hyderabad, India. His research areas include literary history in south and west Asia, postcolonial sexuality studies, and Arabic and Urdu literatures. His most recent book publication is an English translation of a work on the processes of canon formation in modern Hindi: *The Hindi Canon: Intellectuals, Processes, Criticism* (2018). He is currently working on a monograph titled *An Historical Eros: Literary Queerness and the Making of Indo-Persianate Literature*.

René Prieto is the Margaret McDermott Professor in Arts and Humanities at the University of Texas–Dallas. He is a specialist in nineteen- and twentieth-century Latin American and French literature. He is fluent in five languages: English, Spanish, Italian, French, and Chinese. Prior to the University of Texas, he taught at Vanderbilt University, Southern Methodist University, Kwansei Gakuin University, and Middlebury College. He received all of his undergraduate training in Italy and France, and his dissertation on Miguel Ángel Asturias was directed by Roland Barthes and Jean Franco. His interests include European and American literature and literary theory. He has published more than forty articles and reviews and was coeditor of *The Handbook of the Library of Congress* (Central American literature section) for eight years, as well as serving on the editorial board of the *Latin American Literature Journal*. He has received three grants and fellowships from the National Endowment for the Humanities and one from the

Guggenheim Foundation. He has published three books: *Body of Writing: Figuring Desire in Spanish American Literature* (2000); *Miguel Ángel Asturias's Archaeology of Return* (1993); and *Michelangelo Antonioni: A Guide to Reference and Resources* (with Ted Perry, 1986). He is presently completing work on a fourth book, entitled *Blood Ties*, which is an analysis of the role of the father in the nineteenth- and twentieth-century foundational fictions of Latin America.

Gonzalo Robledo is a Colombian producer and journalist and he has lived in Tokyo, Japan, since 1981. He was a visiting professor at the University of Rikkyo and has served as correspondent for the Spanish newspaper *El País*, Televisión Española, and Agencia EFE Spanish News Agency in Tokyo. He has written, directed, and produced reportages, documentaries, and programs for TVE, TeleMadrid, Canal Sur, Agencia EFE-TV, Canal Cuatro, and other Spanish-language TV stations, in addition to Japan's NHK TV, Kansai TV, and the film production company Excellent Films. In Japan his articles have appeared in a number of magazines, such as *Asahi Graph* (*Asahi Shimbun*), *Mainichi Graph* (*Mainichi Shimbun*), *Common Sense* (*Kyoikusha*), *Car Graphic* (*Nigensha*), *NAVI* (*Nigensha*), and *Focus* (*Shinchosha*), among others. In Spain, his articles on Japan and its culture have appeared in such magazines as *GEO*, *Altair*, *Islas*, and *Lonely Planet*. Since 1996, he has been writing a newspaper column in Spanish for *International Press*, a weekly for the Spanish-speaking community in Japan.

Alessandro Rocco is associate professor at the University of Bari (Italy). His main research interests are narrative interactions between literary and audiovisual languages in Spanish American culture, as well as the study of relations between film narratives and human rights, memory, and history. His works focus on the study of screenplays as filmic literature, examining the works of many Spanish American authors, such as Gabriel García Márquez, José Revueltas, José Emilio Pacheco, and Guillermo Arriaga, among others. In this field, he has published the book *Gabriel García Márquez and the Cinema, Life and Works* (2014), and several articles about literary screenplays. He directed a research group on audiovisual narratives within the project "Testimony and Literature in the Cono Sur (1973–2015): New Interpretative and Didactic Models."

María Helena Rueda is associate professor of Latin American literature and culture at Smith College. Her book *La violencia y sus huellas: Una mirada desde la narrativa colombiana* (2011) offers an overview of the treatment of violence in Colombian literature since the early twentieth century. She is the coeditor of *Meanings of Violence in Contemporary Latin America* (2011), a volume that addresses violence and its representation in the region. She has published several articles and book chapters on contemporary literature and visual culture in Latin America, particularly in Colombia.

Álvaro Santana-Acuña is associate professor of sociology at Whitman College (United States). He specializes in the cultural sociology of the arts and literature. Regarding García Márquez's oeuvre, he is the author of award-winning academic articles as well as mass media content published in *The New York Times*, *The New York Times en español*, *Time*, *The Atlantic*, *Nexos*, *El Universal* (Mexico), and *El País* (Spain), among other media. He is the coeditor of *Para una nueva sociología de las artes* (2017) and the author of *Ascent to Glory: How* One Hundred Years of Solitude *Was Written and Became a Global Classic* (2020), to be released in Spanish in 2021, and of the illustrated biography *Gabriel García Márquez: Vida, magia y obra de un escritor global* (forthcoming). He was the first research fellow funded by the Mellon Foundation to work on the García Márquez Archives at the University of Texas at Austin. At the Harry Ransom Center (United States) and Museo de Arte Moderno (Mexico), he curated "Gabriel García Márquez: The Making of a Global Writer," the first international exhibition dedicated to the author's life and career, which featured, among other documents, the manuscripts of all his major works.

Nereida Segura-Rico holds a PhD in Comparative Literature from the University of North Carolina at Chapel Hill. She specializes in literature of the Americas, with a focus on testimonial writing and film in Latin America as well as on African American, Afro-Hispanic, and Caribbean cultural production. Her publications have appeared in a variety of refereed journals and edited volumes. Her current research involves memory studies and crime fiction in Latin America. She is a member of the Department of Foreign Languages at Iona College. Previously she served as chair of the Department of Modern and Classical Languages, as cochair of the Division of the Humanities, and as cofounder and coordinator of the Certificate Program in Latin American and Caribbean Studies at The College of New Rochelle. She also has worked for many years with the AP Spanish Literature and Culture Exam and currently serves as its chief faculty consultant.

Robert Sims is a professor of world studies. He teaches Spanish, French, and Latin American literature at Virginia Commonwealth University in Richmond. He is a specialist in modern literature, the works of Gabriel García Márquez, the Latin American novel, literary theory, postcolonialism, postmodernism, narratology, and topopoetics. He has published articles on Latin American and French literature and two books about García Márquez: *The Evolution of Myth in Gabriel García Márquez from "La hojarasca" to "Cien años de soledad"* (1981) and *The First García Márquez: A Study of His Journalism from 1948 to 1955* (1991). In addition to participating in many national and international conferences, Sims has been a member of the Colombianistas of North America and a Fulbright scholar in Colombia in 1987, 1988, and 1992.

Mariano Siskind is professor of romance languages and literatures and comparative literature at Harvard University. He teaches nineteenth- and twentieth-century Latin American literature, with an emphasis on its world literary relations, as well as the production of cosmopolitan discourses and processes of aesthetic globalization. He is the author of three dozen academic essays and of *Cosmopolitan Desires: Global Modernity and World Literature in Latin America* (2014; translated and published in Spanish as *Deseos Cosmopolitas* in 2016). He has edited Homi Bhabha's *Nuevas minorías, nuevos derechos: Notas sobre cosmopolitimos vernáculos* (2013) and *Poéticas de la distancia: Adentro y afuera de la literatura argentina* (2006) (together with Sylvia Molloy). In 2020, he will publish the monograph *Latin American Literature and World War I: Global*

Modernism and Cosmopolitan Distance; together with Gesine Müller, an edited volume titled *World Literature, Cosmopolitanism, Globality: Beyond, Against, Post, Otherwise*; and with Guillermina De Ferrari, *The Routledge Companion to Twentieth and Twenty-First Century Latin American Literature and Culture*. He is finishing a new book tentatively titled *About the End of the World: The Demise of Cosmopolitanism in Contemporary Culture*.

Philip Swanson is Hughes Professor of Spanish at the University of Sheffield, UK. He has published extensively on Latin American literature, including books on the "New Novel," José Donoso, Gabriel García Márquez, and other aspects of Latin American literature and culture. Titles include *José Donoso: The Boom and Beyond* (1988); *Cómo leer a Gabriel García Márquez* (1991); *The New Novel in Latin America: Politics and Popular Culture after the Boom* (1995); and *Latin American Fiction* (2004). He has edited the following volumes: *Landmarks in Modern Latin American Fiction* (1989 and 2015), *The Companion to Latin American Studies* (2003), and *The Cambridge Companion to Gabriel García Márquez* (2010). He has also published on North American representations of Latin America in film and fiction and on the cinema of Spain. Swanson is a member of various editorial boards and specialist professional advisory bodies, as well as former president of the Association of Hispanists of Great Britain and Ireland. He has taught in a number of universities in Europe and the United States.

Wei Teng received her PhD from Peking University. She is a professor at the South China Normal University. She also serves as director of the Center for Contemporary Cultural Studies of South China Normal University and was a Harvard-Yenching Institute Visiting Scholar (2013–2014). Her research fields include translation studies, cultural studies, and Hispanic literature. She has published several books, including *Border on the South: Latin American Literature and Contemporary Chinese Literature* (2011) and *History of Literary Exchanges between China and Hispanic Countries* (coauthored with Zhenjiang Zhao, 2015), as well as dozens of papers in Chinese. In addition, she has also been invited to contribute papers by internationally renowned publishing houses, including "La traducción y difusión de Don Quijote en China," in *Don Quijote en los cinco continentes: Acerca de la recepción internacional de la novela cervantina* (2016); "On the Depoliticized Politics: Analyzing Roberto Bolaño from the Perspective of Translation History in China," in *Roberto Bolaño as World Literature* (2016); and "Pablo Neruda in Contemporary China: Translation between National and International Politics (1949--1979)," in *Remapping World Literature* (2018).

Marcela Velasco is an associate professor of political science at Colorado State University. She has also taught at the Universidad Javeriana, Universidad del Rosario, and Universidad de los Andes in Bogotá, Colombia. Her areas of specialization include Latin American politics, social movements, environmental politics, and ethnic politics. Her research looks at indigenous and Afro-Colombian contentious organizations and how they shape local politics, including the management of natural resources. She values interdisciplinary work in political science research and is an enthusiastic student of Colombian literature and culture. Her research has been published in *Latin American Research Review*, *Journal of Latin American Studies*, *Journal of Environment and Development*, and *Local Environment*, as well as in various books on social movements and Colombian politics.

Helene C. Weldt-Basson holds a PhD from Columbia University and is currently a professor of Latin American literature at University of North Dakota. She is a noted specialist on the Paraguayan writer Augusto Roa Bastos, about whom she has published two books: *Augusto Roa Bastos's "I The Supreme": A Dialogic Perspective* (1993) and the edited collection *Postmodernism's Role in Latin American Literature: The Life and Work of Augusto Roa Bastos* (2010). She also recently published a translation and critical edition of Roa Bastos's novel *El fiscal: The Prosecutor by Augusto Roa Bastos with Commentary by Helene Weldt-Basson* (2018). Her other books include *Subversive Silences: Nonverbal Expression and Implicit Narrative Strategies in the Works of Latin American Women Writers* (2009); *Masquerade and Social Justice in Contemporary Latin American Literature* (2017); and the edited collections *Redefining Latin American Historical Fiction: The Impact of Feminism and Postcolonialism* (2013) and *Postmodern Parody in Latin American Literature: The Paradox of Ideological Construction and Deconstruction* (2018).

Michael Wood is professor emeritus of English and comparative literature at Princeton University, and the author, most recently, of *Alfred Hitchcock: The Man Who Knew Too Much* (2015): *On Empson* (2017): and *The Habits of Distraction* (2018). He writes regularly for the *New York Review of Books*, the *London Review of Books*, and other journals. He is currently working on a book about crime fiction and film.

Lois Parkinson Zamora is the John and Rebecca Moores Distinguished Professor in the English Department at the University of Houston. She has worked to promote the comparative study of literature of the Americas. *The Inordinate Eye: New World Baroque and Latin American Fiction* (2006) is a comparative study of New World baroque art, architecture, and literature (translated into Spanish, 2011). Zamora's previous books include *Writing the Apocalypse* (1989) and *The Usable Past* (1997), both of which examine the nature of historical imagination and its representations in contemporary US and Latin American fiction. Both have been translated into Spanish and published by the Fondo de Cultura Económica. She has edited the following works: *Magical Realism: Theory, History, Community*, with Wendy B. Faris (1995); *Contemporary American Women Writers: Gender, Class, Ethnicity* (1998); *Image and Memory: Photography from Latin America 1866–1994*, with Wendy Watriss (1998); and *Baroque New Worlds: Representation, Transculturation, Counterconquest* (2010), with Monika Kaup.

INTRODUCTION TO GABRIEL GARCÍA MÁRQUEZ

GENE H. BELL-VILLADA AND IGNACIO LÓPEZ-CALVO

Having published his first novel, *La hojarasca* (*Leaf Storm*), in 1956, Gabriel José de la Concordia García Márquez (affectionately known across the Hispanic world as "Gabo") spent almost two decades struggling to gain a readership as an obscure, if respected, fiction writer, and surviving on ill-paid journalistic jobs, first in Colombia and then in Mexico. In 1967, however, his *Cien años de soledad* (*One Hundred Years of Solitude*) became a huge success among readers as well as critics throughout the Hispanic world. Gregory Rabassa's masterful 1970 translation of the novel (Gabriel García Márquez liked to claim that it surpassed the original in quality) helped popularize it worldwide, eventually earning it the label of "timeless classic." A "total novel,"[1] as Vargas Llosa called it, *One Hundred Years* aims to provide a fully encompassing vision of the entire history of Colombia and, by extension, Latin America. It follows a common thread in dealing with solitude and incest within the seven generations of the fictional Buendía family in the fictional town of Macondo, the latter loosely based on Aracataca, the small town in the Caribbean region where the author was born in 1927 and spent his early childhood. At the same time its general range is vast, with a cast of characters encompassing a full spectrum of recognizable human types; with political conflicts and labor strife sharing space with ribald sex and love stories aplenty; and with comedy and tragedy, outrageous humor and poignant sadness, all present in equal measure.

The swift and amazing diffusion of the book would help popularize the magical realist narrative mode with which previous Latin American authors, such as the Guatemalan Miguel Ángel Asturias and the Cuban Alejo Carpentier, had already experimented in the mid-twentieth century. Magical realism typically blends fantastical events or elements that may seem unreal or magical with a mundane setting and a matter-of-fact narrative voice. Something extraordinary or rationally implausible (apparitions, levitations, telekinesis, clairvoyance) may naturally emerge in an everyday setting, and the characters find it not extraordinary but commonplace; on the other hand, something presumably normal, such as ice or dentures, may seem extraordinary or magical to the—at times naïve—characters.

The sui generis type of magical realism in *One Hundred Years*, which was influenced in part by the worldviews of Colombia's indigenous (the Wayúu maids in Gabito's childhood home)[2] and Afro-Caribbean cultures, would soon become, for numerous authors in postcolonial societies of the Global South, a sort of manual on how to forge a new type of discourse challenging Eurocentric rationalism. It also suggested a useful path for organically blending and erasing the distinction between the real and the fantastical in their narratives, much in the ways many people in and around the Global South (and as García Márquez suggests in his short-story collection *Doce cuentos peregrinos* [*Strange Pilgrims*, 1992], sometimes also in the Global North) experience the world in their daily lives. While the Colombian writer is imitated all over the world, including by fellow Nobel laureates like the American Toni Morrison and the Japanese Kenzaburō Ōe, for some time now younger Latin American authors like those in the McOndo literary movement—in a perhaps Oedipal move—have attempted to break away from the long shadow of this aesthetic approach. They decry it as a fashionable market strategy or, even worse, as an opportunistic, self-exoticizing tropicalism for a Global North readership that expects descriptions of a Latin America dominated by violence, sensuality, superstition, and underdevelopment, aspects that today are quite far from the real-life, daily realities of the region.

Regardless of readers' interpretations, however, there is no doubt that García Márquez, as evident in his journalism and public addresses (including his incisive Nobel acceptance speech, "The Solitude of Latin America"), had a rather different, more realistic image of Latin America than the one described by these younger writers.[3] In his nonfiction writings, we find an engaged activist with an openly anti-Eurocentric outlook, one who demands that the Global North treat Latin America as an equal partner and stop envisioning it through paternalistic lenses. Rather than depicting mythical, magical worlds, in these texts García Márquez bitterly denounces US imperialism and neocolonialism, as well as the omnipresence of social injustice, infant mortality, forced disappearances and exile, genocide, and refugees—among other sociopolitical ills in the region.

In any case, as López-Calvo explains elsewhere, García Márquez's use of magical realism would evolve over time.[4] Thus, in *Del amor y otros demonios* (*Of Love and Other Demons*, 1994), this narrative mode is sometimes used to describe humorous situations, becoming what López-Calvo has termed "pseudo-magical realism." In these passages, which tend to produce comic relief in the midst of tense situations, the unreliable narrator leads readers to expect one of García Márquez's usual scenes of magical realism, only to end up disclosing that they are actually dealing with nothing but a case of mere superstition, religious fanaticism, or sheer ignorance. Traditional scenes of magical realism are therefore mixed with others consisting of an illusory pseudo-magical realism, as if the author, by then perhaps tired of being associated with this literary mode and seeing so many epigones overusing it, were leaving it up to the reader to decide which type of magical realism they might be reading.

The famous opening sentence of *One Hundred Years*, with an analepsis and a prolepsis, announced the formal experimentalism and the creation of a sort of mythical time, which reflected García Márquez's admiration for William Faulkner, Ernest Hemingway, Virginia Woolf, James Joyce, and John Dos Passos, among other English-language modernists. In the remainder of *One Hundred Years*, García Márquez demonstrated that he had already perfected an aesthetic voice and a fictional world—that of a Caribbean Macondo—which he had been exploring in previous, shorter works. As a result, he swiftly became one of the most influential writers of the twentieth century and beyond, to the point that nonspecialists often assume that all Latin American literature is akin to García Márquez's magical realist writing.

Undoubtedly it was this masterpiece in particular that won the Colombian author the Nobel Prize for Literature in 1982. His ensuing novel, another masterwork titled *El otoño del Patriarca* (*The Autumn of the Patriarch*, 1975), would further the tradition of the novel of the Latin American dictator by taking formal experimentalism to even higher grounds, with, for example, an entire chapter comprised of a single long sentence with no punctuation save for commas. Something of a disappointment for many readers and critics, who had expected a sequel to *One Hundred Years*, only time will tell if this "poem on the solitude of power," as the author himself described it, is not arguably his best work. In García Márquez's characteristically indirect fashion, *The Autumn of the Patriarch* poetically connects the long history of colonialism in Latin America, from Columbus to the US Marines: in the first chapter, the aging Patriarch (a synthesis of several Latin American—mostly Caribbean—dictators) sees the arrival of Admiral Christopher Columbus's three caravels from his window, and in the concluding chapter the US Marines pack up the country's ocean waters in numbered boxes and ship them away to Arizona. Resorting to his distinctive, humorous magical realism, García Márquez rewrites Eurocentric historical discourse about the conquest of the Americas, now from the purported perspective of indigenous peoples. Thus, the native folk in the novel explain that the paint on their faces is used as protection against the Caribbean sun, all the while mocking the Spaniards' thick clothing, inappropriate for those warm lands; their nakedness is, therefore, no longer evidence of their savage nature, as Columbus claimed in his letter to Luis de Santángel, but rather of their skillful adaptation to the local climate and environment. Along these lines, Native Americans, in García Márquez's version of this historical episode, are very much aware of the worthless nature of the trinkets received from the conquistadors, but they nonetheless accept them out of courtesy; they are not as naïve as Columbus wanted them to be. In the end, the Admiral appears as a pitiful ghost dressed in Franciscan monk's garb and navigating adrift around the Caribbean islands.[5]

Shifting away from the tone of these two Latin American Boom novels, later works of García Márquez would coincide with post-Boom authors in his acceptance of romantic love as a guiding subject. The most popular among these was *El amor en los tiempos del cólera* (*Love in the Time of Cholera*, 1985). Loosely based on his parents' long courtship, it follows, through a mostly realistic approach, the twists and turns of the story of a couple who at last find love in their seventies. However, *Del amor y otros demonios* (*Of Love and Other Demons*, 1994) and even his last novel, *Memoria de mis putas tristes* (*Memories of My Melancholy Whores*, 2004), can also be considered love stories, despite the major age differences between the respective protagonists (involving young girls in both cases). Some of García Márquez's novellas, such as *El coronel no tiene quien le escriba* (*No One Writes to the Colonel*, 1961) and *Crónica de una muerte anunciada* (*Chronicle of a Death Foretold*, 1981), have also been praised as masterpieces.

The Nobel Committee, in its initial 1982 press release on García Márquez's prize that year, makes a number of references to his "novels *and short stories*" (emphasis added). Indeed, some of the author's twenty-seven or so shorter fictions—whether realistic or magical realist—can be counted among the outstanding instances of the genre in any language. Highly suggestive, at times understated and spare, and on other occasions lavishly exuberant, they were originally gathered in three successive collections: *Los funerales de la Mamá Grande* (*Big Mama's Funeral*, 1962), *La increíble y triste historia de la cándida Eréndira y de su abuela desalmada* (*The Incredible and Sad Tale of Innocent Eréndira and Her Heartless Grandmother*, 1973; henceforth referred to as *Eréndira*), and *Doce cuentos peregrinos* (*Strange Pilgrims*, 1992).[6] Over the years, selected titles from these volumes would become oft-anthologized and frequently taught literary items. Certain pieces—"One of These Days," "Tuesday Siesta," "A Very Old Man with Enormous Wings," "The Handsomest Drowned Man in the World"—may well be a novice student's first in-depth acquaintance with modern, canonical narrative from Latin America (along with well-known stories by Borges, Rulfo, and Cortázar).

García Márquez is the best-known author of the Latin American Boom, having shared that privileged space during the 1960s with three other accomplished novelists: the Peruvian and fellow Nobel laureate Mario Vargas Llosa, the Mexican Carlos Fuentes, and the Argentine Julio Cortázar. Besides their friendship and mutual admiration, one of the things that united these authors initially was their enthusiastic support for Fidel Castro and his Cuban Revolution. In part thanks to the modernization of the publishing industry in Latin America and Spain, the Boom contributed to making Latin American literature among the most influential and respected in the world. Their international success added to the prestige already attained by the Chileans Gabriela Mistral and Pablo Neruda, the first two Latin American Nobel laureates, as well as by the acknowledged genius of the Argentine Jorge Luis Borges and the Mexican Juan Rulfo. Incidentally, Borges and Rulfo were major influences on the Colombian master's writing (in the area of language in the case of Borges, as Bell-Villada points out [*Borges and His Fiction*, 44]).

Although all three fellow Boom writers had become well known before García Márquez and had had masterpieces of their own published some time before his (namely, Fuentes's *La muerte de Artemio Cruz* [*The Death of Artemio Cruz*, 1962], Vargas Llosa's *La ciudad y los perros* [*The Time of the Hero*, 1963], and Cortázar's *Rayuela* [*Hopscotch*, 1963]), none of their novels would alter the course of world literature as has *One Hundred Years*.

García Márquez died of pneumonia in Mexico City on April 17, 2014, at age eighty-seven, leaving a major void in the "World Republic of Letters," but his novels, short stories, speeches, journalistic articles, and screenplays remain an invaluable heritage of the author who put Colombian literature on the map. This volume is our homage to a man and author whom we profoundly admire.

We are pleased to ntroduce thirty-three original essays shedding new light on the larger-than-life phenomenon that is García Márquez. Our first half focuses on broader contexts, our second portion on specific themes and works.

Backgrounds both Sociohistorical and Literary are addressed in the chapters comprising Part I. Biographer Stephen M. Hart proposes not so much to sum up the Colombian author's life as to discuss the problematics of doing so, the choices and emphases a scholar makes—in this case the early roles played by grandfather Márquez, the public memory of the 1928 United Fruit massacre, and the mature novelist's ties with Fidel Castro. Hart concludes with a look at the treasure trove of twenty-seven thousand García Márquez items donated by the author's family to the Harry Ransom Center at the University of Texas, a boon to future researchers. Wendy B. Faris examines Gabo's signature trait, magical realism—its broad range of sources and manifestations and its impact on time and space, emotion, and language—along the way touching on his world influence and its links to the larger process of decolonization. Magalí Armillas-Tiseyra blends literary with socioeconomic analysis in her survey of García Márquez's ties to the Global South, via his own labors as journalist and artist as well as his growing Third World legacy. She brings into relief the international extractive industries that are key to understanding *One Hundred Years* and *The Autumn*, and in turn the impact of these and other novels across Africa and the Muslim world.

Bringing a social science perspective, Marcela Velasco draws striking parallels between the modernization theory of respected Colombian sociologist Orlando Fals Borda and the various fictive accounts of societal development in García Márquez. She traces an unresolved, two-centuries-long clash in Caribbean Colombia between the values of tradition and secularism, capping her performance with close attention to the conflict's effects on several of Gabo's women characters. Juan E. De Castro examines a double dynamic in his look at García Márquez and the world canon. On the one hand, the yet-budding author consciously set out to go beyond regionalism and apply the great modernists' methods to his depiction of Colombian reality. Conversely, the novelist's masterful synthesis of avant-garde techniques with his local material became itself canonical, an achievement that in turn helped lead to an emerging canon of authors from the Global South. Magical realism thus enabled generations of peripheral authors to enter the World Republic of Letters. Lois Parkinson Zamora complements De Castro when (in conscious echo of Borges's famed conceit) she broadens the range of Gabo's "precursors." Taking issue with Harold Bloom's notion of "anxiety of influence," she reminds us that the young author frankly reveled in learning not only from the modernists but also from Catholic folklore as well as from Spanish Golden Age literature. In just one notable instance, *Of Love and Other Demons* cites liberally from the poetry of Garcilaso, thereby creating a precursor.

Aníbal González's erudite meditation on "difficult love" takes on this vast subject in Gabo's oeuvre and reveals its interrelations with writing and reading, society and culture. With Denis de Rougemont's *Love in the Western World* as his point of departure, he not only traces the tensions between *eros* and *agape* in the obvious novels but also notes the divers expressions of the latter among the relatives of the abductee victims (and from an eccentric telepriest) in *News of a Kidnapping*. González's canvas, which ends this section, is rich in reference.

Three essays shed light on issues of Race, Ethnicity, and Gender in the master's writings. Adelaida López-Mejía's chapter notes how, from his early work up to the *Strange Pilgrims* stories, Afro-Colombians are largely associated with stereotypes of sensualism and even raucousness. Some of the bias may be that of a specific character or the narrator, though not necessarily always. Only in *Of Love and Other Demons* does the author provide a fuller, more in-depth and complex view of Black culture and experiences in Colombia's Caribbean. Juan Moreno Blanco in turn breaks new ground on the subject of the Amerindian Wayúu presence and the Guajira peninsula background in both García Márquez's early life and mature work. Boy Gabito was raised with live-in Guajiro servants, as are the four original Buendía children, who as a result grow up bilingual. Moreno traces the underlying shamanic logic and the supernatural in Macondo to the Wayúu, who bring love and loyalty to the solitude-ridden clan in a novel that breaks away from Colombia's national, criollo culture. Nadia V. Celis, for her part, argues that women in Gabo's world are culturally defined by the men to whom they're linked. Well-grounded in feminist theory, and thorough in her analysis of the major works, she notes the limits on women's will and desire, even for powerful female characters like Úrsula and Pilar. In Celis's view, love in García Márquez's romantic tales is more of a redemptive force for older men, and Remedios the Beauty is the only "free woman" in his canon.

The high regard in which Gabo's work is held throughout the Global South and elsewhere comes through in part 3, "World Influences and Legacy." In most all cases, the mature García Márquez soon became required reading in university literature courses and enabled local authors to break away from and go beyond dominant, European literary models.

Regina Janes brings out in impressive detail the Colombian's complex presence in African writing, with its abundance of village chronicles and dictator narratives. "Africa is full of Macondos.... In Mozambique, it isn't magical realism we live.... It's real realism," as Mozambican novelist Mia Couto tellingly states. The 2019 Macondo Literary Festival in Nairobi, Kenya, eloquently emblematizes Gabo's Global South standing. The journalist García Márquez wrote about Lusophone Africa's independence struggles as well as about the Palestinian cause, the latter fact signaled by Heba El Attar's chapter. So revered in the Arab world is the Colombian master's oeuvre that his death reportedly was met with greater public sadness than was the passing, in 2006, of Egypt's Nobel winner, Naguib Mahfouz. Besides the five translations of *One Hundred Years* in as many Arab countries, there was wide acclaim for *Chronicle of a Death Foretold* and the absence in it of Orientalist optics. Lebanese author Elias Khoury even constructed a novel of his own in intertextual response to Gabo's novella. In China, Teng Wei's essay observes, following the turmoil of the Cultural Revolution and the return to relative normalcy, García Márquez's Nobel award offered an example, showing that Third World literature could gain global respect and prominence. Both modernism and magical realism could be refashioned "with Chinese characteristics," as in the instance of Nobel laureate Mo Yan.

Besides being known in English translation throughout South Asia, García Márquez has been rendered into several of the area's many languages—as Sonya Surabhi Gupta and Shad Naved inform us—and exists as a mediating figure who has allowed for differing adoptions of modernity. In the Malayalam-speaking state of Kerala, he has even come to be regarded as a Malayalam author. Two outstanding novelists, Pakistani English Salman Rushdie and Sri Lankan Canadian Michael Ondaatje (who actually made a pilgrimage to Gabo's hometown of Aracataca)[7] are among his most renowned literary offspring. For Japanese writers, Gonzalo Robledo observes, García Márquez provided an incentive for reviving the country's pre-naturalist, folk traditions, and, via Haruki Murakami's novels, for exploring issues of national identity. In addition, Robledo draws parallels between magical realism and the deliberately, vividly realistic fantasy of the Studio Ghibli producers of anime cinema. Finally, García Márquez's very name has been appropriated for Japanese apparel-industry labels, and there is moreover a novel by Yuka Ishii called *A Hundred Years of Mud*.

Gabo's ties with Spain, brought into bold empirical relief by Álvaro Santana-Acuña, are exceptional in various ways: the youthful influence from his grandmother's Galician origins and from the Golden Age classics; the huge Iberian sales of all his titles, beginning with *One Hundred Years*; the extensive if divided book reviewers' responses: the presence of his work on school reading lists; his Barcelona years; and his role in the media as columnist for *El País* and as frequent interviewee. As has happened in other countries, there are voices claiming García Márquez for Spain. And yet his specifically artistic sway seems slight; magical realism seems not to have caught on in Spanish narrative as it has in the non-Western world.

Mercedes López-Baralt opens the section on Key themes and Leitmotifs by arguing that myth and poetry contribute to the ambiguity that helps make *Cien años de soledad* a classic. In her view, interpretations of the work, both optimistic (human beings can change history and embrace solidarity; myth, poetry, and cyclical time open the door to hope) and pessimistic (solitude as man's destiny), can comfortably coexist. In turn, Michael Wood focuses on the deceptive simplicity of the author's prose, in which hints and silences help evoke complex historical circumstances and imagine alternative worlds. The development of his peculiar use of language, according to Wood, can be divided into three different periods. Mariano Siskind, for his part, addresses the politics of García Márquez's travel writing between 1955 and 1959, including the chronicles about his journeys to Eastern Europe, the *Relato de un náufrago* (*Story of a Shipwrecked Sailor*), and short stories from *Doce cuentos peregrinos* (*Strange Pilgrims*) referring to his time in Rome. In Siskind's view, the experience of constant displacement is at the center of García Márquez's writing both as topic and constructive principle.

Turning to ecocriticism, William Flores addresses, via the ideas of dark ecology, hyperobjects, and the Capitalocene, the ways in which *Cien años de soledad* and *El amor en los tiempos del cólera* provide a valuable ecological awareness for the present era. According to Flores, these novels present a global ecological vision that enables the reader to observe a destroyed imaginary world where humanity dies after bringing about an ecocatastrophe. René Prieto looks at the hitherto unexplored topic of alchemy in *Cien años de soledad*, arguing that the novel hides a deeper, esoteric message, an inner teaching grounded in symbolism. There is, in his view, a concealed system of references to alchemy, planets, chemical elements, and mystical symbolism that bolster the novel's message. Next, music as a formal, structuring feature is the focus of Gene H. Bell-Villada and Marco Katz Montiel's essay: phrases from and allusions to boleros, folk songs, children's jingles, Caribbean pop rhythms, *vallenatos*, and classical music, as well as the diegetic roles assigned to musical instruments (a pianola, an accordion, a clavichord), all help provide randomly recurrent markers and organizing structure to the works. In turn, Ignacio López-Calvo explores how, in public speeches and journalism, García Márquez's realistic representation of Latin America is quite different from his famous version of fictional magical realism and the exoticizing tropicalism of which he has been accused by younger Latin American writers. In these nonfiction works, the author openly condemns eurocentrism, neocolonialism, US imperialism, and other sociopolitical ills in the region.

The section dedicated to García Márquez's Key Works opens with María Helena Rueda's essay on how the author's early fictional writings offer a realist approach to the politics and everyday lives of people in the coastal towns of Colombia. More overtly political and directly engaged with local social struggles than his later, best-known books, they provide an acute literary exploration of what it means for a society to live in the shadow of violence. Erik Camayd-Freixas examines the protean viewpoint in *One Hundred Years of Solitude*, which forms the basis for the novel's polyphony: a polyvalent narrator tells what the characters see, producing a multilayered perspectivism, whereby the overlapping worldviews of the modern author, his folk storyteller persona, and the immanent Melquíades are respectively conjugated with each character's ideology.

Mary Lusky Friedman explores one of the most characteristic plotlines in García Márquez's short stories: a vulnerable outsider is received with violence, indignities, or, occasionally, kindness in a community to which he or she does not belong. In Friedman's view, these short stories afford a laboratory in which to observe García Márquez moving toward magical realism and a taste for "monstrous innocence." Philip Swanson looks at fate and free will in *Crónica de una muerte anunciada*, exploring how agency and authorship are mobilized to test the limits of fatalism and convention. As he explains, the investigation undertaken by the detective-like chronicler implies a quest for a kind of "truth," and the final outcome is a not entirely ironic achievement of "true" love, independently chosen by Ángela.

Helene C. Weldt-Basson analyzes how, in *The Autumn of the Patriarch* and *The General in His Labyrinth*, García Márquez employs similar tropes and novelistic elements to develop very different portraits of his two protagonists: the all but nameless Patriarch as a mythic being who epitomizes evil and the abuse of power, and The General as a postmodern historical figure (Bolívar) who combines his power obsession with other mitigating characteristics, such as the love of his continent and the dream of its ultimate unity. She maintains that counterposing these two characters illustrates social-psychological distinctions between the dominance and the functionalist perspectives of power, in addition to clarifying many of the ambiguities inherent in García Márquez's portrait of Bolívar.

Focusing on *Del amor y otros demonios* (*Of Love and Other Demons*, 1994), Nereida Segura-Rico analyzes the subversion of the discourses of power that the narrative voice carries out from within, as it seemingly anchors the action in an identifiable space and time only to dismantle the pretension of progress, historical, or otherwise. The narrator-chronicler intertwines competing philosophies and ideologies by laying bare the binary oppositions enacted by "the lettered city." Segura-Rico conceives of the novel as an extension of death, an ironic chronicling of a progress arrested by its material and moral ruins. Nicholas Birns's examination of García Márquez's later works concentrates on *El general en su laberinto* (*The General in His Labyrinth*), in which the author identifies with Bolívar as a famous man near completion of his work; *Del amor y otros demonios* (*Of Love and Other Demons*), in which the novelist comes close to magical realism and reaffirms the multiracial and Caribbean character of Spanish America; *News of a Kidnapping*, wherein García Márquez ventures into the territory of drug cartels that became the preoccupation of the next generation of Colombian writers; the novel *Memoria de mis putas tristes* (*Memories of My Melancholy Whores*), which testifies to the strangeness of the new territory of extreme old age; and *Vivir para contarla* (*Living to Tell the Tale*), a real memoir that reflects upon the first half of Gabo's own life.

Robert Sims studies the evolution and interaction of writerly, autobiographical, and testimonial selves in García Márquez's work by concentrating on texts from 1955 to 2004. Although, according to Sims, the interplay of these three selves appears at different moments in his fiction as well as his nonfiction, he achieves the most intricate balance between the three in *Crónica de una muerte anunciada*. Closing the volume, Alessandro Rocco considers García Márquez's filmic-literary *production*, consisting of texts written for cinema, as well as the films made by various directors using his film scenarios and/or screenplays. Bearing in mind the distinction between these two textual entities, Rocco outlines the aesthetic characteristics and narrative developments of this production, also highlighting its constant productive process of intertextual interchange and circulation with the author's more strictly literary oeuvre.

Notes

1. In *García Márquez: Historia de un deicidio*, Vargas Llosa, analyzing García Márquez's writing, defines the total novel thus: "a total reality, confronting real reality to an image that is both its expression and negation . . . it is a total novel because of its subject, insofar as it describes a closed world, from its birth to its death and in all the orders that it is made of" ("una realidad total, enfrentar a la realidad real una imagen que es su expresión y negación . . . se trata de una novela total por su materia, en la medida en que describe un mundo cerrado, desde su nacimiento hasta su muerte y en todos los órdenes que lo componen") (480).
2. See Juan Moreno Blanco, "Amerindian Wayúu Legacy and Garciamarquezian Literary Fable," in this volume.

3. For further information, see Ignacio López-Calvo, "Coloniality and Solitude in García Márquez's Public Speeches and Newspaper Articles," in this volume. See also Bell-Villada, "García Márquez as Public Intellectual."
4. See López-Calvo, "Translation, Unreliable Narrators, and the Comical Use of (Pseudo-) Magical Realism in *Of Love and Other Demons*."
5. For more information on the treatment of dictatorship in *The Autumn of the Patriarch*, see chapter 3 in López-Calvo, *"God and Trujillo": Literary and Cultural Representations of the Dominican Dictator*. In addition, see chapter 9 in Bell-Villada, *García Márquez: The Man and His Work*.
6. For a critical survey of these works, see chapter 7, "The Master of Short Forms," in Bell-Villada, *García Márquez: The Man and His Work*.
7. See Ondaatje, "García Márquez and the Bus to Aracataca."

Works Cited

Bell-Villada, Gene. *Borges and His Fiction: A Guide to His Mind and Art*. Rev. ed. U of Texas P, 2000.

Bell-Villada, Gene. "García Márquez as Public Intellectual." *A History of Colombian Literature*, edited by Raymond Leslie Williams, Cambridge, 2016, pp. 311–21.

Bell-Villada, Gene. *García Márquez: The Man and His Work*. 2nd ed., rev. and expanded. U of North Carolina Press, 2010.

Cortázar, Julio. *Hopscotch*. Translated by Gregory Rabassa, Pantheon Books, 1966.

Cortázar, Julio. *Rayuela*. Sudamericana, 1963.

Fuentes, Carlos. *The Death of Artemio Cruz*. Translated by Sam Hileman, Farrar, Straus, Giroux, 1964.

Fuentes, Carlos. *La muerte de Artemio Cruz*. Fondo de Cultura Económica, 1962.

García Márquez, Gabriel. *El amor en los tiempos del cólera*. Bruguera, 1985.

García Márquez, Gabriel. *The Autumn of the Patriarch*. Translated by Gregory Rabassa, Harper & Row, 1976.

García Márquez, Gabriel. *Chronicle of a Death Foretold*. Translated by Gregory Rabassa, Knopf, 1982.

García Márquez, Gabriel. *Cien años de soledad*. Sudamericana, 1967.

García Márquez, Gabriel. *El coronel no tiene quien le escriba*. Vintage Español, [1961] 2014.

García Márquez, Gabriel. *Crónica de una muerte anunciada*. Sudamericana, 1981.

García Márquez, Gabriel. *Del amor y otros demonios*. Mondadori, 1994.

García Márquez, Gabriel. *Doce cuentos peregrinos*. Vintage Español, [1992] 2006.

García Márquez, Gabriel. *I'm Not Here to Give a Speech*. Translated by Edith Grossman, Vintage International, 2014.

García Márquez, Gabriel. *Love in the Time of Cholera*. Translated by Edith Grossman, Knopf, 1988.

García Márquez, Gabriel. *Memoria de mis putas tristes*. Vintage Español, Random House, 2004.

García Márquez, Gabriel. *Memories of My Melancholy Whores*. Translated by Edith Grossman, Knopf, 2005.

García Márquez, Gabriel. *News of a Kidnapping*. Translated by Edith Grossman, Knopf, 1997.

García Márquez, Gabriel. *No One Writes to the Colonel and Other Stories*. Translated by J. S. Bernstein, Harper & Row, 1968.

García Márquez, Gabriel. *Noticia de un secuestro*. Mondadori, 1996.
García Márquez, Gabriel. *Of Love and Other Demons*. Translated by Edith Grossman, Penguin, 1995.
García Márquez, Gabriel. *One Hundred Years of Solitude*. Translated by Gregory Rabassa, Harper & Row, 1970.
García Márquez, Gabriel. *El otoño del patriarca*. Sudamericana, 1975.
García Márquez, Gabriel. *The Scandal of the Century and Other Writings*. Edited by Cristóbal Pera. Foreword by Jon Lee Anderson. Translated by Anne McLean, Alfred A. Knopf, 2019.
García Márquez, Gabriel. *Strange Pilgrims*. Translated by Edith Grossman, Knopf, 1993.
García Márquez, Gabriel. *Yo no vengo a decir un discurso*. Vintage Español, 2010.
López-Calvo, Ignacio. *"God and Trujillo": Literary and Cultural Representations of the Dominican Dictator*. UP of Florida, 2005.
López-Calvo, Ignacio. "Translation, Unreliable Narrators, and the Comical Use of (Pseudo-) Magical Realism in *Of Love and Other Demons*." *Gabriel García Márquez in Retrospect*, edited by Gene H. Bell-Villada, Lexington Books, 2016, pp. 183–94.
Ondaatje, Michael. "García Márquez and the Bus to Aracataca." *Figures in a Ground: Canadian Essays on Modern Literature Collected in Honor of Sheila Watson*, edited by Diane Bessai and David Jackel. Western Producer Prairie Books, 1978, pp. 19–31.
Vargas Llosa, Mario. *La ciudad y los perros*. Seix Barral, 1963.
Vargas Llosa, Mario. *García Márquez: Historia de un deicidio*. Monteávila, 1971.
Vargas Llosa, Mario. *The Time of the Hero*. Translated by Lysander Kemp, Noonday Press, 1966.

PART I

SOCIOHISTORICAL AND LITERARY BACKGROUNDS

CHAPTER 1

SCRIPTING GABRIEL GARCÍA MÁRQUEZ'S LIFE

STEPHEN M. HART

BIOGRAPHY, as Paula R. Backsheider suggests, is the "last literary genre to be read by a very wide cross-section of people" (xiii), and yet, despite its popularity, there is little agreement about the parameters that govern the genre. Gerald Martin's *Gabriel García Márquez: A Life* (2008) is by far the most comprehensive biography written about the great Colombian writer, and yet some reviews of it revealed fundamental disagreement about what the essential ingredients of a biography are. Should the focus be on "the private man's outer self," or should it be, as one reviewer suggested, on García Márquez's "mind-life" (Wilson n.p.)? And if the main aim of a biography is to capture the biographee's "mind-life"—presumably what Backsheider means when she says that the job of the biographer is to get "to the person beneath, the core of the human being" (xvi)—what is the best way to do this? Take the following composite chronology of García Márquez's life as an example:

> Born in the small and remote town of Aracataca in northern Colombia at nine o'clock in the morning on 6 March 1927, to Gabriel Eligio García and Luisa Santiaga Márquez Iguarán, Gabriel José García Márquez went on to become one of the most famous novelists ever to have written in the Spanish language. He lived for the first ten years of his life in the house in Aracataca owned by his grandparents, who doted on him: Colonel Nicolás Márquez Mejía, who had fought in Colombia's Civil Wars of the nineteenth century, and Tranquilina Iguarán Cotes, whose stories of ghosts and omens thrilled and terrified in equal measure the young Gabo, as he was affectionately known. García Márquez began his education in the capital, Bogotá, a city set high up in the Andes that he found cold and unwelcoming. Initially strong-armed by his father into pursuing a legal career, he gave up his law studies at the age of twenty to devote himself to writing. Bitterly disappointed, his father told him: "You will eat paper." In the early 1950s García Márquez worked as a newspaper reporter, first in Barranquilla and Cartagena on the northern coast of Colombia and then for Colombia's most prestigious daily, Bogotá's *El Espectador*. His first short novel,

Leafstorm, was published in 1955. His interest in film grew during this period; in Rome in the 1950s he studied at the Experimental Film School, and while living in Mexico in the 1960s he wrote several film scripts. By the mid-1960s he had published three novels that brought him critical acclaim in Latin America but neither commercial nor international success. His fourth novel, *One Hundred Years of Solitude*, first published in 1967, changed everything. The story of five generations of a Latin American family called the Buendías who lived in the remote town of Macondo, this novel was a runaway success mainly because of its ability to describe magical events in an everyday, down-to-earth style that became known as magical realism. Subsequent successes with *Autumn of the Patriarch* (1975) and *Chronicle of a Death Foretold* (1981) led to the award of the Nobel Prize in 1982, and he continued to beguile readers all over the globe with novels such as *Love in the Time of Cholera* (1985), *The General in His Labyrinth* (1994), and *News of a Kidnapping* (1996). He was diagnosed with lymphoma in 1999 and subsequently began cancer treatment in a clinic in Los Angeles. Undeterred, he began writing his autobiography, and the first volume, *Living to Tell the Tale*, came out in 2002, followed two years later by a short novel, *Memories of My Melancholy Whores* (2004). In 2008 García Márquez's health began to decline, and in 2012 his family confirmed that he was suffering from Alzheimer's disease. He died in Mexico City, surrounded by his family, on Maundy Thursday, 17 April 2014.[1]

One could argue that the main chronological events of García Márquez's life are here: when and where he was born, his education, his interest in journalism and film, the main novels he wrote, his winning of the Nobel Prize, his association with magical realism, the illnesses he suffered from, and when and where he died. But some carping about the details will be inevitable; where, for example, is the reference to García Márquez's politics, his interest in Cuba and close friendship with Fidel Castro? Why is his journalism not given greater emphasis? Why not refer to the real reason he went to Europe in July 1955? Why have the short stories been left out? Why not refer to the rift between García Márquez and Mario Vargas Llosa that led to Mario punching Gabo on the nose after a film screening in Mexico City in 1976? Why not summarize Gabo's Nobel Prize speech? Why not analyze the impact of his magical-realist style on literary writing around the globe? Why is his marriage to Mercedes Barcha on 21 March 1958, in Barranquilla not even mentioned? And how about the birth of his two sons: Rodrigo on 24 August 1959, and Gonzalo on 16 April 1962? One could, of course, ask many more questions, but the important point about this litany of critiques is that they go to the heart of the disagreement about what a biography should and should not include in its narrative, and they revolve around the balance in any account of a given life between the public persona and the private individual. There is, after all, no set formula. As Somerset Maugham once said, "There are three rules for writing biography, but fortunately no one knows what they are" (quoted in Holmes 7).

Before moving on to a discussion of García Márquez's biography, one further point should be made: creative writers often do not like biographers. Alexander Pope, for example, is said to have greeted the announcement of a series of extended obituary-biographies of distinguished contemporaries with the remark, "It gives a new fear to death," while Oscar Wilde once wittily pointed out that "it is usually Judas who writes the biography" (quoted in Backsheider xv–xvi). For his part, James Joyce coined the memorable neologism the "biografiend," which needs no further explanation (Holmes 17). Betrayal is common to all three of these descriptions of the biographer, who is seen according to the Pope-Wilde-Joyce triumvirate as a disciple who betrays his master, someone in on the secret who chooses to spill the beans.[2] This notion of being in on the secret and yet spilling the beans is, for those sitting comfortably outside the battle arena, a source of interest, if not pleasure, even schadenfreude, a joy so unmentionable in English that we refuse to translate it.

While reflecting on how best to not become Judas and thus avoid the pleasures of schadenfreude when writing García Márquez's biography, I thought at one point I had found the solution: I would "shadow" García Márquez's own autobiography, which would have the added bonus of providing direct access to the great Colombian writer's "mind-life." But this solution proved to be a dead end. I soon discovered that *Vivir para contarla* (2002) was clearly not an autobiography in the traditional sense of the word. There were some hostile reviews; Ricardo Bada, for example, argued that Gabo's autobiography reads more like a novel than an objective, personal account of the events of an individual's life (122–26).[3] Clearly, though, there are sections of Gabo's autobiography that describe real places and/or events that occurred in his life, which then found their way into *One Hundred Years*. First, García Márquez uses his biography to clarify that Macondo, the locale where the novel is set, is based on the small real-life plantation of the same name next to Aracataca where he lived for most of his early life (*Living* 19–20; *Vivir para contarla* 28–29). Second, he states that the portrayal of the army's massacre of the three thousand banana plantation workers in the novel is based on the account of the strike that occurred in Ciénaga provided to him by his grandfather. The third helpful "fact" is that the sense of apocalypse that occurs at the conclusion of *One Hundred Years* is based on the mood of decline caused in the 1930s when the United Fruit Company (UFC) pulled out of northern Colombia, and Ciénaga in particular (*Living* 14–18, 27; *Vivir para contarla* 22–27; 38). Even the more trivial events in the novel come from Gabo's experience of life in Aracataca as a young child; thus, the bull bursting into the kitchen in the novel is based on a real-life event (*Living* 36; *Vivir para contarla* 48). Structurally significant events in Gabo's novel also grew out of empirical events; the ancestral guilt of the Buendía family portrayed in chapter one is based on a duel that actually occurred between García Márquez's grandfather and an individual called Medardo Pacheco, who died at the hands of the former (*Living* 37–40; *Vivir para contarla* 48–52).[4]

There are pointers in the autobiography providing insight into seemingly trivial events that, when they appeared transformed in *One Hundred Years*, would have significant repercussions in various literary worlds across the globe. The most important ingredient of magical realism, which led to it being refashioned around the world in novels by Salman Rushdie, Ben Okri, Haruki Murakami, and Mo Yan—namely, the Third-World versus First-World polarity expressed in the idea that what is real in one part of the world is viewed as magical in another part of the world, and vice versa—sprang directly from Gabo's amazed eyes when as a young boy he saw hordes of people from all over the world arriving in Aracataca (*Living* 43; *Vivir para contarla* 56). Finally, the autobiography "proves" that, although the drama of the Buendía family can be described as a metaphor for the genealogy of the human race or as an allegory for the conquest of the Americas, it is also in a very identifiable sense the story of Gabo's own family in Aracataca.

The autobiography is thus very helpful in allowing readers of García Márquez's work to compare the empirical event as it occurred in Aracataca in the 1930s as Gabo was growing up with its novelistic version as recast in *One Hundred Years*. Chapter eleven, for example, contains a description of how Colonel Aureliano Buendía's seventeen illegitimate sons, each named Aureliano, unexpectedly turn up in Macondo on the anniversary of the armistice to pay homage to their father; this is based on a real-life event that occurred one Ash Wednesday when Colonel Nicolás Márquez Mejía's "hijos callejeros" (children born out of wedlock) (*Living* 49; *Vivir para contarla* 64) turned up in Aracataca to wish him well on his birthday. As García Márquez explains in his autobiography, these were the children sired by the colonel during his days warring in the northeastern provinces of Colombia:

> I lived through one of the great fantasies of those years one day when a group of men came to the house, dressed alike in gaiters and spurs, and all of them with a cross of ash drawn on their foreheads. They were the sons fathered by the colonel across the entire length of the Provinces during the War of a Thousand Days, and they had come from their towns almost a month late to congratulate him on his birthday. Before coming to the house they had heard Ash Wednesday Mass and the cross that Father Angarita drew on their foreheads seemed like a supernatural emblem whose mystery would pursue me for years, even after I became familiar with the liturgy of Holy Week (*Living* 66; *Vivir para contarla* 84).[5]

Most readers, when dealing with an event of this kind as described in *One Hundred Years* (see *Cien años de soledad* 176–77; *One Hundred Years* 179–80), will perceive a clear line in the sand between the empirical event that occurred in Aracataca as recounted in the autobiography and the novelistic recreation of the same event in García Márquez's fiction (unlike in the autobiography, for example, the liturgical marking of the Ash Wednesday cross on the illegitimate sons' foreheads occurs in the novel after rather than before their arrival at their father's house, and unlike in "real" life, the cross marked on their foreheads proves to be indelible). But there are a number of cases in the autobiography when the distinction between the unreality of the fiction and the reality of the autobiography breaks down. A good example of this occurs when García Márquez describes how he is walking toward Aracataca from the train station with his mother to visit their old house, which they intend to sell (Stavans 32), and this reminds him of the sequence of events in his short story "La siesta del martes" ("Tuesday Siesta"); he simply comments: "I feel as if I were the thief" (*Living* 23; *Vivir para contarla* 33). His autobiographical self has become fused with the life of his fictional characters.

Pointing in a similar direction, the overlap between the descriptions of the birth of his parents' love affair in *Living* and in his novel, *Love in the Time*, is so pervasive that there is no clear dividing line between the two versions of the event. It is not the case that the account in the autobiography is the real degree-zero version of the love affair while the account in *Love in the Time* is the embellished, literary version.[6] Both versions are as real as they are literary. The famous scene in *Love* when the lovers' eyes meet during Midnight Mass ("in the crowd leaving the church she felt him so close, so clearly, that an irresistible power forced her to look over her shoulder as she walked along the central nave and, a hand's breadth from her eyes she saw those icy eyes, that livid face, those eyes petrified by the terror of love") (García Márquez, *Love in the Time* 68) is in the autobiography, too, but it is more dramatic there because we also learn that Gabriel Eligio García had, in fact, deliberately positioned himself near the nave in order to catch his future wife's gaze; as he told his son: "It was just what I had planned" (*Living* 47).[7]

I soon came to realize as I read the rest of the memoirs that the substratum of historical truth that I was unconsciously searching for was never in fact part of García Márquez's plan. When I interviewed García Márquez at the Fundación del Nuevo Cine Latinoamericano in Havana in December 2007, I told him how much I had enjoyed reading the first volume of the autobiography, and I asked him to sign my copy of the book, which he graciously agreed to do. I then asked him about the sequel, and he told me that he was working diligently on the second volume of his memoirs. In retrospect, I shouldn't have held my breath (Hart, Spanish version 219). The answer to García Márquez's understanding of historical writing, including biography and autobiography, lies in the epigraph to his autobiography, which states as follows: "Life is not what one lived but what one remembers and how one remembers in order to recount it" (*Vivir para contarla*, 1).[8] Biography in García Márquez's work is not a record of the empirical facts, but what is remembered and subsequently recounted. The shaping is more important than the thing itself. It is in writing that reality is born, not vice versa.

As Somerset Maugham hints, there are many ways of writing a biography, but my view is that at the bottom of the Pandora's box of life scripting there are always two blessings, often locked in combat: the Archive and the Narrative. When I finally got around to writing my literary biography, *Gabriel García Márquez*, which was published by Reaktion Books in 2010, there were three central questions I had identified that I wanted my biography to address and hopefully answer. The first was the role played by Gabo's grandfather, Colonel Márquez Mejía, and the house of Aracataca, in the construction of García Márquez's world vision; the second was the role played by the strike that had occurred at the UFC banana plantation in Ciénaga, Colombia, in December 1928 in the construction of García Márquez's novelistic world; and the third was the role played by the Cuban Revolution and Fidel Castro specifically in the construction of Gabo's political universe. These three questions had been addressed, of course, in previous scholarship on García Márquez's work, but I wanted to focus on the interconnection between them; in effect, they became the coordinates that shaped the form the biographical narrative took.

In order to answer my first question, I visited Aracataca in February 2009 and, as a result of an extensive interview with Rubiella Reyes, an attractive young *aracateña* who had a passion for García Márquez's life and offered visitors a tour of the house in Aracataca, I was able to achieve a deeper cultural understanding of the ways in which superstition—the belief in supernatural entities such as local and often tragic ghosts, for example—was imbibed by Gabo as a young child when he lived with his grandparents in Aracataca. One story in particular stuck in my mind, that of a Venezuelan singer who had been successful in Aracataca until he lost his voice and tragically took his own life; his "coughing" could be heard by the neighbors emanating from the nearby house for years after his death. Rubiella took me along to see the still uninhabited house, called "la Casa del Muerto" (the dead man's house), and I used it to construct my own narrative of the world that Gabo had inhabited while growing up in Aracataca (Hart, English version 10–11). This allowed me to see how superstition was itself a type of language that is employed by different people for multifarious ends. There was, for example, a frog-infested pond in the garden of the house in Aracataca where his grandparents lived, and when Gabo's grandmother heard the frogs croaking, she would say that it was one of her husband's "brujas" (witches), a code word for his lady friends. Nicolás Márquez Mejía would then dutifully retrieve his pincers from his workshop, heat them up, go out to the pond, then use them to execute one of the frogs and thereby "atone" for his sin (Hart, English version 10–12).

I also found the grandfather figure to be highly significant in the creation of Gabo's novelistic world in one other way: his siring of between twelve and nineteen illegitimate children during the War of the Thousand Days (17 October 1899–21 November 1902), alongside his three legitimate children (Hart, English version 23–25). Gabo clearly became intrigued by this "other" family when listening as a young boy to his grandfather's stories. Indeed, this fascination even led him to embark many years later—as a young man making a living as a journalist in Barranquilla, in 1952–1953, to be precise—on a trip to discover his roots and meet the members of this "other" family (Hart, English version 41–42). It became clear to me that this obsession lay at the roots of and was one of the hallmarks of his fiction, namely, the "other," which can take a variety of forms ranging from the "writing self" to the "inner self," the "ideal self," the "soul," and the "double." I was able to retrace the leitmotif of the double in García Márquez's work, right back to an early story published in *El Espectador* on 17 January 1948, "Tubal-Caín forja una estrella" (Tubal-Cain Forges a Star), in which García Márquez can be seen confronting his family "doubles" in the form of ghosts, and "La otra costilla de la muerte" ("The Other Side of Death," 1948), which is a meditation on the rivalry between the legitimate child and the *hijo natural* (Hart, English version 44–48). In García Márquez's private symbolic universe, the double of the self was the most authentic when it was mediated by death.

It was when I began to investigate the second question, that is, the role played by the strike that had occurred at the UFC plantation in Ciénaga in December 1928, that I realized there was an intimate connection between the answer to the first and second questions. In February 2009 I consulted the archives of the Biblioteca Luis Ángel Arango in Bogotá, reading all of the available articles that reported on the strike in *El Tiempo* and *El Espectador* in the months before and after the showdown between the strikers and the army, which took place in Ciénaga on 6 December 1928. My idea was to compare and contrast the contemporaneous newspaper reports with the account of the event that appears in chapter fifteen of *One Hundred Years*; in García Márquez's version of the event, more than three thousand striking workers on the banana plantation are machine-gunned and bayoneted to death by the army on the orders of General Carlos Cortés Vargas. A number of things emerged as a result of reading through the daily reports of the conflict. First, the figure three thousand workers, which is an intrinsic ingredient of García Márquez's version of the event, is supported by the contemporaneous reports, which refer again and again to the same number of striking workers (Hart, English version 87). Second, it is abundantly clear, based on all the reports provided by the army and by General Cortés Vargas in particular, that the strike was seen as politically motivated (Hart, English version 87–88). Third, the sequence of events as recounted in the novel—including the order issued by General Cortés Vargas that the strikers must disperse within five minutes, which they refused to do, and the granting of one extra minute to do so—is also supported by contemporaneous accounts (Hart, English version 86–87). The problem starts when we attempt to establish historically what happened next. General Cortés Vargas, in his report on the disturbance that occurred on 6 December 1928, *Los sucesos de las bananeras* (1928), stated that nine people died that day (Hart, English version 86); historians such as Roberto Herrera Soto and Rafael Romero Castañeda have assessed popular reports indicating that one thousand people met their deaths but found no evidence to support the figure of one thousand dead (Hart, English version 93–94), let alone García Márquez's three thousand.

As a result of this huge disparity in the numbers, I decided to travel to Ciénaga myself in March 2009. I visited the site of the old, now disused river port of Ciénaga, where merchandise used to be loaded during the banana boom, and met a resident of the town in his fifties who burst out laughing when I told him that the official report of those killed in the Main Square of Ciénaga on 6 December 1928, was nine. He said it must have been more than three thousand; his grandfather, who was an eyewitness, had told him that the square was ankle-deep in blood after the massacre. He would not allow me to take his name or record an interview with him. I also visited the main square of Ciénaga, where the statue to the Martyrs has been erected. All that is left of the Ciénaga railway station—which originally backed onto the main square and has now been turned into a road packed on both sides with market stalls—is the outer shell of the building itself, which has been converted into a hardware store. I asked the shop assistant what had happened to the rails of the railway line that had once existed nearby, and he pointed to the roof, where I saw that the rails had been reused as buttresses to support the building's roof. I asked for permission to take a photograph of the rails in the roof's structure. The request was taken to the shop owner, who came out to see me; he was taken aback by my request and refused to allow me to take a photograph. He also asked me to leave his shop immediately. The awkwardness of everyone I spoke to in Ciénaga about the events of 6 December 1928, including their reluctance to be identified and their refusal, in some cases, to continue an interview with me or discuss anything relating to those events, suggested to me that what had happened on that day in Ciénaga more than eighty years ago was still an open wound (Hart, Spanish version 260–61).

But how does a novelist express an open wound? The best way of answering this question is to look at what García Márquez does with the aftermath of this event in chapter fifteen of *One Hundred Years of Solitude*. A wound is a gash in the flesh in which the two sides of the skin that surround the gash cannot embrace in order to heal. It is a story in which the two sides of the tale cannot meet and agree about the truth. This gash in the side of Colombian history is precisely what we find in García Márquez's novel. According to one side of the story, José Arcadio Segundo is a banana plantation worker who has worked for the UFC, goes on strike, and is shot dead and "disappeared" by the army on 6 December 1928. According to the other side of the story, José Arcadio Segundo is a ghost who survives the confrontation with the army and now lives in Melquíades's room in the Buendía household. When a soldier demands they open up the room, he uses a lantern to search for revolutionaries, but the ray of his lantern invisibilizes José Arcadio Segundo: "He paused with his glance on the space where Aureliano Segundo and Santa Sofía de la Piedad were still seeing José Arcadio Segundo and the latter also realised that the soldier was looking at him without seeing him" (*One Hundred Years* 254). José Arcadio Segundo is an invisible "double" figure who is mediated by death (since he is a ghost) as much as by politics (since he performs the role of invisible subaltern in the text). And since José Arcadio Segundo is the subaltern, the military and civil authorities can neither see nor hear him; his narrative thereby becomes the reverse side of the official version of history controlled by the Colombian government. García Márquez is, in effect, using this ghost story to destabilize and hollow out from within the epistemic violence of the state. In the section of his autobiography in which he treats this issue, García Márquez discusses the disparity between the official version of the number of deaths and the people's version, and he argues that the fact that in a recent commemoration of the tragedy a senator had referred specifically to the three thousand dead gives greater weight to his version of what happened (*Vivir para contarla* 80).[9]

In order to address the third question—namely, to assess the role played by the Cuban Revolution, and specifically Fidel Castro, in the construction of Gabo's political universe—I set myself the task of interviewing a number of his Cuban colleagues and writers, mainly via the Escuela Internacional de Cine y Televisión, a school that García Márquez, along with filmmakers Tomás Gutiérrez Alea, Julio García Espinosa, and Fernando Birri, had founded and launched on 15 December 1986, and where I worked for a period of ten years (2006–2016) during the summers. García Márquez would often tell his friends that he was a citizen of not one but three countries, which formed between themselves a perfect Caribbean triangle: Colombia (where he was born), Mexico (where he lived), and Cuba (where his heart lived).[10] In 1957 he visited the Communist bloc countries of Eastern Europe, and he was distinctly unimpressed—he quipped that they couldn't get anything right, not even a brothel!—but his journalist's antennae were energized by news of Fidel Castro's attempts to oust Fulgencio Batista in the latter half of 1958. Just days after Fidel Castro came to power in Cuba (1 January 1959), García

Márquez was invited to Havana to attend Castro's Operation Truth, and he arrived there on 19 January 1959. García Márquez was invited to set up the Bogotá office of the recently founded Cuban press agency Prensa Latina, and thus began his love affair with Cuba (Martin, 246–52). He developed a deep and lasting friendship with Cuba's head of state, and he made it very clear that his affiliation was with a Caribbean-style, Fidel Castro–style communism rather than the East European version. Thus he never adopted—nor would it have been logical—Socialist realism as the vehicle for the expression of his art, but the works he wrote from the late 1950s onward began to express a subtly ironic allegorical political message that was no less powerful. His short story "Big Mama's Funeral," for example, was written between May and June 1959 and thus can be seen as a direct response to the ideology of the Cuban Revolution. How can Mamá Grande really be—the narrator of that short story asks—the owner of

> the wealth of the subsoil, the territorial waters, the colors of the flag, national sovereignty, the traditional parties, the rights of man, civil rights, the nation's leadership, the right of appeal, Congressional hearings, letters of recommendation, historical records, free elections, beauty queens, transcendental speeches, huge demonstrations, distinguished young ladies, proper gentlemen, punctilious military men, His Illustrious Eminence, the Supreme Court, goods whose importation was forbidden, liberal ladies, the meat problem, the purity of the language, setting a good example, legal order, the free but responsible press, the Athens of South America, public opinion, the lessons of democracy, Christian morality, the shortage of foreign exchange, the right of asylum, the Communist menace, the ship of state, the high cost of living, republican traditions, the under-privileged classes, statements of political support? ("Big Mama's Funeral" 161)[11]

García Márquez's ideological support of the Cuban Revolution and his personal support of Fidel Castro deepened over the years (Bell-Villada, "Gabriel García Márquez" 17). The fifteenth chapter of *One Hundred Years*, described previously, is a cry of solidarity for Caribbean workers exploited by international capitalism as epitomized by the UFC. In 1968 the Cuban poet Heberto Padilla lost his job as a result of his having eulogized the work of a suspect writer, Guillermo Cabrera Infante, and he was imprisoned in 1971 for counterrevolutionary activities; despite the support for Padilla's release expressed in a letter signed by a number of internationally renowned writers including Jean-Paul Sartre, Mario Vargas Llosa, Juan Goytisolo, Carlos Fuentes, and Octavio Paz, García Márquez stuck to his pro-Castro guns and refused to sign the letter (Hart, English version 105–06). He became more forceful over time in his rejection of dictatorship in Latin America; thus after Chile's government fell to a coup d'état engineered by the Chilean armed forces, García Márquez sent a telegram to General Augusto Pinochet stating: "The Chilean people will never allow itself to be governed by a mob of criminals like you, who are bankrolled by North American imperialism" (Hart, English version 109–10).[12] In 1975 the Colombian writer offered his services to Fidel Castro as the writer of the epic story of the Cuban expedition to Africa, and two years later a set of essays, *Operation Carlota*, was published (Hart, English version 115). His personal diplomacy with Castro resulted in Reinol González's being released from Cuba in December 1977 so he could spend Christmas with his family in Mexico (Hart, English version 115–16). García Márquez asked Castro to read a close-to-final draft of *Chronicle of a Death Foretold* (1981), and Castro drew attention to some errors in the text, which Gabo speedily corrected (Hart, English version 158). When García Márquez won the Nobel Prize, the Cuban government—in harsh contrast to the Colombian government, which seemed almost embarrassed that an award of this kind had even occurred—showered Gabo with gifts, honoring him with the award of the Orden Félix Varela, sending fifteen hundred bottles of rum to Stockholm to help him with the celebrations after the ceremony, and giving him a Protocol House for whenever he stayed in Havana as well as the use of a Mercedes Benz (Hart, English version 123). As a result of having access to the Protocol House, Gabo began making annual visits to Cuba, normally in December so he could also participate in Havana's International Film Festival. He worked with Fidel Castro and a team composed of Gutiérrez Alea, García Espinosa, and Birri to set up a film school in Cuba, and on 15 December 1986, the Escuela Internacional de Cine y Televisión was founded (Hart, English version 137–39). In January 1998, when Pope John Paul II visited Havana, García Márquez was Fidel Castro's special invited guest (Hart, English version 157–58). In 2000 he supported Castro in his stance on Elián González, a boy who had started a political tug of war between Cuba and the United States, and he did so pointedly, even though it meant speaking out against Vargas Llosa, who espoused the anti-Castro stance (Hart, English version 162–63). Right up until he was diagnosed with lymphoma in 1999, Gabo went every year in December to Cuba's International Film and TV School in San Antonio de los Baños to give a seminar, "How to Write a Story," which was much appreciated by the students in the "curso regular." All of this demonstrates the commitment that García Márquez felt for Cuba's style of communism as well as the personal esteem he felt for Fidel Castro.

The crucial figures I used for shaping the narrative of my literary biography of García Márquez, as we have seen, consisted of two people (Colonel Nicolás Márquez Mejía and Fidel Castro), two events (the strike at the UFC banana plantation in December 1928 and the Cuban Revolution), and one object (the house in Aracataca where Gabo was brought up). The archive I had access to consisted of García Márquez's published writings, including his very insightful autobiography, *Vivir para contarla* (2002); key works such as Gerald Martin's above-mentioned biography, *Gabriel García Márquez: A Life* (2008); library holdings in Colombia, Cuba, and Europe; and interviews with a number of the people who had worked with Gabo at the EICTV in San Antonio de los Baños in Cuba.[13] This was the archive I used to create the narrative of my biography, but since the publication of my biography, the field has been revolutionized by the transfer, after García Márquez's death, of the archive of his works to the Harry Ransom Center at the University of Texas. That extraordinary trove, consisting of around 270,000 papers from García Márquez's personal archive, provides a literally inexhaustible archive on his life and work. Manuscript Collection MS-5353 consists of manuscript drafts of published and unpublished works, research material, photograph albums, scrapbooks, correspondence, clippings, notebooks, screenplays, printed material, ephemera, electronic files, thousands of photos, and even Gabo's school reports and his passports. As a result of this exceptional legacy, a number of hoary old chestnuts have been finally laid to rest. For example, rumors had emerged in the years before García Márquez's death that he was working on a new book of fiction. In December 2008 Plinio Apuleyo Mendoza, one of García Márquez's closest friends, announced that Gabo was writing a new novel. It was to be a love story. Mendoza suggested, "He has four versions of it. He told me that he was now trying to get the best from each of them" (Tremlett 23). This was followed by a series of denials and counterdenials in the spring of 2009 (Hart, English version 177) and then, on 29 October 2010, there was a report apparently from García Márquez's publisher in Mexico that the great Colombian writer "in Mexico City, was busy completing his latest novel, *En agosto nos vemos*" (Anonymous n.p.). This story about the missing legacy masterpiece disappeared for a while but then resurfaced with the news that García Márquez had died on 17 April 2014, in articles published in *The Times* of London (18 April 2014) ("Gabriel García Márquez" n.p.) and *The Atlantic* (22 April 2014) (Ohlheiser n.p.). *La Vanguardia* published the text of *En agosto nos vemos* on 20 April 2014 ("La obra inacabada" n.p.), and *The Guardian* provided a report on the new manuscript, published on 23 April 2014, referring to the work as the great writer's "last legacy" (Flood n.p.). Unfortunately, though, it was fake news. As box 37, folders 5–6, in the Harry Ransom Archive prove, *En agosto nos vemos* was the draft of a short story about a fifty-two-year-old woman, Ana Magdalena Bach, who arrives at a Caribbean island to pay her respects at her mother's grave—a ritual she has been performing annually for the last twenty-eight years—and who then sleeps with a man who is staying in her hotel; the short story describes an episode that is clearly seeking to be part of a larger design but is not yet there in the version of the text as published by *La Vanguardia*. Though it is dated 1999, this embryo of a short story has the air of a hybrid work, a rather uncomfortable mix of the lugubrious and overwrought atmosphere of "La siesta del martes" of *Los funerales de la Mamá Grande* (1962) and the sexual directness of *El amor en los tiempos del cólera* (1985). It is neither a novel in embryonic form nor a masterpiece, but rather one of the narratives of a composite text made up of six short stories. The Harry Ransom archive contains another one of the short stories, "La noche del eclipse," in box 37; the latter was destined to be the third story,[14] though it never actually fulfilled its destiny.

What of García Márquez's legacy? There is no doubt that the Harry Ransom archive will be the jewel in the crown of that legacy, and it has the advantage of containing information about Gabo that appeals to the general public as much as university professors. And this is surely the secret to García Márquez's success. Rarely has a writer appealed to popular as well as literary tastes in equal measure as much as Gabo has; his *One Hundred Years* was a selection for Oprah's Book Club in 2004, and his *Love* was chosen in 2007. The proper noun "Macondo," as Gene H. Bell-Villada has pointed out, "has taken on a life of its own"; there is a "Macondo bookstore in New York, a Hotel Macondo in Santa Marta and a Farmacia Macondo in Barranquilla, and there is an excellent Latin pop song called *Los cien años de Macondo*" (Bell-Villada, "Introduction" xvii). Indeed, García Márquez's name has continued to make headlines even after his death. On 2 May 2015, a first edition copy of *One Hundred Years* was stolen from a guarded display case at Bogota's International Book Fair; its owner, Álvaro Castillo, called it a "very painful loss," not least because the copy had been signed by the great Colombian writer himself (Associated Press n.p.). The book, valued at £40,000, was recovered by police on 9 May 2015 ("Colombia Police" n.p.). On 6 March 2018, when Gabo would have been ninety-one years old, his life and work were celebrated by a Google doodle.

García Márquez's fictions, like Borgesian Tlönian objects, have begun to invade the real world. At the end of August 2018 García Márquez's great-niece, Melissa Martínez García, who was thirty-four years old at the time, was kidnapped by a group of armed men who intercepted the car she was driving near the city of Santa Marta, in the northeastern region of Colombia along the Caribbean coast, as she was returning home from her job overseeing work on a banana farm. They subsequently demanded a ransom of $5 million for her release. Martínez García is the granddaughter of Jaime García Márquez, Gabo's brother (Telegraph reporters n.p.). She was released on 17 December 2018, as a result of a special military operation in which a dozen people were detained ("Kidnapped Relative" n.p.).

It is perhaps not surprising that *One Hundred Years* has emerged as the main star in the firmament of Gabriel García Márquez's legacy. Netflix announced on 6 March 2019, that they had acquired the rights to the book and were planning to create the first screen adaptation of the author's 1967 masterpiece. The novel will be adapted into a Spanish-language series and filmed mainly in Colombia; García Márquez's sons, Rodrigo and Gonzalo, will be executive producers. García Márquez's family was initially hesitant about Netflix's offer. As Rodrigo pointed out: "For decades our father was reluctant to sell the film rights to *One Hundred Years* because he believed that it could not be made under the time constraints of a feature film, or that producing it in a language other than Spanish would not do it justice. But in the current golden age of series, with the level of talented writing and directing, the cinematic quality of content, and the acceptance by worldwide audiences of programs in foreign languages, the time could not be better" (Guardian staff and AP n.p.). The first exhibition of the García Márquez collection at the Harry Ransom Center opened on 1 February 2020; a bilingual exhibition entitled "Gabriel García Márquez: The Making of a Global Writer," it focuses on *One Hundred Years* as a global literary phenomenon ("First Exhibition" n.p.). The exhibition is comprised of letters, sketches, photographs, newspaper clippings, artifacts, and manuscripts associated with Gabo's masterpiece and, as Lance Richardson points out, "all the correspondence, edits and dead-end drafts offer a glimpse of what 'genius' actually entails" (Richardson n.p.).

Notes

1. This is a biographical summary of the main events of García Márquez's life that I constructed for the purpose of the argument of this essay.
2. Gerald Martin's biography of García Márquez proves that the Pope-Wilde-Joyce rulebook does not always hold sway, yet I remember an occasion when Gerald told me that he and

Gabo, during one of their lunches in Mexico City, began to discuss in a good-humored way not only who would live longest but also who would finish his biography first—Gabo was writing his autobiography and Gerald finishing off Gabo's biography—and therefore have the last say. There was clearly some one-upmanship going on! As it turned out, Gerald's biography came out six years after the appearance of Gabo's autobiography.

3. Efraín Kristal, in contrast, saw the novelistic qualities of the autobiography as a strength (88–97).
4. The important point here is that this event—that is, Pacheco Medardo's murder—was a crucial stimulus for García Márquez's desire to become a writer: "Fue el primer caso de la vida real que me revolvió los instintos de escritor y aún no he podido conjurarlo" (*Vivir para contarla* 50). Also highly relevant is that the adults all gave him different versions of the events themselves, and it is important to underline that his decision to become a writer was from the beginning intimately connected with the notion of the multiplicity of versions—again a trick/technique that we often find in García Márquez's fiction: "Los adultos lo [el drama] embrollaban delante de mí para confundirme, y nunca pude armar el acertijo completo porque cada quien, de ambos lados, colocaba las piezas a su modo" (*Vivir para contarla* 50–51).
5. "Una de las grandes fantasías de aquellos años la viví un día en que llegó a la casa un grupo de hombres iguales con ropas, polainas y espuelas de jinete, y todos con una cruz de ceniza pintada en la frente. Eran los hijos engendrados por el coronel a lo largo de la Provincia durante la guerra de los Mil Días, que iban desde sus pueblos para felicitarlo por su cumpleaños con más de un mes de retraso. Antes de ir a la casa habían oído la misa del Miércoles de Ceniza, y la cruz que el padre Angarita les dibujó en la frente me pareció un emblema sobrenatural cuyo misterio habría de perseguirme durante años, aun después de que me familiaricé con la liturgia de la Semana Santa" (*Vivir para contarla* 84); for further discussion of this event in *One Hundred Years* and its ramifications, see Hart, English version 85.
6. Compare *Vivir para contarla* 129–32 with *El amor en los tiempos del cólera* 91–108.
7. "Era justo lo que yo había planeado" (*Vivir para contarla* 62).
8. "La vida no es la que uno vivió, sino la que uno recuerda y como la recuerda para contarla" (*Vivir para contarla* 50–53). For an inspirational treatment of these themes, see Martin xix–xxiii.
9. He also refers at the same juncture in the memoirs to his "false memories," one of which is that he was greeted by one of the soldiers as "captain Gabi" (*Vivir para contarla* 80). His view is that he cannot have remembered the event because it cannot have happened. As he concludes: "Múltiples casos como ese me crearon en casa la mala reputación de que tenía recuerdos interuterinos y sueños premonitorios" (*Vivir para contarla* 81).
10. He joked to Julio García Espinosa during a visit to Havana in December 2006 that he would have loved to live in Cuba, but he just couldn't bear the awful internet connection!
11. "La riqueza del subsuelo, las aguas territoriales, los colores de la bandera, la soberanía nacional, los partidos tradicionales, los derechos del hombre, las libertades ciudadanas, el primer magistrado, la segunda instancia, el tercer debate, las cartas de recomendación, las constancias históricas, las elecciones libres, las reinas de la belleza, los discursos trascendentales, las grandiosas manifestaciones, las distinguidas señoritas, los correctos caballeros, los pundonorosos militares, su señoría ilustrísima, la corte suprema de justicia, los artículos de prohibida importación, las damas liberales, el problema de la carne, la pureza del lenguaje, los ejemplos para el mundo, el orden jurídico, la prensa libre pero responsable, la Atenas sudamericana, la opinión pública, las lecciones democráticas, la moral

cristiana, la escasez de divisas, el derecho de asilo, el peligro comunista, la nave del estado, la carestía de la vida, las tradiciones republicanas, las clases desfavorecidas, los mensajes de adhesión" (*Los funerales* 137).

12. It should be noted that, despite his at times outspoken public pronouncements, García Márquez had a shy and extremely private nature; see Williams 154.

13. Other works that formed part of this archive include *El olor de la guayaba: Conversaciones con Plinio Apuleyo Mendoza* (1982); Óscar Collazos, *García Márquez: La soledad y la gloria–su vida y su obra* (1983); Stephen Minta, *Gabriel García Márquez: Writer of Colombia* (1987); Gene H. Bell-Villada, *García Márquez: The Man and His Work* (1990); Dasso Saldívar, *García Márquez: El viaje a la semilla; la biografía* (1997); Jorge García Ustá, *García Márquez en Cartagena: Sus inicios literarios* (2007); Silvia Galvis, *Los García Márquez* (2007); Ilan Stavans, *Gabriel García Márquez: The Early Years* (2010); Philip Swanson, editor, *The Cambridge Companion to Gabriel García Márquez* (2010); and Raymond Leslie Williams, *A Companion to Gabriel García Márquez* (2010).

14. As the note preceding "La noche del eclipse"—which is also included in French translation—suggests: "Este cuento es el tercero de seis, en los que Gabriel García Márquez está trabajando desde hace varios años durante las pausas de sus memorias. Cada uno de ellos podrá leerse en cualquier orden como un relato independiente. Los seis se publicarán junto en un solo volumen cuando estén terminados, y podrán leerse en orden desde el principio hasta el fin, con la continuidad dramática de una novela, y con su título general: *En agosto nos vemos*." The other texts that are included in the same folder, however, are not—as one might have expected—some of the other literary texts that García Márquez was putting together for the composite *En agosto nos vemos*; instead they are either letters or short commissioned journalistic pieces. It is likely, therefore, that *En agosto nos vemos* was only one-third written when Gabo passed away ("Nos vemos en agosto" plus "La noche del eclipse"), and it is unlikely that the other four short stories needed for the six-story format were completed, or indeed, even started.

Works Cited

Anonymous. "García Márquez Publishes Book, Finishes New Novel." *Naharnet*, 29 Oct. 2010, www.naharnet.com/stories/en/721. Accessed 21 Mar. 2020.

Associated Press. "García Márquez's Signed Masterpiece Stolen from Colombian Book Fair." *The Guardian*, 5 May 2015, www.theguardian.com/books/2015/may/05/garcia-marquezs-signed-masterpiece-stolen-from-colombian-book-fair. Accessed 21 Mar. 2020.

Backsheider, Paul R. *Reflections on Biography*. Oxford, 1999.

Bada, Ricardo. "La ficción de la ficción." *Cuadernos Hispanoamericanos*, no. 633, Mar. 2003, pp. 122–26.

Bell-Villada, Gene. "Gabriel García Márquez: Life and Times." *The Cambridge Companion to Gabriel García Márquez*, edited by Philip Swanson, Cambridge, 2010, pp. 7–24.

Bell-Villada, Gene. *García Márquez: The Man and His Work*. U of North Carolina Press, 1990.

Bell-Villada, Gene. "Introduction: García Márquez: His Vast Range, His Varied Legacy." *Gabriel García Márquez in Retrospect: A Collection*, edited by Gene H. Bell-Villada, Lexington Books, 2016, pp. xi–xxvii.

Bell-Villada, Gene H., editor. *Gabriel García Márquez in Retrospect: A Collection*. Lexington Books, 2016.

Collazos, Óscar. *García Márquez: La soledad y la gloria—su vida y su obra*. Plaza y Janés, 1983.

"Colombia Police Recover García Márquez First Edition." *BBC News*, 9 May 2015, www.bbc.co.uk/news/world-latin-america-32670588. Accessed 21 Mar. 2020.

"First Exhibition of Gabriel García Márquez Archive Opens Feb 1," *UT News*, 27 Jan. 2020, news.utexas.edu/2020/01/27/first-exhibition-of-gabriel-garcia-marquez-archive-opens-feb-1/. Accessed 21 Mar. 2020.

Flood, Alison. "Gabriel García Márquez: New Extract Hints at Writer's 'Last Legacy.'" *The Guardian*, 23 Apr. 2014, www.theguardian.com/books/2014/apr/23/gabriel-garcia-marquez-new-extract-legacy. Accessed 21 Mar. 2020.

"Gabriel García Márquez." *The Times*, 18 Apr. 2014, www.thetimes.co.uk/article/gabriel-garcia-marquez-n9d50vtv36x. Accessed 21 Mar. 2020.

Galvis, Silvia. *Los García Márquez*. Arango, 2007.

García Márquez, Gabriel. "Big Mama's Funeral." *No One Writes to the Colonel: Big Mama's Funeral*, Picador, 1979, pp. 153–70.

García Márquez, Gabriel. *Cien años de soledad*. Argos Vergara, 1980.

García Márquez, Gabriel. *El amor en los tiempos del cólera*. Oveja Negra, 2003.

García Márquez, Gabriel. *El olor de la guayaba: Conversaciones con Plinio Apuleyo Mendoza*. Planeta, 1982.

García Márquez, Gabriel. *Living to Tell the Tale*. Translated by Edith Grossman, Jonathan Cape, 2003.

García Márquez, Gabriel. *Los funerales de la Mamá Grande*. Sudamericana, 1977.

García Márquez, Gabriel. *Love in the Time of Cholera*. Translated by Edith Grossman, Penguin, 1989.

García Márquez, Gabriel. *One Hundred Years of Solitude*. Translated by Gregory Rabassa, Picador, 1978.

García Márquez, Gabriel. *Vivir para contarla*. Mondadori, 2002.

García Ustá, Jorge. *García Márquez en Cartagena: Sus inicios literarios*. Planeta, 2007.

Guardian staff and AP. "Netflix to Adapt One Hundred Years of Solitude by Gabriel García Márquez." *The Guardian*, 6 Mar. 2019, www.theguardian.com/books/2019/mar/07/netflix-to-adapt-one-hundred-years-of-solitude-by-gabriel-garcia-marquez#maincontent. Accessed 21 Mar. 2020.

Hart, Stephen M. *Gabriel García Márquez*. Reaktion, 2010.

Hart, Stephen M. *Gabriel García Márquez*. Translated into Spanish by Nadia Stagnaro. Cátedra Vallejo, 2016.

Holmes, Richard. "The Proper Study?" *Mapping Lives: The Uses of Biography*, edited by Peter Frane and William St. Clair, Oxford / The British Academy, 2002, pp. 7–18.

"Kidnapped Relative of Writer Gabriel García Márquez Freed." *AP News*, 17 Dec. 2018, apnews.com/827b2621a8f84063a503128da23f08b3.

Kristal, Efraín. "Lessons from the Golden Age in Gabriel García Márquez's *Living to Tell the Tale*." *A Companion to Magical Realism*, edited by Stephen M. Hart and Wen-chin Ouyang, Tamesis, 2005, pp. 88–97.

Martin, Gerald. *Gabriel García Márquez: A Life*. Bloomsbury, 2008.

Minta, Stephen. *Gabriel García Márquez: Writer of Colombia*. Jonathan Cape, 1987.

Ohlheiser, Abby. "What Will Happen to Gabriel García Márquez's Final Unpublished Manuscript?" *The Atlantic*, 22 Apr. 2014, www.theatlantic.com/culture/archive/2014/04/what-will-happen-to-gabriel-garcia-marquezs-final-unpublished-manuscript/361068/. Accessed 21 Mar. 2020.

Richardson, Lance. "An Exhibition on Gabriel García Márquez's Long Road to Becoming a Writer." *Literary Hub*, 6 Apr. 2020, lithub.com/an-exhibition-on-gabriel-garcia-marquezs-long-road-to-becoming-a-writer/. Accessed 21 Mar. 2020.

Saldívar, Dasso. *Garcia Márquez: El viaje a la semilla; la biografía*. Santillana, 1997.
Stavans, Ilan. *Gabriel García Márquez: The Early Years*. Palgrave-Macmillan, 2010.
Swanson, Philip, editor. *The Cambridge Companion to Gabriel García Márquez*. Cambridge, 2010.
Telegraph reporters. "Colombian Kidnappers Demand Ransom for García Márquez Relative." *The Telegraph*, 31 Oct. 2018, www.telegraph.co.uk/news/2018/10/31/colombian-kidnappers-demand-ransom-garcia-marquez-relative/. Accessed 21 Mar. 2020.
Tremlett, Giles. "Magical and Real: García Márquez Is Writing New Novel, Says Friend," *The Guardian*, 10 Dec. 2008, International section, p. 23.
Vanguardia staff. "La obra inacabada de Gabo." *La Vanguardia*, 20 Apr. 2014, www.lavanguardia.com/cultura/20140420/54405144781/gabo-en-agosto-nos-vemos.html. Accessed 21 Mar. 2020.
Williams, Raymond Leslie. *A Companion to Gabriel García Márquez*. Tamesis, 2010.
Wilson, Jason. "Review, Gabriel García Márquez: A Life, by Gerald Martin." *The Independent*, 24 Oct. 2008, www.independent.co.uk/arts-entertainment/books/reviews/gabriel-garc237a-m225rquez-a-life-by-gerald-martin-5358667.html. Accessed 21 Mar. 2020.

CHAPTER 2

GARCÍA MÁRQUEZ AND MAGICAL REALISM

WENDY B. FARIS

THIS article focuses on why Gabriel García Márquez's novel *One Hundred Years of Solitude* is the ur-magical realist novel, which put magical realism on the world literary map and has inspired its continued global flowering. Homi Bhabha's statement that "'magical realism' after the Latin American Boom, becomes the literary language of the emergent post-colonial world" confirms the prominence of this literary mode in contemporary world fiction, despite the fact that several other writers, including Asturias, Borges, Rulfo, and others, can be seen to have used it somewhat earlier (Bhabha 7). However, during the nearly thirty years since Bhabha's statement, magical realism has continued to flourish and has spread beyond the postcolonial arena to encompass Global North fiction (think of Toni Morrison's *Beloved* or Haruki Murakami's recent *1Q84*), and film (including *The Witches of Eastwick*, *Field of Dreams*, *Ironweed*, *Wolf*, *Thinner*, and, more recently, *Melancholia*, *Beasts of the Southern Wild*, and others), suggesting that García Márquez's text, and magical realism in general, have revitalized all narrative.[1]

As Gene Bell-Villada points out, corroborating John Barth's idea of exhausted and replenished literature, in 1967, fiction in the First World was undergoing something of a crisis, with fears for the death of the novel, and hence was ripe for innovation, provided by *One Hundred Years* (Bell-Villada, *García Márquez*, 7–11, 286–90).[2] Recall also that looking backward at precursors of magical realism—both recent ones such as Günter Grass's *The Tin Drum*, and ancient ones, including *The Odyssey*, and the novels of chivalry cited by García Márquez himself as influential—the mode also predates postcolonial times. What's more, then, from that perspective we might speculate that perhaps *One Hundred Years* partakes of the historically retrospective impulse attributed by Borges to Kafka: that writers create their own precursors and expand it to genre. In other words, once we know about magical realism, it shines backward to illuminate a swath of narratives that span actual and imaginary worlds. Now is an appropriate moment to take stock of *One Hundred Years of Solitude*'s power, since magical realism continues its worldwide growth, despite frequent criticisms of it as politically evasive and commodifying of marginalized cultures. I disagree with Carlos Fuentes's statement (in the 1970s) that magical realism has "been applied indiscriminately as a label to too many Hispanic American novelists, although truly it became the personal stamp of only one: Gabriel García Márquez," but it can serve to confirm the centrality of Márquez's text to the genre (Fuentes 24).

To investigate the idea that *One Hundred Years* has served as a replenishment of international narrative will enable us to discover its essential characteristics, its lasting appeal, and its salient achievement, challenging the dominant tradition of realism in fiction. While they are often intertwined, such characteristics fall under two basic rubrics: literary style—including magical images presented in meticulous detail as real, the use of hyperbole, and distortions of chronological time—and cultural work—integration of ancient indigenous and contemporary culture, communal narrative, and decolonization, among others.

Literary Style

John Barth's enthusiasm often stands for the many testimonials to the enlivening effect of *One Hundred Years*' magical realism, an essential ingredient of which, according to Barth, is the liberating force of its extreme variety and its conjunction of opposites: "the synthesis of straightforwardness and artifice, realism and magic and myth, political passion and non-political artistry, characterization and caricature, humor and terror" (65). Emphasizing a temporal dimension of the text's general style, Raymond Federman reported that he read the novel as if it were written in the conditional tense, even if it were not, because the conditional emanated a sense of possibility, replenishment, and inventiveness; for him, García Márquez was among the writers "who are reinventing the world for us, showing us new possibilities, possibilities that anything can happen" (quoted in Hoffman 242).

In creating a sense of possibility and flexibility, magical realism in general and *One Hundred Years* in particular employ a number of techniques that facilitate the merging of different realms. But before investigating them, we should note what is perhaps García Márquez's most masterful—and influential—technique: the text's descriptions of the ordinary as extraordinary cause the reader to see the world anew, and its portraits of the magical as ordinary suggest that the reader envision alternative realities. This combination is often cited as typical of magical realism; according to Ann Hegerfeldt, "entertaining a completely matter-of-fact attitude towards fantastically implausible or impossible incidents on the one hand, magic realism on the other presents perfectly 'ordinary' reality in such a way that it appears incredible, marvelous, fantastic" (76). Following are a few examples. Upon encountering ice, "an enormous, transparent block with infinite internal needles in which the light of the sunset was broken up into colored stars," José Arcadio Buendía's "heart filled with fear and jubilation at the contact with mystery," and little Aureliano exclaims that "it's boiling" (*One Hundred Years* 25–26).³ Introducing magnets to Macondo, Melquíades goes "from house to house dragging two metal ingots and everybody was amazed to see pots, pans, and braziers tumble down from their places and beams crack from the desperation of nails and screws trying to emerge. . . . Things have a life of their own . . . it's simply a matter of waking up their souls" (*One Hundred Years* 11).⁴ Similarly amazing though real is the iodine circle Colonial Aureliano's doctor paints on his chest: " 'That was my masterpiece,' he said with satisfaction. 'It was the only point where a bullet could pass through without harming any vital organ' " (*One Hundred Years* 171).⁵ In the metaphorical domain, after reading Úrsula's simile of a train as "something frightful, like a kitchen dragging a village behind it," or the narrator's description of movies, in which "the character who had died and was buried in one film and for whose misfortune tears of affliction had been shed would reappear alive and transformed into an Arab in the next one," we can never see these ordinary phenomena in quite the same way again, becoming virtual citizens of Macondo, where "no one knew for certain where the limits of reality lay. It was an intricate stew of truths and mirages" (*One Hundred Years* 210–12).⁶

In a complementary technique to that sense of wonderment at the amazing nature of reality, the magical is frequently presented without narrative comment as real. Ghosts like Melquíades wander the town, the character of Gabriel is "disturbed by the noise of the dead people who walked through the bedrooms [of Aureliano Babilonia's house] until dawn," and at one point "the only thing that was still visible was the ghost of José Arcadio Buendía under the chestnut tree" (*One Hundred Years* 359, 257).⁷ At another the "new gypsies" bring "parrots painted all colors reciting Italian arias, and a hen who laid a hundred golden eggs to the sound of a tambourine, and a trained monkey who read minds, and the multiple-use machine that could be used at the same time to sew on buttons and reduce fevers" (*One Hundred Years* 24).⁸ Similarly, after drinking a cup of hot chocolate, extending his arms, and closing his eyes, "Father Nicanor rose six inches above the level of the ground" (*One Hundred Years* 86).⁹ Rather differently from that frequent brevity of explanation, in some instances the more realistic details an impossible event accumulates, the more magical it appears. The meticulously detailed description of the stream of blood (emanating from José Arcadio's house)—including the particulars of how it negotiates different levels in the streets—together with the name of the street and the exact number of eggs Úrsula is about to crack, as well as ordinary activities like the arithmetic lesson, and perhaps most amazing of all, the implied mental functioning that causes the blood to avoid staining rugs (!): all help make the unrealistically behaving blood real to us, and hence join different realms, such as a world in which blood behaves normally and one in which it has magical properties, weaving a textual connection between the world of the living and that of the dead, because the blood starts in death and then participates in everyday life:

> A trickle of blood came out under the door, crossed the living room, went out into the street, continued on in a straight line across the uneven terraces, went down steps and climbed over curbs, passed along the Street of the Turks, turned a corner to the

right and another to the left, made a right angle at the Buendía house, went in under the closed door, crossed through the parlor, hugging the walls so as not to stain the rugs, went on to the other living room, made a wide curve to avoid the dining-room table, went along the porch with the begonias, and passed without being seen under Amaranta's chair as she gave an arithmetic lesson to Aureliano José, and went through the pantry and came out in the kitchen, where Úrsula was getting ready to crack thirty-six eggs to make bread. (*One Hundred Years* 129–30)[10]

In similar fashion, we hear so many details about the impossible insomnia plague that it too becomes virtually real. In both cases, the magic also encourages particular interpretations. The blood trail between son and mother emphasizes the strong ties within families, the insomnia plague suggests the importance of rest in an overly busy world, and the labels affixed to objects during the loss of memory associated with the insomnia (because people have forgotten their names) suggest the arbitrary nature of language. As Hegerfeldt points out, this duo of contrasting strategies (the real described as so amazing as to seem magical, and the magical described in realistic detail) suggests that "the perception of 'reality' actually depends on pre-existing categories" (77). Furthermore, it erodes our habitual distinctions between the actual and the imagined.

Another technique that facilitates the merging of different realms is that magical realist texts often contain a spectrum of events ranging from the improbable to the impossible, providing, one might almost say, a kind of narrative road readers can travel between them. The number of flowers that fall on the town and smother the animals before José Arcadio Buendía's funeral is improbable but believably real; somewhat less so is the fact that José Arcadio Buendía lives for so many years tied to the tree in the courtyard. Yet what about the report that "during his prolonged stay under the chestnut tree he had developed the faculty of being able to increase his weight at will," or the child born with the tail of a pig at the end of the novel, or the "supernatural proliferation" of Aureliano Segundo's animals (*One Hundred Years* 136, 181)?[11] We have just seen the magical end of the spectrum in the blood trail and Father Nicanor's levitation, and there are many more, like the pot that moves from the center to spill over the table, people riding on "magic" carpets, and Melquíades returning from the dead. Thus from within the text that spectrum joins realistic and fantastic narrative. Enhancing the text's ontological flexibility, its merging of different worlds, is the often idiosyncratic and innovative treatment of time and space. Thus the novel exemplifies a central feature of all magical realism, the disruption of clear temporal and spatial boundaries.

To begin with the temporal scrambling, Melquíades is a primary figure. By the end, we realize that the novel is actually "the history of the family, written by Melquíades, down to the most trivial details, one hundred years ahead of time." It is so ingeniously constructed that "he had concentrated a century of daily episodes in such a way that they coexisted in one instant," mixing up linear and eternal time (*One Hundred Years* 381–82).[12] Elsewhere, Melquíades links normally separate times and spaces, at one point changing from a decrepit old man into his younger self by removing and then replacing his false teeth; at another, his "invisible presence" "continued his stealthy shuffling through the rooms" of the house even after his death (*One Hundred Years* 17, 77).[13]

More generally, the repetition of events and character types (to say nothing of names), together with a number of images regarding time, disrupts our habitual sense of progression and creates a sense of circular rather than chronological time. Úrsula repeatedly expresses that idea, further emphasizing time's circularity, confirming "her impression that time was going in a circle"; "'it's as if the world were repeating itself'"; "'I know all of this by heart,' Úrsula would shout. 'It's as if time had turned around and we were back at the beginning'" (*One Hundred Years* 209, 276, 185).[14] Note how she repeats this idea with virtually the same words, reinforcing the idea textually and almost seeming to enact temporal reversals. Appropriately, then, near her death, "she looked like a newborn old woman" (*One Hundred Years* 315)[15]. Melquíades dies twice and then finds immortality; Aureliano makes his little goldfish repeatedly. Over and over again, characters repeat events from their own or others' lives. On seeing a fleeting vision of her mother, Petra Cotes "felt it was exactly like her, as if she had seen herself twenty years in advance" (*One Hundred Years* 195).[16] Such ubiquitous temporal scrambling keeps readers in a temporally flexible state of mind, open to alternative experiences of time and history, especially to the presence of the past in the present, often cited as a Latin American cultural phenomenon. Furthermore, additional textual repetitions such as the same phrase regarding José Arcadio Buendía taking little Aureliano to see ice, Rebeca's eating earth, and Melquíades's room in which it is always March and always Monday, repeatedly reinforce the sense of temporal circularity and stasis while also textually marking time, charting its passage in the novel, and hence not entirely abolishing all temporal progression. Likewise, the circularity of repetitions, together with the presence of historical events like the discovery of Spanish galleons or the arrival of American fruit companies, means that the novel's symbolic temporal structure resembles neither a circle nor a line but rather a corkscrew, a magical kind of time that both remains and progresses.

This temporal fluidity extends to verbal style as well. According to a brilliant early study by Marta Gallo, the incidence of the future perfect tense ("había de"—"was to"— plus an infinitive) occurs fourteen times more often in *One Hundred Years* than in ordinary speech. It creates a sense of end-stopped progression, a free space within the past in which possibility still exists, but also one in which future action always turns toward the past. In such a flexible narrative space, where ordinary forward-moving chronology needn't apply, "simultaneities, anteriorities, and posteriorities are mixed up" (115).[17] Similarly contributing to the temporal scrambling of chronological time, narrative analepses, in which a past event disrupts a current narrative account (in the midst of the account of Meme Buendía's behavior, "on the night that Fernanda visited [Aureliano Segundo and Meme] in the movies"—which we have witnessed several pages earlier— "Aureliano Segundo felt weighted down by the burden of his conscience and he visited Meme in the bedroom where Fernanda kept her locked up"), and prolepses, in which a future event disrupts a current narrative account (the chapter that narrates the banana company strike and massacre begins thus: "The events that would deal Macondo its fatal blow were just showing themselves when they brought Meme Buendía's son home"), abound (*One Hundred Years* 270, 272).[18]

Such a textual temporal space, according to Gallo, resembles the seemingly miraculous ice that Colonel Aureliano recalls being taken to see in the first sentence of the novel with its future perfect prolepsis: "Many years later, . . . Colonel Aureliano Buendía *was to remember* that distant afternoon when his father took him to discover ice"[19] (Gallo's emphasis). Within such a temporally congealed space we experience—among other phenomena—the impossible longevity of Úrsula and José Arcadio Buendía, as well as Melquíades's room—where it "was always March there and always Monday" (*One Hundred Years* 322).[20] Finally, we must not forget the textual whirl at end of the novel, in which the reader feels enveloped in a temporally telescoping whirlwind that begins amid "the murmurs of ancient geraniums" and that will sweep her away along with the world and the text that she has been reading. There, repetition seems to be destroyed by history, since "races condemned to one hundred years of solitude did not have a second opportunity on earth," which continues on without us, and yet we are reading this, so repetitions will still exist despite the text's assertion of the contrary (*One Hundred Years* 382–83).[21]

García Márquez's treatment of space is also fluid, though slightly less so than that of time, perhaps because of its specific visuality and the novel's location in the particular space of Macondo. Nevertheless, images occasionally merge different spaces, such as when Rebeca's bag of bones is first literally immured in the Buendía house and subsequently discovered and unearthed thanks to its "*cloc-cloc*" sound; when, after Amaranta's death, Macondo's inhabitants give her letters to take to the realm of the dead; or when Melquíades "marked" Macondo "with a small black dot on the motley maps of death," merging the realms of life and death (*One Hundred Years* 79–80).[22] Similarly merging spaces (and times as well) are experienced by Rebeca "in that house where memories materialized through the strength of implacable evocation and walked like human beings through the cloistered rooms" (*One Hundred Years* 152).[23] On a larger scale, space is confusingly scrambled as José Arcadio Buendía and his compatriots search for the sea, at one point unable to return whence they came because "the strip that they were opening as they went along would soon close up with a new vegetation that almost seemed to grow before their eyes."[24] And coming upon an "enormous Spanish galleon . . . adorned with orchids," whose hull, "covered with an armor of petrified barnacles and soft moss, was firmly fastened into a surface of stones," he wonders "how the galleon had been able to get inland to that spot." The galleon and its surroundings project a confusing sense of spatial entrapment and isolation: "[T]he whole structure seemed to occupy its own space, one of solitude and oblivion, protected from the vices of time and habits of the birds" (*One Hundred Years* 20–21).[25]

In the end, whether temporally or spatially oriented, we experience the transformative nature of Garciamarquezian descriptions. They are tied to the real but enlarged by the imaginary. Before hearing their father's metaphor that "light is like water [in the short story of that name], ... you turn on the tap and out it comes," we see his children and their schoolmates flip on the light switch and then navigate at will in the "jet of golden light as cool as water" ("Light" 158). In achieving such a transformation, language seems to play the part assigned it in another metaphor of linguistic empowerment joining the magical and the ordinary in the same story: "[H]ousehold objects, in the fullness of their poetry, flew with their own wings through the kitchen sky" ("Light" 160).[26]

As we have been witnessing in these temporally and spatially overblown and intermingled images, hyperbole, or exaggeration of various kinds is frequent in *One Hundred Years* (as in much magical realism) and contributes to the text's general ebullience, its air of replenishment and creative power.[27] Reality is expanded. Both the natural and the human are enlarged; neither dwarfs the other. Whether it be physical size (José Arcadio's penis is so big he carries it around in a basket) or numerosity ("it rained for four years, eleven months, and two days")—Pilar Ternera stops keeping track of her age at 145; Fernanda finds in her bedroom "so many butterflies that she could scarcely breathe"; and the "supernatural proliferation" of Aureliano Segundo's animals means that "his mares would bear triplets, his hens laid twice a day, and his hogs fattened with such speed that no one could explain such disorderly fecundity except through the use of black magic" (*One Hundred Years* 291, 363, 271, 181)—or exaggerated activities (maniacal warmongering, fanatical housekeeping, manufacturing of hundreds of goldfish or cookies), the numbers are higher than usual, and repeatedly so.[28]

Emotions also run consistently high, often confronting each other, so that the effect is increased: Pietro Crespi kills himself after Amaranta refuses him by saying "I wouldn't marry you even if I were dead" (*One Hundred Years* 109); Colonel Aureliano forbids anyone to come within a ten-foot circle drawn around him; but Úrsula penetrates that circle of solitude and tells him that as soon as she sees the dead body of Gerineldo Márquez, whom Colonel Aureliano plans to execute, "'I will drag you out from wherever you're hiding and kill you with my own two hands,'" with the result that Colonel Aureliano reconsiders and returns to fighting the war (*One Hundred Years* 163).[29] Smaller examples of a generally hyperbolic style pervade the text on virtually every page; we have Amaranta's "measureless love" contrasting with her "invincible cowardice," and Rebeca's "fierce womb" side by side with her "unbridled courage (*One Hundred Years* 234).[30] In contrast to minimalism, the volume and pervasiveness of hyperbole provide a sense of empowerment, imaginative freedom, and expansiveness, characteristics that readers experience positively, despite particular dire events. Paradoxically, we see terrible things happen but are not depressed by them.

Further contributing to the text's general sense of wonder, of the ordinary extending toward the extraordinary, is that it abounds in the nonsystematic and the unexpected, a feature that suggests freedom from constraints and lack of control.[31] Colonel Aureliano seems especially prone to this phenomenon: "[H]is efforts to systematize his premonitions were useless.... On occasion they were so natural that he identified them as premonitions only after they had been fulfilled" (*One Hundred Years* 124).[32] More particularly, over and over again, people try for one thing and end up with another. In the case of Aureliano Segundo and Petra Cotes, "in search of interest he found love, because by trying to make her love him he ended up falling in love with her"; on her return from searching for José Arcadio Buendía after he has left with the gypsies, "Úrsula had not caught up with the gypsies, but she had found the route that her husband had been unable to discover in his frustrated search for the great inventions" (*One Hundred Years* 313, 43).[33] Furthermore, and similarly disruptive of the routine and expected, is that paradoxes abound, perhaps the most central being the simultaneous presence of unifying sexual passion and separating solitude; the text is filled with passionate embraces that often seem to enhance each partner's and the couple's solitude. Petra Cotes and Aureliano Segundo "find the paradise of shared solitude" (*One Hundred Years* 313).[34] Here are Mauricio Babilonia and Meme Buendía: "[S]he lost her mind over him. She could not sleep and she lost her appetite and sank so deeply into solitude that even her father became an annoyance"; here Aureliano and Amaranta Úrsula, who are "secluded by solitude and love and by the solitude of love" (*One Hundred Years* 269, 371).[35]

Finally, with respect to style, it is a simple point, but true, that *One Hundred Years* astounds readers and inspires its descendant texts through the sheer richness of detail and ebullience of prose that piles on such details. Not the least of this general ebullience are enthralling moments, whether of magic or simply extraordinariness, which often proliferate in details that overstep their rationally descriptive qualities, telling us far more than we need to know, delighting in myriad details (as we have seen with the blood trail)—just the opposite of the realistic master Flaubert's advocacy of the mot juste—the one right word for a narrative occasion—and thus forging a post-realist style, one that engenders a sense of delighted surprise in its readers. Such proliferation is baroque, outrageously rich, not efficient. It contributes a new element to the general verbal vim and vigor of the narrative, similar to the verbal liveliness that Joyce's example infused into many Boom (and slightly earlier) writers. Recall the descriptions of the wonders brought by the gypsies, like the magnets that make "pots, pans tongs, and braziers tumble down from their places and beams crack from the desperation of nails and screws trying to emerge"; Nigromanta with "the hips of a mare, teats like live melons, and a round and perfect head armored with a hard surface of wiry hair which looked like a medieval warrior's mail headdress"; or the "traffic" of the numerous dead recalled by the last Buendías: "Úrsula fighting against the laws of creation to maintain the line, and José Arcadio Buendía searching for the mythical truth of the great inventions, and Fernanda praying, and Colonial Aureliano Buendía stupefying himself with the deception of war and the little gold fishes, and Aureliano Segundo dying of solitude in the turmoil of his debauches" (*One Hundred Years* 11, 3, 54, 378).[36] And often the magical and multifarious descriptions seem rather gratuitous, increasing the generalized sense of wonder rather than accurately documenting reality, a characteristic made explicit here: "[E]ven when they brought the ice they did not advertise it for its usefulness in the life of man but as a simple circus curiosity. This time, along with many other artifices, they brought a magic carpet. But they did not offer it as a fundamental contribution to the development of transport, rather as an object of recreation" (*One Hundred Years* 38).[37]

Cultural Work

Latin American magical realism grew from a complex cultural dynamics of European realism, surrealism, and indigeneity. Latin American writers (including Alejo Carpentier, Julio Cortázar, and García Márquez) were glad to see their cultures being appreciated and idealized in Europe and then also wanted to "reterritorialize" the mode, showing it to be an integral growth of indigenous and hybrid Latin American nature and cultures, rather than an artificial construction of opposites (like the surrealist conjunction of an umbrella and a sewing machine on a dissecting table).[38] That same cultural amalgam characterizes other regions of magical realist writing, such as Salman Rushdie's India, Haruki Murakami's Japan, and elsewhere.

In the realm of cultural work, then, stemming from local coloristic narratives, the valorization of New World nature and of indigenous and hybrid cultures attaches texts to their locales as it were, decentering textual authority from abroad. Early on in *One Hundred Years*, the care of the Buendía children is given over to Visitación, "a Guajiro Indian woman who," with her brother, is "so docile and willing to help that Úrsula took them on to help her with her household chores," with the result that "Arcadio and Amaranta came to speak the Guajiro language before Spanish, and they learned to drink lizard broth and eat spider eggs without Ursula's knowing it," facts that fascinate us and deconstruct a colonial environment, as do the proliferating animals in Petra Cotes's house or the powerfully commanding Teófilo Vargas, "a full-blooded Indian, untamed, illiterate, and endowed with quiet wiles and a messianic vocation that aroused a demented fanaticism in his men" (*One Hundred Years* 44, 161).[39] Similarly, tropical American nature provides the intriguing "light rain of tiny yellow flowers falling . . . all through the night in a silent storm, and they covered the roofs and blocked the doors and smothered the animals who slept outdoors" following José Arcadio Buendía's death, and the "four years, eleven months, and two days" of rain that together with its accompanying storms and hurricanes "uprooted every last plant of the banana groves" (*One Hundred Years* 137, 291).[40] We welcome such overturning of harmful colonial culture by nature and dislike the banana company's exploitative practices that change soil and climate, disrupting the formerly harmonious relationship of Macondoans to their land.[41] Similarly, even though it is horrific in a way, a certain celebratory tone pervades the final description of Aureliano and Amaranta Úrsula's whirlwind of passion, during which she "was singing with pleasure and dying with laughter over her own inventions," because it can be seen to sound a warning against human domination of nature (*One Hundred Years* 373).[42] In their atavistic dwelling in which nature devoured culture, with "red ants devastating the garden" and the couple themselves "roll[ing] around in the mud of the courtyard," they "were the only happy beings, and the most happy on the face of the earth" (*One Hundred Years* 291, 371–72).[43] Similarly joyful in a primitivist vein that celebrates proliferating tropical nature is Pilar Ternera's "zoological brothel," with its "large Amazonian camellias," its "herons of different colors, crocodiles as fat as pigs, snakes with twelve rattles, and a turtle with a golden shell who dove in a small artificial ocean.... The atmosphere had an innocent denseness, as if it had just been created," where visitors "felt that time was turning back to its earliest origins"—both invigorating and frightening (*One Hundred Years* 363).[44]

The frequent syncretism resulting from such cultural contact zones in the novel as Rebeca's, Melquíades's, or Gaston's entry into Macondo means that it served to inspire later magical realist border writing and liminality, especially in Latino/a texts, such as Ana Castillo's *So Far from God* and Cristina García's *Dreaming in Cuban*, or texts that play between indigenous and mainstream or other proximate cultures, such as John Nichols's *The Milagro Beanfield War*, Louise Erdrich's *Tracks*, and (in Canada) Robert Kroetsch's *What the Crow Said*, in addition to those of Latin American and postcolonial writers such as Isabel Allende, André Schwartz-Bart, Rushdie, Ben Okri, Wilson Harris, and Toni Morrison.

Such border crossings can be seen as a cultural equivalent of the permeability of times and spaces that I noted earlier in discussing the general temporal and spatial fluidity in *One Hundred Years*. Borders and liminal spaces do play a role in *One Hundred Years*, but less so than in the texts of these successors, because the novel is located in Macondo, which is for the most part a microcosm of both Colombia and Latin America; more than different countries or separate cultures, its liminal spaces are different regions that touch each other and between which characters pass: jungle and village; ocean, "great swamp," and land; indigenous cultures and colonial town; realms of the living and the dead (*One Hundred Years* 19).[45] Close to Macondo is an "enchanted region where [Colonel Aureliano's] father found the fossil of a Spanish galleon" containing "bloody lilies and golden salamanders" (*One Hundred Years* 141, 20).[46] Fernanda takes her daughter Meme back to her own birthplace, which is described as a different realm belonging to the past, a "gloomy city in whose stone alleys the funeral bells of thirty-two churches tolled" (*One Hundred Years* 274) and then returns by train to Macondo, joining those different spaces.[47] Mr. Brown and his gringos "built a separate town across the railroad tracks with streets lined with palm trees, houses with screened windows" (*One Hundred Years* 215).[48] But it is not entirely isolated; such proximity of different regions often produces hybrid phenomena, like Meme's eating "Virginia ham with slices of pineapple," the town's catching the insomnia plague from Rebeca, or a parade containing a diverse mixture of foreigners and animals whose provenance seems uncertain: "a woman dressed in gold sitting on the head of an elephant. He saw a sad dromedary. He saw a bear dressed like a Dutch girl keeping time to the music" (*One Hundred Years* 256, 250).[49] As I have just suggested, such cultural liminality is reinforced at a textually subliminal level by stylistic strategies that merge different realms.

Consonant with such cultural amalgams, *One Hundred Years* is especially rich in a communal imperative, which in much magical realism often highlights group activities rather than focusing on individual ones—though not to their exclusion. Communal phenomena abound: during the insomnia plague, which is experienced by the entire town, "not only did they see the images of their own dreams, but some saw the images dreamed by others" (*One Hundred Years* 51).[50] Throughout the text, the Buendías endlessly repeat family traits, such as fanaticism of one kind or another (for making little goldfish, waging war, cleaning the house, or "the hereditary vice of making something just to unmake it"), a phenomenon further symbolized by the repetition of names through succeeding generations and emphasized by how often we read of it, so that the family itself becomes a kind of collective character (*One Hundred Years* 351).[51] Pilar Ternera reflects that "the history of the family was a machine with unavoidable repetitions" (*One Hundred Years* 364).[52] And again—and again: "With the fierce temerity with which José Arcadio Buendía had crossed the mountains to found Macondo, with the blind pride with which Colonel Aureliano Buendía had undertaken his fruitless wars, with the mad tenacity with which Úrsula watched over the survival of the line, Aureliano Segundo looked for Fernanda" (*One Hundred Years* 197).[53] As Lois Parkinson Zamora notes, one reason for that focus on the communal is that while we certainly see magical realist characters act, we often have no idea why they do what they do, often because they come from places other than our familiar environments; recall the "very old man with enormous wings" in García Márquez's story of that name, whose mode of hanging around in the old dirty chicken coop and then mysteriously departing mystifies the villagers he visits. They—and we—do not see him as an individualized and chronologically developing realistic character. And yet they—and we—are intrigued because in some odd and mysterious way he questions life-as-usual by seeming to represent an insubstantial individual who nevertheless carries a message from a different group (Parkinson Zamora, "Insubstantial Selves," 64–66). Furthermore, occasionally people seem to act as if taken over by forces outside themselves, their individualities obliterated by environments: Colonel Aureliano's "orders were being carried out even before they were given, even before he thought of them," and on meeting his illegitimate sons, "who looked at him with his own eyes, ... he felt scattered about, multiplied, and more solitary than ever" (*One Hundred Years* 161).[54] In a similar but differently inflected point, discussing Latin American film, and speculating that "to kill the subject off" "might be too great a luxury ... for those already marginalized by history," Doris Sommer postulates that "Latin American narrative is busy constructing multiple selves from the margins of postmodern cynicism" (94). Thus at the same time that it forges a communal ethos, magical realism also creates intriguing personalities, a perennial attraction of all fiction, achieving a rich amalgam of the individual and the communal.

Linked to the issue of communal realities is the presence of colonization and decolonization in the novel. Although, as I have been arguing, the continuing viability and present global importance of magical realism still growing out of *One Hundred Years* are due to its applicability *beyond* postcolonial situations, the novel appeared at a time in which its allegory of decolonization resonated powerfully across the decolonizing world. It was the most entertaining, inventive, and baroquely entrancing novel to cast a critical but simultaneously amusing and amused eye on colonization, and that critical and amused stance made it a novel about decolonization as well.[55] And contributing to that decolonizing power is the wealth and specificity of fascinating cultural details—what I have termed "grounding in the ground"—which serves as a kind of counterweight to textual strategies of defamiliarization that describe common items like mirrors or magnets as if they were newly discovered and hence unfamiliar, which makes them into marvels. Perhaps most importantly, then, that oscillation between actual and incredible creates a textual atmosphere that valorizes local culture at the same time that it promotes the imaginative freedom to move beyond it, thus encouraging both the cultural identity and the inventiveness of postcolonial writing, a combination essential to the strength and appeal of the text, both in Colombia and elsewhere, and a reason for its influence on postcolonial fiction.[56] Broadening our view to see how García Márquez's magical realism in *One Hundred Years*, together with its descendants across the globe, corresponds to a more general cultural trend, perhaps we can correlate that simultaneous valuing of local culture and imaginative freedom to move beyond it with Walter Mignolo's idea that "cosmopolitan localism has of necessity to operate on truth in parenthesis and border thinking—cosmopolitan localism means decolonial cosmopolitanism"—a decentered cosmopolitanism, in which an important genre like magical realism comes not from one of the "centers" of culture but from a region that is moving to construct a general cultural mix in which centers and peripheries are dissolving (294). More specifically, from a radical postcolonial perspective, we might consider the two modes of realism and magic, which meet dynamically in the text, in moments—among many others—when magnets pull nails from buildings; matriarchs live to be "between one hundred and fifteen and one hundred and twenty two"; or a mysterious human-animal hybrid with "scales of a remora fish," human parts resembling those of an angel, and "scarred-over and calloused stumps of powerful wings" appears, as an embodied textualization of the process of push and pull that characterizes decolonization itself (*One Hundred Years* 316, 317).[57]

Deeply embedded in both Colombian and Latin American and (in smaller proportion) world culture, then, García Márquez's magical realism stems from a wide variety of sources, including (as he has often stated) his own journalism, with his coverage of events such as the public assassination of a presidential candidate, which people just did not believe could happen—the real was unimaginable. Conversely, nonverifiable events such as the pot moving across the table, the flying carpets, Melquíades's return from the dead, and the blood trail traversing the streets presumably come from his grandmother's stories. Likewise, the inclusion of Catholic traditions, with their belief in nonactual phenomena, such as miracles in scriptures, also leads to presentation of the magical as real—as we have seen with descriptions of Padre Nicanor's levitation or Remedios's rising into the air with the sheets. Such incidents constitute the "faith-based" side of magical realism, which Christopher Warnes contrasts with its "irreverent" aspect, which questions the relationships of words to their referents and is "aware of its own artifice." This is a phenomenon emblematized in the Macondoan period, in which people have forgotten the names of things, so they have affixed labels to objects; the fact that the town's history has been written before the fact by Melquíades; and playful remarks about inspiration from other (sometimes sacred) texts. When Meme's son arrives at the Buendía house in a small basket on the arm of a nun, Fernanda declares: "'We'll tell them that we found him floating in the basket,' she said, smiling. / 'No one will believe it,' the nun said. / 'If they believe it in the Bible,' Fernanda replied, 'I don't see why they shouldn't believe it from me'" (Warnes 96; *One Hundred Years* 277).⁵⁸ Such a statement simultaneously incorporates and distances that sacred text from this secular one that, while not subscribing to any specific doctrine, nevertheless also contains nonverifiable events that loosely conjoin the two.

Therefore, somewhat paradoxically, a potent appeal of García Márquez's magical realism is its nondoctrinal, often even anticlerical stance in combination with the credulous aura that pervades the text, as a result of its small but potent doses of magic from various sources, including ancient beliefs and religious texts, which increase the generalized sense of wonder and marvel. This is a central way in which his text—and the many magical realist texts that continue to follow it—deconstruct the dominant paradigm of the realist novel and the positivist ideology it projects, making room for what I have called a "remystification" of narrative, a small quotient of nonmaterial spirituality within the dominant paradigm of materially based literary realism with its accurate descriptions of actual phenomena (Faris, *Ordinary Enchantments* 63–74). In that sense, it can be seen as corresponding to Franz Roh's early (1925) description of the neorealist European painting that follows expressionism, and which he termed magical realism: "[T]he point is not to discover the spirit beginning with objects but, on the contrary, to discover objects beginning with the spirit," in paintings in which realistically painted objects "nevertheless" exist in "a magic world," and "even the last little blade of grass can refer to the spirit" (Roh 24). Such a combination of factuality and wonder seems like "the reinvention of the world" (to echo the Canadian magical realist Jack Hodgins's novel of that name) for fiction, a revival of fascination with intriguingly odd reality rather than an exhaustion with its predictability.

More generally, the way that García Márquez recenters the world in Macondo, bringing paradigms of Latin American and world history there and playing with them in a nonempirical way, can be seen to decenter the Eurocentric colonial world. Mignolo posits that colonization happened at a moment when aspects of "secularization displaced God as the guarantors of knowledge, placing Man and Reason in God's stead, and centralized the ego" (15). In this context, it may be the case that (as mentioned previously) the festive and nonempirical texts of García Márquez and subsequent magical realists begin to weaken the individual ego in favor of community. Even more importantly, they begin to dismantle that secularism as guarantor of knowledge in favor of making room for small quotients of (if not God-given, then at least suggestive nonsecular) spirit associated (or not) with native cultures.

As we have seen, the verbal inventiveness, irreverence, and flexibility to encompass different realms, together with its valuation of indigenous culture, hybridity, and community, have made *One Hundred Years* the most praised and influential magical realist novel, spearheading this global genre.⁵⁹ And as such, the global continuation of its textual force has contributed to what Brian McHale (optimistically) calls our possible

> genuinely dialogic moment, when the cultures of the world regions exchange memes and models among themselves outside the center/periphery structure of either the old imperial colonialism or Western-centric cultural neocolonialism. We might

imagine these intra- and inter-regional cultural dialogues, not routed through Western metropolitan centers but occurring among the so-called "peripheries," as a series of calls and responses. (363)[60]

As it constitutes such a model, the novel thus both embodies and contributes to this contemporary decentering of literary culture.

Notes

1. For a discussion of numerous texts that reveal the complexities of magical realism as it provides a form for the integration of indigenous and colonist realities in the Pacific, confirming its continuing vitality, see the chapter by Birns on the later work of García Márquez.
2. See Bell-Villada's discussion of the world literary scene and of García Márquez's inheritors in the United States in *García Márquez: The Man and His Work*, final chapter.
3. "Un enorme bloque transparente, con infinitas agujas internas en las cuales se despedazaba en estrellas de colores la claridad del crepúsculo"; "el corazón se le hinchaba de temor y de júbilo al contacto del misterio"; "'está hirviendo,' exclamó asustado" (23).
4. "De casa en casa arrastrando dos lingotes metálicos, y todo el mundo se espantó al ver que los calderos, las pailas, las tenazas y los anafes se caían de su sitio, y las maderas crujían por la desesperación de los clavos y los tornillos tratando de desenclavarse. . . . 'Las cosas tienen vida propia . . . todo es questión de despertarles el ánima'" (9).
5. "'Esta es mi obra maestra,' le dijo satisfecho. 'Era el único punto por donde podía pasar una bala sin lastimar ningún centro vital'" (156).
6. "Un asunto espantoso como una cocina arrastrando un pueblo"; "un personaje muerto y sepultado en una película, y por cuya desgracia se derramaron lágrimas de aflicción, reapareció vivo y convertido en árabe en la película siguiente"; "ya nadie podía saber a ciencia cierta dónde estaban los límites de la realidad. Era un intrincado frangollo de verdades y espejismos" (192–95).
7. "Lo único que seguía siendo visible era el espectro de José Arcadio Buendía bajo el castaño"; "perturbado por el trasiego de los muertos que andaban hasta el amanecer por los dormitorios" (329; 235).
8. "Gitanos nuevos . . . loros pintados de todos los colores que recitaban romanzas italianas, y la gallina que ponía un centenar de huevos de oro al son de la pandereta, y el mono amaestrado que adivinaba el pensamiento, y la máquina múltiple que servía al mismo tiempo para pegar botones y bajar la fiebre" (21).
9. "El padre Nicanor se elevó doce centímetros sobre el nivel del suelo" (77).
10. "Un hilo de sangre salió por debajo de la puerta, atravesó la sala, salió a la calle, siguió en un curso directo por los andenes disparejos, descendió escalinatas y subió pretiles, pasó de largo por la Calle de los Turcos, dobló una esquina a la derecha y otra a la izquierda, volteó en ángulo recto frente a la casa de los Buendía, pasó por debajo de la puerta cerrada, atravesó la sala de visitas pegado a las paredes para no manchar los tapices, siguió por la otra sala, eludió en una curva amplia la mesa del comedor, avanzó por el corredor de las begonias y pasó sin ser visto por debajo de la silla de Amaranta que daba una lección de aritmética a Aureliano José, y se metió por el granero y apareció en la cocina donde Úrsula se disponía a partir treinta y seis huevos para el pan" (118).

11. "En su prolongada estancia bajo el castaño había desarrollado la facultad de aumentar de peso voluntariamente"; "proliferación sobrenatural" (123, 166).
12. "La historia de la familia, escrita por Melquíades hasta en sus detalles más triviales, con cien años de anticipación"; "concentró un siglo de episodios cotidianos, de modo que todos coexistieron en un instante" (349–50).
13. "La presencia"; "continuaba su deambular sigiloso por los cuartos" (70).
14. "Su impresión de que el tiempo estaba dando vueltas en redondo"; "es como si el mundo estuviera dando vueltas"; "'ya esto me lo sé de memoria,' gritaba Úrsula. 'Es como si el tiempo diera vueltas en redondo y hubiéramos vuelto al principio'" (192, 253, 169).
15. "Parecía una anciana recién nacida" (290).
16. "La sintió exactamente igual a ella, como si se hubiera visto a sí misma con veinte años de anticipación" (179).
17. "Simultaneidades, anterioridades y posterioridades temporales se confunden" (Gallo 115).
18. "La noche en que Fernanda los sorprendió en el cine, Aureliano Segundo se sintió agobiado por el peso de su conciencia, y visitó a Meme en el dormitorio donde la encerró Fernanda"; "Los acontecimientos que habían de darle el golpe mortal a Macondo empezaban a vislumbrarse cuando llevaron a la casa al hijo de Meme Buendía" (247, 249).
19. "Muchos años después, . . . el coronel Aureliano Buendía *había de recordar* aquella tarde remota en que su padre lo llevó a conocer el hielo" (*One Hundred Years* 11).
20. "Allí siempre era marzo y siempre era lunes" (296).
21. "Murmullos de geranios antiguos"; "las estirpes condenadas a cien años de soledad no tenían una segunda oportunidad sobre la tierra" (350–51).
22. "El cloc cloc"; "lo señaló con un puntito negro en los abigarrados mapas de la muerte" (79–80).
23. "En aquella casa donde los recuerdos se materializaban por la fuerza de la evocación implacable, y se paseaban como seres humanos por los cuartos clausurados" (139).
24. "La trocha que iban abriendo a su paso se volvía a cerrar en poco tiempo, con una vegetación nueva que casi veían crecer ante sus ojos" (17).
25. "Un enorme galeón español [cuyas jarcias estaban] adornadas de orquídeas"; "José Arcadio se preguntó cómo había podido el galeón adentrarse hasta ese punto en tierra firme"; su "casco, cubierto con una tersa coraza de remora petrificada y musgo tierno, estaba firmemente enclavado en un suelo de piedras. Toda la estructura parecía ocupar un ámbito propio, un espacio de soledad y de olvido, vedado a los vicios del tiempo y a las costumbres de los pájaros" (17–18).
26. "La luz es como el agua . . . uno abre el grifo, y sale"; "Un chorro de luz dorada y fresca como el agua"; "Los utensilios domésticos, en la plenitud de su poesía, volaban con sus propias alas por el cielo de la cocina" (147, 149).
27. For a discussion of this aspect of *One Hundred Years* and an extension of it toward painting, see Faris, "Larger Than Life."
28. "Llovió cuatro años, once meses y dos días"; "tantas mariposas que apenas se podía respirar"; "la proliferación sobrenatural de sus animales"; "sus yeguas parían trillizos, las gallinas ponían dos veces al día, y los cerdos engordaban con tal desenfreno, que nadie podía explicarse tan desordenada fecundidad como no fuera por artes de magia" (267; 333, 248, 166).
29. "Ni muerta me casaré contigo"; "te he de sacar de donde te metas y te mataré con mis propias manos" (98, 148).
30. "Un amor sin medidas"; "una cobardía invencible"; "la del vientre desaforado"; "la valentía sin frenos" (214–15).

31. Jerónimo Arellano places this aspect of *One Hundred Years* in the cultural history of marvels and their trajectories by tracing such sets of heterogeneous images in the novel back to the convention of the *"wunderkammer"* in early modern European history, with its disorderly display, both "producing assemblages of fictitious objects that unsettle modes of experiencing feeling and ordering thought," and which in turn participate in the complex dynamics of colonization and decolonization, in which the colonized realm is *"felt* as a space of enchantment" (372). Both García Márquez's textual and the *wunderkammer's* physical spaces facilitate this sense of wonderment at the real rather than relegating it to a separate realm.
32. "Eran inútiles sus esfuerzos por sistematizar los presagios.... En ocasiones eran tan naturales, que no las identificaba como presagios sino cuando se cumplían" (112–13).
33. "Buscando el interés encontró el amor, porque tratando de que ella lo quisiera terminó por quererla"; "Úrsula no había alcanzado a los gitanos, pero encontró la ruta que su marido no pudo descubrir en su frustrada búsqueda de los grandes inventos" (288, 38).
34. "El paraíso de la soledad compartida" (288).
35. "Se volvió loca por él. Perdió el sueño y el apetito, y se hundió tan profundamente en la soledad, que hasta su padre se le convirtió en un estorbo"; "recluidos por la soledad y el amor y por la soledad del amor" (246, 340).
36. "Los calderos, las pailas, las tenazas y los anafes se caían de su sitio, y las maderas crujían por la desesperación de los clavos y los tornillos tratando de desenclavarse"; "caderas de yegua y tetas de melones vivos, y una cabeza redonda, perfecta, acorazada por un duro capacete de pelos de alambre, que parecía el almófar de un guerrero medieval"; "a Úrsula peleando con las leyes de la creación para preservar la estirpe, y a José Arcadio Buendía buscando la verdad quimérica de los grandes inventos, y a Fernanda rezando y al coronel Aureliano Buendía embruteciéndose con engaños de guerras y pescaditos de oro, y a Aureliano Segundo agonizando de soledad en el aturdimiento de las parrandas" (9, 325, 346).
37. "Inclusive cuando llevaron el hielo, no lo anunciaron en función de su utilidad en la vida de los hombres, sino como una simple curiosidad de circo. Esta vez, entre muchos otros juegos de artificio, llevaban una estera voladora. Pero no la ofrecieron como un aporte fundamental al desarrollo del transporte, sino como un objeto de recreo" (33–34).
38. For a discussion of this issue, see Chanady.
39. "Una india guajira.... Ambos eran tan dóciles y serviciales que Úrsula se hizo cargo de ellos para que le ayudaran en los oficios domésticos. Fue así como Arcadio y Amaranta hablaron la lengua guajira antes que el castellano, y aprendieron a tomar caldo de lagartijas y a comer huevos de arañas sin que Úrsula se diera cuenta"; "un indio puro, montaraz, analfabeto, dotado de una malicia taciturna y una vocación mesiánica que suscitaba en sus hombres un fanatismo demente" (39, 145).
40. "Cayendo una llovizna de minúsculas flores amarillas ... toda la noche sobre el pueblo en una tormenta silenciosa, y cubrieron los techos y atascaran las puertas, y sofocaron a los animales que dormían a la intemperie"; "desenterraron de raíz las últimas cepas de las plantaciones" (126, 267).
41. For the ways in which *One Hundred Years* embodies an ecological imperative, see Holgate and Flores.
42. "Cantaba de placer y se moría de risa de sus propias invenciones" (341).
43. "Hormigas devastando el jardín"; "se revolcaban en cueros en los barrizales del patio"; "eran los únicos seres felices, y los más felices sobre la tierra" (341, 340).

44. "Un burdel zoológico"; "grandes camellias amazónicas, . . . garzas de colores, caimanes cebados como cerdos, serpientes de doce cascabeles, y una tortuga de concha dorada que se zambullía en un minúsculo océano artificial. . . . El aire tenía una densidad ingenua, como si lo acabaran de inventar . . . el tiempo regresaba a sus manantiales primarios " (332–33).
45. "La ciénaga grande" (17).
46. "Región encantada donde su padre encontró muchos años antes el fósil de un galeón español"; "lirios sangrientos y salamandras doradas" (129, 17).
47. "La ciudad lúgubre en cuyos vericuetos de piedra resonaban los bronces funerarios de treinta y dos iglesias" (251).
48. "Un pueblo aparte al otro lado de la línea del tren, con calles bordeadas de palmeras, casas con ventanas de redes metálicas" (197).
49. "A comer jamón de Virginia con rebanadas de piña"; "Vio una mujer vestida de oro en el cogote de un elefante. Vio un dromedario triste. Vio un oso vestido de holandesa que marcaba el compás de la música con un cucharón y una cacerola" (235, 229).
50. "No sólo veían las imágenes de sus propios sueños, sino que los unos veían las imágenes soñadas por otros" (45).
51. "El vicio hereditario de hacer para deshacer" (322).
52. "La historia de la familia era un engranaje de repeticiones irreparables" (334).
53. "Con la temeridad atroz con que José Arcadio Buendía atravesó la sierra para fundar a Macondo, con el orgullo ciego con que el coronel Aureliano Buendía promovió sus guerras inútiles, con la tenacidad insensata con que Úrsula aseguró la supervivencia de la estirpe, así buscó Aureliano segundo a Fernanda" (180–81).
54. "Sus órdenes se cumplían antes de ser impartidas, aún antes de que él se las concibiera . . . [al ver sus hijos adolescentes] que lo miraban con sus propios ojos . . . se sintió disperso, repetido, y más solitario que nunca" (146).
55. For an updating of this association of magical realism with the postcolonial, allying it with the recent perspective of subaltern studies, see Bowers, who astutely notes "the radical connection between the disruption that magical realist narratives can cause to authoritative discourses and how subaltern studies provide alternative accounts of authoritarian history" (35).
56. Nicholas Birns and Juan E. De Castro assert that García Márquez's closeness to an actual place over several generations encouraged contemporary modernist writers to imbricate their innovative modernist fictions in particular localities (5).
57. "Entre los ciento quince y los ciento veintidós años"; "costra de remora"; "los muñones cicatrizados y callosos de unas alas potentes" (291, 292).
58. "'Diremos que le encontramos flotando en la canastilla'—sonrió. / 'No se lo creerá nadie' – dijo la monja. / 'Si se lo creyeron a las Sagradas Escrituras'–replicó Fernanda—, 'no veo por qué no han de creérmelo a mí'" (254).
59. The novel is often reported as read by a wide variety of people. Interesting, in this respect, is that García Márquez is absent from a list of Boom writers frequently termed "Joycean," a designation Brian L. Price considers too narrowly focused on "linguistic pyrotechnics, mythological structures, and narrative games" (182). Perhaps García Márquez's mode belongs to a different branch of the Boom—accessible rather than erudite, a further explanation of its continuing popularity.
60. McHale is referencing the ideas of Christian Moraru in the latter's *Cosmodernism: American Narrative, Late Globalization, and the New Cultural Imaginary*, U of Michigan P, 2011, pp. 206–9.

Works Cited

Arellano, Jerónimo. "From the Space of the *Wunderkammer* to Macondo's Wonder Rooms: The Collection of Marvels in *Cien años de soledad*." *Hispanic Review*, vol. 78, no. 3, Summer 2010, pp. 369–86.
Barth, John. "The Literature of Replenishment: Postmodernist Fiction." *The Atlantic*, vol. 245, no. 1, Jan. 1980, pp. 65–71.
Bell-Villada, Gene H., editor. *Gabriel García Márquez in Retrospect: A Collection*. Lexington Books, 2016.
Bell-Villada, Gene H. *García Márquez: The Man and His Work*. U of North Carolina P, 2010.
Bhabha, Homi. Introduction. *Nation and Narration*. Routledge, 1990.
Birns, Nicholas. "Underdogs and Beautiful Lies: Magical Realism in the Second World." López-Calvo, *Critical Insights*, pp. 146–61.
Birns, Nicholas, and Juan E. De Castro. "Gabriel García Márquez: Writer for the World." Bell-Villada, *Gabriel García Márquez in Retrospect*, pp. 3–19.
Bowers, Maggie Ann. "Magical Realism and Subaltern Studies." López-Calvo, *Critical Insights*, pp. 35–64.
Camps, Martín. "The Plague of Modernity: Macondo, Inc. and the Branding of 'Magical' Latin America." López-Calvo, *Critical Insights*, pp. 84–96.
Chanady, Amaryll. "The Territorialization of the Imaginary in Latin America: Self-Affirmation and Resistance to Metropolitan Paradigms." Zamora and Faris, *Magical Realism*, pp. 125–44.
Faris, Wendy B. "Larger Than Life: The Hyperbolic Realities of Gabriel García Márquez and Fernando Botero." *Word and Image*, vol. 17, no. 4, October–December 2001, Pp. 339–59.
Faris, Wendy B. *Ordinary Enchantments: Magical Realism and the Remystification of Narrative*. Vanderbilt, 2004.
Flores, William. "Satire, Ecocriticism, and Luddite Discourse in *One Hundred Years of Solitude*: Regional Approaches for a Global Economic Crisis." Bell-Villada, *Gabriel García Márquez in Retrospect*, pp. 89–101.
Fuentes, Carlos. *Valiente mundo nuevo*. Mondadori, 1990.
Gallo, Marta "El futuro perfecto de Macondo." *Revista Hispánica Moderna*, no. 38, 1974–1975, pp. 115–35.
García Márquez, Gabriel. *Cien años de soledad*. Sudamericana, 1969.
García Márquez, Gabriel. "Light Is Like Water." *Strange Pilgrims*, translated by Edith Grossman, Knopf, 1993, pp. 157–61.
García Márquez, Gabriel. "La luz es cómo el agua." *Doce cuentos peregrinos*, Vintage Español, 2006, pp. 146–50.
García Márquez, Gabriel. *One Hundred Years of Solitude*. Translated by Gregory Rabassa, Avon, 1971.
Hegerfeldt, Anne "Contentious Contributions: Magic Realism Goes British." *Janus Head: An Interdisciplinary Journal*, vol 5, no. 11, 2002, pp. 62–86. (Special issue on magical realism).
Hoffman, Gerhard. *From Modernism to Postmodernism: Concepts and Strategies of Postmodern American Fiction*. Rodopi, 2005.
Holgate, Ben. *Climate and Crises: Magical Realism as Environmental Discourse*. Routledge, 2019. Routledge Studies in World Literature and the Environment.
López-Calvo, Ignacio, editor. *Critical Insights: Magical Realism*. Grey House Publishing, 2014.
McHale, Brian. "Reconstructing Postmodernism." *Narrative*, vol. 21, no. 3, Oct. 2013, pp. 357–64. (Special issue, Postmodernist Fiction: East and West).

Mignolo, Walter. *The Darker Side of Western Modernity: Global Futures, Decolonial Options.* Duke, 2011.

Parkinson Zamora, Lois. "Insubstantial Selves in Magical Realism in the Americas." *Cambridge Companion to Magical Realism*, edited by Kim Sasser and Christopher Warnes, Cambridge UP, 2020, pp. 64–79.

Parkinson Zamora, Lois, and Wendy B. Faris, editors. *Magical Realism: Theory, History, Community.* Duke UP, 1995.

Price, Brian L. "A Portrait of the Mexican Artist as a Young Man: Salvador Elizondo's Dedalean Poetics." *TransLatin Joyce: Global Transmissions in Ibero-American Literature*, edited by Brian L. Price, César A. Salgado, and John Pedro Schwartz, Palgrave Macmillan, 2014, pp. 181–210.

Roh, Franz. "Magic Realism: Post Expressionism," translated by Wendy B. Faris. Parkinson Zamora and Faris, *Magical Realism*, pp. 15–31.

Sommer, Doris. "Irresistible Romance: The Foundational Fictions of Latin America." Bhabha, *Nation and Narration*, pp. 71–98.

Warnes, Christopher. *Magical Realism and the Postcolonial Novel: Between Faith and Irreverence.* Palgrave Macmillan, 2009.

CHAPTER 3

GARCÍA MÁRQUEZ AND THE GLOBAL SOUTH

MAGALÍ ARMILLAS-TISEYRA

Toward the end of *Cien años de soledad* (*One Hundred Years of Solitude*, 1967; henceforth *One Hundred Years*), Amaranta Úrsula Buendía's Belgian husband, Gaston, writes from Europe with news of the airplane commissioned for his planned airmail service: "a shipping agent in Brussels [*una agencia marítima de Bruselas*] had sent it by mistake to Tanganyika [Tanzania], where it was delivered to the scattered tribe of the Makondos" (406).[1] The reference here is to the Makonde people of southeast and east Africa, who today reside in Mozambique, Tanzania, and Kenya.[2] By this point in Gabriel García Márquez's most famous novel, Amaranta Úrsula has begun a love affair with her nephew, Aureliano Babilonia, which, in one of the novel's many narrative slant rhymes, will result in the birth of a child with the tail of a pig—an outcome originally feared by Úrsula Iguarán in the early months of her marriage to José Arcadio Buendía and before the founding of Macondo. Amaranta Úrsula dies during that birth, and the infant is devoured by ants, unlocking the final key to Melquíades's prophecy, which Aureliano frantically reads as Macondo is wiped out by the wind. This spectacular ending is the final dismantling: once a banana company boom town, Macondo had for years been in decline, slowly abandoned and "forgotten even by the birds," to such an extent that by the time Aureliano's friend Gabriel leaves for Paris, he has to signal for the train to stop and pick him up (404; 456–57). The Belgian shipping agent's (in Spanish, the shipping agency's) mistake, then, can be read as further confirmation of Macondo's isolation—or, in the novel's terms, "solitude"—its anonymity yet another harbinger of the coming annihilation.

But it is necessary to read the dislocating transposition of Macondo, the fictional town, and the Makonde people as more than a comical, if suggestive, error. This is one of the many seemingly minor moments in *One Hundred Years* that serve to locate the narrative within the larger networks of power that condition the existence of Macondo and later bring about its end. The transposition suggests that for the shipping agent—and by extension, for Belgians, Europeans, and the Global North—these very distinct entities of the putative periphery are, for all intents and purposes, indistinguishable and interchangeable; Macondo is "close enough" to the Makonde and vice versa. Gaston's airmail service is itself a repurposing of a venture initially intended for the Congo, where his family has investments in palm oil (another commodity crop, whose destructive history rivals that of the banana). Realizing Amaranta Úrsula wants to stay in Macondo, Gaston decides that "for the purposes of being a pioneer, the Caribbean was about the same as Africa" (my translation).[3] He eventually recovers the airplane in Léopoldville (now Kinshasa, Democratic Republic of Congo) (407; 460). Together with Gaston's arc in the novel, the Belgian shipping agent's transposition of the near-homonymous Macondo and Makonde points to the underlying historical linkages between García Márquez's fictional town, the African continent, and, from there, the world economy at large.

This chapter explores the contours and critical possibilities of such connections, both within the scope of García Márquez's oeuvre as well as through the influence his work has had beyond Latin America. By way of example, in September 2019, more than fifty years after the publication of *One Hundred Years* and the Latin American literary "Boom" of which it was the apex, the Kenyan capital of Nairobi hosted the Macondo Literary Festival. Founded with the aim of breaking down linguistic borders within the African continent, it brought together writers from Anglophone and Lusophone countries under the theme "Re-Imagining Africa's Histories through Literature."[4] The festival website credits García Márquez with its name: "Macondo is a fictional place in the novel *One Hundred Years of Solitude* by Colombian Nobel Laureate Gabriel García Márquez, a place where magical things happen."[5] This formulation was frequently repeated in media coverage of the festival, with one journalist calling Macondo "a literary metropolis of wonder" (Makokha n.p.). In this back and forth (*vaivén*), the emblematic figure of one continent's "solitude"—that is, of its peripheralization within an economic world system designed to extract a maximum amount of profit from those peripheries, a process sustained by histories of colonization and postindependence interference that continue to distort the political cultures of individual nation-states (see García Márquez, "The Solitude of Latin America")—becomes on another, similarly peripheralized continent a symbol of connection, exchange, and the generative potential of literature. This is, of course, just one of the numerous circulations and recodings of the name "Macondo," which range from the adulatory, to the comical, to the critical (as in the McOndo manifesto).[6] Conceding the hyperbole of calling the Macondo of *One Hundred Years* a "metropolis of wonder," I propose that the use made of García Márquez and the name Macondo here is not a misapprehension or misreading. Rather, the resignifications of Macondo in the Macondo Literary Festival help to illuminate the complex world-historical linkages that undergird García Márquez's work and which have shaped its global circulation, particularly in the regions of the world now broadly understood as the Global South.

The reference to the Makonde in *One Hundred Years* and the Macondo Literary Festival in Kenya are two key coordinates for understanding the relationship between García Márquez and the Global South. Even when its focus is ostensibly local, García Márquez's literary output registers the global forces and, specifically, the imbalances of economic, political, and cultural power in the global system that condition those local circumstances. These same forces are the dynamics that define the Global South in the present; that is, "Global South" understood not merely as a place name or post–Cold War substitute for the Third World, but also as a resistant political imaginary and comparative framework within which to consider the cultural production of the so-called periphery. From this perspective, such seemingly minor details as the Belgian shipping agent's mistake become keys for reading García Márquez's work in relation to that Global South. Moreover, as I outline at the close of this article, the immense success and enduring popularity of García Márquez's work means that he is a towering figure not just within Latin American literature, but also in world literature at large (e.g., Moretti). Because of this, his work, and in particular the magical realism of which *One Hundred Years* has served as a global archetype, continues to function as a model for and by which writers and works from other regions of the Global South might gain world literary standing. Without dismissing the hegemonic role that *One Hundred Years* and magical realism have come to occupy, I highlight instances of engagement with García Márquez's work outside the frame of the world literary market but within the scope of the Global South as a transnational collectivity.

Understanding the Global South: A Political Imaginary and Comparative Framework

Despite its ubiquity, the meaning, inflections, and critical utility of the term "Global South" remain questions of heated debate (see Comaroff and Comaroff 49–52; West-Pavlov, "Toward the Global South"). The term originates in the social sciences and developmentalist discourse, where it invokes the notion of a global North-South divide to organize countries according to socioeconomic and political status (cf. Kartha). In popular usage, it predominantly serves to name the same parts of the world that the term "Third World" once did. However, while often invoked as such, the Global South is not simply a place name designating a fixed location, nor it is properly a post–Cold War substitute for the Third World, sometimes taken to also include parts of what was formerly the "Second World." Particularly for scholars in literary and cultural studies, the Global South has come to function as a "deterritorialized geography of capitalism's externalities," a relational concept that emphasizes the connection or interactions between groups rather than steadfast categorization (Mahler, "Global South" n.p.).

The ascent of the term "Global South" around the turn of the twenty-first century was of a piece with a larger shift in the post–Cold War period from East-West rivalries to North-South tensions, where "North" and "South" function as synonyms for economic, social, and political "development" and its opposite. Contrary to the locational specificity of the Third World, where countries were categorized according to relative levels of development, the Global South is not spatially delimited and instead "is to be found everywhere" (Sheppard and Nagar 558). Yet "Third World" was itself a multivalent term: its meanings ranged from serving as a commonly understood synonym for "underdevelopment" to naming a variety of contestatory political projects organized under the broader principle of nonalignment. This latter vision of the Third World was rooted in anticolonial and Cold War radical internationalist movements, nurtured by gatherings such as the Bandung Afro-Asian Conference in 1955 (Indonesia) and the Tricontinental Conference for Solidarity with the Peoples of Asia, Africa, and Latin America in 1966 (Cuba), as well as the Afro-Asian and Tricontinental solidarity organizations established in their wake.[7] Beginning in the 1970s, the global turn toward neoliberalism would effectively dismantle the Third World as a political project (Prashad, *The Darker Nations* 276–81, *The Poorer Nations* 47–83). The Global South, as both a term and concept, thus arises from this collapse and represents an ongoing effort to grapple with the current global disposition by naming its externalities (negative effects) and providing the rubric under which wide-ranging and cross-regional resistance might be imagined.[8] Drawing on this history, scholars such as Alfred López, Vijay Prashad, and Anne Garland Mahler argue for understanding the Global South as a resistant political imaginary arising from the mutual recognition of shared or analogous circumstances by marginalized or dispossessed groups under contemporary capitalism. From here, it becomes possible to speak of a Global South within the Global North, as in the marginalization of indigenous or otherwise racialized populations, as well as of a North within the South, as constituted by an increasingly mobile transnational capitalist class. Recognition is therefore the basis for the creation of Global South consciousness, as the act of coming to awareness of, articulating, and thereby activating solidarities that can then be put into action toward the goal of liberation.

More abstract invocations of the Global South, however, mobilize it as a framework for transregional and specifically South-South comparison, turning attention to shared or analogous experiences of marginalization, dispossession, or oppression without necessarily requiring mutual or even self-recognition, and thereby allowing for looser forms of association (see Armillas-Tiseyra 12–21; Sparke; West-Pavlov, "Toward the Global South"). Here, conceptualization of the Global South as a political consciousness opens up toward its articulation as a comparative framework attuned to underlying connections or similarities between texts and their contexts. Methodologically, this approach is consonant with what Shu-mei Shih describes as "relational comparison," a mode of comparison informed by world or macro history that approaches texts as part of a network connected by a complex of shared or even merely analogous histories. In order to illustrate the concept, Shih, taking inspiration from the work of Édouard Glissant, elaborates the idea of a "plantation arc" stretching from the Caribbean, through the US South, to Southeast Asia, via the Cape and the Indian Ocean ("Comparison as Relation" 86–88; Glissant 63–75). These sites are linked together by historical entanglements with global systems of labor and capital extraction, which serve as the basis for comparative readings of literature emerging from these contexts, whether or not there are material traces of direct contact. In this wider frame, comparison can move along multiple axes and function at various scales; it can—as Shih has written elsewhere of "literary arcs"—both expand and contract. The end of such literary arcs is not a global synthesis, but rather the linking together of multiple nodes so as to shed light on networked interconnections ("World Studies" 434).

Relational comparison, then, is a model for working within the Global South as well as for understanding the constitution of the Global South itself. It does not assume mutual recognition of shared circumstances within the particular sites explored, but rather seeks to illuminate those connections as the basis for comparative analysis. My discussion of the Belgian shipping agent's mistake in *One Hundred Years* is informed by this approach, as is much other scholarship that uses García Márquez's attention to questions of economic dependency and uneven development as the basis for comparison across time and place (e.g., Harford Vargas). This is, as I shall elaborate, the most fruitful approach for understanding the complex connections between García Márquez, his work, and the Global South as a comparative framework. The mode of analysis I enact here combines the principles of relational comparison with attention to the seemingly minor details through which these networks of interconnection are illuminated in García Márquez's work.

The Global South and García Márquez: From Global Engagements to World-Historical Relation

García Márquez's biography, journalism, and political activism offer rich material for linking his work to the Global South. These associations are worth elucidating as a point of contrast for closer analysis of the literature. First, while its literary rendering might be remembered for the emphasis on solitude or isolation, the coastal region of Colombia in which García Márquez was born and raised was very much connected to the world through international circuits of exchange. The early twentieth-century banana boom drew to Aracataca (the town where García Márquez spent his childhood and which would become the model for Macondo, the setting of much of his early work) laborers from the wider Caribbean, South America, and Europe, as well as the Middle East and East Asia, and was accompanied by a dazzling influx of consumer goods—phenomena also registered in García Márquez's fiction (Martin, *Gabriel García Márquez* 21, 39, 47–50).[9] As a young journalist working in Barranquilla, García Márquez became involved with a group of writers and intellectuals who would eventually become known as the Barranquilla Group; as he later explained to Gerald Martin, "Barranquilla enabled me to be a writer. . . . It had the highest immigrant population in Colombia—Arabs, Chinese, and so on. It was like [the Andalusian city of] Córdoba in the Middle Ages" (*Gabriel García Márquez* 126). Such comments locate García Márquez's early development as a writer not in the putative isolation of the periphery, but rather in cosmopolitan spaces of transregional exchange between so-called peripheries, whose contact was only ever partially mediated by the center. "Cosmopolitanism" is, of course, an overdetermined and malleable term (see Lyon). I use it here not so much to link García Márquez's development as a writer to Euro-American modernism writ large (another rich literary-historical and critical vein in the scholarship of his work) as to invoke a cosmopolitan practice as imagined from and in the margins. This is a cosmopolitanism akin to what Ngũgĩ wa Thiong'o invokes when he describes "the postcolonial as the site of globality" as well as what Boaventura de Sousa Santos calls "subaltern insurgent cosmopolitanism" (*Globalectics* 51–55; de Sousa Santos 134–35).

Second, García Márquez's travels, both before and after he became a global star (itself a process marked, first, by the success of *One Hundred Years* in the late 1960s and early 1970s, and second, by the awarding of the Nobel Prize in 1982), attest to a leftist internationalism that would characterize his life as a writer and public figure. While working as a journalist in Paris in the mid-1950s, García Márquez was attuned to the independence struggles in Vietnam and Algeria and became involved with the Algerian National Liberation Front (FLN); often mistaken for Algerian, he was harassed and even arrested by police (Martin, *Gabriel García Márquez* 209–10).[10] This period of exploration culminated with an extended trip into Eastern Europe in 1957, during which García Márquez visited and filed stories from East Germany, Czechoslovakia, Poland, Hungary, and the USSR.[11] Almost two decades after that, García Márquez would celebrate the ways in which a city like London, remade by migration in the wake of empire, could become a crossroads for people from all over the world, such that Oxford Street now resembled a street in Panama, Curaçao, or Veracruz (Martin, *Gabriel García Márquez* 367–68; Visión [staff] 26).

This global consciousness—alternately understood as "cosmopolitanism" or "internationalism" depending on the context in which these questions are engaged—is a crucial facet of García Márquez, his work, and of the so-called Boom more generally. Often overlooked when García Márquez and the Boom writers are engaged outside of Latin America or under the rubric of world literature, this global consciousness is fundamental to understanding their work and its circulation outside of the region (see Franco, "From Modernization to Resistance"; Martin, *Journeys through the Labyrinth* 218–35; Sánchez Prado, "Teaching the Latin American Boom as World Literature"; Sánchez Prado, *América Latina en la "literatura mundial"*; Viñas et al.). One significant exception, perhaps, is the attention paid to García Márquez's well-documented admiration for modernist writers such as William Faulkner.[12] As a young man, García Márquez recognized Faulkner as a fellow writer of the Caribbean; he would later write that it was Faulkner, more than any other writer, who helped him decipher the "demons of the Caribbean" (quoted in Cohn, "Faulkner and Spanish America" 50). Ernest Hemingway, James Joyce, Virginia Woolf, and Franz Kafka were similarly important touchstones for García Márquez and other authors of what would come to be known as the Latin American new novel (*nueva novela*; also the "Boom novel") (see, e.g., Martin, *Journeys through the Labyrinth* 171–74; Williams).

However, García Márquez's inspirations were not exclusively Euro-American. A profile of García Márquez published in the Buenos Aires magazine *Primera Plana* to mark the release of *One Hundred Years* names Faulkner and Kafka as well as François Rabelais as influences, but emphasizes over and above these the foundational importance of *A Thousand and One Nights* for García Márquez's development as a storyteller (cf. van Leeuwen 105; Faris). Appropriately titled "Los viajes de Simbad García Márquez" (The Travels of Sinbad García Márquez), the piece recounts the enchantment felt by the young García Márquez on first encountering these stories (Schóo 52). This experience is recreated in *One Hundred Years* for Aureliano Segundo (later father of Amaranta Úrusula), who finds the stories in what was once Melquíades's room; they are in an unbound book without cover or title, meaning that the reader must recognize the reference from partial sketches of the tales (183 and 213–14).[13] The breadth of García Márquez's interests as a reader is attested to by the myriad allusions that punctuate his work, and which occasionally mislead critics. As García Marquez once commented on the reference to Rabelais in *One Hundred Years*, he placed it as "a banana peel on which many critics slipped" (*El olor de la guayaba* 104; my translation).[14] Recognizing that García Márquez was notoriously cryptic in discussion of his writing, and therefore in his assessment of the critical value of his intertextual allusions, the presence of such references offers the reader a literary map that is nevertheless decidedly and instructively global in scope.

Such forms of global engagement, moreover, existed alongside and in conversation with the development of a Latin American consciousness in the early years of García Márquez's career. This was the elaboration of a sense of cohesive regional or continental identity—what Martin evocatively terms "continental nationalism"—that proved fundamental to the formation and dissemination of the Boom (*Gabriel García Márquez* 180; see also Donoso 38–48; Siskind 85–87). Writing about his time in Paris, immediately after recounting his involvement with the FLN, García Márquez adds that for him the city was also defined by his interactions with fellow Latin Americans:

> When I arrived in Paris, I was little more than a callow *caribe* [caribe *crudo*]. The thing for which I am most thankful to this city, with which I have so many old disputes and even older loves, is that it gave me a new and resolute perspective on Latin America. The overall picture of the continent, which we did not have in any of our countries, became very clear here, sitting around a café table, and one realized that, despite being from different countries, we were crew members on the same ship. ("Desde París, con amor" 354; my translation)[15]

García Márquez's sense of continental solidarity would find myriad expressions over the course of his life: from his allegiance to the Cuban Revolution; to the period spent working in Caracas and the many years he and his family lived in Mexico City; to the promise, made in the wake of the assassination of Salvador Allende (1973), that he would not write fiction until Augusto Pinochet was no longer in power in Chile (eventually rescinded with the publication of *Crónica de una muerte anunciada* [*Chronicle of a Death Foretold*] in 1981); to his vocal denunciations of CIA meddling in the region; to his close friendships with political figures such as Omar Torrijos of Panama and, of course, Fidel Castro of Cuba.[16] The friendship with Castro, itself the topic of much analysis and criticism, was one of several vectors through which García Márquez engaged with Third World–oriented political projects and extended his criticism of First World imperialisms. In later decades, García Márquez would also become involved in the work of international commissions organized by intergovernmental bodies such as UNESCO; examples include his work for the MacBride Commission (International Commission for the Study of Communication Problems, 1977–1980) and his work on the prevention of nuclear proliferation.[17] Such efforts were part of a larger shift from public militancy to diplomacy and mediation beginning in the 1980s (Martin, *Gabriel García Márquez* 390–91). They also brought García Márquez into the same kinds of intergovernmental and international venues from which there emerged initial articulations of what would come to be theorized as the Global South.[18]

Over the course of his life, then, García Márquez moved through a series of spaces and ways of thinking that have come to inform contemporary theorizations of the Global South. But while the various examples presented offer suggestive connections, they do not mobilize the Global South as a comparative framework or, more precisely, as a lens that can inform analysis of García Márquez's literary production. It is therefore necessary to move from biographical précis to more direct engagement with the writing; I will begin with a work of nonfiction. Perhaps the best example of García Márquez's investment in the projects of the Cuban Revolution and tricontinentalism is his account of Cuba's military mission to Angola, Operation Carlota. Named for the enslaved woman who began a revolt in Matanzas in 1843, the mission provided troops and other aid in support of Agostinho Neto and the People's Movement for the Liberation of Angola (MPLA) against the National Union for the Total Independence of Angola (UNITA, backed by the United States and South Africa) beginning in 1975, following Angola's independence from Portugal.

Written at García Márquez's suggestion and with direction from the Cuban government, "Operación Carlota" is uniformly celebratory, framing Cuba's involvement in Angola as part of its long-standing solidarity with liberation struggles elsewhere on the African continent (see Martin, *Gabriel García Márquez* 375–78). As García Márquez declares: "[N]o contemporary African liberation movement has been unable to count on Cuban solidarity, whether expressed in material and arms or in the training of military and civil technicians and specialists" ("Operation Carlota" 126).[19] While Cuba's involvement in African liberation struggles was significant and influential, it existed in tension with the realities of racial essentialism and exclusion on the island. This is what Anne Garland Mahler incisively describes as "Cuba's two-pronged racial discourse— inclusionary discrimination in the domestic sphere and radical antiracism in the international context," which "allowed the communist government to externalize its racial problems, pointing to racism as an expression of U.S. imperialism to which both Cubans and African Americas were subject and denying the presence of racial inequalities within Cuba itself" (*From the Tricontinental* 176).[20] There is no room for such nuanced analysis in García Márquez's triumphalist account, which aims to position Cuba and the Castro brothers as models for international collaboration. In the closing paragraphs, for instance, García Márquez lists changes he has recently noticed in Cuba: short-sleeved suits are in fashion for men, Portuguese words have found their way into everyday slang, and "old African strains [have] reappeared in new popular tunes" (137; 31). These scattered observations are offered as signals of a deeper affiliation between Cubans and Angolans, an emergent political consciousness that shows promise for the future. But no matter how optimistic, drawing on Mahler, this remains a vision for the future as yet unable to confront its internal hierarchies and exclusions in the present.

With this in mind, perhaps the most interesting moments in "Operation Carlota" are García Márquez's fleeting literary flights from the technical language that characterizes the piece as a whole. These are particularly conspicuous when García Márquez turns his attention to the people of Angola, as in the following discussion of Portuguese colonization and the interior of the country:

> Beneath that crust of civilization [the towns constructed by Portuguese settlers] lay a huge, teeming land of misery. The living standard of the native population was one of the lowest in the world, the illiteracy higher than 90 per cent, and the cultural conditions closer to the Stone Age than the twentieth century. Furthermore, in the towns of the interior [*las ciudades del interior*], only the men spoke Portuguese and they lived with as many as seven wives in the same house. Age-old superstitions were a hindrance not only in everyday life but also in the conduct of war. Many Angolans continued to be convinced that bullets could not pierce white skins; they had a magical dread of airplanes; and they refused to fight in trenches saying that tombs are only for the dead. (133)[21]

While such descriptions traffic in ethnographic exoticism, separating the backward Angolans from the forward-thinking Cubans, the language and subtle shift in register in these lines also indexes similarity and opens toward recognition. What begins as a technocratic account of conditions on the ground (discussion of literacy rates), complete with the pejorative implications and paternalism common to so much of that language (the reference to cultural conditions being closer to the Stone Age), shifts in the second sentence. Here, the towns of Angola's interior begin to resemble the world of the fictional Macondo—as a place similarly isolated, riven by superstition and violence. Think, for instance, of José Arcadio Buendía's encounter with the remains of a Spanish galleon in the "enchanted region" around the time of the founding of Macondo, which will later be the place where banana trees are planted and, after that, the ground on which Gaston builds the landing strip for his awaited airplane; or of the amazement expressed by Macondo's inhabitants at the inventions traders (the "gypsies") bring to the town; or, for that matter, of the fourteen assassination attempts, the seventy-three ambushes, and the firing squad survived by Colonel Aureliano Buendía in *One Hundred Years*.

The latent comparison in these lines posits that Cuba (and by extension, the Caribbean and Latin America) and Angola (and the African continent as a whole) are linked not just by the political realities of the Cold War but by the much longer histories of domination and extraction that are the stuff of world-historical and therefore relational analysis. The descriptions sound alike because these places have been subjected to interconnected historical forces. More than by magic or superstition, the towns of the

Angolan hinterland and Macondo are connected by analogous histories of combined and uneven development—that is, of a partial (and conditional) integration in the world economy primarily oriented toward extraction of resources and other forms of wealth, with unequal distribution of the little that is given in return.[22] García Márquez's language, in turn, registers the social and psychological consequences of those material realities. Noting that, a decade earlier, Che Guevara similarly observed this propensity to superstition and took it upon himself to investigate its origins (even learning Swahili), García Márquez explains that it is not a uniquely Angolan or African trait, but the result of "that pernicious force which cannot be vanquished by bullets: mental colonization" (133).[23] Read with this analysis in mind, the enchantments of Macondo, so often romanticized as a place of magic and wonder, are transformed into signals of the novel's underlying critique of the larger capitalist system within which the narrative unfolds. The "magic" of Macondo or even of magical realism, to paraphrase Ericka Beckman, is no more "magical" than the magical thinking that sustains capitalism itself (see "An Oil Well Named Macondo"; see also Wenzel, *The Disposition of Nature* 126–29). Hence García Márquez's oft-repeated claim that the putative inventions of his magical realism were fundamentally rooted in reality (e.g., González Bermejo 10–11; El Manifiesto [staff] 86–87; Dreifus 126–27; Ortega).

The analysis I have outlined through juxtaposition of "Operation Carlota" with *One Hundred Years* relies on an instance of recognition intimated in the text, but which must be activated by the reader and therefore risks being overlooked. Once elucidated, such moments offer rich possibilities for thinking about García Márquez in relation to the Global South. Beyond the suggestive details of the biography, his political work and declarations, or even the points of contact suggested by marks of influence or allusion, this is how one should approach García Márquez's work within a Global South framework. In my usage, therefore, Global South is fundamentally a way of reading, one informed by relational comparison and attuned to the seemingly minor details through which those histories of interconnection, and the analyses they make possible, become manifest.

García Márquez's literary works are filled with gestures toward and references to the larger networks within which his fictional worlds, even the most ostensibly isolated or "magical," are embedded. To put it in slightly different terms, the material substrate of much of García Márquez's fiction invokes the attention to global dynamics and emphasis on interconnection familiar to scholars of capitalism and world-systems analysis. The initial economic boom, the massacre of striking workers, and the ensuing bust unleashed by the banana company in *One Hundred Years* (a thinly veiled fictionalization of the ravages wrought by the Boston-based United Fruit Company) is one immediately recognizable example. Also notable is the Americans' claiming of the Caribbean Sea as repayment for the country's accumulated foreign debt toward the end of *El otoño del patriarca* (*The Autumn of the Patriarch*, 1975; henceforth *The Autumn*). In the latter novel, the Americans carry away the sea in pieces and plant it in Arizona; to replace the ocean winds, the dictator of the unnamed country is forced to install a system of fans (232–34; 265–68). This fantastical scenario provides a canny instantiation of the mechanics of international debt and even anticipates the increasing privatization of natural resources in the present (Beckman, *Capital Fictions* vii–viii). Such attention to political economy is an element of García Márquez's work frequently overlooked in service of celebrating its more marvelous aspects; to quote Martin, "No misreading has been more serious for Latin American literary history than the 'mythreading' of its most celebrated work, *One Hundred Years of Solitude*" (*Journeys through the Labyrinth* 235). In what follows, I offer a series of briefly sketched analyses informed by the Global South as a conceptual framework and intended to counter that tendency to "mythread" García Márquez's fiction.

To return to the episode with which I began, the Belgian shipping agent's transposition of Macondo and the Makonde in *One Hundred Years* points to the underlying historical connections between the fictional town, the African continent, and the global economy. In his autobiography, García Márquez traces the origins of the toponym "Macondo" to a banana plantation near Aracataca. Only years later, after he had begun to use the name in his fiction, would García Márquez learn it was also the name of a tree (*Cavanillesia platanifolia*) and of a people (20; 28–29).[24] Etymologies of the word suggest that the Spanish *macondo* derives from the term for banana (*makondo*) in some of the Bantu languages spoken in Africa and, later, in the Caribbean (see de Granada; Beckman, "An Oil-Well Named Macondo"). Certainly the Spanish and Portuguese term "banana" derives from those in several west and central African languages, mirroring the physical trajectory of the plant (which originates in Asia) from Africa to plantations in the Americas, as well as of the enslaved people taken to work those plantations.[25] These connections are part of a much larger constellation of linkages between Africa and the Americas that includes the Atlantic slave trade, long (and ongoing) histories of extraction (or extractivism, as the extraction of natural resources in an economy that depends primarily on the sale of those resources on the global market is known), and the geopolitical dynamics of the Cold War.[26] Viewed in a world-historical frame, they also point to further links and resonances, such as those between banana cultivation in Latin America and southeast Asia, or rubber extraction across the global tropics (see French; Harp).

Palm oil, invoked in the novel through the reference to Gaston's family's investments, similarly opens up a variety of comparative axes, beginning with the physical "arc" of oil-palm-tree plantations across Latin America, Africa, and Asia. The United Fruit Company was also responsible for the introduction of a West African variety of the oil-palm tree (*Elaeis guineensis*) into Latin America in the 1920s (Taussig n3, 7–8).[27] The farming of the oil-palm stretches back several centuries, particularly in West Africa, where large-scale cultivation of this plant as a commodity crop was propelled by the use of palm oil as a mechanical lubricant during the first Industrial Revolution and, as such, anticipated the discovery and extraction of petroleum in places such as the Niger Delta (Wenzel, "Petro-Magic-Realism" 452; Apter; Lynn). As is suggested by Jennifer Wenzel's analysis of what she calls "petro-magic-realism" in Nigerian fiction—which is informed by Fernando Coronil's work on "petro-magic" in Venezuela—such relational comparative thinking makes possible an analysis of the political ecology not just of Nigerian literature (Wenzel's task) but of the literature of oil-producing regions throughout the Global South.[28] The connections I am drawing here are sustained by the circulation of García Márquez's work, and in particular of the name "Macondo." In an uncanny and suggestive coincidence, the rig responsible for the 2010 Deepwater Horizon oil spill in the Gulf of Mexico was named "Macondo." Per Beckman's analysis of this case, BP's naming of the oil well after García Márquez's fictional town reveals not just capital's reliance on the imaginative apparatuses of fiction, but also its attempts to disavow the history of hypertrophic expansion and catastrophic collapse recounted in *One Hundred Years* itself ("An Oil Well").

Moving to *The Autumn of the Patriarch*, the mechanics of international debt offer a similarly rich comparative arc. Combining attention to the legacies of Latin America's export boom at the turn of the twentieth century with an analysis of the region's political history, García Márquez explicitly frames debt as a tool of capitalist imperialism, as enacted via collaboration with authoritarian regimes, in this dictator novel. The historical reality of exploitative lending practices is registered in *The Autumn* by the unnamed collective narrator who represents the dictator's subjects, as well as by the dictator and his henchmen, in a narrative voice that flows between multiple speakers:

> [W]e're down to our skins general sir, we had used up our last resources, bled by the age old necessity of accepting loans in order to pay the interest on the foreign debt ever since the wars of independence and then other loans to pay the interest on back interest, always in return for something general sir, first the quinine and tobacco monopolies for the English, then the rubber and cocoa monopoly for the Dutch, then the concession for the upland railroad and river navigation to the Germans, and everything for the gringos [. . .] (210)[29]

The country's debts date to the wars of independence, after which it was forced to take out new loans and make commercial concessions to pay the interest on the back interest, and so on, all against the background of boom-and-bust economic cycles. This is a crucial aspect of García Márquez's analysis of dictatorship: while the General has come to seem an all-pervading and "eternal" presence in the lives of his subjects, the novel increasingly emphasizes the limits of his power. Ultimately, the General is subordinate to the desires of the foreign interests (both political and commercial) that have sustained and benefited from his regime. This is a perspective, as I have argued elsewhere, particular to the dictator novel of the Global South. Attention to the role of global political and economic forces in shaping and sustaining dictatorship offers a distinct image of the dictator, who must appease external interests in order to remain in power. The resulting disjunction between the dictator's apparent omnipotence at home and his subjection abroad is often the subject of satire and comedy in the dictator novel of the Global South. In *The Autumn*, while the General might take a contemptuous pride in offering shelter to the deposed dictators of neighboring countries, he is shown to have little more control over his fate than they do (15–17; 23–24).

Emphasis on the links between dictatorship, debt, and capitalist imperialism, particularly in its neoliberal incarnations, remains an important topic in more recent dictator novels from beyond Latin America. In *En Attendant le vote des bêtes sauvages* (*Waiting for the Vote of the Wild Animals*, 1998; Côte d'Ivoire) and *Mũrogi wa Kagogo* (*Wizard of the Crow*, 2006; Kenya), for instance, Ahmadou Kourouma and Ngũgĩ wa Thiong'o respectively turn their attention to the difficulties faced by Cold War–era African dictators after the collapse of the Soviet Union, which effectively removed the geopolitical scaffolding that had sustained such dictatorships on the continent since the era of independence. These (fictional) dictators now find themselves with restricted access to capital and are forced to make significant political concessions in order to receive meager funds. In *Waiting for the Vote of the Wild Animals*, the dictator is eventually ousted and hopes to return to power via elections; in *Wizard of the Crow*, the dictator is killed and replaced by a subordinate who proves more willing to implement the new plan of "corporonialism" (a portmanteau term combining "corporation" and "colonialism") demanded by the Global Bank and Global Ministry of Finance (stand-ins for the World Bank and International Monetary Fund). In neither case does the removal of the dictator signal a significant change in conditions on the ground, as the global systems that conditioned their dictatorships remain in place. Indeed, while *The Autumn* begins and ends with the death of its dictator, the novel itself similarly does not imagine a future beyond dictatorship. So long as those larger interests remain in place, the local reiterations of dictatorship will continue.

Gestures toward the larger systems that condition the fictional worlds in which García Márquez's narratives unfold are not always so explicit or extensively developed as in the examples discussed thus far. But the more subtle indications similarly allow the reader to trace the connections between the local settings of García Márquez's fiction and the larger world. Think, for instance, of the passages in which the pope in Rome learns of the death of Mamá Grande and rushes to Macondo, where the sounds of that town intermingle with those of the Vatican, in "Los funerales de la Mamá Grande" ("Big Mama's Funeral," 1962) (209–11; 159–61); or of the reference to future "passengers on great liners" (*los pasajeros de los grandes barcos*) who will enjoy the sight and smell of the many flowers planted by the town in Esteban's honor in "El ahogado más hermoso del mundo" ("The Handsomest Drowned Man in the World," 1968) (253; 56); or of the US Marines whose presence punctuates the plot of "Blacamán el bueno vendedor de milagros" ("Blacamán the Good, Vendor of Miracles," 1968). In each case, these brief references serve to locate the story in time—the Marines in "Blacamán" come to the deck of their ship to take "colored pictures" with "long-distance lenses" (273; 84)—and place, effectively reframing the narratives in which they appear. In "The Handsomest Drowned Man in the World," for example, the body of a mysterious stranger becomes an object of wonder and desire for the inhabitants of the fishing village where it washes up. Enthralled with the stranger, whom they name Esteban, the villagers decide to give him a marvelous funeral. But both the domestic tensions and enchantment unleashed by the arrival of the dead body only take on meaning when understood in the context of the village's isolation, which is produced by the larger, global systems within which it has been relegated to the margins. The village is, in short, the kind of place otherwise ignored by those great passenger liners.

Similarly isolated are the trading posts of La Guajira, where Eréndira engages in forced sex work in "La increíble y triste historia de la cándida Eréndida y de su abuela desalmada" ("The Incredible and Sad Tale of Innocent Eréndira and Her Heartless Grandmother," 1972), the village where the colonel waits for news of his pension in *El coronel no tiene quien le escriba* (*No One Writes to the Colonel*, 1961), and the coastal backwater that is the setting for *Chronicle of a Death Foretold*, to name just a few examples. In each case, the remoteness or isolation of these spaces is, precisely, produced by systems (the state, the global economy) that have decided to withdraw from or otherwise overlook and exclude the places and people in question. Think, for instance, of the narrator's description of the cursory investigation of the murder of Santiago Nasar in *Chronicle of a Death Foretold*. Twenty years after the murder, the narrator searches for records of the matter in the disordered archives of the Palace of Justice in Riohacha, a decrepit colonial building briefly occupied by Sir Francis Drake during an English invasion of the region in the sixteenth century, where the narrator must now wade through water because the ground floor floods at high tide (98–99; 157–58). The scene is a glimpse of uneven internal development that, once again, recalls García Márquez's description of the villages of the Angolan interior in "Operation Carlota."

What binds all of these examples together is García Márquez's enduring interest in what, in his 1982 Nobel lecture, "La soledad de América Latina" ("The Solitude of Latin America"), he termed "solitude." An allusion to the title of his most famous work, in the lecture the term serves to describe Latin America's condition of dispossession and marginalization, as attested to by long histories of massacre, dictatorship, and disappearances. Crucially, "solitude" is not a given, but rather a condition produced by Latin America's relationship with Euro-America, in which "interpretation of our reality through patterns not our own serves only to make us ever more unknown, ever less free, ever more solitary" (135).[30] Within the scope of the lecture, García Márquez's elaboration of the region's solitude engenders an argument for new forms of representation better suited to conveying Latin American reality. Particularly as this line of argument converges with that of earlier descriptions of a Latin American *real maravilloso* (marvelous real) and *realismo mágico* (magical realism), it has become a touchstone in discussions of the aesthetics of García Márquez's fiction (e.g., Harford Vargas; Sangari). However, García Márquez's elaboration of solitude as a *relational* category that makes visible the global dynamics linking together far-flung regions of the globe, in which "peripheries" are zones of extraction and exclusion produced by the operations of capitalist imperialism, is also a key for reading the world in his literary work. As García Márquez remarked in a 1971 interview: "[T]he book I'm writing isn't the book of Macondo, but of solitude" (González Bermejo 7). Even in his most isolated fictions, the wider world is always there, made present in the seemingly minor details that give the settings texture.

Coda: García Márquez and the Literatures of the Global South

In an essay published on the occasion of García Márquez's death in 2014, Salman Rushdie relays a joke about the outsized influence of *One Hundred Years*: "'I have the feeling,' Carlos Fuentes once said to me, 'that writers in Latin America can't use the word 'solitude' any more, because they worry that people will think it's a reference to Gabo. And I'm afraid,' he added, mischievously, 'that soon we will not be able to use the phrase '100 years' either" ("Magic in Service of Truth" n.p.). Fuentes's bon mot, as reported by Rushdie, captures not just the importance of *One Hundred Years* for Latin American writers, but the extent to which it—and the magical realism of which it came to serve as a global archetype—would determine the international circulation of Latin American literature. The global popularity of *One Hundred Years* engendered what Sylvia Molloy has called a "magic realist imperative," or, per Ignacio Sánchez Prado, a model of "epigonal magical realism," that later generations of Latin American writers would explicitly and sometimes vociferously reject, even as their work continued to be read with those expectations (see Molloy; Sánchez Prado, *Strategic Occidentalism* 79–84; Siskind 85––95; Pollack).[31] The weight of García Márquez's influence is not exclusive to Latin American literature. More than a colossus to be overthrown, however, it offers a means for understanding the narrow place given to literary production from the Global South in the global literary market. By way of conclusion, then, I offer a brief reflection on the role that García Márquez, his work, and its legacies have come to play in the production, circulation, and reception of literary production from elsewhere in the Global South.

Much of García Márquez's international influence is traceable via the dissemination of magical realism as a narrative mode and the critical attention it subsequently received. By the end of the 1980s and into the 1990s, magical realism was being celebrated by some as "the literary language of the emergent postcolonial world" (Bhabha 6–7; see also Slemon; cf. Spivak, Quayson). Such claims are, to an extent, sustained by the clear influence of García Márquez on novels such as Rushdie's multiple Booker Prize–winning *Midnight's Children* (1981), which Rushdie himself has explicitly acknowledged (e.g., "Inverted Realism").[32] The last two decades have seen a wealth of critical work that usefully contravenes the easy declaration that magical realism (itself a contested term) is the literary language of all the postcolonial or Third World or, for that matter, of the Global South. Yet this should not diminish the scope of García Márquez's influence throughout the literatures of the Global South, which extends well beyond the aesthetics of magical realism (see Rincón; Zhang; Jin; and in particular Müller). *The Autumn*, for instance, has shaped global understanding of the dictator novel (as previously discussed), while *Chronicle of a Death Foretold* has served as an intertext in works by writers such as Elias Khoury (*Majma' al-Asrar* [The Collection of Secrets], 1994; Lebanon) and Mohammed Hanif (*A Case of Exploding Mangoes*, 2009; Pakistan).[33] Such engagements with García Márquez's work bypass its predominant association with magical realism by highlighting other—equally defining—formal or thematic elements in his work. *A Case of Exploding Mangoes*, for instance, employs the same narrative structure as *Chronicle*, beginning with a murder (the explosion of an airplane) and then exploring preceding events, highlighting the use García Márquez makes of the procedural, investigative elements of the *crónica* (as a nonfiction narrative genre) in his novel. Finally, Latin American literature and criticism also provide useful critical touchstones for the theorization of literatures elsewhere in the Global South. As Roanne Kantor elaborates, the Latin American literary Boom is a necessary point of reference for understanding the more recent "boom" (and bust) of Anglophone South Asian fiction (466). Building on this work, the same may prove true for analyzing the ongoing eruption of critical and commercial interest in fiction from the African continent.

Given the rise and fall of magical realism as a global (or postcolonial) aesthetic toward the end of the twentieth century, it is surprising the frequency with which García Márquez, and *One Hundred Years* in particular, are invoked in discussions of African writing two decades into the twenty-first. Sweeping historical epics such as Jennifer Nansubuga Makumbi's *Kintu* (2014), Novuyo Rosa Tshuma's *House of Stone* (2018), and Namwali Serpell's *The Old Drift* (2019) have all garnered comparison to García Márquez and *One Hundred Years*.[34] Aside from the question of whether or not these comparisons are fitting (a matter requiring separate analysis), what is striking is the speed with which they are made and reiterated. An early description of Makumbi's *Kintu* as "a Ugandan *One Hundred Years of Solitude*," for instance, has been repeated in multiple reviews as well as promotional materials for the novel.[35] In these more recent invocations, both the name "García Márquez" and "*One Hundred Years of Solitude*," as a literary work and market model, function at a greater degree of abstraction than ever before. They have, in short, become floating signifiers of literary prestige for writing from the Global South. The more easily a work can be compared to either García Márquez or *One Hundred Years*, the more easily it enters the circuits of world literary dissemination.

In one sense, this is hardly a new phenomenon: metropolitan publishers have long sought out African writing that might reproduce the international popularity of Latin American Boom–era writers (see Moudileno 36–37). It was a tendency already parodied by African writers in the 1970s and 1980s, as in Henri Lopès's *Le Pleurer-rire* (*The Laughing Cry*, 1982; Republic of the Congo), a dictator novel that playfully acknowledges its relationship to Latin American precursors such as *The Autumn* and *One Hundred Years*. Toward the end of Lopès's novel, which is ostensibly an account by the dictator's former butler of his time in the autocrat's service, the reader is offered a series of versions of the death of the resistance leader Colonel Yabaka, the last of which depicts Yabaka's surviving multiple salvos from a firing squad. When a character in the novel later finds this fictional manuscript, she chides the unnamed (fictional) writer for the "echo of the Latin American scene" (*une réminiscence de l'actualité latino-américaine*), which to her seems unsuited to "the Africa of today" (*l'Afrique d'aujourd'hui*) (258; 370). This magical-realist turn is a pointed change in register that demonstrates Lopès's familiarity and facility with this narrative mode at the same time that it signals a clear intention to make only limited use thereof, as emphasized in the metanarrative commentary.

At the same time, writers from throughout the African continent have also taken inspiration from the literary experiments of Latin American writers of the Boom era. This affinity was often based on a recognition of shared or analogous circumstances as well as a sense that the two continents had been shaped by analogous historical forces. As the Nigerian critic Chinweizu argued in 1975, the works of Latin American writers "are vibrant, alive, deal powerfully with experiences under imperialized histories and conditions that are, in many significant ways, quite similar to ours in Africa" (105). But in other cases, Latin American writers and their work were simply a source of inspiration. Writers such as Tchichellé Tchivéla and Ngũgĩ wa Thiong'o, for instance, saw in the work of Latin American writers not so much a model to be followed as a signal that the novel form could be bent to new and exciting projects (Tchivéla; Ngũgĩ, "The Language of African Fiction" 64). The Macondo Literary Festival is yet another example of how a comparison that might more often be imposed from without can be productively reclaimed and used to new and generative ends from within. But rather than turn to the kinds of world-historical analysis implied in Chinweizu's comment, the festival borrows the name Macondo and recodes it as a symbol of connection and exchange on the African continent. This is neither the Macondo of *One Hundred Years* nor the Makonde of the Belgian shipping agent's mistake, but another Macondo altogether: one of the many produced by the variegated global circulations of García Márquez's work in the decades since its publication.

And so, when it comes to talking about the influence of García Márquez and his work on the literatures of Global South, it is incorrect to say that these are always models imposed from without. Such dismissals inevitably impoverish the critical conversation, foreclosing the kinds of comparative connections this article has traced. Instead, the task at hand is one of seeking out the traces and discussions of influence (or inspiration) outside the scope of the literary market, in the context of smaller conversations that enact the generative potential of relational thinking. Ultimately, García Márquez's work does not encapsulate the Global South as a clearly delimited totality; this is an impossible task. Rather, it provides crucial cues for thinking about world-historical relation and transregional exchange and, as such, serves to illuminate the Global South as a conceptual category in the present.

Notes

1. The original reads: "una agencia marítima de Bruselas lo había embarcado por error con destino a Tanganyika, donde se lo entregaron a la dispersa comunidad de los Makondos" (459).
2. Makonde people living in Kenya are largely descendants of workers who migrated northward in the first part of the twentieth century; more recent arrivals were displaced by protracted Cold War–era civil war in Mozambique (1977–1992). This community has recently succeeded in gaining legal recognition from the Kenyan government; see www.unhcr.org/ibelong/makonde-in-kenya/ and www.unhcr.org/en-us/news/latest/2018/6/5b361f434/qa-head-kenyas-makonde-people-recounts-long-walk-statelessness.html.

3. My rendering emphasizes valences in the original: "comprendió que las cosas iban para largo, y volvió a establecer contacto con sus olvidados socios de Bruselas, pensando que para ser pionero daba lo mismo el Caribe que el África" (434). By contrast, Gregory Rabassa's translation reads: "[H]e understood that things were going to take a long time and he reestablished contact with his forgotten partners in Brussels, thinking that it was just as well to be a pioneer in the Caribbean as in Africa" (383).
4. Organized by the Macondo Book Society, a Nairobi-based nonprofit founded by the German journalist Anja Bengelstroff and the Kenyan writer Yvonne Adhiambo Owuor, the 2019 Macondo Book Festival featured writers and filmmakers from Angola, Cape Verde, Guinea-Bissau, Kenya, Nigeria, Mozambique, South Africa, and Zimbabwe, as well as Portugal. For more information, see www.macondolitfest.org/.
5. See www.macondolitfest.org/about-us.
6. In the second edition of *Historia personal del boom* (*A Personal History of the "Boom"*, 1972, 1984), José Donoso takes stock of the aftermath of the Boom, noting the ways in which it spurred the institutionalization of Latin American literature outside the continent, as well as the fact that there are now even boutiques called Macondo (143).
7. I am condensing a wealth of scholarship on the Third World, Bandung, tricontinentalism, and the Global South; for further discussion, see Prashad's *The Darker Nations* and *The Poorer Nations*, Mahler's "Global South" and *From the Tricontinental to the Global South*, Dirlik, Klengel and Ortiz Wallner, Lee, Sheppard and Nagar, and Yoon. I also provide a more in-depth discussion of the history of the term in the introduction to *The Dictator Novel*.
8. The World Social Forum, an amalgamation of social and anti- or alter-globalization movements that emerged in 2001 as a response to events such as the World Economic Forum and organized under the rallying cry "Another world is possible!," is one frequently cited example of transnational organizing consonant with this conceptualization of the Global South; for more, see the chapter "A Dream History of the Global South" in Prashad, *The Poorer Nations*.
9. Given García Márquez's stature, there are myriad interviews and biographical sources to reference. I am privileging Gerald Martin's biography *Gabriel García Márquez: A Life* as the most recent and most widely available English-language resource. Unlike García Márquez's autobiography *Vivir para contarla* (*Living to Tell the Tale*, 2002) or Dasso Saldívar's *García Márquez: El viaje a la semilla* (García Márquez: The Journey to the Source, 1997), which end before or just after the publication of *One Hundred Years*, Martin's biography closes with the celebration of the fortieth anniversary of its publication in 2007. Over the years, Plinio Apuleyo Mendoza, a fellow Colombian writer and longtime friend of García Márquez, has published several volumes of conversations, correspondence, and memoirs of that friendship, which are an additional and useful resource (see Works Cited).
10. Here Martin relies on García Márquez's recollection in the article "Desde París, con amor" (From Paris, with Love), published in 1982 as part of his column for the Colombian newspaper *El Espectador* and later reproduced in *Notas de prensa, 1980–1984* (353–55).
11. While some pieces were published immediately, the series as a whole would not appear until 1959, under the title "De viaje por los países socialistas" (Traveling through the Socialist Countries) (Martin, *Gabriel García Márquez* 221). It is currently available in the volume *De viaje por Europa del Este* (2015).
12. The announcement of the acquisition of García Márquez's papers by the Harry Ransom Center at the University of Texas–Austin in 2014, for instance, emphasized that these would now reside alongside those of the authors (namely Faulkner and Joyce) who

influenced García Márquez (www.hrc.utexas.edu/press/releases/2014/gabriel-garcia-marquez-archive.html). García Márquez himself often playfully claimed Faulkner as a Latin American writer, remarking to William Kennedy (to give one of many examples) that "he thought *The Hamlet* was 'the best South American novel ever written'" (72–73) (see also Sauri; Cohn, "'He Was One of Us'"; Doyle).

13. This issue of *Primera Plana* also featured a photograph of García Márquez on the cover, sunglasses in hand and strolling through the Mexico City neighborhood of San Ángel, with the cover line: "La gran novela de América" ("The Great Novel of Americas").

14. The original reads: "En realidad, aquella alusión a Rabelais fue puesta por mí como una cáscara de banano que muchos críticos pisaron" (104). Readers of *One Hundred Years* will remember that Aureliano's friend Gabriel leaves for Paris with "two changes of clothing, a pair of shoes, and the complete works of Rabelais" (404; 456).

15. The original reads: "Cuando llegué a París no era más que un *caribe* crudo. Lo que más le agradezco a esta ciudad, con la cual tengo tantos pleitos viejos, y tantos amores todavía más viejos, es que me hubiera dado un perspectiva nueva y resuelta de Latinoamérica. La visión de conjunto, que no teníamos en ninguno de nuestros países, se volvía muy clara aquí en torno a una mesa de café, y uno terminaba por darse cuenta de que, a pesar de ser de distintos países, todos éramos tripulantes de un mismo barco." The ideas expressed here were frequently repeated in García Márquez's essays and interviews; see, for example, Sheridan and Pereira (4).

16. Martin discusses García Márquez's friendship with Salvador Allende, subsequent declaration of his silence, and eventual reversal of the announcement at length in the biography, alongside attention to García Márquez's close friendships with Torrijos and Castro (see *Gabriel García Márquez*). For an example of García Márquez's criticism of CIA involvement in Latin America, see his review of Philip Agee's *Inside the Company* (1975), "The CIA in Latin America," for the *New York Review of Books*. For more on García Márquez's friendship with Castro, see Esteban and Panichelli.

17. For García Márquez's account of his time on the MacBride Commission, see the article "La comisión de Babel" (The Commission of Babel), in which he compared the experience to "trying to write a book with fifteen people" (my translation). For García Márquez's work on nuclear issues, see the keynote speech "The Doom of Damocles" (*El cataclismo de Damocles*) delivered on the forty-first anniversary of the Hiroshima bombing.

18. I have in mind here the work of the Brandt Commission (International Commission on International Development Issues, 1977–1980) and the South Commission (formed within the Non-Aligned Movement and chaired by Tanzania's Julius Nyerere, 1987–1990). For more on the importance of these commissions for contemporary understandings of the Global South, see Dirlik (12–14) and Prashad, *The Poorer Nations*.

19. The original reads: "Puede decirse que no ha habido en estos tiempos un movimiento de liberación africano que no haya contado con la solidaridad de Cuba, ya fuera con material y armamentos o con la formación de técnicos y especialistas militares y civiles" (12).

20. Such conflicting attitudes are also on display in Jihan El-Tahri's *Cuba: An African Odyssey* (2007), a documentary that explores Cuban support for and involvement in decolonization struggles on the African continent (with thanks to Anne Garland Mahler for the reference).

21. The original reads: "El nivel de vida de la población nativa era uno de los más bajos del mundo, en índice de analfabetismo era superior al 90 por ciento, y las condiciones

culturales eran todavía muy próximas a la edad de piedra. Aún en las ciudades del interior, los únicos que hablaban el portugués eran los hombres, y estos convivían hasta con siete esposas en una misma casa. Las supersticiones atávicas, no sólo eran un inconveniente para la vida diaria, sino también para la guerra. Los angolanos estaban convencidos desde siempre que los blancos no les entraban las balas, tenían un miedo mágico de los aviones y se negaban a pelear dentro de las trincheras porque decían que las tumbas, eran sólo para los muertos" (23–24).

22. The concept of combined and uneven development originates in Leon Trotsky's analysis of the Russian Revolution in 1932. For elaboration of this concept in relation to literature, and world literature in particular, see Warwick Research Collective.
23. The original reads: "una fuerza perniciosa y profunda que se siembra en el corazón de los hombres y que no es posible derrotar a bala: la colonización mental" (24).
24. Martin reports that the Macondo plantation was one of the largest properties belonging to the United Fruit Company, which also controlled the railway in the region (*Gabriel García Márquez* 38).
25. The Spanish *plátano*, by contrast, has Latin roots.
26. For more on the development of the concept of *extractivismo* and its utility as a way of thinking together disparate spaces, see Riofrancos, Gómez-Barris, and Davis.
27. As Taussig explains, while there is an oil palm native to Latin America, it produces oil inferior to that of the West African variety. The initial plantations established by United Fruit were in Guatemala, Panama, and Honduras (n3, 37–38).
28. For an expansion of Wenzel's argument in "Petro-Magic-Realism," see "Hijacking the Imagination: How to Tell the Story of the Niger Delta" in *The Disposition of Nature*; see also Lincoln.
29. The original reads: "estábamos en los puros cueros mi general, habíamos agotado nuestros últimos recursos, desangrados por la necesidad secular de aceptar empréstitos para pagar los servicios de la deuda externa desde las guerras de independencia y luego otros empréstitos para pagar los intereses de los servicios atrasados, siempre a cambio de algo mi general, primero el monopolio de la quina y el tabaco para los ingleses, después el monopolio del caucho y el cacao para los holandeses, después la concesión del ferrocarril de los páramos y la navegación fluvial para los alemanes, y todo para los gringos" (240–41).
30. The original reads: "La interpretación de nuestra realidad con esquemas ajenos solo contribuye a hacernos cada vez más desconocidos, cada vez menos libres, cada vez más solitarios" (n.p.).
31. See, for example, the manifestoes of the "Crack" group in Mexico (Palou et al.) and of the McOndo writers, both issued in 1996 (Fuguet and Gómez, *McOndo*).
32. *Midnight's Children* has, to date, thrice been awarded the Booker: first, upon its publication in 1981; second, as the "Booker of Bookers" on the twenty-fifth anniversary of the prize in 1993; and third, as the "Best of Booker" on the fortieth anniversary of the prize in 2008.
33. Khoury's novel, which is not (as of this writing) available in English or Spanish, takes up the figure of Santiago Nasar in *Chronicle of a Death Foretold*, a member of the wealthy Arab Levantine community in the town (see Civantos); for more on the influence of García Márquez in Arabic fiction, see Nasser and Rodríguez Sierra. In Hanif's novel, one of the characters is reading *Chronicle*, and some of the novel's pages are among the charred remains of the dictator's airplane in this fictionalized account of the assassination of General Muhammad Zia-ul-Haq in 1988.

34. The comparisons are often made in promotional blurbs for the books as well as in reviews; see, for example, Rushdie's review of Namwali Serpell's *The Old Drift* (2019) for the *New York Times*, as well as, for Serpell, Publisher's Weekly (staff), Kirkus Reviews (staff), Athitakis, and Furman, and for Makumbi, Sarasien; see also Attree.
35. The phrase comes from an essay by Lizzy Attree published in the *Los Angeles Review of Books* in 2018 and was repeated in Rushdie's review of *The Old Drift* in 2019 ("Salman Rushdie Reviews").

Works Cited

Apter, Andrew. *The Pan-African Nation: Oil and the Spectacle of Culture in Nigeria*. Chicago UP, 2005.

Armillas-Tiseyra, Magalí. *The Dictator Novel: Writers and Politics in the Global South*. Northwestern UP, 2019.

Athitakis, Mark. "'The Old Drift' Is a Brilliant Literary Response to Generations of Bad Politics." *Washington Post*, 26 Mar. 2019, www.washingtonpost.com/entertainment/books/the-old-drift-is-a-brilliant-literary-response-to-generations-of-bad-politics/2019/03/25/dcc678f2-472d-11e9-90f0-0ccfeec87a61_story.html. Accessed 28 Dec. 2019.

Attree, Lizzy. "Reclaiming Africa's Stolen Histories through Fiction." *Los Angeles Review of Books*, 11 July 2018, lareviewofbooks.org/article/reclaiming-africas-stolen-histories-through-fiction/. Accessed 16 Jan. 2020.

Beckman, Ericka. *Capital Fictions: The Literature of Latin America's Export Age*. U of Minnesota P, 2013.

Beckman, Ericka. "An Oil Well Named Macondo: Latin American Literature in the Time of Global Capital." *PMLA*, vol. 127, no. 1, 2012, pp. 145–51.

Bhabha, Homi K. Introduction. *Nation and Narration*, edited by Homi K. Bhabha, Routledge, 1990, pp. 1–7.

Chinweizu. "African Literary Criticism Today." *Okike*, no. 9, 1975, pp. 89–105.

Civantos, Christina E. "Orientalism and the Narration of Violence in the Mediterranean Atlantic: Gabriel García Márquez and Elias Khoury." *The Global South Atlantic*, edited by Kerry Bystrom and Joseph R. Slaughter, Fordham UP, 2018, pp. 165–85.

Cohn, Deborah. "Faulkner and Spanish America: Then and Now." *Faulkner in the Twenty-First Century*, edited by Robert W. Hamblin and Ann J. Abadie. UP of Mississippi, 2003, pp. 50–67.

Cohn, Deborah. "'He Was One of Us': The Reception of William Faulkner and the U.S. South by Latin American Authors." *Comparative Literature Studies*, vol. 34, no. 2, 1997, pp. 149–69.

Comaroff Jean, and John L. Comaroff. *Theory from the South: Or, How Euro-America Is Evolving toward Africa*. Paradigm, 2012.

Coronil, Fernando. *The Magical State: Nature, Money, and Modernity in Venezuela*. Chicago, 1997.

Cuba: An African Odyssey. Directed by Jihan El-Tahri, BBC Films and Temps Noir, 2007.

Davis, Thomas S. "Perceptual Methods" (Book Review). *Cultural Dynamics*, vol. 31, nos. 1–2, 2019, pp. 144–50.

de Granada, Germán. "Un afortunado fitónimo bantú: *Macondo*." *Thesaurus: Boletín del Instituto Caro y Cuervo*, vol. 26, no. 3, 1971, pp. 485–94.

de Sousa Santos, Boaventura. *Epistemologies of the South: Justice Against Epistemicide* (2009). Paradigm Publishers, 2014.

Dirlik, Arif. "Global South: Predicament and Promise." *The Global South*, vol. 1, no. 1, 2007, pp. 12–23.

Donoso, José. *Historia personal del "boom"* (1972). 2nd ed. Sudamericana, 1984.

Doyle, Laura. "Colonial Encounters." *The Oxford Handbook of Modernisms*, edited by Peter Brooker, Andrzej Gasiorek, Deborah Longworth, and Andrew Thacker, Oxford, 2010, pp. 249–66.

Dreifus, Claudia. "*Playboy* Interview: Gabriel García Márquez" (1982). *Conversations with Gabriel García Márquez*, edited by Gene H. Bell-Villada, UP of Mississippi, 2006, pp. 93–132.

El Manifiesto (staff). "Journey Back to the Source" (1977), translated by Gene H. Bell-Villada. *Conversations with Gabriel García Márquez*, edited by Gene H. Bell-Villada, of Mississippi, 2006, pp. 163–90.

Esteban, Ángel, and Stéphanie Panichelli. *Gabo y Fidel: El paisaje de una amistad*. Planeta, 2006.

Faris, Wendy B. "Scheherazade's Children: Magical Realism and Postmodern Fiction." *Magical Realism: Theory, History, Community*, edited by Lois Parkinson Zamora and Wendy B. Faris, Duke UP, 2005, pp. 407–26.

Franco, Jean. *The Decline and Fall of the Lettered City: Latin America in the Cold War*. Harvard UP, 2002.

Franco, Jean. "From Modernization to Resistance: Latin American Literature, 1959–1976" (1978). *Critical Passions: Selected Essays*, edited by Mary Louise Pratt and Kathleen Newman, Duke UP, 1999, pp. 285–310.

French, Jennifer L. *Nature, Neo-Colonialism, and the Spanish American Regional Writers*. Dartmouth, 2005.

Fuguet, Alberto. "I Am Not a Magic Realist," *Salon*, 11 June 1997, www.salon.com/1997/06/11/magicalintro/. Accessed 29 Dec. 2019.

Fuguet, Alberto. "Magical Neoliberalism." *Foreign Policy*, no. 125, July–August 2001, pp. 66–73.

Fuguet, Alberto, and Sergio Gómez, editors. *McOndo*. Mondadori, 1996.

Furman, Anna. "'The Old Drift' Author Namwali Serpell Shares How Zambian Afronauts Inspired Her Debut Novel." *Los Angeles Times*, 23 Mar. 2019, www.latimes.com/books/la-et-jc-namwali-serpell-old-drift-20190323-story.html. Accessed 28 Dec. 2019.

García Márquez, Gabriel. "El ahogado más hermoso del mundo" (1968). *La increíble y triste historia de la cándida Eréndira y de su abuela desalmada: Siete cuentos*, Sudamericana, 1972, pp. 47–56.

García Márquez, Gabriel. *The Autumn of the Patriarch*. Translated by Gregory Rabassa (1976), Harper Perennial, 2006.

García Márquez, Gabriel. "Big Mama's Funeral" (1962). *Collected Stories*, translated by Gregory Rabassa and J. R. Bernstein (1984), Harper Perennial, 1999, pp. 197–214.

García Márquez, Gabriel. "Blacamán el bueno, vendedor de milagros" (1968). *La increíble y triste historia de la cándida Eréndira y de su abuela desalmada: Siete cuentos*, Sudamericana, 1972, pp. 81–94.

García Márquez, Gabriel. "Blacamán the Good, Vendor of Miracles" (1968). *Collected Stories*, translated by Gregory Rabassa and J. R. Bernstein (1984), Harper Perennial, 1999, pp. 272–82.

García Márquez, Gabriel. *El cataclismo de Damocles/The Doom of Damocles*. Universidad Centroamericana-EDUCA, 1986.

García Márquez, Gabriel. *Chronicle of a Death Foretold* (1981). Translated by Gregory Rabassa (1982), Vintage, 2003.

García Márquez, Gabriel. "The CIA in Latin America," translated by Gregory Rabassa, *New York Review of Books*, 7 Aug. 1975, www.nybooks.com/articles/1975/08/07/the-cia-in-latin-america/. Accessed 15 Nov. 2019.

García Márquez, Gabriel. *Cien años de soledad* (1967). Real Academia Española, 2007.
García Márquez, Gabriel. "La comisión de Babel" (Opinión). *El País*, 21 Nov., 1980, elpais.com/diario/1980/11/21/opinion/343609215_850215.html. Accessed 25 Nov. 2019.
García Márquez, Gabriel. *El coronel no tiene quien le escriba* (1961). Vintage Español, 2010.
García Márquez, Gabriel. *Crónica de una muerte anunciada*. Bruguera, 1981.
García Márquez, Gabriel. "Desde París, con amor" (12 Dec. 1982). *Notas de prensa, 1980–1984*, Mondadori, 1991, pp. 353–55.
García Márquez, Gabriel. *De viaje por Europa del Este* (1957). Literatura Random House, 2015.
García Márquez, Gabriel. "Los funerales de la Mamá Grande" (1962). *Los funerales de la Mamá Grande*, Plaza y Janés, 2006, pp. 141–66.
García Márquez, Gabriel. "The Handsomest Drowned Man in the World: A Tale for Children" (1968). *Collected Stories*, translated by Gregory Rabassa and J. R. Bernstein (1984), Harper Perennial, 1999, pp. 247–54.
García Márquez, Gabriel. "La increíble y triste historia de la cándida Eréndira y de su abuela desalmada" (1972). *La increíble y triste historia de la cándida Eréndira y de su abuela desalmada: Siete cuentos*, Sudamericana, 1972, pp. 90–163.
García Márquez, Gabriel. *Living to Tell the Tale*. Translated by Edith Grossman, Knopf, 2003.
García Márquez, Gabriel. *El olor de la guayaba: Conversaciones con Plinio Apuleyo Mendoza*. Bruguera, 1982.
García Márquez, Gabriel. *One Hundred Years of Solitude* (1967). Translated by Gregory Rabassa (1970), HarperCollins, 2003.
García Márquez, Gabriel. *Operación Carlota*. Prensa Latina, 1977.
García Márquez, Gabriel. "Operation Carlota," translated by Patrick Camiller. *New Left Review*, vol. 1, no. 101, 1977, pp. 123–37.
García Márquez, Gabriel. *El otoño del patriarca* (1975). Sudamericana, 2014.
García Márquez, Gabriel. "La soledad de América Latina" (1982), NobelPrize.org, www.nobelprize.org/prizes/literature/1982/marquez/25603-gabriel-garcia-marquez-nobel-lecture-1982/. Accessed 16 Jan. 2020.
García Márquez, Gabriel. "The Solitude of Latin America: Nobel Lecture, 8 Dec. 1982." *The Georgia Review*, vol. 49, no. 1, 1995, pp. 133–36.
García Márquez, Gabriel. *Vivir para contarla*. Mondadori, 2002.
Glissant, Édouard. *Poetics of Relation* (1990). Translated by Betsy Wing, U of Michigan P, 1997.
Gómez-Barris, Macarena. *The Extractive Zone: Social Ecologies and Decolonial Perspectives*. Duke, 2017.
González Bermejo, Ernesto. "And Now, Two Hundred Years of Solitude" (1971), translated by Gene H. Bell-Villada. *Conversations with Gabriel García Márquez*, edited by Gene H. Bell-Villada, of Mississippi, 2006, pp. 3–30.
Hanif, Mohammed. *A Case of Exploding Mangoes*. Knopf, 2008.
Harford Vargas, Jennifer. "Critical Realisms in the Global South: Narrative Transculturation in Senapati's *Six Acres and a Third* and García Márquez's *One Hundred Years of Solitude*." *Colonialism, Modernity, and Literature: A View from India*, edited by Satya P. Mohanty, Palgrave, 2011, pp. 25–54.
Harp, Stephen L. *A World History of Rubber: Empire, Industry, and the Everyday*. Wiley Blackwell, 2015.
Jin, J. I. "Literary Translation and Modern Chinese Literature." *The Oxford Handbook of Modern Chinese Literatures*, edited by Carlos Rojas and Andrea Bachner, Oxford, 2016, pp. 521–30.

Kantor, Roanne L. "A Case of Exploding Markets: Latin American and South Asian Literary 'Booms.'" *Comparative Literature*, vol. 70, no. 5, 2018, pp. 466–86.

Kartha, Sivan. "Discourses of the Global South." *The Oxford Handbook of Climate Change and Society*, edited by John S. Dryzek, Richard B. Norgaard, and David Scholsberg, Oxford UP, 2011, pp. 504–20.

Kennedy, William. "A Yellow Trolley Car in Barcelona: An Interview" (1973). *Conversations with Gabriel García Márquez*, edited by Gene H. Bell-Villada, of Mississippi, 2006, pp. 59–78.

Khoury, Elias. *Majma' al-Asrar*. Dar al-Adab, 1994.

Kirkus Reviews (staff). "The Old Drift." *Kirkus Reviews*, 15 Jan. 2019, www.kirkusreviews.com/book-reviews/namwali-serpell/the-old-drift/. Accessed 28 Dec. 2019.

Klengel, Susanne, and Alexandra Ortiz Wallner, editors. *Sur/South: Poetics and Politics of Thinking Latin America/India*. Iberoamericana, 2016.

Kourouma, Ahmadou. *En Attendant le vote des bêtes sauvages*. Éditions du Seuil, 1998.

Kourouma, Ahmadou. *Waiting for the Vote of the Wild Animals*. Translated by Carrol F. Coates, U of Virginia P, 2001.

Lee, Christopher J., editor. *Making a World after Empire: The Bandung Moment and Its Political Afterlives*. Ohio UP, 2010.

Lincoln, Sarah L. "'Petro-Magic Realism': Ben Okri's Inflationary Modernism." *The Oxford Handbook of Global Modernisms*, edited by Mark Wollaeger and Matt Eatough, Oxford, 2012, pp. 249–66.

Lopès, Henri. *The Laughing Cry: An African Cock and Bull Story* (1982). Translated by Gerald Moore, Readers International, 1987.

Lopès, Henri. *Le Pleurer-rire* (1982). Présence Africaine, 2003.

López, Alfred J. "Introduction: The (Post)Global South." *The Global South*, vol. 1, no. 1, 2007, pp. 1–11.

Lynn, Martin. *Commerce and Economic Change in West Africa: The Palm Oil Trade in the Nineteenth Century*. Cambridge UP, 1997.

Lyon, Janet. "Cosmopolitanism and Modernism." *The Oxford Handbook of Global Modernisms*, edited by Mark Wollaeger and Matt Eatough, Oxford, 2012, pp. 387–412.

Makokha, Justus Kizito Siboe. "Nairobi Hosts Inaugural Macondo Literary Festival." *The Star*, 4 Oct. 2019, www.the-star.co.ke/sasa/books/2019-10-04-nairobi-hosts-inaugural-macondo-literary-festival/. Accessed 6 Dec. 2019.

Makumbi, Jennifer Nansubuga. *Kintu* (2014). Transit Books, 2017.

Mahler, Anne Garland. *From the Tricontinental to the Global South: Race, Radicalism, and Transnational Solidarity*. Duke UP, 2018.

Mahler, Anne Garland. "Global South." *Oxford Bibliographies Online*, 25 Oct. 2017, www.oxfordbibliographies.com/view/document/obo-9780190221911/obo-9780190221911-0055.xml?rskey=eMzKAW&result=16. Accessed 23 Dec. 2019.

Martin, Gerald. *Gabriel García Márquez: A Life*. Knopf, 2009.

Martin, Gerald. *Journeys through the Labyrinth: Latin American Fiction in the Twentieth Century*. Verso, 1989

Mendoza, Plinio Apuleyo. *Aquellos tiempos con Gabo*. Plaza & Janés Editores, 2000.

Mendoza, Plinio Apuleyo. *Gabo: Cartas y recuerdos*. Ediciones B, 2013.

Molloy, Sylvia. "Latin America in the U.S. Imaginary: Postcolonialism, Translation, and the Magic Realist Imperative." *Ideologies of Hispanism*, edited by Mabel Moraña, Vanderbilt, 2005, pp. 189–200.

Moretti, Franco. *Modern Epic: The World System from Goethe to García Márquez* (1994). Translated by Quintin Hoare, Verso, 1996.

Moudileno, Lydie. "Magical Realism: 'Arme miraculeuse' for the African Novel?" *Research in African Literatures*, vol. 37, no. 1, 2006, pp. 28–41.

Müller, Gesine. "Re-Mapping World Literature from Macondo." *Re-Mapping World Literature: Writing, Book Markets, and Epistemologies between Latin America and the Global South*, edited by Gesine Müller, Jorge J. Locane, and Benjamin Loy, de Gruyter, 2018, pp. 157–73.

Nasscr, Tahia Abdel. "Revolution and *Cien años de soledad* in Naguib Mahfouz's *Layali alf Laylah*." *Comparative Literature Studies*, vol. 52, no. 3, 2015, pp. 539–61.

Ngũgĩ wa Thiong'o. *Globalectics: Theory and the Politics of Knowing*. Columbia, 2012.

Ngũgĩ wa Thiong'o. "The Language of African Fiction." *Decolonizing the Mind: The Politics of Language in African Fiction*, Heinemann, 1986, pp. 63–86.

Ngũgĩ wa Thiong'o. *Wizard of the Crow* (2004–2007). Translated by Ngũgĩ wa Thiong'o, Pantheon, 2006.

Ngũgĩ wa Thiong'o. *Mũrogi wa Kagogo: Mbuku ya Mbere na ya Kerĩ*. East African Educational Publishers, 2004.

Ngũgĩ wa Thiong'o. *Mũrogi wa Kagogo: Mbuku ya Gatatũ*. East African Educational Publishers, 2006.

Ngũgĩ wa Thiong'o. *Mũrogi wa Kagogo: Mbuku ya Kana, Gatano na Gatandatũ*. East African Educational Publishers, 2007.

Ortega, Julio. "Variaciones del Gaborio." *Gaborio: Artes de releer a Gabriel García Márquez*, edited by Julio Ortega, Jorale, 2003, pp. 263–68.

Palou, Pedro Ángel, et al. "Crack Manifesto" (1996), translated by Celia Brotolin and Scott Miller. *Dalkey Archive Press*, www.dalkeyarchive.com/crack-manifesto/. Accessed 29 Dec. 2019.

Pollack, Sarah. "After Bolaño: Rethinking the Politics of Latin American Literature in Translation." *PMLA*, vol. 128, no. 3, 2013, pp. 660–67.

Pollack, Sarah. "Latin America Translated (Again): Roberto Bolaño's *The Savage Detectives* in the United States." *Comparative Literature*, vol. 61, no. 3, 2009, pp. 346–65.

Prashad, Vijay. *The Darker Nations: A People's History of the Third World*. New Press, 2007.

Prashad, Vijay. *The Poorer Nations: A Possible History of the Global South*. Verso, 2012.

Publisher's Weekly (staff). "The Old Drift," *Publisher's Weekly*, 7 Jan. 2019, www.publishersweekly.com/978-1-101-90714-6. Accessed 28 Dec. 2019.

Quayson, Ato. "Fecundities of the Unexpected: Magical Realism, Narrative, and History." *The Novel: History, Geography, and Culture*, vol. 1, edited by Franco Moretti, Princeton UP, 2006, pp. 726–56.

Rincón, Carlos. "Streams Out of Control: The Latin American Plot." *Streams of Cultural Capital: Transnational Cultural Studies*, edited by David Palumbo-Liu and Hans Ulrich Gumbrecht, Stanford UP, 1997, pp. 179–98.

Riofrancos, Thea. "*Extractivismo* Unearthed: A Genealogy of a Radical Discourse." *Cultural Studies*, vol. 31, nos. 2–3, 2017, pp. 277–306.

Rodríguez Sierra, Francisco. "Fictional Boundaries in the 'Journalistic Fiction' of Gabriel García Márquez and Rabee Jaber." *Alif: Journal of Comparative Poetics*, no. 37, 2017, pp. 199–228.

Rushdie, Salman. "Inverted Realism." *PEN America*, 23 Jan. 2007, pen.org/inverted-realism/. Accessed 30 Dec. 2019.

Rushdie, Salman. "Magic in Service of Truth." *New York Times*, 21 Apr. 2014, www.nytimes.com/2014/04/21/books/review/gabriel-garcia-marquezs-work-was-rooted-in-the-real.html. Accessed 30 Dec. 2019.

Rushdie, Salman. "Salman Rushdie Reviews a Sweeping Debut about the Roots of Modern Zambia." *New York Times*, 28 Mar. 2019, www.nytimes.com/2019/03/28/books/review/old-drift-salman-rushdie.html. Accessed 30 Dec. 2019.

Saldívar, Dasso. *García Márquez: El viaje a la semilla*. Alfaguara, 1997.

Sánchez Prado, Ignacio M., editor. *América Latina en la "literatura mundial."* Biblioteca de América, 2006.

Sánchez Prado, Ignacio M.. *Strategic Occidentalism: On Mexican Fiction, the Neoliberal Book Market, and the Question of World Literature*. Northwestern UP, 2018.

Sánchez Prado, Ignacio M. "Teaching the Latin American Boom as World Literature." *Teaching the Latin American Boom*, edited by Lucille Kerr and Alejandro Herrero-Olaizola, Modern Language Association of America, 2015, pp. 121–28.

Sangari, Kumkum. "The Politics of the Possible." *Cultural Critique*, vol. 7, 1987, pp. 157–86.

Sarasien, Amanda. "A Review of Kintu by Jennifer Nansubuga Makumbi." *The Literary Review*, n.d., www.theliteraryreview.org/book-review/a-review-of-kintu-by-jennifer-nansubuga-makumbi/. Accessed 16 Jan. 2020.

Sauri, Emilio. "Faulkner and His Brothers." *Studies in American Fiction*, vol. 40, no. 2, 2013, 259-83.

Schóo, Ernesto. "Los viajes de Simbad García Márquez." *Primera Plana*, vol. 5, no. 234, 20 June 1967, pp. 52–54.

Serpell, Namwali. *The Old Drift*. Hogarth, 2019.

Sheppard, Eric, and Richa Nagar. "From East-West to North-South." *Antipode*, vol. 36, no. 4, 2004, pp. 557–63.

Sheridan, Guillermo, and Armando Pereira. "García Márquez en México (entrevista)." *Revista de la Universidad de México*, vol. 30, no. 6, February 1976, pp. 4–11.

Shih, Shu-mei. "Comparison as Relation." *Comparison: Theories, Approaches, Uses*, edited by Rita Felski and Susan Stanford Friedman, Johns Hopkins, 2013, pp. 79–98.

Shih, Shu-mei. "World Studies and Relational Comparison." *PMLA*, vol. 130, no. 2, 2015, pp. 430–38.

Siskind, Mariano. *Cosmopolitan Desires: Global Modernity and World Literature in Latin America*. Northwestern, 2014.

Slemon, Stephen. "Magic Realism as Postcolonial Discourse." *Magical Realism: Theory, History, Community*, edited by Lois Parkinson Zamora and Wendy B. Faris, Duke, 2005, pp. 407–26.

Sparke, Matthew. "Everywhere but Always Somewhere: Critical Geographies of the Global South." *The Global South*, vol. 1, no. 1, 2007, pp. 117–26.

Spivak, Gayatri Chakravorty. "Marginality in the Teaching Machine." *Outside in the Teaching Machine*, Routledge, 1993, pp. 58–85.

Taussig, Michael. *Palma Africana*. U of Chicago P, 2018.

Tchivéla, Tchichiellé. "Une Parenté outre-Atlantique." *Notre Librairie* 92, 1988, pp. 30–34.

Tshuma, Novuyo Rosa. *House of Stone*. Norton, 2018.

van Leeuwen, Richard. "*A Thousand and One Nights* and the Novel." *The Oxford Handbook of Arab Novelistic Traditions*, edited by Waïl S. Hassan, Oxford UP, 2017, pp. 103–18.

Viñas, David, et al. *Más allá del boom: Literatura y mercado*. Marcha Editores, 1981.

Visión (staff). "Gabriel García Márquez: De la ficción a la política." *Visión: La revista latino-americana*, 30 Jan. 1975, pp. 26–29.

Warwick Research Collective. *Combined and Uneven Development: Towards a New Theory of World-Literature*. Liverpool UP, 2015.

Wenzel, Jennifer. *The Disposition of Nature: Environmental Crisis and World Literature*. Fordham UP, 2020.

Wenzel, Jennifer. "Petro-Magic-Realism: Toward a Political Ecology of Nigerian Literature." *Postcolonial Studies*, vol. 9, no. 4, 2006, pp. 449–64.

West-Pavlov, Russell, editor. *The Global South and Literature*. Cambridge UP, 2018.

West-Pavlov, Russell. "Toward the Global South: Concept or Chimera, Paradigm or Panacea?" *The Global South and Literature*, edited by West-Pavlov, Cambridge, 2018, pp. 1–19.

Williams, Raymond Leslie. *A Companion to Gabriel García Márquez*. Tamesis, 2010.

Yoon, Duncan M. "Bandung Nostalgia and the Global South." *The Global South and Literature*, edited by Russell West-Pavlov, Cambridge UP, 2018, pp. 23–33.

Zhang, Y. P. "The Emergence of the Global South Novel: Red Sorghum, Présence Africaine, and the Third Novelists' International." *NOVEL: A Forum on Fiction*, vol. 52, no. 3, 2019, pp. 347–68.

CHAPTER 4

MODERNIZATION AND CULTURE IN GARCÍA MÁRQUEZ'S CARIBBEAN

MARCELA VELASCO

In Macondo and other fictional towns on the Atlantic coast, Gabriel García Márquez portrays the Colombian Caribbean's experience with the forces of modernization, an open-ended process of technological, political, and economic change that transforms cultures. *La hojarasca* (*Leaf Storm*), his first novel, is set in extraordinary moments of socioeconomic and political disruption that alter the town's prevailing values. The culprit, a foreign banana company, breaks into Macondo, attracts a leaf storm of opportunity seekers, introduces new technologies, and withdraws suddenly, leaving the town destroyed and with scarce resources to recover. The boom and bust cycles of economic development and political instability that befall the Garcíamarquezian Caribbean do not fully uproot the old order or establish the new world announced by the brokers of progress. Instead, people coexist with old norms and emergent values that are thinly supported by the extant social relations.

In the tradition of great works of literature, García Márquez examines the impact of history on individuals, their identities, and the norms that limit their choices. His views of such transformations were inspired by an extraordinary personal life in, and an understanding of, Caribbean culture. Coming of age, García Márquez went through a series of "losses and displacements" that separated him from his Caribbean roots but also brought him face to face with major events, like La Violencia (Bell-Villada, *García Márquez* 45–46), the partisan violence that began in 1948 and brought an end to a "relatively coherent" modernization project initiated by Liberals in the 1930s and 1940s (Melo 27).

As an uninspired and "self-absorbed student of law" in Bogota (Bell-Villada, *García Márquez* 46), García Márquez witnessed the 1948 "Bogotazo": the uprising triggered by the assassination of the popular Liberal Party leader Jorge Eliécer Gaitán, which in turn sparked La Violencia. According to Gilard, the political drama must have swayed the author's appreciation of history. The overt partisan violence unmasked an undemocratic and distraught country that "took a giant step backward"[1] and returned to the barbarism of the civil wars; García Márquez "believes that he witnessed the death of the modern myth [of progress]" (Gilard 53).[2]

Forced to return to his native Caribbean, he chose to rediscover his culture and become a writer of fiction (Bell-Villada, *García Márquez* 46). He took the opportunity to study his land as "a lucid aficionado," doing his best to make this reality known through his journalistic chronicles (Gilard 50). The 1954 chronicles of journeys to La Sierpe—the wetlands in southeast Bolívar (a Caribbean department)—and in Chocó on the Pacific coast, prefigure some of his most memorable fictional narratives. In La Sierpe, he finds a place dominated by superstition, where it was commonplace to avenge an aggression with a curse to grow a monkey inside the attacker, as well as to believe that many years before there lived "la marquesita"—a kind and wealthy Spanish woman who lived two hundred years and was a sort of "great mama" ("La marquesita de La Sierpe" 11, 13–14)— and where social divisions separated people into those believed to be of a higher caste with supernatural and exclusive powers, on the one hand, and those who toiled in life without recourse to the paranormal, on the other ("La herencia sobrenatural de la marquesita" 19). In Quibdó, the capital of Chocó (a department and an economic enclave for Andean gold miners), he finds sixteen thousand well-educated people who know Colombia's civil code by heart and convene weekly to hear the news when the mail arrives with national newspapers. They nevertheless live abandoned in the middle of a rainforest—where it rains continuously—patiently waiting to receive communications from the central government ("Historia íntima" 143).

MODERNIZATION AND CULTURE

Writing during extraordinary times, García Márquez describes the effects of abrupt political and economic change on his fictional characters and communities. In the 1950s and 1960s, Colombia's early social science was also documenting similar concerns. At the time, Orlando Fals Borda, founder of Colombian sociology and one of Latin America's most creative social thinkers, contended that new technologies and urban rationalism were transforming Colombian culture. In his view, values of "class consciousness and ideas of comfort, anonymity and psychological escape" were becoming entrenched in the country ("La teoría" 32).[3] As new worldviews were changing personal behavior, the number of freethinking individuals ready to take risks was increasing (32–33). Fals Borda was describing cultural change by using the predominant modernization theories of the 1950s.

Culture is defined here as a set of widely shared attitudes, values, orientations toward life, and practices that define a particular group, which is communicated from one generation to the next and influences (though does not determine) each individual's behavior (Matsumoto 16; Spencer-Oatey 3-6). Culture also represents the core values normally attributed to specific groups (e.g., Latin Americans, Canadians, Muslims), even though individual members of that group will differ in the extent to which they adhere to or represent the values attributed to that culture (Matsumoto 18). Cultures are relatively stable, but they evolve as a result of new technologies, demographic change, disease, environmental or geographical accidents, or new ideas that influence behavior and values.

Though much of the classical modernization paradigm has now been abandoned by Western social scientists, Fals Borda's assumptions that socioeconomic transformations change people's values and worldviews remain valid today. Contemporary cultural modernization scholarship, by contrast, is concerned with understanding the precise ways in which sustained economic and physical security, the latter a product of economic and technological development, increase the chances that people will engage in a wide range of human aspirations once they take their survival for granted (Inglehart 8). Improvements in material well-being deemphasize *survival* values and enhance *self-expression* values. Furthermore, *traditional* values (e.g., family orientation; religiosity; deference to authority; and rejection of divorce, abortion, or suicide) give way to *secular-rational* values that favor tolerance, trust in abstract institutions, demands for public participation, or gender parity (Inglehart et al. n.p.).

Unlike what modernization theorists once claimed, none of this is the result of immutable laws of historical progress, nor are the pace and scope of change the same everywhere. Furthermore, societies resist or modulate the effects of change, maintaining some essential cultural characteristics. Recent surveys on the values of Latin Americans confirm that many people in the region lean toward self-expression values, while just as many maintain a commitment to traditional values, such as a strong sense of religiosity and deference to authority (Inglehart et al. n.p.). This suggests that Latin America maintains a common cultural core, which is likely informed by comparable histories of socioeconomic and political development, as well as by religious and linguistic traditions.

García Márquez speaks to many of these concerns. His Macondo characters live through major historical events such as the inland settlement of the Caribbean, "the bloody wars of the nineteenth century, the repeated instances of illusory prosperity" and "the hegemonic power of the U.S. economy" (Bell-Villada, *García Márquez* 103-4). As the novelist describes it, the erratic socioeconomic changes associated with this history unevenly improved material well-being and raised—though did not fulfill—expectations and promises for progress. Work of this intellectual caliber—produced when Colombia lacked free speech and robust social science inquiry—should be considered as supportive material to interpret a time and a place in Colombian history.

With the metaphor of the leaf storm, García Márquez reminds us that ephemeral prosperity and violent state- and nation-building failed to improve material conditions, yet exposed people to new technologies, forms of organization, and worldviews. This may be why some of his characters cling to traditional values to survive the maelstrom, while others refuse to let go of the promise of the new knowledge, technologies, or values in order to survive. They are two complementary sides of a coin coexisting in a similar reality.

It Is Better to Talk about History in Poetic Language

In his banquet speech at the Nobel dinner in 1982, García Márquez identified poetry as the secret energy of quotidian life, an energy "that cooks the chickpeas in the kitchen, and spreads the love and repeats the images in the mirrors."[4] The speech "The Solitude of Latin America" offers the region's history as a lesson on life conquering death. A tumultuous record of colonial domination, postcolonial despotism, and ethnocide produced an "outsized reality" that

> lives within us and determines each instant of our countless daily deaths, and that nourishes a source of insatiable creativity, full of sorrow and beauty. . . [The] creatures of that unbridled reality . . . have had to ask but little of imagination, for our crucial problem has been a lack of conventional means to render our lives believable. This, my friends, is the crux of our solitude. . . . In spite of this, to oppression, plundering and abandonment, we respond with life. Neither floods nor plagues, famines nor cataclysms, nor even the eternal wars of century upon century, have been able to subdue the persistent advantage of life over death.[5] (n.p.)

This segment of the speech admits that history shapes individual dispositions and that individuals will survive history while finding ways—some more poetic, some more rational—to cook the chickpeas and spread the love. In this idea lies the cultural spirit of the Colombian Caribbean at a particular moment and as captured by García Márquez in the poetic language of his family home, which reflects the life-affirming truth of his people.

For the author, only poetic language allowed a truthful description of the events that he had seen. García Márquez insisted that he was a realist who portrayed the true "but undocumented pictures of Latin American life" (Palencia-Roth 54). He chose literary fiction once he realized that the genre presented an alternative format to rationalist and academic accounts of the truth and a language that more aptly describes the clash of cultures, worldviews, and sources of imagination that mixed in his Caribbean, where supernatural elements form part of everyday life (Mendoza and García Márquez 31, 52). Ordinary readers of *One Hundred Years of Solitude* (henceforth *One Hundred Years*) confirmed this for him. He found that they were not surprised by the novel, "because, when all is said and done, I'm telling them nothing that hasn't happened in their own lives" (Mendoza and García Márquez, *Fragrance of Guava* 36).[6]

The History of Colombia Is the Story of Macondo

Dauster's proposition that Macondo is a microcosm of human behavior, and that *Leaf Storm* is a microcosm of García Márquez's total work (24), helps justify my selecting these two novels to understand the author's sense of history. Though the routines of the Buendía clan are the "narrative center" of *One Hundred Years*, the novel also successfully "integrates private and public concerns" such as, respectively, family life and romances as well as rebellions, migrations, or political repression (Bell-Villada, *García Márquez* 100). Routines that occur at the interface of family life and major events reveal change and continuity in the values that keep the clan and Macondo together. The center of the narrative in *Leaf Storm*, on the other hand, consists of the perceptions of three members from different generations of the same family about a hated French doctor's death amid the backdrop of larger historical events: civil war and the arrival of the banana company. In the earlier novel, García Márquez highlights the "opposition between traditional practices and relations" in the face of new "collective configurations" brought by modern life (Barreto 47).

Macondo, in *Leaf Storm*, is a town of refugees founded sometime in the late nineteenth century by three hundred settlers. The town replicates some of the boom and bust patterns of urban and demographic collapse experienced by the Colombian Caribbean over a period of two hundred years. Efforts to found cities and towns in the region only began in the eighteenth century after the population had slowly recovered from the destruction of the conquest and ended when the wars of independence once again devastated the population and destroyed the main urban centers of Cartagena, Mompox, and Tenerife. People fled to the hinterland, founded smaller settlements, and "ruralized" the Caribbean region (Zambrano, "Historia" 51).

Demographic revival in the Caribbean was the product of the sanctuary offered by a difficult geography that allowed communities to resist repressive authorities and build subsistence economies. In the eighteenth century, for example, the thriving communities of survivors of indigenous cultures, mestizos and mulattos, poor whites, fugitives, and Black runaways remained entrenched in their *palenques* (maroon societies) or lived *arrochelados* (rambunctiously) in scattered villages outside the scope of the government. Once they were thriving, the colonial Spanish authorities tried to pass measures to contain them within "the social and moral controls of urban life" (CINEP 153).[7] Many of the interethnic societies just described endured well into the twentieth century by adapting to a harsh environment with a mix of hard work and diversion that produced what Fals Borda terms "el dejadismo costeño" (Caribbean abandonment), serving to keep suffering at bay with a blissful, laid-back attitude (Fals Borda, *Historia doble* 158B, 161A).

These settlements helped reproduce morally loose, intercultural, and miscegenated societies, and "constituted a massive disturbance of power structures" (Zambrano,

"Historia" 51).[8] The demographic decline and subsequent population withdrawal into the hinterland that led to the deterioration of urban authority structures replaced Catholic doctrine with personalized worship of individual deities in pagan-like, carnivalesque celebrations of the miraculous (CINEP 227). Centralized authority has thus been historically weak in the Colombian Caribbean. After independence, Bogotá exercised little power over the region, and Caribbean elites undermined centralized powers by practicing contraband or loosening their social morals (CINEP 157; Fals Borda, "Historia" 155A).

Bergquist, however, warns that this reality concealed deep cultural and political tensions (165), such as those reported by the journalist Antolín Díaz, who was commissioned by Liberal president Alfonso López Pumarejo in the 1930s to write a chronicle on the Bolívar province, and who described the abuses of power in the region, where carnivals, music, and dance covered up the despotic nature of local relations. Notwithstanding their character, these societies served as buffers to modernization by either absorbing the excess labor that could never be employed in the embryonic modern economy or taking back the refugees of failed attempts at economic or political modernization.

The Inroads of Modernity

In the fictional Caribbean, progress is illusory, ephemeral, and disruptive and appears in cycles of boom-and-bust activity. *Leaf Storm* sets the tone for the commotion produced by rapid economic change:

> Suddenly, as if a whirlwind had set down roots in the center of the town, the banana company arrived, pursued by the leaf storm. A whirling leaf storm had been stirred up, formed out of the human and material dregs of other towns, the chaff of a civil war that seemed ever more remote and unlikely. The whirlwind was implacable.... In less than a year it sowed over the town the rubble of many catastrophes that had come before it. (García Márquez, "Leaf Storm" 1–2)[9]

The forces of modernity appear as if thrown onto the new town, whose founders nonetheless anticipated that the leaf storm would one day catch up with them. In this story, once the banana company is gone, it leaves a ruined village "occupied by unemployed and angry people who were tormented by a prosperous past and the bitterness of an overwhelming and static present" ("Leaf Storm" 79).[10]

Taking a cue from *Leaf Storm,* the inroads of modernity into Macondo go back to the late 1800s. The novel references the Civil War of 1884–1885, one of five major wars waged in that century. Caribbean political elites from the states of Bolívar and Magdalena were actively involved in this uprising against Conservative efforts to replace the Liberal 1863 Constitution (Bushnell 141–42). The 1863 Constitution reflected the aspirations of a generation of postcolonial elites eager to end the Conservative legacy of the colonial period.

Their ideals were violently crushed by Conservative forces with the defeat of the Liberal forces in La Humareda, on the Magdalena River in 1885.

Opportunities for progress came in the 1870s with the expansion of the world economy and a growing international demand for agricultural commodities like tobacco, quinine, bananas, and coffee (Bushnell 136). This required some reform in order to introduce the necessary institutions and technologies for trade and to access a supply of land and labor. However, the land- and labor-intensive nature of the business of exporting basic agricultural and mineral commodities favored the sort of extractive colonial institutions that had allowed the concentration of land and the repression of peasants. This helped maintain the illiberal socioeconomic relations and extreme inequality that survive to this day (see Coatsworth).

Land dispossession, agrarian counter-reform, and patrimonial politics are thus enduring phenomena in the Colombian Caribbean—and in the rest of the country. As Colombian landowners were wont to do, José Arcadio of the Buendía clan confiscates peasant lands, basing his right on the fact that his father, José Arcadio Buendía, had distributed these properties at the time of the founding of Macondo and that he could prove that he "had been crazy ever since that time" and had dispossessed the family of its patrimony (*One Hundred Years* 118).[11] And as was (and is) the custom of government authorities, his son Arcadio creates institutions to legalize the land grab. This episode anticipates the real strategies of the United Fruit Company in Colombia to acquire rights from the central government and to monopolize the region's land and railways, without meaningful consultation with locals (Abello 234).

Predictably, disagreement over how to develop the economy and who stood to benefit from growth fed into the violent partisan cleavages that had historically divided Liberals and Conservatives over the role of religion and government in public life (Palacios 1–2). In these ideological divisions, the forces of Liberalism were usually defeated, much like the quixotic Colonel Aureliano Buendía, who is aligned with the Liberals and who "organized thirty-two armed uprisings and . . . lost them all" (*One Hundred Years* 107).[12]

The incessant episodes of civil war in the nineteenth century seemed to conclude in the early 1900s, after the Treaty of Neerlandia ended the War of the Thousand Days (1899–1902). The treaty was signed in Santa Marta in 1902 and is attended by Colonel Aureliano Buendía in García Márquez's fictional account of the event. This civil war began as a "gentlemen's affair" but later turned into a guerrilla war that left 150,000 dead; in the end, the Liberals capitulated, the country was ruined, and a year later, the province of Panamá was lost to separatist forces, partly as a consequence of this conflict (Zambrano, "Las guerras"). Colonel Aureliano Buendía returns defeated to Macondo to dedicate the rest of his days to making golden fish. In his retirement he will refuse any government recognition of his legacy.

The first three decades of the twentieth century were relatively peaceful and experienced increased economic growth driven by agricultural exports, industrialization, urbanization, and improved transportation (Melo 181–82). In the Caribbean, growth was driven by the banana enclaves, cattle and agricultural trade with Andean markets, and transportation services for international commerce (Zambrano, "Historia" 54).

Exposure to trade brought new technologies to the region—of the sort displayed by Melquíades or introduced by some of the leaders of Macondo—such as telegraphy, electricity, or photography, while advances in transportation helped connect some regions to domestic and foreign markets. Steam navigation, as an example, introduced in the 1850s, encouraged the settlement of the Magdalena River; later, railroads and modern roads established Barranquilla as the region's main port and industrial sector.

The arrival of the Panama Canal, however, dealt a death blow to the Colombian Caribbean's economic aspirations, as new maritime routes now favored trade through the Pacific town of Buenaventura, a port closer to Colombia's growing coffee-producing regions, which soon replaced Barranquilla as the main center for international commerce. The crisis of the banana industry—so central to the storyline in *Leaf Storm* and *One Hundred Years*—and the loss of the port both sealed the fate of the region until the 1990s: the Caribbean began to lag economically in the period between 1950 and 1990, becoming one of the poorest places in Colombia (Zambrano, "Historia" 55).

The Caribbean, however, was more or less spared from the series of conflicts that began in the 1930s, which devastated the Andean region and led to La Violencia, the bipartisan conflict that left thousands of dead in the countryside and was followed by the dictatorship of Gustavo Rojas Pinilla (1953–1957). The period of civil strife ended with the pacification period of General Rojas Pinilla and the 1958 National Front coalitional governments that brought to power Liberal and Conservative elites in a bipartisan alliance (Palacios 14). However, pacification resembled the tense peace described in *La mala hora* (*In Evil Hour*), whereby ideological cleavages remained, creating an atmosphere of fear and concealed violence, which we now know anteceded Colombia's longest period of armed conflict, which began in the 1960s, when the Revolutionary Armed Forces of Colombia (FARC) as well as other guerrilla forces first appeared, and which was later further complicated by drug-trafficking and paramilitary violence from the right.

The preceding sections have set forth some of the major features of socioeconomic change in Colombia, where the benefits of modernization were concentrated yet were also vulnerable to the vicissitudes of external commodity markets. This, combined with Colombia's notoriously fractured geography that hindered national integration and prosperity (Palacios xiii), produced a stop/go and boom/bust model of economic development and incomplete expansion of liberal political institutions (Bushnell 134). The result was economic growth as well as devastation, socioeconomic inequality, and the periodic demographic collapse of urban centers as people fled to seek refuge from violence, economic failure, or abuse of power.

Modern Politics in Macondo

García Márquez approaches the political dynamics of the Caribbean from a variety of angles and perspectives. He covers the embryonic societies that self-organized in the foothills of the Sierra Nevada de Santa Marta, the emergent caudillos who concentrated local power and replaced organic leaders, the arrival of the banana company, the massacre of labor activists, and the onset of a patchy modern state presence that did little to replace caudillos with modern authorities.

A familiar storyline in Colombian politics also unravels in Macondo. Once refugees set up a cohesive town that could be spotted on the map, the national government or the Catholic Church would send its authorities. This is the story of Apolinar Moscote, the magistrate assigned by the central government to govern Macondo. Moscote's announcement to govern with laws is rejected by José Arcadio Buendía, because "[i]n this town we do not give orders with pieces of paper" (*One Hundred Years* 60).[13] The Christianizing efforts of Father Nicanor Reyna receive a similar response. Macondo is "prospering in the midst of the scandal, subject to the natural law,"[14] and its people believe that many years without a priest have hence allowed Macondo to arrange the "business of their souls directly with God"[15] and lose "the evil of original sin" (*One Hundred Years* 86).[16] Moscote will eventually introduce zoning laws (92), bringing outside norms, armed men, and ideological cleavages, compelling Aureliano Buendía to go to war, while Father Nicanor sets out to construct the greatest church in the world (86).

When an electoral contest introduces Liberal and Conservative ideological cleavages in Macondo, Moscote militarizes the town and commits electoral fraud to ensure a Conservative win (*One Hundred Years* 100–101). In light of the fraud and his nascent sympathies with a newly discovered set of liberal values, Colonel Aureliano Buendía, who is also now Moscote's son-in-law, joins the Liberals in the civil war, entrusting his nephew, Arcadio, with protecting Macondo (108–9). Arcadio quickly becomes a despotic, petty tyrant and is eventually stripped of his powers by his furious grandmother, Ursula Iguarán, who begins to rule the town in his place (*One Hundred Years* 109). During his mandate, Arcadio endorses his father's illegal land grabs and forceful exactions of peasant properties by creating a registry office in exchange for keeping government control over José Arcadio's tax collection initiative (118). It is only after the war that Macondo becomes a proper municipality and General Moncada its first mayor, who undertakes a set of modernization measures (150).

Politics in García Márquez's Macondo is marked with transitions and fickle rules. The story "Los funerales de la Mamá Grande" ("Big Mama's Funeral") is about the death of the despotic, superstitious, and inequitable old order of Big Mama's clan that was nevertheless held together by impossibly weak foundations (Velasco 57). But even as the old order fades away, it leaves no rules to offer guidance, producing a transitional moment when sage doctors and legal alchemists with minds constrained by Big Mama's rules toil away in abstract congressional debates about what to do with her death ("Big Mama's Funeral" 195). The problem is solved when a delirious crowd jubilantly welcomes the traps of an unstable but modern state, as the president and his ministers, the parliament, the Supreme Court, and the representatives of banks, commerce, and industry make their way into the funeral procession (198–99).

This sort of politics—the trappings of the modern state—raises expectations instead of solving collective problems, as in the time-honored tradition of visiting peripheral towns to collect votes during election season, as represented in the story "Muerte constante más allá del amor" ("Death Constant Beyond Love"), in which Senator Onésimo Sánchez promises progress and backs up his speech with the same worn-out paper cutouts of a modern city to a tired and skeptical audience already familiar with the spectacle. Still, they show up for the festivities. In general, none of these political measures do much to improve material conditions in the desolate coastal-desert village, in the town of Macondo, or in other similar settlements in the work of García Márquez a; rather, they sow discord.

Modernity as Spectacle

As we have established so far, in the Caribbean of García Márquez, the forces of modernity are illusory and tend to bring about destruction and collective confusion. Perhaps for this reason, in the storyline they also form part of a wider group of unsettling and inexplicable phenomena, that seemingly arrive from nowhere and attract mobs of spectators who tend to find no difference between the ordinary and the extraordinary, accepting supernatural events as normal and technological phenomena as magical (Bell-Villada, "Labor Strikes"). What the ordinary and the extraordinary have in common is that they reveal the absence of stable or coherent processes, norms, institutions, or values that can help the villagers make sense of what the visits mean for them or how new ideas or technologies can be integrated sustainably.

Macondo at first is so young, for example, that it does not have a cemetery and therefore has no contact with the underworld. This ends with the death of Melquíades, whose spirit traces a route to Macondo and whose ghost begins to appear in the town. Some visitors represent business or political interests (e.g., the banana company's men), some are extraordinary creatures, and others bring new fads or technologies (e.g., Melquíades, the Gypsy or Pietro Crespi, the musician).

Melquíades, the globetrotting gypsy who exhibits fantastical inventions, transforms José Arcadio Buendía, the youthful patriarch and "most enterprising man ever to be seen in the village,"[17] from a man who had neatly organized three hundred people within an "orderly and hard-working"[18] village into someone "lazy in appearance, careless in his dress"[19] and obsessed with outside technologies (*One Hundred Years* 12–13). José Arcadio Buendía, nevertheless, has the foresight to convince the settlers to "open a way that would put Macondo in contact with the great inventions,"[20] perhaps to save them from isolation, or perhaps to condemn them to the vagaries of technological change (14).

A different sort of spectacle is provided by the eponymous "Un hombre muy viejo con unas alas enormes" ("A Very Old Man with Enormous Wings"), found in the mud and kept in a local family's backyard, there inviting the sort of pilgrimage that gives the Caribbean-Colombian town some notoriety. Once the show is replaced by the spectacle of a young woman turned into a spider in punishment for disobeying her parents, the old man's presence becomes routine; without proper guidance from the church or other authorities on how to treat him, the man ends up forgotten like old furniture, abused, and ignored, until one day he flies away on his own ("Un señor muy viejo"). The local priest's vacillation about whether to judge the man as a demon or an angel does not deter a pilgrimage of the curious from Jamaica or Martinique or of the desperately sick seeking miraculous help. Another local crowd is attracted by "El ahogado más hermoso del mundo" ("The Handsomest Drowned Man in the World"), a deceased stranger who washes up at the coastal town; looks unlike anyone in the region; and is effectively integrated into the fabric of that society with a name, a home, a family, and many friends, before receiving a proper burial. Confusion as to the essence of the winged old man is resolved with forgetfulness, whereas the tragedy of a drowned stranger restores a collective sense of solidarity.

In a hopelessly poor and soporific town, a sudden scent of roses that comes from the sea coincides with the arrival of the American Mr. Herbert, reportedly the richest man in the world, who is willing to distribute money to whomever can calculate the amount needed to fix a problem ("The Sea of Lost Time"). People arrive in an atmosphere of carnival; meanwhile, the town's desperate priest, aware of the event's fleetingness, fails to secure money to build a church that will at least give people hope once the money and the smell of roses are gone. The phenomenon is indeed temporary. García Márquez contrasts two views of money in this story: the transactional American visitor for whom spending money is a source of entertainment (despite his claims that he wants to be democratic in how he distributes it) versus the urgent, existential need of his beneficiaries for whom access to the resource is limited and a matter of life and death.

These economic and emotional ebbs and flows produce bounty and scarcity, company and solitude, excitement and boredom, and create a sense of collective existence fettered by material insecurity but inspired by the promise of life. The result is "the blissful, laid back attitude" of ordinary concerns about sex, food, festival, and family described by Fals Borda that comes not from a political economy of sustained material well-being, but the opposite, from a situation of instability that positions people in material and emotional states between life and death, forcing most to choose a rambunctious resilience.

The Solitude of Aureliano Babilonia, the Sacrifice of Santiago Nasar, and the Patience of the Nameless Colonel

The liberating possibilities of new technologies, new values, or new social relations raise individual expectations and increase the number of freethinking individuals, as observed by Fals Borda. But what the sociologist failed to observe, at least in his 1959 work, is that when society fails to absorb such change, freethinking individuals can become lunatics, aspirations turn into eccentric whims, and progress is an illusion. People misinterpret the social cues or work with incomplete and inadequate knowledge that is incompatible with the reality of their societies. The humanities vividly reveal this dynamic in the unencumbered language of poetry. The rudimentary worlds of José Arcadio Buendía and of his great-great-great grandson, Aureliano Babilonia, can scarcely support their intellectual ambition. Santiago Nasar, in *Crónica de una muerte anunciada* (*Chronicle of a Death Foretold*), dies because the townspeople underestimate the grip of atavistic traditions on their society. And the unnamed colonel wastes away while waiting for a pension promised by a spineless bureaucracy.

The frustrations of illusory change are best exemplified by Aureliano Babilonia, the son of Meme Buendía and Mauricio Babilonia. This Buendía, who engenders the pig-tailed child, will learn too late about the secret of his identity and the destiny of his race. It has taken the clan one hundred years to decipher their destiny, and when they finally do so, nothing can be done to avoid it. Aureliano has been reluctantly raised by his conservative grandmother Fernanda del Carpio, who denies him his identity and keeps him hidden in Melquíades's room. There "he learned by heart the fantastic legends of the crumbling book . . . so that he reached adolescence without knowing a thing about his own time but with the basic knowledge of a medieval man" (*One Hundred Years* 355).[21]

Never allowed outside as a child so as to hide the dishonor of his birth, Aureliano only begins to venture out into Macondo as the impoverished young scion of a dying clan trying to sell trinkets to buy food for the house. This newfound freedom brings him into contact with a wise Catalonian bookshop owner and awakens in him some interest in the history of Macondo as he tries to "reconstruct in his imagination the annihilated splendor of the old banana-company town" (383).[22] The Catalonian bookseller provides him the necessary material to decipher Melquíades's parchments, while a budding friendship with a group of arguers teaches him that knowledge has practical applications and that wisdom is "worth nothing if it could not be used to invent a new way of preparing chick peas" (387).[23] Aureliano Babilonia confirms that history is readily forgotten in a town like Macondo, where few people know or care to believe that Colonel Aureliano Buendía had lived, that the striking banana workers had been massacred and disposed of in train wagons, or that the banana company had ever existed (389). The Catalonian wise man and the group of arguers are simply going on with intellectual pursuits "in a town where no one had any interest any more in going beyond primary school" (390).[24] This is a town focused on surviving, where young girls sell themselves in brothels and the children of the founding fathers peddle trinkets. Aureliano Babilonia represents a very modern predicament. In the face of existential crises such as genocide or environmental catastrophe, illumination on the causes and solutions to save the species seems to be wasted on a humanity already trapped in behaviors that limit the applications of science.

Chronicle of a Death Foretold explores the confusion produced in the vacuum of social change as new values seemingly take hold but overlap stubborn older ones. In this novel, Santiago Nasar famously loses his life because no one believes the Vicario brothers' intention of executing the atavistic tradition of avenging the dishonor of their family. The brothers go about town publicly sharpening knives and speaking of assassination. Upon hearing about the threat, the mayor, Colonel Lázaro Aponte, thinks that the brothers are boasting, takes away their knives, and sends them home. Clotilde Armenta, the shop owner who called on the mayor to stop them, has accurately interpreted the brothers' predicament. When the Colonel says that "they haven't got anything to kill anybody with,"[25] she retorts in disappointment that the point was "to spare those poor boys from the horrible duty that's fallen on them" (57).[26] Clotilde Armenta "was certain that the Vicario brothers were not as eager to carry out the sentence as to find someone who would do them the favor of stopping them" (57).[27]

In *El coronel no tiene quien le escriba* (*No One Writes to the Colonel*), a veteran of the War of the Thousand Days has waited for fifteen years for a letter after a law passed by the government without budgetary allocation had entitled him to a war pension. This has fostered in the colonel a mix of hopeful waiting and relative trust in bureaucracy. The colonel patiently waits while trying to maintain his dignity by concealing the abject poverty that he and his asthmatic wife endure. He also hopes to make some economic gains from a prized rooster. This trust in abstract and distant institutions that is only possible in a modern economy is out of line with the colonel's reality. There, raw power, such as that exerted by the wealthy, politically connected, and manipulative Don Sabas, is what determines people's fate.

THE SILENCE OF MEME BUENDÍA: THE WOMEN OF GARCÍA MÁRQUEZ

Women are the least likely to benefit from the forces of modernity. Most female characters in García Márquez are capricious, eccentric, ghostlike, or devotees of tradition. The basic promise of progress—that it will unfetter the individual—is denied to them. Women are constrained to the household and are never at the center of any important historical event. García Márquez holds the view that, in his work, "women keep the world going and stop everything falling apart while men try and push history forward" (Mendoza and García Márquez, *Fragrance of Guava* 76).[28] Such restrictive views of women thus deny them historical agency. In *One Hundred Years*, José Arcadio Segundo organizes the banana workers for the fateful strike that ends with the death of three thousand people in the novel. In the real history, Ignacio Torres Giraldo (1893–1968) and María Cano (1887–1967), labor leaders from the interior of the country, visited the region in advance to prepare the Magdalena activists for the banana strike (Abello 237–38). Cano—along with other activists—was imprisoned in 1928 in Medellin, accused of rebellion and instigating the banana strike. Nicknamed "la flor del trabajo" (labor flower), Cano is widely seen as a main driving force behind Colombia's labor movement (Velásquez n.p.). As a freethinker and female organizer from a wealthy Catholic family when Conservatives had defeated the Liberals, her transgressive identity became a powerful force in support of the civil rights of workers (Velásquez).

Úrsula Iguarán is one of García Márquez's most powerful female characters. However, her social standing is gained from her position as founding member of the town, irreplaceable matriarch, and backbone of her clan. Those who enter public life successfully do so as prostitutes, like Pilar Ternera, who is raped as a young girl, becomes a concubine and mother to Buendía men, has psychic abilities that gain her respect, and runs a brothel. Others earn their independence from their own ambiguous and peripheral social condition, like Petra Cotes, the mixed-race, lower-class concubine of Buendía men, who supports both herself and, eventually, a bankrupt Buendía household, with entrepreneurial skills that are based on her supernatural ability to make crops and animals more productive.

In this constricted universe, Meme is the one woman who dares engage with the new world and test new values—and she pays a high price. Meme is the first Buendía woman to go to boarding school; to fall in love with someone not introduced to her in her household; and to bear a child for the clan, albeit out of wedlock. She seems to be living the promise of a woman's life unregulated by older traditions. She drinks and enjoys the nightlife and finds friends in the American enclave of pools, cars, and parties. She also has a romantic love affair with Mauricio Babilonia, a mechanic for the banana company. When her mother, Fernanda del Carpio, learns about the amour, she determines to avenge her family's honor. The superstitious, Catholic woman sets a trap that leaves Mauricio Babilonia paralyzed and Meme exiled in a convent. From the shock of the tragedy Meme will never speak again. Aureliano Segundo, who lives in concubinage with Petra Cotes, does not defend his daughter, letting Fernanda determine alone the destiny of a child who has resembled him in her pursuit of a bohemian life and free love.

Eréndira, in the novella that bears her name (*Innocent Eréndira and Other Stories*), is perhaps the most tragic representation of the status of women. As is the case with the many anonymous, young, and poor prostitutes who inhabit the brothels of the nightlife enjoyed by the Buendía men or the mobs that come to town, Eréndira enjoys virtually no protections from the church, the family, or the state. She is obedient to her grandmother's orders. Brief refuge offered by nuns at the mission represents another form of confined labor, as she works long hours cleaning the convent. Meanwhile, state authorities, in the person of a senator, serve her grandmother's interests in keeping her enslaved. Like the beautiful Laura Farina, who is offered by her father as a gift to a visiting politician as payback for a favor ("Death Constant Beyond Love"), Eréndira is her family's chattel. Whatever dignity and freedom are enjoyed by Meme, Eréndira, Laura Farina, and the abundant women in the work of García Márquez are ultimately dependent on the unpredictable alliances that they may strike with their families, their men, or generous authorities. No objective norms or values seem to exist for these women.

Conclusions: On the Values of the Caribbean

What do we learn from García Márquez about the values and attitudes that define Caribbean culture? First, individual dispositions in his work are constrained by socioeconomic and political transformations modeled after similar events in Colombian history. These changes go through cycles of boom and bust, an analogy that describes particularly well the march of history in the Caribbean. The region had thrived in the eighteenth century, declined in the nineteenth century, revived again in the early twentieth century with the commercial rise of Barranquilla, and once more, declined between 1940 and 1990 (see Kalmanovitz). The result is a political economy that mostly fails to sustain economic and physical security, but nevertheless exposes people to some of the marvels and benefits of progress.

Second, Macondo and other Garcíamarquezian towns are fictional versions of the fledgling societies that have appeared in various parts of the Caribbean out of the purview of centralized political or religious authorities. In these vacuums of centralized power, they reproduced morally loose, intercultural, and miscegenated societies that prevented demographic collapse and developed resilient, life-affirming practices by adhering to syncretic religious traditions. Modernization in these places is driven by neocolonial relations that strengthen despotic authorities and weaken local life-affirming practices. As in Macondo, their "collective strength" and "capacity for recovery" are eroded by the banana company and by the masses attracted by short-lived progress (*Leaf Storm* 89).

All in all, García Márquez's characters shape their values in an ambivalent space where physical comfort cannot be taken for granted, but where self-expression is also discovered as a powerful survival force. With historical change, new identities that embrace different worldviews appear: the labor unionists and workers of the banana enclave, a Liberal colonel, intellectuals, inventors, entrepreneurs, and an educated woman. However, old identities remain and gain new powers: caudillos, land grabbers, conservative matriarchs, and human traffickers. Cultural transitions in this fictional universe are neither smooth nor complete, and different values coexist in constant tension. This Caribbean, like the real one, follows a messy path to modernity that is at once oppressive and peripheral, but also free and universal.

Notes

1. "Parecía dar un gigantesco paso atrás" (Gilard 53).
2. "Cree presenciar la muerte del mito moderno por antonomasia, que es el del progreso" (Gilard 53).
3. "Tales como la conciencia de clase y las ideas de confort, anonimato y escape psicológico" (Fals Borda, "La teoría" 32).
4. "Que cuece los garbanzos en la cocina, y contagia el amor y repite las imágenes en los espejos" (Banquet Speech).
5. "Vive con nosotros y determina cada instante de nuestras incontables muertes cotidianas, y que sustenta un manantial de creación insaciable, pleno de desdicha y de belleza ... Las criaturas de aquella realidad desaforada hemos tenido que pedirle muy poco a la imaginación, porque el desafío mayor para nosotros ha sido la insuficiencia de los recursos convencionales para hacer creíble nuestra vida. Este es, amigos, el nudo de nuestra soledad. ... Sin embargo, frente a la opresión, el saqueo y el abandono, nuestra respuesta es la vida. Ni los

diluvios ni las pestes, ni las hambrunas ni los cataclismos, ni siquiera las guerras eternas a través de los siglos y los siglos han conseguido reducir la ventaja tenaz de la vida sobre la muerte" ("La soledad de América Latina").

6. "Pues al fin y al cabo no les cuento nada que no se parezca a la vida que ellos viven" (Mendoza and García Márquez, *El olor de la guayaba* 36).
7. "Dentro de los controles sociales y morales que se establecían con la vida urbana" (CINEP 153).
8. "Constituyó una perturbación masiva de las estructuras de poder" (Zambrano, "Historia" 51).
9. "De pronto, como si un remolino hubiera echado raíces en el centro del pueblo, llegó la compañía bananera perseguida por la hojarasca. Era una hojarasca revuelta, alborotada, formada por los desperdicios humanos y materiales de los otros pueblos: rastrojos de una guerra civil que cada vez parecía más remota e inverosímil. La hojarasca era implacable... En menos de un año arrojó sobre el pueblo los escombros de numerosas catástrofes anteriores" (*La hojarasca* 9).
10. "Ocupada por gente cesante y rencorosa, a quien atormentaban el recuerdo de un pasado próspero y la amargura de un presente agobiado y estático" (*La hojarasca* 141).
11. "Estaba loco desde entonces" (*Cien años de soledad* 113).
12. "Promovió treinta y dos levantamientos armados y los perdió todos" (*Cien años* 125).
13. "En este pueblo no mandamos con papeles" (*Cien años* 70).
14. "Prosperaban en el escándalo, sujetos a la ley natural" (*Cien años* 101).
15. "Los negocios del alma directamente con Dios" (*Cien años* 101).
16. "La malicia del pecado mortal" (*Cien años* 101).
17. "Que era el hombre más emprendedor que se vería jamás en la aldea" (*Cien años* 18).
18. "Una aldea más ordenada y laboriosa que cualquiera" (*Cien años* 18).
19. "Aspecto holgazán, descuidado en el vestir" (*Cien años* 18).
20. "Abrir una trocha que pusiera a Macondo en contacto con los grandes inventos" (*Cien años* 19).
21. "Aprendió de memoria las leyendas fantásticas del libro descuadernado... de modo que llegó a la adolescencia sin saber nada de su tiempo, pero con los conocimientos básicos de un hombre medieval" (*Cien años* 403).
22. "Reconstruir con la imaginación el arrasado esplendor de la antigua ciudad de la compañía bananera" (*Cien años* 435).
23. "La sabiduría no valía la pena si no era posible servirse de ella para inventar una manera nueva de preparar los garbanzos" (*Cien años* 440).
24. "En un pueblo donde ya nadie tenía interés ni posibilidades de ir más allá de la escuela primaria" (*Cien años* 443).
25. "Ya no tienen con qué matar a nadie" (*Crónica de una muerte anunciada* 77).
26. "Es para librar a esos pobres muchachos del horrible compromiso que les ha caído encima" (*Crónica de una muerte anunciada* 77).
27. "Tenía la certidumbre de que los hermanos Vicario no estaban tan ansiosos por cumplir la sentencia como por encontrar a alguien que les hiciera el favor de impedírselo" (*Crónica de una muerte anunciada* 77).
28. "Las mujeres sostienen el mundo en vilo, para que no se desbarate mientras los hombres tratan de empujar la historia" (Mendoza and García Márquez, *El olor de la guayaba* 79).

Works Cited

Abello, Alberto. *La isla encallada*. Siglo del Hombre, 2015.

Barreto Viana, Rubén Darío. "La modernidad o la irrupción de lo extranjero: análisis sociocrítico de *La Hojarasca*, de Gabriel García Márquez." *Estudios de Literatura Colombiana*, vol. 37, 2015, pp. 47–64.

Bell-Villada, Gene. *García Márquez: The Man and His Work*. 2nd ed., rev. and expanded. University of North Carolina Press, 2010.

Bell-Villada, Gene. "Labor Strikes, Magic & War; Romantic Love, Sex & Humor; and Some Other Things Novelist García Márquez Brought to His Readers Worldwide." Public Lecture, Colorado State University, Fort Collins, Colorado, 17 Apr. 2015.

Bergquist, Charles. "In the Name of History: A Disciplinary Critique of Orlando Fals Borda's *Historia doble de la costa*." *Latin American Research Review*, vol. 25, no. 3, 1990, pp. 156–76.

Bushnell, David. *The Making of Modern Colombia: A Nation in Spite of Itself*. University of California Press, 1993.

Centro de Investigación y Educación Popular (CINEP). "Región Caribe." *Colombia, país de regiones*, edited by Fabio Zambrano, CINEP, 1998, pp. 143–253.

Coatsworth, John H. "Inequality, Institutions and Economic Growth in Latin America." *Journal of Latin American Studies*, vol. 40, no. 3, 2008, pp. 545–69.

Dauster, Frank. "Ambiguity and Indeterminacy in *Leafstorm*." *Latin American Literary Review*, vol. 13, no. 25, 1985, pp. 24–28.

Díaz, Antolín. *Sinú: Pasión y vida del trópico*. El Garfio, 2006.

Fals Borda, Orlando. *Historia doble de la costa: Mompox y Loba*, vol. 1. Carlos Valencia Editores, 1979.

Fals Borda, Orlando. "La teoría y la realidad del cambio cultural en Colombia." *Monografías sociológicas*, no. 2, Universidad Nacional de Colombia, 1959.

García Márquez, Gabriel. "Banquet Speech: Gabriel García Márquez's speech at the Nobel Banquet," 10 Dec. 1982, www.nobelprize.org/prizes/literature/1982/marquez/speech/. Accessed 12 Dec. 2019.

García Márquez, Gabriel. "Big Mama's Funeral." *Collected Stories*, translated by Gregory Rabassa and J. S. Bernstein, Harper & Row, 1984, pp. 184–200.

García Márquez, Gabriel. *Chronicle of a Death Foretold*. Translated by Gregory Rabassa, Alfred Knopf, 2006.

García Márquez, Gabriel. *Cien años de soledad* (1967). Real Academia Española, 2007.

García Márquez, Gabriel. *Crónica de una muerte anunciada*. Editorial Oveja Negra, 1981.

García Márquez, Gabriel. "Death Constant Beyond Love." *Collected Stories*, Harper & Row, 1984, pp. 237–45.

García Márquez, Gabriel. "The Handsomest Drowned Man in the World." *Collected Stories*, translated by Gregory Rabassa and J. S. Bernstein, Harper & Row, 1984, pp. 230–36.

García Márquez, Gabriel. "La herencia sobrenatural de la marquesita." *Crónicas y reportajes*, Oveja Negra, 1978, pp. 18–24.

García Márquez, Gabriel. "Historia íntima de una manifestación de 400 horas." *Crónicas y reportajes*, Editorial Oveja Negra, 1978, pp. 143–51.

García Márquez, Gabriel. *La hojarasca* (1954). Vintage Español, 1998.

García Márquez, Gabriel. *La increíble y triste historia de la Cándida Eréndira y su abuela desalmada* (1972). Vintage Español, 1998.

García Márquez, Gabriel. "Leaf Storm." *Leaf Storm and Other Stories*, Translated by Gregory Rabassa, Harper & Row, 1972.

García Márquez, Gabriel. *Living to Tell the Tale*. Translated by Edith Grossman, Alfred A. Knopf, 2003.

García Márquez, Gabriel. "La marquesita de La Sierpe." *Crónicas y reportajes*, Oveja Negra, 1978, pp. 11–17.

García Márquez, Gabriel. *No One Writes to the Colonel and Other Stories*. Translated by J. S. Bernstein, Harper & Row, 1979.

García Márquez, Gabriel. *One Hundred Years of Solitude* (1970). Translated by Gregory Rabassa, Alfred A. Knopf, 1995.

García Márquez, Gabriel. "The Sea of Lost Time." *Collected Stories*, translated by Gregory Rabassa and J. S. Bernstein, Harper & Row, 1984, pp. 211–29.

García Márquez, Gabriel. "La soledad de América Latina." Nobel Lecture, 8 Dec. 1982, www.nobelprize.org/prizes/literature/1982/marquez/25603-gabriel-garcia-marquez-nobel-lecture-spanish/. Accessed 10 May 2021.

García Márquez, Gabriel. "The Solitude of Latin America." Nobel Lecture, 8 Dec. 1982, www.nobelprize.org/prizes/literature/1982/marquez/lecture/.Accessed 12 Dec. 2019.

García Márquez, Gabriel. "A Very Old Man with Enormous Wings." *Collected Stories*, translated by Gregory Rabassa and J. S. Bernstein, Harper & Row, 1984, pp. 203–10.

Gilard, Jacques. "Prólogo." *Gabriel García Márquez: Textos costeños. Obra periodística 1 (1948–1952)*, edited by Jacques Gilard, Diana, 1981, pp. 15–71.

Inglehart, Ronald. *Cultural Evolution: People's Motivations Are Changing, and Reshaping the World*. Cambridge UP, 2018.

Inglehart, Ronald, et al., editors. World Values Survey: All Rounds—Country-Pooled Datafile Version. JD Systems Institute, 2014, www.worldvaluessurvey.org/WVSDocumentationWVL.jsp. Accessed 12 Dec. 2019.

Kalmanovitz, Salomón. "Por qué perdió la costa Caribe el siglo XX?" *El Espectador*, 26 June 2011, www.elespectador.com/opinion/por-que-perdio-la-costa-caribe-el-siglo-xx-columna-280179/. Accessed 10 May 2021.

Matsumoto, David. *Culture and Psychology*. Brooks/Cole, 1996.

Meisel Roca, Adolfo. *¿Por qué perdió la costa Caribe el siglo XX?* Banco de la República, 2009, 7 Jan. 2016, www.banrep.gov.co/es/por-que-perdio-costa-caribe-siglo-xx. Accessed 12 Dec. 2019.

Melo, Jorge Orlando. "Algunas consideraciones globales sobre 'modernización' y 'modernidad' en el caso colombiano." *Análisis Político*, vol. 10, 1990, pp. 23–36.

Melo, Jorge Orlando. *Historia Mínima de Colombia*. El Colegio de México, 2017.

Mendoza, Plinio A., and Gabriel García Márquez. *Fragrance of Guava*. Translated by Ann Wright, Verso, 1983.

Mendoza, Plinio A., and Gabriel García Márquez. *El olor de la guayaba: Conversaciones con Plinio A. Mendoza*. Editorial Oveja Negra, 1982.

Palacios, Marco. *Between Legitimacy and Violence: A History of Colombia, 1875–2002*. Duke UP, 2006.

Palencia-Roth, Michael. "Gabriel García Márquez: Labyrinths of Love and History." *World Literature Today*, vol. 65, no. 1, Winter 1991, pp. 54–58.

Spencer-Oatey, Helen. "Introduction." *Culturally Speaking: Culture, Communication and Politeness Theory*. 2nd ed. Edited by Helen Spencer-Oatey, Continuum, 2008, pp. 1–8.

Velasco, Marcela. "García Márquez and Mamagallismo: On Fatigued Roosters, Resistance, Sense of Humor, and the Colombian Personality." *Gabriel García Márquez in Retrospect: A Collection*, edited by Gene H. Bell-Villada, Lexington Books, 2016, pp. 49–63.

Velásquez, Magdala. "María Cano. Pionera y agitadora social de los años 20." *Revista Credencial Historia*, no. 1, 1990, www.banrepcultural.org/biblioteca-virtual/credencial-historia/numero-6/maria-cano-pionera-y-agitadora-social-de-los-a%C3%B1os-20. Accessed 12 Dec. 2019.

Zambrano, Fabio. "Las guerras civiles." *Semana*, 10 July 2010, www.semana.com/especiales/articulo/las-guerras-civiles/109028-3. Accessed 22 Sept. 2019.

Zambrano, Fabio. "Historia del poblamiento del territorio de la región del Caribe de Colombia." *Poblamiento y ciudades del Caribe colombiano*, edited by Alberto Abello and Silvana Giaimo, Observatorio del Caribe Colombiano, 2000, pp. 1–96.

CHAPTER 5

GABRIEL GARCÍA MÁRQUEZ AND THE REMAKING OF THE WORLD CANON

JUAN E. DE CASTRO

For many writers and readers throughout the world, Gabriel García Márquez's *Cien años de soledad* (*One Hundred Years of Solitude*) is the central example of a literature of the Global South—even if this "South" is located mostly to the north of the equator, as is the case with all of Asia and much of Africa. The foundational importance of García Márquez's masterwork to contemporary narrative from this Global South is evidenced by the effusive acknowledgments of his influence by such major writers as the Anglo-Indian Salman Rushdie and the Mozambican Mia Couto. Rushdie, for instance, notes about the relevance of García Márquez's writing to his understanding of the society and history of the Indian subcontinent:

> I knew García Márquez's colonels and generals, or at least their Indian and Pakistani counterparts; his bishops were my mullahs; his market streets were my bazaars. His world was mine, translated into Spanish. It's little wonder I fell in love with it–not for its magic (although, as a writer reared on the fabulous "wonder tales" of the East, that was appealing, too) but for its realism. (n.p.)

Couto makes a comparable comment: "My sources have been fundamentally Latin American.... Africa is full of Macondos, of towns like that, like Gabo's" (n.p.).[1] Rushdie and Couto found in García Márquez's Macondo, the fictional town where most of the plot in *One Hundred Years of Soltiude* is situated, not an exotic location, but rather a world similar to the one they had been born into and raised in. For these and other writers of the Global South, the value of García Márquez's works resides in his ability to represent in his fiction a reality comparable to theirs and to do so at the highest literary level. Like García Márquez's, their writing aims at reflecting in their literature a social and cultural reality that had not been fully represented by earlier writers brought up in European or North American literature, whether realist or high modernist.

Similar ideas were used in justifying the Nobel Prize awarded to García Márquez in 1982. The Colombian master received the prize: "for his novels and short stories, in which the fantastic and the realistic are combined in a richly composed world of imagination, reflecting a continent's life and conflicts" ("The Nobel Prize in Literature 1982" n.p.). Implicit in this statement is the idea that, perhaps for the first time—if not, why grant him the award?—a "world of imagination," that is literature, was able to successfully depict a conflicted reality that had hitherto been at best clumsily represented, if at all. In García Márquez's works, Latin America and, by implication, the Global South as a whole first became identifiable as a distinct region in the World Republic of Letters.

Even if unnamed, one finds in the Nobel Prize communiqué a brief description of the notion of magical realism, the style associated with García Márquez's masterwork. Magical realism is here described, perhaps simplistically, as a writing in which "the fantastic and the realistic are combined" (n.p.). But as we have seen, there is also the implication that by fusing the fantastic and the realistic, that is, by writing in a magical realistic style, an outsized world, characterized by an extremity of life and conflict, is finally represented. Both Rushdie and Couto reaffirm the centrality of magical realism in their apparently successful attempts at representing Indian and African realities. According to Rushdie, "the trouble with the term 'magic realism' . . . is that when people say or hear it they are really hearing or saying only half of it, 'magic,' without paying attention to the other half, 'realism'" (n.p.). Couto adds that "all African writers have a debt with Latin American magical realism because in some way it motivated and authorized us to break with the European model" (n.p.). For these and other novelists and short-story writers, magical realism is a literary style particularly suited to writing about the extreme reality of the Global South. As no less an authority than Homi Bhabha, whose theories of hybridity have often served as the interpretational paradigm with which to read writings from Asia, Africa, and even Latin America, stated in 1990, "'Magical Realism' after the Latin American Boom becomes the literary language of the emergent post-colonial world" (7).[2] One must note that García Márquez himself often stressed the exceptionality of Latin America, at least when compared with Europe and North America, which is precisely what would justify the need for combining fantasy and reality in his writing. As he put it in his well-known interview with Claudia Dreifus: "[T]he Latin American environment is marvelous. Particularly the Caribbean" (112). García Márquez gave the story of a "a man in Aracataca who had the facility of deworming cows . . . by standing in front of the beasts" as an example of Latin America's marvelous reality (112). In a similar vein, in the significantly titled novel ¡Yo!, the Dominican American Julia Álvarez has the eponymous character make the following comment about the Dominican Republic and Latin America: "It's all one big story down here, anyway. The aunts all know that their husbands have mistresses but they act like they don't know. The president is blind but he pretends he can see. Stuff like that. It's like one of those Latin American novels that everyone thinks is magical realism in the States, but it's the way things really are down here" (197).

The banality of the reasons often given to justify a necessary relationship between magical realism and Latin America, as well as the entire Global South, should not be seen as detracting from the value of the magical realist masterpieces by García Márquez,

Rushdie, and others.[3] However, one must note that, as the quotations from García Márquez and Álvarez exemplify, underlying the celebration of magical realism, on occasion even of the exceptionality of Latin America and the Global South, one often finds a view of European and North American societies as rational, ordered, and efficient; needless to say, this is not the case.

Gabo's Canon

Given the influence of *One Hundred Years of Solitude* on postcolonial literature and the stress placed by critics and writers on the particular suitability of magical realism as a style with which to describe Latin America and the Global South, it may surprise the reader to find that the works that influenced Gabriel García Márquez and that are part of the intertextual threads with which he wove *One Hundred Years of Solitude* are nothing less than the modernist canon. Gabo's canon, not only in its meaning of a list of great books, but also in its original sense of works that serve both as models for the artist to follow and as measuring sticks with which to judge new works, is composed precisely of the European and North American masterpieces of the first half of the twentieth century. For instance, reading García Márquez's memoirs, *Vivir para contarla* (*Living to Tell the Tale*, 2002)—truly a *Künstlerroman* or Portrait of the Young Man Becoming an Artist—one learns about the personal and literary evolution that made it possible for him to write his first novel, *La hojarasca* (*Leaf Storm*), published in 1955. Perhaps to the reader's surprise, the intellectual and emotional breakthrough that led García Márquez to become a professional writer is presented as being directly connected to his experiences as a reader of Anglo-European modernist masterpieces. For instance, García Márquez remembers that, shortly before beginning to write his first novel at the age of twenty-three, "I became aware that my adventure in reading *Ulysses* at the age of twenty, and later *The Sound and the Fury*, were premature audacities without a future, and I decided to reread them with a less biased eye. In effect, much of what had seemed pedantic or hermetic in Joyce and Faulkner was revealed to me then with a terrifying beauty and simplicity" (*Living to Tell the Tale* 366). If Rushdie and Couto found in *One Hundred Years of Solitude* the key to being an Indian or Mozambican writer, García Márquez had found the master keys of literature in two of the best-known English-language modernist classics.[4]

Gabo's canon is not only limited to James Joyce and William Faulkner. Franz Kafka is another influence that guided García Márquez's earliest texts. Again, the Colombian master writes about the effects of reading Kafka on his thinking about literature:

> [It] determined a new direction for my life from its first line, which today is one of the great devices in world literature: "As Gregor Samsa awoke one morning from uneasy dreams he found himself transformed in his bed into a gigantic insect." These [and now he's again referring to Joyce and Faulkner in addition to Kafka] were mysterious

books whose dangerous precipices were not only different from but often contrary to everything I had known until then. It was not necessary to demonstrate facts: it was enough for the author to have written something for it to be true, with no proof other than the power of his talent and the authority of his voice. (248)

One must note that this is actually a definition of magical realism, and that it is presented as deriving from the lessons he learned from Kafka and, more generally, from modernism.[5] Of course, one can argue that both Faulkner and Joyce wrote from and about cultural peripheries that had many points in common with Colombia and, in particular, its Caribbean regions. In *Living to Tell the Tale*, García Márquez reminisces that "when I began to read Faulkner, the small towns in his novels seemed like ours" (17). As numerous studies of the last four decades propose, Joyce's novels respond directly to the colonial condition of Ireland in politics and culture. According to Vincent Cheng, "Joyce wrote insistently from the perspective of the colonial subject of an oppressive empire" (i). While Colombia had been independent from Spain for more than 150 years by the time García Márquez began work on *One Hundred Years of Solitude*, it was still very much on the cultural, political, and economic periphery of the West. One could even argue that Colombia's cultural subordination to the West, in particular to the United States, resembled that of Ireland's to England during Joyce's literary heyday, thirty plus years earlier.

A similar argument can be made regarding Kafka, even if García Márquez links his influence to what seems to have been the very beginnings of his magical realist technique. After all, Kafka is the privileged example of a "minor literature," defined as "that which a minority constructs within a major language" (Deleuze and Guattari 16). One could see García Márquez's embrace of Caribbean culture and language, in contrast with the hegemonic putative linguistic purity of Bogota or Madrid, as informing his construction of a "minor literature" in ways analogous to Kafka's.[6]

Faulkner and Joyce were not the only English-language writers who influenced the young García Márquez. Out of many—the list also includes Erskine Caldwell, Robert Nathan, John Steinbeck, and John Dos Passos—two in particular can be singled out: Virginia Woolf and Ernest Hemingway. Woolf, in fact, occupies a central role in García Márquez's development, according to *Living to Tell the Tale*. After receiving a copy of *Mrs. Dalloway* from his friend Álvaro Cepeda, García Márquez, who had till then enjoyed declaiming poetry, began to recite "paragraphs from Mrs. Dalloway and the ravings of its heartbreaking character, Septimus Warren Smith" (339). In fact, García Márquez adopted the byline of Septimus for his journalistic chronicles in homage to Woolf's "heartbreaking character."

Regarding Hemingway, in a widely disseminated essay from 1981, "My Personal Hemingway,"[7] García Márquez writes about his time in Paris in 1957, when he had seen the American author across the street:

> My two greatest masters were the two North American novelists who seemed to have the least in common. I had read everything they had published so far, but not as

complementary reading, but the exact opposite: as two different and almost mutually exclusive forms of conceiving of literature. One of them was William Faulkner. . . . The other was the ephemeral man who just said *adiós* to me from the other side of the street, and had left me with the impression that something had happened in my life, and it had happened forever. (237)

While Hemingway is briefly mentioned in *Living to Tell the Tale*, "My Personal Hemingway" makes clear the central role the author of *The Old Man and the Sea* played in García Márquez's literary development. One must note, however, that while *Living to Tell the Tale* deals with the writerly and personal development that led to the writing of *Leaf Storm*, the brief essay "My Personal Hemingway" refers to the period after the publication of García Márquez's first novel in 1955.[8]

Nevertheless, just as Hemingway's use of Cuban characters and locations in *The Old Man and the Sea* goes unmentioned in "My Personal Hemingway," neither is Woolf's role as an early feminist brought up. With the exception of Faulkner, whose US South setting is seen by García Márquez as resembling that of Caribbean Colombia, the writers included in Gabo's canon are invariably seen as important due to their literary innovations, not for any social reason or political or ideological affinity. In fact, Faulkner's importance resides precisely in his being able to create modernist masterpieces out of Mississippi mud.

Modernism as the Model

Near the beginning of *Living to Tell the Tale*, the young García Márquez, who is struggling with his mother regarding his decision to drop out of school and become a writer, finds, to his surprise, support from an old acquaintance, an elderly doctor still living in Aracataca. When told by the writer's mother that García Márquez aims at becoming a writer, the doctor asks, "Have you read *Doña Bárbara*?" While García Márquez replies that he has read that novel and "almost everything else by Rómulo Gallegos," he hides from the doctor the fact that because of "my fever of 104 degrees for the sagas of Mississippi, I was beginning to see the seams in our native novel" (29). The Venezuelan Gallegos, frequently considered a Latin American classic and, at the time, a perennial Nobel Prize candidate, is described here in terms that clearly criticize his technique as a novelist.[9] It is worth noting that this inability to hide the seams, something that any professional tailor or novelist should be able to do, is not a flaw ascribed only to Gallegos; instead, it is claimed that it is found in the native—in the Spanish original—*vernácula* (*Vivir para contarla* 40), that is, vernacular—novel.

The use of the word *vernácula*, as well as to a lesser degree its translation as "native," raises a number of questions when it comes to García Márquez's rejection of Gallegos. In *Living to Tell the Tale*, is he rejecting the Venezuelan and Colombian novel? The South American novel?[10] Or is he going as far as dismissing all Spanish-language novels? It is true that in his memoirs, he describes himself and his fellow members of the Barranquilla group—Álvaro Cepeda, Germán Vargas, Alfonso Fuenmayor, and their mentor, the Catalonian dramatist Ramón Vinyes—as "early admirers of Jorge Luis Borges, Julio Cortázar, Felisberto Hernández" (111). However, these three authors were best known as short-story writers during the 1950s, the decade when García Márquez's memoirs are set. Cortázar's novels—*The Winners* (1960), *Hopscotch* (1963), *62: A Model Kit* (1968), and *A Manuel for Manuel* (1973)—were yet to be written. In fact, the one Spanish-language novel that gets a pass from the master of Macondo is "Arturo Barea's *The Making of a Rebel*—... the first hopeful message from a remote Spain silenced by two wars" (111). No other contemporary Colombian, Latin American, or Spanish novel is mentioned.[11] For García Márquez, no Latin American or Spanish-language novel was a worthy model.[12] Instead, it is the European and North American novels of the first half of the century that provided examples of a truly professional narrative that had mastered the craft of the invisible seam.

Of the modernist trinity of Joyce, Kafka, and Proust, only the latter is absent from *Living to Tell the Tale*. Proust is present, albeit briefly, in García Márquez's early writings. In an article from 1950 titled "¿Problemas de la novela?" and published under his pen name of Septimus, García Márquez briefly mentions the author of *À la recherche du temps perdu* (*In Search of Lost Time*):

> The novel, undoubtedly and fortunately influenced by Joyce, Faulkner or Virginia Woolf has not yet been written in Colombia. I say fortunately, because I don't believe that Colombians can now be an exception to the flow of influences. In her Prologue to *Orlando*, Virginia Woolf confesses her influences. Faulkner himself could not deny the influence that Joyce has had on him.... Franz Kafka and Proust roam free over the literature of the modern world. If we Colombians were to make the right decision, we would need to irremediably join this current. (213)

Again, though one could read Proust as a queer writer, just as one could see Kafka as a representative of a minor literature or Joyce as an early Commonwealth if not postcolonial writer, Woolf as a feminist, and, as we have seen, even Faulkner as a kind of Caribbean writer, in this specific passage, these authors are seen as modernist masters rather than as representatives of alternative identities. Moreover, these authors are presented as a canon, in its sense of a model that Colombian literature, if it's to be fully modern, must follow. In this text, García Márquez, a young writer himself, is suggesting to other up-and-coming writers to make "the right decision" and begin the study of these European and North American authors rather than Gallegos and others of their ilk.

García Márquez's modernizing bent is far from idiosyncratic; instead, it is characteristic of his literary generation in Latin America. For instance, the other Nobel laureate of the Boom generation, Mario Vargas Llosa, has on many an occasion documented the influence of Faulkner and other modernist novelists on his work. Writing about his apprenticeship as a writer in the mid-1950s in *A Fish in the Water*, his book of memoirs, Vargas Llosa admits to having discovered around this time the author of the saga.

Yoknapatawpha County, which from the first novel of his that I read—*The Wild Palms*—left me so bedazzled that I still haven't recovered. He was the first writer whom I studied with paper and pencil in hand, taking notes so as not to get lost in his genealogical labyrinths and shifts of time and points of view, and also trying to unearth the secrets the baroque construction that each one of his stories was based on. (280)

The fact that Vargas Llosa claims Faulkner as his only English-language influence—his other model at the time was Jean-Paul Sartre—probably reflects the differences between the culture of the Colombian Caribbean, much more directly influenced by that of the United States, and the more traditionally Francophile mores of the Peruvian intelligentsia.[13] However, like García Márquez, Vargas Llosa rejects Peruvian literature, claiming that "the literary world of Lima was rather mediocre" (279), as well as Latin American literature, including, of course, Gallegos, because, as he notes, "I had been forced to read that sort of narrative and its Peruvian equivalent in classes at San Marcos, and I detested it, since it appeared to me to be a provincial and demagogic caricature of what a good novel should be" (293).[14] For both core members of the Boom and future Nobel laureates, the real, rather than caricaturesque, novel was written in Europe and North America.

Faulkner as Temporal Accelerator

While acknowledging the importance of Joyce, whose *Ulysses* is described as "one of the measures of novelistic modernity," Pascale Casanova ("Literature as World" 76) has singled out Faulkner as a central influence on García Márquez, as well as Vargas Llosa and other writers from countries at the margins of Europe and the United States:

Following his international consecration, Faulkner's work played the role of a "temporal accelerator" for a wide range of novelists of different periods, in countries structurally comparable, in economic and cultural terms, to the American South. All of them openly announced their use (at least in a technical sense) of this Faulknerian accelerator; among them were Juan Benet in 1950s Spain, Gabriel García Márquez in Colombia and Mario Vargas Llosa in Peru in the 1950s and 1960s, Kateb Yacine in 1960s Algeria, António Lobo-Antunes in 1970s Portugal, Edouard Glissant in the French Antilles of the 1980s, and so on. (77–78)

As we have seen, this description of Faulkner as a "temporal accelerator," that is, as a model that, if followed, permits writers from marginal countries to fully achieve literary modernity, as defined in Europe and North America, fits the practice and career of García Márquez.[15] It is clear that for the Colombian novelist, Faulkner and modernism in general served as a measuring stick with which to judge the writings of his predecessors and contemporaries, as well as his own literature.

It is necessary, however, to stress that this appropriation of Faulknerian techniques not only allows writers from Spain, Portugal, Colombia, and Peru to write modern literature, but also impacts the reception of these works in the cultural centers of North America and Europe—that is, where modernity is actually defined. As Casanova writes in *The World Republic of Letters*, "the literary Greenwich meridian makes it possible to evaluate and recognize the quality of a work or, to the contrary, dismiss a work as an anachronism or to label it as 'provincial'" (90). In other words, Faulkner's modernism makes the works produced in the peripheries legible by French and, by extension, Western critics for whom modernism is the exclusive example of true literature and the key measuring stick used to judge the value of a literary work since, in this model, outside modernism lies subliterature.

The problem with Casanova's argument is that it goes beyond describing literary practices and seems to uphold the particularities she finds in this World Republic of Letters. Thus, she ultimately identifies literary value with the literature produced in central cultural spaces. While she acknowledges the creative work of the writers who appropriate Faulkner, she seems blissfully unaware of the local dynamics that often help explain the particularities of any work of literature, including that of García Márquez. Ultimately, for her, the literature canonized in "the Greenwich meridian" of Paris and, I would add, in other publishing centers like New York City or London, would by definition be worthy of such canonization. The real and the ideal are thus perfectly compatible in her critical work.

García Márquez as Temporal Accelerator

Be that as it may, Casanova's comment about the appeal of Faulkner among writers from peripheric countries being connected not only to his narrative modernist innovations but also to the fact that they wrote in "countries structurally comparable, in economic and cultural terms, to the American South," is particularly pertinent to the case of García Márquez ("Literature as World" 77–78). As we have seen, unlike his comments about Woolf or Kafka, García Márquez frequently referred to the similarities between Caribbean Colombia and the world depicted by Faulkner. Paraphrasing Couto, one could say García Márquez found Faulkner to be useful in his writing because, for him, Colombia was full of Yoknapatawphas. According to García Márquez, Faulkner is the one major modernist who created masterpieces set in rural, racially divided, and preindustrial cultures and locations.

Mutatis mutandis, what Casanova writes about Faulkner is relevant to a consideration of García Márquez's impact on the literature of the Global South. Colombia is arguably even more "structurally comparable" to the countries of Africa and Asia than to the US.

South, in particular given that by the time, let's say, Rushdie and Couto began to write, the agrarian society depicted by Faulkner lay in the past. Like the Nobel Committee, these and other writers from the Global South found in the magical realism that characterizes *One Hundred Years of Solitude* an appropriate way to represent their societies. This helps explain the influence of García Márquez on so many writers from the Global South, not only Rushdie and Couto, but also Mo Yan (China) and Ben Okri (Nigeria), among others. Even writers who came from subaltern and, frequently, rural ethnic communities, African American writers such as Toni Morrison, or Latinx, such as Rudolfo Anaya, Sandra Cisneros, and Cristina García, found in García Márquez a model. For these writers, García Márquez presented a way of depicting communities and societies characterized by combined and uneven development, as well as by the tensions, hybridizations, and disjunctions present in culturally heterogenous societies. It is not an exaggeration to argue that García Márquez now serves as a temporal accelerator for writers throughout the Global South.

However, as previously mentioned, the impact of Faulkner's or García Márquez's international canonization is not exclusively based on the writer but also on what critics end up considering as modern and even as literature. If the Faulknerian accelerator permitted the critics of the Global North to acclaim *One Hundred Years of Solitude* as a world classic, the prestige acquired by the novel permitted García Márquez to become in turn a model for writers in the Global South and to define what critics in Europe and North America considered valid writing from regions such as Asia and Africa, in addition to Latin America. The centrality of *One Hundred Years of Solitude* in what could be called the world canon is evidenced in García Márquez's influence within and without the Global South. Writers who, in principle, had no need of "modernizing" their literature, such as the Australian Peter Carey, the (US) American Alice Hoffman, or the Canadian William Patrick Kinsella, have written magical realist works.

The temporal accelerator not only helps writers become "modern," it also makes their texts legible as works of literature rather than being dismissed as "anachronisms" or "provincial." Magical realism has become the way for works of literature written in the Global South to be accepted as such by critics in the center—in other words, for them to be included in the world literary canon. In the same way that García Márquez, Vargas Llosa, and Fuentes stormed the World Republic of Letters and its canons by adapting in creative ways the lessons of Faulkner, today writers such as Rushdie, Okri, Mo Yan, and Arundhati Roy are widely acclaimed as major writers, and their works are taught in classes and included in anthologies. In other words, they have entered the world canon by means of magical realism.

Perhaps the best example of the manner in which magical realism helped determine the criteria by which literature from the Global South is read by critics in the United States and Europe is provided by the Chileans Alberto Fuguet and Sergio Gómez in "Presentación del país McOndo," their introduction to *McOndo* (1996), an anthology of short stories by (then) young Latin American writers. As part of their attack on magical realism, Fuguet and Gómez describe the experience of three unnamed Latin American writers at the International Writer's Workshop at the University of Iowa: "Such is the Latin fever that the editor of a prestigious literary magazine hears that there are three

Latin American writers loose on campus, only a few blocks away. The gentleman introduces himself to them and sets up a weekly literary lunch in the cafeteria by the river. His idea is to publish a special issue of his prestigious magazine dedicated to this Latin explosion" (9). However, "the editor reads the Hispanic texts and rejects two. Those discarded are because they 'lack magical realism.' ... [T]hey are discarded due to their disregard for the sacred code of magical realism. The editor stops any discussion by arguing that those texts 'could have been written in any country of the First World'" (10). The unnamed editor, whose views on modern Latin American writing were clearly shaped by *One Hundred Years of Solitude*, reflects the impact of García Márquez on the criteria by which the institutions decide which texts are of value.

García Márquez has exerted a similar influence on the world literary canon. In the section "Contemporary World Literature" of the *Norton Anthology of World Literature*, in addition to the author of *One Hundred Years of Solitude*, magical realists Rushdie, Morrison, Yan, Okri, Leslie Marmon Silko, and Bessie Head, among others, are included. In fact, one of the two post-Boom Latin American authors is García Márquez's disciple Isabel Allende, who is often seen in the Spanish-speaking world as an author of bestsellers. (The second Latin American post-Boom author is, as one would expect, the Chilean Roberto Bolaño.)

Conclusion

The anecdote told by Fuguet and Gómez, as well as the inclusion of Allende in the *Norton Anthology of World Literature*, reflects the tensions between a world literary establishment that, at least until recently, considered magical realism the necessary style in which authors from the Global South were expected to write, and Latin American writers and critics who have never seen magical realism as more than one possible way of writing among many. This, of course, should not be taken as a criticism of García Márquez, whose place in the Spanish-language canon is as solid as ever. In fact, *One Hundred Years of Solitude* was the second book, after *Don Quixote*, to receive a special edition by the Real Academia de la Lengua, in 2007, its fortieth anniversary.

Regardless of the ups and downs of magical realism, it is clear that *One Hundred Years of Solitude* and García Márquez's works as a whole represent the one example of a literature written in the Global South that not only entered the world canon but actually redefined it. Ironically, García Márquez helped shape the world canon by means of his own personal interpretation of the Western canon.

Notes

1. As is the case with all of the books and articles listed in Spanish in the Works Cited, the translation is mine.
2. While a full analysis of Bhabha's misreading of magical realism as characteristic of the Boom as a whole is beyond the scope of this chapter, one must note that the association

of this style with Latin American narrative is also present in numerous other authors, including Couto, Julia Álvarez, and, to a degree, Rushdie, among others. Such was the effect of *One Hundred Years of Solitude* that it spread its magical patina even on literature that could be classified as realist, such as Mario Vargas Llosa's novels of the 1960s (*The Time of the Hero*, *The Green House*, and *Conversation in the Cathedral*), or Carlos Fuentes's best novel of the decade (*The Death of Artemio Cruz*).

3. One can note a stylistic break between Latin American and other literatures from the Global South. Not only was García Márquez the only magical realist among the Boom writers, but a renewed realism, represented by writers such as Alberto Fuguet, Juan Villoro, and Juan Gabriel Vásquez, influenced by such diverse figures as John Updike, Philip Roth, Vargas Llosa, and the Argentine Manuel Puig, is the norm among most Latin American writers. Magical realism is, however, still influential among writers from Asia and Africa.

4. Despite the equal space given to Joyce and Faulkner by García Márquez in this quotation, it is clear from *Living to Tell the Tale*, as well as from his early writings, that the Colombian novelist found in the US American writer a clear model and forerunner. As Gene Bell-Villada writes: "To discuss the presence of Faulkner in García Márquez is to enter a much vaster world of regional likeness, personal affinities, and bonds linking master and disciple" (81).

5. Curiously, García Márquez here veers close to the "tendency to define magical realism in strictly formal terms that overlook its historical, cultural, and political determinations has led many critics to include almost any text featuring a fantastic episode not explainable by the laws of physics, regardless of when or where it may have been produced, within the flexible boundaries of magical realism" (Siskind 82). Against this apolitical and generalized definition of magical realism, Mariano Siskind sees in *One Hundred Years of Solitude* an example of how "magical realism produced a critique (which in certain contexts might very well be called postcolonial) of the social and epistemological relations that give rise to hegemonic modes of symbolizing the real in the margins of global modernity" (85).

6. It is true that García Márquez's sense of a Caribbean identity is not in as dramatic a contrast with Colombia's hegemonic *cachaco* (Andean) culture as Kafka's was with German culture. Nevertheless, the contrast between García Márquez's "Caribbean culture" (*Living to Tell the Tale* 72, 217), "Caribbean localisms" (134), and "Caribbean dialect" (218), and that language and, more generally, the cultures of the Colombian highlands, especially Bogotá, is one of the constants of the Nobel Prize winner's works. An example of this tension between Caribbean language and culture and that of Bogotá, is found in the references to cachacos in *One Hundred Years of Solitude*, in particular in the representation of Fernanda. Unlike the inhabitants of Macondo, whose lives are shaped informally by their vibrant family and social environment, Fernanda is described in García Márquez's masterpiece as the product of an obsolete culture and educational system, delinked from living society. She is presented as being "born and raised in a city six hundred miles away, a gloomy city where on ghostly nights the coaches of the viceroys still rattled through the cobbled streets" (205) and as being educated in a convent, where "after having learned to write Latin poetry, play the clavichord, talk about falconry with gentlemen and apologetics, with archbishops, discuss affairs of state with foreign rulers and affairs of God with the Pope, she returned to her parents' home to weave funeral wreaths" (206).

7. An earlier translation of this essay—originally titled in Spanish "Mi Hemingway personal"—was published by the *New York Times* in 1981, as "Gabriel García Márquez Meets Ernest Hemingway."

8. In fact, writing in 1950, Septimus that is, García Márquez, argued that Hemingway was "much lesser than Dos Passos, Steinbeck, and, of course, the most extraordinary and vital creator of the modern world, William Faulkner" ("Al otro lado del río entre los árboles" 289).
9. In another of his early journalistic pieces, Septimus, noted that "everything seems to indicate that Rómulo Gallegos will be the Nobel Prize winner in 1950," while complaining: "The author of *The Hamlet* will never be a Nobel laureate, for the same reason Joyce wasn't. For the same reason, Proust probably wasn't. For the same reason that English genius named Virginia Woolf wasn't. If the institution of the Nobel Prize were older, we would now be surprised by the fact that it had not been given to Cervantes, Rabelais, or Racine" ("Otra vez el Premio Nobel" 194). Ironically, that same year the author of *The Hamlet*, Faulkner, won the Prize.
10. In "Otra vez el Premio Nobel," an article from 1950, García Márquez describes Rómulo Gallegos as "South American—... our neighbor, almost a relative of Colombian" (195).
11. One must note, however, that if García Márquez rejects Latin American fiction—with the exception of Borges's, Cortázar's, and Hernández's short stories—Spanish-language poetry is embraced. In fact, his first public writing was a series of brief satirical poems published in his high school magazine. Soon he would write carefully crafted sonnets. García Márquez knew by heart Spanish-language poems from the Spanish Golden Age to Pablo Neruda and Colombian master Pablo de Greif. As he writes in *Living to Tell the Tale*, "We not only believed in poetry, and would have died for it, but we also knew with certainty—as Luis Cardoza y Aragón wrote—that 'poetry is the only concrete proof of the existence of man'" (252). His later prose owes much to his obsession with poetry.
12. García Márquez's rejection of Colombian and Latin American supposedly high literary narrative—with the exceptions of the Southern Cone short-story masters Borges, Cortázar, and Hernández—does not imply a rejection of his region's culture in its totality. As we have seen (see note 11), the young Colombian novelist was influenced by Spanish-language poetry. García Márquez was also obsessed with popular music. Writing about Mexican bolero composer Agustín Lara, he states, "For me it was like finding poetry dissolved into the soup of daily life." In fact, not only is García Márquez an admirer of boleros—the pan-Latin American romantic songs of the 1930s, 1940s, and 1950s, which had one of their representatives in composer Lara—he is also an interpreter. Throughout his youth, he sang in bands, tríos, and other popular musical outfits. He played and sang "beautiful serenades of romantic boleros" (*Living to Tell the Tale* 178), adding, "whoever does not sing cannot imagine the pleasure of singing" (*Living to Tell the Tale* 178). But not only boleros exerted their spell on the young novelist; so did the accordion-driven vallenato music of the Colombian Caribbean. He claims to have probably heard Francisco, el hombre (Francisco, the Man), the mythical founder of the style, and a minor character in *One Hundred Years of Solitude*. In *Living to Tell the Tale*, the vallenato is connected to oral storytelling: "Everything that happened to me in the street had an enormous resonance in the house. The women in the kitchen would tell the stories to the strangers arriving on the train, who in turn brought other stories to be told, and all of it was incorporated into the torrent of oral tradition. Some events were first learned through the accordion players who sang about them at fairs, and travelers would retell them and enhance them" (91). García Márquez would later claim that "*One Hundred Years of Solitude* is a vallenato 350 pages long" (Jaramillo n.p.). As Bell-Villada notes, García Márquez singled out "for attention the vallenato songs ... which consist either of love tunes or Iberian style romances (narrative ballads) ... and hence serve as a kind of model for *One Hundred Years of Solitude* and *Love in the Time of Cholera*" (21).

13. The fact that neither García Márquez nor Vargas Llosa knew English at the time they began reading Faulkner (see García Márquez, *Living to Tell the Tale* 352; Vargas Llosa, *A Fish in the Water* 280), and that both mention *Wild Palms* as among the texts they read, serves to highlight the mediating role played by Jorge Luis Borges, who translated the novella, in the dissemination of the (North) American author in Spanish America.
14. Vargas Llosa presents a more academic version of this criticism of earlier Latin American literature in his well-known essay "The Latin American Novel Today." After calling the novels that preceded those of the Boom "primitive novels," Vargas Llosa describes them as "valid geographical testimonials, important documentaries, but their aesthetic significance is nevertheless slight" (8). In one of his Septimus essays, García Márquez had made a similar point when he compared his own literary test with that of "a friend and cordial detractor": "My friend and cordial detractor considers himself as radically different in his aesthetic ideas because I am the supporter of something he calls 'modern decadentism.' Since my favorite authors at the moment are Faulkner, Kafka, and Virginia Woolf, and my greatest aspiration is to write like them, I suppose that is what the writer I'm talking about is why she calls 'modern decadentism.' The favorite writers of my friend are Ciro Alegría and the authors of Marxist treatises. I assume her greatest aspiration is to write like them" ("Memorias de un aprendiz de antropófago" 467). Needless to say, Vargas Llosa classifies Ciro Alegría, together with Rómulo Gallegos and Mariano Azuela, among others, as "primitive."
15. I am, of course, reinterpreting Casanova, since she stresses the central role of Paris as the Greenwich Meridian of the Republic of Letters over that of other editorial centers.

Works Cited

Álvarez, Julia. ¡*Yo!* Plume, 1997.
Bell-Villada, Gene. *García Márquez: The Man and His Work*. U North Carolina P, 2010.
Bhabha, Homi. Introduction. *Nation and Narration*, edited by Homi Bhabha, Routledge, 1990, pp. 1–7.
Casanova, Pascale. "Literature as World." *New Left Review*, vol. 31, 2005, pp. 71–90.
Casanova, Pascale. *The World Republic of Letters*. Translated by Malcolm DeBevoise, Harvard UP, 2004.
Cheng, Vincent J. *Joyce, Race, and Empire*. Cambridge, 1995.
Couto, Mia, "Entrevista a Mia Couto, escritor y poeta mozambiqueño: 'África está llena de Macondos, de pueblos así, como el de Gabo.'" 2014.kaosenlared.net/component/k2/55831-entrevista-a-mia-couto-escritor-y-poeta-mozambiqueño-"áfrica-está-llena-de-macondos-de-pueblos-as%C3%AD-como-el-de-gabo". Accessed 11 Feb. 2020.
Deleuze, Gilles, and Félix Guattari. *Kafka: Toward a Minor Literature*. Translated by Dana Polan, U of Minnesota P, 1986.
Fuguet, Alberto, and Sergio Gómez. *McOndo*. Grijalbo Mondadori, 1996.
García Márquez, Gabriel. "Al otro lado del río entre los árboles." *Obra periodística I: Textos costeños (1948–1952)*, edited by Jacques Girard, vol. 1, Oveja Negra, 1983, pp. 288–90.
García Márquez, Gabriel. *Living to Tell the Tale*. Translated by Edith Grossman, Vintage, 2004.
García Márquez, Gabriel. "Memorias de un aprendiz de antropófago." *Obra periodística I: Textos costeños (1948–1952)*, edited by Jacques Girard, vol. 2, Oveja Negra, 1983, pp. 466–67.

García Márquez, Gabriel. "My Personal Hemingway." *The Scandal of the Century and Other Writings*, translated by Anne McLean, Knopf, 2019, pp. 236–41.

García Márquez, Gabriel. *One Hundred Years of Solitude*. Translated by Gregory Rabassa, Harper Perennial, 2006.

García Márquez, Gabriel. "Otra vez el Premio Nobel." *Obra periodística I*, edited by Jacques Girard, vol. 1, Oveja Negra, 1983, pp.194–95.

García Márquez, Gabriel. "*Playboy* Interview: Gabriel García Márquez." Interview by Claudia Dreifus. *Conversations with Gabriel García Márquez*. Edited by Gene Bell-Villada. U of Mississippi P, 2006, pp. 93–132.

García Márquez, Gabriel. "¿Problemas de la novela?" *Obra periodística I*, edited by Jacques Girard, vol. 2, Oveja Negra, 1983, pp. 212–13.

García Márquez, Gabriel. *Vivir para contarla*. Norma, 2002.

Jaramillo, Juan Carlos. "'Un vallenato de 350 páginas': La magia que comparten '*Cien años de soledad*' y el folclor musical más conocido de Colombia." *BBC.com*, 28 Jan. 2017, www.bbc.com/mundo/noticias-america-latina-38678370. Accessed 11 Feb.2020.

"Nobel Prize in Literature 1982." *NobelPrize.org*. https://www.nobelprize.org/prizes/literature/1982/summary/. Accessed 11 Feb. 2020.

Rushdie, Salman. "Salman Rushdie on Gabriel García Márquez: His World Was Mine." *The Telegraph*, 25 Apr. 2014, www.telegraph.co.uk/culture/books/10787739/Salman-Rushdie-on-Gabriel-Garcia-Marquez-His-world-was-mine.html. Accessed 11 Feb. 2020.

Siskind, Mariano. *Cosmopolitan Desires: Global Modernity and World Literature in Latin America*. Northwestern UP, 2014.

Vargas Llosa, Mario. *A Fish in the Water*. Translated by Helen Lange, Farrar, Straus & Giroux, 1994.

Vargas Llosa, Mario. "The Latin American Novel Today." *Books Abroad*, vol. 44, no. 1, 1970, pp. 7–16.

CHAPTER 6

GARCÍA MÁRQUEZ AND HIS PRECURSORS

LOIS PARKINSON ZAMORA

The Argentine writer Jorge Luis Borges, in his essay "Kafka and His Precursors," challenges the simplicity of our usual ideas about literary influence.[1] Ordinarily, we presume that a writer reads his precursors and is influenced by them. This is true, of course, but there is more. Borges inverts this chronology to propose that influence also flows backward in time because writers *also influence their precursors*. How can a work of literature influence writers who lived before that work was written? Here's how: we read those works *now*.

If, in Borges's example, we read Kafka, we will necessarily read previous works through a Kafkian lens. Thus, Borges finds Kafka's novel *The Castle* haunting Aristotle's account of Zeno's paradox, which argues that a moving object can never reach its goal because it will cover only half the distance, then "half of the half" and then "half of the half of the half, and so on to infinity" ("Kafka" 199). In Aristotle's account, Borges asserts that "the moving object and the arrow and Achilles are the first Kafkian characters in literature" (199). We smile and concede the point. Why not? Other examples follow: Kafka's tone influences a Chinese writer in the ninth century, Kafka's "spiritual affinity" with Kierkegaard influences the Danish thinker's religious fables, and so on. In short, literary history isn't successive but simultaneous. Borges concludes: "The fact is that every writer *creates* his own precursors. His work modifies our conception of the past and it will modify the future" (201).

This is a theory of reading, of course, not of writing. Borges winks and brings his vast and witty erudition to bear on a proposition that in three short pages becomes obvious. Borges's essay occurs to me (after reading Borges, everything is Borgesian) because García Márquez has the same effect as Kafka and Borges: after reading García Márquez, everything is Garcíamarquezian. It doesn't matter whether the text was written centuries before *One Hundred Years of Solitude* or yesterday. Therefore, my title intentionally echoes Borges: I discuss this "Borgesian effect" of retrospective influence because it affects how we read García Márquez, of course, and it also affects his antecedents, most especially those by whom he himself is influenced. In his autobiography *Vivir para contarla* (*Living to Tell the Tale*, 2002), he writes: "I learned and never forgot that we should read only those books that force us to reread them" (137).[2] He mentions William Faulkner, Nathaniel Hawthorne, Virginia Woolf, Kafka, and James Joyce, among many others, and we now reread them under his influence. Entire traditions may also be influential, and influenced. The baroque aesthetic of Spanish Golden Age poetry, theater, and prose is cited by García Márquez as a constant source of inspiration—a word that I consider synonymous with influence: surely to be *inspired* by literary works is to be *influenced* profoundly. Thus, we read the seventeenth-century writers Francisco de Quevedo, Pedro Calderón de la Barca, and Miguel de Cervantes differently because García Márquez adapts their baroque style and sensibilities to serve his twentieth-century purposes. And yet another influence is often mentioned: his grandmother's stories and his deeply religious aunts' accounts of biblical miracles and mysteries. García Márquez's fiction may even influence, or at least intersect with, our reading of the Bible.

I discuss some of these reciprocal influences later, but I start by surveying the tip of this vast iceberg in order to make clear my overarching aim in this essay, which is to complicate our usual understanding of influence. Tracing influences as they move backward *and* forward in time enlarges our understanding of literary relations among authors and enriches our sense of literary traditions as a whole. There is, however, another equally important reason: to study influence is to oppose, indeed cancel, our modern understanding of originality. I have contested Harold Bloom's theory of "the anxiety of influence" elsewhere, and I don't do so here except to say that the desire for originality, which is the apparent cause of Bloomian anxiety, doesn't bother Latin American novelists in the least. Instead, they go out of their way to recognize their shared traditions and precursors, sometimes by explicitly including and revising them in their own work. This practice speaks to the investment of Latin American authors in their collective history and to the political function of literature in creating national and cultural identities. The specifics of these historical conditions are beyond the scope of my discussion, but as a general matter, they help us to understand why precursors are so powerful in Latin America and why traditions tend to be recognized and included in the name of community, rather than evaded or denied in the name of originality.[3]

Another consideration remains. Though Borges says that all texts are influenced by our reading of every text, we aren't Borges, so we will need to set some parameters. The clearest indication of influence is the author's own word for it: (1) if an author says that he or she has read a writer or a text or describes a relevant cultural context, we are justified in assuming that influence operates to a greater or lesser degree; (2) the same is true of *allusions* within the author's work—references, whether explicit or implicit, are clear markers of influence; (3) writers may also *echo* their precursors based on *affinity*—tone, pitch, pace, narrative style, structure, or theme evoke another writer or an entire literary tradition; and finally (4) the *absorption* or *reflection* of cultural conditions and historical settings in an author's work is the most difficult to identify, and the most important, because these influences are likely to inhabit and impel the entire oeuvre. If an author writes about his or her experiences, as García Márquez does in detail in his autobiography, we would be remiss not to pay close attention. These different indicators of influence will necessarily overlap and combine, so here I depend on García Márquez's own account of the intersections.

Living to Tell the Tale

In his autobiography *Living to Tell the Tale*, García Márquez names dozens if not hundreds of writers whom he read avidly during his teens and twenties in Cartagena, Barranquilla, and Bogotá, writers who were important to him then and are still important enough to him fifty-odd years later to name and describe. The effect is sometimes dizzying, so much did he read and so lively were his discussions with friends about their favorite authors. Some of these authors may simply have been appreciated and enjoyed for what they meant to the young reader, but many left an indelible imprint upon the mature writer, as García Márquez makes clear. In either case or both, he seems never to have forgotten a single book or its source, most of them lent to him by friends. Like influence itself, he moves back and forth in this autobiography between the older narrator and his younger self, remembering the circumstances of his youthful discoveries and watching as some of those discoveries mature into "tutelary demons," as he says of Faulkner (*Living* 6). Here, and in innumerable interviews and published conversations, he influences his precursors by recognizing them as such and then considering how he absorbed them into his own literary worldview.

This autobiography is also an account of the places in Colombia that formed the author. As I pick and choose from the seemingly endless library mentioned in this work, I also refer to the Colombian cultures (coastal and Andean) where his library took shape. In fact, there are many temptations for comparatists in this autobiography, so I hope that you, too, will pick and choose, and thus complicate further our understanding of *la tradición gabrielina*.

The Bible and Colombian Catholic Culture

García Márquez was born in 1927 in Aracataca, a small town on the Caribbean coast of Colombia that had suddenly become rich through the establishment of a banana export operation owned by United Fruit. "Gabito" was the oldest of eleven children, and during the first eight years of his life, he lived in Aracataca with his maternal grandparents. His birth parents were in the port city of Barranquilla, struggling to establish a pharmacy (the first of several, all equally unsuccessful), and Gabito saw them only once a year. But in Aracataca he was nonetheless surrounded by family: besides his beloved grandparents, there was an endless supply of aunts who played their different roles in the development of this precocious, timid child.

Despite their huge family, the writer recognizes the solitude of his grandparents' world. They were forced to leave their native Riohacha, a larger coastal city, because his grandfather had killed a man in a duel, and the child senses their longing for home. Nor is the ghost of the dead man ever far from his family circle; when an uncle starts to carry a gun and comments on its weight in his belt, his grandfather says to him by way of warning, "You don't know how much a dead man weighs" (*Living* 74).[4] The sadness is palpable to the boy growing up in what he calls "that earthly paradise of desolation and nostalgia" (*Living* 365).[5]

"Sacred histories" were essential to this world, embellished as they were by his family's Catholic imagination. In *Living to Tell the Tale,* García Márquez describes the large altar in his grandparents' room upon which towered a statue of Christ with real hair, and he remembers the flickering candles illuminating images of martyred saints who terrified him and his mother. But stories of miracles were not to be missed. He writes that as a child, "The voracity with which I listened to stories left me always hoping for a better one the next day, above all those that had to do with the mysteries of sacred history" (*Living* 90–91).[6] These "mysteries" were biblical accounts of miracles, of course, and also hagiographies, that is, the legendary lives of saints, complete with their extraordinary feats and unshakeable beliefs. Every room in his grandparents' house had its saint, with whom his grandmother spoke daily, and we learn that his mother was "inexhaustibly devoted" to Santa Rita de Casia, patron saint of wives with wayward husbands (*Living* 156–57). These legendary human figures with their superhuman capacities and inordinate virtues (and vices) were an integral part of the author's childhood, and they surely influenced the outsized characters in his novels: the extreme patience and devotion of Florentino Ariza in *Love in the Time of Cholera*, the exaggerated appetites of the José Arcadios and exaggerated beauty of Remedios in *One Hundred Years of Solitude*, the diabolical cruelty of the dictator in *The Autumn of the Patriarch*. Because influence moves backward as well as forward, a quick look at any compendium of saints' lives will seem like reading a story by García Márquez.

In his autobiography, García Márquez connects these miraculous figures with the women in his family. Gabito and his grandfather are the only males in the house; his grandfather is treated like a king and Gabito like the heir apparent. The older self, looking back at his childhood, observes that this household now seems to him a perfect example of the machismo of a matriarchal society: his grandfather was king but his grandmother governed. Grandfather Nicolás Márquez possessed a private tenderness that he would have been embarrassed to display in public, and his grandmother devoted herself to his service. Already we see the outlines of Úrsula Iguarán and José Arcadio Buendía in *One Hundred Years of Solitude*. García Márquez says that he owes his way of being and thinking to having grown up among women, and his description of them sometimes feels like hagiography in a secular mode.[7] Clearly, Colombia's Catholic culture is a primary influence and inspiration, and the bedrock of this author's magical realism. It is a short distance from the miraculous to the magical, and García Márquez breaches it by virtue of having lived both.

Colombia signed a concordat with the Vatican in 1887, and again in 1928, whereby the Catholic Church and the Colombian government were essentially a single entity.

Put another way, church and state agreed upon mutual patronage, protection, and shared functions. These agreements were the outcome of years of conflict between anti-Catholic Liberals and pro-Catholic Conservatives, and the concordats were obviously victories for the latter, though the conflict would continue for decades into the twentieth century. All education was Catholic education, bishops and archbishops could be appointed by government officials, and the church was to function as an arm of the government in some civil matters. During the mid-twentieth century, there were only three countries in the world with such an arrangement: Franco's Spain, Colombia, and the Vatican State itself. The Colombian Constitution of 1991 undid the union of church and state, but García Márquez's world was formed long before. That the endless civil wars pervading *One Hundred Years of Solitude* are tied to religious conflict is affirmed by the disillusioned Colonel Aureliano Buendía: "The only difference today between Liberals and Conservatives is that the Liberals go to mass at five o'clock and the Conservatives at eight" (*One Hundred* 228).[8] And when Fernanda proposes to allege that she has found her illegitimate grandson floating in a basket, like Moses in the bulrushes, she justifies her prevarication by saying, "If they believe it in the Bible, I don't see why they shouldn't believe it from me" (277).[9] I don't know whether García Márquez was religious, but I do know that it is impossible to ignore the influence of Colombian Catholic culture in his work.

The arc of biblical history in *One Hundred Years of Solitude* is obvious: Macondo's Edenic beginning, its decline into violence and exploitation, and its ending when "a biblical hurricane" sweeps Macondo away. In this biblical structure, the novel is comparable to William Faulkner's *Absalom, Absalom!*[10] Faulkner's biblical title announces this temporal perspective, as does García Márquez's title. Like St. John of Patmos, the author of the final book of the Christian bible, the narrators of these novels foresee the apocalyptic ending of their stories even as they recount the beginning and middle. Melquíades, like Miss Rosa and Quentin, integrates memory and anticipation, past and future, into the narrative present. Faulkner's novel provided a model for this "retrospective future" narrative technique, as his epic tragedies echo with biblical references that set the tone for *One Hundred Years of Solitude*.

Much has been said about Faulkner's influence on García Márquez, in part because García Márquez himself repeatedly invoked Faulkner as his maestro, his teacher, most notably in his Nobel Prize acceptance speech in 1981. Here, let me point to Faulkner's narrative style and historical sensibility as essential influences. Faulkner's novels are characterized by complex syntax, pages-long paragraphs, multiple perspectives, nonlinear plots, and image-laden prose, for which an American critic dubbed him "the Dixie Gongorist."[11] Long before this "Dixie Gongorist," however, there was the original "Gongorist," the seventeenth-century poet Luis de Góngora, whose poetry gave his name to a literary style that is elegant and elaborate, and sometimes hyperbolic and extravagant. García Márquez and Faulkner share these expansive stylistic tendencies, and they also share the baroque sense of fated history. Both portray political, economic, and cultural forces against which their characters have no recourse. Whether Faulkner was influenced by Spanish baroque literature is questionable, but García Márquez surely was, and his self-conscious revisions of baroque themes and characters make him a neo-baroque writer par excellence.[12] So we go back to seventeenth-century Spain to advance our discussion of García Márquez's precursors.

Golden Age Spanish Literature and the Baroque

García Márquez was emphatic about his love for Spanish Golden Age poetry and drama and for the greatest prose work of the period, *The Ingenious Gentleman Don Quixote de la Mancha*. In a 1969 interview, García Márquez pays homage to the "marvelous origins" of the Spanish baroque, mentioning the novels of chivalry, Don Quixote, and the theater and poetry of the Golden Age: "Style, elegance, luxury, total excess have not been given their due. Young Latin American novelists have known how to be inventive in the best tradition of the Spanish Baroque and, at the same time, to engage in social criticism that is no less telling for being colorful."[13] In 1969, García Márquez would surely have included himself among these "young Latin American novelists," and in *Living to Tell the Tale* he does so explicitly as he looks back upon this younger self. He writes about his six semesters as a university student in Villa de Leyva and Bogotá in the late 1940s, when he was supposed to be studying law. Instead, he tells us, he was dedicating himself "to reading whatever I could get my hands on and reciting from memory the unrepeatable poetry of the Spanish Golden Age" (*Living* 4).[14]

This early fascination with Spanish baroque literature pervades García Márquez's fiction. The poetry of this "golden age" is written in an elaborate metaphorical style and is divided into two branches, referred to as *culteranismo* and *conceptismo*. The former is more ornate than the latter; the former is epitomized by Luis de Góngora and the latter by his contemporary and archrival, Francisco de Quevedo. In his autobiography, García Márquez praises Quevedo, not Góngora. In fact, in a story published in 1970, he inverts the title of Quevedo's sonnet "Amor constante más allá de la muerte" ("Love Constant beyond Death"), changing the positions of "love" and "death" in the title of his story to "Muerte constante más allá del amor" ("Death Constant beyond Love").[15] Whereas Quevedo's poem insists that love survives death, García Márquez's fictional character is terminally ill and "weeps with rage at dying without his lover," certain that death will obliterate his love ("Death Constant" 93).[16] García Márquez thus revises the terms of the baroque sonnet with neo-baroque irony, but despite this reversal (and also because of it), Quevedo's theme will become García Márquez's own.

The Quevedian contest between love's endurance and time's annihilation is present in virtually all of García Márquez's fiction. *El amor en los tiempos del cólera* (*Love in the Time of Cholera*, 1985) describes the battle against aging and death by a lover, Florentino Ariza, who must wait fifty-three years, seven months, and eleven days and nights to possess his beloved. The clock has ticked for decades, and yet the novel ends with the word "forever." In this case, love triumphs over oblivion; time proceeds relentlessly, but love remains.

This battle runs in the family. Florentino's father writes a sentence in a notebook decorated with wounded hearts: "*The only regret I will have in dying is if it is not for love*" (169).[17] It is one of very few italicized sentences in the novel, and it plays with Quevedo's assertion of the power of love over death, though here the suggestion is that the character wants to die *of* love. Further examples of this dynamic are *Crónica de una muerte anunciada* (*Chronicle of a Death Foretold*, 1981), in which a wedding and a murder are set against each other, and *Del amor y otros demonios* (*Of Love and Other Demons*, 1994), which ends with a losing race against death as Sierva María waits in a prison cell for her beloved. In *El general en su laberinto* (*The General and His Labyrinth*, 1989), General Simón Bolívar is dying, but flashbacks replay the battles he has won, not the least of which is with his lover, Manuela Sáenz. And again, the central theme of his late novel *Memoria de mis putas tristes* (*Memories of My Melancholy Whores*, 2005 is the relation between love and aging, desire and death. I leave it to my readers to amplify these discussions, because here I want to return to *Living to Tell the Tale* and Quevedo.

García Márquez writes about his arrival in Barranquilla in 1948 as a young journalist, and the group of friends he established there:

> In the end it was clear to me that my new friends read Quevedo and James Joyce with the same pleasure they derived from reading Arthur Conan Doyle. They had an inexhaustible sense of humor and were capable of spending whole nights singing boleros and *vallenatos* or reciting the best poetry of the Golden Age. By different paths we came to agree that the summit of world poetry are the stanzas of Don Jorge Manrique on the death of his father. (*Living* 337)[18]

Jorge Manrique (1440–1479) precedes the seventeenth-century Golden Age, but García Márquez groups him with the baroque poets whom he and his friends spend "whole nights" reciting. In "Coplas a la muerte de su padre" ("Stanzas on the Death of his Father"), it is the love of a son that conquers death.[19] Of course, it is also Manrique's metaphorical language that captivates, its repeating rhythms and rhymes perfect for reciting by heart.

It is surprising that poetry is so important to García Márquez, given his vocation as novelist, but he writes about his student years in Bogotá:

> It is difficult to imagine the degree to which people lived then in the shadow of poetry. It was a frenzied passion, another way of being, a fireball that went everywhere on its own.... Bogotá was the capital of the country and the seat of government, but above all it was the city where poets lived.... We not only believed in poetry, and would have died for it, but we also knew with certainty—as Luis Cardoza y Aragón wrote—that "poetry is the only concrete proof of the existence of man." (*Living* 252)[20]

Would I have reread Quevedo or discovered Manrique or the Guatemalan poet Luis Cardoza y Aragón without García Márquez's influence? No. His precursors are influenced because, as García Márquez says in the passage quoted earlier, the only books worth reading are worth rereading, now illuminated in a different light.

Baroque drama was also basic to García Márquez's literary education. Plays by the most important Spanish playwright of the period, Pedro Calderón de la Barca, are impelled by flamboyant fatalism and murderous honor—contradictions characteristic of the baroque. Fatalism isn't usually flamboyant, nor honor murderous, but the dynamism of the baroque is generated by this kind of tension, this kind of *coincidentia oppositorum* (coincidence of opposites) in which contraries can be true at once. (Already you will be seeing the baroque *coincidentia oppositorum* in the term "magical realism.") *Chronicle of a Death Foretold* is a Colombian replay of the Calderonian themes of honor, revenge, cruelty, and fate. A bridegroom discovers on his wedding night that his bride is not a virgin, and the bride's brothers vow to kill the man who has disgraced their sister. They stalk Santiago Nasar and murder him the following morning while the whole town looks on. Everyone knows that Santiago will be murdered, everyone but Santiago; his death is "foretold" (*anunciada*), as the title foretells. *The Autumn of the Patriarch* also echoes baroque drama in the monstrous Patriarch, whose cruelty is Calderonian and whose endless reign is also foretold. He is a force, not a face, an embodied archetype of power, as is Faulkner's monstrous Thomas Sutpen in *Absalom, Absalom!*, who is described as "horse-man-demon." García Márquez refers to his youthful attempts to devise a "theory of fatality," and many years later, inspired by both Calderón and Faulkner, he does so in these novels (*Living* 339).

The great novel of the baroque period (arguably the only great one) is Miguel de Cervantes's *The Ingenious Gentleman Don Quixote de la Mancha* (1605, 1615). This work is structured by the illusions and delusions of its main character, a structure that also reflects seventeenth-century aesthetics. Baroque illusionism in art and literature was a reaction to the scientific revolution of the seventeenth century, which exploded received ideas about astronomy, geography, anatomy, and medicine, to name a few areas in which the very nature of reality was thrown into question. In the character of Don Quixote, Cervantes exploits this baroque obsession with the unreliability of perception. Don Quixote constantly mistakes what he sees for what he imagines, thus departing from reality (and realism) in ways that predict the magical realism in *One Hundred Years of Solitude*. Furthermore, Cervantes's pairing of Don Quixote and Sancho Panza embodies the baroque love of coexisting contraries that I have already mentioned: Don Quixote is all intellect and Sancho all appetite; Don Quixote is a deluded dreamer, Sancho a self-interested pragmatist. If this pair reminds you of *One Hundred Years of Solitude* and the bifurcation in the Buendía family between the solitary intelligence of the Aurelianos and the expansive eroticism of the Jose Arcadios, you are not mistaken.

García Márquez recounts his passion for Cervantes's novel in his autobiography. He encounters *Don Quixote* in high school,

> where I was obliged to study it as a requirement, and I had an irremediable aversion to it until a friend advised me to put it on the back of the toilet and try to read it while I took care of my daily needs. Only in this way did I discover it, like a

conflagration, and relish it forward and back until I could recite entire episodes by heart. (*Living* 137)[21]

This description is itself a *coincidentia oppositorum*: aversion and absorption, body and soul, avoidance and embrace, "forward and backward." In these competing energies, we *do* detect a bit of Bloomian anxiety of influence. Perhaps the young García Márquez sensed his affinity for this monumental magical realist text and understood the challenge of meeting, much less matching, Cervantes's masterpiece. Or perhaps he already foresaw, however unconsciously, that he and Cervantes would one day be paired by some as the two greatest writers in the Spanish language.

García Márquez's love of poetry extends back in time to the sonnets of Garcilaso de la Vega. Garcilaso precedes the baroque period per se, but he obviously conspires with Quevedo, Calderón, Cervantes, and others to fuel García Márquez's baroque predilections. This fifteenth-century poet left a small body of work: forty sonnets, assorted songs, elegies, lyrics, and *coplas* (stanzas). Recall that in *Of Love and Other Demons*, García Márquez's characters, the lovers Sierva María and Cayetano Delaura, recite Garcilaso's poems to each other, one reciting a line and the other answering with the line that follows. We are told that they "repeated the lines with the same tenderness, until the end of the book, omitting verses, corrupting and twisting the sonnets to suit themselves, toying with them with the skill of masters" (*Of Love* 126). Here, the characters stand in for their author, influencing their precursor as García Márquez influences his.

Lines from Sonnets I, II, and X are embedded in the narrative of the lovers' furtive meetings. They are quoted in italics, address the relations of love and death (are we surprised?), and reflect the title of the novel. The lines exchanged by the lovers from Sonnet I are the first two lines of Garcilaso's poem: "*When I stand and contemplate my fate and see the path along which you have led me / I reach my end for artless I surrendered to one who is my undoing and my end*" (*Of Love* 126).[22] And in another meeting, they exchange lines from Sonnet II, "*Into your hands at last I have come vanquished where I know that I must die / So that in myself alone it might be proven how deep the sword bites into conquered flesh*" (*Of Love* 127).[23] A phrase from Sonnet X is also recited by Cayetano ("*O sweet treasures, discovered to my sorrow*"),[24] who makes explicit the allusion to Garcilaso:

> Something stirred in the hearts of Sierva María, for she wanted to hear the verse again. He repeated it, and this time he continued, in an intense, well-articulated voice, until he had recited the last of the forty sonnets by the cavalier of amours and arms Don Garcilaso de la Vega, killed in his prime by a stone hurled in battle. (*Of Love* 125)[25]

This is clearly an homage to the "cavalier of amours and arms." *Amor y armas*: another *coincidentia oppositorum* now enacted in a fetid prison cell in the convent of Santa Clara in Cartagena, where one more battle for love is being fought to the death. García Márquez directs us to reread Garcilaso, as Sierva María directs Cayetano, and let our hearts, like Sierva María's, be stirred again.

Franz Kafka and Doña Tranquilina Iguarán

I now turn to more recent precursors. As it happens, the first is the very writer whom Borges selects to exemplify his principle of reciprocal influence, and the second is García Márquez's maternal grandmother. I pair them because García Márquez is specific about their influence: both teach him how to tell extravagant stories without blinking. In 1981, in his *Paris Review* interview, García Márquez praises Kafka,[26] and he does so again in a similar passage in *Living to Tell the Tale* in 2002:

> The book was Franz Kafka's *The Metamorphosis*, in the false translation by Borges published by Losada in Buenos Aires, that determined a new direction for my life from its first line, which today is one of the great devices in world literature: "As Gregor Samsa awoke one morning from uneasy dreams he found himself transformed in his bed into a gigantic insect." . . . It was not necessary to demonstrate facts: it was enough for the author to have written something for it to be true, with no proof other than the power of his talent and the authority of his voice. (*Living* 247)[27]

Needless to say, this technique is the hallmark of García Márquez's "magical realism," and we reread Kafka accordingly.

Doña Tranquilina surely influenced her grandson in many ways, but it is her storytelling that García Márquez's repeatedly credits. Perhaps it was reading the first line by Kafka that made García Márquez look back and realize that his grandmother was Kafkian:

> She was a fabulous storyteller who told wild tales of the supernatural with a most solemn expression on her face. As I was growing up, I often wondered whether or not her stories were truthful. Usually, I tended to believe her because of her serious, deadpan facial expression. Now, as a writer, I do the same thing; I say extraordinary things in a serious tone. It's possible to get away with anything as long as you make it believable. (Ríos, "Some Notes")

The supernatural content of Doña Tranquilina's stories was as riveting as her deadpan delivery. In the same interview, he affirms this fact:

> With my grandmother, every natural event had a supernatural interpretation. If a butterfly flew in the window, she'd say, "We must be careful—someone in the family is sick." When I was a child, my grandmother would wake me in the night and tell me horrible stories of people who, for some reason, had a presentiment of their death, of the dead who appeared, of the dead who didn't appear. Often, our house in Aracataca, our huge house, seemed as if it were haunted. All those early experiences have somehow found themselves in my literature. (Ríos, "Some Notes")

Doña Tranquilina's premonitions foretell death, and they also foretell the theme that I have discussed: the sense that the past is present, that time runs backward and forward, and then runs out.

William Faulkner's Deep South and García Márquez's Caribbean Culture

I have insisted on the importance of Colombia's Catholic culture, but we must also understand the vast differences in Colombia's geographies, topographies, and economies. The Caribbean coast of García Márquez's childhood and the Andean culture of his young adulthood were worlds apart, and although they converge in García Márquez's life and work in some ways, it is the Caribbean world that grounds his discovery of William Faulkner.[28] García Márquez often commented on his attraction to Faulkner's "deep South," which he preferred to call a "coincidence" rather than "influence," and which I call an "awakening." In his *Paris Review* interview, he describes his return to his grandparents' house in Aracataca and gives Faulkner credit for "enabling" him to see that this world will become his literary vocation. He writes:

> I'm not sure whether I had already read Faulkner or not, but I know now that only a technique like Faulkner's could have enabled me to write down what I was seeing. The atmosphere, the decadence, the heat in the village were roughly the same as what I had felt in Faulkner. It was a banana-plantation region inhabited by a lot of Americans from the fruit companies, which gave it the same sort of atmosphere I had found in the writers of the Deep South. Critics have spoken of the literary *influence* of Faulkner, but I see it as a *coincidence*: I had simply found material that had to be dealt with in the same way that Faulkner had treated similar material. (Stone 53; emphasis added)

And in another interview, he tells of his travels through the southern United States because he "wanted to see the country from the small, dusty roads that Faulkner described":

> In Faulkner's country, I remember seeing the small stores along the roadway with people seated out front with their feet up on railings. There was the same kind of poverty contrasting with great wealth. In some ways, it seemed to me that Faulkner was also a writer of the Caribbean. (Ríos, "Some Notes")

In García Márquez's telling, Faulkner becomes a Caribbean writer because the same waters lap the coasts of Mississippi and Colombia. For the sake of cartographic accuracy, Mississippi is on the Gulf of Mexico rather than the Caribbean, but never mind. García Márquez understood this cultural attachment viscerally, as we see in his various terms for his relation to Faulkner's work and world.

Beyond the Caribbean culture that García Márquez shared with Faulkner, there are shared narrative techniques. I have mentioned their use of biblical structures, and here I point to one more bond. García Márquez writes in his autobiography that he was working on a novel to be called *La casa* when he read Faulker's *As I Lay Dying* and was inspired to revise his draft: "I planned to diversify the monologue with voices of the entire town, like a narrative Greek chorus, in the style of *As I Lay Dying*, with the reflections of an entire family interposed around a dying man" (*Living* 366).[29] This novel was eventually abandoned, but we nonetheless sense Faulkner's presence in the communal narrators that intrude in several of García Márquez's novels, for example, in the first-person plural observations of the oppressed community in *The Autumn of the Patriarch*, the collective voice of the townspeople who keep an eye on Fermina Daza and the weather in *Love in the Time of Cholera*, and the villagers who know that Santiago is as good as dead *before* he is dead in *Chronicle of a Death Foretold*. This novel gives us layers of reported conversation: "he told me," "she told me," repeated throughout, which subvert an omniscient narrative perspective in favor of various neighbors trying to figure out what they already know will happen. So García Márquez amplifies Faulkner's "Greek chorus" from "a family interposed around a dying man" to whole communities who must watch from the sidelines as their collective fate unfolds.

I began with Borges's essay on Kafka and his precursors, and I conclude by noting that Borges was not the first writer to consider how influence moves back and forth in time. Before Borges, there was T. S. Eliot. A little-noticed footnote at the very end of Borges's essay acknowledges Eliot as *his* precursor. He cites Eliot's 1941 collection of essays *Points of View*, which contains Eliot's 1919 essay, "Tradition and the Individual Talent." This essay precedes (and influences) Borges in its consideration of how the interactions of writers and readers, past and present, form literary traditions. If Borges focuses on individual writers, Eliot is concerned with the transformation of the tradition as a whole. He asserts that every work of art is part of a transhistorical system that will be influenced by new works of art: "[T]he past is altered by the present, as much as the present is directed by the past."[30] Borges echoes this sentence at the end of his own essay, where we find his footnote: the writer's "work modifies our conception of the past, as it will modify the future" ("Kafka and His Precursors" 201).[31] This echo affirms Borges's argument and also exemplifies it.

No writer has been more deeply embedded in this historical process than Gabriel García Márquez, or more keenly aware of his own role in it. Faulkner famously said that the past is never past, by which he meant that the historical past cannot be undone, and that it will haunt the present unaltered.[32] Similarly, in *One Hundred Years of Solitude*, the repeating generations of Buendías and inherited cycles of violence would seem to align García Márquez with Faulkner. Like Faulkner, García Márquez recognized that the past is always present, and like Borges and Eliot, he also recognized that in literary history, the relations of past and present are reciprocal. By 2002, when he wrote *Living to Tell the Tale*, he knew very well that his work would amplify and alter the baroque tradition to which he was heir. In his autobiography and his fiction, he self-consciously creates his precursors, and in so doing, renovates and reorders that tradition. To read

García Márquez's work in light of his precursors is to enrich our understanding of his themes, his narrative techniques, his characters, and yes, his magical realism. So we enter this polyphonic web of affiliations that he recognized as his own. Call it *la tradición gabrielina*.

Notes

1. This essay first appeared in *La Nación* in 1951 and was collected in *Otras inquisiciones* in 1952.
2. "[A]prendí para no olvidarlo nunca que solo deberían leer los libros que nos fuerzan a releerlos" (*Vivir* 162).
3. See my discussion of this contrast between Latin American and US writers in "Part I: Anxiety of Origins" *The Usable Past* (1–14).
4. "Usted no sabe lo que pesa un muerto" (*Vivir* 87).
5. "Aquel paraíso terrenal de la desolación y la nostalgia" (*Vivir* 432).
6. "La voracidad con que oía los cuentos me dejaba siempre esperando uno mejor al día siguiente, sobre todo los que tenían que ver con los misterios de la historia sagrada" (*Vivir* 107).
7. See, for example, the description of his mother in *Living to Tell the Tale* (6–7).
8. "La única diferencia actual entre liberales y conservadores, es que los liberales van a misa de cinco y los conservadores van a misa de ocho" (*Cien años* 209).
9. "Si se lo creyeron a las Sagradas Escrituras," replicó Fernanda, "no veo por que no han de creérmelo a mi" (*Cien años* 254).
10. I compare these works in some detail in Chapter 1, "Apocalypse and Human Time in the Fiction of Gabriel García Márquez," *Writing the Apocalypse* (32–51).
11. The epithet is attributed to the US critic Allen Tate. It was meant to be pejorative, though I doubt that Faulkner would have minded the comparison to the great Spanish baroque poet, whatever the intention. See Carlos Fuentes on this epithet in "The Novel as Tragedy: William Faulkner."
12. For my discussion of García Márquez as a Neobaroque writer, see *The Inordinate Eye* (214–32, 285–302).
13. Fernández-Braso (75; my translation). Elsewhere in this interview, García Márquez again refers to Spanish baroque literature: "Nosotros arrancamos, estamos muy fundados en el Siglo de Oro español" (78; "Our point of departure, our roots, are in the Spanish Golden Age").
14. "A leer lo que me cayera en las manos y recitar de memoria la poesía irrepetible del Siglo de Oro español" (*Vivir* 4).
15. For Quevedo's poem in Spanish and English, see www.poemas-del-alma.com/amor-constante-mas-alla.htm and www.literarymatters.org/10-2-francisco-de-quevedo-love-that-endures-beyond-death/. Accessed 19 Nov. 2019.
16. "Llorando de la rabia de morirse sin ella" ("Muerte constante" 69).
17. "*Lo único que me duele de morir es que no sea de amor*" (*El amor en los tiempos de cólera* 249).
18. "Al final me quedó claro que mis nuevos amigos leían con tanto provecho a Quevedo y James Joyce como a Conan Doyle. Tenían un sentido del humor inagotable y eran capaces de pasar noches enteras cantando boleros y vallenatos o recitando sin titubeos la mayor

poesía del Siglo de Oro. Por distintos senderos llegamos al acuerdo de que la cumbre de la poesía universal son las coplas de don Jorge Manrique a la muerte de su padre" (*Vivir* 398).

19. Manrique's "Coplas a la muerte de su padre" is comprised of forty stanzas with a repeating rhyme pattern throughout. For Manrique's poem in Spanish and English, see www.uv.es/ivorra/Literatura/Coplas.htm and www.bartleby.com/356/478.html. Accessed 19 Nov. 2019.
20. "Es difícil imaginar hasta qué punto se vivía entonces a la sombra de la poesía. Era una pasión frenética, otro modo de ser, una bola de candela que andaba de su cuenta por todas partes.... Bogotá era la capital del país y la sede del gobierno, pero sobre todo era la ciudad donde vivían los poetas. No sólo creíamos en la poesía, y nos moríamos por ella, sino que sabíamos con certeza—como lo escribió Luis Cardoza y Aragón—que 'la poesía es la única prueba concreta de la existencia del hombre'" (*Vivir* 295–96).
21. "Hice otras tentativas en el bachillerato, donde tuve que estudiarlo como tarea obligatoria, y lo aborrecí sin remedio, hasta que un amigo me aconsejó que lo pusiera en la repisa del inodoro y tratara de leerlo mientras cumplía con mis deberes cotidianos. Sólo así lo descubrí, como una deflagración, y lo gocé al derecho y al revés hasta recitar de memoria episodios enteros" (*Vivir* 162).
22. "Cuando me paro a contemplar mi estado, / y a ver los pasos por do me ha traído, Yo acabaré, que me entregué sin arte / a quien sabrá perderme y acabarme" (Garcilaso Soneto I).
23. "En fin a vuestras manos he venido, / do sé que he de morir tan apretado ... para que sólo en mí fuese probado, / cuánto corta una 'spada en un rendido" (Garcilaso Soneto II).
24. "¡Oh dulces prendas por mi mal halladas" (Garcilaso Soneto X).
25. "Algo se movió en el corazón de Sierva María, pues quiso oír el verso de nuevo. Él lo repitió, y esta vez siguió de largo, con voz intensa y bien articulada, hasta el último de los cuarenta sonetos del caballero de amor y de armas, don Garcilaso de la Vega, muerto en la flor de la edad por una pedrada de guerra" (*Del amor y otros demonios* 169).
26. García Márquez quotes the first line of Kafka's story, then makes the following observation: "When I read this line I thought to myself that I didn't know anyone was allowed to write things like that. If I had known, I would have started writing a long time ago. So I immediately started writing short stories" (Stone 51).
27. "El libro era *La metamorfosis* de Franz Kafka, en la falsa traducción de Borges publicada por la editorial Losada de Buenos Aires, que definió un camino nuevo para mi vida desde la primera línea, y que hoy es una de las divisas grandes de la literatura universal. 'Al despertar Gregorio Samsa una mañana, tras un sueño intranquilo, encontrose en su cama convertido en un monstruoso insecto'.... No era necesario demostrar los hechos: bastaba con que el autor lo hubiera escrito para que fuera verdad, sin más pruebas que el poder de su talento y la autoridad de su voz" (*Vivir* 289–90).
28. García Márquez affirms this cultural connection: "Above all because of the affinities of all kinds that I found between the cultures of the Deep South and the Caribbean, with which I have an absolute, essential and irreplaceable identification in my formation as a human being and as a writer" (*Living to Tell the Tale* 367).
29. "Pensé en diversificar el monólogo con voces de todo el pueblo, como un coro griego narrador, al modo de *Mientras yo agonizo,* que son reflexiones de toda una familia interpuestas alrededor de un moribundo" (*Vivir* 433).
30. I cite from T. S. Eliot's 1919 collection, in which this essay was originally published, (*Sacred Wood* 50). Borges cites Eliot's collection *Points of View* (Faber and Faber, 1941). This

essential essay can be found at www.poetryfoundation.org/articles/69400/tradition-and-the-individual-talent. Accessed 16 Nov. 2019.

31. "Su labor modifica nuestra concepción del pasado, como ha de modificar el futuro" ("Kafka y sus precursors" 89–90).

32. Faulkner's complete phrase, in his novel *Requiem for a Nun,* is this: "The past is never dead. It is not even past" (73).

Works Cited

Primary Sources

Borges, Jorge Luis. "Kafka and His Precursors," translated by James E. Irby. *Labyrinths*, edited by Donald A. Yates and James E. Irby, New Directions, 1964.

Borges, Jorge Luis. "Kafka y sus precursores." *Otras Inquisiciones, Obras completas*, vol. 2, Emecé, 1974.

Eliot, T. S. *The Sacred Wood: Essays on Poetry and Criticism*. Barnes and Noble, 1919.

Faulkner, William. *Requiem for a Nun*. Random House, 1950.

García Márquez, Gabriel. *The Autumn of the Patriarch*. Translated by Gregory Rabassa. Harper & Row, 1975.

García Márquez, Gabriel. *El amor en los tiempos del cólera*. Bruguera, 1985.

García Márquez, Gabriel. *El general en su laberinto*. Diana, 1989).

García Márquez, Gabriel. *El otoño del patriarca*. Diana, 1975.

García Márquez, Gabriel. *Del amor y otros demonios*. Penguin Books, 1994.

García Márquez, Gabriel. *Cien años de soledad*. Sudamericana, 1967.

García Márquez, Gabriel. *Chronicle of a Death Foretold*. Translated by Gregory Rabassa. Alfred A. Knopf, 1983.

García Márquez, Gabriel. *Crónica de una muerte anunciada*. Diana, 1981.

García Márquez, Gabriel. "Death Constant Beyond Love" (1970), translated by Gregory Rabassa. *Innocent Eréndira and Other Stories*, Harper Colophon Books, 1979, pp. 83–93.

García Márquez, Gabriel. *Living to Tell the Tale*. Translated by Edith Grossman, Alfred A. Knopf, 2003.

García Márquez, Gabriel. *Love in the Time of Cholera*. Translated by Edith Grossman, Alfred Knopf, 1988.

García Márquez, Gabriel. *Memoria de mis putas tristes*. Mondadori, 2004.

García Márquez, Gabriel. *Memories of my Melancholy Whores*. Translated by Edith Grossman, Alfred A. Knopf, 2005.

García Márquez, Gabriel. "Muerte constante más allá del amor" (1970). *La increible y triste historia de la Cándida Eréndira y de su abuela desalmada*, Sudamericana, 1973, pp. 57–69.

García Márquez, Gabriel. *Of Love and Other Demons*. Translated by Edith Grossman, Penguin Books, 1995.

García Márquez, Gabriel. *One Hundred Years of Solitude*. Translated by Gregory Rabassa, Harper and Row, 1970.

García Márquez, Gabriel. *The General and His Labyrinth*. Translated by Edith Grossman. Alfred A. Knopf, 1990.

García Márquez, Gabriel. *Vivir para contarla*. Alfred Knopf, 2002.

Secondary Sources

Cohn, Deborah N. "'He Was One of Us': The Reception of William Faulkner and the U.S. South by Latin American Authors." *Comparative Literature Studies*, vol. 34, no. 2, 1997, pp. 49–69.

Cohn, Deborah N. *History and Memory in the Two Souths: Recent Southern and Spanish American Fiction*. Vanderbilt UP, 1999.

Fernández-Braso, Miguel. *Gabriel García Márquez: Una conversación infinita*. Azur, 1969.

Fuentes, Carlos. "The Novel as Tragedy: William Faulkner" (1970). *Baroque New Worlds: Representation, Transculturation, Counterconquest*, edited by Lois Parkinson Zamora and Monika Kaup, Duke UP, 2010, pp. 531–53.

Johnson, Dane. "'Wherein the South Differs from the North': Tracing the Noncosmopolitan Aesthetic in William Faulkner's *Absalom, Absalom!* and Gabriel García Márquez's *One Hundred Years of Solititude*." *Look Away! The US South in New World Studies*, edited by Jon Smith and Deborah Cohn, Duke UP, 2004, pp. 383–404.

Lawrence, Jeffrey. "Uncommon Grounds: The Representation of History in *Absalom, Absalom! One Hundred Years of Solitude*, and *Song of Solomon*." *Anxieties of Experience: The Literatures of the Americas from Whitman to Bolaño*, Oxford UP, 2018, pp. 101–21.

Martínez Gómez, Juana. "El revés de la farsa: Sobre 'Muerte constante más allá del amor.'" cvc.cervantes.es/actcult/garcia_marquez/obra/cuentos/farsa.htm.

Oberhelman, Harley D. "The Development of Faulkner's Influence in the Work of García Márquez." *Gabriel García Márquez: Modern Critical Views*, edited by Harold Bloom, Chelsea House, 1989, pp. 65–79.

Plummer, William. "The Faulkner Relation." *Gabriel García Márquez: Modern Critical Views*, edited by Harold Bloom, Chelsea House, 1989, pp. 33–47.

Ríos, Alberto. "Gabriel García Márquez: Some Notes." www.public.asu.edu/~aarios/resourcebank/garciamarquez/.

Stone, Peter H. "The Art of Fiction No. 69: García Márquez." *The Paris Review*, no. 82, Winter 1981, pp. 44–73. https://www.theparisreview.org/interviews/3196/the-art-of-fiction-no-69-gabriel-garcia-marquez

Zamora, Lois Parkinson. *The Inordinate Eye: New World Baroque and Latin American Fiction*. U of Chicago P, 2006.

Zamora, Lois Parkinson. *The Usable Past: The Imagination of History in Recent Fiction of the Americas*. Cambridge UP, 1997.

Zamora, Lois Parkinson. *Writing the Apocalypse*. Cambridge UP, 1989.

CHAPTER 7

FICTIONS OF DIFFICULT LOVE IN GARCÍA MÁRQUEZ

ANÍBAL GONZÁLEZ

The theme of love is pervasive throughout Gabriel García Márquez's work, from the juvenilia in *Ojos de perro azul* (*Eyes of a Blue Dog*, 1973; Bell-Villada 158–60) through the narratives of the Macondo cycle, including *Cien años de soledad* (*One Hundred Years of Solitude*, 1967), to his autumnal masterpieces, in which love increasingly occupies a central place. This is particularly true of the "amorous triptych" comprised by *Crónica de una muerte anunciada* (*Chronicle of a Death Foretold*, 1981), *El amor en los tiempos del cólera* (*Love in the Times of Cholera*, 1985), and *Del amor y otros demonios* (*Of Love and Other Demons*, 1994). However, love arguably remains a key concept even in other major works of García Márquez's later years, such as *Noticia de un secuestro* (*News of a Kidnapping*, 1996).

As in many works of postmodern fiction, love is present in García Márquez's novels and stories not just as part of the social and psychological portrayal of the characters, but also as a highly symbolic element connected to the novels' self-referentiality, which explores the interrelations among love, writing, and Latin American society and culture. Beyond love's purely thematic function, García Márquez's works examine questions such as: How are love and literary writing connected? Are writing and reading fiction connected to a dynamics of seduction, as Roland Barthes suggested in *The Pleasure of the Text* (1975), as well as to affective elements such as passion or empathy? Can amorous fictions exert a form of "sentimental power" (in Jane Tompkins's phrase) and, by educating the feelings of their readers, promote love and harmony in readers and in society as a whole? The various ways in which love is portrayed by García Márquez, which become more probing and inventive as his work matures, specifically invite readings informed by the ideas of Denis de Rougemont's classic essay *Love in the Western World* (1939), a book about which García Márquez could not have been unaware. Indeed, John Updike once observed, "Denis de Rougemont's analysis of romantic love as a Catholic heresy could scarcely be better illustrated" than in García Marquez's *Of Love and Other Demons*.

De Rougemont's *Love in the Western World*, which may be regarded as a precursor to current critical approaches to feelings and affects in literature, posits the existence of a dichotomy in post-medieval Western culture between two opposing views of love, known by their Greek names: eros and agape. For De Rougemont, the modern idea of passionate love, or eros, derives from the "courtly love" tradition of medieval Provençal lyric poetry. It is in turn rooted in obscure religious sources—the Manichaean and Catharist Christian sects of the Middle Ages—for whom love was a means to achieve transcendence by freeing the soul of its fleshly prison and imbuing it with an "infinite desire" to unite with the divine (61–82). Such "divinization" of love as eros also glorifies passion, that is, the suffering produced by amorous desire, since through suffering the soul is freed from the flesh to connect with the divine. Fundamentally egotistic, in this concept of love the mystical union can only occur between the individual soul and God. The love object, the beloved, fulfills in eros an instrumental function; it is primarily a means to achieve union with the divinity. Paradoxically, in the logic of eros the greater the obstacles are to the lovers' amorous union, the greater are the suffering and the spiritual purification to which the lovers ultimately aspire (50–55).

In De Rougemont's thesis, the notion of love as eros always exists in a tense relationship with the Christian concept of love, or agape. In this concept, through the incarnation of Christ the spirit becomes one with matter, mixing the human with the divine (67–69). Opposed to the passion of eros, agape's ultimate goal is achieving the communion of the faithful, the love of neighbors, instead of the individual soul's union with God. Bringing heaven down to earth, agape also discards suffering as a way to reach transcendence, since it assumes that contact with the divine is God's freely given gift to humanity. The model for agape is the institution of marriage, the link between two beings who love each other equally, without one being superior to the other (311–15).[1]

Focusing primarily on literary sources, De Rougemont begins his book with a brief but striking assertion: "Happy love has no history" (15). He refers to the fact that narrative representations of love, ranging from ancient Greek and Germanic myths to Provençal poetry and modern melodrama, are necessarily based on the trials and tribulations of unfulfilled love. Since narrative is based on action and conflict, the idylls of fulfilled love are generally seen as ephemeral parentheses in love narratives or are confined to lyric poetry. The dominant paradigm of love in the Western tradition would thus be love as eros, a spiritualized love based on suffering as a means to achieve transcendence. In this scheme, agape, a form of brotherly or conjugal love, is regarded as unworthy of representation, save as comedy or satire, due to its restriction to everyday concerns or to the domestic sphere. Although both forms of love generate different modes of narrative, they can coexist in more "mixed" genres such as the novel, in which their contrasting presence often works as an element of the "seduction" exerted by the literary text upon its readers.

If we extend further De Rougemont's implicit view of eros and agape as metaphors of two kinds of writing, we see then that eros is associated with a notion of writing (and by extension, of reading) as an arduous and oppressive activity that is linked to suffering and is afflicted by disjunction, distance, and violence. Writing and reading, in this view, are moved by the perpetually excited as well as perpetually impeded desire of achieving transcendence (whether of intellect or spirit, it matters little). Writing and reading would be in this sense profoundly passionate activities, with a passion moved by the promise that at the end transcendence will be reached as union with a collective or universal knowledge.

On the other hand, the idea of writing as agape emphasizes the communicative aspects of reading and writing and regards the text as a successful mediator and link between writers and readers. Agape does not see writing as problematical (or only to a lesser extent) and underscores instead those elements that simplify the search for the text's meaning: the evocation of orality, acceptance of the conventions of literary genre, personification, and verisimilitude, among many others.

At first, García Márquez's works would seem to follow closely De Rougemont's observed predominance of love as eros in the dichotomy of passionate love versus conjugal love. In the narratives of the Macondo cycle, culminating in *One Hundred Years of Solitude*, this eros/agape antithesis is a major structuring element of the narrative. Certain characters, such as the founders of Macondo José Arcadio Buendía and Úrsula Iguarán, start off as star-crossed lovers who, in order to fulfill their passionate love, must struggle against numerous obstacles and prohibitions. Chief among these is the incest prohibition, since they are cousins, which ultimately leads to tragedy in José Arcadio's murder of Prudencio Aguilar (*One Hundred Years* 29–30). Over time, however, the couple settles into a humorously contrasting domestic arrangement in which José Arcadio Buendía is constantly involved in fantastic and unachievable enterprises outside the home, while Úrsula becomes the levelheaded keeper and increaser of their family's estate.

Another telling example of the tension between eros and agape in *One Hundred Years* is the love between Rebeca and first-born son José Arcadio, which arises with José Arcadio's transgressive love for Rebeca, his sister by adoption. After the "wild passion" of their early days of marriage (96), the couple settles into a quiet, childless, and idyllic existence in their "hospitable home," until José Arcadio's mysterious death from a gunshot wound in his bathroom becomes "the only mystery that was never cleared up in Macondo" (129).[2]

Throughout *One Hundred Years*, love as eros is frequently manifested among the Buendía men as an egotistical penchant for solitude and violence, most dramatically symbolized in Colonel Aureliano Buendía's chalk circle drawn around himself to keep people at a distance (159). Overall, eros predominates in the social world of Macondo; passion, both amorous and political, with its attendant violence and suffering, is dominant in the history of Macondo and its people. Institutional religion, represented by the Catholic Church and the various priests in the town's history, as well as by fanatically religious female characters such as Fernanda del Carpio, appears powerless to promote brotherly love in Macondo. In this context, Remedios the Beauty, whose innocent, virginal, and almost otherworldly attractions make men go mad and die of love for her, appears as an emblem of the deadly effects of passion. When Remedios miraculously ascends to the heavens while picking up the dry laundry in her backyard (223), she clearly becomes a parody of religious figures such as the Virgin Mary, whose cult was instituted in Catholicism after the twelfth century as an attempt to co-opt the love-as-eros concept of the Catharist heresy, so widely disseminated by the courtly love poetry of Provençal troubadours (De Rougemont 111).

At a still deeper level, *One Hundred Years* portrays writing and reading as passionate acts of prophetic vision and decipherment that are akin to the ascetic process promoted by love as eros in its search for transcendence. The story of Melquíades's manuscripts and their ultimate decipherment, which is arguably one of the most continuous narrative threads in this event-filled novel, explores the connections between writing as a hermetic and seductive encoding of transcendent knowledge and reading as an arduous process of decipherment led by an impassioned search for ultimate meaning and revelation (González, "Translation and Genealogy" 75–76). As evidenced in the rhetoric and imagery of mystical poets such as the Spaniards St. John of the Cross and Theresa of Avila, the language of love as eros is given to sublimity, visions (sometimes prophetic in nature), and fantasies, and in this sense writing as eros underlies the miraculous signs and symbols of magical realism in *One Hundred Years*: biblical-style plagues and catastrophes, premonitions, levitating priests, yellow butterflies, galleons shipwrecked in the jungle, and so forth.

Even so, intimations of agape and the more quotidian type of writing associated with it are also present in the novel; *One Hundred Years* is often regarded as the least experimental—perhaps even least intellectual—and most "reader-friendly" of the Latin American Boom novels. Critics have consistently praised its style's resemblance to oral narratives and folktales, as well as its humorous and sentimental elements, which make it a seemingly more approachable text—until one realizes the importance of Melquíades's manuscript and the circularity of the novel's self-reflexive and literally devastating ending, which forces readers to rethink what they have read in a new, more intellectual light (*One Hundred Years* 383).

It is pertinent to note that García Márquez's fictions after *One Hundred Years*, such as *La increíble y triste historia de la cándida Eréndira y su abuela desalmada* (*Innocent Eréndira and Other Stories*, 1972) and *El otoño del patriarca* (*The Autumn of the Patriarch*, 1974), display a style that has been considered much more openly experimental and symbolic, verging almost on the Spanish American "neo-baroque" of writers like the Cubans Alejo Carpentier and José Lezama Lima. The stories in *Innocent Eréndira* are set in a more generically Latin American ambiance than *One Hundred Years*, in nameless towns amid arid desert-like coasts, and they abound in enigmatic figures and images that are closer to mythical and literary symbols than to folktales: winged men, powerful sorcerers, a handsome man's corpse (as in the literary game of the "exquisite corpse"?), as well as references to classics such as the *Odyssey*. Sharp stylistic departures in these stories are their use of pages-long sentences, more complex syntax, more varied and erudite vocabulary, and dreamlike imagery similar to the surrealist-inspired cinema of Federico Fellini and the Brazilian director Glauber Rocha's *Cinema Novo*. More elaborate still is the style of *The Autumn of the Patriarch*, which also incorporates highly erudite allusions to *modernista* poet Rubén Darío and to historical episodes from the lives of various Latin American dictators. Both *Innocent Eréndira* and *The Autumn of the Patriarch* are saturated with the writing of eros and its links to power, particularly in stories such as "Death Constant beyond Love" and "Innocent Eréndira" itself, and in the eponymous Patriarch's obsession with the unreachable Manuela Sánchez.

Perhaps only in the stories from *Innocent Eréndira* "A Very Old Man with Enormous Wings" and "The Handsomest Drowned Man in the World" can one find anything approaching the idea of agape in these texts, as the arrival of ambiguously supernatural figures (the angel-like old man and the drowned man's large and miraculously well-preserved corpse) stirs the imagination of the impoverished townspeople and helps them to develop a sense of community and togetherness based on their multiple fantasies and interpretations about the strange beings in their midst. It is not difficult to see the winged old man and the handsome corpse as emblems of how artistic and literary creations are received by society: the winged old man evokes biblical angels, and his wing feathers are like antique writing instruments, while the incorruptible beauty of the drowned man is reminiscent of sculptures, paintings, and works of visual art in general. In these experimental short stories, García Márquez seems to be obliquely reflecting on literature's capacity to produce empathy and community. Nevertheless, the isolated, desert ambience in which the stories take place also suggests the serious limitations such a project might encounter.

As previously indicated, the theme of love begins to assume a more visible and even central place in García Márquez's fictions of the 1980s and 1990s. Love, is of course, one of the *archthemes* of literature; nevertheless, through much of the twentieth century in Western literature and arts, love and sentimentalism came to be regarded as old-fashioned, even reactionary phenomena that should be banished from the discourses of both high art and revolutionary politics.

García Márquez's renewed attention to love may be linked to major changes in late-twentieth-century society, politics, and culture. Chief among these were the end of the Cold War and the fall of the Soviet Union, the general loss of interest in the revolutionary option, and the worldwide processes of political "redemocratization" and economic "globalization" encouraged by neoliberal economic policies. The generalized "return to love" and the affects in Western culture framed by these phenomena also led to the rise in Spanish America of what may be called "new sentimental narratives," exemplified in works by younger authors such as Isabel Allende, Alfredo Bryce Echenique, Rosario Ferré, and Manuel Puig, as well as in revisionist and self-critical novels penned by Boom authors such as Mario Vargas Llosa, Guillermo Cabrera Infante, Carlos Fuentes, and of course, García Márquez himself (González, *Love and Politics in the Contemporary Spanish American Novel* 3–4).

The novels of García Márquez's "amorous triptych" occupy a salient position among the "new sentimental" narratives of the period. Concerned with an in-depth exploration of love in its social, personal, and literary aspects, each of these novels emphasizes one of these three aspects. Love (and its absence) in contemporary Latin American society is the chief concern of *Chronicle of a Death Foretold*; the individual, subjective experience of love (both as eros and as agape) in a specific epoch in Latin America (the turn of the nineteenth century) is the focus of *Love in the Time of Cholera*; while a more overtly historical reflection on the ancient roots of the Western concept of love is the theme of *Of Love and Other Demons*. In terms of their order of publication and of the three historical periods covered in them, these three novels constitute, it may be argued, a "journey back to the source" of the Western concept of love and its cultural manifestations.

In *Chronicle of a Death Foretold*, García Márquez portrays contemporary Latin American society as caught in a web of violent, ritualistic, and all-encompassing social codes strongly influenced by love as eros and its roots in medieval chivalry. With an epigraph taken from a poem by the medieval Portuguese author Gil Vicente—"The pursuit of love is like falconry"—whose context evokes the quintessential courtly love tradition and the ambience of the so-called Spanish sentimental novels of the fifteenth century,[3] *Chronicle of a Death Foretold* examines the foundations of the sense of community in Hispanic societies with the ironic and skeptical gaze of both the journalist and the detective. This precarious sense of community appears to be based more on the passionate violence of eros than on the peace and tolerance of agape.

In consonance with this approach, the style and structure of *Chronicle of a Death Foretold*, although less challenging than those of *The Autumn of the Patriarch*, still confront readers with a writing-as-eros filled with symbols, enigmas, and paradoxes. A topsy-turvy narrative sequence, in which the crime, the victim, and his victimizers are revealed early on while almost all of the characters' motivations (including those of the author) remain largely obscure, also contributes to the novel's labyrinthine qualities and propels the narrative's implications far beyond its scant one hundred-odd pages.

It is important to note that the atavistic ritual death of Santiago Nasar, in which all the townspeople are involved, takes place just after the bishop's riverboat has gone by the town's dock without landing (*Chronicle* 23–26). Santiago's death resembles not only that of Christ but also the killing of the Commandant by the townsfolk in Lope de Vega's *Fuenteovejuna* (1612–1614).[4] In *Chronicle of a Death Foretold*, García Márquez suggests that contemporary Spanish American societal bonds are based more on a sense of complicity with a violence whose roots lie in passion and in neo-medieval codes of "honor" than on the Christian values of brotherly love that both the political right and left claim to respect. To a certain extent, as in the testimonial narratives it resembles, *Chronicle of a Death Foretold* deals with a world in which the struggle for power and the subjection to social codes and customs predominate over individuals and the expression of their desires and feelings. It is worth remembering that *Chronicle of a Death Foretold* was published a mere six years after García Márquez's "dictator novel" *The Autumn of the Patriarch*, a period of time during which García Márquez increasingly participated in left-wing politics and in human rights campaigns (Bell-Villada 58). This gloomy vision of the lack of communion in the modern world—and also perhaps in the literature the modern world produces—is the point of departure for García Márquez's retrospective inquiry in his triptych into the sources of amorous and sentimental discourse.

In contrast with the narrative styles of *The Autumn of the Patriarch* and *Chronicle of a Death Foretold*, *Love in the Time of Cholera* seeks to explore and portray the passions caused by love as eros from the standpoint of the writing of agape. Hailed as García

Márquez's "return to realism" and to the tradition of intimate, nostalgic evocation of bygone times and places associated with the novels of Marcel Proust (Bell-Villada 191–92; MacAdam 37–38), this novel has become, along with *One Hundred Years*, García Márquez's most widely read masterpiece. With its leitmotifs of disease and medicine, *Love in the Time of Cholera* also pays special attention to the "healing" powers of amorous discourse. In addition, the religious leitmotif of Pentecost—an instance of perfect communication through the Holy Spirit, described in the New Testament (Acts 2)—signifies the novel's intention to further examine how writing can promote agape as a form of friendship or communion between readers.

Based on the parallelisms between literature, religion, and love, *Love in the Time of Cholera* posits that the authority of literary texts, like that of religion and love, arises not from violence but from a kind of seduction. This seduction is achieved by means of a wavering between the writing of eros and that of agape. In its promise to reveal the truth of love, this novel constantly displays the erotic strategy of "intermittence" that Barthes describes in *The Pleasure of the Text* (9–10). Such intermittence can take various forms: it can be the mystery of what caused the suicide of Jeremiah de Saint-Amour (*Love in the Time* 5) or the desire to know what the "true" nature of love is—a revelation with which this novel entices its readers by means of numerous passages offering "definitions" or reflections about love.[5] All this is presented, however, by means of a narrative that flows seemingly without effort and therefore without provoking feelings of passion (and suffering) in its readers. Nevertheless, difficulties do begin to appear when the text's own seductiveness leads readers to go beyond the text's surface to track the meaning of the various erudite allusions offered by the novel, from Saint Thomas Aquinas (*Love in the Time* 118) to Juvenal Urbino's parrot, which evokes Flaubert's "Un coeur simple" (1877; see Franco 147–60).

Significantly, the elderly Florentino Ariza only manages to succeed in his long-awaited seduction of Fermina Daza when he writes her a letter radically different from the "more discursive and more lunatic" letters (*Love in the Time* 69) he had sent her in his youth. It is a typewritten letter that gives barely a glimpse of his passion and appears instead as a meditative discourse on love (*Love in the Time* 292–93, 298–300). In turn, it is by means of these epistles from Florentino that Fermina is "healed" from her subservient relation to Juvenal Urbino and begins to understand herself better (*Love in the Time* 302, 308).

Nevertheless, instead of being a model of conjugal agape, or more generally of communion with one's brethren, the novel's ending underscores the inherent egotism in the two lovers' relationship: still unmarried, surrounded by a devastated nature and the deforestation near the riverbanks caused by steamships like the *New Fidelity*, and overcome by "the horror of real life" (*Love in the Time* 346), Florentino and Fermina decide to continue indefinitely in "this goddamn coming and going" (348).[6] The two protagonists end up literally isolated from the rest of society, turning their backs on the world and without the least desire to reach any destination. It is not only an open ending but also an ambivalent one, since Florentino's and Fermina's "free will" (347) looks too much like a punishment.[7]

One might wonder if this self-absorption of love as eros, this love that lives apart from everyone and everything and reaches the peak of its expression through letters, through writing, is not similar to the condition of writers and their readers, whose only real meeting place is in the letters on a page. At the end of the long journey of *Love in the Time of Cholera* the question arises whether the ideal of agape, unlike eros, is not ultimately inconsistent with the notion of any mediated communication, or even with the idea of communication itself, which already presupposes a gap, a separation between sender and receiver, while the principal commandment of agape is "you must love your neighbor *as yourself*" (Leviticus 19:18, Luke 10:25–37; emphasis added). As De Rougemont's dictum—"Happy love has no history"—implies, happiness in love may well be able to do without writing and literature.

Although *Love in the Time of Cholera* never abandons the ideal of agape—which, among other ways, is nostalgically evoked in Fermina's memories of her lengthy visit to her relatives in the countryside (*Love in the Time* 87)—the novel ultimately recognizes the primacy of eros in a time and place where the world seems to be held in thrall by both cholera (a disease that symbolizes the physical effects of lovesickness) and *cólera*— the Spanish word for "wrath," exemplified in the novel by the Colombian civil wars and the environmental degradation of the country (*Love in the Time* 84, 336). The novel's ending evokes what Plato had observed two millennia before in the *Symposium* and the *Phaedrus*: that love as eros is a *daimon*, a demon, a mediator or go-between, and that as such it is as unreliable and untrustworthy as that other go-between, writing.

Read in Christian terms, the title *Of Love and Other Demons* sounds paradoxical and even a bit shocking. Read in terms of the Platonic view of love, however, to which it openly alludes, it is crystal-clear in its implications. Fully devoted to the exploration of love as eros and its writing, the last novel of García Márquez's amorous triptych is the most patently erudite of the three, the one that most openly flaunts its literary and philosophical sources. This is not surprising, since in the "journey back to the source" of love that this triptych embodies, *Of Love and Other Demons* tries to achieve the closest encounter possible with the very roots of amorous discourse and of the complex relation between love and language.

Unlike the triptych's other two novels, this one begins with a prologue set in the present, in which a first-person narrator who is identified as García Márquez himself narrates the incident that supposedly gave rise to the novel: the exhumation—part looting, part archaeological dig—of the crypts in a convent that was going to be turned into "a five-star hotel" (*Of Love* 3).[8] Although it is totally fictional (Bell-Villada 254), its seemingly realistic setting and tone seek to connect the novel's origins to the journalistic work of the young García Márquez in the 1940s and are the part of the novel that most clearly displays the traits of writing as agape that are always present, to a greater or lesser degree, in the novels of García Márquez's late period. The confessional and affective tone of the prologue is reinforced by the novel's dedication: "For Carmen Balcells, bathed in tears," which conjures up the almost-shocking image of García Márquez's famously feisty literary agent crying her heart out, presumably because of the novel's emotional effect.

The tale told by the novel's third-person narrator takes place in the same slightly fictionalized Cartagena de Indias portrayed in *Love in the Time of Cholera*, and some of its scenes even occur, nearly two hundred years earlier, in the same places as in the earlier novel (the palace of the Marquis of Casalduero, the madhouse of La Divina Pastora). Moreover, the general plot of the novel—the story of a young priest who falls in love with a beautiful maiden—coincides with that of the medieval play *Comédia de Rubena* by Gil Vicente, from which the epigraph of *Chronicle of a Death Foretold* is taken (Hernández de López).

The story begins when the girl Sierva María de Todos los Ángeles, the only child of the Marquis of Casalduero (*Of Love* 7), is bitten by a presumably rabid dog in the city's marketplace. The mistaken belief that his daughter is infected with rabies leads the Marquis to try a series of outlandish remedies. These cause a public scandal so great that it reaches the attention of the asthmatic bishop Don Toribio de Cáceres y Virtudes, who insists the child is possessed by a demon. At the bishop's urging, the Marquis locks up his daughter in the convent of the Poor Clares, while the bishop assigns the task of exorcising her to his most trusted aide, the priest and librarian Cayetano Alcino del Espíritu Santo Delaura y Escudero.

In the convent Sierva María becomes a pawn in the ecclesiastical intrigues between the Poor Clares and the bishop. At the same time, she becomes acquainted with Cayetano, who, after being bitten by Sierva María during their first meeting, falls in love with her. Cayetano, in turn, who is a devotee of the poet Garcilaso de la Vega—to whom he claims to be related—begins to court Sierva María by reading her the sonnets of the great Spanish poet. After a fruitless attempt to free Sierva María from the convent, a remorseful Cayetano Delaura confesses his actions to the bishop, who punishes him severely, depriving him of his authority and sentencing him to help in the lepers' hospital. Cayetano, who "put his trust instead in legal formalities" (135) that would allow him to free Sierva María and marry her, refuses to consider her proposal to flee together to a maroon slave community.[9] When the tunnel through which he visited her is discovered and sealed, Cayetano fails in his last desperate attempt to take her out of the convent in broad daylight and is returned to the lepers' hospital, which he never leaves again. The bishop again tries to exorcise Sierva María, despite the admonitions from other church authorities. After three days of severe exorcism rites, depressed at not being able to see Cayetano, Sierva María is found "dead of love in her bed, her eyes radiant and her skin like that of a newborn baby. Strands of hair gushed like bubbles as they grew back on her shaved head" (147).[10]

It is not difficult to extract from the baroque ossuary of this novel the "remains"—so to speak—of Plato's discourse on love, which, like Sierva María's long red hair, have continued to exist and grow over time. In the *Symposium*, a group of Athenians that includes the philosopher Socrates competes to see which of them discourses most eloquently and persuasively about love (eros). However, it is Socrates's view of love—and the commentary added by Alcibiades—that serves as the point of departure for *Of Love and Other Demons*. Of particular importance is Socrates's retelling of the wise woman Diotima's mythical version of love's origin, in which Love is the child of Abundance and

Need, engendered when Need surprises sleeping Abundance and lies down with him (Plato 555–56).

The parallels between this Platonic vision of eros and the figure of Sierva María de Todos los Angeles in the novel are numerous. As in the myth of Abundance and Need, Bernarda Cabrera, "daughter of one of his [Ygnacio's] father's former overseers who had made a fortune in imported foods" (40), hoping to obtain the fortune of the Marquis of Casalduero, surprises Ygnacio in his hammock one afternoon at naptime "and without glory deprived him of his virginity" (41).[11] In time, Bernarda's pregnancy and the musket in her father's hands force Ygnacio to marry the woman. A product of this violent marriage, Sierva María "had the childhood of a foundling" (*Of Love* 42).[12] Just as Love wanders the streets homeless and in rags, Sierva María is left by her mother in care of the slave nursemaid Dominga de Adviento and is later thrown out of the house and sent to live in the slaves' barracks. Like Love, who is described as "harsh and arid, barefoot and homeless" (Plato 555), despite her long and beautiful head of hair, Sierva María has a "thin body" (*Of Love* 12) and a "forlorn air" (30).[13] In the Platonic myth, Love is "adept in sorcery, enchantment, and seduction" (556), as is Sierva María, with "her vice of lying for pleasure" (*Of Love* 110);[14] her links to the magical beliefs of the slaves (42–43); and her power to communicate by means of dreams and prophecies, as seen in the dream of the snowfall and the bunch of grapes that both she and Cayetano Delaura experience (75, 107). Even Sierva María's illiteracy, which is counterbalanced by her intelligence and her knowledge of African languages and cultures, corresponds to Diotima's description of Love as a being who stands "midway between ignorance and wisdom" (556).

Sierva María's female gender, along with the rest of her qualities, indicates that she is not only a stand-in for eros in the novel but also an emblem of writing, which has often been metaphorized as a woman, at least since the end of the eighteenth century, in a lineage of characters that derive from the child-acrobat Mignon in Goethe's *Wilhelm Meister* (1795–1796).[15] Almost two millennia after Plato, Renaissance Neoplatonism rejects both Plato's disdain for the written word and the less-elitist view of writing found in the Christian Gospels, as in St. Paul's postulation of a script "given life" by the Spirit (2 Corinthians 3:6). Instead, Neoplatonists propose a hermetic and sublime view of the written word in which writing is a privileged medium to achieve a transcendent knowledge. Neoplatonism effectively fuses eros with writing, and does it in a way that is consonant with the troubadours' poetic practice and with the aesthetics of courtly love.

What about rabies? What is its symbolism with regard to Sierva María and throughout the novel? It should first be noted that, ironically, Sierva María never contracts that disease in spite of being bitten by a presumably rabid dog (*Of Love* 63). Rabies can of course be interpreted as an obvious symbol of passion, and it has even been seen in this work as a variation of the same wordplay García Márquez does with the word *cólera* in the triptych's previous novel: *rabia* in Spanish can refer to the disease of rabies, but it is also a synonym for *cólera*, meaning "rage." Undoubtedly, rabies can be understood here as another metaphor of the unbridled—and contagious—passion of *amor hereos* or "lovesickness." In *Of Love and Other Demons* the narrator speaks of an epidemic of rabies just as there is an epidemic of cholera in *Love in the Time of Cholera*. Returning to Plato's

Symposium, however, we find that in Alcibiades's speech, which follows Socrates's, the notion of rage is linked not only to passion but to philosophy. Alcibiades speaks of having been "bitten in the heart or the mind" by Socrates's philosophy, which has filled him with a "philosophical frenzy, this sacred rage" (569).

"Rabies" in this novel thus may also be the lettered wisdom, the literary passion of which Cayetano Delaura suffers and which he passes along to Sierva María by reciting to her the Renaissance verses, laden with Neoplatonic doctrines, of Garcilaso. In this context, the character of the Judeo-Portuguese physician Abrenuncio de Sa Pereira Cao plays a key role. At first his role in the novel would seem to be similar to that of Erixymachus in the *Symposium*, who counsels moderation and balance in one's desires (Plato 540). But the name and attributes of this character also suggest that he embodies in the novel an ironic approach to love and to the religious discourse with which love has also been associated since Plato's *Symposium*. A converted Jew whose name means, in fact, "rejection," Abrenuncio displays an ironic negativity and a dispassionate rationalism that lead him to question everything, even the books he avidly collects but which he does not treat with much respect (28). Reminiscent of Melquiades in *One Hundred Years of Solitude*, Abrenuncio also resembles Gustave Flaubert, who dealt openly with love and letters in novels like *Madame Bovary* (1857) and *L'éducation sentimentale* (1869) and in stories like "The Legend of St. Julian Hospitaller" (1877).[16] Abrenuncio is thus able to diagnose the "Bovaryism" *avant la lettre* of which Cayetano suffers and tries to "cure" him by means of logotherapy, trying to "vaccinate" him with ironic books that will serve as antidotes, such as the eccentric Latin translation of Voltaire's *Lettres philosophiques* (1734; *Of Love* 121).[17] But his efforts are in vain, since the force of writing as eros is too overpowering and, like rabies, it is incurable.

Of Love and Other Demons's ironic narrative about love and literature underscores the predominance of passion in literary writing and marks the instant when that predominance began. Abrenuncio's presence, however, adds a further layer of irony to these observations. Evocative of the hoary topic of the love-medicine relation (first seen in Plato's *Symposium*), Abrenuncio also brings to mind the theme of love as both a prescription and a recipe (two senses of the word *receta* in Spanish). Often appearing as the "love philter" that gives rise to the lovers' passion,[18] in the postmodern context of García Márquez's late narrative this topic is steeped in irony, since postmodern narrative openly accepts the love theme's deeply conventional and codified nature, which turns it into a mere formula or "recipe" for literary creation. Turned into a recipe, the writing of eros becomes "domesticated," so to speak; it becomes less sublime and more accessible, entering the domain of agape. This ironic view of eros as a literary cliché also implies that passionate love is not an unavoidable destiny—as those who suffer from it believe—but rather a conventional code of conduct that has already become a literary myth, a pretext for artistic creation.

However, if passionate love is an illusion of sorts, based as it is on a rejection of mundane reality, it does not necessarily follow that agape, or love of one's neighbor, is any less of an illusion or ideal and any more "real" or effective in lived reality. Although a work of nonfiction, *News of a Kidnapping* is arguably one of García Márquez's last major narrative works, along with his memoir *Vivir para contarla* (*Living to Tell the Tale*, 2002) and his novel *Memorias de mis putas tristes* (*Memories of My Melancholy Whores*, 2004). Both *News of a Kidnapping* and *Memories of My Melancholy Whores* offer autumnal insights into the difficulties of bringing to fruition love of one's neighbor in the sphere of daily life in society.

A powerful blend of journalism with the refined techniques of a master novelist, *News of a Kidnapping* recounts the abductions of several members of Colombia's social elite by the forces of drug kingpin Pablo Escobar to use as hostages in his struggle against extradition to the United States, including the eventual negotiated release of most, though unfortunately not all, of the hostages. As critics have noted, this narrative is intimately linked to the sociopolitical crises Colombia experienced through the 1980s and 1990s (Bell-Villada 268). In the midst of this fragmented, violent society where transaction and lust for power reign supreme, the narrative searches for traces of agape by focusing first on conjugal and filial love. It is this love that leads husbands, wives, parents, and children of the kidnap victims, as well as other members of their large extended families, to fight back despair and keep in touch with their loved ones through the one-way communication afforded by the electronic and print media, while simultaneously negotiating with the kidnappers through back-channel dialogues.

Traces of agape are also visible when both the abductees and their captors search for ways to connect on a human level, even in the darkest moments of their captivity. As the narrator notes, from the early days of their abduction Maruja Pachón and Beatriz Villamizar learned about their constantly masked guardians

> that masks can hide faces but not character. This was how they individualized them. Each mask had a different identity, its own personality, an unmistakable voice. Even more: It had a heart. Without wanting to, they came to share the loneliness of their confinement with them. They played cards and dominoes and helped each other solve crosswords and puzzles in old magazines. (*News of a Kidnapping* 60)[19]

However, the most dramatically effective manifestation of agape in the narrative is directly linked to the Christian religion shared to various degrees by all of the characters, embodied by the eccentric figure of Father Rafael García Herreros, a Eudist or missionary priest who aired a "strange sixty-second program" titled *God's Minute* on Colombia's Televisora Nacional, in which he offered "a reflection that was more social than religious, and often tended to be cryptic" (227–28).[20] Part mystic, part populist TV celebrity, Father García Herreros bridges the divide between eros and agape, although his ultimate success in the negotiations with narco leader Escobar is largely due to his appeal to the popular, homegrown religiosity favored even by the kidnappers, who "worshipped the same Holy Infant and Lady of Mercy worshipped by their captives, and prayed to them with perverse devotion" (60).[21]

Ultimately, however, *News of a Kidnapping* displays a tone and ambience that is closer to literary manifestations of eros in ancient times, particularly to Homer's *Odyssey*. Resemblances to Homer's work include a cast of characters dominated by socially prominent, powerful, and near-legendary individuals; a story featuring the themes of conjugal fidelity and the return to home; and multiple traits evocative of the well-known episode of Odysseus's captivity by the cyclops Polyphemus, all set against a backdrop of war and national crisis. Similar to the epic genre in general, *News of a Kidnapping*'s tone and language are elevated, dignified, and decorous, as is the behavior of most of the characters (with a few exceptions among the lower-echelon kidnappers). In the discourse of eros, violence engendered by passion is often sublimated or ritualized; in this context it is worth remarking on the absence of sexual violence or torture by the kidnappers against their victims (Bell-Villada 270). Rather than a journalistic exposé of the social and political failings that led to the kidnapping of prominent Colombians by Escobar's narcos, *News of a Kidnapping* reads more like an attempt to banish its traumatic events to the past by means of the distancing and healing effects of art, in the hope, as García Márquez's states in the acknowledgments, "that the story it tells will never befall us again."[22]

In contrast to the journalistic actuality and the ultimately failed search for brotherly love in *News of a Kidnapping*, García Márquez's *Memories of My Melancholy Whores*, with its defiantly transgressive title (in the offensive connotations of the word *puta* in Spanish), appears as a paean to both eros and fiction. As well-crafted as any of García Márquez's narratives, this monologue-like novel about love, aging, and literature nevertheless became anachronistic as soon as it was published because of its deeply patriarchal attitudes and ideas about love and sexuality, which have become ethically unacceptable to many readers. The novel begins with the following sentence: "The year I turned 90, I wanted to give myself the gift of a night of wild love with an adolescent virgin" (3).[23] As one reviewer pointed out, this is "a superb opening ... but not, perhaps, the sort of statement that generates waves of good feeling toward the speaker" (Rafferty 14). García Márquez may have felt empowered to write about erotic transgression while displaying a more openly critical view of Colombian society by the example of his countryman Fernando Vallejo, whose rambling novelistic diatribes against Colombian nationalism, religion in general and the Catholic Church in particular, brotherly love, the family, and other societal institutions are voiced by a recurrent curmudgeonly character often referred to as the "old man" (Aristizábal, 11–12, 173–280). However, unlike Vallejo's aggressively contrarian and homosexual narrator, whose savage critique spares no one, even himself, the protagonist and narrator of *Memories of My Melancholy Whores* is on the whole much less self-critical.

The novel's symbolic dimension hinges on the hoary topic of woman as a "blank page," embodied in the novel by the idealized teenaged prostitute the narrator names Delgadina—a literary reference to a sinister medieval Spanish ballad about father-daughter incest. This topic, already sufficiently deconstructed by feminist literary critics from Susan Gubar to Elizabeth Bronfen, objectivizes women's bodies as "works of art" and views heterosexual intercourse as a patriarchal metaphor for the act of writing and literary creation. It is within this archaic framework that García Márquez articulates his exaltation of literary creation as a constant source of artistic renewal.

Memories of My Melancholy Whores is thus built upon a metaphorical association between writing and sexuality, one that furthermore equates artistic writing with a nonreproductive sexuality centered on both passion and pleasure. García Márquez's evocation of his own youthful experience as a boarder in a bordello in his memoirs (*Living to Tell the Tale*, 334–36; see also Martin 133–34) along with the character of María Alejandrina Cervantes, the town's madam in *Chronicle of a Death Foretold*, whose name contains obvious literary allusions, establish a symbolic proximity between sex and writing.

In *Memories of My Melancholy Whores* the link between artistic inspiration and unfulfilled erotic desire that stems from Neoplatonic tradition (as explored in *Of Love and Other Demons*) is dramatized by the protagonist's chaste nocturnal visits to the bordello, during which he watches the nude Delgadina sleep at his side, a scene reminiscent of the courtly test of love in which Tristran and Isolde sleep chastely together separated by Tristran's sword (De Rougemont 29, 31, 34). By no means serene, this difficult contemplation serves to awaken in the novel's protagonist a true and intense amorous passion in the style of the Neoplatonists. At one point he fantasizes about joining a student demonstration with a placard declaring, "I am mad with love" (66).[24]

His passion, linked to the theme of writing as eros, in turn becomes joined to the theme of old age through the promise of renewal and deathlessness present in both eros and writing. Although illiterate, Delgadina is herself an embodiment of writing, just as the old man is both her writer and her reader. Ultimately the narrator, after a life spent scribbling so many trivial columns for the Sunday paper (despite the modest popularity they gave him), realizes—like his author, Gabriel García Márquez—that his love for Delgadina (and for writing) has been his sole and greatest work of art and his best chance at achieving a form of immortality.

Notes

1. For a useful discussion of the contrast between eros and agape, although from a strictly theological perspective, see Nygren.
2. "Pasión tan desaforada," "hogar hospitalario," "el único misterio que nunca se esclareció en Macondo" (*Cien años* 114, 156, 157).
3. The poem is part of a play by Gil Vicente, *Comédia de Rubena* (1521), written with dialogue in both Spanish and Portuguese. The links between the first act of this play and the plot of *Of Love and Other Demons* are highly suggestive (see Hernández de López 209–18).
4. Santiago Nasar, as the autopsy report made by the priest Carmen Amador states, "had a deep stab in the right hand. The report says: 'It looked like a stigma of the Crucified Christ'" (*Chronicle* 87); "tenía una punzada profunda en la palma de la mano derecha. El informe dice: 'Parecía un estigma del Crucificado'" (*Crónica* 99).
5. As in the following few examples: "He just needed a canny interrogation, first to him and then to the mother, to confirm once more that the symptoms of love are the same as those of cholera" (62); "Le bastó con un interrogatorio insidioso, primero a él y después a la madre, para comprobar una vez más que los síntomas del amor son los mismos del cólera" (*El amor* 98); "One night [Fermina] returned from her daily walk stunned by the revelation

that one could not only be happy without love but also against love" (*Love in the Time* 87); "Una noche [Fermina] regresó del paseo diario aturdida por la revelación de que no sólo se podía ser feliz sin amor sino también contra el amor" (*El amor* 134); "Hildebranda had a universalist notion of love, and she thought that anything that happened to one person affected all the other loves in the entire world" (*Love in the Time* 129); "Hildebranda tenía una concepción universal del amor, y pensaba que cualquier cosa que le pasara a uno afectaba a todos los amores del mundo entero" (*El amor* 193); "The widow Nazaret never missed Florentino Ariza's occasional dates, not even in her busiest times, and it was always without aspiring to love nor being loved, although always hoping that she would find something like love but without the problems of love" (*Love in the Time* 150–51); "La viuda de Nazaret no faltó nunca a las citas ocasionales de Florentino Ariza, ni aun en sus tiempos más atareados, y siempre fue sin pretensiones de amar ni ser amada, aunque siempre con la esperanza de encontrar algo que fuera como el amor, pero sin los problemas del amor" (*El amor* 223–24); "nothing in this world was more difficult than love" (*Love in the Time* 223); "nada en este mundo era más difícil que el amor" (*El amor* 326).
6. "El horror de la vida real" (*El amor* 500), "este ir y venir del carajo" (503).
7. "Libre albedrío" (*El amor* 502).
8. "Un hotel de cinco estrellas" (*Del amor* 9).
9. "Confiaba más bien en formalismos legales" (*Del amor* 183).
10. "Muerta de amor en la cama con los ojos radiantes y la piel de recién nacida. Los troncos de los cabellos le brotaban como burbujas en el cráneo rapado, y se les veía crecer" (*Del amor* 198).
11. "Hija de un antiguo capataz [del padre de Ygnacio de Alfaro] venido a más en el comercio de ultramarinos" (*Del amor* 57), "y lo despojó sin gloria de su virginidad" (58).
12. "Tuvo una infancia expósita" (*Del amor* 60).
13. "Cuerpo escuálido" (*Del amor* 20), "aire desvalido" (43). A similar lack of physical attractiveness is also attributed to Florentino Ariza in *Love in the Time of Cholera*. Hildebranda Sánchez's opinion, voiced after she meets Florentino, says it all: "He's ugly and sad . . . but he is all love" (129), "'Es feo y triste . . . pero es todo amor'" (*El amor* 193).
14. "Su vicio de mentir por placer" (*Del amor* 149).
15. See Steedman.
16. The theme of leprosy in *Of Love and Other Demons* could well be linked to this latter text by Flaubert collected in his *Trois contes*, in which the master of Rouen, like García Márquez, recreates a legendary tale from a distant past. In Flaubert's story, the noble Julian, after renouncing his violent life and his success as a warrior, finds sanctity by turning into a hermit. His apotheosis occurs when Julian embraces a leper who asks Julian to warm his dying body with his own (*Three Tales* 86–87).
17. As English Showalter points out, *Lettres philosophiques* (1734) by Voltaire has traditionally been viewed as the first attack launched against the ancien régime (439).
18. See De Rougemont's discussion of the theme of the "love-philter" in the legend of Tristan and Isolde (46–50).
19. "Que la máscara esconde el rostro pero no el carácter. Así lograron individualizarlos. Cada máscara tenía una identidad diferente, un modo de ser propio, una voz irrenunciable. Y más aún, tenía un corazón. Aun sin desearlo terminaron compartiendo con ellos la soledad del encierro. Jugaban a las barajas y al dominó, y se ayudaban en la solución de los crucigramas y acertijos de las revistas viejas" (*Noticia* 71).

20. "Un raro programa de sesenta segundos" (*Noticia* 264), "una reflexión más social que religiosa, y muchas veces críptica" (264).
21. "Vivían aferrados al mismo Divino Niño y la misma María Auxiliadora de sus secuestrados. Les rezaban a diario para implorar su protección y su misericordia, con una devoción pervertida" (*Noticia* 72).
22. "Con la esperanza de que nunca más nos suceda este libro" (*Noticia* 8).
23. "El año de mis noventa años quise regalarme una noche de amor loco con una adolescente virgen" (*Memorias* 9).
24. "Estoy loco de amor" (*Memorias* 67).

Works Cited

Aristizábal, Juanita C. *Fernando Vallejo a contracorriente*. Beatriz Viterbo, 2015.
Barthes, Roland. *The Pleasure of the Text*. Translated by Richard Howard, Hill and Wang, 1975.
Bell-Villada, Gene H. *García Márquez: The Man and His Work*. U of North Carolina P, 2010.
De Rougemont, Denis. *Love in the Western World*. Princeton UP, 1983.
Flaubert, Gustave. *Three Tales*. Translated by Robert Baldick, Penguin Classics, 1987.
Franco, Jean. "Dr. Urbino's Parrot." *Indiana Journal of Hispanic Literatures*, vol.1, no. 2, 1993, pp. 147–60.
García Márquez, Gabriel. *El amor en los tiempos del cólera*. Bruguera, 1985.
García Márquez, Gabriel. *Chronicle of a Death Foretold*. Translated by Gregory Rabassa, Ballantine Books, 1984.
García Márquez, Gabriel. *Cien años de soledad*. Edición Conmemorativa. Real Academia Española, Asociación de Academias de la Lengua Española, 2007.
García Márquez, Gabriel. *Crónica de una muerte anunciada*. Oveja Negra, 1981.
García Márquez, Gabriel. *Del amor y otros demonios*. Norma, 1994.
García Márquez, Gabriel. *Living to Tell the Tale*. Translated by Edith Grossman, Knopf, 2003.
García Márquez, Gabriel. *Love in the Time of Cholera*. Translated by Edith Grossman, Penguin Books, 1989.
García Márquez, Gabriel. *Memorias de mis putas tristes*. Vintage Español, 2004.
García Márquez, Gabriel. *Memories of My Melancholy Whores*. Translated by Edith Grossman, Vintage International, 2005.
García Márquez, Gabriel. *News of a Kidnapping*. Translated by Edith Grossman, Penguin Books, 1998.
García Márquez, Gabriel. *Noticia de un secuestro*. Norma, 1996.
García Márquez, Gabriel. *Of Love and Other Demons*. Translated by Edith Grossman, Vintage International, 2008.
García Márquez, Gabriel. *One Hundred Years of Solitude*. Translated by Gregory Rabassa, Avon Books, 1971.
González, Aníbal. "Translation and Genealogy: *One Hundred Years of Solitude*." *Gabriel García Márquez: New Readings*, edited by Richard Cardwell and Bernard McGuirk. Cambridge UP, 1987, pp. 65–79.
González, Aníbal. *Love and Politics in the Contemporary Spanish American Novel*. U of Texas P, 2010.

Hernández de López, Ana María. "La significación del epígrafe en *Crónica de una muerte anunciada*." *En el punto de mira: Gabriel García Márquez*, edited by Ana María Hernández de López, Pliegos, 1985.

MacAdam, Alfred. "Realism Restored." *Review: Latin American Literature and the Arts*, vol. 18, no. 35, 1985, pp. 34–38.

Martin, Gerald. *Gabriel García Márquez: A Life*. Bloomsbury, 2008.

Nygren, Anders. *Agape and Eros*. Macmillan, 1939.

Plato. *The Collected Dialogues*. Edited by Edith Hamilton and Huntington Cairns, Princeton UP, 1999.

Rafferty, Terrence. "*Memories of My Melancholy Whores*: Client of the Year." *New York Times*, 6 Nov. 2005, www.nytimes.com/2005/11/06/books/review/memories-of-my-melancholy-whores-client-of-the-year.html. Accessed 17 Oct. 2019.

Showalter, English. "1734: Three Editions of Voltaire's *Lettres philosophiques* Are Published and Banned: Intricacies of Literary Production." *A New History of French Literature*, edited by Dennis Hollier. Harvard UP, 1994, pp. 429–35.

Steedman, Carolyn. *Strange Dislocations: Childhood and the Idea of Human Interiority, 1780–1930*. Virago Press, 1995.

Tompkins, Jane P. "Sentimental Power: *Uncle Tom's Cabin* and the Politics of Literary History." *The New Feminist Criticism: Essays on Women, Literature, and Theory*, edited by Elaine Showalter. Pantheon Books, 1985, pp. 81–104.

Updike, John. "Dying for Love: A New Novel by García Márquez." *The New Yorker*, 7 Nov. 2005, www.newyorker.com/magazine/2005/11/07/dying-for-love. Accessed 14 Sept. 2019.

Vicente, Gil. *Comédia de Rubena. Obras completas de Gil Vicente, III*. Libraria Sa da Costa, 1943.

PART II
RACE, ETHNICITY, AND GENDER

CHAPTER 8

IMAGINING THE AFRO-CARIBBEAN IN GARCÍA MÁRQUEZ'S FICTION

ADELAIDA LÓPEZ-MEJÍA

A woman traveling on the same bus as a young Gabriel García Márquez fascinated the new contributor to Cartagena's daily *El Universal* with what he perceived as her carnality and self-assurance: "[T]he black woman travels with all her body ... with the total organism of a woman who knows she is black.... Few things have more plastic beauty than a proud black woman."[1] The budding journalist devoted two of his July 1948 columns to her; in the second one he records his observations of the woman's interaction with a Native-American passenger ("a perfect example of these men, half-primitive, half-civilized, who come down from the Sierra ... with medicinal plants and love potions).”[2] That second column draws to an unexpected close: after requesting a contraceptive from the Indian passenger, the Black woman proceeds to swallow "seeds brought from who knows what corner of witchcraft ... and after each dose a febrile shaking climbs up her possessed body, as if she already felt the steely nips that would scar her dynasty" (98).[3] The woman in these newspaper columns has more than a little in common with the sexually magnetic, eminently practical, and often childless Black female characters of García Márquez's fiction. The novelist would make magical realism a household term, but he was as much of a realist as a magical realist, and it is as products of realism that his Afro-Colombian characters may be studied—not in the sense of an "accurate" portrayal of society and its conflicts, but in the sense of a writer's attempt to describe human types in the context of a certain time and place in history. Realism often reveals a writer's social preconceptions and prejudices; García Márquez's Afro-Colombian characters are no exception. The writer never really shook off the prejudices of an upbringing that valued European ancestry and considered very dark skin undesirable (Saldívar 81; Martin 7, 23). Even so, midway through his novelistic production García Márquez began to seriously address the history of Caribbean slavery and its concomitant legacy of miscegenation.

Jacques Gilard, in his prologue to García Márquez's early journalism, notes that the years the novelist spent in the Caribbean ports of Cartagena and Barranquilla (1948–1950) were definitive in his development as a writer and in his choice of subject matter ("Prólogo" 33). The two passengers described in the Cartagena newspaper encapsulate the multiethnic quality of the Colombian Atlantic Coast.[4] In his 1981 conversations with Plinio Apuleyo Mendoza published as *Fragrance of Guava* (henceforth *Fragrance*), García Márquez drew attention to his own Spanish ancestry in the same breath that he credited his creative manipulation of the supernatural to a familiarity with Afro-Caribbean culture (51; *El olor de la guayaba* [henceforth *Olor*] 73). To Manuel Osorio, moreover, he insisted that his understanding of his own background changed after a 1978 visit to Cuban-supported Angola: "I found that in many of the traditional African art forms there are aesthetic manifestations very much like the one we have in the entire Caribbean area. Because I'm Caribbean, recognizing this fact made me see into myself and realize I'm a *mestizo*."[5] Although the word "mestizo" has described many types of cultural syncretism in Latin America, the rhetoric of *mestizaje* tends to make Blackness invisible; it can be a misleading term to use in discussions of the legacies of the African diaspora.[6] In Nicolás Guillén's preface to *Sóngoro Cosongo*, the Cuban poet deliberately used the word "mulatto" to describe texts infused with Afro-Cuban voices and themes (176). Arguably in the late 1970s and early 1980s, García Márquez was still unsure of how to address what Frantz Fanon had called "the fact of blackness" in the Caribbean.

Leaf Storm, a short novel first published in 1955, is told from a markedly criollo perspective.[7] Based on García Márquez's memories of his childhood in the inland Colombian-Caribbean town of Aracataca, *Leaf Storm* makes Afro-Colombians invisible; so, too, does the work of the early William Faulkner with African-Americans (Erskine 27). García Márquez could get prickly when discussing Faulkner's influence on his fiction; when asked about that influence by Manuel Pereira, García Márquez flippantly responded that, after all, "Faulkner is a Caribbean writer." Surely what the Colombian novelist meant was that he and Faulkner came from societies whose economic foundations had rested on racial slavery.[8] But García Márquez's work before 1975 would not engage in literary evocations of Caribbean slavery.

Two of his short stories from the 1950s portray twentieth-century Afro-Colombian characters as victims of social injustice. In "No Thieves in This Town" a Black man is found guilty of a crime he never committed, and in "Nabo, the Black Man Who Made the Angels Wait," a Black paraplegic lies neglected in a lightless room. García Márquez's *No One Writes to the Colonel* and *In Evil Hour* (henceforth *Evil Hour*), drafted in 1950s Paris, recreate a riverside village based on the Colombian town of Sucre. Readers of *No One Writes to the Colonel* will find an unsympathetic portrayal of a "monumental" Black lawyer working in an office overrun by barnyard ducks (23–27; *El coronel no tiene quien le escriba* 40–46). The suggestion is that this Black character's inability to retrieve his client's military pension stems partly from ineptitude or laziness, although Colombia's impenetrable and corrupt bureaucracy is also at fault.

By contrast, the town that serves as the collective protagonist of *In Evil Hour* is striking in its racial heterogeneity: Syrian immigrants, mestizo policemen, a judge given to remembering "long Sundays of sea and insatiable mulatto women who made love standing up behind the doors of entranceways" (*Evil Hour* 25).⁹ This will not be the writer's sole misstep into racist fantasies in which Black Others enjoy greater access to sexual pleasure.¹⁰ García Márquez's fiction will routinely associate transgressive sexuality with dark-skinned and light-skinned Black women.

The only Black character of *In Evil Hour* is Carmichael, whose name suggests a West Indian origin, and who seems resigned to the vitriol of anonymous lampoons being plastered all over the town: "They've already put mine up. . . . Since my wife is white, the kids have come out all colors. . . . Just imagine, eleven of them . . . the lampoon said that I'm only the father of the black ones" (*Evil Hour* 83).¹¹ Here García Márquez briefly addresses both miscegenation and "ocular" questions of racial identity, touching upon "white" fears that Blacks can look white or that, as Richard Dyer notes, white bodies might not reproduce as white (25). Úrsula, the criolla matriarch of *One Hundred Years of Solitude* (henceforth *One Hundred Years*; *Cien años de soledad*, henceforth *Cien años*), lives in fear that "women of the street" will stain the Buendía bloodline (368).¹²

In the genealogical epic that remains the writer's most influential novel, a nameless "adolescent mulatta with . . . small bitch's teats" constitutes an early example of García Márquez's repeated identification of Afro-Colombian women with prostitution (*One Hundred Years* 51).¹³ She passes through the archetypal village of Macondo as a sex worker exploited by a tyrannical grandmother, and although she may be García Márquez's first (unconscious) evocation of racialized slavery, she seems to exist outside history.¹⁴ The mixed-race sons of Colonel Aureliano Buendía, on the other hand, exemplify how miscegenation and illegitimacy often coincided in both colonial and nineteenth-century Latin America. There is no mention of the skin color of the legitimate Buendías, but the Colonel's illegitimate progeny are initially "children of all ages, all colors" and later men "of all types and colors" (*One Hundred Years* 187).¹⁵ García Márquez never forgot the day when his own maternal grandfather's illegitimate sons passed through Aracataca, their foreheads smudged with the ash of the beginning of Lent (*Living to Tell the Tale* 73; *Vivir para contarla* [84]). The writer transmuted that memory into the language of magical realism: an indelible smudge left on the Colonel's sons' foreheads on Ash Wednesday brands them as Buendías and as Liberals for the rest of their lives. It also stigmatizes their illegitimacy. The most developed of those "men of all colors" is Aureliano Triste, "a big mulatto" who sets up an ice factory and brings the first train to Macondo. Although the character is key to the modernization of the town, it is his criollo grandfather whom readers remember as an ambitious and tragic scientist; Aureliano Triste's attributes include the even temper and "cheerfulness" that are often used to stereotype Colombian Blacks (Wade 243; *One Hundred Years* 217–21; *Cien años* 293–98).

The most striking mulatta character in *One Hundred Years* is Petra Cotes; her face has "the ferocity of a panther, but she had a generous heart and a magnificent vocation for love" (187).¹⁶ Petra belongs to a long line of Black female characters whom García Márquez describes with animal similes. The writer himself suspected that some of his Colombian readers would dismiss her as "a typically Caribbean woman" ("una mujer del Caribe"), but he saw her as a symbol of female strength (*Fragrance* 76; *Olor* 109). Although Petra's "generosity of heart" compares favorably with the criollo Buendías' frequent inability to give of themselves to others, her concubinage with Aureliano Segundo reinforces Colombian stereotypes casting Black women as the adulterous mistresses of Caribbean criollo husbands.[17] Petra's effect on her lover's livestock is another of the novel's magical realist flourishes: her mere presence causes animals to madly reproduce (*One Hundred Years* 191; *Cien años* 268). It may be true that for many non-Black Colombians, "blacks are seen as ... possessed of some special powers, especially magical, sexual, musical, and rhythmic ones" (Wade 23). Since the Buendía family fortune evaporates following the departure of the Banana Company, from a realist perspective it seems evident that Aureliano Segundo's prosperity derived from the economic boom years of the 1920s; these in turn coincided with the United Fruit Company's greatest visibility on the Northern Coast of Colombia. But Petra's lover ascribes his ruin to the waning sexual exuberance of his concubine (*One Hundred Years* 338–39; *Cien años* 412). After the town's economic collapse, Petra makes sure that her lover's family does not go hungry and that his daughter can study abroad (*One Hundred Years* 347, 352; *Cien años* 421, 426). Here her generosity evokes what Toni Morrison called the "limitless" love sometimes given by Black characters to white ones in non-Black writers' fiction (x).

One of the great ironies of the novel is that Petra never has children, in spite of her initial ability to multiply Aureliano Segundo's livestock. And when the narrator compares Petra to her bony mule (*One Hundred Years* 332; *Cien años* 405), readers may remember that the word "mulato" echoed "the debate Euro-Americans engaged in about whether blacks were of the same species as whites. If they were not, the result [of their breeding] would be similar to a mule, ... a being that itself was incapable of producing life" (Christian 116). Arguably Petra's infertility allegorizes the position of Black women in slavery: while prized for their reproductive ability to increase the number of their masters' slaves, as mothers they often were robbed of their offspring. The voices of North American Black women testify that many slave mothers conceived of the fate of children born in slavery as worse than death. García Márquez's childless Black characters perhaps suggest a similar rejection of reproduction.

Mulattas staff the town brothels during the last days of Macondo (*One Hundred Years* 338–39; *Cien años* 405). Nigromanta, the great-granddaughter of a Black West Indian immigrant, turns to streetwalking. With her "body of a wild dog," Nigromanta diverts Aureliano Babilonia's incestuous lust for his aunt and, before the apocalyptic end of García Márquez's novel, she rescues him "from a pool of vomit and tears" (*One Hundred Years* 386; *Cien años* 414).[18] Nigromanta's function is to satisfy Aureliano Babilonia's needs and to succor him in moments of weakness. A Black male character plays a very similar role in García Márquez's *The General in His Labyrinth*.

In 1971 the novelist took a long and purposeful tour of the island and continental Caribbean, for he had been living in Barcelona after the success of *One Hundred Years of Solitude* and had come to feel that only by traveling back to the Caribbean would he be able to incorporate its sensory quality in a new, unfinished novel about a larger-than-life dictator. If we are to believe García Márquez in his interview with Colombian journalist

Juan Gossaín, the sight of a Black woman in the Paramaribo airport was the Proustian moment that reinvigorated the novelist's writing: "In a corner there was a heavy red-scarved black woman selling ginger . . . in that moment I knew that I would be able to return to Barcelona and finish my novel."[19] Seen once, that nameless Black woman will have a long afterlife; in future works similar figures flicker in and out of the writer's imagination, otherized archetypes representative primarily of the body, of the senses, and of public space. In *The Autumn of the Patriarch* (henceforth *Autumn*; *El Otoño del patriarca*, henceforth *Otoño*), Black women sit impassively in a marketplace, "in bright-colored rag turbans . . . fanning themselves without blinking with the canyon-deep calm of sitting idols" (182).[20] In *Love in the Time of Cholera* (henceforth *Love*) a Black woman sells fruit, which she offers lusciously skewered on a butcher's knife [101; *El Amor en los tiempos del cólera* (henceforth *Amor*) 143]. In *Of Love and Other Demons* (henceforth *Of Love*), the parish priest in an eighteenth-century slave district chats with "black matrons . . . like monumental idols beside handmade trinkets" [133; *Del amor y otros demonios* (henceforth *Del amor*) 180].[21] These older, idol-like Black vendors become icons of Caribbeanness; younger, beautiful mulattas do as well. In *Fragrance of Guava* García Márquez claimed that "nowhere in the world do you find the racial mixture and the contrasts which you find in the Caribbean"; as his first example he singled out the region's "honey-colored mulattas with green eyes" (53).[22]

García Márquez published the short stories in *The Incredible and Sad Tale of Innocent Eréndira and Her Heartless Grandmother* (henceforth *Innocent Eréndira*) before finishing *The Autumn of the Patriarch*. References to the island Caribbean dot the collection of short fiction. In "Death Constant Beyond Love," an escaped convict lives with "a beautiful and blasphemous black woman" from Paramaribo; their dark-skinned daughter inherits her mother's beauty (240). The short story that gives its title to the collection, "The Incredible and Sad Tale of Innocent Eréndira and Her Heartless Grandmother" (henceforth "Innocent Eréndira"), reintroduces the child-prostitute of *One Hundred Years* without branding her racially. Antonio Benítez-Rojo and others have argued that the grotesque grandmother who forces Eréndira into prostitution represents colonialism, or in Benítez Rojo's terms, "Europe's law" (Benítez-Rojo 292). But the baroque splendor of the old woman's desert mansion is a legacy left by her husband, "a legendary smuggler" ("Innocent Eréndira" 264). The grandmother's own past lies squarely in the island Caribbean: "The best known version in the language of the Indians was that Amadís the father had rescued his beautiful wife from a house of prostitution in the Antilles" ("Innocent Eréndira" 264).[23] Toward the end of the story Eréndira's grandmother prophesies her granddaughter's identical future in a similar Antillean brothel ("Innocent Eréndira 301; "Cándida Eréndira" 148-49). Both characters exemplify what Michael Dash calls the Caribbean's promiscuous body, "trapped in a discourse that accentuates carnality" (609). No Black characters ever appear in the story, but Eréndira's grandmother carries the attributes of what in García Márquez's writing is becoming a racialized black Caribbean of overwhelming sensual power. Eréndira's flight after murdering her grandmother also evokes a fundamental Afro-Caribbean memory: the maroon, the runaway slave.

In an interview with a group of Colombian reporters in 1975, García Márquez described his new novel *The Autumn of the Patriarch* as the most distinctly Caribbean of all of his works ("El viaje a la semilla" 167). Part of this linguistically complex novel's conflicted exploration of race includes a running phrase that bristles with sexualized racism: "[W]e're leaving you here with *your nigger whorehouse* so let's see if you can put it all together without us" (*Autumn* 25; emphasis added).[24] Gregory Rabassa's translation of "burdel de negros" as "nigger whorehouse" accurately captures North American condescension and racism toward the Caribbean. First uttered by contemptuous US Marines to the dictator, the Patriarch's look-alike Patricio Aragonés quotes it back to the tyrant in a taunting reminder of the latter's dependence on and treatment by the United States. On the one hand, the dictator rapes nameless (often mulatta) women almost daily, be it in the servants' quarters of his presidential palace, in the government house, or in his mother's mansion. Such spaces might stand as a microcosm of an eroticized, racialized nation (*Autumn* 9, 18, 21; *Otoño* 13, 23, 27). Nevertheless, the North Americans' contemptuous phrase echoes painfully in the dictator's thoughts, as an insult both to him and to the people he governs, illustrating what Aníbal Quijano describes as coloniality, that is, a legacy of colonialism (or neocolonialism), in which nations are denigrated sexually and racially, and colonized people are reduced to the color of their skin and placed on the bestial side of a human/animal divide.[25] García Márquez uses the phrase "burdel de negros" ironically, as a pained and bitter reference to the denigrating imbrication of territory, culture, and race. The phrase is a monstrous example of what Dash describes (in another context) as a generalized discourse that eroticizes the Caribbean.

The city in *The Autumn of the Patriarch* is a purposeful palimpsest of Caribbean ports: Santo Domingo, Panama City, La Havana, and Cartagena, among others (Bell-Villada 170). Initially the narrator seems more interested in alluding to British buccaneers, Spanish viceroys, stone cathedrals, and aristocratic nuns (*Autumn* 1, 14; *Otoño* 5, 19). References to riotously painted Black neighborhoods follow. Even after a governmental push toward modernization, "the colors of the Negro shacks on the harbor hills" remain "intact" (*Autumn* 239).[26] Afro-Caribbean culture endures in an arguably stereotyped vitality. The character of Manuela Sánchez, who becomes the dictator's erotic obsession, hails from a similarly brightly painted neighborhood (*Autumn* 72; *Otoño* 83). When the dictator's spies report that she is flitting from one Caribbean dance floor to the next, García Márquez evokes a Caribbean totality through racialized movement and song. Black working-class neighborhoods produced the plena; Papá Montero is the dissolute Black musician of Nicolás Guillén's eponymous poem (*Obra poética* I); Barlovento is a center of Afro-Venezuelan culture, and the lyrics of an eponymous song ("Barlovento") describe Black women dancing: "[T]hey told him that she'd been seen dancing the plena in Puerto Rico,... but it wasn't her ... she'd been seen in the madness of Papa Montero's wake,... but it wasn't her either, in the ticky-tacky of Barlovento ... but none of them was her" (*Autumn* 83).[27] The ever-deferred search for Manuela illustrates the Lacanian idea that desire cannot be satisfied and that it cannot exist outside of language, in this case, outside Afro-Caribbean song. Why García Márquez chooses to leave

Manuela Sánchez's race ambiguous is impossible to tell, but perhaps he could not allow himself to imagine a Black woman as a central object of desire.

In *Fragrance of Guava* García Márquez boasts that he had gone through the Caribbean "island by island, city by city"; he was also struck by learning that British and Dutch pirates had studded women's teeth with diamonds (*Fragrance* 52).[28] The impact of the author's travels can be detected in another of *Autumn*'s extraordinary representations of a Caribbean totality (this time through the sense of sight):

> [H]e had seen from that terrace the line of the hallucinated isles of the Antilles... the perfumed volcano of Martinique,... the gigantic black man with a lace blouse... the infernal market of Paramaribo,... diamonds embedded in the teeth of black grandmothers who sold heads of Indians and ginger roots sitting on their safe buttocks under the drenching rain ... the whole universe of the Antilles from Barbados to Veracruz. (*Autumn* 39–40)[29]

In this magically panoptic view of the sea, the narrator places a jarring stress on racial otherness and gaudiness: the Black man dressed in lace is a feminized figure of excess; the market women selling shrunken heads are a play on stereotypes of the primitive; their teeth evoke an extravagant past and their sturdy buttocks associate them with the body and the earth. The Black ginger-hawker seen by García Márquez in the Paramaribo airport arguably hovers over the scene.

In *Autumn* the author also makes his first explicit allusion to the Caribbean slave trade:

> [T]he sloops ... were anchored in the former slave port loaded with flowers from Martinique and ginger roots from Paramaribo ... around the former slave platform still in use where on another Wednesday of another time in the nation before him they had sold at public auction a captive Senegalese woman who brought more than her own weight in gold because of her nightmare beauty. (*Autumn* 180)[30]

Black bodies continue to overwhelm the senses; the nameless African woman on the auction block embodies racist fantasies of extraordinary, excessive pleasure. The city's modern waterfront remains a space of human traffic, where visitors can watch "shabby sailing ships ... loaded with shipments of unripe whores for the glass hotels of Curacao, for Guantánamo, ... for the saddest and most beautiful islands in the world" (*Autumn* 145).[31] In his interview "Viaje a la semilla," García Márquez evoked his youth in Barranquilla and Cartagena in almost identical words and credited his familiarity with the culture of prostitution to the discovery of his voice as a writer.[32] Whether he would ever acknowledge that his fiction insistently racializes prostitutes' bodies is now impossible to know.

After the publication of *Autumn* in 1975, García Márquez promised that he would not publish anything until democracy was restored in Chile. Nevertheless, during the late 1970s he wrote most of the stories that were to be published in 1992 under the title

Strange Pilgrims. One of these stories, "*Bon Voyage*, Mr. President" (dated 1979), creates the character of a Puerto Rican "mulatta . . . with the eyes of an angry dog"; her name is Lázara Davis.[33] She wears an African dress and santería necklaces during a dinner she serves to the story's protagonist; this is García Márquez's first reference to the religion of santería, born in the Spanish-speaking Caribbean during the time of slavery. Lázara's self-exoticizing attire celebrates the history and culture of the African diaspora. Although the story is set in twentieth-century Geneva, the narrator refers to Lázara as a Yoruban princess ("*Bon Voyage*, Mr. President" 19). There were many Yoruba among the African slaves brought to the Spanish Caribbean, but the description of one of their twentieth-century descendants as a princess seems anachronistic. Be that as it may, the story signals García Márquez's increasing attempt to acknowledge and represent the Afro-centric Caribbean. It also shows a writer reflecting on the legacy of miscegenation in Latin America. The protagonist of the short story, a deposed Caribbean president, speaks pessimistically over dinner of a "continent conceived by the scum of the earth without a moment of love: the children of abductions, rapes, violations, infamous dealings. . . . Mixing the races means mixing tears with spilled blood. What can one expect from such a potion?" ("*Bon Voyage*, Mr. President" 32).[34] He poses the rhetorical question to his unwilling and resentful hostess; Lázara, who is herself the product of racial mixture, does not deign to answer him. Readers are left wondering what she thinks of the question.

In 1982, after seven years of self-enforced semi-silence, García Márquez came out with the highly successful *Chronicle of a Death Foretold* (henceforth *Chronicle*; *Crónica de una muerte anunciada* [henceforth *Crónica*]).[35] It was his third recreation of the Colombian town of Sucre, this time in a retelling of an honor killing. Mulattas staff the town brothels, as in *One Hundred Years of Solitude* (*Chronicle* 64–65; *Crónica* 50–51). The dishonored Bayardo San Román marries a young woman suspected of having lost her virginity with another man. Bayardo's mother is Alberta Simonds, "a big mulatto woman from Curacao, who spoke Spanish with a mixture of Papiamento, [and] in her youth had been proclaimed the most beautiful of the two hundred most beautiful women in the Antilles" (*Chronicle* 33).[36] Readers may recall the beautiful mulattas of the island Caribbean praised by García Márquez in *Fragrance of Guava* (53). In *Chronicle* the author also evokes the history of Caribbean slavery, perhaps as a premonition, when Santiago Nasar, not long before he is murdered, claims to see a ghost from "a slave ship that had sunk with a cargo of blacks from Senegal across from the main harbor mouth at Cartagena de Indias" (67).[37] That port gains greater visibility in García Márquez's final novels; he sets his 1985 *Love in the Time of Cholera* (henceforth *Love*) in a city that corresponds almost exactly to Cartagena itself.

According to the narrator of *Love in the Time of Cholera*, "in the eighteenth century the commerce of the city had been the most prosperous in the Caribbean, owing in the main to the thankless privilege of its being the largest African slave market in the Americas" (*Love* 17; *Amor en los tiempos de cólera*, henceforth *Amor*).[38] Whether the Colombian port of Cartagena could accurately answer to that description is debatable.[39]

In any case, García Márquez's 1985 novel is set in the nineteenth and early twentieth centuries, and the fictional city's Blacks appear to form an instinctual mob prone to noisiness, violence, and orgiastic sex:

> On Saturdays the *poor mulattoes . . . tumultuously abandoned their hovels* of cardboard and tin on the edges of the swamps *and in jubilant assault took over* the rocky beaches of the colonial district. Until a few years ago, *some of the older ones still bore the royal slave brand that had been burned onto their chests* with flaming irons. During the weekend *they danced without mercy, drank themselves blind . . . made wild love among the icaco plants, and broke up their own party with bloody free-for-alls.* During the rest of the week the *same impetuous mob . . .* infused the dead city with *the frenzy of a human fair . . .* a new life.[40] (*Love* 17; emphasis added)

In this visually powerful description, Black bodies seem made for dancing, drinking, fornicating, killing, and being killed; García Márquez's use of a provincial narrator partly excuses the litany of racial stereotypes.

García Márquez continues to be intent on imagining a transnational Caribbean world. The fictional city of *Amor* sits on the South American mainland (like Cartagena) and has close ties to the island Caribbean. Jamaican immigrants live in houses on wooden pilings over a salt marsh; Barbara Lynch and her father, a Black Jamaican pastor, live in a "typical Antillean house," painted brightly, like the Black neighborhoods of *The Autumn of the Patriarch* (*Love* 241; *Amor* 330).[41] Refugees from unnamed islands have fled instability in the Antilles and settled in the narrative's mainland city (*Love* 8; *Amor* 15). Jeremiah de Saint-Amour, whose race and specific origin are never identified, is one of those refugees. He leaves a suicide note, never shared with the reader, confessing to "an atrocious crime" and to having escaped from life imprisonment on the island of Cayenne (*Love* 32; *Amor* 42). This enigmatic character and his Haitian mulatta lover have lived for years in the gossipy narrator's city. For a novel deliberately engaged with the conventions of nineteenth-century realism, too many questions pertaining to Saint-Amour's past and to what became of his lover are left unanswered.

The individualized Black female characters of the novel are vividly drawn, but two of them are stereotypically sexualized and the other one is left unsatisfactorily undeveloped. None of these women seem to have children. Barbara Lynch, a "tall, elegant, large-boned mulatta with skin the color and softness of molasses" gives the impression of possessing a "sex more pronounced than that of other human beings" (*Love* 240–41).[42] Saint-Amour's lover is a "haughty mulatta with cruel golden eyes and hair tight to her skull like a helmet of steel wool"; she resembles "a river idol," has a "serpent's eyes," and follows an independent if not questionable moral code (*Love* 13, 15).[43] The upper-class protagonist Juvenal Urbino concludes that this nameless woman is "irredeemable"; he cannot understand her decision to allow her lover's suicide or her embrace of a clandestine life in a foreign city (*Love* 14–15; *Amor* 25–27). As for Leona Cassiani, when the middle-class protagonist Florentino Ariza first sees her on a trolley, "he could not help thinking what he thought: black, young, pretty, but a whore beyond the shadow of a doubt" (*Love* 182).[44] Which racial stereotypes are the non-Black characters', which the provincial narrator's, and which the author's is not always easy to discern, because authorial efforts to counter the surface racism of the novel are seldom apparent.

In *Love*, the first Black character to receive a name, Gala Placidia, hails from a former runaway slave village. Edith Grossman translates "palenque" as "old slave quarters," but surely the reference is to the historic runaway slave community located close to Cartagena (*Love* 97; *Amor* 137). Although a very minor character, Gala Placidia exemplifies the role that Black female servants (and slaves) could play as intermediaries between overprotected mistresses and urban public space.[45] When Gala Placidia accompanies Fermina Daza into an arcaded market, her young mistress runs from stall to stall in something much like a trance, which a second Black woman cuts short without interrupting the young female protagonist's sensory delight: "[A] good-natured black woman with a colored cloth around her head who was round and handsome offered her a triangle of pineapple speared on the tip of a butcher's knife" (*Love* 101).[46] Arguably, García Márquez's memory of a Paramaribo ginger-hawker is at work here. The appearance of Florentino Ariza puts a stop to Fermina's experience of the sensory pleasures of a Caribbean market; she is chastised for entering a space that blurs the boundaries between adventure and impropriety, one in which Black women appear to enjoy greater "freedom" and mobility than their mistresses.

That type of freedom corresponds to a greater exposure to danger and disease. Open sewage flows through all of the colonial neighborhoods of the city in *Love*, but especially where Blacks work and live (*Love* 12, 108–9; *Amor* 22, 154–55). The criollo physician Juvenal Urbino finds the stench of his city's former slave district unbearable; he only goes there to visit the bereaved lover of his former chess partner, Saint-Amour. The magically tasteful home where the Caribbean refugee lived with his Haitian lover complicates the narrator's insistent description of a neighborhood full of offal and sewage. The description of a cholera epidemic also alludes graphically to the conditions of filth in which the poor Black population works and lives (*Love* 110–12; *Amor* 154–56).

For the upper-class physician's affair with the Jamaican Barbara Lynch, García Márquez turns to exhausted conventions of depicting physical desire as madness. The entire episode provides page after page of stereotypes regarding the "infernal" attractiveness of light-skinned Black women (*Love* 240–50, esp. 246; *Amor* 330–45, 337).[47] In the Jamaican woman's presence Urbino becomes "no longer the best-qualified physician along the Caribbean coastline but a poor soul tormented by his tumultuous instincts" (*Love* 243).[48] Barbara Lynch never refers to herself as mulatta, and twice she refers to herself as Black when articulating her perception of the racist society in which she lives (*Love* 243; *Amor* 333); here the author briefly succeeds in evoking a Black character's subjectivity. Later on, during an exchange between spouses in which Urbino acknowledges his affair to his wife Fermina, García Márquez tentatively addresses the question of hierarchies created by skin-color gradation without probing too deeply into society's bad-faith distinctions between light and dark-skinned Black women:

And worst of all, damn it: with a black woman. He corrected her:
"With a mulatta." But by then it was too late for accuracy. She had finished. "Just as bad,"
she said, "and only now I understand: it was the smell of a black woman."[49] (*Love* 250)

Urbino's insistence that his affair is with a mulatta reads as a feeble "justification" for his infidelity. Certainly, the stereotype of mulatta beauty has never sheltered light-skinned Black women from discrimination or prejudice, and the light-skinned Barbara Lynch knows it.

García Márquez's novel leaves the reader in no doubt regarding the racism of its upper- and middle-class characters. Racism disfigures and dehumanizes Fermina, never more than when she claims that Blacks smell.[50] Her mother-in-law is no different, for Doña Blanca blames her husband's death on his devotion to the city's Black "rabble" during a cholera epidemic.[51] Urbino's exploitative treatment of Barbara Lynch and his attempt to buy her silence appear all the more callous given the racial and social difference between them (*Love* 248, *Amor* 340). The Black character of Leona Cassiani never stops embodying racial and cultural otherness, either for the narrator or for the middle-class protagonist Florentino, thanks to whom Leona gained her first, very low-level position in the River Company of the Caribbean (*Love* 183–84; *Amor* 252).[52] She is the only female character in the novel who is developed in the context of a (slowly) modernizing Latin American workplace. After years of capitalizing on her gift for office politics, Leona "was still the woman she had been, with the same clothes, worthy of an impetuous runaway slave, her mad turbans, her earrings and bracelets made of bone . . . a lioness of the streets" (*Love* 187).[53] Against all odds (and unrealistically, given the racism of the Colombian Caribbean), Leona becomes the brains behind the company: "[Secretly] she had taken control of everything . . . the impassive Florentino Ariza . . . confronted the fascinating spectacle of that *fierce black woman smeared with shit* and love in the fever of battle" (*Love* 187; emphasis added).[54] This is not the first time that the novel associates a Black character with dirt.[55] Leona's own sexuality is deeply masochistic, layered with fantasies recreating a violent rape on the docks. The realist in García Márquez surely intended Leona Cassiani, Barbara Lynch, and Saint-Amour's lover to illustrate the disadvantaged place of Black women in the early twentieth-century Caribbean, but their portrayal too often falls into racist stereotypes, which the author makes few clear attempts to counter.

After publishing *Love*, García Márquez chose to fictionally recreate the last few months in the life of Latin American independence leader Simón Bolívar. The writer's imagination seemed ever more drawn to Latin America's historical past. In *The General in His Labyrinth* (henceforth *The General*; *El general en su laberinto*, henceforth *El general*), the protagonist's relationship with a former slave turned loyal steward is the novel's most complex and intriguing human tie. García Márquez's Bolívar never treats José Palacios as anything other than a subaltern. Nevertheless, his steward is his preferred interlocutor, "his accomplice in everything," the only character who knows the count of the General's women, who stands vigil during his nightmares and cares for him during his final illness (*The General* 216, 228).[56] If in *One Hundred Years* it was Nigromanta who attended to a criollo character's lust and cared for Aureliano Babilonia after his bout of drunken mourning, here it is a Black man who stands at his master's side, attending to his bodily needs, and who, to use Judith Butler's terms, "becomes the master's body."[57]

Bolívar and his steward stand as uncanny reminders of the historical and racialized becoming of Latin America.[58] In highlighting the ex-slave's "whiteness" and the criollo's "Black" ancestry, García Márquez asks his readers to reflect on the unreliability of any racial classification. Palacios "had been born a slave through the misadventure of an African woman and a Spaniard, from whom he had inherited his carroted hair, the freckles on his face and hands, and his light-skinned blue eyes" (*The General* 94).[59] On the other hand, the novel's careful construction of Bolívar as ethnically Caribbean also slowly reveals the General's own African ancestry.[60] According to sociologist Orlando Patterson, "in a multiracial society hair difference is what carries the vital symbolic potency" (61). The significance of Bolívar's "Caribbean curls" in the opening scene becomes more apparent in the subsequent description of his "coarse sideburns and mustache of a mulatto" (*The General* 4, 76).[61] The actual genealogical revelation comes even later, when the General poses for a portrait that will be his last: "[H]e had a strain of African blood through a paternal great-great-grandfather, who had fathered a son by a slavewoman" (*The General* 180).[62] In this slow uncovering of the slave in Bolívar's family tree, García Márquez suggests how disavowed miscegenation can lie at the heart of criollo identity. In a final undermining of fixed racial categorizations, the narrative lends voice to a historical figure for whom Bolívar was both ethnically and politically white: "General Manuel Piar, a hard mulatto from Curacao ... called on blacks, mulattoes, zambos and all the destitute of the country to resist the white aristocracy of the country, personified by the General" (*The General* 229).[63] Bolívar wanted nothing to do with the racially inflected independence movement spearheaded by Piar. Their historical confrontation culminated in Piar's execution and García Márquez shows Bolívar acting ruthlessly in his insistence on a homogenizing rhetoric of *mestizaje*.

García Márquez's Bolívar shows little empathy for characters whose African ancestry he distantly shares. Although his liberation of his family's slaves is described as a sweepingly generous gesture, manumissions in the late eighteenth-century Caribbean were very much the norm (*The General* 189; *El general* 192).[64] The General fails to formally emancipate his steward, leaving him floating in a "civil limbo" (266).[65] Bolívar likes to believe that he seduced a "beautiful mulatta ... with the profile of an idol" on the Venezuelan plains, but in fact this young woman "gave herself not out of desire or love but out of fear" (*The General* 49–50).[66] Indulgence toward rape is not uncharacteristic of García Márquez's fiction. Yet the narrator remains alert to criollo unwillingness to undo the racist structures of Spanish colonialism; Cartagena's former slaves, for example, are set "adrift in a useless freedom" (*The General* 170).[67]

In *El general* García Márquez also relies on fundamental figures in the discourse of Caribbean identity: the sea and the plantation.[68] In "Innocent Eréndira," the young indentured prostitute and her grandmother feel "an urge to live and a knot in their hearts" when approaching the seashore; the grandmother exults in the "light of the Caribbean after half a lifetime of exile" (301).[69] García Márquez's Bolívar feels a similar exaltation, a "strange sensation of freedom.... For there was the sea, and on the other side of the sea was the world" (*The General* 132).[70] The idea that only what lies to the east of the Atlantic is the "world," that only Europe is the site of culture and world-turning events, is also voiced in the 1994 novel *Of Love and Other Demons*.

The figure of the plantation looms even larger than the sea as a locus of identity. Plantations are Bolívar's beginning and his end; they are where he was born and where he dies. When García Márquez's fictional Bolívar arrives at the iconic sugar mill of San Pedro Alejandrino where the historical Bolívar breathed his last, an aroma of burnt sugar transports the fictional character to the "center of his longing," the plantation of his Venezuelan childhood (*The General* 253).[71] In García Márquez's retelling, the sensory impact produced by a Colombian Caribbean sugar mill stirs up Bolívar's long-repressed sadness for the early death of his only wife: "All that could stir her momentary memory was the smell of molasses at San Pedro Alejandrino, the impassivity of the slaves in the mills, who did not cast so much as a pitying glance in his direction" (*The General* 253–54).[72] The slaves' impassivity underscores how little the wars of independence improved the lives of Latin America's Blacks. Yet their presence seems necessary to Bolívar's sense of home. Just before the protagonist expires, the voices of those same slaves appear to offer a promise of redemption; he "began to listen to the radiant voices of the slaves singing the six o'clock Salve in the mills ... the final brilliance of life" (*The General* 268).[73] In a leveling of distinctions, Black voices comfort García Márquez's Bolívar and allow him to feel that he is dying at home. Black bodies, even if unwittingly, facilitate the fulfillment of a primal human desire.

In *Of Love and Other Demons* (henceforth *Of Love*; *Del amor y otros demonios*, henceforth *Del amor*), García Márquez turned again to the framework of the historical novel; the setting is eighteenth-century Cartagena. An "Abyssinian female ... sold for her weight in gold" on the auction block is later made to appear "in the peril of her nakedness" in front of the Spanish viceroy (*Of Love* 8, 98).[74] This woman resembles the Senegalese woman of "nightmarish beauty" sold for more than her weight in gold in *The Autumn of the Patriarch*. Evidently, the figure of an enslaved, uncannily beautiful African woman had taken hold of García Márquez's imagination. Nevertheless, in *Of Love* the writer reverses his previous use of race and herosexuality; in his earlier works, it is usually a Black woman who couples with a non-Black man. Now a Black freeman, Judas Iscariote awakens an obsessive lust in the mestiza character Bernarda; when he dies, she turns to plantation slaves to satisfy her sexual addiction (*Of Love* 46–47; *Del amor* 63–65). The female slave Dominga de Adviento has to control male slaves from "committing calamitous acts of sodomy or fornicating with bartered women" (*Of Love* 11).[75] García Márquez never stopped imagining Black bodies engaged in experiences of prohibited and intense sexual pleasure.

In *Of Love* the author also achieves a richly textured recreation of a city of the eighteenth-century Spanish Caribbean. The book's narrator is finely attuned to the racial categorizations of the Spanish colonial enterprise in the Americas; this is apparent from the opening paragraph with its careful description of a marketplace full of Indian stalls and Black slaves, to which a mulatta servant takes the daughter of a criollo aristocrat

(*Of Love* 7; *Del Amor* 13). Slaves live in the back courtyards of the mansions and convents where they serve; there they create a culturally separate world. Those slaves cannot always communicate with each other; this was a historical fact on many plantations (Klein 63). Rejected at birth by her mestiza mother and her American-born titled father, the twelve-year-old protagonist Sierva María has been raised by household slaves. They have become Sierva María's "true family"; their culture becomes hers.[76] The girl learns "three African languages" in her father's house and can converse in Congolese, Yoruba, and Mandingo. In the convent where she is eventually sequestered, she can "talk with Africans from any nation better than they could among themselves" (*Of Love* 91).[77]

Music and dance form an integral part of the culture that Sierva María absorbs from the slaves who raise her. She "learned to dance before she could speak" and "could dance with more grace and fire than the Africans" (*Of Love* 42, 12).[78] Her singing voice is entrancing. She poses for a portrait "with the exquisite dignity of a black woman" (*Of Love* 105).[79] Although this reduction of culture to dance, song, and elegant carriage is not free from stereotype, the centrality of music and dance to African slave communities in the Americas cannot be called into question.[80] García Márquez knew this, and he knew, too, that aspects of African religion survived in Spanish Caribbean slave quarters, most particularly in the form of Santería, the syncretic faith in which West African Yoruban divinities were worshipped under the guise of Catholic saints. García Márquez's knowledge of the material and ritual culture of Santería was probably enriched during the time he spent in Cuba before and during the 1980s.[81] Santería originated among Cuban slaves, and the island is an important center of its practice today.

García Márquez's young protagonist wears the beads of sixteen gods around her neck (*Of Love* 43; *Del amor* 60); slave women bedecked Sierva María with these necklaces over the course of her childhood. Santería recognizes sixteen major orishas or gods; Michael A. Mason explains how initiatory rites in Santería involve hanging necklaces that represent the more powerful orishas around a novice's neck (29). Three of Sierva María's necklaces correspond to the major orishas Yemayá, Elegguá, and Changó (*Of Love* 131; *Del amor* 178). She also has a string of beads honoring the less well-known divinity of Oddúa, which she eventually gives away as a token of trust and affection (*Of Love* 125; *Del amor* 170). When she is forcibly moved into a Spanish-run convent, the convent slaves recognize her Santería necklaces and welcome Sierva María into their world. The talismanic beads are evidence of the girl's completely constructed identity and also are key to her sense of psychological safety; she responds furiously at any attempt to wrest any necklace from her by force (*Of Love* 68–69; *Del amor* 93–94). Throughout the novel her necklaces are a leitmotif, a material reminder of the religion that slave women taught her and of Sierva María's attachment to those women as well (*Of Love* 125; *Del amor* 170).

Perhaps the most memorable of the slave characters is Sierva María's wet nurse Dominga de Adviento, who has inserted the girl into the religious dimension of culture. Slaves were as open to Catholic beliefs as they were to African ones: "Dominga de Adviento suckled her, baptized her in Christ, and consecrated her to Olokun, a Yoruban deity of indeterminate sex" (*Of Love* 42).[82] It is fitting that a god of uncertain sex serves as the tutelary divinity of a child of similarly liminal ethnicity. When Sierva María's mother declares "the only white thing about that child is her color," García Márquez may be asking his readers to rethink what "race" might really mean (*Of Love* 45).[83] For Bernarda, race seems inseparable from ethnicity. Her postpartum rejection of her daughter soon becomes racially coded fear, for the girl becomes in effect a cultural changeling, an ethnic product of the despised slave culture in which she was raised. Bernarda fears that in the slave quarters Sierva María has learned African witchcraft and will use it against her (*Of Love* 45; *Del amor* 63). The twilight of the eighteenth century in the Caribbean was marked by an intense fear of slave revolt; judicial documents of the period overflow with charges of homicidal attempts by slaves in what is now Northern Colombia (Jaramillo Uribe 56). Don Ygnacio, the aristocratic plantation owner who is Sierva's father, lives in fear that his slaves might murder him (*Of Love* 38, 109; *Del amor* 55, 147). It has not been an uncommon fantasy for parents to imagine that a wet nurse's character traits might be passed on to the nursing child (Shahar 56).[84] Suckled by African slaves, Sierva María could well awaken paranoid parental fantasies.

Narrative suspense hinges first on whether the girl has contracted rabies from a dog that has bitten her ankle in the marketplace and then on whether Catholic authorities will determine that Sierva María is a candidate for exorcism. Although the girl's diagnosis is uncertain, the Spanish bishop sententiously warns Sierva María's father that rabies can mask demonic possession (*Of Love* 55; *Del amor* 76). Cayetano Delaura, the priest who falls in love with Sierva María, expresses his reservations: "[W]hat seems demonic to us are the customs of the blacks, learned by the girl as a consequence of the neglected condition in which her parents kept her" (*Of Love* 91).[85] The religious arm of the Spanish Crown did indeed demonize the people it subjugated; perhaps García Márquez is nudging his readers to consider how people of color can still be demonized today. There is a short-lived moment of hope when Father Narváez, an open-minded inquisitor and an expert in African languages and religions, returns the necklaces that a team of exorcists has wrested from Sierva María; this elder priest speaks to the girl reassuringly in African languages about the orishas and their attributes, which are represented by the color of the beads in her necklaces (*Of Love* 132; *Del amor* 178). Father Narváez's respect for Santería extends to a respect for slave culture in general. He is reaching the conclusion that there is no need for Sierva María to undergo further exorcism, but his unexplained and untimely death leaves the girl once again at the mercy of a retrograde church.

In this novel García Márquez places miscegenation at the center of Caribbean culture and history. Sierva María is the daughter of a mestiza mother and a criollo father. Father Narváez is "the son of a royal solicitor who married his quadroon slave" (*Of Love* 132; *Del amor* 178). At different points in the narrative, two other aging and cultured male characters provide spoken perspectives on the history of race mixture in the Americas. The more pessimistic view is voiced by the Spanish bishop, Don Toribio, who wonders out loud to the visiting viceroy whether Spain has built an evil legacy in the New World, whether "the chaotic mixture of blood that had gone on since the conquest . . . Spanish blood with Indian blood, and both of these with blacks of every sort, even Mandingo Muslims, . . . had a place in the Kingdom of God." The bishop concludes by aggressively asking the viceroy: "What can all this be but snares of the enemy?" (*Of Love* 102).[86] There is an ethical subtext to Don Toribio's diatribe; sexual violence often lay behind colonial miscegenation. This is not the first time such a pessimistic opinion is expressed in García Márquez's oeuvre; the statesman of "*Bon Voyage*, Mr. President" holds a similar view. In *Of Love*, Abrenuncio de Sa Pereira Cao, a Jewish-Portuguese doctor, takes a more forward-looking stance in his conversation with Cayetano Delaura, the priest who is in love with Sierva. Delaura, the son of a New World criolla, complains that "with so much mixing of bloodlines, I am no longer certain where I come from, or who I am," and the erudite Abrenuncio responds: "No one knows in these kingdoms. . . . I believe it will be centuries before they find out" (*Of Love* 114).[87] Abrenuncio conceives miscegenation as an evolving historical process that can culminate in a community's self-knowledge; the optimism of the Enlightenment underlies the Portuguese Jew's words.

The portrayal in *Of Love and Other Demons* of a slave-based society during a time in which there was still little hope of universal emancipation is probably García Márquez's last important novelistic venture. In this work the writer continues to produce descriptions of great visual power and to explore some of the themes at which he excels: the ambivalence at the heart of family relationships, the force of heterosexual passion, the joys of male friendship, and the skeins of Latin American history. Starting out as a writer whose fiction largely ignored the Afro-Caribbean population of his native Colombia, García Márquez increasingly made a space for Black characters in his work. From the 1970s onward he developed a passionate and informed vision of Caribbean history and culture and nudged his readers to reflect on the legacy of slavery and miscegenation in Latin America. Yet it is not unfair to ask whether García Márquez fails to imagine Black characters in a fully human dimension. Too often they are associated with untrammeled sexual instinct or with a servile social position. The author can oscillate between referring to his Black female characters as enigmatic idols (market women in *Autumn*, Saint-Amour's lover in *Love*, the mulatta raped by Bolívar in *The General*) or as animals (Petra and Nigromanta in *One Hundred Years*; Lázara Davis in "*Bon Voyage*, Mr. President"; Leona in *Love*). Probably García Márquez would have known how to defend himself against the accusation that most of his Black characters lack the psychological complexity of which his imagination was capable. Now, alas, he cannot respond to the charge.

Notes

1. All quotations from the June 1948 columns of *El Universal* are from Gabriel García Márquez, *Obra Periodística*, vol. I (henceforth *Obra Periodística*): "la negra viaja con todo el cuerpo . . . con su total organismo de negra convencida. . . . Pocas cosas tienen tanta belleza plástica como una negra engreída" (96). The translations are mine.
2. "Un ejemplar perfecto de estos hombres—mitad primitivos, mitad civilizados—que bajan de la Sierra Nevada . . . cargados de plantas medicinales y de fórmulas secretas para el buen amor" (*Obra Periodística* 97). One wonders whether carrying medicinal plants was in fact routine practice among Native Americans from the Colombian Sierra Nevada.

3. "La negra viene echándose a la boca puñados de semillas traídas de quién sabe qué rincón de la hechicería. Y después de cada dosis, un estremecimiento febril se le trepa por el cuerpo conmovido, como si sintiera en el vientre los acerados mordiscos que van cicatrizando su dinastía" (*Obra Periodística* 98).
4. For an unsurpassed analysis of race in Northern Colombia, see Wade.
5. "Encontré que en muchas formas populares del arte africano se encuentran manifestaciones estéticas muy similares a las que tenemos en toda la zona del Caribe. Como yo soy caribeño, la constatación de este hecho me hizo verme a mí mismo y darme cuenta que yo soy un mestizo" (García Márquez, "Poco Café y mucha política," 182). The translation is from Bell-Villada (22).
6. It began as a term for European and Amerindian racial mixture, and it retains that connotation today; see also Wade (36).
7. Latin American criollos were defined by their Spanish ancestry, of which most were taught to be proud; on *Leaf Storm*'s "patrician" perspective, see Rama (180–81).
8. "Faulkner es un escritor del Caribe" (translation mine). García Márquez, "La revolución cubana" (208). See Klein (83) for the growth of slavery in what is now Caribbean Colombia.
9. "Mulatas insaciables que hacían el amor de pie, detrás del portón de los zaguanes" (*La mala hora* 32.
10. See Evans for an introductory discussion of racism as the fantasy of an Other's access to pleasure.
11. "A mí ya me pusieron el mío, como mi mujer es blanca, los muchachos nos han salido de todos los colores.... Imagínese: son once.... Pues decía el pasquín que yo soy padre solo de los muchachos negros" (*La mala hora* 95–96).
12. "Las mujeres de la calle ... echaban a perder la sangre" (*Cien años* 443).
13. "La mulata adolescente, con sus tetitas de perra" (*Cien años* 128). Part of the discussion of *One Hundred Years* here is derived from Adelaida López-Mejía, "Race and Character in *One Hundred Years of Solitude*," *Theory in Action*, vol. 6, no. 1, 2013, pp. 29–49.
14. The episode is based on one of García Márquez's memories. "[H]e could not imagine their story as a novel—only as a drama in images" (Martin 177).
15. "Niños de todas las edades, todos los colores" (*Cien años* 227); "de los más variados aspectos, de todos los tipos y colores " (*Cien años* 331).
16. "Era una mulata limpia y joven, con unos ojos amarillos y almendrados que le daban a su rostro la ferocidad de una pantera, pero tenía un corazón generoso y una magnífica vocación para el amor" (*Cien años* 266).
17. According to Wade, the Colombian Caribbean is noted for its tolerance of "overlapping unions" and of white men's having Black mistresses (91).
18. "Cuerpo de perra brava"; "lo rescató de un charco de vómito y de lágrimas" (*Cien años* 459, 489).
19. "En un rincón había una negra gorda con una bayeta roja en la frente, vendiendo jenjibre ... en ese momento supe que era capaz de regresar inmediatamente a Barcelona y escribir la novela que quiero" (García Márquez, "El regreso a Macondo," 67).
20. "Las ancianas negras de turbantes de colores radiantes ... abanicándose sin parpadear con una quietud abismal de ídolos sentados" (*Otoño* 202).
21. "Conversando con las matronas negras, sentadas como ídolos monumentales frente a las baratijas de artesanía" (*Del amor* 176).
22. "La síntesis humana y los contrastes que hay en el Caribe no se ven en otro lugar del mundo ... mulatas color de miel, con ojos verdes" (*Olor* 74).

23. "Un contrabandista legendario"; also "La versión más conocida en lengua de indios era que Amadís, el padre, había rescatado a su hermosa mujer de un prostíbulo de las Antillas" (García Márquez, "Cándida Eréndira" 99).
24. "Ahí te dejamos con tu *burdel de negros* a ver cómo te las compones sin nosotros" (*Otoño* 31; emphasis added). See *The Autumn* (120) and *Otoño* (134) for another allusion to the "nigger whorehouse".
25. For a more in-depth discussion of colonialism's racist legacy, see Quijano.
26. "Continuaban intactas las barracas de colores de los negros" (*Otoño* 264).
27. "La vieron en un baile de plenas en Perto Rico, pero no era ella, que la vieron en la parranda del velorio de Papá Montero ... en el tiquiquitaque de Barlovento ... pero ninguna era ella" (*Otoño* 94).
28. "Conozco el Caribe isla por isla, ciudad por ciudad"; "los piratas suecos, holandeses e ingleses ... eran capaces de ... llenar de diamantes las dentaduras de las mujeres" (*Olor* 74).
29. "El había visto desde aquella terraza el reguero de islas alucinadas de las Antillas ... el volcán perfumado de la Martinica, ... el negro gigantesco con una blusa de encajes ... los diamantes incrustados en los dientes de las abuelas negras que vendían cabezas de indios y raíces de jengibre en sus nalgas incólumes bajo la sopa de la lluvia ... el universo completo de las Antillas desde Barbados hasta Veracruz" (*Otoño* 46–48). Benítez-Rojo's conceptualization of the Caribbean as a "repeating island" is apt here.
30. "Los veleros ... fondeaban en el antiguo puerto negrero estibados con flores de la Martinica y rizones de jengibre de Paramaribo ... en torno de la antigua báscula de esclavos todavía en servicio donde otro miércoles de otra época de la patria antes de él habían rematado en subasta pública a una senegalesa cautiva que costó más que su propio peso en oro por su hermosura de pesadilla" (*Otoño* 200).
31. "Los veleros astrosos zarpaban ... cargados de remesas de putas biches para los hoteles de vidrio de Curazao, para Guantánamo, para las islas más bellas y más tristes del mundo" (*Otoño* 163).
32. "It was in the brothels, it was by going back to small towns, in the songs" (my translation of "era en los burdeles, era volviendo a los pueblos, en las canciones") (García Márquez, "Viaje a la semilla" [162]).
33. Grossman translates "perra brava" as "vixen" (*Bon Voyage* Mr. President" 15). But the Spanish is "ojos de perra brava" ("Buen viaje, Señor Presidente" [32]); "eyes of an angry dog" is my translation.
34. "Un continente concebido por las heces del mundo entero sin un instante de amor: hijos de raptos, de violaciones, de tratos infames.... La palabra mestizaje significa mezclar las lágrimas con la sangre que corre. ¿Qué puede esperarse de semejante brebaje?" ("Buen viaje, Señor Presidente" 41).
35. In 1980 he broke his publishing strike with the appearance of a story that would also be included in *Strange Pilgrims*. See Martin (391).
36. "Una mulata grande de Curazao, que hablaba el castellano todavía atravesado de papiamento, había sido proclamada en su juventud como la más bella entre las doscientas más bellas de las Antillas" (*Crónica* 29).
37. "El ánima en pena de un barco negrero que se había hundido con un cargamento de esclavos del Senegal frente a la boca grande de Cartagena de Indias" (*Crónica* 52).
38. "Su comercio había sido el más próspero del Caribe, sobre todo por el privilegio ingrato de ser el más grande mercado de esclavos africanos en las Américas" (*Amor* 29).

39. For a reference to the ports of Panama and and Havana as equally important slave-trade centers, see Klein (82–83).
40. "Los sábados, *la pobrería mulata* abandonaba *en tumulto* los ranchos de cartones y latón de las orillas de las ciénagas ... y se tomaban en un *asalto de júbilo* las playas pedregosas del sector colonial. Algunos, entre los más viejos, llevaban hasta hacia pocos años *la marca real de los esclavos, impresa con hierros candentes* en el pecho. Durante el fin de semana *bailaban sin clemencia, se emborrachaban a muerte*... *hacían amores libres* ... desbarataban sus propios fandangos con *trifulcas sangrientas* de todos contra todos. Era *la misma muchedumbre impetuosa* que el resto de la semana se infiltraba en las plazas y callejuelas de los barrios antiguos, ... *le infundían a la ciudad muerta un frenesí de feria humana olorosa* ... una vida nueva" (*Amor* 29; emphasis added).
41. For a discussion of the immigration of West Indies Blacks into mainland Caribbean countries at the beginning of the twentieth century, see Andrews (136–42).
42. "Una mulata alta, elegante... con la piel del mismo color y la misma naturaleza tierna de la melaza" (*Amor* 330). Part of the description is difficult to translate: "Parecía de un sexo más definido que el resto de los humanos" (*Amor* 330).
43. "Una mulata altiva, con los ojos dorados y crueles, y el cabello ajustado a la forma del cráneo como un casco de algodón de hierro" (*Amor* 23); "parecía un ídolo fluvial ... con los ojos de culebra" (*Amor* 26). In *One Hundred Years*, Nigromanta also has "a hard surface of wiry hair which looked like a medieval warrior's mail headdress" (385).
44. "Él no podía pensar sino lo que pensó: negra, joven y bonita pero puta sin lugar a dudas" (*Amor* 250).
45. See Socolow for a discussion of how colonial Spanish America used Black slaves "as a point of contact between protected elite women and the public space" (132).
46. "La despertó del hechizo una negra feliz con un trapo de colores en la cabeza, redonda y hermosa, que le ofreció un triángulo de piña ensartado en la punta de un cuchillo de la carne" (*Amor* 143).
47. For a brief discussion of stereotypes of mulatta beauty, including how mixed-race slave offspring fetched a higher price on the auction block, see hooks (34, 40).
48. "No ya como el médico mejor calificado del litoral caribe, sino como un pobre hombre de Dios atormentado por el desorden de los instintos" (*Amor* 333). See also the reference to a "mad passion" (*Love* 243); "una pasión enloquecedora" (*Amor* 331).
49. "Y lo peor de todo, carajo: con una negra. Él corrigió: 'Mulata'. ... —Es la misma vaina— dijo—, y sólo ahora lo entiendo: era un olor de negra." (*Amor* 343).
50. For García Márquez's memory of his mother uttering a similar phrase, see *Living to Tell the Tale* (389); *Vivir para contarla* (423–24).
51. "Una montonera de negros" (*Amor* 283).
52. On Black women in the early twentieth-century Latin American workforce, see Andrews (126).
53. "Leona Cassiani seguía siendo igual que aquella tarde en el tranvía, con sus mismos vestidos de cimarrona alborotada, sus turbantes locos ... una leona de la calle" (*Amor* 257).
54. "En medio de aquella guerra *sórdida* dentro de una empresa en crisis perpetua,... el impasible Florentino Ariza no había tenido un instante de paz interior frente al espectáculo fascinante de aquella *negra brava embadurnada de mierda y de amor* en la fiebre de la pelea" (*Amor* 255; emphasis added).

55. See David Marriott's painful discussion of the "absorption of the black body into a fecal object" and the "fantasy of being turned into shit by an organic communion with the black body" (421).
56. "Su cómplice en todo" (*El general* 204); see also *El general* (215–16).
57. In Butler's reading of Hegel, the master/slave relation "requires in effect that the bondsman be the lord's body" (35).
58. On Latin America as "becoming," see Chanady (xxxv–xxxvi).
59. "Era seis años menor que el general, en cuya casa había nacido esclavo por un mal paso de una africana con un español, y de éste había heredado el cabello de zanahoria, las pecas en la cara y en las manos, y los ojos zarcos" (*El general* 94).
60. As González Echeverría states, "the author purports to have presented a truer Bolívar, closer to his Caribbean roots, including his African features" (196).
61. "Asperos rizos caribes" (*El general* 12); "patillas y bigotes ásperos de mulato" (*El general* 78).
62. "Tenía una línea de sangre africana, por un tatarabuelo paterno que tuvo un hijo con una esclava" (*El general* 184).
63. "El general Piar, un mulato duro de Curazao . . . había puesto a prueba la autoridad del general. . . . Piar convocaba a negros, mulatos y zambos, y a todos los desvalidos del país, contra la aristocracia blanca de Caracas encarnada por el general" (*El general* 216).
64. On manumission in the Caribbean during the late eighteenth century, see Klein (221).
65. "Quedó flotando en un limbo civil" (*El general* 249).
66. "Una bella mulata en la flor de la edad . . . no se le entregó por deseo ni por amor, sino por miedo" (*El general* 52–53).
67. "Los antiguos esclavos habían quedado al garete en una libertad inútil" (*El general* 163).
68. Benítez-Rojo uses the term "People of the Sea" (17). On sugar plantations as definitive in Caribbean cultural memory and identity, see Gilroy (47).
69. "Sintieron unas ansias de vida, y un nudo en el corazón, y era que habían llegado al mar . . . la abuela, respirando la luz de vidrio del Caribe al cabo de media vida de destierro" ("Cándida Eréndira" 159).
70. "No era necesario verla para reconocer la potencia inexorable que infundía en los corazones aquella rara sensación de libertad. . . . Pues ahí estaba el mar, y del otro lado del mar estaba el mundo" (*El general* 130).
71. "El centro de sus añoranzas" (*El general* 237).
72. "Lo único que logró remover su memoria por un instante fue el olor de la melaza de San Pedro Alejandrino, la impavidez de los esclavos en los trapiches que no le dedicaron ni siquiera una mirada de lástima . . . el otro ingenio de su vida donde un destino ineludible lo llevaba a morir" (*El general* 238).
73. "Entonces . . . empezó a oír las voces radiantes de los esclavos cantando la salve de las seis en los trapiches, . . . los últimos fulgores de la vida" (*El general* 251).
74. "Cautiva abisinia . . . [con] el precio . . . de su peso en oro" (*Del amor* 14); "el peligro de su desnudez" (*Del amor* 133).
75. "Sólo ella sacaba a escobazos a los esclavos cuando los encontraba en descalabros de sodomía o fornicando con mujeres cambiadas en los aposentos vacíos" (*Del amor* 19).
76. "Su verdadera familia" (*Del amor* 19).
77. "Le permitía entenderse con los africanos de cualquier nación, mejor que ellos mismos entre sí" (*Del amor* 124).

78. "Aprendió a bailar desde antes de hablar" (*Del amor* 60). Also "Bailaba con más gracia y más brío que los africanos de nación, cantaba ... en las diversas lenguas del África" (*Del amor* 19).
79. "Posando con su exquisita dignidad de negra" (*Del amor* 142).
80. See for example Andrews (28–29).
81. On García Márquez in 1970s and 1980s Cuba, see Martin (362–42).
82. "Dominga de Adviento la amamantó, la bautizó en Cristo y la consagró a Olokun, una deidad yoruba de sexo incierto" (*Del amor* 60).
83. "Lo único que esa criatura tiene de blanco es el color" (*Del amor* 63).
84. Blackburn tells us that the word criollo derives from the Spanish word *criada*, "implying that the criollo was suckled as well as born in the Americas, very possibly by an Indian or African nurse" (23).
85. "'Lo que nos parece demoníaco son las costumbres de los negros, que la niña ha aprendido por el abandono en que la tuvieron los padres'" (*Del amor* 124).
86. "Habló del batiburrillo de sangre que habían hecho desde la conquista: sangre de español con sangre de indios, de aquéllos y éstos con negros de toda laya, ... y se preguntó si semejante contubernio cabría en el reino de Dios.... ¿Qué puede ser todo eso sino trampas del enemigo?" (*Del amor* 138–39).
87. "'Con tantas sangres cruzadas, ya no sé a ciencia cierta de dónde soy ... [n]i quién soy.' 'Nadie lo sabe por estos reinos, dijo Abrenuncio, Y creo que necesitarán siglos para saberlo'" (*Del amor* 153).

Works Cited

Andrews, George Reid. *Afro-Latin America 1800–2000*. Oxford UP, 2004.
Bell-Villada, Gene. *García Márquez: The Man and His Work*. U of North Carolina P, 2010.
Benítez-Rojo, Antonio. *The Repeating Island*. Translated by James E. Maraniss, Duke UP, 1996.
Blackburn, Robin. *The Overthrow of Colonial Slavery, 1776–1848*. Verso, 1988.
Butler, Judith. *The Psychic Life of Power*. Stanford UP, 1997.
Chanady, Amaryll. Introduction. *Latin American Identity and Constructions of Difference*, edited by Amaryll Chanady et al., U of Minnesota P, 1994, pp. ix–xlvi.
Christian, Barbara. *Black Feminist Criticism: Perspectives on Black Women Writers*. Pergamon, 1985.
Dash, Michael. "Writing the Body: Edouard Glissant's Poetics of Remembering." *World Literature Today*, vol. 63, no. 4, 1989, pp. 609–12.
Dyer, Richard. *White*. Routledge, 1997.
Erskine, Peter. *William Faulkner: The Yoknapatawpha World and Black Being*. Norwood Press, 1983.
Evans, Dylan. "Jouissance." *Key Concepts of Lacanian Psychoanalysis*, edited by Danny Nobus, Other Press, 1999, pp. 1–28.
Fanon, Frantz. *White Skin Black Masks*. Translated by Charles Lam Markmann, Grove Weidenfeld, 1967.
García Márquez, Gabriel. *El amor en los tiempos del cólera*. Oveja Negra, 1985.
García Márquez, Gabriel. *The Autumn of the Patriarch*. Translated by Gregory Rabassa, Harper & Row, 1976.

García Márquez, Gabriel. "*Bon Voyage*, Mr. President." *Strange Pilgrims*, translated by Edith Grossman, Knopf, 1993, pp. 3–45.
García Márquez, Gabriel. "Buen viaje, Señor Presidente." *Doce cuentos peregrinos*, Mondadori, 2000, pp. 19–52.
García Márquez, Gabriel. *Chronicle of a Death Foretold*. Translated by Gregory Rabassa, Knopf, 1983.
García Márquez, Gabriel. *Cien años de soledad*. Edited by Jacques Joset, Cátedra, 1987.
García Márquez, Gabriel. *Collected Stories*. Translated by Gregory Rabassa and J. S. Bernstein, Harper & Row, 1984.
García Márquez, Gabriel. *El coronel no tiene quien le escriba*. Era, 1990.
García Márquez, Gabriel. *Crónica de una muerte anunciada*. Norma, 1981.
García Márquez, Gabriel. "Death Constant Beyond Love." Translated by Gregory Rabassa. *Collected Stories*, Harper and Row, 1984, pp. 238–45.
García Márquez, Gabriel. *Del amor y otros demonios*. Norma, 1994.
García Márquez, Gabriel. *Doce cuentos peregrinos*. Mondadori, 2000.
García Márquez, Gabriel. "En este pueblo no hay ladrones." *Todos los cuentos*. 1975, pp. 119–47.
García Márquez, Gabriel. *Fragrance of Guava: Plinio Apuleyo Mendoza in Conversation with Gabriel García Márquez*. . Translated by Anne Wright, Verso, 1983.
García Márquez, Gabriel. *García Márquez habla de García Márquez*. Edited by Alfonso Rentería Mantilla, Rentería Mantilla Ltd, 1979.
García Márquez, Gabriel. *El general en su laberinto*. Mondadori, 2000.
García Márquez, Gabriel. *The General in His Labyrinth*. Translated by Edith Grossman, Knopf, 1990.
García Márquez, Gabriel. *La hojarasca*. Sudamericana, 1972.
García Márquez, Gabriel. *In Evil Hour*. Translated by Gregory Rabassa, Harper & Row, 1979.
García Márquez, Gabriel. "The Incredible and Sad Tale of Innocent Eréndira and Her Heartless Grandmother." Translated by Gregory Rabassa, *Collected Stories*, 1984, pp. 262–311.
García Márquez, Gabriel. "La increíble y triste historia de la cándida Eréndira y su abuela desalmada." *La Increíble y triste historia de la cándida Eréndira y su abuela desalmada*. 1972, pp. 97–163.
García Márquez, Gabriel. *La increíble y triste historia de la cándida Eréndira y su abuela desalmada*. Hermes, 1972.
García Márquez, Gabriel. *Leaf Storm and Other Stories*. Translated by Gregory Rabassa, Harper & Row, 1972.
García Márquez, Gabriel. *Living to Tell the Tale*. Translated by Edith Grossman, Vintage, 2003.
García Márquez, Gabriel. *Love in the Time of Cholera*. Translated by Edith Grossman, Knopf, 2007.
García Márquez, Gabriel. *La mala hora*. 1962. Random House, Vintage Español: 2010.
García Márquez, Gabriel. "Muerte constante más allá del amor." *La increíble y triste historia de la cándida Eréndira y de su abuela desalmada*. 1972, pp. 59–69.
García Márquez, Gabriel. "Nabo, el negro que hizo esperar a los ángeles." *Todos los cuentos*. 1975, pp. 75–84.
García Márquez, Gabriel. "Nabo, the Black Man Who Made the Angels Wait." Translated by Gregory Rabassa, *Collected Stories*, 1975, pp. 68–77.
García Márquez, Gabriel. *No One Writes to the Colonel*. Translated by J. S. Bernstein, Harper & Row, 1968.

García Márquez, Gabriel. "No Thieves in This Town." Translated by J. Bernstein, *Collected Stories*, 1984, pp. 111–37.
García Márquez, Gabriel. *Obra Periodística*, vol. I. Edited with a prologue by Jacques Gilard, Bruguera, 1981, pp. 95–98.
García Márquez, Gabriel. *Of Love and Other Demons*. Translated by Edith Grossman, Penguin, 1996.
García Márquez, Gabriel. *Of Love and Other Demons*. Translated by Edith Grossman, Knopf, 2007.
García Márquez, Gabriel. *El olor de la guayaba: Conversaciones con Gabriel García Márquez*. Interviews with Plinio Apuleyo Mendoza. Bruguera, 1982.
García Márquez, Gabriel. *One Hundred Years of Solitude*. Translated by Gregory Rabassa, Harper Perennial, 2006.
García Márquez, Gabriel. *El otoño del patriarca*. Diana, 1986.
García Márquez, Gabriel. "Poco café y mucha política." Interview with Manuel Osorio (1978). *García Márquez habla de García Márquez*, 1979, pp. 179–84.
García Márquez, Gabriel. "El regreso a Macondo." Interview with Juan Gossaín (1971). *García Márquez Habla de García Márquez*, 1979, pp. 65–70.
García Márquez, Gabriel. "La revolución cubana me libró de todos los honores detestables del mundo." Interview with Manuel Pereira (1978). *García Márquez Habla de García Márquez*, 1979, pp. 201–9.
García Márquez, Gabriel. *Strange Pilgrims*. Translated by Edith Grossman, Knopf, 1993.
García Márquez, Gabriel. *Todos los cuentos de Gabriel García Márquez (1947-1972)*. Plaza y Janés, 1975.
García Márquez, Gabriel. "El viaje a la semilla." Interview with El manifiesto (1977). *García Márquez habla de García Márquez*, 1979, pp. 159–67.
García Márquez, Gabriel. *Vivir para contarla*. Norma, 2002.
Gilard, Jacques. "Prólogo." García Márquez, *Obra Periodística*, vol. I, pp. 7–56.
Gilroy, Paul. *The Black Atlantic*. Verso, 1993.
González Echevarría, Roberto. "Archival Fictions." *Critical Theory, Cultural Politics, and Latin American Narrative*, edited by Steven Bell, A. H. LeMay, and Leonard Orr, U. of Notre Dame P, 1993, pp. 183–208.
Guillén, Nicolás. *Obra Poética I*. Instituto Cubano del Libro, 1972.
hooks, bell. *Ain't I a Woman*. South End P, 1992.
Jaramillo Uribe, Jaime. *Ensayos de historia social*. Vol. I. Tercer Mundo 1989.
Klein, Herbert. *African Slavery in Latin America and the Caribbean*. Oxford UP, 1986.
Marriott, David. "Bonding over Phobia." *The Psychoanalysis of Race*, edited by Christopher Lane, Columbia UP, 1989, pp. 417–30.
Martin, Gerald. *Gabriel García Márquez: A Life*. Knopf, 2008.
Mason, Michael Atwood. "I Bow My Head to the Ground: The Creation of a Bodily Experience in a Cuban American Santería Initiation." *Journal of American Folklore*, vol. 107, no. 423, 1994, pp. 23–39.
Morrison, Toni. Preface. *Playing in the Dark*. Random House, 1992.
Patterson, Orlando. *Slavery and Social Death*. Harvard UP, 1982.
Quijano, Aníbal. "Coloniality of Power, Eurocentrism, and Latin America." *Coloniality at Large*, edited by Mabel Moraña, Enrique Dussel, and Carlos A. Jáuregui, Duke UP, 2008, pp. 181–224.

Rama, Ángel. "La narrativa de Gabriel García Márquez: Edificación de un arte nacional y popular." *Texto Crítico*, vol. 10, 1985, pp. 148–245.
Saldívar, Dasso. *García Márquez: Viaje a la Semilla. La biografía*. Alfaguara, 1997.
Shahar, Shulamith. *Childhood in the Middle Ages*. Routledge, 1990.
Socolow, Susan M. *The Colonial Women of Latin America*. Cambridge UP, 2000.
Wade, Peter. *Blackness and Race Mixture*. Johns Hopkins UP, 1993.

CHAPTER 9

AMERINDIAN WAYÚU LEGACY AND GARCIAMARQUEZIAN LITERARY FABLE

JUAN MORENO BLANCO

GABRIEL García Márquez is usually seen as a member of a group of writers known as the Latin American Boom, which impacted world literature in the second half of the twentieth century. Although the members of this group—which also includes Mario Vargas Llosa, Julio Cortázar, and Carlos Fuentes—bear important similarities, it is necessary to call attention to a major difference between the Colombian writer and his three contemporaries: he is the only one who comes from a rural origin, that is, the only one who has links with a nonurban regional culture. From this fact there arise biographical and cultural features of considerable consequence in the literary work of the Colombian-Caribbean Nobel laureate. In this regard, critics have highlighted the crucial role played by orality and memory bequeathed by his maternal grandparents, who raised Gabriel as a child in Aracataca; the stylistic and thematic similarities between his novels and short stories and the stories sung in Vallenato accordion music originating in the banana-growing region of his birth; and the idiosyncrasies his literary characters share with the cultural subjects of the Colombian-Caribbean region. Such perceptions have pointed toward the Amerindian coastal cultural singularity that sociologist Orlando Fals Borda studied in his four-volume *Historia doble de la costa* (Double History of the Coast), published between 1979 and 1986.

Nevertheless, the connections between the regional culture and the imaginary in García Márquez's works pointed out by his critics have made reference solely to anecdotes, semantic preconceptions, and very general contexts (which on many occasions bordered on the obvious or superficial) and above all, have ignored the Amerindian ethnocultural element to which Fals Borda assigned great prominence in reference to the constellations of customs, traditions, and meanings of the region's culture. In fact, critics' views regarding the culture of the author of *Cien años de soledad* (*One Hundred Years of Solitude*) lean heavily on the clues that link his literary imaginary to a vast written culture, namely the "national" history of his country or the political-ideological activism of Latin American intellectuals during the Cold War era (a time when the writers of the Boom had both of these factors in common), even as the writer's regional culture remained terra incognita. In contrast to these perspectives (which included some critics and biographers who noted that in those cultural contexts, "the Indians were lost in oblivion"), I take a different approach to the historical-biographical context of the Colombian writer, one that allows us to see the relationship between his work and the regional Amerindian coastal culture from which he comes.

CHILDHOOD IN A HOUSE DEEP IN THE CARIBBEAN REGION

Culture is typically acquired in the universe of childhood, and it is commonplace to state that that of our writer was extraordinary. Therefore, his biographers, Dasso Saldívar and Gerald Martin, have offered detailed descriptions of the house where he lived those first years; in this article—seeking to shed light on the indelible marks left by the words that first nourished García Márquez—I give full consideration to the colloquial expression that states that in this circumscribed space, the only child of the house would go around "as if he owned the place." Undoubtedly, to see him coming and going in that domestic atmosphere during the early development of his intellect and imagination will allow us to better understand his cultural roots. To do so, I turn now to three of the writer's childhood memories.

In the first one, the inveterate storyteller traces a link between the sense of smell and the moment he met his mother for the first time in that house:

> "What did you experience, being such a young child, the first day you saw your mother?"
>
> "What I remember most is the perfume, it was a perfume that if I were to smell it now, I would probably recognize. We lived in Aracataca; my mother had gone with her husband, my father, to live in Barranquilla and my earliest memory related to her is that they told me, 'Your mother lives in Barranquilla and your father lives in Barranquilla.' There were no photos, nothing of the kind . . . and I had an image of her, an image of her that. . . ."
>
> "And what did they explain to you? What would they tell you about them living in another place?"
>
> "No . . . those things were not explained to children. I was a very young child when they moved to Barranquilla . . . and suddenly I began to hear, 'Your mother is coming; your mother is going to come.' And I could not imagine how that encounter would be and had no idea how old she could be. . . . But I remember that *I came from. . . . It was a house with a very large corridor and a very deep courtyard* and they said to me, 'Your mother has arrived; she is there.' And I went in and everyone was in the living room; there were many women sitting on chairs placed against the wall, and I saw her

and recognized her right away and she was dressed like the characters in the films of those years ... late twenties, early thirties ... with a bell hat.... I remember perfectly her silk suit with beige embroidery, the straw hat of the same color, and then she said to me, 'Ay!' and she hugged me and I sensed the smell." (Navarro n.p.; emphasis added; translation by Juan Fernando Merino and Jenny Petrow)[1]

The wealth of allusions from the indefatigable narrator show the scene in a dwelling that was rather large. From a space in the back part of the house, the young "master" approaches through a "very large corridor" that connects with the part of the house where the living room is located, as well as the bedrooms and the kitchen, and where, after a long and sweltering trip from Barranquilla, the only daughter has been welcomed by her parents, freshened up, given and received news, arranged her personal effects, and participated in the setting of an entire scenography to wait for the son she has not seen for years. They don't call him; they wait until he himself comes. The young child spends all that time, hard to measure precisely, in the "very deep courtyard!" What happens there that keeps him so busy? Is it possible that his family leaves him on his own in that courtyard? Why does that seem normal? Photographs taken by Indira Restrepo show that "very large corridor" from two opposite angles (see figure 1), before the unfortunate "reconstruction" of the house when it was converted into a museum. In those photos one can clearly see the separation of the front and the back of the house, as if the corridor were a bridge that joined two separate universes. If in one of them the child finds his family, what attracts him and keeps him for such a long time—and apparently on a regular basis—in the other?

Two more memories of the adult that this young "master" became draw the cultural map of that house in the deep Caribbean that will answer our questions. One is from an interview in 1994:

> The house in Aracataca was full of Guajiro Indians, indigenous people from that ethnic group, not inhabitants of the department of La Guajira. They were different people, who brought to that house of Spaniards a way of thinking and a culture that the elders did not appreciate or believe. But I lived more at the level of the Indians, and they taught me history and shared with me their superstitions, ideas that I noticed that my grandmother didn't have.[2] (Cardona and Flórez 35; translation by Juan Fernando Merino and Jenny Petrow)

Another is recounted in his memoirs:

> Their [his maternal grandparents'] closest friends were, before anyone else, those who came from the Province [Padilla, in the south of La Guajira]. Their domestic language was the one their grandparents had brought from Spain across Venezuela in the previous century, revitalized by Caribbean localisms, the Africanisms of slaves, and fragments of the Guajiro language that filtered into ours, drop by drop. My grandmother would use it to conceal things from me, not realizing I understood it better than she did because of my direct dealings with the servants. I still remember

Figure 1. Photos of the house in Aracataca where García Márquez was born, prior to its "reconstruction" (and perhaps invention) for conversion to a museum-house. From two opposite angles are visible the long corridor connecting the front of the dwelling—where the bedrooms, the kitchen, the office, and the living room of the author's maternal family were located—to the large rear patio, where the Guajiro Indians lived and performed a variety of labors.
Source: Courtesy of Indira Restrepo.

many terms: *atunkeshi*, I'm sleepy; *jamusaitshitaya*, I'm hungry; *ipuwots*, the pregnant woman; *aríjuna*, the stranger, which my grandmother used in a certain sense to refer to the Spaniard, the white man, in short, the enemy.[3] (*Vivir para contarla* 64; emphasis added; translation by Juan Fernando Merino and Jenny Petrow)

"I lived more at the level of the Indians . . . my direct dealings with the servants . . . they taught me history and shared with me their superstitions." These are statements that suggest that the Guajiro Indians,[4] in that "very deep courtyard," had adopted from the beginning the *aríjuna* child born in that house, he whose intelligence and time in the world were to grow out of an extended family with parallel lexicons. Thus the boy received two ancestral memories: that of the Colombian criollo majority and that of an ancient Amerindian culture.[5] His childhood was so extraordinary because it was bilingual and bicultural; in that childhood were forged the gifts bestowed upon a child who, from his earliest memories, understood that reality is a narrative construction, that it is the word that creates the world, and that many worlds fit, side by side, within a single universe.

LITERARY FABLE AND AUTOBIOGRAPHICAL CHILDHOODS

In García Márquez's literary oeuvre the first mentions ever of Macondo, a place where criollos and Guajiro Indians coexist, occur in the short story "Monólogo de Isabel viendo llover en Macondo" ("Monologue of Isabel Watching It Rain in Macondo," 1955; initially published with the title "El invierno" [Winter] in 1952), and in the novella *La hojarasca* (*Leaf Storm*, 1955). In both narratives, the Guajiros are almost voiceless and are presented through the eyes of the criollos (it was an aristocratic gaze, as observed quite rightly by Vargas Llosa in *García Márquez*). It is not trivial that, in *Leaf Storm*, it is the voice of the Guajira woman Meme that invokes, in front of the young daughter of the colonel ("with an accent mixed with precision and vagueness, as if there was a lot of incredible legend in what she was recalling"; 24)[6] the memory of the family's migration from La Guajira to the banana-growing region:

> Their wild and burdensome cargo was everywhere; the trunks full of clothing of people who had died before they'd been on earth . . . and even a trunk filled with the images of saints, which they used to reconstruct their family altar everywhere they stopped. It was a strange carnival procession with horses and hens and the four Guajiro Indians [Meme's companions] who had grown up in the house and followed my parents all through the region like trained circus animals. (25)[7]

As biographers have remarked, this migration is more or less the same as that of the writer's maternal grandparents to Aracataca, where they arrived with Guajiro Indian servants, coming from the town of Barrancas, in the southern part of the department

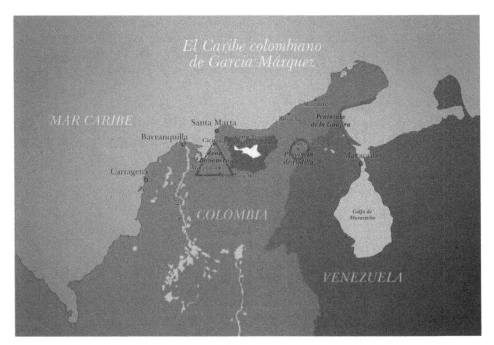

Map 1. Gabriel García Márquez's Caribbean Colombia
Source: Map by Juan Moreno.

of La Guajira (which coincides geographically with the "settlement of peaceful Indians" from *One Hundred Years of Solitude*), in the second decade of the twentieth century. The birth of their grandson Gabriel in 1927 thus took place in an environment where two cultures and two languages coexisted, as is the case in the house of the colonel in the novel. After the mother and grandfather, the third monologue that sustains this narrative is that of a young boy whose autobiographical features the writer would point out in an interview many years later. "That is an image of myself that is already in *La hojarasca*. . . . The image of the child sitting, scared to death, is indeed a recurring theme in my books . . . and it is an image that I remember perfectly from the house in Aracataca" (Castro Caycedo n.p.; translation by Juan Fernando Merino and Jenny Petrow).[8]

"I have not invented anything" is the answer García Márquez always gave when asked about the origin of his imagined worlds. Therefore, it should not be surprising that in the Buendías' novel-saga, which appeared twelve years later, we find again, in a house very similar to that of Aracataca, not only Guajiro Indians next to criollos but also bilingual *aríjuna* children, like the boy who went around the house as if he owned the place—as the writer describes himself in his childhood. In the third section of the novel, the Guajiro Indians are mentioned ten times, and in the first paragraph we read that "Arcadio and Amaranta came to speak the Guajiro language before Spanish" (*One Hundred Years of Solitude* 19).[9] There are multiple mentions of the Indians' ancestral territory, that is, the Guajira, where there occurred the remote event giving rise to the origin of the lineage "when the pirate Sir Francis Drake attacked Riohacha" (19) and whence, from a "settlement of peaceful Indians," the future founders of Macondo migrated. The Buendías and all the founders of the village are originally from La Guajira. Rebeca, the adoptive daughter who has arrived from Manaure, another locality in La Guajira, also speaks the language of the Indians, and other Buendías from later generations will also grow up next to the household servants and will speak their language. The first Buendía offspring "learned to drink lizard broth and eat spider eggs without Ursula's knowing it, for she was too busy with a promising business in candy animals" (19); meaning that the children were nourished by the food and spoken rituals of the Amerindian, in the Amerindian language, sitting during long stretches at the table in a space not frequented by the parents.

In *La increíble y triste historia de la cándida Eréndira y de su abuela desalmada* (*The Incredible and Sad Tale of Innocent Eréndira and Her Heartless Grandmother*), a novella that takes place in the desert of La Guajira, the young Ulises speaks with his Wayúu mother in Wayuunaiki, with his Dutch father in his tongue, and with Eréndira in the language of the criollo majority. In a house in colonial Cartagena de Indias, which is also divided into two cultural and linguistic universes, the young girl Sierva María de Todos los Ángeles, in the novel *Del amor y otros demonios* (*Of Love and Other Demons*, 1994), speaks the language of the Spanish Empire with her parents in the front part of the house, while in the slave yard she speaks various African languages. As metaphors of his childhood—and of his own writing—the children in the Garciamarquezian literary fable move about as they please through the organic cultural heterogeneity of the American continent.[10]

Wayúu Shamanic Logic and Supernatural Image in *One Hundred Years of Solitude*

The emphatic testimony leaves no doubt: "They were different people, who contributed a way of thinking and a culture to that house ... which the elders did not appreciate or believe" (quoted in Cardona and Flórez 35; translation by Juan Fernando Merino and Jenny Petrow), meaning that on a day-to-day basis, as a member of the Wayuunaiki language community, the future novelist—who appreciated the Wayúu company enough to spend much of his time in that courtyard and, being the child that he was, believed everything they told him—acquired a legacy in the form of a language of the world. With the language he received from his mother's family and that of the Wayúu, his personal reality merged with very deep memories that would feed his literary imagination. As Jorge Luis Borges once said about relating literature and memory: "We can also think of what the great Irish poet William Butler Yeats called the Great Memory, the idea that in each of us lives the memory of all of our ancestors. We are infinite. Therefore, the poet cannot stick only to his personal ideas and when he writes he receives this Great Memory" (n.p.; translation by Juan Fernando Merino and Jenny Petrow).[11] Thus, contrary to the usual ways of examining what links our writer's verbal creation has with the "national" culture and with the galaxies of written verbal creation, to understand in particular how the Wayúu world language would nourish his work, we are led toward a heuristic that abandons the presupposition of canonical interpretations. We undertake a perspectivist[12] approach to compare the very present supernatural image in the most famous novel by García Márquez with the hierophantic images of the Amerindian narrative tradition that nurtured the orality in his childhood at the home of his maternal grandparents in Aracataca.

All Amerindian societies are characterized by shamanic logic; this is the feature that defines their common ancestry: before being the West of the West, America was the East of the East, that is, the destiny of the various migratory vectors that arrived thousands of years ago from Asia or Oceania, continents inhabited without exception by cultures of shamanic logic. The anthropologist Michel Perrin, in one of his many works on Wayúu shamanism, explains how this logic works: "In oral societies, the world, let us remember, is divided into two spaces: this world and the world-other. . . . The 'sacred' or the 'supernatural' is characterized by the Guajiros as *pülashu*, as opposed to what they consider to be *anasü*, that is to say, banal, not dangerous, allowed" (*Les praticiens du rêve* 99–100; translation by Juan Fernando Merino and Jenny Petrow).[13] In the Wayúu cosmovision, the world is made up of two complementary orbs or hemispheres, one of them natural and the other supernatural, and the shaman—though not only he—is the one who interrelates them. The Wayúu language lives and recounts the world as an interrelation between the two orbs; the *pülashu* manifests itself in the *anasü* via the phenomenon that Mircea Eliade called hierophany (11). When narrating the world, every Wayúu story constructs a plot in which, while hierophany is occurring, the human being comes into contact with a cosmic dimension that suspends or subverts merely human historical time so as to bring into existence a time-other and articulates to the time of myths all realities built by the narration. In other words, the Wayúu integrate reality and unreality into their story of the world or, to go even further, for them there is no reality without unreality (the idea of a world of reality and nothing else would baffle them).

Let us look at three types of manifestations of the *pülashu* in the *anasü* as cataloged by Michel Perrin. First, the dead next to the living:

> The Guajiros have an extraordinary conception of death. . . . They have imagined a kind of life cycle that demonstrates that dying is not useless. When one dies one goes first to Hepira [home of the specters of the dead]. In that land of the dead the Wayúu meet again in the form of *Yoluhas*. Their souls follow them but return to the world in the dreams of the living to disturb them. The *Yoluhas* are also seen at night[14]. (Perrin, "Viajes de las almas" 21; translation by Juan Fernando Merino and Jenny Petrow)

Second, messages from the world-other while dreaming: "The Guajiros have the idea of a temporary time lag between this world and the world-other, which anticipates what will happen in this world. The dream predicts. Then the shamans or 'the good dreamers' will say what needs to be done so that the event announced by the dream does not reach us, is diverted"[15] (Perrin, "Entretien avec Michel Perrin" 29; translation by Juan

Fernando Merino and Jenny Petrow). Third, divination of the future: "The cultures which obey these logics have assumed that it is possible to have a two-way communication between this world and the other-world, which indirectly communicates with the first through special languages, such as those of divination"[16] (Perrin, *Les praticiens du rêve* 102; translation by Juan Fernando Merino and Jenny Petrow).

Let us now turn to the narrative art of our *aríjuna* child imbued with that logic, and with which, in his adulthood, he will profoundly alter the calm waters of Colombian literary tradition. In Jorge Isaacs's novel *María* (1867), Creole landowners live side by side with voiceless African slaves, who are happy in a happy Catholic Republic; in José Eustasio Rivera's *La Vorágine* (*The Vortex*, 1924), the alterity of the literate criollo is the American nature that ends up devouring him; and—if for a moment we imagine a quiet continuity—in *One Hundred Years of Solitude* we would read the history of a country in which a criollo family emigrates to its banana-growing region from a nondescript place, a family that arrives with Indian servants without a voice and where, throughout the generations, we witness an endless parade of civil wars, foreign domination, and the greed of a political elite—all so that in the "national" literary tradition, a naturalist-realistic language could carry on, uninterrupted: a criollo literature for criollos. But no, García Márquez could not offer a calm continuity to the criollo literary tradition. He does not belong solely to that social and economic majority resulting from interracial mixing, whose major cultural markers are those inherited from the empire that conquered and colonized the Latin American continent: namely, the Spanish language and religious fundamentalism. As with his autobiographical characters, he finds himself in a place where several languages of the world intertwine, and he could not write the literature associated with the white-Catholic religiosity (with its created and unmovable reality) and with the monological spirit of the "national" culture. From the beginning of his oeuvre, "The Third Resignation," a short story from 1947 in which a child is in transit from his first death to the second Wayúu death, all the way to his next-to-last novel, *Of Love and Other Demons*, in which a girl, like the Wayúu shaman, practices dreaming at will, the assault of *pülashu Wayúu* on a bland reality makes his literary art[17] the sounding board for the polyphony of languages that Latin American literature became during the twentieth century.

Let us now see how the intervention of *pülashu Wayúu* in its narrative makes *One Hundred Years of Solitude* become the novel that it is. In the first event of the timeline, the ancestor of Úrsula Iguarán flees from Riohacha to "a settlement of peaceful Indians" (where the great-granddaughter will meet José Arcadio Buendía) because Úrsula's great-grandmother believed that the pirates she dreamed of would come to torment her in her waking hours. Far from the sea, her Aragonese husband builds for her "a bedroom without windows so that the pirates of her dream would have no way to get in" (20).[18] For these characters, dreams predict or anticipate reality; the same logic operates in the founding of Macondo: the patriarch José Arcadio Buendía dreams of the village and founds it when he wakes up. Without this oneiromancy of undoubted Wayúu provenance that guides the actions of the characters, neither the birth of the Buendía lineage nor the foundation of Macondo would have taken place. A dead Prudencio Aguilar frightens the couple who had founded the lineage and forces them to migrate;

Melquíades returns from the dead to save the inhabitants of Macondo from the plague of insomnia. Without these dead people who are not *really* dead, but return to live next to the living, there would have been neither a founding caravan of Macondo nor an escape from the disease of oblivion; they are *Yoluhas*, specters of the first Wayúu death. A feature that differentiates the Aurelianos from the José Arcadios is that the former can foretell the future (the first Aureliano predicts that a pot of boiling broth will fall, and it does fall; that someone is about to arrive, and Rebeca arrives; that a woman who visits him in one of his war camps and has turned her back on him is getting ready to shoot him, and in effect, his anticipation disarms her). Pilar Ternera also predicts another attempt on Colonel Aureliano Buendía's life: "I don't know what it means, but the sign is very clear. Watch out for your mouth" (138).[19] However, the one who has the greatest mastery of the art of prediction is Melquíades, and if he had not known the destiny of the lineage, the novel would not have been written, for he is its narrator, in Sanskrit. His existential role model is more than evident: the Wayúu shaman who serves as a bridge between this world and the world-other (where knowledge of the future lies).[20]

Standing quite far from the language of the Colombian literary tradition, in this novel García Márquez found, after two decades of searching, the stylistic-verbal creation not only of the form of representation but also, above all, of the mode of transmission of the literary invention of the Colombian history that had been obsessing him. He had understood that he should dispense with the view and the way of thinking that confine themselves to a very normalized idea of the natural-real, and that he needed a stylistic rearrangement, a combinatorial art language in which the supernatural-unreal is not announced, does not stand out, and does not conform to the comparative intentionality with relation to the natural-real. We are forced to verify: no matter how much he would have looked to the oeuvre of the masters and the models of great literature, it was not there that he found the language that he had always known quite well: the Wayúu[21] narrative style that depicts the presence of the dead, the realization of dreams, and the divination of the future in the most natural way. Everything was in his Great Memory, in the Amerindian way of thinking and culture that, as a child, he had appreciated and believed in.

Writing the Criollo Destiny in Humboldt and Melquíades

It is well known that between the dictionary of the Royal Academy and that of María Moliner, our writer preferred the *Diccionario de uso del español* (Dictionary of Spanish Usage) compiled by Moliner. In fact, the semantic tone and accentuation that the latter gives to the entry for *estirpe* ("Family of someone who belongs to the nobility or is illustrious / Line of descent, ancestry, caste, lineage, race";[22] 1227) has a closer correspondence with the parodic-sarcastic intentionality of the cervantine narrative of *One Hundred Years of Solitude*, which consists of decentralizing the storytelling of the "national" and dethroning the criollo. Accordingly, from the simple status of family, the Buendías are elevated to that of a lineage, a lineage that represents the very high self-inventions of the Colombian ethnic-cultural majority. The intentionality of the narrative perspective can be emphasized by placing the writing of the novel, that is, the writing of Melquíades, in parallel with that of Humboldt, parodying it. Even though what Melquíades writes is an enigma, on one occasion the first Aureliano, "thought he understood something of what Melquíades was saying . . . the only thing that could be isolated in the rocky paragraphs was the insistent hammering on the word equinox, equinox, equinox, and the name of Alexander von Humboldt" (74). And at the end of the novel we learn that the manuscripts in Sanskrit written by the gypsy, much the same as Humboldt's writing in French, dealt with the destiny of the criollos in territories where, in the sky over the equator, the equinox takes place; yet in the case of Melquíades's writings they deal with a very different criollo destiny than the one foreseen by Humboldt.

In fact, we owe to Alexander von Humboldt the bird's-eye view that traces the border dividing the civilized and the uncivilized in the American territory; for him the criollos were the destiny of America and the Indians its anti-destiny. The Humboldtian view that classifies the population in a given space and establishes hierarchies among cultures would be an inspiration for the criollos who founded the Latin American nations, or at least the nation that eventually would become Colombia. It is as if the implementation of the criollo project of establishing a nation were the pragmatic dimension of Humboldt's texts[23]: they will design a "national" society where cultural alterity (mainly Amerindians and Latin Americans of African ancestry) is given a peripheral place or simply ignored. The national narrative considers that the "national" culture is, of course, the set of significant artifacts produced by that "we" that, through the written word, exercises political and economic power, whereas beyond the limits of civilization, culture does not exist. In the coherence of this framework, a literary tradition idealizes a "national" cultural subject defined by essentialities: Catholic, Spanish-speaking, literate property owners, heterosexual, but above all, "white." The meaning of the subjects of cultural alterity remains static: they are called savages, barbarians, primitives. The impermeable frontier that separates the civilized from the noncivilized moves in favor of the former; the civilized republic of the criollos is a machine that perpetuates the conquest and colonization.

In *One Hundred Years* the point of view and perspective expressed about the criollo and his role in the destiny of the continent are very different. Through the Melquíades's writing the reader perceives the vision of an author who does not write from the nation's criollo center but instead builds that center as an alterity. The contrasts between García Márquez and the Buendía characters of his novel-saga are considerable (which is why they are not entirely autobiographical). While in his literary imaginary he remained loyal to his legacies, the *aríjuna* children of Macondo do not remain loyal when they become adults. Another difference is that none of these characters can claim to have done something "in order to be loved more," which was the reason, as he explained so many times, the Colombian Nobel laureate crafted his literary oeuvre. On the contrary, these characters have not sought love. Colonel Aureliano Buendía is the father of children conceived but not intended; he is the only one who does not see the specter of his father, living in death while tied to the chestnut tree in the courtyard. The virgin Amaranta has experienced so much hatred that she has not had time to feel love. José Arcadio's death appears to be just retribution for his appropriation of the entire land of Macondo. The erotic attraction that Remedios the Beauty arouses is something that she herself has never experienced, and therefore her ascent to heaven is confirmation of her indifference to human love. Divided between Petra Cotes and Fernanda del Carpio, Aureliano Segundo behaves like a scared child who loves only the one who happens to be absent. It is only fitting that in this arid geography of affections the only member of the Buendía family conceived in love—albeit a love drowned in one's own blood—is also "the mythological animal that was to bring the line to an end."[24]

However, that does not mean that, in the geography of affections, love does not flourish in Macondo; it blooms, but outside of the lineage. Since the beginning, the Indians have accompanied the growth of the family and have nourished the children with their diet and their legacy; they are faithful. The Guajiro Cataure will return to Macondo—in spite of the fear of the insomnia plague—for the funeral of the founder, José Arcadio Buendía, whose death his arrival announces ("I have come for the exequies of the king"; 144).[25] Aureliano Amador has escaped—at least provisionally—from the extermination of the Buendías, marked with the indelible ash cross on his forehead because he received help: "[He] was lost in the labyrinth of the mountains, which he knew like the back of his hand thanks to the friendship he maintained with the Indians" (284).[26] There are also the living dead and their fidelity to human love: Prudencio Aguilar returns from the dead to visit the founder of the lineage because he "had ended up loving his worst enemy" (79);[27] Melquíades returns from death to again meet his friend in Macondo "because he could not stand the loneliness" (50).[28] Friendship, love, and loyalty, although they do not exist among the Buendías, do exist among the neighbors around them. With the increasing complexity of the geography of affections, the Garciamarquezian literary imaginary establishes in the Macondo metaphor of America an arc of the extended community beyond the narrow limits of criollo identity.

It is evident that to represent his Buendía creatures, the writer has gone overboard. They no longer see the community they were part of or the ties that link them to their own tradition from La Guajira, their genealogical and cultural background. Permanently afflicted by the plague of oblivion, the Buendía descendants have forgotten that as children their first language was that of the Indians; their longing for prestige has wreaked havoc with their memory. They are Caribbean and have sought to blend in with the threads that govern social time from the capital and with institutions such as political parties and the Catholic Church.[29] The second José Arcadio undertakes for his petty benefit the first agrarian reform of Macondo, and Arcadio validates it by registering in the official deed the nullification of collective land ownership; the first Aureliano will wage thirty-three wars on behalf of the Liberal Party to finally understand in his loneliness and old age that "the only difference . . . today between Liberals and Conservatives is that the Liberals go to mass at five o'clock and the Conservatives at eight" (248); however, many generations later, the father of the last Buendía will want to repeat the story with his newborn son: "We will name him Aureliano and he will win thirty-two wars" (417). Úrsula, who will be affected by a real and metaphorical blindness, forbids that the accordion—the main instrument of *vallenato* music—be played in the house, but she wants her great-granddaughter to become a clavichord virtuoso; Aureliano the Second brings from the highlands the most beautiful woman in the world but will have to replace her later on with Petra Cotes; and the great-grandson leaves for the seminary, where he will begin his career to become a pope, dressed in stifling and ridiculous clothes in the heat of the Caribbean. In other words, in addition to not knowing how to love, having forgotten their origins and being surrounded by loneliness, the storyteller from Aracataca overwhelms the Buendías with the unforgivable sin of inauthenticity. But the greatest tension between the Garcíamarquezian and the Humboldtian narratives is that in the Colombian novel, the lineage of cultural mimicry, affective self-isolation, loneliness, and oblivion perishes in the end and leaves the scene where American continuity is woven.

The fable of Macondo has not been written as a mimicry of colonialist narratives, the latter of which not only centered on a discourse of action, but also irradiated the reference to values that essentialized the singular meanings of a singular story. In this way, a landscape of an American world was built in which the alterities of the ethnic majority did not form part of "the" history or were included only as stragglers lagging behind on the road that led humanity toward the universal promotion of progress. There is a very different understanding of American historical experience in the Garciamarquezian literary imaginary: historical time is interrupted and altered by mythical time; the time of a dominant social group intersects with the time of another minority group. In that rainbow of temporalities—incompatible with the idea of a singular social time—the Promethean mythology of the Greco-Humboldtian lineage is pulverized: those who do not know human love and suffer from the plague of oblivion will deplete the time of historical experience.

The Conquest of a Language

"One of the most intense adventures of my life was the experience that you and I lived in San Francisco when, taking turns, we read aloud *One Hundred Years of Solitude*. That was not a mere reading experience, although it also was, in that way in which a book manages to become a hedonistic pleasure, a means of amusement, a poem. It was also the occasion when I could understand, thanks to this book, the way in which mysteries are understood, in bursts, during a moment of lucidity, what is the homeland, and the ancestral history of each one of us, because after all, the history of a nation is the history of each of its inhabitants. It was the only time in my life that I felt patriotism without any touch of sentimentality or shame" (Jaramillo Agudelo 55–56; translation by Juan Fernando Merino and Jenny Petrow).[30] These are words of the narrator of the novel *La muerte de Alec* (The Death of Alec), a reading experience that combines joy, poetry, collective memory, and autobiography, but above all, that depicts the encounter of the subjectivity of a Colombian reader with a startling and unique act of self-discovery. And if it is self-congratulatory, it is because the reader-narrator recognizes himself in this story that he has carried hidden within him and of which he was part, but that no one had previously known or been able to tell through using the words of the tribe. The character, an alter ego of Jaramillo, feels exposed, objectified, and at the same time subject to an emancipation, a liberation, an independence. At last, a narrative has woven together the threads of language and history in a voice that spoke from within the Great Memory to belie and definitively fissure the teleological and ethnocentric stories about his own universe.

After *One Hundred Years of Solitude*, neither Colombian literature nor Colombia would be the same. By discarding the point of view and perspective of the stories that are told from a supposed center, this literary narrative of a society's past revealed that it was different, compelled it to give of itself the authenticity of its meaning, and opened up new possibilities for the future. It is not that a truth was discovered; the truth is not found in what is recounted but rather in the framework and accentuation of the words that narrate. With his storytelling artistry, García Márquez gained a mastery of the language in such a way that he was able to remove the limitations of temporality and bring into existence those voices that colonialism had left in oblivion. It is perhaps the conquest of that language by our fabulist of Aracataca that is most admired by other writers, who, faithful to his legacy, in their novels are providing a narrative for the Great Memory of their respective worlds.

Note: Translated from the Spanish by Juan Fernando Merino and Jenny Petrow.

Notes

1. "¿Qué experimentó, siendo tan niño, el primer día que vio a su madre?" / "Lo que más recuerdo es el perfume, es un perfume que probablemente si lo siento ahora, lo reconozco. Nosotros vivíamos en Aracataca; mi madre se había ido con su marido, mi padre, a Barranquilla y la memoria más antigua que tengo en relación con ella es que me decían: 'Tu mamá vive en Barranquilla y tu papá vive en Barranquilla.' No había fotos, nada de eso. . . . Y yo tenía una imagen de ella, una imagen de ella que . . . " / "¿Y qué le explicaban? ¿Qué por qué vivían en otra parte?" / "No . . . a los niños no se les explican esas cosas. Era yo muy niño cuando ellos se fueron a Barranquilla . . . y de pronto empecé a oír: 'Que viene tu mamá, que va a venir tu mamá.' Y yo no me imaginaba cómo podía ser aquello ni tengo idea de qué edad podía tener . . . pero recuerdo es que yo *venía de . . . era una casa con un gran corredor y un patio muy profundo y yo venía* y me dijeron: 'Ya llegó tu mamá, está ahí.' Y yo entré y estaban en la sala, sentadas con las sillas pegadas a la pared muchas mujeres, y yo la vi y la reconocí enseguida y estaba vestida como los personajes de las películas de esos años . . . finales de los veinte, principios de los treinta . . . con el sombrero de campana . . . recuerdo exactamente su traje de seda con bordados color beige, el sombrero de paja del mismo color, y entonces ella me dijo: 'Ay', y me abrazó y yo sentí el olor" (Navarro n.p.).

2. "La casa de Aracataca estaba llena de guajiros –de indios de la Guajira, no de habitantes del departamento de la Guajira. Eran gente distinta, que aportaba un pensamiento y una

cultura a esa casa que era de españoles, y que los mayores no apreciaban ni creían. Pero yo vivía más a nivel de los indios, y ellos me contaban historia y me metían supersticiones, ideas que yo notaba que no tenía la abuela" (Cardona and Flórez 35).

3. "Sus amistades [las de los abuelos maternos] eran antes que nada las que llegaban de la provincia [la Provincia de Padilla, en el sur de la Guajira]. La lengua doméstica era la que sus abuelos habían traído de España a través de Venezuela en el siglo anterior, revitalizada con localismos caribes, africanismos de esclavos y retazos de la lengua guajira, que se iban filtrando gota a gota en la nuestra. La abuela se servía de ella para despistarme sin saber que yo la entendía mejor por mis tratos directos con la servidumbre. Aún recuerdo muchos: *atunkechi*, tengo sueño; *jamusaitshi taya*, tengo hambre; *ipuwots*, la mujer en cinta; *aríjuna*, el forastero, que mi abuela usaba en cierto modo para referirse al español, al hombre blanco y en fin de cuentas al enemigo" (*Vivir para contarla* 81–82).

4. This is how the criollo majority refers to the Wayúu, an Amerindian society that speaks Wayuunaiki, a language of the Arawak linguistic family, whose ancestral territory is located east of the banana-growing region, on the Guajira peninsula, between Colombia and Venezuela. For the contexts, the regional juncture, and the migratory vectors that explain the presence of Wayúu Indians in that house, see Moreno Blanco, "Migración y contacto transculturizador Wayúu."

5. Silvia Galvis's book of interviews with almost all the Nobel Laureate's brothers, *Los García Márquez*, provides testimonies about the Wayúu influence on the other children of that family who periodically spent some time in that house. In it, she cites Eligio García Márquez, the youngest of the brothers: "Regarding superstitions in the family, Jaime has his own theory: he says that it is based on Guajiro Indian culture, which has a Wayúu origin, and that must be true, because I am very, very superstitious, and I think that all of us, in that sense, are the same, including Gabito" (256). In the house-museum of Aracataca, in the large courtyard next to the enormous tree, is the room where the Wayúu servants slept. Aída García Márquez, sister of the novelist, included in her own book a photograph of "The room of the Guajiros" (*Gabito* 86). When in 1997 Dasso Saldívar presented his biography in the city of Cali, I asked him why he had not included that room in the patio in the plan of the house (annex 13), and he replied that he had forgotten it.

6. "Con un acento mezclado de precisión y vaguedad, como si hubiera mucho de increíble leyenda en lo que recordaba" (García Márquez, *La hojarasca* 52).

7. "A todas partes llevaron su extravagante y engorroso cargamento; los baúles llenos con la ropa de los muertos anteriores al nacimiento de ellos mismos . . . y hasta el baúl lleno de santos con los que reconstruían el altar doméstico en cada lugar que visitaban. Era una curiosa farándula con caballos y gallinas y los cuatro guajiros (compañeros de Meme) que habían crecido en casa y seguían a mis padres por toda la región, como animales amaestrados en un circo" (*La hojarasca* 53).

8. "Esa es una imagen de mí mismo que está ya en *La hojarasca* . . . la imagen del niño sentado, muerto de miedo es efectivamente un tema recurrente en mis libros . . . y es una imagen que yo recuerdo perfectamente en la casa de Aracataca" (Castro Caycedo n.p.)

9. "Arcadio y Amaranta hablaron la lengua guajira antes que el castellano" (*Cien años de soledad* 53).

10. Although in reality, the first bilingual and bicultural child is Isabel's son, who offers the third monologue in *La hojarasca*, because according to the colonel, "los cuatro guajiros . . . se han criado en mi casa." In turn, regarding the doctor and the guajira Meme, Isabel says, "ambos compartían la casa de mi padre, ella como hija de crianza y él como

huésped permanente," which implies that the guajiros have lived, since their childhood, in the colonel's house; that is, they were there before the grandson was born. Therefore, having grown up between two cultures he is, in fact, beyond what the writer declares, the first character in all his work that has autobiographical cultural belongings.

11. "On peut penser aussi à ce que le grand poète irlandais William Butler Yeats appelait la great memory, l'idée que dans chacun de nous vit la mémoire de tous nos ancêtres. Nous sommes donc infinis. Donc le poète ne peut pas s'en tenir à ses idées personnelles; il reçoit quand il écrit cette grande mémoire" (Borges n.p.).

12. Perhaps the first to carry out this type of exercise was the anthropologist Jean-Guy Goulet in one of his works on the Wayúu: "[I]t is said about the Jinnu, Ipuana, Uliana de Aliu [wayúu clans] that they have their homeland in another part of the peninsula [Guajira peninsula]. In a dialogue in the novel *One Hundred Years of Solitude* by Gabriel García Márquez a couple expresses a concept of homeland analogous to the Guajiro concept discussed here. García Márquez's heroine, Úrsula, opposes her husband José Arcadio who wants to move from their place of residence. Úrsula says, 'we won't leave. We will not leave.... We will stay here, because we have had a son here'. José Arcadio Buendía: 'We have still not had a death, he said. A person does not belong to a place until there is someone dead under the ground.' Therefore, the Epieyu of Aliu who did not have a cemetery and had not buried the remains of any of their uterine relatives are without a homeland in the Guajiro sense of the word" (Goulet 59).

13. "Le 'sacré' ou le 'surnaturel' est pour les Guajiro tout ce qu'ils qualifient de pülashü, par opposition à ce qu'ils considèrent comme anasü, c'est-à-dire banal, non dangereux, permis" (Perrin, *Les praticiens du rêve* 99–100).

14. "Los guajiros tienen una extraordinaria concepción de la muerte.... Han imaginado una suerte de ciclo vital que demuestra que morir no es inútil. Cuando uno muere va primero a Hepira [lugar de residencia de los espectros de los muertos]. En esa tierra de muertos los wayúu se reencuentran bajo la forma de *Yoluhas*. Sus almas los siguen pero vuelven al mundo en los sueños de los vivos a inquietarlos. También se ve a los *Yoluhas* en la noche" (Perrin, "Viajes de las almas" 21).

15. "Les Guajiros ont l'idée d'un décalage temporel entre ce monde-ci et le monde-autre, lequel anticipe ce qui se passera dans ce monde-ci. Le rêve prédit. Alors des chamanes ou des 'bons rêveurs' diront ce qu'il faut faire pour que l'événement annoncé par le rêve ne nous atteigne pas, soit dévié" (Perrin, "Entretien avec Michel Perrin" 29).

16. "Les cultures qui obéissant à ces logiques ont supposé possible une communication à double sens entre ce monde-ci et le monde-autre, lequel communique indirectement avec le premier par le biais de langages spéciaux, tels ceux des divinations" (Perrin, *Les praticiens du rêve* 102).

17. Concerning the semantic effectiveness of the *pülashu Wayúu* in the poetic narrative of García Márquez, see Moreno Blanco, "*Transculturación narrativa*."

18. "Un dormitorio sin ventanas para que no tuvieran por donde entrar los piratas de sus sueños" (*One Hundred Years of Solitude* 32).

19. "No sé lo que quiere decir, pero la señal es muy clara: cuídate la boca" (166).

20. Critic Stephan Minta envisioned this trait of the character in one of his works on García Márquez: "Melquíades, too, is a kind of eternal priest-king. He has many of the attributes of a shaman, the traditional priest-doctor among the American Indians: shamans are preeminent in their knowledge of myths and of the meaning of myths; they are able to maintain close contact with the world of spirits, to travel to the spirit world, and to return with

their knowledge enhanced; they have the power of bilocation, enabling them to be seen simultaneously in different places; they have skill in divination, in poetry, and in magical medicine, and, in general, they serve as the repository of a wisdom beyond ordinary people's power to attain" (151). Because we focus primarily on *One Hundred Years of Solitude*, we do not address here the shamanic attributes of other characters in his short stories; with respect to this, see Guerra Overton.
21. This language distinctive of the Wayúu thought and culture can be seen in the stories included in Michel Perrin's first book devoted to this Amerindian society: *The Way of The Dead Indians*. It can also be found in the books of traditional Wayúu stories published by the bilingual Wayúu writer Miguel Ángel Jusayú (see Works Cited).
22. "Familia de alguien cuando pertenece a la nobleza o es ilustre / Abolengo, alcurnia, casta, linaje, raza" (Moliner 1227).
23. I was inspired by Edward Said, for whom Western imperialist domination over the countries of the East is the pragmatics of orientalist texts. On Humboldt's civilizing narrative and its relationship to the story of the Colombian nation in the nineteenth century, see Moreno Blanco, "Del *Viaje a las regiones equinocciales*."
24. "El animal mitológico que había de poner fin a la estirpe" (*One Hundred Years of Solitude* 484).
25. "He venido al sepelio del rey" (172).
26. "Se perdió en los laberintos de la sierra que conocía palmo a palmo gracias a la amistad de los indios" (284).
27. "Había terminado por querer al peor de sus enemigos" (100).
28. "Porque no pudo soportar la soledad" (100).
29. "La única diferencia . . . entre liberales y conservadores es que los liberales van a misa de siete y los conservadores van a misa de ocho" (287).
30. "Una de las más intensas aventuras de mi vida fue la experiencia que vivimos tú y yo en San Francisco cuando, turnándonos, leímos en voz alta *Cien años de soledad*. No fue aquella una simple experiencia de lector, aunque también lo fue, de ese modo en que un libro logra convertirse en placer hedonista, en una diversión, en un poema. Fue también la ocasión en que yo pude entender, gracias a este libro, de esta manera como se entienden los misterios, a ráfagas, por un momento de lucidez, lo que es la patria, y la historia ancestral de cada uno de nosotros, pues al fin y al cabo, la historia de una nación es la historia de cada uno de sus habitantes. Ha sido la única vez en mi vida que sentí patriotismo sin ningún toque de sentimentalismo o de vergüenza" (Jaramillo Agudelo 55–56).

Works Cited

Borges, Jorge Luis. *La création poétique selon BORGES*. Collège de France, 1983, www.youtube.com/watch?v=AJdFLGec_h8&t=379s. Accessed 4 Dec. 2019.

Cardona, Mateo, and Miguel Flórez. "La edad de las palabras." *Gaceta*, no. 22, 1994, pp. 34–38.

Castro Caycedo, Germán. *Gabriel García Márquez con RTI y Germán Castro Caycedo*. RTI, 1976. www.youtube.com/watch?v=F2_ga0730J0&t=7s. Accessed 4 Dec. 2019.

Eliade, Mircea. *The Sacred and the Profane*. Translated by Willard R. Trask, Harcourt Brace Jovanovich, 1987.

Fals Borda, Orlando. *Historia doble de la costa*, vols. I and II. Carlos Valencia, 1979, 1980.

Galvis, Silvia. *Los García Márquez*. Arango-Peisa, 1996.

García Márquez, Aída. *Gabito, el niño que soñó a Macondo*. Ediciones B, 2013.
García Márquez, Gabriel. *Cien años de soledad* (1967). Norma, 1996.
García Márquez, Gabriel. *Del amor y otros demonios* (1994). Norma, 2008.
García Márquez, Gabriel. *La hojarasca* (1955). Norma, 2003.
García Márquez, Gabriel. *Leaf Storm and Other Stories*. Translated by Gregory Rabassa, Harper & Row, 1972.
García Márquez, Gabriel. *Living to Tell the Tale*. Translated by Edith Grossman, Knopf, 2003.
García Márquez, Gabriel. *One Hundred Years of Solitude*. Translated by Gregory Rabassa, Penguin, 1973.
García Márquez, Gabriel. *Vivir para contarla*. Norma, 2002.
Goulet, Jean-Guy. "El universo social y religioso guajiro." *Revista Montalbán*, no 11, 1981, pp. 3–458.
Guerra Overton, James. *El chamanismo y la perspectiva chamánica en el análisis de la obra magicorrealista: Estudio aplicado a dos cuentos de García Márquez*. U of Michigan, PhD dissertation, 1994.
Jaramillo Agudelo, Darío. *La muerte de Alec* (1983). Alfaguara, 1999.
Jusayú, Miguel Ángel. *Achi'ki. Relatos guajiros*. Universidad Católica Andrés Bello, 1986.
Jusayú, Miguel Ángel. *Aquí están mis relatos: Anu Taku'jalairrua*. Carbones de Zulia, 1995.
Jusayú, Miguel Ángel. *Autobiografía*. Dirección de Cultura de la Universidad de Zulia, 1993.
Jusayú, Miguel Ángel. *Wané Takü'jalayaasa*. Universidad Nacional Experimental Rafael María Baralt, 1992.
Martin, Gerald. *Gabriel García Márquez: A Life*. Bloomsbury, 2008.
Minta, Stephan. *García Márquez: Writer of Colombia*. Harper & Row, 1987.
Moliner, María. *Diccionario de uso del español*. Gredos, 2002.
Moreno Blanco, Juan. "Del *Viaje a las regiones equinocciales* . . . de Alexander de Humboldt al atlas de las narrativas civilizatorias en la nación colombiana." *La nación imaginada: Ensayos sobre los proyectos de nación en Colombia y América Latina en el siglo XIX*, edited by H. Quiceno, Universidad del Valle, 2015, pp. 295–320.
Moreno Blanco, Juan. "Migración y contacto transculturizador Wayúu en la Aracataca de Gabriel García Márquez." *Diálogos latinoamericanos Journal*, no. 5, 2002, pp. 24–39.
Moreno Blanco, Juan. *Transculturación narrativa: La clave wayúu en Gabriel García Márquez*. Universidad del Valle, 2015.
Navarro, Ana. *Entrevista a Gabriel García Márquez*. TVE, 1995. www.youtube.com/watch?v=2FW4K2Npjlg&t=132s. Accessed 4 Dec. 2019.
Perrin, Michel. "Entretien avec Michel Perrin, Enthnologue." *Revue Synapse*, no. 92, 1993, pp. 25–38.
Perrin, Michel. *Les praticiens du rêve: Un exemple de chamanisme*. Presses Universitaires de France, 1992.
Perrin, Michel. "Viajes de las almas, prácticas del sueño. Entrevista con Michel Perrin." *Juan Moreno Blanco, Huellas Journal*, no. 41, 1994, pp. 19–27.
Perrin, Michel. *The Way of the Dead Indians: Guajiro Myths and Symbols*. Translated by Michael Fineberg in collaboration with the author, U of Texas P, 1987.
Said, Edward. *Orientalism*. Routledge & Kegan Paul, 1978.
Saldívar, Dasso. *García Márquez: El viaje a la semilla; La biografía*. Santillana, 1997.
Vargas Llosa, Mario. *García Márquez: Historia de un deicidio*. Barral, 1971.

CHAPTER 10

THE POWER OF WOMEN IN GABRIEL GARCÍA MÁRQUEZ'S WORLD

NADIA CELIS-SALGADO

The Paradox of Women's Power

A palette of vibrant and resilient female characters populates García Márquez's world. His heroines are the material and spiritual axes of families and communities, the survival of which depends as much on women's most ordinary skills as on the supernatural expressions of their strength, fecundity, and knowledge. Yet echoing the tensions surrounding women and women's power in Caribbean and Latin American cultures, most of García Márquez's protagonists are primarily defined by their roles in the lives of the men they are intimately linked to. The surrendering of self-determination on behalf of love is the precondition of the limited influence that even the most powerful of García Márquez's female characters exert over others.

García Márquez's narrative voices are known for their irreverence toward the political institutions and the moral grounds of hegemonic power. This irreverence does not extend to a demystification of the privileges men hold over women. Traditional gender hierarchies that equate masculinity with active sexuality, instinctive aggressiveness, intellectual pursuits, and public authority, while reducing femininity to caretaking and domestic roles, are a naturalized feature of García Marquez's world. Paradoxically, the indomitable character of his female roles is also a distinctive feature of his narrative. García Márquez's women are not naturally submissive or happily compliant. In his depiction of women's attempts to break from patriarchal expectations of femininity, García Márquez's world betrays the contradictions inherent to gender and power in Caribbean and Latin American cultures.

The tensions elicited by the requirement to comply with patriarchal gender roles are central to García Márquez's major works, both to those more obviously concerned with social power, such as *One Hundred Years of Solitude* (1967) and *The Autumn of the Patriarch* (1975), and to those openly devoted to love, namely *Love in the Time of Cholera* (1985) and *Of Love and Other Demons* (1994). In this chapter I document major trends in these novels' portrayals of gender, sexuality, and love, as a means to examine the extent of women's power in García Márquez's world. In light of gender studies in the Caribbean, I explore the female characters' strategies to assert autonomy, agency, and influence on others, with an emphasis on their intimate relations, rendered both as the setting for women's resistance and as the preferred means to co-opt women's power. I argue that although women's capacity to perform the affective and erotic care that allows humans to exist and to become subjects—in a word, the power of love—is the force that sustains García Márquez's universe, at the same time sexual and affective relations in his works play the role of securing the supremacy of men. By studying affective and sexual relations in García Márquez's fiction, this article ultimately documents the intimate anchors of social and political power.

García Márquez's spectrum of daughters, wives, mothers, mistresses, and prostitutes rests heavily on the patriarchal classification of women, which cements their value on the degree of access to their sexuality and on their utility in men's exchanges for social recognition and capital. As Luce Irigaray establishes in her Marxist critique of patriarchy, becoming a "normal woman" within the patriarchal sexual economy requires that women's bodies be transformed into objects carrying men's values in a social relation among men that enables the circulation of power (171). Women are valuable commodities, yet they are not expected to participate as subjects or to choose their value in men's exchanges (169). While the latent sexuality of the virgin makes the bodies of younger women desired as "pure exchange value," once those bodies are secured for motherhood, they cease to be interchangeable and publicly desirable. Meanwhile, non-marriageable women, often identified with "lower" classes or races, are primarily valued for their availability for sexual consumption. Women are persuaded to comply with the transformation of their bodies into objects because both the fulfillment of their sexual drives and their social existence continue to depend on their relationships with men. A complex hierarchy of women, and men, emerges from those relationships.

As Irigaray remarks, in none of their assigned positions are women expected to exercise the right to pleasure. The double standard that anchors males' privilege to receive self-fulfillment and public authority through sex and love prevails in Macondo and beyond. Regardless of the female characters' willingness to enter into men's homosocial transactions, sexual encounters tend to result in a denigration of women, whose resilience in the face of men's impetuous drives accentuates the enjoyment and the virility of their partners. Women perform, in the intimate realm, the care and sexual labor that allow men to venture into public domination. When seduction or social pressures fail to secure the rendering of those services by women, violence comes readily to secure compliance with gender roles and to ratify men's privilege to dominate sexually, affectively, and socially. Women's access to power in García Márquez's work is by default mediated by their ability to negotiate autonomy and social influence through intimate relationships.

Competing notions of power that surface in García Márquez's work contribute to the paradoxical depiction of the power of women. Women's ability to influence others in the private realm is celebrated, and the public exercise of such power is tolerated, provided that women surrender control of their destinies and subordinate their agency to the needs of their partners and children. Centering on the last of the Buendía women, the first section of this article illustrates the predicaments of women's power in Macondo. I discuss the revered matriarchs of *One Hundred Years of Solitude*, Úrsula Buendía and Pilar Ternera, in light of Amaranta Úrsula's synthesis of their legacy. Despite the madonna-whore dichotomy they embody, both Úrsula and Pilar are self-effacing mothers praised for the use of their prodigious strength in the service of the Buendía clan. Úrsula's dominion as the head of her household and a business owner still does not entitle her to men's ubiquitous privilege to assert themselves via the control of others. While the sympathetic deployment of Pilar Ternera, among other mistresses, may be mistaken as a defense of women's sexual freedom, these women do not escape the devaluation of their bodies. Sexual workers further emphasize the disposability of sexually available women, as well as the naturalization of this condition despite the poverty, marginalization, and sexual violence that make it possible. Next to the faithful wives and mothers, the mistresses and prostitutes provide the affective and sexual care, as well as the tutelage that enables men to extend their domination from the intimate into the public realm.

At the same time, the sympathetic deployment of the "joyful" sexuality of the "other" women does not extend to women in the middle and upper classes. García Márquez's novels are full of stubborn young women whose reluctance to compromise their self-determination is key to the development of these novels' plots. That is the case for the Buendía daughters in *One Hundred Years of Solitude*, Ángela Vicario in *Chronicle of a Death Foretold* (1981), Fermina Daza in *Love in the Time of Cholera*, and the ferocious Sierva María in *Of Love and Other Demons*. Their thirst for freedom is revealed by a variety of symptoms, from their refusal to comply with the incest and virginity taboos to their rejection of marriage. As I illustrate in the second section, women's self-determination is privately discouraged and publicly punished in Macondo and beyond. The interplay of sexual violence and the promises of ideal love are key to understanding the ultimate defeat of most of the young women's ambitions.

Other powerful women in García Márquez's world further illustrate, by contrast, the centrality of the control of women's sexuality in the circulation of hegemonic power. In the third section I focus on Leticia Nazareno, the wife of the decadent dictator in *The Autumn of the Patriarch*, and Bernarda Cabrera, the venomous mother of Sierva María in *Of Love and Other Demons*, as samples of the terrible matriarchs who capitalize on their intimate connections to pursue public control over others. The deformation of these female characters' bodies, rendered as savage and disgusting, speaks of the corrosive condition that the author attributes to the pursuit of power by women. Moreover, neither the good nor the bad "matriarchs" dare to question the privileges of men, and none of these powerful women enjoy autonomy. In the fourth section of this essay, I examine the possible exceptions to this rule, delving into two characters who rebel in their inability to surrender to the traps of love: Fermina Daza, in *Love in the Time of Cholera*, and the mythical Remedios the Beauty.

The Power of Mothers' Love

In the penultimate chapter of *One Hundred Years of Solitude*, Aureliano Babilonia cries in the lap of Pilar Ternera, who promptly infers the source of his tears and asks who the object of his love is:

> When Aureliano told her she let out a deep laugh, the old expansive laugh that ended up as a cooing of doves. There was no mystery in the heart of a Buendía that was impenetrable for her because a century of cards and experience had taught her that the history of the family was a machine with unavoidable repetitions, a turning wheel that would have gone spilling into eternity were it not for the progressive and irremediable wearing of the axle. (402)[1]

The deteriorated axle that can no longer delay the family's destruction is the female side of the lineage, whose ideal embodiment is Úrsula Iguarán. The women of Macondo are the unyielding source that allows the Buendías to survive over a century of rumbling solipsism and cyclical violence. The patriarchal classification of women works to secure their compliance with that role, placing below Úrsula the virgin Buendía daughters and the legitimate wives of the Buendía men, followed by their mistresses, Pilar and Petra Cotes, and by the many anonymous bodies that contribute to the assertion of the Buendía men's ability to rule Macondo. In spite of the apparent naturalization of women's subordination, the novel also betrays the intimate battles that the surrendering of their strengths on behalf of gender hierarchies presents to these women.

The rise and decline of Úrsula's influence on her family is emblematic of the tensions surrounding women's power in García Márquez's world. Úrsula is certainly far more than the ideal mother or the moral compass of Macondo. Beyond the supernatural strength that keeps her alive over 120 years, she is the provider in her household, the first entrepreneur of the village, and the herald of Macondo's modernization. While immersed in her frenetic business career, Úrsula even delegates the raising of children to several substitute mothers. Mimicking the contradictions surrounding women's power in Caribbean societies, Úrsula is both the steward of patriarchal values and the embodiment of its fallacies. Úrsula challenges male monopoly of power privately and publicly, yet she is a fervent defender of the privileges of her men, and she fails to conceive any path for her daughters other than her own self-effacing fate. The precariousness of Úrsula's power is further illustrated by her descendants' disregard for the aging matriarch, the dramatic shrinking of her body that precedes her death, and the rapid erasure of her memory that follows it. Unsurprisingly, most of the young Buendía women refuse to replicate her model.[2]

"Active, small, and indomitable like Úrsula," Amaranta Úrsula, the source of Aureliano Babilonia's tears, is the first to inherit both Úrsula's extraordinary strength and her devotion to the house. Her return from Europe is a turn of events that amuses even the novel's imperturbable narrator: "[I]t was incomprehensible why a woman with that spirit would have returned to a dead town burdened by dust and heat, and much less with a husband . . . who loved her so much that he let himself be led around by her on a silk" (384).³ The great-great-granddaughter's return resembles Úrsula's own as a young mother, when after a five-month disappearance she came back to open the route that would bring capitalism, the state, and the United Fruit Company to Macondo.

Yet as her name suggests, Amaranta Úrsula is not only Úrsula's descendant but that of her grand-aunt Amaranta, whose legacy includes her public resistance to marriage and a secret rebellion against the suppression of women's erotic drives. While Úrsula has been the adamant antagonist of incest, Amaranta has been its priestess, the one nurturing in the Buendía men a desire for the family women. Unlike Amaranta, and unlike her sister Meme, who has paid with a life of confinement for her out-of-wedlock affair, Amaranta Úrsula manages to enact her passion within marriage. Her open defiance of patriarchal hierarchies is complemented by the explosive erotic life she enjoys with her European husband. However, reenacting the story of her other grand-aunt, Rebeca, Amaranta Úrsula will eventually withdraw her love from Gastón, a man who has shown no desire to control her, to surrender to her hypermasculine relative's will.

Beyond the antagonistic forces embodied by her name, Amaranta Úrsula bears the dilemmas of all the Buendía women. She is also the great-granddaughter of Pilar Ternera, the unsung matriarch, whose passionate blood runs through six generations of Buendías. But not even the incarnation of the power of the archetypical mothers of humanity, Eve and Mary, could defeat the Buendías' rush into destruction. García Márquez's women may resemble goddesses, but they lack the power to preserve themselves from their love for men and from their men's love affair with power. In fact, women's power is instrumental to the completion of the self-destructive itinerary prophesized by Melquíades for the Buendía line. Úrsula has vanished just in time to free the young Amaranta Úrsula and her nephew from the memories of the ancestor engendered by incest that had terrorized generations of Buendías. Similarly, Pilar Ternera lives just long enough to mobilize Aureliano Babilonia's willingness to possess Amaranta Úrsula. Prompted to console his tears, Pilar announces, "Wherever she is right now. . . . She is waiting for you" (402).⁴

Pilar's words are the last of her interventions on behalf of the Buendía lineage. Both as the willing mistress and the other mother, Pilar has enabled the extension of the family, by giving birth to Úrsula's grandchildren, Arcadio and Aureliano José, and by mediating their descendants' access to other sexual partners. Complementing Úrsula's domestic reign, Pilar is at the top of the women whose bodies facilitate the satisfaction of the Buendías' sexual needs and their training in sexual domination, while preserving the women of the house from the urges of their relatives and their own.

The myth of the joyful and open eroticism of Caribbean men and women resonates in Pilar's expansive laughter. The lighthearted tone that characterizes García Marquez's depiction of sexual labor may be partly explained in the documented history of transactional sexuality in Caribbean societies. As Kemala Kempadoo illustrates in *Sun, Sex and Gold: Tourism and Sex Work in the Caribbean*, from the times of slavery, sexual transactions have been a common and tolerated realm of negotiation of material conditions, personal autonomy, and social power in the Caribbean, predominantly for women racialized under colonial hierarchies and their legacies. However, just as in Caribbean societies, the "normality" that García Márquez's narrator assigns to these women's sexual availability does not save them from marginalization or grant them control over their own bodies or pleasure. In the case of Pilar, it is Úrsula herself who, enacting her moral superiority, excludes Pilar from the house and erases her from the memory of her descendants.

Next to Pilar, Petra Cotes, the emblematic mulatto lover, and Nigromanta, the daughter of a black Antillean migrant, among other racialized women, perform the complementing roles that allow the Buendía men to extend their dominion. Aureliano Segundo's absurd opulence is built on Petra Cotes's supernatural influence on the fertility of animals. Echoing a history of free labor by African descendants in the Caribbean, Petra continues to work to maintain the family, among them Fernanda del Carpio, the white, legal wife of her lover, even after all but one of the animals engendered by her magic have perished. Pilar and Petra, in their role as mistresses, as well as Nigromanta and the many workers of Macondo's brothels, exemplify the decisive role of sexual labor in the constitution of gender roles. As Jacqui Alexander discusses in her critique of prostitution in Caribbean countries, the "anomalous" sexuality of sexual workers has defined, by contrast, the borders of respectability that entitle good women and men to the rights of citizenship ("Not Just Any [Body]" 7). García Márquez's characters also point to the economic grounds of the co-optation of women's "erotic autonomy" critiqued by Alexander ("Erotic Autonomy" 85–88).

Pilar's words to Aureliano Babilonia bring to an end the battle between the subjugation of desire to the demands of respectability and patrimony and the apparent liberation of such desire, embodied by the two matriarchs. But neither the battle nor its conclusion defies the patriarchal sexual economy that governs García Márquez's world. The resilience attributed to the matriarchs, as much as the "freedom" celebrated in Macondo's lovers and prostitutes, obscures the fact that these women's power is limited to the selfless authority they put in the service of "their" men. Most importantly, the narrative obscures the means that secure the surrendering of these women's will to the patriarchal sexual economy. Both Pilar, as the fourteen-year-old victim of an older man, and Úrsula, as a young wife refusing to have intercourse with her cousin, have been initiated into sex, love, and masculine domination by sexual violence.

Between Violence and Love

By the time the once secluded Aureliano Babilonia confesses his love for his aunt, he has received—assisted by his group of irreverent friends, and in the sheltered Eden of the brothels—an expedited introduction to patriarchal masculinity. He is now ready to stop crying and run back to possess Amaranta Úrsula. The "waiting" announced by Pilar is far from literal. What begins as a "fierce fight" turns into a "savage and ceremonious battle," until Amaranta Úrsula, "suddenly, almost playfully ... dropped her defense, and when she tried to recover, frightened by what she herself had made possible, it was too late" (365).[5] The encounter that finally enables the incest is a rape. Just as José Arcadio Buendía, after killing Prudencio Aguilar, possessed Úrsula against her will to erase the shadow of his rival's questioning of his masculinity, Aureliano Babilonia is now ready to enact the violence that will seize Amaranta Úrsula from her husband. The patriarchal equation of sexuality with domination, sexual violence, and the projections of male fantasies on women's eroticism justifying such violence are all commonplace in García Márquez's work. Another persistent trend is the assignment of responsibility for the violence to the victim. The quoted scene reproduces also the classic "rape myth" prevalent among García Márquez's works. As in the emblematic case of Leona Cassiani in *Love in the Time of Cholera,* violence is concealed by the attribution of pleasure to the victim and further effaced by the conversion of her feelings for the rapist into "love."

The allegedly "only real love" of the Buendía line accentuates the solitude of both the men and the women of Macondo:

> Although Aureliano was as ferocious a lover as his rival, it was Amaranta Úrsula who ruled in that paradise of disaster with her mad genius and her lyrical voracity, it was as if she had concentrated in love the unconquerable energy that her great-great-grandmother had given to the making of candy animals. And yet, while she was singing with pleasure and dying with laughter over her own inventions, Aureliano was becoming more and more absorbed and silent, for his passion was self-centered and burning. (*One Hundred Years* 411)[6]

Amaranta Úrsula's erotic power is the last expression of women's role in *One Hundred Years* as the axle that allows life to prevail, yet as with Úrsula's or Pilar's power, Amaranta Úrsula's willpower is not only insufficient against the line's self-destructive journey, but is also instrumental to its completion. Amaranta Úrsula, whose "passionate blood was insensible to any artifice that did not come from love" surrenders to a bleeding caused by childbirth in the face of her lover's abandonment of hope in saving her (418).[7] Aureliano Babilonia leaves the house to cry in the arms of his black lover long enough for the ants to claim the body of the baby. Withholding love and embracing solitude allow Aureliano to reassert the intellectual power that is the ultimate dominion of the Buendía men. Meanwhile, Amaranta Úrsula's solitary end speaks of the greatest predicament faced by García Márquez's women. In Macondo, and all through his world, love is both the fundamental source of, and the fundamental threat to, the power of women.

The contradictory expectations that love poses for men and women in patriarchal societies are invoked in García Márquez's work in order to justify the privileges that male protagonists exercise on "their" women and to grant women's willing concession of their autonomy to male authority. The typical "love" arrangement portrays men "conquering" women's will through various forms of seduction. As is suggested by the most emblematic of his love stories, *Love in the Time of Cholera*, access to the love object may be delayed, but the usual outcome still consists of the surrendering of women to men's desire to possess them. At the core of this depiction of intimacy there is a hierarchical classification of gendered identities that reduces women to passivity and upholds men as the active subjects both in the intimate and in the social scene. Even more, the sustained affair with power of García Márquez's male characters reveals an androcentric and solipsistic understanding of subjectivity, expressed emblematically in the Buendías' solitude. In her critique of the psychoanalytic narrative of self-development, Jessica Benjamin frames this predicament. The idealization of separation and the denial of human interdependence fostered by male-centered views of personality development condemn women to the subexistence associated with the dependence on others and leave no option to men but domination:

> Since the child continues to need the mother, since man continues to need woman, the absolute assertion of independence requires possessing and controlling the needed object. The intention is not to do without her but to make sure that her alien otherness is either assimilated or controlled, that her own subjectivity nowhere asserts itself in a way that could make his dependency upon her a conscious insult to his sense of freedom. (80)

The Buendía men are condemned to solitude because they don't know how to be or how to "love" without dominating. Such notions of subjectivity and love also illuminate the trap that desire represents for García Márquez's women. According to Benjamin, "woman's propensity toward ideal love" is at the core of "the intricate relationship between woman's desire and woman's submission," and it explains women's role in both "criticizing and complying with the elevation of masculine individuality and the devaluation of femininity" (78). Inasmuch as "love," and its legitimate expression within marriage, constitutes in García Márquez's world the privileged channel for "good women" to pursue self-fulfillment, his female characters cannot satisfy their desire without surrendering self-determination. The attribution of enjoyment to violent subjugation leaves room to wonder whether pleasure is even possible for García Márquez's women. The idealization of love provides both the promise of fulfillment and a compensatory device for women's potential loss of pleasure.

Eudine Barriteau sheds further light on the relation between female desire, love, and power in her assessment of contemporary gender relations in Caribbean societies. Barriteau argues that "male dominated society is produced and reproduced by means of appropriative practices or exploitation of women's love power" (61). Expressions of such power include "modes of sexual intimacy, caretaking, and parenting, along with the material conditions shaping these activities" that allow not only the reproduction of humans but also their transformation into socially competent individuals (71). As most of García Márquez's young female characters illustrate, women pursue the erotic dimension of "love power" in many activities, but in the process, Barriteau notes, they are often either forced to surrender their "love power" or have it extracted from them (64). The displacement of romantic love toward love for their children among García Márquez's matriarchs further demonstrates Barriteau's point:

> In practice, men's "rights" to appropriate women's sexual resources, especially their capacities for love, continues. . . . Women and men as sociosexual beings constitute the main parties of a particular exploitative relationship, a relationship in which men tend to exploit women's capacities for love and transform these into individual and collective modes of power over which women lose control. (62)

Amaranta Úrsula's voracious eroticism is the synthesis of all the capacity for love and care of life the Buendía women possess and of all the traps that constrain women's ability to exercise that power without relinquishing desires and ambitions of their own. Choices to assert agency among Macondo's women are strictly sanctioned. Either they subordinate their will to the demands of their partners and children, or they conduct their desire in "illegitimate" sexual exchanges at a high cost. After releasing her sexual urge with her foster brother José Arcadio, Rebeca spends her long life as a widow confined and isolated; Meme's defiance of her mother's tyranny in the arms of a man of a "lower" class ends with her being buried alive in a cloister away from Macondo. Although Amaranta's refusal of marriage and her sustained foreplay with her nephews suggests that she does not fully surrender her desire, and indeed chooses autonomy over love, her perpetual resentment betrays her dissatisfaction.

The struggle over women's desire and willpower is key to the plots of several of García Marquez's post-Macondo narratives as well. The violation of the taboo of virginity by Ángela Vicario is the trigger of both the crime and the love story of *Chronicle of a Death Foretold*. In *Love in the Time of Cholera*, Fermina Daza's assertion of her right to choose her lover against her father's will nurtures Florentino Ariza's five-decades-long obsession. In *Of Love and Other Demons*, the alleged rabies that Inquisitors mistake for a demoniac possession is the furious expression of Sierva María's commitment to self-determination. A combination of violence and "love" secures the substitution of these women's active desire for their compliance with being objects of male desire. Physical punishment and exile compel Ángela Vicario to eventually seek the husband who rejected her on their wedding night.[8] Cloistering and torture prepare Sierva María to surrender to the illusion of freedom in the arms of Cayetano, the older priest who courts her. Age disparity accentuates the inequity that frames sexuality and "love" in a number of García Márquez's works. In a paradigmatic expression of the affair of patriarchal masculinity with domination, young girls succumb to the desires of the elderly protagonists of *The Autumn of the Patriarch*, *Love in the Time of Cholera*, and *Memories of My Melancholy Whores* (1998). "Love" operates in these cases as a redemptive force for the older men, helping to obscure their dubious seduction strategies and the consequences of such affairs for the young girls.[9]

Patriarchal power in García Márquez's world is only truly defied by women who refuse the spell of "ideal love."

In Love with Power

The clash of women's ambitions with the social expectation of male-exclusive access to public power results in the grotesque representations of the women who dare to pursue power of their own. In *The Autumn of the Patriarch*, hundreds of mistresses and prostitutes feed the voracious will for power of the decadent dictator, up to the appearance of the Antillean nun who becomes his wife, Leticia Nazareno. Kidnapped and kept captive for two years before she surrenders to his desires, Leticia sells her care services at a high cost. Through a combination of mother's and mistress's skills, Leticia remakes the omnipotent, hoary man to her will. She teaches him sexual etiquette, hygiene, and manners, and she initiates him into the pleasures of reading. Most importantly, she teaches him tenderness and mutual care, motivating the happy surrender of the omnipotent ruler to the pleasures of dependence. Leticia learns in exchange the hunger for power.

By means of a series of "bedroom law[s] which she had promulgated in secret without consulting anybody and which he had approved in public so it would not appear to anyone's eyes that he had lost the oracles of his authority" (166),[10] Leticia manages to withhold "the key to his power" (173).[11] While love humanizes the aberrant patriarch, Leticia's progressive infatuation with power transforms her into a dreadful woman. The same woman who had brought beauty to the debased government palace and whose hands had carefully bathed her partner as if he were a baby causes degradation and scandal when her power moves into the public spaces:

> [B]ursting as he himself would not have dared into the motley gallery of the bird and vegetable market followed by the uproar of street dogs ... she moved with the insolent domination of her authority through slender columns of ironwork ... where she chose the most delicious fruits ... unaware of the evil virtue of her hands which made mold grow of bread still warm and had blackened the gold of her wedding ring, so that she heaped curses on the vegetable women for having hidden their best wares. (181)[12]

Although Leticia's abuses fall short in comparison to the violent assertions of men's authority under her husband's regime, her power is depicted as particularly corrosive, "worse than the locust, worse than a hurricane" (180).[13] The grotesque description of her body, through the accentuation of her loud voice, vulgar demeanor, and "devil virtues," echoes the characterization of other "ugly" matriarchs in García Márquez's work, such as the monumental protagonist of "Big Mama's Funeral" and Bernarda Cabrera, Sierva María's mother in *Of Love and Other Demons*. Obesity in the first two, and various addictions in Bernarda, betray these women's voracious appetite for power.

The power of both the good and the ugly matriarchs in García Márquez's world may be better understood in the light of studies of Caribbean "matrifocal" societies. A long history of working-class women's autonomy and of persistent labor migrations explains the profusion of mothers acting as heads of households and providers for generations of

Caribbean families. Far from fostering a rearrangement of gender hierarchies, the power of mothers and grandmothers that has fueled their depiction as overstrained heroines has fostered, as Janet Momsen suggests, "the paradox of patriarchal family values within a matrifocal and matrilocal society" (51). García Márquez's patriarchal "matriarchs" display a further paradox, the fact that "the contemporary patriarchy of Caribbean societies is often patriarchy in absentia" of the men (51). Úrsula's power in *One Hundred Years* clearly illustrates such paradoxes, while pointing to the distinction that makes the public display of authority by the good matriarchs tolerable and the power of the ugly ones degenerating and grotesque. While Úrsula's willingness to put her agency to the service of the family makes her occasional incursions into public power an appreciated extension of her domestic kingdom, the displacement of the authority of the patriarch on behalf of Leticia's own ambitions is depicted as a threat in need of contention and reprisal. Similarly, in *Of Love and Other Demons,* the entrepreneurial skills that allow Bernarda to regenerate the fortune that she seizes from the hands of her useless husband are associated with greed, linked to the eventual ruin of her family, to the scapegoating of her daughter, and to her own physical and moral deterioration.

The protagonist of "Big Mama's Funeral" may at first seem the exception to García Márquez's equation of "good" public authority with patriarchal values. Feminizing power allows in this short story the extension of García Márquez's critique of the state, typified as masculine, into the nation, imagined as a mother. As the enumeration of her patrimony reveals, the monumental Big Mama's power relies not only on her ownership of the land and the servitude of those exploiting it—the colonial legacy—or on her monopoly of political power, which she continues to balance through her intervention in "democratic" elections; this embodiment of the nation rules also on private and public morality, on the bodies and the consciousness of her subjects, keeping for herself the privilege to sanction everything from marital associations to scientific knowledge. Like all other matriarchs, Big Mama holds attributes and privileges usually associated with traditional masculinity, but her control comes from capitalizing on rather than questioning hegemonic power.

Sexuality continues to be key to these women's access to power. Remaining unmarried and a virgin is the condition to preserve Big Mama's ability to administer her patrimony, while her niece's choice to become a nun brings her ability to extend it to an end. In contrast, Leticia Nazareno and Bernarda are characterized by and punished for their use of sexuality to enact control over men. Whereas Leticia has established her position by awakening the patriarch to love, Bernarda gains it by raping the Marques and rousing him from his apathy. Bernarda's introduction further illustrates the degradation that comes with the collusion of women's power and sexual domination:

> She had been an untamed mestiza of the so-called shopkeeper aristocracy: seductive, rapacious, brazen, with a hunger in her womb that could have satisfied an entire barracks. In a few short years, however, she had been erased from the world by her abuse of the fermented honey and cacao tablets. Her Gypsy eyes were extinguished and her wits dulled, she shat blood and vomited bile, her siren's body became as bloated and

coppery as a tree-day old corpse, and she broke wind in pestilential explosions that startled the mastiffs. (8–9)[14]

Racialization comes hand in hand with the distinctive voracity and with the disgusting effluvia attributed to the bodies of the illegitimate "matriarchs." Bernarda's vices are further elaborated by her depiction as a hateful wife and mother, invested in an unscrupulous business career and destroyed by sex addiction.

The despicable matriarchs in García Márquez's world can be read as an embodiment of the archetypical fear of a mother's sexuality, whose sexual feelings, returning to Jessica Benjamin, "with their threat of selfishness, passion, and uncontrollability, are a disturbing possibility that even psychoanalysts would relegate to the 'unnatural'" (84). Outlandish ends will eventually confirm both the degeneration that love for power inflicts on mothers and the need to neutralize such "unnatural" power. Bernarda sees "the final step in her degradation" after the death of her favorite lover, giving "herself over to unrestrained fornication with the slaves on the plantation . . . until she became swollen and ugly, and they did not have the courage to take on so much body" (141).[15] Leticia Nazareno and her son are "torn to pieces and eaten [alive] by the stray dogs at the public market," slowly sinking "in a hellish whirlpool," in the face of "the impassable horror of the totemic vegetable women spattered with hot blood" (185–86).[16] A threat against themselves and their descendants, the corruption of these monstrous mothers concludes—as is also the case with Amaranta Úrsula—not only with their destruction but with the death of their children.

Power beyond "Love"

Does García Márquez's work account for intimate relationships that do not demand women's subordination? Is it possible for women in García Márquez's world to escape sexual or affective domination? I close by testing these possibilities in the case of two rebellious daughters, Fermina Daza in *Love in the Time of Cholera* and the legendary Remedios the Beauty in *One Hundred Years of Solitude*.

The competition for Fermina's willpower between her two suitors, Florentino Ariza and Juvenal Urbino, is an extension of her relationship to her father, Lorenzo Daza, who has invested his hopes for social climbing in the prospective marriage of his only child. Disappointed by Fermina's first choice, Florentino, a telegraph operator without name or fortune, Lorenzo attempts to counteract his romantic spell by sending Fermina on a hazardous trip. At first her father's opposition fuels Fermina's desire to affirm herself through forbidden love, unknowingly repeating her own young mother's rebellion against her family's will. With the complicity of her cousin Hildebranda, who shares both Fermina's "imperial haughtiness" and her devotion to an impossible love, Fermina remains in touch with Florentino. But the trip also provides her with the unexpected opportunity to explore a new kind of freedom and love. Under the tutorship of her "troop of cousins," she "learnt about herself, she felt free for the first time, she felt befriended and protected, her lungs full of the air of liberty" (*Love in the Time of Cholera* 87). Her cousins are also accomplices in Fermina's explorations with self-pleasure. These experiences lead her to "the revelation that one can be happy not only without love, but despite it" (87).[17] When Fermina sees Florentino again, she recognizes her delusion. Asking herself "how she could have nurtured such a chimera in her heart for so long and with so much ferocity," she dismisses Florentino (102).[18]

In sharp contrast with Florentino's reliance on romantic letters, the second suitor, Juvenal Urbino, resorts to his social reputation to defeat Fermina's initial rejection. Lorenzo Daza's excitement about the new suitor nurtures Fermina's resistance. Her cousin Hildebranda comes to Fermina's rescue again by framing Juvenal as a desirable object for Fermina's ambitions. Fermina embraces the comforts of marriage to a "modern" man, "a physician with family and fortune, with an extraordinary reputation for a man of his years" (137),[19] who devotes himself to patiently gaining her compliance with her duties as a wife.

Fermina and Juvenal's relationship illustrates a notion of "love" as shared power that, starting in their intimate exchanges, extends to the public recognition of the wife's role in the existence of her socially prominent partner. The description of the long foreplay that leads to their first sexual intercourse is exceptional in García Márquez's work. Juvenal encourages Fermina's exploration of his body for "a lesson in love" and waits for Fermina to release her tension until it is she who takes the initiative and gives herself "without fear, without regret, with the joy of an adventure" (159).[20] Although the narrative voice clarifies that Juvenal married Fermina knowing that he did not love her, their physical contact confirms that "there would be no obstacle to their inventing true love" (159).

"True love" appears in this context associated not only with the sharing of sexual power but also with the self-assertion of both lovers: "they both made love well" and because "he was a man of strong impulses, and well disciplined besides, and she was not one to let anyone to take advantage of her . . . they had to be content with sharing power in bed" (160).[21] By the time they return from a long honeymoon in Europe, their "invention" has brought about a radical transformation in the couple. They are the heralds of "a new conception of life, bringing with them the latest trends in the world and ready to lead" (160).[22] The rendering of their story accounts for challenges to Juvenal and Fermina's balance of power, and the narrative voice continues to question the feasibility of such invention. Nevertheless, their bond grows with the recognition of each other's strengths and vulnerabilities and with the sustained autonomy of both partners within the context of mutual dependence.

Meanwhile Florentino, conscious of his inferiority in the face of his rival, conceives of the plan of becoming a man of means while waiting for Juvenal's death. Initiated in the brothels "into the secrets of loveless love" (75),[23] Florentino finds the courage to remain loyal to his "true love" in his sexual affairs, rigorously collected in a series of notebooks titled *Women* and accounting for "six hundred twenty-two entries of long-term liaisons, apart from the countless fleeting adventures that did not even deserve a charitable note" (152).[24] I have discussed elsewhere the contradictions in the depiction of Florentino as the loyal ideal lover (Celis "Del amor, la pederastia y otros crímenes literarios"). I will add here that, although the original "love" nurtured by romantic literature is nothing but the projection of Florentino's ideal onto Fermina, the love that he is able to offer her fifty years later is that of an astute conqueror, capable of shaping himself into the image of women's desire. The narrative voice privileges Florentino's love, presenting his reunification with Fermina as "beyond the pitfalls of passion, beyond the brutal mockery of hope and the phantoms of disillusion: beyond love" (345).[25] However, it is up to readers to decide how Florentino's conquest compares to the life and love Fermina has experienced with her husband, or whether Fermina's life with a second man is the solution to her long-lasting battle for freedom.

Returning to Macondo, there is certainly one truly free woman in García Márquez's world, Remedios the Beauty, so odd that the narrative voice declares her "not a creature of this world" (*One Hundred Years* 202).[26] Armed by a nature that "resisted all manner of convention" (202),[27] Remedios arrives at the age to be a suitable wife with no knowledge and no interest in any of the features that would make her desirable, and no sexual desire of her own. While some of her family members consider her "mentally retarded," Colonel Aureliano Buendía identifies in her a "penetrating lucidity," "as if she's come back from twenty years of war," suggesting an association between his own disillusion with power and Remedios's natural distrust of authority (202).[28] Remedios's refusal to wear anything but a coarse cassock exemplifies, by contrast, the technologies of the body by means of which, as Michel Foucault puts it, power "applies itself to immediate everyday life, categorizes the individual, marks him by his own individuality, attaches him to his own identity, imposes a law of truth on him that he must recognize and others have to recognize in him" (781). Furthermore, Remedios's dismissal of the preferred marks of femininity points to the gendered nature of such technologies.

Remedios unfolds the myth of the provoker that cements the patriarchal notions of both women's and men's sexuality. The less she cares about men's interest, "the more disturbing her incredible beauty became and the more provocative she became to men" (236).[29] The Macondo men's obsession with Remedios highlights the projection of their own desires that lead to patriarchal notions of women's sexuality. Moreover, Remedios's refusal to channel her ambitions through being desired makes her immune to the appropriation of her willpower. Exemplified by the ritual of self-care that she performs through her long baths, Remedios's true will is being of herself, and her power lies in her immunity to the domination others may perform on her through sexual control. No wonder the men of Macondo interpret Remedios's freedom as a dangerous power. The tragic deaths of those who attempt to conquer her lead to "the legend that Remedios Buendía did not give off a breath of love but a fatal emanation" (240).[30]

Both Úrsula and Amaranta try to "make her into a useful woman" (241). They also entertain hopes for the miracle of a man with enough patience to search "for the weak point of her heart" (241).[31] The "trap" that love means to women's subjectivity is betrayed by the narrator's assessment of the failure of Macondo men to domesticate Remedios: "Perhaps, not only to attain her, but also to conjure away her dangers, all that was needed was a feeling as primitive and simple as that of love, but that was the only thing that did not occur to anyone" (241).[32] The connection between love and care labor is also remarked by Úrsula's attempts to gain Remedios's interest in domestic affairs: "'Men demand much more than you think,' she said enigmatically. 'There's a lot of cooking, a lot of sweeping, a lot of suffering over little things, beyond what you think'" (241). Úrsula is dissuaded by her own disbelief in men's ability to love beyond love. "Once his passion was satisfied" no man on earth, the matriarch concludes, would be amenable to Remedios's "negligence" (241).[33] The useless Remedios the Beauty is left "wandering through the deserts of solitude, bearing no cross on her back," until the longed miracle arrives in the form of the "delicate wind of light" that raises her (242).[34]

In light of the repressed rebelliousness of the women of her lineage, the ascension of the indomitable Remedios, the only one immune to desire and love, might be read not as the climax of her purity but as her escape from a world that could not accept such a powerful woman. Either way, the magic powers of the writer come to rescue Macondo from Remedios's "powers of death" (240),[35] enabling the reparation of the patriarchal order.

Conclusion

Although female characters in García Márquez's world demonstrate plenty of unruly desires, betraying perhaps aspirations that escape the narrator's imagination, there is no "successful" life for women that is not tied to the men they love. Whether we think of power as the freedom to pursue desires and ambitions of their own, or as the ability to affect the actions of others, including the agency to work within patriarchal gender constraints to gain such control, the power of women in García Marquez's world is defined by their sexual and affective ties to the men who oppress them. Is the unviability of women's power over their own lives an expression of Caribbean and Latin American social and cultural realities? Or is it also an expression of the author's own vision of power?

García Márquez's works are built upon the recognition of women's extraordinary capacity to sustain life. Sexual desire is key to the fulfillment of such a powerful role. As Remedios the Beauty's useless life suggests, women have to engage in some desire of their own in order to engage with men's desires. Hence, the key to the containment of women's power is not so much the repression as the domestication of their sexuality. While women's engagement with productive enterprises may be compatible with their main form of power, other ambitions—the search for self-realization through creative or intellectual fulfillment, the need for gratifying relations with people beyond their families, the hope for the recognition of their contributions to society beyond their role in the lives of their partners and children—are implausible and incompatible with women's "real" power. The social devaluation of their bodies faced by women who conduct their sexuality outside of marriage and the ubiquitous threat of sexual violence play a role in encumbering "love" as the most suitable option for the realization of at least some of women's desires and for the enactment of the limited power allowed to them.

Although in alignment with trends present in Caribbean cultures of his time, and even of today, García Márquez's portrayal of women's power reveals a distinctive understanding of gender and subjectivity. While establishing privately and displaying publicly control over others is the naturalized expression of masculinity, women can only access power privately and through public subordination to men's control. It is worth adding that García Márquez's world is a heteropatriarchal heaven where other gender expressions are scarce, and "love" other than from men to women does not appear viable. As the male-centered notion of subjectivity betrayed by the Buendías' solitude reveals, the equation of manhood with domination is in itself a technology of power. García Márquez's male characters lack the self-awareness needed to understand the power that, in their relationship to themselves and their loved ones, makes them agents in their own subjugation. In consequence, men are in love with power even when they are in love.

Framed by such an understanding of love and power, women's freedom is restricted to the control they can seize in their private relationships. Within those limits, García Márquez's women expose an arrangement of extraordinary abilities that exceed the expectations of their traditional roles. By recognizing women's resilience in face of the suppression of their freedom, García Márquez has drawn an extraordinary portrait of the existing and latent potencies of women. Women may not be the "main characters" in García Márquez's world because their services to family, their communities, and society are taken for granted and not deemed equal to men's contributions, but women and their power make García Márquez's world possible.

Notes

1. "Cuando Aureliano se lo dijo, Pilar Ternera emitió una risa profunda, la antigua risa expansiva que había terminado por parecer un cucurrucuteo de palomas. No había ningún misterio en el corazón de un Buendía que fuera impenetrable para ella, porque un siglo de naipes y de experiencia le había enseñado que la historia de la familia era un engranaje de repeticiones irreparables, una rueda giratoria que hubiera seguido dando vueltas hasta la eternidad, de no haber sido por el desgaste progresivo e irremediable del eje" (343).
2. See Celis, "La Soledad de Úrsula" for an extensive study of Úrsula Iguarán.
3. "No era comprensible que una mujer con aquel espíritu hubiera regresado a un pueblo muerto, deprimido por el polvo y el calor, y menos con un marido . . . que la amaba tanto que se había sometido a ser llevado y traído por ella con el dogal de seda" (328).
4. "En cualquier lugar en que esté ahora, ella te está esperando" (343).
5. "De pronto, casi jugando, como una travesura más, Amaranta Úrsula descuidó la defensa, y cuando trató de reaccionar, asustada de lo que ella misma había hecho posible, ya era demasiado tarde" (344).
6. "Aunque Aureliano era un amante tan feroz como su rival, era Amaranta Úrsula quien comandaba con su ingenio disparatado y su voracidad lírica aquel paraíso de desastres, como si hubiera concentrado en el amor la indómita energía que la tatarabuela consagró a la fabricación de animalitos de caramelo. Además, mientras ella cantaba de placer y se moría de risa de sus propias invenciones, Aureliano se iba haciendo más absorto y callado, porque su pasión era ensimismada y calcinante" (350).

7. "la sangre apasionada de Amaranta Úrsula era insensible a todo artificio distinto del amor" (356).
8. See Celis, "Entre el 'crimen atroz' y el 'amor terrible'" for an in-depth analysis of power and love in *Chronicle*.
9. See Celis, "Del amor, la pederastia y otros crímenes literarios" and Luiselli for more about girls in García Márquez's novels.
10. "por una ley de alcoba como tantas otras que ella expedía en secreto sin consultarlo con nadie y que él aprobaba en público para que no pareciera ante los ojos de nadie que había perdido los oráculos de su autoridad" (144).
11. "las claves de su poder" (146).
12. "irrumpía" como no se hubiera atrevido él mismo en la galería abigarrada del mercado de pájaros y legumbres . . . se movía con un dominio procaz de su autoridad entre las esbeltas columnas de hierro bordado . . . donde escogía las frutas más apetitosas y las legumbres más tiernas . . . inconsciente de la mala virtud de sus manos que hacían crecer el musgo en el pan todavía tibio y habían renegrido el oro de su anillo matrimonial, así que se soltaba en improperios contra las vivanderas por haber escondido el mejor bastimento" (148–49).
13. "peor que la langosta, peor que el ciclón" (148).
14. "Había sido una mestiza brava de la llamada aristocracia de mostrador; seductora, rapaz, parrandera, y con una avidez de vientre para saciar un cuartel. Sin embargo, en pocos años se había borrado del mundo por el abuso de la miel fermentada y las tabletas de cacao. Los ojos de gitana se le apagaron, se le acabó el ingenio, obraba sangre y arrojaba bilis, y el antiguo cuerpo de sirena se le volvió hinchado y cobrizo como el de un muerto de tres días, y despedía unas ventosidades explosivas y pestilentes que asustaban a los mastines" (15).
15. "Se había entregado a la fornicación sin freno con los esclavos del trapiche . . . [hasta que] se volvió hinchada y fea y los ánimos no le alcanzaron para tanto cuerpo" (190).
16. "se los habían comido a pedazos los perros cimarrones del mercado público . . . ahogándose junto con los perros en un torbellino de infierno . . . ante el horror impasible de las verduleras totémicas salpicadas de sangre caliente" (162).
17. "Fermina Daza se reconoció, se sintió dueña de sí misma por primera vez, se sintió acompañada y protegida, con los pulmones colmados por un aire de libertad . . . la revelación de que no sólo se podía ser feliz sin amor sino también contra el amor" (123).
18. "cómo había podido incubar durante tanto tiempo y con tanta sevicia semejante quimera en el corazón" (143–44).
19. "un médico de alcurnia y fortuna, educado en Europa y con una reputación insólita a su edad" (189).
20. "sin miedo, sin dolor, con la alegría de una aventura de alta mar" (220).
21. "Él era un hombre de buenos ímpetus, y además bien entrenado, y ella no estaba hecha para dejarse tomar ventaja de nadie, de modo que tuvieron que conformarse con el poder compartido en la cama" (220).
22. "Volvieron con una concepción nueva de la vida, cargados de novedades del mundo, y listos para mandar" (221).
23. "los secretos del amor sin amor" (108).
24. "seiscientos veintidós registros de amores continuados, aparte de las incontables aventuras fugaces que no merecieron ni una nota de caridad" (210).
25. "más allá de las trampas de la pasión, más allá de las burlas brutales de las ilusiones y los espejismos de los desengaños: más allá del amor" (470).
26. "no era un ser de este mundo" (175).

27. "su naturaleza se resistía a cualquier clase de convencionalismos" (175).
28. "Parecía como si una lucidez penetrante le permitiera ver la realidad . . . no era en modo alguno retrasada mental . . . 'Es como si viniera de regreso de veinte años de guerra'" (175–76).
29. "más perturbadora resultaba su belleza increíble y más provocador su comportamiento con los hombres" (203).
30. "la leyenda de que Remedios Buendía no exhalaba un aliento de amor, sino un flujo mortal" (205).
31. "convertirla en una mujer útil . . . un hombre lo bastante intrigado como para buscar con paciencia el punto débil de su corazón" (207).
32. "Tal vez, no sólo para rendirla sino también para conjurar sus peligros, habría bastado con un sentimiento tan primitivo y simple como el amor, pero eso fue lo único que no se le ocurrió a nadie" (207).
33. "'Los hombres piden más de lo que tú crees-le decía enigmáticamente. Hay mucho que cocinar, mucho que barrer, mucho que sufrir por pequeñeces, además de lo que crees.' . . . estaba convencida de que una vez satisfecha la pasión, no había un hombre sobre la tierra capaz de soportar así fuera por un día una negligencia que estaba más allá de toda comprensión" (207).
34. "vagando por el desierto de la soledad, sin cruces a cuestas . . . un delicado viento de luz" (208).
35. "poderes de muerte" (205).

Works Cited

Alexander, Jacqui M. "Erotic Autonomy as a Politics of Decolonization: An Anatomy of Feminist and State Practice in the Bahamas Tourist Economy." *Feminist Genealogies, Colonial Legacies, Democratic Futures*, edited by Chandra Talpade Mohanty and M. Jacqui Alexander, Routledge, 1997, pp. 63–100.

Alexander, Jacqui M. "Not Just (Any) Body Can Be a Citizen: The Politics of Law, Sexuality and Postcoloniality in Trinidad and Tobago and the Bahamas." *Feminist Review*, vol. 48, 1994, pp. 5–23.

Barriteau, Eudine. "Coming Home to the Erotic Power of Love and Desire in Caribbean Heterosexual Unions." *Love and Power: Caribbean Discourses on Gender*, edited by Eudine Barriteau, U of West Indies P, 2012, pp. 72–104.

Benjamin, Jessica. "A Desire of One's Own: Psychoanalytic Feminism and Intersubjective Space." *Feminist Studies/Critical Studies*, edited by Teresa de Lauretis. Indiana UP, 1986, pp. 78–101.

Celis, Nadia. "Del amor, la pederastia y otros crímenes literarios: América Vicuña y las niñas de García Márquez." *Poligramas. Revista Literaria*, vol. 33, June 2010, pp. 29–55.

Celis, Nadia. "Entre el 'crimen atroz' y el 'amor terrible': Poder y violencia en *Crónica de una muerte anunciada* de Gabriel García Márquez." *Revista de estudios de género y sexualidades*, vol. 44, no. 1, 2019, pp. 19–36.

Celis, Nadia. "La soledad de Úrsula: Intimidad y violencia en Macondo, ayer y hoy." *Cien años de soledad cincuenta años después: Gabriel García Márquez, Literatura y memoria II*, edited by Juan Moreno Blanco, Programa Editorial de la Universidad del Valle, 2017, pp. 337–56.

Foucault, Michel. "The Subject and Power." *Critical Inquiry*, vol. 8, no. 4, 1982, pp. 777–95.

García Márquez, Gabriel. *El amor en los tiempos del cólera*. Oveja Negra, 1985.
García Márquez, Gabriel. *The Autumn of the Patriarch*. Translated by Gregory Rabassa, Harper and Row, 1976.
García Márquez, Gabriel. *Cien años de soledad* (1967). Sudamericana, 1976.
García Márquez, Gabriel. *Del amor y otros demonios*. Norma, 1994.
García Márquez, Gabriel. *Love in the Time of Cholera*. Translated by Edith Grossman, Alfred Knopf, 1988.
García Márquez, Gabriel. *Of Love and Other Demons*. Translated by Edith Grossman, Alfred Knopf, 1995.
García Márquez, Gabriel. *One Hundred Years of Solitude*. Translated by Gregory Rabassa, Harper and Row, 1970.
García Márquez, Gabriel. *El otoño del patriarca* (1978). Oveja Negra, 1985.
Irigaray, Luce. *This Sex Which Is Not One*. Translated by Catherine Porter, Cornell UP, 1985.
Kempadoo, Kamala. *Sun, Sex and Gold: Tourism and Sex Work in the Caribbean*. Rowman and Littlefield, 1999.
Luiselli, Alessandra, "Los demonios en torno a la cama del rey: Pederastia e incesto en *Memoria de mis putas tristes* de Gabriel García Marquez." *Espéculo. Revista de estudios literarios*, vol. 32, 2007, webs.ucm.es/info/especulo/numero32/camarey.html. Accessed 28 Dec. 2019.
Momsen, Janet. "The Double Paradox." *Gendered Realities: Essays in Caribbean Feminist Thought*, edited by Patricia Mohammed, U of the West Indies P, 2002, pp. 44–55.

PART III

WORLDWIDE INFLUENCES AND LEGACY

CHAPTER 11

GARCÍA MÁRQUEZ IN AFRICA

REGINA JANES

GABRIEL García Márquez first visited Africa in the late 1970s when he was almost fifty years old, drawn by Cuban military interventions in Angola and Congo, which he celebrated in his journalism about Africa. Decades later, looking back, African writers were not so celebratory. From 1979, traces of *Cien años de soledad* (*One Hundred Years of Solitude*, 1967; henceforth *One Hundred Years*), *El otoño del patriarca* (*The Autumn of the Patriarch*, 1975), and *Crónica de una muerte anunciada* (*Chronicle of a Death Foretold*, 1981) begin to appear in African writings. The modern African canon had already emerged (Senghor, Tutuola, Achebe, Beti, Soyinka, Ngũgĩ), when, as Syl Cheney-Coker observes, *One Hundred Years* dangled its formal alternatives to an "Achebean... sociological" or "Ngũgĩan... political" vision before writers tasked with representing societies in which magic was more real than their own disbelief (quoted in Cooper, *Magical* 119). The original phrase describing the achievement of *One Hundred Years*, "marvelous American reality," was soon overtaken by "magical realism." "Marvelous American reality" had been coined, under Parisian surrealist inspiration, to describe the Francophone African diaspora of Haiti (Alejo Carpentier, *The Kingdom of This World*, 1949 [Scarano 9–11]). "Marvelous reality" was African all along, as García Márquez came to recognize. To magical beliefs represented without apology or frame, *One Hundred Years* added playful hyperbole and intertextual invention. Attuned to the Caribbean and Brazilian diasporas, Africans in turn reappropriated their mingled magic and modernity. "Magical realism" floated down over African writers like a net capturing a sea of creatures that have nothing in common, threatening to drown them all in a single soup pot, but ultimately to benign effect. As the British-Ghanaian writer Nii Parkes observed, "*One Hundred Years of Solitude* taught the West how to read a reality alternative to their own" (Parkes and Unigwe n.p.).

Africa—West, East, Central, and Southern, below the Sahara (for Arabic-speaking North Africa, see El Attar's chapter in this volume)—comprises forty-eight of Africa's fifty-four nations, 1.078 of its 1.273 billion people, and most of its 750 to 3,000 languages. As a Sony Labou Tansi character scoffs, "All this talk of white minorities, when the whole of Africa is teeming with black minorities" (*Antipeople* 108). Literacy rates in 2016 range from 95 percent in Equatorial Guinea to 22 percent in Chad; the region averages 64 percent, with Angola at 71 percent (World Bank). García Márquez estimated Angolan literacy in 1976, the year after its independence from Portugal, at 10 percent, with only 2 percent able to read and write Portuguese ("Angola" 167). Access to García Márquez requires literacy in one of Africa's colonial-imperial languages: Spanish, Portuguese, English, French, Italian, German, Dutch, or Arabic. His work has been translated into no sub-Saharan language: not Kiswahili, Gĩkũyũ, Wolof, Twi, Shona, Afrikaans, Tigrinya, Sango, Kirundi, Tswana, Kinyarwanda, Igbo, Hausa, Yoruba, Malinké, Fulani, or any other. Traveling principally in Spanish, English, Portuguese, and French, his works surfaced in African bookshops as well as university and school libraries through the spotty colonial distribution networks established to serve colonial administrators and the multilingual indigenous educated, the latter fluent—as Yambo Ouologuem (51) observes (for Mali)—in French, Arabic, and seven vernaculars. Many African writers discovered him while they were studying or living abroad: Alain Mabanckou in France and Syl Cheney-Coker in the United States (Stevenson 12; Palmer and Cole 25).

Four pieces constitute García Márquez's own African corpus: "Operación Carlota" ("Operation Carlota," 1976) and "Angola, un año después: Una nación en la escuela primaria" ("Angola a Year Later: An Entire Nation in Primary School," 1977), both on Cuban intervention in the Angolan civil war; "Los meses de tinieblas: El 'Che' en el Congo" (Shadowy Months: Che in the Congo, 1977), on Che Guevara's frustrated Congolese sojourn of 1965 (first published in, respectively, *El Espectador*, Bogotá; the *Washington Post*, Washington, D.C.; and *Alternativa*, Bogotá [in *Por la libre*]); and finally "Esposas alquiladas" (Rented Wives, 1983 [in *Notas*]), on the pulchritude of first ladies.[1] Widely circulated and reprinted, "Operation Carlota" recounts the Cuban airlift that enabled Agostinho Neto's MPLA to repel the combined forces of Mobutu's Zaire, supporting Holden Roberto; Jonas Savimbi's US-supported UNITA; and apartheid South Africa. "Carlota" celebrates Cuba's outfoxing of Henry Kissinger in its first sentence and concludes with Cuba's need for triumphs after such setbacks as the death of Che Guevara in Bolivia and the coup against Salvador Allende in Chile. "Angola a Year Later" marked García Márquez's first visit to Africa and his surprise at the smell, the wreckage, the rags, and the intellectuals in charge of ministries. "Che in the Congo" relates Che's journeys to and from Congo but provides no details of his activities there. Che did advise the nameless "tall and well-built black man" responsible for his security to paint himself white to attract less attention ("Los meses" 191).[2]

"Rented Wives" speculates about the rumor that African rulers with homely wives outfit themselves in public with statuesque ebony beauties who make white wives invisible and their husbands breathless. Wondering about the rulers' rights in private, García Márquez concludes that women should have the same right vis-à-vis horrid husbands, from John Kennedy to Idi Amin Dada (451). (In Ngũgĩ wa Thiong'o's 2006 novel *Wizard of the Crow*, the antagonist's wife, not wanting to bother being empress, authorizes a hostess substitute, contingent on there being no sexual hanky-panky.) Apart from Neto, who compliments Cuba's military generosity ("Operación Carlota" 127) and acknowledges compromises over Gulf Oil and diplomacy ("Angola" 170, 171,

173, 175), García Márquez quotes only one African, the "charismatic" Julius Nyerere of Tanzania: "Tanzania . . . is not a country on the 'road to development,' as the current facile translation of the English phrase 'developing country' has it, but an underdeveloped country that has not even begun to find the road to ceasing to be so" (*Notas* 176).[3] (Registering Nyerere's charisma, the heroine of *Wizard of the Crow* attributes a saying to Nyerere, but is corrected: it's a common Kiswahili proverb, quoted by Nyerere [120].) Elsewhere, García Márquez refers to the innumerable languages of Oceania and India but allows "Swahili" to stand in for all of Africa's languages (*Notas* 25). Congratulating Che for learning it, he inadvertently turns Che's code name Tatu, Swahili for "three," into "two" to echo the Argentine novel's eponymous protagonist Don *Segundo* Sombra (emphasis added; *Changing* 53; "Operación Carlota" 147; Guevara 251; "Los meses" 193).

"Operation Carlota" reports that some Cubans and Angolans look so much alike that to tell them apart, it is necessary to feel the tips of their noses; Angolans have a flabby cartilage from nuzzling their mothers' backs as infants, an explanation last seriously proposed in *Gulliver's Travels* (1726), in which it explains why natives and Yahoos have flatter noses than Europeans. Culturally backward, Angolans are 90 percent illiterate, polygamous, living in conditions "closer to the Stone Age than the twentieth century" (*Changing* 54; "Operación Carlota" 146–47).[4] Terrified of airplanes, many thought bullets could not pierce white skin, and they refused to fight in trenches; tombs are for the dead. They wore necklaces, bracelets, and charcoal smudges as protection from bullets. (Such *naparama* warriors reappear in Mia Couto's *Sleepwalking Land* [1992, 20] and *Under the Frangipani* [1996, 111], Mozambique; Paulina Chiziane's *First Wife* [2002, 218], Mozambique; and as a disguised Cuban in José Eduardo Agualusa's *A General Theory of Oblivion* [2012, 146], Angola.) In a UNITA minister's comfortable home, MPLA men found "in his refrigerator jars of viscera and bottles of frozen blood taken from the war prisoners he had eaten."[5] In sum, "Mercenaries and snakes, rockets and cannibals" threaten the Cubans as magical beliefs impede military effectiveness (*Changing*, 53–55; "Operación Carlota" 149, 148).[6]

In "Angola, a Year Later," García Márquez was impressed by Luanda's modernity after the desolation and smell of Guinea. Alberto Moravia had told him Africa had a distinctive smell, and it turned out to be true ("Angola" 162).[7] (Agualusa revisits the famous smell of Africa as the smell of piss in *My Father's Wives* [2007], 19–20, 203.) That week there were no matches to be had, nor soap, milk, aspirin, or razor blades, and nothing works. The Portuguese had disabled, burned, and demolished as they left, taking even the doorknobs and the screens, and no one knows anything ("Angola" 161, 163–67). Mail carriers cannot read addresses; a smiling young hotel worker does not know how to change a light bulb, and a telephone operator asks what country New York is in (169). (A telephone operator in New York who knows what country Luanda is in probably hails from Kampala or Maputo, Brazzaville or Kinshasa.) Naming ministers of state, from the president down to culture and justice, García Márquez counts their years spent in Portuguese prisons (six to fourteen). Manuel Pacavira was imprisoned as an illiterate seventeen-year-old; Marxist poet António Jacinto saw to his education, and Pacavira is now minister of transport and an elegant writer and historian. A poet, Fernando Costa

Andrade, directs the *Jornal de Angola*; poet and cartoonist Henrique Abranches, the museums; and novelist Luandino Vieira, the television (172–73). In prison Agostinho Neto wrote the poems of *Sagrada Esperanza* and smuggled them out two verses at a time, rolled in cigarettes offered to his visiting wife (175). With ironic, exotic detail, humor, and hyperbole, García Márquez marks the sociocultural gaps in intercivilizational regard. Wanted is "a new society" that combats "tribalism and racism" and foments "free education and public health" (148).[8] Quoting Che, García Márquez deplores "the colonization of the mind" ("Operación Carlota" 147).[9] Socialism, like white supremacy, has a civilizing mission, but takes it seriously. Ngũgĩ called for "decolonising the mind."

In 1977 no one knew that a quarter century of civil war had begun, which would end in 2002 with Jonas Savimbi's death. Carlota's world was shredded. Agostinho Neto (1922–1979) died in office, succeeded by José Eduardo dos Santos, who became the second longest serving African president until he stepped down in 2017. In December 1982, Costa Andrade (1936–2009) was arrested for a satirical play that President Santos had seen performed in August and was held without trial for two and a half years. He died in Lisbon. Jacinto (1924–1991) also died in Lisbon, retiring from politics in 1990. Pacavira (1939–2016), once ambassador to Italy and UN agricultural agencies, died in Lisbon. Abranches (1932–2004) died in South Africa. Luandino Vieira (1935–) has lived since 1992 in northern Portugal.

As early as 1982, novelist and former prime minister Henri Lopes (Republic of Congo, 1937–) cast a cool eye on celebrations of Angola. In *The Laughing Cry*, Daddy the dictator stages the live spectacular *ANGOLA*, dramatizing precolonial culture, interrupted by Portuguese colonialism, white domination, and Black servitude imposed with Senegalese assistance. Then Daddy's own armed forces liberate Angola from Portugal: "Looking carefully at the soldiers, one could distinguish among them some whose dress and headgear evoked the bearded Cubans" (69). The Portuguese flag is pulled down, that of the Angolan resistance raised above that of the Organisation of African Unity and above "our own." Visiting heads of state thought Daddy's efforts "the didactic, militant and realist art that Africa needed" (69). In Angola, Pepetela (1941–), once an MPLA guerrillero, ends his novel *Yaka* (1984) before liberation, when a generous Cuban mulatto named Rigoberto dies along with his trainees at the disastrous battle of Catengue, the defeat (a South African victory) that induced Operation Carlota (301–2).

Thirty years later, Lopes's compatriot and fellow novelist Alain Mabanckou (1966–) noted some ambiguous consequences of Cuban intervention. García Márquez had praised Che's fleeting visit to Congo as "sowing a seed that will never be eradicated" and cited the Cuban instructors based in Brazzaville ("Operación Carlota" 135–36).[10] Some of them planted less metaphorical seeds. In Mabanckou's *Black Moses* (2015), abandoned Congolese-Cuban children are cared for in a hospital funded by Fidel Castro, and a Zairean priest is more attractive than the socialists, intent though they may be on combating tribalism, nepotism, and racism. (In his dazzling *Broken Glass* [2005, 136], Mabanckou places a tribute to *One Hundred Years* between his tributes to Camara Laye and Sony Labou Tansi, native sons, and Victor Hugo, imperial inspiration, a generosity reaffirmed in *Memoirs of a Porcupine* [2006, 104].) Emmanuel Dongala criticizes the new socialism as equally ingenious, syncretic, and lethal in the stories of *Jazz and Palm Wine* (2003, Republic of Congo), especially "The Astonishing and Dialectical Downfall of Comrade Kali Tchikati," "Old Likibi's Trial," and "The Ceremony." "A Love Supreme" balances that perspective against America's model, where white police so frequently shoot young black boys.

The most intricate trajectory over Cuba, Angola, and García Márquez comes from the Angolan José Eduardo Agualusa (1960–). An early short-story collection, *D. Nicolau Água-Rosada e outras estórias verdadeiras e inverosímeis* (D. Nicolau Água-Rosada and Other True and Unbelievable Stories, 1990), evokes García Márquez. His later novels allude cheekily to the Colombian author and the Lusophone canon. *The Book of Chameleons* (2006) reports on what the chameleons read in their previous lives: "[N]o one had read Shakespeare. A cardinal liked Gabriel García Márquez" (40). In *My Father's Wives* (2008), a narrator, self-chiding for easy weeping, cites in a footnote *Love in the Time of Cholera*; the reference to the "smell of Africa" is mockingly revisited, and one of "my father's [promiscuous] wives" paints portraits of herself every decade. From ages twenty to fifty, she paints herself reading Camilo Castelo Branco's *Love of Perdition* (Anglophone readers may know Raúl Ruiz's beautiful, desolate film version of *Mysteries of Lisbon* [2010]); at sixty, with twelve grandchildren and three great-grandchildren, "she's reading *A Hundred Years of Solitude* by Gabriel García Márquez" (*My Father's Wives* 63). In her eighties she still paints, but at seventy stopped painting herself because she doesn't "like painting old ladies" (63). In Agualusa's *A General Theory of Oblivion*, Cubans shoot a Portuguese mercenary, through whom the bullet passes as miraculously as in Colonel Aureliano Buendía's suicide attempt; a monkey is named Che Guevara for his haughty, rebellious look; and Cabrera Infante's Havana disappears with Joyce's Dublin in a book burning that catches *Three Trapped Tigers* and *Ulysses*. A retired torturer dies installing a satellite dish for his wife's television soap operas; he had meant to "spend his final years rereading Jorge Amado, Machado de Assis, Clarice Lispector, Luandino Vieira, Ruy Duarte de Carvalho, Julio Cortázar, and Gabriel García Márquez" (209).

By contrast, Agualusa's earlier *Rainy Season* (1996) repurposes a structural device from *Chronicle of a Death Foretold*, combines it with the political scope of *One Hundred Years*, and reproduces lyrical riffs from all over García Márquez's oeuvre to critique Angolan history. A journalist attempts to reconstruct the disappearance of his subject, the poet and historian Lídia do Carmo Ferreira (as in *Chronicle*). That attempt turns into an account of the nation from Lídia's birth in 1928 (like the book's dedicatee, Mário Pinto de Andrade, an MPLA cofounder who broke with Neto in 1974) through independence and the civil war thereafter (as in *One Hundred Years*). Dreaming of the sea is to dream of death, a wise grandmother says, as independence brings a night of victory and of defeat for Lídia. "[A] story of a desperate love" (*Rainy Season* 9) segues into a heroine who thinks her grandfather's house is the largest in town and then cannot identify it years later. Educated like the heroine in *Of Love and Other Demons*, she can recite poems by St. Francis of Assisi, knows the secrets of the Bible, conjugates the most obscure Latin verbs, and eats roses. The author seems to be working his way through a serious case of García-Márquez-imitativitis, until a chapter epigraph pulls up "Operation Carlota," written almost twenty years earlier: "'It was a terrible war [the Angolan civil war], in which one had to defend oneself against both the mercenaries and the snakes, both cannons and cannibals,' Gabriel García Márquez, in *Operation Carlota*, Mosca Azul publishers, Peru, 1977"(113). It then becomes clear that a far more complicated relationship than imitation is in play. The novel ends with a line as dramatic, flat, and hopeless as the last line of *No One Writes to the Colonel*, but in an altogether different key: "'This country's dead.' *Lisbon/Luanda* 1994" (192).

For García Márquez himself, twenty more-hopeful years earlier, Angola brought home how African his Caribbean was. Rebounding came "the world of my childhood . . . my whole childhood, things I had forgotten. . . . I even had again the nightmares I had as a child" (*El olor* 73).[11] Anticipating a world "strange, totally strange," he found instead the familiar one of Aracataca and its nearby banana plantation Macondo, a Bantu word for "banana" (Bell-Villada 19). Customs that were indigenized in Caribbean Colombia had arrived long ago through the slave port of Cartagena in chains, "forced, outrageous, but lucky" for the "magical syncretism" of the coast's culture (*Notas* 120).[12] One trace was the legendary Marquesita of La Sierpe (*Entre cachacos* 117–21, 136–40, 145–53, 161–65). Able from a distance, with only a description and a location, to heal a dying person or to send snakes to kill an enemy, she is the prototype of Big Mama (119), but her initial beneficence more closely resembles Ben Okri's Madame Koto (*The Famished Road*, 1991; *Songs of Enchantment*, 1993, Nigeria). She divides her powers among her heirs, who cannot take money for exercising their single inherited power, yet may accept gifts (136), like the diviners in Ngũgĩ's *Wizard of the Crow* (295). In Ouologuem's *Bound to Violence* (1968), readers learn how carefully asp-handlers train their snakes to kill. García Márquez, it turns out, was part of the African diaspora, or the African diaspora was part of him, without his having known it. That knowledge, which he described as splitting his life in two, he took back into his own writing (Amor; Deandrea 210). (See López-Mejía on the African diaspora in this volume.)

When *One Hundred Years* appeared in 1967, a flourishing Western-accessible, pan-African canon had already established itself. Representing imbricated discursive registers and realities, it had emerged in English and French in the mid-twentieth century, with Portuguese trailing thereafter, its longer literary tradition hobbled by the Salazar dictatorship (Rodrigues and Sheldon 79; Hamilton 240). Superstition and modernity coexisted in overlapping layers. Animist and Western religious traditions competed and combined. Violence persisted as a condition of order, and writers had equal access to Western literary and musical traditions as to indigenous oral and written alternatives. Written literature in Ethiopia dates from the fifth century CE, in Swahili from the seventeenth century, and in many other African languages from the nineteenth century. Currently, publication is often more robust in indigenous languages than in colonial languages (Barber 129).

Leading off the anglophone canon, Amos Tutuola (1920–1997, Nigeria) had published six novels before 1967, including *The Palm-Wine Drinkard* (1946, published in 1952) and

My Life in the Bush of Ghosts (1954), repurposing Yoruba folktales and earning Wole Soyinka's praise in 1963 for gathering material from two cultures and "exploiting them in one extravagant confident whole" (Soyinka 390). Soyinka later described his childhood (*Aké: The Years of Childhood*) as a "'Tutuolaic' world of daemons and wood spirits... as real and as intrusive [as] parents, Hausa traders, missionaries, 'babalawos,' educators, administrators, Hitler War (Ogun Hitila) and the women's uprising in Egbaland" (quoted in Awoyinfa n.p.). Silent between 1967 and 1981, Tutuola later published another half dozen works.

Chinua Achebe (1930–2013, Nigeria) had completed four novels anticipating the historical scope of *One Hundred Years*: colonialism's arrival in *Things Fall Apart* (1958), modern corruption through the earlier protagonist's grandson in *No Longer at Ease* (1960), theo-ideological conflict in *Arrow of God* (1964), and postcolonial satire in *A Man of the People* (1966). Uche Atuma describes *One Hundred Years* as the great Latin American novel: "That is, it is taken as their own *Things Fall Apart*, if you like" (n.p.) Wole Soyinka (Nigeria, 1934–) put modern villagers, forest spirits, the dead, and an ancient court on stage in *A Dance of the Forest* (1960). *The Swamp-Dwellers* (1958) and *The Lion and the Jewel* (1959) dealt with the strains of modernity and tradition, satirically in *Trials of Brother Jero* (1960). As *One Hundred Years* was being written, Soyinka sat in a Nigerian prison for his activism during the Biafran civil war, and in 1968 he published his translation of the Yoruba writer D. O. Fagunwa's *Forest of a Thousand Daemons* (1938; 1903–63). So vibrant was "marvelous" Yoruba writing that a British colonial committee in 1954 sponsored a competition for "realistic" rather than "spirit-in-the-forest" stories (Barber 143; Òkédìjí 33). Down in Lesotho, young Zakes Mda (1948–) concluded that African writing in English, rather than isiXhosa or Sesotho, had to be set in Nigeria (*Sometimes* 149).

In Anglophone Kenya, James Ngugi (1938–) set contending belief and political systems against each other in *Weep Not, Child* (1964), *The River Between* (1965), and *A Grain of Wheat* (1967), the last memorializing Kenya's Uhuru-winning Mau-Mau, who had terrified white Africa in the 1950s. Having abandoned his Leeds University thesis on Barbados's George Lamming and finished both his fourth novel *Petals of Blood* (1977) and a term of imprisonment, Ngũgĩ wa Thiong'o began to write under his African name and in Gĩkũyũ. Equally in the Anglo-realist tradition were (notwithstanding its title) Nadine Gordimer's *The Soft Voice of the Serpent* (1952; South Africa, 1923–2014) and Bessie Head's *When Rain Clouds Gather* (1968; Botswana, 1937–1986). Taking a hint from Brazil's João Guimarães Rosa, Angola's Luandino Vieira innovated linguistically, using Angolan-Portuguese street dialect for narration and in dialogue to tell realistic fables of the underclasses. The only moment "close to magic" in *Luuanda* (1964, 108) is a boy's rooster whistle that excites a chicken to escape soldiers' confiscation. After Lisbon's venerable Portuguese Writers Society awarded the book its Grand Prize in 1965, the book was banned, and the society was shut down, its offices wrecked (Ngũgĩ, *In the Name* 103).

West Africa's Francophone authors rendered folk beliefs as active realities, perhaps encouraged, like the Latin American pioneers of the marvelous real, by Parisian surrealism or, in Mongo Beti's case, by Voltairean irony (Cameroon, 1932–2001). In *Poor Christ of Bomba* (1956), Beti's innocent altar-boy narrator exposes, by his unwavering support, colonial Christianity as (ultimately, literally) the pox. *Mission to Kala* (1957) and *King Lazarus* (1958) mingle "wonder and participation" (Soyinka 396). Mali's Yambo Ouologuem (1940–2017) traverses 750 years of magic, sexuality, and deracination in *Bound to Violence* (1968), though charges that intertextual citations from Graham Greene and André Schwarz-Bart were plagiarism damaged his reputation.

Most strikingly, Guinea's Camara Laye (1928–1980) wove together the double perception of mysterious wonders and later knowledges, both African and European, in *L'Enfant noir* (*The Dark Child*, 1953). *Dramouss* (*A Dream of Africa*, 1966) represents as equally real, hard times in Paris, globalism's destruction of native crafts, guardian black snakes in the wall, and rules for dreaming the future with the white ball kept in a cowrie shell.[13] Ahmadou Kourouma (Ivory Coast, 1927–2003), also rendering beliefs as realities, opens *The Suns of Independence* (1968) on a death announced in both ordinary French and a translated Malinké idiom. The shade of the dead man rises and undertakes the journeys the dead make until he returns for his funeral (3-4). Thereafter, the novel shifts to the living dying, a sterile, beggarly, dispossessed prince and his desperate wife, her initiatory excision graphically described. Africa has been "démystifié" (149; "unmagicked" 100). Magic and realism seamlessly interlace when magic is an alternative ontology, as entirely a human creation as "realism."

To writers enmeshed in incommensurable belief systems and contentious histories, *One Hundred Years* offered intertextuality, hyperbole, allegory, and sometimes, its author lamented, a rhetoric. The Bible and Bunyan's *Pilgrim's Progress* figure in D. O. Fagunwa (and Fagunwa in Tutuola); Soyinka multiplies Fagunwa's four hundred divinities into a thousand daemons, but *One Hundred Years* opened all history, literature, and autobiography to appropriation and reinvention. Recognition was the source of its power. Mia Couto observes, "Africa is full of Macondos.... In Mozambique it isn't magical realism we live. It's real realism" (quoted in Quiroz; Fernández Quincoces n.p.).[14] Peter Kimani (Kenya) cites *One Hundred Years* as a "decisive inspiration" for *Dance of the Jakaranda* (2017) in its evocation of "narratives of my own community," even as he accords equal importance to Ngũgĩ and overlaps Colson Whitehead's *Underground Railroad* (2016) (Kimani, n.p.). Moses Isegawa (Uganda) called *One Hundred Years* his "model" for *Abyssinian Chronicles* (2000): "In Uganda also you hear stories as fantastic as those García Márquez tells. In fact, you live them daily" (quoted in Gámez n.p.). Syl Cheney-Coker (1945–, Sierra Leone) tells the best story. In 1972, pursuing his passion for the poets Pablo Neruda and César Vallejo, he recognized, astonished, the gypsies in *One Hundred Years*. Those were no gypsies; they were Tuaregs, who came from the north, spread out their things, told about the road having eyes and visions, and dug cowrie shells from the ground (Palmer 25–26). Mia Couto sums up: all African writers have a debt to Latin America's magical realism; it "encouraged us and authorized our breaking from European models" (quoted in Quiroz n.p.).[15]

García Márquez rapidly became canonical. Transforming the University of Nairobi's literature department in the mid-1970s, Ngũgĩ wa Thiong'o put García Márquez ahead of Richard Wright, George Lamming, Balzac, Dickens, Shakespeare, and Brecht, and in the middle of the list after Achebe, Sembène, Lu Hsun, and Alex La Guma (*Decolonising* 95, 105). Soyinka brought the Colombian to the University of Ife's students in his 1981 inaugural lectures (Awoyinfa n.p.). Achebe included García Márquez in his list of world writers to read, along with Joyce, Hemingway, and new writers from the Caribbean (173). In 2009, Britain's *Wasafiri*, a magazine for international contemporary writing, asked twenty-five authors to name the book that had most shaped world literature over the previous twenty-five years. *One Hundred Years* was the only book named more than once, by one Indian and two African writers (Chika Unigwe and Nii Parkes). Of other authors named, three had been influenced by *One Hundred Years* (Rushdie, Morrison, Okri). When García Márquez died, African journalists outside South Africa emphasized his political commitments over his literary accomplishments, often echoing his rhetoric (Osundare, "Gabriel"; "Adieu, Gabo"). He told stories like their own, such as passing a dead man on the street, and he had lived in a dangerous country, Colombia (Macha).

Not everyone channels García Márquez. Women writers once appreciated but ignored him—there are no traces of him in Mariama Bâ's groundbreaking *So Long a Letter* (Senegal, 1981), Nadifa Mohamed (*Orchard of Lost Souls*, 2013, Somalia), or Tsitsi Dangarembga (*Nervous Conditions*, 1988, Zimbabwe). Chika Unigwe's *On Black Sisters' Street* (2007, Nigeria) hinges on a prophecy so natural that the pig's tail in *One Hundred Years* would never come to mind had Unigwe not said that every writer she knows has felt the influence of *One Hundred Years* (Parkes and Unigwe n.p.). Her *Night Dancer* (2012) evokes Bâ's *So Long a Letter*. Tsitsi Dangarembga's opening line challenges any novel for most stunning first sentence, but it is hers alone: "I was not sorry when my brother died" (*Nervous Conditions*, 1). Her intertextuality stays home. The omnivorous reading and name of her heroine, Tambudzai, suggest Dambudzo Marechera, a fellow Zimbabwean writer who died in 1987. Feminine Tambudzai means "Give trouble," unisex Dambudzo "Trouble." In *The Book of NOT*, clueless Tambudzai supposes *A Grain of Wheat* is an agricultural, not revolutionary, novel by some "starving Kenyan author" (117). Novuyo Rosa Tshuma's *House of Stone* (Zimbabwe, 2018), with its eerie doubling and historical ambition, recalls Marechera's title, *House of Hunger* (1978). Marechera favored the term "fantastic realism," but his own explosive practice evokes less García Márquez than, inadvertently, Guillermo Cabrera Infante. (Impatient with a García Márquez-adoring Swedish girlfriend, a Binyavanga Wainaina narrator demands: "What is it with you white people and magic realism?" He reads Dambudzo Marechera "when he is alone" [104, 106; Kenya, 1971–2019].)

Chimamanda Ngozi Adichie (Nigeria) claims Achebe in the first sentence of *Purple Hibiscus*: "Things started to fall apart at home" (3). The way things fall apart, however, in manly violence and womanly assertiveness, looks to Dangarembga's *Nervous Conditions*, while fire-colored flower petals recall Ngũgĩ's *Petals of Blood* (Cooper, *New* 122, 126). In this intertextual stew of writers absorbing each other, women writers have begun to exploit García Márquez, particularly Namwali Serpell, *The Old Drift* (Zambia, 2019) and Jennifer Nansubuga Makumbi, *Kintu* (Uganda, 2014). Yet Serpell's magic mosquitoes also hark back to Sony Labou Tansi's ferocious flies (*Life and a Half,* 1979). In Makumbi, the curse, first man (Kintu), and echoing names evoke the Buendías for readers of García Márquez, while Achebe's readers will find Ikemefune, precolonial chronicle, and modern religious tensions. With a rational, if terrifying, explanation for the mysteriously fated deaths of the opening, Makumbi keeps her multiple lines of affiliation braided.

Although García Márquez has not been translated into any African language, his influence may extend to writers in African languages who remain untranslated and do not, like Ngũgĩ, translate themselves. The observation is speculative, but the structure of the Yoruba writer Oládèjo Òkédìjí's *Atótó Arére* (After That, 1981), as described by Karin Barber, suggests *One Hundred Years*: an execution by firing squad from which the narrative backtracks, comes forward and reaches again, and then passes, adding new characters and episodes. In *Atótó*, a man in a crowd anxiously scans birds overhead as his friend is executed for an act he himself committed. Retracing the steps leading to that moment, the novel reaches that day and moves on. The opening scene is "the structural turning point of the novel towards which and out of which all the narrative flows" (Barber 157). The execution having been retold, the narrative splinters into multiple perspectives, "and the last point of view of all is that of one of the vultures, waiting impatiently for làbá to die" (Barber 157). Òkédìjí cannot be asked, inasmuch as he died in April 2019, but he read English and practiced an "intense intertextual allusiveness" (Barber 159) that included American crime thrillers. One may read colonial languages and write in Yoruba, Shona, or Ndebele. Conversely, such authors as Mia Couto and Zakes Mda have seen to their own translations into African languages (Chikwava n.p.; *Sometimes* 505).

The Francophone playwright Sony Labou Tansi (Republic of Congo, 1947–1995) was among the first writers worldwide to adopt and adapt García Márquez. (Toni Morrison's *Song of Solomon* was earlier, 1977.) Equally affined to Ionesco, Artaud, and Jarry, Sony moves from random echoes (*Life and a Half,* 1979) through obtrusively appropriated structural devices (*The Shameful State,* 1981; *The Seven Solitudes of Lorsa Lopez,* 1985) to a springboard for antithetical arguments. In *Les yeux du volcan* (Eyes of the Volcano, 1988), a gigantic stranger, "the colossus," arrives in a town, arousing curiosity and then adulation, to foment revolution, but he is murdered, a grim twist on "El ahogado más hermoso del mundo" ("The Handsomest Drowned Man in the World"). Sony's final novel, *Le commencement des douleurs* (The Beginning of Sorrow, 1995), also untranslated, reworks a premise of *Love in the Time of Cholera,* an inappropriate and deferred love affair, that persists. Sony's appropriations vindicate his posthumously published note: "[S]omeday somebody will say 'I influenced him.' To them all I say, yes, you've influenced me, and I've gone further than you" (*L'autre monde* 11).

Darkly, violently inventive, Sony's *Life and a Half* begins as a daughter watches the Providential Guide carve up and eviscerate her father, the dissident Martial. An eating contest resembles Aureliano Segundo's when the Providential Guide bests the famous Kanawamara, who said he had come from where the sun came, as well as Kopa the soup pot, Samou the terrible, Ansotoura the son of buffaloes, Gramanata the paunch, and others (13) The heroine outdoes Eréndira with 363 men in one night (49). Upon his succession, Jean-Heart-of-Stone decrees blue the color of the nation, and everything must be blue, including clothing, cars, and houses (100). When Jean-Heart-of-Stone weeps for his children, the townsfolk buzz, "At last, he's learned how a cadaver weighs" (109). A doctor tortured to death with a fork ponders, "Solitude. Solitude. Man's greatest reality is Solitude" (24). In a forest of constant rain, a pair come to a clearing, which they name, where Jean Calcium years later will discover the sound machine with sounds from thirty-nine pygmy civilizations going back millions of years; there he builds his fifth fly factory to wage war against Katamalanasia and the foreign power that supplies the guides (61). Closer to *Autumn of the Patriarch*, a dissident is imprisoned for 88 years, the time for his ideas never comes, and he dies at age 133. Buried by Jean-Heart-of-Father, he does not decompose. Some observations García Márquez should have invented but did not: to have a pretty woman, one need only claim she was one of Martial's mistresses, in "this new technique of seduction without regrets" (18). In the first week of the third month of the second year of another reign, the period of hunting pygmies to integrate them was at an all-time high, and three thousand pygmies were imprisoned in an amusement park (71). As he is murdered, and when he reappears, Martial repeats, with dignity, "I do not want to die this death" (6, 7). Something of that subject position reappears in the protagonist of Ngũgĩ's *Matigari* (1987), the rare fictional character to have his arrest actually ordered by an irate dictator, Kenya's Daniel arap Moi (Isaacson).

If *Life and a Half* recycles certain instants that cling to memory, *Shameful State* and *Seven Solitudes* appropriate more deliberately. *The Shameful State* (1981) embraces the communal jubilation of "Big Mama's Funeral" and the shifting voices of *Autumn of the Patriarch*, sliding from dialogue to monologue to commentary within a sentence, as the dictator Colonel Lopez celebrates National Mom, redraws the national boundaries as a square, and strokes his herniated testicle. Turds begin appearing in mugs, beds, caviar; the national parrot is executed, and every government employee resigns one day, unwilling to leave in this shameful state the country "to the children of our children of our children" (46).

In *The Seven Solitudes of Lorsa Lopez* (1985), "Lorsa Lopez" is almost Gabriel García Márquez: an initial letter repeats (GG, LL), as do the first vowel (GarMar, LorLop) and the first and final syllables (cia/sa, quez/pez), and the name itself is egregiously Hispanic in a Francophone text, sidestepping, or swiping, Sony's fellow Congolese novelist Henri Lopes. The first sentence evokes *Chronicle of a Death Foretold*: a murder will occur on a predicted day, for infidelity, motivated by sexual jealousy. A corpse arrives in a trunk, sweetly arranged, like Fernanda's father. But this corpse has been murdered, and we never learn by whom. A character is named the beauty of beauties, and the Virgin Mary's image floats in a quadriga (a four-horse chariot)—but no one believes it. Remedios the Beauty's sheet-gripping floating off to heaven recalls once again the Assumption of the Virgin Mary, August 15 (when everything closes, even the Bibliothèque Nationale in allegedly secular republican Paris). The novelist found that interpretation so ludicrous he remembered its source, "a Catholic schoolteacher" (*Notas* 53–54).[16] In *Lorsa Lopez*, before José Saramago's *Stone Raft* set sail (1986) or Kojo Laing's and Mia Couto's countries vanished into the abyss in *Major Gentl* (1992) and *Last Flight of the Flamingo* (2000), a city disappears out to sea. Aristophanes contributes a sex strike; the barely visible first-person narrator is female. Before the police arrive, forty-seven years elapse, by which time no one remembers much about the crime, but the parrot is shot and the photographer incarcerated. Sony sacrifices parrots while Ngũgĩ's professors of parrotology persist (*Matigari, Wizard of the Crow*). Ngũgĩ repeats the title "shameful state" in his translation of *Wizard of the Crow* (2006).

Neither Sony nor Syl Cheney-Coker (nor García Márquez) cares for the term "magical realism."[17] Sony's intense spirituality finds "[i]t's all magic," from the sun itself to what professors would call "magical literature," but "my mother or my grandmother" considered simply ordinary reality ("La magie" 58–59; Clark). Cheney-Coker calls magical realism "intellectual humbug" because West Africa's reality is marvelous (*Sacred* vii). He adopted *One Hundred Years* as a formal framework for a marvelous historical epic of Sierra Leone, as Virgil rewrote Homer for Rome.

Cheney-Coker's *The Last Harmattan of Alusine Dunbar* (1990) transforms Melquíades into Sulaiman the Nubian, who returns anagrammatized as Alusine Dunbar, to foresee the history of Malagueta from before its founding by former slaves, through its colonial struggles, into the corrupt present. In a final affiliative gesture, the novel reproduces the metafictional self-reference and Caribbean hurricane that bring an end to *One Hundred Years*. The last harmattan (a West African wind) takes Alusine Dunbar away on a flying carpet, defenestrates the president, and pinions a corrupt couple copulating like dogs forever in the air, in the pages of his book, named in italics. As with Sony, the echoes signify most in the differences they reveal. Much like *One Hundred Years*, *The Last Harmattan* begins with an imprisoned military officer "[t]wo nights after his failed coup," expecting death. The mirage of *One Hundred Years* materializes. The general hangs. Like Mongo Beti, who reminds readers that the parallel to African magic is neither Western magic nor witchcraft but Western religion, the prologue links African djinn and Portuguese Black Madonna. Cheney-Coker retells Tutuola's story of the proud girl who marries a demon, borrows magic carpets from Arabia (as did *One Hundred Years*), and invents folklore of his own, like the Arab woman transformed into an elephant with ten identical little girls under her skirts, a Nutcracker ballet that explains Lebanese fecundity (Palmer 262–64). Certain motifs appearing in García Márquez reverse their meanings. A herniated testicle glows, a divining tool. Ants devour the last abandoned Buendía; Cheney-Coker's trails of black ants lead to life and illumination.

In *Sacred River* (2014), evidently rankled that his affiliative gesture had been designated "derivative" (Gaylard 40), Cheney-Coker responded with aggressive intertextuality. His chapter titles include "The River Between," "The Unbearable Loneliness of Being Chief Justice," "Of Mice and Men," "The Not-so-Discreet Charm of the Bourgeoisie," "A Man of the People," "Professor of Desire," "Return of the Native," and "Beasts of No Nation." Textual citations range from Mariama Bâ through Breyten Breytenbach's *Confessions of an Albino Terrorist* and Soyinka's *Strong Breed*, to James Baldwin and Alusine Dunbar. Reaffirming the Afro-Caribbean connection, the novel focuses on a democratically elected African dictator-to-be, inspired by his dreams of Haiti's Henri Christophe. Tankor Satani builds a Xanadu to answer Christophe's Sans Souci; vultures swoop into and out of the presidential palace. There are secrets that everyone knows, including the vengeful mermaid deprived of her comb; the magic airplane of Palo the Eunuch (recalling Laing's *Woman of the Airplanes*); and Samson, the excrement-throwing chimp, finally released by a crowd invading the palace. This inspired exuberance is enclosed by a prologue recounting a rape in time of civil war, its only magical element being the victim's survival, and an epilogue in which nature's marvelous reality exacts retribution. Threading through the politics are generations of men and women making choices about their lives and loves, ultimately sustained in spite of corruption and disasters of war by the earth and its rivers.

Ngũgĩ also rejected "magical realism" as an influence on his *Wizard of the Crow* (2006), naming instead orature (Isaacson). Always stylistically protean, from the modernism of *Petals of Blood* to the devastating imitative orality of *Matigari*, Ngũgĩ's *Wizard* adds to his repertoire a tragicomic allegorical invention, including Fanon's "white-ache" and withering money bushes, yet oral storytelling is its base and frame. *Devil on the Cross* (1980) is linked by Oliver Lovesey to García Márquez's magical realism (65), as *Wizard* is by Joseph McLaren (58). By the time Ngũgĩ turned to the novel of the dictator, such inventions had been naturalized in African fiction. Anticipated by Augusto Roa Bastos's *Yo el Supremo* (1974) and *The Autumn of the Patriarch* (1975) (Armillas-Teseyra 187), comic-satirical novels taking on the dictator included Henri Lopes's *The Laughing Cry* (1982; its narrator's innocence Beti-inspired), Sony's *Life and a Half* (1979) and *Shameful State* (1983), Kojo Laing's *Major Gentl and the Achimota Wars* (1992), and Ahmadou Kourouma's *Waiting for the Vote of the Wild Animals* (1998). Ngũgĩ's brilliant recursive structure and genial didacticism lead to neither apocalypse nor transcendence, but to a side-by-side moving on of ordinary people, disconnected, isolated, though maintaining multiple communities by telling stories. Ngũgĩ also gently intimates that his readers may need to learn something. Whether in Gĩkũyũ or in English translation, he leaves his Kiswahili untranslated, like Henry Fielding sporting a Latin tag. In Fielding's day, Latin, like Kiswahili now, separated the literate from the illiterate, those who can read it from those who cannot, in a hierarchy of readership.

Brenda Cooper's *Magical Realism in West Africa: Seeing with a Third Eye* (1998) led the way in designating as "magical realist" works so diverse as to have nothing in common except, as novelist J. M. Coetzee puts it, "the elision of the *either-or* holding 'fantasy' and 'reality' apart" (263). Coetzee was rescuing García Márquez from "the tag 'magic realist' attached to him," describing as now "commonplace... [what] caused such stir when *One Hundred Years of Solitude* came out in 1967" (263). Cooper links Cheney-Coker, who happily intertextualizes with García Márquez but detests "magical realism"; Ben Okri (1959–) in whose early works García Márquez left some traces, as Faulkner left traces in García Márquez and was then left behind; and B. Kojo Laing (1946–2017, Ghana), who resembles García Márquez not at all in his whimsical verbal pyrotechnics. Cooper has since identified her "magical realism" with Harry Garuba's "animist materialism" (Garuba; Cooper, *New* 20), yet no terms can catch the variety of literary practices coruscating through modern African fiction or the slippery meanings of belief, and not only in Africa.

In Ben Okri's book of stories *Stars of the New Curfew* (1988), his fourth volume, "Worlds That Flourish" recalls "Monologue of Isabel Watching It Rain in Macondo" and Juan Rulfo's *Pedro Páramo*. On the second day of a rain that keeps falling, "I went to the window, my ears reverberating with persistently dripping water, and looked out. That was when I discovered I had temporarily lost the names of things" (21). When the narrator emerges, a tumultuous journey takes him to—and from—the land of the dead, where he recognizes his missing neighbor and flees again, sounding a warning that goes unheeded. Other stories—"In the Shadow of War," "City of Red Dust," and "When the Lights Return"—adhere to a devastatingly rigorous realism, like García Márquez's early stories, while "What the Tapster Saw" presses a Tutuolan fable into new territory. The title story mingles the realistic and the nightmare-oneiric. Much as "Big Mama's Funeral" discovered the attitude that enabled *One Hundred Years*, so "Stars of the New Curfew" achieves the stylistic breakthrough that sustains *The Famished Road* (1991) and *Songs of Enchantment* (1993). Okri animates the masquerades, alive, breathing, threatening, juxtaposed with the bitter dust of every day. Such later novels as *Starbook* (2007) take yet another direction. The powerful visionary world Okri calls up has no parallel or ties with *One Hundred Years* or Latin America or, indeed, anything anywhere else. His is its own African Genesis (Altares n.p.; Oliva 178).

B. Kojo Laing's brilliant comedy is verbal. *Search Sweet Country* (1986), *Woman of the Airplanes* (1988), *Major Gentl and the Achimota Wars* (1992), and the theological *Big Bishop Roko and the Altar Gangsters* (2006) invent words and proverbs, sport flying witches overseeing the welfare of Accra, define an "optimist, [as] the monkey that believed he could climb down his own tail in an emergency," and describe the persuasive Dr. Boadi as "an expert in ironing out moral creases" (*Search* 45, 48). Laing's glossaries in the first two novels designate the words he has himself invented, but *Major Gentl* remakes the glossary crib more purposefully: "I believe that more parochial areas of the world need a broadening of vocabulary.... Some [words] are invented, most are direct translations from Akan and Ga and sometimes Hausa. It is usual in Ghana (with such a cosmopolitan mix of cultures) to intersperse one language with words from another. This ought to be done universally" (vi). "Lungulungu" for convoluted or labyrinthine; "Wasa," Akan for "it is finished"; "Kwee" for fart? Or, a useful reminder in this time of invented afterlives, and remote from García Márquez: "Especially for the poor and the powerless what greater horror was there than a Godless universe without true normative concerns?" (*Big* 44).

Laing's imbricated languages or Okri's hallucinatory powers represent, as Akwaeke Emezi (*Freshwater*, 2018; lineage of Okri) observes, alternative realities, or ontologies. Engaging the fantastic, Mia Couto and Kojo Laing reinvent the proverb's frozen dialectic, restoring to European languages a form of eloquence. In *Memoirs of a Porcupine*, Alain Mabanckou shifts his style to animate belief, fabulating without allegory, in a tale that turns inside out to reveal a terrifyingly realistic portrait of resentment and isolation. Isegawa's magical realism debunks its wonders, like Toni Morrison's flying Solomon or Carpentier's Mackandal. A priest flies from his steeple while installing a cross, but sadly kills both himself and a woman hit by the ladder. Isegawa catches Idi Amin Dada's appeal and Africa's diversity, as a character protests an absurdity: "[W]hoever heard of a woman getting circumcised?" (19). Answer: Ngũgĩ and Kourouma, and they do not like it. In Ngũgĩ's *River Between,* her circumcision kills a girl, though Africans defend the practice from Europeans in *A Grain of Wheat.* Kourouma in *Suns of Independence* depicts female circumcision as horror.

Appreciation of García Márquez and other Latin American writers has been generous among African authors. Ungulani Ba Ka Khosa (Mozambique, 1957–) complains that Ngũgĩ wa Thiong'o, Sembène Ousmane, and Mongo Beti were all saying "no"; theirs was a protest literature that rejected continental realities. From Latin America came "that breath of freedom, as if it were saying: 'You can write, don't be ashamed to talk about witchcraft. You can write about that.' And so, although it may not appear so, this breath of freedom came from outside the country. Write at will. Accept your own country. Accept your diversity" (Leite 232). Mozambique's first woman novelist, Paulina Chiziane (1955–), whose astonishing novel *The First Wife: A Tale of Polygamy* (*Niketche* 2002) is more delightful than any book on its topic should be, credits for her literary formation the Portuguese Florbela Espanca and the Brazilian Jorge Amado (Leite 219); her marvels flash no trace of García Márquez. By contrast, Marcelo Panguana (1951–) singles out García Márquez for enabling him to discover his own Mozambique: "[A]t the time I was fascinated with Gabriel García Márquez and magical realism, and so I wrote *A Balada dos Deuses* (Ballad of the Gods, 1991) as an attempt to get to know this magical reality that we have here in Mozambique. . . . recovering the magic of reality—magical realism . . . allows us to see that we haven't moved very far from this magical world [that] distinguishes us and makes our social and cultural reality much richer" (Leite 159).

Going further, Ungulani cited the Angolan Pepetela's *Yaka* (1984) and Senegal's Sembène Ousmane's *Xala* (1974) as, respectively, "a reading of a cultural reality of which one is not organically part" or of an "urban world as if to say: 'This is not quite mine'" (Leite 232). Paradoxically, in Ungulani's *Ualalapi* (1987), "No" is Ualalapi's final cry as he vanishes from a world caught between a lethal African king and deadlier Portuguese colonels and functionaries (Leite 21). The only traces of *One Hundred Years* are temporal moments anticipated though never represented and miraculously flowing blood (Matusse 102). Both *Yaka* and *Xala*, however, compared to their authors' earlier works, gesture toward the new freedom Ungulani cites, writing about witch doctors and inventing myths. Moving from the realism of *God's Bits of Wood*, Sembène's *Xala* (1974) sends an elegantly suited, villa-dwelling, Europeanized Muslim to healers, seers, marabouts, and witch doctors to cure an impotency curse, ending with a visitation out of Luis Buñuel's *Viridiana* (1961). Sembène made a film of his novel (1975).

In *Yaka* (1984), the Angolan revolutionary Pepetela (nom de guerre of Artur Carlos Maurício Pestana dos Santos) put a perceiving, speaking, invented Yaka statue at the center of an otherwise realistic historical narrative. There had been nothing magical in *Mayombe* (1971, published 1980), his account from within the guerrilla war, its narrative shifting between third and multiple first persons. A decade later, *Return of the Water*

Spirit (1995) embraced a magical realist conceit against postrevolutionary Angola's socialist and capitalist corruptions and invoked Vieira's authority. High-rise apartment buildings on the lagoon, in the best part of town, collapse, gently, suddenly, and irresistibly.[18] The authors Vieira and Santos debate how to explain the lagoon's turning red when the water spirit's tree was cut down—blood, insists Vieira; chemical interactions, replies Santos (*Return of the Water Spirit* 37). Pepetela has since moved on to a parodic detective, with a big bottom: *Jaime Bunda, Secret Agent: Story of Various Mysteries* (2001).

There is sustained critical attention worth paying to García Márquez relative to Africa. His journalism belongs with the "nay-sayers" Beti, Ngũgĩ, and Sembène. His fascination with power challenges comparison with Soyinka's (*You Must Set Forth at Dawn* [2006]) and demands a deconstruction like Kourouma's (*Waiting for the Vote of the Wild Animals*). He never felt Mia Couto's desire to invent a translator, displacing Black ventriloquism (*The Last Flight of the Flamingo*). It would be good to learn how much he knew about the Makonde (of Tanzania, Mozambique, and Kenya), to whom the Belgian's airplane is misdelivered in *One Hundred Years*, or what owner gave the name Macondo to that banana plantation near Aracataca. That information may never be available, but since García Márquez claimed, "My starting point has to be a real fact. That is how I function as a writer" (Bahgat n.p.), it seems well to end on "a real fact" that marks his continuing contribution to stimulating African writers to engage with each other and their art, across languages and nations.

The real name "Macondo," visible on maps of the banana zone near Aracataca, displaced the real name of a nearby town, turning both into an invention and a metaphor for invention. It has been attacked at home (*McOndo* [1996]) but has found a happier afterlife traveling. It now names a literary society that sponsors a literary festival dedicated to promoting African writers and their communication within and among nations, across one continent and on to other continents.

In September 2019, the Kenyan novelist Yvonne Adhiambo Owuor (*Dust*, 2013) and the journalist Anja Bengelstorff, cofounders of the Macondo Book Society, Nairobi, organized the Macondo Literary Festival, bringing together Anglophone and Lusophone authors from Angola, Brazil, Cape Verde, Guinea-Bissau, Zimbabwe, South Africa, Kenya, Mozambique, Portugal, Nigeria, and Portugal-UK. The French were left out, but Mozambique's Mia Couto implies they would have been welcome:

> Separated by official languages, geography and strategic regions, our continent is unknown to itself today more than ever. In the field of literature, we know little of what our neighbors are debating and publishing. Even worse, what we know comes from Europe, through old and untouchable colonial circuits. African literary festivals can be a way to break this isolation and reciprocal ignorance (Macondo Book Society n.p.).

The festival's organizers explained the name: "Macondo is a fictional place in the novel *One Hundred Years of Solitude* by Colombian Nobel Laureate Gabriel García Márquez, a place where magical things happen" (n.p.). That a word of African origin, domesticated and disseminated across the ocean, should return to bring Africans of different languages together in mutual discovery, is a little magical and very real.

Notes

1. *Por la libre* dates "Angola, un año después: Una nación en la escuela primaria" as 30 May (161); it actually appeared in two parts on 27 and 28 May 1977 in the *Washington Post*. *Por la libre* omits the *Post*'s parenthetical demurrals to allegations of Portuguese destructiveness: one source claimed that colonials' trucks, far from being destroyed, were carried away to Cuba. "Operación Carlota—Cuba en Angola" is available in translation online at a site dedicated to Rhodesian [sic] history; in print in García Márquez, *Changing the History of Africa*; and extracted in the *Washington Post*, 10, 11, and 12 Jan. 1977. Except for the first paragraph, the section "Cuban Internationalism" is reprinted in Guevara, *Congo Diary* (3–4). García Márquez, "Los meses de tinieblas—El 'Che' en el Congo" expands anecdotal material from "Operación Carlota" (134–35), but omits Che's study of "cultural absurdities" ("estos absurdos culturales"; 147). All translations are the author's unless a translated work is cited.
2. "Un negro alto y bien plantado ... Un hombre tan vistoso que llamaba la atención por todas partes, hasta el punto de que el Che Guevara le ordenó en broma que se pintara de blanco para no despertar tanta curiosidad a su paso" (191).
3. "'Tanzania', dijo, 'no es un país en vías de desarrollo, come se dice ahora por una traducción fácil del inglés (developing country), sino un país subdesarrollado que ni siquiera ha empezado a encontrar las vías para dejar de serlo'" (*Notas* 176).
4. "Las condiciones culturales eran todavía muy próximas a la Edad de Piedra" ("Operación Carlota" 146–47).
5. "En la casa de un ministro de la UNITA que vivía con el confort propio de su rango, los hombres del MPLA encontraron dentro de un refrigerador las vísceras sobrantes y varios frascos con la sangre congelado de los prisioneros de guerra que se habían comido" ("Operación Carlota" 149). Africans' horror of cannibalism, visible in Mali's thirteenth-century epic *Sundiata*, the evil sorcerer's severed heads, and human drumskins, continues (*Sundiata* 39; Mūchiri 221–23).
6. "Era una guerra atroz, en la cual había que cuidarse tanto de los mercenarios como de las serpientes, y tanto de los cañones como de los caníbales" ("Operación Carlota" 148). "Las supersticiones atávicas no solo eran un inconveniente para la vida diaria, sino también para la guerra" (147).
7. "Con todo, nunca lo hubiera imaginado. Era un olor virulento, con una cierta índole sobrenatural, que no parecía ser el olor de las cosas, ni de los animales ni de la gente, sino el olor ineluctable de la vida en el otro lado del mundo" (162). Versus Luanda: "Era todo lo contrario de la imagen convencional del África negra. Tampoco tenía nada del Portugal soñoliento y católico de las canciones portuguesas sino que parecía más bien un balneario de moda de la Riviera italiana con un malecón interminable de palmeras iguales y rascacielos de vidrios azules frente a un mar juvenil" (162).
8. "En los territorios liberados se elevaba el nivel político y cultural de la población, se combatía el tribalismo y el racismo y se fomentaba la educación gratuita y la salud pública. Era la simiente de una nueva sociedad" (148).
9. "[L]a colonización mental" (147).

10. "Aquel paso fugaz y anónimo del Che Guevara por el África dejó sembrada una semilla que nadie había de erradicar. Algunos de sus hombres se trasladaron a Brazzaville y allí instruyeron unidades de guerrillas por el Partido Africano de Independencia de Guinea y Cabo Verde (PAIGC), que dirigía Amílcar Cabral, y en especial para el MPLA" (135–36).
11. "Yo esperaba encontrarme en un mundo extraño, totalmente extraño, y desde el momento en que puse los pies allí, desde el momento mismo en que olí el aire, me encontré de pronto en el mundo de mi infancia. Sí, me encontré toda mi infancia, costumbres y cosas que yo había olvidado. Volví a tener, inclusive, las pesadillas que tenía en la niñez" (73). He dates his visit to 1978.
12. "Un sincretismo mágico cuyo interés artístico y cuya propia fecundidad artística son inagotables. La contribución Africana fue forzosa e indignante, pero afortunada" (120).
13. Christopher L. Miller is anxious to make Camara's *L'enfant noir* an "as-told-to" book written by an undetermined white Frenchwoman (25, 31, 90–103, 209n16), without evidence and without appearing to have read Camara's other fictions, which, unlike *The Radiance of the King*, clearly share authorship with *L'enfant noir*. *Radiance of the King* (1954), published under Camara's name, is arguably a deliberate hoax in collaboration with a white Belgian, and affords an interesting case study in white and Afro-American critical response, viz. the preference for a white male protagonist, not a Black one, who submits to an African king.
14. Fernández Quincoces cites Quiroz, but the sentences after the ellipsis are not in the Quiroz interview.
15. "Además pienso que todos los escritores africanos tenemos una deuda con lo que se conoce como realismo mágico latinoamericano porque creo que de alguna forma nos alentó y nos autorizó a romper con el modelo europeo. Fue importante y toda una referencia'" (Quiroz n.p.)
16. "Un maestro católico enseñaba que la subida al cielo de Remedios la Bella era una transposición poética de la ascensión en cuerpo y alma de la virgen María" (53–54).
17. García Márquez seems to have endorsed the term only once, when he referred angrily to the "magic-realist novel that is present-day life in Colombia" at the time of his 1981 flight from the country; "esa gran novela de realismo mágico que es la vida real de Colombia" (*Notas* 295).
18. The human anti hcroine of *Water Spirit* is a staunch Marxist who turns corrupt capitalist; she is not the president's daughter. From January 20 to 26, 2020, the *New York Times* ran a series of articles alleging that Isabel dos Santos, daughter of former president José Eduardo dos Santos, siphoned billions of dollars from state revenues through shell companies with the assistance of American and European banks, financial advisers, and consulting firms (Boston Consulting Group, McKinsey & Company, PwC [PricewaterhouseCoopers]). Forsythe (1) through "When Firms Profit from Poor Nations" (12). The first story appeared online "How U.S. Firms Helped Africa's Richest Woman Exploit Her Country's Wealth." The lead author for the *Times* was Michael Forsythe.

Works Cited

Achebe, Chinua. *Conversations with Chinua Achebe*. Edited by Bernth Lindfors, U of Mississippi P, 1997.

Adichie, Chimamanda Ngozi. *Purple Hibiscus*. Algonquin Books of Chapel Hill, 2012.

"Adieu, Gabo: Gabriel García Márquez, Father of Magic Realism" and "Reflections." *Lagos Sun*, 1 Aug. 2014.

Agualusa, José Eduardo. *The Book of Chameleons* (2004). Translated by Daniel Hahn, Arcadia, 2006.

Agualusa, José Eduardo. *D. Nicolau Água-Rosada e outras estórias verdadeiras e inverosímeis.* Vega, 1990.

Agualusa, José Eduardo. *A General Theory of Oblivion* (2012). Translated by Daniel Hahn, Harvill Secker, 2015.

Agualusa, José Eduardo. *My Father's Wives* (2007). Translated by Daniel Hahn, Arcadia, 2008.

Agualusa, José Eduardo. *Rainy Season* (1996). Translated by Daniel Hahn, Arcadia, 2009.

Altares, Guillermo. "La Voz de África: Interview with Ben Okri." *El Pais*, 29 Dec. 2007, //elpais.com/diario/2007/12/29/babelia/1198889418_850215.html. Accessed 3 Mar. 2019.

Amor, Aouini. "África y los negros en la obra de Gabriel García Márquez." *AnMal Electrónica*, no. 31, 2011, pp. 123–45, www.amuafroc.wordpress.com. Accessed 1 Apr. 2019.

"Angola to Charge Africa's Richest Woman with Financial Crimes." *The New York Times*, 24 Jan. 2020, Sect. A, p. 8.

Armillas-Teseyra, Magalí. "Marvelous Autocrats: Disrupted Realisms in the Dictator Novel of the South Atlantic." *The Global South Atlantic*, edited by Kerry Bystron and Joseph R. Slaughter, Fordham UP, 2018, pp. 186–204.

Atuma, Uche. "Politics in a Game of Free Kicks?" *Lagos Sun*, 9 Mar. 2017.

Awoyinfa, Mike. "My Soyinka Satori Moment." *Lagos Sun*, 27 July 2019.

Bahgat, Elnadi, Adel Rifaat, and Miguel Labarca. "Gabriel García Márquez: The Writer's Craft (Interview)." *The Unesco Courier*, Feb. 1996, en.unesco.org/courier/febrero-1996/gabriel-garcia-marquez-writers-craft-interview. Accessed 12 Jan. 2020.

"Bank Opens Investigation of Africa's Richest Woman." *The New York Times*, 21 Jan. 2020, Sect. A, p. 9.

Barber, Karin. "African-Language Literature and Post-Colonial Criticism." *Imagined Commonwealths: Cambridge Essays on Commonwealth and International Literature in English*, edited by T. J. Cribb, St. Martin's Press, 1999, pp. 125–65.

Bell-Villada, Gene. *García Márquez: The Man and His Work*. U of North Carolina P, 1990.

Cheney-Coker, Syl. *The Last Harmattan of Alusine Dunbar*. Heinemann, 1990.

Cheney-Coker, Syl. *Sacred River*. Ohio UP, 2014.

Chikwava, Brian. "Mia Couto Talks to Brian Chikwava." *Wasafiri*, 22 Mar. 2017, www.wasafiri.org/article/mia-couto-talks-brian-chikwava/. Accessed 15 Mar. 2019.

Chiziane, Paulina. *The First Wife: A Tale of Polygamy*. (*Niketche*, 2002). Translated by David Brookshaw, Archipelago, 2016.

Clark, Phyllis. "Passionate Engagements: A Reading of Sony Labou Tansi's Private Ancestral Shrine." *Research in African Literatures*, vol. 31, no. 3, 2000, pp. 39–68.

Coetzee, J. M. *Inner Workings: Literary Essays 2000–2005*. Viking, 2007.

Cooper, Brenda. *Magical Realism in West African Fiction: Seeing with a Third Eye*. Routledge, 1998.

Cooper, Brenda. *A New Generation of African Writers: Migration, Material Culture & Language*. Boydell and Brewer, 2008.

Couto, Mia. *The Last Flight of the Flamingo* (2000). Translated by David Brookshaw, Serpent's Tail, 2004.

Couto, Mia. *Sleepwalking Land* (1992). Translated by David Brookshaw, Serpent's Tail, 2006.

Couto, Mia. *Under the Frangipani* (1996). Translated by David Brookshaw, Serpent's Tail, 2001.

Dangarembga, Tsitsi. *The Book of NOT: A Sequel to Nervous Conditions*. Ayebia Clarke, 2006.

Dangarembga, Tsitsi. *Nervous Conditions*. Seal Press, 1989.

Deandrea, Pietro. "'History Never Walks Here, It Runs in Any Direction': Carnival and Magic in the Fiction of Kojo Laing and Mia Couto." *Coterminous Worlds: Magical Realism and Contemporary Post-Colonial Literature in English*, edited by Elsa Linguanti, Francesco Casotti, and Carmen Concilio, Rodopi, 1999, pp. 209-25.

Dongala, Emmanuel. *Jazz and Palm Wine* (2003). Translated by Dominic Thomas, Indiana UP, 2017.

Emezi, Akwaeke. "Nurturing Possibilities by Casting Spells." Interview with Concepción de León, *The New York Times*, 13 Sept. 13, 2019, p. C16.

Fernández Quincoces, Sonia. "Gabriel García Márquez y los escritores africanos." 17 Apr. 2014, www.literafrica.wordpress.com/2014/04/17/gabo-y-los-escritores-africanos/. Accessed 1 Apr. 2019.

Forsythe, Michael, et al. "Earning Riches by Exploiting a Poor Nation." *The New York Times*, 20 Jan. 2020, Sect. A, p.1+.

"Gabriel García Márquez (1927-2014)." *Lagos Sun*, 2 May 2014.

Gámez, Pablo. "[Moses Isegawa] A la Feria del Libro de Bogotá llega el hombre que escribió el testamento de África del Sur," www.noticiasliterarias.com/articulos_literarios/articulos%20literarios%2012.htm. Accessed 17 June 2019.

García Márquez, Gabriel. "Angola, un año después: Una nación en la escuela primaria." *Por la libre/Obra periodistica 4 (1974-1995)*, edited by Jacques Gilard. Norma, 1999, pp. 161-75.

García Márquez, Gabriel. *Changing the History of Africa: Angola and Namibia*. No translator credited. Ocean Press, 1990, pp. 41-60.

García Márquez, Gabriel. *Cien años de soledad*. Edited by Jacques Joset, Cátedra, 1984.

García Márquez, Gabriel. *Crónica de una muerte anunciada*. Bruguera, 1981.

García Márquez, Gabriel. "La Marquesita de la Sierpe," "La Herencia Sobrenatural de la Marquesita," "La Extraña Idolatría de la Sierpe," "El Muerto Alegre." *Entre cachacos I/Obra periodistica 2 (1954-1955)*. Edited by Jacques Gilard, Bruguera, 1982, pp. 117-21, 136-40, 145-53, 161-65.

García Márquez, Gabriel. "Los meses de tinieblas—El 'Che' en el Congo." *Por la libre/Obra periodistica 4 (1974—1995)*, edited by Jacques Gilard, Norma, 1999, pp. 189-95.

García Márquez, Gabriel. *Notas de prensa 1980-1984*. Edited by Jacques Gilard, Mondadori, 1991.

García Márquez, Gabriel. *El olor de la guayaba: Conversaciones con Plinio Apuleyo Mendoza*. Sudamericana, 1982.

García Márquez, Gabriel. "Operación Carlota—Cuba en Angola." *Por la libre/Obra periodistica 4 (1974-1995)*, edited by Jacques Gilard, Norma, 1999, pp. 127-56.

García Márquez, Gabriel. *El otoño del patriarca*. Sudamericana, 1975.

García Márquez, Gabriel. *Por la libre/Obra periodistica 4 (1974-1995)*. Edited by Jacques Gilard, Norma, 1999.

Garuba, Harry. "Explorations in Animist Materialism: Notes on Reading/Writing African Literature, Culture, and Society." *Public Culture*, vol. 15, no. 2, 2003, pp. 261-85.

Gaylard, Gerald. *After Colonialism: African Postmodernism and Magical Realism*. Wits University P, 2005.

Guevara, Ernesto Che. *Congo Diary: Episodes of the Revolutionary War in the Congo*. No translator credited. Ocean Press, 2011.

Hamilton, Russell G. "Portuguese-Language Literature." *A History of Twentieth-Century African Literatures*, edited by Oyekan Owomoyela, U of Nebraska P, 1993, pp. 240–84.

"How U.S. Firms Helped Africa's Richest Woman Exploit Her Country's Wealth." *The New York Times*, 19 Jan. 2020, www.nytimes.com/2020/01/19/world/africa/isabel-dos-santos-angola-html. Accessed 27 Jan. 2020.

Isaacson, Maureen. "Ngũgĩ's Life of Reversals and Essential Connections." *Sunday Independent* [South Africa], 25 Mar. 2007, p. 18.

Isegawa, Moses. *Abyssinian Chronicles*. Knopf, 2000.

Khosa, Ungulani Ba Ka. *Ualalapi: Fragments from the End of Empire* (1987). Translated by Richard Bartlett and Isaura de Oliveira, foreword by Phillip Rothwell, Tagus P, 2017.

Kimani, Peter. "El keniano Peter Kimani, el nuevo 'heredero' de García Márquez en África," by Pedro Alonso, 11 Dec. 2018, www.efe.com/efe/espana/cultura. Accessed 15 Mar. 2019.

Kourouma, Ahmadou. *Les soleils des indépendances* (1968). Editions du Seuil, 1970.

Kourouma, Ahmadou. *The Suns of Independence* (1968). Translated by Adrian Adams, Africana, 1981.

Kourouma, Ahmadou. *Waiting for the Vote of the Wild Animals* (1998). Translated by Carrol F. Coates, UP of Virginia, 2001.

Laing, Kojo. *Big Bishop Roko and the Altar Gangsters*. Woeli, 2006.

Laing, Kojo. *Major Gentl and the Achimota Wars*. Heinemann, 1992.

Laing, Kojo. *Search Sweet Country* (1986). Introduction by Binyavanga Wainina, McSweeney, 2011.

Leite, Ana Mafalda, Sheila Khan, Jessica Falconi, and Kamila Krakowska, editors. *Speaking the Postcolonial Nation: Interviews with Writers from Angola and Mozambique* (2012). Peter Lang, 2014.

Lopes, Henri. *The Laughing Cry: An African Cock and Bull Story* (1982). Translated by Gerald Moore, Readers International, 1987.

Lovesey, Oliver. *Ngũgĩ wa Thiong'o*. Twayne, 2000.

Mabanckou, Alain. *Black Moses* (*Petit Piment*, 2015). Translated by Helen Stevenson, New Press, 2017.

Mabanckou, Alain. *Broken Glass* (2005). Translated by Helen Stevenson, introduction by Uzondinma Iweala, Soft Skull, 2010.

Mabanckou, Alain. *Memoirs of a Porcupine* (2006). Translated by Helen Stevenson, Serpent's Tail, 2011.

Macha, Freddy. "How Is Colombia Writer Marquez Relevant to East Africa?" *The Citizen*, Dar es Salaam [Tanzania], 25 Apr 2014, freddymacha.blogspot. Accessed 15 Mar. 2019.

Macondo Book Society. Macondo Literary Festival, Nairobi, 27–29 Sept. 2019, organized by Yvonne Adhiambo Owuor and Anja Bengelstorff, www.macondolitfest.org. Accessed 27 Sept. 2019.

Matusse, Gilberta. "The Construction of Mozambican Identity in Ungulani Ba Ka Khosa," translated by Niyi Afolabi. *Emerging Perspectives on Ungulani Ba Ka Khosa*, edited by Niyi Afolabi, Africa World Press, 2010, pp. 99–103.

McLaren, Joseph. "Ngũgĩ's Wizard of the Crow: Women as 'The Voice of the People' & the Western Audience." *New Novels in African Literature Today*, 27, edited by Ernest N. Emenyonu, James Currey, 2010, pp. 55–64.

Mda, Zakes. *Sometimes There Is a Void*. Farrar, Straus, and Giroux, 2011.

Miller, Christopher L. *Impostors: Literary Hoaxes and Cultural Authenticity*. U of Chicago P, 2018.

Mũchiri, Ng'ang'a. "'A Nation of One's Own': Fictional Indictment of Cannibalistic African States." *Unmasking the African Dictator: Essays on Postcolonial African Literature*, edited by Gichingiri Ndĩgĩrĩgĩ, U of Tennessee P, 2014.

Ngũgĩ wa Thiong'o. *Decolonising the Mind: The Politics of Language in African Literature*. James Currey, 1986.

Ngũgĩ wa Thiong'o. *In the Name of the Mother: Reflections on Writers & Empire*. James Currey, 2013.

Ngũgĩ wa Thiong'o. *Wizard of the Crow*. Translated by Ngũgĩ wa Thiong'o, Pantheon Books, 2006.

Òkédìjí, Oládèjo, and Karin Barber. "Oládèjo Òkédìjí on His Writing Life." *Research in African Literatures*, vol. 37, no. 3, Autumn, 2006, pp. 28–44.

Oliva, Renato. "Re-Dreaming the World: Ben Okri's Shamanic Realism." *Coterminous Worlds: Magical Realism and Contemporary Post-colonial Literature in English*, edited by Elsa Linguanti, Francesco Casotti, and Carmen Concilio, Rodopi, 1999, pp. 171–96.

Osundare, Niyi. "Gabriel García Márquez: Farewell to the Magic Muse." *Lagos Sun*, 26 Apr. 2014. Proquest.

Ouologuem, Yambo. *Bound to Violence* (*Le devoir du violence* 1968). Translated by Ralph Manheim, Harcourt Brace Jovanovich, 1971.

Palmer, Eustace. *Of War and Women, Oppression and Optimism: New Essays on the African Novel*. Africa World Press, 2008.

Palmer, Eustace, and Ernest Cole, editors. *Emerging Perspectives on Syl Cheney-Coker*. Africa World Press, 2014.

Parkes, Nii, and Chika Unigwe. "25 Acclaimed Writers Select the 25 Most Influential Books." *Wasafiri: International Contemporary Writing*, 15 Jan. 2013, www.wasafiri.org/article/25-acclaimed-writers-select-the-25-most-influential-books/. Accessed 10 Sept. 2019.

Pepetela. *Return of the Water Spirit* (1995). Translated by Luís R. Mitras, Heinemann, 2002.

Pepetela. *Yaka* (1984). Translated by Marga Holness, Heinemann, 1996.

Quiroz, Sandra. "Mia Couto: África está lleno de Macondos, de pueblos así, como el de Gabo." *Afribuku*, 29 Apr. 2013, www.afribuku.com/miacouto/. Accessed 17 June 2019.

Rodrigues, Isabel Fêo P. B., and Kathleen Sheldon. "Cape Verdean and Mozambican Women's Literature: Liberating the National and Seizing the Intimate." *African Studies Review*, vol. 53, no. 3, Dec. 2010, pp. 77–99.

Scarano, Tommaso. "Notes on Spanish-American Magical Realism." *Coterminous Worlds: Magical Realism and Contemporary Post-Colonial Literature in English*, edited by Elsa Linguanti, Francesco Casotti, and Carmen Concilio, Rodopi, 1999, pp. 9–28.

Sony Labou Tansi. *The Antipeople*. Translated by J. A. Underwood, Marion Boyars, 1983.

Sony Labou Tansi. *L'autre monde: Ecrits inedits*. Edited by Nicolas Martin-Granel and Bruno Tilliette, Revue Noire, 1997.

Sony Labou Tansi. *Life and a Half* (1979). Translated by Alison Dundy, introduction by Dominic Thomas, Indiana UP, 2011.

Sony Labou Tansi. "La magie des quotidiens." *Magie et Écriture au Congo*, edited by Jean-Michel Devesa, L'Harmattan, 1994, pp. 57–59.

Sony Labou Tansi. *The Shameful State* (1981). Translated by Dominic Thomas, introduction by Alain Mabanckou, Indiana UP, 2016.

Sony Labou Tansi. *The Seven Solitudes of Lorsa Lopez* (1985). Translated by Clive Wake, Heinemann, 1995.

Soyinka, Wole. "From a Common Back Cloth: A Reassessment of the African Literary Image." *The American Scholar*, vol. 32, no. 3, Summer, 1963, pp. 387–96.

Stevenson, Helen. "Alain Mabanckou in Conversation," *Wasafiri*, vol. 27, no.1, 2012, pp. 11–17.

Sundiata: An Epic of Old Mali. Edited by D.T. Niane, translated by G.D. Pickett, Pearson Longman, 1965.

Vieira, José Luandino. *Luuanda* (1964). Translated by Tamara L. Bender with Donna S. Hill, Heinemann, 1980.

Wainaina, Binyavanga. "Ships in High Transit." *The Granta Book of the African Short Story*, edited by Helon Habila, Granta, 2011, pp. 92–121.

"When Firms Profit from Poor Nations." Editorial, *The New York Times*, 26 Jan. 2020, Sect. A, p. 12.

World Bank. World Bank Open Data. data.worldbank.org. Accessed 29 Dec. 2019.

CHAPTER 12

THE ARABS AND GABRIEL GARCÍA MÁRQUEZ

HEBA EL ATTAR

An Arab Requiem

When Gabriel García Márquez (1917–2014) died, the Tunisian writer Kamal Ryahi claimed that the Arabs' sadness for his passing was stronger than for the death of Naguib Mahfuz, the only Arab Nobel laureate in literature (Salman n.p.). There are Latin American authors, such as Jorge Luis Borges, Julio Cortázar, and Carlos Fuentes, to name a few, who are as well-known across the Arab world as was García Márquez, but none have elicited such a strong reaction. Therefore, Ryahi's claim poses some questions: Why does this Latin American author in particular have such an impact in the Arab world? Is his impact confined to Arab literary circles or shared by the Arab public at large? And what are the implications, if any, of that impact?

A good starting point to answer these questions might be the film *al-sfārï fi al-ʿmārï* (The Embassy in the Building), released by Egyptian filmmaker Amr Arafa in 2005. A political comedy, the movie quickly became a hit across the Arab world and continues to be widely watched today, especially because it stars the famous Egyptian actor Adel Imam. In one of its scenes, Imam's character visits an Egyptian family of leftist activists and discusses politics with all the family members save one of the sons, who is busy reading a book. When Imam inquires what book it is, the young man says: "*Love in the Time of Cholera*. Gabriel García Márquez's masterpiece." Amr Arafa, the filmmaker, must have been confident that major sectors of the audience across the Arab world would note the link between that reference to García Márquez's work and leftist politics. His confidence in that regard must have stemmed from the fact that Arabs are avid readers of García Márquez. It is true that the Colombian author's work has universal appeal, but for Arabs, there is something more to it. Gabo's writing depicts tensions that are too similar to everyday realities in the Arab world. And the mixture of leftism and anti-imperialism in his work brings back to mind nostalgic memories of nationalist and populist eras. The

Egyptian filmmaker must have known also that García Márquez was acclaimed by the general public—be it in Arabia, the Gulf, the Levant, or North Africa—as much as by the leading Arab literary circles. Amr Arafa definitely ascertained this correctly, because in the Levant, for instance, Syrian novelist and screenwriter Khaled Khalifah affirms that Arab readers are drawn to Gabo's work inasmuch as they find in it reverberations of canonical Arab literature such as *The Thousand and One Nights*. Lebanese writer Jabbour Douaihy attributes García Márquez's popularity among the Arab readership to the endless affinities between ancient and modern histories and politics in the Arab world and Latin America. In Jabbour's view, Gabo's work was able to influence how Arab readers deal with the finest and most forgotten details of their daily lives as much as it has influenced how Arab authors write about dictatorships (Ashour n.p.). In North Africa, Tunisian novelist Messaouda Boubaker concurs that Gabriel García Márquez was influenced by canonical Arab literature and draws further attention to how his work guided Arab authors to turn local realities into universal ones (Salman n.p.).

Additionally, the film director Amr Arafa must have known that García Márquez engaged not only with Arab literature and culture but also with critical issues that matter to Arabs, such as anticolonialism in North Africa and the Palestinian question. Indeed, it was Arab politics that resulted in young Gabo's incarceration when he was exiled in Paris. At the time, the National Liberation Front (NLF) of Algeria had intensified its struggle against French colonialism, and Gabo's interest in and support of the right of all people to freedom was drawing him to closely follow the activism of the NLF in France. At one point, the French police decided to launch raids against those activists; Gabo, who was frequenting their neighborhoods and the locations of their reunions, was racially profiled and mistaken for an Arab and hence put in jail along with Algerians. Twenty-five years later, García Márquez noted: "When I was invited for the anniversary of the Algerian Independence, I confessed to one of the reporters an unbelievable fact: the Algerian revolution was the only one for which I was jailed" ("Desde París" n.p.).[1]

The Colombian author did not let that incident deter him, though. He continued to follow thoroughly other critical issues in the Arab world, namely the Palestinian question. In this respect, the Kuwaiti author and journalist Talib Alrefai observes:

> Although he belongs to Latin America and is far from Palestine, the Colombian writer Gabriel García Márquez was one of the authors who manifested a vehement solidarity with the Palestinian people, and who wrote and defended their righteous cause. For instance, in the 80s, when Zionism was in control of the international media ... the author rented, at his own expense, a page in a newspaper ... to write an article in support of the Palestinians and their cause. (Ashour n.p.)

As García Márquez's attention to Arab culture and the Arab world was growing, the Arabs' interest in him was peaking as well, thanks mainly to an ardent effort to translate his work into Arabic since the 1970s (Civantos 165). The 1967 novel *Cien años de soledad* (*One Hundred Years of Solitude*) alone was translated into Arabic at least five times between 1989 and 2005 (Molina 109). This translation effort was not confined to his fiction but rather included his nonfiction writing. A translation into Arabic of the 2010 compilation of his formal speeches, *Yo no vengo a decir un discurso* (*I Am Not Here to Give a Speech*), was published in Egypt in 2011.[2] Also, a translation into Arabic of the 1999 compilation of his journal articles, *Por la libre: Obra Periodística 4 (1974–1995)* (Freely: Journalistic Work [1974–1995], vol. 4), was published in Beirut in 2018.[3]

Thus, the Tunisian writer Kamal Ryahi might not have been exaggerating in saying that the Arabs' sadness over García Márquez's passing was stronger than over Naguib Mahfuz's. Indeed, the impact of his death on the Arab world was such that it drew the attention of the media across the Spanish-speaking world. Among other newspapers that took interest in the phenomenon, *La Vanguardia*, in Spain, reported the solemn tribute paid to the Colombian author in Saudi Arabia, which at the time was hosting the Third Summit of Arab and Latin American Ministers of Culture: "'Our sadness for the loss of the prestigious García Márquez in Saudi Arabia and the entire Arab world shows the convergence of cultural and civilization ties between our peoples,' said Abdelaziz al Joya, the Saudi Minister of Culture, in his opening speech" (Rubio n.p.).

LATIN AMERICA AND THE ORIENT

Many other Latin American authors, as indicated elsewhere in this essay, are well-known across the Arab world, but none were celebrated quite as García Márquez was. However, like the Colombian author, their literature became popular among Arabs for its postcolonial and/or anti-imperialist discourses and, at times, for its deviation from traditional orientalism. The latter, mainly associated with Europe and the United States, "is wedded to an ideology of colonial mastery that constructs a hierarchy of superior and inferior cultures" (Hassan 279). This deviation derives from the fact that postindependence Latin American literature strove to carve a unique identity for the continent by revisiting, questioning, and rearticulating its history, and by redefining its relations with all hegemonic powers and subalterns, be they inside or outside the continent's borders. In that process, according to Tyutina, reexamining the relation with the Orient and/or East was inevitable, especially because the image of and relationship with the Orient, particularly the Arab Muslim Other, had migrated with Spaniards upon their reconquest of Iberia and conquest of the New World. That relationship/image was orientalist in nature, and religion gave it grounds by shaping the dichotomy of the peninsular/ "us" versus the oriental/"them," which, in turn, is still shaping peninsular literature and politics in the twenty-first century. Nonetheless, with its independence, Latin America started shifting away from that peninsular orientalism by transcending the traditional concept of the oriental as Moor (Muslim or Arab) and also by including the Far East (71, 233). During the first few stages of that shift, however, Latin American authors who wrote about the Orient—such as Rubén Darío, then later Pablo Neruda and Octavio Paz, among others—though they did not have direct imperial motivations, were still indirectly reinforcing the colonial hierarchy, which favors Europe not only against the Orient but even against Latin America itself (Nagy-Zekmi 15–16). Even when the traditional exoticization of the oriental Other manifested some veneration toward the Orient, as in the case of Borges, such reverence preserved a lingering hierarchical structure with the Other and hence kept overlapping with traditional orientalism. It was only later, around the mid-twentieth century, that there was a growing tendency to reexamine the relationship between East and West in the past and the present, not with "the purpose of domination of the Other, but rather to create a distinction from the traditional image of the subaltern" (Tyutina 282–84, 311).

It is worth noting, however, that the consistent and steady growth of that deviating tendency does not automatically mean that it has completely dissociated itself from traditional orientalism. In his study of Brazilian orientalism in twenty-first-century media in Brazil, Hassan observes that it deviates from Euro-American orientalism in that it replaces the traditional depiction of the West as the embodiment of freedom versus an oppressive East/Orient with a self-critique of Brazilian identity itself. In his view, Brazilian orientalism also veers away from the Euro-American variety, which insists that East and West shall never meet, since it sustains that the two can and do meet. Despite these important differences, Hassan notes that Brazilian orientalism still overlaps with the nineteenth-century European version whenever it engages in facile exoticizations of the Arab Other (285, 287, 293). In her approach to the depiction of the Arab Other in some of the literary works by Santiago Gamboa, Omar Toson reaches similar conclusions and further finds links between such an exoticization and the peaking anti-Arab and anti-Muslim prejudice in the wake of the September 11, 2001, attacks (218, 234). These limitations should definitely be taken into account. However, they do not override Latin American orientalism's divergence from traditional orientalism. And it is within this diverging trend, which could be viewed as anti-orientalist or dis-orientalist, that García Márquez's work, in which the Arab Other is a constant feature, could be rightfully placed. The Colombian author not only discerned the nonphysical presence of that Other in the transatlantic peninsular heritage, but he also ascertained its physical presence and visibility in modern-day Latin America, as is the case in *Cien años de soledad* (*One Hundred Years of Solitude*).

Fiction

Jorge García Usta contends that even though the depiction of the Arab Other in modern Latin American literature is more frequent than not, it was in *One Hundred Years* that the Arab Other became an integral part of the ethnic fabric and memory of the continent. The novel focused on the history of Macondo, a mythical town that signifies the Caribbean and/or Latin America. Among other things, it includes the story of Arab immigrants in Macondo and how they start out as peddlers before establishing businesses and expanding their ownership to real estate properties, thereby shaping the town's recent history by contributing to its economic survival, revolutionization, and prosperity (106). This chronicling of Arab immigrants' presence and ascension in social strata in *One Hundred Years* echoes García Márquez's own familiarity with Arab migratory waves to the Caribbean, where he grew up and socialized with many of said migrants, to the point of marrying the daughter of an Egyptian immigrant. Such familiarity and closeness granted him a (semi)insider position from which to observe and portray the community.

The legitimate question, however, would be whether such a portrayal retained (or not) traditional orientalism between its lines. And an answer to that could be found in the Arabic translations of *Cien años de soledad*. Molina, who studied five of these translations published in Lebanon, Syria, Egypt, Kuwait, and Iraq, looked at how some of the words that purposefully appear in the original text in reference to the Arab world and/or culture (e.g., *mezquita* [mosque] and *chillaba* [jillab]), were sometimes semantically modified and/or omitted in the Arabic version. This modification or omission, she noted, was often due to the Arab translators' mindfulness of the cultural weight of some of these words, which, if left intact as they appear in the original Spanish version, might be misconstrued by the Arab readership. Though Molina covers many examples, two in particular can be useful for the purpose of this essay, since they relate to past and present identities of the Arab Other. The first example is the synonymous use of the words "Turks" and "Arabs" in the original text: "Three of the five translations neutralise the association between Arabs and Turks" (111). Thus, Arab translators preferred to neutralize the generalization of the Arab Other who, in the Latin American host societies, was indistinguishably seen as Turk. When Arabs started migrating from Syria, Lebanon, and Palestine in the mid-nineteenth century, the Middle East was still under the Ottoman rule of the Turks; hence those immigrants held Ottoman documentation, and the host societies generalized the reference to them by identifying them as "Turks." From such generalization stemmed the Turkophobic (anti-Arab) prejudice in Latin America, which García Márquez aims to deconstruct. If left intact in the Arabic version, that reference would be confusing to the Arab readership, especially because in the Arab world today, Ottoman rule does not exist and the words "Arab" and "Turk" have almost opposite meanings.

The second example relates to that Arab Other's identity during medieval times. It is embedded in "the sadness of a Saracen" (García Márquez, *One Hundred Years* 245), which, according to Molina, all five translations sought to distance "from target readers" (120). This is because the Saracen's sadness mentioned in the novel capitalizes more on how the interaction between the Spaniards and the Arabs/Moors in medieval Spain ended in the latter's defeat. The Arab audience's collective memory, however, cherishes the positive aspects of the medieval interaction between Moors and Christians in Al-Andalus. If left intact in the Arabic version, this description would not be palatable to an Arab readership, hence the alterations. It could be inferred, then, that Arab translators cared that some of the words and/or descriptions employed by the author in reference to Arab culture and/or history should not be mistaken for traditional orientalism by Arab readers. This would subsequently suggest that the translators might have found such references in the original text to be rather anti-orientalist. If this suggestion were true, it would not necessarily mean that most of García Márquez's representation of the Arab Other is devoid of traditional orientalism. But if compared to other portrayals of Arabs in other works by the author, it can shed light on whether dis-orientalism outweighs conventional orientalism in his work. And for this purpose, it would be ideal to look at his 1981 novella *Crónica de una muerte anunciada* (*Chronicle of a Death Foretold*), in which García Márquez has deliberately allotted an Arab ethnicity to the main character.

Chronicle builds upon the portrayal of Arabs in *One Hundred Years*. While the latter described how those immigrants became peddlers and/or real estate owners in the Caribbean, *Chronicle* narrates how they became ranchers and cattle breeders and touches upon their migratory waves, religious affiliation, and gradual loss of their heritage language:

> The Arabs comprised a community of peaceful immigrants who had settled at the beginning of the century in Caribbean towns, even in the poorest and most remote, and there they remained, selling coloured cloth and bazaar trinkets. They were clannish, hardworking, and Catholic. They married among themselves, imported their wheat, raised lambs in their yards, and grew oregano and eggplants, and playing cards was their only driving passion. The older ones continued speaking the rustic Arabic they had brought from their homeland, and they maintained it intact in the family down to the second generation, but those of the third, with the exception of Santiago Nasar, listened to their parents in Arabic and answered them in Spanish. (81)

Chronicle tells the story of a newlywed, Bayardo San Román, who returns his bride, Ángela Vicario, to her family upon discovering that she is not a virgin. When the family beats her to learn who took her virginity, she gives the name of Santiago Nasar, an affluent man of Arab origin. His ethnic background suffices to legitimize Ángela's brothers' decision to avenge the family's honor by killing Santiago without bothering to verify their sister's story. It also legitimizes the townspeople's inaction, since they collectively decide not to stop the crime, even though Ángela's brothers announce their homicidal intentions publicly around town, whether in defiance of everyone and everything, or in the hope that someone would stop them. Furthermore, it legitimizes the townspeople's bias. Bayardo San Román is a stranger to the community, he is a non-Arab, and the townspeople seem predisposed to accept and like him. At the same time, they are predisposed to doubt Santiago Nasar's ethics in business and in love and determined to ignore that he is no stranger to their faith, Catholicism, or to their language, Spanish. *Chronicle* stresses how the townspeople are inexplicably resentful of the power of Santiago, the signifier of Arab immigrants. Such power is not only economic but political, since *Chronicle* mirrors Arab immigrants' involvement in Colombian politics. This is especially implied by the author's emphasis on the alertness that has led Santiago and his father to always keep a gun under their pillows. Such alertness could only be justified in light of the Arab immigrants' actual participation, locally and nationally, in Colombian politics, since many of them were affiliated with the Partido Liberal and later became, directly and/or indirectly, part of the bloody clash between Liberals and Conservatives that shook the country for an entire decade (El Attar 923).

The story of Santiago Nasar and the Arab community in *Chronicle* shows that those immigrants not only contributed to the society but were also increasingly integrated therein. This notion per se subverts the anti-Arab prejudice, and the violence against Santiago in the novella does not contradict such subversion but rather supports it. The townspeople know that Ángela's brothers are going to kill Santiago. However, no one cares to stop the homicide because the removal of that man, Santiago, who bears Arab blood is, implicitly, a relief for everyone. His death will end the individual cognitive dissonance with which the townspeople have to deal. His death is easier than the effort of admitting that the affinities surpass the discrepancies between that Oriental Other/ "them" and the townspeople/"us." The latter's cognitive consonance in regard to the Arab Other, whom they view as lacking in basic human values and mores, is never going to be restored unless the cause of that cognition—that is, Santiago Nasar—is made to disappear. Therefore, the author decided that Santiago would be killed from the onset of the novella. Once the homicide is perpetrated, the burden of the situation shifts to the townspeople, and their values, mores, and perceptions become the object of scrutiny. In other words, the author was momentarily numbing the orientalist prejudice that was still persisting in the Hispanic society and that, in the novella, was embodied in the townspeople's attitude. This numbness could be viewed as an initial step that permitted the author to deconstruct the layers upon which their prejudiced cognitive consonance regarding the Arab Other was grounded. Therefore, it could be argued that Santiago Nasar's Arab identity, along with the portrayal of the Arab community in *Chronicle*, could be viewed as a deconstruction of the prejudice against the oriental Other. This argument would be supported, among other things, by the contrast drawn between the townspeople's unjustifiable fear of the Arab community and the actual help provided by the same to one of the two homicidal brothers:

> Colonel Aponte, worried by the rumors, visited the Arabs family by family and at that time, at least, drew a correct conclusion. He found them perplexed and sad, with signs of mourning on their altars, and some of them sitting on the ground and wailing, but none harbored ideas of vengeance. The reaction that morning had grown out of the heat of the crime, and even the very leaders admitted that in no case would it have gone beyond a beating. Furthermore, it was Susana Abdala, the centenarian matriarch, who recommended the prodigious infusion of passion flowers and absinthe that dried up Pablo Vicario's diarrhea and unleashed at the same time his brother's florid flow. Pedro Vicario then fell into an insomniac drowsiness and his recovered brother earned his first sleep without remorse. (*Chronicle* 82)

Not only was *Chronicle* widely acclaimed by the Arab readership, but it has also inspired the writings of some Arab novelists. In her comparative study of the Lebanese author Elias Khoury's novel *Majma'al-asrar* and *Chronicle of a Death Foretold*, Civantos underscores how Khoury built his narrative intertextually around *Crónica*. In his work, she explains, Khoury imagines the life of Ibrahim Nasar, a cousin of Santiago Nasar, who did not migrate to the New World but rather kept living in Beirut. In her comparative analysis, Civantos acknowledges that García Márquez's novella has successfully critiqued many aspects of anti-Arab essentialism. Nevertheless, she notes that aspects of that essentialism inhere in *Chronicle*. For example, she notes that the narrator's reference to Santiago's Arab eyelids and curly hair "marks Santiago as visibly biologically different. In racializing Santiago, the narrator establishes his own perspective as a non-Arab and draws a line of difference between them" (174). However, as Hassan rightly observes, difference does not automatically imply negativity or inferiority, for it may be neutral unless it carries a negative connotation (286). Thus, the narrator's comment on Santiago's biological differences does not automatically bear a connotation of the dominance implied in the racialization that Civantos suggests.

Also, Civantos views the narrator's depiction of the town madam as sitting naked while enjoying a large Babylonian plate stacked up with food to bear clear aspects of an odalisque. Such portrayal may well be part of the overall deconstruction of the anti-Arab prejudice in the novella. Nevertheless, Civantos underscores the fading line between the real author and the narrator. Specifically, she argues: "This narrator, given that he is not only called García Márquez, but, like the author, grew up in the town in which the murder took place and was friends with the victim, carries an authoritative voice within the text" (174). She insists on this fading line when she underscores the narrator's reference to Santiago's Arab eyelids and his odalisque depiction of the town madam. Then she concludes that the novella regenerates, in spite of itself, essentialist perceptions of the Arab Other. Now, even if we take these aspects as drawbacks to the anti-Arab critique in *Crónica*, still one basic question will remain: Do they supersede the anti-orientalism in the novella, or do they outweigh the value of the actual critique of the anti-Arab prejudice? To answer such a question, several considerations may be taken into account.

The first consideration could be the revisionist trend that, as indicated elsewhere in this essay, had started in postindependence Latin America with the aim of gradually, rather than drastically, reassessing its vision of and its relation with the Other in general and the oriental Other in particular. This re-evaluation started to better ascertain that relation from the mid-twentieth century onward. *Crónica*, which was published in 1981, seems to be in line with that *evolving* shift. Another consideration would be the persuasive aim of the narration, which stems from the author's own background as a former law student and a journalist who wrote many articles of opinion and columns. He was then clearly aware, by experience and profession, that a text that is too argumentative is often less persuasive. Hence, what may be deemed as a limitation to the critique of anti-orientalism in the novella could rather be a well-crafted counterargument deliberately aimed at balancing out such a critique. An additional consideration is the dialogue that *Crónica* succeeded in establishing with that oriental Other, as evidenced by Elias Khoury's decision to write a novel inspired by/in response to Gabo's novella. A final consideration is the Arab ethnicity chosen for *Crónica*'s main character and marked by his family name: Nasar. It was the family name of Lydia Nasar, the girlfriend of Cayetano Gentile, who was the victim in a real crime perpetrated in Sucre; this event was the inspiration for García Márquez's novella (Hart 31). The family name Nasser, with its variants (e.g., Nasr, Nazar, and Nasar), is associated with Levantine immigrant families in Latin America. Khoury traced its origin to Lebanon (Civantos 176). Ambrozio, however, traced the origin of this family name back to Nazareth, Palestine (33). In Colombia, the bulk of Palestinian immigrants first established themselves in the department of Magdalena, whereas the Syrian and Lebanese ones headed primarily to Sucre (García Usta 106). Even though the first migratory waves brought more or less equal numbers of Lebanese, Syrians, and Palestinians, the subsequent ones brought more immigrants from Palestine. This is especially true since 1948, in the wake of the UN Resolution on the Israel/Palestine question. It could be inferred, then, that the time frame of the novella corresponds to a time of influx of Palestinian immigrants to the Caribbean; hence the author, when he decided to use the name "Nasar," may well have been associating its origin with Palestine rather than Lebanon. If such an inference were true, then García Márquez was not generalizing the reference to the Arabs living in this Caribbean region but rather diligently discerning their subethnicity. Also, if that inference were valid, then the probability of any ambivalence in the anti-orientalist critique in *Crónica* is less than the likelihood of the author's conscious and consistent commitment to the anti-orientalist critique. And so the question here should be: Why would such an inference be at all true? And the answer to that, as will be further discussed, could be García Márquez's thorough deference to factual details related to that Arab Other, be it within or outside of Latin American borders.

Nonfiction

In 1981, the same year in which *Crónica* was published, Ikram Antaki, a Syrian Mexican journalist working for the Palestinian-Lebanese newspaper *Al Karmel*, conducted an interview with the Colombian author, in which the latter expressed his views regarding the Palestinians' cause:

> I support the Arabs, and, in France, they arrested me for my support of the Algerian war of liberation... And I have been supporting Palestine since... since forever. There is no other cause that is more legitimate and more just. People cannot continue to suffer like this. The war must end. There must be some political solution to the matter. (quoted in Rohana n.p.)

A year after that interview was published, García Márquez wrote an article titled "Beguin y Sharon, premios Nobel de la muerte" (Begin and Sharon, Nobel Laureates of Death), about which Gerald Martin writes the following:

> The Nobel season was approaching once more and, as in previous years, García Márquez's name was being mentioned again, only this time even more insistently.

All the more surprising, then, that he chose, less than a month before the award was announced, to launch a withering attack on Israeli leader Menachem Begin—and, by direct implication, the Nobel Foundation which had awarded the Nobel Peace Prize in 1978. In early June Begin had ordered the invasion of neighboring Lebanon and his military commander General Ariel Sharon had neglected to protect Palestinian refugees from the attack, thereby enabling the massacres in the Sabra and Chatila camps in Beirut on 18th of September. García Márquez suggested that Begin and Sharon should be awarded a Nobel Death Prize. . . . But there is every sign he had been on his own candidacy too. (426)

Even though General Sharon, at the orders of Prime Minister Begin, had launched the Israeli offensive in Southern Lebanon primarily against Palestinian refugees and the headquarters of the Palestine Liberation Organization (PLO), Martin here seems to suggest that the military operation was mainly targeting Lebanon, and that Sharon only "neglected" to protect Palestinian refugees during the attack. More importantly, Martin seems to suggest that the article was rather an anomaly on García Márquez's part and an attempt at generating controversy intended by the author to gain attention from the Nobel Prize institution. Nonetheless, a few years prior to the publication of that article, the Nobel Peace Prize had been awarded jointly to Begin and President Sadat, in 1978, for reaching a peace agreement between Egypt and Israel. Thus, in the aforementioned article, Gabo invoked the memory of the Nobel Peace Prize awarded to Begin and contrasted its symbolism against the excessive use of force by Israel, at the orders of Begin, in that attack against Southern Lebanon. García Márquez specifically lamented the silence of many intellectuals and authors who feared being accused of anti-Semitism. While being vocal in favor of the Palestinians, however, the Colombian author did not imply any anti-Semitism. Quite the contrary; his article maintains a balanced deference toward the different stakeholders evidenced, among other things, in statements like the following: "The truth is that no one has been abandoned more than the Jewish people and the Palestinian people in midst of so much horror."

Regardless of any political controversy, it could be argued that both examples, the 1981 interview published in *Al Karmel* and the 1982 article that Gabo himself wrote, display a deep level of consciousness on his part regarding the most critical conflict in the Middle East, which is also one of the most persistent conflicts in modern history. Such awareness suggests, once again, that the anti-orientalism in his work—in general and in *Chronicle* in particular—outweighs its limitations. Also, it suggests that the author's attention to Arab subethnicity is not accidental. This would be supported by the fact that, a few years later, in 1986, he published a nonfiction book, *La aventura de Miguel Littín: Clandestino en Chile (Clandestine in Chile: The Adventures of Miguel Littín in Chile)*, about the Chilean filmmaker Miguel Littín. Even though Littín is of Greek-Palestinian descent, his Palestinian heritage in particular could not be downplayed. On the one hand, Chile is not merely a host society for immigrants of Palestinian descent; rather it is home to the largest Palestinian (Christian) diaspora outside of the Middle East. On the other hand, Littín himself is vocal about that heritage, as evidenced in his

1991 novel *El viajero de las cuatro estaciones* (*The Traveler and the Four Stops*), his 2001 documentary *Crónicas palestinas* (Palestinian Chronicles), and his 2005 feature film *La última luna* (The Last Moon), among other things.

In 1986, García Márquez met in Madrid with Miguel Littín, a longtime friend and a devout supporter of Salvador Allende. The meeting resulted in García Márquez writing *Clandestine in Chile*, in which he not only documented the filmmaker's adventurous activism but also captured the creativity of a descendant of Arabs (and Greeks) in challenging a dictatorship in Latin America. In the wake of the Pinochet coup, Miguel Littín had been exiled from Chile. Years later he managed to infiltrate the country in disguise and coordinated the work of several groups of European cinematographers who, under his lead, filmed critical aspects of Chilean life under the dictatorship. Littín succeeded in fleeing the country with precious footage, which he edited in 1986 into an internationally acclaimed documentary titled *Acta general de Chile* (*General Report on Chile*). García Márquez, himself a leftist and admirer of Allende, was among the interviewees featured in the documentary. This, however, seems to have happened without the author knowing, at the time, the details behind the documentary's creation:

> Early in 1986 in Madrid, when Miguel Littín told me what he had done and how he had done it, I realized that behind his film there was another film that would probably never be made. And so he agreed to a grueling interrogation, the tape of which ran some eighteen hours. It encompassed the full human adventure in all its professional and political implications, which I have condensed into ten chapters. (*Clandestine in Chile* ix–x)

In 1988 the Pinochet regime was strongly shaken, and Littín was able to return from exile. This return marked his reunion with his Chilean self, but he was still in pursuit of a similar reunion with his Greek and Palestinian selves. García Márquez was aware of that identity quest. Therefore, in his book he draws attention to the filmmaker's dual heritage, both the Greek and the Arab; in doing so, he is not merely showing awareness of the filmmaker's Arab ethnicity, but rather of his Palestinian subethnicity: "Next was the hair on my head. Mine is pitch-black, inherited from a Greek mother and a Palestinian father who also passed on to me my tendency to premature baldness... The change made me look more Oriental, in fact, closer to how I ought to have looked, considering my ancestry" (*Clandestine in Chile* 5).

IMPLICATIONS

Even though it was often silenced, ignored, or suppressed, the Arab Other became part of Latin America beginning in 1492. Centuries later, there was a growing tendency on the continent not to distance the West from the East, but rather to underscore cultural and literary affinities between the two (Kushigian 169). In other words, there was a growing trend toward anti-orientalism. This trend, which has been growing since the mid-twentieth century, developed in tandem with the continent's need for "establishing a more autonomous national identity and defining a place for Latin America in a decentered contemporary world" (Tyutina 324). This renders Hispanic orientalism potentially different today from traditional European orientalism. And like other Latin American authors whose works fall within the framework of that trend, García Márquez's fiction and nonfiction persistently display anti-orientalism. However, among the authors of that trend, the case of the Colombian author stands out.

The examples from Gabo's works discussed in this essay suggest that he consistently deviates from traditional orientalism by deconstructing prejudicial portrayals of the Arab Other and engages with that Other as an active and equal interlocutor. Nonetheless, for the sake of argument, even if none of the examples discussed throughout this essay sufficed to prove it, could there be better evidence than what happened in Algeria, the Arab country for which he was imprisoned?

Among the people who solemnly paid tribute to the author upon his death across the Arab world was Algerian president Abdelaziz Bouteflika. In 2014, the Algerian Press Services (APS) reported that Bouteflika's formal message of condolence to the Colombian embassy praised Gabo for courageously championing change. Ironically, the Algerian president himself was far from implementing any change. Only two years later, in 2016, in presidential elections held in Algeria, Bouteflika, despite his incapacitating illness, he still won the presidency for a fourth consecutive term. Instead of quoting Naguib Mahfuz or the work of any other Arab novelist, Algerians did not find a better inspiration than García Márquez's powerful novel *El otoño del patriarca* (*The Autumn of the Patriarch*) to describe the absurdity of the political panorama in Algeria:

> The elections were held in surrealist conditions similar to the ones described in García Márquez's works such as *The Autumn of the Patriarch*. The candidate, and current president Abdel Aziz Bouteflika, won for a fourth term despite his barely visible presence since he was unable to utter a single word due to his illness which kept him on a wheelchair while other officials and ministers were speaking in his name on the campaign trail, such as the First Minister Abdelmalek Sellal who once announced: "President Bouteflika is married to Algeria ... or maybe Algeria is married to him. ... I don't know ... but he has to be elected." (Talib)

NOTES

1. All translations from Arabic and Spanish are mine unless a published translation is listed in Works Cited.
2. García Márquez, *mā ǧ'it lilqā' ḥtbï*.
3. García Márquez, *blā qiūdd*.

Works Cited

Ambrozio, Leonilda. "Morte/Nao morte: O mito de Cristo em Crônica de uma morte anunciada." *Revista Letras*, no. 35, 1986, pp. 17–36.

APS. "Death of Garcia Marquez: Yousfi Offers Algeria's Condolences." *Egypt Today*, 28 Apr. 2016, www.egypt-today.com/en/amp/248/death-of-garcia-marquez-yousfi-offers-algerias-condolences. Accessed 5 Jan. 2020.

Arafa, Amr. *al-sfārī fi al-'mārī*. Essam Imam Productions, 2005.

Ashour, Radwa. " mārkīz kmā īrāh rā'īūn 'rb" ["Márquez as Seen by Arab Novelists]. *Thaqafiat*. 19 Apr. 2014, claudeabouchacra.wordpress.com/ 2014/ 04/ 19/ماركيز-كما-يراه-روائيون-عرب/. Accessed 15 Jan. 2021.

Civantos, Christina. "Orientalism and the Narration of Violence in the Mediterranean Atlantic: Gabriel García Márquez and Elias Khoury." *The Global South Atlantic*, edited by Kerry Bystrom and Joseph R. Slaughter, Fordham UP, 2018, pp. 165–85.

El Attar, Heba. "Orientalismo hispanoamericano en *Crónica de una muerte anunciada* de Gabriel García Márquez y *La turca* de Jorge Luis Oviedo." *Hispania*, vol. 91, no. 4, 2008, pp. 914–24.

García Márquez, Gabriel. *La aventura de Miguel Littín clandestino en Chile*. Diana, 1986.

García Márquez, Gabriel. "Beguin y Sharon, premios 'Nobel de la muerte.'" *El país*, 28 Sept. 1982, https://elpais.com/diario/1982/09/29/opinion/402102007_850215.html. Accessed 15 May. 2021.

García Márquez, Gabriel. *blā qīūdd*. Translated by Heba El Attar and Gihan Hamid, Al Farabi, 2018.

García Márquez, Gabriel. *Chronicle of a Death Foretold*. Translated by Gregory Rabassa, Knopf, 1983.

García Márquez, Gabriel. *Cien años de soledad*. Mondadori, 1967.

García Márquez, Gabriel. *Clandestine in Chile: The Adventures of Miguel Littín*. H. Holt, 1987.

García Márquez, Gabriel. *Crónica de una muerte anunciada*. La Oveja Negra, 1981.

García Márquez, Gabriel. "Desde París, con amor." *El País*, 29 Dec. 1982, elpais.com/diario/1982/12/29/ opinion/409964412_850215.html. Accessed 5 Jan. 2020.

García Márquez, Gabriel. *mā ǧ'it lilqā' ḥṭbī*. Translated by Ahmed Abdel Latif, Rawafid, 2011.

García Márquez, Gabriel. *One Hundred Years of Solitude*. Translated by Gregory Rabassa, Avon, 1971.

García Márquez, Gabriel. *Por la libre: Obra periodística 4 (1974–1995)*. Mondadori, 1999.

García Márquez, Gabriel. *Yo no vengo a decir un discurso*. Grijalbo Mondadori, 2010.

García Usta, Jorge. "Árabes en Macondo." *Aguaita*, no. 26, Dec. 2014, pp. 104–15.

Hart, Stephen M. *Gabriel García Márquez, Crónica de una muerte anunciada*. Grant & Cutler in association with Tamesis Books, 1994.

Hassan, Waïl. "Carioca Orientalism. Morocco in the Imaginary of a Brazilian Telenovela." *The Global South Atlantic*, edited by Kerry Bystrom and Joseph R. Slaughter, Fordham UP, 2018, pp. 274–94.

Khoury, Elias. *Majma' al-asrar*. Dar al Adaab, 1994.

Kushigian, Julia. "*El primero sueño y las mil y una noches*: Sor Juana Inés de la Cruz, orientalista." *Moros en la costa: Orientalismo en Latinoamérica*, edited by Sylvia Nagy-Zekmi, Iberoamericana, 2008, pp. 167–86.

Littín, Miguel, director. *Acta General de Chile*. Alfil Uno Cinematográfica and TVE, Televisión Española, 1986.

Littín, Miguel, director. *Crónicas Palestinas*. Pepe Torres, 2001.
Littín, Miguel, director. *La última luna*. Latido Films, 2005.
Littín, Miguel. *El viajero de las cuatro estaciones*. Mondadori, 1990.
Martin, Gerald. *Gabriel García Márquez. A Life*. Bloomsbury, 2009.
Molina, Lucía. "The *Mahjar* Comes Home: Arab References in Arabic Translations of *One Hundred Years of Solitude*." *Traducción, interpretación y estudios interculturales*, edited by Lucía Molina and Laura Santamaría, Comares, 2016, pp. 109–25.
Nagy-Zekmi, Silvia, editor. *Moros en la costa: Orientalismo en Latinoamérica*. Iberoamericana, 2008.
Omar Toson, Ghada. "La presencia árabe e islámica en *El síndrome de Ulises* y en *El cerco de Bogotá* de Santiago Gamboa." *eHumanista/Ivitra*, no. 6, 2014, pp. 218–34.
Rohana, Shadi. "Una entrevista peregrina." *Revista Al Zeytun: Revista iberoamericana de investigación, análisis y cultura palestina*, no. 1, 2017, p. 52.
Rubio, Enrique. "Árabes convierten el duelo por García Márquez en nuevo vínculo con Suramérica." *La Vanguardia*, 29 Apr. 2014, www.lavanguardia.com/cultura /20140429/ 54406466745/arabes-convierten-el-duelo-por-garcia-marquez -en-nuevo-vinculo-con-suramerica.html. Accessed 5 Jan. 2020.
Salman, Hassan. " rṯā' 'rbi ġīrmktml lġābryil ġārsīā mārkīz" ["Incomplete Arab Eulogy for Gabriel García Márquez"]. *Al Quds Al Arabi*, 18 Apr. 2014, www.alquds.co.uk/رثاء-عربي-غير-مكتمل-لغابرييل-غارسيا-ما/. Accessed 15 Jan. 2021.
Talib, Jamal Eldin. " īūm a'tql mārkīz bā'tbārh ğzā'iriā" ["The Day Marquez Was Arrested for Being Mistaken for an Algerian"]. *Al Arabi Al Jadid*, 28 Apr. 2016, www.alaraby.co.uk/يوم-اعتقل-ماركيز-باعتباره-جزائرياً/. Accessed 15 Jan. 2021.
Tyutina, Svetlana. *Hispanic Orientalism: The Literary Development of a Cultural Paradigm from Medieval Spain to Latin America*. 2014. Florida International U, PhD dissertation, digitalcommons.fiu.edu/etd/1592/. Accessed 5 Jan. 2020.

CHAPTER 13

GARCÍA MÁRQUEZ IN CHINA

WEI TENG

During the 1950s and 1960s, the newly founded China adopted a "highly selective policy" (Hong, *History of Chinese Modern Literature* 228–29): there were clear guidelines about what could and could not be translated and what should be translated first. By the end of the 1970s, after ten years of silence during the Cultural Revolution, people longed for an end to cultural shortage and self-closure, as well as a prompt importation of Western culture, all with an open mind to diversity. Meanwhile, to bring order out of the chaos of the Cultural Revolution, China "restarted the process of modernization"[1] in the hope of "rejoining the world"; thus, "The Four Modernizations" (agriculture, industry, national defense, and science and technology) became the most effective slogan for social integration. It was deemed an overall solution or remedy and was constructed as a social consensus making people believe that, under these guidelines, China would bid farewell to poverty, stagnation, autocracy, and ignorance, and therefore enter a prosperous new era. This appeal sent China back into the historical binary frame East/West, underdeveloped/developed, and shed light on "the Other"—"learn from the West." The 1980s thus saw another growth in translations, with a focus on the West along the lines of the May Fourth Movement (五四运动, 1919) in twentieth-century China.

In this process, foreign literature, especially modern genres, took on an unprecedented legitimacy[2] as a formerly forbidden area and as a "victim" of the Cultural Revolution. In fact, foreign literature directly participated in the construction of new Chinese literature in the 1980s. Almost every significant change in 1980s literature in China was "connected directly with the collision and integration brought about by the influence from outside" (Hong, *History of Chinese Modern Literature* 228–29). In the 1980s the upsurge in translations of foreign literature, including Latin American literature and especially works of "magical realism," exerted a widespread and long-lasting influence on contemporary Chinese letters. Thus, Li Tuo, one of the most remarkable critics in 1980s China, highlighted in his essay "Pay Attention to Latin American Literature's Development Model": "In my opinion, the most significant event in recent decades when it comes to the translation and introduction of foreign literature should be one of the Latin American contemporary literatures" (282–87). When we reflect today on China's contemporary literary history and discuss "Root-Seeking Literature" (寻根文学)[3] as well as avant-garde novels (先锋小说),[4] one of the topics that should be discussed is the influence of Latin American fiction. Gabriel García Márquez, Jorge Luis Borges, Juan Rulfo, Mario Vargas Llosa[5]—all of these contemporary Latin American authors became well known among Chinese literary circles, and *Cien años de soledad* (*One Hundred Years of Solitude*; henceforth *One Hundred Years*) was heralded as the new Bible for writing. As a scholar on China's contemporary literature asserted:

> Apart from Márquez, there has never been any Nobel laureate that has caused such a long-term interest in Chinese authors. *One Hundred Years of Solitude* appeared on almost every writers' desk, and in literature gatherings, big or small, the participants kept mentioning the name "Márquez." He indeed shook the Chinese literary circle in the 1980s and became an inspirational figure. (Li Jiefei 103)

When will Chinese writers be awarded the Nobel Prize in Literature, as was García Márquez? When will Chinese literature be globally accepted, as Latin American literature has been? Literary circles in the 1980s posed questions of this sort; as Liu Xinwu once said: "Chinese literature should aspire to build a unique charming modern literary system . . . just like what Latin American literature did, winning international recognition with its system meanwhile making an influence on the development of the world. That's what we call a contribution to humanism" (quoted in Duan 261). This opinion is typical of literary circles in the 1980s. García Márquez was treated not only as a brilliant writer, but also as an icon of success and an example for Chinese literature to learn from in order to "embrace the world."

CHINESE TRANSLATION OF GARCÍA MÁRQUEZ'S WORKS

Before García Márquez was awarded the Nobel Prize for Literature, Hispanic literary circles in mainland China had already noticed him. A restricted publication, *Foreign Literature Affairs*,[6] founded by the People's Literature Publishing House during the Cultural Revolution, introduced the "Colombian novel of the new genre *One Hundred Years of Solitude*" in the special issue "Latin American Literature" in January 1975. In February 1976, the same magazine introduced *El otoño del patriarca* (*The Autumn of the Patriarch*), recently published by the writer. After the Cultural Revolution, Chen Guangfu published "One Glimpse on the Contemporary Latin American Novels" in *New Perspectives on World Literature* in 1979, in which he again mentioned both this new genre, magical realism, and *One Hundred Years* by García Márquez. Lin Yi'an published "Colombian Magical Realist Author García Márquez and His New Work *El otoño del Patriarca* (*The Autumn of the Patriarch*)" in *World Literature Recent Developments* in 1979. These articles show the change in mainstream cultural logic: Cold War ideology was dying out, and reviews from American media were quoted positively. The third issue of *Foreign Literature and Art* in 1980 published "Four Short Stories by García Márquez": "Los funerales de la Mamá Grande" ("Big Mama's Funeral") "En este pueblo no hay ladrones" "(No Thieves in This Town), "La siesta del Martes" (Tuesday Siesta), and "Rosas artificiales" (Artificial Roses)".

These were the first of García Márquez's works to be translated into Chinese. In the sixth issue of the same magazine in 1982, his novel *Crónica de una muerte anunciada* (*Chronicle of a Death Foretold*), co-translated by Li Deming et al, appeared in its entirety. Acknowledging the author's importance, *World Literature* decided to publish the translated sections of *One Hundred Years* by Shen Guozheng et al. in the sixth issue of 1982. During proofreading there came news of the announcement of García Márquez's Nobel Prize, and Lin Yi'an, who was the Spanish-language literature editor of the magazine, added "laureate of 1982 Nobel Prize in Literature" to the published translation. At the same time, *Foreign Literature and Art* also ran the news item "García Márquez Won Nobel Prize in Literature of 1982" as well as advertisements for his upcoming short-story collections by Shanghai Translation Publishing House. In the second issue of *Foreign Literature and Art* of 1983 there also appeared the complete text of García Márquez's award ceremony speech, "The Solitude of Latin America." García Márquez thus became the first Nobel literary laureate introduced to China entirely by Chinese media.

Due to the sensational effect of the Nobel Prize, García Márquez and Latin American literature gained fame exponentially in China. From 1982 to 1989 128 articles were published in Chinese periodicals related to the Nobel Prize in Literature, among which fifty-one were about García Márquez; they were published in *World Literature, Dushu, Journal of Latin American Studies, People's Daily*, and others. Therefore, García Márquez became the most introduced and translated Nobel literary laureate in China in the 1980s. Most of these articles were gathered together and issued in 1984 as *Nobel Prize Laureate in Literature 1982: Research Materials on García Márquez*.

On May 5–11, 1983, the Asociación China del Estudio de la Literatura Española, Portuguesa y Latinoamericana held a national conference on "García Márquez and Latin American Magical Realism." This was the first academic conference on Latin American literature since the founding of the society. At the meeting, fourteen essays about García Márquez or magical realism written by researchers in Spanish-language literature were presented. Xinhua News Agency, China Radio International, *China Daily*, and media from Hispanic countries, such as Agencia EFE from Spain, released news about this symposium. In the course of the 1980s, García Márquez's chief works, such as *Cien años de soledad* (*One Hundred Years of Solitude*), *El otoño del patriarca* (*The Autumn of the Patriarch*), *Crónica de una muerte anunciada* (*Chronicle of a Death Foretold*), *El coronel no tiene quien le escriba* (*No One Writes to the Colonel*), *El amor en los tiempos del cólera* (*Love in the Time of Cholera*), and *El general en su laberinto* (*The General in His Labyrinth*); collections of short stories; *Research Materials on García Márquez*, and conversations with García Márquez in *El olor de la guayaba* (*Fragrance of Guava*) were all translated and published in China.

Master of Magical Realism

Along with García Márquez, the new literary concept of magical realism was introduced to Chinese readers. In the very beginning, both *One Hundred Years* and magical realism were severely criticized from an ideological point of view. *Foreign Literature Affairs* released a special issue in January 1975 about Latin American literature, and the editor, Wang Yangle, set forth in the preface:

> The realism emerging among the Latin American literature in the 1930s and 1940s died out in the 1950s. In the middle of complicated national class struggles and two-line struggles under the corrupting influence of modern revisionism and Western bourgeois ideology. Some of the progressive writers now escape from reality and the progressive tradition of Latin American literature. Some are degenerating and giving in to the dominance of Western declining bourgeois culture. (1)

The article claimed *One Hundred Years* "to be of a new genre called 'fantasy literature'(幻想文学) or 'magical realism' (魔术现实主义)" (1). Although describing the sensation caused by *One Hundred Years* in world literary circles, it criticized the novel severely. The criticism was not about the novel but about how "The Soviet Union revisionism, following closely the West, had glorified *One Hundred Years of Solitude* and touted it as a novel with true humanism" (1). Hence it aimed at unmasking a Soviet Union that was "trying to woo Latin American writers over by despicable means" (1). In February 1976 the same journal reviewed García Márquez's latest work, *The Autumn of the Patriarch*, claiming that the author used magic realism to magicalize the Latin American dictatorship instead of analyzing its roots from a political and class struggle perspective (34).

After the Cultural Revolution, Chen Guangfu, in "One Glimpse on the Contemporary Latin American Fiction," adopted the same translation, "Moshu Xianshi Zhuyi" (魔术现实主义), used by, Wang Yangle in the mid-1970s, but the tone was milder, and he emphasized the fact that magical realism, in his view, did represent reality. However, since "the absurd isn't inferior to that of some West European or American modernism" (Chen Guangfu, "One Glimpse" 37–60) and since at that time China had not yet finally decided how to judge Western modernist literature, the author was still inclined to celebrate the traditional realist novel.

Soon thereafter, *New Perspectives on World Literature* published in one issue two articles about contemporary Latin American novels: "Colombian Magical Realist Writer García Márquez and His New Novel: *The Autumn of the Patriarch*" by Lin Yi'an and "Mexican Writer Juan Rulfo with His Magical Realist Novel *Pedro Páramo*" by Duan Ruochuan. This was the first time the word "magical realism" appeared in Chinese as Mohuan Xianshi Zhuyi (魔幻现实主义).[7] According to the first article, magical realism dates back to the late 1920s; in its narrative, the piece said, "realistic scenes and plots coexisted and entangled with pure imagination" (Lin 23–32), emphasizing that the "magical" effect lies behind "turning the reality into fantasy without damaging the veracity"

(23–32). Moreover, this article explained the origin of the Spanish phrase *realismo mágico* and listed several so-called magical realist writers: Rulfo, Donoso, Carpentier, García Márquez, Fuentes, Asturias, Roa Bastos, and even Borges and Cortázar. It was a completely different attitude after three years, although both reviews were about *The Autumn of the Patriarch* and were published in a restricted journal. In 1976, although there had been differing opinions, those articles cited only the negative reviews from foreign media, declaring that "nothing stays in my mind after reading the book" (Wang Yangle, "Lating American Literature in 1975" 34). In contrast, the 1979 review quoted the recommendation of the American magazine *Time* and praise of the Latin American literary circle. García Márquez's gesture of donating the cash award from the 1971 Rómulo Gallegos International Novel Prize to the Venezuelan left-wing political organization Movement toward Socialism was used to "expose Soviet revisionism" in 1976 (34), but to salute the author for his social-critical standpoint in 1979. The other article, by Duan Ruochuan, basically focused on the novel, examining the characteristics of magical realism and abandoning the ideological-critical method that had been in use for a long time when discussing Latin American literature.

In 1980 Chen Guangfu wrote another article on magical realism. This time he pointed out that magical realism was constructed

> on the base of American Indian classical literature . . . taking in narration method from both the Western and Eastern myths plus methods such as alienation, absurd, dream from Western modernism thus reflecting or insinuating Latin America's reality and accomplishing the mission of mocking, condemning, revealing, satirizing or attacking the status quo. ("Comments and Introduction of Magical Realism" 131)

This endows magical realism with a certain quality similar to critical realism and thus becomes a deeper realism that has been learned from Western modernist literature. It not only keeps some distance from modernism but also meets mainland China's advocacy for critical realism.

In this process of introduction, one must notice the evolution of the translation of the term *realismo mágico*. Although Mosh (魔术)/Mohuan (魔幻) is only one Chinese character different, the meaning varies. 魔术现实主义 Moshu leaves an impression that it is an art method that deforms reality. 魔术 Moshu is linked with forms or tricks. On the other hand, Mohuan is contrary to reality, which means it is not real and is different from pure realism. By putting these two words—Mohuan and reality—together, Mohuan Xianshizhuyi presents a rich ambiguity and is a paradox that leads to a quest for the essence of realism. However, perhaps it is the paradoxical combination of Mohuan 魔幻 and reality that allows magical realism to stray, though not too far from the realist tradition, which thereby gains for it a legitimate space for acceptance and dissemination.

From 1982 to 1983 almost forty articles about García Márquez were published in China; without exception, all of them mentioned magical realism. In the aforementioned 1983 conference, the Hispanic circle had reached a consensus that magical realism was a new phase or a new current within Latin American realism. But at that time barely any other Chinese writer or critic of Chinese contemporary literature agreed with this; instead, they boldly emphasized the realistic side of magical realism. In 1984 the Chinese translation of *One Hundred Years* from the Spanish version was published, and Chinese readers started to have a more direct understanding of magical realism. From that point, this new genre began having an impact on Chinese literature, reaching its apex in the glory of Root-Seeking as well as that of avant-garde literature during 1985–1987. Although these two genres are not opposed to each other, there are profound differences in their ideas and practice, stemming from their divergent understandings of the "modernity" component in magical realism.

In the 1980s, the Latin American literature introduced into China included realism, pastoral romanticism, regionalism, revolutionary novels, indigenism, fantasy fiction, avant-garde fiction, and the like. There were various genres and ideas, but when introduced to China, regardless of the differences between the styles and genres of the authors or works, they were all designated "magical realism." The term represented by *One Hundred Years* in the 1980s became the name for Latin American literature in China.

"The Boom" and "Latin American Experience"

As mentioned earlier, García Márquez is important not only because he was awarded the Nobel Prize for Literature, but also because he set an example, sending a message to Chinese novelists that it is possible for Third World literature to command a world literary circle. The 1982 Nobel brought García Márquez to Chinese readers; moreover, it also brought with it the trend of magical realism and the legend of the Latin American Boom.

By the end of the Cultural Revolution, the term "Boom" had been translated into Chinese but was considered as a current "created by Western bourgeois intellectuals" (Wang Yangle, "Latin American Literature in 1975" 34).[8] In 1980 Chang Cheng published an article titled "Boom Literature," one of the earliest articles to introduce the phenomenon to Chinese readers, which was based on compiling foreign materials, considering the Boom as a literary genre of magical realism. It provided a superficial description of some individual figures and their masterpieces, as well as negative criticism. The author claimed that, although the Boom had got rid of the pattern of the "Novela de la Tierra," it copied the various styles of some new Western genres; thus, it had not completely eradicated the old tradition. The "Boom writers," it continued, were trapped in their petit-bourgeois limits, hence their works were not only pessimistic but also too highbrow, and "out of the reach of the vast majority of working class" (18). In his 1981 article "Latin American Literature Updates," Wang Yangle considered the Boom the fourth high point of Latin American literary history and argued that the word "Boom" could be translated to "literary sensation," Wenxue Hongdong (文学轰动), or "explosive literature," Baozha

Wenxue (爆炸文学), in Chinese. With García Márquez's 1982 Nobel Prize, the Boom immediately entered the limelight of the Chinese literary stage, and its Chinese name (文学爆炸) also came into fixed expression. China's Latin American literature fever in the 1980s derived from and focused on the Boom.[9] From 1979 until June 1989 more than forty novels or collections by Boom authors were published in China; over one hundred novels or short stories from the 1960s and 1970s and more than two hundred reviews on the Boom were released in magazines or newspapers. With García Márquez's award, the Boom, in the Chinese context, attained fame and glory, a landmark signifying the global recognition and admiration of some (trans)national literatures. Amid this fever for translation and introduction, there was no retrospection on how the name "Boom" had come into being. Obviously it is an English word, and Wang Yangle also mentioned that it was used by British and American critics. But no question was asked about the intention of using it to designate the 1960s literary flourishing in Latin America, nor was anybody interested in some Latin American writers' rejection of this term. Chilean writer José Donoso once said of this label:

> This English word is not neutral; on the contrary, it has many meanings: apart from the meaning of "voluminous", the rest are either negative or doubtful. "Boom" is an onomatopoeia that stands for "explosion;" but as time went by, it carries with it a meaning of "falsity." What explodes from nothing is nothing and leaves behind less. This short process of the void without question lacks quality and originality which leads only to deception and corruption. (3)

The poet Octavio Paz also considered this word with distaste, as "a horrid term," "a business glossary" (536). Carpentier criticized with outrage: "[N]aming Latin American literature as a Boom is casting an evil spell on it" (19). Some Latin Americans thought that the initiator had chosen this word not with praise or admiration, but rather to describe the emergence of Latin American literature as a flash in the pan and to predict its early death. That is why Latin American literary circles, including the writers who are named after the Boom, did not consider the word a declaration of success. Instead, they perceived the prejudice implied by the word and rejected this West-centered naming.

At that time, Chinese articles that discussed the Boom either ignored the etymology of the word or regarded it as a compliment to Latin American literature. Chen Zhongyi even declared that China did not care about the meaning of the word but focused only on how to reach a Boom:

> However, how come Latin American literature apex is called a "Boom"—maybe because the explosion vividly describes the sudden rise and prosperity of Latin American literary–is not one of our major concerns. What we want to know is the reason for the Boom. (60)

"Boom" implies the shock that the 1960s Latin American novel brought to Western-centered and European/American culture, yet it is the recognition and admiration of the West that caught Chinese literary circles' eyes. Without a doubt, this is a process to reacquaint the self and the other, through the mediation of the West.

It is noteworthy that at that time, Chinese Hispanists did not intend to hide the connection between the Boom and Latin American political movements. As an example, this is how a scholar analyzed the background of the Boom:

> The reason why Latin America experienced a literary thrive has everything to do with the flourish of revolutions. . . . The development path of Latin American literature sets a good example for the rest of the world, especially for Asian and African countries. It should be put this way: the world literature's hope consists of the development of the broad Third World literature. (Ni 23)

In the context of the 1980s, however, this kind of rhetoric and speech brings to people's mind the memory of "highly politicized literature" from Mao's era. In the "New Era" (新时期), by contrast, when writers wanted to free themselves from the idea that "literature should serve politics" and longed for complete autonomy of literature, speech of this sort was indeed "inappropriate" and it was thus hard to find approval for it in China. What needs to be pointed out is that, in the 1980s, the de-revolutionizing of 1960s Latin American literature was not unique in Latin American or Chinese contexts of that time, but rather an organic part and distant echo of a worldwide "depoliticized politics" of "farewell revolution" and "farewell to the 60s."

To sum up, because in the 1980s Chinese literary circles placed too much emphasis on the sensation caused by the Boom and overlooked the inevitable connection between the literary flowering and its revolutionary culmination under the influence of the Cuban Revolution, they treated the rise of Latin American literature as the outcome of the internal development of literature. They also considered the globalization of Latin American literature the result of its own opening and reform. This discursive practice of de-revolutionizing and depoliticization of 1960s Latin American novels is the reason Chinese writers, when they would read these works, overfocused on the innovations of skills, styles, and language, overlooking the fact that none of these innovations came from a purely formalist revolution. Nor did they ask: Without the 1960s, would there still be a "Boom"? In the 1980s, when the global landscape had seen a megashift and the global market had replaced Third World revolutions as the main interest of the world, would Chinese literature be able to restore glory to Third World literature by replicating the Latin American experience from the 1960s?

APPRENTICES OF GARCÍA MÁRQUEZ: ROOT-SEEKING LITERATURE AND AVANT-GARDE LITERATURE

Among 1980s Chinese fiction, the two most eye-catching tendencies are Root-Seeking literature (寻根文学) and avant-garde literature (先锋文学). To Root-Seeking writers such as Han Shaogong, Ah Cheng, Li Hangyu, Zheng Wanlong, and Zheng Yi, magical realism gave their lingering doubts an answer at that time: besides their aspiration to "embrace the world," more importantly, it showed them the way to do so. In their opinion, Latin America was the same as China, part of the Third World. But in the 1960s and 1970s, Latin America went through a rapid modernization, absorbing rich local cultural resources (such as Amerindian culture and Black culture). Eventually, Latin American writers won Western recognition with their uniquely national modern literature—this is the inspiration that the Root-Seeking writers gained from the success of *One Hundred Years*. However, this does not mean that Root-Seeking authors were being utilitarian when they were learning from Latin American culture; that would be an oversimplified judgment. A critic ironically described the Root-Seeking writers thus:

> We seek the root of "Root-seeking" while exaggerating the anxiety of the "root": through the veil of the metropolis, not without pretension we look far into the distant poor hometown trying to "remember" its cultural "sediment" which is not poor; we imagine the glorified future of Root-seeking literature and we seem to see a Chinese Root-seeking writer, joyfully on his/her way to Stockholm to be awarded Nobel Prize. (Yin 23–44)

Root-Seeking consciousness and Root-Seeking narrative, without a doubt, were the result of the appeal of "embrace the world" and the reflexion on Western modernist fever of that time. As He Guimei explained,

> At least according to the initiators of this trend, Root-seeking was the reply to Western modernism or even to certain doubts or critics generated in the process of China's modernization. Through reorganizing national cultural resources, it tried to re-establish Chinese culture's subject position and produce a new discourse which can be called cultural nationalism. (164)

With regard to writing, what the Root-Seeking novelists need to solve is the selection of the path of novel writing at the crossroads. At the end of the 1970s and beginning of the 1980s, some literary works gained fame overnight. But critics have pointed out their aesthetic shortcomings; even the better ones were simply replicating the traditions or forms that had been suppressed by the norms of socialist realism, and that is why they were described as serving to "make up the lessons"[10] (Li Zehou 311). In the early 1980s, novels in China still had the heavy burden of reflecting on history, but they had made progress in narrative. Under the shock of Western modernist writing, Chinese literature was facing a new question: Besides tears, sad stories, and realism, what can novels do in the New Era? Where are they heading? To further realism, or to imitate Western modernism? Is there an alternative for Chinese literature? (Hong, *Writer's Attitude* 54–66).

Those who were involved in Root-Seeking also expressed the same attitude when they later recalled that movement. Han Shaogong said he was against accepting modernism— taking imitation and duplication as creation—which he called "transplanting foreign 'Model Opera' (样板戏)." He was also not content with the so-called anti–Cultural Revolution literature that "was still using the same concept as in the old-time, only exaggerating the politics. In those works, there were only political characters, no cultural ones; only political coordinates, no cultural ones" (Han, quoted in Wang Rao 107). In this context, as Han Shaogong argued, "how to understand China's conditions, how to organize our cultural legacy, how to create with all the cultural resources from China and West in the process of opening to the world, and pave a unique Chinese literature development path, become the main concern of some writers and me" (107). Li Tuo also agreed that Latin American magical realism "offered a new horizon"; it "combined modernism with local culture, creating a new version of Latin American modernist novel instead of European modernism. It is unique to Latin America" (quoted in Wang Rao 107). Literary critics at that time looked up to magical realism as an example for Chinese literature, to show them the way to modernization with national characteristics.

However, in speaking of the connection between Root-Seeking and magical realism, the people involved in the movement ended up with different memories. In 1984, the Hangzhou Meeting was started; it was later considered the beginning of Root-Seeking literature.[11] One of the organizers, Cai Xiang noted, "At that time, Latin American Boom, especially *One Hundred Years* by Márquez made a great impact on Chinese contemporary literature" (91) and it "sent a message to the new-reborn Chinese literature: to base ourselves on local culture" (quoted in Wang Rao 107). But when Han Shaogong was interviewed in 2004, he denied that there was a "Latin America Fever" at the Hangzhou Meeting or that the participants had read any work by García Márquez (quoted in Wang Rao 107). This discrepancy reveals the metacognition of historical narrative. On the one hand, the people involved felt slightly disgusted at the idea of considering "literary Root-Seeking" as a utilitarian way to "embrace the world" (that is, looking to the West) and going after the Nobel Prize in Literature. On the other hand, since the 1990s in China there have been reflections on Western modernization, and as a result, the writers from that time "magnified" their reflections on literary modernization. According to Han Shaogong, the idea of Root-Seeking was a response to modernity and to the desire to have a conversation with the world, but what was more important to them was the subjectivity of Chinese writers; not only having self-consciousness, but also gaining foresight into the exploration of a unique Chinese literary modernization path with both local and external resources. This is to say that they had "a backward tendency when they move forward" (Dai, *Landscape* 16):[12] they did not reject modernity but rather attempted to find a way, much like what so-called Latin American magical-realist literature was doing, to go beyond simple imitation and enter the modern world (He 169).

However, Chinese writers' Root-Seeking journey did not go as well as that of García Márquez. It did leave a remarkable trace on local literary concepts and future writings, but it did not last long, nor did it have a global influence like that of magical realism. On the one hand, Root-Seeking authors' premature "backward" tendency could hardly gain general recognition in the Westernizing modernization of the early and mid-1980s. Some people "threw an almost irredeemably evil reproach on the face of Root-seeking writers," which is "reaction"; they "considered Root-seeking as a historical, philosophical and aesthetic regress of contemporary literature which was already in the process of modernization" (Li Jiefei 104). To the literary people of that time, history meant nightmare, "a runaround of death" (Dai, *Invisible Writing* 48); any attempt at returning to history or restoring tradition would be suppressed. For them, five thousand years of Chinese history were an ultra-stable structure, a suffocating "iron house," and the greatest obstacle to modernization. The movements of historical and cultural reflection in the 1980s were based on this concept. Root-Seeking literature was nostalgic about the abandoned or damaged traditional culture and the disapproval of the extreme action of the New Culture Movement of 1919, which made even more angry and alert the 1980s enlighteners who compared themselves to the May Fourth intellectuals. All in all, before Root-Seeking exploration had been systematized or theorized, it was already submerged by the wave of questioning and condemning. Literati at that time could not see that "Root-Seeking" was proposed within the problematic of modernity or that it "was a type of writing in response to modernity" (Cai 92).

On the other side, under the banner of Root-Seeking, there were too many different kinds of miscellaneous discourses that elicited ridicule. The Root-Seeking "manifesto"[13] and other major problems brought about questioning and controversy. The cultural fracture zone caused by May Fourth, the modern meaning of the integrated Confucian-Taoist-Buddhist tradition, the value of folk "indigenous culture," and the like have been the major topics for almost a century in Chinese philosophical and cultural circles. The Root-Seeking writers, however, are not capable of embarking on the task. As Cai Xiang argued, the Hangzhou Meeting was a representation of the complex mentality of Chinese writers and critics: they embraced Western modernism, but at the same time they were trying to struggle against being West centered; they highlighted the value of national culture and local culture while rejecting any kind of retroism or conservatism (Cai 92). In an emphatic era when modernism was expanding, this kind of paradox was not welcome and thus left no room for further discussion.

There is no denying that Root-Seeking novelists followed magical-realist literature and tried to accomplish modernization through nationalization, as their Latin American pioneers had done. Their aspirations were at one time very similar to those of the so-called magical realist Latin American writers. But as mentioned earlier, cultural nationalism did not exceed the modernity of enlightenment, so a new narrative was not to be constructed by the national subject, as Juan Rulfo or García Márquez had done in Latin America. Among their works, some Root-Seeking writings that claimed to return to local culture were merely describing a poor, remote countryside, demons, and spirits; they successfully avoided becoming "pseudo-modernists" but instead turned into "pseudo-magical" and "pseudo-folklore" writers, with suspicion of "self-orientalism." After 1985, several comparative literature theses on Root-Seeking literature and Latin American magical realism only offered a comparison of skills. Some of them were even trying to do some analysis from the perspective of magical realism in classical Chinese canons, such as poems by Qu Yuan, *Strange Stories from a Chinese Studio* (《聊斋志异)》by Pu Songling, and *A Dream of Red Mansions* (《红楼梦)》and *A Journey to the West* (《西游记). At that time writers from minority areas such as Tibet, Yunnan, Guizhou, Sichuan, and Guangxi province, believing that their hometowns were very similar to Latin America in geography and culture, paid a lot of attention to magical realism. In the Root-Seeking fever, the Flower Mountain 花山 writers' group came up with the slogan "Baiyue Realm" 百越境界, which to a certain extent is a local attempt at magical realism (Mei and Yang 71–72). The Yunnan People's Publishing House classified the Latin American literature series as a priority and applied to join the National Eighth Five-Year Publishing Plan. It was believed that China shared a great number of similarities in cultural traditions with Latin America, that "the two of them have the same blood type" and "thus there won't be rejection in their cultural communication" (Liu and Tang 107). In 1988 the book *Selection of Magical Realist Fictions* was published in China, with eight works, including "Red Sorghum" and "Dog Ways" by Mo Yan, "Homeward Bound I Go" by Han Shaogong, "Tibet, Mysterious Years" and "Souls Tied to the Knots on a Leather Cord" by Tashi Dawa, and "Five Women and One String" by Ye Weilin. The reason they were viewed as magical realist was that "they applied the techniques of hyperbole, metaphor, symbolism, absurdism, and inserted myths as well as legends" (Meng 10). However, these similarities are merely superficial; that is why Meng Fanhua, who wrote the preface to the book, did not admit to a Chinese magical realism. When "magical realism" became a common critical term in China, it was used arbitrarily. Several novels were designated as magical realist only because they depicted episodes such as "the Beauty flew to the sky on bedsheets" or "the dead walking around in the yard." As Liu Zhenyun stated, "[W]e took them for essence, as our guidelines. What would Márquez think about it?" (218–19).

Certainly Chinese Root-Seekers also had the intention of conceptualizing social issues through literature, but the link between Latin American magical realism and political reality was neglected in the depoliticized cultural context of the 1980s, either consciously or not. In 2004 Han Yuhai, together with some other young critics, was trying to recover the left-wing aspect of Latin American writers, and they published a series of essays titled "Revaluating Latin America" on the website https://m.douban.com/mip/group/topic/1185290/?author=1. Light was not shed on this until twenty years later, which serves as proof of Dai Jinhua's argument that this kind of "rediscovering" or "filling" history was not meant to complete the original history, but rather to change the entire historical narrative because of the emergence of the forgotten and the forbidden (*Through a Glass Darkly* 32–33). This change, without a doubt, is the outcome of the new discursive/political practice in a new historical context.

Despite the problems existing within the miscellaneous Root-Seeking discourse system, it still can be seen to some extent as a "renovated start." Some critics argued that it "inspired the stylistic revolution of novels in the mid-80s" (Li Jiefei 113). In other words, "it added into the literary circle's agenda the revolution of novel language and skills" of Chinese contemporary literature (113). As Nan Fan points out, "It doesn't matter whether if they found the Root or described the traditional culture accurately; a new imagination was inspired by the Root-seeking slogan: isn't that enough for literature?" (108). Pioneers such as Wang Zengqi 汪曾祺 and later Jia Pingwa 贾平凹, Han Shaogong 韩少功, Ah Cheng 阿城, Mo Yan 莫言, and others, created, in their textual practice using local cultural resources, a unique "modern fiction" instead of copying the

Western classics. In particular Mo Yan, who is considered the true Chinese disciple of magical realism, became one of the earliest Chinese writers in the 1980s to be translated and published in the West, with his "national" characteristics as shown in the "Red Sorghum" 红高粱 series. This seems to prove that learning from Latin American magical realism has been effective in terms of stylistic renovation.

Chinese avant-garde writers who held a leading position after 1985 also applauded magical realism, which had become belletristic in the local context. They endowed *One Hundred Years* with the value of the construction of a new concept of time and space in narrative. The first sentence alone, "Many years later, as he faced the firing squad, Colonel Aureliano Buendía was to remember that distant afternoon when his father took him to discover ice," prompted countless interpretations and was re-employed in numerous texts. "Many years ago" and "after many years" at that time became standard lines in avant-garde novels. García Márquez had started the parable of Latin American modernization history with an outstanding opening sentence and thus completed a reflexion on modern civilization. But unfortunately, many avant-garde writers who reflected on modern China's history from the perspective of new historicism were filling in the blanks of the history with folk tales, legends, and myths that in the end overturned and rewrote the entire revolutionary past. Take *Red Sorghum* as an example: in this personal heroic legend, no political power plays any significant part, which clearly shows its ideological appeal in this depoliticized writing. And this is exactly why Mo Yan is like García Márquez yet will never become García Márquez. It is a fine example, serving to demonstrate how Chinese writers accepted Latin American magical realism but not without reservation, leading to a bifurcation in the end.

Conclusion

Examining the past forty years, it can be said that without García Márquez, the contemporary Chinese novel would have a different look. The Colombian author's "success"—and that of the Boom—from the beginning took Chinese literary circles by shock: we thought we were familiar with Latin American literature, but our view changed overnight. We were not familiar with European and American literature because of the Cold War from the 1950s to the 1970s; but how then to explain our "ignorance" of Latin American literature? Worse still, this seems to suggest that Chinese literature "fell behind" not only to Western but also Latin American literature, in the former European colonies for which China had expressed support constantly from the 1950s to the 1970s. Latin Americans had gained recognition from the world literary mainstream, whereas Chinese literature, with its over two-thousand-year history, had not contributed any writer with global fame. At that time many articles about the Boom focused on how could it happen in Latin America. Someone came up with the question: "How did the little guy in the village become a millionare"? (Wen Ren, "Reconsideration" 132). Some were desperate for a Chinese Boom in the world after the Latin American one. They were asking, "Why is it that Latin America could make world literature history? Why can't it be China?" (Zhao Deming 39). They were full of pride and confidence, in the 1980s style: "There is no doubt that very soon we will have our own Boom" (Wen Ren, "Reconsideration" 104).

Represented by García Márquez, Latin American literature became an example of how to finally catch up with the top students from Europe and America; using Luis Harss and Barbara Dohmann's words, to enter *Into the Mainstream*. It was thus a body of work admired by Chinese literary people, who were enthusiastic to learn from the example and thus spread the high fever in the 1980s to translate, publish, and read Latin American literature.

But the fact is that the reflections and thoughts on history and reality of 1960s Latin American literature were considered irrelevant to literature itself. In China it was abandoned for belletristic discourse; the only thing left was imitation and taking over the techniques. Referring to that literature with the Western name of the "Boom" and making allusions to "magical realism" led to the translations of this kind of literature, "literatura comprometida" (engaged literature), to take part in the discursive construction of "farewell revolution" in Chinese society in the 1980s.

At the beginning of the new century, Li Tuo, among others, brought up the topic of rethinking belletrism. He also noticed the deviation of the Chinese reception of Latin American writing in the 1980s. That literature, he argued, was highly political; to some extent, it was the culmination of the literature of the twentieth century, yet scholars did not pay enough attention to its complexity (Li Tuo, quoted in Dong 138). Still, this late comment cannot stop the momentum that took shape in the process of depoliticized translation of García Márquez. In 2011, Thinkingdom Media 新经典文化 finally cracked the hard nut after a lengthy negotiation and launched the first official Chinese version of *One Hundred Years*, authorized by García Márquez and newly translated by Fan Ye 范晔. Fan's version is the bestseller among all the roughly forty Chinese editions of this work since 1984, with sales of over one million copies. All of a sudden a new low fever over García Márquez had started in China. Within the coming year, several books relating to García Márquez were published, including *I'm Not Here to Give a Speech* (《我不是来演讲的》, 2012), a new edition of *Love in the Time of Cholera* (《霍乱时期的爱情》, 2012), and *Gabriel García Márquez: The Early Years* by Ilan Stavans (《加西亚·马尔克斯传：早年生活》[1927-1970], 2012).

However, this comeback of García Márquez in the new century is still depoliticized. Even when his lifetime left-wing opinions are mentioned, they are taken as an unbelievable "stain." Only when deemed nonrevolutionary and depoliticized could a work become a "new classic," and perhaps the "old classics" that are set aside are the revolutionary classics from the socialist period.

The translation history of García Márquez into Chinese serves as an example that demonstrates the "depoliticized politics" and "Cold War logic in the post–Cold War era" in Chinese society since the Economic Reform and the Opening Up.

Notes

1. In 1978, the Third Plenary Session of the Eleventh Central Committee of the Communist Party of China passed a resolution: "The Party's focus from 1979 should be on the socialist modernization construction." ("Communiqué of the Third Plenary 1).
2. Feng Zhi stated in his speech in the Third Enlarged Meeting of the Third Session of National Committee of China Federation of Literary and Art Circles: "(during the Cultural Revolution) Newspapers didn't publish reviews on foreign literature; presses rarely published translations of foreign literature; libraries didn't allow readers to view or borrow foreign literature books; literature departments in universities cancelled courses of foreign literature; as a result, this generation is ignorant of foreign affairs. Some English graduates work as translators and don't know whether Shakespeare is a place or a person. Chinese textbooks for middle school students were not allowed to include 'Petrel', because nobody dared to study the relation between Lu Xun and foreign literature" (Feng 4). *Yilin* magazine, founded in November 1979, started the foreword to the first issue, titled "Open a Window to Know the World" with this: "The Gang of Four negated the cultural legacy from home and abroad and forbid reading or studying foreign literature, resulting in our ignorance of the matter" (*Yilin* Editorial Board 7). As He Guimei concluded: "Without the blockade, negation and rejection towards the Western 'modern' literature during the 1950s to 70s, there won't be such a huge desire in the 80s. It's a deprivation caused by taboo" (118).
3. Root-Seeking Literature (寻根文学) is a literary movement in mainland China that began in the mid-1980s. From 1983 to 1984, some young and middle-aged writers, including Han Shaogong, Li Tuo, A Cheng, and others, began to exchange ideas on the roots of literature through meetings and discussions. In 1985, Han Shaogong published the article "The Root of Literature," which was regarded as the manifesto of Root-Seeking movement. Then Zheng Wanlong, Li Hangyu, and A Cheng also published articles to support Han. They expressed similar point of views: Chinese literature should be rooted in the nation's extensive and profound cultural traditions, and it is necessary to explore our own traditions in order to have a dialogue with world literature. Root-seeking literature has stimulated contemporary Chinese writers' interest in regional, traditional, folk, minority culture, and even writing in dialects. In the 1980s, when the whole society was learning from the West, the movement turned to China's own multiculture and tradition instead (Hong, *History of Chinese Modern Literature* 321–22).]
4. Avant-garde novels (先锋小说), also known as experimental novels (实验小说), were produced by a new literary school that emerged in mainland China in the mid-1980s, starting with Ma Yuan's "Goddess of the Lhasa River," published in 1984. Later, more young novelists, including Hong Feng, Yu Hua, Ge Fei, Sun Ganlu, and Ye Zhaoyan, published dozens of works of fiction and novels in succession. Their common point is "narrative first." Compared to content, they care more about form, that is, how to tell a story. They take delight in deconstructing the grand narrative of the mainstream; refuse to offer meaning to the story; and prefer gloomy themes such as death, violence, or sex. Therefore this literary school is regarded as a formalist revolution in Chinese contemporary literature (Hong, *History of Chinese Modern Literature* 338–39).
5. According to custom in Spanish-speaking countries, García Márquez should not be abbreviated as "Márquez," nor should Vargas Llosa be shortened to "Llosa." However, direct quotations are provided verbatim; no changes have been made to the names.
6. *Foreign Literature Report* was founded by People's Literature Publishing House during the Cultural Revolution. It was meant to provide information on foreign literature for internal

circulation, as were *World Literature Recent Developments*, from the Institute of Foreign Literature of the Chinese Academy of Social Sciences, and *Foreign Literature News*, from the Institute of Information/Literature of Shanghai Academy of Social Sciences. Wang Yangle, alias Wei Hua, was in charge of the editing and translation of the Latin American literature report.

7. Lin Yi'an was the first person to translate *realismo mágico* into 魔幻现实主义, and the translation was disseminated. But Chen Guangfu seems to have reservations about it (*Magical Realism* 8–9).
8. As mentioned in "Latin American Literature in 1975." It pointed out the fact that the name came from the West, but when the Latin American Boom was officially introduced to China in the 1980s, such a description was considered as typical Cultural Revolution speech and thus omitted.
9. Liu Xiliang, Spanish literature translator and former vice-minister of State Administration of Radio, Film, and Television, once said that 1980s' Latin American literature fever was indeed Boom fever (279).
10. In the 1980s, Chinese literary circles often borrowed the term "make-up lessons" proposed by Li Zehou in his study of the history of Chinese modernization.
11. The contemporary novel seminar was co-organized in 1984 by *Shanghai Literature*, Zhejiang Literature and Art Publishing House, and *West Lake* magazine. Among the attendants there were writers and critics, including Zhou Jieren, Cai Xiang, Ji Hongzhen, Huang Ziping, Li Tuo, Ah Cheng, Chen Jiangong, Zheng Wanlong, Han Shaogong, Li Hangyu, Li Qingxi, Chen Cun, Wu Liang, Chen Sihe, Nan Fan, Xu Zidong, Lu Shuyuan, and Song Yaoliang.
12. Dai Jinhua came up with this description when criticizing the root-seeking practice of contemporary cinema, the Fourth Generation directors' works (Dai, *Landscape in the Mist* 16).
13. The so-called manifesto refers to articles published in the second half of 1985, such as "Literary Root" by Han Shaogong (2–4); "My Roots" by Zheng Wanlong (44–46); "To Sort Out Our 'Roots'" by Li Hangyu (75); "Culture Restricts Humanity" by Ah Cheng; and "Stride across Cultural Fracture Zone" by Zheng Yi.

Works Cited

Ah Cheng. "Culture Restricts Humanity." *Literature and Art Newspaper*, 6 July 1985.
Alejo Carpentier. "The Origin of Latin American Novels." *Novel Is a Must*, translated by Chen Zhongyi, Yunnan People's Publishing House, 1995, pp. 1–22.
Cai, Xiang. "Before and after Hangzhou Meeting." *Aspects of Chinese Contemporary Writers: Conversation Between Souls*, edited by Lin Jianfa and Xu Lianyuan, Zhejiang Literature and Art Publishing House, 2004, pp. 88–93.
Chang, Cheng. "Boom Literature." *World Books*, no. 1, 1980, pp 18–20, and no. 2, 1980, pp 13–15.
Chen, Guangfu. "Comments and Introduction of Magical Realism." *Literature and Art Studies*, no. 5, 1980, pp. 131–38.
Chen, Guangfu. *Magical Realism*. Flower City Publishing House, 1986.
Chen, Guangfu. "One Glimpse on the Contemporary Latin American Novels." *New Perspectives on World Literature*, no. 3, 1979, pp. 37–60.
Chen, Zhongyi. "The Emergence of Latin American Literature." *Foreign Literature Studies*, no. 4, 1984, pp. 59–64.

"Communiqué of the Third Plenary Session of the Eleventh Central Committee of the Communist Party of China." *Selected Documents since the Third Plenary Session of the Eleventh Central Committee*, Peoples' Publishing House, p. 1.

Dai, Jinhua. *Invisible Writing: Cultural Studies in China in the 1990s*. Jiangsu People's Publishing House, 1999.

Dai, Jinhua. *Landscape in the Mist: Chinese Film Culture(1978-1998)*. Peking UP, 2000.

Dai, Jinhua. *Through a Glass Darkly: Interviews with Dai Jinhua*. Knowledge P, 1999.

Dong, Zhilin. "Sidelights on Symposium of Contemporary Literature and 'Mass Culture Market.'" *Literary Review*, no. 1, 2003, pp. 131–38.

Donoso, José. *The Boom in Spanish American Literature: A Personal History*. Translated by Duan Ruochuan, Yunnan People's Publishing House, 1993.

Duan, Ruochuan. *Eagles on the Andes: Nobel Prize and Magic Realism*. Wuhan Publishing House, 2000.

Feng, Zhi. "Bring Order out of Chaos, Restore Foreign Literature Study: Speech on the Third Enlarged Meeting of the Third Session of National Committee of China Federation of Literary and Art Circles." *World Literature*, no.3 (internal issue), 1978, pp. 4–20.

García Márquez, Gabriel. *The Autumn of the Patriarch*. Translated by Yi Xin, Shandong Literature and Art Publishing House, 1985.

García Márquez, Gabriel. "*Chronicle of a Death Foretold*." Translated by Li Deming et al. *Foreign Literature and Art*, no. 6, 1981, pp. 68–142.

García Márquez, Gabriel. *Collections of Short Stories*. Translated by Zhao Deming et al., Shanghai Translation Publishing House, 1982.

García Márquez, Gabriel. *Fragrance of Guava*. Translated by Lin Yi'an, SDX Joint Publishing, 1985.

García Márquez, Gabriel. *The General in His Labyrinth*. Translated by Shen Baolou et al., Nanhai Publishing, 1990.

García Márquez, Gabriel. *I'm Not Here to Give a Speech*. Translated by Li Jing, Thinkingdom Media, 2012.

García Márquez, Gabriel. *Love in the Time of Cholera*. Translated by Jiang Zongcao et al., Hei Longjiang People's Publishing House, 1987.

García Márquez, Gabriel. *No One Writes to the Colonel*. Translated by Tao Yuping, Commercial P, 1985.

García Márquez, Gabriel. *One Hundred Years of Solitude*. Translated by Huang Jinyan et al., Shanghai Translation Publishing House, 1984.

García Márquez, Gabriel. "*One Hundred Years of Solitude* (Excerpts)." Translated by Shen Guozheng et al. *World Literature*, no. 6, 1982, pp. 33–116.

Han, Shaogong. "Literary Root." *Writer Magazine*, no. 4, 1985, pp. 2–5.

Harss, Luis, and Barbara Dohmann. *Into the Mainstream: Conversations with Latin American Writers*. Harper & Row, 1969

He, Guimei. *Knowledge Archives of the "New Enlightenment": On Chinese Culture of the 1980s*. Peking UP, 2010.

Hong, Zicheng. *History of Chinese Modern Literature*. Peking UP, 1999

Hong, Zicheng. *Writer's Attitude and Self Consciousness*. Shanxi People's Education P, 1991.

Institute of Party Literature. *Selected Documents since the Third Plenary Session of the Eleventh Central Committee*. People's Publishing House, 1982.

Li, Hangyu. "To Sort Out Our 'Roots.'" *Writers Magazine*, no. 6, 1985, p. 75.

Li, Jiefei. "Root-Seeking Literature: A Renovated Start (1984–1985)." *Contemporary Writers Review*, no. 4, 1995, pp. 101–13.

Li, Tuo. "Pay Attention to Latin American Literature's Development Model." *World Literature*, no. 2, 1987, pp. 282–87.

Li, Zehou. *Modern Chinese Thoughts*, Peoples' Publishing House, 1979, 311.

Lin, Yi'an. "Colombian Magical Realist Writer García Márquez and His New Novel: *The Autumn of the Patriarch*." *World Literature Recent Developments*, no. 8, 1979, pp. 23–32.

Liu, Shu'e, and Bing Tang. "On Chinese New Era Literature's Reception of One *Hundred Years of Solitude*." *Journal of Hubei University (Philosophy and Social Science)*, no. 3, 1993, pp. 105–11.

Liu, Xiliang. "Reflections on Latin American Literature Fever." *World Literature*, no. 6, 1989, pp. 279–82.

Liu, Zhenyun. "Monologue." *Aspects of Chinese Contemporary Writers*, edited by Lin Jianfa and Wang Jingtao, Time Literature and Art Press, 1991, pp. 218–19.

Mei, Shuaiyuan, and Ke Yang. "Baiyue Realm: Flower Mountain Culture and Our Creation." *Guangxi Literature*, no. 3, 1985, pp. 71–72.

Meng, Fanhua. "Chinese Magical Realism." *Selection of Magical Realist Fiction*, Time Literature and Art Press, 1988, p. 10.

Nan, Fan. *Literature in Conflict*. Shanghai Academy of Social Sciences P, 1992.

Ni, Luo. "Starting from the Boom." *World Affairs*, no. 9, 1985, pp. 22–23.

Paz, Octavio. "The Irrational Part of Human: The Poetry." *Selected Works of Paz*, vol. 2 (in Chinese), translated by Zhao Zhenjiang, Writer's P, 2006, pp. 532–539.

Wang, Fan. "Asturias and Magical Realism." *Yihai*, no. 2, 1981, pp. 204–6.

Wang, Rao. "Before and after 1985 'Fiction Revolution'—Tracing Avant-Garde and Root-Seeking Discourse." *Contemporary Writers Review*, no. 1, 2004, pp. 102–12.

Wang, Yangle. "Latin American Literature in 1975." *Foreign Literature Affairs* (Restricted Publication), no. 2, 1976, pp. 34..

Wang, Yangle. "Latin American Literature Updates." *Social Sciences Abroad*, no. 7, 1981, pp. 31–36.

Wang, Yangle. "Preface." *Foreign Literature Affairs* (Restricted Publication), no. 1, 1975, p. 1.

Wen, Ren. "The Inspiration from Latin American Contemporary Novels." *Dushu*, no. 95, 1987, pp. 48–51.

Wen, Ren. "Reconsideration on the Inspiration from Latin American Contemporary Novels." *Dushu*, no. 104, 1987, pp. 144–60.

Weng, Jiaxi. "Magical Realism." *Guangzhou Literature*, no. 7, 1981, pp. 59–60.

Wu, Liang. *Selection of Magical Realist Fiction*. Time Literature and Art P, 1988.

Yang, Ke, and Mei, Shuaiyuan. "Re-embark on Baiyue Realm." *Guangxi Daily*, 12 Nov. 1985.

Yilin Editorial Board. "Open a Window to Know the World." *Yilin*, No.1, 1979, p. 7.

Yin, Changlong. *1985: Extension and Twist*. Shandong Education Press, 1998.

Yuan, Haoyi. "About Latin American Magical Realist Fiction." *Modern Literary Magazine*, no. 12, 1985, pp. 61–64.

Zhang, Guopei. *Research Materials on García Márquez*. Nankai UP, 1984.

Zhao, Deming. "The Boom: Latin American New Fiction." *University Students Series*, no.1, 1981, p. 39.

Zheng, Wanlong. "My Roots." *Shanghai Literature*, no. 5, 1985, pp. 44–46.

Zheng, Yi. "Stride across Cultural Fracture Zone." *Literature and Art Newspaper*, 13 July 1985.

CHAPTER 14

SOUTH ASIAN READINGS OF GABRIEL GARCÍA MÁRQUEZ

SONYA SURABHI GUPTA AND SHAD NAVED

The linguistic imperialism of Spain and Portugal in the Americas does not match the experience of South Asian societies that developed in a hierarchical proximity to English. It is only with the late twentieth-century emergence of writers of "non-mimetic" persuasions, to use Kumkum Sangari's phrase, that English in their work becomes an "Indian" or "Pakistani" or "Bangladeshi" language. As the Marxist feminist critic Kumkum Sangari notes in her comparative essay on Gabriel García Márquez and Salman Rushdie, there was no comparable settler colonialism in the South Asian colonies of Europe, and therefore the sense of hybridity in the two writers' work is not similar. On his part, Salman Rushdie, whose novel writing has been compared and contrasted with García Márquez's fiction, places all such comparisons in the transnational dialogue between spaces that constitute the imaginary of the "Third World." But with the rise of Brazil and India (key members of BRICS) as "major emerging national economies" in the current millennium, the classification of "those parts of the world which one could loosely term the less powerful, or the powerless" (Rushdie 68) has been somewhat blunted as a ground for global comparisons through a Third World imaginary. Today García Márquez is read as a world literary, translated writer in South Asia with little memory of an earlier mode of transcontinental politics that might bring formal concerns of settler colonialism into dialogue with the direct colonialism of the British variety.

That this transnational comparison has even become possible between the Latin American Boom and the various booms in Indian, Pakistani, Bangladeshi, and Sri Lankan English from the 1980s onward is inevitably the result of the novel as the privileged genre and site for the expression of modern ideas about the self, history, literature, and culture in these former colonial societies. From the colonial period, the novel enables a global comparativity (particularly in the humanities classroom) such that trends in the Euro-American novel have become the touchstone for the literariness of the so-called vernacular languages of the subcontinent. Thus, when the phenomenon of magical realism announced a break within the "Western" novel technique, it created ripples in all those "peripheries" that had been forced into a literary, cultural, and economic simultaneity with Euro-America. In Homi Bhabha's words, "'Magical realism' after the Latin American Boom, becomes the literary language of the emergent post-colonial world" (7). Aijaz Ahmad, however, counters this view by noting the prepackaging of Latin American works for readerships in ex-colonies such as South Asia, which serves to orchestrate the encounter between the authors and their readers in translation (45). Sangari also signals the literary-theoretical subsumption of these works through varieties of "postmodernist" theory that determine the terms of "access" to a writer such as García Márquez. Gayatri Spivak's view on the absence of decolonization in Latin America is a stark reminder of the entrenchment of literary style *as* decolonization, which she contends is the reason magical realism has become paradigmatic of "Third World literary production" (57). Before we compare magical realist modes in Latin America and South Asia, Spivak suggests, we need to decolonize the magical realist style itself.

Thus, the magical realist departures of García Márquez's fiction invite non-Western readers to reflect on the connectivity of various "global" literatures (say, between global Spanish and global English); the relation between theory (largely located in the Western academy) and students, critics, and readers in the ex-colonies; and, what is not always stressed by South Asian theorists, the relation between forms of global culture (such as world literature and its subset, the Latin American novel) and the thousands of "vernaculars," not just in the "Old World" but also in the very spaces of magical realist writing in Latin America. No account of the world literary significance of García Márquez is possible without giving an account of the afterlives of García Márquez's fiction in the inferiorized vernaculars of the Global South. Whether these literary spaces are to be called the Third World, the Global South, or the ex-colonies, South Asia, with its linguistic and subnational plurality, mediated by an increasingly global English translation industry, offers an exemplary ground for giving such an account of the worldly trajectories of García Márquez's work.

The Circulation of García Márquez's Works in South Asia

While the theoretical positions on the circulation of magical realism, and more specifically García Márquez's works, in non-Western literary contexts come from postcolonial debates in the 1990s, the ground for this circulation was in the making since at least the 1960s. It is a little-known fact that García Márquez visited India as a part of the delegation from Cuba led by Fidel Castro to attend the seventh summit of the Non-Aligned Movement in New Delhi in March 1983 (Singh 224). Today, the forgotten collective spirit of the 1955 Bandung conference of Afro-Asian nations, the Non-Aligned Movement, and the energies of the Cuban Revolution worldwide all must be recalled if we are to begin recounting the circulation of García Márquez and his fiction within the various South Asian literary cultures.

South Asian readers outside of the English-dominated city read in vernaculars, languages with robust literary traditions in India, Nepal, Pakistan, Bangladesh, and Sri Lanka. It is in these languages, with millions of speakers, that avid readers in the smaller towns particularly discovered García Márquez's fiction in translation. From among the Latin American writers whose works have been circulating through cheaply priced, often unauthorized, translated editions, García Márquez is undoubtedly the most translated and most widely read (followed by Juan Rulfo, Jorge Luis Borges, and Mario Vargas Llosa), and predictably *Cien años de soledad* (*One Hundred Years of Solitude*) is the one Latin American novel translated into several languages of the subcontinent, including Malayalam, Sinhala, Urdu, Bengali, Tamil, Kannada, Gujarati, and Hindi. These translations, mainly from the English version, except for a few cases from the original Spanish, have been instrumental in making García Márquez a familiar name in the middle-class intellectual culture of many regions of the subcontinent. English translations of his works are equally ubiquitous, featuring in the syllabi of graduate and undergraduate courses of numerous departments of English, which during the 1980s and 1990s were opening up to a new curricular (decolonizing and decanonizing) agenda under the postcolonial critique.

García Márquez's works were already known to many in the subcontinent even before he was awarded the Nobel Prize for literature in 1982 and was elevated into a world literary sensation. Malayalam readers and writers in the southern Indian state of Kerala, for example, were introduced to him in the early 1970s by M. T. Vasudevan Nair, the doyen of Malayalam literature, who, in his travelogue *Aalkkoottathil Thaniye* (Alone in the crowd, 1982), mentions how during his journey in the United States in the 1970s he had read *Cien años de soledad* in English translation (21). In the late 1970s, and also in an essay-travelogue titled "Garcia Marquez and the Bus to Aracataca" (1978), Michael Ondaatje, the Booker Prize–winning diasporic Sri Lankan writer, wove his brilliant reading of the same novel into an English-language chronicle of his pilgrimage to Aracataca. The travelogue surprises the reader as Ondaatje's arrival at the writer's Colombian hometown takes him back to the text of the "bible book of the twentieth century, *One Hundred Years of Solitude*" (21), and instead of a report of the journey undertaken, what Ondaatje presents is a lyrical account amalgamating the narration of his passage through the town that was transformed into the famed Macondo of *Cien años de soledad*, with reflections on that novel and its formal strategies. However, it was through translations of the Colombian's short fiction that had begun circulating in translation in local literary magazines in the 1970s that García Márquez first became known in the other languages of the subcontinent. In the same decade, his short stories were also circulating in Malayalam and Bangla translations in India, and *Cien años de soledad* was included as prescribed reading in literature programs at some Indian universities as early as 1971.

The literary-critical world took note of the already palpable effects of Latin American magical realist writing, through the figure of García Márquez, in such important publications as the special issue "Marquez and Latin America" (1985) of the *Journal of Arts and Ideas* (India), in which many of the above-mentioned theoretical positions first appeared in print. A notable contribution to García Márquez studies in Urdu appeared in a special number (1991) of *Aaj* (Pakistan), a journal dedicated to the latest trends in literary Urdu and world literatures in Urdu translation. In his editor's introduction, Ajmal Kamal (3) refers to García Márquez as a *"qissa-go"* (a storyteller of the traditional Urdu oral tale), and the five-hundred-page volume of the journal carries complete translations of *El coronel no tiene quien le escriba* (*No One Writes to the Colonel*), *Crónica de una muerte anunciada* (*Chronicle of a Death Foretold*), selections from *Cien años de soledad* and *El amor en los tiempos del cólera* (*Love in the Time of Cholera*), and dozens of short stories and pieces on García Márquez's biography as well as criticism. Monographs and single-author studies of the writer, on the other hand, are rarer in the various subnational languages of the subcontinent. Prabhat Ranjan in Hindi (2014) and Khalid Javed in Urdu (2009) are two notable examples of literary studies of García Márquez in the two respective languages, Javed himself being part of a generation of young Indian Urdu fiction writers who have been deeply influenced by García Márquez.

THE CREATIVE AND LITERARY RECEPTION OF GARCÍA MÁRQUEZ'S WORKS IN SOUTH ASIA

Critics have identified elements of magical realism in the works of several South Asian writers. This identification is strongest for diasporic South Asian writers such as Salman Rushdie, Hanif Kureishi, and Chitra Banerjee Divakaruni, who have engaged with its techniques in differing degrees. The most explosive effects of this novelistic technique on societies in the subcontinent and beyond was the *Satanic Verses* controversy (1989), beginning with the religious condemnation of Salman Rushdie by the Ayatollah Khomeini of Iran, which revealed the tension of avant-garde writing in relation to the politics of national identity and faith in the non-West, a conjuncture that astonished Western critics and commentators. In South Asia, despite the banning of *The Satanic Verses* in India, Pakistan, and Bangladesh, Indian English writers invariably turned to the possibilities of the magical realist mode for their debut novels (most notably Amitav Ghosh, I. Allan Sealy, Kiran Nagarkar, Rukun Advani, and Shashi Tharoor). While several of these writers have moved toward more sober versions of realism, the stamp of magical realism can be found in South Asian English writers across national borders even today. The most recent trends in Pakistani fiction, especially the novels of Nadeem Aslam and Mohammed Hanif, show elements of the magical realist mode. Beginning with Rushdie, one crucial aspect of magical realism may be summed up not as the mere presence of the non-real but as the pulsating presence of the sounds, images, and structures of feeling associated with the so-called vernacular cultures that have traditionally been excluded from the citadel of English writing. It is no surprise therefore that writers in these latter languages have found their own modes of engagement with magical realism, particularly through the mediating figure of García Márquez.

Beyond the well-established comparisons and connections between García Márquez and Rushdie (and some other South Asian writers in English), recent comparative studies underline the affinity of literary practices and modes of representation between writers in the South Asian vernaculars (*bhashas*) and García Márquez, tracing parallels of Garciamarquezian non-mimetic realism in South Asian literary heritage (Harder; Vargas). They also recognize that writers from the subcontinent are drawn to García Márquez's narrative technique because of its enabling potential for retrieving alternative or local visions of modernity in places where modernity remains an unfinished project given the colonial intervention (Ramakrishnan). Jennifer Vargas compares the nineteenth-century Indian novel *Six Acres and a Third* (serialized between 1897 and 1899 and translated into English in 2005) by the Oriya writer Fakir Mohan Senapati and García Márquez's *One Hundred Years*, arguing that they share startlingly similar critical-realist forms employing "under-ground types of storytelling—mainly oral, ironic, dialogic, and parodic ones," producing a "literary realism rooted in local vernaculars and epistemologies" (27–28). Such narrative transculturation of the novel form with parodic vernacular oral forms as is seen in both the novels, she argues, interrogates Eurocentric representational paradigms and foregrounds "subaltern consciousness as an organising narrative perspective" (36). Popular wisdom in Urdu criticism also compares the civilizational sweep of Qurratulain Hyder's archetypal South Asian novel *Aag ka dariya* (River of Fire, 1959) to García Márquez's novel on the solitude of Latin America, even considering her the Indian García Márquez (Hussein xxii), but the comparison is more in terms of the stature of the two novelists than of particular elements of style or politics in their work. E. V. Ramakrishnan, in an essay on García Márquez and his influence on Malayalam fiction, focuses on Garciamarquezian traits in the work of two contemporary Malayalam writers and similarly argues that "by shifting the optics of narration from the print directed page to the oral context of storytelling," García Márquez's magical realist narrative mode effected an "epistemological leap," and this is where the fascination with him lies for writers of Kerala, a state with a high literacy rate in comparison to the rest of India, where colonial modernity had alienated writers from their precolonial oral traditions (157–58).

Several major works in South Asian languages that came out around the time of the publication of *Cien años* show affinity with its magical realist preoccupations. One of the leading figures of Malayalam literature whose style has been associated with the Colombian writer is O. V. Vijayan (1930–2005). His novel *Khasakinte Itihasam* (1969; the English translation by the author himself, *The Legends of Khasak*, was published in 1994) has drawn comparisons with *Cien años*. The novel is set in the fictional town of Khasak, in the backwaters of Kerala, with myriad characters whose incredible life stories crisscross in a narrative web of myth, magic, fable, and reality, reminiscent of life in Macondo. The translation of *Cien años* into Malayalam (*Ekanthatayude Nooru Varshangal*) in 1984, the earliest in this part of the world, transported the

Garciamarquezian world to many readers in this region. Such is the popularity of Malayalam translations of García Márquez's works in Malayalam that N. S. Madhavan (1948–), one of the important current writers in Malayalam, when once asked who the most popular Malayalam novelist was, answered that it was García Márquez (Satchidanandan).

Some of the founding figures of the modern Bengali novel of Bangladesh too have produced epic novels on the scale of *Cien años*, with the 1947 partition of India, the 1971 War of National Liberation, and the turmoil preceding the war as a backdrop. Among the several works of Syed Waliullah (1922–1971), for example, who wrote both in Bengali and English, *Kando Nodi Kando* (1968; English translation, *Cry, River, Cry*, 2015) is considered a canonical magical realist novel of Bengali literature. Poet and novelist of the postliberation era, Syed Shamsul Haque (1935–2016), is similarly considered by critics to be a magical realist, and in his novels from the 1990s he created the fictional town of Jaleshwari, which is again reminiscent of García Márquez's Macondo (Haque, "Syed Shamsul Haq"). Also writing in Bengali, but in West Bengal in India, Syed Mustafa Siraj (1930–2012) is considered yet another practitioner of magical realism (Chaudhuri 122; Haque, "Syed Mustafa Siraj"), especially as evidenced in his novel *Aleek Manush* (1988; English translation *Mythical Man* published in 2005). The novel, set in his native Murshidabad, in rural North Bengal, oscillates between past and present, from the turn of the nineteenth century to more recent times, as it narrates the tale of Murshidabad's Muslim communities and the anti-British struggles via its two central protagonists. Akhtaruzzaman Elias's (1943–1995) *Khowabnama* (The dream chronicle, 1997) is an epic spanning an expansive line of history of subaltern resistance extending synchronically from the Fakir rebellion, an uprising of Muslim mendicants against the British in 1770s, to the beginning of the Tebhaga peasant rebellion of 1947–1948, one of the key moments in the history of agrarian struggles in modern South Asia. Set in rural Bangladesh, the novel opens with Tameejer Baap trying to chase away the grey clouds in the sky to catch a glimpse of Munshi Barkatullah Shah, one of the mendicant leaders of the eighteenth-century rebellion, who was killed by a bullet from the gun of an officer of the East India Company, and who since his death has ruled the marsh perched on a Pakur tree, with iron chains around his body and the hole the bullet made in his neck never having closed. Combining myth and history, the novel creates a dreamlike time frame as the poor fisherfolk and the landless peasants live the past of the Fakir rebellion in their present through myths and legends of their heroes. In her study of the Bengali novel, Supriya Chaudhuri has considered this work "possibly the greatest modern Bengali novel," indicating how Elias draws on "indigenous traditions of folk narrative, memory and legend, as on subaltern history," to create a singular narrative technique which, while being magical realist, is "not imitative of the Latin American masters he so admired" (122).

These key twentieth-century works in Malayalam and Bengali share the impulse for social critique and utopia that the alternative rationality of the Garciamarquezian mode carries within itself. In the debates on modernity during the 1980s, Aníbal Quijano had argued that in Latin America, colonial domination led to a "metamorphosis" of modernity because of which the relation between history and time in Ibero-America is completely different than that in Europe or the United States: "What in Europe were stages of the history of capital . . . here constitute both historical stages and the present structural grounds for capital. . . . Time in this history is simultaneity and sequence at the same time" (150). Given this different history of time or a time different from history, he argues, a rationalism with a "unilinear perspective of time" or a "unidirectional perspective of history" cannot support a cognitive matrix for a historical identity in Latin America. Quijano goes on to say that it was García Márquez, not a social scientist, who, through his "aesthetic-mythic" mode, found a way to give an account "of this simultaneity of all historical times in the same time" (150). His "strange way of revealing the untransferable identity of history," Quijano writes, "proves to be a kind of rationality, which makes the specificity of *that* universe intelligible. . . . The real is rational only inasmuch as rationality does not exclude its magic" (150–51). It is this alternative rationality and its mythic time, its nonlinear relation between the past and the present, that South Asian writers share with García Márquez. The latter's achievement lies in forging a transcultural idiom to express in his works what Quijano has characterized as "the tensile character of Latin America subjectivity" in "a permanent note of dualism" (149).

A younger generation of writers in the 1990s and afterward thus saw in the Garciamarquezian mode the emancipatory promise of an alternative rationality. Many of these writers read García Márquez in translation. Bengali, Malayalam, Urdu, and Sinhala are the South Asian languages into which his works have been translated most extensively, and not surprisingly it is among the writers of these languages that we can see a major legacy of García Márquez. The translations of his works by Gamini Viyangoda in Sri Lanka in the 1990s, such as those of *El amor en los tiempos del cólera* and *Crónica de una muerte anunciada*, became crucial in familiarizing a younger generation of Sinhala writers with García Márquez's works and played an important role in the shift in the 1980s and 1990s in modern Sinhala literature, from the social realist writing of masters like Wickramasinghe, to the post-realists such as Simon Navagattegkama, Ajith Tilaksena, and Daya Dissanayake, among others, whose discovery of Garciamarquezian magical realism occasioned a "rediscovery . . . of those non-realist and anti-realist aspects of classical Buddhist literature that had been overlooked and marginalized by the dominant realism of Wickramasinghe and the generation of writers inspired by his writing" (Mohan 211). In Bangladesh, newer writers such as Syed Manzoorul Islam (1951–), Shaheedul Zahir (1953–2008), and Nasreen Jahan (1966–) are deeply influenced by García Márquez's works. For example, in his preface to Jahan's debut novel, *The Woman Who Flew* (2012; original title in Bengali, *Urrukoo*, published in 1993), translator Kaiser Haq mentions how the author lists García Márquez, whom she read in Bengali translation, as one of her admired writers (ix).

Among bilingual writers, Syed Manzoorul Islam, a professor of English, uses elements of a García Márquez–like universe to present stories from the groundswell of life in postcolonial and postindependence Bangladesh. In his collection of English short stories *Daedalus's Kite* (2018), Manzoorul Islam shows the micro-voices of modern life in moments of tender connection with each other and violent confrontation with the larger forces of capitalism, state oppression, and national myths. His storytelling eschews a straightforward realism for moments of banal wonder (either the banalization of such nature-defying events as a man flying or the ascription of wonderment to perfectly banal, criminal actions of the corrupt). These moments are not always exuberant or comical, and they often turn toward the wretchedly tragic, confronting us with the harsh realities of the disenfranchised people of the Third World. Manzoorul Islam's fictional universe teems with events and characters that do not follow the logic of bourgeois-nationalist realism: character development, seamless narration, and conclusive endings. The narrator is distant from the happenings yet seems to belong to the world he is narrating. This neatly encapsulates the self-consciousness of an English-language writer of non-English realities in Bangladesh and South Asia at large.

Among the more recent writers in Malayalam, Subash Chandran's (1972–) debut novel, *Manushyanu Oru Amukham* (2010), translated into English as *A Preface to Man* (2018), has been compared to *Cien años*. Chandran, winner of the Kerala Sahitya Akademi (The Academy of Letters of the state of Kerala) award on two occasions, is one of the most celebrated and widely read contemporary writers in Malayalam. *A Preface to Man* is set in the fictional village of Thachanakkara and recounts the family saga of three generations of a feudal Nair family.

Uday Prakash (1952–) is a notable voice in contemporary writing in Hindi, whose short stories and novellas, appearing in the late 1980s and 1990s, were so starkly different in form and style from anything being written in Hindi at that time that influential critics initially dismissed them as a mere "concoction of Marquez-Borges" (Gupta 60; translation ours). Well versed in Latin American writing in general—his translations of Neruda's poetry into Hindi have been widely read and appreciated—Uday Prakash has vehemently denied having imitated the Garcia Marquezian magical realist style, but has acknowledged the proximity he feels between the world of his own childhood in a village in central India and life as it went by in Macondo. In one of the several autobiographical essays that he has written, Prakash recalls that his "village was not different from Marquez's Macondo in *One Hundred Years of Solitude*" ("Exiled from Poetry and Country" n.p.), and the lack of electricity, roads, and bridges prompted him and other adolescents in the town to attempt small technological discoveries and invent "like Colonel Buendia from Marquez's Macondo, innumerable games of lenses and sun and focus and fire" (n.p.). One of his early stories, "Tirich," published for the first time in 1988, is considered a key example of magical realism in Hindi fiction. The story moves along two planes, village and urban, the real and the unreal, as the narrator recounts the hallucinatory journey to the city of an old man bitten in the village jungle by a tirich, a poisonous lizard, whose bite it is believed is impossible to survive. Critics have compared its nonlinear structure and the motif of a preannounced death to García Márquez's *Crónica de una muerte anunciada*. "Tirich" and some of his later novellas and stories, such as "Heeralal's Ghost" and "Mongosil" (2003, 2016), generated a rich debate on magical realism and García Márquez in the leading literary journals of Hindi till the late 1990s (Gupta 42–56).

With the appearance of García Márquez's late works, South Asian writers too have kept up with their changing themes, mood, and style. The Pakistani short-story writer

Mohammed Hameed Shahid (1957–) represents a younger generation of Urdu writers less interested in catching up with the trends of world literature than in absorbing these influences in new experiments with form and technique. His short story "Semantics of Lust" (*Shakh-e-ishtiha ki chatak*, 2013) develops its narrative through the narrator's reading of an Urdu translation of *Memoria de mis putas tristes* (*Memories of My Melancholy Whores*; translated by Muhammad Umar Memon as *Apni sogwar beswaon ki yaden* in 2008). Shahid is interested less in the obvious stylistics of magical realism than in the difficulties of translating erotic states and feelings from a Western text into an Urdu one. And yet the story is a tribute to the travails of erotic love as these shape and destroy lives and cannot be contained in the confines of realist narrative. Shahid's recent adaptation of the Garciamarquezian stance on erotic love points to the afterlife of the writer's less political preoccupations in South Asian literatures.

Translations of García Márquez's Works

English has been the source language for most of the translations of García Márquez in South Asia. This is mostly because of the linguistic constraint, namely, a lack of knowledge of Spanish. But the reason is more historical and cultural as well, since English plays the role of the pivot language for translations between the various languages of the subcontinent in India, where in most cases, English translations are the source texts for translating regional language texts into other regional languages. Thus, twice removed from the original, translations in the subcontinent are more retellings or transcreations, sometimes not just of literary texts, but also of narrative modes such as magical realism that became popular in regional writings through translations of the works of García Márquez (Chandran, "Dancing in a Hall of Mirrors"), as has been noted in the case of Gamini Viyangoda's translations in Sri Lanka. Mini Chandran bluntly notes about the Malayalam translations: "The *One Hundred Years of Solitude* that is read by the Malayali reader is a translation of Gregory Rabassa's translation-interpretation of Marquez and not the Latin American Colombian culture that Marquez depicts" (98). And yet as previously noted, according to N. S. Madhavan, García Márquez could well be the most popular writer in Malayalam! Meena Pillai situates this criticism on the level of global knowledge production, following Lawrence Venuti, again addressing the Malayalam translations: "If the Malayalam translator has used the English translation, is he equipped to translate the inscriptions of the original Spanish text or has he been forced to adopt the English version as 'the transparent vehicle of universal truth, thus encouraging a linguistic chauvinism, even a cultural nationalism?'" (49) If we move beyond the question of English in the translation of García Márquez's works, we can note other uses of Garciamarquezian texts in translation precisely in relation to questions of universalism, linguistic identity, and nationalisms.

With nearly four hundred million speakers in Bangladesh and West Bengal in India, Bengali is the language that has the maximum number of translations of García Márquez's works. In the case of *Cien años*, there have been multiple translations, five in Bengali (between West Bengal and Bangladesh) and two in Sinhala (a partial list is given in the "Works Cited"). While a synopsis of these translations would require careful comparative reading, some of the titles in Bengali translation, for example, Shahabuddin Bhuiyan's leaving the title "One Hundred Years of Solitude" untranslated, point to the untranslatability of the stature of García Márquez's greatest novel, almost like a famous brand name. Along with Bengali, Urdu is another language that cuts across national borders (between India and Pakistan), and when a novel, say, *Cien años de soledad*, is intercepted in translation in either of these languages, its readership, critical reception, and broad influence reach beyond precisely those borders that are meant to create national readerships and national literary traditions. Many of these translations travel across borders in unauthorized versions, and thus their circulation cannot be mapped using traditional means of publishing history or distribution networks. Thus, when translation scholars complain that García Márquez translations seldom announce their source texts and thus "situate themselves in an ambivalent space between two languages and cultures" (Pillai 49), it is precisely this "ambivalent space," in which non-English creative writers find themselves in an ambivalent relation to English as recounted in the previous section, that enables them to forge their own localized trajectories of reimagining García Márquez.

Hindi, on the other hand, is purported to be the "national" language of India, yet it has the fewest translations of García Márquez's works. The reasons for this could be the splitting of the language into two almost identical variants, Hindi and Urdu, with Urdu as the more transnational entity now spread across India and Pakistan and Hindi remaining a more regional version while claiming a larger national space for itself. Also, the Hindi public sphere has a working bilingualism with English and thus requires fewer translations of García Márquez and other Latin American writers. Yet translations of *Cien años de soledad* and other Spanish-language writers, such as Camilo José Cela, have appeared in Hindi from the original and have sold out quickly, which shows the demand for translated works from the originals among the Hindi readership.

In her provocatively titled essay on García Márquez translations into Malayalam, "Is Gabriel Garcia Marquez a Malayali?," Meena T. Pillai reiterates the problem central to world literatures that the translation of *One Hundred Years of Solitude*, and reviews and studies accompanying it, fail "to anchor the text in its historical and cultural context, resulting in a translation which appears free-floating and unhinged from the specificities of history to occupy a universal realm which transcends linguistic and cultural differences" (50). Without discarding the critical point about translation in a world literary moment here, we can treat this "free-floating" and "unhinged" quality of deracinated translations of García Márquez in South Asia as a moment with different resolutions in the several literary and linguistic contexts of South Asia. A thorough appreciation of this moment, however, requires a comparative analysis of the various receptions of

García Márquez in the South Asian languages, including by critics and theorists writing in English, preliminary directions for which have been the subject of this survey article.

The South Asian reception of Gabriel García Márquez inaugurated a theoretical encounter between postcolonial thought and Latin American magical realism as a possible literary mode for ex-colonial literary cultures (whether "Third World", "non-Western," or "postcolonial"). This encounter predates and was elaborated by a steady absorption of García Márquez's oeuvre into the so-called vernaculars of South Asia, precisely those languages left out of the literary world by the imperialism of global English. The media for this absorption are both the transcreation of Garciamarquezian worlds, devices, and resolutions in novels and short stories into the major languages of South Asia and their readers' interception in translation. The translation medium bears the marks of inequality of a world literature mediated by English alone, yet an inequality that has resulted in a proliferation of unofficial and distanced renditions of the writer's key works, especially in Bengali, Malayalam, Urdu, and Hindi. These vernacular translations can be conceived of as the many South Asian afterlives of an icon of twentieth-century Latin American literature.

Works Cited

Ahmad, Aijaz. *In Theory: Classes, Nations, Literature.* Oxford UP, 1992.

Bhabha, Homi. *Nation and Narration.* Routledge, 1990.

Chandran, Mini. "In the Marketplace: Publication of Translations in Regional Indian Languages." *Textual Travels: Theory and Practice of Translation in India,* edited by Mini Chandran and Suchitra Mathur, Routledge, 2015, pp. 92–111.

Chandran, Mini. "Dancing in a Hall of Mirrors: Translation between Indian Languages." *A Multilingual Nation: Translation and Language Dynamic in India,* edited by Rita Kothari, Oxford UP, 2018, pp. 273–290.

Chandran, Subash. *A Preface to Man.* Translated by E. V. Fathima, Harper Perennial India, 2016.

Chaudhuri, Supriya. "The Bengali Novel." *The Cambridge Companion to Modern Indian Culture,* edited by Vasudha Dalmia and Rashmi Saldana, Cambridge UP, 2012, pp. 99–123.

Elias, A. *Khowabnama.* Naya Udyog. 1997.

García Márquez, Gabriel. *Cien años de soledad* (1967). Various translations. Malayalam: *Ekanthatayude Noor Varshangal,* translated by S. Velayudhan Nair, D C Books,1984. Bengali: (1) *Nishongoter Eksho Bochor,* translated by G. H. Habib, Batighar, 2001; (2) *Nishongoter Eksho Bochor,* translated by Zulfiqar Newton and Dilip Kuman Halder, The Universal Academy, 2016; (3) *One Hundred Years of Solitude* (the English title was retained and printed in Roman letters), translated by Shahabuddin Bhuiyan, Jonaki Prokashoni, 2016; (4) *Nishongoter Eksho Bochor,* translated directly from the original in Spanish by Anisuzzaman, Anyaprakash, 2018. Hindi: *Ekant ke Sau Varsh,* translated directly from the original in Spanish by Sonya Surabhi Gupta, Rajkamal, 2003. Sinhala: (1) *Hudekalave Siyavasarak,* translated by Sahara Wijesinghe, Nipuna Enterprises, 2003; (2) *Siyak Vasaka Hudekalava,* translated by Abe Dissanayake and Pasan Kodikara, Vidarshana, 2003. Kannada: *Nooru Varshada Ekaanta,* translated by A. N. Prasanna, Foreword by N. Manu Chakaravarthy, Anandakanda Publications, 2005. Tamil: *Thanimaiyin Nooru Aandugal,* translated by Sukumaran and Gnalan Subramaniyan, Kalachuvadu Publications, 2013. Urdu: *Tanhai ke Sau Saal*, translated by Naeem Klasra, Fiction House, 2011.

García Márquez, Gabriel. *La mala hora* (1962). Gujarati translation by Niranjana Tripathi, Gurjar Granthratna Karyalay, 1991.

García Márquez, Gabriel. *Memoria de mis putas tristes* (2004). Urdu translation: *Apni sogwar besvaon ki yaden*, translated by Muhammad Umar Memon, Shaharzad, 2006.

Gupta, Shambhu. *Dibiya mein Dhup: Uday Prakash: Ek Adhyayan*. Vani Prakashan, 2017.

Haque, Junaidul. "Syed Mustafa Siraj: A Writer's Writer. . . ." *The Daily Star*, 15 Sept. 2012, www.thedailystar.net/news-detail-249758. Accessed 29 Aug. 2019.

Haque, Junaidul. "Syed Shamsul Haq: Our Finest Literary All-Rounder." *Dhaka Tribune*, 5 Oct. 2017, www.dhakatribune.com/magazine/arts-letters/2017/10/05/syed-shamsul-haq-finest-literary-rounder/. Accessed 30 Aug. 2019.

Harder, Hans. "Bangla Sahiter Jaadu Bastob." *Prothom Alo*, 6 Apr. 2018.

Hussein, Aamer. "That Little Bird: Remembering Qurratulain Hyder." *Fireflies in the Mist*, translated by Qurratulain Hyder, New Directions Books, 2008.

Hyder, Qurratulain. *Aag ka dariya*. Educational Publishing House, 2019.

Jahan, Nasreen. *The Woman Who Flew*. Translated by Kaiser Haq from the original in Bengali, Penguin, 2012.

Javed, Khalid. *Marquez: Fun aur Shakhsiyat*. Karnataka Urdu Academy, 2009.

Kamal, Ajmal. *"Jawaz" Aaj: Khususi shumara* (special issue): *Gabriel Garcia Marquez*. Mar.–Apr. 1991.

Manzoorul Islam, Syed. *Daedalus's Kite*. Rubric Publishing, 2018.

Mohan, Anupama. *Utopia and the Village in South Asian Literatures*. Palgrave Macmillan, 2012.

Nair, M. T. Vasudevan. *Aalkkoottathil Thaniye*. DC Books, [1982] 2018.

Ondaatje, Michael. "García Márquez and the Bus to Aracataca." *Figures in a Ground*, edited by Diane Bessai and David Jackel, Western Prairie Books, 1978, pp. 19–31.

Pillai, Meena T. "Is Gabriel Garcia Marquez a Malayali?" *Translation Today*, vol. 5, nos. 1–2, 2008, pp. 41–53.

Prakash, Uday. "Exiled from Poetry and Country." *Pratilipi*, no. 13, June 2008, http://pratilipi.in/2008/06/01/exiled-from-poetry-and-country-uday-prakash/. Accessed 17 Dec. 2019.

Prakash, Uday. *Rage, Revelry and Romance. . . .* Translated by Robert A. Hueckstedt, Srishti, 2003.

Prakash, Uday. *The Walls of Delhi: Three Novellas*. Seven Stories Press, 2016.

Quijano, Aníbal. "Modernity, Identity, and Utopia in Latin America." *Boundary 2*, vol. 20, no. 3, 1993, pp. 140–55.

Ramakrishnan, E. V. "Modernity, Memory and Magic Realism: Gabriel Garcia Marquez and Malayalam Fiction." *Indigenous Imaginaries: Literature, Region, Modernity*, edited by E. V. Ramakrishnan, Orient Blackswan, 2017, pp. 156–83.

Ranjan, Prabhat. *Márquez: Jadui Yathartha ka Jadugar*. Vani Prakashan, 2014.

Rushdie, Salman. *Imaginary Homelands: Essays and Criticism 1981–1991*. Penguin Books, 1991.

Sangari, Kumkum. "The Politics of the Possible: The Narrative Modes in Gabriel García Márquez and Salman Rushdie." *Cultural Critique*, no. 7, 1987, pp. 157–86.

Satchidanandan, K. "Language into Language: On the Translation Scenario in Malayalam." https://blog.ilfsamanvay.org/2016/08/14/language-into-language/. Accessed 22 Mar. 2019.

Shahid, Mohammed Hameed. "Semantics of Lust." *In Search of Butterflies*, edited and translated by Saeed Naqvi, Oxford UP, 2017, pp. 1–14.

Singh, Natwar K. *One Life Is Not Enough*. Rupa, 2014.

Siraj, Syed Mustafa. *Mythical Man*. Sahitya Akademi, 2005.
Spivak, Gayatri Chakravorty. *Outside in the Teaching Machine*. Routledge, 1993.
Vargas, Jennifer Harford. "Critical Realisms in the Global South: Narrative Transculturation in Senapati's *Six Acres and a Third* and García Márquez's *One Hundred Years of Solitude*." *Colonialism, Modernity, and Literature*, edited by Satya P. Mohanty, Palgrave Macmillan, 2011, pp. 25–54.
Vijayan, O. V. *The Legends of Khasak*. Penguin, 1994.
Waliullah, Syed. *Cry River Cry*. Translated by Osman Jamal, Writers Ink, 2015.
Zahir, Shaheedul. *Jibon o Rajnoitik Bastobota* (Life and Political Reality). Maula Brothers, 1988.
Zahir, Shaheedul. *She Rate Purnima Chhilo* (That Was a Moonlit Night). Maula Brothers, 1995.

CHAPTER 15

ONE HUNDRED YEARS OF SOLITUDE AND ITS INFLUENCE IN JAPAN

GONZALO ROBLEDO

THE Japanese publication of *Cien años de soledad* (*One Hundred Years of Solitude*; *Hyakunen no Kodoku*) in 1972 was a cultural milestone in Japan. Its influence is still felt today. From literature and cinema to plays and anime films, prominent Japanese creators have pointed to García Márquez's masterpiece as a source of inspiration or a turning point in their careers. Writers such as Kenzaburō Ōe, Nobel laureate for Literature in 1994, and Natsuki Ikezawa, awarded the Akutagawa prize in 1988, have affirmed that they were influenced by *One Hundred Years of Solitude* (henceforth *One Hundred Years*) in the creation of their own imaginary landscapes, thus helping them challenge Japan's official history. Magical realism has also been pointed out as Haruki Murakami's main technique for exploring the identity crisis of Japanese individuals born after World War II. The publication of García Márquez's work in Japan helped to identify parallels between magical realism and the themes and style of Japanese literature written since the late nineteenth century, after Japan had ended more than two hundred years of voluntary isolation from the outside world, adopting Western naturalism in lieu of its own older traditions of the fantastic nourished by legends and folklore.

FIRST AND ONLY TRANSLATION IN 1972

One of the first literary works in Spanish translated into Japanese was *The Ingenious Gentleman Don Quixote of La Mancha*. The work began to be translated toward the end of the nineteenth century, though from languages other than the Spanish original. In the twentieth century, however, a dozen translators offered their own renditions, directly from Spanish into Japanese, of Cervantes's masterwork. By the twenty-first century, translating *Don Quixote* has become a professional challenge for many Japanese Hispanists. *One Hundred Years,* by contrast, was first translated directly from Spanish into Japanese in 1972, five years after the original version. Although revised several times by its now deceased translator, it remains the only translation into Japanese almost a half century hence. The idea of translating *One Hundred Years* into Japanese is attributed to the Hispanist Yoshio Masuda (1928–2016). He recommended it to Shinchosha Publishing, suggesting as a translator a colleague, Professor Tadashi Tsuzumi (1930–2019). Tsuzumi, who had never visited Colombia, faced the challenge of translating an unusual and innovative novel from a Western language whose initial contact with Japan dates back to the sixteenth century. This was the period of evangelization by European Jesuits that led to Japan's so-called Christian Century (1549–1650), during which Japan tried to initiate stable commercial exchanges with the West.

In 1613, Japan sent a diplomatic mission via New Spain (Mexico) that visited Cuba, Spain, France, and the Vatican. In the middle of their journey, though, Christianity was banned in Japan. Some members of the Japanese delegation who had been baptized now chose to live in the Andalusian town of Coria del Río rather than return to their homeland. Hundreds of their Iberian descendants still bear the surname "Japón." For the next two centuries, Japan would maintain a limited trade with the West while remaining closed to contacts with Spanish-speaking countries. This situation would not change until the second half of the nineteenth century, when Japan signed international trade agreements with, and Japanese nationals first started emigrating to, countries in Southeast Asia, the United States, and Mexico. In the twentieth century, Japanese seeking a better life emigrated to Latin American republics such as Peru, Brazil, Bolivia, Argentina, and Colombia. Contact between those overseas Japanese settlers and their country of ethnic origin remained minimal up until 1990, when Japan's labor shortages led to a policy of admitting descendants of Japanese to work in factories. From this moment on, the Spanish language became a factor in Japan's foreign relations while European football and salsa music made an impact on Japanese culture. Japanese media outlets started reporting on the Latin American countries of origin of these new immigrants, while publishers brought out Spanish textbooks and updated bilingual dictionaries.

When Tsuzumi was first translating *One Hundred Years,* however, it was still two decades before this boom of things Spanish. There were not yet any Latin supermarkets where Japanese could taste and see the flavors and colors of the tropics. And since Tsuzumi was translating in the pre-internet era, seeking out the definition of nouns that few Japanese had ever heard of—such as *guava*—required a laborious search outside Japan's linguistic field. Inasmuch as Japan had remained isolated culturally and ideologically by its indigenous language, spoken solely in the archipelago, it was only natural that, for his version of Macondo, Tsuzumi would resort to the domestication of the original text. Japanese grammar reverses the verb-object word order of Western languages such as Spanish, and its readers perceive the sequence in which the elements of a scene appear in an order opposite to the one used by a foreign author.[1] García Márquez introduces us to Macondo in a kind of landing in which we see the "twenty adobe houses" then the "river of clear water" that flows in a bed of "polished stones which were white and enormous like prehistoric eggs" (*One Hundred Years* 11).[2] But the reader of the Japanese translation arrives in Macondo sailing upriver, and the first thing he or she sees is the stones/eggs belonging to a "prehistoric monster" that does not appear in the original text. In revised versions the "monster" was replaced by a "beast." In his translation Tsuzumi resorts to onomatopoeia, which is used frequently in Japanese to describe sounds, actions, textures, moods, or situations. Japanese onomatopoeia can take the form of adverbs or adjectives with repeated syllables. The abundance of stones that form the bank of the river in Macondo is expressed, for example, with the sound *goro-goro*, while the smooth touch of those polished stones is *sube-sube*. For the title of the book the translator chose an exotic touch, using the Spanish word order and putting the "hundred years" at the beginning of the sentence: *Hyakunen no kodoku*, which in Japanese grammar would be equivalent to saying "The loneliness of one hundred years." A more domestic translation of the title would have been *Kodoku no Hyakunen*. Tsuzumi made at least three revisions for the successive editions of the book. His colleagues praised his extensive vocabulary that served to convey in a rich and fluid Japanese the warm and compelling tone of the oral narration in García Márquez's text. Tsuzumi's translation continues to play an important role in the dissemination of Spanish-speaking culture in Japan today and in the perception of Latin American culture. In addition, it has had a persistent influence on other well-known creative endeavors that followed its publication.

Moment of the Publication of *One Hundred Years* in Japanese

While it became a must-read novel for Japanese intellectuals, *One Hundred Years* also encouraged many young people to know and study the language spoken in Hispanic America. Until the 1970s, Spanish books translated into Japanese were, above all, Golden Age novels and Federico García Lorca's poetry, as well as works by Camilo José Cela, Juan Goytisolo, and other realist authors from Spain. In Japan at that time, Latin America was perceived as a continent rich in natural resources that had remained in constant political effervescence since the 1959 socialist revolution in Cuba. The confrontation of the small Caribbean island with the United States also served as an inspiration to leftist movements from the main universities of Japan. For them, one of the main issues had become the US military's occupation and control of Okinawa, Japan's southernmost and westernmost prefecture, following Japan's defeat in World War II. The United States was using Okinawa as a base for supporting its war in Vietnam and for keeping Japan's Communist neighbors—China, the Soviet Union, and North Korea—under surveillance. In the anti-American environment of the 1970s, Japanese intellectuals identified closely with the militancy found in Latin American literature. These socially committed novels in Spanish aligned with other similarly themed literary works coming out of Africa and Southeast Asia. Although some non-Japanese authors saw

Macondo's story as apolitical,[3] the denunciation of the abuse of political power and corruption present in *One Hundred Years*, along with the way García Márquez portrayed the genesis of the Latin American continent via a single remote village, contributed to its appeal for intellectuals and other readers. They also found in the novel a template for an irreverent vision of Japan's own national history that up until then had been almost inconceivable.

Kenzaburō Ōe, the Great Admirer of Spanish-Speaking Culture

The three authors on which I focus here have all proclaimed their enthusiasm for *One Hundred Years*. One wrote a book paying tribute to García Márquez, and another described his contact with the universe of Macondo as close to an epiphany. Kenzaburō Ōe (1935–), who studied French literature and speaks English fluently, learned about García Márquez's work through those two languages. He used *One Hundred Years* as a reference for his own novel *Dojidai Gemu* (*The Game of Contemporaneity*, 1979), a story of an imaginary remote town that serves as a pretext to explain the modern history of Japan.[4] Thanks to his numerous trips abroad as an academic, Ōe had firsthand experience of life in other countries, a background that contributed to his politically committed writing. In 1976 Ōe traveled to Mexico for six months as a visiting professor at the Colegio de México. There he became acquainted with the Mexican muralists and was inspired by works such as *Dream of a Sunday Afternoon in the Central Alameda* by Diego Rivera. Painted between 1946 and 1947, it synthesized Mexican history since the arrival of the Spanish conquistadores, using a wide cast of characters (Wilson n.p.).

Ōe has been described by Fumiaki Noya as ideologically Sartrean, though thematically closer to Mario Vargas Llosa than to García Márquez[5] (Zambrano, *El horizonte de las palabras* 14). His ethical concerns range from pacifism to human rights, seen through the prism of the antinuclear movement. After he received the Nobel Prize for Literature in 1994, Ōe used this recognition to advance a political agenda that focused on questioning the Japanese imperial system and Japan's responsibility in World War II. Following the triple tragedy of an earthquake, a tsunami, and the nuclear accident in Fukushima in 2011, Ōe has reinforced his opposition to atomic energy. In *The Game of Contemporaneity*, he recreates the microcosm of an alternative, fantastical, and often grotesque Japan. Its setting is a town that, like Macondo, could have existed in the vicinity of its author's remote homeland, allowing it to be connected to the outside world and at the same time to have its own foundational myth. If, as Alonso notes, Macondo's creation evokes the biblical Genesis,[6] Ōe draws on Japanese mythology. The founders of his village have as their mission to question the origin of the Japanese imperial family. Susan J. Napier explains, "While García Márquez's text implicitly equates the founders of Macondo with Adam and Eve, *The Game of Contemporaneity* explicitly positions the founders of the village in opposition to the ruling Japanese mythology of the Sun Goddess by suggesting that they are the descendants of the "dark gods" expelled from heaven by Amateratsu, the sun goddess and progenitrix of the Japanese imperial house (8) *Dojidai Gemu*'s narrator makes explicit references to existing themes in *One Hundred Years* such as incest, or a war that, much like "The Thousand Days War" in Macondo-Colombia, is remembered for its duration: "The Fifty Days War." Yet while García Márquez narrates portentous events with great plausibility, Ōe resorts to fantastic hyperbole. Huge creatures appear throughout his story to intervene supernaturally in the struggle for independence or to facilitate the escape of rebels by moving rocks in the mountains. While García Márquez describes class struggle, the exploitation of a colonial power, and the corruption of Latin American governments, Ōe focuses on disputing the legitimacy of the Japanese imperial family. This is a high-risk political stance in Japan, where much of the public still reveres what is considered the oldest reigning dynasty in the world. Although Ōe's prose lacks the fluidity of *One Hundred Years*, Napier gives him a prominent place in Japanese literature for his own questioning of the country's history and for his attempt to retell it from the beginning: "*The Game of Contemporaneity* lacks the color and enchantment of *One Hundred Years of Solitude*, or many of Ōe's own novels for that matter, perhaps because its anti-emperor ideological agenda is so strident. It remains a landmark in Japanese literature however, an attempt to retell Japanese history 'from the ground up' by emphasizing the energy and potentiality of the people, encapsulated in the protean figure of the Destroyer " (8).

Naturalism and Fantastic Literature

The great receptivity toward the magical realism of *One Hundred Years* of Ōe and other contemporary Japanese authors is attributed, in part, to a reaction to the naturalism of the first literature imported from the West at the end of the nineteenth century. For Napier, the Westernization of Japanese society that started with the Meiji era (1868–1912) transformed its literature and created a marked dichotomy between Western-style realism and the long tradition of fantasy present in Japan. Influential Japanese authors of the first part of the twentieth century such as Jun'ichirō Tanizaki (1886–1965), Yasunari Kawabata (1899–1972), Osamu Dazai (1909–1948), and even Yukio Mishima (given name Kimitake Hiraoka; 1925–1970) adhere to that modernity and emulate naturalism through confessions written in the first person, in a literary genre called *Shishosetsu* or the "I Novel." Although this genre produced works of great sociological or philosophical depth, some of its authors departed from naturalistic description and ventured into fantastic narrative in order to give free rein to their imaginations. Napier states, "Indeed a surprising number of Japan's greatest writers, including those famous for their powerful mimetic portrayals of modernizing Japan, also used the genre of the fantastic to create visions of a chaotic, fascinating, occasionally marvelous, but more frequently uncanny, fictional world. Such works were even more memorable than their mimetic fictions" (8).

A prominent feature of Japanese authors who eschew naturalism is their frequent use of the grotesque in the form of a metamorphosis or mutilations and an eroticism that crosses over into the macabre. In its most sinister version, the grotesque received a strong input of ideas and visual references from the nuclear bombing of Hiroshima and Nagasaki at the end of World War II. The atomic explosions demonstrated the vast destructive power of science and ingrained forever the sinister imagery of its misuse in the national memory of Japan. Numerous manga and anime works have been inspired by the experiences of atomic bomb survivors, contributing to masterpieces such as *Hotaru no Haka* (Grave of the Fireflies), an anime film by Isao Takahata released in 1988. The fear of mutations caused by radioactivity gave birth to cinematic archetypes such as Godzilla, the monster created in 1954, which has in turn spawned a number of sequels that new generations continue to watch. Another traumatic event of World War II that affected many Japanese creators born after the conflict was the written renunciation by Emperor Hirohito of his supposed divine principles,[7] as demanded by the US-led Occupation Forces. Hirohito's message shook one of the main pillars of Japanese tradition, empowering artists, intellectuals, and of course politicians to question the "truth" as defined by official history. No postwar Japanese writer has received more world attention for combining in his work the grotesque with a harsh critique of the imperial system than Kenzaburō Ōe. His questioning of official history through a reality distorted by irony and exaggeration reflects García Márquez's magical-realist synthesis of Colombia's turbulent history via Macondo. Napier's assessment of the universe of Ōe in *Dojidai Gemu* could be applied to the Colombian reality described in *One Hundred Years*: "Ōe's fictional Japan is a place marked by confrontation rather than harmony, violence rather than peace, and repression rather than freedom" (Napier 8).

Other Japanese writers of great influence, such as Hisashi Inoue (1934–2010), have employed the literary form of an isolated village that confronts the central power. His work *Kirikiri-jin* (*The People of Kirikiri*, 1981) recounts in a satirical tone and with fantastic touches the rebellion for independence of the inhabitants of a town located in the Tohoku region, in the northeast of Japan. The origin of the revolt is discontent with the agricultural policy of the central government. The protagonist is a writer traveling through the area who becomes involved in the uprising and, after receiving Kirikiri's first literary prize, becomes president of the new nation. Inoue, an intellectual voice who wrote and directed numerous plays during his life, questioned not only Japan's official history but also the way it was taught in schools. According to the author, the school calendar itself was designed to avoid having to explain to students the role of Japan in helping to start World War II.[8]

Natsuki Ikezawa, Creator of Another Macondian World

Natsuki Ikezawa (1945–), is the author of another important Japanese novel of Macondian inspiration, *Mashiasu Giri no Shikkyaku* (*The Navidad Incident: The*

Downfall of Matías Guili, 1993). The work received the Tanizaki Prize, one of the highest literary awards in Japan, in the year it was published. The plot begins with the disappearance of a bus full of Japanese travelers on an imaginary Micronesian island called Navidad, governed by one Matías Guili, himself an Asian parody of Latin American dictators. Japan's literary critics highlighted the eclecticism of the novel's different genres and its stylistic rupture with the naturalistic and introverted fiction that had dominated Japanese literature for more than half a century (Zambrano, *El horizonte de las palabras*; translation mine). Fumiaki Noya, a Hispanic scholar and disciple of Tsuzumi (the translator of *One Hundred Years*), identifies Garciamarquezian references in Ikezawa's work in a conversation with the author published in *Shincho Magazine*. He points out both the choice of a peripheral setting and an omniscient narrator as an attempt to break free from the first-person autobiographical narrative so prevalent in previous Japanese literature. Ikezawa acknowledges his admiration for Latin American writing and in particular for the work of García Márquez, to whom he pays homage with an episode with butterflies evocative of the ones that always accompany Mauricio Babilonia. After explaining his interest in what he calls "dictators' literature," Ikezawa confesses his inability to create a tyrant characterized by the same infamy as Latin American dictators, due to the absence in Micronesia of an Iberian religious culture that would propitiate such evil rulers: "The evil of my dictator reaches, at best, that of a corrupt Japanese politician" (Noya 14; translation mine). Ikezawa is an active promoter of the work of the Colombian author in Japan. In his opening speech at the First García Márquez Congress, which took place at the Cervantes Institute in Tokyo in October 2008, he reiterated his debt to the Colombian author from whom he learned how to "defy the laws of cause and effect" (Zambrano, *Hacer el mundo con palabras*, 112).

KŌBŌ ABE, THE LATE READER OF *ONE HUNDRED YEARS OF SOLITUDE*

The most famous homage to the author of *One Hundred Years* that exists in the Japanese language is, without a doubt, the speech entitled *Chikyūgi ni sumu Garushia Marukesu* (*García Márquez, inhabitant of the Globe*), delivered by the writer Kōbō Abe at Sophia University in Tokyo in 1983. Abe was one of the most prominent writers of the second half of the twentieth century. His international reputation is attributed in part to the ambiguity of his characters, located in abstract spaces and situations easily transferable to any other contemporary culture. Although his work can be read as a satire of modern Japan, Abe rejected giving his novels a local specificity; like Ōe and Ikezawa, he avoids the mimetism of Japanese literature of the first half of the twentieth century. Growing up in the Chinese territory of Manchuria, occupied by Japan between 1932 and 1945, Abe's lack of a direct connection with his Japanese roots has been cited by critics as the reason for his ambiguous settings. The metamorphoses undergone by some of his characters allow him to be placed closer to Franz Kafka (Scott-Stokes, n.p.). His recurring themes are the lack of freedom of the individual and the alienation of modern man. His protagonists are isolated prisoners of a work routine that is broken by unexpected and fantastic turns.

Although Abe is often associated with magical realism in Japan, his work and his connection to García Márquez are focused on the creation of a particular universe whose realistic appearance alternates with situations that go beyond logic. In "The Woman of the Dunes" (1962), one of his best-known short stories thanks to the award-winning film version that followed its publication, Abe presents a normal male character (a schoolteacher who loves entomology) in a realistic setting (the deserted coastline of a village that can be reached in a few hours from Tokyo), and a mundane situation (collecting bugs for research). When the teacher misses the last bus home, the villagers take him to spend the night in a house at the bottom of a sand pit where a young widow lives. From there the logic of his world begins to crumble. With small realistic details, the teacher, the rational man who symbolizes modernity, is informed that he has fallen into a trap and that his life will never be the same as before. After several failed escape attempts, he finally accepts the destiny of being the woman's companion whose job it is to take out sand daily to sell. The protagonist builds a logic that allows him to integrate into the new reality and resign himself to his new life.

Abe's 1983 speech reflects the appreciation of a sophisticated and witty fan who encourages his countrymen to embrace the novels of an author who is still not well known. He started his famous presentation by confessing that he had learned too late that there was a Japanese version of *One Hundred Years* and had asked its publisher to increase promotion of the book. He also claimed that García Márquez was not strictly Latin American and that his literary universe was better described in terms of time rather than geography. Abe then cited his own peculiar remedy for his countrymen's "excessive" seriousness, which was to stimulate the right side of his brain by eating spicy food. To properly enjoy *One Hundred Years*, he said, the Japanese should eat sushi; the spiciness of the wasabi would perfectly complement the work of the Colombian author (Robledo n.p.) Abe's widow later said that after reading *One Hundred Years* her husband had entered a period of depression and writer's block that lasted until 1982. Only when he heard the news that García Márquez had been awarded the Nobel Prize for Literature could he recover and continue writing, inasmuch as he believed the Colombian author was now "among the immortals" and had ceased to be a direct competitor.[9]

Murakami and Magical Realism

Haruki Murakami, the most translated and read Japanese author in the world thus far, has stated in press interviews that his literature is "realistic" because, in order to find situations or magical things in a civilized place like Tokyo, he has to look inside himself, where "everything is natural, logical, realistic and reasonable"[10] (Anderson n.p.).

Murakami's use of a porous border between the real and the magical connects his technique with that of García Márquez. Critics like Matthew C. Strecher, however, state that Murakami's work uses magical realism without resorting to the Latin American literary fascination with its surroundings, described by Alejo Carpentier as *lo real maravilloso* ("the marvelous real"). Nor does Murakami pursue a political agenda that, according to Ángel Flores, employs magical realism as a postcolonial discourse rejecting rationalism and positivism and fostering the coexistence of reality and magic; Murakami uses the techniques of magical realism without the various political attachments that Carpentier and Flores would insist upon. In short, Murakami's use of magical realism, while closely linked with the quest for identity, is not the least bit involved with the assertion of *an* identity. To put it another way, magical realism in Murakami is used as a tool to seek a highly individualized personal sense of identity in each person rather than a rejection of the thinking of one-time colonial powers or the assertion of a national (cultural) identity founded on indigenous beliefs and ideologies (Strecher 269). Strecher places Murakami at the "apex of Japanese postmodern Literature" and highlights how his work has helped erase the barriers between "art and entertainment." It is precisely through a modern entertainment medium such as anime that postwar Japanese have access to what can be considered a popular use of the techniques of magical realism (Strecher 23).

Magical Realism in Anime

The creation of hyperrealistic worlds in which characters, circumstances, or elements seem fantastic but at the same time plausible is a mark of Studio Ghibli, the award-winning Japanese producer of anime cinema in which castles can walk, and teenage witches or monstrous creatures hold normal jobs and interact naturally with others. When scholar and translator Keizuke Dan describes García Márquez's literary technique as "telling big lies with a serious or severe attitude" (quoted in Zambrano, *El horizonte de las palabras* 115), he could be paraphrasing Hayao Miyazaki, one of the founders of Studio Ghibli, when he explains his creative philosophy: "Anime may depict fictional worlds but I nonetheless believe that at its core it must have a certain realism. Even if the world depicted is a lie, the trick is to make it seem as real as possible. Stated another way, the animator must fabricate a lie that seems so real viewers will think the world depicted might possibly exist." (Miyazaki). Miyazaki challenges the conventions of Western realism by introducing into scenes of daily life—these drawn with naturalistic detail—the iconography and concepts of Shintoism, Japan's indigenous religion, whose animistic and pantheistic beliefs connect it to African and Native American religious traditions. Lacking sacred texts, dogmas, or doctrines, Shintoism offers a set of vague beliefs that lend themselves to multiple interpretations and artistic appropriation. It was one of Miyazaki's films most heavily imbued with Shinto symbolism that won the Academy Award for Best Animated Feature in 2003. *Spirited Away* (*Sen to Chihiro no Kamikakushi*, 2001) has now been translated into dozens of languages. Many episodes in *One Hundred Years* that have been described as "magical"—such as the dialogue with the dead, the ascension into the sky of Remedios the Beauty, and the luminous discs that appear before Úrsula's death—have visual equivalents in scenes from Ghibli movies. Scholars of the Ghibli universe refer to its "immersive realism," a label that could be applied to any great work of art that, through its story and narrative technique, captivates readers and disconnects them from other realities (Isbrucker n.p.).

One Hundred Years of Solitude's Place in Japan

In addition to *One Hundred Years*, most of García Márquez's other works have been translated into Japanese by academics such as Eiichi Kimura (*Memoria de mis putas tristes* [*Memories of My Melancholy Whores*], *El amor en los tiempos del cólera* [*Love in the Time of Cholera*], *El general en su laberinto* [*The General in His Labyrinth*], *El otoño del patriarca* [*The Autumn of the Patriarch*]), Keizuke Dan (*Vivir para contarla* [*Living to Tell the Tale*], *Del amor y otros demonios* [*Of Love and Other Demons*]), and Fumiaki Noya (*Crónica de una muerte anunciada* [*Chronicle of a Death Foretold*], short stories). Some of these translators, including the aforementioned writer Natsuki Ikezawa, participated in the First García Márquez Congress at the Cervantes Institute in Tokyo in 2008. The conference was held to commemorate a hundred years of diplomatic relations between Colombia and Japan, the fortieth anniversary of the original publication of *One Hundred Years of Solitude*, and the eightieth birthday of its author. A review of the presentations by Venezuelan professor Gregory Zambrano in his book *Hacer el mundo con palabras* (Making the World with Words) gave a broad overview of the challenges faced by translators. Regarding the complication of multiple regional meanings not found in dictionaries when reading literary masterpieces whose geographical scope makes them rich and varied, Zambrano quotes the philologist and lexicographer Margareth de Oliveira, who referred to the challenges posed by Colombian idioms in García Márquez's work. She equated untranslatable terms such as *gordolobo* (the nickname of a rum) and *alijuna* (an outsider in the language of the Wayúu tribe in Colombia's Guajira province) with Japanese words such as *yukata* (a kimono-style light cotton gown), *origami* (the art of folding paper), or *seppuku* (ritual suicide by disembowelment) (Isbrucker 25). Academic and translator Keizuke Dan also spoke of the challenge presented in translating humor because of its strong dependence on the original language's nuances and contexts: "Many believe that there is a style that is coupled exclusively with magical realism but in my opinion this has been exaggerated.... In Spain and Latin America jokes are often told to make people laugh but García Márquez tells extravagant tales without preparing the reader for a joke that is coming. Through his works I can see García Márquez laughing furtively. That is the feeling I try to communicate in my translation" (quoted in Zambrano, *Hacer el mundo con palabras*, 113–15).

García Márquez the Writer and Japan

The special relationship that García Márquez had with Japan resulted in his writing two works inspired by a novel by Yasunari Kawabata (Nobel Prize for Literature 1968) and a conversation with director Akira Kurosawa on adapting literature to film. Kawabata is remembered for his forays into the absurd, incorporating improbable situations into the daily life of his protagonists. An often cited example is his story *Kataude* (One Arm, 1961), featuring a man who borrows a young woman's arm and takes it home to spend the night with it. Once at home he removes his own arm, replaces it with that of the girl, and falls asleep. A slightly less fantastic premise in *The House of the Sleeping Beauties* (*Nemureru Bijou*, 1961) inspired García Márquez to write a newspaper article that later turned into the short story "Sleeping Beauty and the Airplane" (1982) and served as the basis for his last novel, *Memories of My Melancholy Whores* (2004). The plot of Kawabata's book revolves around a brothel where the elderly pay to sleep beside a young virgin who has been drugged but whom they must not touch. García Márquez evoked his fascination with Kawabata's work in an article published in Bogota's daily *El Espectador*, describing a transatlantic flight that the narrator spends admiring the beauty of a stranger sleeping in the seat next to him: "Before landing, when they handed me the immigration form, I filled it in with a feeling of bitterness. Profession: Japanese writer. Age: 92 years old" (García Márquez, "El avión de la bella durmiente" n.p.). The article later became the short story included in his *Strange Pilgrims* collection. In *Memories of My Melancholy Whores*, the premise of the Japanese book is reset in the Caribbean. The protagonist, an inveterate bachelor, announces in the opening lines his desire to celebrate his ninetieth birthday by spending the night with a teenaged virgin. Writing in the form of a first-person confession with a realistic tone reinforced by his profession as newspaper journalist, the narrative has resonances of the Japanese genre of the "I Novel" (*Shishosetsu*). Renowned Japanese instances of that genre, such as *Shinsei* (*New Life*, 1919) by Toson Shimazaki and *Sukyandaru* (Scandal, 1986) by Shuzaku Endo, focused on the relationship of older men with much younger women.

Another key person in Japanese culture whom García Márquez greatly admired was the director Akira Kurosawa, whom García Márquez hoped would adapt one of his novels to cinema. Traveling to Tokyo in 1990 at the invitation of the Japan Foundation, García Márquez scheduled meetings with the veteran filmmaker. Citing his advanced age, however, Kurosawa rejected the idea of making a movie based on *The Autumn of the Patriarch*, a literary work that would require a radical readaptation or filming outside of Japan (García Márquez, "Esperando el tifón" n.p.). In their conversation the Colombian novelist spoke of his well-known reluctance to have his works made into movies, and Kurosawa in turn explained how some filmmakers manage to capture and express in images messages that were evident only to their authors. García Márquez had previously rejected an adaptation of *One Hundred Years* by the transgressive poet, theater director, and filmmaker Shūji Terayama (1935–1983) in the 1980s. Terayama failed to convince the Colombian author to allow him to use the title of the novel in his film launch, which had to be reedited; it then premiered at the 1985 Cannes festival as a posthumous work with the title *Saraba no Hakobune* (*Farewell to the Ark*). Like the universe of Ikezawa, the Macondo of Terayama is impregnated with Japanese folklore and is nourished by García Márquez situations such as the disappearance of all the clocks of the town, handwritten signs stuck on things to identify them, and the suffering of a woman punished with a chastity belt in the form of a crab.

THE LEGACY OF *ONE HUNDRED YEARS OF SOLITUDE*

Googling García Márquez's name in Japan today brings up, in addition to the Colombian writer's books, a series of women's apparel products such as jackets, bags, and necklaces bearing the label GARCIA MARQUEZ, though without the Spanish accent marks and with an added label saying "Made in Japan." When searching *Hyakunen no Kodoku* (*One Hundred Years of Solitude*), in addition to the novel itself, there appears an expensive barley liquor made by using a hundred-year-old distilling method (Robledo n.p.). The buyer who is unfamiliar with the novel will not discover the origin of the title because nothing on the bottle or its packaging connects the whisky to the original work. The sole reference to the passage of time is a pocket watch and chain drawn in black ink on the brown label. Still, in Japan the literary impact of *One Hundred Years* remains alive and well. In 2018 the Akutagawa Prize, Japan's highest award for serious literature, was given to *Hyakunen Doro* (*One Hundred Years of Mud*) by the writer Yuka Ishii. The author attributes the title to her admiration for the creator of Macondo, to whom she pays tribute with her own use of magical realism. Based on Ishii's experiences in India, the novel tells of the protagonist's relationship with people and objects that have disappeared, but which return in a sea of mud following a flood that takes place every hundred years.

The consensus of Japanese translators of Latin American literature is that the rendering of *One Hundred Years* by Tadashi Tsuzumi has more than fulfilled its function of spreading Latin American culture and promoting the Spanish language within Japan. However, the technological limitations of linguistic research forty-eight years ago, compared with the more dynamic commercial and cultural relationship between Japan and Spanish-speaking countries today, makes one think that the time may have arrived for a new version. Tsuzumi himself referred to the vertiginous changes of a Japanese language that almost every day welcomes neologisms, invents onomatopoeia, and takes in new words borrowed from other cultures. The ever-changing renditions of *One Hundred Years of Solitude* in Japanese and other languages, as made by successive generations, will keep it alive and current. As such, it continues to be a bridge that brings cultures closer together.

Note: Translated from the Spanish by Gonzalo Robledo and Robert Wallis.

Notes

1. "In the Japanese language the adjective goes before the noun. In other languages it can be placed before or behind the noun. In addition, in the case of Spanish there is a tendency to use relatives, which allow one phrase after another to be put together. García Márquez uses this technique, which consists of putting together long sentences chained through relatives." Lecture by Professor Keizuke Dan, translator, at the First García Márquez Congress, held at the Cervantes Institute in Tokyo in October 2008 (quoted in Zambrano, *Hacer el mundo con palabras* 114; translation by Gonzalo Robledo).
2. "Veinte casas de barro y cañabrava." "Río de aguas diáfanas." "piedras pulidas, blancas y enormes como huevos prehistóricos" (*Cien años* 51).
3. "Its political element is ultimately an apolitical condemnation of both the abuse of political power and of the dressing of such abuse in the trappings of democracy. This apolitical aspect is significant in that García Márquez, as a self-identified socialist, might hypothetically have wished to include in his novel an overtly ideological agenda" (Shattuck O'Keefe).
4. "Exactly right now, I am preparing a work that gathers the daily experiences of a Japanese town to concretely understand the modern history of Japan; I do it under the influence of García Márquez and I consider that work will be a summary of everything I have written to date" (Kenzaburō Ōe, quoted in Sologuren; translation by Gonzalo Robledo).
5. "Ōe is more like Vargas Llosa, both are Sartreans, but García Márquez is not, he likes more authors like Kafka" (Fumiaki Noya, quoted in Zambrano, *El horizonte de las palabras* 14; translation by Gonzalo Robledo).
6. "First, he creates Macondo, probably mocking some of the biblical foundational myths recalled by those countries that try to lend an aura of magnificence to their identity as nations" (Alonso Alonso).
7. "The ties between Us and Our people have always stood upon mutual trust and affection. They do not depend upon mere legends and myths. They are not predicated on the false conception that the Emperor is divine, and that the Japanese people are superior to other races and fated to rule the world" ("Emperor, Imperial Rescript Denying His Divinity").
8. "The main problem is our education system. Japanese children learn Japan's history starting from the ancient period and moving toward modern days. Normally, in other countries, they learn history starting with the present and moving into the past to learn where things come from. But in practice in Japan, history teachers generally teach up to, and including, the Meiji Era [1868–1912] and they don't teach about the Showa Era [1926–1989]. Often this is because they run out of time to cover the curriculum—which includes the Showa Era. This means that the government has not settled what is Japanese history yet, so history lessons stopped at the point where they suspend judgment on the Showa Era. So they never talk about the responsibility of starting the war" (Nobuko Tanaka, quoted in Inoue).
9. Rush, p. 122.
10. "'I live in Tokyo,' he told me, 'a kind of civilized world—like New York or Los Angeles or London or Paris. If you want to find a magical situation, magical things, you have to go deep inside yourself. So that is what I do. People say it's magic realism—but in the depths of my soul, it's just realism. Not magical. While I'm writing, it's very natural, very logical, very realistic and reasonable'" (Anderson).

Works Cited

Alonso Alonso, María. *Diasporic Marvellous Realism: History, Identity, and Memory in Caribbean Fiction*. Brill Rodopi, 2015.

Anderson, Sam. "The Fierce Imagination of Haruki Murakami." *The New York Times Magazine*, 21 Oct. 2011, www.nytimes.com/2011/10/23/magazine/the-fierce-imagination-of-haruki-murakami.html. Accessed 3 Apr. 2020.

"Emperor, Imperial Rescript Denying His Divinity (Professing His Humanity)." National Diet Library, 3-1, www.ndl.go.jp/constitution/e/shiryo/03/056shoshi.html. Accessed 27 Jan. 2020.

García Márquez, Gabriel. "El avión de la bella durmiente," *El Espectador*, 19 Sept. 1982.

García Márquez, Gabriel. *Cien años de soledad*. Edited by Joaquín Marco, Espasa-Calpe 1983.

García Márquez, Gabriel. "Esperando el tifón." Interview with director Akira Kurosawa. *El País*, 9 June 1991.

García Márquez, Gabriel. 百年の孤独 [*Hundred Years of Solitude*]. Shinchosha Publishing, 1983.

García Márquez, Gabriel. *One Hundred Years of Solitude*. Translated by Gregory Rabassa, Avon, 1971.

Inoue, Hisashi. Interview with Nobuko Tanaka. *The Japan Times*, 1 Oct. 2006.

Isbrucker, Asher. *The Immersive Realism of Studio Ghibli*. http://asherkaye.com/portfolio/the-immersive-realism-of-studio-ghibli/ Accessed 28 Jan. 2020.

Miyazaki, Hayao. "Starting Point." *Viz Media*. Shogakukan, 1996.

Napier, Susan J. *The Magic of Identity: Magic Realism in Modern Japanese Fiction*. Duke UP, 1995.

Noya, Fumiaki, Ikezawa Natsuki. 独裁者 マシアス・ギリの選択 ["Why Did I Choose Dictator Matias Guili"], *Shincho Magazine*, Aug. 1993, pp. 266–78.

Robledo, Gonzalo. "'Cien años de soledad' a la japonesa." *El Espectador*, 5 June 2017, www.elespectador.com/noticias/cultura/cien-anos-de-soledad-la-japonesa-articulo-696982. Accessed 3 Apr. 2020.

Rush, Norman. "Enduring Honors," in "Shouts and Murmurs" section. *The New Yorker*, 12 Apr. 1993, p. 122.

Scott-Stokes, Henry "Japan's Kafka Goes on the Road." *The New York Times*, 29 Apr. 1979, www.nytimes.com/1979/04/29/archives/japans-kafka-goes-on-the-road-kobo-abe-the-celebrated-surrealist.html. Accessed 3 Apr. 2020.

Shattuck O´Keefe, Arthur. "The Role of Politics in Gabriel García Márquez *One Hundred Years of Solitude*." Showa Women´s University, Institute of Modern Culture No. 931, June 2018, pp. 53–60, swu.repo.nii.ac.jp/?action=pages_view_main&active_action=repository_view_main_item_detail&item_id=6538&item_no=1&page_id=15&block_id=24. Accessed 30 Mar. 2020.

Sologuren, Javier. "Gravitaciones y tangencias." *Obras completas*, vol. 7, edited by Ricardo Silva-Santisteban, Pontificia Universidad Católica, Peru, 2005, pp. 120–22.

Strecher, Matthew C. "Magical Realism and the Search for Identity in the Fiction of Murakami Haruki." *The Journal of Japanese Studies*, vol. 25, no. 2, Summer 1999, pp. 263–98, www.jstor.org/stable/pdf/133313.pdf?refreqid=excelsior%3A16dc15af9dcdde6b4f4b4bcf7555812e. Accessed 3 Apr. 2020.

Suna no Onna [*Woman in the Dunes*]. Directed by Hiroshi Teshigahara, script by Kobo Abe, Teshigahara Productions, 1962. (Special Jury Prize at the 1964 Cannes Film Festival).

Wilson, Michiko N. *The Marginal World of Ōe Kenzaburō: A Study of Themes and Techniques*. Routledge, 2015.

Zambrano, Gregory. *Hacer el mundo con palabras*. Universidad de los Andes, 2011.

Zambrano, Gregory. *El horizonte de las palabras: La literatura hispanoamericana en perspectiva japonesa; Conversaciones con académicos y traductores*. Instituto Cervantes de Tokio, 2009.

CHAPTER 16

SPAIN IN THE MAKING AND RECEPTION OF GARCÍA MÁRQUEZ'S WORKS

ÁLVARO SANTANA-ACUÑA

The Spanish Connection

For someone born in Colombia, who absorbed his home country's culture from an early age, the major influence Spain had on García Márquez's literary education and professionalization is remarkable. He first experienced this influence at home, especially through his maternal grandmother, whose family came from the Spanish region of Galicia. "I remember her very well," the writer said in an interview, "she spoke an extraordinary Castilian Spanish, full of archaisms, dazzling images, which has been my starting point for writing.... I grew up with those words... as if they were part of the natural language of the people, which was the one she spoke... with that language I write my books."[1] García Márquez then encountered other agents of Spanish culture that influenced him between the early 1940s and the mid-1960s. As he put it, "from the first letters... my teachers, my friends in Colombia and then in Mexico were Spanish republicans."[2] Thanks to them, as he said often over the years, "I knew really well the history of the Spanish Civil War [and] really well the literature of Spain." For example, "I remember," he said, "the fields of Azorín... the fields of Machado... those rivers with the poplar trees on their banks."[3] Indeed, not only did the adolescent García Márquez read literature from Spain, but also later, when he was writing his early works, Spanish exiles who had fled the Civil War and the Franco dictatorship were among his closest collaborators. In the 1950s and 1960s, these collaborators shaped the literary imagination of the budding writer and even his politics, to the point that, as he recalled years later in an interview on Televisión Española, Spain's national television network, "I was already completely a Spanish republican."[4] When he left Latin America in 1967, recalling his arrival in Spain and especially in Barcelona, he said, "I arrived as if I had lived there a long time ... and then I found that those affinities that I had with my Spanish teachers, with Spanish friends, with the Spanish butcher, with the Spanish fisherman, with the Spanish blacksmith, with the Spanish shoemaker, among whom we grew up, still existed there [in Spain]."[5]

This Peninsular component of García Márquez's education, outlook, and professionalization favored his successful reception in Spain in ways that call for further research. Based on the large print runs of his books in this country, one notes that it is the Spanish-speaking territory where, historically, most copies were put on sale, with first editions that were often twice as large as those sold in Argentina, the second Spanish-language market for his works.

García Márquez's first encounter with Spanish literature happened during his school years in Barranquilla between 1940 and 1942. There he read works from the Spanish Golden Age by Miguel de Cervantes, Luis de Góngora, and Pedro Calderón de la Barca, as well as nineteenth-century romantic poets (García Márquez, *Vivir* 192). These Spanish writers offered him models he wished to imitate. As his friends recall, he would brag about writing something as good as *Don Quixote* (Martin 148). After a short stay in Bogotá, he moved to Cartagena in 1948 to work as a newspaper columnist. With Colombian colleagues, he continued to read Spanish authors, including Ramón Gómez de la Serna, an important literary influence (García Usta 144ff). In Cartagena, he met Dámaso Alonso, the Spanish poet and Góngora scholar, with whom García Márquez shared some of his writing. Later on he lived in Barranquilla, where, as a budding journalist, he joined another group of amateur artists and writers, the so-called Barranquilla Group, led by Ramón Vinyes. He became one of García Márquez's mentors, offering advice on his projects, including his first ideas and manuscripts for "La casa" ("The House"), the original rough draft of what eventually evolved into *One Hundred Years*. Famously, Vinyes "warned" García Márquez during one of their meetings "that nobody would believe my story if I set it in Barranquilla. Furthermore, he reproached me that it was an anti-literary name."[6] Following his mentor's advice, the aspiring writer opted for a place name that would change world literature: Macondo.

An occasional member of the group was Lluís Vicens, another Spanish exile, with whom García Márquez had long conversations about cinema and who participated in the making of his first film, *La langosta azul* (*The Blue Lobster*, 1954). Another Spanish expatriate who marked García Márquez in his early years was the critic Guillermo de Torre. A reader for the prestigious Argentine press Losada, he turned down for publication García Márquez's first novel *Leaf Storm*, using aesthetic arguments in doing so. Saddened at first, this rejection helped García Márquez to understand early in his career that his style had to please gatekeepers of the book industry if he hoped to get his work published.

His journalistic writings, especially during his formative years between 1947 and 1953, contain numerous references to Spanish works, including the already mentioned *Don Quixote*, Juan Ramón Jiménez's *Platero y yo*, Gustavo Adolfo Bécquer's *Rimas*, and writers such as Lope de Vega, Federico García Lorca, and Ramón Gómez de la Serna. They also mention films such as Luis García Berlanga's *Bienvenido, Mr. Marshall* and Luis Buñuel's *Los olvidados* and *Robinson Crusoe*.[7]

In 1955, García Márquez arrived in Paris, where he lived until 1957. His closest companion was the Spaniard Tachia Quintana, after whom he modeled the female character in *El coronel no tiene quien le escriba* (*No One Writes to the Coronel*, 1961). An ex-partner of Basque poet Blas de Otero, Quintana was also knowledgeable and actively involved in Spanish culture. In 1961, García Márquez arrived in Mexico City, which had been a preferred destination for Spanish exiles since the 1930s. One of them, the writer Max Aub, offered García Márquez his first job in town in 1961. Four years later, Aub was quoted in the prestigious French newspaper *Le Monde* as saying that García Márquez would be one of the voices of the new Latin American literature (Piatier 13). Another two Spaniards in Mexico who influenced García Márquez's imagination and professional trajectory were filmmaker Buñuel and scriptwriter Luis Alcoriza. García Márquez sent film ideas to Buñuel, who was even a character in the movie directed by Alberto Isaac, *En este pueblo no hay ladrones* (*There Are No Thieves in This Town*, 1965), based on a short story of the same name by García Márquez. Alcoriza and García Márquez were collaborating on several scripts when the latter decided to commit all his time and energy to writing *One Hundred Years*.

Arguably, the peak of Spanish influence on García Márquez was the imagination, production, and reception of *One Hundred Years*. He attributed to his grandmother's Spanish (specifically Galician) ancestry the fantastic tales that had shaped his way of telling the stories in the novel (Chao 25). As homage to Vinyes for his mentorship, the latter became the character of the wise Catalan in the work. In 1964, in the months prior to starting the writing of the novel, García Márquez recommended to a friend that he should write his book "as Cervantes wanted it."[8] That is, García Márquez was recommending his friend to follow Cervantes's style. He ended up doing the same himself in *One Hundred Years* a few months later. As he explained to another friend who listened to him read the first chapter of the book, "[T]he best way to tell all these crazy things is to assume the same style of the Spanish narrators of chivalry novels."[9] Among those who listened to him was Spanish exile and writer Federico Álvarez, to whom García Márquez explained in detail how he was crafting the novel's distinctive language. When he was writing the novel between 1965 and 1967, Spanish migrants María Luisa Elío and Jomí García Ascot, and Carmen Miracle Feliú, daughter of a Spanish exile, were among his closest collaborators. The three, along with Colombian poet Álvaro Mutis, met regularly in García Márquez's home and checked on the progress of the novel (Santana-Acuña, *Ascent* 134, 136–37). By then, Elío and García Ascot had already made *En el balcón vacío* (*On the Empty Balcony*, 1961), a movie about a woman who recalls her childhood prior to her exile. In this movie, one can find the kinds of imaginary elements, especially childhood memories, that helped García Márquez to write *One Hundred Years*.

Regarding Spanish influence on the publication of the novel, he had first promised it to Ediciones Era, cofounded by Neus Espresate Xirau, member of an exiled Catalan family. In 1963, Era had started to promote new editions of García Márquez's early works. However, García Márquez decided instead to publish *One Hundred Years* with Editorial Sudamericana, whose acquisitions editor was the Spanish-born Francisco Porrúa and editor-in-chief was Antonio López Llausàs, an exiled Spaniard. Spanish literary agent

Carmen Balcells brokered the publishing contract with Sudamericana. She first learned about García Márquez around 1962, thanks to a tip from Spanish political dissident and poet José Manuel Caballero Bonald, who was then living in Bogotá. He informed Balcells about a promising writer who had just won Colombia's award for best novel, the ESSO Prize. The award-winning novel was *La mala hora* (*In Evil Hour*, 1962). That year Balcells first signed a contract with García Márquez to represent him in the foreign rights market. Three years later, in 1965, they signed another contract, now to represent him in all languages; García Márquez's Catalan friend Vicens acted as witness to the deal. When García Márquez finished the novel, he gave the galley proofs to Alcoriza as a gift and dedicated the book to Elío and García Ascot. Another Spanish exile, the artist Vicente Rojo, designed the novel's iconic cover. Before Argentine Sudamericana press bought the publication rights, *One Hundred Years* was offered, unsuccessfully, to the leading publisher of New Latin American Novels, Spanish press Seix Barral. Yet other Spanish publishers (especially Círculo de Lectores, which sold hundreds of thousands of copies) helped make this novel into a long-term bestseller (Santana-Acuña, *Ascent* 57, 65–66).

Reception of García Márquez's Works in Spain before *One Hundred Years of Solitude*

Via friends, collaborators, and gatekeepers, Spanish culture influenced the early works of García Márquez. Yet despite this Spanish connection, these works were poorly received in Spain before 1967. The earliest known reference to García Márquez in a Peninsular book dates from 1961, when Cuban writer Gastón Baquero published in Madrid the volume *Escritores hispanoamericanos de hoy* (Today's Spanish American Writers), sponsored by the Instituto de Cultura Hispánica as part of its *Nuevo Mundo* collection. Baquero wrote it especially for "young Spanish students." This volume listed García Márquez as one of the region's key writers, along with famous names such as Rubén Darío and Jorge Luis Borges, as well as lesser-known figures such as Francisco Romero and Ignacio B. Anzoátegui. To young Spanish readers, Baquero said he could not understand how *La hojarasca* (*Leaf Storm*, 1955), the only work by García Márquez he mentioned, had not received more attention. "It is," he said, "one of the great literary documents of America, compelling admiration not only for the doses of exoticism it contains, but also for its literary wisdom." He added, "it has . . . a lot of gold inside its wonderful structure."[10]

Thus, the poor reception of García Márquez's works in Spain before *One Hundred Years* had nothing to do with the fact that they were completely unknown or had received no praise there. Neither was such a scant response due to the fact that he had not attempted publication of his work in Spain. In 1962, he approached Editorial Vergara in

Barcelona to put out *In Evil Hour*, though only Ediciones Iberoamericanas in Madrid agreed to do so. Yet again, as had happened with the manuscript of *Leaf Storm* sent to Losada, García Márquez faced criticism about his style from another Spanish gatekeeper. The publisher did not reject the novel (winner of the ESSO Prize), but the proofreaders translated the author's original text into perfect "Castilian" without informing him. When the book came out, García Márquez protested, and a controversy ensued. The Instituto Nacional del Libro Español had to publicly state that the government's Censorship Office had had nothing to do with the incident. The publisher apologized and offered to pulp the first edition and reprint one at no cost in the author's Colombian Spanish ("Respecto" 69). García Márquez refused the offer and instead released a conciliatory statement in which he hoped that "in the future, all Latin American writers [would] be treated as adults by Spanish publishers."[11] A day after his statement, he wrote in a letter to a friend that the controversy actually had helped to sell out the first edition of 5,000 copies (García Márquez, Letter to Mendoza, June 14, [1963], 1). Yet the reality is that this edition of *In Evil Hour*, printed in Spain for export to the Latin American book market, went unnoticed by most critics and readers in Spain itself.

García Márquez must have kept in mind this new incident with aesthetic gatekeepers, because in his next work, *One Hundred Years*, he refurbished his style, using, among other sources of inspiration, the classic language of Cervantes (Santana-Acuña, *Ascent* 133). The result was quite positive; the novel cleared censorship in less than two weeks and without any stylistic changes. In his reader's report, the censor in Spain concluded: "As a novel, it is very good."[12]

Inasmuch as book publication and distribution in Spain was under strict surveillance by Franco's censors, it is possible to know how much of García Márquez's work was imported before *One Hundred Years* arrived on the scene. Except for *In Evil Hour*, all books by García Márquez consumed by readers on the Peninsula before *One Hundred Years* had been imported products. In 1967, the year this novel was issued in Argentina, Spain imported twenty-five copies of *In Evil Hour*, twenty-five of *No One Writes*, fifty of *Big Mama's Funeral*, and just fifty of *One Hundred Years*.

Yet García Márquez could not have written his masterpiece at a better moment. A modernizing book industry in Spain facilitated its success. During the 1960s, the country increased by 327 percent the number of titles published per year (Santana 43). In 1966 and 1967, that is, during the final production and publication of *One Hundred Years*, over fifteen thousand literary titles were released in Spain. There was also an important change in terms of aesthetics: namely, the collapse of social realism, a sober style of storytelling that was popular among Spanish writers at the time though in decline among readers. Simultaneously, the New Latin American Novel was booming. In Spain, print runs of Mario Vargas Llosa's books rose by 7,600 percent. This extraordinary increase happened between 1959—the year he published his first book, a collection of stories entitled *Los jefes* (*The Leaders*), with a print run of 1,300 copies—and 1973, when 100,000 copies of the first edition of *Pantaleón y las visitadoras* (*Captain Pantoja and the Special Service*) were put on sale. The success of *One Hundred Years* in Spain built on the success of the country's rapidly modernizing book industry, with hundreds of thousands of members of the rising urban middle class making novel reading one of their hobbies and choosing García Márquez as one of their favorite authors (Santana-Acuña, *Ascent* 46–48).

Reception of *One Hundred Years of Solitude*

Sudamericana published this novel in June 1967 in Buenos Aires. For more than a year, Spanish readers only had access to it via imported copies from Argentina. This changed in 1969, when the Franco government authorized EDHASA, Sudamericana's branch in Spain, to print and sell copies on Peninsular soil. Print runs skyrocketed. In January 1969, *One Hundred Years* was sold out, and EDHASA applied for permission to print 5,000 copies at a sales price of 180 pesetas (US$2.50). Three months later it requested approval for a reprint of 10,000 copies. And just a week later, it sought to issue another reprint. Requests kept coming throughout 1969 and always with the same arguments: "[G]iven the success achieved by the work of GABRIEL GARCÍA MÁRQUEZ, 'One Hundred Years of Solitude'" in Argentina, given "the haste with which our clients request more copies of it," and given the delay in shipping them from Argentina, "we ask that a new printing be printed in Spain."[13] In five years, more than 100,000 copies of the EDHASA edition were sold (Santana-Acuña, *Ascent* 163).

The first known reviews in Spain were published on October 14, 1967. Catalan poet Pere Gimferrer claimed that this novel was yet another example of "the current vitality of Latin American narrative," and critic Rafael Conte noticed that its author was "one of the peaks of current Latin American narrative."[14] They both agreed that García Márquez was mostly unknown in Spain. To solve this, the same month, critic Joaquín Marco ("Gabriel" 124) called García Márquez a "young maestro" in a review, published in the weekly magazine *Destino*, that introduced Spanish readers to all his works prior to *One Hundred Years*. In 1968, and especially after its publication in Spain the following year, this novel was amply reviewed in national, regional, and local media. These media targeted both highbrow and popular audiences, from the readers of specialized publications such as *Reseña de literatura, arte y espectáculos*, *Cuadernos para el diálogo*, and *Revista de Occidente* to those of more general venues, among them *Índice* and *Meridiano*. One can also find book reviews across the ideological spectrum of Francoist Spain, including the monarchist *ABC*, the Catalan *La Vanguardia Española*, the Falangist *Diario SP*, the Christian-Democratic *Informaciones*, the Catholic *Ya*, the leftist *Triunfo*, and the Francoist *Pueblo*.[15]

Leading journalists, critics, and writers endorsed the novel. Writer Carmen Laforet said in an interview in national media, "[I] deeply admire [it]" (Gómez-Santos 123). In "Repaso de lecturas de 1968," a piece about the best books of the year included in the cultural magazine *El Ciervo*, journalist Rosario Bofill stated that it was "the best book

I have read in recent years."[16] Even writers with differing aesthetic agendas praised it. For social realist Miguel Delibes (quoted in Tola de Habich and Grieve 130), García Márquez's work was "extraordinary," and for experimentalist José María Guelbenzu (48), it was "superb." Writer Juan Benet (57) put in words the feelings of thousands of readers when he wrote, "DO NOT DISTURB ME. I'M IN MACONDO."[17] Poet Lorenzo Gamis was also impressed by "how a man can create a world, and how thousands of men and women–the readers–can talk about that world for hours."[18] This quotation summarizes what happened in Spain not only to *One Hundred Years* but also to most of García Márquez's works from 1969 onward: they reached large and diverse audiences.

At a time when writers, critics, and readers were accusing the European novel of being too experimental, readers of *One Hundred Years* were impressed by its traditional storytelling. In her book review, historian Carmen Llorca argued, "with García Márquez, the novel becomes the novel again: with its human beings, its environment, its plot, its wonderful language, its incredible clarity."[19] This was also the opinion of Gimferrer: it was a "return to narrative imagination."[20] Likewise, as they wrote in their reviews, for journalist Pascual Maisterra this novel was "a narrative feat," for writer Luis Izquierdo it was "an atmospheric purifier," and for writer Domingo Pérez Minik it was "pure narration."[21] Critic Andrés Amorós believed that this "authentic masterpiece" was successful because the writer "*narrates*."[22] And for Guillermo Díaz-Plaja (22), García Márquez could narrate because he went back to the "medieval origins" of the novel as a genre.

Whereas reviewers agreed on the novel's narrative power, there was no agreement about its narrative genre. This is an important and yet underappreciated fact about the book's initial reception. Considering that the novel is now regarded as the key work of the genre known as magical realism, it is remarkable that none of its early readers in Spain called García Márquez a magical realist or thought that the novel was an example of that approach (Santana-Acuña, "Reviewing"). Rather, they referred to "unreality" and noticed that "surrealism operates with real events," as writer Jorge Campos put it.[23] Similarly, according to critic Dámaso Santos, "fantasy and reality merge," and writer Luis Goytisolo said this novel was "a curious case of mythical realism."[24]

Unfavorable criticism, from subtle to harsh, has accompanied *One Hundred Years* ever since its publication (Santana-Acuña, *Ascent* 167–68). In his review for the leading Spanish literary journal *Papeles de Son Armadans*, Mexican writer Francisco Cervantes (327) insisted that the novel, contrary to what many people said, was not "easy to read." For him, it was full of confusions, and characters' names repeat themselves. Such was also Benet's opinion. As praise for *One Hundred Years* grew, there were Spanish writers who felt threatened by it, while some critics tried to set the record of literary history straight. Critic de Torre (who years earlier had rejected *Leaf Storm*) belittled the rapid success of *One Hundred Years* because the story was, in his opinion, "anachronistic, given its structure and contents" and more importantly because praise for this novel ignored the key historical fact that the boom of Latin American dated from the 1930s, not just from the 1960s.[25] On the contrary, Llorca (14) wrote, forecasting the future, that García Márquez was going to become "one of the classics of Spanish-American literature." For Santos, "Many Spanish novelists could achieve something like this [novel] if they did not feel crushed by their faith in the traditional novel or go around in circles for having chosen the path of rupture."[26] Yet *One Hundred Years* did not help them. At least, this is what an anonymous reviewer for *Informaciones* thought: "I know writers who have stopped writing" because of the impact it had had on them.[27]

At a moment when Spain was expanding its educational system nationwide, *One Hundred Years* entered the lives of thousands of students either via textbooks or as curricular reading. Regarding textbooks, the second edition of the popular *Historia universal de la literatura* (History of World Literature, 1969), by Cuban-born and Catalan writer Ramón D. Perés (1863–1956), stated that *One Hundred Years* was "an eagerly awaited book, because it is said that it will become one of the pillars of the new America."[28] Regarding the curriculum, the novel became required reading for generations of high school and university students, despite the opposition of ordinary citizens like José Vernet Mateu. In 1972, the latter wrote to the Ministry of Information and Tourism, in charge of the Censorship Office, to complain about the popularity of this "repugnant . . . disgusting book." He lamented that it was "required for sixteen-year-old boys, whom it literally corrupts and brutalizes."[29] As further proof, he attached to his letter photocopies of what he believed were several controversial pages of *One Hundred Years*.

Along with students, many of García Márquez's readers were also grown-up members of Spain's rising urban middle class, who were among the main consumers of Latin American novels. Thousands of middle-class families got books via the Círculo de Lectores. Thanks to this book club founded in 1962, thousands of households saw New Latin American Novels delivered to their doorsteps for the first time ever. Círculo published its first edition of *One Hundred Years* in 1970 at 98 pesetas (US$1.40), just over half the price of the EDHASA edition. During the 1970s, the Círculo edition sold over 400,000 copies.[30] Yet successful as it was, this edition was just one among many others. By 1987, on its twentieth anniversary, out of a total of 7.2 million copies sold worldwide, *One Hundred Years* had sold 3.4 million in the Spanish language. And of these copies in Spanish, eleven publishers in Spain had sold 46 percent, that is, 1.5 million copies (Balcells 2–3).

More than five decades after its release, this novel continues to be available in multiple editions, from scholarly editions such as Cátedra's collection *Letras Hispánicas*, to mass market editions such as *El País*'s volume in *Biblioteca García Márquez*, to hybrid versions such as the Real Academia Española edition with the participation of another nineteen academies in Latin America. In 2007, this edition sold half a million copies in its first two months. It was the second title in the *Ediciones Conmemorativas* collection, dedicated to Spanish-language classics. The first title was *Don Quixote*, a novel that Spanish audiences often compare to *One Hundred Years* (Santana-Acuña, *Ascent* 233, 237).

Reception of Works beyond *One Hundred Years of Solitude*

Following the success of this novel, García Márquez's previous works started selling quite well in Spain. In October 1968, he wrote in a letter to a friend: "I don't know for how long: not only *One Hundred Years*, but my other books, have occupied the first rows of sales in Spain for three months."[31] The government kept receiving requests to print more copies of his early works.[32] Reviews were enthusiastic, too. In his 1968 piece on *In Evil Hour*, critic Conte said that the writer was "already famous in all Spanish-America and profusely translated."[33] Upon the publication of a new edition of *Leaf Storm* in Barcelona in 1969, leading national newspaper *ABC* noticed that García Márquez was "alarmingly turned into 'fashionable writer.'"[34] Indeed, almost every work published after *One Hundred Years* became a major cultural event in Spain. Each new work was reviewed in print, was covered on radio and TV, had sales of thousands of copies, and was a bestseller. In addition, all kinds of audiences, including celebrity artists, read them. For example, musician Joan Manuel Serrat said that García Márquez "is a great writer" (Iparraguirre 137). Praises such as "brilliant author of *One Hundred Years of Solitude*" and "splendid novel" became the norm over the years.[35]

In 1970, Catalan publisher Tusquets Editores released in paperback format the writer's journalistic reportage *Relato de un náufrago* (*The Story of a Shipwrecked Sailor*), which since its publication has gone through more than sixty reprints. Its release also initiated a trend that affected most works issued in the wake of *One Hundred Years*: they were compared to the latter novel, even if they were works he had written previously, like *Shipwrecked Sailor*. In his review, poet Enrique Badosa warned that "the reader will not encounter the magical realism of *One Hundred Years of Solitude*," and yet he added that the book "is a jewel of literature and journalism."[36] Likewise, critic Juan Antonio Masoliver Ródenas wrote, "We are no longer in Macondo" and suggested that the shipwrecked sailor was "somehow the writer himself," lost in the success of *One Hundred Years*.[37] In their coverage of the release, even regional media such as *El Noticiero* of Zaragoza and *El Correo de Andalucía* reminded readers that García Márquez was first and foremost the author of *One Hundred Years*.[38]

By then he was becoming a divisive figure in Spanish letters. Novelist José María Gironella attacked him and fellow writers of the Latin American Boom in a six-page article in *ABC* in 1970, claiming that their language was full of "idiomatic baroqueness."[39] The same year, writer Alfonso Grosso criticized several Latin American authors. He called García Márquez a "bluff" and said that *One Hundred Years* was unreadable after two pages (quoted in Marco and Gracia García 136). Spanish media also became a platform for Latin American writers to criticize García Márquez and his work. In 1973, the magazine *Cuadernos para el diálogo* ran an interview with Borges, who, after being asked whether he had read García Márquez, replied, "I have not read him because I lost my sight in 1955" and added elsewhere, "literature is going through a very unpleasant commercial stage.... Nobody thinks that the books that sell a lot are good. It's all a matter of fashion, a kind of mania to read what others read."[40]

While throughout the 1970s Spanish writers, critics, and readers were taking sides on the worth of García Márquez as an author, he published two new books. The first was the collection of short stories *La increíble y triste historia de la cándida Eréndira y de su abuela desalmada* (*The Incredible and Sad Tale of Innocent Eréndira and Her Heartless Grandmother*, 1972). As happened with most of his books from then onward, the first edition was released in four countries simultaneously. Spain was always one of them.

Upon reading this new book, many started to question whether García Márquez could ever write something as good as *One Hundred Years*. Critic Marco turned his review into an analysis of why this novel had succeeded as it did and reached the conclusion that in this novel's case, as in the new book, the oral tradition merged with chivalric novels. In that sense, for Marco, García Márquez was more an "integrator and adaptor, more than innovator,"[41] as shown, for example, by the strong presence of the work of Gómez de la Serna, a Spanish author who had influenced him in his early works. Other critics received García Márquez's new short stories as residual materials that he could not include in *One Hundred Years*.

The second new book was *El otoño del patriarca* (*The Autumn of the Patriarch*, 1975). His first novel after *One Hundred Years* was much anticipated by readers and critics. But it was not what most of them had expected: a second part or continuation of the Macondo and Buendía saga. Rather, reviewers alerted readers that the author had written a long and complex reflection on the solitude of power. Some reviewers celebrated this book as a major literary achievement, though an imperfect one. "Narrative prose," as Marco put it, "has been transformed into artistic prose."[42] In *Triunfo*, Luis Íñigo Madrigal praised "the greatness and impossibility of García Márquez's attempt."[43] Other readers dutifully mentioned the novel's connections with Spanish culture. Juan Pedro Quiñonero found in this book "the sentimental tenderness of Ramón Gómez de la Serna" and, since this work was "a titanic project," it had the airs of a political pamphlet like Cervantes's historical play *Numancia* and Valle-Inclán's dictator novel *Tirano Banderas*.[44]

Given that García Márquez was already a divisive figure, harsh criticism of *Autumn* spread widely, and thus some potential readers hesitated to read it. This also happened to writer Carmen Martín Gaite. She said that colleagues and friends in Spain had cautioned her that this novel was "more of the same ... the author returned, in the end to the usual."[45] Yet she read *Autumn* and believed that it was better than *One Hundred Years*. Her stance was not unusual; it exemplifies a long-term tendency to judge whether a new work of fiction by García Márquez was to be superior or inferior to the Macondo book, pointing out similarities and differences between the works. Precisely because of this, some reviewers started to warn readers that the work of García Márquez should not simply be reduced to *One Hundred Years*.

For its toughest critics, especially those against the Latin American Boom—a trend that had grown enormously in the literary establishment by the mid-1970s—the publication of *Autumn* (and its disappointing sales) marked the end of the New Latin American Novel. This was the opinion of Spanish-born writer José Blanco Amor. In his essay "El final del 'boom'" ("The End of the 'Boom'"), he attacked García Márquez for belonging to a literary mafia that only promoted the works of its members. His criticism echoed that of Spanish scholar Manuel Pedro González, who claimed that Latin American novels were pure copies of older works of fiction and products of propaganda. In Spain, Blanco Amor's essay was published in *El País*, and soon afterward he turned it into a book (Santana-Acuña, *Ascent* 184–86). Though time has shown this kind of criticism to be excessive, the perception at the moment was that, even for partisans of García

Márquez like Gimferrer ("García" 40), the publication of *Autumn* proved that there was no longer a Boom in Latin American literature. By the early 1970s, when the Boom was coming to an end, García Márquez's works started to consolidate as a topic of scholarly research in Spanish universities (see, e.g., Camacho Delgado; García Ramos; Salvador). Furthermore, national as well as regional writers started to imitate his style and themes, including the controversy prompted by Gonzalo Torrente Ballester's award-winning novel *La saga/fuga de J. B.* (The Saga/Flight of J. B., 1972). He had to declare that he had not read *One Hundred Years*, given the similarities between García Márquez's novel and his own (see, e.g., Landín Carrasco 15).

In 1981, after six years of literary silence, García Márquez published *Crónica de una muerte anunciada* (*Chronicle of a Death Foretold*). Reviews of this short novel exploded in Spain. One could find them not only in national, mainstream media but also in more and more regional and local outlets, such as *Faro de Vigo*, *El Personal*, *Diario de Barcelona*, *El Adelantado de Segovia*, *El Norte de Galicia*, *El Correo Catalán*, *El Diario Vasco*, *Diario de Cuenca*, *Nueva España*, *El Heraldo de Aragón*, and *La Voz del Penedés*. Indeed, the publication of this short novel was a turning point in the reception of García Márquez in Spain. Leading newspapers such as *El País* and *Diario de Barcelona* announced its release months in advance, indicating that the initial printing would be one million copies. To this date, it remains the largest initial print run of a book written by a Spanish-language author. Almost one-third of this edition (300,000 copies) was released in Spain at a price of 375 pesetas (US$4.25) (Conte, "Gabriel" n.p.). In its first twenty hours, *Chronicle* sold 35,000 copies—that is, more than 10 percent of the print run (Ceberio 29).

While reviewers of *Chronicle* continued to talk about *One Hundred Years* as a "narrative monument," several praised this new book as a "Chronicle of a Success Foretold," as Florentino Martínez Ruiz (47) put it. For poet Luis Suñen ("Gabriel" 1), this novel was a return to "the best García Márquez," the one of *One Hundred Years*. For critic Marco ("Crónica" 41), it was "an extraordinary work." According to conservative politician Joaquín Calomarde, its author was an "enormous Spanish American writer."[46] These and other reviewers again insisted on two features that others already had done for *One Hundred Years*: namely, the novel's connection with Spanish culture and the writer's storytelling powers. Critic Andrés Amorós highlighted these in his review. He found connections between this "chronicle" and García Lorca's *Bodas de sangre* (*Blood Wedding*) and underscored that García Márquez's merit was that he "narrates" (Amorós, "El arte" IV). Negative comments appeared, too. For journalist and writer Luis Blanco Vila, it was "a minor work, [not] a work of art."[47] Readers, however, felt otherwise. *Chronicle* was already the number one bestselling work of fiction in its first week, as reported by *Diario 16* ("Los libros más" n.p.).

New works by García Márquez continued to appear, but surveys and other types of cultural activities kept reminding old and new generations of readers about the importance of *One Hundred Years*. In 1984, *Disidencias*, the cultural supplement of *Diario 16*, asked thirty prominent figures in Spanish-American literature and culture to vote for their favorite novel in the Spanish language published after 1939. *One Hundred Years* was ranked number one, with Cortázar's *Rayuela* (*Hopscotch*, 1963) and Martín-Santos's *Tiempo de silencio* (*Time of Silence*, 1962) as numbers two and three, respectively ("En lengua castellana" I–VIII).

The following year, in 1985, García Márquez published *El amor en los tiempos del cólera* (*Love in the Time of Cholera*). It was much awaited because it was the first novel he had written after receiving the Nobel Prize. It was released on December 4, to cash in on the Christmas shopping season. *La Vanguardia* sent a special correspondent to cover the book release in the Colombian city of Cartagena (Ibarz 53). In Spain, the first edition had a print run of 250,000 paperback copies at a list price of 1,000 pesetas (US$6.23). The book immediately reached the number one spot in the bestseller list for fiction ("Libros" XII). At this point, given García Márquez's Nobel status, media were gossiping about the amounts he received for his book contracts. For *Love*, they reported that he "will receive a fixed amount of 25 million pesetas" (US$160,440) and ten percent in royalties ("Las caras" 13; "Bruguera" n.p.). As usual, things involving García Márquez would inevitably lead to controversy. On the issue of payment, he said that he found it "offensive" that people thought he had transformed his literature into "merchandise" (Arroyo 27).

Along with ample coverage in national media during the preceding weeks in *El País* and *Diario 16* (including interviews and reportage), the customary short notices and book reviews appeared in regional and local newspapers across Spain, such as *Época*, *Álcazar*, *Avui*, *El Món*, and *El Norte de Castilla*. Several of them conveyed the idea that García Márquez had written a "telenovela" ("soap opera"). Overall, praise outdid disparagement of the book. Anonymous commentators in *Ya*, *ABC*, and *El Periódico de Cataluña* referred to it as a novel of "rare quality" and as "almost required reading," and to its author as "Colombian *magician* and Nobel Prize," respectively ("Selecciones" 30; "Gabriel García Márquez, color" 7; "Amor" 107). In *Cambio 16*, writer Javier Goñi (100) dubbed it "a splendid novel." Along with the usual comparison between the new novel and *One Hundred Years* (for Marco ["García" 27], this "love novel" was different from his now classic book), "masterpiece" was a recurrent way of designating *Love*. So did critic Suñen, who added that García Márquez has "absolute control . . . of the narrative form."[48] According to scholar Nora Catelli, "masterpieces, those of García Márquez, have been or will be something else."[49] José García Nieto, of the Spanish Royal Academy, wrote for *ABC* that it was "one of the best novels of the century written in the Spanish language."[50] Mexican Carlos Monsiváis went a step further and asked his readers in his review for *Diario 16*: "How can we not realize on every page that we are facing one of the great living classics of our language?"[51]

But even *Love*'s most enthusiastic reviewers had some reservations. For Suñen, the ending was too abrupt. Catelli in turn thought that there were irregularities and that the second half was better than the first. Some criticized the language, which was "dense text, overly scented," according to Adrián Monroy.[52] Others took issue with García Márquez as a narrator. For instance, critic Santos Sanz Villanueva had no doubt that the "vigorous narrator" was still in great shape and that the novel was a nice homage to old forms such as the "literatura de folletín" ("feuilleton literature") but said that the narrator's voice was more typical of an apprentice than of a canonical writer (Sanz Villanueva 11).

As García Márquez had started doing in the 1970s, he took advantage of the release of his latest book to announce the next one: his autobiography. Yet what he wrote after *Love* turned out to be a different kind of autobiography: *El general en su laberinto* (*The General in His Labyrinth*, 1989). His first historical novel was released at a time when Spain's institutional preparations for the five-hundredth anniversary of Columbus's first voyage to the Americas were underway. With a clear political intent, García Márquez focused his novel on the man who had freed the region from Spanish rule three centuries hence: Simón Bolívar. According to the book contract, signed with publishing giant Mondadori, the first edition consisted of 175,000 hardcover copies at a sales price of 1,450 pesetas (US$12.60), for which García Márquez received an advance payment of 60 million pesetas (US$522,000), plus royalties now starting at 12 percent, rather than the customary 10 percent.[53]

An interview appeared in the conservative *ABC* (Samper VII–IX) to announce the novel's release, and the left-leaning *El País* ran in full the first chapter in two consecutive installments (García Márquez, "El general" 1–4 and 12–13). Upon its publication in Latin America, the book was caught in the middle of a heated controversy. Historians, politicians, and critics accused García Márquez of making deliberate historical errors and lamented that he had exalted the figure of Bolívar and denigrated that of his rival, Colombian General Santander. Other critics were outraged by the presentation of the *libertador* as "an everyday man," which was something that the Colombian critic for *Diario 16*, Dasso Saldívar, rather considered one of the novel's positive traits.[54] This was also the opinion of former Colombian president Belisario Betancur in a two-full-page essay published in *El País*. It is a book, he wrote, that "is going to enter history because [Bolívar] is a credible hero; and therefore, people are going to like it, even though it is painful."[55]

Although mainstream Spanish national media such as *Diario 16* and *El País* mentioned the controversy, this was not the way the book was received in Spain. Instead of debating its historical accuracy and ideological message, reviewers paid more attention to its aesthetic merits. Here again unanimity was almost the norm. Once more, the themes that had appeared in previous book coverage resurfaced: the immensely popular writer, the masterful novel, the connections to Spanish culture, and the shadow cast by *One Hundred Years*. Critic Conte wrote that García Márquez was "not just a writer: he is a living myth of the universal literature of our times."[56] As such, according to critic Fernando Valls, García Márquez had become a writer whom even those who "deal little with books" read, adding that this novel confirmed him as "one of the best [writers] of the century."[57] Journalist and writer Juan Cruz highlighted a potential connection with the poetry of García Lorca and noted, "like the characters of *One Hundred Years of Solitude*, the general in his labyrinth knows that there will never be a second opportunity on earth."[58] Some critics, however, started to show fatigue with his style. Writer Miguel García Posada lamented the author's "verbal 'pyrotechnics,'" which at times reminded him of García Lorca's poetry. He believed that the Colombian was a "master," but "literature is more than a verbal question." And he concluded, "García Márquez has become his own imitator."[59] Likewise, writer Laura Freixas said, "a good novel, that's all it is ... quality, by itself, does not sell."[60]

García Márquez's most "Spanish" work came out in 1992: *Doce cuentos peregrinos* (*Strange Pilgrims*). It included twelve short stories, several of which he had conceived while living in Barcelona in the late 1960s and early 1970s. The author, who had done no book presentations for decades, traveled to Spain, presenting the volume at the Universal Exposition of Seville during the day dedicated to Colombia. He was given a rock star's welcome. Since he was going to be there for just two hours, media reported that police forces had to intervene and monitor attendees, upon fears of an avalanche of anxious fans seeking autographs during the book signing ("García Márquez presentó" n.p.). In his review of the volume, the director of the Royal Spanish Academy, Fernando Lázaro Carreter, wrote that these were "splendid short stories," but also wanted to "forewarn those who run to this book with the merry illusion of finding the never-seen-before."[61] The stories were known already, he said. Some had been released by the same publisher less than a year before, he lamented.

In 1994, the covers of cultural supplements and coverage on radio and TV programs announced the publication of *Del amor y otros demonios* (*Of Love and Other Demons*). To *El País*, in an interview published just days before the book release, the author confessed, "with none of my books have I felt as insecure as with this novel."[62] Despite García Márquez's ties to Castro's Communist Cuba, conservative newspaper *ABC* dedicated the cover of its cultural supplement to him, posing with a *red* jacket and his new book. "All about the latest novel by the Colombian Nobel," read the cover caption. *ABC* also published four pages of excerpts, decorated with illustrations both in color and black and white, given "the book's journalistic, editorial, and literary interest" ("Del amor" 16). Released on World Book Day, this issue of the newspaper, which bragged about having had access to the entire book, claimed that it was going to be a commercial success. Months later, *ABC* asked fifteen male figures, mostly critics and writers, to vote for the best book of the year. The winner was *Of Love* ("Los mejores libros del año" 16–18). This new volume had managed to convince those disappointed by the previous one, such as Lázaro Carreter. He was critical but had to concede. In this novel, "a strange thing in García Márquez, the harmony is balanced with the plot. But its beauty is such for long stretches that it is almost impossible to deny this work the right to be part of the best written by the maestro."[63] *Of Love* reached the number one spot on the bestseller list for fiction during its second week on the market ("Libros más vendidos de la semana" 6).

Two years later, in a piece about García Márquez's writing "manias," the weekly *Interviú* announced three months in advance the release of his next book, the journalistic account *Noticia de un secuestro* (*News of a Kidnapping*, 1996) ("Nueva novela" 6). *Interviú* reported in June that the book, published in April with an initial print run of 150,000 copies (Mora, "He escrito" 1), had been a number one bestseller on the nonfiction list for several weeks ("Libros" 81; "Libros" 87). *El País* published the book's first chapter in its Sunday edition, just four days before its release (García Márquez, "Noticia" 1–4), and on January 4, 1996, *Diario 16* announced to its readers an exclusive interview with the writer about his new work. These and other readers were informed that it was not a novel but a reportage in response to the violent events in Colombia that occurred during the years of drug lord Pablo Escobar, who died in 1993. Readers learned from various media that, as García Márquez revealed, "it is the hardest and saddest book I have written."[64]

As early as four years before its publication, Spanish media started to announce the coming of the writer's memoir, *Vivir para contarla* (*Living to Tell the Tale*, 2002). *El País* published advance excerpts in 1998, 2001, and 2002 (García Márquez, "Relato" 1–4). It was a long-awaited book, on this occasion because it was known that the writer was recovering from lymphatic cancer. In Spain, Mondadori launched a first edition of 300,000 copies at 25.50 euros (Obiols 31; R. M. n.p.). As usual, national and regional print and TV media (now with their budding online and internet services) covered its publication. With the headline "Gabo Takes Stock of His Life," the Canarian newspaper *La Provincia-Diario de Las Palmas* announced the imminent release of the memoir on the cover of its cultural supplement.[65] This was also the mood among some reviewers. Journalist and economist Joaquín Estefanía (3) took the book as an opportunity to reflect on the presence of García Márquez in his life. Similarly, *El País* featured Carlos Fuentes's (2–3) essay, in which he recalled his discovery of García Márquez's works and their old friendship. Another one of his friends, critic and novelist Tomás Eloy Martínez, said "the book should have been called, *Living to Enjoy It*, because even the worst misfortunes of poverty, hunger and disease are narrated with invincible humor."[66] Others preferred to go back and rethink their own understanding of the author's works. The veteran García Márquez critic Masoliver Ródenas said that this memoir was "required reading" and also used his review as an opportunity to assess the writer's opus: "[I do not] share the almost unanimous enthusiasm for the García Márquez of *One Hundred Years of Solitude* . . . with each new reading, the magic fades away." For him, only *Shipwrecked Sailor*, *No One Writes*, and *Chronicle*, were "classic pieces."[67]

Two years after the memoir came out, Spanish readers had in their hands *Memoria de mis putas tristes* (*Memories of My Melancholy Whores*, 2004). This was, as the media announced, García Márquez's return to the novel after a ten-year lapse. Of the first edition of 400,000 copies, 255,000 were released in Spain for 17 euros (Pacheco Colín 33). As was customary, *El País* (García Márquez, "El año" 33) published an excerpt from the novel. Reviewers who for decades had helped shape the writer's reception among Spanish readers reviewed what became García Márquez's last published novel in his life. One of them was Masoliver Ródenas and the other was Rafael Conte, who called García Márquez "the most popular novelist—and one of the best—in the world." For him, this novel about love was "a great work."[68]

Unlike previous books, *Memories* was not met with overwhelming admiration and endorsement. *Babelia*, *El País*'s cultural supplement, ranked it among the best books of 2004, yet the description was unenthusiastic: "[T]he story itself does not progress, one misses a solid plot and the narrator's monologue becomes monotonous and predictable."[69] Nonetheless, even García Márquez's rivals had to acknowledge the writer's capacity to create linguistic fashion. In *El País*, writer Vargas Llosa used the title of the new book to write an opinion column against Castro's government, "Las 'putas tristes' de Fidel" ("Fidel's 'Melancholy Whores'"). Vargas Llosa charged that "intellectuals, politicians, or governments . . . agree to play the pitiful role of . . . 'melancholy whores'—to use a current term—of the Caribbean dictatorship."[70]

Memories was the last book finished and published by García Márquez. Yet some of his work in progress was also released in Spain before his death. In 2003, *El País* (García Márquez, "La noche" 1–3) premiered "La noche del eclipse" ("The Night of the Eclipse"), which was a chapter from his novel in progress at the time, *En agosto nos vemos* (*We'll See Each Other in August*). Three days after his passing, *La Vanguardia* (García Márquez, "En agosto" 1, 46–50) released as a world exclusive the first chapter from this novel, which he had left unfinished. Also incomplete was the awaited second volume of his memoirs, in which he was supposed to tell readers about, among other experiences, his years in Spain.

García Márquez as an Icon

Many Spaniards were to become acquainted with García Márquez not through his books, but rather via his regular appearances in newspapers and magazines and on TV and radio programs. For decades he was a kind of pop icon; toward the end of his life, he was regarded as a legendary figure. His statements on the most diverse topics made headlines in print and visual media. He was a writer praised by critics who also appeared in celebrity magazines such as *¡Hola!* ("Entrega" n.p.) and sensationalist publications such as *Playboy España* ("Entrevista" 15–26) and *Interviú*,[71] which, like its American counterpart, also featured semi-nude and nude photographs of women on its cover. In García Márquez's personal archives, one can find photos of him with major Spanish cultural and political figures like sovereigns Juan Carlos I and Felipe VI of Spain; prime ministers Felipe González, José Luis Rodríguez Zapatero, and Mariano Rajoy; politicians Javier Solana, Pasqual Maragall, and Alberto Ruiz-Gallardón; businessman Jesús de Polanco; and artists Raphael, Miguel Bosé, Luis Buñuel, Pedro Almodóvar, and Luis Eduardo Aute, among numerous others.

Arguably, a telling sign of the successful reception of García Márquez in Spain is that he was appropriated as a Spanish writer (Santana), including efforts to locate his ancestors in Galicia. In 1974, this region's leading newspaper, *La Voz de Galicia*, called him "our Colombian writer" and turned into a headline García Márquez's statement "my work is Galician," in clear reference to the influence of Galician culture on *One Hundred Years*. This newspaper highlighted that his maternal grandmother's family was from Galicia. The journalist noted that she not only had fed the little Gabo with Galician food, but also, speaking in an old Castilian Spanish, had "told him strange and mysterious stories" that shaped his literary imagination from early on. And when he was living in Spain from 1967 onward, he discovered that the "legends [in his works] were ours [from Galicia]."[72] Spain's appropriation of García Márquez increased over the decades. In the mid-1990s, Televisión Española introduced him to its hundreds of thousands of viewers at the beginning of an hour-long interview in this way: "Galician is his fascination with the supernatural, and Basque [is] the unconditional loyalty to his friends. Of the Andalusians he has the taste for exaggeration and embellishing words. And he reminds us of Castile in that wise way of seeing life."[73]

At first, media exposure of García Márquez was prompted by the success of *One Hundred Years*. As he stated in an interview, "What do I do with this fame? How can I not (I told myself) spend it on politics?"[74] And he began to do so from Spain. He arrived in Barcelona in 1967 and lived there until 1975 (Ayén). Months after his arrival, he started granting interviews in which, along with opinions about literary issues, he talked about politics between the lines, since he was living in a country with a dictatorship. In 1968, Miguel Fernández-Braso (35–38) interviewed him for the leading Francoist newspaper *Pueblo*, which portrayed him as a major exponent of Latin American literature and *One Hundred Years* as its best example. A year later, this interview appeared as a book entitled *La soledad de Gabriel García Márquez: Una conversación infinita* (Gabriel García Márquez's Solitude: An Infinite Conversation, 1969). Just a year after the release of *One Hundred Years*, the magazine *Índice* ("Gabriel García Márquez en *Índice*" 25) published a fourteen-page feature article, including an interview calling him "Lord of Macondo." General interest magazine *Meridiano* ("Un libro condensado" 130–44) published a series of excerpts from *One Hundred Years*, which was presented as a bestseller in Spain.

By 1970, he was being asked for opinions on issues beyond those of his books. Popular Catalan newspaper *Tele|eXpres* asked him what the future of literature would be in 1984; in that future year, the interviewer noted from the beginning, readers would continue to read *One Hundred Years*, *No One Writes*, and many other works of his. During the interview García Márquez said, "the book, as an object, is the most rudimentary and uncomfortable thing that humanity has invented" and predicted that "as long as there is a scared man, there will be poetry. And I have the impression, as things are going, that in 1984 men will be more scared than ever."[75]

As Spain was transitioning to democracy following Franco's death in 1975, old and new media welcomed the opinions of García Márquez, who had by now openly embraced revolutionary, leftist politics. One of his preferred outlets was the anti-Francoist magazine *Triunfo*. It interviewed him as early as 1970 and continued to do so for the rest of the decade, publicizing his political statements, such as "writing well is our revolutionary duty"[76] and "it is a crime not to have active political participation,"[77] and his reasons for writing a book about daily life in Cuba under the embargo. In another *Triunfo* interview, he warned that "the information war has begun" (Chao and Ramonet 36). This magazine also published his reportage endorsing Cuba's intervention in Angola against European and US imperialism, as well as other pieces of his political journalism up until 1979.[78]

In the 1980s, *El País* (founded in 1976) became the new medium that best channeled the socialist politics of García Márquez. Eventually this daily (thanks to its link to the Prisa and Santillana groups) became pivotal to the successful reception of García Márquez's works over the next four decades. The connection between the writer and the newspaper started early. In 1978, in a long interview with journalist Ángel S. Harguindey, García Márquez opened with a statement about his commitment to the cause of socialism in general and to the Cuban Revolution in particular, while attacking European intellectuals (especially the French) for abandoning the revolution and for acting as "cultural colonizers in relation to Latin America."[79] Starting in 1980 and on through 1984, *El País* published in its Sunday edition the writer's weekly column on many topics and with catchy titles: "Seamos machos: Hablemos del miedo al avión" ("Let's Be *machos*: Let's Talk about Fear of the Airplane"), "Cuento de horror para la Nochevieja" ("Horror Story for New Year's Eve"), and "Me alquilo para soñar" ("I Rent Myself Out for Dreaming"). It was an auspicious collaboration. In 1980, *El País* had become the country's leading newspaper, with a circulation of over 150,000 copies on weekdays and double that on Sundays. If his books were yet unknown to readers, this column helped turn him into a household name among new generations and increased his popularity among older ones.

Along with *El País*, Spanish media diligently reported not only the release of new works but also information concerning the life and initiatives of García Márquez. These media informed their readers, of course, about the quarrel between the writer and his friend Vargas Llosa, who had punched him in the face for reasons that Spaniards have argued about for years (de Bethencourt 43). In the 1980s, García Márquez collaborated with King Juan Carlos I of Spain in a campaign in favor of human rights.[80] (They met again several times until 2007.) The media covered his Nobel Prize for literature in 1982, which Spain's cultural and political establishment celebrated as if it had been awarded to a Spanish writer. The country's national television network dedicated several programs to the new Nobel laureate. One of them was a special twenty-five-minute interview in which, among other things, he expressed his admiration for the Spanish people, who had just elected Socialist politician Felipe González as prime minister ("Especial" 20:10). *La Vanguardia* dedicated a full cover to the laureate, too ("García Márquez, un Nobel" 1). Even the celebrity magazine *¡Hola!* joined in the celebration with three pages of coverage of the Nobel Prize ceremony, highlighting the fact that the writer had worn during the celebration a fashionable *liqui liqui*.

Until then, García Márquez had attracted people's attention in Spain mostly through his literary works. But now, with a Nobel Prize in his hands, his public statements and media coverage of his numerous conversations with world leaders made him a familiar name and face for millions of Spaniards. In particular in the 1980s, Spanish media punctually reported on his meetings with Fidel Castro, François Mitterrand, and Mikhail Gorbachev, among others. These three leaders expressed in public their admiration for *One Hundred Years*, and Gorbachev thanked García Márquez for the invitation to travel to Latin America (Bonet 1). Regarding Spanish politics, he repeatedly stated his commitment to Felipe González's vision of a socialist Spain after the latter governed the country from 1982 until 1996, when he lost the general election to Jose María Aznar, the country's new, conservative prime minister. "I'm a Felipista," the writer declared to *El País* and laughed at the fact that some were now calling his rival Vargas Llosa "the García Márquez of Aznar."[81]

As if García Márquez were a world leader, in the 1980s and 1990s, Spain's newspaper readers, radio listeners, and TV spectators publicized his statements, such as "I am a commercial writer";[82] "More than making money, what I want is to be read";[83] "Let them say whatever they want";[84] "I am obsessed with the idea of Spain becoming European";[85] and "I will never return to Spain."[86] The first and second statements date from 1981, during the release of *Chronicle*, and from 1996, during the publication of *News*. The third statement was in reference to accusations against him about his political initiatives, after writers Jorge Edwards and Octavio Paz called him "a great novelist, but a mediocre politician" and "an apologist for tyrants," respectively.[87] He made the fourth and fifth statements to complain that Spain was mistreating Latin Americans as a strategy to prove its strong desire to fully integrate into the European Union. By 1992, its integration would entail citizens from other Spanish-speaking nations would need a visa in order to visit Spain. García Márquez highlighted that this was a paradox, as the quincentennial of Columbus's discovery of the Americas was approaching, and "we [Latin Americans] need a visa to go celebrate it" in Spain (García Márquez, "No volveré" n.p.). Of course, he was thankful to Spain and expressed his gratitude several times. Not only did he take pride in the fact that some of the most important people in his literary education were Spaniards who had gone into exile after the coup d'état against the Second Republic and that he was a "Spanish republican," but he also enjoyed the Spanish way of life. "Still now they ask me," he said in an interview in 1995, "What are you coming to do in Spain? As always, to 'fight' with my Spanish friends, because together we kick up a tremendous 'ruckus' and have tremendous pig-outs, and one lives in a permanent volcanic eruption."[88]

An area that deserves further research is García Márquez's long and fruitful relationship with Spain's cultural establishment (Ayén; Martin; Santana-Acuña, *Ascent*). Leading artists such as Imanol Arias, Pilar Bardem, José Sacristán, Javier Bardem, Ana Belén, and Carlos Saura have performed or adapted his works.[89] He also engaged in famous controversies with this establishment, especially with the Royal Spanish Academy. In one of his numerous public statements, he accused the academy of being at "war with the Spanish language": "[Academicians] have the language imprisoned . . . they don't let it flow [like] living languages do."[90] On two occasions, in 1994 and 1997, he declined the highest honor proposed by the academy's plenary: the Cervantes Prize for lifetime literary achievement. He argued that, after being awarded the Nobel, he could accept no other literary honors. He clashed with some academy members in 1997, when, during the first Congreso Internacional de la Lengua Española, he gave the controversial address "Jubilemos la ortografía" ("Let's Retire Spelling"), calling for a radical simplification of spelling norms, which disagreed with what the academy had intended.

Yet this and other controversies were forgotten by 2007, when the academy published its own edition of *One Hundred Years*, whose text García Márquez revised in full for this special occasion, including the addition of small changes. Spain's most watched television newscast, Telediario, reported to its millions of viewers that the printing of this edition involved "Macondian figures . . . magical realism": "500,000 copies . . . 350 tons of paper, 30 tons of cardboard, 1,000 kilos of ink [and] 1,000 of glue" (Telediario 1:49–2:00). The same year, García Márquez was the major star of the fourth Congreso Internacional de la Lengua Española in Cartagena, Colombia, attended by the king and queen of Spain and politicians, artists, and scholars from all over the world. Attendees celebrated the writer's eightieth birthday, the sixtieth anniversary of the publication of his first short story, the fortieth anniversary of *One Hundred Years*, and the twentieth-fifth anniversary of his Nobel Prize. This and other homages, such as the one organized by PEN America in New York in 2003, were dutifully covered by print, visual, and digital media in Spain.

In 2009, the news that he could no longer write brought about deep sadness to numerous fans in Spain, which was only surpassed by the news of his death in 2014. His face occupied most of the cover of the national newspapers *ABC*, *El País*, *El Periódico de Catalunya*, and *La Razón*. His passing was also reported on the covers of regional and local newspapers. And it was one of the day's major stories on radio and TV newscasts. Among the headlines were "Goodbye to Gabo," "The Genius of World Literature," "A Universal Narrator Is Dead," "Macondo Cries," "The Master of Magical Realism Dies," "Magic Loses Gabo," "Goodbye to a Genius of Literature," "We Have Macondo Left," and "Gabo Leaves Us All by Ourselves."[91] And these headlines were followed for more than a week on news media, radio, and TV programs as well as social media by an avalanche of columns, testimonies, and messages across the political and cultural spectrum. Gone was the person who had become a writer with the help of Spanish expatriates, who had found in Spain's literature the inspiration for several of his major works, who had lived in Spain during a key historical moment, and who had had in Spain his largest number of readers in the Spanish language. More than seven years after his death, García Márquez's figure and works continue to enjoy extraordinary popularity and wide circulation in Spain.

Notes

1. "Recuerdo muy bien" and "hablaba un castellano extraordinario, lleno de arcaísmos, de imágenes deslumbrantes, que ha sido el punto de partida mío para escribir . . . yo crecí con esas palabras . . . como si fuera la lengua natural de la gente, que era la que ella hablaba . . . con ese idioma escribo yo mis libros" ("Especial dedicado" 9:20–9:58).
2. "Desde las primeras letras . . . mis profesores, mis amigos en Colombia y luego en México eran republicanos españoles" (Harguindey VI).
3. "Conocía muy bien la historia de la Guerra Civil [y] muy bien la literatura española," "los campos de Azorín . . . los campos de Machado," and "esos ríos con los chopos en sus orillas" (Navarro 4:39–5:19).
4. "Era ya completamente republicano español" (Navarro 4:29).
5. "Llegué como si hubiese vivido ahí mucho tiempo . . . y luego encontré que esas afinidades que tenía yo con mis maestros españoles, con los amigos españoles, con el carnicero español, con el pescador español, con el herrero español, con el zapatero español, entre los cuales nos criamos, seguían existiendo allá [en España]" (Navarro 6:54–7:16).
6. "Me advirtió . . . que nadie me creería esa historia si la ubicaba en Barranquilla. Además, me reprochó diciéndome que era un nombre antiliterario" (García Márquez quoted in Santana-Acuña, *Ascent* 57).
7. For references to Spanish culture in his early journalism, see, for example, García Márquez, *Textos costeños*: "Anteayer puso París" (June 1948), "Nada hay más difícil" (June 1948), "El derecho a volverse loco" (Jan. 1950), "La orfandad de Tarzán" (Mar. 1950), "Mientras duermen los capitalistas" (May 1950), "Ilia en Londres" (July 1950), "Sexto relato del viajero imaginario" (Feb. 1951), "Décimo relato: teatro parroquial" (Mar. 1951), "Un poeta en la

ciudad" (June 1952), "Misterios de la novela policíaca" (Aug. 1952), "Los piratas se volvieron locos" (Aug. 1952), "Elegía" (Sept. 1952).
8. "Como lo quiso Cervantes" (García Márquez, Letter to Mendoza, [Dec. 1964], 4).
9. "La mejor forma de contar todas estas locuras es asumiendo el mismo estilo de los narradores españoles de los relatos de caballería" (José Font Castro, quoted in Santana-Acuña, *Ascent* 133).
10. "Es uno de los grandes documentos literarios de América, obligante a la admiración no solo por las dosis de exotismo que contenga, sino en razón de su sabiduría literaria," and "tiene... mucho oro dentro de su maravillosa estructura" (Baquero 113).
11. "En el futuro todos los escritores latinoamericanos seremos tratados como mayores de edad por los editores españoles" (García Márquez, Declaración del escritor 1).
12. "Como novela, muy buena." Censorship file on *One Hundred Years*, Archivo General de la Administración, sig. 66/02529, exp. 1184, p. 1.
13. "Dado el éxito alcanzado por la obra de GABRIEL GARCÍA MÁRQUEZ, 'Cien años de soledad'"; "la premura con que nuestros clientes nos solicitan más ejemplares de la misma"; and "pide que se imprima una nueva impresión en España." Quotations in letters from EDHASA to Censorship Office, 29 Jan., 29 Apr., and 25 Nov. 1969, Archivo General de la Administración, sig. 66/02529, exp. 1184, sig. 66/03060, exp. 4946, and sig. 66/03638, exp. 11838.
14. "La actual vitalidad de la narrativa latinoamericana" (Gimferrer, "Sobre" 125) and "una de las cumbres actuales de la narrativa latinoamericana" (Conte, "La soledad" 14).
15. Examples of the reception of *One Hundred Years* in García Márquez, Scrapbooks and papers, Harry Ransom Center, MS-5353, osb. 7 and osb. 13.
16. "El mejor libro que he leído en estos últimos años" ("Repaso" 14).
17. "NO ME MOLESTEN. ESTOY EN MACONDO" (capitals in original).
18. "Cómo un hombre puede crear un mundo y millares de hombres y mujeres –los lectores– hablar de ese mundo durante horas" ("Repaso" 13).
19. "Con García Márquez la novela vuelve a ser novela: con sus seres humanos, su ambiente, su argumento, su maravilloso lenguaje, su increíble claridad" (Llorca 14).
20. "Retorno a la narrativa de la imaginación" (Gimferrer, "Sobre" 125).
21. "Una hazaña narrativa" (Maisterra 16), "un purificador atmosférico" (Izquierdo 14), and "una narración monda y lironda" (Pérez Minik 3).
22. "Auténtica obra maestra" and "*narra*" (Amorós, "*Cien años*" 58; emphasis in original).
23. "Irrealidad" and "el surrealismo opera con hechos reales" (Campos, quoted in Santana-Acuña, *Ascent* 166).
24. "Se confunden fantasía y realidad" (Santos 23) and "un caso curioso de realismo mítico" (Goytisolo, quoted in Tola de Habich and Grieve 125).
25. "[Un libro] anacrónico, atendiendo a su estructura y contenido" (de Torre 3).
26. "Muchos novelistas españoles podrían alcanzar triunfos así de no sentirse encogidos por hallarse incluidos en la fe de la novela tradicional o dándole vueltas a la manera por haber elegido el camino de ruptura" (Santos 23).
27. "Conozco a escritores que han dejado de escribir" ("Nacimiento de Macondo" 3).
28. "Libro esperado con afán, pues se asegura que constituirá, asimismo, uno de los pilares de la nueva América" (Perés, quoted in Santana-Acuña, *Ascent* 215).
29. "Repugnante... libro soez" and "texto obligatorio a muchachos de 16 años, a los que literalmente corrompe y embrutece" (Vernet Mateu 1).

30. Santana-Acuña (*Ascent* 47). See also Letter from Círculo de lectores to Ministry of Information and Tourism, 12 Mar. 1971, Archivo General de la Administración, sig. 73/00681, exp. 2632.
31. "No sé por cuanto tiempo: no solo Cien años, sino mis otros libros, ocupan los primeros renglones de venta en España desde hace tres meses" (García Márquez, Letter to Mendoza, 28 Oct. 1968, 4).
32. See, for example, Archivo General de la Administración, sig. 66/03060, exp. 4945.
33. "Famoso ya en toda Iberoamérica y profusamente traducido" (Conte, "García" n.p.).
34. "Alarmantemente convertido en 'escritor de moda'" ("García Márquez, Gabriel: 'La hojarasca'" 63).
35. For these and other examples of praise, see García Márquez, Scrapbooks and papers, Harry Ransom Center, MS-5353, osb. 13.
36. "El lector no se encontrará con el realismo mágico de *Cien años de soledad*" and "es una joya de la literatura y el periodismo" (Badosa 14).
37. "Ya no estamos en Macondo" and "es, de algún modo, el propio escritor" (Masoliver Ródenas, "*Relato*" 59).
38. See García Márquez, Scrapbooks and papers, Harry Ransom Center, MS-5353, osb. 13.
39. "Barroquismo idiomático" (Gironella 8).
40. "No lo he leído porque perdí la vista en 1955" and "la literatura está pasando por una etapa comercial muy desagradable. . . . Los libros que se venden mucho nadie piensa que sean buenos. Es todo una cuestión de moda, una especie de manía de leer lo que los demás leen" (Borges, quoted in Santana-Acuña, *Ascent* 178).
41. "Integrador y adaptador, más que innovador" (Marco, " La imaginación" 52).
42. "La prosa narrativa ha sido transformada en prosa artística" (Marco, "Mito" 53).
43. "La grandeza y la imposibilidad de la tentativa de García Márquez" (Madrigal 72).
44. "La ternura sentimental de Ramón Gómez de la Serna" and "un proyecto titánico" (Quiñonero 8–9).
45. "Otro golpe a lo mismo . . . el autor volvía, en fin a lo de siempre" (Martín Gaite 82).
46. "Enorme escritor hispanoamericano" (Calomarde I).
47. "Una obra menor, [no es] una obra de arte" (Blanco Vila 43).
48. "Un dominio absoluto . . . de la forma narrativa" (Suñén, "Amor" 5).
49. "Las obras maestras, las de García Márquez, han sido o serán otra cosa" (Catelli 44).
50. "Una de las mejores novelas del siglo escritas en lengua castellana" (García Nieto 1).
51. "¿Cómo no darse cuenta a cada página de que se está ante uno de los grandes clásicos vivos de la lengua?" (Monsiváis I).
52. "Texto denso, demasiado perfumado" (Monroy 22).
53. Contract between Latimer, S. A. and Mondadori, 23 Feb. 1989, Harry Ransom Center, MS-5353, cont. 66. See also Sorela 38.
54. "Un hombre cotidiano" (Saldívar 1).
55. "Va a entrar a la historia porque [Bolívar] es un héroe creíble; y, por tanto, le va a gustar a la gente, a pesar de que sea doloroso" (Betancur 44).
56. "Ya no tan solo un escritor: es un mito viviente de la literatura universal de nuestro tiempo" (Conte, "El sueño" 13).
57. "Poco trato con los libros" and "uno de los mejores [escritores] del siglo" (Valls 37, 39).
58. "Como los personajes de *Cien años de soledad*, el general en su laberinto sabe que nunca habrá una segunda oportunidad sobre la tierra" (Cruz 14).

59. "'Pirotecnia' verbal" and "García Márquez se ha convertido en su propio imitador" (García Posada III).
60. "Una buena novela 'a secas' . . . la calidad, por si sola, no vende" (Freixas 37).
61. "Espléndidos relatos" and "prevenir a quienes corran hacia este libro con la ilusión alborozada de encontrar lo nunca visto" (Lázaro Carreter, "Doce" 7).
62. "Con ninguno de mis libros me he sentido tan inseguro como con esta novela" (Mora, "La nueva" n.p.).
63. "Cosa extraña en García Márquez, la armonía se equilibra con el argumento. Pero es tanta su hermosura en largos trechos que resulta casi imposible negarle el derecho a alinearse entre lo mejor del maestro" (Lázaro Carreter, "Del amor" 7).
64. "Es el libro más duro y triste que he escrito" (Mora. "He escrito" 1).
65. "Gabo hace balance" ("Gabo" 1).
66. "El libro debería haberse llamado, *Vivir para gozarla*, porque hasta los peores infortunios de la miseria, el hambre y las enfermedades están narrados con un humor invencible" (Martínez 4).
67. "Lectura obligada," "no comparto el entusiasmo casi unánime por el García Márquez de 'Cien años de soledad' . . . a cada nueva lectura, la magia se va desvaneciendo," and "piezas clásicas" (Masoliver Ródenas, "García Márquez" 6).
68. "El novelista más popular—y uno de los mejores—del mundo" and "una gran Obra" (Conte, "Paso" 9).
69. "La historia misma no progresa, se extraña un argumento sólido y el monólogo del narrador se vuelve monótono y predecible" ("Los mejores libros de 2004" 3).
70. "Intelectuales, políticos o Gobiernos . . . acepten jugar el lastimoso papel de . . . 'putas tristes'—para emplear un término de actualidad—de la dictadura caribeña" (Vargas Llosa 19).
71. See, for example, *Interviú*'s early coverage of García Márquez: "Festival de Cine de Moscú," no. 174, 13–19 Sept. 1979; "El escritor García Márquez nos explica su huida de Colombia," no. 256, 9–15 Apr. 1981; "Exclusiva mundial: Gabito jamás se emborrachará de fama," no. 337, 27 Oct.–2 Nov. 1982; and "Exclusiva mundial: García Márquez habla por primera vez tras el Nobel," no. 346, 29 Dec.–4 Jan. 1982.
72. "Nuestro escritor colombiano," "mi obra es gallega," "le contaba historias extrañas y misteriosas," and "sus leyendas eran nuestras" (Chao 25).
73. "Gallega es su fascinación por lo sobrenatural, y vasca la lealtad incondicional por los amigos. De los andaluces tiene el gusto por la exageración y el adorno en la palabra. Y recuerda a Castilla en esa manera sabia de ver la vida" (Navarro 2:20–2:39).
74. "¿Qué hago con esta fama? ¿Cómo no (me dije) me la gasto en política?" (Márquez 46).
75. "El libro, como objeto es lo más rudimentario e incómodo que ha inventado la humanidad" and "mientras haya un hombre asustado, habrá poesía. Y tengo la impresión, como van las cosas, que en 1984 los hombres estarán más asustados que nunca" ("1984: Un análisis" 4).
76. "Escribir bien es deber revolucionario nuestro" (Gilio 44–45).
77. "Es un crimen no tener participación política activa" (Márquez 46).
78. For García Márquez pieces in *Triunfo*, see "Operación Carlota" (1), no. 730, 22 Jan. 1977, pp. 19–23; "Operación Carlota" (2), no. 731, 29 Jan. 1977, pp. 27–31; "La CIA en América Latina," no. 640, 4 Jan. 1975, pp. 11–12; "Los cubanos frente al bloqueo," no. 831, 30 Dec. 1978, pp. 29–31; and "Vietnam por dentro," no. 883, 29 Dec. 1979, pp. 45–54.
79. "Colonos culturales en relación con América Latina" (Harguindey VI).

80. Meeting with Juan Carlos I of Spain, in García Márquez, Scrapbooks and papers, Harry Ransom Center, cont. 64.1 and osb. 10.
81. "El García Márquez de Aznar" (Mora, "He escrito" 1, 32).
82. "Soy un escritor comercial" (Falowell VI).
83. "Más que ganar dinero, lo que quiero es que me lean" (Mora, "He escrito" 32).
84. "Que digan lo que quieran . . . " (García Márquez, "Que digan" 1).
85. "Me obsesiona la idea de que España se vuelva europea" (García Márquez, "Me obsesiona" 22–23).
86. "No volveré nunca a España" (García Márquez, "No volveré" n.p.).
87. "Gran novelista, pero mediocre político" and "apologista de tiranos" (García Márquez, "Que digan" 19).
88. "Todavía ahora me preguntan, ¿qué viene a hacer a España? Como siempre a pelear con mis amigos españoles porque armamos unas broncas tremendas y unas comilonas tremendas y vive uno en permanente erupción volcánica" (Navarro 7:15–7:30).
89. See, for example, García Márquez, Scrapbooks and papers, Harry Ransom Center, cont. 54.2.
90. "Guerra en contra del castellano" and "ellos tienen preso el idioma . . . no lo dejan que fluya [como] los idiomas vivos" (Navarro 8:30–9:25).
91. Main lines on covers for 18–19 Apr. 2014: "Adiós a Gabo" (*El Heraldo de Aragón*), "El genio de la literatura universal" (*El País*), "Muere el narrador universal" (*ABC*), "Llora Macondo" (*El Correo*), "Muere el maestro del realismo mágico" (*La Voz de Galicia*), "La magia pierde a Gabo" (*El Mundo*), "Adiós a un genio de la literatura" (*Canarias 7*), "Nos queda Macondo" (*El Periódico de Catalunya*), and "Gabo nos deja solos" (*La Razón*).

Works Cited

Primary Sources

Balcells, Carmen. Letter to García Márquez, 5 May 1987. Harry Ransom Center, MS-5353, cont. 66.9.

Censorship files, *One Hundred Years of Solitude* (1969–1976), Ministry of Information, Archivo General de la Administración (Spain), sig. 66/02529, exp. 1184; sig. 66/03060, exp. 4945; sig. 66/03060, exp. 4946; sig. 66/03638, exp. 11838; sig. 73/00681, exp. 2632; sig. 73/02026, exp. 6990; sig. 73/04801, exp. 4717; sig. 73/04878, exp. 6660; sig. 73/05017, exp. 9674; sig. 73/05253, exp. 209; sig. 73/05484, exp. 5469.

García Márquez, Gabriel. "En agosto nos vemos." *La Vanguardia*, 20 Apr. 2014, pp. 1, 46–50.

García Márquez, Gabriel. "El año de mis noventa años." *El País*, 20 Oct. 2004, p. 33.

García Márquez, Gabriel. Book contracts. Harry Ransom Center, MS-5353, cont. 66.

García Márquez, Gabriel. Declaración del escritor colombiano Gabriel García Márquez en relación con las adulteraciones que una editorial española hizo a su novela "La mala hora," 13 June 1963. Harry Ransom Center, MS-5353, osb. 6.

García Márquez, Gabriel. "El general en su laberinto." *Domingo*, supplement of *El País*, 5 Mar., pp. 1–4, and *El País*, 6 Mar., pp. 12–13.

García Márquez, Gabriel. Letter to Plinio Apuleyo Mendoza, 14 June [1963]. Harry Ransom Center, MS-5367.

García Márquez, Gabriel. Letter to Plinio Apuleyo Mendoza, [Dec. 1964]. Harry Ransom Center, MS-5367.

García Márquez, Gabriel. Letter to Plinio Apuleyo Mendoza, 28 Oct. 1968. Harry Ransom Center, MS-5367.
García Márquez, Gabriel. "Me obsesiona la idea de que España se vuelva europea." *El País*, 2 Sept. 1990, pp. 1, 22–23.
García Márquez, Gabriel. "La noche del eclipse." *El País*, 25 May 2003, pp. 1–3.
García Márquez, Gabriel. "Noticia de un secuestro." *Domingo*, supplement of *El País*, 12 May 1996, pp. 1–4.
García Márquez, Gabriel. "No volveré nunca a España." *Excelsior* (Mexico), 28 Mar. 1989.
García Márquez, Gabriel. "Que digan lo que quieran." *Diario 16*, 1 Sept. 1990, pp. 1, 19.
García Márquez, Gabriel. "Relato de un náufrago." *Domingo*, supplement of *El País*, 6 Oct. 2002, pp. 1–4.
García Márquez, Gabriel. Scrapbooks and papers. Harry Ransom Center, MS-5353. Containers 52.4, 52.5, 53.2, 53.3, 54.2, 64.1, 66 and oversize boxes 5, 6, 7, 9, 10, 12, 13.
García Márquez, Gabriel. *Textos costeños*. Penguin Random House, 2015.
García Márquez, Gabriel. *Vivir para contarla*. Mondadori, 2002.
Vernet Mateu, José. Letter to Ministry of Information and Tourism, 24 Sept. 1973. Archivo General de la Administración, sig. 73/2026, exp. 6990.

Secondary Sources

"1984: Un análisis del futuro. Literatura; Opina Gabriel García Márquez." *Tele|eXpres*, 20 July 1970, p. 4.
"Amor en tiempos de cólera." *ABC*, 20 Dec. 1985, p. 107.
Amorós, Andrés. "El arte de contar." *Sábado Cultural*, supplement of *ABC*, 9 May 1981, p. IV.
Amorós, Andrés. "*Cien años de soledad*." *Revista de Occidente*, no. 70, Jan. 1969, pp. 58–62.
Arroyo, Francesc. "Editorial Bruguera publicará en España la última novela de Gabriel García Márquez." *El País*, 24 Oct. 1985, p. 27.
Ayén, Xavi. *Aquellos años del Boom: García Márquez, Vargas Llosa y el grupo de amigos que lo cambiaron todo*. RBA, 2014.
Badosa, Enrique. "Un 'marginal' de García Márquez." *El Noticiero Universal*, 1 July 1970, p. 14.
Baquero, Gastón. *Escritores hispanoamericanos de hoy*. Instituto de Cultura Hispánica, 1961.
Benet, Juan. "De Canudos a Macondo." *Revista de Occidente*, no. 70, Jan. 1969, pp. 49–57.
Betancur, Belisario. "García Márquez en el laberinto del general." *El País*, 10 Mar. 1989, pp. 44–45.
Blanco Vila, Luis. "Crónica de un éxito anunciado." *Ya*, 8 May 1981, p. 43.
Bonet, Pilar. "García Márquez pide a Mijail Gorbachov que viaje a Latinoamérica." *El País*, 17 July 1987, p. 1.
"Bruguera a recuperarse con lo último de García Márquez." *Cinco Días*, 17 Dec. 1985.
Calomarde, Joaquín. "G. Márquez: Crónica de una muerte anunciada." *Artes y Letras*, supplement of *Las Provincias*, 7 May 1981, p. I.
Camacho Delgado, José Manuel. *Césares, tiranos y santos en* El otoño del patriarca: *La falsa biografía del guerrero*. Diputación Provincial de Sevilla, 1997.
"Las caras de la noticia." *ABC*, 18 Dec. 1985, p. 13.
Catelli, Nora. "El último García Márquez." *La Vanguardia*, 19 Dec. 1985, p. 44.
Ceberio, Jesús. "García Márquez: 'Crónica de una muerte anunciada' es mi mejor novela." *El País*, 1 May 1981, p. 29.

Cervantes, Francisco. "*Cien años de soledad*." *Papeles de Son Armadans*, no. 166, Jan. 1970, p. 327.

Chao, Ramón. "García Márquez: 'Mi obra es gallega.'" *La Voz de Galicia*, 24 Jan. 1974, p. 25.

Chao, Ramón, and Ignacio Ramonet. "La guerra de la información ha comenzado." *Triunfo*, no. 874, 27 Oct. 1979, pp. 36–40.

Conte, Rafael. "Gabriel García Márquez publica su novela 'Crónica de una muerte anunciada.'" *El País*, 22 Jan. 1981.

Conte, Rafael. "García Márquez o las fuentes de la violencia." *Informaciones* [1968]. García Márquez, Scrapbooks and papers, Harry Ransom Center, MS-5353, osb. 13.

Conte, Rafael. "Paso frente al amor y la muerte." *Babelia*, supplement of *El País*, 23 Oct. 2004, p. 9.

Conte, Rafael. "La soledad de Gabriel García Márquez." *Informaciones*, 14 Oct. 1967, p. 14.

Conte, Rafael. "El sueño de Simón Bolívar." *Domingo*, supplement of *El País*, 19 Mar. 1989, p. 13.

Cruz, Juan. "El prestigio del tiempo." *Domingo*, supplement of *El País*, 19 Mar. 1989, p. 14.

de Bethencourt, Gonzalo. "El 'caso Vargas Llosa-García Márquez': Una bofetada política." *Pueblo*, 16 Feb. 1976, p. 43.

de Torre, Guillermo. "Anverso y reverso de la novela hispanoamericana." *ABC*, 11 Sept. 1969, p. 3.

"'Del amor y otros demonios': El último García Márquez." *ABC Literario*, supplement of *ABC*, 8 Apr. 1994, pp. 16–19.

Díaz-Plaja, Guillermo. "*Cien años de soledad*, de Gabriel García Márquez." *ABC*, 18 July 1968, p. 22.

"En lengua castellana y desde 1939: Las diez novelas 10." *Disidencias*, supplement of *Diario 16* no. 175, 6 May 1984, pp. I–VIII.

"Entrega de los Premios Nobel por los soberanos suecos." *¡Hola!*, no. 2000, 25 Dec. 1982.

"Entrevista con Gabriel García Márquez." *Playboy España*, no. 51, Feb. 1983, pp. 15–26.

"El escritor García Márquez nos explica su huida de Colombia." *Interviú*, no. 256, 9–15 Apr. 1981.

"Especial dedicado a Gabriel García Márquez." Radio Televisión Española, 1982, www.rtve.es/alacarta/videos/escritores-en-el-archivo-de-rtve/especial-dedicado-gabriel-garcia-marquez-1982/353148/. Accessed 13 May 2021.

Estefanía, Joaquín. "El mejor oficio del mundo (todavía)." *Babelia*, supplement of *El País*, 12 Oct. 2002, p. 3.

"Exclusiva mundial: Gabito jamás se emborrachará de fama." *Interviú*, no. 337, 27 Oct.–2 Nov. 1982, pp. 100–103.

"Exclusiva mundial: García Márquez habla por primera vez tras el Nobel." *Interviú*, no. 346, 29 Dec.–4 Jan. 1982.

Falowell, Duncan. "Soy un escritor comercial." *Disidencias*, supplement of *Diario 16*, no. 175, 6 May 1984, pp. VI–VIII.

Fernández-Braso, Miguel. "3 horas de compañía infinita. Gabriel García Márquez." *Pueblo*, 30 Oct. 1968, pp. 35–38.

"Festival de Cine de Moscú." *Interviú*, no. 174, 13–19 Sept. 1979.

Freixas, Laura. "Una buena novela." *La Vanguardia*, 31 Mar. 1989, p. 37.

Fuentes, Carlos. "Gabo: Memorias de la memoria." *Babelia*, supplement of *El País*, 12 Oct. 2002, pp. 2–3.

"Gabo hace balance." *Cultura*, supplement of *La Provincia-Diario de las Palmas*, 7 Nov. 2002, p. 1.

"Gabriel García Márquez, color, olor, sabor." *Ya*, 22 Dec. 1985, p. 7.

"Gabriel García Márquez en *Índice*." *Índice*, no. 237, May 1968, pp. 23–37.
"García Márquez, Gabriel: 'La hojarasca.'" *ABC*, 4 Dec. 1969, p. 63.
"García Márquez presentó en la Expo sus 'Doce cuentos peregrinos.'" *El País*, 31 July 1992.
"García Márquez, un Nobel joven para Iberoámerica." *La Vanguardia*, 22 Oct. 1982, p. 1.
García Nieto, José. "El amor en los tiempos del cólera." *Sábado Cultural*, supplement of *ABC*, 21 Dec. 1985, p. 1.
García Posada, Miguel. "El general en su laberinto." *ABC Literario*, supplement of *ABC*, 18 March 1989, p. III.
García Ramos, Juan-Manuel. *Una teoría de la lectura: Cien años de soledad*. Universidad de La Laguna, 2016.
García Usta, Jorge. *Cómo aprendió a escribir García Márquez*. Lealón, 1995.
Gilio, María Esther. "García Márquez: Escribir bien es deber revolucionario nuestro." *Triunfo*, no. 752, 25 Jun. 1977, pp. 44–45.
Gimferrer, Pere. "García Márquez y *El otoño del patriarca*." *Destino*, 14 June 1975, pp. 40–41.
Gimferrer, Pere. "Sobre *Cien años de soledad*." *Destino*, 14 Oct. 1967, p. 125.
Gironella, José María. "Viaje en torno al mundo literario español." *Los Domingos de ABC*, supplement of *ABC*, 22 Feb. 1970, pp. 8–13.
Gómez-Santos, Marino. "24 horas de Carmen Laforet." *ABC*, 14 July 1968, pp. 122–23.
Goñi, Javier. "Del amor y otras soledades." *Cambio 16*, no. 740, 3 Feb. 1986, p. 100.
Guelbenzu, José María. "Literatura, una insoportable soledad." *Cuadernos para el diálogo*, extraordinario, no. 6–7, Feb. 1968, pp. 47–50.
Harguindey, Ángel S. "Franco tuvo una muerte que hubiera sido irreal en literatura." *Arte y pensamiento*, supplement of *El País*, 2 Apr. 1978, pp. I, VI–VII.
Ibarz, Joaquim. "Cartagena de Indias en fiesta por la nueva novela de García Márquez." *La Vanguardia*, 3 Dec. 1985, p. 53.
Iparraguirre, Enrique. "Juan Manuel Serrat." *ABC*, 1 June 1969, pp. 135–37.
Izquierdo, Luis. "El universo de Macondo: *Cien años de soledad*, de Gabriel García Márquez." *El Ciervo*, no. 179, 1969, p. 14.
Landín Carrasco, Amancio. "Cuadernos de la romana." *ABC*, 7 Sept. 1976, p. 15.
Lázaro Carreter, Fernando. "Del amor y otros demonios." *ABC Literario*, supplement of *ABC*, 15 Apr. 1994, p. 7.
Lázaro Carreter, Fernando. "Doce cuentos peregrinos." *ABC Literario*, supplement of *ABC*, 31 July 1992, p. 7.
"Un libro condensado: *Cien años de soledad* de García Márquez." *Meridiano*, Mar. 1969, pp. 130–44.
"Libros." *Diario 16*, 12 Jan. 1986, p. XII.
"Libros más vendidos." *Interviú*, 17 June 1996, p. 81.
"Libros más vendidos." *Interviú*, 24 June 1996, p. 87.
"Libros más vendidos de la semana." *ABC Literario*, supplement of *ABC*, 6 May 1994, p. 6.
"Los libros más vendidos de la semana." *Disidencias*, supplement of *Diario 16*, 7 May 1981.
Llorca, Carmen. "Las novelas de García Márquez." *Diario SP*, no. 165, 20 Mar. 1968, p. 14.
Madrigal, Luis Íñigo. "García Márquez: Una reflexión sobre el poder." *Triunfo*, no. 662, 7 June 1975, p. 72.
Maisterra, Pascual. "*Cien años de soledad*: Un regalo fabuloso de Gabriel García Márquez." *Tele|eXpres*, 28 Nov. 1968, pp. 16–17.
Marco, Joaquín. "'Crónica de una muerte anunciada', la extraordinaria novela de Gabriel García Márquez." *La Vanguardia*, 14 May 1981, p. 41.

Marco, Joaquín. "Gabriel García Márquez: Un joven maestro de la literatura colombiana." *Destino*, 14 Oct. 1967, pp. 124–25.

Marco, Joaquín. "García Márquez presenta su paseo romántico por el amor y la muerte." *El Periódico de Cataluña*, 28 Dec. 1985, p. 27.

Marco, Joaquín. "La imaginación desbordante: Los últimos cuentos de Gabriel García Márquez." *La Vanguardia Española*, 22 June 1972, p. 52.

Marco, Joaquín. "Mito y poder: *El otoño del patriarca*, de Gabriel García Márquez." *La Vanguardia Española*, 19 June 1975, p. 53.

Marco, Joaquín, and Jordi Gracia García, editors. *La llegada de los bárbaros: La recepción de la narrativa hispanoamericana en España, 1960–1981*. Edhasa, 2004.

Márquez, Bernardo. "García Márquez: 'Es un crimen no tener participación política activa.'" *Triunfo*, no. 708, 21 Aug. 1976, pp. 44–46.

Martin, Gerald. *Gabriel García Márquez: A Life*. Alfred A. Knopf, 2009.

Martín Gaite, Carmen. "Un libro y un autor: *El otoño del patriarca* o la identidad irrecuperable." *Revista de Occidente*, no. 2, Dec. 1975, pp. 82–83.

Martínez, Tomás Eloy. "La imagen ante un espejo." *Babelia*, supplement of *El País*, 12 Oct. 2002, p. 4.

Martínez Ruiz, Florentino. "García Márquez: Crónica de un éxito anunciado." *ABC*, 3 May 1981, p. 47.

Masoliver Ródenas, Juan Antonio. "García Márquez: Años de formación." *La Vanguardia*, 9 Oct. 2002, pp. 6–7.

Masoliver Ródenas, Juan Antonio. "*Relato de un náufrago*, por Gabriel García Márquez." *La Vanguardia Española*, 5 Nov. 1970, p. 59.

"Los mejores libros de 2004." *El País*, 31 Dec. 2004, pp. 1–3.

"Los mejores libros del año." *ABC Literario*, supplement of *ABC*, 30 Dec. 1994, pp. 16–18.

Monroy, Adrián. "Una historia de amor y de muerte." *La Gaceta del Libro*, Jan. 1986, p. 22.

Monsiváis, Carlos. "García Márquez, al margen del Nobel." *Culturas*, supplement of *Diario 16*, 29 Dec. 1985, pp. I–II.

Mora, Rosa. "He escrito mi libro más duro, y el más triste." *El País*, 15 May 1996, pp. 1, 32.

Mora, Rosa. "La nueva novela de García Márquez." *El País*, 15 Apr. 1994.

"Nacimiento de Macondo." *Informaciones*, 29 May 1969, p. 3.

Navarro, Ana Cristina. *La vida según . . . Gabriel García Márquez*. Radio Televisión Española, 1995, www.rtve.es/alacarta/videos/personajes-en-el-archivo-de-rtve/vida-segun-gabriel-garcia-marquez/2488243/. Accessed 13 May 2021.

"Nueva novela de García Márquez." *Interviú*, 15 Jan. 1996, p. 6.

Obiols, Isabel. "Las memorias de García Márquez salen a la calle con un millón de ejemplares." *El País*, 10 Oct. 2002, p. 31.

Pacheco Colin, Ricardo. "Arrasa en ventas nuevo libro de García Márquez." *Crónica* (Mexico), 29 Oct. 2004, p. 33.

Pérez Minik, Domingo. "La provocación en la novela hispanoamericana." *El Día* (Santa Cruz de Tenerife), 25 Aug. 1968, p. 3.

Piatier, Jacqueline. "Le Congrès de Valescure." *Le Monde*, 8 May 1965, p. 13.

Quiñonero, Juan Pedro. "*El otoño del patriarca*, la nueva novela de Gabriel García Márquez: Tras una estética del panfleto." *Informaciones*, 15 May 1975, pp. 8–9.

R. M. "Mondadori publicará las memorias de Gabriel García Márquez en octubre." *El País*, 28 June 2002.

Radio Televisión Española, Archivo Histórico, García Márquez (1982–2014).

"Repaso de lecturas de 1968: ¿Cuáles son los libros que más te han interesado en 1968?" *El Ciervo: Revista mensual de pensamiento y cultura*, no. 178, 1968, pp. 13–15.

"Respecto a una denuncia de un novelista colombiano." *ABC*, 13 June 1963, p. 69.

Saldívar, Dasso. "La victoriosa derrota." *Libros*, supplement of *Diario 16*, 16 Mar. 1989, p. 1.

Salvador, Gregorio. *Comentarios estructurales a* Cien años de soledad. Universidad de La Laguna, 1970.

Samper, María Elvira. "Mi libro es una venganza." *ABC*, 18 Mar.1989, pp. VII–IX.

Santana, Mario. *Foreigners in the Homeland: The Spanish American New Novel in Spain, 1962–1974*. Bucknell UP and Associated U Presses, 2000.

Santana-Acuña, Álvaro. *Ascent to Glory: How* One Hundred Years of Solitude *Was Written and Became a Global Classic*. Columbia UP, 2020.

Santana-Acuña, Álvaro. "Reviewing Strategies and the Normalization of Uncertain Texts." *American Journal of Cultural Sociology*, 2021. doi.org/10.1057/s41290-021-00128-z Accessed 13 May 2021.

Santos, Dámaso. "*Cien años de soledad*." *Pueblo*, 16 July 1968, p. 23.

Sanz Villanueva, Santos. "El derecho al amor." *Dossier 16*, supplement of *Diario 16*, 19 Dec. 1985, pp. 1, 11.

"Selecciones." *El Periódico de Cataluña*, 14 Dec. 1985, p. 30.

Sorela, Pedro. "García Márquez recrea en Bolívar, protagonista de su última novela, el desencanto tras el poder." *El País*, 16 Mar. 1989, p. 38.

Spanish periodicals: *ABC* (1963–2014), *Álcazar* (1985), *Avui* (1985), *Cambio 16* (1986), *Canarias 7* (2014), *Cinco Días* (1985), *Cuadernos para el diálogo* (1967–1968, 1973), *Diario de Barcelona* (1981), *Diario de Cuenca* (1981), *Diario SP* (1968), *Diario 16* (1981–1996), *Destino* (1967–1975), *Dossier 16* (1985), *El Adelantado de Segovia* (1981), *El Ciervo* (1968–1969), *El Correo* (2014), *El Correo Catalán* (1981), *El Correo de Andalucía* (1975), *El Día* (1968), *El Diario Vasco* (1981), *El Heraldo de Aragón* (1981, 2014), *El Món* (1985), *El Norte de Castilla* (1985), *El Norte de Galicia* (1981), *El Noticiero* (1975), *El Noticiero Universal* (1970), *El País* (1978–2014), *El Periódico de Catalunya* (1985–2014), *El Personal* (1981), *Época* (1985), *Faro de Vigo* (1981), *¡Hola!* (1982), *Índice* (1968), *Informaciones* (1967–1975), *Interviú* (1979–1982, 1996), *La Gaceta del Libro* (1986), *La Provincia-Diario de las Palmas* (2002), *Las Provincias* (1981), *La Razón* (2014), *La Vanguardia* (1970–2014), *La Voz de Galicia* (1974, 2014), *La Voz del Penedés* (1981), *Meridiano* (1969), *Nueva España* (1981), *Papeles de Son Armadans* (1970), *Playboy España* (1982), *Pueblo* (1968, 1976), *Reseña de literatura, arte y espectáculos* (1967), *Revista de Occidente* (1967, 1969, 1975), *Tele|eXpres* (1968–1970), *Triunfo* (1975–1979), *Ya* (1981–1985).

Suñén, Luis. "Amor y Caribe." *Babelia*, supplement of *El País*, 19 Dec. 1985, p. 5.

Suñén, Luis. "Gabriel García Márquez, el placer de lo fatal." *Libros*, supplement of *El País*, 17 May 1981, p. 1.

Telediario. "Congreso de la lengua española: Homenaje a García Márquez." Radio Televisión Española, 2007. www.youtube.com/watch?v=xyhNmp-O2X8. Accessed 13 May 2021.

Tola de Habich, Fernando, and Patricia Grieve, editors. *Los españoles y el boom*. Tiempo Nuevo, 1971.

Valls, Fernando. "Un mundo de historia, fantasia y tradición." *La Vanguardia*, 31 Mar. 1989, pp. 37, 39.

Vargas Llosa, Mario "Las 'putas tristes' de Fidel." *El País*, 31 Oct. 2004, p. 19.

PART IV
KEY THEMES AND LEITMOTIFS

CHAPTER 17

MYTH AND POETRY IN MACONDO

MERCEDES LÓPEZ-BARALT

One Hundred Years of Solitude (henceforth *One Hundred Years*) has frequently been approached from a historical perspective, focusing on the colonial imprint in Latin America's destiny. Yet in his Nobel Prize acceptance speech, Gabriel García Márquez made it clear that he wished to be remembered for the poetry that permeates his writing. This essay (a short and revised version of my 2013 book *Una visita a Macondo: Manual para leer un mito*) is inspired by this assertion, as well as by a quotation by Ernesto Sabato, who claims that, for philosophers and artists, myth and poetry are keys to access the Absolute (*Resistencia* 58). Taking into account the few previous attempts to pursue these motifs in the novel, I decided to undertake a search of the traces of both myth and poetry in García Márquez's magnum opus. The faces of myth in the work are many: Oedipus, prophecies, magic, utopia, the mandala of the tree of life, cyclical time, alchemy, one-dimensional characters (known as actants), genesis, and apocalypse. On the other hand, poems and metaphors are ever present in the novel. This search led me to a new reading of *One Hundred Years*, opening my eyes to a twofold conclusion. The novel ends with the destruction of Macondo and the solitary Buendía dynasty, but the notion of cyclical time opens a window to hope. This celebration of ambivalence confirms my favorite definition of a classic. As well said by Italo Calvino, a classic is a book that never finishes saying what it has to say.

Being a classic, *One Hundred Years* has been described by Carlos Fuentes in "García Márquez: La segunda lectura" (The Second Reading) as the Latin American equivalent of Cervantes's *Don Quijote* (65). Translated into some forty languages, it is undoubtedly the reason for our author's chief awards: the Rómulo Gallegos Prize (1972) and the Nobel (1982). An early critical anthology (*Nueve asedios a García Márquez*, 1969); Mario Vargas Llosa's monumental book-length study of the novel (*García Márquez: Historia de un deicidio*, 1971); Helmy Giacoman's homage volume (1972); the 2007 canonical edition of the novel by the Academies of the Spanish Language, with a selection of critical essays; and its first screen transformation into a television series in the upcoming Netflix adaptation, which will be filmed mainly in Colombia, all help confirm *One Hundred Years*' status as a classic.

I would like to point out, from the outset, two factors that launched the novel to such an enthusiastic and immediate acclaim. The first one drew a line between the novelists of the narrative boom, evidencing the heterogeneity of the new literary phenomenon. On one side were Carlos Fuentes, Julio Cortázar, Mario Vargas Llosa, and others; on the opposite side was García Márquez. Almost all of them engaged in experimenting with narrative techniques, such as temporal and spatial dislocation; multiplicity of points of view; a story within another story (Chinese boxes); parallel scenes that contaminate each other (communicating vessels); and the hidden fact, which the novel silences in order to enhance it in its due moment to shed light on the story (*el dato escondido*).[1] The purpose was to create "a new novel," whose complications would demand a "second reading." On the other side of the ring, García Márquez evidenced his paradoxical originality by imitating the ancestral oral art of storytelling, exempt from narrative twists, as noted by Ricardo Gullón. Contrary to Cortázar, who aims in *Rayuela* to reach the "male" or active reader, as opposed to the "female," passive one (500), our author democratizes the new novel, providing immediate gratification to the reader—unisex, of course, and never giving up complexity, submerged in the text. The words of Gene Bell-Villada attest to García Márquez's success: *One Hundred Years* has reminded us that "literary novels could be not just beautiful, moving and profound but also exciting, entertaining, and fun" (Introduction 6).

Another key to the popularity of *One Hundred Years* is its ambiguity. The novel is based on polarizations that coexist harmonically: history/myth, history/poetry, sadness/joy, humor/lyricism, clarity/complexity, linear time/cyclical time, destruction/hope. I return to the issue of ambiguity later in the chapter, but concerning the surprising joy that attracts the reader in a story of solitude, I must stress the playful aspect of the novel as explained by Luce López-Baralt. Its male characters are not children (this is not a Bildungsroman), but adults who behave as such: they do not work, and they address sex, war, and politics as play.

But there are two other important elements that contribute to *One Hundred Years*' haunting quality: myth and poetry. Let us consider both.

Myth in *One Hundred Years of Solitude*

The mythical dimension of this famous book has attracted critics and writers. In "García Márquez: La segunda lectura," Carlos Fuentes characterized it as a "mythical novel" (59). Other mythical approaches have been proposed by Plinio Apuleyo Mendoza, Álvaro Mutis, Carmen Arnau, Luis Beltrán Almería, Roberto González Echevarría, Iván Ivanovici, and Aníbal González, among others. And, *ça va sans dire*, García Márquez himself. It is interesting to note the author's mythical aura as a man of the people, an average citizen who motivates his readers to address him by his nickname, Gabo—to such a degree of familiarity that one of his critical anthologies is titled *Gaborio* (roughly, "Gaboriana"). Beyond the anecdote, however, García Márquez acknowledged the importance of myth in his magnum opus, when, in his 1982 interview with Mendoza, he stated that the novel was inspired by the mythical oral tradition of Aracataca, brought to life in his grandmother's tales. The presence of myth in the text suggests that the author is conversant with Ovid, Vladimir Propp, Claude Lévi-Strauss, and Mircea Eliade, as we shall see.

Let us address the mythical elements that contribute to the enchantments of García Márquez's masterpiece. First of all, it is evident that the Bible is its endless source of mythmaking, as it stages such essential episodes as genesis, original sin, exodus, the plagues, the universal flood, and the apocalypse. In a recent book, Aníbal González suggests that *One Hundred Years* applies religious notions (the sacred, creation, eternity, belief, prophecy and quest) to seek revelations about human life (x, 126, 141).

But beyond the Bible, Mircea Eliade's definition of myth and mythical time fits the novel to a T. Myths are magical stories that go back to the dawn of the earth. In the case of *One Hundred Years*, such beginnings are those of the Buendía dynasty. According to Mircea Eliade, *Mito y realidad*, mythical time is divided into sacred and profane: sacred time, the time of creations by supernatural entities, is perfect; profane time, by contrast, is an imperfect time, in which humans try to imitate the deeds of the gods. With their rituals, men intend to recreate instances of sacred time. In *One Hundred Years* we recognize sacred time as utopia. The very word is ingrained in one of the names of the founding father, José *Arcadio*, who—in the spirit of Theocritus's and Virgil's notion of paradise—creates the idyllic village of Macondo. Work, justice, peace, joy, and a sense of community characterize this happy town in its origins, when old age and death are unknown. Naturally, in this bucolic village the mandala of the tree of life is essential. A metaphor for the totality of the universe, it is present in the biblical Genesis and the crucifixion of Christ, and it reappears in America as the cosmic ceiba tree of the Maya and Aztec codices. In *One Hundred Years*, we recognize it as the chestnut tree beside which José Arcadio decides to construct the family home. Later on, when he becomes senile, his son Aureliano ties him to the tree with a rope. In "García Márquez: La segunda lectura," Fuentes sees in this fusion between man and tree the transformation of José Arcadio into the dynasty totem (63). As the reader well knows, later on Macondo will deteriorate; its inhabitants will inherit the names of the founding family and, in emulation of the sacred time of creation, engage in Sisyphean efforts to create and then destroy.

Prophecy emerges in the novel as linked to Melquíades's manuscript and to the master of cards, Pilar Ternera, who reads in them Macondo's future: the Buendía dynasty is "a machine with unavoidable repetitions, a turning wheel that would have gone on spiraling into eternity were it not for the progressive and irremediable wearing of the axle" (*One Hundred Years* 396).[2] Incest, the core of the Oedipus myth, is related to the origins of the Buendía family, inasmuch as its founding couple, José Arcadio and Úrsula, are cousins. It also triggers its destruction, when Aureliano Babilonia and his aunt, Amaranta Úrsula, become lovers. Both bear a child marked with the stigma of punishment: a pig's tail. Thus, the novel's story mirrors the structure of fairy tales and myths, which, as conceived by Vladimir Propp and Claude Lévi-Strauss, is threefold: prohibition-transgression-happy ending, due to rewards and/or punishment; in other words, order-disorder-new order.

Propp and Lévi-Strauss have also dwelled on the nature of characters in popular tales and myths. Unlike the characters in a novel, which are ambivalent, changing, and unpredictable, those in oral tradition—technically referred to as actants—are simple and lack introspection. In *One Hundred Years*, aside from Fernanda del Carpio, Amaranta, and Úrsula Iguarán, who have their dose (be it large or small) of interior monologues, the male characters may be defined by a single quality.

Examining the role of alchemy in the novel, Josefina Ludmer proposes that its central theme is that of the *homo duplex*. If alchemy strives to restore the harmonious unity of the world (*omnia in unum*), its goal is not to find gold, but to achieve human fulfillment. The first Buendía, José Arcadio, is complete, for he blends imagination (mind, reduced to a metonymy: eyes) with sexual potency (body, reduced to another metonymy: penis). His sons and male descendants are incomplete: the José Arcadios are bodies; the Aurelianos are minds. But the novel has a "happy" ending, in the sense that the last Buendía, begotten with love, is born big and husky and with his eyes wide open. Curiously, females are ignored in Ludmer's *homo duplex* hypothesis. But they are admired in the novel, in the paradigm of Úrsula, the ultimate source of strength for the Buendías. And let us not forget that García Márquez has paid homage to women in his memoirs, when he states that they sustain the world, while men, with their predictable ruthlessness, turn it upside down (*Living* 77).

Interestingly, the myth of the return to origins has a literary version in our novel. For, as noted by Arturo Echavarría Ferrari, García Márquez and Marcel Proust have something in common: for both, childhood memories become the origins of fiction. In his memoirs, the Colombian novelist emulates Proust's emblematic madeleine scene, when the dormant world of infancy wakes in his mind while sipping a creole soup in Aracataca (Echavarría Ferrari 259).

As we have seen, myth is ever present in *One Hundred Years*, but there is one instance that has been particularly cherished in our contemporary Latin American imaginary, that of Macondo, also imbued in ambiguity by its multiple meanings: solitude, madness, anarchy, revolution, underdevelopment, and neocolonialism. Any crisis in Latin America is popularly adjudicated to the Buendías' way of life and condensed in an angry phrase: "This is Macondo!"

García Márquez as a Poet

Let us address the presence of poetry in *One Hundred Years*, a book that in 2017 was canonized by the editors of Colombia's newspaper *El Tiempo* as the great national poem of his author's homeland. Well said, for among the many literary strategies that contribute to García Márquez's originality is his surprising combination of poetry and humor, something not often seen in a novel. Like the Peruvian writer José María Arguedas, García Márquez is a poet who chose to tell stories. This is the true vocation that he has confessed to over and over again in his interview with Mendoza, as well as in his Nobel address and in his memoirs. In the famous conversation with the former, he admits to treasuring the letter in which Losada's editor turned down *La hojarasca*, because it acknowledged his excellent sense of poetry. He also says that he would have loved to have Petrarch as a friend (*Fragrance* 55, 125). In his Nobel speech he states that this prize was awarded to him as an homage to poetry. He also acknowledges his fervent admiration for Homer, Dante, and Pablo Neruda, and endorses an idea of his friend, the poet Luis Cardoza Aragón, who proclaims that poetry is the only concrete proof of the existence of man. In his memoirs, *Living to Tell the Tale*, García Márquez recognizes his addiction to poetry, states that the best poem in the world is Jorge Manrique's medieval elegy, and recognizes the lyrics of Mexican composer Agustín Lara's popular songs as verses dissolved in the soup of daily life (*Living* 220, 223, 371). This vocation for poetry, evident in the published and unpublished poems of his youth, as commented by José Luis Díaz-Granados, has been acknowledged by writers and critics such as Vargas Llosa, Claudio Guillén, Luis Rafael Sánchez, Víctor García de la Concha, Daniel Torres, and Juan Gustavo Cobo Borda, the latter of whom dubs García Márquez "the poet he always was" (497a; my translation). As for the author himself, when he declared in his memoirs that the initial manuscript version of *One Hundred Years* lacked poetic truth, he was suggesting that the definitive version would be a landmark thanks to poetry (*Living* 401–2).

The first critic who examined with a close-up lens the poems imbedded in the narrator's discourse in his famous novel is Daniel Torres, who discovered many of them, giving each an appropriate title: "Remedios," "Los ruidos nocturnos" (Night rumors), "Los cuartos infinitos" (The infinite rooms), "El extraviado" (The lost one), "El desfile del circo" (The circus parade). Torres refers to passages that, because of their beauty, their synthetic brevity, their metaphors, and their rhythm, may be extracted from the novel as poems.

One of the most touching love declarations in *One Hundred Years* is the poem that Aureliano dedicates to Remedios Moscote (the child), with its rhythmical anaphoras and homespun, nostalgic images: "Remedios in the soporific air of two in the afternoon, Remedios in the soft breath of the roses, Remedios in the water clock secrets of the moths, Remedios in the steaming morning bread, Remedios everywhere and Remedios forever" (65).[3] It is evident that this passage, quoted by one of his critics as an example of the author's mastery of poetry (Cobo Borda 503), may be scanned into verse.

"Viendo llover sobre las begonias" (Watching it rain on the begonias) evokes García Márquez's short story "Isabel viendo llover en Macondo." The family's old house, after the vicissitudes of war, becomes a metaphor for the humiliations of time. It is contemplated with resignation and melancholy by Colonel Aureliano Buendía, who knows that the end of Macondo is not far off. The poem—as many others—is produced by the narrator: "He was not pained by the peeling of the whitewash on the walls or the dirty, cottony cobwebs in the corners or the dust on the begonias or the veins left on the beams by the termites or the moss on the hinges or any insidious traps that nostalgia offered him. He sat down on the porch, wrapped in his blanket and with his boots still on, as if only waiting for it to clear, and he spent the whole afternoon watching it rain on the begonias" (*One Hundred Years* 172).[4]

But what for me constitutes García Márquez's most haunting poem is the most mysterious one of them all. Minimalist and surrealistic, in its powerful synthesis it serves as a preview of forthcoming attractions in the narrative: the destruction of Macondo. Here is the context of the poem. Aureliano Babilonia and Amaranta Úrsula begin to play rough like children (her husband Gastón, oblivious to their flirting, is in the adjacent room). Suddenly, to put it in the eloquent words of Jorge Amado, love happens.[5] Aureliano penetrates her, and Amaranta's erotic delirium invades, in the mode of Flaubert's free indirect discourse, the voice of the narrator: "A huge commotion immobilized her in her center of gravity, planted her in her place, and her defensive will was demolished by the irresistible anxiety to discover the meaning of the orange whistles and the invisibles globes that awaited her on the other side of death" (397).[6] The embrace of Eros and Thanatos in the poem recalls a metaphor used by the author in his memoirs, when he refers to intercourse as an "exquisite death" (*Living* 77).

The two recurrent avant-garde metaphors of this poem—the orange whistles and the invisible globes—come brimming with meaning. Both constitute what Carlos Bousoño has named visionary or impossible images. The whistle—the wind's caress or the lover's call—is a renowned metaphor in Spanish poetry, present in San Juan de la Cruz's "*Cántico espiritual*" (The Spiritual Canticle) and in Miguel Hernández's *El silbo vulnerado* (The Wounded Whistle). The rupture of logic in both metaphors (orange air and intangible globes) expresses the hallucinatory madness of orgasm, an ecstasy that permits the lovers' access to the ultimate mystery: death (no wonder the French phrase for orgasm is *petite mort*).

Interestingly, these images of flying spheres and whistles reverberate in other instances of the novel. They appear first when Úrsula fears that her son Aureliano may have been murdered: "At dusk through her tears she saw the swift and luminous *disks* that crossed the sky like an *exhalation* and she thought that it was a signal of death" (*One Hundred Years* 178). She might be right, for the word *exhalation* suggests a dying whistle, the last breath. Later on they reappear to announce Úrsula's death, when Santa Sofía de la Piedad one night "saw a row of luminous *orange disks* pass across the sky" (*One Hundred Years* 342). In another moment, Aureliano Babilonia and Amaranta Úrsula are in bed, and in their embrace, they ignore the signs of destruction that surround them: "[T]hey were not frightened by the *sublunary* explosions of the ants or the noise of the moths or the constant and clear *whistle* of the growth of the weeds in the neighboring rooms" (*One Hundred Years* 411). The last time the image emerges in the novel is when, just after Amaranta Úrsula's death in childbirth, Aureliano Babilonia, weeping desperately and trying to find consolation in Pilar Ternera's brothel, overlooks "the luminous *orange disks* that were crossing the sky and that so many times on holiday nights he had contemplated with childish fascination" (*One Hundred Years* 413).[7]

These instances lead the reader to infer that death is summoned in the novel by three metaphors: disks in the sky, the orange color, and whistles. The disks may refer to the stars, the orange color to twilight and fire, and whistles to the wind. Stars and dusk evoke night or finality; wind and fire evoke destruction. Thus, we infer that these metaphors not only point to death (as Úrsula had wisely foreseen), but also become omens of the apocalypse that will destroy Macondo.

THE REIGN OF AMBIGUITY: TWO INTERPRETATIONS OF THE NOVEL.

The ambivalence of *One Hundred Years* has much to do with myth, poetry, and Cervantes's legacy. *Don Quixote*'s mark is evident in García Márquez's novel in the volatile notion of time, the unreliable narrator, and the topos of the ciphered manuscript—but most important, in the celebration of the freedom of the reader, which opens the door to ambiguity. Narrating the adventures of the Cave of Montesinos in the second part of *Don Quixote* (chapter XXIV), Cide Hamete Benengeli says: "It is impossible for me to believe that Don Quixote could lie, since he is the most truthful gentleman and the noblest knight of his time.... If, then, this adventure seems apocryphal, it is not fault of mine. So, without declaring it false or true, I write it down. Use your own wisdom, reader, to decide as you see fit, for I am not required, nor is it in my power, to do more" (558).[8] It is obvious that García Márquez has learned this invaluable lesson, which incidentally anticipates by more than three centuries Umberto Eco's 1962 notion of *opera aperta* ("open work").

At the same time, both myth and poetry are essential to the ambiguity of *One Hundred Years*. Ovid's ancient definition of myth as constant metamorphosis pervades the text (as proved by the evolution of wind and mirror). As for poetry, Roman Jakobson states that its ambivalence results in polysemy. And the novel's corpus of poems attests to this.

All of the above leads to a dilemma: two possible readings of *One Hundred Years*—which recalls the challenging moment that Borges describes in "The Aleph," when his narrator reaches the center of the story and faces his perplexity as a writer. I proceed to prove textually that two opposite interpretations (pessimistic and optimistic) can coexist comfortably in the novel, not only because the text allows it, but also because it encourages the reader to choose one or to accept both. This duality of interpretations was inaugurated by two future Nobel laureates: Vargas Llosa and García Márquez, who engaged in a public dialogue on *One Hundred Years* in Lima the very same year of its publication, 1967. The underlying question was: Is utopia possible? Their answers may surprise us today. García Márquez bets for solitude as man's destiny, while Vargas Llosa tries to convince him that solitude is not inherent in man, and that in Latin America it is a consequence of alienation (from which we can infer that colonized people can rise to change history and embrace solidarity). Inspired by this dialogue, I propose my own elaboration of this twofold view of the novel, based on textual evidence.

Apocalypse Now: Crime and Punishment

Macondo and the Buendía dynasty are destroyed for their shortcomings: incest, lack of work ethic, childhood regression, selfishness, solitude. It is not by chance that the last Buendía (the child with the pig's tail) and his father share the name of Babilonia. An ominous name in the biblical Apocalypse, it is a metaphor for all the sins that will drive Macondo to the worst of punishments: destruction.

This is the usual and predictable reading of the book. For solitude is irrevocable and is ever present in the twenty chapters of the novel; suffice it to pick one example for each, in chronological order: José Arcadio begins to speak to himself, and Úrsula tells him to go crazy alone; in search of Pilar Ternera, José Arcadio suffers the pain of solitude; Aureliano feels terribly lonely in a brothel; being dead, the ghost of Prudencio Aguilar feels the need for company; Amaranta takes charge of Aureliano José to relieve her loneliness; Úrsula feels lonely when her husband lies under the chestnut tree; Aureliano returns from war more lonely than ever; Coronel Buendía's seventeen illegitimate children all have in common an air of solitude; Amaranta locks herself into her room to weep for her solitude till she dies; Aureliano Segundo and José Arcadio Segundo retain the air of solitude of the Buendías; Rebeca conquers the privilege of solitude; Remedios wanders in the desert of solitude; Úrsula lives the unfathomable solitude of old age; Mauricio Babilonia dies alone of old age; José Arcadio Segundo takes refuge from the military repression in the solitude of Melquíades's room; Aureliano Babilonia exhibits the Buendías' air of solitude; Aureliano Segundo and Petra Cotes find paradise in shared solitude; Aureliano and José Arcadio are two solitaries of the same lineage; Aureliano Buendía is marked by the smallpox of solitude; near the end of Macondo, Aureliano Babilonia and Amaranta Úrsula hide in the Buendías' house, protected by love and loneliness and by the solitude found in love.

The theme of loneliness is also present in García Márquez's Nobel speech, precisely titled "The Solitude of Latin America." There he examines its historical nature, for he sees it as the consequence of colonization and neocolonization, though in his dialogue with Vargas Llosa he had seen it as inherent to man. Another testimony of his obsession, this time in his famous interview: when Mendoza asks him what, if he were to write a book that would comprise all of his works, he would call it, he replies: *The Book of Solitude* (*Fragrance* 53).

In the novel, solitude is linked to the Buendías' capital sin of incest, a sin with two faces—solitude and lack of solidarity—for it is not only a biblical sin, but a social one. If the incest taboo contributes to the exogamic imperative that is the basis of society, creating alliances between diverse groups, as Lévi-Strauss has proposed in his *Structural Anthropology* (19), then the Buendías are antisocial: closed off in endogamy, they are a paradigm of solitude. Carmen Arnau, feeling certain that García Márquez had read *Les structures élémentaires de la parenté* (1949)—in which Lévi-Strauss states that the incest prohibition turns out to be a gift for society—suggests that the Buendías' vocation for incest causes their lack of social solidarity (124). She is right, although this want is present within the family as well. When Aureliano sees the scars of more than half a century of suffering in the face of his aging mother, Úrsula, he becomes aware that they do not provoke in him the least feeling of mercy, because in his heart there are no affections left (*One Hundred Years* 173).

Aside from incest, two other topics link García Márquez to Lévi-Strauss: repetitions and apocalypse. In *Tristes tropiques* (*Tristes trópicos* 446) the anthropologist states that man has done nothing but repeat himself. And in *The Naked Man*, (*El hombre desnudo* 627–28) he concludes that the final destiny of man is apocalypse, because, as he had said in *Tristes tropiques*, the world began without man and will end without him (*Tristes trópicos* 466). As if this weren't enough, in "García Márquez: La segunda lectura," Carlos Fuentes confirms the desolation of the novel, when he states that *One Hundred Years* is a terrifying metaphor for man's orphanhood on earth" (64). As the reader may see, there are many reasons to interpret the novel's ending as a final cataclysm. And yet ....

THE DAWN OF A NEW ERA

I propose here a new reading of the novel, in which myth and poetry open the door to hope. But before following the rational road of reason, let us give credit to intuition, the ultimate trigger of interpretation: namely, intuition of hope based on the joy of reading. Several factors contribute to the delight of the reader of García Márquez's magnum opus. First of all, there is Caribbean humor, as distinct from satire and moral redemption, as seen by Jorge Mañach in his *Indagación del choteo* (An Inquiry into Joking, 1928). As a tactic for survival in adverse circumstances, Caribbean humor abolishes solemnity and mocks the establishment, but above all, it cherishes joie de vivre (a good example: the character known as Heathen Chinky or *la China Hereje* "singing in the rain" of her shower in Luis Rafael Sánchez's *La guaracha del Macho Camacho* [*Macho Camacho's Beat*, 1976]). And its collateral effect, laughter, kills fear, to evoke Umberto Eco's famous line in *Il nome della rosa* (*The Name of the Rose*, 1980). The intuition of hope is also sustained by an intertext suggested by the novel's title. I refer to the most optimistic of Spanish proverbs: "There's no harm that lasts a hundred years, nor a body that can survive it."[9] To utter it in the context of *One Hundred Years* causes an unexpected shudder in the reader, for a delightful hunch seems to knock at his door, saying: solitude may well have an expiration date. Other factors for joy are freedom and imagination: both result from the narrative strategy of magical realism, as well as from the ludic attitude of the male Buendías, who act like spoiled children.

We have taken note of a proverb, but there is another intertext from popular tradition that deserves attention. I refer to a beloved Latin American bolero titled *Historia de un amor* (Love Story). It has gone viral, since 1955, in the voices of popular vocalists like Libertad Lamarque, Los Panchos, Lucho Gatica, and Marco Antonio Muñiz. The song claims that there is no story of love that can challenge the one it cherishes. But its uniqueness has a literary equivalent: the last romance of our novel, a love that borders on the absolute, aspires to transcend death, and deserves a poem. Obviously, I refer to the incestuous affair of Aureliano Babilonia and Amaranta Úrsula. The narrator states that both lovers were not only the happiest, but indeed the only happy couple in the world. And he adds that solidarity is the key to the strength of their love (404, 407-8). This is the very first appearance of the word *solidarity* in the story of the Buendías, brimming with hope in a novel marked by solitude. Hope incarnated in the fruit of love: the last Buendía is welcomed with enthusiasm by the narrator, when he describes the baby as the savior of the dynasty because of its being engendered with love. The passage may be read as the unquestionable clue to a happy ending. The destruction of Macondo, however, cancels this possibility.

Yet we shall not despair. Two critics have glimpsed the chance of hope in *One Hundred Years*. Beltrán Almería states that the notion of time in the novel implies optimism. Melquíades's tiny room, in which it is always Monday and Tuesday, contains an eternalized fraction of time, a fact that attests to the existence of a marvelous, harmonious, and unified world on this earth (33). On the other hand, Aníbal González proposes that the pessimistic ending of the novel is subdued because it encourages readers to return to the beginning, prompting them to read it in another way, and intending "to change all who read it" (144).

Well said, yet following the premise that the final words of the novel limit the target of punishment to "the races condemned to a hundred years of solitude" (*One Hundred Years* 417), I argue that the mythical notion of cyclical time, hand in hand with an essential subtext (an ancestral myth reformulated by a contemporary poem) will lead us to hope. Let us open the door.

Two Mythical Allegories: An Intertext and a Subtext

Readers and critics agree in considering the Bible the most important intertext of García Márquez's novel. Two good reasons for this consensus are its explicitness and the fact that the Bible is the sacred book of the Western world. I agree, but there are two—not only one—mythical allegories that coexist in the novel: the biblical one, linked to linear time and visible as an intertext, and another one, linked to cyclical time and submerged in the novel as a subtext—an invisible story that leaves, without being mentioned, eloquent traces. Its source is Native American. I refer to the Aztec myth of Quetzalcóatl.

This ancient tale—whose main sources in Nahuatl are the *Anales de Cuauhtitlán* and the *Códice Matritense de la Real Academia* (León Portilla 302)—tells the story of the constant struggle between two of the sons of the Creator-God, Ometéotl: Tezcatlipoca (the black, smoking mirror, related to conflict and war) and Quetzalcóatl (the plumed serpent, associated with peace, art, and civilization, and also known as Ehécatl, the wind). One of its versions narrates that as the Toltec god of Tula, Quetzalcóatl abolished human sacrifice, repudiated war, and was keen on teaching his people science and the arts. Defeated by his enemies and summoned by the sun, he flees to the East, disappears into the sea, and is transformed into Venus, the morning star. Another version recounts that Tezcatlipoca shows Quetzalcóatl his tricky mirror twice, to destabilize him. His image appears first as old and dirty, and then as radiant. Then he prepares maguey wine to intoxicate him. Drunk, Quetzalcóatl seduces his own sister. After sleeping, he regrets the deed and throws himself into a pyre. But from the ashes of his heart, his spirit, turned into a star, ascends into the realm of the sky.

The story is essentialized in the novel, for it has been stripped of the anecdote, the names of its protagonists, its region, and its culture. But it may be recognized by several signs: two metonymic incarnations (Quetzalcóatl as the wind and Tezcatlipoca as the mirror); their final fight, in which Quetzalcóatl is the victor; and the destruction of a deficient humanity.

The reader may ask, why did the author reduce such an important myth to the traces of a subtext, while the Bible served explicitly as an intertext? The answer is obvious. The biblical allegory is useful because this sacred book is not associated with a particular nationality. Rather, it is an essential part of the Western imaginary and belongs to us all. To quote explicitly the Quetzalcóatl legend, however, would have wielded the flag of a Mexican identity, invalidating the purpose of the novel, which attempts to be both Caribbean and universal.

Yet another question lingers. Why Quetzalcóatl? Let us mention a few facts. First of all, it is the most cherished of Latin American indigenous myths. Also, our author had been living in Mexico from 1961 to 1967. There he wrote the most mythical of his novels, *One Hundred Years*; there he embraced fame. To live in a nation so intensely proud of its rich pre-Columbian legacy, without being aware of the existence of this legend, would have been difficult, and for a writer with the cultural baggage of García Márquez, impossible. His interest in Mexican mythology was attested by Carlos Fuentes in 2007 in his essay "Para darle nombre a América" (To Name America), in which he recalled their visit to the Anthropological Museum of Mexico in 1962. Contemplating the monolith of the Mexican goddess of love and war, Coatlicue, García Márquez exclaimed: "Now I understand Mexico!" (xviii). Fuentes, incidentally, is the author of *Tiempo mexicano* (1971), in which he exalts the figure of Quetzalcóatl for having ingrained in Mexicans *a circular suspicion*: that of the Aztec hero´s return to earth, bringing an imminent resurrection. In his poem *Quetzalcóatl* (1985), Ernesto Cardenal revisits this messianic issue. One last fact: this hope of a collective rebirth is consistent with García Márquez's vocation of utopia. As a man of the 1960s, he embraced the Marxist concept of the new man (*el hombre nuevo*).[10]

For our author, the two most accessible sources for the Quetzalcóatl myth would have been Miguel León-Portilla's *La filosofía náhuatl* (*The Nahuatl Philosophy*, 1956), a bestseller in Mexico in the 1960s, and Octavio Paz's extraordinary, lengthy poem *Piedra de sol* (*Sun Stone*, 1957). As for Paz, it is well known that his lengthy reflection on Mexico,

El laberinto de la soledad (*The Labyrinth of Solitude*, 1950), was an important inspiration for *One Hundred Years*. We infer that the same has occurred with *Piedra de sol*, García Márquez being an avid reader of poetry. In addition, his novel and the poem share three important elements: the coexistence of linear and cyclical time, the presence of Quetzalcóatl as a link between a world that ends and another that begins, and solidarity as the key to hope.

The first traces of the subtext—two incarnations of mythical heroes as dominant symbols, the wind and the mirror—appear early on in the novel, and finally close it. I draw this useful notion of a persistent and ambivalent symbol, meaningful of important values or ideas for the story told in the text, from Victor Turner's *The Forest of Symbols* (1967).

The mirror enters the novel in an oblique way. On the front cover of the second edition (1967), the letter E of the word *soledad*, in the title, is emphasized. Let us remember that it is the first letter of *espejo* (mirror). This emphasis assumes a curious form: the E is inverted, as seen in a reflection. Arnau sees it as a symbol of the introverted life of the Buendías, enclosed in the family and distanced from the rest of the world (71). The mirror appears also in the first sentence of the novel, in the form of ice, and then in José Arcadio Buendía's dream of a city with walls of glass. It also appears as mirages (*espejismos*), in the new name given to Macondo at the very end of the novel: "the city of mirrors (or mirages)" (*One Hundred Years* 417). If a mirage deceives the spectator, the mirror may have a negative side. Associated with illusion and dreams, it repeats images that we can neither touch nor possess. And it serves to have us look at ourselves, not at others. Hence the mirror may very well be a metaphor for solitude. Having lost his beloved Amaranta Úrsula, the last Aureliano sees himself in Melquíades's manuscript "as if he were looking into a speaking mirror" (416), facing at the end of the novel—as Quetzalcóatl did—a mirror that will lead him to death. The manuscript has taken the place of Tezcatlipoca's deceitful mirror.

As for the wind, it has a rich story as symbol. Animated as a living entity in *One Hundred Years*, it begins as a witness, follows as a luminous breeze, turns resolute, becomes a prophet, and ends as an avenging judge. Its first appearance is in the founders' bedroom. Oblivious to their incestuous sin, the newlyweds make love until dawn, indifferent to the presence of a vigilant wind. This wind reappears when Remedios the Beauty rises to heaven. In the form of "a delicate wind of light," it turns into "a determined wind" (236), which Úrsula recognizes. The latter adjective suggests that the wind still has something important to do, although the reader cannot imagine that it will have the quality of a quest. Later, toward the end, when describing the ruins of Macondo after almost five years of rain, the narrator bestows on the wind a solemn role, when he says that the city seemed devastated "in an anticipation of the prophetic wind that years later would wipe Macondo off the face of the earth" (331).[11]

The wind also emerges in an erotic context, in the form of whistles—but with a destructive purpose, for they are the heralds of death, like the orange whistles in Amaranta Úrsula's delirium. Near the very end of the novel, she and Aureliano Babilonia shut themselves off into the family home that is at the edge of collapsing even by a mere breath, and they hear the whistle of the weeds that surround them (41, 411). They never think the breeze might turn into a hurricane.

The wind metaphor is so powerful that, aside from the mythical subtext that we are following, we may add to it two other sources. On the one hand, and taking into account García Márquez's passion for the seventh art, there is the title of one of the most popular American movies, which synthesizes superbly the end of the novel: *Gone with the Wind*. On the other, there is the author's well-known aerophobia, associated with his fear of flying and an incident in Cadaqués, Barcelona, when he experienced, hermetically shut off in his hotel room, a fierce episode of La tramontana wind.

THE CLASH OF THE TITANS

In the final words of the novel, the reader becomes a spectator of the struggle between Quetzalcóatl and Tezcatlipoca, turned into their mythical metonymies. Their polarity as good and evil is transformed in the novel into the clash between solitude and solidarity. Or **soledad** versus **solidarid**ad. I emphasize the similarity between the two words in Spanish, for it confirms the Manichaean bipolarity of myth. Interviewed in 1982 by Mendoza, García Márquez states that the Buendías were not capable of love, except for the last couple, and that the opposite of loneliness is solidarity (*Fragrance* 75).

The biblical intertext and the Aztec subtext embrace on the last page. The hurricane that destroys Macondo is described as "biblical," but the final struggle is in the hands of the Aztec heroes, with Quetzalcóatl (in his mask of Ehécatl, the wind) as victor over Tezcatlipoca (Macondo, "the city of mirrors"). Deciphering Melquíades's manuscript, Aureliano Babilonia reckons that he is doomed, for "it was foreseen that the city of mirrors (or mirages) would be wiped out by the wind" (*One Hundred Years* 417).[12] The redeeming will of this wind enhances the mythical structure of the story—order, disorder, and new order—this time reestablished by punishment. Quetzalcóatl's quest has opened the way to a new era.

From the mythical perspective of cyclical time, as explained by Eliade, each era of mankind is provisional, being created, nurtured, and destroyed for its deficiencies by the gods. In the Aztec tradition, this succession of eras is known as the "Legend of the suns" (Leyenda de los soles). Taking this into account, let us complete that concluding quotation: "it was foreseen that the city of mirrors (or mirages) would be wiped out by the wind *and exiled from the memory of men*" (417).[13] I have emphasized the final phrase, for it has a clue that has been overlooked by readers and critics. It is of the utmost importance, for it assures the reader that after the destruction of Macondo the world has not been deserted. In Franz Kafka's words: "We were expelled from Paradise, but Paradise was not destroyed" (29).[14] Because there remains—or has emerged—another mankind, which judges and reproaches sternly the solitude of the Buendías, condemning them to the most terrible and inevitable consequence of destruction: oblivion. In brief, there is a new mankind marked by solidarity, like the one yearned for by Octavio Paz in *Piedra de sol*: "the kingdom of pronouns intertwined" (32).[15]

Walt Whitman Has the Last Word

In closing, it is time to recall Cervantes, who ordered the reader to draw his own conclusions. Choosing, however, is always paradoxical. A supreme act of liberty, it takes away the wings of freedom, by discarding options. Yet the rich complexity of *One Hundred Years* makes it impossible to restrict the reader's alternatives. García Márquez leaves contradiction untouched to its very last, as a signal of polyphony: plurality of conscience, or the coexistence of opposing points of view within a novel (Bakhtin 5–6, 17). Let us recall what the narrator says at the end about the last Buendía infant: that he was "predisposed to begin the race again from the beginning and cleanse it of its pernicious vices and solitary calling, for he was the only one in a century who had been engendered with love" (*One Hundred Years* 411–12)[16]. This declaration leads the reader to entertain hope—though only for a fleeting moment, the destruction of Macondo being imminent. Now, let us consider contradiction as an ultimate: in his 1967 conversation with Vargas Llosa on *One Hundred Years*, García Márquez declared that a writer who does not contradict himself is a dogmatic writer, and that if necessary, he would not refuse to rewrite the novel and resurrect Macondo (*La novela* 55).

One contradiction on top of the other triggers questions: Is the apocalyptic ending of the novel final and firm? Or does it convey a hidden hope for a better world? The reader must decide—without thinking, not even for an instant, that the chosen interpretation is definitive, for García Márquez's unbridled imagination will always render it provisional. As for myself, I embrace, in awe, the two readings nurtured by this great *opera aperta*. And I bow to Walt Whitman, who deserves the last word:

Do I contradict myself?
Very well, then I contradict myself.
(I am large —I contain multitudes).

("Song of Myself," *Leaves of Grass*, 1885)

Acknowledgments

I wish to express my gratitude and admiration to the editors of *Una visita a Macondo: Manual para leer un mito*, the source of this essay: the late Elizardo Martínez and Neeltje Van Marissing. I also thank Kevin Matos for his indispensable help in formatting the essay in the MLA mode, and Beatriz Cruz Sotomayor for helping me with the manuscript correction method.

Notes

1. For more information on "cajas chinas", "vasos comunicantes" and "dato escondido", see Vargas Llosa's *Cartas a un joven novelista*.
2. All passages from *One Hundred Years of Solitude* are from Gregory Rabassa's 2003 English translation (1st ed., 1970). In Rabassa's translation I have substituted one word: "spilling" is replaced by "spiralling." Original version: "un engranaje de repeticiones irreparables, una rueda giratoria que hubiera seguido dando vueltas hasta la eternidad, de no haber sido por el desgaste progresivo e irremediable del eje" (448). Throughout this article, I quote the Spanish original from the 2007 Real Academia edition.
3. Original version: "Remedios en el aire soporífero de las dos de la tarde, Remedios en la callada respiración de las rosas, Remedios en la clepsidra secreta de las polillas, Remedios en el vapor del pan al amanecer, Remedios en todas partes y Remedios para siempre" (82).
4. "No le dolieron las peladuras de cal en las paredes, ni los sucios algodones de telarañas en los rincones, ni el polvo de las begonias, ni las nervaduras del comején en las vigas, ni el musgo de los quicios, ni ninguna de las trampas insidiosas que le tendía la nostalgia. Se sentó en el corredor, envuelto en la manta y sin quitarse las botas, como esperando apenas que escampara, y permaneció toda la tarde viendo llover sobre las begonias" (201).
5. The English translation renders trivial the phrase: "Liking just happens" (20). I prefer my translation, for it fits perfectly the original in Portuguese: "Bem-querer acontece" (28). Literally, "love happens."
6. My translation. In this case, and with all due respect to Rabassa's translation, I prefer mine, because he interprets Amaranta Úrsula's curiosity as a desire to know *how* the whistles and globes were, whereas in the Spanish original, her desire is to understand *what* they were, which is the same as what they meant (my emphasis). Here is the original in Spanish: "Una conmoción descomunal la inmovilizó en su centro de gravedad, la sembró en su sitio, y su voluntad defensiva fue demolida por la ansiedad irresistible de descubrir qué eran los silbos anaranjados y los globos invisibles que la esperaban al otro lado de la muerte" (450).
7. I have emphasized these words: disks, exhalation, sublunar, and whistle. Here are the quotations from the original: "Al anochecer vió a través de las lágrimas los raudos y luminosos discos anaranjados que cruzaron el cielo como una exhalación, y pensó que era una señal de la muerte" (208); "vió pasar por el cielo una fila de luminosos discos anaranjados" (389); "no los amedrentaban las explosiones sublunares de las hormigas, ni el fragor de las polillas, ni el silbido constante y nítido del crecimiento de la maleza en los cuartos vecinos" (464); and "los luminosos discos anaranjados que cruzaban por el cielo, y que tantas veces había contemplado con una fascinación pueril, en noches de fiesta" (467).
8. "Pero pensar yo que don Quijote mintiese, siendo el más verdadero hidalgo y el más noble caballero de sus tiempos, no es posible; . . . y si esta aventura parece apócrifa, yo no tengo la culpa; y así, sin afirmarla por falsa o verdadera, la escribo. Tú, lector, pues eres prudente, juzga lo que te pareciere, que yo no debo ni puedo más" (Cervantes, *Don Quijote* 734).
9. In Spanish: "No hay mal que cien años dure ni cuerpo que lo resista."
10. Though differing from my hypothesis, Víctor Ivanovici has recognized an analogy between the destruction of Macondo and that of the second Aztec sun by a hurricane wind. He does not elaborate on the subject, nor does he mention Quetzalcóatl (24).
11. "Por una anticipación del viento profético que años después había de borrar a Macondo de la faz de la tierra" (375).
12. "Estaba previsto que la ciudad de los espejos (o los espejismos) sería arrasada por el viento" (471).

13. "Estaba previsto que la ciudad de los espejos (o los espejismos) sería arrasada por el viento y desterrada de la memoria de los hombres" (471).
14. In his short essay titled "Paradise," Kafka asserts: "In a sense our expulsion from Paradise was a stroke of luck, for had we not been expelled, Paradise would have had to be destroyed" (29). Luis Rafael Sánchez suggested the pertinence of the Kafka quote to back up my interpretation of the last page of García Márquez's magnum opus.
15. In the original version: "el reino de pronombres enlazados."
16. "Predispuesto para empezar la estirpe otra vez desde el principio y purificarla de sus vicios perniciosos y su vocación solitaria, porque era el único en un siglo que había sido engendrado con amor" (465).

Works Cited

Amado, Jorge. *Teresa Batista, cansada de guerra*. Losada, 1976.
Amado, Jorge. *Tereza Batista, cansada de guerra*. Companhia das Letras, 2008.
Amado, Jorge. *Tereza Batista: Home from the Wars*. Translated by Barbara Shelby, Alfred A. Knopf, 1975.
Arnau, Carmen. *El mundo mítico de Gabriel García Márquez*. Península, 1971.
Bakhtin, Mikhail. *Problems of Dostoevsky's Poetics*. Edited and translated by Caryl Emerson, U of Minnesota P, 1984.
Bell-Villada, Gene H. Introduction. *Gabriel García Márquez's "One Hundred Years of Solitude": A Casebook*. Oxford UP, 2002, pp. 3–16.
Beltrán Almería, Luis. "La revuelta del futuro: Mito e historia en *Cien años de soledad*." *Cuadernos Hispanoamericanos*, no. 535, 1995, pp. 23–38.
Benedetti, Mario, editor. *9 asedios a García Márquez*. Editorial Universitaria, 1969.
Borges, Jorge Luis. *El Aleph* (1947). Alianza, 1971.
Bousoño, Carlos. *Teoría de la expresión poética*. 2 vols. Gredos, 1985.
Calvino, Italo. *Por qué leer los clásicos*. Translated by Aurora Bernárdez, Tusquets, 1994.
Cardenal, Ernesto. *Quetzalcóatl*. Nueva Nicaragua, 1985.
Cervantes, Miguel de. *Don Quijote de la Mancha*. Edited by Francisco Rico, Real Academia de la Lengua Española y las Academias de la Lengua, 2004.
Cervantes, Miguel de. *Don Quixote*. Translated by John Ormsby, edited by Joseph R. Jones and Kenneth Douglas, Norton, 1981.
Cobo Borda, Juan Gustavo. "El patio de atrás." *Cien años de soledad*, Real Academia de la Lengua Española / Asociación de Academias de la Lengua, 2007, pp. 495–510.
Cortázar, Julio. *Rayuela*. Sudamericana, 1963.
Díaz-Granados, José Luis. "La poesía de Gabriel García Márquez, una faceta poco conocida." *Prensa Bolivariana*, 21 June 2015.
Echavarría Ferrari, Arturo. "El tiempo recobrado (en Aracataca y Combray): En torno a *Vivir para contarla* de Gabriel García Márquez." *Gaborio: Artes de leer a García Márquez*, edited by Julio Ortega, Jorale, 2003, pp. 253–61.
Eco, Umberto. *The Name of the Rose*. Translated by William Weaver, Harcourt, 1983.
Eco, Umberto. *Obra abierta*. Translated by Roser Berdagué, Planeta-De Agostini, 1992.
"Editorial: *Cien años de soledad*." *El Tiempo*, , 3 Feb. 2017, www.eltiempo.com/opinion/editorial/cien-anos-de-soledad-editorial-el-tiempo-4-de-febrero-de-2017-54544. Accessed 11 Oct. 2019.

Eliade, Mircea. *El mito del eterno retorno*. Translated by Ricardo Anaya, Alianza/Emecé, 1972.
Eliade, Mircea. *Mito y realidad*. Translated by Luis Gil, Guadarrama, 1973.
Fuentes, Carlos. "García Márquez: La segunda lectura." *La nueva novela hispanoamericana*, Joaquín Mortiz, 1967, pp. 58–67.
Fuentes, Carlos. "Para darle nombre a América." *Cien años de soledad*, Real Academia de la Lengua Española / Asociación de Academias de la Lengua, 2007, pp. xv–xxiii.
Fuentes, Carlos. *Tiempo mexicano*. Joaquín Mortiz, 1971.
García de la Concha, Víctor. "Gabriel García Márquez, en busca de la verdad poética." *Cien años de soledad*, Real Academia de la Lengua Española / Asociación de Academias de la Lengua, 2007, pp. lix–xcv.
García Márquez, Gabriel. *Cien años de soledad*. 2nd ed. Editorial Sudamericana, 1967.
García Márquez, Gabriel. *Cien años de soledad*. Edición conmemorativa. Real Academia de la Lengua Española / Asociación de Academias de la Lengua, 2007.
García Márquez, Gabriel. *The Fragrance of Guava*. Translated by Ann Wright, Verso, 1983.
García Márquez, Gabriel. "Isabel viendo llover en Macondo." *Isabel viendo llover en Macondo*, Estuario, 1969, pp. 8–20.
García Márquez, Gabriel. *Living to Tell the Tale*. Translated by Edith Grossman, Vintage, 2004.
García Márquez, Gabriel. *La novela en América Latina: Diálogo con Mario Vargas Llosa*. Carlos Milla Batres, Ediciones-UNI, 1968.
García Márquez, Gabriel. *El olor de la guayaba: Conversaciones con Plinio Apuleyo Mendoza*. Bruguera, 1982.
García Márquez, Gabriel. *One Hundred Years of Solitude*. Translated from the Spanish by Gregory Rabassa, HarperCollins, 2003.
García Márquez, Gabriel. "La soledad de América Latina (Discurso de aceptación del Premio Nobel de Literatura 1982)." Ciudad Seva, ciudadseva.com/texto/la-soledad-de-america-latina/. Accessed 25 Aug. 2019.
García Márquez, Gabriel. *Vivir para contarla*. Sudamericana, 2002.
Giacoman, Helmy. *Homenaje a García Márquez*. Anaya, 1972.
González, Aníbal. *In Search of the Sacred Book: Religion and Contemporary Latin American Novels*. U of Pittsburgh P, 2018.
González Echevarría, Roberto. "*Cien años de soledad*: The Novel as Myth and Archive." *Modern Language Notes*, vol. 99, no. 2, 1984, pp. 358–80.
Guillén, Claudio. "Algunas literariedades de *Cien años de soledad*." *Cien años de soledad*. Real Academia de la Lengua Española / Asociación de Academias de la Lengua, 2007, pp. xcvii–cxxvi.
Gullón, Ricardo. *García Márquez o el olvidado arte de contar*. Taurus, 1970.
Ivanovici, Victor. "Gabriel García Márquez y el mito." *Gaborio: Artes de leer a García Márquez*, edited by Julio Ortega, Jorale, 2003, pp. 213–25.
Jakobson, Roman. "Lingüística y poética" (1960). *Ensayos de lingüística general*. Translated by Josep M. Pujol and Jem Cabanes, Seix Barral, 1975.
Kafka, Franz. "Paradise." *Parables and Paradoxes*. Translation based on the restored text (The Schocken Kafka Library), Schocken Books, 1961.
León-Portilla, Miguel. *La filosofía náhuatl*. UNAM, 1974.
Lévi-Strauss, Claude. *El hombre desnudo*. Translated by Juan Almela, Siglo Veintiuno, 1976.
Lévi-Strauss, Claude. *Mitológicas: Lo crudo y lo cocido*. Translated by Juan Almela, Fondo de Cultura económica, 1972.

Lévi-Strauss, Claude. *Structural Anthropology*, vol. 2. Translated by Monique Layton, Basic Books, 1966.
Lévi-Strauss, Claude. *Tristes trópicos*. Translated by Noelia Bastard, Paidós, 1997.
López-Baralt, Luce. "Algunas observaciones sobre el rescate artístico de la niñez en *Cien años de soledad* y *El tambor de hojalata*." *Sin Nombre*, vol. 1, no. 4, 1971, pp. 55–67.
López-Baralt, Mercedes. "Del tiempo abolido por los signos en rotación: Octavio Paz en *Piedra de sol*." *Para decir al Otro: literatura y antropología en nuestra América*, Iberoamericana/ Vervuert, 2005, pp. 270–85.
López-Baralt, Mercedes. *Una visita a Macondo: Manual para leer un mito*. Callejón, 2013.
Ludmer, Josefina. *Cien años de soledad: Una interpretación*. Tiempo contemporáneo, 1972.
Mañach, Jorge. *Indagación del choteo*. Revista de Avance, 1928.
Mutis, Álvaro. "Lo que sé de Gabriel." *Cien años de soledad*, Real Academia de la Lengua Española / Asociación de Academias de la Lengua, 2007, pp. xiii–xiv.
Ovidio Nasón, Publio. *Metamorfosis*. Translated by Ana Pérez Vega, Orbus Dictus, 2002.
Paz, Octavio. "Piedra de sol." *Configurations*, translated by Muriel Rukeyser, New Directions Publishing Corporation, 1971.
Propp, Vladimir. *Morfología del cuento* (1928). Translated by Lourdes Ortiz, Fundamentos, 1977.
Sabato, Ernesto. *La resistencia*. Seix Barral, 2007.
Sánchez, Luis Rafael. "Fragmentos de un hechizo." *El Nuevo Día*, 4 Mar. 2007.
Sánchez, Luis Rafael. *La guaracha del Macho Camacho*. La Flor, 1976.
Sánchez, Luis Rafael. *Macho Camacho's Beat*. Translated by Gregory Rabassa, Pantheon, 1988.
Torres, Daniel. *Los poemas inéditos del coronel Buendía rescatados del discurso de "Cien años de soledad"*. Monografías del Maitén, 1985.
Turner, Victor. *Forest of Symbols. Aspects of Ndembu Ritual*. Cornell UP, 1967.
Vargas Llosa, Mario. *Cartas a un joven novelista*. Alfaguara, 2011.
Vargas Llosa, Mario. *García Márquez: Historia de un deicidio*. Monte ́Ávila, 1971.

CHAPTER 18

STYLE AND SURPRISE IN GARCÍA MÁRQUEZ

MICHAEL WOOD

CERTAIN features of the language of Gabriel García Márquez's fiction remain constant throughout his career. There is his fondness for cliché, often put to ironic or lyrical use, but sometimes played quite straight, and in any case connecting his writing to older narrative traditions.[1] Both *Los funerales de la Mamá Grande* ("Big Mama's Funeral") and *El general en su laberinto* (*The General in His Labyrinth*), for example, end with the words "por los siglos de los siglos" (200), translated in the first case as "forever and ever" (195) and in the second as "through all eternity" (273).

There is, as many critics have noticed, a sparsity of dialogue in the fiction, so that conversations tend to be epigrammatic, as if they were mini-dramas or sketches within a more discursive context. García Márquez likes his sentences to multiply, like branches on a tree, so that assertions or descriptions often get second or third chances to say what they mean. And finally, key words keep recurring, as characters recur in Honoré de Balzac or William Faulkner. The verb *llegar* (to arrive, to come, to get to, to reach, to manage, to end up) would be an instance, hinting at a swerving, recurring story that runs through the word's various meanings. A letter doesn't arrive, but ghosts do. Historians arrive to destroy the world of myth. A character arrives at an insight; another arrives at a fiction. A bishop arrives in a small town.

What changes over his career is chiefly the mode of meaning, the practices of reference and implication. Very bluntly we could say that García Márquez starts out as a realist with a playful touch and ends up as a writer of fantasy entangled in realism. This is all, as we shall see, part of a long dialogue between fiction and history.

The constancies and changes I have just described will be visible everywhere in what follows and, for clarity's sake, I have grouped their exploration under the topics competing stories, deferred meanings, subdued voices, and singing along. The works I look at most closely are "Big Mama's Funeral" (1962), *Cien años de soledad* (*One Hundred Years of Solitude*, 1967), *El otoño del Patriarca* (*The Autumn of the Patriarch*, 1975), *Crónica de una muerte anunciada* (*Chronicle of a Death Foretold*, 1981), and *El amor en los tiempos del cólera* (*Love in the Time of Cholera*, 1985).

Competing Stories

García Márquez said in an interview that the duty of writers is not to conserve language but to open a way for it in history.[2] The context is that of his earlier attack on scholars who doggedly wish to preserve old-fashioned spelling, as if that were what mattered most about language, but I want to concentrate on the metaphor of "the way" or the road. Why does it need to be opened? Are the old roads closed, or is history generally short of roads for writing? And where does fiction, for example, situate itself "in history"?

A good place to look for the beginning of an answer to these questions is the early story "Big Mama's Funeral." The work opens by addressing "all the world's unbelievers" and announcing itself as "the true account of Big Mama, absolute sovereign of the Kingdom of Macondo" (184) who ruled for ninety-two years and died last September.[3] The pope attended the funeral. The next paragraph lavishly sets a scene and makes a recommendation:

> Now that the nation, which was shaken to its vitals, has recovered its balance; now that the bagpipers of San Jacinto, the smugglers of Guajira, the rice planters of Sinu, the prostitutes of Caucamayal, the wizards of Sierpe, and the banana workers of Aracataca have folded up their tents to recover from the exhausting vigil, and the President of the Republic and his Ministers and all those who represented the public and supernatural powers on the most magnificent funeral occasion recorded in the annals of history have regained their serenity and taken possession again of their estates; now that the Holy Pontiff has risen up to heaven in body and soul; and now that it is impossible to walk around in Macondo because of the empty bottles, the cigarette butts, the gnawed bones, the cans and rags and excrement that the crowd which came to the funeral left behind; now is the time to lean a stool against the front door and relate from the beginning the details of this national commotion, before the historians have a chance to get at it.[4] (184–85)

The structure of the proposition is simple—now that x is happening, it is time to do y—but the details threaten the stability of the structure at every moment. The three "now that"s (four in English for good measure) introduce the recovery of order and calm (or disorder and calm) for three different groupings of persons: the nation; various none too reputable professionals, including prostitutes and the president of the republic; the pope in heaven; and the people of Macondo unable to get on with their lives because of the mess the celebration of the funeral has left. Words like "balance" and "serenity" sound ironic as synonyms for normality, and they are, but it's not clear the narrator intends any irony. Gerald Martin suggests that the "voice and point of view steer just shy of outright sarcasm and rest content with an almost Swiftian irony" (44). This is a subtle reading, although we might also think the irony belongs to the author, while the narrator is rather more direct on his or her own terms, very casual, not averse to self-contradiction (invoking annals, attacking historians), and generally rather muddled in the attempt to list the facts and promote the myth.

The last lines of the story make clear that the awaited historians are not part of any memorial action, but the reverse. They are the agents of oblivion, metaphorical companions of the cleaners, and they will be here tomorrow. The parallel implication that the true story is trash is plainly not intended—or at least not by the narrator within the text:

> The only thing left then was for someone to lean a stool against the doorway to tell this story, lesson and example for future generations, so that not one of the world's disbelievers would be left who did not know the story of Big Mama, because tomorrow, Wednesday, the garbage men will come and sweep up the garbage from her funeral, forever and ever.[5] (200)

The "account" of the work's first paragraph and "this story" of the last paragraph are both translations of the word *historia*, but neither of them is what any historian will write. In English we distinguish between story and history. In Spanish people do too, but they use the same word twice, which is either confusing or a wonderful invitation to think about what we actually mean. A true story, in the language of García Márquez's fiction, means an oral or written account of what happened, with many material details and whatever elements of mythography and exaggeration are inseparable from the experience. History is the record of the same event, constructed with a pretense of objectivity, mitigated (or enhanced) by forgetfulness, sloth, and the political interests of those who have commissioned the report. The narrator's apparently naïve juxtaposition of the bagpipers and their working colleagues with the country's politicians and clergy appears in Spanish in an elegant grammatical inversion: the relevant verb forms follow the first set and precede the second. The device separates the groups only to connect them again. They are all part of history, and for the moment, history has gone home, leaving the coast clear for story. But history will be back. It always is. That's why language has to find a way for itself there; it can't rest in mythology, however true the myths are.

The mention of unbelievers and future generations in the earlier quotations recalls the many defenses of the incredible we find in Cervantes and his predecessors. They, like García Márquez, are playing with words. But they are also creating an intellectual platform for sophisticated debates about truth and falsehood, without seeming to do anything of the kind. This mode of not seeming, or seeming to be what is not, is an essential feature of García Márquez's style and part of his literary inheritance.

Deferred Meanings

The tangled myth of origin told about Macondo has many elements, and the initial sequence is of special interest. Because of a prophecy, Úrsula Iguarán is afraid that her marriage to a cousin will cause her to give birth to an iguana or a child with a pig's tail, and she wears a sort of chastity belt to prevent this from happening. This arrangement gives rise to the rumor that her husband, José Arcadio Buendía, is impotent, which in turn is used by a poor loser in a cockfight as an insult to the winner. The winner, José Arcadio, kills the offensive loser, Prudencio Aguilar. We are almost but not yet quite on the road that leads to the creation of Macondo. This happens when both José Arcadio Buendía and Úrsula Iguarán start seeing the ghost of Prudencio trying to clean up his wounds.

When Úrsula first sees the ghost, José Arcadio Buendía dismisses it as a projection of guilt: "This just means that we can't stand the weight of our conscience" (*One Hundred Years of Solitude* 22).[6] And when he himself sees the ghost, his initial reaction is to offer to renew the killing: "Just as many times as you come back, I'll kill you again"[7] (22). But then José Arcadio Buendía sees an "immense desolation" in the dead man's gaze and moves immediately to an identification with Prudencio's feelings themselves: his nostalgia, his anxiety.

This whole cluster of thoughts and emotions—the painful liveliness and loneliness of death—returns when Prudencio Aguilar's ghost catches up with José Arcadio Buendía in another place. This is where an attention to language is especially revealing. José Arcadio Buendía has become a great inventor and amateur scientist, and again, he can't sleep. He doesn't recognize the shaky, white-haired man who comes into his room in the early hours:

> It was Prudencio Aguilar. When he finally identified him, startled that the dead also aged, José Arcadio Buendía felt himself shaken by nostalgia. "Prudencio," he exclaimed. "You've come from a long way off!" After many years of death the yearning for the living was so intense, the need for company so pressing, so terrifying the nearness of that other death which exists within death, that Prudencio Aguilar had ended up loving his worst enemy. He had spent a great deal of time looking for him. He asked the dead from Riohacha about him, the dead who came from the Upar Valley, those who came from the swamp, and no one could tell him because Macondo was a town that was unknown to the dead until Melquíades arrived and marked it with a small dot on the motley maps of death. José Arcadio Buendía conversed with Prudencio Aguilar until dawn.[8] (77)

José Arcadio Buendía is "startled" at the aging of his visitor: *asombrado*, usually translated as "amazed." I'll come back to this word. And now it is José Arcadio Buendía who succumbs to nostalgia. His greeting to the ghost is jovial and intimate, which makes the sudden switch to indirect speech for the ghost's report almost shocking, the register of a distance no one can reduce, however close the two figures are otherwise. The next sentence has the signature of García Marquez written all over it: the phrase "many years," the list of conditions (longing, the need for company, the proximity of death), the crisis-loaded adjectives (intense, urgent, terrifying), the logical connection "so . . . That." For the rest, we note the names and places on the maps of death, the return of Melquíades, and the faintly formal suggestion of José Arcadio and Prudencio "conversing," rather than just talking, until dawn.

Prudencio's ghost can ask his way of those who share his condition but can learn of the living only through the dead. This idea echoes two thoughts we heard near the beginning of the novel, the first uttered by José Arcadio Buendía himself: "A person does not belong to a place until there is someone dead under the ground"[9] (13). This line in turn refers back (for the reader) to an earlier one: "It was a truly happy village where no one was over thirty years of age and where no one had died"[10] (9). Macondo was, or thought it was, a kind of paradise, but it was also a kind of nowhere. Death is the condition not of life, but of history and knowable habitation.

But now the ghost who could talk only to the dead is talking to the living, even if we don't hear his direct speech. I don't know whether Prudencio's ghost is aware that José Arcadio Buendía is on the edge of madness, or whether the ghost's arrival in any way triggers the tipping over the edge, but after that long conversation, José Arcadio Buendía decides that every day is Monday, destroys his laboratory, and starts "barking in a strange language" that turns out to be Latin. He dies two chapters later, and Prudencio's ghost has "for a long time" been the only person he remained in touch with, a figure "almost pulverized by the profound decrepitude of death."

A story of guilt and haunting, of penance insufficiently served, becomes a story of knowledge, a story about what Úrsula and José Arcadio Buendía learn rather than what they have done. Death is their instructor; it tells them everything they didn't know about sorrow and solitude, about death within life and life within death. In this perspective, the bad consequences of superstition and violence seem relatively minor. Even the killing of Prudencio is perceived as more (and less) than a killing. It is a banishment from life that no one has the right to impose on another, an exile that includes many of the characteristics of living—having to keep cleaning one's wounds, an awareness of one's condition, getting older, dying one day—but not that of being alive.

Asombro, the "capacity for surprise," is the key element in one of García Márquez's most interesting theoretical interventions in a fiction. Ghosts are not the only source of amazement in *One Hundred Years of Solitude*, and we should note that José Arcadio Buendía is amazed not at seeing a ghost but at seeing a ghost who has aged. The inhabitants of Macondo are faced with surprises that are no longer any surprise to us. They have to deal with the arrival of electric light, a railway, moving pictures, the gramophone, the telephone—modernity itself, we might say. They are "dazed by so many and such marvelous inventions" and can't tell "where their amazement began" (223).[11] The narrator translates this into a kind of speculative theology: "It was as if God had decided to put to the test every capacity for surprise and was keeping the inhabitants of Macondo in a permanent alternation between excitement and disappointment, doubt and revelation, to such an extreme that no one knew for certain where the limits of reality lay"[12] (224).

This is the game of belief and unbelief that is played in "Big Mama's Funeral." Only here the technological takes on the role of the fabulous. What is important to understand, across the playful historical ironies, is that not knowing the limits of reality is a dilemma but not a misfortune. It may save us from the lies of historians, even if we don't yet have anything we can put in their place. The attraction of myth is not that it tells us the truth. It tells us to keep looking.

Subdued Voices

Many sentences in *The Autumn of the Patriarch* are structured around seeing, and especially the verb form *vimos*, "we saw." But those who have seen are now talking; this is their narrative. Who are they? The narrative persona in García Márquez is always in some sense plural, even when the grammatical form is singular—a voice haunted by other voices, a sort of ventriloquist. But the effect is mostly rather discreet, and here it is out in the open. First and most simply, the narrators of the novel are the people who enter the palace after the president's death, or presumed death. This means that they are literally and symbolically "the people" of the unnamed country but also that various shifts are required. Already in the second chapter—the work has six untitled chapters, all consisting of long, sometimes extremely long sentences—the voice says "none of us was old enough" to have been there for the scene narrated in the first chapter, so that "we" means persons in a similar position rather than the same persons. This second set is more skeptical, too: "[B]ut we knew that no evidence of his death was final, because there was always another truth behind the truth. Not even the least prudent among us would accept appearances" (45).[13] The "we" also takes all kinds of liberties with tone and character. It addresses figures in the fiction as well as the reader; it describes the mental processes of persons and sets of persons, takes up their point of view. The result is a sort of narrative consortium, well represented in the novel's many tour de force sentences.

This voice does remarkably well, and more systematically, what the narrators of other works do only in brief epigrams or leave to the characters, as in the wonderful exchange that takes place (twice) in *One Hundred Years of Solitude*. The first speaker says, "What did you expect?" [or What did you want?] Time passes" (124). The second speaker says, "That's how it goes, but not so much[14] (335). There is a game with logic here and in all the many cases of such riddles in García Márquez. The notion that time passes more than it is supposed to doesn't correspond to any clock or calendar but makes perfect sense as a feeling about time at any given moment.

In *Autumn of the Patriarch*, the same style of remark takes on a strongly political tinge, as if politics were a real-life nonsense we can't escape, and that can be caught verbally only by strange, apparently simple, illogical claims. Gerald Martin shrewdly suggests, thinking both of the novel and its real-life models, "It was not that myth had triumphed over history but that history itself always becomes mythologized" (66). A good example here is the suggestion that the Patriarch's much-deferred autumn had "begun forever that night"[15] (*Autumn of the Patriarch* 36). I don't think the idea is that the autumn kept beginning; rather, it is that it began and never ended. This is impossible for any autumn we know, but it is close, as a concept, to the Patriarch's term of life, which is scarcely a term at all. He dies at an indefinite age somewhere between 107 and 232 years. That's a long life by any standards, but the estimated gap is itself more than a lifetime.

It's not often that a mythological statement confesses to its mythological basis so clearly. As with what "not even the most prudent" would accept, we are getting a whiff of the climate of outrageous authoritarian rule, and the theory of this response is brilliantly hinted at in the following political imperative. A government has to take action "so that no one would discover that everybody knew" (literally "what everybody knew")[16] (81). The prevention of knowledge is the prevention of any declarable claim to the possession of knowledge, a measure all the more necessary because everybody possesses it. You can't keep secrets, but you can enforce secrecy. `

It's worth comparing these riddling formulations to more open, declarative statements about the politics and psychology of this unnamed country. In one of them the narrators quote an American ambassador's claim that inertia is behind many reactions of the people: "The regime wasn't being sustained by hope or conformity or even by terror, but by the pure inertia of an ancient and irreparable disillusion" (229).[17] And something like this condition afflicts the patriarch himself:

> [A]s he discovered in the course of his uncountable years that a lie is more comfortable than doubt, more useful than love, more lasting than truth, he had arrived without surprise at the ignominious fiction of commanding without power, of being exalted without glory and of being obeyed without authority when he became convinced in the yellow trail of yellow leaves of his autumn that he had never been master of all his power, that he was condemned not to know life except in reverse. (250)[18]

We may think the ambassador's view is too purely practical. He is after all telling the Patriarch (no doubt correctly) that the people will not be behind him if he tries to renege on his agreement to sell his country's portion of the Caribbean to the United States—or indeed if he seeks their support in any other venture. But then we remember that the people's disillusion is fueled by everything we hear in the narrative voice: disarray certainly, even despair, but also an endless, ironic attention to detail, and a tireless will to keep talking in those long sentences. There is a form of understanding here, however chaotic, and any understanding, even of one's helplessness, is something other than inertia.[19]

As for the Patriarch himself, there is too much self-pity in his diagnosis for us to take it at face value: his "ignominious fiction" is a brutal fact for thousands of people. But his sense of the value of lies (their comfort, their uses, their endurance) may in the end correspond quite closely to the people's more sophisticated suspicion, evoked earlier, that "there was always another truth behind the truth.." If this is a binary proposition, the first truth is the appearance, and the second is the reality. But if we allow "always" its full force, then every truth is shadowed by another, and every shadow converts its predecessor into a sort of lie, even if it's true. This is pretty much García Marquez's view of Latin American history, and it is the reason why fiction (a departure from known reality but not a lie) can correct a mangled portrait of the world. Fiction doesn't speak truth to power, as the saying goes, it tells the stories power doesn't want to hear. The supposedly inert people of *Autumn of the Patriarch* are doing just this. But who will listen?

Singing Along

The young magistrate examining the crime in *Chronicle of a Death Foretold* becomes

> so perplexed ... that he kept falling into lyrical distractions that ran contrary to the rigor of his profession. Most of all he never thought it legitimate that life should make use of so many coincidences forbidden literature, so that there should be the untrammeled fulfillment of a death so clearly foretold. (99)[20]

It's very literary of the judge—the narrator speaks of the magistrate's reading of the classics and his familiarity with Nietzsche—to be surprised that truth can be stranger than fiction, and he is perhaps being a little too professional in thinking about legitimacy, but he speaks distinctly, if discreetly, for García Márquez the writer when he complains about an "untrammeled fulfillment," a completion *sin tropiezos*, literally without acts of stumbling. Obstacles, we know from countless literary theoretical pronouncements, and especially from Roland Barthes's book *S/Z*, are the life of narrative. They keep multiplying, and they keep getting overcome or circumvented. That's what a story is. *Chronicle of a Death Foretold* both confirms and inverts this proposition. The obstacles are there, and they structure the tale. But then they vanish with magical ease. They don't serve as obstacles to anything, least of all to death.

The language of the novella tracks the inaction of many characters and the helplessness of narrative, indeed the helplessness of knowledge when it comes too late or too early, or comes without force or instruments of persuasion. But the language itself is not helpless. It represents the phenomenon very well. And more often than not in García Márquez, it does a few other things too. Most frequently, and especially in the later work, it tells a better story than reality, because it knows what it is doing, and reality doesn't. But in telling such a story, it also invites us to look back at reality and measure the gap between the fiction and what may be the facts. One of the writer's most subtle forms of issuing this invitation is to stylize, or crystallize, the work fiction is doing by making it seem like a sort of song.

García Márquez spoke to Plino Apuleyo Mendoza about the effects he was trying for in *One Hundred Years of Solitude* and about his indebtedness for one of them to the popular song form known as the bolero. This is an interesting acknowledgment, but his real bolero novel, less generally recognized as such, is a later one, *Love in the Time of Cholera*. Critics have spoken about the roman-feuilleton as a model for this book, and also of the telenovela, and there is no disputing these influences, the first acknowledged within the text.[21] I am thinking of something else, though, which speaks more directly to the interaction of style and sentiment.

We may turn to the moment when Fermina Daza, our heroine, asks Florentino Ariza, our seventy-six-year-old hero, why he is not known to have had any romantic affairs during the long spell of their separation from each other, and this in a "city where everything was known even before it happened." He speaks "without hesitation in a steady voice," telling Fermina that he remained a virgin for her. This assertion provokes a remarkable commentary, a paraphrase of what is going on in Fermina's lucid and subtle mind: "She would not have believed it in any event, even if had been true, because his love letters were composed of similar phrases whose meaning mattered more than their brilliance. But she liked the spirited way in which he said it"[22] (339). It's hard to think of a better example of the truth of romance, the sense that lies can be truer than truth when they need to be. It's also a good instance of what is needed for this form of truth to work: a talented performer and an audience that knows how to combine skepticism and faith. But then the whole novel is saturated with the mood of the bolero, even when the effect is more subdued.

This is not the place for an essay on the musical form as it developed in the twentieth century, but a few titles will help us to see (or hear) where we are. "I Will Return," "You Said You Loved Me," "When I Return to Your Side," "If I Don't See You Again," "Why Remember," "You Don't Love Me Now," "That's a Lie," "My Secret"—all these songs are by the Mexican composer Maria Grever. The third of these works is well known in its English-language version, "What a Difference a Day Makes." Time, love, separation, memory, truth, concealment, the end of the affair: these are the elements of many romantic novels (and quite a few unromantic novels too), but they have a special valence in song, and this is what García Márquez is borrowing for his own purposes.

Here is what Fermina's house looks like shortly after her husband has died. He fell from a ladder while trying to recapture a pet parrot—hence the expression on his dead face:

> The house was under the rule of death. Every object of value had been locked away for safekeeping, and on the bare walls there were only the outlines of the pictures that had been taken down. Chairs from the house, and those lent by the neighbors, were lined up against the walls from the drawing room to the bedrooms, and the empty spaces seemed immense and the voices had a ghostly resonance because the large pieces of furniture had been moved to one side, except for the concert piano which stood in its corner under a white sheet. In the middle of the library, on his father's desk, what had once been Juvenal Urbino de la Calle was laid out with no coffin, with his final terror petrified on his face, and with the black cape and military sword of the Knights of the Holy Sepulcher. At his side, in complete mourning, tremulous, hardly moving, but very much in control of herself, Fermina Daza received condolences with no great display of feeling until eleven the following morning, when she bade farewell to her husband from the portico, waving goodbye with a handkerchief[23] (46–47).

There is nothing here that would be out of place in a realist novel, and the bolero effect is very quiet indeed. It is there, though: in the empty spaces and ghostly voices, in the allusion to the absurdity of the husband's mode of death, in Fermina's slightly too stylish self-control. The song doesn't mock the realism; it just reminds us how conventional the real can be, how it can make us feel we have been there once too often:

> Fermina finally catches sight of Florentino at the end of the vigil for her husband.
>
> She saw Florentino Ariza, dressed in mourning and standing in the middle of the deserted drawing room. She was pleased, because for many years she had erased him from her life, and this was the first time she saw him clearly, purified by forgetfulness. But before she could thank him for the visit, he placed his hat over his heart, tremulous and dignified, and the abscess that had sustained his life finally burst.
>
> "Fermina," he said, "I have waited for this opportunity for more than half a century, to repeat to you once again my vow of eternal fidelity and everlasting love."
>
> Fermina Daza would have thought she was facing a madman if she had not had reason to believe that at that moment Florentino Ariza was inspired by the grace of the Holy Spirit.[24] (49–50)

Boleros like forgetfulness, but only if there are memories in the offing. It's interesting that Florentino here attracts the word "tremulous," as Fermina had done a little earlier; both uses are connected not so much with emotion as with shakiness within a sustained pose. The abscess is a little too much for the world of romantic song, but even great lyricists slip at times. And here, as at the end of the novel, the account of Fermina's response is wonderfully clear and includes what she would have thought as well as what she does.

She is not quite ready for the Holy Spirit, though, and this is why Florentino's speech is unacceptable—for the moment. She kicks him out of the house. Full of grief for her husband, she goes to bed still dressed and hopes she may die in her sleep. She is finally "awakened by the despised sun of the morning without him. Only then did she realize that she had slept a long time without dying, sobbing in her sleep, and that while she slept, sobbing, she had thought more about Florentino Ariza than about her dead husband" (51).[25]

In one sense the novel is already over, and we are only on page 51 of a 450-page book. She will stop sobbing, and she and Florentino will live happily ever after, or *toda la vida*, as Florentino puts it in the final line. But then the bolero is not a long form, even if it can color a whole lengthy work, and with the bolero as with other myths and fictions, what can't be said is interesting, too.

And what has language been doing all this while in these competing stories, these realms of deferred meaning, in these helpless rambling voices and these conversions into song? Too many things to count, probably. But at the very least it has been seeming to attack or deny history while setting up a dialogue with it, exploring human amazement and the lessons to be learned from an intimacy with living death, and going on when all other social institutions have quit—this is a large part of what those long sentences of *The Autumn of the Patriarch* are about: refusing to leave reality alone, or merely copy it.

All of these activities have something to do with language's relation to fiction. Of course language is not a fiction, it is a fact and a practice. But it is, by its nature, implicated in the possibility of fiction. Because words are not things, they can name both what is the case and what isn't, and in García Márquez's work they do both. They report on reality and on what is missing from reality as we know it. They have another virtue, too: they report, implicitly but constantly, on their own reporting.

Notes

1. See José María Pozuelo Yvancos (481–93).
2. "El deber de los escritores no es de conservar el lenguaje sino abrirle camino en la historia" ("García Márquez dice" n.p.).
3. "Esta es, incrédulos del mundo entero, la verídica historia de la Mamá Grande, soberana absoluta del reino de Macondo" (167).
4. "Ahora que la nación sacudida en sus entrañas ha recobrado el equilibrio; ahora que los gaiteros de San Jacinto, los contrabandistas de la Guajira, los arroceros de Sinú, las prostitutas de Guacamayal, los hechiceros de la Sierpe y los bananeros de Aracataca han colgado sus toldos para restablecerse de la extenuante vigilia, y han recuperado la serenidad y vuelta a tomar posesión de sus estados el presidente de la republica y sus ministros y todos aquellos que representaron al poder publico y a las potencias sobrenaturales en la mas esplendida ocasión funeraria que registran los anales históricos; ahora que el Supremo Pontífice ha subido a los Cielos en cuerpo y alma, y que es imposible transitar en Macondo a causa de las botellas vacías, las colillas de cigarrillos, los huesos roídos, las latas y trapos y excrementos que dejo la muchedumbre que vino al entierro, ahora es la hora de recostar un taburete a la puerta de la calle y empezar a contar desde el principio los pormenores de esta conmoción nacional, antes de que tengan tiempo de llegar los historiadores" (167–68).
5. "Sólo faltaba entonces que alguien recostara un taburete en la puerta para contar esta historia, lección y escarmiento de las generaciones futuras, y que ninguno de los incrédulos del mundo se quedara sin conocer la noticia de la Mamá Grande, que mañana miércoles vendrán los barrenderos y barrerán la basura de sus funerales, por todos los siglos de los siglos" (195).
6. "Lo que pasa es que no podemos con el peso de la conciencia'" (26).
7. "'Cuantas veces regreses volveré a matarte'" (27).
8. "Era Prudencio Aguilar. Cuando por fin lo identificó, asombrado de que también envejecieran los muertos, José Arcadio Buendía se sintió sacudido por la nostalgia. 'Prudencio'—exclamó—, '¡cómo has venido a parar tan lejos!' Después de muchos años de muerte, era tan intensa la añoranza de los vivos, tan apremiante la necesidad de compañía, tan aterradora la proximidad de la otra muerte que existía dentro de la muerte, que Prudencio Aguilar había terminado por querer al peor de sus enemigos. Tenía mucho tiempo de estar buscándolo. Les preguntaba por él a los muertos de Riohacha, a los muertos que llegaban del Valle de Upar, a los que llegaban de la ciénaga, y nadie le daba razón, porque Macondo fue un pueblo desconocido para los muertos hasta que llegó Melquíades y lo señaló con un puntito negro en los abigarrados mapas de la muerte. José Arcadio Buendía conversó con Prudencio Aguilar hasta el amanecer" (74–75).
9. "Uno no es de ninguna parte mientras no tenga un muerto bajo la tierra" (19).
10. "Era en verdad una aldea feliz, donde nadie era mayor de treinta anos y donde nadie había muerto" (16).
11. "Deslumbrada por tantas y tan maravillosas invenciones, la gente de Macondo no sabía por dónde empezar a asombrarse" (197).
12. "Era como si Dios hubiera resuelto poner a prueba toda capacidad de asombro, y mantuviera a los habitantes de Macondo en un permanente vaivén entre el alborozo y el desencanto, la duda y la revelación, hasta el extremo de que ya nadie podía saber a ciencia cierta dónde estaban los límites de la realidad" (198).

13. "La segunda vez que lo encontraron carcomido por los gallinazos en la misma oficina, con la misma ropa y en la misma posición, ninguno de nosotros era bastante viejo para recordar lo que ocurrió la primera vez, pero sabíamos que ninguna evidencia de su muerte era terminante, pues siempre había otra verdad detrás de la verdad. Ni siquiera los menos prudentes nos conformábamos con las apariencias" (47).
14. "—¿Qué esperabas? —suspiró Úrsula—. El tiempo pasa.
    —Así es —admitió Aureliano—, pero no tanto" (114).
    "—Qué quería —murmuró—, el tiempo pasa.
    —Así es —dijo Úrsula—, pero no tanto" (291).
15. "Que aquella noche había empezado para siempre" (37).
16. "Para que nadie descubriera lo que todo el mundo sabía" (77).
17. "El régimen no estaba sostenido por la esperanza ni por el conformismo, ni siquiera por el terror, sino por la pura inercia de una desilusión antigua e irreparable" (247).
18. "A medida que descubría en el transcurso de sus años incontables que la mentira es más cómoda que la duda, más útil que el amor, más perdurable que la verdad, había llegado sin asombro a la ficción de ignominia de mandar sin poder, de ser exaltado sin gloria y de ser obedecido sin autoridad cuando se convenció en el reguero de hojas amarillas de su otoño que nunca había de ser el dueño de todo su poder, que estaba condenado a no conocer la vida sino por el revés" (270).
19. For two very interesting discussions of this aspect of the novel see Ortega and Labanyi.
20. "Tan perplejo . . . que muchas veces incurrió en distracciones líricas contrarias al rigor de su ciencia. Sobre todo, nunca le pareció legítimo que la vida se sirviera de tantas casualidades prohibidas a la literatura, para que se cumpliera sin tropiezos una muerte tan anunciada" (130).
21. See Fiddian (192–94).
22. "Ella no lo hubiera creído de todos modos, aunque fuera cierto, porque sus cartas de amor estaban hechas de frases como esa que no valían por su sentido sino por su poder de deslumbramiento. Pero le gustó el coraje con que lo dijo" (490).
23. "La casa quedó bajo el régimen de la muerte. Todo objeto de valor se había puesto a buen recaudo, y en las paredes desnudas no quedaban sino las huellas de los cuadros descolgados. Las sillas propias y las prestadas por los vecinos estaban puestas contra las paredes desde la sala hasta los dormitorios, y los espacios vacíos parecían inmensos y las voces tenían una resonancia espectral, porque los muebles grandes habían sido apartados, salvo el piano de concierto que yacía en su rincón bajo una sábana blanca. En el centro de la biblioteca, sobre el escritorio de su padre, estaba tendido sin ataúd el que fuera Juvenal Urbino de la Calle, con el último espanto petrificado en el rostro, y con la capa negra y la espada de guerra de los caballeros del Santo Sepulcro. A su lado, de luto íntegro, trémula pero muy dueña de sí, Fermina Daza recibió las condolencias sin dramatismo, sin moverse apenas, hasta las once de la mañana del día siguiente, cuando despidió al esposo desde el pórtico diciéndole adiós con un pañuelo" (77).
24. "vio a Florentino Ariza vestido de luto en el centro de la sala desierta. Se alegró, porque hacía muchos años que lo había borrado de su vida, y era la primera vez que lo veía a conciencia depurado por el olvido. Pero antes de que pudiera agradecerle la visita, él se puso el sombrero en el sitio del corazón, trémulo y digno, y reventó el absceso que había sido el sustento de su vida.
    —Fermina—le dijo—: he esperado esta ocasión durante más de medio siglo, para repetirle una vez más el juramento de mi fidelidad eterna y mi amor para siempre.

Fermina Daza se habría creído frente a un loco, si no hubiera tenido motivos para pensar que Florentino Ariza estaba en aquel instante inspirado por la gracia del Espíritu Santo" (82).
25. "La despertó el sol indeseable de la mañana sin él. Sólo entonces se dio cuenta de que había dormido mucho sin morir, sollozando en el sueño, y que mientras dormía sollozando pensaba más en Florentino Ariza que en el esposo muerto" (83).

Works Cited

Barthes, Roland, *S/Z*. Editions du Seuil, 1970.

Fiddian, Robin. "A Prospective Postscript: Apropos of *Love in the Time of Cholera*." McGuirk and Cardwell, *Gabriel García Márquez: New Readings*, pp. 192–94.

García Márquez, Gabriel. *El amor en los tiempos del cólera*. Bruguera, 1985.

García Márquez, Gabriel. *The Autumn of the Patriarch*. Translated by Gregory Rabassa. Avon Books, 1976.

García Márquez, Gabriel. *Chronicle of a Death Foretold*. Translated by Gregory Rabassa. Vintage, 1982.

García Márquez, Gabriel. *Cien años de soledad*. Sudamericana, 1967.

García Márquez, Gabriel. *Collected Stories*. Harper & Row, 1984.

García Márquez, Gabriel. *Crónica de una muerte anunciada*. La Oveja Negra, 1981.

García Márquez, Gabriel. *Los funerales de la Mamá Grande*. Sudamericana, 1962.

García Márquez, Gabriel. "García Márquez dice que no fue bien comprendido." *El Tiempo*, 14 May 1997.

García Márquez, Gabriel. *El general en su laberinto*. Vintage Español, 1989.

García Márquez, Gabriel. *The General in His Labyrinth*. Translated by Edith Grossman, Vintage, 1990.

García Márquez, Gabriel. *Love in the Time of Cholera*. Translated by Edith Grossman, Penguin Books, 1988

García Márquez, Gabriel. *One Hundred Years of Solitude*. Translated by Gregory Rabassa, Harper & Row, 1970.

García Márquez, Gabriel. *El Otoño del Patriarca*. Plaza & Janes, 1975.

Labanyi, Jo. "Language and Power in *The Autumn of the Patriarch*." McGuirk and Cardwell, *Gabriel García Márquez: New Readings*, pp. 135–49.

Martin, Gerald. *The Cambridge Introduction to Gabriel García Márquez*. Cambridge UP, 2012.

McGuirk, Bernard, and Richard Caldwell, editors. *Gabriel García Márquez: New Readings*. Cambridge UP, 1987.

Mendoza, Plinio Apuleyo. *El olor de la guayaba*. Bruguera, 1982.

Ortega, Julio. "*El otoño del partriarca*, texto y cultura." *Gabriel García Márquez*, edited by Peter Earle, Taurus, 1981, pp. 214–35.

Pozuelo Yvancos, José María. "García Márquez y el estilo del cuento tradicional." *Teoría e interpretación del cuento*, edited by Peter Fröhlicher and Georges Güntert, Peter Lang, 1997, pp. 481–93.

CHAPTER 19

GARCÍA MÁRQUEZ'S GLOBAL TRAVEL WRITING BEYOND THE IRON CURTAIN, 1955–1959

MARIANO SISKIND

ALTHOUGH travel figures prominently in the writing of Gabriel García Márquez, the critical tradition has paid very little attention to the cultural-political functions of travel and its narrative articulations in his work. And yet not only did García Márquez author a travelogue that narrates and fictionalizes his journeys across Eastern Europe between 1955 and 1957, but he also wrote hundreds of pages as a traveler (from *crónicas* and reportages to on-the-road recordings that involved note-taking, correspondence, and photography).[1] The figure of the traveler arriving from overseas is, moreover, distinctly meaningful in his fiction. A possible reason for this omission might be that when García Márquez writes about his own travels, or about fictional travelers who never shake off their foreign difference (like Melquíades in *Cien años de soledad*), or whose estranged gaze reinvents and denaturalizes the places they visit (like Antonio Pigafetta in "La soledad de América Latina" [*The Solitude of Latin America*], his Nobel lecture), the characters' displaced and displacing presences shake up whatever is fixed and stable in the narrative where they are inserted, including, most specifically, readerly expectations. The writing of travel and of the figure of the displaced global traveler is one of the most fruitful textual sites in which to examine the misrecognitions that surround the cultural identities of the traveler, as well as the symbolic structures represented through his eyes (Bartkowski xvi), and in the case of García Márquez, the status of his own authorship. In this chapter, I examine figures and narratives of global travel in García Márquez's writing. My idea is that by displacing our critical attention from the rootedness of Macondo's creative foundation to these images of mobility and foreignness, we get a divergent idea of his authorial figure and his texts, particularly when comparing them to the ones resulting from the enthronement of magical realism as the aesthetic form meant to define the differential identity of the region's literature in the context of the relational, uneven making of world literature. A critical examination of his writing of global travel as a textual site, in which the arrival of the foreigner shakes up stable or reified forms of identity (including his own) and opens them up to new forms of signification, is particularly urgent today in a world defined by the proliferation of migratory crises across the globe.

García Márquez's writing of travel dislocates an established, monolithic authorial mode of analysis in which everything the Colombian has ever written is positioned within a teleological interpretation that begins and ends in Macondo as metaphor for the Latin Americanist determination of the region's cultural politics. Foucault explains that an author is "the ideological figure by which one marks the manner in which we fear the proliferation of meaning" (119). Indeed, authorship is a contingent function of a text's singularity, and García Márquez's writing about travel (be it travelogue or the narrative moment when a global wanderer disrupts the stability of any given cultural structure) reveals an epistemological divergence from that other García Márquez who pens identitarian narratives of Latin American Macondism (it is important to point out that this divergence can be registered between *or* within texts).[2] The author function that emerges from the accounts of his visits to such places as the Nazi concentration camps of Auschwitz, Buchenwald, and Mauthausen, or the site of the razed Warsaw ghetto, or the mausoleum containing the embalmed bodies of Lenin and Stalin on Red Square in Moscow, or of the days he spent in Budapest searching for signs of the 1956 Hungarian Revolution ten months after it was quashed by the Soviet army, is different from the author- function in the scene of Remedios the Beauty ascending to heaven amid white bed sheets. His writing of global travel is the discursive site of "proliferations of meanings" that becomes rather illegible if we fix the meaning of the García Márquez textual formation to a preexisting author who is always identical to his 1960s Latin Americanist self.

Understood as a voluntaristic, particularistic, and agonistic discourse on the region's differential cultural identity, Latin Americanism was the aesthetic ideology of some of the most important novels of the Latin American Boom, and found in García Márquez's magical realism (which he had derived from Alejo Carpentier's idea of *lo real maravilloso*) its most perfect literary form (Siskind 72–75 and 87–88). Beyond the formalist drive to naturalize marvels and to get a glimpse into the supernatural core that is constitutive of the real, magical realism is meant to express a Latin American identity (and in its most general formulations, the cultural difference of geopolitically varied subaltern formations). This identity emerges from the collective and combined experiences of colonial, capitalist, racist, or gender oppression and from the way the literary protocols that had been institutionalized in Latin America since the 1940s were capable of working through these traumatic experiences.[3] But even within the foremost magical realist novel, *Cien años de soledad*, there are tropes that effectively disrupt the Latin Americanist construction of Macondo as a cultural place whose identity with itself and difference from the outside world explains the naturalization of the marvelous and the supernaturalization of the real as the logic of its symbolic order. The global travels of

Melquíades are one of these tropes. Buried underneath the story of the Buendías and Macondo lies the unrealized potency of a novel of fantastic transatlantic voyages and an implied narrative theory of global travel centered around the figure of Melquíades, the bearded, aging gypsy (though later rejuvenated, dead, and revived), whose periodic arrivals from distant lands disrupt the family's relation with itself and its sense of purpose.

The beginning of the novel seems to be not so much the story of a village, the house of its founding family, and their trials and tribulations, but the novel of Melquíades. Indeed, Melquíades's arrivals structure the narrative of the first chapter, from the disruption of linear time performed by the iconic opening line, when José Arcadio Buendía takes Aureliano to see the block of ice exhibited by the gypsies on the outskirts of Macondo, to the astonished reactions elicited by the other novelties brought by Melquíades (magnetic ingots from Macedonia, a telescope and a magnifying glass made by the Amsterdam Jews, Portuguese maps and navigation instruments, and several other miraculous and technical implements, among others). In these beginning scenes, the novel seems bent on exploring the dislocations enacted by the successive arrivals of a traveler, a stranger who has survived "pellagra in Persia, scurvy in the Malayan archipelago, leprosy in Alexandria, beriberi in Japan, bubonic plague in Madagascar, an earthquake in Sicily, and a disastrous shipwreck in the Strait of Magellan" (10);[4] it appears to be a novel about global travel and the local inscriptions of its displacements.

In "The Storyteller," Walter Benjamin laments the loss of the kind of embodied, artisanal narrative skill that disappeared with the emergence of a technical modernity marked by the radical impoverishment of experience and its lived immediacy (incidentally, this coincides precisely with Macondo's mythical time of prehistorical experiential fullness, at least until the temporal breakdown effected by the arrival of the state representative and the banana plantation massacre). Benjamin presents the theoretical fiction of two archetypical modalities of storytelling ("the resident tiller of the soil, and the trading seaman . . . who has come from afar," 84–85) that stand for the structures that once organized the practice of narration before the emergence of modernity and, according to him, the degradation of experience. Even though in the first chapter of *One Hundred Years of Solitude*, the lived worlds of both these narrative types are interwoven, it is the successive arrivals from afar of Melquíades that disrupt the symbolic order of Macondo, mostly but not exclusively, through his influence over José Arcadio Buendía. It is only after the first death of Melquíades, announced by the Armenian merchant, that the novel swerves toward the Buendías' fantasy of foundation and rootedness and away from the death drive introduced by the foreign words and deeds of Melquíades as he returns from the dead and becomes a permanent resident of Macondo. No longer the passing traveler who brought the world into the town only to disappear immediately thereafter, he now invokes the names of travelers like Alexander von Humboldt in conversation while leading a sedentary life in his room in the Buendías' house, instead of crossing worlds and oceans himself.[5] His foreignness (once again, the death drive inscribed in his otherness) survives in the illegibility of his parchments, and it is only at the end of the novel that his opaque, otherworldly writing becomes transparent to

Aureliano Babilonia at the very instant in which Macondo is sucked into "a fearful whirlwind of dust and rubble being spun about by the wrath of the biblical hurricane" (399).[6] When the foreigner's knowledge finally becomes intelligible to Aureliano Babilonia, it does not result in the assimilation of his radical otherness but, paradoxically, in the moment of utter apocalyptic transparency, in a confirmation of all its dislocating (in this case, destructive) force. The novel of Melquíades buried deep in *Cien años de soledad*, the novel of a radical difference brought about by the experiential otherness of the global traveler, bookends the novel of the Buendías.[7]

However, as I explained earlier, the writing of global travel—both its dislocation of symbolic structures and its inertial cultural forces—can be traced back to the moment before García Márquez became García Márquez (and before he adopted Latin Americanism as his predominant ideological place of enunciation). This writing can be found in the chronicles he published in magazines recounting his three journeys to Eastern Europe between 1955 and 1957, and in a montage of texts that became his travelogue *De viaje por los países socialistas* (*Travels across Socialist Countries*, reissued in 1978 by the independent Ediciones Macondo in Cali as part of a mad dash to reissue every single uncollected page written by the by then world-famous author of *Cien años de soledad*). In the later edition, he manipulates the dates and itineraries of his travel to make it seem like it was one single excursion across most of Eastern Europe and fictionalizes the identities of his travel companions, the people he meets, several scenes and encounters, and the motives behind each of his trips.

On July 16, 1955, García Márquez arrived in Paris as a European correspondent for the Bogotá newspaper *El Espectador* to cover a summit in Geneva that was to convene the presidents and premiers of the United States, the Soviet Union, France, and England, as well as to report on that year's Venice Film festival. At the time, he was an accomplished journalist and storyteller widely recognized in Colombia, but not yet an established writer: "Gabriel was a very well-known journalist in his country, but he still remained a clandestine writer" (Mendoza *The Fragrance of Guava*).[8] Besides a handful of uneven short stories published in newspapers and magazines between 1947 and 1955, and his many unfinished, proliferating manuscripts, his first book, the fully modernist, Faulknerian novella *La hojarasca* (*Leaf Storm*), had just appeared in April in Colombia, published by Samuel Lisman Baum's independent press, four years after he had finished writing it. (Guillermo de Torre, editorial director of Losada in Buenos Aires, had rejected it with a hurtful letter in 1952.) In April, *El Espectador* had published his fourteen-part reportage series on the story of the Colombian navy sailor Luis Alejandro Velasco, the only survivor of the shipwreck of the *ARC Caldas*, a disaster brought about by the Colombian Navy's negligence and corruption. The series, titled "La verdad sobre mi aventura" ("The Truth about My Adventure"), displayed García Márquez's astonishing narrative talent (the accidental displacement and survival of a castaway in the Caribbean sea can be read as his first incursion into the writing of global displacement) and revealed the cover-up organized by the military government then led by General Gustavo Rojas Pinilla. García Márquez's investigation and the testimony of the shipwrecked sailor had "challenged the ruling system more effectively than any of his more vocal leftist colleagues" (Martin 170) and made him persona non grata during the dictatorship. The newspaper decided to protect him by sending him to Europe as a correspondent.

And yet the decision to spend a few years in Europe must also be understood in light of García Márquez's own sentimental education as a young aspiring artist.[9] He wanted to spend time in Rome, study filmmaking at the Centro Sperimentale di Cinematografia, explore the possibility of interning in Cinecittá with his admired Césare Zavattini, and be in close proximity to his Italian neorealist film heroes (Martin 186–87).[10] But most of all, like so many writers before him, he had the by now unoriginal desire to live and write in Paris, to be a starving artist in the city that had been the capital of the World Republic of Letters (in Casanova's phrase) and that was now in decline, about to concede its pre-eminent global position (at least as far as Latin American literature was concerned) to Barcelona, New York, and London, but also to Buenos Aires and Mexico City. In any event, the twenty-eight-year-old journalist who arrived in Paris and was eager to see the cities he had read about and seen in movies had already found his voice as a reporter by writing for the Colombian press. Over the next two and a half years he would write seventy-seven articles and *crónicas* about European politics, everyday life, culture, and art from Geneva, Rome, Venice, Vienna, Paris, and London for the Colombian readers of *El Espectador* and *El Independiente* and the Venezuelan audiences of the Caracas magazines *Elite* and *Momento*.[11]

García Márquez's first eastward journey was from Vienna to Warsaw, Krakow, and the Auschwitz concentration camp memorial and museum in October 1955, after having spent almost three months in Rome. During his second journey in June 1957, he traveled from Paris (where he was permanently in residence) to the German Democratic Republic with his close friend Plinio Apuleyo Mendoza and the latter's sister, Soledad. They drove to Frankfurt, and then across West and East Germany to West and East Berlin, and finally visited Leipzig and Weimar before returning to Paris. Soledad Mendoza went back to South America, and the two friends started planning their next trip, this time to Moscow, where they were planning to participate in the Sixth World Youth Congress in Moscow. García Márquez had attempted and failed to get a visa to visit the Soviet Union because he lacked an official sponsor. While in Paris, however, he met an old acquaintance from Bogotá and Cartagena, the Afro-Colombian novelist Manuel Zapata Olivella, who "was accompanying his sister Delia, an expert practitioner of Colombian folklore, who [in turn] was taking a troupe of mainly black Colombians from Palenque and Mapalé to the Moscow Festival. García Márquez was a reasonably convincing singer, guitarist and drummer, and he and Mendoza signed up, then travelled to Berlin to meet the rest of the party" (Martin 214–15). They headed to Moscow, then to Leningrad and Kiev, where García Márquez parted ways with Mendoza to go on his own to Budapest, where he would survey the Hungarian capital's political landscape ten months after it had been crushed by Soviet tanks and troops on November 4, 1956: "[W]e wanted to know exactly what had happened in Hungary, without political distortions."[12]

García Márquez wrote the travelogue as soon as he returned to Paris in the fall of 1957, in an attic that a friend had lent him in the Parisian suburb of Neuilly, using notes and photographs from three separate trips he had taken between the summers of 1955 and 1957. He wrote eleven articles conceived as chapters of one longer narrative piece. He hoped to publish the entire series in *El Independiente* in Bogotá, the newspaper launched by his friend Guillermo Cano along with Alberto Lleras Camargo in February 1956, after the dictatorship of Rojas Pinilla had shut down *El Espectador*. Although Rojas Pinilla had been ousted a few months earlier, and even though García Márquez was critical of the immediate post-Stalinist transition and approved of Nikita Khrushchev's official process of de-Stalinization, *El Independiente* decided to pass on the articles, out of fear of a renewed bout of censorship for being associated with a discussion of the socialist Eastern European bloc. Still, his friend Mendoza was able to help, offering to publish only a selection of the most current and urgent sections in his magazine in Caracas. Thus, on November 15, *Momento* ran "Yo visité Hungría" ("I Visited Hungary") followed by two parts of "Yo estuve en Rusia" ("I Was in Russia"), with selections and versions of his texts on Budapest and Moscow on the November 22 and 29. He eventually only published ten of the eleven parts of the travelogue (the whole series minus the Hungarian chapter) during ten consecutive weeks between July 27 and September 28, 1959, when he was already back in Colombia, living in Bogotá. One of the reasons that might explain the decision to insist on the publication of the travelogue two years after his having written it might be the beginning of his political-ideological affiliation with the Cuban Revolution. At the end of January 1959, while living in Caracas, he had traveled to Havana, again with Mendoza, and they had met Fidel Castro less than a month after the establishment of his revolutionary government. A few months later, they took charge of the Bogotá offices of the Cuban news agency, Prensa Latina.[13] According to Jacques Gilard:

> In order for the complete series, except for the Budapest report, to finally appear in *Cromos,* a very particular interest that García Márquez had in publishing those texts had to come into play.... Above all, the military victory of the Cuban Revolution and its first reforms had heralded a new historical era on the continent ... [and] this long report-reflection on European socialism became more current for Latin America in 1959 than when it was written in a loft in Neuilly.[14]

Gilard's political interpretation is convincing, particularly because it underscores the ideological crystallization of García Márquez's shift toward Latin Americanism during 1959 in connection with his support for the Cuban Revolution and his work for Prensa Latina, which he began to process during his time in Paris: "When I arrived in Paris I was nothing but a raw Caribbean. What I am most grateful to this city for . . . is that it gave me a new and resolute perspective on Latin America. The broader view, which we didn't have in any of our countries, became quite clear here" (García Márquez, "Desde París, con amor").[15]

Although the Cuban Revolution/Latin Americanist ideological formation may have influenced his desire to publish "90 días en 'La Cortina de Hierro'" ("90 days behind the Iron Curtain"), I believe his financial needs in 1959, his writerly investment in the literary procedures of the text, and his cultural-aesthetic ambitions were the principal motivations behind his efforts to see it published; after all, for Latin American writers and intellectuals since the nineteenth century, the publication of their travel narratives across Europe had served as a shibboleth that offered entry into the world of letters. Even though his journalistic pieces had functioned as prose laboratories for his literary projects since the late 1940s, his travel writing should be squarely inscribed within the realm of fiction, not because of the lack of formal reportage and views that directly reflected García Márquez's own, but because of the literary criteria that oriented the literary constructive principles of the text itself.

Perhaps the most salient of these literary procedures was the decision to turn three separate and rather short West-to-East-and-back-to-the-West itineraries into the fiction of one long, continued eastward Grand Tour heroic narrative. For students and scholars of travel literature, there is nothing surprising here. Any writer's experience of travel is always mediated by literary constructive protocols, because, among other reasons, the anticipation of its future narration mediates the traveler's lived experience, investing it with the kind of transcendent meaning that in turn (in a circular logic typical of modernist processes of intellectual and aesthetic subjectivation) justifies and authorizes the social place of the writer *as* traveler. In other words, the writer's experience of travel is determined by the proleptic effect of its future narration.

In the case of García Márquez's travelogue, the constitutive gap that binds and separates the experience and the writing of travel exists as an echo or a trace that can be found in numerous places: in its highly tropological language; in the fictionalized dialogues with colorful secondary characters that highlight the tensions surrounding existing socialism and the varied stages of the process of de-Stalinization; and in the detached narrative persona García Márquez gives his narrator, a true *costeño* whose sense of fun, lack of solemnity, and distanced stance (very much modeled on the figure of the *pícaro*, perhaps with the exception of some passages in Poland and Hungary) allows him to ironize, and at times mock, everything he encounters. This narrator invokes rural, popular Colombian signifiers not as markers of nationality but rather of marginality, and positions himself as a provincial cosmopolitan who is constantly negotiating his distance from and proximity to the backward, socialist realities he intends to criticize.

A privileged aspect of the literary status of García Márquez's travelogue can be found in the invention of markedly narrative settings that do not coincide with what took place during the trips and in the fictional construction of actual travel companions and friends met along the way. In "90 días en la 'Cortina de Hierro,'" Plinio Apuleyo Mendoza becomes a certain Franco, "a wandering Italian, occasional correspondent for Milanese magazines, taking up residence wherever the night finds him [donde lo sorprende la noche],"[16] and Soledad Mendoza becomes "Jacqueline, French of Indo-Chinese origin, a layout artist at a magazine in Paris."[17] Gilard argues that these changes were meant to protect their identities (21–22), but for the reader, the textual evidence is overwhelming: García Márquez, an avid reader of travel books and adventure novels, wrote a travel narrative based on his experiences in Eastern Europe, yet took all the liberties necessary to produce an engaging narrative and to construct the narrator as a literary hero on-the-go, in the tradition of the books he knew so well. Nevertheless, the choice of an Italian journalist and a French-Vietnamese designer is worth looking into.

Franco is the narrator's sidekick, and the narrative is full of scenes of male camaraderie, almost as if Franco were a projection of the narrator (Rome and Venice were two of the privileged destinations of the European tour of García Márquez, and in fact, back in Bogotá he had dreamt about being immersed in Italian culture). A perfect example of their masculine sociability takes place in Leipzig, in East Germany, where they go (along with the Chilean student "Sergio" and another of their fictionalized acquaintances, the Colombian exiled intellectual Luis Villar Borda) to a decrepit brothel, "a state-run cabaret . . . a labyrinthine hodgepodge of the Divine Comedy and Salvador Dalí. Men and women weakened by drunkenness played out scenes of love, slowly and without imagination."[18] They dance with the locals while they make fun of the latter's looks and the ways they dress; they meet a German who confesses to have been happier when he was in a Nazi concentration camp—he doesn't say whether he was there as a Nazi guard or as a prisoner, and neither the narrator nor his buddies care to ask. The description of the setting underscores the oneiric and pathetic overtones of the place and very effectively conveys to the reader the estranged experience of the foreign travelers. The narrator specifies that this is a scene that he had never encountered in the *other Europe*: "I hadn't seen anything like it in Saint Germain-des-Prés" and "there's more authenticity in the bars of Via Margutta in Rome" (28).[19] And just as in the rest of the travelogue, the narrator does not waste an opportunity to delight in the strangeness of the places he visits. The text is meant to take the Colombian reader of *Cromos* beyond familiar lands through the looking glass—again, global travel as the experience of dislocation.

The relationship between Franco and the narrator—or rather, the presence of Franco as a projection of the narrator's own masculine traveling subjectivity—begs the question of why García Márquez chose to alter the identity of the third member of the touring party, Jacqueline. The fictional version of Soledad Mendoza, who journeyed with them during the spring of 1957, is present during the first half of the travelogue. The choice of a French-Asian identity suggests an erotic exoticizing of the female companion that is confirmed at different turns of the narrative; for instance, when they are in East Berlin and they enter a dining hall: "Our entrance brought an end to the murmur. I, who have little awareness of my moustache and my checkered red and black coat, attributed that suspension to the exotic physique of Jacqueline".[20] Yet even though Jacqueline is with them almost all of the time, she is frequently an afterthought for the male protagonists, not even a secondary character; always in the background of the narrator and Franco's main action, she is only given voice to make rather trivial remarks: "Franco and I had forgotten about Jacqueline. The whole day she walked behind us, straggling, observing without interest the dusty shop windows where second-rate items are displayed at outrageous prices. At lunch she showed signs of life: she complained about the lack of Coca-Cola" (*Cromos*, 3 Aug. 1959, 31).[21] Many more passages could be compiled to show that, rather than "rezagada" (straggling), Jacqueline is constantly excluded and shut out of the narrative.[22] In spite of all the fictional licenses, the narrative sends her back to Paris before they cross into Czechoslovakia, confirming that the narrative, structured as a masculine escapade, does not need Jacqueline. In García Márquez, border-crossing adventures undoubtedly belong to the realm of male sociability, and one of the sole cultural institutions that survives the dislocating symbolic procedures at the center of the writing of global travel is the patriarchal distribution of narrative gender roles.

Indeed, outside of the not-so-subtle insistence on the narrator's gendered identity, from a geopolitical perspective he eschews any reified or stable subject position other than the perspective of the foreigner. As I explained earlier, Gilard, Molina Fernández, and the very few critics who have studied García Márquez's travel writing see in his travelogue the first formulations of the Latin Americanist aesthetico-political identity that García Márquez would embrace after 1959, during the 1960s, and throughout the rest of his writing life.[23] However, nothing in the text points to a Latin Americanist perspective intent on instrumentalizing the encounter with Eastern European social and political difference to affirm a collective identity, particularly one seeking to metaphorize nonexistent essentialized regional cultural commonalities, or to express a common political destiny or forms of transregional solidarity based on supposedly similar challenges and ideological horizons. Neither Latin Americanist nor Europhilic, the narrator is determined not to be pinned down to an identitarian locus of enunciation. His self-representation is distinct from those typical of Latin American leftist travelers to the Soviet Union and the Soviet-controlled bloc "who travel to become acquainted with a concrete reality that is important not only because of what it constitutes in itself, but also because it represents the materialization of a general theory that is thought to be transmissible and transferable to other spaces, nations and cultures."[24] Back in Colombia, García Márquez had not been formally affiliated with the Communist Party (even though he had many close friends who were), but his leftist inclinations were evident and undisguised. However, when traveling across Eastern Europe he is constantly disappointed, bored, and made indignant by the realities he finds along the way. He is attentive to the urban traces of the de-Stalinization process that Khrushchev had recently announced ("The removal of the portraits of Stalin is being done in a very discreet way, without substituting them with portraits of Khrushchev")[25] and notices the population's fear of expressing themselves ("we didn't encounter anyone who roundly declared themselves against Stalin").[26] He explains that only his interpreter was willing to speak freely about Stalin's terror: "He spoke to us of horrifying crimes, of rigged trials, of mass executions. He claimed that Stalin was the most vicious, sinister and ambitious figure in the history of Russia. I had never heard such terrifying stories expressed with such candor."[27]

On several occasions, the narrator and Franco request permission to visit the mausoleum containing the embalmed bodies of Lenin and Stalin, and they convince a guard to let them in two days before their departure. They are even more impressed by the monumentality of the underground catacomb, its red and black marble walls, and red lighting (he confesses to be absorbed by the "glacial atmosphere"[28]) than by the actual cadaver of Stalin: "I became disillusioned: he looks like a wax figure.... Stalin is submerged in a dream without remorse.[29] The narrator builds a crescendo of anticipation only to be let down in the anticlimactic moment of the encounter with the dictator's dead body. Faced with the figure of the feared and bloody strongman, the narrator is significantly more interested in his own disappointment and boredom. By creating expectation in the reader as he and Franco descend into the underground chamber underneath Red Square, he prepares the scene of his own disillusionment: he, and not Stalin's embalmed corpse, is at the center of this awaited scene.

When considering Soviet culture, once again, he is disappointed and bored by its backwardness, a perspective seen in passages such as "we have basic concepts that the Soviets can't wrap their heads around"[30] and "an untenable feeling arises when, after making a joke about Marilyn Monroe, the audience is completely lost. I didn't encounter a single Soviet who knew who Marilyn Monroe was."[31] Nothing could be further from a Latin Americanist discursive formation than a traveler who constantly belittles the people with whom he interacts ("We looked at them passing by with their provincial shyness, like unhurried geese, never daring to bother us").[32] The same might be said for the protagonist who, when traveling across Eastern Europe, is often happy to place himself in the narrative as a spokesman for a vague and undifferentiated notion of Western capitalist modernization, lecturing from a position of moral superiority to naive Russians, who are presented as having a hard time comprehending the intricacies of the capitalist social institutions that are so familiar to him:

> Just as the radios have but one button, the newspapers—which are property of the state—have only one wavelength: "Pravda."... It's understandable that even the journalist's thoughts get all jumbled up when I explain our concept of journalistic news. A group of employees that came to the door of our hotel with an interpreter asked me how a newspaper functions in the West. I explained it to them. When they realized that there was an owner involved, they made incredulous comments.[33]

At the same time, when visiting West Berlin the narrator denounces the American occupation, which he accuses of turning a city that is in the process of being rebuilt twelve years after the end of the war into "a fake city ... aseptic, where things have the disadvantage of seeming too new," where "the big advertisements for Coca-Cola," "the North American tourists [that] invade in summer," and whose "five radio stations have never broadcast a word in German" all lead him to conclude that this "small island nestled in the iron curtain ... is a huge agency for capitalist propaganda."[34] Here I would like to return to the idea that the writing of global travel in García Márquez is structured around the foreigner's drive toward the radical dislocation of any stable place of enunciation. Again, the writing is neither pro-capitalist nor pro-socialist, but rather a constantly shifting point of view that displaces common perceptions and cultural myths.

The demystification of American/Western capitalism and of Soviet/Eastern European socialism is not performed in the name of a Latin Americanist version of nonaligned Third Worldism. The concept of "Tiers Monde," coined by the French demographer and anthropologist Alfred Sauvy in *L'Observateur* in 1952, was widely known in Latin America by the time García Márquez set off to Europe and more so by 1957, when he wrote the travelogue; and the Bandung conference on the future of the decolonized nations in Asia and Africa, which had given political substance to the notion of a Third World, had taken place in April 1955. Still, neither the concept of the Third World, nor Bandung, nor even Juan Domingo Perón's doctrine of the Third Position is ever mentioned in the travelogue or in García Márquez's journalistic pieces from the 1950s. Nor does one find any suggestion of an ideology or "structure of feeling" (Williams) akin to a Third Worldism "that condensed emancipatory political expectations" in the context of a paradoxical internationalism, expressed as a national-popular political unit (Bergel 132–33), and which mediated its inscription within the discursive sphere of Latin Americanism, particularly during the 1960s and 1970s. Nothing is seen but radical political disidentification.

There are two moments in the travelogue that disrupt this detached stance of disidentification (one, subtle and pithy; the other, momentous and surprising). Both are based on García Márquez's visits to the razed site where once stood the Warsaw ghetto and to Auschwitz in October 1955, a few months after the tenth anniversary of the defeat of Hitler. Both of these moments dislocate the figure of the traveler as ironist, and the humanist pathos they display breaks down the ironic distance between the traveler and his experience: an ironic distance that, throughout the travelogue, is meant to preserve his condition as stranger, his sovereignty over his own text, and at times, his moral superiority.

Soon after arriving in Europe, García Márquez covered the Venice Film Festival for *El Espectador*. Prior to returning to Rome, he managed to get himself invited as the Colombian representative to the International Federation of Film Critics Awards that was being organized in the context of the Warsaw Film Festival in October. On his way to Poland he decided to spend a few days in Vienna, where he wanted to recreate the trajectories of Orson Welles and Joseph Cotten's characters from Carol Reed's film version of Graham Greene's novel *The Third Man* (García Márquez, *De Europa a América* 251, 257–61). While in Austria, before leaving for Warsaw, he visited the Nazi concentration camp of Mauthausen, but he left no record of his impressions there other than the mention of the "stairs of death," the twelve hundred steps that Jews had had to climb with heavy rocks on their backs, from the quarry to the camp. In Warsaw, he visited the vacated lot where the ghetto had been, and after he was done with the Film Festival he traveled to Krakow. It was during his two days in the medieval city that he decided to join an organized excursion to the memorial and museum located in the Auschwitz I section of the Auschwitz-Birkenau concentration camp, where he stood inside the gas chambers, barracks, crematoria, administrative offices, and memorial galleries (later, in 1957, while in East Germany, he would also visit the site of Buchenwald).

As opposed to the ostensibly ironic, light, impish, and self-assured tone of the rest of the travelogue, in Auschwitz and in the brief line he writes about the Warsaw ghetto, García Márquez's narrator is overtaken by anguish and a sense of the historical gravity of these places. The pathetic, earnest register of the narrative reads as deliberate disruption of the discourse of the travelogue. His description of the ghetto as an absent presence ("The Ghetto is now a deserted and bare plaza, smooth as a butcher's table"[35]) offers up his writing as a sort of memorial to the carnage of the Shoah, embedding with historical and rhetorico-poetic meaning (the "mesa de carnicería" [butcher's table]) what in 1955 was an empty lot.

In Auschwitz he faces not a void but instead an overwhelming amount of remains and vestiges of the Holocaust, which the narrative lists in detail: "the unending barbed wire of the concentration camp," "the crematory ovens," "a small bathroom with poison gas showers," "the stretchers on which they placed corpses to burn," "a laboratory for the production of human substances [which] set up a thriving industry of human leather, textiles, human hair, and derivatives of human fat," "a suitcase made with human leather."[36] The narrator hopes that the description of the spaces, tools, and engineered systems of genocide can convey the pathos of the Shoah as he walks through the concentration camp. Yet time and time again he runs into the impossibility of making sense of Auschwitz: "In Germany . . . I racked my brain trying to understand the concentration camps. At the concentration camps I racked my brain but still couldn't understand the Germans."[37] Again and again, the narrator says that he does not understand, that what took place there is incomprehensible: "When the commissions of the International Red Cross inspected the camp, the Nazis showed them those innocent rooms [the gas chambers' showers] in order to convince them of the hygiene arrangements. One can't explain how those commissions didn't get it."[38] The writing of the visit itself is symptomatic of the impossibility of properly accounting for Auschwitz: García Márquez systematically misspells the German name of the camp; not once but the six times that the name is invoked, he writes "Auswisch."[39]

In *Remnants of Auschwitz*, political philosopher Agamben thematizes the paradoxical status of post-Holocaust testimonial narratives through his reading of Primo Levi's idea that survivors cannot be true witnesses precisely because they survived, and that the dead, "those who saw the Gorgon, have not returned to tell about it" (quoted in Agamben 33). Following Levi, Agamben explains that the survivor embodies the responsibility of bearing witness to the event of mass death he has outlived, thereby rendering testimony impossible. García Márquez's momentarily undone and dislocated *costeño* narrator is a mere tourist, but he nevertheless is affected by the impasse that Auschwitz opens up in the history of modern discursivity; the language of affect and frustration ("I was grinding down a deaf rage because I had the desire to cry"[40]), the pathos he had not experienced before, disrupts the traveler's place of enunciation and points to the impossibility of mourning.

His tears in Auschwitz (but wait, did he cry or not?) mark the limits of irony for García Márquez's narrator, who in turn journeys across Eastern Europe enacting the promise or threat to displace every stable discursive formation he encounters. This series of dislocations is constitutive of García Márquez's writing of global travel apart from the politics of ironic disidentification and particularistic misrecognition. Rather than as a genre, global travel can be seen as a series of discrete events of writing that hold the potential to displace, within and beyond "90 días en la Cortina de Hierro," foundationalist forces and reified identities or authorial figures, as well as to shed light on new and unstable cartographies unfamiliar to the geopolitics of a Latin Americanism that García Márquez's writing overflows with. Global travel is the possibility of reading García Márquez against himself.

Notes

1. The most important historical reconstructions of García Márquez's journeys to Eastern Europe can be found in Gerald Martin's remarkable biography and in the preface Jacques Gilard wrote for García Márquez's collected journalistic chronicles. When Penguin Random House relaunched his journalistic pieces, there was a flurry of reviews in the press, but the absence of critico-theoretical studies of his travel writing is noteworthy. One exception is Carolina Molina Fernández's "Y Gabriel García Márquez descubrió Europa," which is heavily based on Gilard's preface. For an interesting essay on the uses of Antonio Pigafetta's travels in García Márquez's Nobel lecture, see Humberto E. Robles. I would like to thank Anna White-Nockleby for her brilliant suggestions for this essay.
2. I take the idea of Macondism as a specific and historically situated form of Latin Americanism from Erna von der Walde's essay "El macondismo como latinoamericanismo" (227).
3. I take this characterization of magical realism from Irlemar Chiampi's classic definition: "a naturalização do irreal e a *sobrenaturalização* do real" (26). García Márquez himself expresses the dilemma that led him to magical realism thus: "My main problem was that I wanted to destroy the separation between what appeared to be real and what appeared to be fantastic because, in the world I was trying to evoke, that barrier did not exist" ("Mi problema más importante era destruir la línea de demarcación que separa lo que parece real de lo que parece fantástico. Porque en el mundo que trataba de evocar esa barrera no existía") (quoted in Palencia-Roth 69).
4. "La pelagra en Persia, al escorbuto en el archipiélago de Malasia, a la lepra en Alejandría, al beriberi en el Japón, a la peste bubónica en Madagascar, al terremoto de Sicilia y a un naufragio multitudinario en el estrecho de Magallanes" (*Cien años de soledad* 17).
5. The transformation of Melquíades the traveler into a sedentary, secluded, and venerably patriarchal Melquíades is quite striking: "When Úrsula undertook the enlargement of the house, she had them build him a special room next to Aureliano's workshop, far from the noise and bustle of the house. . . . The new place seemed to please Melquíades, because he was never seen any more, not even in the dining room. . . . Aureliano ended up forgetting about him, absorbed in the composition of his poems, but on one occasion he thought he understood something of what Melquíades was saying in his groping monologues, and he paid attention. In reality, the only thing that could be isolated in the rocky paragraphs was the insistent hammering on the word equinox, equinox, equinox, and the name of Alexander von Humboldt" (73–74). ("Cuando Úrsula dispuso la ampliación de la casa, le hizo construir un cuarto especial contiguo al taller de Aureliano, lejos de los ruidos y el trajín domésticos. . . . El nuevo lugar pareció agradar a Melquíades, porque no volvió a vérsele ni siquiera en el comedor... Aureliano terminó por olvidarse de él, absorto en la redacción de sus versos, pero en cierta ocasión creyó entender algo de lo que decía en sus bordoneantes monólogos, y le prestó atención. En realidad, lo único que pudo aislar en las parrafadas pedregosas, fue el insistente martilleo de la palabra equinoccio equinoccio equinoccio, y el nombre de Alexander Von Humboldt") 61).

6. "Un pavoroso remolino de polvo y escombros centrifugado por la cólera del huracán bíblico" (*Cien años de soledad*, 288).
7. García Márquez's literature is full of local, rather than global, travel and displacement that I do not analyze here because these instances fall outside of the purview of the critical argument I am trying to think through, and because this article is not meant to be exhaustive. My idea is that, as opposed to the investment of the writing of global travel in the creative force of dislocation and destabilizing, local travel follows an identitarian logic of foundation and reterritorialization. Local travel can be seen in José Arcadio Buendía's search for a path to the sea through the jungle and the swamp that resulted in the foundation of Macondo, and in García Márquez's memories of his youthful days on board a steamer on the Magdalena River (an itinerary that is fictionalized in *El amor en los tiempos del cólera*). In his autobiography, *Vivir para contarla*, García Márquez reminisces about his trips back and forth to Bogotá as a young student: "Today, I can dare to say that the only reason why I would want to be a boy again is to enjoy that voyage once more. I had to take the trip back and forth several times, . . . and each time I learned more about life than I did in school, and learned it better than in school. . . . The ships had easy, basic names: *Atlántico, Medellín, Capitán de Caro, David Arango*. Their captains, like those of Conrad, were authoritarian, good-natured men who ate like savages and did not know how to sleep alone in their regal cabins. The voyages were slow and surprising (*Living to Tell the Tale* 175). ("Hoy me atrevo a decir que por lo único que quisiera volver a ser niño es para gozar otra vez de aquel viaje. Tuve que hacerlo ida y vuelta varias veces . . . y cada vez aprendí más de la vida que en la escuela, y mejor que en la escuela. . . . Los buques tenían nombres fáciles e inmediatos: *Atlántico, Medellín, Capitán de Caro, David Arango*. Sus capitanes, como los de Conrad, eran autoritarios y de buena índole, comían como bárbaros y no sabían dormir solos en sus camarotes de reyes. Los viajes eran lentos y sorprendentes") (*Vivir* 212). In a future article I might extend the hypothesis of this essay to the fiction of Western European travel, migration, and displacement in some of the short stories of *Doce cuentos peregrinos (Pilgrim Stories)*.
8. "Gabriel era un periodista muy conocido en su país, pero todavía seguía siendo un escritor clandestino" (105). This translation, and all subsequent translations (unless otherwise noted), are by Anna White-Nockleby.
9. "Traveling to Europe was an old dream of García Márquez's; some signs of his intentions can be found in his Barranquilla journalistic production. Journalism was a mere pretext" ("La intención de viajar a Europa era un viejo sueño de García Márquez, del que aparecen algunas señales en la producción periodística de Barranquilla. El periodismo fue el pretexto.") (Gilard 26).
10. "García Márquez had arrived in Europe looking for cinema rather than literature" ("García Márquez había llegado a Europa buscando el cine más que la literatura") (Saldívar 302).
11. During the second half of 1955 García Márquez wrote forty-five articles for *El Espectador*, but the initial agreement with his former employers ended in December. For the Bogotá newspaper *El Independiente* he wrote seventeen articles between March and April 1956. He resumed his paid work for Latin American publications only late in 1956, when he started writing for the Venezuelan magazine *Elite* (he only sent them fifteen articles between September 1956 and March 1957). Thanks to his close friend and travel companion Plinio Apuleyo Mendoza, shortly before his departure from Paris to return to South America, he was able to publish in November 1957 three articles based on the longer travelogue recounting the Soviet and Hungarian portions of his trip. I have reconstructed the sequence and quantity of García Márquez's periodical publications using the detailed edition of García Márquez's *crónicas* edited by Jacques Gilard .

12. "Queríamos saber qué pasó en Hungría, a ciencia cierta y sin mistificaciones políticas" (*Momento*, 15 Nov. 1957, 10).
13. García Márquez explains to Plinio Apuleyo Mendoza that his friendship with Fidel Castro was politico-ideological when they first met and became personal only several years later: "[M]y very close and affectionate friendship with Fidel Castro began through literature. I'd known him casually when you and I were working for Prensa Latina in 1960 but I'd never felt we had much in common. Later on, when I'd become a famous writer and he was the best-known politician in the world, we met several times but still, in spite of mutual respect and goodwill, I never felt there could be more to the relationship than political affinity. However, in the very early hours one morning . . . I suggested that he relieve the tedium of required reading with something lighter but which, at the same time, was great literature. I gave him a few examples and was surprised to find that he'd read them all and, what's more, had a good appreciation of them. That night I discovered what few people realize—that Fidel Castro is a voracious reader, that he loves good literature from all periods and that he is a serious connoisseur of it (*Fragrance of Guava* 121). "[M]i amistad con Fidel Castro, que yo considero muy personal y sostenida por un gran afecto, empezó por la literatura. Yo lo había tratado de un modo casual cuando trabajábamos en Prensa Latina, en 1960, y no sentí que tuviéramos mucho de qué hablar. Más tarde, cuando yo era un escritor famoso y él era el político más conocido del mundo, nos vimos varias veces con mucho respeto y mucha simpatía, pero no tuve la impresión de que aquella relación pudiera ir más allá de nuestras afinidades políticas. Sin embargo, una madrugada . . . yo le sugerí que leyera algunos libros que unían a su valor literario una amenidad buena para aliviar el cansancio de la lectura obligatoria. Le cité muchos, y descubrí con sorpresa que los había leído todos, y con muy buen criterio. Esa noche descubrí lo que muy pocos saben: Fidel Castro es un lector voraz, amante y conocedor muy serio de la buena literatura de todos los tiempos" (*El olor de la guayaba* 195).
14. "Para que en 1959 terminara apareciendo en *Cromos* la serie completa, menos la crónica de Budapest, tuvo que entrar en juego un interés muy particular de García Márquez por publicar esos textos . . . sobre todo el triunfo militar de la Revolución Cubana y sus primeras reformas anunciaban una nueva era histórica en el continente . . . [y] ese largo reportaje-reflexión sobre el socialismo europeo llegaba a ser más actual para Latinoamérica en 1959 que cuando fue escrito en una buhardilla de Neuilly" (57–58).
15. "Cuando llegué a París yo no era más que un caribe crudo. Lo que más le agradezco a esta ciudad . . . es que me hubiera dado una perspectiva nueva y resuelta de Latinoamérica. La visión de conjunto, que no teníamos en ninguno de nuestros países, se volvía muy clara aquí" (n.p.).
16. "Un italiano errante, corresponsal ocasional de revistas milanesas, domiciliado donde lo sorprende la noche" (*Cromos*, 27 July 1959, 32).
17. "Jacqueline, francesa de origen indochino, diagramadora en una revista de París" (*Cromos*, 27 July 1959, 32).
18. "Un cabaret de estado . . . una laberíntica mescolanza de la Divina Comedia y Salvador Dalí. Hombres y mujeres postrados de la borrachera protagonizaban escenas de amor, lentas y sin imaginación" (*Cromos*, 10 Aug. 1959, 28).
19. "Yo no había visto nada igual en Saint Germain-des-Pres" and "hay más autenticidad en los bares de Vía Margutta, en Roma" (*Cromos*, 10 Aug. 1959, 28).
20. "Nuestra entrada puso fin al murmullo. Yo, que tengo muy poca conciencia de mis bigotes y de mi saco rojo a cuadros negros, atribuí aquél suspenso al tipo exótico de Jacqueline" (*Cromos*, 27 July 1959, 35).

21. "Franco y yo nos habíamos olvidado de Jacqueline. Todo el día anduvo detrás de nosotros, rezagada, observando sin interés las polvorientas vitrinas donde se exhiben a precios escandalosos artículos de pacotilla. Al almuerzo dio muestras de vida: protestó por la falta de Coca-cola" (*Cromos*, 3 Aug. 1959, 31).
22. Many critics have written about the masculine hegemony of travel writing genres in Latin American literature, despite there being a varied and rich repository of women travelers that only started to be recuperated and read critically in the late 1980s and during the 1990s. In her excellent book *Women in Argentina: Early Travel Narratives*, Mónica Szurmuk explains that "an overwhelming majority of travel writers were men, and the genre was defined within marked male categories such as the privileging of the gaze and freedom of movement" and underscores the scholarly need to "challenge the widely held assumption that women's travel writing is a purely personal interior venture" (2, 6). Of course, Jacqueline is a female character in García Márquez's travelogue and not the author or narrator of her own travel narrative; however, García Marquéz's lack of interest in exploring the specificity of his female companion's experience of estrangement is quite striking.
23. Take, for example, this passage: "The certainty that García Márquez had nothing to look for in Europe because he already held his cultural convictions; he was not aware of the fact that the already possessed the keys to his art. He traveled to Europe only to confirm what he already knew. Before his departure, he was fully Latin American. Intellectuals from previous generations had taken advantage of their stays in Europe to cultivate themselves and consolidate their Latin American interests and experiences, which demonstrated that the necessity of the journey. García Márquez's case is different as a result of his own labors and reflections: he takes the leap with fully formed convictions" ("La certidumbre de que nada tenía que buscar García Márquez en Europa, porque ya disponía de sus convicciones culturales; las claves que por entonces ignoraba, ya las poseía en realidad, sin saberlo. A Europa viajó, cuando más, a confirmar lo que ya sabía. Antes de partir era ya todo un latinoamericano. Los intelectuales de generaciones anteriores habían aprovechado su estadía en Europa para enriquecer o cuajar sus preocupaciones y experiencias americanas, lo cual demostraba que les era necesario el viaje. En cambio, con García Márquez, como efecto de sus propios esfuerzos y reflexiones, se da un caso de nuevo cuño: el de quien da el salto con sus convicciones ya forjadas" (Gilard 26–27).
24. "Que viajan para conocer una realidad concreta que es importante no sólo por lo que constituye en sí misma, sino porque representa la materialización de una teoría general que se piensa transmisible y trasladable a otros espacios, a otras naciones, a otras culturas" (Saítta 17).
25. "El retiro de los retratos de Stalin se está haciendo de una manera muy discreta, sin sustituirlos por retratos de Kruschev" (*Momento*, 29 Nov. 1957, 10).
26. "No encontramos a nadie que se pronunciara rotundamente contra Stalin" (*Momento*, 29 Nov. 1957, 10).
27. "Nos habló de crímenes espantosos, de procesos acomodados, de ejecuciones en masa. Aseguró que Stalin era la figura más sanguinaria, siniestra y ambiciosa de la historia de Rusia. Yo nunca había escuchado relatos aterradores expresados con tanto candor" (*Cromos*, 21 Sept. 1959, 32).
28. "Atmósfera glacial" (*Cromos*, 21 Sept. 1959, 33).
29. "Sufrí una desilusión: parece una figura de cera. . . . Stalin está sumergido en un sueño sin remordimientos" (*Cromos*, 21 Sept. 1959, 33).

30. "Nosotros tenemos nociones elementales que a los soviéticos no les caben en la cabeza." (*Cromos*, 14 Sept.1959, 37).
31. "Es indefendible la sensación que produce hacer un chiste sobre Marilyn Monroe y que la concurrencia se quede en las nubes. Yo no encontré un soviético que supiera quién es Marilyn Monroe" (*Cromos*, 14 Sept. 1959, 37).
32. "Nos miraban pasar con su timidez aldeana, con su parsimonia de ganso, sin atreverse a perturbarnos" (*Cromos*, 14 Sept. 1959, 37).
33. "Así como los aparatos de radio no tienen sino un solo botón, los periódicos—que son de propiedad del estado—tienen una sola onda: 'Pravda' . . . Es natural que inclusive los periodistas se formen un embrollo en la cabeza cuando les explico nuestro sentido de la actualidad periodística. Un grupo de empleados que vino a la puerta de nuestro hotel con un intérprete me preguntó cómo funciona un periódico en Occidente. Yo les expliqué. Cuando se dieron cuenta de que había un propietario de por medio hicieron comentarios de incredulidad" (*Cromos*, 14 Sept. 1959, 37).
34. "Una ciudad falsa . . . aséptica, donde las cosas tienen el inconveniente de parecer demasiado nuevas" ; "los grandes anuncios de Coca-cola"; "los turistas norteamericanos [que] la invaden en verano"; "cinco emisoras que nunca se ha transmitido una palabra en alemán"; "islote enclavado en la cortina de hierro . . . es una enorme agencia de propaganda capitalista" (*Cromos*, 3 Aug. 1959, 30).
35. "El Ghetto es ahora una plaza desierta y pelada, lisa como una mesa de carnicería." (*Cromos*, 31 Aug. 1959, 36).
36. "Las interminables alambradas del campo de concentración"; "los hornos crematorios"; "una pequeña sala de baño con dos duchas [de] gas venenoso"; "las parihuelas en que metían a asar los cadáveres"; "un laboratorio de elaboración de substancias humanas [donde] se organizó una próspera industria de cuero humano, de textiles, de cabellos humanos, de derivados de la manteca humana"; "una maleta fabricada con cuero de hombre" (*Cromos*, 31 Aug. 959, 39).
37. "En Alemania . . . yo me rompía la cabeza tratando de entender los campos de concentración. En los campos de concentración me rompía la cabeza sin poder entender a los alemanes." (*Cromos*, 31 Aug. 1959, 39).
38. "Cuando las comisiones de la Cruz Roja Internacional inspeccionaban el campo los nazis les mostraban aquellos cuartos inocentes [the gas chambers' showers] para convencerlos de la organización de la higiene. Uno no se explica cómo esas comisiones no se daban cuenta" (*Cromos*, 31 Aug. 1959, 39).
39. Incredible as it may seem, García Márquez's shocking, erroneous spelling of Auschwitz as "Auswisch" in *Cromos* was not corrected in the first edition of the travelogue in book format in Colombia in 1978; it was only corrected later in 1983 when a second edition of the book was published in Spain by Editorial Bruguera.
40. "Estaba moliendo una cólera sorda porque tenía deseos de llorar" (*Cromos*, 31 Aug. 1959, 39).

Works Cited

Agamben, Giorgio. *Remnants of Auschwitz: The Witness and the Archive*. Translated by Daniel Heller-Roazen, Zone Books, 1999.

Bartkowski, Frances. *Travelers, Immigrants, Inmates: Essays in Estrangement*. U of Minnesota P, 1995.
Benjamin, Walter. "The Storyteller." *Illuminations*, translated by Harry Zohn, edited by Hannah Arendt, Schocken Books, 1968, 83–110.
Bergel, Martín. "Futuro, pasado y ocaso del 'Tercer Mundo.'" *Nueva Sociedad*, no. 284, Nov.–Dec. 2019, pp. 130–44.
Casanova, Pascale. *The World Republic of Letters*. Translated by Malcolm DeBevoise, Harvard UP, 2004.
Chiampi, Irlemar. *O realismo maravilhoso: Forma e ideologia no romance hispano-americano*. Perspectiva, 1980.
Foucault, Michel. "What Is an Author?" *The Foucault Reader*, edited by Paul Rabinow, Pantheon Books, 1984, pp. 101–20.
García Márquez, Gabriel. *Cien años de soledad*. Alfaguara / Real Academia Española / Asociación de Academia de la Lengua Española, 2007.
García Márquez, Gabriel. *De Europa y América: Obra periodística 3, 1955–1960*. Edited by Jacques Gilard, Bruguera, 1983.
García Márquez, Gabriel. "Desde París, con amor." *El País*, 28 Dec. 1982, elpais.com/diario/1982/12/29/opinion/409964412_850215.html. Accessed 14 Aug. 2020.
García Márquez, Gabriel. *De viaje por los países socialistas: 90 días tras la "Cortina de Hierro"*. Macondo, 1978.
García Márquez, Gabriel. *Living to Tell the Tale*. Translated by Edith Grossman, Knopf, 2003.
García Márquez, Gabriel. "90 días en la Cortina de Hierro I: La cortina de hierro es un palo pintado de rojo y blanco." *Cromos*, no. 2198, 27 July 1959, pp. 34–35.
García Márquez, Gabriel. "90 días en la Cortina de Hierro II: Berlín es un disparate." *Cromos*, no. 2199, 3 Aug. 1959.
García Márquez, Gabriel. "90 días en la Cortina de Hierro III: Los expropiados se reúnen para contarse sus penas." *Cromos*, no. 2200, 10 Aug. 1959, pp. 28–29.
García Márquez, Gabriel. "90 días en la Cortina de Hierro VI: Con los ojos abiertos sobre Polonia en ebullición." *Cromos*, no. 2203, 31 Aug. 1959, pp. 35–39.
García Márquez, Gabriel. "90 días en la Cortina de Hierro VIII: Moscú, la aldea más grande del mundo." *Cromos*, no. 2205, 14 Sept. 1959, pp. 28–29.
García Márquez, Gabriel. "90 días en la Cortina de Hierro IX: En el mausoleo de la Plaza Roja Stalin duerme sin remordimientos." *Cromos*, no. 2206, 21 Sept. 1959, pp. 32–33.
García Márquez, Gabriel. *One Hundred Years of Solitude*. Translated by Gregory Rabassa, Avon Books, 1970.
García Márquez, Gabriel. *La soledad de América Latina*. Corporación Editorial Universitaria de Colombia, 1983.
García Márquez, Gabriel. *Vivir para contarla*. Mondadori, 2002.
García Márquez, Gabriel. "Yo estuve en Rusia II." *Momento*, vol. 6, no. 72, 29 Nov. 1957, pp. 8–17.
García Márquez, Gabriel. "Yo visité Hungría." *Momento*, vol. 6, no. 70, 15 Nov. 1957, pp. 8–19.
Gilard, Jacques. "Prólogo." Gabriel García Márquez, *De Europa a América: Obra periodística 3, 1955–1960*, edited by Jacques Gilard, Random House, 2015, pp. 19–89.
Martin, Gerald. *Gabriel García Márquez: A Life*. Vintage Books, 2008.
Mendoza, Plinio Apuleyo. *The Fragrance of Guava*. Translated by Ann Wright, Verso, 1983.
Mendoza, Plinio Apuleyo. *El olor de la guayaba*. Norma, 2005.
Molina Fernández, Carolina. "Y Gabriel García Márquez descubrió Europa." *Per Abbat*, no. 4, 2007, pp. 121–27.

Palencia-Roth, Michael. *Gabriel García Márquez: La línea, el círculo y las metamorfosis del mito*. Gredos, 1983.

Robles, Humberto E. "The First Voyage around the World: From Pigafetta to García Márquez." *Gabriel García Márquez. Modern Critical Views*, edited by Harold Bloom. Chelsea House, 1989, pp. 183–201.

Saítta, Sylvia. "Hacia la revolución." *Hacia la revolución: Viajeros argentinos de izquierda*, edited by Sylvia Saítta, Fondo de Cultura Económica, 2007, pp. 11–44.

Saldívar, Dasso. *García Márquez: El viaje a la semilla*. Alfaguara, 1997.

Siskind, Mariano. "The Global Life of Genres and the Material Travels of Magical Realism." *Cosmopolitan Desires: World Literature and Global Modernity in Latin America*. Northwestern UP, 2014, pp. 59–100.

Szurmuk, Monica. *Women in Argentina: Early Travel Narratives*. UP of Florida, 2000.

von der Walde, Erna. "El macondismo como latinoamericanismo." *Cuadernos Americanos* vol. 1, no. 67, 1998, pp. 223–37.

Williams, Raymond. *Marxism and Literature*. Oxford UP, 1977.

CHAPTER 20

DARK ECOLOGY IN *ONE HUNDRED YEARS OF SOLITUDE* AND *LOVE IN THE TIME OF CHOLERA*

WILLIAM FLORES

Using the theory of dark ecology and other twenty-first-century developments in ecocriticism, this essay explores how *Cien años de soledad* (*One Hundred Years of Solitude*; henceforth *One Hundred Years*) and *El amor en los tiempos del cólera* (*Love in the Time of Cholera*; henceforth *Love*) present a valuable, global, ecological vision. For this purpose, I use the following definitions. *Ecocriticism* is the study of the relationship between human beings and their natural environment within the diverse cultural manifestations in which this relationship presents itself, such as literature and the arts. Within ecocriticism, *dark ecology* is a theory that proposes that ecology is dark, meaning that the relationship between humans and their natural environment is toxic and that this reality needs to be accepted and presented, including the fact that all humans are causing it. The main difference between dark ecology and traditional theories within ecocriticism is in the emphasis placed by dark ecology on presenting the raw reality of the environmental crisis, rather than focusing on hopeful, unrealistic ways in which the world could become less toxic. Before delving into the analysis of the novels, the essay provides a review of recent scholarship and a brief examination of new developments in ecocritical theory.

In the following section, I explain how a number of scholars have acknowledged environmental themes that are relevant to my main thesis, which is that *One Hundred Years* and *Love* both evidence ecological wisdom consistent with twenty-first-century notions of dark ecology. Examining the apocalyptic imagination in *Love*, David Buehrer points out that the novel is a traditional and even post-apocalyptic work in its assumption that old age and love can survive the apocalypse as portrayed in the narrative.[1] Buehrer posits that in García Márquez's telling, humanity does get a second chance of survival that comes with a return to traditional humanistic values; if such is the case, however, then the message of *Love* is in direct opposition to that of *One Hundred Years*, in which humanity does not get a second chance on earth. This essay examines the apparent paradox by focusing on the textual portrayals presented in *Love* through the lens of dark ecology.

Focusing on the theme of romance in *Love*, Gerald Martin sees hope and an affirmation of life through the portrayal of enduring love in the text:

> The book is undoubtedly, for García Márquez himself, a reconciliation with people and cities he has been estranged from.... The first half of his literary trajectory, then, deals more with solitude, power and death; the second, more with love, acceptance and the affirmation of life. In fact, the ingredients are the same; it is the distribution and the emphasis which has changed. Here, in a novel which ought, given its elements, to be sombre and discouraging, we find García Márquez affirming life. (10)

Vicente Cervera Salinas is another critic who notes the novel's emphasis on the theme of hope, reading *Love* as a narrative in which García Márquez now trades the tragic fate of Macondo for the hopeful destiny of characters filled with grace and undying hope. Concurrently, Gene Bell-Villada examines the subject of love and further analyzes the novel, stating that "*Love* is in some ways a serene compendium of García Márquez's life experiences and wisdom" (*García Márquez* 211). I use these prior findings and further explore what this wisdom in the novel is in environmental terms.[2] In like manner, I take into consideration Bell-Villada's examination of names and narrative patterns in *One Hundred Years*, as he posits that García Márquez's system of names and narrative patterns is a rigorous and consistent construct whereby personalities and family resemblances are uniquely depicted and an ample variety of names are applied as self-contained rubrics to convey so commonplace a topic as that of family existence ("Names"). I take into consideration this examination of names and narrative patterns while providing an ecocritical reading of *One Hundred Years* that applies the theory of dark ecology.

Another scholar who has noted environmental themes that are relevant to my proposal is Josefa Lago Graña, who explores how representations of nature in *One Hundred Years* connect with masculine and feminine traits. While Lago Graña's work identifies gender representations in *One Hundred Years*, Eman ElSherief explores political ecology and finds that the struggle in the novel is based on ruthless monopolistic practices that a minority imposes on the rest of the population. According to ElSherief, these monopolistic practices are what bring about the destruction of Macondo. Support for this premise is based on García Márquez's Nobel Prize speech, in which the novelist states his desire for "a new and sweeping utopia of life ... where love will prove true and happiness be possible, and where races condemned to one hundred years of solitude will have, at last and forever, a second opportunity on earth" (cited in Ortega 91). ElSherief suggests that this utopia, based on fraternal love that opposes monopolistic practices, is a major implication in the novel. I take into consideration the researches presented by ElSherief, Lago Graña, and other scholars to provide an original examination of *One Hundred Years*.

Providing a distinct ecocritical reading of *One Hundred Years*, Diva Marcela Piamba Tulcán explores the relationship between the Macondo community and its natural environment; her examination discusses how *One Hundred Years* effectively evokes the close emotional and physical interdependence that exists among Colombian Caribbean living beings. Additionally, Raymond L. Williams points out that *One Hundred Years* is "the total story (and history) of Macondo from an oral, prewriting society to its development as a sophisticated writing culture in the final chapters" (116). García Márquez at first describes Macondo as a natural paradise where inhabitants live together with nature, respecting it. Concerning this utopian world, Rosario Curiel notes that, during Macondo's earlier years, people and nature live in harmony; she also posits that the anthropocentric rule over nature is a reason for the utopia described in the first stages of Macondo. This essay further explores the literary representation of the Anthropocene and Capitalocene while taking into consideration such prior findings.

In ecocritical studies, the concept of the Anthropocene is understood as the age that begins with the Industrial Revolution, continues until the present, and is characterized by increased human contamination and irreversible impact on the environment (Morton, "Poisoned Ground" 2013).[3] Since the notion of the Anthropocene began to be applied in cultural studies, many critics have identified some possible flaws in the theory itself. Ecotheorist Jason Moore critiques the theory of the Anthropocene on its foundational assumption that the Industrial Revolution is not a pivotal change in capitalist practices; rather, the Industrial Revolution is an augmentation of these practices ("The Capitalocene Part II"). In his studies that identify possible logical flaws in the theory of the Anthropocene, Moore points out that the theory of the Capitalocene is a more precise and workable theory than the Anthropocene, inasmuch as the Capitalocene identifies the root problem for the modern ecological crisis as the rise of capitalist practices (Farrier). Moore posits that "the Industrialization Thesis on ecological crisis [to support the Anthropocene] is dangerous because it blinds us to the early modern remaking of planetary natures" (Moore, "The Capitalocene, Part I" 621). To state, then, that the current ecological crisis is part of the Anthropocene era can well be interpreted as proposing that human activity, or at least all human industrial activity, is the root of the crisis. Thus, the most often cited theory for current environmental studies reduces all humanity to a single entity acting like a selfish unit that, by nature, will unrestrictedly destroy the planet. The assumptions that support the Anthropocene era undermine efforts in ecofeminism, postcolonial studies, and second-wave ecocriticism, all of which attempt to identify specific problems in human behavior and Anthropocentric practices that have caused human oppression, exploitation, and abuse of other humans and the environment.

Whether the Anthropocene Age begins with general human activity or with the Industrial Revolution, the problem would still remain that of human impact on the environment. I propose, however, that Moore's Capitalocene is more applicable to the Latin American reality because it uncovers a specific type of human impact, the vices of capitalism throughout the historical exploitation of the Latin American space and of many of its underprivileged inhabitants as the root cause of the current environmental crisis.

Nonetheless, the vast majority of modern academic entries in environmental, cultural studies in the *MLA International Bibliography* utilize or allude to the Anthropocene, and only a few include the Capitalocene, which, as this study points out, is a more applicable theoretical approach.

Other concepts that I use in this essay are those of hyperobjects and dark ecology. *Hyperobjects* are "massively distributed entities that can be thought and computed, but not directly touched or seen" (Morton, "Poisoned" 37), such as "global warming, nuclear radiation, tectonic plates, biosphere, evolution" (39). Hyperobjects encompass visible entities that are intrinsically interconnected with other entities, such as the effects of plastics on animal and human health. These effects in turn become part of procreation, producing a cycle that makes the effect of plastics a constant element surpassing time and space limitations, and so large that it merits the label hyperobjects. A fourth important theory is dark ecology, which proposes that the environmental movement should no longer focus on making the world less toxic but rather on accepting and presenting the current dark reality and the fact that humans are also causing it. According to dark ecology, humans are all part of the environmental dilemma, and the world is indeed dying (Aretoulakis). Timothy Morton critiques traditional environmentalism by suggesting that an apocalyptic environmental imagination provides a catharsis that encourages inaction. His pessimistic, dark ecology, conversely, attempts to provide a vivid, realistic portrayal of the current environmental dilemma that denies readers a catharsis and instead offers an urgent call for a change in behavior. Consequently, "ecological politics has a noir form. We start by thinking that we can 'save' something called 'the world' 'over there,' but end up realizing that we ourselves are implicated" (Morton, *Ecology* 187). This dark ecology hence differentiates itself from deep ecology in that the latter depicts representations of survival and continuation of life. Such representations provide false hope for the future survival of humanity, whereas in dark ecology, humans are slowly buried through their own destructive practices, leaving readers with a better sense of the current environmental reality.

As previously noted, in dark ecology, we are all part of the problem, and the world is indeed dying. Thus, "we should be finding ways to stick around with the sticky mess that we're in and that we are, making thinking dirtier, identifying with ugliness, practicing 'hauntology' (Derrida's phrase) rather than ontology" (Morton, *Ecology* 188). Dark ecology focuses on the present reality of environmental displacement from the ideal, pristine environment and the resulting feelings of loneliness and separation, instead of the fantasies of a hopeful, ideal relationship with nature. By focusing on the present, dark ecology attempts to be an applicable theory, examining the literature for its symptomatic value as works that portray the realities of the current environmental dilemma in all its manifestations, including the feelings of despair, and as works that do not necessarily provide a solution to the environmental crisis (Morton, *Ecology*).

The next section of this essay offers a reading of *One Hundred Years of Solitude* and *Love in the Time of Cholera* through the lens of dark ecology to explore how these novels offer a valuable ecological awareness. Moreover, this article explores how García Márquez's works provide a global ecological vision. *Love*, for example, uses the voice of the almost one-hundred-year-old character Uncle Leo XII to present what I find to be a constant concern in the novels of García Márquez that this essay examines: namely, that the economy managed by locals should not be transferred to overtly ambitious people from larger cities who will sell the businesses and their surrounding environments to overtly ambitious foreign entrepreneurs. While expressing this constant concern, the near-centenarian goes on to state that "we are still in colonial times" (*Love* 266),[4] suggesting that a way by which centralized governments preserve the coloniality of power is by transferring local enterprises and their natural environment to foreign businesses. By advocating for local management of sustainable living with the natural environment and by defending local minority communities, the novel evidences environmental wisdom that attempts to forestall the adoption of multinational, liberal capitalism in rural areas and the resulting environmental transformation. *Love* thus makes a clear distinction between local, sustainable economies and a multinational, unsustainable capitalism, which in the novel is represented by the possible acquisition of river navigation by German capital. The text further states that Florentino Ariza, one of the protagonists of the novel, "based his thinking [that prevented the sale of river navigation to foreign entrepreneurs] on the experience of the German commodore Johann B. Elbers, whose noble intelligence had been destroyed by excessive personal ambition" (*Love* 267).[5] In context, the passage explains Florentino Ariza's opposition to monopolies and the boundless avidity of foreign and national entrepreneurs. *Love* consistently manifests how such greed and ambition destroy not only the most gentle and intelligent people, but also the natural environment, namely, the Magdalena River and its surrounding forest.

In another episode, *Love* portrays nature as a collective living being that responds to human interaction. Its fourth chapter depicts a magical episode in which nature itself reciprocates a kind act on the part of Florentino Ariza by providing extraordinary growth and abundant fruit. In that episode, Florentino Ariza plants two small rose bushes to commemorate the death of his lover, Olimpia Zuleta. Later in *Love*, nature responds to this benevolent action by multiplying the two rosebushes into a dense rose garden that overwhelms a cemetery. In the wake of this episode, the garden is then destroyed by authoritative, centralized power, represented by the city's mayor, who belongs to the Republican faction. This latter action highlights a selfish act; it is important to note that it is the Republican faction that commits this destruction, a bloc that acts against minority groups. *Love* thus offers a narrative that defends minorities; exposes the abuses of centralized governments; and depicts nature as an important, collective living being.

In an examination of the portrayal of centralized governments and minority groups in *One Hundred Years*, I find that this novel presents an instance of abuses committed by a multinational company in rural areas, namely, abuses by an unnamed banana firm in the Caribbean region and the unconditional support that the multinational company has received from the central government. *One Hundred Years* presents these abuses, first, with the arrival of a representative from the central state; this representative, called Apolinar Moscote, is appointed by the central authorities to become the mayor of Macondo. He comes uninvited to rule over a people who have not elected him and immediately begins to change their way of life. As the narrator states, "Don Apolinar Moscote, the magistrate, just arrived in Macondo very quietly.... His first order was for all the houses to be painted blue in celebration of the anniversary of national independence" (*One Hundred Years* 57).[6] The passage portrays common abusive practices in which a central government attempts to assert its newly imposed authority by forcing a minority to do something that truly has no value for them: to paint their houses blue, a color that represents the Colombian Republican faction and an action that celebrates the independence of a nation that has not yet been identified with this rural community, given that there is no helpful national, institutional presence in the village. The passage presents circumstantial irony in that, by forcing the people of Macondo to celebrate the independence of a nation in which they have neither representation nor a meaningful belonging, the people of Macondo in fact are deprived of their liberty and independence. Through the use of this circumstantial irony, *One Hundred Years* subverts the imposition of power that centralized governments enforce over rural communities.

Besides subverting this imposition of central power through the use of irony, *One Hundred Years* defends the rights of local minorities through the voice of the diligent leader of Macondo, José Arcadio Buendía, stating the following: "Facing Don Apolinar Moscote, he [José Arcadio Buendía] gave a detailed account of how they had founded the village, of how they had distributed the land, opened the roads, and introduced the improvements that necessity required without having bothered the government and without anyone having bothered them.... They were happy that up until then it [the government] had let them grow in peace" (57–58).[7] Through the voice of José Arcadio Buendía, conscientious leader of the early stages of Macondo, the novel defends the rights of local communities to govern themselves without the influence of the state. Furthermore, the text provides specific reasons why local communities should retain their rights to govern themselves, such as the fact that they have successfully "founded the village," "distributed the land," "opened the roads," and "introduced the improvement that necessity required without" intrusion from the government (*One Hundred Years* 57–58). The text goes on to describe this influence of the central government as a "bother" in order to highlight the exploitative, abusive practices of central authority over rural communities and the self-sufficiency of local governments. At the same time, the text describes the localized improvements as "necessity required" (57–58), rejecting excessive ambition and capitalist abuse of the natural environment, a perspective that is also present in *Love*, as I have pointed out in this essay.

The representations of centralized government continue in the text while the narrator describes a confrontation that is threatening to become, as the narrator states, "a bloody and unequal civil war" in which the abusive side is formed by fictional, centralized forces overpowering the resistance of Liberals, formed mainly by rural communities (*One Hundred Years* 309).[8] The abuses of centralized government are also exposed in the text through a detailed account of how the authorities deceived union workers into coming to a negotiation meeting, only to be massacred (311). Through these and other fictitious, textual representations of the historical struggle between Liberals and

Conservatives that took place throughout the nineteenth and twentieth centuries in Latin America, *One Hundred Years* provides a fictional representation that exposes historical abuses committed by centralized government over rural communities and their natural environment.

Consequently, I find that *One Hundred Years* and *Love* provide valuable, solid representations of unrestrained central government committing abuse toward rural communities and against their natural environment—in order that these abuses may be considered and, hopefully, may not be repeated. Concurrently, both novels indicate that self-sufficient rural communities and economies are capable of attaining a sustainable relationship with nature. In so doing, both *One Hundred Years* and *Love* provide a global, ecological perspective that is consistent with the development of local, sustainable, peaceful economies.

In addition, *One Hundred Years* and *Love* contain portrayals of what can be construed as hyperobjects. Hyperobjects encompass visible entities that are intrinsically interconnected with other entities. In *Love*, pollution, food supply, and health are omnipresent themes. As contaminated elements enter the food supply and then affect animal and human health, this in turn produces cholera, other illnesses, and animal extinction, all of which are vividly depicted in the narrative. Through illness, procreation, and death, a cycle is created that makes pollution a constant element surpassing time and space limitations, and that is so massive it merits the label hyperobjects.

Moreover, the extreme contamination and deforestation of the Magdalena River region, including the massive animal extinction depicted in *Love,* produce imbalanced ecosystems that have a large effect on the biosphere, consequences that can also be thought of as hyperobjects. The environmental imagination portrayed in *Love* depicts a somber world in which animal species become progressively extinct and vegetation is destroyed. Such actions produce a chain reaction whereby the biosphere becomes unrestorable as the extinction of some species produces an overpopulation of other species. At the same time, this overpopulation results in the extinction of other species amid an unbalanced ecosystem where vegetation has been devastated. It is a chain reaction that can lead only to a barren, destroyed environment, as depicted in *Love*.

As happens in *Love*, excessive human interference produces a natural disaster in *One Hundred Years*; after the fruit company "changed the pattern of the rains" (233),[9] constant rain becomes the destruction for that company in Macondo. This destructive rainstorm begins in the wake of the massacre of banana workers at the end of chapter fifteen. As the beginning of the next chapter indicates, "It rained for four years, eleven months, and two days. . . . The sky crumbled into a set of destructive storms and out of the north came hurricanes that . . . uprooted every last plant of the banana groves" (320).[10] The novel goes on to describe how this inundation changes the livelihood of the community: "Petra Cotes sent him word that the horse pastures were being flooded, that the cattle were fleeing to high ground, where there was nothing to eat and where they were at the mercy of jaguars and sickness . . . the deluge was pitilessly exterminating a fortune that at one time was considered the largest and most solid in Macondo, and of which nothing remained but pestilence" (326).[11] The text goes on to portray how the rain lays waste to the town; in the end, most of the working population has left once the rain forced the banana company to leave Macondo, but also through the latter's abandonment, nature reclaims its territory by reclaiming the town.

The alteration of rain patterns for the purpose of satisfying economic ambitions, it can be said, triggers a series of events leading to the overall destruction. First, it brings about extraordinary rains that last for almost five years. Then, the alteration of rain cycles causes livestock and crops to die, resulting in hunger and death. The chain of events includes hurricanes, mass migration, poverty, and illness. This series of disasters is so massive and long-lasting that it surpasses perceivable time and space, a definition consistent with Timothy Morton's hyperobjects. The same imagination that creates Mr. Brown, who is able to alter the climatological cycle of a geographical Macondo, is also the imagination that creates Macondo's environmental destruction through a catastrophic sequence corresponding to hyperobjects. García Márquez portrays an eco-catastrophe that could occur as humans continue to manipulate the environment for economic ends.

Furthermore, I find that *One Hundred Years* evidences ecological wisdom consistent with twenty-first-century ecotheory. At the end of the novel, Aureliano finds his son being dragged away by ants even as he reads the epigraph of Melquíades's parchments, which states that "the first of the like is tied to a tree and the last is being eaten by the ants" (420). It is no accident that the first Buendía dies tied to a tree while ants devour the last Buendía, both being symbols of nature. Thus, nature becomes the executioner of the Buendía family and of Macondo itself as nature reclaims the world that was damaged irremediably by ambition, represented in the abusive practices of the banana company, as the following passage indicates:

> Macondo was already a fearful whirlwind of dust and rubble being spun about by the wrath of the biblical hurricane. . . . The city of mirrors (or mirages) would be wiped out by the wind and exiled from the memory of men at the precise moment when Aureliano Babilonia would finish deciphering the parchments . . . because races condemned to one hundred years of solitude did not have a second opportunity on earth. (422)[12]

With these words, the people who allowed the banana company to alter nature's cycles come to a hopeless end that is congruent with dark ecology, inasmuch as there is no opportunity for humanity to survive.

In *Love*, I also find relevant ecological wisdom. The first chapter of the novel, for example, depicts the escape of a pet parrot owned by one of the main characters, Dr. Juvenal Urbino—just one of several caged pets that are the property of his wife Fermina Daza. The novel, however, does not depict an appreciation for the animals accounted because of the intrinsic value of the animals per se, but rather it vividly represents the human utilization and abuse of these caged creatures. *Love* shows how the entire lives of animals are valued only for bringing laughter to humans. The parrot is able to escape from the cage and climbs over a patio mango tree that is also being utilized to tie down a monkey.

When Fermina Daza calls firemen to get the parrot back into its cage, the firemen destroy the tree and also part of the house; the narrator goes on to state that "on their way out they muddied the interior terrace and the drawing room and ripped Fermina Daza's favorite Turkish rug" (*Love* 39).[13] The narrative describes this destruction as "[n]eedless disasters, all of them, because the general impression was that the parrot had taken advantage of the chaos to escape to neighboring patios" (*Love* 39).[14] All these disasters caused by humans trying to control and subdue nature are described as needless because nature, as represented in the animal, is able to escape and manages to obtain its freedom. Just as the multinational banana company in *One Hundred Years* tries to manage and control the natural environment but at the end, this environment is able to free itself and destroy the Buendía world, so human beings in *Love* try to control nature and create "needless disasters," while nature is again portrayed as a living entity that manages to free itself.

There is also dark, circumstantial irony in this episode of *Love*, since Dr. Juvenal Urbino, who has been trying to keep this parrot in a cage, after a struggle with the bird, dies on Pentecost Sunday, the same day when many Catholics commemorate the coming of the Holy Spirit to earth. The circumstantial irony resides in the fact that Dr. Juvenal Urbino, who abuses animals and has a disregard for nature, dies, according to the text, without confession. The dark irony resides in the fact that according to Catholic belief, dying without confessing sin leads to eternal condemnation. Thus, on the same day on which many celebrate a believed blessing on earth, he is separated and dies, going into punishment, at least according to the prevailing worldview. The novel can be seen as presenting a judgment against those who mistreat animals and practice abuse toward nature; in so doing, the book demonstrates consistency with basic environmental principles, such as the recognition of the right of every life form to flourish and reach a positive development and the appreciation of nature for its intrinsic value (Devall and Sessions; Foucault).

Furthermore, *Love* explicitly exposes crimes of eco-injustice as it depicts and condemns illegal fishing that continues to take place in the Colombian-Caribbean region, such as using the mullein plant for indiscriminate, unsustainable fishing and utilizing dynamite in like manner. *Love* not only describes the practices but also highlights that they have been illegal since colonial times, presenting a clear position against them. On a positive note, the third chapter of *Love* also narrates how the captain of a ship named *Pius V Loayza* keeps the peace on his ship during a civil war, protects its passengers from contracting cholera even while traveling through cholera-infested territories, and prevents illegal hunting from taking place. *Love* goes on to state that this captain, who is commanding the ship on which Florentino Ariza is a passenger, is "inflexible even with the British minister who, on the morning following their departure, appeared in a hunting outfit, with a precision carbine and a double-barreled rifle for killing tigers" (*Love* 141).[15] In context, this quotation presents a mindful ship captain and consistency in the representations of the treatment of animals so that when the latter is present, a hero, the captain, prevents an antihero from harming the creatures. Thus, *Love* also evidences representations that are consistent with basic environmental principles.[16]

Years after the death of Dr. Juvenal Urbino, his widow Fermina Daza commits additional acts of cruelty: cutting down the fruitful patio mango tree to its roots and keeping caged the parrot that many times had tried to escape. *Love* goes on to state that the selfish reason for these actions is to obtain "the kind of house she had always dreamed of: large, easy, and all hers" (*Love* 302). By so stating, *Love* portrays a selfish character who only seeks her comfort regardless of the hurt experienced by other living beings. Such a passage could be interpreted as representing human exploitation of animals and nature with total disregard for the feelings that animals and plants may have. This is the same parrot who has come back to the house presenting, according to the narrator, sadness for the death of Dr. Juvenal Urbino. Fermina Daza takes advantage of the opportunity to cage and keep the bird for years after her husband's death, only to surrender the bird to a museum for continual entrapment. Paradoxically, the same living entities that have given their life providing fruit and company to Fermina Daza are the entities that are discarded and destroyed even while continuing to supply the benefits for which they have been appreciated throughout their lives. The paradox can be construed as a representation of human anthropocentric practices that plagued Latin America throughout the twentieth century and continue to damage the natural environment in the twenty-first, even as this natural environment continues to provide life and nourishment to humans.

Just as *One Hundred Years* and *Love* contain representations of hyperobjects and ecological wisdom, both novels also depict the influence of the Capitalocene era in rural communities and nature. *Love*, for example, highlights in its last chapter how boundless ambition, including the arrival of various steamboat companies from larger cities in the Magdalena region, produces an ecocatastrophe in the Magdalena River and its surrounding area. The narrative depicts a Magdalena region that faces uncontrolled deforestation, a polluted watercourse, extinct alligators and manatees, dead monkeys and parrots, and destroyed foliage. Part of this destruction is caused by hunters whom the text describes as "hunters for sport" (*Love* 331).[17] *Love* emphasizes the fact that it is not sustainable hunting nor hunting for needs, but rather hunting for the sake of hunting that causes the destruction of nature in the Magdalena region.

In *Love*, the arrival of various steamboat companies from larger cities can be understood as the foretold menace that the wise Uncle Leo XII had warned would arise if the steamboat economy opened up to overtly ambitious people from the larger cities. The narrator goes on to clarify that it is not the delta that has been destroyed, but rather the entire river. The text states that the waterway became "only an illusion of memory. Captain Samaritano explained to them [Florentino Ariza and Fermina Daza] how fifty years of uncontrolled deforestation had destroyed the river: the boilers of the riverboats had consumed the thick forest of colossal trees" (*Love* 331).[18] Unlike anthropocentric narratives that put the blame on all humanity, singling out imperialism and the coloniality of power as if they were part of human nature, this account pinpoints the arrival of various steamboat companies from larger cities and overweening ambition as the reason for environmental destruction. Such an analysis thus suggests that Moore's Capitalocene is more applicable to an ecocritical reading of *Love*, inasmuch as the novel exposes the excessive ambition and capitalist abuse of the natural environment, vices that are characteristic of the historical exploitation of Latin American space and of many of its underprivileged inhabitants. *Love* thus evidences an environmental imagination, vividly portraying the current ecological crisis while human beings continue with destructive anthropocentric practices that have plagued the twentieth and twenty-first centuries.

Love brings out the vices of capitalist abuse through the arrival of various steamboat companies to a rural region from large cities and those companies' excessive ambition; concurrently, *One Hundred Years* presents these vices through the arrival of merchants, the fascination with alchemy and gold, and the resulting change in the way of life of rural populations. *One Hundred Years* describes the beginning of Macondo as "a village that was more orderly and hard-working than any known . . . a truly happy village" (9).[19] The early settlement is further described as "a village of twenty adobe houses, built on the bank of a river of clear water that ran along a bed of polished stones, which were white and enormous, like prehistoric eggs" (1).[20] The narrative depicts an environment in which the population lives happily in rudimentary houses, made of biodegradable materials amid a natural paradise, where society respects and appreciates the natural environment. This description could be interpreted as a preindustrial, idyllic society within the construct of the Anthropocene. If such were the case, then the change would begin with the arrival of the innocent yellow train, which in turn is a leitmotif of the advance of the Industrial Revolution into rural Latin America. Nonetheless, the change in Macondo does not take place with the arrival of the machine, but rather with the arrival of the gypsies, the fascination with alchemy and gold, and the change in the way of life in Macondo, as the text indicates "that spirit of social initiative disappeared in a short time, pulled away by the fever of the magnets, the astronomical calculations, the dreams of transmutation, and the urge to discover the wonders of the world" (10).[21] This change in Macondo is congruent with the adoption of liberal capitalism as the basis of the transformation of Macondo from an organized, happy village into a place of solitude and destruction.

Moreover, *One Hundred Years* portrays the early days of Macondo as a place in which the inhabitants coexist with nature without damaging it—a depiction that is consistent with a pre-Capitalocene era in rural Macondo prior to the arrival of capitalism, as shown in the following passage: "José Arcadio Buendía at that time did not believe in the honesty of gypsies, so he traded his mule and a pair of goats for the two magnetized ingots. Úrsula Iguarán, his wife, who relied on those animals to increase their poor domestic holdings, was unable to dissuade him" (2).[22] The passage describes how the arrival of capitalism in the novel continues to transform the way of living of the inhabitants as they give away their livelihood for trinkets. It is important to note that the gypsies are depicted as an enlightened people in the novel, bringing knowledge and new technology to the village; nonetheless, the text also indicates that the spirit of social initiative, characteristic of Macondo prior to the arrival of the gypsies, disappears almost immediately, as I have pointed out in this essay. It can be inferred, therefore, that this mixture of advanced knowledge and trading practices is the beginning of capitalism in Macondo and, as the text indicates, a departure from the communal, social spirit that characterized the early settlement.

Even though *One Hundred Years* presents the recently founded village as an orderly place, as the plot unravels, the development of capitalism provides for the greedy exploitation of a rural society; in other words, the arrival of the Capitalocene in Macondo is what brings about the destruction of the otherwise happy village, beginning with the introduction of capitalist practices and increasing with the arrival of the banana firm in Macondo. The greedy, abusive practices of the company transform the natural world, rather than Aureliano Triste's bringing the innocent train to the town. As the narrator puts it in reporting the arrival of the Americans:

> No one knew yet what they were after, or whether they were actually nothing but philanthropists, and they had already caused a colossal disturbance, much more than that of the old gypsies, but less transitory and understandable. Endowed with means that had been reserved for Divine Providence in former times, they changed the pattern of the rains, accelerated the cycle of harvests, and moved the river from where it had always been. (233)[23]

It is interesting that *One Hundred Years* even compares the transformation now occurring with the arrival of the banana company to that of the arrival of the gypsies, since both arrivals transform the town into a market system. The arrival of the banana company, however, brings more than just detrimental capitalism. Again, as the novel indicates, the company "changed the pattern of the rains, accelerated the cycle of harvests, and moved the river from where it had always been" (233). Thus, there occurs in Macondo a transformation of the entire ecosystem. García Márquez portrays a world that is completely impacted and exploited for capitalist ends, a world in which one alteration in nature produces a chain reaction of events that irreversibly destroys the natural environment.

In conclusion, *One Hundred Years* and *Love* can be read through the lens of dark ecology, the Capitalocene, and hyperobjects, and as a result, the two works evince a valuable global, ecological vision. The environmental consciousness in *One Hundred Years* is consistent with dark ecology because the novel portrays a certain end to humanity in Macondo with no second opportunity for survival. *One Hundred Years* also enables the reader to observe a destroyed Macondo, an imaginary world where all humanity perishes in the wake of an ecocatastrophe produced by the manipulation of rain patterns. This alteration of the climate produces a series of events that, through this essay, I point out is a hyperobject. *One Hundred Years* is not, therefore, a narrative of an idealized primordial past or a catharsis that immerses us in the natural world to cleanse our minds of a guilty environmental reality; rather, the novel portrays characteristics of dark ecology, which aims to provide a vivid portrayal of the current environmental crisis. Hence *One Hundred Years* can be read through the lens of dark ecology as a novel that evidences closeness to the earth, a novel in which the unifying theme of solitude enables the reader to be in tune with nature, more than a mere presentation of an idealized interconnection with the environment.

In the Capitalocene, greedy interference is irreversible to the point that the destruction of humanity is unstoppable; I reveal in this essay that this irreversible greedy interference is present in *One Hundred Years* through the transformation that Macondo suffers following the arrival of merchant gypsies and the banana company. The change in the way of life in Macondo provides for the adoption of a liberal capitalism that transforms an organized, happy, village into a place of solitude and destruction. I also demonstrate how in the novel harmful capitalism deceptively takes advantage of a primitive rural society based primarily on barter, and also how this capitalism transforms the happily functioning village of Macondo's beginnings. *One Hundred Years* is thus a portrayal of a world that is completely impacted and exploited for capitalist purposes, a world in which one alteration in nature produces a chain reaction of events that irreversibly despoils the natural environment.

Similarly, I show in this essay how *Love* also portrays a valuable ecological perspective bringing to mind dark ecology, the Capitalocene, and hyperobjects. Although hope is a main theme present in *Love*, through the lens of dark ecology, *Love* can be seen as demonstrating that human beings are all part of the current environmental dilemma; as this essay indicates, even the main character Florentino Ariza contributes, although inadvertently, to the pollution and destruction of the environment by going against the wise advice of his old uncle and opening the region to a variety of companies that bring various steamboats to the area and produce an ecocatastrophe in the Magdalena region. The ecocatastrophe causes polluted elements to enter the food supply and affect animal and human health, including the outbreak of a cholera epidemic, other illnesses, and animal extinction. The representation of the cycle of illness, procreation, and death that I present in this essay is altogether a portrayal of a hyperobject carefully depicted in *Love*.

Furthermore, the extreme contamination and deforestation of the Magdalena region and the massive animal extinction portrayed in *Love* produce imbalanced ecosystems that have a large effect on the biosphere, which, as I indicate, is also a hyperobject. In the narrative, animal species become progressively extinct and vegetation is destroyed, producing a chain reaction whereby the biosphere becomes unrestorable as the extinction of some species produces an overpopulation of other species, resulting in an unbalanced, desolate, destroyed environment. Applying the theory of the Capitalocene, I also demonstrate that *Love* points at the vices of capitalism in its destruction of the natural environment and in its exploitation of underprivileged inhabitants as the root cause of a Magdalena region made barren.

Additionally, this essay presents several instances in which two main characters, Fermina Daza and Dr. Juvenal Urbino, contribute to the environmental crisis depicted in *Love* by hurting animals and vegetation alike for anthropocentric reasons. *Love* thus portrays a reality of environmental displacement from the ideal, pristine environment and the resulting feelings of loneliness and separation instead of the fantasies of a hopeful, ideal relationship with nature. *Love* is therefore a valuable novel to be seen through the lens of dark ecology inasmuch as it focuses not on making the world less toxic, but rather on accepting and presenting the current grim reality and the fact that all humans are also causing it.

The essay also finds that *One Hundred Years* and *Love* present a global, ecological vision enabling the reader to observe a destroyed imaginary world in which humans die in the wake of an ecocatastrophe in turn produced by excessive human interference in nature. According to dark ecology, human beings are all part of the environmental dilemma, and the world is indeed dying; this is precisely the reality depicted in *One Hundred Years* and *Love*, a vivid, valuable portrayal that, instead of producing an illusory catharsis, presents the reality of a dying world. Such a perspective is consistent with the pessimistic idea in dark ecology of the unstoppable self-destruction of humanity. As Morton points out, "If we get rid of the grief too fast, we eject the very nature we are trying to save" (*Ecology* 185).

Notes

1. David Buehrer points out that in *Love*, humanity gets a second chance of survival amid an apocalyptic environment by presenting the following arguments: after presenting the novel as an apocalyptic narrative, "a novel refreshingly traditional (or, one might say, post-apocalyptic) in its assumption that 'old age, love and death' as human virtues can survive the 'blast' (here, the metaphor for apocalypse being the cholera epidemic), that subsurface feeling can incubate in and be unearthed from the fallout ashes, that the resources for self-renewal, contrary to the inevitablist theories, are possible" (16), Buehrer states: "After decimation—environmental, cultural, social, even personal—what can possibly remain to revive a world spent by abuse and its own historical exhaustion?" (21). He then responds by stating that "human love, in all its manifestations" can remain to revive the world, for according to Buehrer, "the 'blast' may have devastated the environment, but paradoxically, it has served only to purify the emotions that have endured" (21). Buehrer then goes on to interpret the river in *Love* as "a vision of humanistic hope amidst the fallout of historical apocalypse" (23) and as "the depthless reservoir that symbolizes the rebirth of human emotions" (24). Thus Buehrer posits that in the novel, humanity does get a second chance at survival, but one that comes with a return to traditional humanistic values.
2. In a relevant criticism of *Love*, Manuel Cabello Pino explores the transposition of the novel from literature to the film version and finds: "If there is something that defines Florentino Ariza throughout the almost five hundred pages of García Márquez's novel is his hermetic personality and his taste for secrecy in everything that concerns his love life. He is not a Don Juan who conquers to show off his conquests, but quite the opposite. . . . It is that secrecy and that distancing from Don Juan's own behavior that manages to redeem the character of Florentino Ariza in the eyes of the readers of the novel, and that secrecy and distancing from the Don Juan also make the readers forgive his excessive promiscuity and allow readers to continue to identify with him as a romantic hero" (my translation). ("Si hay algo que define a Florentino Ariza a lo largo de las casi quinientas páginas de la novela de García Márquez es su carácter hermético y su gusto por el secretismo en todo lo que respecta a su vida amorosa. Él no es un don Juan que conquista para presumir de sus conquistas, sino todo lo contrario. . . . Son ese secretismo y ese alejamiento del comportamiento propio del don Juan los que logran redimir al personaje de Florentino Ariza a

los ojos de los lectores de la novela y los que hacen que estos le perdonen su desmesurada promiscuidad y se sigan identificando con él como héroe romántico" [n.p.]). Through a different reading, Robert Nana Baah suggests that in *Love*, García Márquez problematizes "the past, both at the personal and collective levels, and he does so by matching the disadvantages of remembering . . . against the benefits of forgetting. . . . At the collective level, García Márquez exposes the relative inadequacies of the old ways of doing things, whether they refer to customs, traditions, hygiene, medicine, technology, or politics, in light of new values fostered by modernity" (211). Baah then goes on to propose that *Love* "shares the view that no harm is done by forgetting our questionable past so we can forge new identities in the journey of life and nation building" (212). Though examining *Love* from an ecocritical perspective, this essay takes into consideration Baah's study on the value of the novel in terms of nation building. Exploring environmental consciousness in literary works written by Colombian authors Gabriel García Márquez, José Eustasio Rivera, Laura Restrepo, Héctor Abad Faciolince, and Candelario Obeso, scholar Ana María Mutis finds that the literary rivers in these works "channel the deterioration of the environment with the marginalization of certain sectors of the community, with violence, with foreign intervention, and with exclusion and social inequality, within a vision of nature in which it is recognized as an integral part of the community" (181).
3. The concept of the Anthropocene was coined by Nobel laureate scientist Paul Crutzen in 2000, when the unprecedented magnitude of anthropogenic environmental transformation since the advent of the Industrial Revolution led him and scientist Eugene Stoermer to publish their "proposal for the designation of a new geological time period called the 'Anthropocene,' a term intended to capture the 'central role of mankind' in planetary geological and ecological processes since at least the eighteenth century" (Anderson ix).
4. "Seguimos en la Colonia" (*El amor en los tiempos de cólera* 355).
5. "Florentino Ariza fundaba sus razones en la experiencia del comodoro alemán Juan B. Elbers, que había estropeado su noble ingenio con la desmesura de su ambición personal" (356).
6. "Don Apolinar Moscote, el corregidor, había llegado a Macondo sin hacer ruido. . . . Su primera disposición fue ordenar que todas las casas se pintaran de azul para celebrar el aniversario de la independencia nacional" (148).
7. "Ante la impavidez de don Apolinar Moscote, [José Arcadio Buendía] hizo un pormenorizado recuento de cómo habían fundado la aldea, de cómo se habían repartido la tierra, abierto los caminos e introducido las mejoras que les había ido exigiendo la necesidad, sin haber molestado a gobierno alguno y sin que nadie los molestara. . . . Se alegraba de que hasta entonces [el gobierno] los hubiera dejado crecer en paz" (149).
8. "La situación amenazaba con evolucionar hacia una guerra desigual y sangrienta" (419).
9. The Spanish edition of this passage indicates what the managers of the unnamed banana firm did: "modificaron el régimen de lluvias" (337).
10. "Llovió cuatro años, once meses y dos días. . . . Se desempedraba el cielo en unas tempestades de estropicio, y el norte mandaba unos huracanes que . . . desenterraron de raíz las últimas cepas de las plantaciones" (431).
11. "Le mandó a decir que los potreros se estaban inundando, que el ganado se fugaba hacia las tierras altas donde no había qué comer, y que estaban a merced del tigre y la peste . . . el diluvio fue exterminando sin misericordia una fortuna que en un tiempo se tuvo como la más grande y sólida de Macondo, y de la cual no quedaba sino la pestilencia" (437).

12. "Macondo era ya un pavoroso remolino de polvo y escombros centrifugado por la cólera del huracán bíblico . . . la ciudad de los espejos (o los espejismos) sería arrasada por el viento y desterrada de la memoria de los hombres en el instante en que Aureliano Babilonia acabara de descifrar los pergaminos . . . porque las estirpes condenadas a cien años de soledad no tenían una segunda oportunidad sobre la tierra" (547–48).
13. "De paso embarraron la terraza interior y la sala, y desgarraron una alfombra turca" (61).
14. "Desastres inútiles, además, porque la impresión general era que el loro había aprovechado el desorden para escapar por los patios vecinos" (61).
15. "Fue inflexible inclusive con el ministro británico, que desde el día siguiente de la partida amaneció vestido de cazador, con una carabina de precisión y una escopeta de dos cañones para matar tigres" (192).
16. Since *Love* exposes crimes of eco-injustice, including condemning indiscriminate practices of illegal fishing and hunting, the novel evidences representations that are consistent with basic environmental principles, such as the recognition of the right of every life form to flourish and reach a positive development (Devall and Sessions; Foucault), the appreciation of nature for its intrinsic value, and the recognition of excessive human interference in balanced ecosystems (Devall and Sessions).
17. The Spanish version of the novel identifies the type of animal hunters that contribute to the destruction of the environment using the title "los cazadores de placer" (*El amor en los tiempos de cólera* 439).
18. "Solo una ilusión de la memoria. El capitán Samaritano les explicó cómo la desforestación irracional había acabado con el río en cincuenta años: las calderas de los buques habían devorado la selva enmarañada de árboles colosales" (439).
19. "Una aldea más ordenada y laboriosa que cualquiera de las conocidas . . . una aldea feliz" (91).
20. "Una aldea de veinte casas de barro y cañabrava construidas a la orilla de un río de aguas diáfanas que se precipitaban por un lecho de piedras pulidas, blancas y enormes como huevos prehistóricos" (81).
21. "Aquel espíritu de iniciativa social desapareció en poco tiempo, arrastrado por la fiebre de los imanes, los cálculos astronómicos, los sueños de transmutación y las ansias de conocer las maravillas del mundo" (92).
22. "José Arcadio Buendía no creía en aquel tiempo en la honradez de los gitanos, así que cambió su mulo y una partida de chivos por dos lingotes imantados. Úrsula Iguarán, su mujer, que contaba con aquellos animales para ensanchar el desmedrado patrimonio doméstico, no consiguió disuadirlo" (82).
23. "Nadie sabía aún qué era lo que buscaban, o si en verdad no eran más que filántropos y ya habían ocasionado un trastorno colosal, mucho más perturbador que el de los antiguos gitanos, pero menos transitorio y comprensible. Dotados de recursos que en otra época estuvieron reservados a la Divina Providencia, modificaron el régimen de lluvias, apresuraron el ciclo de las cosechas, y quitaron el río de donde estuvo siempre" (337).

Works Cited

Anderson, Mark. "Introduction: The Dimensions of Crisis." *Ecological Crisis and Cultural Representation in Latin America: Ecocritical Perspectives on Art, Film, and Literature*, edited by Mark Anderson and Zélia M. Bora. Lexington Books, 2016, pp. ix–xxxii.

Aretoulakis, Emmanouil. "Towards a PostHumanist Ecology." *European Journal of English Studies*, vol. 18, no. 2, 2014, pp. 172–90.

Baah, Robert Nana. "Return to the Past in García Márquez's *El amor en los tiempos del cólera*." *Romance Notes*, vol. 53, no. 2, 2013, pp. 203–12.

Bell-Villada, Gene H. *García Márquez: The Man and His Work*. 2nd ed. U of North Carolina P, 2010.

Bell-Villada, Gene H. "Names and Narrative Pattern in *One Hundred Years of Solitude*." *Gabriel García Márquez in Retrospect: A Collection*, edited by Gene H. Bell-Villada. Lexington Books, 2016, pp. 67–76.

Buehrer, David. "'A Second Chance on Earth': The Postmodern and the Post-Apocalyptic in García Márquez's *Love in the Time of Cholera*." *Critique*, vol. 32, no. 1, 1990, pp. 15–26.

Cabello Pino, Manuel. "La transposición cinematográfica de *El amor en los tiempos del cólera* o la fidelidad a la letra escrita como objetivo." *Espéculo: Revista de Estudios Literarios*, no. 44, 2010, n.p.

Cervera Salinas, Vicente. "Génesis y contextos de *El amor en los tiempos del cólera*, o cuando Gabo se despidió de Macondo." *Cartaphilus: Revista de investigación y crítica estética*, no. 13, 2014, pp. 84–93.

Curiel, Rosario. "Carpentier y Gabriel García Márquez: maravilla y magia de la utopía." *Quinientos años de soledad: actas del Congreso "Gabriel García Márquez" celebrado en la Universidad de Zaragoza del 9 al 12 de diciembre de 1992*, edited by Rosa Pellicer and Alfredo Saldaña Sagredo, Navarro and Navarro, 1997, pp. 443–52.

Devall, Bill, and George Sessions. *Deep Ecology: Living as if Nature Mattered*. Gibbs M. Smith, 1985.

ElSherief, Eman Mohammed. "Political Ecology in Gabriel García Márquez's *One Hundred Years of Solitude*." *Advances in Languages and Literary Studies*, vol. 7, no. 2, 2016, pp. 13–17.

Farrier, David. "Disaster's Gift, Interventions." *Interventions: International Journal of Postcolonial Studies*, vol. 18, no. 3, 2016, pp. 450–66.

Foucault, Michel. *The Order of Things: An Archaeology of the Human Sciences*. Anonymous translation, Vintage Books, 1994.

García Márquez, Gabriel. *El amor en los tiempos del cólera*. Vintage Español, 2003.

García Márquez, Gabriel. *Cien años de soledad*. Cátedra, 2001.

García Márquez, Gabriel. *Love in the Time of Cholera*. Translated by Edith Grossman, Vintage International, 2003.

García Márquez, Gabriel. *One Hundred Years of Solitude*. Translated by Gregory Rabassa, Perennial Classics, 1998.

Lago Graña, Josefa. "La colmena y el hormiguero: una lectura eco-crítica de *Cien años de soledad*." *Red de Revistas Científicas de América Latina y el Caribe, España y Portugal*, vol. 34, no. 1, 2015, pp. 141–51.

Martin, Gerald. "Chapter 7 Love in the Time of Cholera (1985): The Power of Love." *The Cambridge Introduction to Gabriel García Márquez*, Cambridge UP, 2012, pp. 90–101.

Moore, Jason W. "The Capitalocene, Part I: On the Nature and Origins of Our Ecological Crisis." *The Journal of Peasant Studies*, vol. 44, no. 3, 2017, pp. 594–630.

Moore, Jason W. "The Capitalocene Part II: Accumulation by Appropriation and the Centrality of Unpaid Work/Energy." *The Journal of Peasant Studies*, vol. 45, no. 2, 2018, pp. 237–79.

Morton, Timothy. *Ecology without Nature: Rethinking Environmental Aesthetics*. Harvard UP, 2009.

Morton, Timothy. "Poisoned Ground: Art and Philosophy in the Time of Hyperobjects." *Symploke*, vol. 21, no. 1, 2013, pp. 37–50.

Mutis, Ana María. "Del río a la cloaca: la corriente de la conciencia ecológica en la literatura colombiana." *Revista de Crítica Literaria Latinoamericana*, vol. 40, no. 79, 2014, pp. 181–200.

Ortega, Julio. *Gabriel García Márquez and the Powers of Fiction*. U of Texas P, 1988.

Piamba Tulcán, Diva Marcela. "La flora y la fauna de Macondo: un asunto de interpretación." *Cuadernos del Caribe*, no. 22, 2016, pp. 26–44.

Williams, Raymond L. *The Colombian Novel, 1844–1987*. U of Texas P, 1991.

CHAPTER 21

REPETITION AND ALCHEMY IN *ONE HUNDRED YEARS OF SOLITUDE*

RENÉ PRIETO

PUBLISHED in 1967, *One Hundred Years of Solitude* is both humorous and deadly serious, racy and yet deeply moral. If ambiguity presupposes a lack of clarity, and lack of clarity is an irreducible feature of narrative deceit, Gabriel García Márquez's masterpiece can be summarily described as deceptively ambiguous. Deceptive because although the author dwells on two subjects—a family history in which names and behaviors are duplicated, and the discipline of alchemy—he details neither the reason for the obsessive repetitions in the one nor the hidden significance of the other. *One Hundred Years* has both an exoteric, literal meaning and an esoteric, inner teaching; grounded on a symbolic seedbed, its deeper message is not readily available. The same is true of alchemy; in this arcane science, the transmutation of metals into gold is only the tip of the iceberg. In fact, the material liberation of philosophic gold from vulgar metal is a metaphor for the psychological processes concerned with the liberation of man from life's basic contradictions. As Carl Jung points out, "from its earliest days alchemy had a double face: on the one hand the practical chemical work in the laboratory, on the other a psychological process, in part consciously psychic, in part unconsciously projected and seen in the various transformations of matter" (*Psychology and Alchemy* 258). In his masterpiece, the Colombian author also sets forth a number of contradictions, namely between proliferation and decay, and between the Buendías' ostensible gregariousness and their equally widespread tendency toward solitude. As alchemy teaches the resolution of opposites, García Márquez suggests that humanity's perpetual wavering between contradictory tendencies could be mitigated, perhaps even resolved, on the way toward higher self-development.[1]

The fact that he is seeking to resolve differences is not readily apparent when we start reading, however. Dazzled by his storytelling, readers tend to focus on the plot and not on the tangled threads deployed to convey meaning. The Buendías' family saga contains both an obvious and a well-concealed system of references to alchemy that bolster its meaning and ruefully convey it. As happens with many of Aesop's fables, or La Fontaine's, the anecdotal level of this family's colorful capers is the spoonful of sugar that helps the medicine go down. All three writers entertain without making readers consciously aware of hidden truths that turn their writings into riddles, prompting the narrator's wisecrack: "[L]iterature was the best plaything that had ever been invented to make fun of people" (*One Hundred Years* 388).[2]

That García Márquez enjoys playing with readers' expectations explains why deceit and equivocation are ubiquitous in his writings and most particularly in this novel. For example, Melquíades's freakish and seemingly unassuming scribble, speciously described as "pieces of clothing put out to dry on a line" turns out to be Sanskrit encoded "in a Lacedemonian military code" (349, 415).[3] Characters who appear to be wise, such as the patriarch José Arcadio Buendía, turn out to be fools, and those who seem foolish—like Petra Cotes, Pilar Ternera, and José Arcadio Segundo—are among the most sensible. Although García Márquez does not shy away from practical jokes, these are never gratuitous; carefully read, his often ribald tales turn out to contain instructive *exempla* purposely designed to remain veiled until, like the last Aureliano in the novel, readers figure out a way to unravel the baffling threads that wind their way through this family saga. The threads are baffling because García Márquez as well as Melquíades—ostensible author of the manuscript—make readers only superficially aware of the sober message contained in the novel. That being said, although many important concepts are concealed, the narrative ground is littered with crumbs: bits and pieces of knowledge, half-truths, and oracular sophistry. Enough bits and pieces to provide readers with an understanding of the storyline, even if understanding is fragmentary until we reach the cryptic end. At that point, exegesis turns into illumination, although the illumination is still in code. Why do the members of this family keep repeating the behaviors of their ancestors, and why, despite their raging hormones, are they "armored by the same impermeability of affection" (262)?[4] Why is solitude portrayed as such a blemish, and, more importantly, why is the city of Macondo "wiped out by the wind and exiled from the memory of men" (417)?[5]

The only character who may be able to answer these questions is the next to the last family member to be introduced. Aureliano Babilonia finds answers to the riddles because he can read and understand the whole saga of the Buendía family in one fell swoop. Comparing the behavior of the first José Arcadio to that of the many José Arcadios and Aurelianos, Amarantas, and Ursulas that follow, he grasps what should be obvious: most Buendías live fully, but neither wisely nor well. With their compulsion for repeating themselves in both name and deed, each generation makes the same mistakes and indulges in the same vices as their ancestors.[6] Why such insistence on repetition, one wonders? Why are characters in this novel so unable or unwilling to evolve? These questions are never answered, although they are insistently raised each step of the way. In view of García Márquez's political beliefs, I argue that he viewed egotism as the root of social inequality, and the isolation that results from self-centeredness as the effective force that wreaks havoc on the social contract. He stated as much in his Nobel Prize acceptance speech when he declared: "[T]he immeasurable violence and pain of our history are the result of age-old inequities" (46). Tracing the rationality of the social contract down to its roots, that is, to the relationship one ought to have with one's functions, one's activities, and one's obligations, became part of his hidden agenda, and because he wanted to come up with a vehicle to suggest that human limitations could be overcome only if we made up our minds to do so, he latched onto alchemy as a way to convey this idea without bringing in religious dogma.

Understanding our social responsibilities is necessary before human rights can be protected and promoted. As Plutarch took pains to point out, "one will not be able to rule if one is not oneself ruled" (89). But ruling themselves is exactly what the Buendías fail to do, beginning with the youthful patriarch José Arcadio. We are told that before meeting Melquíades, he had "collaborated with everyone . . . for the welfare of the community" (*One Hundred Years* 17).[7] Once he develops an appetite for the contraptions the gypsies bring to town, however, "those who had known him since the foundation of Macondo were startled at how much he had changed" (17).[8] The spirit of social initiative that characterizes him early in the novel fades further with each passing generation of Buendías. Most José Arcadios in the family start off as enterprising, only to turn randy, bellicose, or greedy; most Aurelianos were "withdrawn," Amaranta lives "isolated from everyone," and Rebeca's once burning heart ends up "turned to ash" (181, 276, 156).[9] "Expansive and cordial" when young, they soon become "wrapped up in [them]selves," with "a solitary character and an impenetrable heart" including those, like Meme and Aureliano Segundo, who start off being gregarious and congenial (28, 283, 62).[10] Even Ursula, the beating heart at the center of the Buendía household for over one hundred years, is eventually drawn into "the impenetrable solitude of decrepitude" (248).[11] Summing up the problem while referring to them as a collective entity, the omniscient narrator speaks of "the solitary fate of the family" (259).[12] And not just solitary but exclusive, like Fernanda, or secluded, like the Colonel, who "locked himself up inside himself" and grew to view his home as "a strange house where nothing and no one now stirred in him the slightest vestige of affection," a veritable "cloister of solitude" (263, 240, 347).[13] All this is to say that in spite of the frequent sexual romps that shake the Buendía house and Pilar Ternera's room down to their foundations, Macondo is the "community which had been singled out by misfortune" for "the hardness of the inhabitants," and strange though this may sound, the Buendía household is the cynosure of that emotional hardness (305, 81).[14]

But why such insistence on behaviors that are isolating, reprehensible, and keep turning up in each new generation of family members? Comparable in many ways to the *hupomnemata* of ancient Greece, García Márquez's novel is set up to enable the formation of the self out of the collected examples of others.[15] Didactic, his work is also spiritual because it concerns itself with the sovereignty that one exercises over oneself and that, for lack of a lay term, we call the life of the soul. As I've already suggested, removing all religious connotations, he grafts the Buendías' development onto a pseudoscientific vehicle, avoiding dogmatism through indirection.[16] This is why seven generations of family members are cast as a single organism whose development mirrors the formation of the ethical subject in the doctrine of alchemy.

Mystical Symbolism in *One Hundred Years of Solitude*

In our day and age alchemy is no longer held in high esteem, but we will soon see its suitability for García Márquez's purpose. Most modern dictionaries lend currency to popular misconceptions by dismissing this pseudoscience as an immature, empirical, and speculative precursor of chemistry that had as its object the transmutation of base metals into gold. The fact is that chemistry evolved from alchemy, but the two fields have very little in common. Whereas chemistry deals with scientifically verifiable phenomena, alchemy pertains to a hidden reality of the highest order, one that constitutes the underlying essence of all religions. This reality proposes that individuals be involved in a process of continuous transmutation during which consciousness is radically altered. For the adept to achieve higher consciousness means, in the first place, acquiring "golden understanding" (*aurea apprehensio*) of his own microcosm and of the macrocosm in which it fits. It is in the course of his pursuit of the Philosopher's Stone that he or she acquires this new awareness. Thus, the quest is more important than the reward; as a matter of fact, the quest *is* the reward. Alchemy is nothing other than an instrument of knowledge—of the total knowledge that aims to open the way toward total liberation. Only by acquiring this "golden understanding" will the adept succeed in achieving the higher consciousness that is the first stage toward the reconstitution, at a higher level, of the unity of his divided self. Jung terms this psychological process "individuation," and he defines it as "the centralizing processes in the unconscious that go to form the personality" (*Psychology and Alchemy* 462). He then goes on to say, "I hold the view that the alchemist's hope of conjuring out of matter the philosophical gold, or the panacea, or the wonderful stone, was only in part an illusion, an effect of projection; for the rest it corresponded to certain facts that are of great importance in the psychology of the unconscious" (462).

Transmutation then, is the essence of the so-called Great Work[17] that is at one and the same time a material and a spiritual realization. The dual nature of this Great Work is very often overlooked, however. Some commentators claim alchemy to be a wholly spiritual discipline, while others seem interested only in finding out whether gold was actually made, and by whom. Both attitudes are misleading. It is essential to keep in mind that there are precise correspondences, fundamental to alchemy, between the visible and the invisible, matter and spirit, planets and metals. Gold, because of its incorruptible nature and its remarkable physical characteristics, is to alchemists the sun of matter, an analogy to the ultimate perfection they seek to attain by helping base metals reach its lofty state. Symbolically speaking, the Great Work is about the creation of man by himself, that is to say, about the full and entire conquest of our faculties and future. To conquer our faculties, we must confront ourselves, implement a whole network of ethical obligations and services to the soul, exercise what Foucault calls "a technology of the self" (46).

Seeking to enlighten those who read his novel, García Márquez lays bare the sick organism of the world by holding a mirror to the lives of a representative family in an arguably representative town in Latin America. Once the setting is circumscribed and the character flaws are delineated, he sets out to illustrate how the spirit is led through a number of stages or generations of what should be a perfecting journey that culminates in self-discovery. In alchemy there are seven stages on the path to self-realization, stages that are symbolically represented by the planetary spheres of the Ptolemaic cosmos, each of which is assigned specific properties. "There is nothing in the being of all beings," wrote alchemist Jacob Boehme, "that does not contain these seven properties; for they are the wheel of the center" (34–35). Lead, the grossest element, corresponds to Saturn, as Boehme goes on to say, "the outermost sphere known as 'the sullied garment of the soul'" (36). Passing through this sphere meant physical death and the putrefaction of matter that is a prerequisite to transformation. In alchemy each of the seven metals is taken to represent various degrees of maturity or illness of the same basic material on its way to gold; symbolically speaking, reaching the Sun is tantamount to attaining the goal that alchemists describe as "discovering the Philosopher's Stone" (Roob 19).

As I set out to demonstrate from this point onward, the concordance between planets and chemical elements was very much in García Márquez's mind when he wrote *One Hundred Years*. For instance, when furnishing Melquíades's laboratory in the opening pages of the novel, he makes a point of including "samples of the seven metals that corresponded to the seven planets" (7).[18] Since this concordance drew his attention, it is not surprising that, as there are seven planetary spheres in the Ptolemaic cosmos, there are seven generations of Buendías in *One Hundred Years of Solitude*. In the first, the founding couple—José Arcadio Buendía and Ursula Iguarán—are brought together. The second comprises their children, Colonel Aureliano Buendía, José Arcadio, Amaranta, and Rebeca. In the third, both Aureliano José, son of the Colonel, and Arcadio, son of the José Arcadio who was "so well-equipped for life," are illegitimate and born of the same woman, Pilar Ternera (25).[19] Illegitimacy rears its ugly head once again in the fourth generation with the birth of Remedios the Beauty, Aureliano Segundo, and José Arcadio Segundo to Arcadio and Santa Sofía de la Piedad, but it is held in check in the fifth with the birth of Meme, José Arcadio, and Amaranta Úrsula to Aureliano Segundo and his arrogant wife, Fernanda del Carpio. Finally, incest returns with a vengeance when they bring home Aureliano—the son of Meme and Mauricio Babilonia—as well as in the seventh generation, with the birth of Aureliano Babilonia Buendía, whose mother, Amaranta Úrsula, turns out to be Aureliano Babilonia's aunt (416).

The correspondence between the seven generations of Buendías and the seven spheres of the Ptolemaic cosmos provides us with the first indication that García Márquez borrowed notions of the Great Work to assemble his own great work. As James Joyce arrayed colors, numbers, musical instruments, parts of the body, and times of day to orchestrate *Ulysses*, García Márquez cast planets, chemical elements, and their spheres of action to piece together his family saga. First-time readers of this novel pay little attention to the fact there are seven generations of Buendías (in fact, the initial review of the novel in *The New York Times Book Review* refers to "five generations of descendants of Jose Arcadio Buendia and his wife Ursula"; Kiely 3). Many may think that García Márquez didn't choose this number, that it was mere happenstance. However, as we shall see, "coincidences" between the lore of alchemy and the structure and design of *One Hundred Years* are consciously although not always conspicuously found at each step of the novel's development.

For instance, is it a coincidence that Colonel Aureliano Buendía and his eponymous children and grandchildren should be goldsmiths? Not only is "Au" the symbol for gold in the periodic table, in addition, many of the attributes of this metal match the behavior of García Márquez's Aurelianos. Gold is hard, resilient, long-lived, and most importantly, *isolated*. Most Aurelianos in the novel are impervious to emotion and suffer from chronic solitude; like gold, they form no compounds. Chemical elements readily match the names of other Buendías. For instance, Rebeca mirrors the attributes of rhenium ("Re" on the periodic chart). Silvery white and with a metallic luster, this element evokes Rebeca's pale skin and fair hair. Like uranium, rhenium has "a long life" and is "resistant to poisoning from other elements," as is Rebeca, who cannot be blotted out by her sister Amaranta, no matter how hard she tries (Liu, Takahashi, and Bassett). In addition, the metal dust of rhenium "presents an explosion hazard," a proclivity that brings to mind the unexplained death of Rebeca's husband, José Arcadio, from an exploded bullet that has left no hole in his body and is "the only mystery that was never cleared up in Macondo" (Huheey, Keiter, and Keiter; *One Hundred Years* 131).[20]

The longest-lived family member in the novel is Úrsula, a feature that invites a comparison with the equally long-lived uranium ("U" on the periodic chart, element no. 92). Interestingly, when uranium ceases being radioactive, it becomes lead. In alchemy, lead is paired with the planet Saturn (José Arcadio Buendía, Úrsula's husband, is likewise linked with Saturn, as we shall see). In addition, symbolically speaking, "passing through Saturn" means to undergo physical death, a process involving the putrefaction of matter required in the course of transformation. Fittingly, when Úrsula dies (or in other words, when uranium turns to lead), the cycle of proliferation and growth she emblematizes in the novel comes to an end; from that point onward, the Buendía family speeds relentlessly onward to its doom.

I have just mentioned how lead is associated with the founder José Arcadio. Despite his willingness to learn alchemy, the young patriarch misinterprets the teachings of Melquíades. As referred to by those who practice this science, he is a "puffer" who strays from the community-minded role he fulfills early on in the action to focus entirely on "the formulas of Moses and Zozimus for doubling the quantity of gold" (7).[21,22] Seeking to follow "the processes of the Great Teaching that would permit those who could interpret them to undertake the manufacture of the philosopher's stone," José Arcadio ends up fusing part of Ursula's inheritance with "copper filings, orpiment, brimstone, and lead" and reduces it to something that looks like "a large piece of burnt hog cracklings" (7).[23] In short, once seduced by "the formulas to double the quantity of gold," he starts to fumble; furthermore, we are told that he, "the most enterprising man ever to be seen in the village," had lost his wits looking for the philosopher's stone (7, 9).[24] Before that time, José Arcadio Buendía had impressed everyone with his sharpness of mind and the accuracy of his decisions, qualities that invite a comparison between the youthful patriarch and Saturn, embodiment of analytical intelligence.

When he first meets Melquíades, the Buendía patriarch combines a childlike curiosity with the behavior of a sage. Sharp-witted and resourceful, he quickly becomes "an expert in the use and manipulation of his instruments" (4).[25] His discoveries are so impressive that Melquíades "gave public praise to the intelligence of a man who from pure astronomical speculation had evolved a theory that had already been proved in practice . . . and as a proof of his admiration he made him a gift . . . : the laboratory of an alchemist" (5).[26] Like the mythical Saturn, José Arcadio Buendía's ferocious mind soon renders him self-absorbed and solitary, however. He "acquired the habit of talking to himself, of walking through the house without paying attention to anyone . . . as if he were bewitched, softly repeating to himself a string of fearful conjectures without giving credit to his own understanding" until, finally, "that spirit of social initiative disappeared" (4, 9).[27] Forsaking community involvement includes cutting himself off from his children and soon elicits Úrsula's reproach: "Instead of going around thinking about your crazy inventions, you should be worrying about your sons . . . Look at the state they're in, running wild just like donkeys" (14).[28] But instead, "always too absorbed in his fantastic speculations," José Arcadio becomes "alien to the existence of his sons" (15).[29] This alienation invites yet another comparison with the god Saturn, one that will require what may at first seem like a digression.

The great mystic William Blake saw our passage through life as a process of purification at the end of which lay the overcoming of man's "raw nature," which he refers to as the "old Adam" (Bedard plate 15). In Blake's work, the term "paradise" is not to be taken literally but as a symbol of happiness in life, the aim and object of an ongoing spiritual quest. Like García Márquez in *One Hundred Years*, Blake, a committed alchemist, sought to summarize spiritual progress from birth to death. With this end in mind, he began *The Gates of Paradise* by portraying an old man—the biblical Adam—as someone who, like José Arcadio Buendía, strays from the path. Adam embodies the male principle or "seed" at the beginning of the Great Work; as far as Blake was concerned, he was "raw" because inexperienced, a man-child because totally unaware of his purpose in the world. Pointedly, and again like José Arcadio Buendía, Blake's raw male principle or seed was to be "found . . . beneath a tree in the Garden" (Bedard 10). In the Great Work the character that corresponds to Blake's old man is Saturn, who, like the patriarch José Arcadio in García Márquez's tale, is an "enormous old man," and like Blake's man-child, is found beneath a tree: it takes twenty men to drag José Arcadio Buendía "to the chestnut tree in the courtyard, where they left him tied up" (*One Hundred Years* 80, 78).[30] Blake's engraving of the water element portrays the raw and inexperienced Adam not just seated beneath a tree but also with rain pouring down on him (Bedard 11), a description that mirrors both the setting and circumstances of founder José Arcadio "soaked with rain and in a state of total innocence" or "discolored by the . . . rain" in García Márquez's novel (*One Hundred Years* 78, 80).[31] For Blake, as it was for the Neoplatonists, water was a symbol of matter, that is, "the material world into which Man has been born" (Bedard 11). Like García Márquez, Blake was pained by human limitations; he felt, most particularly, that the process of selfhood was never accomplished, and portrayed this failure in symbolical means by showing how "the watery shore" of the physical world constantly leads human beings to engage in foolish behavior and keeps them from self-fulfillment (11). Isn't it likely, then, that the epigraph to Melquíades's manuscript—"The first of the line is tied to a tree"—is a direct reference to Blake, for whom "the birth of Man is represented as taking place under a ... tree, symbolic of the unhappy vegetable world we inhabit" (*One Hundred Years* 415; Bedard 11)?[32]

If José Arcadio Buendía is meant to symbolize "the unhappy world we inhabit," his antithesis in *One Hundred Years* is Melquíades, who seems to stay perpetually young and is a harbinger of joy and renewal. From the start of the novel, Melquíades is conspicuously connected with mercury. Soon after being introduced to the reader, the gypsy breaks a flask of bichloride of mercury when Úrsula enters his laboratory. Irked by him because he keeps filling her husband José Arcadio's head with crazy notions, Ursula snaps, "it's the smell of the devil" (*One Hundred Years* 6).[33] Melquíades wastes no time in correcting her: "[N]ot at all," he insists, "it has been proven that the devil has sulphuric properties and this is just a little corrosive sublimate" (6).[34] Undeterred by Melquíades's assurances, Úrsula goes about her business while readers are told, "that biting odor [i.e., of mercury] would stay forever in her mind linked to the memory of Melquíades" (6).[35] In addition, readers will likely recall that before he dies, Melquíades instructs José Arcadio Buendía "to burn mercury in his room for three days"; true to his promise, the youthful patriarch "puts a kettle of mercury to boil next to the body" (72).[36]

The unrelenting association between Melquíades and this chemical element invites us to explore the connection between the gypsy, the eponymous classical god, and the planet named after him. In one of the late Renaissance's key works about universal knowledge, Achille Bocchi's emblem book, *Symbolicae quaestiones*, we find a picture of Hermes-Mercury, god of trade and communication, pointing his index finger to his lips to urge silence (74).[37] Hermes's gesture illustrates how the spiritual center—referred to in alchemy as "Unit" or *Monas*—is inaccessible to the expressive possibilities of language. This image also sheds light on the hermetic qualities of Melquíades's manuscript. The manuscript that we come to know as *One Hundred Years of Solitude* is filled with revelations, but its spiritual center—its truth—is inaccessible, described in the novel as "flaky stacks of paper covered with *indecipherable* signs," so indecipherable that the marks in the manuscript look "like pieces of clothing put out to dry on a line" (74–75, 349; emphasis added).[38]

Researching the role of Mercury as background for his characterization of Melquíades, García Márquez must have also made note of the link between the winged messenger of the gods, Hermes (whose Latin name is Mercurius), and Thoth. In late classical Egypt, Thoth was the god of writing and magic, worshipped, like Hermes, as the souls' guide through the underworld. Guiding the perpetually straying Buendías happens to be Melquíades's task in *One Hundred Years*. In addition, the gypsy's role as educator—he goes to great lengths to introduce each generation of Buendías to his arcane erudition—finds an echo in the mythical figure of Hermes Trismegistus. The wise Trismegistus was supposed to have taught Egyptians all their knowledge of natural and supernatural things, including their grasp of hieroglyphic script. The alchemists saw him as their Moses, who had handed down the divine commandments of their art in the "Emerald tablet." This *Tabula Smaragdina*—believed to date back to the sixth to eighth centuries AD—is clearly the model for the manuscript that eventually reveals to the hapless Buendías the pernicious nature of their commitment to solitude.

As did Joyce, García Márquez sees writing as *fons et origo*. In fact, Melquíades's scribbling echoes Joyce's ingenious "allaphabed" or "amphybed" to refer to the body of inscription, the body of letters with which the world is described, that is to say, *created* through writing (*Finnegans Wake* 18, 619). Whenever García Márquez brings into action the character of Melquíades—or his tribe of gypsies, for that matter—he has alchemy in mind. We are repeatedly told, for instance, that Melquíades "wore a large black hat that looked like a raven (or crow) with widespread wings" (*One Hundred Years* 6, 184, 262, 348).[39] This description appears to be just a suitable simile until we learn from Trismegistus's *Tractatus aureus* that "the principle of the art [i.e., of alchemy] is the raven, who flies without wings in the blackness of night and in the brightness of day" (12).

The first invention Melquíades brings to Macondo, the magnet, is another important reference to alchemy that is not readily evident. The magnet, which Melquíades describes as "the eighth wonder of the learned alchemists of Macedonia" (*One Hundred Years* 1), is likened to the imagination by no less an apostle of the hermetic doctrine than Paracelsus in his *De Virtute Imaginativa* (*Hermetic and Alchemical Writings* S 14:309–19).[40] Such a comparison is predicated on the notion that the magnet's power of attraction draws elements of the external world within man in order to reshape individuals—that is to say, in order to alter their spiritual path. In Paracelsus's own words: "[M]an is that what he thinks. If he thinks fire, he is fire . . . it all depends merely on that the whole of his imagination becomes an entire sun; i.e. that he wholly imagines that which he wills" (S 14:317). Stated otherwise, if men and women can think themselves differently, they can actually bring about that difference and transform their behavior; the power of the imagination is capable of stimulating what Paracelsus calls man's "divine nature" and can "raise up" that nature.

One could argue that raising reader's consciousness to aspire to become responsible members of the human community is, in many regards, García Márquez's aim. This is why casting a failed prototype, a model of misbehavior that stubbornly repeats itself for seven generations, is so essential to his master plan. Unable or unwilling to evolve from one generation to the next, the Buendías, repeating the behavior of their ancestors ("condemned to one hundred years of solitude"), head irrevocably to their doom, blind to the possibility of change (*One Hundred Years* 417).[41] Their loss is presented as a paradigm for readers whose behavior may be altered in response to the relentlessly self-absorbed, lonely human beings they confront in this novel. I am fully aware that ascribing an intention—or at least, *this* intention—to the repetition compulsion in *One Hundred Years* may sound far-fetched. But when I see how many allusions to Paracelsus's, William Blake's, and Carl Jung's esoteric writings, not to mention to classical sources, are present in the novel, I cannot help but pursue this line of thought. As a case in point, Paracelsus argued that "man is a twofold being, having a divine and an animal nature. If he feels, and thinks, and acts as divine beings should act"; he went on to say, "he is a true man; if he feels and acts like an animal, he is then an animal, and the equal of those animals whose mental characteristics are manifested in him" (S 14:318). Beginning with the patriarch José Arcadio and up until Mauricio Babilonia, the Buendías demonstrate a profound inability, some might call it a reluctance, to rise above their baser instincts; time and again, their desire for and commitment to all that drags them down (self-absorption, violence, rancor, and cupidity) become the reason Macondo does not have "a second opportunity on earth" (*One Hundred Years* 417).[42]

The only exception to this commitment is Úrsula, whose perpetually renewed ability to take the house in hand and breathe new life against the perpetual onslaught of age and decay casts her as evidence that renewal *is* possible, that giving, and sharing, and keeping doors perpetually open is a matter of choice. The fact that she ends up grotesquely coiffed and painted by her own great-great grandchildren, who delight in torturing her and finally convince her that she is dead, serves to make the point that her always propitious lessons are not heeded (275). Her significance as a potential family redeemer is clear, in fact, when we learn that she dies "the morning of Good Friday" and that, with her death, "the house ... fell into a neglect from which it could not be rescued" (342, 345).[43]

As he drafted his own *Gran Magisterio*, it is difficult to think that García Marquez was not striving to uplift the imagination by bringing the full impact of alchemical symbols into play. He suggests as much in the conclusion of his Nobel Prize acceptance speech when he states: "[W]e, the inventors of tales, who will believe anything, feel entitled to believe that it is not yet too late to engage in the creation of the opposite utopia ... where love will prove true and happiness be possible" (43). In fact, the ritual and tools of alchemy upon which García Márquez relies in this novel are designed to stimulate the subconscious minds of those exposed to them and quicken what Paracelsus referred to as the higher potential of human beings. I suggest that raising readers' consciousness to an awareness that choice was possible, and that sliding into self-absorption and solitude was not an irreducible fact, was exactly what García Márquez had in mind. This is why he designed a novel that relies so heavily on symbols and that acts so forcefully upon the imagination. Paracelsus compares the imagination to a sun that acts variously on things and on people. As he sees it, imagination has agency; it can transform minds and affect behavior, ignite a virtue comparable to alchemical fire. Melquíades's words echo those of Paracelsus when he declares, "things have a life of their own ... it's simply a matter of waking up their souls" (11).[44] If things have "a life of their own," human beings stand a good chance of having an awakening; that is to say, we have the potential of transforming and renewing ourselves even if, as is made amply clear in this novel, we tend to sell ourselves short. Clearly relevant to the overall message, the preamble to this moral fable on the limitations that human beings put on their enormous gifts is the tale of the once "kind and youthful patriarch who ... collaborated with everyone ... for the welfare of the community ... the most enterprising man ever to be seen in the village," only to give up all social initiative as he became "too absorbed in ... fantastic speculation" which ultimately drives him, and all those he begets, into a wasteland of solitude (8, 9, 15).[45]

Time and Space in *One Hundred Years*

Another feature that links García Márquez's moral fable with alchemy is the time of year when the action opens. "Every year during the month of March," we are told on the opening page, "a family of ragged gypsies would set up their tents" (1).[46] More significant than having the action of *One Hundred Years* begin in March is the fact that the gypsies return to Macondo at the same time *every year* and that in the isolated room where Melquíades's manuscripts are stored for a hundred years, both José Arcadio Segundo and Aureliano Babilonia claim, "it was always March . . . and always Monday" (2, 348).[47] Colonel Aureliano Buendía is born in March, and he marries Remedios Moscote "one Sunday in March" (14, 79)."[48] March falls in Aries, first sign of the zodiac; significantly—although by no means surprisingly at this point—according to the teachings of alchemy, "the Work may only be begun in the spring, under the signs of Aries, Taurus and Gemini (the most favorable time to begin being in Aries, the celestial hieroglyph of which corresponds, in the esoteric or steganographic language, to the name of the *Materia Prima*" (Klossowski 10). The action of García Márquez's saga doesn't just begin under the sign of Aries; he also makes us conspicuously aware that the very important couple portrayed at the tail end of the family line, Aureliano Babilonia and Amaranta Úrsula, make love in April for the first time (*One Hundred Years* 397). In other words, *One Hundred Years* both opens and begins its last revolution under the sign of Aries, giving the novel a circular structure, as we are reminded when Ursula proclaims, "It's as if time had turned around and we were back at the beginning" (193), or when Aureliano Babilonia reveals to Pilar Ternera the name of the woman he loves, and she laughs knowingly because "a century of cards had taught her that the history of the family was a machine with unavoidable repetitions, a turning wheel that would have gone on spilling into eternity were it not for the progressive and irremediable wearing of the axle" (396).[49]

The Buendías' time machine is curiously reminiscent of the "machinery" that according to William Blake represents two contrasting expressions of time. The first type includes those that "Wheel within wheel, in freedom revolve in harmony and peace" ("Jerusalem"). Blake believed this kind of machinery duplicated the creative time of Eden in which all events of the cosmic year exist concurrently. Designed to copy this creative time, the intertwined structures of Blake's own poems are based on a view of the simultaneity of events in space and time, one that is diametrically opposed to teleological time. The various levels or dimensions in which events occur in Blake's poems are both parallel to and flowing into one another with startling shifts of perspective. The chronological structure that García Márquez crafts for his novel mirrors Blake's conception, one borrowed lock, stock, and barrel from the doctrine of alchemy. Many critics have remarked on the very unusual handling of time in *One Hundred Years*, but few have paused to ponder over the mechanisms that make it so unusual. To understand the way that events unfold in this unique novel, we need to picture multiple stories, each told in linear or historical progression. García Márquez takes each of his storylines and cuts it into segments, segments that could be labeled—for the sake of clarity—from A to Z. After breaking the stories into segments, he chooses one in particular from the many he has in store. The segment he chooses is not usually from the beginning, moreover. Let us say, for the sake of argument, that he chooses the third or fourth narrative segment from a storyline that we shall call master plot one. He then places this fragment—describing, for example, the day when, "as he faced the firing squad, Colonel Aureliano Buendía was to remember that distant afternoon when his father took him to discover ice"—as part of his opening sentence (1).[50] Instead of developing master plot one in chronological order from that point onward, however, he cuts away from it and inserts another segment—one likewise from the middle or end sections of a master plot—as a sequel to the first.

The novel unfolds not as a sequence of stories told from beginning to end, but as a patchwork of middles, endings, and beginnings stitched together in apparent disarray and mirroring "the Past, Present and Future existing all at once" of Blake's poems, which is no more and no less than the way Melquíades "concentrated a century of daily episodes in such a way that they coexisted in one instant" (415).[51] As in a puzzle, each of these segments is eventually pieced together with other segments from the same master plot until the whole story is assembled, bit by bit, even as we read. In other words, each master plot develops by skipping back and forth between later events in a given story to earlier ones—or, stated otherwise, from the narrative future to the narrative past. Readers learn what happens in a given master plot before they know anything about any of the characters in that particular story. Because the narrative future of each tale is disclosed before the events leading up to it, one could refer to García Márquez's handling of time as *retroactive progression*: the action moves forward by telling readers what will happen before it does.

The consequences of this cunning manipulation of time are manifold. To begin with, whenever we come upon the second and each succeeding segment of a given master story, instead of stumbling onto something new, we recognize it as something with which we are already familiar. García Márquez doesn't just interweave narrative segments to give the effect of simultaneity, as does Blake; he also diminishes the effect of surprise because we know what is going to happen in each of the master plots before it actually happens. We know, for instance, that Colonel Aureliano Buendía will face the firing squad at some point in his life (an action described on pages 80, 103, 112, and 128) because we are told that he will on page 1, that is, thirteen pages before the scene describing his birth on page 14. Knowing what will happen gives readers an illusion of omniscience and invites our identification with Melquíades, the all-knowing author of the manuscript. We have the feeling of knowing the future because we know the outcome of many stories before their respective beginnings are taken up in linear fashion during the hundred-year saga of the Buendía family.

Retroactive progression can be readily compared to the eidetic reductions of future misfortune developed by the Stoics. Seeing the worst that can happen in the future reveals not something bad but what must be accepted. It allows those who confront truths "to get prepared," precisely what the Greeks termed *paraskeuazo*. Confronting the unavoidable future before its time, one can transform truths into a permanent principle of action. Assimilated, the lessons taught by García Márquez's *exempla* work as a salutary treatment designed to steer readers away from the forces that wreck the lives of his misguided characters. Grasping the art of existence portrayed in the dystopian society of *One Hundred Years*, we, the readers, are invited to question our own lives and, if all goes well, to attain *askesis*, not the renunciation, but the progressive mastery over ourselves obtained through the acquisition and assimilation of truths.

The most fundamental truth readers hopefully assimilate is that individuals need to play an active role in shaping the ethical path their lives will follow. Naturally, tending to this path takes time as well as sustained effort. Furthermore, the work of oneself on oneself is not a narcissistic activity, but a lifelong endeavor that entails communicating with others. In the words of Foucault, "[T]he activity devoted to oneself... constituted, not an exercise in solitude, but a true social practice" (51). Social practice is what most Buendías turn their backs to when they make a centenary commitment to solitude. Substituting social feasting for the bonds of fellowship, family members choose wealth, power, and sensual gratification over the wholesome companionship that García Márquez exalts as a crucial component of the art of living. The characters of his timely saga exert themselves to please the body while doing nothing to develop the spirit. Once again borrowing words from Joyce, we could say they choose "sinse" over sense, letting the spirit wilt until the sixth generation of Buendías, when Aureliano and his aunt Amaranta Úrsula fall into each other's arms (*Finnegans Wake* 313).[52]

The importance of the last relationship portrayed in *One Hundred Years* cannot be overstated. Typical of the process alchemists refer to as the first stage of the *coniunctio*, during which soul and spirit are symbolically united, Aureliano and Amaranta Úrsula are melded together; "they were becoming a single being," readers are told (*One Hundred Years* 410).[53] In alchemy, uniting soul and spirit separates them from the body, however, and amounts to the body's death in a second phase likewise transposed into *One Hundred Years* when "Amaranta Úrsula was bleeding in an uncontainable torrent" (412).[54] Immediately before this happens, readers are told that the last Buendía couple is "predisposed to begin the race again from the beginning and cleanse it of its pernicious vices and solitary calling" (411–12).[55] In other words, the body's "death" is a necessary step in a process of renewal, one that will culminate in a veritable transformation, since we are told that their child "was the only one in a century who had been engendered with love" (412).[56] That love is an essential ingredient in the synthesis with which *One Hundred Years* concludes is evident from the two first syllables of Amaranta Úrsula's name. *AMAR* spells out the verb "to love" in Spanish and conveys the nature of her "passionate blood," which, readers are told, "was insensible to any artifice that did not come from love" (379).[57]

Referring to the alchemical conjunction that points to the union of opposites and the birth of new possibilities, Carl Jung suggests that since the body must die in order to be born again, the second union of the mind with the body "shows forth the wise man, hoping for and expecting that blessed third union," one referred to in alchemy as the *unus mundus* (*Collected Works: Mysterium*, vol. 14, 465). The climax of the entire process of transmutation, this last stage of the *coniunctio*, is a veritable "integration to the world" (ARAS). That being said, it is not easy to get the mind to embrace the body during the second stage (or *unus mentalis*) since it has previously devoted all its efforts to separating from it. An *enantiodromia*—the Greek notion of things turning into their opposite—needs to take place, and that is not an easy process because what had previously been seen as a bundle of greed, lust, power striving, and unconscious negatives (i.e., the body) must now be invited back. The emergence of what Jung described as "an unconscious opposite in the course of time" entails or requires coming to terms with the self, which is in every way what takes place in *One Hundred Years* when, alone and emotionally unhinged by Amaranta Ursula's death, Aureliano turns to Melquíades's manuscripts (Jung, *Collected Works: Two Essays*, 72). He discovers, at long last, that the manuscript contains his family's history. The epic saga of the Buendías includes, of course, the full details of Aureliano's origins, details that have remained a mystery to him up to that point. After learning his identity, Aureliano proceeds to read the tale of his life from the beginning. In other words, having first achieved a fusion with AMAR and then losing her enables him to return to himself, to place the whole of his past life before his eyes.

Fundamental to both Stoics and Epicureans, the knowing, or more exactly, the care, of the self is equally significant in the Great Work of alchemy. In the Alexandrian treatise of Krates, it is perfect knowledge of the soul that enables adepts to understand the different names that philosophers give to the arcane substance (Jung, *Collected Works: Mysterium*, vol. 7, 460). Aureliano Babilonia is the only member of the Buendía family to be given the opportunity of knowing himself, a discovery cast, as we have seen, in the language of alchemy. Extracting knowledge about his ancestors as well as about his own origins from Melquíades's manuscripts, which he can suddenly read "without the slightest difficulty, as if they had been written in Spanish," Aureliano discovers the family's pernicious pact with solitude (*One Hundred Years* 415).[58] How to rescind this pact is the question the novel tacitly addresses to all readers. Those who would find the answer must begin by taking a hard, unblinking look within. If they are honest, García Márquez is saying, they will see that the root of our trouble lies in an almost total ignorance of that which matters most. Seemingly taking his cue from Platonic thought as expressed at the end of the *Alcibiades*, García Márquez suggests the problem for the individual soul is to recognize itself in what it is (*One Hundred Years* 588–95). Moral and spiritual growth is the consequence of self-knowledge and a condition for understanding the text: what Augustine calls *quis facit veritatem*, "to make truth in oneself" (243).

Regrettably, the Buendías begin to make truth in themselves while remaining steadfastly self-absorbed; even the passion of a soon to be enlightened Aureliano Babilonia, we are told, "was self-centered" (406).[59] Preferring "death to separation," he and his aunt end up "floating in an empty universe" from which everyone else is excluded (404, 417).[60] In contrast with the self-absorption and consequent solitude of the Buendías, the third stage of the *coniunctio* foregrounds the ultimate union in the alchemical process: only after spirit, soul, and body are brought together in the second stage does it become possible to be united with the world. But clearly these "solitary lovers" are barred from attaining such unity, which is why they are "wiped out by the wind and exiled from the memory of men" at the precise moment when Aureliano Babilonia prophesizes himself in the act of deciphering the last page of the parchments, "as if he were looking into a speaking mirror" (411, 417, 416).⁶¹

A mirror is an instrument that allows us to recognize ourselves. In the last page of Melquíades's manuscript we are led to believe, at first, that Macondo is a place where characters have the possibility of discovering who they are because the town is first described as a noisy place "with houses having mirror walls" and, much later, as "the city of mirrors" (24, 417).⁶² That they fail to fulfill this possibility becomes apparent when mirrors are likened to delusions in the parenthesis that follows Macondo's epithet: "the city of mirrors (*or mirages*)" (417; emphasis added).⁶³

Mirrors in Macondo fail to do what they are supposed to. What shows up on their surface—the drunken revelries and wild romps of the Buendías—is a mirage because, to quote Seneca, there is no "return to oneself" in this godforsaken family (66, 45). Each generation in this novel repeats the errors of its ancestors in an incessant repetition compulsion that includes the loving couple at the end, "secluded by solitude and love and by the solitude of love" (404).⁶⁴ The accursed search for gold, the sweaty embraces in Pilar Ternera's hammock, the searing jealousy (between Amaranta and Rebeca, Amaranta and Fernanda, Fernanda and Petra Cotes)—all Buendía actions, in fact—are fleeting and futile. For them, self-knowledge only comes when the winds of destruction have begun blowing apart this Babylon of solitude. It comes too late.

Significantly, mirrors enter the writings of Plato (558, 591–92) and Aristotle (*Magna Moralia* 132c–133c) whenever the subject of self-knowledge is discussed, and it is undoubtedly to these writings that García Márquez is referring when he brings mirrors into his portrayal of self-discovery. In the *Alcibiades* Socrates asks his pupil, "let us think of something that allows us to see both it and ourselves when we look at it" (591). The youth readily answers "the mirror," forgetting, all too quickly, that the eye also fulfills both roles (592). In the dialogue that ensues, Socrates reminds Alcibiades that the eye will also see itself if it observes "the best part" of another eye (i.e., the pupil); using this analogy, he links self-reflection to soul searching: "Then if the soul, Alcibiades, is to know itself," says Socrates, "it must look at a soul, and specially at that region in which what makes a soul good, wisdom, occurs" (592). This exchange between Socrates and Alcibiades touches upon the focal point of García Márquez's novel. In order to know ourselves we need to shape ourselves, and while shaping ourselves we must surpass our own limitations, which is to say, we need to master the appetites that threaten to overwhelm us. Isn't this what the Buendías never manage to do? Isn't one of the points García Márquez is making with his insistence on repetition that the members of this family never surpass themselves, that they fall prey to the same passions and appetites that brought ruin to their ancestors?

Recognizing the Self

In sum, then, I am suggesting that *One Hundred Years of Solitude* is a didactic vehicle designed to keep us from straying any longer from the essential task of self-realization.

But how could an author who despises both proselytes and sermons convey the idea of healing the spirit without sounding like a pedant or a preacher? It is for this reason that alchemy enters his design. The quest for self on which García Márquez embarks entails peeling off everything that is not essential, renouncing covetousness, vanity, and pride. With typical wit, he portrays the painful process of sloughing off layers not as some sort of mystical renunciation but as a walloping hurricane that wipes the Buendías from the face of the earth in a burst of wind, begonias, and ants. Using the members of this family as role models, *One Hundred Years* urges the transformation, or more exactly, the amelioration, of each individual, a process equivalent in the symbolic language of alchemy to the discovery of the Philosopher's Stone.

Preparing or "discovering" the Philosopher's Stone is the culmination of the alchemic process, one that follows the *coniunctio*. Jacob Boehme sums up the outcome of the first two stages with a succinct formulation: "[T]his is nothing," he writes, "but knowledge of oneself" (20). Seeing self-knowledge as prerequisite for any other intellectual endeavor, alchemy takes up a notion that had been of paramount importance since antiquity. In his comments about Plato's *Alcibiades*, Proclus states: "Let . . . knowledge of ourselves. . . be the start of philosophy" (557). But what is this self that needs to be cultivated? As Proclus goes on to say, "It is his soul, the ruler of his body. The virtues of the soul that he needs to acquire are the intellectual skills that give it the authority to rule, over its body and over other people as well" (557). Because of its emphasis on self-knowledge as the necessary foundation of any other knowledge, the *Alcibiades* held pride of place in later antiquity as the ideal work with which to begin the study of Platonic philosophy, and this same emphasis fills the pages of alchemists and thinkers who have pondered how to rule ourselves. Knowledge of oneself develops a social conscience and, eventually, devotion to a common weal. As García Márquez plainly put it: "Solidarity with our dreams will not make us feel less alone, as long as it is not translated into concrete acts of legitimate support for all the peoples that assume the illusion of having a life of their own in the distribution of the world" (Nobel Speech). If we continue to live self-absorbed lives, there is little hope of establishing an egalitarian society. After all, solitude is defined as the state of being "remote from society" (*Webster's* 1098). Remoteness breeds self-interest, and concern for number one promotes the establishment of tyranny because it threatens the freedom of others.

Before industrialism took a grip on the world, in the days when individuals were taught to think before they learned to govern (the very subject of Plato's *Alcibiades*), some were fortunate to have teachers who shaped their understanding. In our own age, telling stories designed to educate is rare, but fortunately for us, not entirely outmoded. For decades we have entertained ourselves with the ordinary and extraordinary adventures of a legendary family living in a town emblematic of all Latin America, a story about everyone living anywhere south of the Rio Grande. Much has been written about the Buendías' zest for life, but not enough has been said about their unskillfulness in the art of living. Their problem is not just that they cling to solitude, but that they never learn to do otherwise. The point incessantly made by repetition in their life saga is, once a Buendía, always a Buendía. Their charm, feistiness, and lust for life must not obscure their voracious cravings and their tendency to ignore the needs and wishes of others in order to more fully satisfy their own. The Buendías' self-absorption leads to their ruin, and their ruin is presented to readers as food for thought.

In every sense, then, *One Hundred Years* is a rite-of-passage novel in which the coming of age is designed for readers who learn from characters. García Márquez conveys his lesson in and through writing, and writing has, as Ricardo Gutiérrez Mouat rightly points out, "bewitching powers" in this novel (275). Developing notions that Derrida explores in "Plato's pharmacy," Gutiérrez Mouat suggests that Melquíades is the *farmakeus*, the speaking subject who "bewitches when he speaks" (276). Like Melquíades, García Márquez bewitches readers into realizing that individuals who allow selfishness and greed to rule their lives will "not have a second opportunity on earth" (*One Hundred Years* 417).[65] This meaning is not readily apparent, as I have taken pains to point out. Like most alchemical texts, *One Hundred Years of Solitude* contains elaborate devices to deter the unprepared. Couched in a language that is frequently obscure and impenetrable, the literature of alchemy requires years of devoted attention, of reading and rereading, before its exegesis can be attempted. In short: secrecy is inextricably woven into its fabric. The hermetic quality of the alchemical texts poses a challenge to those who seek to *innerstand*. Like Theseus, enquirers seeking to find alchemy's hidden message enter a labyrinth. Like all labyrinths, *One Hundred Years of Solitude* defies linear logic; only through reliance on inspired intuition—the golden thread of Ariadne—can its puzzling mystery fall into place.

Notes

1. In a book published in 2004, Shannin Schroeder dedicates a fifteen-page section to exploring in what way the alchemical experiments of the Buendías rely on "the balance of the magical and the real" and are interconnected with "the future of Macondo" (47). Although a number of interesting notions about alchemy are brought forth, her overall emphasis is on the relationship between alchemy and magical realism; consequently, our two readings follow different paths. She rightly argues that "[t]o consider this novel a macrocosmic alchemy in and of itself, we would need to be able to see the methodology of the science at work within the text itself, and, indeed, GM creates a text in which the literal and fictional worlds are coordinated into one such process. Just as characters in *One Hundred Years of Solitude* attempt transmutations on both the physical and the spiritual planes, García Márquez attempts a dual-level alchemy of his own with the town (and the novel) he creates" (51). I completely agree with the need to study "this novel [as] a macrocosmic alchemy in and of itself"; regrettably, as I see it, Schroeder fails to convincingly explain the transmutation that takes place in what she calls "the spiritual plane."
2. "La literatura era el major juguete que se había inventado para burlarse de la gente" (312).
3. "Piezas de ropa puestas a secar en un alambre" (281); "con claves militares lacedemonias" (333).
4. "Acorazados por la misma impermeabilidad a los afectos" (212-13).
5. "Arrasada por el viento y desterrada de la memoria de los hombres" (334)
6. Addressing the issue of what she calls "self-defeating repetition" in *One Hundred Years* in her *Foundational Fictions*, Doris Sommer traces its causes to "the bad fits between developmentalist assumptions and Latin American history" (2-3). Sommer sets out limits on

the scope of García Márquez's project that are simply not there, however. Individual development is not linked to a national project in this novel but to an ontological one. The errors perpetuated by the Buendías are universal and should not be seen as the exclusive domain of "Latin American history."

7. "Colaboraba con todos... para la buena marcha de la comunidad" (13).
8. "Quienes lo conocían desde los tiempos de la fundación de Macondo, se asombraban de cuánto había cambiado" (13).
9. "Retraído..." (149); "apartada de todos..." (223); "convertido en cenizas" (130).
10. "Expansivos y cordiales..." (28); "ensimismados..." (283); "con un corazón imprenetrable..." (57).
11. "La impenetrable soledad de la decrepitud" (201).
12. "El sino solitario de la familia" (210).
13. "Se encerró con tranca dentro de sí mismo..." (213); "una casa ajena donde ya nada ni nadie le suscitaba el menor vestigio de afecto..." (196); "el encierro y la soledad..." (279).
14. "Aquella comunidad elegida por el infortunio..." (305); "la aridez de los habitantes" (72).
15. Michel Foucault recalls the ancient Greek concept of the *hupomnemata* or notebooks that contained narratives of the self in the form of memorable quotations and thoughts for rereading or future use. In Foucault's view, this practice contributed to the formation of individual selfhood (*Care of the Self* 46).
16. Roberto González Echevarría has delved into the relationship between literature and scientific discourse in his pellucid *Myth and Archive*. González explains how a number of foundational novels in Latin America describe nature and society "through the conceptual grid of nineteenth-century science" (12). As the epitome of the foundational novel, *One Hundred Years* turns—like so many of its illustrious predecessors—to the hegemonic discourse of science as a framework in order to structure and deliver its message. In fact, as far back as Rome's imperial period, ethical principles could not be assimilated without a theoretical framework such as science, as we see, for example in Lucretius's *The Nature of Things*.
17. The Great Work (or magnum opus in Latin) is an alchemical term for the process of working with the *prima materia*, a legendary substance capable of turning base metals into gold in order to create the philosopher's stone. As Schroeder points out, "in its literal sense, this stone is a physical object that alchemists sought to synthesize in their labs, using mercury and sulfur. That being said, the stone also represented a veritable spiritual transformation, the act of making the soul 'golden'" (72). If the *materia prima* serves as the root of the alchemical process, then the philosopher's stone can be considered the end product. Both terms describe personal and spiritual transmutations in the Hermetic tradition as well as being attached to the laboratory processes of alchemists. In *One Hundred Years*, García Márquez refers to the Great Work as "The Great Teaching," and to the philosopher's stone as "the philosopher's egg" (7).
18. "Muestras de los siete metales correspondientes a los siete planetas" (11).
19. "... tan bien equipado para la vida..." (26).
20. "El único misterio que nunca se esclareció en Macondo" (110).
21. "Puffer" is the name given to aspiring alchemists who spent all their time blowing on the bellows to bring about the transformation of base metals into gold. Puffers failed to see that alchemy was a spiritual doctrine and that gold was not an end unto itself but was ascribed a symbolic (and spiritual) role.
22. "Las fórmulas de Moisés y Zózimo para el doblado del oro" (11).

23. "Los procesos del Gran Magisterio, que permitían a quien supiera interpretarlos intentar la fabricación de la piedra filosofal," "raspadura de cobre, oropimente, azufre y plomo," "chicharrón carbonizado" (11, 12).
24. "Fórmulas para doblar el oro" (12); "el hombre más emprendedor que se vería jamás en la aldea" (13).
25. "Experto en el uso y manejo de sus instrumentos..." (9).
26. "Exaltó en público la inteligencia de aquel hombre que por pura especulación astronómica había construido una teoría ya comprobada en la práctica y como una prueba de su admiración le hizo un regalo...: un laboratorio de alquimia" (10).
27. "Sin hacer caso de nadie... como hechizado, repitiéndose a sí mismo en voz baja un sartal de asombrosas conjeturas, sin dar crédito a su propio entendimiento" (9–10); "Aquel espíritu de iniciativa social desapareció" (14). José Arcadio's lack of consideration for others and self-absorption are highlighted on pages 13–14; his sons display the same sort of behavior on pages 28, 30, 32, 34, 39, etc.
28. "En vez de andar pensando en tus alocadas novelerías, debes ocuparte de tus hijos.... Míralos como están, abandonados a la buena de Dios, igual que los burros" (17).
29. "Absorto en sus propias especulaciones químicas," "ajeno a la existencia de sus hijos" (18).
30. "Enorme anciano" (71); "Hasta el castaño del patio... donde lo dejaron atado" (69).
31. "Empapado de lluvia y en un estado de inocencia total" (69); "descolorido por... la lluvia" (71).
32. "*El primero de la estirpe está amarrado en un árbol*" (332).
33. "Es el olor del demonio" (11).
34. "En absoluto.... Está comprobado que el demonio tiene propiedades sulfúricas, y esto no es más que un poco de solimán" (11).
35. "Aquel olor mordiente quedaría para siempre en su memoria, vinculado al recuerdo de Melquíades" (11).
36. "Quemen mercurio durante tres días en mi cuarto," "puso a hervir un caldero de mercurio junto al cadáver..." (64).
37. In alchemical texts, representations of alchemical processes were often encoded in pictorial language, "an additional barrier [to understanding the texts] was erected in the shape of an extensive structure of pictorial symbolism and allegorical expression" (Glidewell 38). A unique example of this is *The Wordless Book*, a collection of fifteen engraved plates that gives the alchemical process in its entirety using symbols and drawings of the alchemists at work (Powell 70).
38. "Quebradizos papeles apretados de signos indescifrables" (63); "parecían piezas de ropa puestas a secar en un alambre" (281).
39. "Usaba un sombrero grande y negro, como las alas extendidas de un cuervo" (11, 212, 184, 262, 348).
40. "La octava maravilla de los sabios alquimistas de Macedonia" (7).
41. "Estirpes condenadas a cien años de soledad" (334).
42. "Una segunda oportunidad sobre la tierra" (334).
43. Curiously, the Spanish original reads "el jueves santo" (27), but the point is well taken in either case. "La casa volvió a caer en... abandono" (278).
44. "Las cosas tienen vida propia... todo es cuestión de despertarles el ánima" (7).
45. "Patriarca juvenil, que... colaboraba con todos... para la buena marcha de la sociedad" (13); "el hombre más emprendedor que se vería jamás en la aldea" (13); "demasiado absorto en sus propias especulaciones químicas" (18).

46. "Todos los años, por el mes de marzo ... una familia de gitanos desarrapados plantaba su carpa cerca de la aldea ..." (7).
47. "Siempre era marzo y siempre era lunes" (8, 280).
48. "Un domingo de marzo" (18, 70).
49. "Es como si el tiempo diera vueltas en redondo y hubiéramos vuelto al principio" (159); "un siglo ... de experiencia le había enseñado que la historia de la familia era un engranaje de repeticiones irreparables" (318).
50. "Frente al pelotón de fusilamiento el coronel Aureliano Buendía había de recordar aquella tarde remota en que su padre lo llevó a conocer el hielo" (7).
51. "Concentró un siglo de episodios cotidianos, de modo que todos coexistieran en un instante" (333).
52. Joyce's pun bringing together "sin" and "sense."
53. "se iban convirtiendo en un ser único" (328).
54. "Amaranta Ursula se desangraba en un manantial incontenible" (330).
55. "Predispuesta para empezar la estirpe otra vez por el principio y purificarla de sus vicios perniciosos y su vocación solitaria" (330).
56. "Era el único en un siglo que había sido engendrado con amor" (330).
57. "Sangre apasionada ... insensible a todo artificio distinto del amor" (331).
58. "Sin la menor dificultad, como si hubieran estado escritos en castellano" (333).
59. "Su pasión era ensimismada" (325).
60. Incestuous couples show up in each of the seven generations of Buendías, making incest a constant and clearly significant element in this novel. In alchemy, the prototype of the alchemical marriage happens to be the brother-sister incest, in which, according to Jung, "the Brother-Sister pair stands allegorically for the whole conception of opposites" (*Psychology and Alchemy*, 317). Delcourt convincingly argues that "the union of the incestuous pair symbolizes 'the return to the primordial unity' " (124; my translation). In short then, alchemical incest is the ideal mythical model for the state in which, after all contradictions have been resolved, individuation is achieved and creation becomes possible. The union of the incestuous brother-sister (or coniunctio oppositorum) reconstitutes the original unity of the primordial being. "Preferían la muerte a la separación" ; "flotando en un universo vacío" (*Cien años* 326).
61. "Amantes solitarios," (329); "la cólera del huracán bíblico," "de la memoria de los hombres" (334); "como si se estuviera viendo en un espejo hablado" (334).
62. "Con casas de paredes de espejo" (25); "la ciudad de los espejos" (334).
63. "La ciudad de los espejos (o los *espejismos*)" (334).
64. "Recluidos por la soledad y el amor y por la soledad del amor" (324).
65. "No tenían una segunda oportunidad sobre la tierra" (334).

Works Cited

ARAS (The Archive for Research in Archetypal Symbolism). *Threefold Coniunctio*. Catalogue of Online Books.
Aristotle. *Magna Moralia*. Translated by W. Rhys Roberts, Franklin Classics, 2018.
Augustine. *Confessions*. Translated by Henry Chadwick, Oxford UP, 2009.
Bedard, Michael. *William Blake: The Gates of Paradise*. Tundra Books, 2006.

Blake, William. "Jerusalem: I See the Four-Fold Man, the Humanity in Deadly Sleep." *Jerusalem: The Emanation of the Giant Albion*, CreateSpace Independent Publishing Platform, 2015.
Bocchi, Achille. *Symbolicae quaestiones. Achille Bocchi and the Emblem Book as Symbolic Form*, by Elizabeth See Watson, Cambridge UP, 2004.
Boehme, Jacob, *The Signature of All Things*. Facsimile reprint of original. Kessinger Publishing, 2005.
Delcourt, Marie. *Hermaphrodite: Mythes et rites de la bisexualité dans l'antiquité Classique*. Presses Universitaires de France, 1958.
Foucault, Michel. *The History of Sexuality*, vol. 3, *The Care of the Self*. Translated by Robert Hurley, Vintage, 1988.
García Márquez, Gabriel. *Cien años de soledad*. Argos Vergara, 1980.
García Márquez, Gabriel. *I'm Not Here to Give a Speech*. Vintage International, 2019.
García Márquez, Gabriel. *One Hundred Years of Solitude*. Translated by Gregory Rabassa, Harper Perennial Modern Classics, 2006.
Glidewell, Marvin E. *Alchemy and Symbols*, reprinted from *The Hexagon*, 1940, vol. 31, no. 2.
González Echevarría, Roberto. *Myth and Archive: A Theory of Latin American Narrative*. Duke UP, 1998.
Gutiérrez Mouat, Ricardo. "*Cien años de soledad* y el mito farmacopéyico del realismo mágico." *Revista de Estudios Hispánicos* (Puerto Rico), nos. 17–18, 1990–1991, pp. 267–79.
Huheey, J.E., Keiter, E.A., and Keiter R.L. *Inorganic Chemistry: Principles of Structure and Reactivity*. 4th ed., Harper Collins, 1993.
Joyce, James. *Finnegans Wake*. Wordsworth Classics, 2012.
Jung, C. G. *The Collected Works: Mysterium Coniunctionis*, vol. 14, *An Inquiry into the Separation and Synthesis of Psychic Opposites in Alchemy*. 2nd ed. Translated by Gerhard Adler and R. F. C. Hull, Routledge, 1963.
Jung, C. G. *The Collected Works: Mysterium Coniunctionis*, Vol. 7, *Two Essays on Analytical Psychology*. 2nd ed. Translated by Gerhard Adler and R. F. C. Hull, Routledge, 2014.
Jung, C. G. *Psychology and Alchemy (Collected Works of C. G. Jung)*. 2nd ed. Translated by Gerhard Adler and R.F.C. Hull, Routledge, 1980.
Kiely, Robert. Review of *One Hundred Years of Solitude*. *The New York Times Book Review*, 8 Mar. 1970, p. 3.
Klossowski de Rola, Stanislas. *Alchemy, the Secret Art*. Reprint ed. Thames and Hudson, 2013.
Liu, L.G., Takahashi, T., Bassett, W.A. "Effect of pressure and temperature on lattice parameters of rhenium." *Journal of Physics and Chemistry of Solids*, vol. 31, no. 6, 1970, pp. 1345–1351.
Lucretius. *The Nature of Things*. Translated by A. E. Stallings, Penguin Classics, 2007.
Paracelsus. *The Hermetic and Alchemical Writings of Paracelsus*. Edited by Arthur E. Waite, Merchant Books, 2015.
Plato. *First & Second Alcibiades*. Translated by Benjamin Jowett, independently published, 2020.
Plutarch. *To an Uneducated Ruler* in *Moralia*, Vol. X/10 (Loeb Classical Library). Translated by Harold North Fowler, Harvard UP, 1960.
Powell, Neil. *Alchemy, the Ancient Science*. Doubleday and Company, 1976.
Proclus Diadochus. *Plato, Complete Works*. Edited by John M. Cooper, Hackett Publishing, 1997.
Roob, Alexander. *Alchemy and Mysticism: The Hermetic Museum*. Taschen, 2020.
Seneca, Lucius Annaaeus. *Moral Letters to Lucilius: Epistulae Morales ad Lucilium*. Translated by Richard Mott Gummere, CreateSpace Independent Publishing Platform, 2018.
Schroeder, Shannin. *Rediscovering Magical Realism in the Americas*. Praeger Publishers, 2004.

Sommer, Doris. *Foundational Fictions: The National Romances of Latin America*. 1st ed. U of California P, 1993. Latin American Literature and Culture, vol. 8.

Trismegistus, Hermes. *The Golden Work (Tractatus aureus)*. 1st ed.. edited by Philip N. Wheeler, translated by William Salmon, CreateSpace Independent Publishing Platform, 2015. The R.A.M.S. Library of Alchemy, vol. 4.

Webster's New Collegiate Dictionary. G. & C. Merriam, 1981.

CHAPTER 22

MUSIC AS FORMAL AND SIGNIFYING FEATURE IN GARCÍA MÁRQUEZ'S MATURE FICTION

GENE H. BELL-VILLADA AND
MARCO KATZ MONTIEL

In his mature work, García Márquez makes frequent use of music as a formal, structuring device or as a signifying motif. A passing musical reference might function as part of a larger given setting or time frame, complementing the visual descriptions or broader actions. Allusions to a musical instrument, to a taste in musical styles, or to a musical piece can help represent and round out specific characters, can suggest something about their backgrounds, inclinations, status, or roles within the plot—thereby serving as "identity markers" (Katz Montiel 8). Alejo Carpentier, who theorized the "Marvelous Reality" that led to the literary milieu in which García Márquez and other exponents of the Latin American Boom flourished, expounded on such markers in a 1933 article on radio production. Among the various techniques employed by Carpentier, classical and romantic chamber and orchestral works, he notes, can "fix an idea, immediately, in the mind of the listener" (552). Bringing up examples from the nineteenth and twentieth centuries, the author points out how "[t]he opening theme of *Fingal's Cave* by Mendelssohn can always represent the sea, the beginning of *In the Steppes of Central Asia* by Borodin recreates the desert or plains, *Scheherazade* the East, a jazz composition could synthesize Harlem, the song of the Lorelei could evoke the Rhine" (552).[1] While recognizing differences in the musical formation and listening experiences of readers from diverse backgrounds, one can still understand how musical references can support interpretations of authorial intent or lead to profound readings that the author never imagined.

In a notable instance, García Márquez has acknowledged his adoption of the six string quartets of Hungarian composer Bela Bartók while drafting the literary architecture of *The Autumn of the Patriarch*.[2] That narrative of dictatorship, we shall further see, brings into play a variety of musical formulas and allusions, as do García Márquez's two subsequent, highly idiosyncratic, and innovative novels of male-female romance, *Love in the Time of Cholera* and *Memories of My Melancholy Whores*. Columbia University philosophy professor Lydia Goehr, who writes extensively about philosophies of music, provides a demonstration of the power of bringing music into a written text. Referential description, she observes, moves beyond the data, the facts so beloved by those intent on making humanities disciplines more "scientific," into evocative readings of artistic creations. Her list includes ways "[t]o render absent things as if both present and real served purposes broader than that of 'mere' classification: to legitimize the present state of things by bringing the past state of things back, as it were, to life; to generate material, literary, and mythological histories and traditions" (394). Indeed, just as introductory literature courses teach students about intertextual literary references, professors can impart lessons on how musical texts enrich textual meaning. Readers of García Márquez can listen to the works mentioned in his novels (almost all of these, the classic and the popular, can be easily found free of charge on music-sharing sites), but instead of playing them in the background, one can focus aurally in order to hear what these works bring to one's mind and soul and how that helps one think about the writing in new ways.

Although García Márquez frankly admitted to having no technical knowledge of music (Bell-Villada, "Building a Compass" 138), in his fiction and journalism he demonstrates an ample, detailed, and intimate knowledge of both the European-classical repertory and the popular folk elements of northern Colombia, of a broader Caribbean and Latin America, and of Spain as well. When Bell-Villada interviewed the author in Mexico City in June 1982, he noted the presence of perhaps thousands of LP records lining the shelves of the future Nobel laureate's writing studio (134).

One grassroots musical tradition that crops up from time to time in García Márquez's work is that of the *vallenato*. The name means literally "of the valley born," owing to the music's reported roots in Valledupar, a city in northeastern Colombia situated between two snowcapped ranges. The art itself is a fusion of African and indigenous percussion rhythms with Spanish lyric practices and German technology. A "classic" *vallenato* ensemble consists of a small drum (known as a *caja*), a ribbed scraping-stick (a *guacharaca*), an accordion for melody and harmonies, and a vocalist (usually the accordionist). From its mid-nineteenth-century origins the musicians had the role of troubadours, minstrels who wandered about Caribbean Colombia, performing love songs and narratives and bringing news—all roughly along the lines of the Spanish *romance* (ballad) tradition and, later, the salsa *pregonera* made world famous by Héctor Lavoe. Over the years, the music has become subjected to commercialization, and since 2006 the Latin Grammy awards have even included a *vallenato* category.

From his earliest years as a cub reporter, when writing about, among other things, Colombia's folk culture, García Márquez was conscious of the potential of *vallenato*.

Thus, in one of his very first articles as a twenty-year-old columnist at Cartagena's *El Universal*, he praised the accordion as a "proletarian instrument," and he would do so again in later pieces (*Obra periodística* vol. I, 79). In his maturity, he was often quoted as describing *One Hundred Years of Solitude* as "a 350-page *vallenato*," a way of signaling the novel's rootedness, in part, in folk narrative.

The work itself contains *vallenato* allusions, some quite explicit. In a paragraph in chapter three, we read of occasional visits to Macondo by Francisco el Hombre, a two-hundred-year-old vagabond who brings tidings and tells stories with his aging, out-of-tune voice, accompanying himself "with the same archaic accordion that Sir Walter Raleigh had given him in the Guianas" (*One Hundred Years of Solitude* 57).[3] Incidentally, the latter detail may be a bit of playful anachronism on the author's part, since the instrument reportedly was not invented, by Friedrich Buschmann in Berlin, until 1822. Francisco el Hombre, on the other hand, is an actual figure in Caribbean-Colombian mythology, a *vallenato* bard who, legend has it, traveled from town to town, bringing news via singing duels, which he would always win. There are statues of Francisco el Hombre throughout the region; the allusion to him in Gabo's epic is thus part of that (as it were) "Franciscan" subculture.

On the other hand, in the final chapter of the novel, just four pages from the end, a lonely, bereaved Aureliano Babilonia drifts aimlessly about the streets of Macondo, and we read: "In the last open salon of the tumbledown red-light district an accordion group was playing the songs of Rafael Escalona," the latter characterized as "heir to the secrets of Francisco el Hombre" (380).[4] In real life, Escalona (1926–2009) was probably the most renowned composer of *vallenato* music and, it is worth noting, a sometime friend and an almost exact contemporary of the novelist. In this passage, moreover, Escalona is being linked directly to Francisco el Hombre, the two figures thus serving as quasi-bookends within the purported *vallenato* that is the history of Macondo.

Without employing the generic term, García Márquez also assigns apparent *vallenato* music to a major Buendía character. In chapter ten, bon-vivant-to-be Aureliano Segundo wins an accordion in one of Petra Cotes's early raffles, eventually becoming and remaining a virtuoso on the instrument. Over the course of his existence of unbridled revelry, he will perform at several festivities (for his mistress Petra, for the Colonel, for the seventeen illegitimate Aurelianos); during the five-year-rainstorm; and as old-age solace for the last raffle, where he "played the forgotten songs of Francisco el Hombre on the accordion" (324).[5] When, toward the end of chapter seventeen, an elderly Aureliano Segundo departs his lover's side for the Buendía household in order to die close to his wife Fernanda, he brings with him "his wandering trunks and wastrel's accordion" (326).[6] *Vallenato* music thus punctuates and plays an unstated role in Aureliano Segundo's unfetteredly hedonistic and dissipated lifespan.

By contrast, the pianola and piano rolls that arrive accompanied by "Italian expert" (64)[7] Pietro Crespi, and that will liven up the Buendía household with music and dance, all stand for the European cultural imports helping to symbolize the family's rising local status and acceptance of bourgeois values. Pietro will also open a musical instruments store, stocking all manner of gadgets capable of playing Asian pentatonic scales as well as European diatonic music; these include "reproductions of the tower of Florence that told time with a concert of carillons, and music boxes from Sorrento and compacts from China that sang five-note melodies when they were opened" (108).[8] Moreover, Crespi "donated a German harmonium to the church, organized a children's chorus, and prepared a Gregorian repertory [i.e., chant] that added a note of splendor to Father Nicanor's quiet rite" (108).[9] On the other hand, when Amaranta rejects Crespi's love, he will sing to the accompaniment of a zither before tragically committing suicide. The Italian immigrant thus brings the trappings of European sophistication, technology, and modernity to small-town Macondo. The memory of the pianola will maintain a lingering presence throughout much of the Buendía clan's history.

In a kind of latter-day musical counterpart, in chapter thirteen Fernanda's daughter Meme returns from school "with a clavichord, which took the place of the pianola" (236).[10] Primarily to appease her mother and to stave off boredom, she will receive a diploma that "certified her as a concert clavichordist" (251)[11] and play for family feasts, for Amaranta's farewell, and even for "gringo" gatherings. It is of course fitting that a compliant, dutiful Meme would gain proficiency on an instrument of late medieval vintage, associated with Europe's aristocratic court—precisely the milieu that Fernanda's parents and their vice-regal forebears would idealize and to which they would aspire. Significantly, years later, when raising money for their younger daughter Amaranta Ursula's Belgian education, Aureliano Segundo will sell off the pianola and the clavichord "and other junk that had fallen to disrepair" (324).[12] The two European instruments thereby function as both parallel and mutually contrasting kin.

For his next novelistic masterpiece, *The Autumn of the Patriarch*, García Márquez deployed his musical materials in differing ways. Each of the six chapters of this one-of-a-kind novel, as readers know, is made up of a single paragraph some fifty pages in length. Other than the proper names, there are no traditional markers such as indentations or separate dialogues, no quotation marks or dashes, no punctuation signs other than periods or commas (save for a single dramatic instance of an exclamation point). The obvious danger of such an experimental literary approach is that the prose could become rambling and amorphous.

García Márquez counters this danger through various means, the poetical and the musical among them. On more than one occasion, the author has characterized the book as a long prose poem on the subject of power. Indeed, the narrative is sprinkled throughout with poetic rhymes and repetitions (quasi-refrains such as "pobre hombre" ["poor man"], said by the dictator about each one of the rivals whom he dispatches) as well as political slogans ("el progreso dentro del orden," a play on a nineteenth-century, Mexican positivist formula, "Orden y Progreso"). Rhetorical devices shape the prose from time to time—the several instances of anaphora, either with "Vimos" ("We saw") in chapter one, or with "Vio" ("He saw") in later passages, or the aging General's pair of "*Ubi sunt?*" ("Where are they?") dirges in his declining phase. There are the countless, humorous children's ditties with which the illiterate, mature Patriarch is taught to read in chapter five. There are lengthy quotations from Rubén Darío's famous poem "Marcha triunfal," recited by the Nicaraguan poet on his public visit to the unnamed capital city.

And in true epic poem fashion, there is the catalog of Caribbean locations viewed by the lordly General from his seaside balcony at the end of chapter one.

For like reasons, the language of *Patriarch* presents numerous musical allusions to and quotations from folk tunes and popular melodies, along with formulaic kinds of phrases typical of such styles of music. Many of these references are common fare and may be familiar to Hispanic or Caribbean browsers of García Márquez's generation and after, who would recognize them outright. Unfortunately, the language as well as the allusions are precisely what is lost on even the most learned *non*-Hispanic reader; they are, to all accounts, untranslatable. Hence the analysis that is to follow in the following pages.

By contrast, the refined, cultured, Frenchified thug José Ignacio Sáenz de la Barra is given a couple of musical associations of his own. A formidable figure, he goes about regularly accompanied by his Doberman named Lord Köchel. Ludwig Ritter von Köchel (1800–1877) was an Austrian aristocrat and independent polymath, today remembered for having cataloged the entirety of Mozart's oeuvre. The "K" that customarily follows the title of a Mozart work (e.g., *Don Giovanni*, K. 527; Symphony no. 40, K. 550) is the opus number assigned by Herr von Köchel. Incidentally, the cataloger was awarded a knighthood for his labors (the "Ritter" in his name signifies "Knight")—and thus the "Lord" attributed to Sáenz de la Barra's fearsome hound is an accurate cognomen! In addition, Sáenz's numerous torture sessions are accompanied by recordings of music by Anton Bruckner (1824–1896), the Austrian organist and composer, renowned for his nine symphonies that are inordinately long and loud—traits fully appropriate for drowning out the cries of Sáenz's hapless victims. García Márquez thus suggests that a love of European high culture and cold-hearted cruelty, a pairing seen extensively during the Second World War, are not necessarily incompatible traits.

To return to the popular music elements of *Patriarch*: they are legion, and it is worth singling out at least some of them. Many are the novel's phrases in the style of boleros, Latin-Caribbean love-ballads. In an early episode of Rabelaisian ribaldry, when the still young Patriarch succeeds in inebriating rival General Adrián Guzmán, the latter loses control and exposes himself, peeing on banquet guests as he croons, "soy el amante desairado que riega las rosas de tu vergel, oh rosas primorosas" (65) ("I'm the gallant swain who waters the roses of your bower, oh lovely rose in bloom" [52]). Having searched fruitlessly for a previous incarnation of the lyric, we have concluded that this was an invention of the author.

Later in chapter two, the General falls madly in love, sight unseen, with beauty queen Manuela Sánchez. When invoking her name, he will often allude to her with dolorous tag-phrases suggestive of wistful boleros. On just a single page, for instance, he refers to "Manuela Sánchez de mi mala hora," "de mi desastre," "de mi locura," and "de mi potra" (79) ("of my evil hour," "of my disaster," "of my madness," and "of my rupture" [63–64]). At one point the General finds a secluded spot in the presidential palace to actually sing, "para que no me olvides, cantaba, para que sientas que te mueres si me olvidas" (83) ("so you won't forget me, he sang, so you'll feel you're dying if you forget me" [67]). By sheer chance—or not—a bolero entitled "Para que no me olvides," by singer-songwriter Lorenzo Santamaría, appeared in 1975, the year of publication of the Spanish original of *Patriarch*—though, in what would have been a wonderful real-life imitation of Jorge Luis Borges's "Pierre Menard, autor del Quijote," the piece does not contain the line intoned by the General.

Similarly, in the course of the Patriarch's protracted, bizarre pursuit of and relationship with future wife Leticia, analogous sorts of formulas crop up, though not as many. Hence, "Leticia Nazareno de mi desconcierto" (182) ("Leticia Nazareno of my bewilderment" [152]), he reflects rhymingly to himself in the initial stages of his outré courtship of the erstwhile nun. Later, during his widowhood, the now-literate General will write on a piece of paper, "Leticia Nazareno de mi alma mira en lo que he quedado sin ti" (181) ("Leticia Nazareno of my soul look at what has become of me without you" [151]).

The prose of *Patriarch* is further peppered, here and there, with casual quotations from real songs readily recognizable to Hispanic readers. Early on, in a lengthy, pained soliloquy, the dictator's public double Patricio Aragonés refers to one of the boss's concubines as "de las que saben de dónde son los cantantes mi general" (19) ("one of those who knows where the tune comes from general" [12]). The original Spanish is a direct echo of the second line from "Son de la loma" ("They're from the Hills"), a lively *guaracha* song by the well-known popular composer Miguel Matamoros (1894–1971). The piece starts out with "Mamá yo quiero saber / de dónde son los cantantes" ("Mom, I want to know / Where the singers are from"). Over time, however, the modified quotation, "yo sé / él sabe de dónde son los cantantes" ("I know / He knows" etc.) would become quasi-proverbial, roughly akin to the English-language expression, "I know/He/She knows what the score is"—precisely the sense intended here by the Patriarch's double.

In another instance in chapter two, we read that Saturno Santos, the Patriarch's "full-blooded Indian" bodyguard who can play the folk harp, is celebrating his boss's birthday along with a chorus singing "Las mañanitas," "la canción de las mañanitas que cantaba el rey David" (68) ("the morning serenade King David sang" [54]). A song in Mexican folk-tune style written by composer Manuel M. Ponce in 1914, this beautiful alternative to "Happy Birthday" is customarily performed in observance of a loved one's birthday or saint's day. Not coincidentally, the reference in *Patriarch* is followed immediately thereafter by a flash-forward to a brief recollection of Consul Hanneman's cylindrical recording of "Happy Birthday."

Much later, when the General finds himself in decline, his henchman José Ignacio Sáenz de la Barra having reduced his life to emptiness and desolation, we are informed that the girls at the nearby school no longer sing at recess the melody about "la pajarita pinta paradita en el verde limón' (248) ("the petite painted bird perched on the green lemon limb" [211]). The line cites in slightly modified form one of the most famous Latin American children's songs, known to almost any Hispanic youngster:

Estaba la pájara pinta /sentada en un verde limón
con el pico cortaba la rama / con la rama cortaba la flor...
(The painted she-bird was / Perched on the green lemon tree.
With her beak she cut off the twig / With the twig she cut off the flower...)

Some sixteen lines further down, we read "la vida era un soplo" (248) ("life was a breath of fresh air" [212]), an oblique allusion to "Volver" ("Return"), a renowned 1934 tango by Carlos Gardel and Alfredo LePera that evokes a doleful return to the site of one's first love; it features the unforgettable, somber sequence, "Sentir / que es un soplo la vida / que veinte años no es nada" ("To feel / That life is but a breath / That twenty years is nothing"), etc. The absence of the singing girls and the reminder of life's fleeting nature both serve to accentuate the General's darkly autumnal mood.

Toward the end of chapter two, in the wake of Manuela Sánchez's magical disappearance during the General's gift of a solar eclipse, his lost love-object is reportedly sighted at various Caribbean locations, these musically tagged. The ensuing musical series, with its refrain-like line "pero no era ella" ("but it wasn't her"), is among the most richly, densely allusive passages in all of García Márquez's oeuvre. It quotes three specific songs plus referencing two musical genres from across the Hispanic Caribbean.

The first, "allá donde cortaron a Elena" (96) ("there where they cut Elena" [79]), cites a well-known *plena* (a national dance-rhythm of Puerto Rico), a succinct tale about a victim of a crime of passion:

Cortaron a Elena/(Repeat)
(Repeat)/y se la llevaron
pa'l hospital ...
(They cut Elena [Repeat]
[Repeat] and took her
T' the hospital ...)

The song was composed by Mario Jiménez (1895–1975), a multifaceted Puerto Rican musician who first recorded it in 1932.

Next comes "la parranda del velorio de Pepe Montero, zumba, canalla rumbero" (96) ("the madness of Papa Montero's wake, tricky, lowlife rumba bunch" [79; the line's verbal rhythms, alas, defy translation!]). From a 1940s Cuban song—now quasi-folklore—reportedly written by pianist and composer Eliseo Grenet (1893–1950), the piece laments the death of an eponymous Afro-Cuban trickster who, steeped in an ever-vital joy, loved and lived to dance with *mulata* women.

The third of these allusions invokes "Barlovento," perhaps the second-most-famous song from Venezuela, composed in 1936 by Eduardo Serrano (1911–2008). The originating piece starts out "Barlovento, Barlovento / tierra ardiente y del tambor" ("Barlovento ... / Ardent land of the drum") and captures the beat and dance rhythms of Afro-Venezuelans. Its most oft-quoted line is in fact "el tiquiquitaque / de Barlovento sobre la mina" (96) ("the ticky-tacky of Barlovento / over the mine" [79]), precisely as appears verbatim in García Márquez's Caribbean-music travelogue. Barlovento itself is the name of a town located some sixty miles east of the capital city, Caracas.

The following allusion, "la cumbiamba de Aracataca" (96) ("the dance of Aracataca" [79], as rendered, truncated and nonspecifically, by the translator Gregory Rabassa) is of a more generic cast yet happens to single out the novelist's very own village of birth and early childhood. The *cumbiamba*, a dance music native to Gabo's Caribbean region and of diasporic African roots, is performed by holding candles in both hands and serves as the basis for the *cumbia*, Colombia's best-known musical dance form, with popular adaptations throughout the continent, notably in Mexico.

The concluding reference in the series, "el bonito viento del tamborito de Panamá" (96) ("the pretty wind of the little drum of Panama" [79]), both signals a national genre and hints at a concrete song. The noun *tamborito* denotes an Afro-Panamanian music and dance form performed during Carnival season and featuring a female chorus decked out in elegant formal wear; the choristers respond to a soloist's highly suggestive chants, even as a couple dances provocatively on the open floor. Conversely, "Bonito viento pa' navegar" ("Pretty/nice wind fer sailing") is the title of a specific instance of the genre, dating probably from the 1920s. Owing perhaps to its collective, stylized nature, the *tamborito* is scarcely known outside Panama; García Márquez's allusion gives it a moment's visibility.

As the foregoing discussion demonstrates, *The Autumn of the Patriarch* holds a rich variety of musical materials, fully integrated and subtly imbedded within its densely poetical text. The allusions and quotations have a signifying function in their own right, while adding extra solidity to the novel's vast experiment in prose and structure. And, it goes without saying, Hispanic readers can derive a special pleasure from recognizing the words themselves and sensing the sources whence these myriad musical markers flow.

Music, introduced and developed throughout these earlier works, breaks out into florid counterpoint in the later novels. Music suffuses *Love in the Time of Cholera* in ways that define character and suggest rationales for seemingly inexplicable behaviors and actions. Both the protagonist and his antagonist fill their lives with music, while the woman they both love sometimes supports and at other moments subverts the sonic arts. The two men will come together in *Memories of My Melancholy Whores* to create a character almost entirely explained by his participation in and reactions to the music of his time and place. Although the two novels generally invite varied critical approaches, it is hard to see how either of these can be profoundly understood without a close reading of their successive musical moments.

Juvenal Urbino, the antagonist, appears first in *Love in the Time of Cholera*. A medical man and pillar of his city's upper social set, the young cosmopolitan (as his name suggests) marries Fermina Daza, daughter of a nouveau riche man with a dubious background, creating a union that endures throughout most of the years of her life. Florentino Ariza, a flowering force of nature (also suggested by his name), only appears in the plot after Juvenal leaves Fermina widowed, but the novel then goes on to reveal that he was her first as well as last love, effectively sandwiching the longer relationship with Juvenal.

Florentino and Juvenal both employ music to captivate Fermina Daza, the one communicating directly via his idiosyncratic violin playing and the other including her in classical and romantic musical productions staged for the community and more intimate social gatherings. While courting her, the doctor also produces a serenade performed with a grand piano under the damsel's balcony. Under Fermina's veiled—if perhaps unconscious—direction, her two lovers spend their lives weaving a florid counterpoint that only Florentino recognizes.

Fermina receives Florentino's music in live performance, direct from the source. In a demonstration of his obsession, Florentino only acts, in music as in everything else, to capture the heart of Fermina: "The only reason he was interested in accompanying Lotario Thugut on his violin from the privileged vantage point in the choir was to see how her tunic fluttered in the breeze raised by the canticles" (64).[13] Going to church while still a schoolgirl, she "knew that he was one of the musicians in the choir, and although she never dared raise her eyes to look at him during Mass, she had the revelation one Sunday that while the other instruments played for everyone, the violin played for her alone" (66).[14] Not long afterward, she hears the violin again, right outside her bedroom window, "playing the same waltz over and over again" (70).[15] Hardly believing his audacity, the young woman feels great relief when, the following morning, her Aunt Escolástica manages to offer an anodyne explanation of the performance to Fermina's father, who still knows nothing of this affair. Later that day, the young man confirms his responsibility for the musical intervention, letting his intended know "that he had composed the waltz, and that it bore the name that he called Fermina Daza in his heart: 'The Crowned Goddess'" (70),[16] a *vallenato* that the author anachronistically employs in this setting. Not daring to return to the immediate vicinity of her home, Florentino employs his remarkable comprehension of meteorology to make his notes follow the winds directly to her bedroom, in this way guiding his music to her from any distance or direction.

Focused on his own musical and poetic output, Florentino appears seldom in the company of friends or acquaintances, leaving an impression of a solitary life save for the hundreds of conquests listed in his record book. In this, the music to some extent defines the musician; like his creative output, Florentino remains directed inward, making his musical mentor, Lotario, a notable exception. Among the vast German migration to the Americas during the nineteenth century, "the ubiquitous presence of German music teachers" led to educational opportunities for numerous impecunious aspiring players, and many of these young musicians eagerly incorporated the wildly popular sounds of European romanticism into their eclectic American innovations (Katz Montiel 134). As one of these young musicians, Florentino "attracted the attention of the telegraph operator, the German émigré Lotario Thugut, who also played the organ for the important ceremonies in the Cathedral and gave music lessons in the home. Lotario Thugut taught him the Morse code and the workings of the telegraph system, and after only a few lessons on the violin Florentino Ariza could play by ear like a professional" (54).[17] Either by Morse or by music, Lotario's student can deliver a message. Up on the latest musical fashions as well as on the music imparted by Lotario, Florentino "was always willing to play violin serenades to his friends' sweethearts" (54).[18] Years later, "Lotario Thugut would also say of him that he had been his worst voice student, and still he could make even tombstones cry" (167).[19] With this indifferent training and what the novel clearly presents as an extra-large dose of talent, Florentino makes a strong impression with his music.

After learning of Fermina's engagement to Juvenal, Florentino quietly prepares to depart from the city and leave his music behind. Aside from his mother, he says goodbye to no one, but goes to the street where Fermina lives to play their secret waltz for her one final time. "He played, murmuring the words, his violin bathed in tears, with an inspiration so intense that with the first measure the dogs on the street and then the dogs all over the city began to howl, but then, little by little they were quieted by the spell of the music, and the waltz ended in supernatural silence" (138).[20] None of this elicits any response from Fermina, the neighbors, or even the night watchman, a figure who normally shows up to elicit a gratuity from serenaders. Having determined to leave and never return, Florentino leaves "behind his violin, for he identified it too closely with his misfortune" (139).[21] The music, like everything else he had to offer, had been for her; after this, readers scarcely see him play again.

After leaving Fermina and his hometown, Florentino continues to hear music. On his first trip up the river to Caracolí, a band composed of crew members and a fireworks display entertains the passengers. A minister from Great Britain shows up at the party "wearing the tartans of the MacTavish clan, and he played the bagpipe for everyone's entertainment and taught those who were interested how to dance his national dances" (146).[22] The rejected suitor's itinerary contrasts, musically as well as geographically, with the journey enjoyed by Fermina and Juvenal, whose wedding reception ends "after midnight on board the brightly lit ocean liner, with a Viennese orchestra that was premiering the most recent waltzes by Johann Strauss on this voyage" (155).[23] In this moment, when both the protagonist and antagonist temporarily remove themselves from the original scene of the novel's action, music begins to highlight the different situations and outlooks of both men, with one restricting his travels to areas closer to home and the corresponding autochthonous sounds, while the other heads across the Atlantic Ocean to hear what Europe has to offer.

In Europe, Juvenal and Fermina begin to figure out how to love each other at the same time that they make cultural discoveries. After attending what would be remembered as the historic opening night of Jacques Offenbach and Jules Barbier's *Tales of Hoffman*, the couple returns "with a new conception of life, bringing with them the latest trends in the world and ready to lead" (160). In addition to checking out new works dealing with literature, plastic arts, and science, Juvenal arranges with a bookseller in Paris to receive music: "The same bookseller agreed to mail him the most attractive scores from the Ricordi catalogue, chamber music above all, so that he could maintain the well-deserved title earned by his father as the greatest friend of concerts in the city" (160).[24] Juvenal's inheritance as a cultural benefactor establishes another difference with Florentino. While the latter creates music for himself and turns inward, the former must, if he will follow his progenitor's path, look outward to others for cultural production. Thus, when Juvenal serenades his love with live music, he must resort to intermediaries. His connections make it possible for him to contract a touring pianist with the promising name of Romeo Lussich to perform under his intended's balcony. With this performer under contract, he requisitions "the piano from the Music School placed in a mule-drawn wagon and brought a history-making serenade to Fermina Daza" (122).[25] Not exactly like playing one's own music, but certainly a way to make an impression.

Early in life, Juvenal abandons his own musical practice in favor of opening up spaces for other performers: "Next to the dining room, the space that had originally been designed for gala suppers was used as a small room for intimate concerts where famous performers came to the city" (19).[26] Amid the room's furnishings, there remains "the piano that Dr. Urbino had not played for many years" (19).[27] Even so, he will occasionally give voice to his own music, even though these intentions are sometimes thwarted. At a party thrown by Don Sancho, a concert band "began a popular tune that had not been announced on the program" and "once again, after so many long years, he felt like singing. And he would have no doubt, on the urging of the young cellist who offered to accompany him, if one of those new automobiles had not suddenly driven across the mudhole of the patio, splashing the musicians and rousing the ducks in the barnyards with the quacking of its horn" (38).[28] After so many years, the doctor cannot raise a musical voice against the sounds of new technologies.

Albeit clearly preferring music considered high art, Juvenal does not shun popular offerings, even if these sometimes appear dated. Returning from one of his trips to Europe, he brings back recordings with "the songs of [chanteuse] Yvette Guilbert and [performer and café owner] Aristide Bruant, who had charmed France during the last century" (20).[29] Sometimes his discoveries of more widely disseminated sounds cause him to miss serious chamber music, as in the instance in which "he surrendered to the diaphanous and fluid lyricism of the final piece on the program, which he could not identify. Later the young cellist, who had just returned from France, told him it was a quartet for strings by Gabriel Fauré, whom Dr. Urbino had not even heard of, although he was always very alert to the latest trends in Europe" (37).[30] His somewhat eclectic tastes are thus shown to remain a bit disorganized, as might be expected of one fitting this into a medical career.

Through this mix of eras and genres, readers get more of a sense of time and place from the musical references than they are likely to comprehend from many other details set out in the story. In an interview with Raymond Leslie Williams, García Márquez acknowledges a writerly process "quite disrespectful of real time and space" (136). Although, by the author's admission, people and places do not always coincide accurately in *Love in the Time of Cholera*, musical details provide a sense of the late nineteenth- and early twentieth-century setting of the novel in an urban space much like Cartagena, with borrowing from other world-renowned metropolitan areas.

Within this Caribbean city, Juvenal enjoys a great deal of prestige among the segments of society. For the entire population, he brings innovations in sanitation and health care, along with a great deal of diverse music, including musical scores, pedagogical programs, visiting artists, chamber ensembles, and full-blown operas made available to a population that otherwise would have seen and heard few, if any, such offerings. In what the narrator calls "Urbino's most contagious initiative," a French opera production featuring a Turkish soprano causes an "opera fever" that "infected the most surprising elements in the city and gave rise to a whole generation of Isoldes and

Otellos and Aïdas and Siegfrieds" (44).³¹ The appropriateness of the author's insertion of medical terminology into these discussions of music highlights the manner in which Florentino's unknowing antagonist brings together the arts of sound and healing: "Do you like music?" he asks new patients and acquaintances. When confronted with this query, Fermina, who first knows him as a medical man treating her, thinks he has made a joke and responds interrogatively, "What is the point of that question?" Far from joking, it turns out that the doctor genuinely considers music "important for one's health." In fact, "she was going to know very soon, and for the rest of her life, that the topic of music was almost a magic formula that he used to propose friendship" (118).³² Early in the novel, the narrative provides an example of this magic, when Urbino resolves his bitterness over his friend Jeremiah de Saint-Amour's deception and suicide, realizing that it wasn't his own wife's arguments that won him over, "but rather a miracle of the music" (38).³³ In contrast with the sounds of Florentino, Juvenal's music brings him into contact with people and helps preserve the friendships that result from those acquaintances.

As the two men mature, so to speak, and move on in their lives, their differing interactions with music continue to mark them. Florentino inherits the exuberant musicality, unlike the refined noblesse-oblige patrimony handed down to Juvenal, of his uncle Don Leo XII Loayza. Similarly inspired by European musical sources, the uncle employs them in ways that would have been inconceivable in the Urbino family circle. "He had the voice of a galley slave, untrained but capable of impressive registers" (166).³⁴ Hearing that Enrico Caruso could shatter glass with his voice, Leo spends years trying to recreate this feat at gatherings of friends. Although never successful with this party trick, "in the depth of this thundering there was a glimmer of tenderness that broke the hearts of his listeners as if they were the crystal vases of the great Caruso" (166).³⁵ Florentino's uncle has several other amusing musical escapades. On an early trip up the Magdalena River, he decides to "awaken the creatures of the jungle by singing a Neapolitan *romanza* from the Captain's balustrade" (264).³⁶ Attesting to his success, Leo's companions "could hear the flapping wings of the cranes in the marshes, the thudding tails of the alligators, the terror of the shad as they tried to leap onto dry land, but on the final notes, when it was feared that the singer would burst his arteries with the power of his song, his false teeth dropped out of his mouth with his last breath and fell into the water" (264).³⁷ After stopping the journey so that an emergency replacement can be made, Leo demonstrates the act to the ship's captain and promptly loses the new set of dentures.

Upon reaching the age of ninety-two, Uncle Leo turns the business over to Florentino. At his farewell ceremony, the uncle gets up to make a short speech, concluding, "The only frustration I carry away from this life is that of singing at so many funerals except my own" (268).³⁸ Having selected "Addio Alla Vita" (Goodbye to Life), the hugely popular excerpt from the opera *Tosca* by Giacomo Puccini, to conclude the occasion, Leo "sang it a capella, which was the style he preferred, in a voice that was still steady. Florentino was moved, but he showed it only in the slight tremor in his voice as he expressed his thanks" (268).³⁹ Leo combines hard work, business acumen, and musical ability and exuberance in ways that make him a powerful figure along the river. Surprisingly, his nephew will follow a similar path to business success, although his aim remains more focused on impressing Fermina rather than the world at large.

Among the hundreds of women that Florentino succumbs to, seduces, or violates, the "best loved of them all" plays music on an instrument held between her legs:

> He remembered Ángeles Alfaro, the most ephemeral and best loved of them all, who came for six months to teach string instruments at the Music School and who spent moonlit nights with him on the roof of her house, as naked as the day she was born, playing the most beautiful suites in all music on a cello whose voice became the human between her golden thighs. From the first moonlit night, both of them broke their hearts in the fierce love of inexperience. But Ángeles Alfaro left as she had come, with her tender sex and her sinner's cello, on an ocean liner that flew the flag of oblivion, and all that remained of her on the moonlit roofs was a fluttered farewell with a white handkerchief like a solitary dove on the horizon, as if she were a verse from the Poetic Festival. With her Florentino Ariza learned what he had already experienced many times without realizing it: that one can be in love with several people at the same time. (270)[40]

The cellist, more than any other woman, including Fermina, breaks his heart.

For her part, Fermina accepts the music of both lovers in turn. When forced by her mother-in-law to engage in her own musical studies, she manages to turn even a harp, "the instrument of the angels,"[41] into a subversive tool of death and destruction. With striking language, the narrative shows how Fermina's harp teacher from Mompox unexpectedly dies within two weeks of the commencement of lessons, and the new teacher's "gravedigger's breath distorted her arpeggios."[42] When the mother-in-law's god finally answers her prayers for death, the harp goes to the "Museum of the City until it and all it contained were consumed in flames" (208).[43] In the novel, the music lessons lead directly into the most miserable part of Fermina and Juvenal's married life, a period of misery only to be alleviated long afterward when the doctor undergoes an extended process of penitence for an extramarital affair. Aside from the episode with the harp, readers learn little about Fermina's thoughts on music or anything else; the narrator reveals little about her mental processes even as he writes copiously about what Fermina's two contenders think and feel. In one other revelation worth noting, however, the novel contrasts Juvenal's ears with Fermina's nose: "The truth is that her sense of smell not only served her in regard to washing clothes or finding lost children: it was the sense that oriented her in all areas of life, above all in her social life" (237).[44] While Juvenal listens to the world, his wife smells it.

Florentino meets his rival just once in the novel: "This was during a time that Dr. Juvenal Urbino had overcome the pitfalls of his profession, and was going from door to door, almost like a beggar with this hat in his hand, asking for contributions to his artistic enterprises. Uncle Leo XII had always been one of his most faithful and generous contributors, but just at that moment he had begun his daily ten-minute siesta" (189).[45] The two lovers of Fermina "had seen each other on various occasions, but they had never before been face to face as they were now" (190).[46] When they finally meet, Florentino feels inadequate in the face of Juvenal's urbanity. Then the doctor asks, "Do you like music?" This question catches his interlocutor feeling unprepared even though he attends every available concert and opera performance. His "weakness for popular music, above all sentimental waltzes, whose similarity to the ones he had composed as an adolescent" causes him to demur in giving "a serious answer to a serious question put to him by a specialist" (190).[47] Instead, he says simply, "I like Gardel,"[48] a guarded reference to the popular tango singer and composer that launches Juvenal into a rambling commentary in which he deprecates popular tastes, current performance practices, and lack of government support for the arts. The normally penetrative narrative stays on the surface here, leaving readers to wonder how Juvenal might have responded if he had known about Florentino's own compositions or his remarkable ability to remember an entire piece of music after hearing it only once.

During this disquisition, Juvenal also reveals his love of Fermina and his admiration for her crucial role in bringing culture to the city; "Without her I would be nothing,"[49] he declares (191). This combination of musical expertise and open affection for his wife causes Florentino to identify with his rival. "For the first time in the interminable twenty-seven years that he had been waiting, Florentino Ariza could not endure the pangs of grief at the thought that this admirable man would have to die in order for him to be happy" (191–92).[50] Shortly afterward, he shares these feelings with his one true confidant, Leona Cassini. "What hurts me is that he has to die." When she points out that all people pass away, he replies in the affirmative and then, inexplicably to her, "but he more than anyone else" (192).[51] Although Florentino proceeds with his long plan of conquest, the feelings that he has for Juvenal touch upon the readers' sensibilities, especially in the way that they coincide with the way that Efraín feels about his unwitting rival Carlos in a scene, also filled with music, from the classic Colombian novel *María* (Isaacs 124–57), which forms the basis for this reenactment in *Love in the Time of Cholera*.

A break "in the formal silence achieved for the opening bars of Mozart's 'La Chasse,'" caused in part by "the intrusions of Don Sancho's black servants" (36),[52] subtly reminds readers that an entire realm of sound exists outside the ken of the criollo world inhabited by Florentino and Juvenal. With some exceptions, notably Leona Cassini and Juvenal's lover Barbara Lynch, people of African descent appear only fleetingly in the novel, and in the world outside as well as inside this book, several decades will pass before large numbers of white people take more than a passive interest in black music. In rare moments the narrator mentions Florentino hanging out with his mentor "in the taverns around the port," an area that, much like Harlem during the 1920s to 1940s Renaissance, attracted slumming socialites as well as the social gamut of people from the neighborhood: "Lotario Thugut was in the habit of going there after the last shift at the telegraph office, and dawn often found him drinking Jamaican punch and playing the accordion with the crews of madmen from the Antillean schooners" (62–63).[53] Some of these sounds might seep into the soul of Juvenal, as well, as he visits the home of his friend Jeremiah in the city's "wretched and desolate" old slave quarters and hears "the thunder of riotous music, the godless drunken celebration of Pentecost by the poor" (12–13).[54] No one in the novel connects quite so well with the music of people of African descent as does Florentino's Uncle Leo, who "liked nothing better than to sing at funerals" (166).[55]

These offerings enjoy a gratifying reception among mourners until the time "when he thought it a good idea to sing 'When I Wake Up in Glory,' a beautiful and moving funeral song from Louisiana, and he was told to be quiet by the priest, who could not understand that Protestant intrusion in his church" (166).[56] Although a later version, with a lyric penned by Mahalia Jackson, became popular in the mid-twentieth century, the song has a long history and would have likely been known to popular music cognoscenti in Colombia, even if it had far wider dissemination in the southern United States.

"There is still a great deal left for us to say about music,"[57] says a newspaper editor in *Memories of My Melancholy Whores* (50). Imploring the ninety-year-old protagonist to reconsider his retirement plan, this statement makes the point that even after all that has been published to date, García Márquez has not exhausted the potential of sound creation in his novels. In his final novel, García Márquez fuses the protagonist and antagonist of *Love in the Time of Cholera* with an idea taken from one of the author's short stories, "Sleeping Beauty and the Airplane," from the collection *Strange Pilgrims*.

In a book made up of first-person narration, the protagonist of *Memories of My Melancholy Whores* starts out by arranging to have a fourteen-year-old girl, drugged and naked, made available to him as a celebration of the vespers of his ninetieth birthday. Given the protagonist's own origins in the bourgeoisie and the date of his birth, "August 29, the day of the Martyrdom of St. John the Baptist" (28),[58] we can accurately refer to him as don Juan. He uses what little money he has left to purchase women, who make him feel socially superior by remaining in every way beneath him. "I have never gone to bed with a woman I didn't pay," he explains in the book's first-person narration, "and the few who weren't in the profession I persuaded, by argument or by force, to take money even if they threw it in the trash" (11–12).[59] In this way, he lives diametrically opposed to the protagonist in *Love in the Time of Cholera*, who "could not conceive of anything more contemptible than paying for love: he had never done it" (182).[60] Throughout these texts, García Márquez does a beautiful job of demonstrating the exploitation that results from both approaches.

In the absence of conversation, musical sounds permeate the relationship, of sorts, between the protagonist of *Memories of My Melancholy Whores* and the girl he makes up in his mind as she sleeps. With her clothes exchanged for drugs, the girl sleeps during all of their encounters. "I ran the tip of my index finger along the damp nape of her neck," he recalls, "and she shivered inside, along the length of her body, like a chord on the harp, turned toward me with a grumble, and enveloped me in the ambience of her acid breath" (27). After she turns away again, he tries to separate her legs and meets with resistance: "I sang into her ear: *Angels surround the bed of Delgadina*. She relaxed a little" (28). Taking the power given to Adam to label the flora and fauna that surround him, the protagonist chooses her name from the song he has just sung to her: "Delgadina." During a conversation that takes place after more of these meetings, Rosa Cabarcas, the madam of the house, "was surprised when I mentioned the name Delgadina. That isn't her name, she said, her name is.... Don't tell me, I interrupted, for me she's Delgadina" (68).[61] Rosa merely shrugs at this, the right of denomination apparently being yet another service of the establishment.

"Delgadina," with a lyric based on an old Spanish *romance* (ballad), has since migrated to the *corrido* format. Assuming the adolescent pays any attention to this performance, she must wonder why her admirer has chosen to recount this tale of a girl driven to suicide for refusing to marry her own father.[62] "And so I began to dry her with a towel while I sang in a whisper the song about Delgadina, the king's youngest daughter, wooed by her father," recalls the protagonist:

> As I dried her she was showing me her sweaty flanks to the rhythm of my song: *Delgadina, Delgadina, you will be my darling love*. It was a limitless pleasure, for she began to perspire again on one side as I finished drying the other, which meant the song might never end. *Arise, arise, Delgadina, and put on your skirt of silk*, I sang into her ear. At the end, when the king's servants find her dead of thirst in her bed, it seemed to me that my girl had been about to wake when she heard the name. Then that's who she was: Delgadina. (56)[63]

Conveniently, he sees *his* girl respond, catlike, to the pet name that he has given her.

From his position of power and privilege, the narrator moves from naming to making up an entire life around the girl's sleeping form. Changing details about her appearance to suit his moods, he imagines their lives together over decades: "We sang Puccini love duets, Agustín Lara boleros, Carlos Gardel tangos, and we confirmed once again that those who do not sing cannot even imagine the joy of singing. Today I know it was not a hallucination but one more miracle of the first love of my life at the age of ninety" (60).[64] Before this, he had looked in the mirror, not liking the image reflected there, especially the "thin, lank hair that had once been my musician's mane" (27).[65] Now, with the girl under his power, he feels as though he is not as old as he thought he was and believes his real life has begun in these imagined moments. Ninety, it turns out, is the new thirty.

Having found true love and life, he makes arrangements with Rosa Cabarcas for what amounts to the permanent transfer of the perpetual sleeping beauty. Don Juan—or, given his maternal Italian heritage, Don Giovanni—plans his happy ending, with one of the funniest lines ever penned by García Márquez: "It was, at last, real life, with my heart safe and condemned to die of happy love in the joyful agony of any day after my hundredth birthday" (115).[66] No one in the narrative wakes up Delgadina to ask for her opinion on the matter.

Although lost a bit in translation, the narrator goes to some lengths to demonstrate the Italian roots that form his own lifelong passion for music. Early on, he introduces his readers to "Florina de Dios Cargamantos, a notable interpreter of Mozart, a multilingual Garibaldian, and the most beautiful and talented woman who ever lived in the city: my mother" (5).[67] In fact, the protagonist continues to occupy the house where his "mother would sit on March nights to sing love arias with other girls, her [Italian] cousins" (5–6).[68] After his parents passed away, Don Juan had done what many offspring do, getting rid of everything he "didn't need to live, which turned out to be almost everything but the books and Pianola rolls" (6).[69] Don Juan does more than reach back to his lineage. Books he keeps within his reach include "the *Vocabolario della lingua italiana*, by Nicola Zingarelli, to help me with my mother's language, which I learned in the cradle" (32).[70] His employment of musical language does not please everyone, however; at the newspaper offices, the censor "had a personal aversion to me, either because of my grammarian's airs or because I would use Italian words without quotation marks or italics when they seemed more expressive than Spanish, which ought to be legitimate practice between Siamese languages" (41–42).[71] The Italian background, slightly backgrounded in the translation, explains his attraction to music, an unavoidable element in his life. Although the protagonist earns nothing for the music and theater criticism he writes "when notable performers come to town" (7),[72] he gains local fame for his cultural expertise.

Like Juvenal Urbino, the narrator develops a reputation as a cosmopolitan lover of the arts. Having retired, he has little to do but to devote himself to the arts by fulfilling "other obligations that have a certain significance: concerts at Bellas Artes, painting exhibitions at the Centro Artístico, of which I am a founding member, an occasional civic conference at the Society for Public Improvement, or an important event like Fabregas's engagement at the Teatro Apolo" (15–16).[73] Meanwhile, he finds some solace in recordings of orchestral and chamber music. On the eve of his ninetieth birthday, for example, having arranged for a supposed virgin in a brothel, the narrator turns to the baroque era as he agonizes with nerves and anticipation: "At four o'clock I tried to calm my spirit with Johann Sebastian Bach's six Suites for Unaccompanied Cello in the definitive performance by Don Pablo Casals. I consider them the most accomplished pieces in all of music, but instead of soothing me as usual they left me in an even worse state of prostration" (17).[74] On another occasion he disconnects "the phone in order to take refuge in an exquisite program of music: Wagner's Rhapsody for Clarinet and Orchestra, Debussy's Rhapsody for Saxophone, and Bruckner's String Quintet, which is an Edenic oasis in the cataclysm of his work" (53).[75] Briefly, he manages to bring this music into Delgadina's room, pleased to hear that "Brahms's First Sonata for Violin and Piano was being diluted at half volume on the radio" (91).[76] Later in the story, after Rosa Cabarcas calls with a proposal for reconciliation, he lies "down in the hammock, trying to restore my serenity with the ascetic lyricism of Satie" (101).[77] Ever the musical expert, he almost always provides not just the name of the work and its composer, but also a brief evaluation of the piece mentioned.

The music that the protagonist chooses for his listening at home contrasts with the sounds forced on him as he goes about in the world. "A brass band played a languid waltz"[78] the first time he goes to see the girl he will call Delgadina (19). From earlier visits to houses of prostitution, he remembers Castorina, a prostitute he had known years earlier, and the music associated with her. "Her last steady stud, a fortunate black from Camagüey called Jonás the Galley Slave, had been one of the great trumpet players in Havana until he lost his entire smile in a catastrophic train collision" (111).[79] One can only try to imagine our Don Juan taking in a performance by Jonás and his compatriots from the Cuban capital.

Art and popular music come together, as they do in *Love in the Time of Cholera*, in boleros. Following the madam to his assigned room, he hears one of the women listening to the Mexican actress and bolero stylist "Toña la Negra singing a song of failed love on the radio. Rosa Cabarcas sighed: The bolero is life. I agreed, but until today I haven't dared to write it" (25).[80] This signals a crucial transformation for Don Juan, who until this day has enjoyed this style of music in relative secrecy. On another visit to Delgadina, he reaches her room, and "at top volume, I heard the warm voice of Don Pedro Vargas, the tenor of America, singing a bolero by Miguel Matamoros. I felt as if I were going to die. I pushed open the door, gasping for breath, and saw Delgadina in bed as she was in my memory" (62).[81] In an acknowledgment of musical acceptance that coincides with his new life, he hears popular music instead of the Mozart quartets he had programmed for the girl's room: "It was her preference, no doubt, and I accepted this without sorrow, for I had cultivated the same preference in my better days" (71).[82] Boleros signify youth for both of them, even if that youth takes place seventy-six years apart.

When the girl disappears for an extended period of time, don Juan takes "refuge in the peace of boleros. That was like a lethal potion: every word was Delgadina. I always had needed silence to write because my mind would pay more attention to the music than to my writing. Now it was the reverse: I could write only in the shade of boleros" (82).[83] As a result of this musical contact, his columns become so popular that the managing editor cannot deal with all of the mail the paper receives. In spite of this acclaim, the protagonist remains despondent over the girl's absence and begins to avoid listening to any type of music.

Having despised himself for most of his life, the protagonist has difficulty inciting admiration in others. Potential triumphs turn into defeats, such as when he appears as a "guest of honor at the concert in Bellas Artes by Jacques Thibault and Alfred Cortot, whose interpretation of the Sonata for Violin and Piano by César Franck was glorious, and during the intermission I listened to improbable praise. Maestro Pedro Biava, our gigantic musician, almost dragged me to the dressing rooms to introduce me to the soloists"[84] (45). Even so, this possible new beginning ends comically when the narrator misnames a work in the performance, leading to public humiliation. Behind these social missteps lies a presentiment of death that has lasted for decades. At a Bellas Artes concert, he recalls,

> The air-conditioning had broken down, and the elite of arts and letters was cooking in a bain-marie in the crowded hall, but the magic of the music created a celestial climate. At the end, with the Allegretto poco mosso, I was shaken by the stunning revelation that I was listening to the last concert fate would afford me before I died. I did not feel sorrow or fear but an overwhelming emotion at having lived long enough to experience it. (106)[85]

In spite of the drama of the moment, the narrator has had this feeling before, forty years earlier. Dancing "an apache tango," shortly before his fiftieth birthday, he "was shaken for the first time and almost knocked to the ground by the roar of death. It was like a brutal oracle in my ear: No matter what you, this year or in the next hundred, you will be dead forever" (107–8).[86] During those first ninety years, however, he finds some comfort in the fact that his impending doom will finally end a mostly unwanted life.

With the advent of his ninetieth birthday and the new feelings of love it brings come the rising popularity of his newspaper columns and his newfound sense of belonging in the world. In order to make the most of these unexpected developments, he reorganizes his life, and perhaps more crucially, his library, discarding "the player piano as a historical relic, along with more than a hundred rolls of classical music, and bought a used record player that was better than mine, with high-fidelity speakers that enlarged the area of the house. I was on the verge of ruin but well-compensated by the miracle of still being alive at my age" (64).[87] In short, "I became another man" (65).[88] He then goes back to the romantic literature that his mother adored and discovers new understandings of love. And then, "When my tastes in music reached a crisis, I discovered that I was backward and old, and I opened my heart to the delights of chance" (65–66).[89] As he does not place this discovery of chance precisely in music or in love, readers can only speculate on the possibility of any involvement by the works or philosophies of Edgard Varèse.

As a culmination, he begins to enjoy the activities of his own youth. Riding a bicycle for the first time in years, "I began to sing. First to myself in a quiet voice, and then at full volume, with the airs of the great Caruso, in the midst of the public market's garish shops and demented traffic" (72).[90] Later that week, this exuberant display leads him to write "another bold column: 'How to Be Happy on a Bicycle at the Age of Ninety'" (72).[91] On the evening of her fifteenth birthday, Don Juan sings the song from the market "to Delgadina, and I kissed her all over her body until I was breathless" (72).[92] Gratifyingly, "her body resonated inside with an arpeggio" (72),[93] making it clear that the instrument he plays upon responds well to its master's touch.

Even more than Fermina, the sought-after prize in *Love in the Time of Cholera*, the girl called Delgadina remains a mystery. Readers cannot know if she feels any of the emotions attributed to her by the man who could be her great-great-grandfather or if those imaginings are merely in the same category as the changing of her eyes and hair and the duets she sings during his daydreams. About the man, however, the text reveals a great deal, especially in those musical moments that appear throughout the book. As seen in two of his love novels, García Márquez elevates music to a position in which readers with any listening experience can take the time to appreciate the amplified sense of reading words and notes while seeing and hearing simultaneously. For those willing to put in the effort, it makes for an extraordinary cultural experience.

Notes

1. "Fragmentos de obras conocidas, que fijan una idea, inmediatamente, en el cerebro del oyente. El tema inicial de Las grutas de Fingal, de Mendelssohn, representará siempre el mar; el principio de Las estepas del Asia Central, de Borodine, figurará el desierto, la llanura; Scherezada, el oriente; *un jazz hot*, será la síntesis de Harlem; el canto de la Lorelei evocará el Rhin" (552; translation by Katz Montiel).
2. For a detailed examination of this feature, see Bell-Villada, *García Márquez*, pp. 182–85.
3. "Con el mismo acordeón arcaico que le regaló Sir Walter Raleigh en la Guayana" (García Márquez, *Cien años de soledad* 106).

4. "En el último salón abierto del desmantelado barrio de tolerancia un conjunto de acordeones tocaba los cantos de Rafael Escalona, . . . heredero de los secretos de Francisco el Hombre" (444).
5. "Tocó en el acordeón por última vez las canciones olvidadas de Francisco el Hombre" (386).
6. "Sus baúles trashumantes y su acordeón de perdulario" (388).
7. "Un experto italiano" (114).
8. "Reproducciones del campanario de Florencia que daban la hora con un concierto de carillones, y cajas musicales de Sorrento, y polveras de China que cantaban al destaparlas tonadas de cinco notas" (159).
9. "Le regaló al templo un armonio alemán, organizó un coro infantil y preparó un reperetorio gregoriano que puso una nota espléndida en el ritual taciturno del padre Nicanor" (159–60).
10. "Con un clavicordio que ocupó el lugar de la pianola" (294).
11. "La acreditaba como concertista de clavicordio" (309).
12. "La pianola, el clavicordio y otros corotos caídos en desgracia" (386).
13. "Por lo único que le interesaba entonces acompañar con el violín a Lotario Thugut en el mirador privilegiado del coro, era por ver cómo ondulaba la túnica de ella con la brisa de los cánticos" (92).
14. "También sabía que era uno de los músicos del coro, y aunque nunca se había atrevido a levantar la vista para comprobarlo durante la misa, un domingo tuvo la revelación de que mientras los otros instrumentos tocaban para todos, el violín tocaba sólo para ella" (95).
15. "Una noche, sin ningún anuncio, Fermina Daza despertó asustada por una serenata de violín solo con un valse solo" (99).
16. "Florentino Ariza confirmó que era él quien había llevado la serenata, y que el valse había sido compuesto por él y tenía el nombre con que conocía a Fermina Daza en su corazón: *La Diosa Coronada*" (100).
17. "Llamó la atención del telegrafista, el emigrado alemán Lotario Thugut, que además tocaba el órgano en las ceremonias mayores de la catedral y daba clases de música a domicilio. Lotario Thugut le enseñó el código Morse y el manejo del sistema telegráfico, y bastaron las primeras lecciones de violín para que Florentino Ariza siguiera tocándolo de oído como un profesional" (78).
18. "Estaba siempre a disposición de sus amigos para llevar a sus novias serenatas de violín solo" (78).
19. "Pues también de él decía Lotario Thugut que había sido su peor alumno de canto, y sin embargo hacía llorar hasta las lápidas de los cementerios" (224).
20. "Lo tocó murmurando la letra, con el violín bañado en lágrimas, y con una inspiración tan intensa que a los primeros compases empezaron a ladrar los perros de la calle, y luego los de la ciudad, pero después se fueron callando poco a poco por el hechizo de la música, y el valse terminó con un silencio sobrenatural" (187–88).
21. "Había dejado el violín, que se identificaba demasiado con su desgracia" (189).
22. "La víspera de la llegada al puerto de Caracolí, que era el término del viaje, el capitán ofreció la fiesta tradicional de despedida, con una orquesta de viento formada por los miembros de la tripulación, y fuegos de artificios de colores desde la cabina de mando" (198). "Con el traje escocés del clan MacTavish, y tocó la gaita a placer y enseñó a todo el que quiso a bailar sus danzas nacionales" (198–99). (We must point out a false note in an otherwise admirable translation. An *orquesta de viento* would not have been a woodwind

ensemble, as stated in the translation, but more likely some type of brass ensemble, possibly with some woodwind instruments.)
23. "Pues la fiesta terminó después de la medianoche a bordo del transatlántico iluminado, con una orquesta de Viena que estrenaba en aquel viaje los valses más recientes de Johann Strauss" (210).
24. "Con una concepción nueva de la vida, cargados de novedades del mundo, y listos para mandar. Él con las primicias de la literatura, de la música, y sobre todo las de su ciencia... El mismo librero se comprometió a mandarle por correo las partituras más seductoras del catálogo de Ricordi, sobre todo de música de cámara, para mantener el título bien ganado por su padre de primer promotor de conciertos en la ciudad" (217). "Llevaban, además, tres recuerdos imborrables: el estreno sin precedentes de *Los Cuentos de Hoffman*, en París" (218).
25. "El doctor Juvenal Urbino hizo subir el piano de la Escuela de Música en una carreta de mulas, y le llevó a Fermina Daza una serenata que hizo época" (167).
26. "El espacio concebido en sus orígenes para las cenas de gala, a un lado del comedor, fue aprovechado para una pequeña salsa de música donde se daban conciertos íntimos cuando venían intérpretes notables" (32).
27. "El piano que el doctor Urbino no había vuelto a tocar en muchos años" (33).
28. "La banda de vientos inició un aire populachero, no previsto en el programa ... otra vez, al cabo de tantos y tantos años, tenía ganas de cantar. Lo hubiera hecho, sin duda, a instancias del joven chelista que se ofreció para acompañarlo, de haber sido porque un automóvil de los nuevos atravesó de pronto el lodazal del patio, salpicando a los músicos y alborotando a los patos en los corrales con su corneta de pato, y se detuvo frente al pórtico de la casa" (59). (Again, there is a problem here in translating *vientos*. Although it will generally contain flutes, clarinets, and saxophones, a *banda de vientos* could be a concert band, brass band, or just plain band, but not a woodwind band.)
29. "Las canciones de Yvette Guilbert y Aristide Bruant, que habían hecho las delicias de Francia en el siglo pasado" (35).
30. "Se abandonó al lirismo diáfano y fluido de la última pieza del programa, que no pudo identificar. Más tarde, el joven chelista del conjunto, que acababa de regresar de Francia, le dijo que era el cuarteto para cuerdas de Gabriel Fauré, a quien el doctor Urbino no había oído nombrar siquiera, a pesar de que siempre estuvo muy alerta a las novedades de Europa" (57).
31. "La iniciativa más contagiosa del doctor Urbino, pues la fiebre de la ópera contaminó hasta los sectores menos pensados de la ciudad, y dio origen a toda una generación de Isoldas y Otelos, y Aidas y Sigfridos" (67).
32. "¿Le gusta la música? . . . ¿A qué viene la pregunta? . . . La música es importante para la salud. . . . Lo creía de veras, y ella iba a saber muy pronto y por el resto de su vida que el tema de la música era casi un a fórmula mágica que él usaba para proponer una amistad" (162). (A small, but potentially revelatory detail, is worth noting here: the translator has decided that she will know this for the rest of *her* life even though the text written by García Márquez takes advantage of the gender-neutral third person singular possessive pronoun to leave it open as to whether she remembers it for the rest of *his* life.)
33. "Al decirlo sintió que la compasión había vuelto a prevalecer sobre la amargura de la carta, y no se lo agradeció a su mujer sino a un milagro de la música" (58).
34. "Tenía una voz de galeote, sin ningún orden académico, pero capaz de registros impresionantes" (122).

35. "Sin embargo, en el fondo de su trueno había una lucecita de ternura que agrietaba el corazón de sus oyentes como a las ánforas de cristal del gran Caruso" (122).
36. "Que era capaz de despertar a las criaturas de la selva cantando una romanza napolitana desde la baranda del capitán" (352).
37. "En las tinieblas del río se sentían los aleteos de las garzas en los pantanos, el coletazo de los caimanes, al pavor de los sábalos tratando de saltar a tierra firme, pero en la nota culminante, cuando se temió que al cantor se le rompieran las arterias por la potencia del canto, la dentadura postiza se le salió del boca con el aliento final, y se hundió en el agua" (352).
38. "La única frustración que me llevo de esta vida es la de haber cantado en tantos entierros, menos en el mío" (358).
39. "Cantó el aria del *Adiós a la Vida*, de Tosca. La cantó *a capella*, como más le gustaba, y todavía con voz firme. Florentino Ariza se conmovió, pero apenas si lo dejó notar en el temblor de la voz con que dio las gracias" (358).
40. "Ángeles Alfaro, la efímera y la más amada de todas, que vino por seis meses a enseñar instrumentos de arco en la Escuela de Música y pasaba con él las noches de luna en la azotea de su casa, como su madre la echó al mundo, tocando las suites más bellas de toda la música en el violonchelo, cuya voz se volvía de hombre entre sus muslos dorados. Desde la primera noche de la luna, ambos se hicieron trizas los corazones con un amor de principiantes feroces. Por Ángeles Alfaro se fue como vino, con su sexo tierno y su violonchelo de pecadora, en un transatlántico abanderado por el olvido, y lo único que quedó de ella en las azoteas de luna fueron sus señas de adiós con un pañuelo blanco que parecía una paloma en el horizonte, solitaria y triste, como en los versos de los Juegos Florales. Con ella aprendió Florentino Ariza lo que ya había padecido muchas veces sin saberlo: que se puede estar enamorado de varias personas a la vez" (360).
41. "El instrumento de los ángeles" (278).
42. "Empezó con un maestro de maestros que trajeron a propósito de la ciudad de Mompox, y que murió de repente a los quince días, y siguió por varios años con el músico mayor del seminario, cuyo aliento se sepulturero distorsionaba los arpegios" (278).
43. "Museo de la Ciudad, hasta que lo consumieron las llamas con todo lo que tenía adentro" (278).
44. "La verdad es que el olfato no le servía sólo para lavar la ropa o para encontrar niños perdidos: era su sentido de orientación en todos los órdenes de la vida, y sobre todo de la vida social" (316).
45. "Era la época en que también el doctor Juvenal Urbino había superado los escollos de la profesión, y andaba casi de puerta en puerta como un pordiosero con el sombrero en la mano, buscando contribuciones para sus promociones artísticas. Uno de sus contribuyentes más asiduos y pródigos lo fue siempre el tío León XII, quien en aquel momento justo había empezado a hacer su siesta diaria de diez minutos" (253).
46. "Se habían visto en diversas ocasiones, pero nunca habían estado así, frente a frente, y Florentino Ariza padeció una vez más la náusea de sentirse inferior" (253).
47. "—¿Le gusta la música? . . . Tenía la sangre dulce para la música de moda, sobre todo los valses sentimentales, cuya afinidad con los que él mismo hacía de adolescente. . . . Pero esa no sería una respuesta seria para una pregunta tan seria de un especialista" (254).
48. "—Me gusta Gardel—dijo" (254).
49. "Dijo: 'Yo no sería nadie sin ella'" (255).
50. "Por primera vez en los veintisiete años interminables que llevaba esperando, Florentino Ariza no pudo resistir la punzada de dolor de que aquel hombre admirable tuviera que morirse para que él fuera feliz" (256).

51. "Lo que me duele es que se tiene que morir.... Sí—dijo él—, pero éste más que todo en el mundo" (257).
52. "El grupo de la escuela de Bellas Artes inició el concierto, en medio de un silencio formal que alcanzó para los compases iniciales de *La Chasse* de Mozart. A pesar de las voces cada vez más altas y confusas, y del estorbo de los criados negros de Don Sancho" (56).
53. "Lotario Thugut solía irse por allí después del último turno del telégrafo, y muchas veces amanecía bebiendo ponche de Jamaica y tocando el acordeón con las tripulaciones de locos de las goletas de las Antillas" (90).
54. "Todo tenía un aspecto miserable y desamparado, pero de las cantinas sórdidas salía el trueno de música de la parranda sin Dios ni ley del Pentecostés de los pobres" (24).
55. "Nada le gustaba más que cantar en los entierros" (222).
56. "Salvo en uno, en el que tuvo la buena idea de cantar *When wake up in Glory*, un canto funerario de la Luisiana, hermoso y estremecedor, y fue hecho callar por el capellán que no pudo entender aquella intromisión dentro de su iglesia" (222). (Note: the translator changes the song title, probably correctly, to "When I Wake Up in Glory.")
57. "Todavía nos queda mucho por hablar de la música" (52).
58. "29 del agosto, día del Martirio de San Juan Bautista" (31).
59. "Nunca me ha acostado con ninguna mujer sin pagarle, y a las pocas que no eran del oficio las convencí por la razón o por la fuerza de que recibieran la plata aunque fuera para botarla en la basura" (16).
60. "No podía concebir nada más indigno que pagar el amor: no lo hizo nunca" (243).
61. "Se sorprendió cuando mencioné el nombre de Delgadina. No se llama así, dijo, se llama. No me lo digas, la interrumpí, para mí es Delgadina" (69).
62. "Delgadina" lyric:

>Delgadina se paseaba de la sala a la cocina
>con su vestido de seda, que a su cuerpo le ilumina
>Levántate Delgadina, ponte tus nahuas de seda
>porque nos vamos a misa a la ciudad de Morelia
>Luego que salió de misa su papá le platicaba
>Delgadina hijita mía yo te quiero para dama
>No permita Dios del cielo ni la reina soberana
>Esta ofensa para Dios y traición para mi mama
>Júntense los once criados y encierren a Delgadina
>remachen bien los candados, que no se oiga voz ladina
>Papacito de mi vida, tu castigo estoy sufriendo
>regaladme un vaso de agua, que de sed me estoy muriendo
>Júntense los once criados llévenle agua a Delgadina
>en vaso sobredorado, vaso de cristal de china
>Cuando le llevaron la agua, Delgadina estaba muerta
>tenía sus brazos cruzados, tenía su boquita abierta
>La cama de Delgadina de ángeles está rodeada
>la cama del rey su padre de demonios apretada
>Ya con esta me despido tengo una cita en la esquina
>aquí se acaba el cantando versos de la Delgadina.
>English translation:
>Delgadina walks from the parlor to the kitchen
>with her silk dress, that illuminates her body
>Wake up Delgadina, put your silk clothes on

because we're going to attend mass at the city of Morelia
Right after mass, her father told her
Delgadina, my daughter, I want you as my wife
God of Heaven and the sovereign queen forbid
this offense to God, and treason to my mother
Eleven servants, gather around and lock up Delgadina
Tighten up the locks, so that no soft voice may be heard
Dear father of my life, your punishment I am suffering
Give me a cup of water, for I am dying of thirst
Eleven servants, gather around give water to Delgadina
in a gold cup, a cup of crystal china
When they went to give her water, Delgadina was dead
she had her arms crossed, she had her mouth closed
The bed of Delgadina is surrounded by angels
The bed of her father the king, of demons tightened
And with this I say goodbye, I have an appointment in the corner
Here ends the singing of the verses of "La Delgadina"

63. "De modo que empecé a secarla con la toalla mientras le cantaba en susurros la canción de Delgadina, la hija menor del rey, requerida de amores por su padre. A medida que la secaba ella iba mostrándome los flancos sudados al compás de mi canto: *Delgadina, Delgadina, tú serás mi prenda amada*. Fue un placer sin límites pues ella volvía a sudar por un costado cuando acababa de secarla por el otro, para que la canción no terminara nunca. *Levántate, Delgadina, ponte tu falda de seda*, le cantaba al oído. Al final, cuando los criados del rey la encontraron muerta de sed en su cama, me pareció que mi niña había estado a punto de despertar al escuchar el nombre. Así que era ella: Delgadina" (58).
64. "Cantábamos duetos de amor de Puccini, boleros de Agustín Lara, tangos de Carlos Gardel y comprobábamos una vez más que quienes no cantan no pueden imaginar siquiera lo que es le felicidad de cantar. Hoy sé que no fue una alucinación, sino un milagro más del primer amor de mi vida a los noventa años" (62).
65. "Desmirriadas las crines que habían sido mi melena de músico" (30).
66. "Era por fin la vida real, con mi corazón a salvo, y condenado a morir de buen amor en la agonía feliz de cualquier día después de mis cien años" (109).
67. "Florina de Dios Cargamantos, intérprete notable de Mozart, políglota y garibaldina, y la mujer más hermosa y de mejor talento que hubo nunca en la ciudad: mi madre" (11).
68. "Se sentaba en las noches de marzo a cantar arias de amor con sus primas italianas" (11). Translations for audiences who purchase trade publications have their own purposes, which do not always coincide with those of scholarly research, so we have reintroduced the adjectival Italian left out of the text in English.
69. "Empecé a subastar cuanto me iba sobrando para vivir, que terminó por ser casi todo, salvo los libros y la pianola de rollos" (11). Strictly speaking, he kept the player piano. Although García Márquez's text in Spanish does not say so, the protagonist likely held onto the rolls as well, as the instrument would have had little use without them.
70. "El *Vocabolario della lingua italiana* de Nicola Zingarelli, para favorecerme con el idioma de mi madre, que aprendí desde la cuna" (36).
71. "Tenía una aversión personal contra mí, por mis ínfulas de gramático, o porque utilizaba palabras italianas sin comillas ni cursivas cuando me parecían más expresivas que en castellano, como debiera ser de uso legítimo entre lenguas siamesas" (44).
72. "En que vienen intérpretes notables" (12).

73. "U otros empeños de cierta monta: conciertos en Bellas Artes, exposiciones de pintura en el Centro Artístico, del cual soy socio fundador, alguna que otra conferencia cívica en la Sociedad de Mejoras Públicas, o un acontecimiento grande como la temporada de la Fábregas en el teatro Apolo" (20).
74. "A las cuatro traté de apaciguarme con las seis suites para chelo de Juan Sebastián Bach, en la versión definitiva de don Pablo Casals. Las tengo como lo más sabio de toda la música, pero en vez de apaciguarme como de sólito me dejaron en un estado de la peor postración" (21).
75. "El teléfono para refugiarme en la música con un programa exquisito: la rapsodia para clarinete y orquesta de Wagner, la de saxofón de Debussy y el quinteto para cuerdas de Bruckner, que es un remanso edénico en el cataclismo de su obra" (54).
76. "En el radio se diluía a medio volumen la sonata número uno para violín y piano de Brahms" (88).
77. "Me eché en la hamaca, tratando de serenarme con la lírica ascética de Satie" (97).
78. "Una banda de cobres tocaba un valse lánguido" (23).
79. "Su ultimo machucante de planta, un negro feliz de Camagüey a quien llamaban Jonás el Galeote había sido un trompetista de los grandes en La Habana hasta que perdió la sonrisa completa en una catástrofe de trenes" (106).
80. "Toña la Negra cantaba en el radio una canción de malos amores. Rosa Cabarcas tomó aire: El bolero es la vida. Yo estaba de acuerdo, pero hasta hoy no me atreví a escribirlo" (28).
81. "A volumen más alto, distinguí la voz cálida de don Pedro Vargas, el tenor de América, con un bolero de Miguel Matamoros. Sentí que iba a morir. Empujé la puerta con la respiración desbaratada y vi a Delgadina en la cama como en mis recuerdos" (63).
82. "Era el gusto de ella, sin duda, y lo asumí sin dolor, pues también yo lo había cultivado con el corazón en mis mejores días" (71).
83. "Me refugié en la paz de los boleros. Fue como un bebedizo emponzoñado: cada palabra era ella. Siempre había necesitado el silencio para escribir porque mi mente atendí más a la música que a la escritura. Entonces fue el revés: sólo pude escribir a la sombra de los boleros" (80–81).
84. "Fui invitado de honor al concierto de Jacques Thibault y Alfred Cortot en la sala de Bellas Artes, con una interpretación gloriosa de la sonata para violín y piano de César Frank [sic], y en el intermedio escuché elogios inverosímiles. El maestro Pedro Biava, nuestro músico enorme, me llevó casi a rastras a los camerinos para presentarme a los intérpretes" (47).
85. "El aire acondicionado había fallado y la flor y nata de las artes y las letras se cocinaban al bañomaría en el salón abarrotado, pero la magia de la música era un clima celestial. Al final, con el *Allegretto poco mosso*, me estremeció la revelación deslumbrante de que estaba escuchando el último concierto que me deparara el destino antes de morir. No sentí dolor ni miedo sino la emoción arrasadora de haber alcanzado a vivirlo" (101).
86. "Que bailaba un tango apache" (102). "Cuando me derribó por tierra el frémito de la muerte. Fue como un oráculo brutal en el oído: Hagas lo que hagas, en este año o dentro de ciento, estarás muerto hasta jamás" (103).
87. "Por ultimo rematé la pianola como reliquia histórica con sus más de cien rollos de clásicos, y compré un tocadiscos usado pero mejor que el mío, con parlantes de alta fidelidad que engrandecieron el ámbito de la casa. Quedé al borde de la ruina pero bien compensado por el milagro de esta vivo a mi edad" (65).
88. "Me volví otro" (66).
89. "Cuando mis gustos en música hicieron crisis me descubrí atrasado y viejo, y abrí mi corazón a las delicias del azar" (66).

90. "Empecé a cantar. Primero para mí mismo, en voz baja, y después a todo pecho con ínfulas del gran Caruso, por entre los bazares abigarrados y el tráfico demente del Mercado público" (72).
91. "Esa semana, en homenaje a diciembre, escribí otra nota atrevida: *Como ser feliz en bicicleta a los noventa años*" (72).
92. "La noche de su cumpleaños le canté a Delgadina la canción completa, y la besé por todo el cuerpo hasta quedarme sin aliento" (72).
93. "Ella resonó por dentro con un arpegio" (72).

Works Cited

Bell-Villada, Gene H. "Building a Compass" (Interview with García Márquez). *Conversations with Gabriel García Márquez*, edited by Gene H. Bell-Villada, UP of Mississippi, 2006, pp. 133–40.

Bell-Villada, Gene H. *García Márquez: The Man and His Work*. 2nd ed., rev. and expanded. U of North Carolina P, 2010.

Carpentier, Alejo. "La radio y sus nuevas posibilidades." *Crónicas*, 17 December 1933, Letras Cubanas, 1985.

García Márquez, Gabriel. *El amor en los tiempos del cólera* (1985). Vintage, 2003.

García Márquez, Gabriel. *The Autumn of the Patriarch*. Translated by Gregory Rabassa, Harper, 1999.

García Márquez, Gabriel. "El avión de la bella durmiente." *Doce cuentos peregrinos*, Vintage, 1992, pp. 50–57.

García Márquez, Gabriel. *Cien años de soledad*. Austral, 1983.

García Márquez, Gabriel. *Love in the Time of Cholera*. Translated by Edith Grossman, Vintage, 2003.

García Márquez, Gabriel. *Memoria de mis putas tristes*. Vintage, 2004.

García Márquez, Gabriel. *Memories of My Melancholy Whores*. Translated by Edith Grossman, Vintage, 2005.

García Márquez, Gabriel. *Obra periodística*, vol. 1, *Textos costeños*. Edited with an Introduction by Jacques Gilard, Bruguera, 1981.

García Márquez, Gabriel. *One Hundred Years of Solitude*. Translated by Gregory Rabassa. Avon Books, 1979.

García Márquez, Gabriel. "Sleeping Beauty and the Airplane." Translated by Edith Grossman, *Strange Pilgrims*, Penguin, 1993, pp. 54–61.

Goehr, Lydia. "How to Do More with Words. Two Views of (Musical) Ekphrasis." *British Journal of Aesthetics*, vol. 50, no. 4, Oct. 2010, pp. 389–410.

Isaacs Ferrer, Jorge. *María* (1867). Edited by Donald McGrady, Cátedra, 1993.

Katz Montiel, Marco. *Music and Identity in Twentieth-Century Literature from Our America: Noteworthy Protagonists*. Palgrave Macmillan, 2014.

Katz Montiel, Marco. "Popular Music Genres." *A Companion to Popular Culture*, edited by Gary Burns, Wiley-Blackwell, 2016, pp. 123–43.

Williams, Raymond Leslie. "The Visual Arts, the Poetization of Space and Writing: An Interview with Gabriel García Márquez." *PMLA*, vol. 104, no. 2, Mar. 1989, pp. 131–40.

CHAPTER 23

COLONIALITY AND SOLITUDE IN GARCÍA MÁRQUEZ'S PUBLIC SPEECHES AND NEWSPAPER ARTICLES

IGNACIO LÓPEZ-CALVO

GABRIEL García Márquez's magical realist narrative mode has been criticized by some scholars and younger Latin American writers as resorting to a certain tropicalism, an approach that exoticizes Latin America as a region where violence and sensuality dominate every aspect of daily life. They have accused the Nobel laureate of selling a magical Third World underdevelopment full of superstition, mythical legends, popular folklore, and distortions of time aimed at the Global North's reading markets, which is quite different from everyday reality in the region. Chilean writer and filmmaker Alberto Fuguet, for instance, strategically distanced himself in 1997 from García Márquez's approach to Latin American reality. Instead, he laid his claim to

> something much closer to what I call "McOndo"—a world of McDonald's, Macintoshes and condos. In a continent that was once ultra-politicized, young, apolitical writers like myself are now writing without an overt agenda, about their own experiences. Living in cities all over South America, hooked on cable TV (CNN en español), addicted to movies and connected to the Net, we are far away from the jalapeño-scented, siesta-happy atmosphere that permeates too much of the South American literary landscape. (n.p.)

In turn, Colombian writer Juan Gabriel Vásquez, talking about his 2013 novel *The Sound of Things Falling*, stated:

> I want to forget this absurd rhetoric of Latin America as a magical or marvelous continent. In my novel there is a disproportionate reality, but that which

is disproportionate in it is the violence and cruelty of our history and of our politics. Let me be clear about this. . . . I can say that reading "One Hundred Years of Solitude" . . . in my adolescence may have contributed much to my literary calling, but I believe that magic realism is the least interesting part of this novel. I suggest reading "One Hundred Years" as a distorted version of Colombian history. (quoted in White n.p.)

Actually, it would be wrong to associate García Márquez's entire fictional opus with this literary mode, since he never resorts to it in testimonial works like *La aventura de Miguel Littín clandestino en Chile* (*Clandestine in Chile: The Adventures of Miguel Littín*, 1986) or, for the most part, in love novels such as *El amor en los tiempos del cólera* (*Love in the Time of Cholera*, 1985). In any case, whether or not one agrees with these critical assessments, in his journalism and public speeches García Márquez undoubtedly offers a highly different assessment of Latin American reality from the one censured by the disparagers of his fiction.[1] And it is there, perhaps, that one can find his true image of Latin America, which was indeed far from tropicalism and exoticization. This essay compares and contrasts the author's magical-realist image of Latin America in some of his fictional works with the typically more realistic one (there are some exceptions) set forth in his speeches collected in the volumes *Yo no vengo a decir un discurso* (*I'm Not Here to Give a Speech*, 2010) as well as in his newspaper articles collected in *El escándalo del siglo: Textos en prensa y revistas* (*The Scandal of the Century and Other Writings*, 2018). In particular, it reveals García Márquez's grasp and denunciation of what decolonial thinkers have termed "coloniality."

Without mentioning the term, in his speeches against Eurocentric interpretations of Latin America and in favor of the region's right to determine its own sociopolitical destiny beyond Western, universalist, grand narratives, García Márquez is implicitly criticizing the persistence of "the coloniality of power." The term, coined by Peruvian sociologist Aníbal Quijano, refers to a specific form of domination that takes place after formal colonization is over. It is a discriminatory discourse that originated during colonial times and is still reflected in the socioeconomic structures of modern postcolonial societies. Reproduced not only in sociopolitical and racial orders (i.e., social and racial discrimination) but also in forms of knowledge, it is the living legacy of colonialism. Moreover, coloniality, according to Quijano and Walter Mignolo, is a constitutive part of Western modernity: there is no modernity without coloniality since they are two sides of the same coin. According to decolonial thought, the colonial project and European modernity worked hand in hand, constructing their hegemonic power through the control of cultural means that ultimately became colonizing tools, such as Western alphabetic writing. Modernity, according to Mignolo, has always been intricately linked to what he calls "the colonial matrix of power."

Whereas explicit imperialism and political domination may for the most part be gone, the imposition of Eurocentric worldviews stubbornly remains, leaving behind or subalternizing the Other as racially or ethnically marked, and moreover as female, nonbinary, oppressed, and/or poor. This universalist episteme continues to impose the values (including racial, patriarchal, and class values, and our relationship with the natural world) of European modernity in postcolonial societies. Therefore, a formally sovereign nation in the postcolonial world, which is no longer controlled by an imperial colonial power, may still operate under these power patterns and relations, as well as under the epistemic impositions that were established during the colonial process. I argue, then, that coloniality is, for García Márquez in these speeches, the source of Latin America's solitude. In other words, in my view, one could change the title of his Nobel acceptance speech, "La soledad de América Latina" ("The Solitude of Latin America") to "Coloniality in Latin America" without significantly changing the intended message. In fact, the word "solitude," used in different passages in the speech, is somewhat cryptic and enigmatic, leaving the listener or reader to figure out its meaning. It is first mentioned in relation to the failure of language to describe Latin America's immeasurable reality. In turn, in the second passage, the source of Latin America's solitude seems to be Europe's denial of the region's right to search for original paths to and methods for social change and justice, always considering the different circumstances. The third and last solitude is used arises in connection with Latin Americans' right to dream of a utopia where no one can decide for them any longer, where love and happiness are finally possible. This utopia or second opportunity, as he calls it, is nothing other than the end of the coloniality of power.

The author not only blames the Global North's colonial gaze, which is still negatively affecting Latin America, but also the omnipresence of these same Eurocentric views in Latin American societies themselves, which have not yet managed to articulate an independent regional identity and worldview. It could be argued that his attempts at creating a united Latin American film industry and a coherent Latin American journalism (including his creation of numerous journals and magazines, such as *Cambio* and *Alternativa*),[2] documented in several speeches in *I'm Not Here to Give a Speech*, are his own expressions of leadership in search of such a pan–Latin American worldview and identity, finally liberated from coloniality. Among these attempts, he donated the $22,000 he had received from the Rómulo Gallegos Novel Prize to the Venezuelan Movimiento al Socialismo (MAS; Movement to Socialism), the latter of which in turn used it to start the newspaper *Punto*; in Cuba, he was the president of the Foundation for a New Latin American Cinema, which was responsible for the founding of the Escuela Internacional de Cine, Televisión y Video (EICTV; International School of Cinema, Television, and Video) in 1986; and he was also the founder and president of the Foundation for a New Ibero-American Journalism. Created in 1994, this foundation organizes workshops and seminars to promote the continuing education of journalists in Latin America.

The coloniality of power, a hegemonic model inaugurated during the conquest of the Americas that articulates the understanding of race, labor, and space for the benefit of capital and European colonizers, still persists today in the global structures of power. García Márquez suggests that if Latin America is ever going to rid itself of its economic and political dependence, it must first eradicate this Eurocentric colonial difference in the areas of epistemology and culture. He reminds Latin Americans that they can and must also produce valuable knowledge—accepting indigenous (see Juan Moreno Blanco's essay on the Wayúu influence on García Márquez's fiction, included in this volume) and Afro-Latin American knowledges—based on their own particular experiences. This advice is, in fact, reminiscent of Mignolo's concept of "the geopolitics of knowledge," a term introduced to counter the idea that knowledge is universal, that it has no location. Knowledge, according to Mignolo, is always located and situated in the colonial matrix of power, according to racial, sexual, and gender classifications. In this context, García Márquez declares that Europe must accept Latin America's ways of being in the world as well as its struggles for liberation, including decolonization.

As is well known, García Márquez has openly condemned contemporary US imperialism. For instance, in his 2003 speech "La patria amada aunque distante" ("The Beloved though Distant Homeland"), he states:

> [T]here are still some puerile souls who look to the United States as a polestar of salvation with the certainty that in our country we have used up even the sighs to die in peace. However, what they find there is a blind empire that no longer considers Colombia a good neighbour, or even a cheap, trustworthy accomplice, but only another target for its imperial voracity.[3] (128)

The presence of a critique of imperialism and colonialism in García Márquez's discourse is not, however, the object of study in this essay; rather, I am more interested in his early intuition and denunciation of the persistence of coloniality in Latin America. Thus, in his 1982 speech "La soledad de América Latina," given during his Nobel Prize in Literature acceptance, as well as in his 1995 speeches "América Latina Existe" ("Latin America Exists") and "Dreams for the Twenty-First Century," one finds an openly decolonial and anti-Eurocentric stance, with which he calls on Europe to try to conceive of Latin America in a different, less paternalistic way. He demands that peripheral, non-Eurocentric worldviews and ways of being in the world be respected on equal terms. Moreover, a sober, realistic denunciation of injustice, infant mortality, forced disappearances, genocide, the abundance of forced exiles and refugees, and other social evils pervades many of these speeches and newspaper articles. In all, I consider these texts essential not only for understanding García Márquez's fiction but, more important, for gaining insight into how he really saw Colombia and Latin America, their social problems, and the obstacles to liberation, and what he perceived as possible solutions.

García Márquez begins his 1982 acceptance speech for the Nobel Prize for Literature, "La soledad de América Latina," by presenting as a predecessor of magical realism the imaginative description of natives, as well as of the flora and fauna of the Americas, by Antonio Pigafetta, a Florentine navigator who served as Magellan's official chronicler during their historic, first circumnavigation of the planet. The author then proceeds to mention the testimonies of Latin American reality provided by the chroniclers of the Indies, including the imagined El Dorado (according to him, used—in a clear example of early resistance—by witty indigenous people to rid themselves of the invaders) and the Fountain of Youth, as well as the explorations of Álvar Núñez Cabeza de Vaca, followed by the mad deeds of several Latin American dictators. Yet after these first four paragraphs, somehow reminiscent of the tone and content of his magical realist texts, the speaker dives into the tragic reality of the Latin America of the early 1980s, marked by coups, dictators, civil wars, ethnocide, child deaths, stolen children, exile, refugees, and disappearances, claiming along the way his literature's attachment to these harsh circumstances: "[A]ll of us who are creatures of that disordered reality have had to ask very little of our imaginations, because the greatest challenge for us has been the insufficiency of conventional devices to make our lives believable" (21).[4] The Nobel laureate then modestly presumes that it is this unforgiving Latin American reality that has attracted the attention of the Swedish Academy of Letters, rather than his literary representation thereof.[5]

It is at this point that García Márquez suddenly moves from thankfulness and modesty to an open condemnation of Eurocentric interpretations of Latin America's plight and of European refusal to allow Latin Americans to build their own type of modernity. He even resorts to a thinly veiled touch of sarcasm:

> [I]t is not difficult to understand that the rational prodigies of this side of the world, enraptured by the contemplation of their own culture, have been left without a valid method for interpreting us. It is understandable that they insist on measuring us with the same yardstick they use to measure themselves, not remembering that the ravages of life are not the same for everyone, and that the search for identity is as arduous and bloody for us as it was for them. The interpretation of our reality using foreign systems only contributes to making us more and more unknown, less and less free, more and more solitary. Perhaps venerable Europe would be more understanding if it tried to see us in its own past.[6] (22)

Sarcastically calling Europeans, or perhaps the Swedish academy in particular, "talentos racionales" (rendered as "rational prodigies") brings to mind the Spanish colonial differentiation between *gente de razón* (people of reason, or rational people), a term that was used—in the context of the *sistema de castas* (caste system)—to designate people who had been culturally Hispanicized, as opposed to indigenous people who maintained their culture in *repúblicas de indios* or mixed-race people in urban areas. This way, the speech is subtly framed, from then on, within the context of historical European colonialism in the Americas. The passage hints at the idea that contemporary Europeans still refuse to see Latin Americans as equals, as *gentes de razón*, simply because they do not think or act like them, because they are not Europeanized enough.

At the same time, despite the accusation of ethnocentrism, García Márquez may be falling, in this paragraph, into the Eurocentric colonial trap of seeing the Global South as a historical stage behind Europe, or perhaps of conceiving its peripheral histories as mere variations of a purported master narrative of Europe's history or of European modernity. In this sense, in his *Provincializing Europe: Postcolonial Thought and Historical Difference* (2000), Indian historian and theorist of postcolonial and subaltern studies Dipesh Chakrabarty denounces this type of stagist and historicist contrast between the modern and the nonmodern by which European colonizers propose their "'waiting-room' version of history" to justify their "denial of 'self-government' to the colonized" (9). It was by convincing the colonized that they were "not yet" civilized enough to rule themselves, claims Chakrabarty, that European colonizers kept them waiting in an imagined waiting room of history.

In fact, García Márquez denies again coevalness to Latin America and the Caribbean in other speeches such as "Palabras para un nuevo milenio" ("Words for a New Millennium") delivered at the headquarters of the Casa de las Américas—the most prestigious cultural institution in Cuba, which was founded by the government in 1959 with the goal of extending sociocultural relations with the rest of the Caribbean, Latin America, and the world—in Havana, Cuba, on November 29, 1985, during the Second Meeting of Intellectuals for the Sovereignty of the Peoples of Our America, in front of three hundred Latin American intellectuals, including Frei Betto, Ernesto Cardenal, Juan Bosch, Daniel Viglietti, and Osvaldo Soriano:

> Any decision in the medium term made in these twilight times is a decision for the twenty-first century. And yet, we Latin Americans and people from the Caribbean approach it with the devastating sense that we've skipped the twentieth century: we've passed through it without having lived it. Half of the world will celebrate the dawn of the year 2001 as the culmination of a millennium, while we're beginning to catch glimpses of the benefits of the Industrial Revolution. (33–34)[7]

Within the context of the Cuban Revolution, the participants at the meeting were demanding their right to decide their own nations' political destinies without the intervention of the Global North and, more specifically, of the United States.

García Márquez, toward the end of the speech, emphasizes an early culture of resistance in the region, which has been preserved in "the dangerous memory of our peoples" (35).[8] He argues that one can find signs of resistance to colonization in Latin America's rich cultural patrimony: in its language, cuisine, fashion, nostalgic music, and mulatta Madonnas, which the Colombian master sees as "true miracles of the people against the *colonizing* clerical power" (35; emphasis added).[9] One can also find indigenous protest tactics in defense of their identity and sovereignty in, for instance, artisanal angels in Catholic churches. Insurgence and transgression, García Márquez continues, are further reflected in Latin American and Caribbean cultures of the fiesta, which break with reality in order to reconcile reason and imagination. In what the aforementioned later generations of Latin American writers would perhaps consider an example of tropicalism, García Márquez claims that "[t]his is the strength of our backwardness" (36),[10] thus proudly owning what in other contexts could be perceived as a source of shame. These early strategies of defiance, proclaims the speaker, "cannot be domesticated by imperial voracity" (36).[11]

The text closes with what I interpret as yet another denunciation of a centuries-old coloniality: "It would be, in brief, a decisive contribution to the political determination, which cannot be deferred, to leap over five alien centuries and enter, with a firm step and a thousand-year horizon, the imminent millennium" (37).[12] It is nothing other than an unnamed coloniality of power that—in García Márquez's poetical words of longing for a sovereign region without foreign interference or internal oppressors—has kept Latin Americans alienated. Glimpsing "new forms of practical organization" (37)[13] by channeling the uncontainable imagination of Latin Americans and the fruitful solidarity of the region's intellectuals will, according to the author, one day eradicate these dark forces of alienation and coloniality.

The Nobel laureate insists, in "La soledad de América Latina," that Europe needs to revise the way it looks at Latin America, learning to respect its right to independence, originality (several speeches celebrate Latin Americans' amazing imagination), and the pursuit of its own dreams: "Why is the originality granted to us without reservation in literature denied us with every kind of suspicion when we make our extremely difficult attempts at social change? Why think that social justice, which advanced Europeans strive to establish in their own countries, cannot also be a Latin American objective using distinct methods under different conditions"[14] (23). Presumably, when making these remarks García Márquez had in mind historical cases such as the CIA-backed coup d'état against Salvador Allende in Chile nine years earlier and the ongoing US blockade against Cuba (he always supported the Cuban Revolution and was a personal friend of Fidel Castro).[15] But his overall message continues to refute supposedly universalist (read European and US) solutions for particular Latin American problems and conditions. Inspired by his leftist political leanings, therefore, he argues that Latin America should be allowed to seek social justice on its own terms, independently from the two superpowers of the time, the United States and the USSR.

In reality, halfway through his Nobel Prize speech, the topic of literature, for which he is receiving the prestigious award, becomes secondary to that which concerns him much more deeply: Latin America's sociopolitical and economic ills, its right to choose its own destiny, and the persistence of coloniality in the region. In fact, it would not be too far-fetched to conclude that perhaps even García Márquez's decision to break with tradition and deliver his Nobel speech dressed in a *liquiliqui* (a typical outfit—a pair of traditionally white, beige, cream, or ecru full-length linen or cotton trousers and a jacket—from the Llanos, a geographical region between Colombia and Venezuela, which is mostly worn at social events, fiestas, and the joropo dance) instead of the formal white tie and tails was yet another way to claim Latin America's right to break away from coloniality and to do things its own way.

Along these lines, in his speech "Latin America Exists," which was supposed to address mainly peace, democracy, and drug trafficking in the region, at a meeting of Latin American politicians on the island of Contadora, Panama, on March 28, 1995, García Márquez continues to unmask, from a decolonial perspective, European ethnocentrism. Thus, in a reaction to Italian, pro-Mussolini writer Giovanni Papini's (1881–1956) affirmation, during the 1940s, that Latin America had contributed nothing to humanity, not even a saint, García Márquez remarks, after clarifying that there was indeed one saint (Saint Rosa of Lima):

> His statement illustrated very well the idea that Europeans have always had of us: everything that doesn't resemble them they think is an error, and they do everything they can to correct it in their own way, like the United States. Simón Bolívar,

exasperated over so much advice and so many prescriptions, said: "Let us have our Middle Ages in peace." (88)[16]

Once again, immediately after demanding, as in the previously discussed speech, Latin America's right to political independence, freedom, and originality, García Márquez concedes the view of Latin America as a sort of earlier historical stage of Europe or as a sui generis, anachronistic version of the European master narrative of human history.

In any case, he reminds us that from the very inception of the independence process, Simoón Bolívar was constantly pressured by Europeans to choose one of the main European governing models and dogmas of the time: either a monarchical or a republican system; they would not allow him, García Márquez laments, to choose his own path for Latin America. Interestingly, in this speech delivered in Panama, the Colombian-Caribbean speaker seems not to have given up on Bolívar's dream of Latin American political and economic integration. In fact, he believes that the first major needed step, cultural integration, is already being achieved by the region's writers and artists:

> When political and economic integration are achieved, and they will be, cultural integration will be a long-standing, irreversible fact. Even in the United States, where enormous fortunes are spent on cultural penetration, while we, without spending a cent, are changing their language, their food, their music, their education, their styles of living and loving. That is, the most important thing in life: their culture. (90–91)[17]

Therefore, regional integration and unity (including Brazil in this text) are destined to contain US cultural imperialism—as well as other forms of imperialism—in Latin America. The tone of the speech then switches to a sort of cultural triumphalism that is reminiscent of the Uruguayan José Enrique Rodó's emphasis on Latin American regional and cultural identity as well as of his denunciation of US utilitarianism and positivism in his iconic essay *Ariel* (1900). A century after Rodó's secular sermon to Latin American youth, a purportedly materialistic and pragmatic United States is now being conquered by a Latin America that is supposed to be more idealistic, spiritual, and inclined toward the arts and beauty.[18] Meanwhile, García Márquez concludes, the region continues with its eternal search for identity and an ethics of life.

A third speech, "Ilusiones para el Siglo XXI" ("Dreams for the Twenty-First Century"), delivered in Paris on March 8, 1999, within the context of the seminar "Latin America and the Caribbean Facing the New Millennium," organized by the Inter-American Bank for Development and UNESCO, insists again on the need for Latin America to free itself from European cultural colonialism. As in the previously discussed speech, García Márquez quotes both Bolívar's plea to let Latin America have its Middle Ages in peace and Giovanni Papini's disdainful descriptions of Latin America: "Papini infuriated our grandparents in the 1940s with a venomous sentence: 'America is made with the waste of Europe.' Today we not only have reasons to suspect that it is true, but also something even sadder: that the fault is ours" (122).[19] The Colombian master then proceeds to sadly describe Latin America as a laboratory of failed dreams where foreign doctrines are constantly reheated and where other people's wars are fought. The solution? Young Latin Americans must imagine and build their own twenty-first century according to their own circumstances, instead of following foreign, universalist dogmas: "A century that doesn't come factory-made but ready to be forged by you in our image and likeness, and that will only be as peaceful and as much as our own as you are capable of owning it" (124).[20] As is well noted, he never loses his optimism and hopes for a more prosperous and autonomous future.

At this point, it is important to call attention to the fact that, parallel to these nonfictional proclamations, García Márquez has defended, through his fiction and magical realist mode, the value and importance of non-Western knowledges and ways of being in the world. Several critics have considered his magical realist writing (and magical realism in general), with its incorporation of subaltern indigenous and Afro-descended, ethnicized knowledges, a type of literary response to hegemonic Western modernity and rationalism. Thus, Maggie Bowers sees magical realism as "a way to discuss alternative approaches to reality to that of Western philosophy, expressed in many postcolonial and non-Western works of contemporary fiction" (1). In her view, magical realism has provided agency to non-Western writers to question Eurocentrism. Similarly, Lois Parkinson Zamora and Wendy B. Faris underscore the counterhegemonic potential of the magical realist mode: "Magical realist texts are subversive: their in-betweenness, their all-at-onceness encourages resistance to monologic political and cultural structures, a feature that has made the mode particularly useful to writers in postcolonial cultures and, increasingly, to women" (6). While it is unclear whether García Márquez himself envisioned magical realism as a liberating tool for Latin American ethnicized groups in postcolonial contexts trying to defend their right to heterogeneity, it is at minimum a faithful literary reflection of the demands he has made in his public addresses.

In addition to the subversive potential of García Márquez's version of the magical realist mode, the very topics of his fiction reflect his commitment to sociopolitical issues in the region. Thus, as Gene Bell-Villada points out:

> Many of his novels and stories deal with themes of social conflict and political power. Thus, *One Hundred Years of Solitude* in its central episodes depicts a civil war, an exploitative agribusiness firm, a workers' strike, and a military massacre. *The Autumn of the Patriarch* anatomizes two, or perhaps five, centuries of Latin American dictatorship, going back to Columbus, while *Crónica de una muerte anunciada* (1981, *Chronicle of a Death Foretold*) shows readers the ages-old, Iberian family honor- and-virginity code as the destructive force it can be–and not just for women. *El general en su laberinto* (1989, *The General in His Labyrinth*), in turn, paints an up-close, highly realistic portrait of Bolívar, the continent's most mythologized and sanctified political-military leader. And the otherwise beautiful *Del amor y otros demonios* (1994, *Of Love and Other Demons*) also evokes the ravages of Afro-Hispanic slavery and of the colonial Spanish Inquisition. (319)

And on several occasions, García Márquez's activism and advocacy went beyond his writing profession, reacting directly to political events. Thus, in September 1973, he fired off a telegram to the new military junta in Chile, dubbing them "a gang of criminals in the pay of North American imperialism." In addition, with this latest "big" novel now completed, in 1975 he started to serve, as elected vice-president, on the Second Bertrand Russell Tribunal that investigated war crimes, an association he maintained until 1980. (Bell-Villada 315)

As with his public speeches, García Márquez's newspaper articles reveal not just the process of formation of his peculiar rhetorical style—full of hyperbole, humor, and irony—but also his true perception of the harrowing reality of Latin America and the Caribbean. As Bell-Villada accurately indicates, "In the case of García Márquez, doing journalism was an essential complement to his literary labors, a part of his personal vocation to tell as well as poeticize the truth–and of his lifelong role as public intellectual" (316–17). Unfortunately, English-language readers will not have access to the full spectrum of García Márquez's political commitment in his journalistic writing, since, as Tony Wood complains, the English-language article collection *The Scandal of the Century* only includes three articles from the 1970s, a period of intense political activity for the author: two pieces from 1977 and 1978 on the early days of revolutionary Cuba and the effects of the US blockade, and a third one, also from 1979, on the Sandinista takeover of the National Palace in Managua. Instead, one-third of the volume is dedicated to lighthearted, less politically engaged articles published during the 1980s in the prestigious Spanish daily *El País*. According to Wood, this type of selection may offer a misguided image of his journalistic opus: "The effect is a dramatic scaling back of our sense of García Márquez's political commitments—their intensity and urgency as well as their geographical breadth and their significance in his political and intellectual development" (n.p.).

Some of these pieces from the 1980s are, in fact, reminiscent of his magical-realist fiction. For instance, in "Una equivocación explicable" ("An Understandable Mistake") an inebriated man jumps out of a hotel window in Cali, Colombia, after seeing tiny silvery fish fall from the sky. Furthermore, in some of these articles, such as "Fantasmas de carreteras" ("Ghosts of the Road"), the action takes place in Europe, thus bringing García Márquez's magical realism outside its "natural" Caribbean context. Notwithstanding these examples of magical-realist writing in his nonfiction, most of his newspaper articles reflect not an exoticized, tropicalized, or essentialized vision of Latin American societies, but rather a heartbreaking reality of injustice, suffering, and inequality. Still, the journalist defends the existence—and the right to exist, in the face of hegemonic, rationalistic, Western impositions—of a not fully Western realm (because of indigenous and African influences) to which he belongs.

It is apparent that García Márquez enjoys introducing his readers to the alternative, sometimes subalternized reality that became a source of inspiration for his fiction. One of the articles in which the journalist proudly identifies with a non-Western worldview is "Algo más sobre literatura y realidad" ("Something Else on Literature and Reality"), published in *El País* on July 1, 1981. In it, he categorizes what he considers a "very homogeneous cultural area,"[21] namely, the Caribbean, which extends, culturally, from the southern United States to Brazil. The author twice highlights the magical nature of this syncretic reality, which is also marked by its boundless freedom and its artistic proliferation:

> In the Caribbean, the original elements of the primal beliefs and magical conceptions previous to the discovery are joined by the profuse variety of cultures that came together in the years following it in a magic syncretism the artistic interest and actual artistic fecundity of which are inexhaustible. The African contribution was forced and infuriating, but fortunate. In that crossroads of the world, a sense of endless liberty was forged, a reality with neither God nor laws, where each person felt it was possible to do what they wanted without limits of any kind. (233)[22]

This fruitful ethnocultural and religious syncretism have therefore produced a type of godless freedom and lawlessness that is an essential component of the region's endless creativity and originality.

To add verisimilitude to the passage, the journalist reminds us that he was born and raised in this Caribbean basin and that he knows each of its countries and islands. The Caribbean is so beyond measure, he adds, that it is hard to find the appropriate words to describe it. Hence, if we take these claims at face value, his writing is not as hyperbolic as it may at first seem. For this reason, the Colombian master rhetorically admits, he has never been able to write anything more astonishing than what was already present in the region's everyday reality. His only merit, he modestly avers, has been to adorn it with poetic overtones: "But there is not a single line in any of my books that does not have its origin in a real event" (233).[23] García Márquez closes the article by warning his fellow writers that Latin American reality, and especially Caribbean reality, is a much better writer than they, the writers, are; the only thing they can aspire to do is to humbly imitate it as much as they can.

Curiously, while in his speeches García Márquez blames Europe for misunderstanding Latin America and for trying to impose its Eurocentric worldviews, he admits that, like his admired friend Julio Cortázar, it was in Paris where he was finally able to attain a wide-ranging image of Latin America and the Caribbean and thus achieve a fuller understanding of their respective realities. Thus, in "Desde París, con amor" ("From Paris, with Love"), published in *El País* on December 29, 1982, he recalls:

> When I arrived in Paris, I was nothing but a raw Caribbean. I am most grateful to that city, with which I have many old grudges, and many even older loves, for having given me a new and resolute perspective on Latin America. The vision of the whole, which we didn't have in any of our countries, became very clear here around a safe table, and one ended up realizing that, in spite of being from different countries, we were all crew members of the same boat. (281)[24]

This paragraph brings to mind the famous polemical debates between Peruvian writer José María Arguedas and the Argentine Julio Cortázar from 1967 through 1969. In 1967, invited to contribute to the Cuban magazine *Casa de las Américas*, Cortázar, in an open letter to Roberto Fernández Retamar, criticizes what has been known as *telurismo* in literature—which focused on the influence the geographical area people inhabit has on their lives—as narrow, parochial, and provincial. The Argentine author rejected what he perceived as an exalted localism or regionalism that praised only local values and thus inevitably would lead to the negativity of nationalism; he proposed in its stead a totalizing vision of culture and history facilitated by his long experience of living abroad. Arguedas, as is well known, drastically rejected, in an article published by the Peruvian magazine *Amaru,* this supranational or cosmopolitan preference, defending instead his regional, *indigenista,* and transcultural approach to literature, with his affinity for local, indigenous knowledges that have been oppressed, first, by European colonialism and, to this day, by an internal version thereof. Though the Peruvian novelist and fellow Latin American Boom writer Mario Vargas Llosa supported Cortázar's perspective, to my knowledge García Márquez never publicly intervened in the debate. Still, the aforementioned quotation seems to indicate that he too would have sided with Cortázar.

Be that as it may, whether from a cosmopolitan and urban abroad or from the narrower viewpoint of one's own native homeland, it is clear that García Márquez validates any tactic that is able to contest coloniality, proposing—in his nonfiction speeches and newspaper articles as well as in his magical-realist fiction—an alternative, non-Eurocentric, nonrationalistic way of conceiving of Latin American reality. Only this locally grown (even if it is with the help of a wider perspective from Paris) decolonial approach will finally cure that recurrent solitude that was to become the axis mundi in much of his discourse.

In conclusion, García Márquez's public speeches and newspaper articles help us dispel some critics' suspicion that the Nobel laureate attempted to sell a facile, commodified, and shallow tropicalized image of Latin America and the Caribbean in order to meet the expectations of a Global North readership. The decolonial approach to Latin American reality in his nonfiction writing suggests, instead, that it would be more appropriate to conceive of his novels and short stories as a fictionalized version of Colombian, Caribbean, and Latin American history, devoid of pamphletary political didacticism and often enriched by his beautifully suggestive lyricism, understanding of myth (see Mercedes López-Baralt's essay in this volume), and not fully Western worldviews. Rather than an exoticizing demagogue, therefore, he was—as demonstrated by his sociopolitical commentary delivered as a public intellectual—an anti-imperialist visionary and an advocate for a liberated and independent Latin America in which nations may, once and for all, decide their own destinies without the hindrance of foreign political intervention or pressure.

Notes

1. For a deeper discussion of the reception of Magical Realism in Latin America, see López-Calvo, "A Postmodern plátano's Trujillo" and the introduction to López-Calvo, *Critical Insights.*

2. García Márquez risked his own life with these initiatives. As Bell-Villada explains, in 1975 a bomb exploded at the headquarters of *Alternativa* (316).
3. "Pero todavía quedan almas pueriles que miran hacia los Estados Unidos como un norte de salvación, con la certidumbre de que en nuestro país se han agotado hasta los suspiros para morir en paz. Sin embargo, lo que encuentran allá es un imperio ciego que ya no considera a Colombia como un buen vecino, ni siquiera como un cómplice barato y confiable, sino como un espacio más para su voracidad imperial" (127–28).
4. "Todas las criaturas de aquella realidad desaforada hemos tenido que pedirle muy poco a la imaginación, porque el desafío mayor para nosotros ha sido la insuficiencia de los recursos convencionales para hacer creíble nuestra vida. Este es, amigos, el nudo de nuestra soledad" (168)
5. Later, in his speech "A Toast to Poetry," delivered in Stockholm on December 10, 1982, during the royal banquet offered by the king and queen of Sweden in honor of those who have received Nobel Prizes, García Márquez presumes that it is the poetry in his fiction that must have attracted the attention of the Swedish Academy of Letters.
6. "No es difícil entender que los talentos racionales de este lado del mundo, extasiados en la contemplación de sus propias culturas, se hayan quedado sin un método válido para interpretarnos. Es comprensible que insistan en medirnos con la misma vara con que se miden a sí mismos, sin recordar que los estragos de la vida no son iguales para todos, y que la búsqueda de la identidad propia es tan ardua y sangrienta para nosotros como lo fue para ellos. La interpretación de nuestra realidad con esquemas ajenos sólo contribuye a hacernos cada vez más desconocidos, cada vez menos libres, cada vez más solitarios. Tal vez la Europa venerable sería más comprensiva si tratara de vernos en su propio pasado" (25–26).
7. "Que cualquier decisión a mediano plazo que se tome en estos tiempos de postrimerías es ya una decisión para el siglo XXI. Sin embargo, latinoamericanos y caribes nos acercamos a él con la sensación desoladora de habernos saltado el siglo XX: lo hemos padecido sin vivirlo. Medio mundo celebrará el amanecer del año 2001 como una culminación milenaria, mientras nosotros empezamos apenas a vislumbrar los beneficios de la revolución industrial" (39). In his 1993 speech "In Honor of Belisario Betancur on the Occasion of His Seventieth Birthday," he again argues that "Colombia entered the twentieth century almost half a century late because of poetry" (63).
8. "La peligrosa memoria de nuestros pueblos" (40).
9. "Verdaderos milagros del pueblo en contra del poder clerical colonizador" (40).
10. "Ésta es la fuerza de nuestro retraso" (41).
11. "Que no podrá ser domesticada ni por la voracidad imperial" (41).
12. "Sería, en fin, un aporte decisivo a la inaplazable determinación política de saltar por encima de cinco siglos ajenos y de entrar pisando firme, con un horizonte milenario, en el milenio inminente" (42).
13. "Nuevas formas de organización práctica" (41–42).
14. "¿Por qué la originalidad que se nos admite sin reservas en la literatura se nos niega con toda clase de suspicacias en nuestras tentativas tan difíciles de cambio social? ¿Por qué pensar que la justicia social que los europeos de avanzada tratan de imponer en sus países no puede ser también un objetivo latinoamericano con métodos distintos en condiciones diferentes?" (27).
15. The US blockade against Cuba is addressed in his newspaper article "Los cubanos frente al bloqueo" (Cubans and the Blockade).

16. "Su afirmación ilustraba muy bien la idea que siempre han tenido de nosotros los europeos: todo lo que no se parece a ellos les parece un error y hacen todo por corregirlo a su manera, como los Estados Unidos. Simón Bolívar, desesperado con tantos consejos e imposiciones, dijo: 'Déjennos hacer tranquilos nuestra Edad Media'" (93).
17. "Cuando la integración política y económica se cumplan, y así será, la integración cultural será un hecho irreversible desde tiempo atrás. Inclusive en los Estados Unidos, que se gastan enormes fortunas en penetración cultural, mientras que nosotros, sin gastar un centavo, les estamos cambiando el idioma, la comida, la música, la educación, las formas de vivir, el amor. Es decir, lo más importante de la vida: la cultura" (94–95).
18. By contrast, in a different speech, "Words for a New Millennium," García Márquez bemoans the fact that in the last one hundred years Latin Americans "have lost the best human virtues of the nineteenth century: fervent idealism and the primacy of feeling: the shock of love" (34).
19. "El escritor italiano Giovanni Papini enfureció a nuestros abuelos en los años cuarenta con una frase envenenada: 'América está hecha con los desperdicios de Europa'. Hoy no sólo tenemos razones para sospechar que es cierto, sino algo más triste: que la culpa es nuestra" (123).
20. "Un siglo que no viene hecho de fábrica sino listo para ser forjado por ustedes a nuestra imagen y semejanza, y que sólo será tan glorioso y nuestro como ustedes sean capaces de imaginarlo" (124).
21. "Un área cultural muy homogénea" (282).
22. "En el Caribe, a los elementos originales de las creencias primarias y concepciones mágicas anteriores al descubrimiento, se sumó la profunda variedad de culturas que confluyeron en los años siguientes en un sincretismo mágico cuyo interés artístico y cuya propia fecundidad artística son inagotables. La contribución africana fue forzosa e indignante, pero afortunada. En esa encrucijada del mundo, se forjó un sentido de libertad sin término, una realidad sin Dios ni ley, donde cada quien sintió que le era posible hacer lo que quería sin límites de ninguna clase" (282).
23. "Pero no hay una sola línea en ninguno de mis libros que no tenga su origen en un hecho real" (282).
24. "Cuando llegué a París, yo no era más que un Caribe crudo. Lo que más le agradezco a esta ciudad, con la cual tengo tantos pleitos viejos, y tantos amores todavía más viejos, es que me hubiera dado una perspectiva nueva y resuelta de Latinoamérica. La visión de conjunto que no teníamos en ninguno de nuestros países, se volvía muy clara aquí en torno a una mesa de café, y uno terminaba por darse cuenta de que, a pesar de ser de distintos países, todos éramos tripulantes de un mismo barco" (330).

Works Cited

Bell-Villada, Gene H. "García Márquez as Public Intellectual." *A History of Colombian Literature*, edited by Raymond Williams. Cambridge UP, 2016, pp. 311–21, doi:10.1017/CBO9781139963060.017.

Bowers, Maggie Ann. *Magic(al) Realism*. Routledge, 2004.

Chakrabarty, Dipesh. *Provincializing Europe: Postcolonial Thought and Historical Difference*. Princeton UP, 2000.

Dussel, Enrique. *Postmodernidad, transmodernidad*. Universidad Iberoamericana, 1999.

Fuguet, Alberto. "I Am Not a Magic Realist!" *Salon.com*, 11 June 1997, https://www.salon.com/1997/06/11/magicalintro/. Accessed 4 April 2021.

García Márquez, Gabriel. "Algo más sobre literatura y realidad." *El escándalo del siglo*, pp. 280–84.

García Márquez, Gabriel. "América Latina Existe." *Yo no vengo a decir un discurso*, Vintage Español, 2010, pp. 91–98.

García Márquez, Gabriel. *El amor en los tiempos del cólera*. Penguin Random House, 1985.

García Márquez, Gabriel. *La aventura de Miguel Littín clandestino en Chile*. Plaza & Janés, 1993.

García Márquez, Gabriel. "Los cubanos frente al bloqueo". *Bohemia. Revista Cubana de Actualidad General*. 18 Oct. 2016. http://bohemia.cu/nacionales/2016/10/gabriel-garcia-marquez-los-cubanos-frente-al-bloqueo/ Accessed 4 April 2021.

García Márquez, Gabriel. *Del amor y otros demonios*. Diana, 1994.

García Márquez, Gabriel. "Desde París, con amor." *El escándalo del siglo*, pp. 328–31.

García Márquez, Gabriel. "Dreams for the Twenty-First Century." *I'm Not Here to Give a Speech*, pp. 122–24.

García Márquez, Gabriel. *El escándalo del siglo: Textos en prensa y revistas*. Prologue by Jon Lee Anderson, edited by Cristóbal Pera. Vintage Español, 2018.

García Márquez, Gabriel. "Fantasmas de carreteras." Opinión. *El País*. 18 Aug. 1981. https://elpais.com/diario/1981/08/19/opinion/367020007_850215.html Accessed 4 April 2021.

García Márquez, Gabriel. "From Paris, with Love." *Scandal of the Century and Other Writings*, pp. 279–82.

García Márquez, Gabriel. "Ghosts of the Road." *Scandal of the Century and Other Writings*, pp. 242–45.

García Márquez, Gabriel. "Ilusiones para el Siglo XXI." *Yo no vengo a decir un discurso*, pp. 123–24.

García Márquez, Gabriel. *I'm Not Here to Give a Speech*. Translated by Edith Grossman, Vintage International, 2014.

García Márquez, Gabriel. "In Honor of Belisario Betancur on the Occasion of His Seventieth Birthday." *I'm Not Here to Give a Speech*, pp. 61–66.

García Márquez, Gabriel. "Latin America Exists." *I'm Not Here to Give a Speech*, pp. 96–95.

García Márquez, Gabriel. "Palabras para un nuevo milenio." *Yo no vengo a decir un discurso*, pp. 35–42.

García Márquez, Gabriel. "La patria amada aunque distante." *Yo no vengo a decir un discurso*, pp. 125–30.

García Márquez, Gabriel. *The Scandal of the Century and Other Writings*. Edited by Cristóbal Pera, foreword by Jon Lee Anderson, translated by Anne McLean, Alfred A. Knopf, 2019.

García Márquez, Gabriel. "'La soledad de América Latina,' Discurso de aceptación de Gabriel García Márquez del Premio Nobel 1982". Libro y Lectura, Nacional. Ministerio de la Cultura, las Artes y el Patrimonio. Gobierno de Chile. 20 April. 2014. https://www.cultura.gob.cl/agendacultural/la-soledad-de-america-latina-gabriel-garcia-marquez/ Accessed 4 April 2021.

García Márquez, Gabriel. "The Solitude of Latin America." *I'm Not Here to Give a Speech*, pp. 16–24.

García Márquez, Gabriel. "Something Else on Literature and Reality." *Scandal of the Century and Other Writings*, pp. 231–35.

García Márquez, Gabriel. "A Toast to Poetry." *I'm Not Here to Give a Speech*, pp. 26–28.

García Márquez, Gabriel. "An Understandable Mistake." *Scandal of the Century and Other Writings*, pp. 8–10.

García Márquez, Gabriel. "Una equivocación explicable." *Obra periodística 1. Textos costeños*. Sudamericana, 1993. 201-03.

García Márquez, Gabriel. "Words for a New Millennium." *I'm Not Here to Give a Speech*, pp. 29-37.

García Márquez, Gabriel. *Yo no vengo a decir un discurso*. Vintage Español, 2010.

López-Calvo, Ignacio, editor. *Critical Insights: Magical Realism*. Salem Press, 2014.

López-Calvo, Ignacio. "A Postmodern plátano's Trujillo: Junot Díaz's *The Brief Wondrous Life of Oscar Wao*, More Macondo Than McOndo." *Antípodas*, vol. 20, 2009, pp. 75-90.

Mignolo, Walter. *The Darker Side of Western Modernity. Global Futures, Decolonial Options*. Duke UP, 2011.

Parkinson Zamora, Lois, and Wendy B. Faris, editors. *Magical Realism: Theory, History, Community*. Duke UP, 1995.

Quijano, Aníbal. "Colonialidad del poder, eurocentrismo y América Latina." *Cuestiones y horizontes: de la dependencia histórico-estructural a la colonialidad/descolonialidad del poder*. CLACSO, 2014.

Rodó, José Enrique. *Ariel*. Biblioteca Virtual Universal, 2013. https://biblioteca.org.ar/libros/70738.pdf Accessed 4 April 2021.

White, Edmund. "Requiem for the Living." *The New York Times*, 1 Aug. 2013, www.nytimes.com/2013/08/04/books/review/the-sound-of-things-falling-by-juan-gabriel-vasquez.html. Accessed 30 Dec. 2019.

Wood, Tony. "Reality Is the Better Writer: The Nonfiction of Gabriel García Márquez." *The Nation*, 13 Jan. 2020, www.thenation.com/article/archive/gabriel-garcia-marquez-journalism-and-politics-book-review/. Accessed 23 Jan. 2020.

PART V
KEY WORKS

CHAPTER 24

WRITING AND POLITICS IN GARCÍA MÁRQUEZ'S EARLY WORKS

MARÍA HELENA RUEDA

Before *Cien años de soledad* (*One Hundred Years of Solitude*, 1967), the book that propelled him to world fame, Gabriel García Márquez had published numerous journalistic pieces, a few short stories, and three short novels—*La hojarasca* (*Leaf Storm*, 1955), *El coronel no tiene quien le escriba* (*No One Writes to the Colonel*, 1961), and *La mala hora* (*In Evil Hour*, 1962).[1] Written at a pivotal time for the author and his country of birth, these early works have been studied primarily as heralds of his best-known novels, which came later. Praised by critics and devoured by readers at the time, however, these early texts established the author's reputation in Latin America, years before he gained worldwide recognition. As such, they merit an interpretation that goes beyond their status as precursors. They belong to a period when García Márquez was actively involved in politics and saw his writing as participating in a process of social change. This chapter focuses on the trio of short novels he published during these years, examining how they were shaped by their context of writing and by the author's views on the social impact of his craft.

Leaf Storm, *No One Writes to the Colonel*, and *In Evil Hour* offer a realist approach to the mechanisms and effects of the practice of violence, at a time when Colombia was experiencing the aftermath of a deadly armed conflict. Focused on the everyday lives of people in the country's coastal towns, these novels portray men and women struggling with complex emotions in a provincial landscape marked by oppressive social norms, political rivalries, economic exploitation, governmental abuse, and a general sense of unfairness that elicits resentment and various forms of resistance. Although these works include almost no descriptions of violent acts, their characters remember instances of past violence that have shaped their present lives. The memory of those killed for political or economic reasons persists among the living, threatening the order established by such violence, an order that benefits the rich and powerful.

From a technical standpoint, these novels constitute early examples of the author's fruitful experimentation with narrative time—a feature that would earn him much praise in *One Hundred Years of Solitude*. The three novels recount events situated in the past from the perspective of a present that foresees the time to come. This technique is particularly visible in the first book, *Leaf Storm*, but also noticeable in the two others, which are more linear. Rather than just a technical resource, in these works such experimentation allows for a reflection on how the past shapes the present and projects it into the future. More specifically, the author here uses these narrative strategies to articulate how dramatic events of the past, such as the rise of the banana plantation economy and the fighting of multiple civil wars, shape the present and future lives of the inhabitants of his native land.

These works also interrogate how literature can intervene in such a context. Such intervention consists mainly of exploring how writing can articulate the damage caused by violence and the factors that propel its practice. Violence is understood in these works as a phenomenon with deep roots, tied to massive economic forces that benefit only a few, leaving all others in a state of powerlessness and abandonment. There are barely any depictions of violent events in these novels; for García Márquez, the description of cruel and deadly events was not an adequate way to write about violence and its effects on the population. In these works, violence is a behavior that leaves people at the mercy of powerful economic and political interests. The author at this stage was far more interested in how writing could denounce and resist those forces than he would be at any other point in his literary career. This interest was directly linked to events in his local context at the time.

Writing in a Landscape of Conflict

García Márquez started his literary career during an intensely politicized and violent time in Colombia. Growing up in the small town of Aracataca, on the Caribbean coast, he knew of the radical transformation brought to the region by the United Fruit Company. He became particularly interested in the massacre of striking banana workers that was perpetrated by the Colombian army in 1928. A popular leftist leader named Jorge Eliécer Gaitán, who had denounced the massacre, was assassinated in Bogotá in 1948, while García Márquez was a law student in the city. This was one of the most decisive events in Colombian politics of the twentieth century, giving way to deadly riots in the urban center and then to La Violencia: a brutal confrontation between members of the Liberal and Conservative Parties that ravaged the country for almost a decade. At the time, García Márquez had started publishing short stories in local newspapers and would soon abandon his law studies to become a full-time journalist for *El Espectador*, a major Colombian newspaper. His articles in that venue became popular with readers, and his short stories gained him critical acclaim.

In 1955, García Márquez published *Leaf Storm*, a book that cemented his literary standing in Colombia. That same year *El Espectador* sent him to Paris as its European correspondent. The assignment would not last for long. In 1956, the dictator Gustavo Rojas Pinilla shut down the newspaper for political reasons, and García Marquez was left without a job or income. Penniless and writing his novels, he stayed in Europe until 1958, when he moved to Venezuela to work for the magazine *Momento*. After the triumph of the Cuban Revolution he went to Havana, where he became a reporter for the government news agency Prensa Latina. He worked with the agency for two years, opening offices in New York and in Bogotá, before moving to Mexico City with his family in 1961.

During these years, while the Cuban Revolution was shaping the political life of the continent, Colombia experienced the aftermath of La Violencia. In 1957 an agreement between the two parties, called the Frente Nacional (National Front), put a partial end to the atrocities, but the social ills behind them were far from resolved. Like elsewhere on the continent, the idea of socialism as a viable alternative to structural inequalities was strengthened in Colombia by the success of the Cuban Revolution, leading in the mid-1960s to the formation of leftist guerrilla armies that would remain active for decades. A member of the Communist Party in his youth, García Márquez was part of a group of left-leaning intellectuals paying close attention to this unrest, discussing together how to write about it and what role literature could play in a process of social change. His participation in such discussions left an important mark on his early novels, particularly *In Evil Hour* and *No One Writes to the Colonel*.

Many scholars have studied how García Márquez's early writings were influenced by his reading of modernist European and North American novelists, William Faulkner in particular, but also Franz Kafka, Virginia Woolf, James Joyce, and Ernest Hemingway.[2] García Márquez himself frequently said in interviews that these authors were important to his formation as a writer.[3] The impact of contemporary local writers and intellectuals on his work has been less explored, in part because García Márquez tended to dismiss it or to talk about it mostly in negative terms. During his formative years in Colombia, however, he did read the series of novels known as Novelas de la Violencia. He also actively participated in debates on how literature could best articulate the wounds caused by the conflict, its origins, and its long-term effects on society. Therefore, while García Márquez was an avid reader of those world-renowned authors, and their mark is palpable in his early works, the political aspects of his early writings were more decisively impacted by his local historical context. Most significantly, this context influenced how his first novels explored the role of literature in a landscape of violence.

How to Write about Violence

While working at the office of Prensa Latina in Bogotá, García Márquez published two articles on Colombian literature that offer some clues to his thinking about the role of his own writing with regard to the situation of violence in his country. These articles are

"Dos o tres cosas sobre la novela de la violencia" (Two or Three Things about the Novels of La Violencia), published in October 1959, and "La literatura colombiana, un fraude a la nación" (Colombian Literature, a Fraud to the Nation), published shortly thereafter, in April 1960.[4] Written shortly before the publication of *In Evil Hour* and *No One Writes to the Colonel*, they most likely reflected the creative and intellectual process that had accompanied these novels. They also possibly made reference to what the author accomplished in *Leaf Storm*, which had become a popular book among readers in Colombia.

At the time, García Márquez was well known locally as a reporter and an author. He actively participated in local debates about writing and politics. During La Violencia, and for a few years after its nominal conclusion in 1957, most literary writing in Colombia had been highly politicized, with novels explicitly defending one of the two opposing parties and attacking the other. In the above-mentioned articles, García Márquez was critical of this tendency, revealing both his desire to intervene in the local context and his intention to transcend it with his writing.

When García Márquez attained world fame, he would often be asked for his thoughts on the role of a writer in a process of social change. During a period marked by the success of the Cuban Revolution, when authors were often questioned about the political impact of their writing, his answer was that "the main political duty of a writer is to write well."[5] This statement would become one of his most famous quotations and over time would receive many differing and opposing interpretations. It is sometimes cited as a sign of the author's lack of interest in politically engaged writing and sometimes as evidence of the opposite. His early reflections on how to write about violence in Colombia shed some light on his understanding of the subject.

His 1959 essay "Two or Three Things about the Novels of La Violencia" starts with a reference to political activists, particularly those on the left, who pressed writers to produce political literature. He described this pressure as deriving from a questionable presumption: "Literature, they assume without questions or admonitions, is a powerful weapon that must not remain neutral in political quarrels."[6] The choice of the word "weapon" could be interpreted as a concern over the idea that literature should be a participant in confrontation. His criticism is not directed at this postulate itself but at the fact that it is accepted as true, without questioning or reflecting on the precise way in which literature can impact society.

García Márquez's response in this article is twofold. On the one hand, he argues that with regard to writing, honesty to life experience should prevail over political commitment: "It may be more valuable to tell what one honestly feels capable of telling because one experienced it, than to tell . . . what our political position indicates that should be told."[7] On the other, he explains that experience by itself is not enough, questioning the quality of some novels on La Violencia. In his view, these authors "did not have the serenity or the patience, yet not even the cunning, to take the time they needed to learn how to write [those novels]."[8] He goes on to say that writers should first and foremost perfect the craft of writing, in order to produce novels with social significance. As he saw it, to have political impact, a writer should be an honest observer of social reality and take the time to learn how to convey that reality in writing.

The author also criticized the excess of macabre description in the novels of La Violencia, suggesting that with their disproportionate attention to brutality, writers had missed the real drama of violence: "The novel was not in the dead who had their guts taken out, but in the living who must have sweated ice in their hiding place, fearing that with every heartbeat they ran the risk of having their guts taken out."[9] The idea of paying attention to the drama of survival is perhaps the most important point of the article.[10] It reveals the author's emerging interest in violence not as a problem in and of itself, but as a practice that had a dramatic effect on the survivors who lived with its impact. He saw that violence allowed people in power to increase their wealth and influence while leaving others powerless, destitute, and unable to seek justice. In his view, an effective writer could have a political impact by exposing such abuses, against a push toward denial or oblivion—justified by the powerful as something that was necessary to leave behind the horrors. García Márquez's local context of writing would have made him particularly attentive to this situation.

In the years of the National Front, the government in Colombia had proclaimed an end to the confrontations. Leaders of the opposing parties decided to forego prosecution of those responsible for the wounds of La Violencia. García Márquez problematized both the idea of staying silent and the opposing tendency of hyper-representing the horrors. He argued instead for placing the focus on the effects and the motivations of the practice of violence, with literature working to denounce and resist the structures that allowed and promoted such violence. To achieve this goal, writers had to become masters of their craft. The author would further develop this idea in the second piece he published on the subject.

The article he published in April 1960 questioned the effectiveness of not only the writers of La Violencia, but also practically all Colombian writers. With the revealing title "Colombian Literature, a Fraud against the Nation," the piece describes the nation as a community of readers that has been "defrauded" by its literary authors. García Márquez begins the article with a reference to a recent Colombian book festival at which 300,000 copies of books by Colombian authors quickly sold out, taking that as proof of a significant interest in national literature among Colombian readers.[11] He points out that Colombian authors have not hitherto responded effectively to this audience because so far they "have lacked an authentic sense of the national."[12] He goes on to say that such a sense could be articulated in specific reference to violence.

In the same article, García Márquez links the possibility of meeting the needs of the national community of readers with the development of literary strategies deployed specifically to narrate the events of La Violencia. The author refers to this violence as "the first national drama we were aware of"[13] and says that the novels of La Violencia were "the only literary explosion of legitimate national character we have had in our history."[14] His assessment of these books is, however, as negative here as in the previous article. Here too he attributes the failure of these novels to the fact that previous Colombian authors had not mastered the craft of literary writing. García Márquez talks about the writing of novels as exacting physical work, something that requires commitment, training, and expertise: "Great writers have confessed that writing is a demanding task, that there is a carpentry of literature, and that it is necessary to face it with courage and even some muscular energy."[15] In his view, this task was implicitly political, as it could lead to a consequential collective awareness of the significance of a transformative national drama.

García Márquez wrote in the two articles with well-founded confidence in his ability to communicate effectively with his readers. Before publishing his best-known literary works, he was already practically a bestselling author in Colombia, where several journalistic pieces he published in El Espectador—including the famous "Story of a Shipwrecked Sailor"—considerably increased sales of the newspaper (Saldívar 316). In 1959, Leaf Storm was republished in a ten-thousand-copy second edition, which was considered an extraordinary feat at the time (Saldívar 319). This popularity reveals him to be an author who was attuned to the expectations of his local reading public. These readers would at the time have found themselves accustomed to hearing daunting stories about the confrontations of La Violencia. The need to reflect on those events and understand their implications, beyond the horrors of the atrocities, would be politically consequential.

García Márquez believed that a writer had to respond to the needs of the reader. This belief oriented an inquiry into the social effects of writing that would continue throughout his life, but which is particularly visible in *In Evil Hour* and *No One Writes to the Colonel*, the two novels in which he deals more clearly with the theme of La Violencia. The popularity achieved by the already published *Leaf Storm* provides some evidence for the effectiveness of his approach. In this early novel he experimented with narrative time as a way to talk about economic forces that violently altered a community and its landscape, affecting people's lives in the present and the future.

The Transformative Force of the Banana Plantation in *Leaf Storm*

His first published novel, *Leaf Storm*, is prefaced by a poetic two-page account of the radical transformations brought upon a town by the arrival and growth of the banana company, a phenomenon that receives the name of a leaf storm, giving the novel its title. In this short account, marked as written in Macondo in 1909, the storm is said to have "sowed over the town the rubble of many catastrophes that had come before it, scattering its mixed cargo of rubbish in the streets" (9). In the pages of the novel, we find the stagnation left behind by such a storm, with characters left in a permanent state of waiting for another storm to come, passively watching their unfulfilling lives unfold before their eyes, devoid of any feeling of solidarity toward others, and lacking a sense of agency over the situations they confront.

Published in 1955, before García Márquez went on his pivotal trip to Europe, it was written while Colombia was in the midst of La Violencia. During those years the country endured the brunt of repressive regimes and violent confrontations that sowed a generalized sense of powerlessness among the population. The author meanwhile worked as a reporter and had started to receive praise for his short stories. The Argentinian publishing house Losada rejected a first version of the novel in 1950, in a now infamous letter in which the editor advised the young author to take up a different profession (Saldívar 314). With the support of his friends from the legendary Barranquilla Group, García Márquez revised the manuscript, publishing it as a small edition in a local press in 1955.[16] It was praised by critics and would eventually be selected to be included in the first Colombian book festival, which led to the much larger edition published in 1959. The novel's numerous readers were apparently receptive to its experimental style, which was unusual in the local scene at the time.

There are three distinct narrative voices in the novel, each representing the past, the present, and the future of the town. The voice of a ten-year-old boy starts the narration, followed by those of his mother, Isabel, and his grandfather, a retired colonel who is a veteran of the last civil war.[17] They are gathered at the house of an old doctor who has hanged himself, and are preparing for his funeral. The grandfather is fulfilling via this funeral a promise he had made to the now-deceased doctor after the latter had healed him following a near-fatal injury. There is fear that the townspeople will attack the funeral procession, as they had vowed never to let anyone bury the doctor, because years ago he had refused to treat those wounded in a deadly assault by an unidentified armed group. The doctor's refusal to help on that occasion was in turn the result of his vow never to help the town residents, since they had stopped using his services after the banana company brought in its own doctors and lured all his patients to its offices.

Resentment over past wrongs and lack of compassion toward the suffering of others mark the lives of everyone in the town, leading to a generalized sense of isolation and abandonment. An eccentric character who only ate grass, did not believe in God, and had no problem performing an abortion on his lover, the doctor had lived a life of loneliness, buried in his house for years. The colonel and his wife, Isabel's stepmother, had received him when he first arrived in the town, and he had lived for years in their house, but left when it was discovered that he was sleeping with their indigenous servant, Meme. He moved in with her to a separate house, where they were chastised by the rest of the town for living together out of wedlock. Only they showed some defiance in a town where everyone seemed unable to break a series of unwritten rules that kept them all in check.

Most characters in the novel act as if they had no agency over their lives. Isabel goes to the funeral because her father tells her to attend, and the son because his mother asked him to accompany her. The colonel himself organizes the burial only out of a sense of obligation, linked to a tragic sense of fate by the inclusion of a quotation from Sophocles's *Antigone* as an epigraph to the work. Many of the important events in the novel seem to happen without the approval of its participants, who are left only with resentment or desolation as they carry on with their lives. The best example is perhaps Isabel's wedding to Martín, a newcomer who ends up abandoning her and their first child, after arranging the wedding with her father without consulting her and later stealing their money.

Isabel goes through the motions as if participating in someone else's wedding. When Martín leaves, nobody offers support or even acknowledges the abandonment. While recalling the events in her monologue, she participates in the collective denial of their significance, recalling Martín as an "unreal" (98) fiancé and husband.[18]

An inability to assume agency over events of the past or to break free from the entrapment created by those events leaves characters stuck in a suspended present, where they feel powerless over their past and future. Their apparent obliviousness to the passage of time is contrasted with the precise reference to years and historic events included in the novel. The preparation of the doctor's body before leaving for the funeral procession takes place between 2:30 and 3:00 p.m., on Wednesday, September 12, 1928.[19] The events recalled by the characters cover a span of about forty years. The date of the burial is significant, as the banana massacre happens shortly thereafter, on December 5–6 of that same year. Together with the preface about the wreckage created by the arrival of the banana company and the multiple references to its impact throughout the novel, García Márquez invites readers to reflect on its historical impact beyond and before the massacre.

Leaf Storm, however, was not as purposely political as the author's next two novels, *In Evil Hour* and *No One Writes to the Colonel*, which explicitly denounced the abuse and corruption that accompanied the practice of violence in rural Colombia. Those two novels were written in the late 1950s. Both of them take place in an unnamed town that, per the author's own comments (in interviews), was not Macondo. They are both focused on the drama of survival, that is, on how people who live in communities that were wracked by violence in the past suffer the effects of the abuse for a long time to follow. In these novels, though, characters have a greater sense of agency and exert more resistance than the characters did in *Leaf Storm*.

Writing and the Disruption of a Corrupt Order in *In Evil Hour*

Possibly García Márquez's most overtly political novel, *In Evil Hour*, looks explicitly into the motivations and consequences of the practice of violence. It also explores the power of writing to intervene in a situation where violence has become normalized. Written in a realistic, almost cinematic style, the narrative relies mainly on dialogue, with an objective narrator providing only bare, present-time descriptions of the characters' actions and surroundings. This novel has received less attention from critics and readers than other works by the author. This is in part the result of García Marquez's own negative judgment of the work. He often disdained it as a novel in which he was excessively concerned with the immediate reality of his country (Mendoza and García Márquez 56).

The story takes place in a town that has lived for two years in a purportedly peaceful situation, after a long period of brutality. It is now governed by a corrupt military mayor, who belongs to the political faction responsible for much of the killing. The only jail is empty, and there is no overt repression, but there are frequent references to a recent past of violence that has left a profound mark on the community. Characters often mention a time when members of the opposition were murdered or were forced to leave, resenting the mayor for his part in the atrocities. There are also several references to how the authorities and people of means increased their wealth and power as a result of such violence.

The violent past appears in the characters' conversations as an indelible memory that inspires constant resistance. People obey, though reluctantly, or only in appearance, as if showing that violence can incite obedience but cannot control their inner will. At one point, the mayor compels a woman to serve him a bowl of soup. She complies, but tells him: "May God give you indigestion" (67).[20] When the mayor in reply asks how much longer townspeople like her will maintain their defiant attitude, she responds: "Until you people bring back to life the dead that you killed" (67).[21] Her reference to this unattainable condition essentially tells him that the people they tried to eliminate through violence remain ever present, sustaining the defiance of survivors. Her comeback also shows that those who stay in power through violence alone are destined to feel forever threatened by the people they govern.

The novel's main plot is centered on how some lampoons (anonymous flyers) destabilize the town. Posted at night on the doors of the wealthiest households, the lampoons contain gossip about those families that everyone in the town has been passing on one to another. Although the reader never knows exactly what the lampoons say, dialogues in the novel show that they expose the hypocrisy that reigns in the town. The characters declare that the lampoons reveal true or false episodes of sexual misconduct, which are known by everyone but become disruptive only when put into writing and posted on doors. Husbands murder their presumed rivals, men are no longer certain of being the real fathers of their heirs, families abandon the town, threats circulate, and fears flow. All this happens even though no one reads the lampoons, except the person on whose door one gets posted, because people in the town become so paranoid that the lampoons are always removed by the owner of each house at dawn, before anyone can read them.

Some of the lampoons, we learn, talk about the dark or violent origins of the fortunes amassed by the wealthy. There is one, for instance, that denounces one of the wealthiest men in town, Don Sabas, for amassing part of his fortune by selling donkeys and then surreptitiously killing them, so their owners would be forced to buy from him again. In talking to someone about the crime, Sabas speaks one of the many memorable lines included in the novel: "There isn't a single fortune in this country that doesn't have some dead donkey behind it" (90).[22] The characters' conversations confirm that all the wealthy people in the town made their money through some form of exploitation based on the practice of violence. Describing how one of them, José Montiel, amassed his fortune, the town's barber says: "A fine business: my party gets in power, the police threatens my political opponents with death, and I buy up their land and livestock at a price I set myself" (43).[23] We learn that anyone who questioned the legality of this scheme would suffer consequences.

At one point, the town's judge notes that the mayor is "getting rich" (156)[24] from the situation inherited from the violence of the past. In this case, his wealth comes from his ability to abuse the authority awarded him through the martial law imposed by the governing party. This state of exception—which has become the norm—is shown here as a strategy that allows a circumvention of the laws and enables corruption. In one instance, the mayor must appoint a deputy of the public ministry to certify the legitimacy of a corrupt operation that will allow him to make lots of money by selling his own land to the municipality. The judge, in the presence of his secretary, indicates that martial law authorizes him for this appointment, which would normally be undertaken by the town's council. We read that "the secretary had an observation of an ethical nature to make concerning the procedure recommended by his superior . . . [but] Judge Arcadio insisted: it was an emergency procedure under an emergency regime" (63).[25]

These and other forms of abuse are well known to the townspeople, who have learned to live with the exploitation as a result of the fear imposed by past practices of violence. That fear is a powerful deterrent to any action on the part of those who suffer the effects of the atrocities. One character describes it as the horror of "getting up every morning with the certainty that they're going to kill you and ten years pass without their killing you" (156).[26] It is a situation of naturalized violence in which people have no desire to take action—until the lampoons wreak havoc in the town. People react to their mere existence, the fact that they put common knowledge into writing, and also to their being publicly exposed outside the private space of the house.

Besides the lampoons, there are other types of writing in the novel. The priest writes letters in which he updates an unidentified recipient about everything that happens in the town. The reader has very few indications of the contents or the recipient of these letters. But ultimately the addressee and the content are not as important as the fact that the priest writes those letters. Putting things into writing is what has an effect, a negative one in this case, as it seems to facilitate the repression. The writing that appears in the newspapers, by contrast, is significant for what it does not say, inasmuch as the government censors the papers' contents. The characters develop strategies to make up for the lack of information, distributing clandestine flyers and communicating the news in person. The lampoons also serve this purpose.

The priest and the mayor initially pay little attention to the lampoons. As the chaos initiated by their appearance grows, however, the priest convinces the mayor to respond with repressive measures. When this occurs, members of the opposition become active in their resistance, and lampoons are no longer posted. Instead, there is an increased circulation of clandestine political flyers that directly invite people to take up arms against the government. The covert and silent incitation of the lampoons is replaced with a direct appeal to action from members of the opposition. The novel ends when the town is again taken over by overt violence. The police persecute conspirators, and the town's men join guerrilla groups in the mountains. There is a feeling that violence announces the advent of important changes for the town and the nation.

Beyond its attention to the effects of writing as a mechanism to denaturalize the practice of violence, *In Evil Hour* also makes references to certain modalities of violence implicit in actions that do not require weapons. The priest uses it when he tolls the church bells to approve or disapprove of attendance at the films shown in the town's projection hall, or when he condemns couples who live together without having been married by the church. Even the incapacity of the central government to respond to citizens' needs is referred to as violence. As the barber puts it, "The state of abandonment we are in is a persecution too" (44).[27] Each of these forms of violence appears, however, as inseparable from the one that was exercised with weapons before the events represented in the novel, establishing fear as a motivation for obedience.

The lampoons are the point at which the diverse conceptions of violence presented in the novel converge. Their capacity to ignite reactions derives from the same method used by violence: both provoke fear. The judge notes that the disturbing power of the lampoons is strange, since the majority of them are removed before dawn, when people in the town are still in their homes. His secretary replies "It isn't the lampoons that won't let people sleep; it's fear of the lampoons" (65).[28] Although nobody knows exactly what the lampoons say or who writes them, awareness of their presence creates fear and is capable of transforming the town's life. It is not by chance that one of the characters speaks of the lampoons as a novel: "I don't want to die without finding out how this novel comes out" (88).[29] *In Evil Hour* offers an exploration into the power of writing and literature to intervene in a situation where violence has become normalized, affecting people who have been rendered powerless by the assault of violence but who are nonetheless resilient and capable of changing their imposed fate.

ENDURANCE AND RESISTANCE IN *NO ONE WRITES TO THE COLONEL*

Originally written as an episode of *In Evil Hour* that took on a life of its own, *No One Writes to the Colonel* is particularly admired for economically describing life in a rural town, where people live under the shadow of violence. It tells the story of a veteran colonel who lives in poverty with his wife, after many years of waiting for the arrival of a war pension. He lets time go by, hoping the government will finally respond, mourning a son who was killed by the authorities, and caring for a fighting rooster that once belonged to the deceased young man. There is no description of the battles the colonel fought or the way in which his son was killed. We only get the painful and long-lasting effects of those events in the life of this old man, who, the novel tells us, "[f]or nearly sixty years—since the end of the last civil war—... had done nothing else but wait" (3).[30]

At the start of the work, a single reference to a funeral for the first person to die a natural death in several years gives an indication of what the town has gone through. Throughout the novel there are other references to the horrors of the past, as well as abundant evidence of the repression imposed through such violence. The narrative focuses on describing the scarcity in the colonel's life, but there are indications that the whole town lives in a permanent state of siege as a result of the civil wars. Their legacy also includes widespread resentment and resistance that turns most people in the town into conspirators who distrust the government and the official sources of information. Censorship is prevalent and interpreted as another form of violence. Members of the opposition circulate mimeographed copies of a clandestine news bulletin, containing, as described by one of them, "What the newspapers didn't print yesterday . . . [r]evelations about the state of the armed resistance in the interior of the country" (16).[31]

The lingering presence of people killed by violence is a particularly powerful source of resistance. Agustín, the colonel's son, who was murdered while distributing clandestine political flyers, is referred to as someone who is still around and supporting the forces of rebellion. His friends and former comrades are now part of the resistance. Every time a new dispatch of their news bulletin is released, they announce it to their political allies by saying "Agustin wrote" (32).[32] When the colonel hears that sentence, he asks, "What does he say?" (32),[33] talking about the news included in the bulletin in the present tense, which may be intriguing for readers who are aware that Agustín is no longer alive. With this subtle subversion of the conventions of narrative time, the novel indicates how present-day resistance is sustained by the memory of those who were killed in the past.

Violence is seen here as a presence with which people have become accustomed to live, to the point of no longer taking notice, even if they continue to suffer from its effects. When a funeral procession is ordered not to pass in front of the police barracks, one of the characters says, "I always forget that we are under martial law" (9).[34] As in *In Evil Hour*, the state of exception allows here for a circumvention of institutional obligations. The colonel, who still trusts the state for which he fought in the war, seems content to just wait for the promised pension. But the reality, which the reader and practically all other characters realize, is that the pension will never come and that the legal order will not allow him to make his claim effective, because governmental rules are vitiated by what has become a permanent state of siege imposed through violence.

What remains is an order of survival in which those who have no scruples enrich themselves, and all others live in poverty. Don Sabas, who also appears in *In Evil Hour* as one of the wealthy residents of the town, is described in this novel as the only leader of the opposition who escaped persecution. We learn that he became rich by denouncing the other political leaders of his party and buying up their properties for close to nothing when they were imprisoned, killed, or forced to leave. His prosperity is contrasted with the poverty in which the colonel lives and seen as a sign of how the current order benefits those who have no qualms about acting in an unethical way, with complete disregard for the well-being of their fellow human beings.

The colonel's relentless waiting for the arrival of his pension is by contrast consistent with the rules of acceptable social behavior and could be seen as an act of resistance to the corrupt norm. His perseverance affirms the state's obligation to offer some form of restitution to those who have suffered from the practice of violence. We see that the lives of the colonel and his wife were dramatically affected by the violence of war and the absence of reparations. The colonel, however, exerts only a passive form of resistance. His main purpose is to endure, hoping that the government will one day respond to his many letters and demands, even while remembering his dead son and taking care of his rooster. He projects onto this animal his own battle for survival, to the exasperation of his wife, who would rather have him sell the rooster so they can get something to eat.

The colonel's wife constantly confronts her husband about his confidence in a government that only shows disdain for the needs of the population. For her, the main issue is to find a tangible source of income, and she resents her husband for relying on monetary claims that do not materialize. When he tells her that they will make money from bets at the cockfighting ring, because as the owner of the animal he is entitled to 20 percent of the earnings, she tells him: "You were also entitled to the veteran's pension after breaking your neck in the civil war. Now everyone has his future assured and you are dying of hunger" (60).[35] The very idea of "being entitled" to certain benefits from the state is disallowed in the state of siege, and people are left to fend for themselves. If the colonel has done nothing but wait, the only thing his wife has done is live day to day, always looking for ways to find money and get food, selling every item of value they have or borrowing from others.

As in *In Evil Hour*, we have here several references to the role of writing in a situation of naturalized violence. The clandestine newspapers and flyers are the most obvious examples of how an organized resistance relies on writing to oppose an oppressive regime, but there are other forms of writing in *No One Writes to the Colonel*, among them the letters that the colonel writes to the government regarding his claim. In a way, this writing is part of how he exerts his own personal form of resistance. More significant, though, is the fact that the government never responds to his claims, as the reader well knows. The letter that the colonel never receives moves the plot forward, evoking in its absence the damage caused by a government that has failed its citizens—appealing to them only as victims or perpetrators of civil wars.

García Márquez said on occasion that in the colonel of this short novel he projected his own struggles as a young writer who had been left to fend for himself in Paris, where he wrote the story. Deprived of his only source of income by the violent actions of a dictator who shut down a newspaper because it had dared to denounce his abuse of power, the author probably suffered from the same sense of deprivation and unfairness we find in *No One Writes to the Colonel*. Perhaps he wrote this story as he pondered how his situation was part of a much larger pattern of abandonment, in which people were seen as expendable in a violent social order that benefited only a few. He possibly reflected also on how his writing could have an effect on this order. Those questions would accompany his literature for many years, but these early works offer a particularly transparent window into his reflections on the politics of his craft.

Notes

1. Throughout this chapter these three works are referred to as novels or short novels, since they have been studied as such by the majority of scholars and critics. It should be noted, though, that in most English editions, *Leaf Storm* and *No One Writes to the Colonel* are

categorized as novellas, or simply as stories, and are published alongside other short texts by García Márquez. The majority of Spanish editions have them as self-standing books.
2. For a study on García Márquez's early reading and its impact, see Bell-Villada 70–92.
3. García Márquez talked about the influence of these authors in many interviews. See, for instance, Mendoza and García Márquez 47, 54.
4. Both articles were reprinted in Spanish in a three-volume compilation of journalistic pieces by García Márquez, under the title *Obra periodística* (1997). As I have shown elsewhere (Rueda), the first article was in part responsible for the denomination of the group of novels that dealt with the Colombian civil war of the 1950s as "Novelas de La Violencia." It was part of a heated and consequential local debate about the merits of these novels.
5. "El principal deber político de un escritor es escribir bien" (Vargas Llosa and García Márquez 19). The idea was repeated with variations in several interviews the author gave over the years. The quote comes from a well-known conversation he held with writer Mario Vargas Llosa in 1967.
6. "La literatura, suponen sin matices preguntantes y reprochadores, es un arma poderosa que no debe permanecer neutral en la contienda política" (561; my translation). Henceforth, for every Spanish quotation that does not include an English version in the list of works cited, the translation is mine.
7. "Acaso sea más valioso contar honestamente lo que uno se siente capaz de contar por haberlo vivido, que contar . . . lo que nuestra posición política nos indica que debe ser contado" (562).
8. "No tuvieron la serenidad ni la paciencia, pero ni siquiera la astucia, de tomarse el tiempo que necesitaban para aprender a escribir las [novelas]" (562).
9. "La novela no estaba en los muertos de tripas sacadas, sino en los vivos que debieron sudar hielo en su escondite, sabiendo que a cada latido del corazón corrían el riesgo de que les sacaran las tripas" (563).
10. García Márquez would go back to this idea in interviews he gave over the years. A relatively elaborate commentary on the subject appears in his conversation with Mario Vargas in 1967. See Vargas-Llosa and García Márquez 23.
11. García Márquez mentions that the collection comprised a representative selection of Colombian literature since the late nineteenth century. It included books such as the classic novels *María* (1867), by Jorge Isaacs, and *La vorágine* (*The Vortex*, 1924), by José Eustasio Rivera.
12. "Han carecido de un auténtico sentido de lo nacional" (578).
13. "El primer drama nacional de que éramos conscientes" (578).
14. "La única explosión literaria de legítimo carácter nacional que hemos tenido en nuestra historia" (578).
15. "Grandes escritores han confesado que escribir cuesta trabajo, que hay una carpintería de la literatura que es preciso afrontar con valor y hasta con cierto entusiasmo muscular" (578).
16. Barranquilla Group was the name given to the gathering of writers, journalists, artists, and intellectuals who converged in the Colombian city of Barranquilla in the mid-twentieth century, convening initially around a now-legendary bookstore run by exiled Catalan writer Ramón Vinyes. Alongside García Márquez, some of its most notable members were Álvaro Cepeda Samudio, Germán Vargas, and Alfonso Fuenmayor, all of whom would appear as the "four friends" of Macondo in *One Hundred Years of Solitude*.
17. This civil war is most likely the Thousand Days' War, which is also the war fought by the titular colonel in *No One Writes to the Colonel*.

18. "Irreal" (*Leaf Storm* 91).
19. All narrative voices note the time in their initial monologues, and the colonel indicates the date at the end of the first chapter (35).
20. "Quiera Dios que se le indigeste" (*In Evil Hour* 53).
21. "Hasta que nos resuciten los muertos que nos mataron" (53).
22. "En este país no hay una sola fortuna que no tenga a la espalda un burro muerto" (70).
23. "Lindo negocio: mi partido está en el poder, la policía amenaza de muerte a mis adversarios políticos, y yo les compro tierras y ganados al precio que yo mismo ponga" (35).
24. "Se está volviendo rico" (118).
25. "El secretario tuvo una observación de carácter ético al procedimiento recomendado por su superior ... [pero] el juez Arcadio insistió: era un procedimiento de emergencia bajo un régimen de emergencia" (50).
26. "Levantarse todas las mañanas con la seguridad de que lo matarán a uno, y que pasen diez años sin que lo maten" (118).
27. "El abandono en que nos tienen también es persecución" (36).
28. "Lo que quita el sueño no son los pasquines, sino el miedo a los pasquines" (52).
29. "No me quiero morir sin saber como termina esta novela" (69).
30. "Durante cincuenta y seis años—desde cuando terminó la última guerra civil—... no había hecho nada distinto a esperar" (3).
31. "Lo que no decían los periódicos de ayer ... Revelaciones sobre el estado de la resistencia armada en el interior del país" (18).
32. "Escribió Agustín" (36).
33. "¿Qué dice?" (36).
34. "Siempre se me olvida que estamos en estado de sitio" (10).
35. "También tenías derecho a tu pensión de veterano después de exponer el pellejo en la guerra civil. Ahora todo el mundo tiene su vida asegurada y tú estás muerto de hambre" (71).

Works Cited

Bell-Villada, Gene H. *García Márquez. The Man and His Work*. 2nd ed. U of North Carolina P, 2010.
García Márquez, Gabriel. *El coronel no tiene quien le escriba*. Oveja Negra, 1978.
García Márquez, Gabriel. "Dos o tres cosas sobre la novela de la Violencia." *Obra periodística 3*, edited by Jacques Gilard, Norma, 1997, pp. 561–65.
García Márquez, Gabriel. *La hojarasca*. Oveja Negra, 1978.
García Márquez, Gabriel. *In Evil Hour*. Translated by Gregory Rabassa, Harper & Row, 1979.
García Márquez, Gabriel. *Leaf Storm and Other Stories*. Translated by Gregory Rabassa, Avon Books, 1973.
García Márquez, Gabriel. "La literatura colombiana, un fraude a la nación." *Obra periodística 3*, 575–79. Edited by Jacques Gilard. Norma, 1997.
García Márquez, Gabriel. *La mala hora*. Oveja Negra, 1979.
García Márquez, Gabriel. *No One Writes to the Colonel and Other Stories*. Translated by J. S. Bernstein, Harper & Row, 1968.
Mendoza, Plinio Apuleyo, and Gabriel García Márquez. *The Fragrance of Guava*. Translated by Ann Wright, Verso, 1983.

Rueda, María Helena. *La violencia y sus huellas: Una mirada desde la narrativa colombiana.* Iberoamericana Vervuert, 2011.

Saldívar, Dasso. *García Márquez: El viaje a la semilla.* Alfaguara, 1997.

Vargas Llosa, Mario, and Gabriel García Márquez. *Diálogo sobre la novela latinoamericana (1967).* Perú Andino, 1988.

CHAPTER 25

THE PROTEAN VIEWPOINT IN *ONE HUNDRED YEARS OF SOLITUDE*

ERIK CAMAYD-FREIXAS

In the years surrounding the publication of *Cien años de soledad* (*One Hundred Years of Solitude*, 1967), there appeared a number of significant theoretical studies about point of view in fiction (e.g., Lubbock; Booth; Scholes and Kellogg; Todorov; Rico, *Novela picaresca*; Genette; Prince; Friedman; Uspensky). Critics generally agree that viewpoint is a primary category of narrative discourse, given that other elements such as characterization, description, language, worldview, structure, and even genre, if they are to be convincing, need to be consistent with the adopted vantage point.[1] Narrative experimentation since modernism provided a fertile ground for theoretical development, which in turn stimulated further innovations.

The history of the novel as genre acquired the semblance of a dramatic stage wherein all prescribed unities would be shattered. It began with the unities of time, space, and action, prescribed by Aristotle in the *Poetics*, where drama was to represent a life's turning point in a single day, place, and plot. The idea was meant to bolster verisimilitude by presenting the spectator with an uninterrupted whole and nothing to hide. Any hiatus would open the door for sophistry and prestidigitation. At the same time, such rules were more like rubrics meant to provide a framework for authors to compete and show their prowess, much like athletes in the Olympiads. The advent of the printing press, however, meant that by the end of the fifteenth century plays could then be read and not just represented. Drama began to approach narrative as it became freer from the material constraints of the stage. Fernando de Rojas's *La Celestina: Tragicomedia de Calisto y Melibea* (*Celestina: The Tragicomedy of Calisto and Melibea*, 1499)—to which is owed the fact that both *Don Quixote* and *One Hundred Years of Solitude* parody epic and embrace tragicomedy—set out to subvert the three unities, resulting in a hybrid between theater and romance, written entirely in dialogue, with twenty-one acts, amenable for reading but impractical to represent. Mannerist and baroque theater, from the commedia dell'arte to Shakespeare and Lope de Vega, adapted historical, legendary, and popular tales to the stage (Chevalier). They are the distant precursors of narrative film.

Unity of plot was challenged by the many subplots of the realist novel. And when modernism seemed to run out of unities to break, Virginia Woolf did the unthinkable: she exploded the unity of character and personal identity in *Orlando: A Biography* (1928), in which the hero changes from man to woman and lives through three centuries of social history. There remained the essential unity of narrative viewpoint, already made flexible in theater by the voices of the characters and the absence of a narrator. A similar flexibility has been noted in the polyphonic novel, from Cervantes to Dostoyevsky, in which the narrator's single vision is refracted by the characters (Bakhtin).[2] Polyphony is understood as variety of perspectives and unity of style. Radical experiments with perspectivism, however, began in earnest with cubism's absorption of non-Euclidean geometry into the principles of fragmentation and simultaneity. In prose narrative this led to the same events being told from the conflicting perspectives of different characters. A prime Latin American example is Carlos Fuentes's *La muerte de Artemio Cruz* (*The Death of Artemio Cruz*, 1962), in which extreme fragmentation and simultaneity, conveyed via stream of consciousness, result in a seemingly chaotic narration that stretches the reader's competence. In contrast, *One Hundred Years of Solitude* subtly explodes perspective through the sophisticated pretense of naïve storytelling by a layered narrator who reports what the different characters see, think, and say, all the while preserving coherence, readability, and unity of style (Gullón). García Márquez's accomplishment is akin to Virginia Woolf's and no less significant. It is equivalent to turning the protean Orlando into a concealed yet omniscient narrator: Melquíades.[3]

Narrative voice in García Márquez is, however, singular in tone, supporting the unity of style. Finding such a voice is one of the hardest and most crucial goals that an author must attain. In this regard, Franz Kafka's *The Metamorphosis* was an avowed epiphany: " Kafka ... recounted things in German the same way my grandmother used to.... When I saw how Gregor Samsa could wake up one morning transformed into a gigantic beetle, I said to myself, 'I didn't know you could do this, but if you can, I'm certainly interested in writing'" (García Márquez, 30).[4] Going into the greatest disproportions of the story without any explanation forces a ludic pact with the reader, who has little choice but to accept the literary game, moved by the metanarrative challenge of deciphering its rules.

The author's grandmother, Tranquilina Iguarán Cotes, loosely represented in the novel by Úrsula Iguarán, had the gift of the folk storyteller who projected a firm belief in all the enormities she heard from the townsfolk, becoming a repository of folk tales—exactly what the author needed as a model of an archaic narrator who shares the same worldview as his characters: "She used to tell me about the most atrocious things without turning a hair, as if it was something she'd just seen. I realized that it was her impassive manner and her wealth of images that made her stories so credible. I wrote *One Hundred Years of Solitude* using my grandmother's method" (30).[5] Of course, the grandmother's method was augmented by the technical complexities inherited from the modernist novel and enriched by his continuing contact with the folklore of his native region.[6]

Studies of viewpoint have shed light on the complexities of voice, tone, focus, distance, phraseology, multiple and simultaneous perspectives, as well as diegetic levels. All aspects of viewpoint are useful for literary analysis, but particularly revealing of magical realism is the concept of an *ideological* point of view in the composition of the novel, proposed by Boris Uspensky. He defines ideology as the "general system of viewing the world conceptually" (8). It serves to examine the standpoint the narrator and the characters adopt when perceiving and evaluating the narrated world. This optic may belong at any given time to the normative system of the author, the narrator, or any of the characters. In the disposition and articulation of the various ideological viewpoints there resides, according to Uspensky, the fundamental problem in the composition of the literary work. He insists that, far from explicit, the ideological viewpoint is revealed at the phraseological level of the text, where the minutiae of language reveal the underlying ideology—thus marking a return to rhetorical criticism.

The characters' worldview, in particular, depends on the milieu. In this case, it is the rustic village of Macondo in the Latin American hinterland. The ideology of the village is conveyed mainly by the founders, José Arcadio and Úrsula, with Colonel Aureliano Buendía representing the second generation. Many other characters will enrich the ideological portrait of the village throughout the seven generations of the Buendía family—another collective character—finally zeroing in on the last adult Aureliano. The José Arcadios are collectively taciturn dreamers, while the Aurelianos are more inclined to be men of action. All are perfectly flat, devoid of any deep psychology, which allows the author to treat them dispassionately, from an extreme affective distance, almost like ancient relatives we never knew, staring at us from a daguerreotype. The absence of anguish and grief supports the unworried good humor of a bedside story, in imitation of *Don Quixote*. But here too is where Cervantes shows his true prowess: his characters are profoundly human; there is something of them in each of us. The Buendías' dominant trait, however, is that they are mostly unaware of and unencumbered by the tribulations of the industrial world that comes knocking at their door like a grim reaper. They are naïve quixotic characters from an archaic, pastoral world that has disappeared as much as the world of the knights errant. As such they are unrepeatable. Melquíades, the author's puppet master, and his "new inventions" help to delineate a contrast with the remote Macondo as a collective character in itself, with its tribal organization and homogeneous clan identity.

There is yet another contrasting perspective: that of the modern reader, who may see the transactions of trinkets for gold between the "gypsies" and the "natives" as part of a satirical allegory of (neo-)colonization. Macondo is a microcosm of Latin America, given its analogous historical stages: the sighting of the Spanish galleon and suit of armor; the age of piracy with Sir Francis Drake; the scientific expeditions through the jungle in the Age of Enlightenment; the endless wars between Liberals and Conservatives that consumed the nineteenth century; and the arrival of the banana company in the early twentieth century, a reference to the United Fruit Company. It is, in short, an allegory of five centuries of Latin American history. Whereas pure allegory, such as fable, personifies abstract ideas, historical allegory functions inversely; the alien world, Macondo, is the abstraction that personifies a concrete historical reality. Yet the novel is also a satire of underdevelopment. Immersed in its solitude, ignorant of the world, the Buendía clan was unwittingly destined to repeat the history of mankind, from Genesis to Apocalypse. Hence the novel's lapidary ending: "[R]aces condemned to one hundred years of solitude did not have another opportunity on earth" (383).[7] It echoes José Martí's dictum in his seminal essay, "Our America": "What remains of the village in America *is to* awaken."[8]

The novel links the microhistory of Macondo to great biblical deeds. In the middle of the Genesis-like jungle, the foundational couple, defying the original sin of incest, builds an Adamic village where things lack names and no one has yet died. The founding expedition is also an Exodus from Ríohacha to a land that no one had promised them, through a swampy jungle that will bring upon Macondo the plagues of Egypt and the Great Flood, until its extinction by a "biblical hurricane" (*One Hundred Years* 383).[9] Melquíades's parchments are an apocryphal scripture. This is Macondo viewed *sub specie aeternitatis*. The biblical totalization of time provides the referential framework whereby the official history of Latin America is parodied and rewritten from the people's perspective as a barefoot myth, along the lines of Lévi-Strauss's *Structural Anthropology* (1963), yet mimicking the feverish gaze of the Discoverers and the amazement of the conquistadors *conquistados* ("conquered").

The ideological distance between the modern author and the archaic world of his characters is a crucial gap that must be bridged somehow in order to establish authority, that is, to make credible the author's claim to knowledge of that alien world. García Márquez's precursors in what came to be known as the Latin American Boom offered him a succession of experiments in this regard. First there was Alejo Carpentier, who coined the literary myth of the marvelous real (*lo real maravilloso*) in Latin America, which soon morphed into magical realism. Influenced by existentialism, in which authenticity was king, Carpentier's narrator was always himself, an erudite author who presented the narrated world from the perspective of a researcher scrutinizing a case study. His seminal novel *El reino de este mundo* (*The Kingdom of This World*, 1949) was exactly that, a researcher's case study meant to substantiate his theory of *lo real maravilloso*, outlined in the prologue to the first Spanish edition. The novel is narrated in the author's own erudite voice and phraseology, but from the vantage point of Ti Noel (petit Noel), a slave boy who grows up to die of old age while witnessing the Vodou-inspired Haitian Revolution of 1791 and its gradual betrayal, culminating with a new, Black emperor, the Napoleonic Henri Christophe; his fall; and the final succession by the no less tyrannical regime of the republican mulattoes. Careful not to usurp the voice of the Other, Carpentier opts to focalize in parallel with his character. Like a camera pointed over the witness's shoulder, the erudite narrator tells what his character perceives. García Márquez will do the same, but with an omniscient folk narrator as his implied author, speaking both from within and from without his many characters. Carpentier's own ideology is that of an avant-garde artist and amateur anthropologist who zeroes in on the clash of ideologies and imaginaries between the Europe of the Age of Reason—which provides a mere veneer of civilization—and the throbbing, erupting undercurrent of Vodou as an alternate system of thought inspiring the revolution. The optic is that of the modern Western explorer observing the "primitive" Other in awe. But for García Márquez's purpose, Carpentier's narrator, as an outsider, would always have too limited a perspective, like one who looks over the fence at an unknown mansion and wonders what lies inside.

The view from inside the characters' world is represented by Guatemalan Nobel laureate Miguel Ángel Asturias, Mexican neoregionalist Juan Rulfo, and García Márquez himself. Asturias, who was the only one of these writers to label himself a magical realist, studied Mayan texts and anthropology in Paris and participated in the surrealist movement, marrying both perspectives in his early poems as well as the poetic prose of his *Leyendas de Guatemala* (*Legends of Guatemala*, 1930). In the process, he cultivated a personal myth for himself as the *Gran Lengua* (Grand Interpreter) of the ancient Maya, a role reserved for the prophetic high priest and royal scribe (*Chilam Balam* or *Its'at*), who interpreted the pictograms of the sacred codices, such as the *Popol Vuh* and the *Libros del Chilam Balam* (Books of Chilam Balam). In his landmark novel, *Hombres de maíz* (*Men of Maize*, 1949), Asturias attempts to rescue that enigmatic Mayan mythology and to posit an aspirational continuity into the modern age. Mediated by the surrealist clash of disparate images, chance encounters, and automatic writing, Asturias turned his mythologizing of history into a denunciation of the modern expropriation of sacred indigenous lands (Camayd-Freixas, *Etnografía imaginaria*). But having run its course through the heyday of Mesoamerican archaeology, Asturias's personal myth as the poetic voice of the Maya would eventually be perceived merely as a marketing persona.

Juan Rulfo found a different solution. He wrote a five-hundred-page manuscript and cropped it to scarcely a hundred, eliminating the narrator altogether. His brief masterpiece, *Pedro Páramo* (1955), was based on the author's return to his hometown after thirty years, only to find it abandoned. In his novel it would become the fictional Comala, a remote desert village in the author's home state of Jalisco. The first narrator is Juan Preciado, illegitimate son of Pedro Páramo, who returns to the village in search of his father in order to exact vengeance for his mother, Dolores Preciado, who has sent him on a mission to make his father pay for the abandonment in which he left them all those years. Dolores and other characters will also tell their own stories in their own words, providing background information and filling in portions of the plot, as in a mosaic, with its fragmented timeline and overlapping perspectives of the same events. Well into the novel, the reader discovers that all the characters are dead, relating their own memories simultaneously, in the form of ghostly murmurs from beyond the grave. Each character can only hear murmurs from nearby graves, while the focus moves freely to different clusters of tombs, establishing an order of exposition and weaving the plot like a patchwork quilt of all the stories that compose the village of Comala as a collective character, like Macondo, inspired by William Faulkner. Instead of dialogue, Rulfo's novel is a mosaic of monologues. Yet by making the setting rural and provincial, instead of primitive or tribal, and modeling it after his own hometown, the author closes his distance from his narrated world, bolstering his authority and credibility. Rulfo's greatest achievement—capturing the rural language of Jalisco toward the end of the Mexican Revolution (1910–1928)—was simply the language he had learned in his youth from his elders and townsfolk, a language endowed with folk poetry, which the author in turn artistically refines. The orality of his regional speech permeates each of the monologues, supporting the unity of style.

García Márquez, on the other hand, is eminently a storyteller with little inclination to dialogue, notwithstanding his novel being inspired by his grandmother's stories and his own hometown of Aracataca: "[D]ialogue doesn't ring true in Spanish. I've always said that in this language there's a wide gulf between spoken and written dialogue. A Spanish dialogue that's good in real life is not necessarily good in a novel. So I use it very little" (García Márquez and Mendoza, 33).[10] Presumably, the regional variations of Spanish pronunciation and colloquialisms would almost require phonetic transcription to sound genuine, whereas the formality of written Spanish would sound generic and contrived. In any case, Rulfo's solution, namely to suppress the narrator, was not viable for the Colombian. And instead of claiming a personal myth like Asturias, García Márquez opts for an old device dear to mannerism: he deflects the personal myth onto his protean narrator and authorial mask, the figure of Melquíades. This is the same operation practiced by Cervantes when he claimed to have bought the manuscript of *Don Quixote* at the market of Toledo from a dubious Moor named Cide Hamete Benengeli, an unreliable narrator. It is the same as Velázquez painting himself into *Las meninas*, the play within a play in *Hamlet*, or Hitchcock featuring himself in a corner of his films. Finally, unlike Carpentier, whose narrator comments on and dramatizes the clash between modern and archaic ideologies explicitly in the text, García Márquez's great realization is that the reader already supplies the modern viewpoint without any help from the narrator, who assumes instead the ideology of the characters, while the author seals the ludic pact with his frequent winks, inviting the reader to a game of make-believe. It proved to be a felicitous formula.

Magical realism feeds on this clash between the modern (Western) and the archaic (Other) as collective ideologies, siding with the latter as a way of enticing the reader into seeing from the Other's perspective and questioning his or her own cultural norms. However, as in Thomas More's *Utopia*, the appeal to a primitive innocence always entails a critique of modernity. When we talk about collective ideologies and cultural norms, we enter the public square of social convention. The expectation of everyday normality is a construct that depends on time and place: "the socially given text that is taken as the 'real world'" (Culler); "the text of the natural attitude of a society" (Heath); a "general and diffuse text which might be called 'public opinion'" (Todorov); a "collective, anonymous voice, whose origin is a general human knowledge" (Barthes); a view from a "middle distance" determined by "the fictional creation of *people*, of individual characters and lives informed by what in any one age is agreed to constitute a certain integrity and coherence" (Stern); and an "ideology" or a "body of maxims and prejudices which constitute both a vision of the world and a system of values" (Genette) (all of the preceding are cited in Culler 138–44.). In magical realist novels, the socially given text of habitual reality is that of the Other, producing a double effect: the denaturalization of the real and the naturalization of the marvelous (Chiampi). This requires that the narrator's worldview coincide with that of the characters, while allowing the author to remain in touch with the modern reader, whose vanity is stroked, privileged by the author's invitation to join him in Olympus with its godly bird's-eye view over the novelistic world below.

The phraseology initially reveals these two opposing perspectives merged into a single style: a folk, archaic narrator, a believer, who narrates from inside the characters' worldview, while from the outside, the modern author slips in his ironic winks to the modern reader, thereby modifying the simple style of the folk tale with the complex technical toolbox of contemporary narrative. The ideological viewpoint of the archaic storyteller is the novel's primary support, transmitted by the subtlest dimensions of narrative voice—the calm, placid, and disinterested tone of the entire novel, in normalizing contrast with the Gargantuan vagaries and portents it relates—and then there is the colloquial rhythm of the prose, which affords it the orality of a folk tale, an olden-times anecdote, or a children's story. Its imperturbable authority is buttressed by a richness of imagery and a meticulous precision that goes beyond the Kafkian verisimilitude of detail to a hyperbolic and parodic sense of exactitude: It rains for four years, eleven months, and two days; José Arcadio's stream of blood traces a precise trajectory down to his mother's house; he will need a special coffin measuring two meters and thirty centimeters long and one meter and ten centimeters wide; and the Colonel escapes thirty-two armed uprisings, fourteen assassination attempts, seventy-three ambushes, and a firing squad. This hyperbole of detail, worthy of Melquíades, is the modern author's tongue-in-cheek way of claiming a fictional proximity to the legendary events and compensating for any perceived ideological distance toward the narrated world.

Here the author has abandoned any attempt to negate his own presence in the text, and instead of disguising it he deliberately calls attention to it with those winks that secure the reader's complicity. Such are all the "new inventions" that bedazzle Macondo, which the reader recognizes as the ridiculous anachronisms they really are. Narrator and characters make indirect metanarrative comments about the very mechanisms of fiction. When the town is filled with noisy birds, Úrsula covers her ears so as not to lose her sense of reality; when she sees the family fates repeated with each generation, the matriarch declares that time runs in a circle, adumbrating the novel's own narrative time structure. In the end, Aureliano Babilonia discerns that "Melquíades had not put events in the order of man's conventional time, but had concentrated a century of daily episodes in such a way that they coexisted in one instant" (*One Hundred Years* 382).[11] This is an allusion to "The Aleph" by Jorge Luis Borges, the aesthetic father of the Boom generation, who first experimented with the bifurcation and circularity of narrative time. Borges's influence was cemented by the stories collected in *Ficciones* (1955), written between 1939 and 1953. And let us not forget our author's playful references to characters from other contemporary novels: Julio Cortázar's Rocamadour from *Rayuela* (*Hopscotch*, 1963), Carlos Fuentes's Artemio Cruz (1962), and Alejo Carpentier's Víctor Hugues from *El siglo de las luces* (*Explosion in a Cathedral*, 1962). Rather than being true intertextuality, these passing references are part of the novel's construction of an allegory of reading, which culminates with Aureliano Babilonia deciphering Melquíades's parchments.

The old seafaring, barnacle-encrusted gypsy is finally revealed to be that third narrative voice that helps to bridge the first two, the cosmopolitan and the folk, the author and his grandmother, with her straight face and her fabulous children's stories, in which Melquíades may have been one of the characters. This vignette helps to configure a virtual reader, not only by evoking the child García Márquez listening to his grandmother's tales but also by appealing to the child in every reader. The novel, written by the adult author remembering his childhood, constantly addresses the reader both as an adult and as a child. Both temporal perspectives are reenacted by the characters:

> Many years later, as he faced the firing squad, Colonel Aureliano Buendía was to remember that distant afternoon when his father took him to discover ice. At that time Macondo was a village of twenty adobe houses, built on the bank of a river of clear water that ran along a bed of polished stones, which were white and enormous, like prehistoric eggs. The world was so recent that many things lacked names, and in order to indicate them it was necessary to point. Every year during the month of March a family of ragged gypsies would set up their tents near the village, and with a great uproar of pipes and kettledrums they would display new inventions. (*One Hundred Years* 11)[12]

The phraseology and particularly the verb tenses and moods are carefully chosen for their ambiguity and duration. The three narrative voices are superimposed from the start. The first sentence begins with the standard perspective of the modern author as the Colonel faces the firing squad. However, the verbal form "was to remember" reads like an ancient prophecy already fulfilled, suggesting Melquíades's authorship and absolute control over the fate of his characters. The predicate that follows implies the folk storyteller launching a children's story about the discovery of ice. The opening formula "Once upon a time" has been transposed as "Many years later" and then reclaimed as a "distant afternoon." The second sentence again starts with the modern author (and the echo of Melquíades) describing Macondo, but ends with the folk narrator's childlike parlance describing the river stones as "white and enormous, like prehistoric eggs." This prepares the third sentence, which introduces with sleight of hand a pivotal phrase, the moment when the wording radically turns to the naïve perspective of the child: "The world was so recent [for the child Aureliano] that many things lacked names, and in order to indicate them it was necessary to point." Here the folk narrator appeals to the reader child, while the author winks at the adult reader—all of which seems like an antic belonging to the old gypsy trickster. Now the stage is set for introducing the fabulous Melquíades, his gypsies, and new inventions in a more convincing fashion, as characters in a children's story.

The fact that the three narrative viewpoints converge and overlap raises an important problem. In any story, the reader's first task, in order to get oriented, is to determine the point of enunciation, the narrator's present from which the story is told. Here, all three narrators are blended, sending the reader reeling in different directions: Melquíades (past), the oral storyteller (present), and the modern author (future). There is a floating narrative viewpoint as the point of enunciation remains undetermined, immersing the reader in a timeless, mythical world. The characters' ideological point of view, which normally is mediated by a single narrator, is now inflected by any combination of the three. There are in fact seven possible combinations of the three narrative viewpoints that may converge on any given phrase, variously coloring each character's perception.[13] García Márquez shows true mastery in maintaining this complex phraseological consistency for almost four hundred pages, hiding behind its readability a sophisticated naiveté, which flows so naturally that even highly competent readers often overlook the artifice.[14] In a Russian-dolls effect, the three narrators together narrate three or more metadiegetic levels; for example, the three narrate the adult Colonel narrating his story as a child who tells the story of his father telling the story of Melquíades—a story within a story four times over. In addition, the parchments and the novel reflect each other in a mise en abyme or parallel mirror effect. The narrative focus, initially presided over by Colonel Aureliano's memories, will henceforth stroll freely among the different narrators and characters, with frequent pivots and overlays where the different viewpoints at times become indistinguishable.

The beginning in medias res, in the middle of the matter, plays a central role in the narrative time structure, and hence in the composition of the novel. In the typical in medias res scheme, the writer begins in the middle of the action, preferably at a climactic moment, here the Colonel facing the firing squad. Suspense will build up as the narration loops back through memory lane to explain the origin of how that initial knot or complication came to be (Bland). In our novel this means going back to the childhood memory of the Colonel meeting Melquíades. In chapter two, the narration reaches as far back as the origin of the Buendías and the founding of Macondo, before working its way forward to the starting point in subsequent chapters. Finally, the writer will stretch that loop at will and eventually return to cross the starting point, unravel the knot in the denouement, and advance the action into the future, like a tango that takes two steps back and three steps forward along the timeline of the plot. The author will keep us wondering about that firing squad for the entire first half of the novel. Let us not forget that the text also supports the possibility that the whole first half was all the Colonel's recollection as his life flashed before his eyes, an instant that is stretched out indefinitely in narrative time. Once the firing squad is disbanded and the Colonel escapes with his life, the narrative advances further until the end of the first half. Then the second half of the novel (chapter ten) begins with the same rhetorical device: "Years later on his deathbed Aureliano Segundo *would remember* the rainy afternoon in June when he went into the bedroom to meet his first son" (*One Hundred Years* 174).[15] This will be the point in medias res that begins a second memory loop, but this second half covers the last five generations of Buendías, as the narration accelerates toward the end as though time were running out. The same memory loop structures each chapter. The first one ends where it started: "Those hallucinating sessions," referring to Melquíades's stories, "remained printed on the memories of the boys in such a way that many years later, a second before the regular army officer gave the firing squad the command to fire, Colonel Aureliano Buendía saw once more that warm March afternoon on which his father" took him to discover ice (24).[16] The novel will return sporadically to the firing squad in a manner of quilting points that connect the three temporal planes of enunciation: Melquíades's, the storyteller's, and the implied author's (Booth). Any element in one chapter can become the starting point in medias res of the next chapter's narrative loop, and so forth, forming a loop chain that reveals the novel's mode of composition. This loop chain will become García Márquez's signature time structure, with which to organize scene, chapter, and book.

José Arcadio Buendía, the father, already under Melquíades's spell, oversells the wonder of that block of ice and becomes yet another prism that will color the narration, starting with the children's perception and the reader's expectations of the event. The matter is resolved in the most insignificant way when "Aureliano, on the other hand, took a step forward and put his hand on it, withdrawing it immediately. 'It's boiling,' he exclaimed, startled" (*One Hundred Years* 26).[17] Yet the childhood memory grows over time to become a cherished moment, remembered in the face of death, as a return to the origins, to the lost Golden Age of innocence, happiness, and plenitude. García Márquez's matter-of-fact, unsentimental narration and flat characters, devoid of angst and pathos, offer the reader a blank slate on which to project our own human sentiments and readerly identification, filling in our own self-image as though "looking into a speaking mirror" (383).[18]

One thing is certain. At the end, the tricked reader is prompted to start again from page one, to verify Melquíades's presence in the text. The resulting circular reading would be the mirror image of Scheherazade's circular narration in the ancient folk tales of the *One Thousand and One Nights*, reintroduced by Borges onto the Latin American literary scene since the 1950s. In a very real sense, Borges and Carpentier were the masters of the Latin American narrative Boom. Carpentier and *lo real maravilloso americano* represented a trend of *littérature engagée*, issuing from André Malraux and Jean-Paul Sartre's existentialism, together with a nativist call for Latin American artists to forsake European models and return to their own, authentic national treasures, in a sort of Rediscovery of America. Borges, on the other hand, represented the more technical, Europolitan, and formalistic side of literature—in short, the opposite pole. García Márquez achieves a harmonious blend of the two. Yet both Borges with his conceptual fictions and Carpentier with his returns to the origins and to recurring revolutions posit a circularity of cultural and historical time, greatly popularized after *One Hundred Years of Solitude* under the banner of *el eterno retorno*, following mythologist Mircea Eliade (*Mythe*).

The rereading of the novel shows that the first chapter begins and ends with the discovery of ice. It has a circular time structure, like the novel itself. It is an embryonic first chapter that already contains all the main topics and themes to be developed later, perhaps following Cervantes, who wrote Don Quixote's first sally as a microcosm of his masterwork, giving rise to the theory that he had tested the waters with the short novellas he wrote starting in 1590, eventually collected in his *Novelas ejemplares* (*Exemplary Novels*, 1613), until he realized the novelistic potential of the knight errant as soon as he added the latter's sidekick, Sancho Panza, only then committing to his magnum opus. García Márquez also experimented for years with both short stories and journalistic chronicles, until he found a voice and a perspective from which to narrate the larger work. His short story "Un señor muy viejo con unas alas enormes" ("A Very Old Man with Enormous Wings," 1968) appears like a character sketch in search of Melquíades.[19]

One Hundred Years of Solitude shows that despite finding a unique voice, the author saw the potential of a movable narrative perspective, one that mimics Euro-American modernism, but with the elusive, mestizo difference of the colonized. A polyvalent and layered diegesis is verified from the beginning, endowed with an as yet unexplained omniscience. In the end it is suggested that Melquíades was the source of that omniscience, and that the point of enunciation was the deciphering of his mysterious parchments, when the last adult Aureliano goes back to the beginnings, like Tristram Shandy, in search of his own origin. But this is just an Escher-style illusion not consistent with the phraseology of the novel. The author will never reveal either of them, the source of the omniscience or the point of enunciation. In reality, the novel will have multiple narrative presents. This allows the narrator to pretend to be contemporaneous with the point in medias res from which he begins each chapter. It also creates the sensation of orality, that the present of the narrative is the same as the present of the reading, that is, the illusion that one is listening in person to the storyteller himself.

Children's stories are in fact the first of several genres of the marvelous that the novel simulates. The anticipated conventions of genre provide in themselves a perspective that helps to naturalize the narrative, supplying "a specifically literary and artificial *vraisemblance*" (Culler 140). That is, the marvelous is rendered acceptable because it is traditionally expected of that genre. Fittingly, four pages into the novel, Melquíades himself assumes the role of storyteller: "The children were startled by his fantastic stories. Aureliano, who could not have been more than five at the time, would remember him for the rest of his life as he saw him that afternoon, sitting against the metallic and quivering light from the window, lighting up with his deep organ voice the darkest reaches of the imagination. . . . José Arcadio, his older brother, would pass on that wonderful image as a hereditary memory to all of his descendants" (*One Hundred Years* 15–16).[20] The genre expectations of the children's story will be reinforced throughout the novel, in cases such as the circus man turned monster for disobeying his parents or the innkeeper whose hand was burned for having raised it against his mother. The novel is indeed full of adult children, including the Colonel, who plays at his thirty-two civil wars. Úrsula will save him from the firing squad, scolding and disbanding the rest of the soldiers and her son, like neighborhood brats caught in an act of mischief and sent home to their parents.

The orality and the reality expectations of myths, legends, folk tales, fairy tales, and children's stories coalesce in the narrative, reinforcing each other. Similarly, the written historiographical models provided by the chronicles of mariners and discoverers; the travelogues of merchants, adventurers, missionaries, naturalists, and explorers;

and the accounts of ethnography are all genres that share historically and discursively a family resemblance and as such converge indistinctly in the novel's polyphony and heteroglossia (Bakhtin, *Dialogic Imagination*). The modes of persuasion and seduction, of pact and complicity with the reader, which make these genres viable, come into play in orchestrated fashion, as though in a totalizing attempt to attack on all fronts the problem of the novel's own credibility. This overlay of genres serves to bolster the verisimilitude of magical-realist narrative (Camayd-Freixas, "Theories," "Primitivism"). Melquíades is an amalgam of these—mariner, merchant, alchemist, scientist, prophet, and chronicler: "That prodigious figure, said to possess the keys of Nostradamus" (*One Hundred Years* 15).[21] It is he, with his stories, instruments, and Rennaissance maps, who inspires the navigation through the jungle in search of an impossible route out to sea; while he works on his parchments, he can be heard murmuring the name "Humboldt," oblivious to the caricature of science enclosed in his anachronistic trade as an alchemist. The parchments are the chronicle of his expeditions to Macondo.

In his 1982 Nobel Lecture, García Márquez highlights the importance of the chronicles of the Indies for *One Hundred Years of Solitude* and evokes, as a model for his hyperbolic narrator, Magellan's fantastic and imaginative chronicler, Antonio Pigafetta, who scrupulously reported on their South American lower passage "that he had seen hogs with navels on their haunches, clawless birds whose hens laid eggs on the backs of their mates . . . a misbegotten creature with the head and ears of a mule, a camel's body, the legs of a deer and the whinny of a horse. He described how the first native encountered in Patagonia was confronted with a mirror, whereupon that impassioned giant lost his senses to the terror of his own image."[22] By the same token, it is not difficult to see Melquíades as the ethnographer who comes every year to live among the villagers and write a treatise linking their deeds to universal myths. They will only decipher the parchments after many "premature" attempts, once they are able to see themselves from without and historical self-awareness breaks down their archaic notion of cyclical time. This entails a loss of innocence and the end of the villagers' mindset. The arrival of the ethnographer is already a first contact with the modern world. His account traces the route map for a new foreign penetration and conquest, much as the "gypsies" pave the way for the banana company, a paradise lost, and a rude awakening from the village slumber. The company colonizes, depletes the soil, and moves on, turning the town's fleeting splendor and illusion of progress into ruins.

In the final scene, Melquíades's prophetic parchments appear to coincide with the novel, as though they were one and the same. Yet the novel could not be a simple translation of the parchments. That perspective merely offers the reader an easy way out of the novel's labyrinthine game. Certainly, when Aureliano Babilonia deciphers his own present as in a "speaking mirror," the parchments converge for an instant with the novel, and the reader with Aureliano, who finish the reading together as though it were the Apocalypse at the end of the world. But the novel and the parchments are not identical. Many details contradict that assumption. Melquíades wrote not only in Sanskrit but also in verse. The novel refers to the parchments in the third person: "Melquíades . . . refused to translate the manuscripts. 'No one must know their meaning until he has reached one hundred years of age,' he explained" (*One Hundred Years* 177).[23] We read that the last adult Aureliano, before deciphering the instant he was living, skipped ahead in his reading, impatient to know his own origin. Had he read about his jumping forward in the parchments, he would have already and prematurely deciphered his own present. The novel speaks about Melquíades in the third person. He is described and quoted in a ladipary voice and a pontificating tone different from those of the folk storyteller. From the very first page, with the introduction of the magnet, the conventions of reality are inverted, as in Sebastian Brant's *Ship of Fools* and the Rabelaisian carnival. Meanwhile, Melquíades's distinctive voice is established: "[E]verybody was amazed to see pots, pans, tongs, and braziers tumble down from their places and beams creak from the desperation of nails and screws trying to emerge.... 'Things have a life of their own,' the gypsy proclaimed with a harsh accent. 'It's simply a matter of waking up their souls'" (11).[24] The parchments are supposed to contain only the history of the family, which is merely the center line of the much broader history of Macondo, Latin America, and humanity.

In retrospect, the suspenseful episode of the firing squad and all the ruckus about the ice only serve to distract the reader from the true reason for the Colonel's remembrance, which was not an insignificant block of ice, but rather because it was on that trip that they found out from the gypsies that by the time the novel started, Melquíades, after sailing the Seven Seas and surviving every ailment known to man, had finally "succumbed to the fever on the beach at Singapore and that his body had been thrown into the deepest part of the Java Sea" (25).[25] But his hereditary memory and the alchemy laboratory and parchments he bequeathed to the family return time and again throughout the novel, creating the illusion that he was still alive and immanent in the story.

Who, then, is that genie in the lamp of the parchments that the last Aureliano rubbed; who that omnipresent witness who traverses seven generations of Buendías, as well as Latin American and universal history? The reader will search in vain for the answer to this and other mysteries, but ultimately will be left with the precursors hinted at by García Márquez himself: Scheherazade, Cide Hamete Benengeli, Nostradamus, Magellan, Pigafetta, Humboldt, Orlando, and of course Proteus, son of Neptune, whom Homer called the Old Man of the Sea, also known as the shepherd of the oceans. Like Melquíades, Proteus had the gift of prophecy, but morphed at will in order not to reveal it.

Notes

1. Modern theorization on viewpoint was initially spurred by Heisenberg's "uncertainty principle" (1927) in quantum mechanics and its influence on epistemology. Among other things, it showed that the measurement or results of any two codependent variables will depend on and be relative to the observer's position. The more precisely a particle can be located in space, the less precisely its momentum can be predicted, and vice versa. Since the 1970s, critical studies have additionally gravitated toward Saussurean linguistics and epistemology: "Far from it being the object that antedates the viewpoint, it would seem that it is the viewpoint that creates the object" (Saussure 7).

2. Cervantes's polyphony has long been noted (Ortega y Gasset, *Meditaciones de Quijote*; Castro). E. C. Riley writes, "*Don Quixote* is a novel with multiple perspectives. Cervantes observes the world created by him from the points of view of the characters and the reader in the same measure as the author's" (71).
3. Here we have an unrecognized narratological phenomenon, the case of the narrator gone rogue. I am referring to the rogue or picaro of the picaresque novel, the antihero who comes from the lower echelons of society, blending with the world of the gypsies. *Lazarillo de Tormes* (1554) founded this figure and genre, whose key feature is being a servant of many masters, capable of knowing the intimacies of different types across society and exposing its hypocrisies. It is an attempt at a justified though limited omniscience. Even more apropos is *El Diablo Cojuelo* (1641) by Luis Vélez de Guevara: Don Cleofás opens a bottle, and the mischievous Little Limping Devil of Castilian folk tales leaps out to take the bewitched student on an astral voyage across the buildings and houses of Madrid, satirically exposing (now with full omniscience) the whole carnival of deceit, in accordance with the baroque poetics of *desengaño*, unmasking, undeceiving, but also ascetic disillusionment with the vanities of the world. With Melquíades as author, the picaro becomes the coveted third-person omniscient narrator. The subversive underdog is now on top, in charge of the carousel—a reenactment of the satirical world-upside-down of the medieval carnival.
4. The young García Márquez read the Spanish edition, *La metamorfosis* (Losada, 1938), with a prologue by Jorge Luis Borges and a translation wrongly attributed to the Argentine master as well. By his own admission, Borges ("Un sueño eterno") imitated Kafka in some of his early short stories, later compiled in his landmark collection, *Ficciones* (1955). Borges's engagement with Kakfa's works spanned seven decades, and while he did translate several of Kafka's stories, eventually it was established that *The Metamorphosis* was not one of them (Sorrentino). This came as a disappointment to many readers, including the later García Márquez. There appears to have been a disagreement between Borges, who insisted that *Die Verwandlung* should be translated as "The Transformation," and the editor, who noted that the title, *The Metamorphosis*, was already famous. In the end, an unnamed Spanish translator was chosen over Borges and his Argentine inflection.
5. "Me contaba las cosas más atroces sin conmoverse como si fuera una cosa que acabara de ver. Descubrí que esa manera imperturbable y esa riqueza de imágenes era lo que más contribuía a la verosimilitud de sus historias. Usando el mismo método de mi abuela, escribí *Cien años de soledad*" (*El olor* 30).
6. Until age nine García Márquez lived with his maternal grandparents in the river town of Aracataca, Colombia, founded in 1885. His grandparents had been there from the very beginning. In the novel, which covers roughly from the founding to the author's birth in 1927, he would imagine his grandparents fleeing Ríohacha after a crime of passion and founding Macondo as José Arcadio Buendía and Úrsula Iguarán. The author's birth in 1927 suggests the teasing possibility of his being the novel's postapocalyptic baby born with a pig's tail, the corkscrew that opens the bottle to let out the spiral of history. Even though, proverbially, the author credits only his grandmother, his grandfather, Nicolás Márquez, was also a storyteller. Due to her senility, her tales were no doubt more colorful and fantastic. However, they were not the only influence. In his youth, the author scraped a living selling encyclopedias on foot in the towns along the Magdalena River, which was for him like the Mississippi for Mark Twain and his character Huck Finn. In his travels, García Márquez picked up an abundance of stories and listened to the love tales and legends of the local folk music: *vallenato* (valley-born), which married the tradition of the old Spanish *juglares*

(minstrels) with that of the West African *griots* (bards) who served as community historians and storytellers. Later, García Márquez started his journalistic career at *El Heraldo de Barranquilla*, covering all manner of strange happenings in the region and proposing clever and amusing explanations for the unexplained (gabo.elheraldo.co).

7. "Las estirpes condenadas a cien años de soledad no tenían una segunda oportunidad sobre la tierra" (*Cien años* 351). All English quotations from the novel refer to the translation by Gregory Rabassa (*One Hundred Years*).
8. My translation and emphasis here are meant to highlight the prophetic tone of the verbal form, *is to* (indicative + infinitive), with usage in the potential and imperative moods. "*Lo que quede de aldea en América* ha de *despertar*" (José Martí, "Nuestra América," *La Revista Ilustrada*, 1 Jan. 1891). García Márquez uses the same form of prophetic command throughout his novel (e.g, "was to remember"/"*había de recordar*"), especially to begin the first and second halves of his novel (see note 16), in order to agree with the perspective of Melquíades's prophetic parchments. This is an example of the masterful selection of person, tense, mood, and voice that supports the novel's overlapping perspectives.
9. This "huracán bíblico" (*One Hundred Years* 350) mimics the apocalyptic hurricane-of-history that ends Alejo Carpentier's seminal novel, *The Kingdom of This World* (1949).
10. "El diálogo en lengua castellana resulta falso. Yo siempre he dicho que en este idioma ha habido una gran distancia entre el diálogo hablado y el diálogo escrito. Un diálogo en castellano que es bueno en la vida real no es necesariamente bueno en las novelas. Por eso lo trabajo tan poco" (*El olor* 33–34).
11. "Melquíades no había ordenado los hechos en el tiempo convencional de los hombres, sino que concentró un siglo de episodios cotidianos, de modo que todos coexistieran en un instante" (350).
12. "Muchos años después, frente al pelotón de fusilamiento, el coronel Aureliano Buendía había de recordar aquella tarde remota en que su padre lo llevó a conocer el hielo. Macondo era entonces una aldea de veinte casas de barro y cañabrava construidas a la orilla de un río de aguas diáfanas que se precipitaban por un lecho de piedras pulidas, blancas y enormes como huevos prehistóricos. El mundo era tan reciente, que muchas cosas carecían de nombre, y para mencionarlas había que señalarlas con el dedo. Todos los años, por el mes de marzo, una familia de gitanos desarrapados plantaba su carpa cerca de la aldea, y con un grande alboroto de pitos y timbales daban a conocer sus nuevos inventos" (9).
13. The seven combinations of the three narrative voices are A, B, C, ABC, AB, BC, and AC.
14. For example, critic J. S. Brushwood asserts that this novel "presents a very strange reality, but one that is entirely accessible to the reader, because there are no barriers created by difficult narrative techniques. . . . The author seems to write from inspiration, using what he remembers combined with what he thinks during the writing process. His novel possesses a high degree of spontaneity, not a carefully wrought pattern of meaning" (cited in Levitt 227–28).
15. Emphasis added. Note that the English translation erroneously replaces the prophetic imperative "was to" with the past future "would": "Años después, en su lecho de agonía, Aureliano Segundo había de recordar la lluviosa tarde de junio en que entró en el dormitorio a conocer a su primer hijo" (159).
16. "Aquellas alucinantes sesiones quedaron de tal modo impresas en la memoria de los niños, que muchos años más tarde, un segundo antes de que el oficial de los ejércitos regulares diera la orden de fuego al pelotón de fusilamiento, el coronel Aureliano Buendía volvió a vivir la tibia tarde de marzo en que su padre" (21).

17. "Aureliano, en cambio, dio un paso hacia adelante, puso la mano y la retiró en el acto. 'Está hirviendo', exclamó asustado" (23).
18. "Como si se estuviera viendo en un espejo hablado" (350).
19. García Márquez envisioned Macondo early on. In 1946 at age nineteen, he started writing *La hojarasca* (*Leaf Storm*, 1955), featuring Macondo for the first time. Then came his columns in *El Heraldo de Barranquilla* starting in 1950. The first one, titled "The Giraffe," provided a wealth of vignettes and character studies; the second one, "The House of the Buendías," ran until 1952. Following *La hojarasca*, several of his short works tried different approaches to the world of Macondo, but it was not until he saw Melquíades in the mirror that he found his Sancho Panza, a dialogic parallax from which to narrate his masterwork. "A Very Old Man with Enormous Wings," the personification of a fallen condor caught in a deluge, shares a key element with Melquíades. Both figures pay tribute to Julio Cortázar's signature paradigm: the sudden chance irruption of an extraneous agent that subverts a quiet sanctum—a derivation of surrealism. In 1972, *La hojarasca* appeared in English as *Leaf Storm, and Other Stories*, among them "A Very Old Man." Secondary sources erroneously began dating it to 1955, the publication date of *La hojarasca*, which had not included any additional stories. In 1968 a standalone version of "A Very Old Man" appeared in a periodical, with the explanatory subtitle "A Children's Story." Finally, it was anthologized and dated "(1968)" in *La cándida Eréndira* (1972), a collection comprised of updated artist proofs that never made it into the masterpiece. They were probably written or already in the inkwell before 1965, when the author immersed himself in his pièce de résistance. However, *Innocent Eréndira, and Other Stories* (1978) gathered later tales and excluded "A Very Old Man," because the same publisher had already printed it in *Leaf Storm, and Other Stories* (1972). The original Spanish collection of *La cándida Eréndira*, printed in 1972, channels Cervantes's *Novelas ejemplares* (1613), filled with scenes that never made it into *Don Quixote* (1605, 1615).
20. "Los niños se asombraron con sus relatos fantásticos. Aureliano, que no tenía entonces más de cinco años, había de recordarlo por el resto de su vida como lo vio aquella tarde, sentado contra la claridad metálica y reverberante de la ventana, alumbrando con su profunda voz de órgano los territorios más oscuros de la imaginación.... José Arcadio, su hermano mayor, había de transmitir aquella imagen maravillosa, como un recuerdo hereditario, a toda su descendencia" (13).
21. "Aquel ser prodigioso que decía poseer las claves de Nostradamus" (13). As opposed to the legendary "said to possess" of the English translation, in the original it is Melquíades who claims to possess the keys of Nostradamus, thus preserving his role as unreliable narrator, befitting a circus gypsy, soothsayer, and snake-oil peddler.
22. See www.nobelprize.org/prizes/literature/1982/marquez/lecture/: "Contó que había visto cerdos con el ombligo en el lomo, y unos pájaros sin patas cuyas hembras empollaban en las espaldas del macho ... un engendro animal con cabeza y orejas de mula, cuerpo de camello, patas de ciervo y relincho de caballo. Contó que al primer nativo que encontraron en la Patagonia le pusieron enfrente un espejo, y que aquel gigante enardecido perdió el uso de la razón por el pavor de su propia imagen." On Pigafetta and *One Hundred Years of Solitude*, see Robles; on the *Chronicles of Indies*, Zavala, "*Cien años de soledad*"/; on travelogues, Pratt; on Alexander von Humboldt, González Echevarría; and on ethnography and magical realist narrative, Camayd-Freixas, "Primitivism" and "Theories."
23. "Melquíades ... se negó a traducir los manuscritos. 'Nadie debe conocer su sentido mientras no hayan cumplido cien años', explicó" (161). Note that the English translation refers to Melquíades's age, whereas the original refers to the age of the manuscripts.

24. "Todo el mundo se espantó al ver que los calderos, las pailas, las tenazas y los anafes se caían de su sitio, y las maderas crujían por la desesperación de los clavos y los tornillos tratando de desenclavarse. . . . 'Las cosas tienen vida propia'—pregonaba el gitano con áspero acento—, 'todo es cuestión de despertarles el ánima' " (11).
25. "Melquíades había sucumbido a las fiebres en los médanos de Singapur, y su cuerpo había sido arrojado en el lugar más profundo del mar de Java" (22).

Works Cited

Primary Sources

Asturias, Miguel Ángel. *Hombres de maíz*. Losada, 1949.
Asturias, Miguel Ángel. *Legends of Guatemala*. Translated by Kelly Washbourne, Latin American Literary Review P, 2012.
Asturias, Miguel Ángel. *Leyendas de Guatemala*. Oriente, 1930.
Asturias, Miguel Ángel. *Men of Maize*. Translated by Gerald Martin, Pittsburgh UP, 1995.
Borges, Jorge Luis. *Ficciones* (1955). Emecé, 1956.
Borges, Jorge Luis. *Ficciones*. Translated by Anthony Kerrigan et al., Grove Press, 1962.
Borges, Jorge Luis. "Un sueño eterno." *El País* (Madrid), 3 July 1983, p. 3.
Carpentier, Alejo. *The Kingdom of This World*. Translated by Harriet de Onís, Knopf, 1957.
Carpentier, Alejo. *El reino de este mundo*. EDIP, 1949.
García Márquez, Gabriel. *Cien años de soledad*. Sudamericana, 1967.
García Márquez, Gabriel. *La hojarasca*. Ediciones SLB, 1955.
García Márquez, Gabriel. *Leaf Storm, and Other Stories*. Translated by Gregory Rabassa, Harper & Row, 1972.
García Márquez, Gabriel. *La increíble y triste historia de la cándida Eréndira y de su abuela desalmada*. Barral, 1972.
García Márquez, Gabriel. *Innocent Eréndira, and Other Stories*. Translated by Gregory Rabassa, Harper & Row, 1978.
García Márquez, Gabriel. *El olor de la guayaba: Conversaciones con Plinio Apuleyo Mendoza*. Oveja Negra, 1982.
García Márquez, Gabriel. *One Hundred Years of Solitude*. Translated by Gregory Rabassa, Avon, 1971.
García Márquez, Gabriel, and Plinio Apuleyo Mendoza. *The Fragrance of Guava*. Translated by Ann Wright, Verso, 1983.
Rulfo, Juan. *Pedro Páramo*. Fondo de Cultura Económica, 1955.
Rulfo, Juan. *Pedro Páramo*. Translated by Margaret Sayers, Peden, Grove Press, 1994.
Vélez de Guevara, Luis. *El Diablo Cojuelo: Novela de la otra vida, traducida a ésta* (1641). Castalia, 1988.

Secondary Sources

Bakhtin, Mikhail M. *The Dialogic Imagination: Four Essays*. Translated by Michael Holquist and Caryl Emerson, U of Texas P, 1981.
Bakhtin, Mikhail M. *Rabelais and His World*. Translated by Hélène Iswolsky, MIT Press, 1968.
Barthes, Roland. *S/Z*. Tel Quel, 1970.
Barthes, Roland. *S/Z: An Essay*. Translated by Richard Miller, Hill and Wang, 1975.

Bland, D. S. "Endangering the Reader's Neck: Background Description in the Novel." *Criticism*, vol. 3, no. 2, 1961, pp.121–39.
Booth, Wayne. "Distance and Point-of-View: An Essay in Classification." *Criticism*, vol. 11, no. 2, 1961, pp. 60–79.
Camayd-Freixas, Erik. "Narrative Primitivism: Theory and Practice in Latin America." *Primitivism and Identity in Latin America: Essays on Art, Literature and Culture*, edited by Erik Camayd-Freixas and José E. González, U of Arizona P, 2000, pp. 109–34.
Camayd-Freixas, Erik. *Etnografía imaginaria: Historia y parodia en la literatura hispanoamericana*. F&G Editores, 2012.
Camayd-Freixas, Erik. "Primitivism, Ethnography and Magical Realism." *Magical Realism and Literature*, edited by Christopher Warnes and Kim Sasser, Cambridge UP, 2019, pp. 30–48.
Camayd-Freixas, Erik. "Theories of Magical Realism." *Critical Insights: Magical Realism*, edited by Ignacio López-Calvo, Salem Press, 2014, pp. 3–17.
Castro, Américo. "Cervantes y Pirandello." *La Nación* (Buenos Aires), 16 Nov. 1924.
Chevalier, Maxime. *Folklore y literatura: El cuento oral en el Siglo de Oro*. Grijalbo, 1978.
Chiampi, Irlemar. *O realismo maravilhoso: Forma e ideologia no romance hispanoamericano*. Perspectiva, 1980.
Culler, Jonathan. *Structuralist Poetics*. Cornell UP, 1975.
Eliade, Mircea. *Le mythe de l'éternel retour: Archétypes et répétition*. Gallimard, 1949.
Eliade, Mircea. *The Myth of the Eternal Return: Or, Cosmos and History*. Translated by Willard R. Trask, Princeton UP, 1954.
Friedman, Norman. "Mimetic and Didactic." *Form and Meaning in Fiction*, U of Georgia P, 1975, pp. 102–15.
Genette, Gérard. *Figures III*. Seuil, 1972.
González Echevarría, Roberto. "*Cien años de soledad*: The Novel as Myth and Archive." *MLN*, vol. 99, no. 2, 1984, pp. 358–80.
Gullón, Ricardo. "Gabriel García Márquez and the Lost Art of Story-Telling." Translated by José G. Sánchez. *Diacritics*, vol. 1, no. 1, 1971, pp. 27–32.
Levitt, Morton P. "From Realism to Magic Realism: The Meticulous Modernist Fictions of García Márquez." *Gabriel García Márquez*, edited by Harold Bloom, Chelsea House, 1989, pp. 227–42.
Lubbock, Percy. *The Craft of Fiction*. Viking, 1957.
Ortega y Gasset, José. *Meditaciones del Quijote*. Residencia de Estudiantes, 1914.
Ortega y Gasset, José. *Meditations on Quixote*. Translated by Evelyn Rugg and Diego Marín, Norton, 1963.
Pratt, Mary Louise. *Imperial Eyes: Travel Writing and Transculturation*. Routledge, 1992.
Prince, Gérald. "Introduction á l'étude du narrataire." *Poétique*, no. 14, 1973, pp. 178–96.
Rico, Francisco. *La novela picaresca y el punto de vista*. Seix Barral, 1970.
Rico, Francisco. *The Spanish Picaresque Novel and the Point of View*. Cambridge UP, 1984.
Riley, E. C. *Cervantes's Theory of the Novel*. Clarendon P, 1962.
Robles, Humberto E. "The First Voyage around the World: From Pigafetta to García Márquez." *Gabriel García Márquez*, edited by Harold Bloom, Chelsea House, 1989, pp. 183–201.
Saussure, Ferdinand de. *Cours de linguistique générale* (1916). *Course in General Linguistics*, edited by Charles Bally and Albert Sechehaye, translated by Wade Baskins, Philosophical Library, 1959.
Scholes, Robert, and Robert Kellogg. *The Nature of Narrative*. Oxford UP, 1966.

Sorrentino, Fernando. "La metamorfosis que Borges jamás tradujo." *La Nación* (Buenos Aires), 9 Mar. 1997, pp. 6, 4.

Todorov, Tzvetan. *The Fantastic: A Structural Approach to a Literary Genre*. Translated by Richard Howard, Cornell UP, 1975.

Todorov, Tzvetan. *Introduction à la littérature fantastique*. Seuil, 1970.

Uspensky, Boris. *A Poetics of Composition*. Translated by Valentina Zavarin and Susan Wittig, U of California P, 1983.

Zavala, Iris. "*Cien años de soledad: Crónica de Indias.*" *Homenaje a Gabriel García Márquez*, edited by Helmy F. Giacoman. Las Américas Publishing Company, 1972, pp. 3–11.

Zavala, Iris. "*One Hundred Years of Solitude* as Chronicle of the Indies." *Gabriel García Márquez's* One Hundred Years of Solitude: *A casebook*, edited by Gene H. Bell-Villada, Oxford UP, 2002, pp. 109–26.

CHAPTER 26

MONSTROUS INNOCENCE AND ITS EXPRESSION IN GARCÍA MÁRQUEZ'S TALES

MARY LUSKY FRIEDMAN

GABRIEL García Márquez cannot let go of the motif of the vulnerable outsider. Each of the three books of tales he published between 1962 and 1992 offers more than one telling of a newcomer's reception in a community to which he does not belong. "La siesta del martes" ("Tuesday Siesta") and "Un día después del sábado" ("One Day after Saturday") in *Los funerales de la Mamá Grande* (*Big Mama's Funeral*, 1962); "Un señor muy viejo con unas alas enormes ("A Very Old Man with Enormous Wings") and "El ahogado más hermoso del mundo" ("The Handsomest Drowned Man in the World") in *La increíble y triste historia de la cándida Eréndira y de su abuela desalmada* (*The Incredible, Sad Tale of Innocent Eréndira and Her Heartless Grandmother*, 1972); and nearly all of the texts in *Doce cuentos peregrinos* (*Strange Pilgrims*, 1992) narrate the indignities, outright violence, and occasionally, kindness with which new arrivals to a community are met.[1]

Surely García Márquez's fellow feeling with his vulnerable protagonists underlies his retellings of what amounts to a paradigmatic Garcíamarquezian plot. Facile though it is to identify this empathetic impulse, one can study the many versions of this single fiction to a further end: to explore García Márquez's evolution as a writer of tales, as a stylist, and as a sensibility. From a lapidary realist bent on exposing social ills in a Colombian town similar to the Aracataca of his birth, he becomes the genius of magical realism and the poetic grotesque in the mid-1960s. Then, in a third phase of his career, he de-emphasizes magical realism, distilling from his earlier writings what might be called "monstrous innocence." Monstrous innocence is a crucial feature of García Márquez's texts.

Previous critics have done much to characterize what is distinctive in García Márquez's work. Stephen Hart, in a recent essay focusing on the Colombian's short fiction, identifies five features of García Márquez's finest narrative:

1. Magical realism . . .; 2. the portrayal of time as a truncated, or dislocated reality rather than an historical continuum . . .; 3. the use of punchy dialogue often

characterized by lapidary one-liners . .; 4. the use of a humor which is often absurd and sometimes black; 5. the portrayal of events in such a way that they may be interpreted as a political allegory. (129–30)

Although magical realism counts as only one of the five attributes that Hart points out, he lists it first, and one may note that two other techniques—the treatment of time and the use of allegory—also lead away from realism. In a similar vein, a great many critics of García Márquez´s tales explore his debt to nonrealistic narrative genres like myth, legend, fairy tale, and the archetypes found in religion.[2] Though not all of these studies elucidate stories that are magical realist, taken altogether they imply that what is most "Garcíamarquezian" in García Márquez´s writing is its assimilation of culturally significant nonrealistic works.

In what follows, I take a different tack. To my mind, what is most singular in García Márquez´s work—realistic and magical realist texts alike—is not his linking of incongruent registers of thought (the magical and the real). It is his conjoining of two incongruent moral categories, on the one hand innocence and on the other the monstrous. As we shall see, each of these categories finds multiple expression in his writings. The purpose of this essay is to reveal different avatars of monstrous innocence in parallel stories of outsiders written at three stages in García Márquez´s career, and to ask why García Márquez found monstrous innocence so compelling.

"Monstrosity" and "innocence," as García Márquez conceives them, are terms that bear defining, but it is best to proceed by seeing how their meaning changes over time. A good place to start is "Tuesday Siesta," written in 1958, one of the first outsider narratives he composed. The town the story depicts does violence to two outsiders, first a thief and then the thief´s mother. By the time the story begins, the thief has been killed, shot in the face by Rebeca, the old woman whose house he was trying to rob. The story's protagonist, however, is a second outsider, the bereaved mother who travels to the town with her twelve-year-old daughter to lay flowers on the young man's grave. Too poor to stay in the town overnight, she must visit the cemetery during the heat of the day so as to catch the train when it returns later in the afternoon, and she goes straight to the priest's house to borrow the graveyard's key. He has already lain down for his siesta and must get up to receive her. In no mood to extend pastoral sympathy, he offers the mother no condolence but asks instead why she did not impart better morals to her son and presses her for alms she cannot give. The woman does not wither under his assault. When she adds her own surname "Ayala" to "Carlos Centeno" as she identifies her son, she quietly affirms her bond with him, and she rebuts the priest's criticism. As the mother and girl prepare to leave for the cemetery, the priest's sister realizes that a crowd has gathered outside, with self-righteous nosiness, to gawk at the criminal's kin. The story ends at its dramatic peak as mother and daughter, their dignity intact, emerge from the curate's house to brave the people's censure and the stifling midday heat, a metaphor for the town's opprobrium.

Where is innocence in "Tuesday Siesta," and where monstrosity? It is easy to see that no one character embodies both. The priest's callousness is monstrous. Like the mayor in "Un día de estos" ("One of These Days," 1962) and the eponymous Big Mama in other tales from the same book, he abuses his power. The mother and daughter embody innocence, and not merely because they are blameless. The woman's vulnerability—to poverty, to grief, and to the mistreatment by the priest—is an essential component of Garcíamarquezian innocence. As for her daughter, she is innocent because she is a child. So unworldly that she has never before that day traveled on a train, she seems not quite attuned to the enormity of the moment. Unselfconsciously, she unbuckles the strap on her Mary Jane as she waits for her mother to finish with the priest.

Blameless, vulnerable, and childlike. "Tuesday Siesta" permits us to link these three attributes to Garciamarquezian innocence. To uncover further insight about innocence in "Tuesday Siesta," one must compare the story to the opening passage of García Márquez's autobiography, *Vivir para contarla* (*Living to Tell the Tale*, 2002). There García Márquez recounts an experience that without any doubt inspired the story, a journey he took with his mother in 1950 to Aracataca so that she could sell the house where he was born. Gabo's journey back to his source holds pride of place in his memoir because it detonated in him deep nostalgia for the childhood he had lost. "That innocent journey of only two days," he reflects, "would prove so decisive for me that the longest and most diligent of lives wouldn't be enough for me to finish telling about it" (*Vivir* 11; my translation,).[3]

What are the parallels between memoir and tale? Like the girl in "Tuesday Siesta," Gabo accompanies his mother on a very hot train on which they are the only passengers. Both Carlos Centeno's mother and Luisa Santiaga de Márquez are prematurely aged and wear mourning. And like her fictional counterpart, Gabo's mother is poor, so poor she has asked her impecunious son to pay for their trip. Yet she is "imperturbable" (*Living* 20). "Seeing her endure that brutal journey without complaint," García Márquez recalls, "I wondered how she had been able to confront so quickly and with so much dignity the injustices of poverty" (*Vivir* 14; my translation).[4] Carlos Centeno's mother, similarly unbowed with her back held erect against the seatback, "bore the conscientious serenity of someone accustomed to poverty" (100).[5]

García Márquez uses several of the same phrases in both accounts. The train traverses "un trepidante corridor de rocas bermejas" (*Todos* 135; *Vivir* 24) ("a bone-shaking corridor of bright red rock" [*Living* 16]), then passes among rows of banana trees that are "simétricas e interminables" ("symmetrical and interminable"), and trundles through identical villages as soot drifts into the third class car. When both sets of travelers reach their destination, they get off the train in an "estación abandonada cuyas baldosas empezaban a cuartearse por la presión de la hierba" (*Todos* 137; *Vivir* 30) (a "deserted station whose tiles were beginning to crack under the pressure of the grass" [*Living* 21].) The phrase is identical in autobiography and tale, though in the story, which of course was written first, the triumph of grass over paving tile presages the mother's quiet insistence, which the priest cannot turn aside. In contrast, the crumbing tiles in the memoir are one index of Aracataca's economic woes. The withdrawal of the United Fruit Company decades before has plunged the region into depression.

In his autobiographical account, it is at this point that García Márquez thought of the thief—he really existed—whose death he retells in "Tuesday Siesta" and of the robber's mother and sister. Taking stock for the first time of the "drama of the woman and the girl" and of the woman's "imperturbable dignity" (*Living* 23), he walks with his own mother down the same street the woman had trod, and at the same sweltering time of day. "The feeling of being forsaken [*desamparo*] became unbearable," he reports. "Then I saw myself and I saw my mother just as I saw, when I was a boy, the mother and sister of the thief whom María Consuegra had killed with a single shot one week earlier, when he tried to break into her house" (*Living* 22).[6]

Although, as this passage shows, he first identifies with the girl, soon he tells his mother, "'I feel as if I were the thief'" (*Living* 23).[7] Perhaps he means that at this moment, when both he and his mother report experiencing fear, he feels annihilated by stress; the thief was the first dead body he had ever seen. But is Gabo a thief? The memoir flirts with this idea. On the way to the Márquez house, his mother and he visit an old friend of hers. The woman's husband had terrified Gabo when he was a boy because he had caught Gabo stealing mangoes. But this petty thievery, which, after all, Gabo remembers *after* he felt like the thief, only hints at the real thing the twenty-two-year-old García Márquez was trying to make off with: nothing less than his own future.

The *cantus firmus* underlying the entire account of Gabo's journey to Aracataca with his mother is his father's extreme displeasure that his oldest son had dropped out of law school to become a writer. She has enlisted his company not just for moral support on what was no doubt a painful mission, but also, and especially, to insist that he return to his father's good graces by earning his degree. The rebellious Gabo's rift with his father threatens to be irreparable, for he stubbornly resists his mother's arguments each of the many times she pressures him. He is determined to be a writer.

Moreover, the loss of family relationships looms over the journey for a second reason. The house of Colonel Nicolás Márquez, Gabo's grandfather and his first great friend, was the place where Gabo had been happy until the age of eight. He had not set foot in it since his grandfather died. Now his mother intended to sell it. Small wonder that on the journey Gabo evokes key memories of his grandfather, one of them the sound of a nighttime brawl in which, he later found, his grandfather might have been killed. Pain at family separation thoroughly imbues the journey to Aracataca that García Márquez will later fictionalize in "Tuesday Siesta." We shall see that nearly all of his stories about vulnerable outsiders foreground the loss, and, in happier texts, the recovery of family ties.

In "Tuesday Siesta," the mother's loss of her son stands at the story's core. That is to say, the widow Rebeca's lethal reception of Carlos Centeno Ayala and, later, his mother's mistreatment by the priest, do not altogether capture the essence of their vulnerability as Garcíamarquezian outsiders. Yet this story conveys a triumph of maternal love, and García Márquez uses four evocations of a vulnerable outsider, expressed as the image of a supplicant at a door, to enact in physical terms the mother's solidarity with her son. Both Carlos Centeno and his mother have problems getting into a house. The young man is killed as he tries to pick a lock. His mother, standing at the priest's door, finds herself in the same posture as her son, as she peers through an opaque screen and tries to persuade the priest's sister to let her in. The cemetery's gate is still another entrance she needs to get through. And since the cemetery's large, rusty keys are made to invoke those of Saint Peter, we are drawn to imagine Carlos Centeno's soul standing at heaven's portal, his admittance to the precinct of the blessed barred.

"Tuesday Siesta," then, repeats the image of a vulnerable outsider in order to reaffirm the affective tie between a mother and her dead son. The other story in *Big Mama's Funeral* that inscribes the motif of the vulnerable outsider is "One Day after Saturday" and it, too, centers on a young man's suddenly impaired relationship with his mother. He has left home for the first time in his life to act as his mother's advocate as she applies for a pension. Entrusted with the documents needed to process her claim, he inadvertently betrays his mother's trust by leaving the papers on the train when he gets off in a strange town for lunch. The train leaves without him. So heedless is he that it takes him many hours to realize he has made a terrible mistake.

The nameless boy's sin against his mother is monstrous. At the same time, however, he exemplifies innocence. Crucially, it is in this text that García Márquez first combines the two traits in a single vulnerable outsider. To appreciate that García Márquez views the feckless newcomer as innocent, one must widen one's view of the story. A rambling, disconcertingly long tale, "One Day after Saturday" develops material that García Márquez will later consolidate in *Cien años de soledad* (*One Hundred Years of Solitude*, 1967). Of the story's three main characters—the boy, a cranky old woman, and a senile priest—the latter two will reappear in the novel as Rebeca Buendía and Father Antonio Isabel. The lives of the three abut only slightly against one another. Yet on the last page what we have taken as a series of character studies suddenly coheres, and the boy emerges as the key figure.

Both the querulous Rebeca and the foggy-headed priest appear in the story long before the boy does. García Márquez describes how each of the two takes belated cognizance of a plague of birds that are falling out of the sky because of the heat. The story opens as Señora Rebeca, in high dudgeon, storms into the mayor's office to complain that someone has ruined her window screens. Rebeca's outrage and self-centeredness keep her from seeing at first that the mayor is mending his own screens. But he tells her that heat-struck birds, not vandals, have crashed through screens all over town, seeking respite from the heat in the coolness to be found indoors. The birds are the story's first-mentioned vulnerable outsiders.

We meet Father Antonio Isabel as he finds a dead bird on a bench at the train station, where he habitually goes to meet arriving trains. It is the third dead bird he has found. In a flash of lucidity, he connects the three, but it is not until a fourth bird falls at his feet that he takes action. This bird, he sees, is still alive, and he knocks on the nearest door—Rebeca's—to sue for help. He asks her to help him revive the expiring creature, but the hard-hearted widow dunks the bird in a glass of water and then shakes it roughly. The bird dies under her ministrations.

At first, the plight of the birds has not struck the priest as something worthy of a sermon. Then, when he detects the stench of their corpses, he wonders (hilariously) whether he should compose a homily about sins of olfaction. More and more, however, he feels that the birds portend something ominous. An earthquake? A storm? The Apocalypse? Suddenly, with a jolt of misguided recognition, he exclaims, "The

Wandering Jew!" Seized by the conviction that the birds presage a visitation of the Wandering Jew, he sets out to write the sermon of his life. He will tell his flock he has seen that monster of depravity, an outcast cursed to wander the world because he is guilty of mocking Jesus on the way to Calvary.

It is now, at the story's halfway point, that the boy descends from the train and enters the tale. We will come to associate him both with the helpless birds (he has enjoyed tending his mother's chickens, and his hat has "alas," which means both "hat brim" and "wings") and with the Wandering Jew, but first we follow him to the hotel, where he orders lunch, is pestered by a young girl, and realizes he has lost his mother's papers. Despite the heat, he keeps tight hold of his hat, a birthday gift from his mother. In fact, when he goes to Mass the following day, he offends Father Antonio Isabel by not removing the hat in church. But the priest does perceive how forlorn the boy is. He tells his acolyte to collect an offering from the congregation and to say it will be used "to expel the Wandering Jew." Then, he tells his assistant, he should give the alms to the hapless boy sitting in the back pew: "'You tell him that it's from the priest, and that he should buy a new hat'" ("One Day after Saturday" 172).[8] The reader, partly because of the priest's two-part instruction and partly because of the boy's guilt, connects the boy with the Wandering Jew. And we feel how terribly the priest's intended empathy miscarries. Precisely when the boy is panicked at having caused a breach with his mother, the priest proposes he give up the tangible symbol of her love.

These two realistic stories from *Big Mama's Funeral* cast both innocence and monstrosity as traits of individual characters. With García Márquez's advance into the magical realism of *One Hundred Years of Solitude*, he conceives of innocence in a new way. Drawing on his rediscovery of Aracataca, he compounds the folk beliefs of his grandmother and great aunts with the naiveté that was his as a small child. From these two sources, he forges a fictional, premodern worldview whose innocence attaches to the town as a whole. Newly founded, "Macondo was a village of twenty adobe houses, built on the bank of a river of clear water that ran along a bed of polished stones, which were white and enormous, like prehistoric eggs. The world was so recent that many things lacked names, and in order to indicate them it was necessary to point" (1).[9] Only a stern anthropologist could fail to be seduced by this pure, apparently prelapsarian community whose people, still inventing language itself, point like children. Macondo's youthful patriarch, José Arcadio Buendía (his name contains "Arcadia" and "good") is both moral—he locates each house the same distance from the river—and capable of wonder at something as simple as ice. What is more, the storytelling voice shares the ingenuousness of Macondo's residents. The pleasure we derive from magical realism arises from that ingenuousness and the comic dissonance it creates between Macondo's innocence and our own worldview.

One Hundred Years chronicles the arrival in Macondo of scores of outsiders. And, it must be said, a few of them—the orphaned Rebeca and Pietro Crespi, to name two– resemble vulnerable outsiders in the mold of the Garcíamarquezian paradigm I am examining here. Other newcomers, most notably the North Americans with their Banana Company, are sinister and exploit the town. However, it is not outsiders who embody monstrous innocence in the novel; it is the Buendías themselves. The family is cursed with incest, and each member has a fatal idiosyncrasy that damns him or her to solitude. Amaranta's self-destructive guilt, Colonel Aureliano Buendía's shyness and pride, and Aureliano Segundo's self-indulgence are among the most salient examples.

Monstrous innocence appears not just in the novel's characters but in the prose itself. García Márquez employs countless stylistic techniques in *One Hundred Years*. One of them, I think, inscribes monstrous innocence on the level of language by juxtaposing the poetic and the grotesque. Here is one example: as José Arcadio Buendía and his men hacked their way through an enchanted jungle looking for a route to the outside world, they "felt overwhelmed by their most ancient memories in that paradise of dampness and silence, going back to before original sin, as their boots sank into pools of steaming oil and their machetes destroyed bloody lilies and golden salamanders" (11–12).[10] Bloody lilies! Lilies and salamanders! This is an unpleasant paradise indeed. The passage continues with further juxtapositions of the gorgeous and the spoiled. Still in the jungle, the men awake from a deep sleep to behold a ship lodged in the midst of the forest. "Before them, surrounded by ferns and palm trees, white and powdery in the silent morning light, was an enormous Spanish galleon. Tilted slightly to the starboard, it had hanging from its intact masts the dirty rags of its sails in the midst of its rigging which was adorned with orchids. The hull, covered with an armor of petrified barnacles and soft moss, was firmly fastened into a surface of stones" (12).[11] The wondrous powdery morning light, the orchids and soft moss, coexist with dirty, tattered sails and petrified barnacles.

In *One Hundred Years*, poetic grotesqueness most often appears in descriptions of sexuality and death. Meme receives her lover, Mauricio Babilonia, "trembling with love among the scorpions and butterflies" (297).[12] And the delicate yellow flowers that rain down as nature mourns the death of José Arcadio Buendía smother animals in the street. Remedios the Beauty ascends to heaven amid "beetles and dahlias" (243),[13] and the putrefying corpse of Fernanda's father, long dead and covered with evil-smelling sores, simmers in his coffin "in a frothy stew with bubbles like live pearls" (219).[14]

García Márquez's habit of conjoining the repulsive and the beautiful as a kind of stylistic shorthand for monstrous innocence is particularly evident in the next two iterations of his paradigm of the vulnerable outsider. The title of one, "The Handsomest Drowned Man in the World," illustrates this oxymoronic technique. Both that story and "A Very Old Man with Enormous Wings" bear the composition date of 1968 in García Márquez's next volume of tales, *Innocent Eréndira*. Both texts figure among the most arresting and successful works of García Márquez's magical realism. They are related narratives. Not only does each portray the arrival in a small coastal town of a magical real creature—a decrepit angel in one case and an enormous drowned man in the other—but each focuses on the host community and on the failings and strengths of its Caribbean popular culture. Moreover, the theme of each tale is the importance of experiencing wonder. One of the towns fails to wonder sufficiently or in the right way at a winged being who, for all his squalor, is divine. The other village does come to wonder at the corpse and awakens imaginatively as a result.

The opening of "A Very Old Man" establishes right away the cultural innocence of the speaker and of the story's fictional world:

> On the third day of rain they had killed so many crabs inside the house that Pelayo had to cross his drenched courtyard and throw them into the sea, because the newborn child had a temperature all night and they thought it was due to the stench. The world had been sad since Tuesday. Sea and sky were a single ash-gray thing ["una misma cosa de ceniza"] and the sands of the beach, which on March nights glimmered like powdered light ["polvo de lumbre"], had become a stew of mud and rotten shellfish. The light was . . . weak ["manso"] at noon. (*Collected* 203)[15]

The matter-of-fact syntax of the first sentence leads us to accept that, after a storm, crabs do scrabble into seaside homes in an unmanageable tide, that people will swat them, and that the smell of their rotting bodies may sicken a child. This is vintage magical realism. Animistic descriptions of the bad weather and the light endow the natural world with human qualities, as premodern cultures might do: "The world had been sad since Tuesday." The midday light was "tame." The sea and sky, both gray, are described with poetic but childlike stiltedness as "a single ashen thing." And the sand, as beautiful on calm March nights as "polvo de lumbre"—a ravishing phrase and one that locates the tale among those who think light can crumble—has become a revolting "stew of mud and rotten shellfish." A single thing, the sand, is both lovely and monstrous.

Grotesque, too, is the fallen stranger whom Pelayo finds stuck in the mud of his courtyard. The winged old man is only one degree more extraordinary than the profusion of crabs of which Pelayo and his wife are struggling to dispose. (We may compare the crabs to the plague of birds in "One Day after Saturday," which anticipates the arrival of the boy.) Pelayo, frightened at first, shows his wife Elisenda the helpless creature and, with "mute stupor" they take stock of his bald head, his nearly toothless mouth, his ragged clothes, and his "huge buzzard wings." He looks nothing like an angel. Before long, they "overcame their surprise and in the end found him familiar" (*Collected* 204).[16] When they do not recognize his language, they exert common sense and conclude he is a castaway from a foreign ship sunk in the storm.

The old woman who lives next door tries to set them right. He's an angel, she tells them, come for the child but too weak to carry him off. (The notion that the Angel of Death tumbles from the sky, too feeble to execute his fearful mission, is an inspired comic idea.) Nothing in the rest of the story contradicts the neighbor's insight; once the angel is grounded, the health of the baby improves, and the visitor really is supernatural, for he takes flight at the end of the story. In this comic inversion of the Garcíamarquezian paradigm, the vulnerable newcomer is not a child but the grim reaper manqué, and a child is restored to, not severed from, his parents.

Before the angel can escape, he confronts three kinds of ill use. First, townspeople who get wind that Pelayo and Elisenda are harboring an angel rush to see the prodigy. They begin an avalanche of pilgrims from all over the Caribbean who come to express devotion but do so frivolously and without reverence. They peer at the angel, ask him to perform miracles for them, pelt him with fruit peel and stones, and when they fear he may have died, burn his side with a branding iron. They believe so readily in the supernatural that they do not wonder at it. When a circus comes to town, they shift their interest to another spectacle, a spiderwoman. In a world where acrobats fly and a disobedient girl has been changed into a tarantula with a human head, it is hard to tell the freakish from the holy.

The second kind of abuse comes, ironically, from the village priest Father Gonzaga, who fails to recognize God's messenger. Suspicious when the angel knows no Latin, the language of the Catholic Church, the curate warns away his overcredulous flock and undertakes a hairsplitting theological correspondence with ecclesiastical higher-ups. Pedantically following Aquinas, they ask him to specify how many of the winged creature would fit on the head of a pin.

The third kind of mistreatment comes at the hands of Pelayo and Elisenda. They cage him in their chicken coop, reasoning, no doubt, that his wings make him kin to barnyard fowl. What is worse, when they see that a curious multitude has come to see the angel, they build a wall around him and charge admission. Enriching themselves by exploiting their captive, they build a new house but neglect his cleanliness and care.

"A Very Old Man with Enormous Wings," unlike most of García Márquez's works, paints an unsavory picture of Caribbean popular culture, with its ready eye for the supernatural and its carnivalesque penchant for exuberant street life. The last paragraph of the story, it is true, reaffirms the loveliness of the narrator's magical realism. As the angel scrabbles his way into the sky, he digs up the garden with his flailing fingernails "and he was on the point of knocking the shed down with the ungainly flapping that slipped on the light and couldn't get a grip on the air" (*Collected* 210).[17] Nevertheless, the characters prove imaginatively stunted and, in consequence, cruel. Emma Speratti-Piñero has noted this link between the townspeople's imaginative deficiency and their inhumanity. The story, she perceives, "shows . . . that the lack of imagination in recognizing or accepting the extraordinary leads necessarily to a repellent dehumanization or to an increase in the negative aspects of humanity" (551; my translation).[18] Yet a burden of this story is that imagination is hard won; it is very hard for the characters, or for that matter for us, to discern the true nature of something new. Fugitive of a celestial conspiracy? A decrepit hen? A Norwegian with wings? An epistemology class or, in our own day, a student of politics might study this narrative with profit.

"A Very Old Man with Enormous Wings" recounts an opportunity lost, as though the fisherman in the fairy tale who pulls a magic fish from the sea would throw it back with the by-catch. Its sister story, "The Handsomest Drowned Man in the World," uses the same formula of the vulnerable outsider, but to opposite effect. The monstrous innocent, an outsize cadaver crusted over with exotic sea muck, inspires wonder in a tiny town of simple folk; from that wonder flow many salutary effects.

It is the most creative of the residents, the children, who first espy the drowned man's floating form. They cannot make out what it is but, fancifully, they hope it is an enemy ship, and then, detecting no mast, they think it may be a whale. Once it washes up on the beach, they unsqueamishly pick off "the clumps of seaweed, the jellyfish tentacles, and the remains of fish and flotsam" (*Collected* 230)[19] and discover it is a drowned man. Even then, undeterred from inventive play, they spend the afternoon burying and unburying the corpse.

The adult men who find them take charge of the body and sound the alarm but, like the children, evince imaginative innocence; hefting the heavy corpse, they wonder whether it drifted for so long that water has seeped into its bones. Then, taking stock of its hugeness, "they thought that maybe the ability to keep on growing after death was part of the nature of certain drowned men" (*Collected* 230–31).[20] The simplicity of their ideas, which charms the reader, stems from the rudimentary nature of their town, a scant twenty wooden houses perched on an arid cliff. The wind from the sea, so strong that mothers fear it will carry off their children, has scoured away much of the soil. No flowers grow in the stone courtyards, and the dead must be pushed into the sea instead of being buried underground.

While the men make inquiries in neighboring towns to find out who the drowned man is, the women prepare the body for a wake. As they pick "underwater burrs" (my translation)[21] from his tangled hair and scrape his body with fish-scaling tools to remove mud and debris, the women have ample time to think about the drowned man's underwater odyssey: "They noticed that the vegetation on him came from faraway oceans and deep water and that his clothes were in tatters, as if he had sailed through labyrinths of coral" (*Collected* 231).[22] He has traveled widely, while they have not. When they finish cleaning the body, they are breathless with admiration. "Not only was he the tallest, strongest, most virile, and best built man they had ever seen, but even though they were looking at him there was no room for him in their imagination" (*Collected* 231).[23]

Their imagination, however, expands as they sew his burial clothes. Seated in a circle around him, they contemplate his beauty and quietly think. The prose emphasizes their reverie with phrases like "it seemed to them," "they supposed," and (twice) "they thought" (*Collected* 232).[24] They conjure up for themselves what might have been. If the dead man had lived among them, he would have had the finest house, his wife would have been the happiest woman, he would have summoned fish from the sea and water from the rocks, and he would have sown flowers on the cliffs. The women's musings lead them through a "maze of fantasy" (*Collected* 232)[25] until the oldest among them, suddenly compassionate, remarks, "He has the face of someone called Esteban" (*Collected* 232).[26]

The reader laughs out loud at the unexpectedness of her pronouncement, and at its seeming arbitrariness. But the plain name "Esteban" suits the forthright character that the women imagine for the man who lies before them. Collectively, they endow him not just with a name but with an identity. It occurs to them that Esteban's hugeness must have been a burden to him. As their empathy blossoms, the prose changes character, abandoning for the rest of the tale the omniscient third person and flowing from voice to voice without quotation marks to convey the new mental freedom of the women, a freedom later shared by the whole town:

> They could see him in life, condemned to going through doors sideways, cracking his head on crossbeams, remaining on his feet during visits, not knowing what to do with his soft, pink, sea lion hands while the lady of the house looked for her most resistant chair and begged him, frightened to death, sit here, Esteban, please, and he, leaning against the wall, smiling, don't bother, ma'am, I'm fine where I am, ... just to avoid the embarrassment of breaking up the chair, and never knowing perhaps that the ones who said don't go, Esteban, at least wait till the coffee's ready, were the ones who later on would whisper the big boob finally left, how nice, the handsome fool has gone. (*Collected* 233)[27]

Ultimately, the women pass from compassion to grief. When their husbands return with the news that no one is missing from the surrounding towns, they find their wives sobbing and wailing for a man they never knew. Though the men are jealous, they quickly join their wives in pitying Esteban: "[T]here he was, stretched out like a shad [my translation], shoeless, wearing the pants of an undersized child" (*Collected* 235).[28] They mourn him sincerely and arrange a splendid funeral. Their vulnerable outsider has, of course, lost his own family, but rather than consign him to the sea in this orphaned state, the villagers appoint parents, aunts, uncles, and cousins for him. Then, bound together by this adoptive consanguinity, they resolve to become worthy of their guest; wonder has spawned magnanimity and corrected the "narrowness of their dreams" (*Collected* 236).[29] The town forges a sympathy so profound with the being who, in the story's first line, is described as a "dark, secret promontory" (my translation), that it becomes itself a "promontory of roses" (*Collected* 236).[30]

These two "outsider" stories from *Innocent Eréndira* are at base about the capacity for wonder, and wonder is integral to the aesthetic experience. One reason García Márquez prizes monstrous innocence is that, for him, it has to do with the making and appreciating of art. As he continues to deploy his paradigm in his last book of stories, *Strange Pilgrims* (1992), his focus shifts somewhat. Unlike his earlier collections, *Strange Pilgrims* has a unifying idea. As García Márquez notes in his prologue, all have Latin American protagonists who experience "strange things" in Europe (viii). Each of the twelve stories, in this sense, centers on a vulnerable outsider prey to unexpected harm at the hands of Spaniards, Swiss, Italians, Germans, or French: a Colombian bride pricked by a rose on her wedding day bleeds to death in a Paris hospital; a Colombian father whose daughter's corpse does not decay gets the runaround from the Vatican when he tries to have her canonized; and a young Mexican woman whose car breaks down near Barcelona is interned by mistake in a mental hospital. Throughout the book, García Márquez endows his Latin Americans with attractive imaginative éclat and casts Europeans as inflexible or hidebound. However, beyond trying to cope with cultural rigidities, his "pilgrims"[31] from the New World contend with death. The critic Rubén Pelayo notes, "Of the twelve short stories comprising this collection, only three do not portray death itself," and tallies the book's "total death toll" as sixty-eight (141). One can see that García Márquez processes in these texts a preoccupation with humankind's ultimate vulnerability.

Two of the *Pilgrim* stories, "Buen viaje, señor presidente" ("*Bon Voyage*, Mr. President") and "Diecisiete ingleses envenenados" ("Seventeen Poisoned Englishmen"), restate in its complete form the Garcíamarquezian paradigm of the vulnerable outsider. "*Bon Voyage*, Mr. President," in fact, resembles so closely "A Very Old Man with Enormous Wings" that it seems like a remake with a happier ending. The main character, an elderly dictator from a fictional Caribbean country, deposed long before and living in exile in Martinique, travels to Geneva for medical treatment, vulnerable because of his illness but monstrously cavalier in his sense of entitlement. (He steals flowers from the public gardens and leaves miserly tips.)

His Swiss doctors, after exhaustive diagnostic tests, recommend a costly and life-threatening surgery. As he digests his baleful prospects, the once-powerful ex-president encounters only half by chance a genial countryman named Homero Rey. Unbeknownst to him, Homero, an ambulance driver well placed to ferret out medical secrets, has been shadowing him, hoping to profit from his death; Homero supplements his meagre income with commissions earned as intermediary between the very sick and the funeral business. Partly out of sincere fellow-feeling but partly out of self-interest, Homero invites his prospective client to a Caribbean dinner at his home.

Homero and his wife, a fiery Puerto Rican named Lázara Davis, stand poised to assume the same mercenary role as Pelayo and Elisenda in "A Very Old Man." Lázara, in particular, is ill-disposed toward her guest, whose unlikable arrogance she at once detects. Little by little, however, she relents toward the sick old man as she discovers how destitute he really is. When the dictator, to save his own dignity, asks Homero to pawn the jewelry that is the only residue of his fortune, it is Lázara who haggles for the best price with a jeweler who points out that all of the gemstones are fake. And when she sees that the president launders his own underwear and hangs it to dry in the mansard that is the only accommodation he can afford, she gives in to pity and takes home his wet clothes to iron them herself. In the end, Homero and Lázara dip into monies earmarked for their own children in order to help pay the president's medical bills. That is to say, they treat him as family. The story ends as they send him back to the Caribbean and wish him bon voyage.

This dictator, unlike his counterpart in *El otoño del patriarca* (*The Autumn of the Patriarch*, 1975), triumphs temporarily over his mortality. A second story that treats with comic grace a Latin American's attempt to manage death is "María dos Prazeres." Although only traces of the outsider paradigm figure in this narrative, its first scene reprises the encounter at the front door of a young man and an old woman that proved so lethal to Carlos Centeno in "Tuesday Siesta." The story begins as María, a retired Brazilian prostitute who has lived most of her seventy-six years in Barcelona, opens the door of her well-appointed flat to "a timid young man wearing a checked jacket and a tie with birds in different colors" (*Strange* 97).[32] (We recall that birds in "One Day after Saturday" are pitifully vulnerable, and this young visitor wears no overcoat though it is a cold spring day.) Although his punctuality—it is 8:00 in the morning—has brought him to their appointment before María has finished her toilette, she has the advantage of him, with her "pitiless yellow eyes" and "laugh sharp as hail." As he meekly wipes his feet on her jute welcome mat and bows ceremoniously to her, María strikes him as "a merciless old lady who at first glance seemed a madwoman" (*Strange* 97).[33]

However, unlike Rebeca Buendía, she is neither fey nor dangerous, and the young man has come not to steal from her but to sell her a burial plot. That is to say, García Márquez here softens (or parodies) his own schema, as he does in "Bon Voyage, Mr. President." María has summoned him because she has had a presentiment that she will die before Christmas and is taking methodical steps to put her affairs in order. We smile both at the mundane commercialization of death that purchasing a gravesite implies and at María's requirements for a resting place. Most important to her is to be buried lying down, and on a site high enough so that it will never flood. Vividly, she "remembered with an ancient horror the graveyard in Manaus under the October rains, when tapirs splashed among nameless tombs and adventurers' mausoleums.... One morning, when she was a very little girl, the Amazon in flood had become a sickening swamp, and in the courtyard of her house she had seen the broken coffins floating with pieces of rag and the hair of the dead coming through the cracks" (*Strange* 99).[34] Small wonder that María is eager to control her own burial! The young salesman, equipped with his collapsible pointer, unfolds on the dining room table a huge diagram of Montjuic Cemetery and locates hilltop graves. He offers a civilized, European death, sans tapirs.

María's other pressing task is to make provision for her little dog, Noi. From the name of her pet—"Noi" means "boy" in Catalan—we see that the dog is María's surrogate child, her sole family. She finds a suitable neighbor to adopt Noi after she dies. Even more importantly, she trains the little dog to cry, and to find his own way to Montjuic Cemetery so that he can visit her grave and mourn. This touch of magical realism in a largely realistic text bears testament to María's solitude.

The story ends unexpectedly. As it has opened with a doorstep scene, it ends with one, as well. María has been caught in a storm on her way home from the cemetery. Drenched, carrying Noi in her arms, she looks in vain for a taxi or bus. Suddenly, "when even a miracle seemed impossible" (*Strange* 111),[35] a sleek, grey limousine stops for her. The window rolls down "as if by magic"[36] and the chauffeur asks where she is going. "'To Gracia,'" she replies (*Strange* 112)[37]. That is her neighborhood, but her destination, we already sense, is a different state of grace. As, on her way home, María takes stock of her rescuer, she admires his curly hair and "profile of a Roman bronze" (*Strange* 113).[38] He is an adolescent, and she thinks to herself that "his mother must feel very happy when she heard him walk in the door" (*Strange* 113).[39] Self-conscious, she feels old and bedraggled, and when they reach her address she clambers out of the car "with as much dignity as her body would allow" (*Strange* 113).[40] To her astonishment, when she turns to thank her benefactor, he is staring at her with desire. "'Can I come up?'" he asks (*Strange* 113).[41]

At this point the reader must decide whether the young man personifies Death (as she climbs the stairs to her door, María feels "choked by a fear she would have thought possible only at the moment of death" (*Strange* 114)[42] or offers a moment of passion that it has been worth her life, "so many years, ... so much suffering in the dark, if only to live that moment" (*Strange* 115).[43] Whichever is the case, the story ends with a marvelous and unsought experience of pleasure.

Another story that upends our expectations of how death arrives is "Miss Forbes's Summer of Happiness."[44] We immediately identify the innocents in this work as two boys, nine and seven years old, the elder of which narrates the tale. Their father is a Latin American writer reminiscent of García Márquez himself. He permits his sons delightful freedoms when the family summers on Pantellaria, an island just south of Sicily. Happy under the tutelage of a young diving instructor name Oreste, the boys learn to deep-sea dive, and with their father explore sunken torpedoes and underwater classical ruins. (Here, as in other Garcíamarquezian texts, the sea contains wonders, not the least of which is the handsomest drowned man, Esteban.) Each night after dinner the family's cook, the joyous, unruly, and extravagantly named Fulvia Flaminea, invites the boys to her house to listen to the sounds that waft over the water from nearby Tunis. Her husband takes the boys on evening adventures hunting rats.

This heady regimen comes to an abrupt end when the boys' parents depart for a five-week cruise, leaving them in the charge of a German governess. The draconian Señora Forbes is a monster: "She arrived in that southern heat wearing combat boots, a dress with overlapping lapels, and hair cut like a man's under her felt hat. She smelled of monkey urine" (*Strange* 148).[45] In one of *Strange Pilgrims*'s many jibes at Europeans, their father tells them, "'That's how every European smells, above all in summer.... It's the smell of civilization'" (*Strange* 148).[46] Curtailing the boys' every pleasure and subjecting them instead to Shakespeare and good table manners, she imposes iron discipline. Though she makes splendid desserts, she withholds them if, according to the strict point system she institutes, the boys have not met muster. What is worse, she is a hypocrite. When the boys go to bed, she indulges herself with sybaritic pleasures: her own desserts, their father's wine, forbidden films, and midnight swims. The boys hear her singing and sobbing without restraint and declaiming Schiller in German until dawn.

One day the boys return from the beach to find an "enormous sea serpent nailed by the neck to the door frame. Black and phosphorescent, it looked like a Gypsy curse with its still-flashing eyes and its sawlike teeth in gaping jaws" (*Strange* 141).[47] The boys are terrified. In their panic, they do not pause to think that Oreste, whom they have seen spearing octopuses with his knife, may have left the creature as a frightful practical joke. Señora Forbes, too, is taken aback when she sees the corpse, so much so that she speaks to the children in German. To regain her own composure, she scolds the boys for screaming. Then, at dinner that night, the monstrous governess compels them to eat the other monster, the one from the sea. The narrator's brother throws up. That night, with childlike clarity of conscience, the seven-year-old makes up his mind to kill the sadistic Señora Forbes.

The boys have dredged up from the seabed a Roman amphora containing ancient wine, which their father has pronounced poisonous. Together, the brothers fill their father's decanter with the potion, and watch in suspense for several days. Finally, Señora Forbes drinks it. The following morning, the boys rise early and go to the beach, certain to be free of their nemesis. Sure enough, when they return to the house hours after no one has summoned them to lunch, the police have arrived and the neighbors have assembled for a wake. With a sudden pang of guilt, the boys approach Señora Forbes's bedroom and, before Fulvia Flaminea can intercept them, catch a glimpse of the woman they are convinced they have murdered. To their (and the reader's) surprise, she is covered in blood, stabbed twenty-seven times "with the fury of a love that found no peace" (*Strange* 156).[48] Oreste has been her lover, and it is he who has killed her. Although the children never implicate their young diving instructor as the murderer, the reader infers that Oreste, who wears six knives on his belt during deep-sea dives, is responsible both for Señora Forbes's summer of happiness and for her death. She has confided to the children's parents that "it was impossible to imagine a more beautiful human being" than Oreste (*Strange* 142).[49] What is more, the name "Oreste" brings to mind Aeschylus's matricidal Orestes, a young man who kills a woman older than he. Whoever kills her, Señora Forbes plays the role of monster, but in her need for love proves innocent as well. Vulnerability, here as always in García Márquez's work, renders innocent the most heinous of villains.

Most of the *Pilgrim* stories, like the three examined here, treat death with wry humor and, insofar as García Márquez does recur to his paradigm of the outsider, he undercuts its menace. Both in its preoccupation with death and in its mellowness, this collection resembles *El amor en los tiempos del cólera* (*Love in the Time of Cholera*, 1985).

What can we learn from examining the series of tales, written over a span of thirty years, in which García Márquez tells again and again about a vulnerable outsider who arrives in a strange town? First, that he identifies unreservedly with the outsider. In the touchstone autobiographical event from which his paradigm sprang, he *was* an outsider re-encountering Aracataca. Equally important, though, we can observe García Márquez developing a personal habit of mind—a predisposition to conjoin the innocent and the monstrous—that becomes the hallmark of his sensibility and his art. During the emotionally fraught journey to Aracataca, Gabo found both qualities in himself. Sudden nostalgia for a privileged childhood made him feel with immediacy the innocence of his first eight years. At the same time, he hardened his defiance of his father. Whether he felt (monstrous) guilt at rebelling against his father's wishes, we will never know. But he might have sensed that the artist he aspired to be would need to transgress, at least in spirit, as well as to cultivate the imaginative innocence that permits the experience of wonder. The fictional artists García Márquez would later create confirm this intuition. Baltazar, maker of the world's most beautiful birdcage, is an innocent, and Melquíades, author of Macondo's history, is benevolent. But Jeremiah de Saint-Amour, the chess master and photographer of children who kills himself in the first chapter of *Love in the Time of Cholera*, has eaten human flesh. And the magician who narrates "Blacamán the Good, Vendor of Miracles" ("Blacamán el bueno, vendedor de milagros") uses his supernatural powers to torture the mentor who has betrayed him.

Yet García Márquez's early versions of the "outsider" paradigm do not connect monstrous innocence to his artistic métier. They locate innocence in the new arrivals and the source of harm in individual townspeople. Quickly, García Márquez defines innocence not just as absence of guilt but also as childlikeness and, crucially, "desamparo" (vulnerability). What is more, by the paradigm's second iteration, "One Day after Saturday," he fuses monstrosity and innocence in a single person, the flustered but guilty boy cast as the Wandering Jew.

Then García Márquez takes a giant step. He extends both innocence and monstrosity to a whole community, Macondo. With his turn to magical realism in *One Hundred Years of Solitude*, he mines Colombian folk culture to create a *collective* innocence shared by characters and narrator alike. When he again takes up the "outsider" paradigm in his magical realist stories "A Very Old Man with Enormous Wings" and "The Handsomest Drowned Man in the World," monstrous innocence attaches both to the vulnerable new arrival and to the town that receives him. It is the towns' behavior that García Márquez explores.

These two stories cast the extravagant outsiders as a cause for wonder and introduce the idea that a wholesome community fosters imaginativeness. *Strange Pilgrims*, which depicts Latin Americans as imaginatively superior outsiders prey to European hosts, continues this idea. Although this use of the "outsider" paradigm unifies the volume, one feels that the original urgency of his schematic story has faded away. The real topic of *Strange Pilgrims* is man's need for dignity in the face of death. In the three stories I have discussed, García Márquez deploys his "outsider" paradigm in unexpected, comic ways to deflect the menace of mortality.

A vignette in one of the *Pilgrim* stories sums up a good deal about García Márquez´s fascination with two kinds of monstrous innocence: one afforded by the spectacle of death and the other, a countervailing one, by art. "Seventeen Poisoned Englishmen" begins as Prudencia Linero, an unworldly Colombian widow on a pilgrimage to Rome, arrives in Naples. Never before, in her seventy-two years, has she ventured outside her native Riohacha, and as her ship pulls into port, she feels more and more alone and ill at ease, "[suffering] for the first time in her life the sharp pain of being a foreigner" (*Strange* 118).[50] Suddenly, her gaze falls upon a drowned man in the water. "Señora Prudencia Linero saw him drifting faceup, a mature, bald man of rare natural distinction with open joyful eyes the color of the sky at dawn" (*Strange* 118).[51] He is dressed for a wedding, a gardenia in his lapel, but his "pale iron fingers" clutch at the bow of a small, square gift "which was all he had found to hold on to at the moment of his death" (*Strange* 118).[52] Though no one around her seems much concerned, Prudencia Linero is horrified. Immediately thereafter, however, she catches sight of an old magician doing tricks on the crowded pier. From the pockets of his shabby coat he pulls a profusion of baby chicks, which pour onto the dock as the heedless crowd tramples them. But unlike the wedding guest, many of the chicks do not die. They are magical.

Like these vulnerable magic chicks, the outsider stories that García Márquez lets loose into the world have a life of their own. We should wonder at them.

Notes

1. References to García Marquez´s stories will be to *Todos los cuentos* with the exception of citations from *Doce cuentos peregrinos*.

2. Among those who relate García Márquez's short stories to these nonrealistic genres are Antonio Benítez Rojo ("Eréndira" [fairy tale]) and, with Hilda Benítez, "Eréndira liberada" (archetype); Emma Speratti-Piñero (rituals of Tammuz, Adonis, and Osiris); Paloma Martínez-Carbajo (ancient Greek myth of Achilles and Penthesilea); Susan Mott Linker (the Bible, myth of Dionysis); Arnold M. Penuel (the subversión of the fairy tale form); and Robin Fiddian.

3. "Aquel cándido paseo de sólo dos días iba a ser tan determinante para mí, que la más larga y diligente de las vidas no me alcanzaría para acabar de contarlo" (11).

4. "Viéndola sobrellevar sin inmutarse aquel viaje brutal, yo me preguntaba cómo había podido subordinar tan pronto y con tanto dominio las injusticias de la pobreza" (14).

5. "Tenía la serenidad escrupulosa de la gente acostumbrada a la pobreza" (*Todos* 156).

6. "La sensación de desamparo se me hizo insoportable. Entonces me vi a mí mismo y vi a mi madre, tal como vi de niño a la madre y la hermana del ladrón que María Consuegra había matado de un tiro una semana antes, cuando trataba de forzar la puerta de su casa" (*Vivir* 32).

7. "Me siento como si yo fuera el ladrón" (*Vivir* 33).

8. "Di que es para desterrar al Judío Errante . . . le dices que ahí le manda el padre para que se compre un sombrero nuevo" (*Todos* 218).

9. "Macondo era entonces una aldea de veinte casas de barro y cañabrava construidas a la orilla de un río de aguas diáfanas que se precipitaban por un lecho de piedras pulidas, blancas y enormes como huevos prehistóricos" (*Cien años* 7).

10. "Se sintieron abrumados por sus recuerdos más antiguos en aquel paraíso de humedad y silencio, anterior al pecado original, donde las botas se hundían en pozos de aceites humeantes y los machetes destrozaban lirios sangrientos y salamandras doradas" (*Cien años* 17–18).

11. "Frente a ellos, rodeado de helechos y palmeras, blanco y polvoriento en la silenciosa luz de la mañana, estaba un enorme galeón español. Ligeramente volteado a estribor, de su arboladura intacta colgaban las piltrafas escuálidas del velamen, entre jarcias adornadas de orquídeas. El casco, cubierto con una tersa coraza de rémora petrificada y musgo tierno, estaba firmemente enclavado en un suelo de piedras" (*Cien años* 18).

12. "Temblando de amor entre los alacranes y las mariposas" (*Cien años* 305).

13. "Los escarabajos y las dalias" (*Cien años* 250).

14. "[E]n un espumoso y borboritante caldo de perlas vivas" (*Cien años* 226).

15. "El mundo estaba triste desde el martes. El cielo y el mar eran una misma cosa de ceniza, y las arenas de la playa, que en marzo fulguraban como polvo de lumbre, se habían convertido en un caldo de lodo y mariscos podridos. La luz era . . . mansa al mediodía" (*Todos* 245i).

16. "Callado estupor"; "alas de gallinazo granado"; "se sobrepusieron muy pronto del asombro y acabaron por encontrarlo familiar" (*Todos* 245–46).

17. "Y estuvo a punto de desbaratar el cobertizo con aquellos aletazos indignos que resbalaban en la luz y no encontraban asidero en el aire" (*Todos* 252).

18. "Muestra . . . que la carencia de imaginación para reconocer o aceptar lo extraordinario desemboca necesariamente en una repelente deshumanización o en un acrecentamiento de los aspectos negativos de la humanidad" ("De las fuentes," *Collected* 551).

19. "Los matorrales de sargazos, los filamentos de medusas y los restos de cardúmenes y naufragios" (*Todos* 273).

20. "Pensaron que tal vez la facultad de seguir creciendo después de la muerte estaba en la naturaleza de ciertos ahogados" (*Todos* 273).
21. "Abrojos submarinos" (*Todos* 274).
22. "Notaron que su vegetación era de océanos remotos y de aguas profundas, y que sus ropas estaban en piltrafas, como si hubiera navegado por entre laberintos de corales" (*Todos* 274).
23. "No sólo era el más alto, el más fuerte, el más viril y el mejor armado que habían visto jamás, sino que todavía cuando lo estaban viendo no les cabía en la imaginación" (*Todos* 274).
24. "Les parecía"; "suponían"; "[p]ensaban que" (*Todos* 274–75).
25. "Dédalos de fantasía" (*Todos* 275).
26. "Tiene cara de llamarse Esteban" (*Todos* 275).
27. "Lo vieron condenado en vida a pasar de medio lado por las puertas, a descalabrarse con los travesaños, a permanecer de pie en las visitas sin saber qué hacer con sus tiernas y rosadas manos de buey de mar, mientras la dueña de la casa buscaba la silla más resistente y le suplicaba muerta de miedo siéntese aquí, Esteban hágame el favor, y él recostado contra las paredes, sonriendo, no se preocupe, señora, así estoy bien . . . sólo para no pasar por la vergüenza de desbaratar la silla, y acaso sin haber sabido nunca que quienes le decían no te vayas, Esteban, espérate siquiera hasta que hierva el café, eran los mismos que después susurraban ya se fue el bobo grande, qué bueno, ya se fue el tonto hermoso" (*Todos* 276).
28. "Allí estaba tirado como un sábalo, sin botines, con unos pantalones de sietemesino" (*Todos* 277).
29. " La estrechez de sus sueños" (*Todos* 278).
30. "Promontorio oscuro y sigiloso" (*Todos* 273); "promontorio de rosas" (*Todos* 279).
31. The word "pilgrim" in the title *Strange Pilgrims* refers not only to the protagonists but also to the texts themselves, an idea patent in the Spanish title *Doce cuentos peregrinos*. Notes and early drafts of these stories traveled widely with their author. During the eighteen years he worked intermittently on them, García Márquez moved several times, carrying the project with him.
32. "Un joven tímido con una chaqueta a cuadros y una corbata con pájaros de colores" (*Doce* 137).
33. "Ojos amarillos y encarnizados"; "carcajada de granizo"; "a primera vista le pareció una loca" (*Doce* 138).
34. "Se acordó con un horror muy antiguo del cementerio de Manaos bajo los aguaceros de octubre, donde chapaleaban los tapires entre túmulos sin nombres y mausoleos de aventurEros. . . . Una mañana, siendo muy niña, el Amazonas desbordado amaneció convertido en una ciénaga nauseabunda, y ella había visto los ataúdes rotos flotando en el patio de su casa con pedazos de trapos y cabellos de muertos en las grietas" (*Doce* 139).
35. "Cuando ya parecía imposible hasta un milagro" (*Doce* 152).
36. "Por un soplo mágico" (*Doce* 152).
37. "A Gràcia" (*Doce* 153).
38. "Perfil de bronce romano" (*Doce* 153).
39. "Su madre debía ser muy feliz cuando lo sentía volver a casa" (*Doce* 153).
40. "Con tanta dignidad como el cuerpo se lo permitiera" (*Doce* 154).
41. "—¿Subo?" (*Doce* 154).
42. "Sofocada por un pavor que sólo hubiera creído posible en el momento de morir" (*Doce* 155).
43. "Tantos y tantos años, y haber sufrido tanto en la oscuridad, aunque sólo hubiera sido para vivir aquel instante" (*Doce* 155–56).

44. The title in Spanish is "El verano feliz de la Señora Forbes." Following Hispanic custom, the children address their caretaker as "señora" as a title of respect. Edith Grossman has translated "Señora" as "Miss" because the governess is not married.
45. "Llegó con unas botas de miliciano y un vestido de solapas cruzadas en aquel calor meridional, y con el pelo cortado como el de un hombre bajo el sombrero de fieltro. Olía a orines de mico" (*Doce* 196–97).
46. "Así huelen todos los europeos, sobre todo en verano. . . . Es el olor de la civilización" (*Doce* 197).
47. "Una enorme serpiente de mar clavada por el cuello en el marco de la puerta, y era negra y fosforescente y parecía un maleficio de gitanos, con los ojos todavía vivos y los dientes de serrucho en las mandíbulas despernancadas" (*Doce* 189).
48. "Con la furia de un amor sin sosiego" (*Doce* 206).
49. "Era imposible concebir un ser humano más hermoso" (*Doce* 190).
50. "Padeciendo por primera vez en su vida la punzada de ser forastera" (*Doce* 161).
51. "La señora Prudencia Linero lo vio flotando bocarriba entre dos aguas, y era un hombre maduro y calvo con una rara prestancia natural, y sus ojos abiertos y alegres tenían el mismo color del cielo al amanecer" (*Doce* 161).
52. "Dedos de hierro lívido"; "que era lo único que encontró para agarrarse en el instante de morir" (*Doce* 161).

Works Cited

Benítez Rojo, Antonio. "Eréndira, o la Bella Durmiente de García Márquez." *Cuadernos Hispanoamericanos*, no. 448, Oct. 1987, pp. 31–48.

Benítez Rojo, Antonio, and Hilda O. Benítez. "Eréndira liberada: La subversión del mito del macho occidental." *Revista Iberoamericana*, vol. 50, nos. 128–29, July–Dec. 1984, pp. 1057–75.

Fiddian, Robin. "Legend, Fantasy and the Birth of the New in *Los funerales de la Mamá Grande* by Gabriel García Márquez." *A Companion to Magical Realism*, edited and introduced by Stephen M. Hart and Wen-Chin Ouyang, Tamesis Books, 2005, pp. 210–21.

García Márquez, Gabriel. *Cien años de soledad*. Editorial Diana, 1986.

García Márquez, Gabriel. *Collected Stories*. Translated by Gregory Rabassa and J. S. Bernstein, Harper Perennial, 1991.

García Márquez, Gabriel. *Doce cuentos peregrinos*. Sudamericana, 1992.

García Márquez, Gabriel. *Living to Tell the Tale*. Translated by Edith Grossman, Alfred A. Knopf, 2003.

García Márquez, Gabriel. *One Hundred Years of Solitude*. Translated by Gregory Rabassa, Harper Perennial, 1991.

García Márquez, Gabriel. *Strange Pilgrims*. Translated by Edith Grossman, Penguin Books, 1993.

García Márquez, Gabriel. *Todos los cuentos*. 2nd ed. Debolsillo, 2012.

García Márquez, Gabriel. *Vivir para contarla*. Diana, 2002.

Hart, Stephen. "García Márquez's Short Stories." *The Cambridge Companion to Gabriel García Márquez*, edited and introduced by Philip Swanson, Cambridge UP, 2010.

Linker, Susan Mott. "Myth and Legend in Two Prodigious Tales of García Márquez." *Hispanic Journal*, vol. 9, no. 1, Fall 1987, pp. 89–100.

Martínez-Carbajo, Paloma. "Aquiles y Pentesilea o la señora Forbes y el deseo insatisfecho." *Hispanet Journal*, no. 3, 2010, pp. 1–17.

Pelayo, Rubén. "The Magic of Love, the Horrors of Death and Other Themes in the Short Stories of Gabriel Gracía Márquez." *Gabriel García Márquez in Retrospect: A Collection*, edited and introduced by Gene H. Bell-Villada, Lexington Books, 2016, pp. 129–45.

Penuel, Arnold M. "A Contemporary Fairy Tale: García Márquez' 'El rastro de tu sangre en la nieve" *Studies in Twentieth Century Literature*, vol. 19, no.2, Summer 1995, pp. 239-55.

Speratti-Piñero, Emma. "De las fuentes y su utilización en 'El ahogado más hermoso del mundo.'" *Homenaje a Ana María Barrenechea*, edited by Lia Schwartz Lerner and Isaías Lerner, Castalia, 1984, pp. 549–55.

CHAPTER 27

FATE AND FREE WILL IN *CHRONICLE OF A DEATH FORETOLD*

PHILIP SWANSON

WHILE there is a degree of critical excess with regard to the notion of magical realism as manifested in the works of Gabriel García Márquez, the debates around the concept largely boil down to the binary tension inscribed in the term. For some, the *magical* is associated with fantasy, myth, literariness, and the unknowability of reality. For others, the idea of *realism* suggests the need to see through fictitious versions of reality as constructed by hegemonic social, political, historical, and philosophical discourses. *Crónica de una muerte anunciada* (*Chronicle of a Death Foretold*, 1981) is very much about fate, religion, and ambiguity, but it also seems to encourage the challenging of convention and the assertion of an independent identity. Thus, the "magic" of the human imagination and its ability to imagine alternative ways of being is a potential pathway to a new reality. The novel's title suggests both the entrapping circularity of an almost mystical destiny ("a Death Foretold") and the investigative desire to recuperate historical truth ("Chronicle"). The death at the heart of this novel is inevitable because of an honor code rooted in religious and social conformity, and there is a strong performative, as well as ritualistic or sacrificial, dimension to the planning of the death. Behind all this is the idea that the magic of love itself has become little more than a social contract and, in that sense, has ceased to be "real." The investigation of the detective-like chronicler (into a real event now being transformed into a fiction) implies a quest for a kind of "truth," and the final outcome is the achievement of a species of "true" love, independently chosen. It appears that agency and authorship are mobilized in *Chronicle of a Death Foretold* to test the limits of fatalism and convention. However, that testing is also "con-tested" and ultimately opened to further questioning and rendered uncertain.

As is well known, *Chronicle of a Death Foretold*, is based on real events and is presented as an attempt to reconstruct and illuminate those events. On January 22, 1951, in the town of Sucre, a young student from a well-off family, Cayetano Gentile Chimento, was hacked to death by two brothers, Víctor and Joaquín Chica Calas. They were avenging their family honor after their sister, Margarita, was returned to her family on the night of her wedding by her new husband, Miguel Reyes Palencia. Cayetano was accused of relieving her of her virginity prior to the marriage. García Márquez had family connections with some of the protagonists of the scandal, but in his rendering of it, the identities and some of the details are changed.[1] In the novel, in an unnamed town, a young heir to a substantial family fortune, Santiago Nasar, is murdered by the Vicario brothers, Pablo and Pedro, following the doomed marriage of their humble sister Ángela to wealthy Bayardo San Román. The narrator—seemingly a version of García Márquez himself—returns to the case nearly thirty years later in an attempt to understand, chronicle, and explain what happened and why. García Márquez, of course, had a long and distinguished career as a journalist (often an investigative one) and had already published, for example, his documentary narrative exposé *Relato de un náufrago* (*The Story of a Shipwrecked Sailor*) in 1970, based on a series of investigative articles originally composed in 1955 for the newspaper *El Espectador*.[2] *Chronicle of a Death Foretold* may be a novel, or a fictionalized version of reality, but it carries the weight of the techniques of investigative journalism and presents itself as a project to try to get to the bottom of what really took place.

Yet the investigative journalistic approach is offset by ambiguity, uncertainty, and the language of magical realism. The narrative is not fantastic as in *Cien años de soledad* (*One Hundred Years of Solitude*), nor linguistically hyperbolic as in *El otoño del patriarca* (*The Autumn of the Patriarch*). If anything, the style is methodical, full of closely observed detail, relatively accessible and essentially realistic. Yet the story of Santiago Nasar's death is an unlikely tale of how virtually everyone in the town (except the victim) knows he is going to die, and how, either by accident or occasional design, they fail to warn him. Moreover, Ángela, who had no time for Bayardo San Román, actually falls in love with him after his rejection of her, and even more improbably, following a seventeen-year campaign of nearly two thousand love letters, eventually wins him back. The exaggeration of magical realism is also present in the description of the "delirious" extravagance of the wedding, with its massive scale, imported ballet company, two waltz orchestras, and two thousand bottles of liquor, or in, say, the breakfast of the local brothel madam, consisting of "a Babylonic platter of things to eat: veal cutlets, a boiled chicken, a pork loin, and a garnishing of plantains and vegetables that would have served five people" (*Chronicle* 38, 77–78).[3] Ángela Vicario weeps for three days straight (93), while her brother Pedro does not sleep for eleven months (80). In a classic instance of the deadpan narration of extraordinary occurrences, a young servant girl shakes the pillow case of Santiago's father (in which he conceals his gun) "and the pistol went off as it hit the floor and the bullet wrecked the cupboard in the room, went through the living room wall, passed through the dining room of the house next door with the thunder of war, and turned a life-size saint on the main altar of the church on the opposite side of the square to plaster dust" (4).[4] Soft magical elements abound, such as Santiago's mother's "well-earned reputation as an accurate interpreter of other people's dreams, provided they were told her before eating" (2)[5] or the narrator's mother's own ability to know already how things will turn out before she is told (21). Also, there are various other references to the supernatural, such as when the soul of the widow Xius's dead wife confirms in her own handwriting during a séance that she has been pilfering knickknacks from their old family home (87–88).

There is something mildly comical about these magical tropes, in a way jarringly at odds with the darkness of the subject matter. Of course, one conventional view of magical realism is that it is empowering, privileging the worldview of a remote semirural community over that of metropolitan rationality. Here, though, many of the gnomic magical utterances come across as inconsequential, gesturing at a depth of meaning that they simply do not have: Plácida Linero's observation that her son, Santiago, "was always dreaming about trees" (1);[6] her remark that "any dream about birds means good health" (4);[7] the advice of Ángela's mother, Purísima del Carmen, to her daughters not to "comb your hair at night" so as not to "slow down seafarers" (31).[8] And what is the significance of Santiago Nasar's "magical talent for disguises" (66)?[9] Anything at all? As Raymond Leslie Williams has noted (Williams 119), the investigative journalistic chronicle abounds in facts and details (obvious examples are the often rigorous fixing of the time of day in the chronology of the crime or the semiclinical documentation of Santiago's autopsy [75–76]), but omits answers to questions of crucial importance: most notably, who did take Ángela's virginity? Williams even goes so far as to see *Chronicle of a Death Foretold* as a "postmodern" text, about its own narrative process and resolution, about "the story's coming into being" (121). This echoes Carlos Alonso's earlier characteristically theoretically sophisticated, if rather self-serving, quasi post-Structuralist reading of the novel as, on the one hand, a structural re-enactment of the crime and, on the other, a text "guided primordially by a performative rather than a logical or teleological drive" (Alonso 153).

While reading against the grain may be entertaining, it might be more helpful to see García Márquez's fictional works rather as an unresolved tension between sincerity and human inconsistency. The journalistic dimension is clearly present in the present narrative. Indeed, García Márquez has often stressed the value of the journalistic aspect of his career, waxed lyrical about the links between journalism and literature, and claimed that his 1981 novel represented the perfect coming together of the two (see, for example, Hart 14). This suggests a desire to apprehend reality while at the same time inevitably blurring reality and fiction. The investigative journalist, who has so far depended largely on inherently ambiguous spoken testimonies, finally locates the judge's brief—but he only gets access to 322 pages of a document that must have been more than 500 pages long. Not only is the evidence incomplete, it is possibly of limited reliability, since a reading of it reveals that the "judge was a man burning with the fever of literature," who, with reference to the Nasar case, "never thought it legitimate that life should make use of so many coincidences forbidden [to] literature" (*Chronicle* 100).[10] Reality may be distorted by the human imagination, it seems, yet equally, fact may be stranger than fiction.

Fact and fiction are also the stuff of the detective novel, and it has been widely remarked that *Chronicle of a Death Foretold* emulates this genre, as it pursues its investigative path. Does the detective format suggest the pursuit of truth? Well, the embrace of popular genres such as detective fiction has been seen as a characteristic feature of the

Latin American post-Boom as it, to some degree, reacts against the complexity and tortuous ambiguity of the New Novel of the Boom. Established New Novelists like Carlos Fuentes, Mario Vargas Llosa, José Donoso, and García Márquez, alongside emerging figures like Manuel Puig and Luisa Valenzuela, all produced experimental variations on the crime novel between the late 1970s and early 1990s. This development represents both a movement away from fantasy toward reality in a post-Boom context, but also promotes a questioning of the mystery-resolution model of traditional detective fiction in the context of a lack of confidence in the notion of justice in many parts of Latin America, as well as a residual sense of metaphysical or at least epistemological and, increasingly, ontological anxiety.[11] This heady combination of resolution and the lack thereof is very much at the heart of *Chronicle of a Death Foretold*.

Detection often depends on evidence (which may or may not exist, be found, or be properly understood) and witnesses (whose memories of events may or not be accurate or at least reliable). Ángela states that Santiago Nasar was the one who took her virginity, but there is no evidence for this; it seems an unlikely pairing, and it is not clear if the act was consensual or one of rape. The truth is never established. Santiago's death is delayed because he leaves his house, unusually, from the opposite door to that at which the Vicario brothers are lying in wait for him: "[I]t was for such an unforeseen reason that the investigator who drew up the brief never did understand it" (50).[12] One of the narrator-investigator's first interviews is with Plácida Linero. She is lost in old age and confuses the narrator with "the memory of Santiago Nasar" (5).[13] The narrator reflects that he has "returned to this forgotten village, trying to put the broken mirror of memory back together from so many shattered shards" (5).[14] When he later tries to establish the facts of the story of Bayardo San Román's first encounter with Ángela Vicario from his former landlady and her clients, "three people who had been in the boarding house confirmed that the episode had taken place, but four others weren't sure" (28).[15] The motif of the unreliability of memory (and therefore of the investigative process) is perhaps most consistently brought out by the disagreements about the weather on the day of Santiago's murder. Right from the start until near the end, there are repeated references to conflicting recollections: some think it was radiantly sunny, while others think it was grey and rainy. Again, the truth is never established. Even the evidence of the eyes cannot be trusted. Detection is often linked to close observation. However, time after time, various townsfolk observe the Vicario brothers preparing for the crime, talking about it and lying in wait for Santiago, yet they repeatedly discount this evidence and do not believe their own eyes and ears. Santiago's mother looks out of the door and blocks it when she sees the Vicario twins launch their attack, not realizing that she is actually blocking the escape route of her own son, who is just outside her field of vision. Even the probably innocent Santiago does not seem to understand what he is witnessing or why this is happening to him when he looks down at the entrails he clutches to his stomach and observes his own death (102). And, of course, the evidence of the unstained matrimonial bedsheet and the broken hymen is visual evidence of Santiago's offence to the Vicarios' honor—only it is not: the visual proof tells us nothing about the perpetrator of the act, and that truth remains unknown.

The detective also traditionally connotes mastery, authority, and control. In the classical model, he solves the mystery, identifies the culprit, and restores normality in the wake of the fissure opened in the social order. Even in the North American hard-boiled model, the moral integrity of the near-chivalric private eye and the intellectual knowledge of resolution remain intact despite the societal corruption that surrounds the detective. García Márquez said of *Chronicle* that he was able to "exercise a rigorous control" over it (Mendoza 89).[16] Indeed, the novel is very tightly constructed, and on top of the careful assembly of testimony, the narrator-investigator actually displays full omniscience on a few occasions (for example, when he appears to penetrate the inner thoughts of Ángela and Santiago [47, 101–2]). Yet despite this power, the narrator does not appear to be a particularly good detective. He fails to identify Ángela's real lover or rapist and fails to identify the person who delivered an anonymous note attempting to warn Santiago of what was going to happen. He even falls asleep during the crucial run-up to the crime and misses the opportunity to witness anything (69). In any case, the "detective" has no real case to crack; the identity of the killers is known in advance and made clear from the outset. The authority of the investigator is even further undermined by the possibility of his own complicity. Critics have drawn attention to García Márquez's fascination with Sophocles's *Oedipus Rex* as the detective story par excellence, and in which the hero discovers his own guilt or the detective discovers that he is the murderer (see, for example, Corwin 88, 96 via Pellón). This destabilizing of the innocence and external perspective of the detective has something of a tradition (even in the likes of Agatha Christie), but was to become a prominent feature of postmodern detective fiction like, say, Juan José Saer's *La pesquisa* (*The Investigation*, 1994). In *Chronicle*, the detective is not revealed as the assassin, but some have argued—after noticing close parallels between the narrator and Santiago, some ambiguity of language, and signs of excessive narratorial distancing from events—that he is compromised by being the possible deflowerer of Ángela Vicario (see Hart and Zaidi among others). Given that the narrator must also be identified with García Márquez (there are multiple personal and family allusions, including reference to his future wife Mercedes Barcha), this goes beyond mere unreliable narration and radically problematizes the authority of the author himself.

The reliability of the detective genre as a conduit to reality is tempered anyway by its very generic or literary quality. It is, above all, a fictional form. In fact, the Vicarios' crime is itself something of a fiction in that it is a species of performance: the twins clearly do not want to kill Santiago and therefore act out their plans and intentions very publicly in the hope of being dissuaded or prevented from executing them (e.g., 49, 57). Moreover, if the preexistence of generic conventions implies a lack of full authorial control, there is even a hint that the author or narrator figure is not fully in command of the genre he appears to be manipulating. In a sense, the detective genre is displaced or usurped by the love story genre, as the narrative slips into the tale of Ángela Vicario's passionate endeavors to woo Bayardo San Román back to her. After all the scandal, anguish, and drama, it turns out that the couple love each other anyway, thus rendering the entire murder plot pointless.[17] This turn to extravagant sentimental romance (foreshadowing *El amor en los tiempos del cólera* [*Love in the Time of Cholera*] and perhaps revealing García Marquez's true vocation as a novelist of love) rather corrodes the framing narrative of hard-nosed journalistic investigation of reality.

The romantic coming together of the lovers despite the formidable barriers that separate them not only returns us to the realm of literary precedents rather than ones based on concrete external reality, it also raises the idea of destiny and inevitability. The famous "sino solitario" or solitary fate of the Buendía family in *One Hundred Years of Solitude* always risks undermining the novel's social or political charge by implying that life is predetermined or fundamentally unchangeable. Fate is central to this novel, too. The text begins with the phrase, "On the day they were going to kill him" (*Chronicle* 1).[18] Santiago Nasar's fate is sealed before the action even begins, and the phrase is immediately followed by a reference to ill omen in the form of his dream of a happy stroll through a grove of trees before being "completely spattered with bird shit" (1).[19] The bird imagery builds up a fatalistic sense of inevitability. Santiago goes around like "a chicken hawk..., nipping the bud of any wayward virgin" (90).[20] Yet, echoing the novel's epigraph in which medieval Portuguese playwright and lyric poet Gil Vicente warns of "haughty falconry," the narrator cautions Nasar, with a portentous, further citation from Vicente: "*A falcon who chases a warlike crane can only hope for a life of pain*" (65).[21] Toward the end, at the moment of his death, it is said that Santiago "looked like a little wet bird" (116).[22] He is a dead man walking from the start. A victim of "fatal coincidences" (10), his grip is "like the hand of a dead man" (12) and "he already looked like a ghost" (13).[23] In fact, the narrator-investigator at one stage appears to state that his motivation is not "to clear up mysteries" but to achieve "an exact knowledge of the place and the mission assigned to us by fate" (97).[24] The magical, mystical apprehension of fate overshadows everything and undermines the thrust toward realism and illumination.

However, is the very tension between investigation and fate a challenge to magical thinking? That is, is it an implied exhortation to see through all the myth and superstition and countenance historical reality? To use, in other words, the magic of the imagination not for fantastical thought but to envisage an alternative way of perceiving reality? After all, the death of Santiago Nasar is only preordained in the sense that his "fate" is merely a manifestation of the concrete reality of social tradition and the honor code. The Vicario brothers' actions are simply an effect of "the horrible duty that's fallen on them" (57).[25] The idea of a shared destiny, then, is the complicity of the whole of the community with their actions. This is "a death for which we all could have been to blame" (82).[26] Something happens that nobody, including the perpetrators, wants to happen, because they are driven by social conventions that could be challenged but have taken on the quality of immutable givens. Indeed, the entire novel is drenched in notions of ritual behavior: honor, courtship, marriage, religion, class, gender, and ethnicity. Santiago's identity is predetermined because of hereditary factors: he has inherited the characteristics of his Arabic father and Latin mother (6). Yet this dual "inheritance" is really a matter of social codes; he is a victim of ethnic prejudice and Catholic morality. In particular, gender and class norms are the determining factors in this community. With regard to the Vicario family: "The brothers were brought up to be men. The girls had been reared to get married" (30).²⁷ Even emotions are socially constructed. When Ángela is forced into a loveless engagement with a suitable match (described disingenuously as "a prize of destiny" [34]²⁸), she is told: "Love can be learned too" (34).²⁹ Her lower social class is what obliges her to marry the moneyed Bayardo San Román, just as that same class is what makes a dalliance with Santiago Nasar so unlikely. Bayardo's status is such that he can effectively buy Ángela Vicario (38). And there is an implicit political criticism of this status. When he displays his credentials by bringing his family to the town, the star attraction is his father, "General Petronio San Román, hero of the civil wars of the past century, and one of the major glories of the Conservative regime for having put Colonel Aureliano Buendía to flight in the disaster of Tucurinca" (33).³⁰ Readers of García Márquez's earlier works will see this as an allusion (albeit to a fictional character) to an association with negative social and political values. The narrator's mother continues the theme by declining to "shake hands with the man who gave the orders for Gerineldo Márquez to be shot in the back" (13).³¹

The novel's blurring of fiction and reality seems designed, at one level, to draw attention to the essentially fictitious or performative nature of a socially and politically constructed reality. The socially motivated crime at the heart of the novel is itself a fiction, in the sense that the brothers are acting out the preparations in an exaggerated manner precisely so that they can be stopped. Yet the community misreads the signs that the young men exhibit, some thinking that this is no more than a parade of bravado, with the result that the tragedy is not prevented. Is this a hint that it is important not to be blinded by false, fictitious values, not to misread reality? The crime is a public spectacle (like a Greek tragedy), but the viewers are essentially complicit partners in the performance. The viewer, or in this case the reader, needs to break out of that complicity and see through the haze of magical thinking and confront social reality. Perhaps, then, it is the reader (the people, as it were) who must ultimately assume the role of investigator or detective, who must be, in the real world outside the world of fiction, the seeker of truth.

Magic and realism, nonetheless, go side by side or are intertwined in this novel. In a sense, the blending of the two tells us that there is no such thing as incontrovertible reality and no such thing as total fiction. What remains is culture, where performance and reality are hard to separate. An obvious example is the "mourning" of Bayardo San Román's womenfolk:

> They came on a cargo boat, locked in mourning up to their necks because of Bayardo San Román's misfortunes, and with their hair hanging loose in grief. Before stepping onto land, they took off their shoes and went barefoot through the streets up to the hilltop in the burning dust of noon, pulling out strands of hair by the roots and wailing loudly with such high-pitched shrieks that they seemed to be from joy. I watched them pass from Magdalena Oliver's balcony and I remember thinking that distress like that could only be put on in order to hide other, greater shames. (85–86)³²

Emotional life is public here and thus part of culture. Culture is a reality but also a fiction. Hence in this novel real people and events are turned into fictional versions. Thus, as Michael Bell has conjectured (97–98), it is not individual psychology that matters here so much as the collective psyche: the murderous brothers in García Marquez's novel are made to be twins, different individuals who are forced to act collectively despite what their deeper instincts may be telling them.

One obvious manifestation of a collective psyche is attachment to ritual. In *Chronicle*, there are framing concentric circles of ritual: the ritual slaughter of Santiago Nasar, the ritual of a wedding ceremony, the ritual blessing of the bishop on his passing fluvial visit. Within this structure are the embedded rituals of social customs and behaviors, in which even love is expressed through rituals of courtship and honor. The references to the bishop's visit from the start (Santiago goes to witness the bishop's blessing while the twins lie in wait for him on his return) frame the whole of what follows from the perspective of religious ritual in particular. The novel is saturated with religious insinuations: the Spanish title hinting at the annunciation, the surname Vicario (referring to a type of clergyman), the apostolic Christian names of Pedro and Pablo (Peter and Paul), the saintly connotations of San Román, the friend Cristo (Christ) Bedoya, the narrator's sister the nun, the Nasar family's ranch called Divino Rostro (Divine Face), the maid Divina Flor (Divine Flower). Santiago's first name recalls St. James the "Moor Slayer," while his family name Nasar posits him as kind of Nazarene and his ethnicity may hint at a Middle Eastern provenance. If he is a kind of Jesus Christ figure, the public spectacle of his journey from the bishop's boat to his death could be a species of ironic Calvary. The cocks crow as his journey begins (12), and the journey ends with him being nailed to the wood of the door like Jesus on the cross (121). His death cry is like "the moan of a calf" (connoting religious sacrifice), and a knife wound in his hand "looked like the stigmata of the crucified Christ" (120, 76).[33] And like the story of Christ, his story had been "foretold." But Christ's sacrifice brought redemption, and this is what comes to Ángela as she finds feelings of love for another and a kind of spiritual rebirth. Interestingly, she is the Judas figure who betrays the Christ substitute, while those bearing the names of Christ's disciples, Peter and Paul, are his crucifiers. This inversion perhaps points to a rejection of conventional Christian morality and the social codes it supports. At a stretch, the inside-out biblical framework may also situate this "chronicle" as a kind of new gospel, revealing the good news or truth but in inverted form, encouraging the reader and the general populace to see through myth and confront reality.

Ángela Vicario's redemption is arguably the core of the novel's proposed reimagination of human reality. Bell and Mark Millington both read Ángela, to different degrees, as embodying some kind of will to subversion or independence. She has made an active choice (probably) in choosing to have sexual intercourse with a man before marriage; she chooses not to try to cover up the loss of her virginity on her wedding night; she chooses to impose her own version of reality by naming Santiago Nasar (possibly, as her surname hints, vicariously assuming an active and avenging role for all women who have been abused by "chicken hawks" like Nasar, even if he was not literally the cause of her loss of virginity); and she decides to win back Bayardo San Román and succeeds. Reversing the cult of inevitability, "she was reborn" and became "mistress of her fate" (93–94).[34] She is rewarded with true love when she rejects the false or fictional love of conventional marriage and embraces the genuine love of her own free choice. It is worth noting that Ángela was rejected by San Román because of the formality of wounded honor (not necessarily because of a lack of love). Her discovery by herself of the truth of love displaces the male obsession with form and codes, and she is able therefore to lead Bayardo back to a relationship based not on the falseness of convention but on the real thing.

Ángela Vicario, then, can be seen as triumphing by facing reality, facing the truth, and abandoning mindless conformism to the phoniness of customary and internalized behaviors. Interestingly, her pathway to success is also by becoming an author: she takes up intensely creative letter writing to achieve her goal of winning back and enjoying love with Bayardo San Román. Does her epistolary fervor get closer, then, to the "real" than the implied author's chronicle? She is the author figure's creation; she is "authored" by him. Indeed, when she accuses Santiago Nasar, she famously uses the phrase "Fue mi autor" (literally "He was my author," that is, the author of my fate [106][35]). The figure of the submissive, passive, female victim, the "authored" woman is effectively inverted when Ángela becomes mistress of her own fate and becomes an author herself. Has she (vicariously?) usurped the power of the male author and assumed his authority? The male author figure seeks the truth, via his investigative process, but fails to find it. However, the female author does find the truth. Perhaps the real figure of authority or at least authenticity is the one who is willing to see through the magic and find that which is real.

This revelatory insight into reality would be a pleasing way to end. However, García Marquez's texts are never that neatly reductive. Millington would argue, legitimately, that it is important to read against the grain, to offer a "resistant reading," "one not sanctioned by the novel" ("The Unsung Heroine" 162). Unveiling the unconscious omissions, assumptions, and even prejudices behind a text can be revealing. Equally, reading against the grain can dissolve into the over-reading of small pieces of evidence and can stretch credulity. For example, identifying the narrator as the writer of the anonymous letter or the perpetrator of Ángela's "dishonor" may be a clever reading, but there is no real evidence for this, and it is not a necessary position to take. Similarly, to read Santiago Nasar as a Christ figure has a degree of validity, but such a reading is limited in scope: the description of Santiago's death ends the novel, not Ángela's redemption, and Nasar himself does not undergo a symbolic resurrection or emerge as an emblem of salvation like the murdered son in *El coronel no tiene quien le escriba* (*No One Writes to the Colonel*), who is resurrected in the clandestine newsletter that bears his name, *Agustín*, and in the resilient prize cock that fights on in the ring where opponents of the system gather and the newsletter is distributed. In fact, the Christian religious imagery of *Chronicle* alluded to earlier is rather scattered and not really part of any systematic pattern of symbolism. The anxiety-ridden humanities of the twenty-first century often seek to turn literature into a productive form of "useful" social or political commentary. But literature is much more than that, and García Márquez's literature especially so. García Márquez is very much a political figure. He famously once declared that he would not publish another book until Chile's then military dictator, General Augusto Pinochet, left power. When Pinochet did not oblige, the Colombian eventually published *Chronicle*. Yet this does not mean he is insincere or a political fraud. It means he is a writer of literature and a human being, full of strong views, inconsistencies, contradictions, and good and bad points. *Chronicle* is many things at the same time. It is concerned with society and external reality, but it does have an air of metaphysical gloom. It is interested in the idea of truth but is also evasive and occasionally even ingenuous. It is, in other words, a very human novel. It does have social and political bite, but it is above all else a work of literature.

Notes

1. Details are provided, for example, by Hart and Williams based on Roca and Calderón and Roca.
2. For a useful account of García Márquez's journalistic career, see, for example, Sims.
3. "Delirio," "un platón babilónico de cosas de comer: costillas de ternera, una gallina hervida, lomo de cerdo, y una guarnición de plátanos y legumbres que hubieran alcanzado para cinco" (*Chronicle of a Death Foretold* 44, 84). All subsequent references to *Chronicle of a Death Foretold* are followed by page number(s) only.
4. "Y la pistola se disparó al chocar contra el suelo, y la bala desbarató el armario del cuarto, atravesó la pared de la sala, pasó con estruendo de guerra por el comedor de la casa vecina y convirtió en polvo de yeso a un santo de tamaño natural en el altar mayor de la iglesia, al otro extremo de la plaza" (11).
5. "Reputación muy bien ganada de intérprete certera de los sueños ajenos, siempre que se los contaran en ayunas" (9).
6. "Siempre soñaba con árboles" (9).
7. "Todos los sueños con pájaros son de buena salud" (12).
8. "No se peinen de noche que se retrasan los navegantes" (37).
9. "Talento casi mágico para los disfraces" (71).
10. "Era un hombre abrasado por la fiebre de la literatura," "nunca le pareció legítimo que la vida se sirviera de tantas casualidades prohibidas a la literatura" (105, 106).
11. For more on the post-Boom and detective fiction, see Swanson.
12. "Fue por una razón tan imprevista que el mismo instructor del sumario no acabó de entenderla" (57).
13. "El recuerdo de Santiago Nasar" (12).
14. "Volví a este pueblo olvidado tratando de recomponer con tantas astillas dispersas el espejo roto de la memoria" (12).
15. "Tres personas que estaban en la pensión confirmaron que el episodio había ocurrido, pero otras cuatro no lo creyeron cierto" (34).
16. "Ejercer un control riguroso." The English translation is mine.
17. Of course one might argue that this love is one-sided in that Bayardo himself never explicitly expresses his feelings verbally. For more on love, see, for example, Millington, "García Márquez's Novels of Love," and Bell-Villada.
18. "El día en que lo iban a matar" (9).
19. "Por completo salpicado de cagada de pájaros" (9).
20. "Él era un gavilán pollero. Andaba solo . . . cortándole el cogollo a cuanta doncella sin rumbo empezaba a despuntar por esos montes" (96).

21. "*Halcón que se atreve con garza guerrera, peligros espera*" (71).
22. "Un pajarito mojado" (120).
23. "Tantas coincidencias funestas" (17), "como una mano de muerto" (18), "Ya parecía un fantasma" (20).
24. "No lo hacíamos por un anhelo de esclarecer misterios, sino porque ninguno de nosotros podia seguir viviendo sin saber con exactitud cuál era el sitio y la misión que le había asignado la fatalidad" (103).
25. "El horrible compromiso que les ha caído encima" (63).
26. "Una muerte cuyos culpables podíamos ser todos" (88).
27. "Los hermanos fueron criados para ser hombres. Ellas habían sido educadas para casarse" (36).
28. "Premio del destino" (40).
29. "También el amor se aprende" (40).
30. "El general Petronio San Román, héroe de las guerras civiles del siglo anterior, y una de las glorias mayores del régimen conservador por haber puesto en fuga al coronel Aureliano Buendía en el desastre de Tucurinca" (39).
31. "Darle la mano a un hombre que ordenó dispararle por la espalda a Gerineldo Márquez" (39). Gerineldo Márquez is a character in *One Hundred Years of Solitude*. He is the friend and ally of the great Liberal war hero Colonel Aureliano Buendía and the great-great-grandfather of a semiautobiographical character named Gabriel Márquez.
32. "Vinieron en buque de carga, cerradas de luto hasta el cuello por la desgracia de Bayardo San Román, y con los cabellos sueltos de dolor. Antes de pisar tierra firme se quitaron los zapatos y atravesaron las calles hasta la colina caminando descalzas en el polvo ardiente de mediodía, arrancándose mechones de raíz y llorando con gritos tan desgarradores que parecían de júbilo. Yo las vi pasar desde el balcón de Magdalena Oliver, y recuerdo haber pensado que un desconsuelo como ése sólo podia fingirse para ocultar otras vergüenzas mayores" (91–92).
33. "Un quejido de becerro" (123–24), "parecía un estigma del Crucificado" (82).
34. "Nació de nuevo," "dueña por primera vez de su destino" (99).
35. Unfortunately, the official English translation reads: "He was my perpetrator" (101).

Works Cited

Alonso, Carlos. "Writing and Ritual in *Chronicle of a Death Foretold*." *Gabriel García Márquez: New Readings*, edited by Bernard McGuirk and Richard Cardwell, Cambridge UP, 1987, pp. 151–67.

Bell, Michael. *Gabriel García Márquez*. Macmillan, 1993.

Bell-Villada, Gene. *García Márquez: The Man and His Work*. U of North Carolina P, 2010, pp. 204–5.

Corwin, Jay. *Gabriel García Márquez*. Palgrave, 2016.

García Márquez, Gabriel. *Chronicle of a Death Foretold*. Translated by Gregory Rabassa. Penguin, 2014.

García Márquez, Gabriel. *Crónica de una muerte anunciada*. Mondadori, 2002.

Hart, Stephen. *Gabriel García Márquez: Crónica de una muerte anunciada*. Grant and Cutler, 1994.

Mendoza, Plinio Apuleyo. *Gabriel García Márquez: El olor de la guayaba*. Bruguera, 1982.

Millington, Mark. "García Márquez's Novels of Love." *The Cambridge Companion to Gabriel García Márquez*, edited by Philip Swanson, Cambridge UP, 2010, pp. 113–28.

Millington, Mark. "The Unsung Heroine: Power and Marginality in *Chronicle of a Death Foretold*." *García Márquez*, edited by Robin Fiddian, Longman, 1995, pp. 161–79.

Pellón, Gustavo. "Myth, Tragedy and the Scapegoat Ritual in *Crónica de una muerte anunciada*." *Revista Canadiense de Estudios Hispánicos*, vol. 12, no. 3, 1988, pp. 397–413.

Roca, Julio. "Sí, la devolví la noche de bodas." *Al Día*, no. 3, May 1981, pp. 24–27.

Roca, Julio, and Camilo Calderón. "García Márquez lo vio morir." *Al Día*, no. 1, Apr. 1981, pp. 52–60.

Sims, Robert L. "García Márquez's Non-fiction Works." *The Cambridge Companion to Gabriel García Márquez*, edited by Philip Swanson, Cambridge UP, 2010, pp. 144–59.

Swanson, Philip. "Authority, Identity and the Latin American Detective." *Studies in Latin American Literature and Culture in Honour of James Higgins*, edited by Stephen M. Hart and William Rowe, Liverpool UP, 2005, pp. 216–27.

Swanson, Philip. *The New Novel in Latin America: Politics and Popular Culture after the Boom*. Manchester UP, 1995.

Williams, Raymond Leslie. *A Companion to Gabriel García Márquez*. Tamesis, 2010.

Zaidi, Ali Shehzad. "The Hidden Depths of *Crónica de una muerte anunciada*." *Annals of Ovidius University Philology Series*, vol. 23, no. 2, 2011, pp. 107–16.

CHAPTER 28

PATHOLOGY, POWER, AND PATRIARCHY IN *THE AUTUMN OF THE PATRIARCH* AND *THE GENERAL IN HIS LABYRINTH*

HELENE C. WELDT-BASSON

THE theme of power has been at the center of Gabriel García Márquez's work since its inception. Despite the extensive bibliography on the Nobel laureate, to date there is no study that compares his two most important novels on the theme of power: *The Autumn of the Patriarch* (1975; henceforth *The Autumn*) and *The General in His Labyrinth* (1989; henceforth *The General*). I suggest that García Márquez implicitly invites this very comparison through a parallel construction of both works; in other words, each novel contains the same series of elements, but each develops them in the opposite direction. These elements include the physical and mental deterioration of the protagonists, their numerous relationships with women, a dislike for losing at games, the respective protagonists' belief in their own immortality, their attitude toward personal wealth, their intimate knowledge of the lives of the individuals they govern, the assassination attempts on their lives, their solitude, and a series of other minor motifs that connect the two protagonists.

The multiple connections between *The Autumn* and *The General* suggest that there exists a dialogic relationship between these two novels. According to Mikhail Bakhtin:

> Two discourses equally and directly oriented toward a referential object within the limits of a single context cannot exist side by side without intersecting dialogically, regardless of whether they confirm, mutually supplement or (conversely) contradict one another, or find themselves in some other dialogic relationship (that of question and answer, for example). (188–89)

The multiple similarities between the two novels suggest that García Márquez wished to create a dialogue on the topic of power. I show here how each novel reflects on power through the use of the same elements but develops a different vision or type of power.

The Autumn illustrates what social psychology experts term a dominance perspective of power (the exertion of power over people), while The *General* illustrates a functionalist perspective of power (the ability or power to influence people) (Overbeck 21–30).

Before we can examine how García Márquez develops his protagonists in these opposite directions, we should first consider a general definition of power. According to Ana Guinote and Theresa K. Vescio, power is:

> The potential to influence others in psychologically meaningful ways ... through the giving or withholding of rewards and or punishments ... Psychologically meaningful influences include ... effects on the way people feel, think, or behave ... power may be exerted by means of "soft" influence tactics (rewards, charisma, knowledge) or "hard" tactics (e.g., physical punishment). In its strongest form, power confers the ability to control completely outcomes that are valued by others. (2–3)

Jennifer Overbeck refines this definition by delineating the different uses or goals of power: "How is power used and to what end? ... Answers tend to fall into two categories: dominance perspectives, which emphasize a more sinister use of power aimed at coercion and exploitation, and functionalist perspectives, which argue for constructive use aimed at mutual benefit" (21).

García Márquez's two generals (both protagonists are called "El General" in their respective novels, but I use "the Patriarch" for the dictator in *The Autumn* and "the General" for Simón Bolívar in *The General* for purposes of distinguishing between the two here) are constructed as complete opposites despite their mutual obsession with power. The Patriarch is constructed as a mythic figure who allegedly lives to up to 250 years, while the General is based on the life of the hero of Latin American independence, Simón Bolívar, a historical figure who died at age forty-six. While the Patriarch is the illegitimate son of a prostitute, origins he desperately tries to hide in the chapter in which he attempts to have his mother canonized as a saint, the General is a landowner born into high society with great personal wealth. The Patriarch is illiterate, signing documents with his thumbprint until his old age, when Leticia Nazareno finally teaches him to read, whereas we are told that the General is an avid reader "of imperturbable voracity" (92).[1] Although both protagonists fail to remember their wives, in the case of the Patriarch it is because he becomes senile, while the General simply refuses to remember his wife in order to shield himself from pain, until he is on his deathbed: "[H]e had buried her at the bottom of watertight oblivion as a brutal means of living without her" (253).[2] While the Patriarch ruthlessly has the dogs killed in Manuela Sánchez's neighborhood, in the later novel, when street dogs are being poisoned to prevent the spread of rabies, we are told that the General is upset by this because he loves dogs as much as he does "horses and flowers" (172).[3] Finally, whereas the Patriarch refuses to contemplate a successor, the General tries to groom his friend Sucre to carry out his work once he is gone. These numerous inverted parallels pave the way for an analysis of how García Márquez contemplates two opposite visions of power in these two novels.

The first and most central element related to power in both novels is the deterioration that each protagonist undergoes throughout the narrative. In the case of the Patriarch, his deterioration is both physical and mental, whereas in the case of the General, it is only physical. The extensive bibliography on both novels has discussed some aspects of how physical deterioration functions in these works. Patricia Mohen Hart examines the relationship between the Patriarch's incontinence (his herniated testicle and lack of bowel control as elements of incontinence) and the Patriarch's loss of potency and power (1–3). This same connection is made in Mario Vargas's dictator novel, *The Feast of the Goat* with regard to the Dominican dictator Rafael Trujillo.[4] Both Tim Richards and Rosalía Cornejo-Parriego examine the grotesque elements of *The Autumn* in Bakhtinian terms to illustrate how the deteriorating body is used to demystify and critique the protagonist.[5] Olivia Vázquez-Medina explores how the General's body in *The General* "has an organic connection with the 'cuerpo de la nación' [body of the nation]" (555), showing how the novel uses the language of health and disease to describe not only the protagonist's physical decline but also that of Latin American countries.

I suggest that in addition to the loss of power related to physical deterioration that Hart has so aptly signaled in her article, the loss of power experienced by the Patriarch is more strongly associated with his mental pathology. The Patriarch's senility is portrayed as grotesquely as is his physical deterioration, casting a negative light on his power. In contrast, although the General's decline in *The General* is also associated with loss of power, his death from tuberculosis contributes to his presentation as a romantic, melancholic figure, creating a more positive view of his power.

In *The Autumn*, senility and loss of power are associated in various episodes, the first of which is the one dealing with lottery. The schoolchildren who have been instructed to choose the coldest balls, which always correspond to the dictator's ticket, are executed by the Patriarch's mandate, to avoid discovery of the trick. This mandate is clearly attributed to the Patriarch's senility:

> Because General Rodrigo de Aguilar had collected the most unimpeachable evidence that I spent my nights conversing with vases and oil paintings of patriots ... that I had a tomb built for an admiral of the ocean sea who did not exist, except in my feverish imagination ... and that during an attack of senile dementia I had ordered 2,000 children put on a barge ... that was dynamited at sea ... and it was on the basis of that solemn testimony that General Rodrigo de Aguilar and the high command decided to intern him in the asylum for illustrious old men. (122–23)[6]

Similarly, the dictator's senility leads him to seduce a schoolgirl whose identity he forgets after the first encounter. Unable to distinguish one schoolgirl from the next because they all wear the same uniforms, "he replaced her with a different one every afternoon" (221).[7] When his henchmen discover what he has done, they send the original schoolgirl away, move the school to another location, and have prostitutes dress as schoolgirls to fool him. His officials clearly manipulate everything surrounding the dictator, including printing a newspaper just for him with the news he likes to read (239) and videotaping him to make him appear on national television without his knowledge (234). The senile dictator first relinquishes power to his wife, Leticia Nazareno, who makes him return privileges to the clergy, and then to José Ignacio Sáenz de la Barra, who becomes the terrorist arm of the government, sending him a series of decapitated heads of his so-called enemies. This all leads the Patriarch to reflect that "he had arrived at the ignominious fiction of commanding without power ... and of being obeyed without authority when he became convinced in the trail of yellow leaves of his autumn that he had never been the master of his power" (268).[8]

It is not a coincidence that the Patriarch's senility is associated with a massacre of schoolchildren and then later with pedophilia. The fact that the victims of his senility are innocent children exacerbates the grotesqueness of his mental decline, granting it a singularly negative and unsympathetic character that is communicated to the nature of his power.

In direct contrast with this portrayal of the Patriarch is the physical deterioration suffered by the protagonist in *The General*. Although we do witness some grotesque details of the General's illness (his vomiting blood, foul-smelling gas, and so forth), the character and his illness are to a large degree romanticized in the novel and, as Isabel Vergara has pointed out, his suffering until his death, stopping at various locations along the Magdalena River, is presented in religious terms that liken him to Christ and the stations of the cross (71–72). The parallel between illness and loss of power is emphasized in various passages, such as the following: "That night he composed his resignation, under the demoralizing effect of an emetic prescribed by a chance physician. ... The simple knowledge that he was no more than an ordinary citizen intensified the devastating effects of the emetic" (21–22).[9] Similarly, we are told: "That dawn he officiated at the daily mass of his ablutions with more frenetic severity than usual trying to purge his body and spirit of twenty years of fruitless wars and the disillusionments of power" (5).[10] The flip side is that when the General is faced with the possibility that he might be able to return to power, he suddenly feels better: "It had been a long while since José Palacios could remember his master's health as stable as it was during this time, for the headaches and twilight fevers surrendered their weapons as soon as the news of the military coup was received" (200).[11] Power and health are related, but the General's illness, at the same time that it humanizes him, also casts a positive light on his power in various ways.

According to Carlos Alonso, *The General* "depicts for us a Bolívar trapped in the somber labyrinth of his personal and historical melancholy, so that our cultural melancholy will recognize itself in the written mirror and will transform itself into beneficent mourning so that the lost object of modernity may cease to rule" (260). Alonso equates, therefore, the General with modernity through his project to create a united Latin America and argues that the death of this project has been viewed with melancholy for centuries by Latin American intellectuals. By tracing Bolívar's death in the novel, Alonso posits, using Freud's distinction between melancholia and mourning, that the people of Latin America can pass from one to the other, and put the dream of modernity to rest (257–58). For our purposes, what is interesting about this theory is that it emphasizes the aura of melancholy that surrounds the General until it is finally destroyed via his death. Melancholy is a characteristic associated with romanticism and, according to Susan Sontag, it has also historically been associated with the illness Bolívar was thought to have suffered, tuberculosis. The following montage of quotations from Sontag's *Illness as Metaphor* explains this traditional view of tuberculosis:

> Having tuberculosis was imagined to be an aphrodisiac, to confer extraordinary powers of seduction.... Tuberculosis is a disease of time; it speeds up life ... spiritualizes it.... For over one hundred years, tuberculosis remained the preferred way of giving death a meaning—an edifying, refined disease.... Tuberculosis takes on qualities assigned to the lungs, which are part of the upper, spiritualized body.... It was very possible, through fantasies about tuberculosis, to aestheticize death.... Tuberculosis was thought of as a decorative, often lyrical death.... According to the mythology of tuberculosis, there is generally some passionate feeling which provokes, which expresses itself in a bout of tuberculosis. But the passions must be thwarted, the hope blighted, and the passion, although usually love, could be a political or moral passion.... Tuberculosis was one index of being genteel, delicate, sensitive.... Sadness and tuberculosis became synonymous. The myth of tuberculosis constitutes the next to the last episode in the long career of the ancient idea of melancholy. (13–26)

Although many details of the illness given in the novel are far from romantic, others clearly adhere to this concept of tuberculosis as a "romantic" and elevating disease. For example:

> Don Joaquín de Mier would remember ... the dreadful creature carried ashore ... wrapped in a woolen blanket ... with hardly a breath of life ... his burning hand, ... *the supernatural elegance* with which he left the litter and stood, holding himself upright with the help of his aides-de-camp to greet them all. (*The General* 246; emphasis added)[12]

In addition to emphasizing the General's elegance within his illness, other passages signal the connection between his physical and spiritual status, thus confirming Sontag's association of tuberculosis and moral passion: "Because of ... the contraction of his chest and the yellowness of his face, the doctor thought it a case of damaged lungs ... *the physician attributed as much importance to moral torment as to physical calamities*" (248; emphasis added).[13] In summary, while the Patriarch is cast as grotesquely senile, the General is seen as suffering a romantic illness that spiritualizes him.

The second way in which the two protagonists are set in contrast is through their relationships with women. Although both employ their power to initiate sexual relationships with the opposite sex, the Patriarch uses what Theresa K. Vescio et al., in "Power and Sexism," term "harsh tactics," while The General employs "soft tactics": "Men may exert power in gender interactions by means of soft influence tactics (e.g., praise, reward) versus harsh influence tactics (e.g., coercion, aggression, hostility)" (363). Although both are negative and involve using power to obtain sex, the use of harsh tactics is clearly worse than the use of soft tactics, thus allowing the reader to maintain a more sympathetic vision of the General than of the Patriarch.

The Patriarch consistently rapes women, except for Leticia Nazareno, although she was kidnapped by his henchmen in an effort to please the dictator, itself also a violent act for which the Patriarch is ultimately responsible. Among these women is Francisca Linero, who states: "Although I was dying of fear, I maintained enough lucidity to realize that my only means of salvation was to let him do anything he wanted to me on the dinner table" (*The Patriarch* 96).[14] The dictator subsequently has his henchmen murder her husband because "he would have been a mortal enemy for the rest of his life" (96).[15] Similarly, he aggressively assaults his concubines and the mulatto servant girl who has come to collect eggs (111). We are also told that during siesta time "he would take refuge in the shade of the concubines, he would choose one by assault" (9)[16]. Rape, murder, and assault are the harsh techniques employed by the dictator in his sexual relationships. In contrast, the General uses praise and words of love in his sexual conquests. The only partial exception to this rule is Queen María Luisa. Although Bolívar uses "soft" techniques to exert power over her, she still consents out of fear:

> The sight of him frightened her. . . . He embraced her with all his strength, holding her so she could not move while he nibbled with soft kisses at her forehead, her eyes, her check, . . . until he had quieted her . . . and she gave herself to him not out of desire or love but out of fear. (*The General* 50)[17]

However, after this episode, the General "rewards" María Luisa, when, upon learning she is a slave, he grants her freedom. Bolívar also uses "soft" tactics with the five women from the Garaycoa family, whom he leaves with the promise of "eternal love and a prompt return" (150).[18]

Similarly, the General tells the Bedouin woman whom he shaves head to toe that he loves her "more than anyone else in this world" (213).[19] So, whereas the Patriarch is raping and assaulting women, the General is kissing and whispering words of love to them. Both are clearly womanizers (we are told that the General had thirty-five lovers, and that was "not counting the one night birds, of course" (154),[20] clearly using his position to obtain sex, but on the other hand, in contrast to the Patriarch, whose partners are even more numerous, his tactics are less aggressive and less violent.

Other dimensions that underscore a more positive side to the General's power in contrast with that of the Patriarch is the attitude of both men toward losing games. Neither one enjoys losing, or as Adelaida López-Mejía puts it, "Like Bolívar in García Márquez's recent novel, *El general en su laberinto*, the patriarch cannot abide losing; their pathological need for mastery both tarnishes and constitutes their political genius" (310). Winning at games is another form of power, as Gene Bell-Villada points out with regard to the Patriarch playing dominos with the former dictators: "The Spanish dominó can be taken as a pun: 'he dominated'" (172). However, although neither protagonist likes to lose, there is a marked difference in their comportment. The Patriarch does not allow anyone except Rodrigo de Aguilar and José Ignacio Sáenz de la Barra to beat him at dominoes. He mandates that everyone else lose: "[H]e grew bored on domino nights because even though he faced the sharpest opponents, try as he might to set up the best traps against himself, he couldn't lose" (213).[21] In contrast, the General does not win by decree, but rather insists on playing cards until he begins to win. General Carreño recalls the night they waited for the results of the Ocaña Convention as "the longest night of his life,"[22] in which they played cards from 9:00 p.m. until 11:00 a.m. the next day, "when his companions agreed to let the General win 3 games in a row" (64–65).[23] Although the General is angry at Colonel Wilson, who keeps beating him at the game (until he finally decides to lose on purpose), instead of holding a grudge, the General eventually forgives him, thus showing that he is not such a bad person after all.

The Patriarch and the General also stand in direct contrast regarding their attitude toward personal wealth. While the Patriarch fixes the lottery to gain the national funds for his own personal fortune, the General uses his personal fortune on behalf of the nation and others, giving his earnings to disabled war veterans and the wives of soldiers killed in the line of duty. In addition, he wills his house to his sister, his sugar plantation to his nieces and nephews, and his lands to freed slaves. Finally, he refuses to accept the large sum of money offered to him by Lima's Congress after he has liberated Peru (189). A certain populism characterizes the protagonists of both novels. The Patriarch, we read,

> would not let a single detail go by without some explanation in his talks with men and women he had called together using their names and surnames as if he had a written registry of inhabitants and statistics and problems of the whole nation in his head, so he called me without opening his eyes, come here Jacinta Morales, he said to me, tell me what happened to the boy he had wrestled with himself and given a fall the year before so he would drink a bottle of castor oil. (*The Autumn*, 87)[24]

This passage is very similar to the following excerpt from *The General*: "On his journeys the General was in the habit of making casual stops to inquire about the problems of the people he met along the way. He asked about everything: the age of their children, the nature of their illness, the condition of their business, what they thought about everything" (168). However, once again, there is a fundamental difference in the relationship between each protagonist and the populace. In *The Autumn*, these encounters with ordinary people cease to be authentic because the Patriarch "didn't even suspect that the assault at the waterfront may have been spontaneous but that the ones that followed had been organized by his own security services in order to please him without any risks" (15),[25] while the protagonist in *The General* is genuinely approached by the common people, who would grab his horse's halter to stop him in order to request favors or offer complaints about public services (40).

Nonetheless, despite García Márquez's emphasis on the dominance aspect of the Patriarch's power, it is important to note that even this type of coercive power contains elements of consensus. According to Bernd Simon and Penelope Oakes, "most power relations involve elements of both consensus and conflict" (211). As they note in their study, "Beyond Dependence," any given group may simultaneously identify with "inclusive identities" (such as national identity), which lead them to cooperate with coercive power, at the same time that they do not identify with less inclusive identities that characterize that power (e.g., they may belong to a minority group not supported by that power). This leads to elements both of consensus and of conflict vis-à-vis the coercive leader. Such a concept is particularly interesting when applied to *The Autumn*, because although the novel is tilted overwhelmingly toward elements of conflict between the Patriarch and the populace, the reader does perceive some elements of consensus. For example, there is the aforementioned episode at the waterfront in which a group of people spontaneously cheer him: "[I]t's him, she exclaimed with surprise, hurray for the stud, she shouted, hurray, shouted the men the women, the children who came running out of the Chinese bars and lunchrooms, hurray, shouted the ones who held the horses' legs and blocked the coach's way so they could shake the hand of the power that was" (15).[26] Furthermore, this tug-of-war between consensus and conflict extends to the Patriarch's death. According to Adelaida López-Mejía, the novel communicates a certain ambivalence on the part of the narrating "we" that finds the dictator's corpse:

> Such insistence on doubt and disbelief not only evokes dictatorial society in which information is always rumor and nothing can be believed, it also suggests a wish to deny the patriarch's death. Denial, in fact, constitutes part of the work of mourning. . . . Nonetheless, the fear that the dictator has not died coexists with a not-so-unconscious desire that he come back to life and control the nation. (305)

However, for the most part, elements of consensus in *The Autumn* are sparse, and the distinction between the Patriarch's coercion and the General's ability to influence still stands as a major distinction between their respective powers.

These inverted parallels are the technique that García Márquez employs to suggest that in the dialogue between his earlier version of power (*The Autumn*) and his more recent contemplation of power (*The General*) there are some key differences. The softer tactics and "nicer" behaviors of the General (romanticized figure through tuberculosis; seducer, not rapist, of women; sore loser but not winner by decree; generous with personal wealth; and possessor of a genuinely populist attitude requited by the masses and not imposed by henchmen) all suggest that there is a fundamental difference in the power he assumes vis-à-vis that of the Patriarch. This difference, as previously mentioned, has its roots in the dichotomy dominance versus functionalist perspective.

Each of the six chapters of *The Autumn* focuses on a different way in which the Patriarch employs his power in coercive, destructive, aggressive, and violent manners. In chapter two, he has all the local caudillos (except for Saturno Santos) murdered in order to consolidate his own power and eliminate any threats to it. In chapter three, he suspects Rodrigo de Aguilar of treason and has him killed, serving his garnished body on a plate at a banquet of functionaries. In chapter four, in which he attempts to canonize his mother, Bendición Alvarado, the dictator destroys all the property of the clergy and banishes them from the country when the papal representative does not cooperate with his plan. In chapter five, he has the supposed perpetrators of Leticia's and his son's murders executed. Not satisfied that he has punished the true culprits, he hires José Ignacio Sáenz de la Barra and authorizes him to punish the guilty parties. Sáenz de la Barra symbolizes the secret police, decapitating all of the government's "enemies." He is an instrument of dominance that resembles the description offered by Simon and Oakes:

> Extremely coercive power relations may attempt the destruction of agency in various ways, but the point is that this then ceases to be a relationship of power (ceases to recruit agency and becomes violence or even war). There is no relationship of power between victims and agents of plain violence and war, although the latter may well be involved in a power relationship with a third party that recruited them as "willing executioners." (114)

In contrast, although several passages of *The General* describe Bolívar's obsession with power, there are many other passages that focus on the relationship between this power and the General's goal to unify the Latin American countries. These passages illustrate how the historical Bolívar exerted his power to influence people to support his cause. They also focus on the fact that his power was goal-oriented for what he viewed as the common good, thus distinguishing it from the Patriarch's coercive power for personal gain.

One passage that emphasizes this goal describes the General's feud with Vice-President Santander, insisting that their rift was caused not by attempts at absolute power on the part of Bolívar, but rather by Santander's disagreement with the General's goal of unification: "'The real reason was Santander could never assimilate the idea that this continent should be a single nation,' said the General" (117).[27] Similarly, the following paragraph, in which Bolívar responds to the many contradictions of which he has been accused, including promoting Spain's spirit while he simultaneously led the war of independence against her, illustrates that Bolívar's power is purely goal driven:

> "Well, all of that is true, but circumstantial" he said, "because everything I've done has been for the sole purpose of making this continent into a single, independent country, and as far as that's concerned, I've never contradicted myself or had a single doubt." And he concluded in pure Caribbean: "All the rest is bullshit!" (202–3)[28]

In other instances, toward the end of the novel, several passages show how, when Urdaneta seizes power to fight the Venezuelan separatists in Bolívar's name, the General enlists men who willingly join the fight because they support his agenda (199). Moreover, Bolívar insists he will only assume power if this assumption of power is somehow legitimized: "I do not want to be the leader of rebels or be named by dint of the victors' military might.... As long as there was no clear mandate from a legitimate source, there was no possibility of his assuming power" (203–4).[29] The fact that the General is concerned with the issue of legitimacy implies that he does not want to assume a coercive power over others, but rather to adopt a cooperative power through consensus. These and other passages of *The General* illustrate what has been termed a functionalist perspective of power. The General, in contrast to the Patriarch, may have assumed dictatorial powers, but he does so for the achievement of an agenda seen as favorable to the nation and that is clearly shared by a constituency.

This comparison of *The Autumn* and *The General* suggests that perhaps García Márquez had the former novel in mind during the construction of the latter to create a supplemental dialogue between the two on the topic of power. García Márquez examines power from a dominance perspective in *The Autumn* and from a functionalist perspective in *The General*. Nonetheless, despite their many shared motifs, the two novels reflect distinct aims largely related to the time periods in which they were produced. *The Autumn* presents a dictator who although he is the composite of multiple historical dictators, is primarily characterized as a hyperbolic myth, through the use of experimental narrative techniques, such as long chapters with stream-of-consciousness narration and minimal punctuation. For example, we are told that the people believe a bullet would go right through the Patriarch without harming him (45), that he had fathered five thousand children (46), that his mother had conceived him through immaculate conception (47), that he made the torrential rains cease with a wave of his hand (101), that those who were ill and licked the salt he distributed regained health immediately (244), and that he grew a third set of teeth between ages 100 and 150 (45). This focus on myth and narrative experimentation is characteristic of the Latin American Boom period, at the very end of which the novel appears. Moreover, the 1970s was the era of historical dictatorships in Latin America, so that the novel, despite humanizing the dictator to a certain extent, has a primary function of denunciation and sociopolitical criticism.

In contrast, *The General* is a historical novel published in 1989 during what is now seen as the postmodern period. As I have shown elsewhere, the novel relies heavily on information from the collection of Bolívar's letters published and annotated by Eugenio Gutiérrez Cely and Fabio Puyo Vasco titled *Bolívar día a día* (Weldt-Basson, "The Purpose," 96–108). There is only a minor alteration of historical facts in the novel, as well as some important omissions that have been pointed out by Bell-Villada, such as Bolívar's repudiation of Francisco de Miranda in 1812 and a private meeting with San Martín in Guayaquil in 1822 (236). According to Bell-Villada, these episodes do not reflect favorably on Bolívar and thus their omission "tilts the scales ever so slightly in favor of the national hero" (236). Nonetheless, as Bell-Villada points out, García Márquez's novel is one of the first Colombian works that demystifies Bolívar by humanizing him rather than presenting him as the perfect hero (220). Thus, because of both the focus on history and the postmodern time period, the ultimate concerns and purposes of *The General* are quite different from those of *The Autumn*.

The novel's focus on a historical figure and its creation during the rise of postmodernism both converge in creating a postmodern dialogue on the figure of Simón Bolívar. (Was he a power-hungry dictator or a national patriot? Was he an invincible general or simply a vulnerable human being?) The father of Latin American independence is humanized and thus desacralized in the novel. In addition, the work manipulates historical facts in much the same way historiography does, thus illustrating a postmodern view of both history and fiction. As Hayden White states:

> No given set of casually recorded historical events can itself constitute a story; the most it might offer to the historian are story elements. The events are made into a story by the suppression or subordination of certain of them and the highlighting of others, by characterization, motific repetition, variation of tone and point of view,

alternate descriptive strategies, and the like—in short, all of the techniques that we would normally expect to find in the emplotment of a novel or play. (84)

García Márquez essentially creates his own "history" of Bolívar, to emphasize, as White indicates, the parallels, and thus perhaps the overlap, between history and fiction. He even goes so far as to speak of "the exactitude of this novel" (273) in the "My Thanks" section, when historical rigor or "exactitude" is not normally a criterion for fiction but rather historiography. This is very similar to what other novelists have done, such as Augusto Roa Bastos in his trilogy on the "monotheism of power," in which he shows the ambiguities inherent in such nineteenth-century Paraguayan historical figures as the dictator José Gaspar Rodríguez de Francia and President Francisco Solano López (Weldt-Basson, "Augusto Roa Bastos" 341–44). Thus, the time period of postmodernism takes us beyond historical criticism and denunciation to what Bakhtin would term a polyphonic view of historical figures in which different visions of them intersect to create ambiguity and multiple versions of the truth regarding their identity. As major theorists of postmodernism such as Linda Hutcheon (3–53) and Jean-François Lyotard (34) assert, postmodernism views all knowledge as a subjective, human construct, thus questioning the transparent relationship between history and reality. This is the ultimate purpose of *The General*.

Notes

1. "De una voracidad imperturbable" (100). All Spanish quotations from *The General in His Labyrinth* are taken from García Márquez, *El general en su laberinto* (1989).
2. "Pues la había sepultado en el fondo de un olvido estanco como un recurso brutal para poder seguir vivo sin ella" (255).
3. "Los caballos y a las flores" (179).
4. Although this is an important aspect of *The Feast of the Goat*, the novel is more focused on the psychosocial effects of the Trujillo dictatorship on the Dominican people, with subtle hints to the parallel between Trujillo and Alberto Fujimori. See Weldt-Basson, "*La fiesta del chivo*" (113–30).
5. See Richards (111–18) and Cornejo-Parriego (59–64).
6. "El general Rodrigo de Aguilar había acumulado testimonios del mayor crédito de que yo me pasaba las noches sin dormir conversando con los floreros y los óleos de los próceres . . . que había hecho construir una tuba de honor para un almirante de la mar océana que no existía sino en mi imaginación febril . . . y que en un ataque de demencia senil había ordenado meter a dos mil niños en una barcaza cargada de cemento que fue dinamitada en el mar, . . . y era en base en aquellos testimonios solemnes que el general Rodrigo de Aguilar y el estado mayor de las guardias presidenciales en pleno habían decido internarlo en el asilo de ancianos ilustres" (139). All Spanish quotations of *The Autumn of the Patriarch* are taken from García Márquez *El otoño del patriarca* (1999).
7. "Él la había olvidado al segundo día en que no la vio entrar por la claraboya . . . la sustituía por una distinta todas las tardes porque ya para entonces no distinguía muy bien quién era quién en el tropel de colegialas de uniformes iguales" (246).

8. "Había llegado sin asombro a la ficción de ignominia de mandar sin poder, de ser exaltado sin gloria y de ser obedecido sin autoridad cuando se convenció en el reguero de hojas amarillas de su otoño que nunca había de ser el dueño de todo su poder" (297).
9. "Aquella noche redactó su renuncia bajo el efecto desmoralizador de un vomitivo que le prescribió un médico ocasional para tratar de calmarle la bilis... La sola certidumbre de no ser más que un ciudadano corriente agravó los estragos del vomitivo" (28–30).
10. "Aquella madrugada oficiaba la misa diaria de la limpieza con una sevicia más frenética que la habitual, tratando de purificar el cuerpo y el ánima de veinte años de guerras inútiles y desengaños de poder" (13).
11. "José Palacios no recordaba a su señor en mucho tiempo con una salud tan estable como la de aquellos días, pues los dolores de cabeza y las fiebres del atardecer rindieron las armas tan pronto como se recibió la noticia del golpe militar" (203–4).
12. "Don Joaquín de Mier había de recordar... la criatura de pavor que desembarcaron en andas... envuelto en una manta de lana... apenas con un soplo de vida... la mano ardiente,... la prestancia sobrenatural con que abandonó las andas para saludarlos a todos" (248).
13. "Por... la contracción del pecho y la amarillez del rostro, pensó que la causa mayor eran los pulmones dañados... atribuyó tanta importancia a las calamidades del cuerpo como al tormento moral" (250).
14. "Y aunque yo estaba agonizando de miedo conservaba bastante lucidez para darme cuenta de que mi único recurso de salvación era dejar que él hiciera conmigo todo lo que quiso sobre el mesón de comer" (111).
15. "Porque iba a ser enemigo mortal para toda la vida" (111).
16. "Se refugiaba en la penumbra de las concubinas, elegía una por asalto" (15).
17. "Se asustó al verlo... La abrazó con toda su fuerza, manteniéndola impedida para moverse mientras la picoteaba con besos tiernos en la frente, en los ojos, en las mejillas... hasta que logró amansarla.... y ella no se le entregó por deseo ni por amor, sino por miedo" (57–58).
18. "De amor eterno y pronto regreso" (158).
19. "Más que a nadie jamás en este mundo" (217).
20. "'Sin contar las pájaras de una noche, por supuesto'" (162).
21. "Se aburría en las veladas de dominó hasta cuando se enfrentaba con los cuartos mas diestros pues no lograba perder una partida por mucho que intentaba las trampas mas sabias contra sí mismo" (237).
22. "La noche más larga de su vida" (72).
23. "Cuando sus compañeros de juego se concertaron para dejar que él ganara tres partidas continuas" (72).
24. "No dejaba sin esclarecer un solo detalle de cuanto conversaba con los hombres y mujeres que había convocado en torno suyo llamándolos por sus nombres y apellidos como si tuviera dentro de la cabeza un registro escrito de los habitantes y las cifras y los problemas de toda la nación, de modo que me llamó sin abrir los ojos, ven acá Jacinta Morales, me dijo, cuéntame qué fue del muchacho a quien él mismo había barbeado el año anterior para que se tomara un frasco de aceito de ricino" (101).
25. "Él ni siquiera sospechaba que el asalto del puerto había sido espontáneo pero que los siguientes fueron organizados por sus propios servicios de seguridad para complacerlo sin riesgos" (22).
26. "Es él, exclamó asustada, que viva el macho, gritó, que viva, gritaban los hombres, las mujeres los niños que salían corriendo de las cantinas y las fondas de chinos, que viva, gritaban los que trabaron las patas de los caballos y bloquearon el coche para estrechar la mano del poder" (22).

27. "'La verdadera causa fue que Santander no pudo asimilar nunca la idea de que este continente fuera un solo país,' dijo el general" (125).
28. "Lo acusaban ... de que hacía la guerra a muerte contra España y era un gran promotor de su espíritu, ... de que había sido masón y leía a Voltaire en misa, pero era el paladín de la iglesia ... 'Pues bien: todo eso es cierto, pero circunstancial,' dijo, 'porque todo lo he hecho con la sola mira de que este continente sea un país independiente y único, y en eso no he tenido ni una contradicción ni una sola duda.' Y concluyó en caribe puro: ¡Lo demás son pingadas!" (206-7).
29. "No quiero pasar por jefe de rebeldes y nombrado militarmente por los vencedores ... hasta no disponer de un mandato diáfano emanado de una fuente legitima, no había posibilidad alguna de que asumiera el poder" (208-9).

Works Cited

Alonso, Carlos. "The Mourning After: García Márquez, Fuentes and the Meaning of Postmodernity in Spanish America." *MLN*, vol. 109, 1994, pp. 252–67.

Bakhtin, Mikhail. *Problems of Dostoevsky's Poetics*. Edited and translated by Carly Emerson, U of Minnesota P, 1984.

Bell-Villada, Gene H. *García Márquez: The Man and His Work*. 2nd ed. U of North Carolina P, 2010.

Cornejo-Parriego, Rosalía. "The Delegitimizing Carnival *of El otoño del patriarca*." *Structures of Power: Essays on Twentieth-Century Spanish-American Fiction*, State U of New York P, 1996, pp. 59–64.

García Márquez, Gabriel. *The Autumn of the Patriarch*. Translated by Gregory Rabassa, HarperPerennial, 1991.

García Márquez, Gabriel. *El general en su laberinto*. 6th ed. Editorial Sudamericana, 1989.

García Márquez, Gabriel. *The General in His Labyrinth*. Translated by Edith Grossman, Penguin Books, 1990.

García Márquez, Gabriel. *El otoño del patriarca*. Mondadori, 1999.

Guinote, Ana, and Theresa K. Vescio. "Power in Social Psychology." *The Social Psychology of Power*, edited by Ana Guinote and Theresa K. Vescio, Guilford P, 2010, pp. 1–16.

Hutcheon, Linda. *A Poetics of Postmodernism*. Routledge, 1988.

Hart, Patricia Mohen. "Potency vs. Incontinence in *The Autumn of the Patriarch* of Gabriel García Márquez." *Rocky Mountain Review*, vol. 33, no. 1, 1979, pp. 1–6.

López-Mejía, Adelaida. "Burying the Dead: Repetition in *El otoño del patriarca*." *MLN*, vol. 107, no. 2, 1992, pp. 298–320.

Lyotard, Jean-François. *The Postmodern Condition: A Report on Knowledge*. Translated by Geoff Bennington and Briam Massumi, U of Minnesota P, 1984.

Overbeck, Jennifer R. "Concepts and Historical Perspectives on Power." *The Social Psychology of Power*, edited by Ana Guinote and Theresa K. Vescio, Guilford P, 2010, pp. 19–45.

Richards, Tim. "El patriarca rabelesiano: La mistificación de la dictadura a través del cuerpo grotesco." *La palabra y el hombre*, vol. 67, 1988, pp. 111–18.

Simon, Bernd, and Penelope Oakes. "Beyond Dependence: An Identity Approach to Social Power and Domination." *Human Relations*, vol. 59, no. 1, 2006, pp. 105–39.

Sontag, Susan. *Illness as Metaphor and AIDS and Its Metaphors*. Picador, 1990.

Vázquez-Medina, Olivia. "The Patria's Ravaged Body: Bolívar's Illness in *El general en su laberinto*." *Bulletin of Hispanic Studies*, vol. 88, 2011, pp. 553–70.

Vergara, Isabel. "Representación paródica en *El general en su laberinto*." *Crítica Hispánica*, vol. 14, nos. 1–2, 1992, pp. 69–80.

Vescio, Theresa K., Kristine Schlenker, and Joshua G. Lenes. "Power and Sexism." *The Social Psychology of Power*, edited by Ana Guinote and Theresa K. Vescio, Guilford P, 2010, pp. 341–62.

Weldt-Basson, Helene C. "Augusto Roa Bastos's Trilogy as Postmodern Practice." *Studies in Twentieth Century Literature*, vol. 22, no. 2, 1998, pp. 335–55.

Weldt-Basson, Helene C. "*La fiesta del chivo*: History, Fiction or Social Psychology?" *Hispanófila*, vol. 156, 2009, pp. 113–30.

Weldt-Basson, Helene C. "The Purpose of Historical Reference in Gabriel García Márquez's *El general en su laberinto*." *Revista Hispánica Moderna*, vol. 47, no. 1, June 1994, pp. 96–108.

White, Hayden. "The Historical Text as Literary Artifact." *Tropics of Discourse: Essays in Cultural Criticism*, Johns Hopkins UP, 1978, pp. 81–100.

CHAPTER 29

MODERNITY AND ITS RUINS IN *OF LOVE AND OTHER DEMONS*

NEREIDA SEGURA-RICO

On the opening page of the first chapter of *Of Love and Other Demons* (1994), a dog runs through a market biting four people—one of them the novel's central character, Sierva María de Jesús—just outside the neighborhood of Getsemaní, where the arrival of a ship from the Compañía Gaditana de Negros (a real entity that operated in Cartagena de Indias in the second half of the eighteenth century) has caused quite a stir. The commotion is not so much because of the anticipation that the arrival of such ships means for the city, but rather because of an illness that had killed much of the human cargo, which was then thrown overboard. As the bodies float off in the bay, it will finally be determined that the slaves had died not from some African plague, as had been originally feared, but from food poisoning. The surviving slaves are being auctioned off at a lower price, except for a woman of impossible beauty, for whom the governor pays her weight in gold.

In its rampage, the dog brings together for the reader the chaos of the harbor, creating a semantic unity from a diversity of textual signs. Of course the dog's path only becomes visible through the narrative eye that tracks the movement and, by doing so, establishes that unifying thread. By situating side by side the lively activities of the market and the stillness of bodies, dead or displayed for sale, the narrator offers an unequivocal vantage point for the story that has started to unfold. In developing that unique narrative perspective through the rest of the novel, Gabriel García Márquez undermines from within the discourse of progress and civilization in the Spanish colonies even as he places marginal elements of colonial life at the very center. This viewpoint is reinforced when, just a few pages later, it is determined that the dog has rabies; the threat and spread of the disease functions as a counterpoint to the promises of modernization and rational change in the Age of Enlightenment. As this opening scene reveals, the location of the events is critical, in that it also functions as a site of enunciation. The historical narrative takes place in a very specific, yet unnamed and allegorical, urban center. Similarly, the voice of the narrator is both omniscient and deeply personal, resembling an urban chronicler, a sort of modern *letrado*—a transfiguration of the colonial man of letters—who constructs that city as emblematic in order to expose its moral and structural ruins.

As noted, references to specific events in the neighborhood of Getsemaní situate the narrative in eighteenth-century Cartagena de Indias. Founded in 1533 and established in 1615 as the main port for the slave trade in Spanish South America, the city underwent a social and economic decline in the early 1700s. In *El fracaso de la nación: Región, clase y raza en el Caribe colombiano (1717–1821)*, Colombian historian Alfonso Múnera provides a novel approach to correlating disparate sociohistorical and economic components of the eighteenth century in New Granada, and more specifically in Cartagena de Indias, in order to dismantle some of the myths about the founding of the nation—namely, the idea that there was political unity in the region as well as a creole elite that led the independence movement in the face of the passivity of blacks and an indigenous and mixed population of color (*castas*) (13–14). The Viceroyalty of New Granada, established only in 1739, evidenced the internal weakness and fragmentation that had been a constant throughout the colonial period and that were to determine the character of events at the beginning of the nineteenth century. As Múnera points out, citing documents that use words such as "desolation" to describe the socioeconomic reality in the region at the beginning of the eighteenth century, New Granada was defined throughout the 1700s by its economic backwardness, a situation that not even the Bourbon reforms of the second half of the century were able to change (46–47).

However, the latter half of the 1700s saw a rise in commerce and investment in the military, which revived the city of Cartagena de Indias as an important fortress for the defense of the American colonies for the new Bourbon dynasty in Spain. That bustling activity is captured in the opening page of the first chapter of the novel, reminiscent of the height of the city as a slave port that drew all sorts of foreigners. The Crown had already established there in 1610, as Múnera explains, the Tribunal of the Inquisition for the Caribbean and Northern South America in order to "repress the activities of Jews, Protestants and other heretics of different nationalities that the port attracted with its business possibilities" (78).[1] It is through the contradictory specificities of this time and place that García Márquez's urbane narrator creates an allegory of competing forces that could never be integrated.

***

Published in 1994, *Of Love and Other Demons* (henceforth *Of Love*) is at first glance vintage García Márquez, with its cast of eccentric characters, events that defy logic and reason, and abundance of both inter- and intratextual references as well as metafictional elements. However, it is also quite different from previous works by the author, due not only to its historical referentiality but also because of a narrative approach that is at odds with magical realism as an inclusive mode of interpretation of a heterogenous reality. Even though when it was first published *Of Love* did not receive the same critical attention as García Márquez's other novels, this rather brief work has subsequently elicited a numerous and wide range of responses and critical studies.² Many of those studies address the issue of hybridity represented by the main character, a twelve-year-old girl named Sierva María de Jesús, born of a criollo aristocrat and a mestiza woman and raised in the African traditions by the slaves of the household: "Transplanted to the courtyard of the slaves, Sierva María learned to dance before she could speak, learned three African languages at the same time, learned to drink rooster's blood before breakfast and to glide past Christians unseen and unheard, like an incorporeal being" (42).³ This incorporeality notwithstanding, Sierva María embodies in a very material way the conflicts that result from the opposition between the written word and orality, between subject and object positions that are defined by the authority of a Western epistemological discourse vis-à-vis alternative forms of knowing.⁴ In this regard, many of the critical approaches to the novel focus on the representation of a Western discourse that confronts the ideology of Enlightenment with the fanaticism of religious beliefs. This essay takes as its point of departure those studies as I consider how the text constitutes itself as a hybrid composition highlighting its own narrative construct, inscribing itself within the artifices of power that the novel continually illuminates as "demonic."⁵

In this regard, Julio Ortega has remarked that "this is the most emotional novel by the author, but it is also the most literary" ("Sujeto" *El sujeto dialógico* 300).⁶ Ortega's analysis of the novel is part of a volume in which he studies a series of texts to explore what he has termed a "conflictive modernity," in which the colonies little by little produced the formation of subjects that respond to colonization through "narrative strategies, negotiations and regroupings, required appropriations and trans-codifications and debates that form part of the cultural practice of hybridization and *mestizajes*" (*El sujeto dialógico* 17).⁷ Within that theoretical framework, Ortega studies the character of Sierva María de Jesús as "an American sign" that is born in the discourse of the New World and "that cannot be reduced to the dominant discursive logic" (*El sujeto dialógico* 304).⁸ For the Peruvian writer and critic, the novel evinces the misunderstanding in the reading of the codes that subjects human life to an arbitrary interpretation of those codes within a senseless rationality (*El sujeto dialógico* 298). Whereas Ortega focuses on the multiple and intertwining readings that are both produced and reproduced in the novel, and whereas these layered acts of reading cannot be understood separated from their obverse, writing—that is, the novel as "a complex act of the formidable task of writing reading" (*El sujeto dialógico* 302)⁹—I propose to explore further that very function of writing in *Of Love*. It is through a textual inscription and rewriting that the novel engages, at the end of the twentieth century, not only the institutionalization of power in the Spanish-American colonies but also the novel's very position as a literary genre vis à vis authoritative discourses of power. As a chronicler of the city, the narrator anchors the narrative action in an identifiable space and time, only to dismantle the pretension of progress, historical or otherwise.

In analyzing the position of the narrator in *Of Love*, I find Julio Ramos's discussion of the function of the chronicle genre in relation to the urban experience quite productive. Neither the utopian place for "an ideally modern society and rationalized public sphere" (118) that would be the epitome of civilization for intellectuals such as Sarmiento, nor what Martí saw as "the scenery in which the fragmentation of discourse that distinguishes modernity would come to be represented" (118–19), the colonial urban space of Cartagena de Indias needs to be thought of, using Ramos's words, "as the field of signification itself" (119). In this space, the temporal connection between the past and present is effectively rescued from the breakage with the past that modernity enacts. García Márquez's narrator deliberately collapses distances in time and between disparate elements to show them as coexistent. By positing what is, ultimately, a chronicle of death, the characters cannot but succumb to the fate of history, in which they are doomed to fulfill an existence made also of ruins.

***

In considering the sociohistorical context in which the novel is published, Margaret Olsen points out that *Of Love* contributes to the reflection in the historical novel of phobias embedded in the national formation of contemporary societies, pathologies that, in the case of Colombia, she identifies with its failure to acknowledge all the different elements of its cultural composition (1068). Olsen adds that it is also through the mechanisms of the historical novel that Spanish-American writers have confronted a conception of modernity that was imposed on a reality not corresponding to expectation (1068).[10] Viewed from the perspective of historical fiction, García Márquez is not alone in locating the failure of a modernity that does not result in an inclusive independence project. It is especially telling that García Márquez travels back to the eighteenth century instead of to the formation of the Colombian nation in the nineteenth century. The year of the publication of *Of Love* saw also the release of *El camino de Yyaloide* by Edgardo Rodriguez Juliá, which, along with *La noche oscura del niño Avilés* (Niño Avilés's Dark Night, 1984) and two others, was to form his *Crónicas de Nueva Venecia* tetralogy. The Puerto Rican eighteenth century is also the temporal framework for his novel *La renuncia del héroe Baltasar* (1974; *The Renunciation* 1997). As Carolina Sancholuz points out, these novels echo the work being carried out by what is known as "the new Puerto Rican historiography," which focused on areas of investigation such as slavery and its cultural legacy, a subject that had been relegated to the margins by official historiography (2–3). In conversation with Julio Ortega, Rodríguez Juliá highlights the importance of the eighteenth century as a foundational era not only for Puerto Rican nationhood but also for the rest of Latin America, "a mix of rationality and irrationality, a fascinating mix of the Enlightenment and Goya's monsters and of Piranesi" (*Reapropiaciones*129–30).[11]

Both Rodriguez Juliá and García Márquez depict the eighteenth century as textualized constructs. For the latter, it is not a utopia in the manner in which Rodríguez Juliá portrays black populations who debunk colonial hierarchy in order to establish their own city. Rather, by juxtaposing an archaeology of the present—a function of the chronicle genre, according to Susana Roetker (106)—with an archaeology of the past, the narrator offers a romantic story and a national history that need to be mourned both for what they were but also for what they could have been. The ultimate transgression of the narrative is not the subversion of official historical discourse, but its refusal to redeem the ruins of which it writes. In *The Writing of History*, Michel de Certeau declares that "death obsesses the West" and explains the task of historiography as denying "loss by appropriating to the present the privilege of recapitulating the past as a form of knowledge. A labor of death and a labor against death" (5). For de Certeau, the gesture that accomplishes this feat, and that has "at once the value of myth and ritual," is *writing* (5). Against the mythical view of the discourse of historical progress as an antidote against death, through which Western historiography, according to de Certeau, brings back to life "the perishable data," *Of Love* enacts its own form of ritualistic writing in order to do the opposite, that is, to negate such historical progress by not letting go of death, even as it resuscitates the fictional corpses of Colombian history.

The prologue to the work ostensibly provides forensic evidence for the story that is to unfold in the novel proper. That evidence is further sustained by seeming references to historical characters and events that ground the novel in the spatial and temporal context of Cartagena de Indias in the Age of Enlightenment. In this regard, the historicism of *Of Love* resembles the historical narratives of Alejo Carpentier in his two seminal novels of the eighteenth century, *El reino de este mundo* (*The Kingdom of This World*, 1949) and *El siglo de las luces* (*Explosion in a Cathedral*, 1962). The textual fabrications in Carpentier's novels are carefully embedded in a historical referentiality as well as in a historical sense to reflect on a concept of time in relation to the idea of progress. Contrary to this, in García Márquez's novel the temporal framework is not so clearly established, notwithstanding the inclusion of specific dates and historical references. Historical events either do not quite follow a plausible chronology, have been displaced, or have been plainly invented.[12] The chronological development of events exists paradoxically in an arrested time subjected to the plotting devices of the novel and the colony through what Ortega has described as a story "unleashed by death and retraced by fiction" (*El sujeto dialógico* 302). It is, indeed, through the very act of writing, or better, rewriting, that the novel manages to camouflage its ahistorical historicity. That rendering of history is not so much the product of the construction of the text as a "ritualistic repetition" of history (141)—as Roberto González Echevarría's study of Carpentier's *The Kingdom of This World* posits—but rather a result of the intervention of a chronicler who acts, in between the lines, as a counterpoint to the omniscient narrator.

After witnessing, as a journalist, the opening of the tombs of the convent of Santa Clara, García Márquez confesses in the prologue that "*[a]lmost half a century later, I can still feel the confusion produced in me by that terrible testimony to the devastating passage of the years*" (4; emphasis in original).[13] However, such an avowal constitutes, as I explore later, another textual deceit, one that allows the author to underscore the link between his journalistic work and his narrative fiction, a connection that most of the writers of the Latin American Boom generation share. In this regard, the historical revisionism in the aforementioned novels by Rodriguez Juliá is profoundly influenced by the development of the Latin American chronicle as a journalistic genre, which is, in Susana Roetker's characterization, "a hybrid product" (199). Yet that hybridity, or heterogeneity, does not necessarily imply a "discursive heteronomy," as Julio Ramos has remarked, but rather "the chronicle reflects a discursive field contested by competing subjects and authorities" (87). If Carpentier in *The Kingdom of This World* presents what

González Echevarría has portrayed as an all-encompassing fiction that ends up showing the artifice of the author's own claim regarding the historical interpretation of Latin America, the radical presence in *Of Love* of an eyewitness limits that totalizing vision. In chronicling this history of Cartagena from the point of view of an observer immersed in his milieu and transformed into a historical actor of sorts, García Márquez abandons the approach of magical realism to offer, so to speak, its limitations and to dispute Carpentier's famous claim about Latin American narrative as a chronicle of the region's inherently marvelous reality. I agree with Ortega's view of the narrator of the novel as a "pilot in the ship of reading" (*El sujeto dialógico* 308) but would take that characterization further to fully implicate him in the act of writing as a chronicler not only *of* the city that he resurrects, but *in* that city, fully participating in the articulation of the discourses of power of what the Uruguayan critic Ángel Rama has called *la ciudad letrada*, "the lettered city."[14]

***

In the same year that the novel was published, the Gabriel García Márquez Foundation for New Ibero-American Journalism was launched in Cartagena de Indias. As Jon Lee Anderson explains in his foreword to *The Scandal of the Century: And Other Writings* (2019), a selection of García Márquez's journalistic work, the Colombian writer had a "vision of a future hemispheric fraternity of reporters and chroniclers" that, apart from elevating "the standards of Latin American's journalism" would "also help to fortify its democracies" (xix). Thus, García Márquez claims the unique role of journalism in building and sustaining a democratic consciousness comprised of multiple readings of the national space. The public discourse of journalism as a methodological critique of modernity in combination with a private novelistic discourse transforms *Of Love* into a reflection, a metanarrative, about authoritative, as well as authorizing, forms of representation.

As Anderson mentions, Cartagena de Indias is where the Colombian writer started his journalistic career. It is in those beginnings at *El Universal* that the prologue to *Of Love* situates the writer when he explains that the origins of the novel we are about to read are to be traced to the end of October in 1949—more specifically, October 26—when the editor of the newspaper learns that the tombs in the crypt of the convent of Santa Clara were being unearthed to make way for a hotel and asks the young reporter to stop by and see what he can come up with. However, despite such precise chronological references, and as some critics have remarked, there is no article published by García Márquez around that time that covers the opening of the crypt in the convent of Santa Clara, nor is there a historical register that can verify the identity of the names in the tombs, and of course there is no girl whose hair has been growing since the time of her death to measure over twenty-two meters. And as if these inventions were not enough, the opening of the tombs in preparation for the transformation of the convent into a luxury hotel did not take place until more than forty years later, making it coeval to the novel.[15] By situating this event at the beginning of his career as a journalist, the author constructs an "I" that bridges a gap not only between the present and the past of the city, but also between his own present and past. This move allows him to craft a memory that will give both temporal and physical dimensions to "the devastating passage of the years" (4).

García Márquez thus creates an authoritative support for the story we are about to read. At the same time, he uses the support of what purportedly is a testimonial account to unite reality and legend by rescuing, once again, the memory of his grandmother and her oral stories and making them the seed of the book.[16] In this regard, the immediate present that is the subject matter of journalism and the popular memory of the past form the basis of the novel to create a narration that seemingly renounces its own authoritative position.[17] And yet the act of recording the present is transposed to the act of recording the past enacted in the novel, not as a historical text, as I pointed out earlier, but as a chronicle of an epoch. Starting with the detailed description of the events in the harbor and continuing with the topographical situatedness of the narrative voice in a city that is never mentioned by name (a common practice in García Márquez's fiction), apart from the reference in the prologue, there is an "I" that posits itself as part of the society it describes, again bridging the separation between the "now" and "then," and that, as a good chronicler, incorporates the reader into that (a)temporality. The clearest examples of this are the geographical references by the narrator in different parts of the novel, in which certain locations are described in relation to the "here" of the city that the narrator and, by virtue of that positionality, also the reader occupies: "a cattle ranch in Mompox and another in Ayapel, and two thousand hectares in Mahates, just two leagues from *here*" (38); "When she spent time *here*, even before the crises, she seemed like another caged mastiff" (45); "He [Father Tomás de Aquino de Narváez] had been born *here*, the son of a royal solicitor who married his quadroon slave" (132); "She had once told Cayetano that she would like to take refuge with him in San Basilio Palenque, a settlement of fugitive slaves twelve leagues from *here*" (135, emphases added in all quotations).[18]

The narrative voice also refers to a historical memory that would constitute the basis of the chronicle (*his* chronicle) as the history of Cartagena de Indias. The seemingly arbitrary decision on the part of Bishop Toribio de Cáceres y Virtudes that Father Cayetano Delaura should undertake Sierva María's exorcism transforms the latter into a central figure in the narrative and, hence, in the life of the city: "This was how Cayetano Alcino del Espíritu Santo Delaura y Escudero, at the age of thirty-six, entered the life of Sierva María and the history of the city" (77).[19] His decision to obey the Bishop, which will forever change his destiny, is consonant with Delaura's previous decision to follow him to Yucatán after having been his student in Salamanca. After being shipwrecked, they end up in Santa María la Antigua in Darien until, as the narrator explains, "de Cáceres was named interim bishop of *these* lands, whose see was left vacant at the sudden death of the titular bishop" (79; emphasis added). Thus, Father Cayetano Delaura becomes the librarian in the Bishop's palace and custodian of books banned by the Inquisition. By arriving, in a twist of fate, at the New Kingdom of Granada, he traces back his mother's birthplace in the province of Mompox and discovers an "inherited nostalgia" for a place he had never visited before (77). The narrator creates further textual evidence for

Delaura's presence in Cartagena de Indias, such as the verses that he writes to calm the desires of his body and that were supposedly discovered a century later when the library was dismantled (99). As with the dismantling of the crypt of the Convent of Santa Clara, the novel presents these fictional records as a mode of appropriation of the past, as an intervention in the official discourse of history.

Thus, the city constitutes a shared referential point that appeals to a shared system of meaning on the part of the reader. In order to inscribe the system of signs that constitutes the city as the center of power, García Márquez develops a narrative voice that conjures up many of the elements of chronicle, as I have argued, inscribing it within the *letrado* discourse that the Rama has described in *The Lettered City* (1982) as an instrument of control on the part of the metropolis in colonial Latin America. Regarding the role of the cities in the viceroyalty of New Granada, Múnera points out that even though the Colombian territory was colonized as a de facto proposition rather than as the result of the designs of law and reason, the cities within the colonial plan were still the symbol of power, the lack of urban development in the Caribbean region notwithstanding (50–51). The Cartagena de Indias depicted by the novel is configured as a unity out of the landmarks that are its recurrent spatial referents: the palace of the Marquis of Casalduero, the palace of the Bishop, and the Convent of Santa Clara.

In that sense, this imagined landscape mirrors Rama's conception of the lettered city as a system of signs where writing is sacred:

> We can visualize the two cities—the real one and the ideal one—as entities quite distinct yet also inescapably joined. . . . The first exists on the physical plane, where the common visitor can lose himself in an increasing multiplicity and fragmentation. The second exists on the symbolic plane that organizes and interprets the former, rendering the city meaningful as an idealized order. There is a labyrinth of streets penetrable only through personal exploration and a labyrinth of signs decipherable only through the application of reason. (Rama 27)

With its detailed topographical references, the novel draws a map of divisions and exclusions, of real and symbolic signs, where the physical and ideal city collide. In this play of signs, the former contests the homogenizing power of the latter: "The resounding courtyard of the slaves, where Sierva María's birthday was being celebrated, had been another city within the city in the time of the first Marquis. . . . Now all that splendor was a thing of the past. Bernarda had been extinguished by her insatiable vices, and the slave yard reduced to two wooden shacks with roofs of bitter palm, where the last scraps of greatness had already been consumed" (11).[20] As a city within a city, the slave quarters encapsulate the contradictions of the Enlightenment, inasmuch as they constitute a symbol of progress as well as of its own undoing, of its impossibility as a modernity project due to the enslavement of human beings, as British sociologist Paul Gilroy discusses in his seminal work *The Black Atlantic: Modernity and Double Consciousness* (1993).[21] Bernarda Cabrera, Sierva María's mestiza mother, succumbs to the very excesses born of the slave trade and her own success in the business of trafficking in slaves and, especially, in flour, as she flouts the regulations for the importation of both. Having repudiated her own daughter, she falls victim to the moral and material decadence of the city, a ruin that her own physical deterioration mimics. She had married Ygnacio, Marquis of Casalduero, after becoming pregnant, in a plot devised by her father, an *indio ladino*,[22] who had worked for the Marquis as an overseer and who had been economically successful as a merchant. In a strong indictment of the power of the Spanish aristocracy in the colony's class divisions, the novel presents Ygnacio as a hapless man devoid of any skills. Even if his lack of interest in pursuing his father's lucrative activities as a trafficker of slaves could be considered a redeeming quality, his indolence and passivity contribute as much to his daughter's as to the city's eventual demise.[23]

The narrator-chronicler resuscitates the city from the ruins as the stage for the configuration of power in the colony, with the tension between the centers of that power and the areas relegated to the margins: Divina Pastora asylum, Abrenuncio's house, the neighborhood of Getsemaní, Amor de Dios Hospital, and the Mahates sugar plantation.[24] The Portuguese Jew, Abrenuncio de Sa Pereira y Cao, an outlier in his rational approach to the rabies that Sierva María may or may not have contracted, is also unorthodox in his healing practices and beliefs. He is a doctor amid the domains of the Holy Office, with a vast library that Father Cayetano cannot help but envy. Abrenuncio is also a man of letters, albeit a freethinking one—a *liberto letrado* (27). All these marginal places are united by the common denominator of heterogeneity presented most notably through the elaborate superimposition of the signifiers of illness, madness, blackness, and witchcraft.[25] (For all his enlightened ideas, the doctor has a reputation for necromancy.) In this context, the body of Sierva María constitutes another symbolic location of the internal divisions of the colony. Sierva María's biggest sin is to become an "other" of herself, confirming the fears expressed by the Bishop regarding the loss of a sense of self and of purpose, which are both deeply tied to and defined by the absolute power of the imperial metropolis. In a conversation with Cayetano Delaura, the Bishop voices his nostalgia for Spain not only in geographical terms but also in terms of identity: " 'How far we are!' . . . 'From ourselves' " (95). He is alluding to a disassociation from within that threatens a static and monolithic conception of identity, based on a production of knowledge that Aníbal Quijano, in his discussion of what he terms "the coloniality of power," links to a subject-object relation that denies "intersubjectivity and social totality as the production sites of all knowledge" (173). This idea is again stressed when the Bishop reiterates the futility of the colonial enterprise to the new viceroy, don Rodrigo de Buen Lozano, who has just arrived in Cartagena de Indias with much more "progressive" views: "He spoke of the chaotic mixing of blood that had gone on since the conquest: Spanish blood with Indian blood, and both of these with blacks of every sort, even Mandingo Muslims, and he asked himself whether such miscegenation had a place in the kingdom of God" (102).[26] Similarly, Bernarda's sarcasm in describing the Marquis's newfound love for his daughter alludes to the monstrous outcomes of the sin of incest as a metaphor for the sin of miscegenation, of the mixing of blood: " 'Not a bad little business: You could breed American-born marquises with chicken feet and sell them to the circus' " (26).[27]

As a heterogenous sign, Sierva María is condemned from the first page of the novel not to survive in a space where the application of a unifying discourse on a fragmented reality negates, in the context of the novel, her very possibility of existence. The irony here is that Sierva María is an outward sign that represents not only the stigmatization of the culture of slaves, as Fajardo Valenzuela points out (126), but also the fears of the ruling elites of the same processes of transculturation that become demonized in order to be readily exorcized.[28] Delaura dares to offer an explanation to Bishop Cáceres y Virtudes regarding the girl's behavior that highlights this association between, on the one hand, the customs and cultural practices of the black population—which Sierva María learned after being abandoned by her parents—and witchcraft on the other (126). When the priest voices his doubt regarding the girl's demoniac possession and thus whether they would be exorcizing a "healthy creature," the Bishop accuses him of rebellion, which here carries connotations of heresy, for it is clear that, by virtue of her hybridity, Sierva María is not and cannot be under any circumstance "healthy." The portrayal of Cayetano Delaura as the voice of reason against the Bishop and also against María Josefa, the Abbess of the convent—whom he accuses of being the one possessed by the demon in her rancor, intolerance, and ignorance (94)—is the result of a dialogic intervention on the part of the narrator, the contemporary *letrado*, to offer an alternative interpretation of the sign of the city in order to undermine its sanctioned configuration of knowledge.

∗∗∗

In speaking of the longevity of the city of letters, Rama attributes such endurance to its "conservative influence" as well as the fact that it was "relatively static in social makeup and wedded to aesthetic models that kept the *letrados* constantly harkening back to the period of their collective origin" (21). That origin is located in the Baroque sensibility that, as Rama points out, has "permeated the colony, then extended its influence well beyond, at least to the middle of the twentieth century" (21). Hence the continuum in the form of that written language during the more than three centuries of Spanish colonial rule in the Americas that, as Rama argues, needed to be mastered by illiterate communities, since "all attempts to deter, defy, or negate the imposition of these functions of writing must, inescapably also be formulated in writing. One might go so far as to assert that writing eventually looms over all human liberty, because new emerging groups can effectively assail positions of social power only on a two-dimensional battlefield of line and space" (37). As a chronicle of that colonial rule focusing on the power of the Church and, more specifically, of the Inquisition, *Of Love* adopts the aesthetic of the Baroque in its linguistic expression and its conceptualization of the spirit of the Counter-Reformation. In this regard, it also shares this formal approach with the historical novels of Rodríguez Juliá. However, whereas the subversive use of a Baroque expression in Rodríguez Juliá's *Niño Avilés* results in an overt parody of colonial discourse, the Baroque in García Márquez's novel, while also parodic, is highly self-referential and at the service of the internal structure of the work. The conservative design of the lettered city serves well the worldview of the narrative in its portrayal of a decadence that undermines any claim of revolutionary change in the Age of Reason.

In her study of the Baroque in the work of García Márquez, Lois Parkinson Zamora has coined the term *barroco gabrielino* to refer to "a transculturated Baroque, a New World Baroque that . . . serves as a mode of historical recovery and cultural remembering such as Alejo Carpentier predicted and described" (230). She highlights García Márquez's "ironic engagement of hagiographic history and its conventions of ecstatic subjectivity" in *Of Love* as Neobaroque and his dramatization of "the heterogenous cultures and belief systems in colonial Cartagena" as New World Baroque (230). In the process of "historical recovery and cultural remembering," the different narrative discourses of the novel also make use of the Baroque to claim the validity of these discourses as artifice. The focus on the artifice of the narrative discourse reflects, in turn, the arbitrariness of the reading of signs claimed by the novel versus absolute notions of truth. This particular use of the Baroque in the text, which mimics the colonial Baroque rather than directly engaging and transforming it through the Neobaroque (the ironic and dramatic elements of the narrative notwithstanding), is what, in my view, cancels out the use of magical realism in *Of Love* as a form of transculturated knowledge.

All the tensions in the novel are the product of the very same Baroque worldview that the narrator develops in his liminal location between the contemporary and colonial world. He eschews a syncretic narrative voice that would incorporate non-Western forms of knowledge in order to reflect on those very expressions of cultural syncretism as subaltern forms of control of the lettered city. The Bishop denounces the futility of the colonial enterprise to conquer souls, hence acknowledging the deceit carried out in outward expressions of faith: "He spoke of Yucatán, where they had constructed sumptuous cathedrals to hide the pagan pyramids, not realizing that the natives came to Mass because their sanctuaries still live beneath the silver altars" (102).[29] And yet the novel foregrounds the artifice, the decentering of meaning, the unreliability of perceptions. The reality of the novel is the reflection of many other realities as in a never-ending hall of mirrors, or in the portrait of Sierva María in which the artist depicts her on a cloud surrounded by adoring demons and which she describes as a true reflection of her real self, "a mirror" (105). Cayetano Delaura, who observes her as she poses for the painter, does not perceive such supernatural attributes but instead sees her "covered in precious gems and with her hair spilling down to her feet, posing with the exquisite dignity of a black woman for a celebrated portrait painter from the Viceroy's entourage" (105).[30] Rather than positing magic as a form of knowledge, the novel, stressing its own narrative construct as the direct participation of a chronicler/*letrado*, calls attention to the issue of perception, to what it means to see in order to apprehend reality. Many examples sustain this thematic focus, such as when Cayetano's vision in one eye is temporarily impaired by the eclipse, only to have Abrenuncio remove the priest's eyepatch and remark that the only thing wrong with the eye is that it sees more than it should (113). From this perspective, other episodes of seeing/not seeing that would be deemed magical or fantastic constitute allegorical representations of cognitive processes that uncover individual and collective states of mind and their epistemological limitations rather than instances of magical realism.[31] An example is when Delaura, with his eyes closed, witnesses "Sierva María's hair coiled with a life of its own, like the serpents of Medusa, and green spittle and a string of obscenities in idolatrous language poured out from her mouth" (118); another is when the guard comes into her cell and, after making a routine inspection, "left without seeing Cayetano in the bed" (126).[32]

In this Baroque consciousness of mirrors, the references to lying on the part of the slaves point to a subaltern assertion of agency in the face of colonial power. When the Marquis explains to Cayetano Delaura that "'the blacks lie to us but not to each other'" (110),[33] he is admitting to an epistemological challenge to the knowledge of Western subjectivity that, in the universe of the novel, is deeply embedded in the appearances and illusions of sensorial perceptions of the Baroque. The novel references the complex signification of African-influenced traditions by alluding to an alternative space of epistemological subversion. And yet that space exists mostly on a symbolic plane, as a counternarrative to the powers of the Church, much like the banned books in both Abrenuncio's house and the library overseen by Cayetano or the poetry of Garcilaso.[34] In fact, rather than being unified in the aesthetic syncretism of the Baroque,[35] these spaces exist side by side as the narrator-chronicler intertwines competing philosophies and ideologies, laying bare the binary oppositions enacted by "the lettered city." In this accumulation of meanings, the narrative reveals, on the one hand, the contradictions and fragmentations of the modernity project, and on the other, the normative power of writing, represented here by the records (*actas*) from the convent based on firsthand observations of Sierva María's behavior. Even if in practice the laws in the colonies change rapidly—as Abrenuncio states regarding Cayetano's eventual banishment to the leper hospital because of his inappropriate relations with Sierva María, and as further suggested in the Bishop's questioning of the reliability of the *actas*—the authority of colonial rule is sustained by the symbolic power of the law. Notably, that construction of colonial power in the novel does not entirely correspond to the society of the Caribbean coast of Colombia in the eighteenth century, which Múnera characterizes as peripheral in its lack of rule of law or religious control (71).[36]

In this system of signs that form the city within the novel, the narrative makes visible the complexities of Santería practices as a form of knowledge that defies the unifying control of the *letrados*. The description of Santería practices in the novel constitutes an amalgamation of elements from diverse religious systems. As with the novel's other cultural and historical representations—its ahistorical historicity—the portrayal of African-influenced traditions incorporates local realities without aiming for ethnographic precision. In fact, as amalgamations, these portrayals should strike the reader as deliberately artificial.[37] Against the Catholic Church's Counter-Reformation ideology of death, the syncretism of Santería functions in the novel as a life force.[38] The only parts of the city that seem to be alive are those associated with black culture, such as the slave quarters where Sierva María has grown up and the neighborhood of Getsemaní: "In that oppressive world where no one was free, Sierva María was: she alone, and there alone. And so that was where her birthday was celebrated, in her true home and with her true family" (11–12).[39] Ortega describes Sierva María as premodern in her education and ethnicity, as well as in her refusal of writing (*El sujeto dialógico* 306). For Gilroy "premodern images and symbols" acquire "an extra power in proportion to the brute facts in modern slavery" (56). Those symbols appear in the novel in the form of vernacular languages and cultural practices, such as cures for rabies, that escape the totalizing control not only of the Church but also of a modernity project. The threat to colonial rule is articulated not within those cultural manifestations, however, but rather in the total absence of discourse, with the depiction of the slaves lurking in the shadows of the palace of the Marquis and "the congenital fear of American-born nobles that their slaves will murder them in their beds" (38).[40] With this clear allusion to slave rebellions in the colonies, especially to the slave rebellion at the end of the century in Haiti, the novel invokes another scenario for the independence process in Latin America, a possibility of escaping the mechanisms of the lettered city. Still, this alternative cannot materialize within the parameters of the novel.[41]

Rama states that one of the important roles of the lettered city is "overseeing the transculturation of an indigenous population numbering in the millions. In the universe of signs, the native people could be made to acknowledge, with satisfactory formalism, European values that they embraced only tepidly and may, at times, hardly have understood" (19). The hybridity of Sierva María, developed under the tutelage of head slave Dominga de Adviento, explodes the understanding of transculturation as a civilizing practice through the act of writing the city and its subjects, highlighting once again, in the Baroque construction of the novel, the artificiality of signs. Sierva María infiltrates this discursive world by parodying those efforts of civilization, appropriating its excesses and exploiting its fears and irrationality to show that the evil, the monstrous, is created in the eye of a fanatical beholder. She may succumb to the traps of European courtly love through the poetry of Garcilaso, but she does so by making the verses her own through her own orality, "corrupting and twisting the sonnets to suit themselves, toying with them with the skill of masters" (126).[42] In this sense, Sierva María also signals the appropriation of Western cultural expressions to suit a particular (American) reality.[43] However, doomed from the beginning of the novel to an early death, the girl's radical interventions and appropriations are ultimately rendered futile.[44]

***

In the rewriting of the colony carried out in *Of Love*, the historical processes are presented as inevitable, already determined by the forensic evidence of the present. For a story allegedly born out of García Márquez's chance visit to the convent of Santa Clara as a young journalist, the fatalistic reading of those corpses as evidence of failed progress for Latin America may seem paradoxical in its overdetermination. In a novel in which nothing is happenstance, the mention of Leibniz on the part of the viceroy constitutes a metareference to the transition from the Renaissance and Baroque to a different concept of Fate in modernity that redefines it as a "contingency" rather than a "necessity."[45] Yet within the dominant system of beliefs in the novel, the fateful rendering of events undermines the claims to both the liberating power of reason and the control of human beings over circumstances not necessarily of their own making. The unexplained death of Father Tomás de Aquino de Narváez could be interpreted as a contingent event, but one that it is ultimately a necessary plot development within the novel's narrative design. Father Aquino, whom the Bishop chooses as Sierva María's exorcist to replace Father Cayetano, can communicate with her in three African languages and, because of his enthusiastic knowledge of African religions and life among slaves, together with his position as former prosecutor for the Inquisition, can mediate between the girl and the Abbess. It is clear that such a character, who would have saved the girl, could not himself survive. The narrator-chronicler cannot but transmit a sense of doom in the face of events that seem to be governed by outside forces and that undermine his own narrative agency. Of course this avowed lack of authorial control is inscribed in the very fictionality of a novel that, in its prologue, negates such fabrication; everything is determined in the act of writing that sustains a Baroque perspective of fate, rather than a modern one, in order to highlight the erasure carried out by the passing of time. As he surveys the city's material and moral ruins, the depiction of the chronicler brings to mind Quevedo's "Salmo XVII," in which the gaze of the poetic voice can find nothing in its material surroundings that is not a reminder of death.

Sierva María's fate is determined by the very conditions of her birth that deny her the possibility of life, only to be saved by the faith of a slave: "That was when Dominga de Adviento promised her saints that if they granted the girl the grace of life, her hair would not be cut until her wedding night. No sooner had she made the promise than the girl began to cry" (42).[46] When Dominga proclaims that the girl will be a saint, the Marquis contradicts her, saying that the girl will be a whore (42). Right from the beginning Sierva María becomes a site of contested interpretations, a symbol of an already plotted destiny that can only be fulfilled. That fate is further reaffirmed in the dream she uncannily shares with Cayetano Delaura, in which she is sitting in front of a window—Cayetano's window in Salamanca—overlooking the fields covered in snow and eating a bunch of grapes. Because a new grape comes out each time she consumes one, Sierva María does not hurry to eat up all of the grapes, as she will die as soon as she eats the last one in the bunch. This is the dream she has at the end of the novel, just before she is to face another exorcism session. In this instance, she hurries to devour the whole cluster, finally in charge of her destiny by cutting short the rituals of exorcism to die instead, as the narrator proclaims, because of love. Hence, the novel cannot but be an extension of death, an ironic chronicling of a progress arrested by its material and moral ruins, highlighting its own narrative construct to make it inseparable from the artifices of power. Having been born from the bones discovered in the crypt of the convent, the whole narrative becomes a memento mori, its development punctuated by instances of illness and demise, as with the corpses of the slaves afloat in the harbor, or the annihilation of reason, both literally and metaphorically, embodied in a diagnosis of rabies.

At the end, the novel can only invoke modernity's demons, as its title suggests, with love in modern form as the most monstrous and destructive among them. The concluding lines, which document the rebirth of Sierva María's hair, revert back to the opening of the narrative. In retrospect, we see the work's fundamental tension already laid out from the very beginning. The first words of the text are an epigraph by Thomas Aquinas suggesting that hair, unlike other parts of the body, has a limited material afterlife. The prologue that immediately follows contradicts Aquinas's claim even as Sierva María's hair—in Baroque excess—overflows her tomb when it is opened two hundred years later. Such excess undermines the tenets of Aquinas's Scholasticism, repeatedly invoked throughout the novel by the representatives of colonial authority. That hair is what stands out as newsworthy for the author-journalist, not just because of its strangeness but because it makes present a popular memory and culture surviving to bear witness to the ruins of the past. In contrast to the cataclysmic wind that sweeps away Macondo at the end of *One Hundred Years of Solitude*, the narrator-chronicler of *Of Love and Other Demons* recovers the remains of a city with historical accounts made anew in the present moment of writing/narrating. Thus, the novel inscribes through the same fateful discourse that condemns the past its own possibilities of redemption.

Notes

1. "La ciudad se llenó de extranjeros—especialmente portugueses y holandeses ligados al negocio de la esclavitud—hasta tal punto, que la corona decidió establecer allí el Tribunal de la Inquisición para el Caribe y el norte de Suramérica, con el objetivo principal de reprimir las actividades de los judíos, protestantes y herejes de distintas nacionalidades, atraídos al puerto por las posibilidades de hacer negocios" (78) (translation mine).
2. According to Gene Bell-Villada, one reason for this relative lack of immediate attention is the novel's "recondite contents," which include "black slavery, African folk-beliefs and religious practices, church-state relations, Catholic hierarchy politics, and, most tellingly, an intense amour between a love-struck thirty-six-year-old Jesuit cleric and an alienated twelve-year-old girl" (238).
3. "Traspuesta en el patio de los esclavos, Sierva María aprendió a bailar desde antes de hablar, aprendió tres lenguas africanas al mismo tiempo, a beber sangre de gallo en ayunas y a deslizarse por entre los cristianos sin ser vista ni sentida, como un ser inmaterial" (60). All English quotations from the novel are from Edith Grossman's 1995 translation.
4. See Aníbal González for a detailed analysis of the act of writing in the novel in connection with the expression of a subaltern identity.
5. An objective of this chapter is to represent and engage existing scholarship on the novel, which is wide ranging. I identify a number of those works in the essay.
6. "Ésta es la novela más emotiva del autor, pero es también la más literaria." All translations from this source by Ortega are mine.
7. "Estrategias narrativas, negociaciones y reagrupamientos, apropiaciones y transcodificaciones demandas y debates que son toda una práctica cultural de la hibridación y los mestizajes" (17).
8. "Ella sólo puede ser un signo irreductible a la lógica discursiva dominante " (304).
9. "Un acto complejo de la formidable empresa de escribir leyendo " (302).
10. As she connects the novel to current events in Colombian society in the 1990s, Olsen includes an interesting reference to the Colombian constitution of 1990, noting its recognition and protection of all the different ethnicities that compose the Colombian nation.
11. "Esa mezcla de racionalidad e irracionalidad, esa mezcla tan fascinante del siglo de las luces y los monstruos de Goya y de Piranesi " (129–30) (translation mine).
12. Edwin Carvajal Córdoba and María Eugenia Osorio refer to the fictionalization of historical characters as well as the anachronisms in the novel as elements of the "New Historical Novel" (49). But even if García Márquez takes some historical liberties, such elements are

not necessarily anachronistic. For example, what these critics see as a modern rendering of the animosity and open confrontation among the different religious authorities is the setting forth of a historical background in chapter three of the novel in order to explain it as the result of a conflict in the seventeenth century between the Franciscan bishop of the city and Clarissan nuns that led the former to retaliate against them.

13. "*Casi medio siglo después siento todavía el estupor que me causó aquel testimonio terrible del paso arrasador de los años*" (10; emphasis in original).
14. I deliberately refer to the narrator as male, not to conflate "him" with García Márquez but rather to highlight the extent to which *letrados* were assumed to be men.
15. Gene Bell-Villada points out that the novelist's inventions begin in the prologue, since there is no historical documentation of the people buried in the crypt of the convent. He also references the essay by José Manuel Camacho Delgado that notes that the dismantling of the convent of Santa Clara took place at the beginning of the 1990s. My research into the transformation of the convent into a hotel also points to the last decade of the twentieth century instead of the 1940s. Like Bell-Villada, Camacho Delgado considers the prologue a sort of "chapter 0" of the novel (130).
16. For Camacho Delgado, the reference to the writer's grandmother "places us in the realm of myth and legend, it takes us back to his childhood experiences, to the very center of his creative impulse" (130) (translation mine).
17. Isabel Rodríguez Vergara sees the narrator as a writer-historian as well as an archaeologist who interprets and makes possible the communication among the different power sectors that include the state, the church, and the texts. Rodríguez Vergara discusses the 1613 trial of Lorenza de Acereto, accused of witchcraft by the Holy Office, as the historical basis for García Márquez's rewriting of the cultural conflicts in the colony.
18. "Una hacienda de ganado en Mompox y otra en Ayapel, y dos mil hectáreas en Mahates, a solo dos leguas de aquí" (54); "En el tiempo que pasaba aquí, aun antes de las crisis, parecía otro mastín enjaulado" (62); "Había nacido aquí, hijo de un procurador del rey que se casó con su esclava cuarterona" (181); "Le había dicho a Cayetano en alguna ocasión que le hubiera gustado refugiarse con él en San Basilio de Palenque, un pueblo de esclavos fugitivos a doce leguas de aquí" (185).
19. "Fue así como Cayetano Alcino del Espíritu Santo Delaura y Escudero, a los treinta y seis años cumplidos, entró en la vida de Sierva María y en la historia de la ciudad" (106–7).
20. "El fragoso patio de los esclavos, donde se celebraban los cumpleaños de Sierva María, había sido otra ciudad dentro de la ciudad en los tiempos del primer marqués.... Ahora todo esplendor pertenecía al pasado. Bernarda estaba extinguida por su vicio insaciable, y el patio reducido a dos barracas de madera con techos de palma amarga, donde acabaron de consumirse los últimos saldos de grandeza" (18).
21. As Gilroy succinctly expresses it, "racial terror is not merely compatible with occidental rationality but cheerfully complicit with it" (56).
22. Edith Grossman translates "indio ladino" (58) as "astute Indian" (41). I believe "ladino" in the original Spanish has a cultural meaning (indigenous people who have assimilated certain cultural traits of Spanish culture), rather than referring to a personal characteristic.
23. The palace of the Marquis of Casalduero and its adjacent asylum of Divina Pastora are first mentioned in *El amor en los tiempos del cólera* (*Love in the Time of Cholera*), published nine years earlier. It is the ancestral residence of the Urbino de la Calle family. Juvenal Urbino finds the family home in a state of decrepitude when he returns to it after his father's death (147). This novel also depicts Cartagena de Indias in a state of permanent decay (152).

24. See Fernández Merino for an insightful analysis of the role of the configuration of the space of the city as well as of the issue of voice in the novel.
25. For an in-depth discussion of these themes in the novel, see Vázquez-Medina, Reati, Rodríguez Vergara, Utley, and Olsen.
26. "Habló del batiburrillo de sangre que habían hecho desde la conquista: sangre de español con sangre de indios, de aquellos y estos con negros de toda laya, hasta mandingas musulmanes, y se preguntó si semejante contubernio cabría en el reino de Dios" (141).
27. "No sería mal negocio parir marquesitas criollas con patas de gallina para venderlas en los circos" (38). Mireya Fernández Merino has pointed out that Bernarda's words echo the description of the character of Eréndira in "La increíble y triste historia de la cándida Eréndira y de su abuela desalmada" (116). Certainly the reference to "circuses" entails an anachronistic reference.
28. Múnera points to the Inquisition records as evidence that criollos and even Spaniards had adopted elements of the black population's social and religious practices (81).
29. "Habló de Yucatán, donde habían construido catedrales suntuosas para ocultar las pirámides paganas, sin darse cuenta de que los aborígenes acudían a misa porque debajo de los altares de plata seguían vivos sus santuarios" (140).
30. "Cubierta de joyas legítimas y con la cabellera extendida a sus pies, posando con una exquisita dignidad de negra para un célebre retratista del séquito del virrey" (145).
31. Ignacio López-Calvo analyzes these episodes as examples of pseudo-magical realism that, with their comedic effect, make fun of the commercialization and proliferation of magical realism in narratives at the end of the twentieth century. For López-Calvo, the novel satirizes Latin American colonial society with the use of a "corrosive humor" (192). For Reati there is an implied critique of magical realism in the novel.
32. "La cabellera de Sierva María se encrespó con vida propia como las serpientes de la Medusa, y de la boca salió una baba verde y un sartal de improperios en lenguas de idólatras" (160–61); "salió sin ver a Cayetano en la cama" (173)
33. "Los negros nos mienten a nosotros, pero no entre ellos" (151).
34. See Penuel for an in-depth analysis of the symbolic meaning of places and cultural expressions in the novel.
35. Sierva María, as the main exponent of syncretism in the novel, with her suffering and her copper hair can be associated with Mary Magdalene, especially in the portrait by Baltasar de Echeve Ibía, as Parkinson Zamora shows. Both Corwin and de la Cruz García focus on her connection to the Yoruba orisha Oshún and her Catholic counterpart, la Virgen de la Caridad del Cobre, the patron saint of Cuba.
36. Reati also cites Múnera's work to support his insightful analysis of the conflicts between Cartagena and Bogotá in the contexts of both regional colonial power and the independence process.
37. See Tedio and Steenmeijer for further discussions of the discursive function of blacks in the novel.
38. Múnera highlights the vitality of a black and mulatto culture in contrast to a weak cultural production by the white elites. The last decades of the eighteenth century will be a time of transition, with a new generation of criollos who are more intellectually active (106). This enlightened criollo class continues to regard the colonial ethnic others as inferior (74).
39. "En aquel mundo opresivo en el que nadie era libre, Sierva María lo era: sólo ella y sólo allí. De modo que era allí donde se celebraba la fiesta, en su verdadera casa y con su verdadera familia" (19).

40. "El miedo congénito de los nobles criollos de ser asesinados por sus esclavos durante el sueño" (55).
41. For Bell-Villada the rigid, Catholic belief system presented in the novel is subtly challenged by the Enlightenment forces that will eventually sweep it away—under Simón Bolívar's leadership, among others (243). Yet I believe the novel's less optimistic view of modernity's redeeming powers in a Latin American context portrays a historical time that still needs to be redeemed.
42. "Pervirtiendo y tergiversando los sonetos por conveniencia, jugueteando con ellos a su antojo con un dominio de dueños" (173).
43. My analysis here echoes, to some extent, Gustavo Verdesio's critique of the lettered city in its dependence on a model of writing as expression of hegemonic control. For Verdesio, Rama's analysis could have been much more productive had he included the traces of orality in those hegemonic texts (244).
44. For López-Calvo the ending of the novel "signals the end of a potential utopian impulse and points to a pessimistic, allegorical view of reconciliation in a dystopian country" (192). I would argue that this pessimistic fatalism cancels out any utopian readings of the novel.
45. My understanding of Leibniz's concept of Fate has benefited greatly from Franzisca Rehlinghaus's insightful analysis of the change of meaning of Fate in connection to modernity.
46. "Fue entonces cuando Dominga de Adviento le prometió a sus santos que si le concedían la gracia de vivir, la niña no se cortaría el cabello hasta su noche de bodas. No bien lo había prometido cuando la niña rompió a llorar" (60).

Works Cited

Anderson, Jon Lee. Foreword. *The Scandal of the Century: And Other Writings*, by Gabriel García Márquez, translated by Anne McLean, Knopf, 2019, pp. ix–xix.

Bell-Villada, Gene H. "The Unending Love Story." *García Márquez: The Man and His Work*, U of North Carolina P, 2010, pp. 237–66.

Camacho Delgado, José Manuel. "La religión del amor en la última narrativa de Gabriel García Márquez." *Boletín Cultural y Bibliográfico*, vol. 35, no. 48, 1998, pp. 128–36.

Carvajal Córdoba, Edwin, and María Eugenia Osorio. "Historia y ficción en *Del amor y otros demonios*." *Taller de Letras*, no. 60, 2017, pp. 39–52.

Corwin, Jay. "*Del amor y otros demonios* and the Aesthetic Trajectory of García Márquez." *Theory in Action*, vol. 12, no. 4, 2019, pp. 7–19, doi:10.3798/tia.1937-0237.1930. Accessed 4 Apr. 2020.

De Certeau, Michel. *The Writing of History*. Translated by Tom Conley, Columbia UP, 1988.

De la Cruz García, Katia. "Elementos y simbolismo del arquetipo filosófico afrocaribeño de Oshún en la obra *Del amor y otros demonios*." *Literatura: teoría, historia, crítica*, vol. 21, no. 2, 2019, pp. 229–64, dx, doi.org/10.15446/lthc.v21n2.78644. Accessed 24 June 2020.

Fajardo Valenzuela, Diógenes. "El mundo africano en *Del amor y otros demonios* de Gabriel García Márquez." *América Negra*, no. 14, 1997, pp. 101–24.

Fernández Merino, Mireya. *Escrituras híbridas: Juego intertextual y ficción en García Márquez y Jane Rhys*. Comisión de estudios de Posgrado, Facultad de Humanidades y Educación, Universidad Central de Venezuela, 2004.

García Márquez, Gabriel. *El amor en los tiempos del cólera*. Vintage Español, 1985.

García Márquez, Gabriel. *Del amor y otros demonios*. Diana, 1994.
García Márquez, Gabriel. *Of Love and Other Demons*. Translated by Edith Grossman, Knopf, 1995.
Gilroy, Paul. *The Black Atlantic. Modernity and Double Consciousness*. Harvard UP, 1993.
González, Aníbal. "Viaje a la semilla del amor: *Del amor y otros demonios* y la nueva narrativa sentimental." *Hispanic Review*, vol. 73, no. 4, 2005, pp. 389–408.
González Echevarría, Roberto. *Alejo Carpentier: The Pilgrim at Home*. U of Texas P, 1990.
López-Calvo, Ignacio. "Translation, Unreliable Narrators, and the Comical Use of (Pseudo) Magical Realism in *Of Love and Other Demons*." *Gabriel García Márquez in Retrospect: A Collection*, edited by Gene H. Bell-Villada, Lexington Books, 2016, pp. 183–94.
Múnera, Alfonso. *El fracaso de la nación: Región, clase y raza en el Caribe colombiano (1717-1821)*. Banco de la República/El Áncora Editores, 1998.
Olsen, Margaret. "La patología de la africanía en *Del amor y otros demonios* de Gabriel García Márquez." *Revista Iberoamericana*, vol. 68, no. 201, 2002, pp. 1067–80.
Ortega, Julio. *El sujeto dialógico: Negociaciones de la modernidad conflictiva*. Instituto Tecnológico y de Estudios Superiores de Monterrey/Fondo de Cultura Económica, 2010..
Ortega, Julio. *Reapropiaciones: Cultura y nueva escritura en Puerto Rico*. Editorial de la Universidad de Puerto Rico, 1991.
Parkinson Zamora, Lois. *The Inordinate Eye: New World Baroque and Latin American Fiction*. U of Chicago P, 2006.
Penuel, Arnold. "Symbolism and Clash of Cultural Traditions in Colonial Spanish America in García Márquez's *Del amor y otros demonios*." *Hispania*, vol. 80, no. 1, 1997, pp. 38–48.
Quijano, Aníbal. "Coloniality and Modernity/Rationality." *Cultural Studies*, vol. 21, no. 2, 2007, pp. 168–78.
Rama, Ángel. *The Lettered City*. Translated by John Charles Chasteen, Duke UP, 1996.
Ramos, Julio. *Divergent Modernities. Culture and Politics in Nineteenth-Century Latin America*. Translated by John D. Blanco. Duke UP, 2001.
Reati, Fernando. "Andes españoles, costa africana: Multiculturalismo e identidad en *Del amor y otros demonios* de García Márquez." *Proceedings of 1998 Jornadas Andinas de Literatura Latinoamericana (JALLA)*, Universidad Andina Simón Bolívar, 1998, pp. 91–96.
Rehlinghaus, Franzisca. "Farewell to Fortuna-Turning Towards Fatum." *The End of Fortuna and the Rise of Modernity*, edited by Arndt Brendecke and Peter Vogt, De Gruyter Oldenbourg, 2017, pp. 151–74.
Rodríguez Vergara, Isabel. "*Del amor y otros demonios*: Incinerando la colonia." *Apuntes sobre literatura colombiana*, compiled by Carmenza Kline, www.javeriana.edu.co/narrativa_colombiana/contenido/bibliograf/kline/isabel.htm. Accessed 10 May 2020.
Roetker, Susana. *La invención de la crónica*. Letra Buena, 1992.
Sancholuz, Carolina. "Sobre los comienzos: *La renuncia del héroe Baltasar* y sus proyecciones en la narrativa de Edgardo Rodríguez Juliá." *Orbis Tertius*, vol. 12, no. 13, 2007, pp. 1–17.
Steenmeijer, Maarten. "Racismo utópico en *Del amor y otros demonios* de Gabriel García Márquez." *Espéculo: Revista de Estudios Literarios*, no. 27, 2002, www.ucm.es/ info especulo/numero27/delamor.html. Accessed 30 Dec. 2019.
Tedio, Guillermo. "*Del amor y otros demonios* o las erosiones del discurso inquisitorial." *Espéculo: Revista de Estudios Literarios*, no. 29, 2005, www.ucm.es/info/especulo/ numero29/delamor.html. Accessed 30 Dec. 2019.
Utley, Gregory. "Exorcism, Madness and Identity in Gabriel García Márquez's *Del amor y otros demonios*." *Hispanófila*, no. 162, 2011, pp. 79–90.

Vázquez-Medina, Olivia. "Reading Illness in Gabriel García Márquez's *Del amor y otros demonios.*" *The Modern Language Review*, vol. 108, no. 1, 2013, pp. 162–79.

Verdesio, Gustavo. "Revisando un modelo: Ángel Rama y los estudios coloniales." *Ángel Rama y los estudios latinoamericanos*, edited by Mabel Moraña, Instituto Internacional de Literatura Iberoamericana, Universidad de Pittsburgh, 1997, pp. 235–48.

CHAPTER 30

THE LATER WORK OF GABRIEL GARCÍA MÁRQUEZ

NICHOLAS BIRNS

The Astute Devices of Poetry

Two observations within pages of each other in the first volume of Gabriel García Márquez's never-completed autobiographical trilogy *Living to Tell the Tale* display the delicate interweave between García Márquez's art and life that characterizes his later work. One observation is of a political nature. He describes the 1940s Colombian president Alberto Lleras Camargo as "a writer gone astray" (221),[1] in a way clearly sympathetic to a moderate liberal who is supposed to create and strengthen mainstream regional institutions such as the Organization of American States. Earlier, the author had made clear his distaste for the Conservative Party, which had dominated Colombian politics for so long, and his emotional allegiance to the liberalism of figures such as Lleras Camargo and the martyred Jorge Eliécer Gaitán, who was kept from the presidency by the conservative establishment. Although by the time García Márquez reached adulthood this liberal tradition had broken down in frustration and disillusionment and new, more radical approaches as expressed in the Cuban Revolution were gaining prominence, García Márquez as a writer is almost a mirror image of his portrait of Lleras Camargo: humane, reformist politics forced into imagination as the only arena in which it can achieve not just victory but sustenance and survivability. This residual Liberal theme looms in all of the Colombian master's work; even in *Memories of My Melancholy Whores*, the nameless elderly male narrator muses on his grandfather telling him about the Thousand Days' War and the treaty of Neerlandia, events in the early twentieth century that ended the residue of the nineteenth-century Colombian Liberal dream, entrenched the Conservative Party in power, and transferred the Panamanian isthmus into more or less a protectorate of the United States, making politically literal the economic dominance that the latter half of *One Hundred Years of Solitude* shows US economic and corporate interests already achieving in Macondo.

These are the political basics of García Márquez. Yet they are political basics with imaginative consequences. A few pages earlier in *Living to Tell the Tale*, García Márquez speaks of the *Arabian Nights* and the supposition of his youthful self that "the marvels recounted by Scheherazade really happened in the daily life of her time" (219).² He goes on to say that if those sorts of miraculous events stopped happening, it was because of the intimidation and demoralization of the people. In this way, marvel and miracle in the imagination can also serve as a form of political liberation and of liberalism that can, paradoxically, be more readily realized than can the actual election of a liberal figure such as Gaitán. García Márquez as a writer is formed by the weird necessity that, as it were, "Scheherazade Sí, Gaitán No" is a slogan that was practicable in the world in which he grew up and indeed, for him as a writer, was the only practicality.

What Mariano Siskind terms the "idiosyncratic hyperlocalism" (87) of Aracataca/Macondo, the way it is only a small city in a peripheral vision that is not necessarily representative of the entire country, unburdens García Márquez from the task of literal national representation, even if it frees him to take up the task on a higher, more metaphorical level, and in a way that extends the task past the national to the international and transnational. The author is defining the name as a sign for a plantation, a home, a dwelling, not a larger community; that he himself speculates about the possible antecedents of and causation of the name in his own unconscious allows an element of randomness reminiscent of the surrealist even as, on another level, it deeply responds to experiential prompts.

For those accustomed to only seeing the work of García Márquez through the lens of magical realism, the later work is apt to seem anticlimactic and even inert. The tendency has been to see the later work, as instanced by *News of A Kidnapping* and *Living to Tell The Tale*, as more journalistic and more tending toward nonfiction. Yet not only is *Memories of My Melancholy Whores* very much a fictional narrative, but conversely, one of García Márquez's earliest works, *The Story of a Shipwrecked Sailor*, is a (ghost-written) nonfictional autobiography, and *Clandestine in Chile*, published just before the beginning of the late phase, is a nonfiction narrative. García Márquez's muse has always been one that hovered delicately in the neighborhood of fact, on the other hand always seeing a sort of inherent or found poetry in the given and the apparent. Along with V. S. Naipaul, his fellow Caribbean writer and fellow Nobel laureate, and to a degree the Polish writer Ryszard Kapuściński, García Márquez may be said to have invented the nonfiction novel about the Global South. These three writers are comparable despite their very different political affiliations: Kapuscińki was a Pole who during the communist era was at least tacitly critical of the regime, and Naipaul was a great scourge of the international left who was at least received hospitably in conservative quarters even if never overtly identifying as a conservative, yet whom García Márquez nonetheless acclaimed as a "maestro of the novel" (193).³ Unlike the other two, García Márquez is perceived very much as a man of the left internationally. Yet all practiced literary reportage that went beyond the headlines and regime changes of the Global South to look at how conjunctions of political power, incidences of daily life, and quirks of personality intersected.

Literary reportage also enabled García Márquez to go beyond the memories of the Aracataca of his childhood. *News of a Kidnapping*—in its focus on the drug trade, the Medellín cartel, and its kingpin, Pablo Escobar, and more widely, on violent deeds committed by nonstate actors, including interests such as the drug cartels that are clearly benefiting from global neoliberalism, without which the demand for cocaine in the United States would have been smaller—heralds the world of the Latin American novel of the early twenty-first century and even of television dramas such as *Sicario*. Indeed, two major Colombian books by writers of the next generation deal with these issues: Héctor Abad Faciolince's *Oblivion*, a memoir about the killing of his father in Medellín by paramilitaries, and Juan Gabriel Vásquez's *The Sound of Things Falling*, which features, in the days of its later abandonment, the same personal zoo of Pablo Escobar that García Márquez mentions in the days of its flourishing. *News of a Kidnapping* disallows any binary divides between the Nobel Prize winner and the Colombian writers of the generation who followed him. That Vásquez's book is fiction and Abad's nonfiction shows how gossamer the line between them is in *News of a Kidnapping*, despite nothing in the latter being made up.

Thus the proximity to fact in the later work of García Márquez does not mean it is without an aesthetic component. First, the concession and verbal austerity of a certain mood of reportage can be very close to poetry, and this is seen in such writers as Ernest Hemingway, Albert Camus, and Stephen Crane. García Márquez has a much more florid and exfoliating style than any of these, but he has a similar eye for the revelatory detail or the immaculately turned phrase that is true to life on the substantive level, yet true to art on a stylistic one. Second, *News of a Kidnapping*—the most overtly nonfictional of the later work—is novelistic in its initial focus on the figure of Maruja Pachón and its intimate portrayal of her experience of being kidnapped, as is its broadening out to tell the story of a good number of people and how they were involved in the web of the kidnappings. Not just the victims but Escobar himself and the conservative president César Gaviria are described with a combination of neutrality and empathy—with a sense of how they felt, not how García Márquez, in a biographical sense, felt about them. Small details are included, like Gaviria not turning on his bedroom light on the day of the announcement of Maruja Pachón's release, so as not to wake his wife; the level of genuine personal respect Escobar feels for Father García Herreros, who acts as an intermediary and negotiator to free the hostages, or for Maruja's husband, Luis Alberto Villamizar, whom Escobar praises as "a man of your word" who he knew "wouldn't fail me" (275). It is not just a matter of the author being a good reporter but of his having insight into psychology and narrative shape. This is made explicit at the end of the book when Maruja receives a package with the ring she had been wearing the night of the abduction: "One diamond chip was missing, but it was the same ring" (291). This final image lends the book a sense of unity and a slight dialectical or redemptive fillip to counteract the unimpassioned detachment of the author's tone. The facts are all true. But the focus on character and experience is novelistic. This is true of *Living to Tell the Tale* as well. It not only adheres to the very literary conventions of an autobiography but is also the story of its author becoming the writer he has to be in order to compose the book; it is not just a *Bildungsroman* but also a *Künstlerroman*. It makes clear that the life of its author is preeminently a life of art.

Strange Pilgrims is a collection of stories García Márquez wrote largely in the 1970s but which were published in the 1990s. It thus belongs to the period of the later work, with its atmosphere of observed anecdote leading to radical love or loss without any graduation. In his prologue to the collection, García Márquez speaks of the stories in the book as "based on journalistic facts that would be redeemed from their mortality by the astute devices of poetry" (ix).[4] García Márquez said *Strange Pilgrims* was his only deliberately composed book of short stories. He also says he originally wrote sixty-four, ended up with only twelve that were satisfying, and revised them very quickly, giving them the forcefulness and improvisation of a sketch and the unity of feeling of a lyric poem. Several of them were treatments of film scripts, some of which were actually realized. They thus are interstitial not only in setting but also in genre; this in-between quality pervades the stories. In "Sleeping Beauty and the Airplane," the third story in the collection, the narrator writes of his encounter with a beautiful woman who sits next to him on a flight from New York to Paris after the flight was delayed by many hours. Though he never even knows her name, the many hours of physical proximity give him a tantalizing sense of her presence, yet even though they "lay together, closer than if we had been in a marriage bed" (59), her veil of anonymity and mystery is never pierced. This is not only a realistic story of the practical hardships and accidental rencontres of globalization, but a lyric encounter with a romantic object at once tangibly close and perceptually far. Kathleen McEvoy points out that this can be seen as the germ of the unconsummated romantic relationship in *Memories of My Melancholy Whores*. That literary works by Gerardo Diego and Yasunari Kawabata are mentioned in the story heightens this sense of it being at once a nugget of fact and an imaginative parable. Some stories, such as "Light Is Like Water," are pure parables, with the mystical light that at first seems salvific being in fact menacing. "The Ghosts of August" is a rather straightforward parable. It is set in Arezzo, in the villa once owned by the real-life Venezuelan writer Miguel Otero Silva. Here, the presence of the past in all its palpable menace breaks into the present, in a way that might have been rendered in their own ways by Henry James or Nathaniel Hawthorne. But most of the stories are an uncanny juxtaposition of parable and anecdote, phantasmagoria and realism, that takes full advantage of what Julio Ortega calls the author's "combinatory freedom" (4).

No writer has been as burdened by being claimed representative as García Márquez, and no writer has had the reach of their career more overshadowed by their most famous book. *Strange Pilgrims* is a good antidote to stereotypes about the Colombian writer, because the stories are all set in Europe and are all about the storied Old World being seen through the New World prism. The Europe of *Strange Pilgrims* is the same Europe that will later be pictured in the novels of Roberto Bolaño, a Europe of exile and displacement, cosmopolitan opportunities, and fascist ghosts. It is the Europe that García Márquez first visited as a young newspaper correspondent in the 1950s, when he traveled to Italy, France, and even Hungary, and continued to experience as a visitor and traveler in the following decades. It is a Europe that beneath its serene present harbors an often-disturbing past that is also the past of the colonial side of Latin America.

This is rendered very literally in "The Ghosts of August," when a family on a vacation visit to Italy finds the presence of the past far more literal in its haunting than realistic presuppositions would indicate. We get a glimpse of late Franco-era Spain in "Maria dos Prazeres," in which a Brazilian woman who surreptitiously honors the grave of the slain anarchist Buenaventura Durruti lives in fear of the realization of the dreams of death, only to find an astonishing realization of love. That instead of death, our author gives her an unexpected, late-in-life love, shows also that there is political hope beyond the decaying authoritarianism of the Franco regime. Romantic hope is, or can also be, political hope.

Manipulation and Astonishment

Some of the stories in *Strange Pilgrims* are anecdotal and reportorial: some end with shocking deaths—such as "Seventeen Poisoned Englishmen," in which seventeen English tourists die, appallingly, unpreventably, and almost en passant, in Naples. A more pointed critique of European complacency occurs in "Tramontana," when self-styled Swedish sophisticates mock and try to discourage the superstitious fears of a Caribbean man, only for him to kill himself because he was being forced to go to a place, Cadaqués, which he feared. In "Bon Voyage, Mr. President" an exiled Colombian president in Geneva appears to be down on his luck and on his last legs. The exiled president corrals a working-class Colombian man, the ironically named Homero Rey de la Casa, and his wife Lázara David into taking care of the exiled leader and helping him put on his last possessions. At the end of the story, though, the former president has returned to the Western Hemisphere and is seeking once again the political role in his own country. There is a sense of trickery here. The president may have played up his situation with the couple; on the other hand, it may just be an incident of happenstance. He may have thought he was near the end but in fact had more life in him, one of the sheer and strange accidents of ongoing life.

The overtones of power and manipulation in this story become darker in "I Only Came to Use the Phone." Here, the symbolically named María de la Luz Cervantes goes into a hospital in Spain just to try, as the title proclaims, to make a telephone call, but is incarcerated as a mental patient. Her lover tries to visit her but is unable to get her released. At the end of the story she actually becomes insane, having been driven mad by confinement, and dies. The story can be read as parabolic of the torture inflicted by authoritarian governments in Latin America as well as a more subtle critique, in the style of Michel Foucault, of the institutional constraints in seemingly neutral power systems such as hospitals and schools. The story exudes a profound sense of helplessness of an individual who unexpectedly loses her autonomy and is no longer in control of her circumstances. Much in the manner of *News of a Kidnapping*, it suggests that, potentially, such a fate could happen to us all, that we cannot assume we will live in a liberal world. "The Trail of Your Blood in the Snow" is another hospital story, or ends up being one.

The honeymoon of Billy Sánchez and Nena Daconte ends up tragically. Nina incurs what seems at first a minor wound, noticed when she and Billy cross the border from Spain to France. The wound quickly deteriorates and ends up sending her to the Paris hospital, where she dies, with her husband missing both her death and her burial. This is the story of a future being foretold, but also of innocent young people growing through tragedy. His wife's condition, her hospitalization, and, it is revealed, pregnancy, lead Billy "to be an adult" (182). The story, at the end, provides a sort of catharsis, with the specter of snow without blood or promising some sort of transcendence, even if Billy is still too enraged and brave to realize that yet. His pilgrimage is toward a heart-wounding experience that will at once abrade and crystallize the hope with which he had started out.

In "Miss Forbes's Summer of Happiness," a German governess with an English last name is hired by a Caribbean writer living on the Italian island of Pantelleria to teach his children and make them as Northern European as possible. Miss Forbes is hated and mocked by the children, who look down on her. But beneath her repressed exterior, she is filled with deep erotic yearning for Oreste, a handsome, youthful scuba diver. Because she cannot reconcile her lust with her conscious personality, she plays a cat and mouse game with Oreste, finally arousing so much rage that he stabs her to death. The real drama of the story, though, is the children's realization that Miss Forbes is less in control of herself than she seems, as well as the way they yearn for and anticipate her grisly end, even if they do not cause it or understand its sexual sources. There is also a kind of inversion in that the Caribbean family looks down on the Northern European as an "other" the same way Northern Europeans have traditionally done to Iberians and Latin Americans. In another way, the European tradition that the children's father so eagerly seeks comes back to haunt the family in the violent death of the governess and the exposure of the façade of civilization. That Miss Forbes's favorite poet is Schiller, the father of *Bildung*, is no accident. Further, the name Oreste plays with Greek tragedy, and the classical remains on the island are a key part of the atmosphere. The title, with its reference to the governess's summer of happiness that is also the summer of her cruel death, also operates by iconic inversion. But it does allow the woman some autonomy and some moments of actual happiness in her limited and truncated life. The poetry of Schiller serves as a metaphor for her unrequited love, whose absurdity she eventually realizes. Yet even though she is stabbed to death by her would-be lover, there still is a sense in which the idea of her summer of happiness is not a sarcastic or empty one. She actually has had some real happiness and some sense of her life mattering in an erotic sense. She has felt her body to be not just superfluous or expendable. This experience is almost worth her tragic end.

This effect is both one of intense realism and gory, disturbing mystery. To comprehend this duality is important for analyzing García Márquez's vision and practice. In the stories set in Latin America it might be, and has been, tempting to see this effect as saying something about the asymmetries and aborted development of the region. Yet Miss Forbes is in Europe and very much associated with Northern European signifiers. This reversal deprovincializes the aforementioned formula, making us see even the self-purporting universal as vulnerable to the pain of being alive. Here, García Márquez is less testifying to the distinct trauma of the oppressed than registering how the basic situation of humanity is one of suffering. This is true notwithstanding how, as a governess, the dependent position of Miss Forbes is noted, and even though, as a middle-aged woman long past her peak of sexual attractiveness, her ephemeral happiness and permanent sadness stem inexorably from a lack of physical and affective power.

Similarly, in "Light Is Like Water" there is an inversion of privilege. The parents are leftists who leave the children at home so they can see the Gillo Pontecorvo movie *Battle of Algiers*. The drowning at the end of the story is somehow linked to the landlocked status of Madrid and its lack of sea access to the Americas. Just as light ends up being a variation of water in its ability to bestow both life and death, Europe and the Americas hold analogous positions and powers, even if their external forms are different.

In "The Saint," a Colombian man, Margarito Duarte, seeks canonization for his dead daughter, whose body has remained uncorrupted for twenty years. Margarito tries to meet the pope through a series of papacies, dying before he can do so. The narrator of the story pronounces that the father, Margarito Duarte, not the daughter, is the real saint because his selfless persistence and perseverance is truly worthy of veneration. A question in this story is what it has to say about the papacy or the Catholic Church, inasmuch as the last pope that he aspires to meet is John Paul I, who died only weeks into his papacy, and whom he thus does not see. The story makes no explicit mention of the more conservative John Paul II, who would have disagreed with García Márquez on several issues. That García Márquez, when visiting Poland in the 1950s, disliked Cracow, the pope's ecclesiastical home base, as "full of inherent conservatism and regressive Catholicism" (Martin 192) and that García Márquez, in 1983, "was brooding" (Martin 447) about anti-Communist Polish union leader Lech Walesa winning the Nobel Peace Prize, suggests there may also be criticism of John Paul II in the latter's seeming refusal to ever see Margarito, in contrast to his Italian predecessor's willingness to do so. García Márquez's remarks on wanting to go to Poland in 1980—"I would very much like to write on Poland. I think if I could describe exactly what is now going on, it would be a very important story" (Stone n. p.)—suggests that the two eminencies also might have had some attitudes in common. García Márquez was capable of seeing saints and sinners in and outside of political allegiance. "The Saint" tantalizes with these possible implications but finally withholds them from the reader through its astute fabulist devices.

"I Sell My Dreams" is the one story in *Strange Pilgrims* not fully set in Europe, taking place mainly in Havana, Cuba. It inverts the general pattern of the stories by portraying the protagonist, whose occupation was selling dreams, as a Colombian woman, now retired in the New World following years spent living in Vienna and Porto. The tale also explicitly mentions García Márquez's great Latin American literary peers, Pablo Neruda (encountered in Barcelona) and Jorge Luis Borges. There seems to be an analogy to the dreams of the woman of the title and the labyrinthine fictions of Borges, a comparison that is much friendlier to the Argentine writer than, for instance, García Márquez's article on the Nobel Prize in 1980, in which he indicates that Borges's support for the Chilean dictatorship undermined his chances to win the prize and that his name, once prominent in predictions of the winner, had, as of 1980, "disappeared" (*Scandal of the*

Century 190) from them. García Márquez's tacit posture here is one of lamentation and empathy. Indeed, he speaks admiringly of Borges in several places. The labyrinths of *Strange Pilgrims*, though less ramified than those of the Argentine master, still have their intricacies.

García Márquez's attitude to the trajectories of his pilgrims within what Mercedes Cano Pérez calls "European labyrinths" is at various times compassionate, ironic, or even morbid, but their journeys are never decisively differentiated from his own. He always remained a kind of pilgrim. García Márquez easily could have spent his last two decades in the realm of orotund literary celebrity, writing position papers, orating on issues allegedly important to us all, and positioning himself as a weathervane testing the wind in the large gap between his two friends Fidel Castro and Bill Clinton. Instead, his writing became more intimate, more recursive, more fine-grained and to the point. García Márquez took the road less traveled of immediacy and attention over the more frequently trod highway of public intellectual pronouncements. Very few writers had won the Nobel Prize for Literature at so young an age, as is illustrated by a writer of essentially the same generation, Mario Vargas Llosa, winning the prize twenty-eight years later. Few of the younger winners of the prize stayed more loyal to the structures of literary art than the Colombian writer, for all that his fame might have threatened to hinder that achievement. García Márquez largely took positions identified with the revolutionary left and was sympathetic to Marxism, even though he never officially became a Communist or intellectually identified with Marxist systems of thought. But his road to these positions was through the liberalism of his literal and metaphorical ancestors. He felt the impact of the promise of that liberalism being tragically unfulfilled. For all that he could have been a privileged radical, he remained to the end a wounded liberal.

Circling Back to Macondo

But García Márquez, literally and figuratively, remained what he always was, a writer too much on the move to settle down into complacency. Much of *Living to Tell the Tale* has to do with journeys within Colombia, as we get to see our author-protagonist go between Aracataca and Barranquilla, Medellin and Bogotá, Sucre and Cartagena, in peregrinations that are both peripatetic and hyperlocal, glamorous and mundane. This shows the writer as a novice on the move, getting to know both himself and his country, almost like a musician might do while on tour. The title has two aspects. One is simply that the writer has lived long enough to tell the tale, and we think of Ishmael at the end of *Moby-Dick*, or perhaps someone like Antonio Pigafetta on Ferdinand Magellan's voyage (Pigafetta's account cited in García Márquez's 1982 Nobel Prize lecture), a voyager who lived long enough to tell his own story.

The second aspect of the title *Living to Tell the Tale* is a writer's vocation. This is the significance of the first chapter, chronicling the story of a journey that the author and his mother made, when the author was in his twenties, from Barranquilla to Aracataca to sell the family's old house. On the journey, the mother consistently tries to dissuade the young Gabo from pursuing a career as an author, mainly on the basis that his father wants him to take a degree and have a remunerative vocation. García Márquez describes how the plantation called Macondo that he passed by on the train ride inspired him to name his fictional territory, his version of Faulkner's Yoknapatawpha. When reencountering the sign as an adult, García Márquez realizes that his fictional voyage is already underway, and there is nothing his parents' discouragement can do to stop him. His life will be as a storyteller, that is his vocation, and the first chapter of the book shows how he came to the certainty that he would have pursued a literary career no matter what the obstacles. He would live, and love, to tell the tale.

Bogotá, although clearly the center of Colombian politics and culture, does not exert the centripetal force that London or Paris did in nineteenth-century England and France, in the model proposed by Franco Moretti. This also swerves from the traditional model of Colombian culture in which Bogotá, as the "Athens of South America," was inevitably, in the words of Raymond L. Williams, "Colombia's cultural center" (55). García Márquez's Caribbean aspects go outside of the Eurocentric tradition of Colombian culture as a model of propriety and civilization for the rest of the region. Thus the model of a young man from the provinces seeking self-realization in the capital (Moretti 63–65) is not available to García Márquez. But nor is he simply a man of his region. Barranquilla, Aracataca, Bogotá, Cartagena, Rome, and Budapest are just the apt arenas for his literary self to unfold. It certainly would have been different in Peru or Argentina, for the young writer would have inevitably gravitated to Buenos Aires or Lima. The young Gabo eddies between various Colombian metropolises and regional centers, his peregrinations having some of the enlightening randomness of the picaresque.

We learn unexpected nuggets of information about the writer's sources and inspirations. An early short story in high school was occasioned by reading one of Freud's clinical cases, and one of the two records he listened to while writing *One Hundred Years of Solitude* was the Beatles' "A Hard Day's Night." Often, and perhaps as an epiphenomenon of their haste to enshrine him among the great authors of the canon, critics have seen García Márquez as somebody not particularly in touch with either the advanced theory or pop culture of the twentieth century. *Living to Tell the Tale* reveals García Márquez to be very much part of the international culture, high and low, of his time, and could be read as a tacit reminder to the groups of younger writers that had emerged by the time the book was written—for instance the Crack writers in Mexico and the McOndo writers in Chile—that they were not the first Latin American writers to be global and contemporary. García Márquez indeed at an early age had international ambitions and wrote into international literary space. As revealed in his fragmentary essay, "I Visited Hungary," included in *The Scandal of the Century* (112–18), García Márquez was among the first sets of journalists admitted into Hungary after the suppression of the 1956 revolution, where, he observed, "fear and distrust appear everywhere" (117).[5] Likewise, *Living to Tell the Tale* ends with him leaving Colombia to go to Europe in order to cover the Geneva summit between Eisenhower and Khrushchev. Although, as Gerald Martin reveals, García Márquez, as a leftist, was "pleased to be given arguments" (227) that the repressive state apparatus of the Soviet-supported Janos Kádár was not as awful as it in fact was, his interest was always far more exploratory and reportorial than propagandistic or polemical. García Márquez's early work as a journalist introduced him to quirky incidents and unforgettable personalities of Colombia, but he also wrote into the matrix of Northern Hemisphere global tension in the Cold War and into global space generally; the "scandal of the century" that provided its name to his posthumous collection of essays transpired in mid-1950s Rome. Even though the young Gabo "had no languages but Spanish" (482)—albeit, when pressed, he spoke a bit of English in Hungary in 1957—he went out into the world. Yet *Living to Tell the Tale* is not a triumphalist story of the writer's ascent from the provincial to the cosmopolitan. When he is leaving for Geneva, he decides to formally tell Mercedes Barcha, "slim and distant" (483)[6] with an "intense stillness," of his love for her.

As he is changing planes in Montego Bay, Jamaica, the young Gabo puts the love letter in the box, then embarks on his flight for Geneva. This complex mixture of home and away, ambition and romance, and the outer and inner self emblematizes the multiple structures of feeling that anchor the memoir. That García Márquez's illness left him unable to write the second volume leaves this volume on its own, and that what was intended as a transitional ending is the only ending we have, fortifies, through the accidents of time, embodiment, and fate, its compelling ambivalence. The last sentence of the book finds the young Gabo in Geneva, walking into his hotel after covering "another useless day of international disagreements" (484), and then he finds Mercedes's "letter of reply." Though he does not tell the reader whether Mercedes's response is negative or affirmative, we know, not just from our knowledge outside the book that Gabo and Mercedes were eventually married, but also from a certain affirmation inside the writer's reticence, that the answer was positive. Beneath the caginess and matter of factness, there is an intense romantic idealism that is both remembered and lived in line with the recursivity of the autobiographical narrative and the general way in which García Márquez's later work tends to be both summation and retrospect.

Open reticence, straightforward ascesis, is at the heart of García Márquez's later work. Through its accounts of the germination of García Márquez's journalistic and fictional practices, it also gives us a good sense of ways in which good practices in one genre can help inform another. The young García Márquez hears of a "legendary treasure" (479) that had belonged to Simon Bolívar, most likely gold that he had left behind in his final journey from Cartagena. There is not enough evidence to make it into a plausible newspaper story, but the germ of the writer's much later Bolívar novel was already there.

Yet by the time he comes to write the novel, García Márquez still does not feel he can deploy the legend of the missing gold, even though literary license would certainly permit him to do it. Not only is the older author further distancing himself from any reputation for flagrant magical realism, he is insisting that the best fiction is one that is extrapolatable from truth and stays within the confines of truth, even though not limited or constrained by truth. Even though the story of the gold "would have been essential" (48), the writer nonetheless "could not obtain enough facts to make it credible" (48).[7] This tension—between the narratively essential and the factually credible—is a vertebral tension in the later work and makes the redemptive, reparative love of the old man for Delgadina in *Memories of My Melancholy Whores* at once a triumph of storytelling and of psychological plausibility.

In a discussion between the young Gabo and his journalistic colleagues in Cartagena in which "the ingredients common to the novel and feature articles" (*Living to Tell the Tale*, 336)[8] are discussed, García Márquez says he admires the reportorial directness of Defoe's *Journal of the Plague Year*, but one of his colleagues reminds him that the English writer was too young to thoroughly recall the events of the plague. His colleague Germán Vargas observes that Alexandre Dumas wrote about sailors without realizing many people on a ship in past centuries could not swim. The "grains of pepper" that Vargas puts into the discursive stew to prevent imagination from running riot are very much emulated by the older García Márquez in both factual and fictional narrative, as any incipient flights of fancy are always speckled with grains of reality, there at once for fidelity to reality and deliberate narrative effect.

Love and Politics

The later work of García Márquez begins in 1990, after the fall of the Berlin Wall and the approach of the "Special Period" in Cuba, after the novelist had ended his sixties, and after his work had begun to reflect back on itself. Yet the book in which this latter development first commences, *The General in His Labyrinth*, is not only not overly about García Márquez but very much about someone else: Simon Bolívar. Indeed, as a historical novel about somebody who was not only world famous but whose deeds are very comprehensively recorded, the book does not offer García Márquez much room to innovate, beyond of course speculating how the great leader might have felt about or viewed the final scenes of his life. There is a potential doubling between Bolívar and García Márquez himself, as both are great Colombians coming to the end of their lives and reflecting; in a sense the author is using the general as his surrogate. Equally, although Bolívar is not seen as the direct ancestor of the Latin American dictator, his status as a still admired liberator inevitably slipping into compromise and authoritarianism can be read as a twinned celebration and critique of García Márquez's friend, the Cuban leader Fidel Castro.

Even in *Living to Tell the Tale*, his first and, as fate would have it, only volume of autobiography, García Márquez's late work reveals him as a consummately anti-egocentric writer, whose impulses are scrupulous and matter of fact. By his sixties, he has learned that his creativity and imagination are so extraordinary that he need only let it unfold, with no fireworks, no adornments. This is particularly notable in the book that commences the later phase, *The General in His Labyrinth*. This novel about the last weeks of the life of Simón Bolívar displays the greatest Colombian writer representing the greatest Colombian political figure, although for Bolívar the very idea of Colombia itself was a truncation of his continent-wide dreams. Yet some American reviews—most notably John Leonard's in *The Nation*—were disappointed in how documentary the novel seemed to be, how much it adhered to the historical record. It is true that in this novel García Márquez seems to feel a deep sense of responsibility—he mentioned in *Living to Tell the Tale* that he would have included the talk of Bolívar's lost gold if he felt it had any credence, as it was so promising novelistically. This responsibility is to Bolívar, as a complex historical figure whose memory he respects and wishes to honor. As García Márquez put it, "[y]ou can invent or reinvent if you are writing about Byzantium, but not about General Bolívar" because of the amount of documentation on him. And yet in his afterword to the novel, García Márquez says he had chosen the general's final voyage down the Magdalena River because it was "the least documented period in his life" (271). Fidelity and inventiveness receive equal attention. On top of this is another responsibility the author feels, to Álvaro Mutis, his fellow Colombian novelist, who was planning a book about Bolívar's final voyage but died before he could complete it. As a contemporary who lived significantly longer than Mutis and a writer who achieved international acclaim the way Mutis did not, García Márquez is at pains to honor his colleague's contribution, and perhaps to write a novel slightly less flamboyant than he might have if he felt, as he clearly did with *The Autumn of the Patriarch*, that he was free to reinvent a genre, in that case one perfected by Miguel Ángel Asturias. But *The General in His Labyrinth* has in common with the earlier novel that it is what Gene H. Bell-Villada calls "a novel that aspires to the condition of poetry" (*Gabriel García Márquez: The Man and His Work* 185).

The General in His Labyrinth is not a dictator novel per se, but Bolívar is poised between hero and villain, success and failure. That García Márquez makes frequent references to Agustín de Iturbide, the founding "emperor" of Mexico, allows him to both show Bolívar being anticipatorily ironic when he says that he will be deterred from trying to establish a monarchy because he has Iturbide "there to remind me" (11) and to show how, even though Bolívar shies away from being a monarch, he is not thoroughly democratic either. The end of the general's life is bitter, as he realizes he has lost the greatest part of his best, most true self. The book thus heeds simultaneously clock-time, remembered time, and what Michael Wood calls "the time of the human body" (in Bell-Villada, *Gabriel García Márquez in Retrospect* 118). His last journey down the Magdalena is as compact and emblematic as the Admirable Campaign from Cúcuta to Caracas that unfolded Bolívar's insurgent challenge to the colonial authorities. It is a reenactment and recapitulation of his life, but also an attempt to regain his own individuality and rescue his soul even as the body decays from disease. Manuela Sáenz, his paramour, is ever present in his memories as companion and muse, a comforter but also an index of the hero's own disappointment in himself. In this way, the fact of Bolívar's being trapped in a labyrinth out of which the only possible way is death is analogous to the subject position of the aging writer himself, an analogy that would not be possible if the writer could not estimate he was of equal stature with the general and have that not be seen as egocentric or deluded. There is a sense the author is remaking Bolívar in his own image. But if he had not done so, the reader's sense of letdown would have been understandable.

Despite Bolívar being a public man par excellence, the novel focuses on his private and inner life and measures how it is at once quickened and marred by his public persona. Wandering at night in Puerto Real, he sees a woman "who turned to look at him as he passed" (90), leaving him surprised "by her lack of surprise at his nakedness" (90).[9] She sings under her breath "it is never too late to die of love" (91).[10] On an inexorable journey toward death, Bolívar still has the option to die of love—to die as a private person, an individual—and not die without love, a mere political symptom. Whether she is "a dream, a hallucination, or an apparition" (91) is never solved, but no one else but the general sees her. The woman might seem a ghost, but her presence is the opposite of a haunting: it is the possibility of transcendence in a story that would otherwise be totally pathetic and anticlimactic. This elusive sense of transcendent love reveals the imaginative, poetic dimension of the novel, beneath its unobtrusive, documentary surface. The key charge for critics of García Márquez is to analyze the love theme and the social justice theme as both connected and disconnected, allied and contradictory, but both participating in a movement of desire for a better world. This in turn might lead to understanding why he seems able to be so factual and so fictive at the same time, in the same gesture. "The astute devices of poetry"—to cite again Garcia Márquez's characterization, in the prologue to *Strange Pilgrims*, of what was additional to the anecdotal in his stories—as a phrase does not connote flagrantly fictionalizing, unleashing an impasto of imagination upon reality, but consciously brings out poetic aspects that are already there in the material, elucidating them, foregrounding them, and capitalizing upon them.

The same astute devices forestall any dogmatic sense of the political. García Márquez was willing to let his friendship with and affinity to Fidel Castro be the dominant impression of him held by many causal followers of literature, culture, and politics. Many have had their opinion of the Colombian writer lessened by what Gerald Martin calls García Márquez's tendency "to be intoxicated by direct access to the powerful" (226). But one has to say the relationship with Castro did not leave a huge impression on his written work. For instance, Neruda, in his Nobel speech, specifically lauded the Allende regime, whereas García Márquez in his own Nobel speech criticized the United States—indeed wondering if Washington was behind the air crashes that had killed Ecuador's president Jaime Roldós Aguilera and Panama's Omar Torrijos Herrera. None of his last books display this sort of political partisanship, and they concentrate much more on the internal polices and cultural topography of Colombia itself than on mounting larger arguments about the wider world. If the Bolívar novel is a reflection of Castro—as liberator/dreamer/tyrant/tragic hero—it is at best an ambivalent portrait. The same is true if Bolívar is a figure for the author himself. The author seems to agree with Bolivar that Spanish America not uniting is a tragedy, even though such a "golden dream of continental unity" (21)[11] not only would have had to deal with Brazil, huge and at that time still a monarchy, protruding into its core but might eventually have found that unity threatened by reassertions of indigenous identity. The dream of unity is mainly a jab at the United States of the late twentieth century, one with which Fidel Castro would have heartily agreed. Yet all this is only suggestive, a phantom playfulness beneath and around the book's pseudo-documentary surface.

The later García Márquez likes to play with his own sense of identity. The protagonist of *Memories of My Melancholy Whores* is a García Márquez manqué. He is a nonagenarian who has never really grown up. Indeed, he still lives in the house of, and frequently refers to, his parents. He is a writer who has dabbled in journalism and musical performance reviews but has never achieved any success or fame outside of local and unappreciated newspaper columns. His voice is deliberately flat. Reviewers such as Alberto Manguel, in his review in the *Guardian*, criticized this as a fault of the novel. But García Márquez is trying to portray a man of limited sensibility despite his literary interests, someone who despite being second rate in terms of world creative hierarchies has the capacity to change, to grow, and to love. Where the character betrays the excellence that he has otherwise left unmanifested is in his reading: he makes astute comments about an idiosyncratic mix of authors from Thornton Wilder to Álvaro Cepeda Samudio, and the way he reads to his suddenly found beloved, from the *Arabian Nights* to Perrault's fairy tales, is an index of how genuinely open and compassionate he is to her. Whereas the character's sexual experience is merely cumulative, his readerly experience is actually additive. This willingness to attend as a reader to the works of others betokens his late conversion in an emotional and moral sense. He changes from being a man who has never had sex he has not paid for—he feels he has to corrupt even a voluntary encounter with some cash reimbursement—and who has physically exploited at least 514 different women, to being someone who selflessly loves the young girl he has called Delgadina. Like the central characters who reaffirm love late in life in *Love in the Time of Cholera*, *Memories of My Melancholy Whores* shows that it is possible to change even in old age. Rather than the long-delayed romantic fulfillment of *Love in the Time of Cholera*, though, *Memories* portrays a true change of heart, a metanoia in a radical sense. Rosa Cabarcas, the brothel keeper who brings together the narrator and Delgadina, in another story would be a panderer, in the literal sense. But here she is kind of a helping figure who guides the narrator to transcendence.

Some discomfort with the gender politics of the book is understandable. Even though we are told the story of a man who late in life discovers selflessness and true love over erotic exploitation, the extreme age and power asymmetries between him and Delgadina, in addition to the fact that her real name is never revealed and he calls her by a name that is not only redolent of medieval romance but infantilizing—"the little thin one"—make their love more an idiosyncratic blessing than something that can be postulated as a universal example. As in *Of Love and Other Demons*, *Memories of My Melancholy Whores* shows the possibility of an unconsummated love between a man and a woman being, even though within the network of desire, outside the relations of patriarchy and dominance. García Márquez's intent is less to show an undoing of the patriarchy in one fell swoop by a late swerve in the life of a limited old man than to show the possibilities afforded by longevity.

Longevity was also always a theme in García Márquez's work. Indeed, one of the shorthands to describe the magical realism of *One Hundred Years of Solitude* when it first came out was to speak of the incredulity of characters living for a hundred years. With the average human lifespan increasing and with more people able to live with continuing lucidity and purpose in their eighties and nineties than ever before, the late reversal of the main character in *Memories of My Melancholy Whores* is something more realistic now than in previous eras. Indeed, our expectations about age frame our initial expectation of the title: that it will consist of a recounting of past erotic incidences, rather than a new chapter, a new revelation, which make all the purely transactional erotic experiences seem melancholy by comparison. The force of this revelation is accentuated by the deeply particular and indelibly Colombian cast of the action. For all the novella's parabolic qualities, the chief character is no Everyman, but a man embedded and limited by time, place, and character who nonetheless wins out to a rare, cathartic emotional breakthrough.

If the love theme in the later works has made some commentators see García Márquez as a latter-day version of the nineteenth-century Colombian romancer Jorge Isaacs (Palencia-Roth 54), his determination to tell the tale within the labyrinth, to lay out facts real or imagined with the astute devices of poetry, supplies a bracing austerity. García Márquez's ability to adapt his genius to circumstances and constraints can be seen in an anecdote he relates toward the end of *Living to Tell the Tale*, about the story that became the basis of *The Story of a Shipwrecked Sailor*. In researching the story for a write-up in the Bogotá newspaper *El Espectador*, the young journalist found that there had been no storm, and the ship had in fact capsized because of an excess of cargo, improperly arranged on the ship. The story of the shipwrecked sailor, originally perceived as a dramatic scoop, could not be reported as the fact that had organically been conceived. The writer adjusted to the task and produced a moving and engaging account that has reached more readers by its generic oddity than a conventional rescue story ever would have. The moral is both that reality is always stranger than we think and that the writer has to cope with reality as they find it—factual, social, moral, psychological—and work within those limits to their greatest levels of talent and ingenuity, always armed with the astute devices of poetry.

Notes

1. "Escritor extraviado" (244).
2. "Para mí fue como encontrar la poesía disuelta en una sopa de la vida diaria" (224).
3. "gran maestro de la novela," (240).
4. "basados en hechos periodísticos pero redimidos de su condición mortal por las astucias de la poesía," (x).
5. "la desconfianza y el miedo," (154).
6. "alta y delgada,"(502).
7. "habría sido esencial", (56); "no logré los suficientes datos para hacerla creíble" (56).
8. "sobre los ingredientes comunes de la novela y el reportaje" (397).
9. "que se volvió a mirarlo a pasar" (91); ella no se sorprendiera de su desnudez, (91).
10. "dime que nunca es tarde para morir de amor," (107).
11. "sueño casi maniático de la integración continental," (94).

Works Cited

Ashton, Katherine. "Interview with Gabriel García Márquez." *Harvard Advocate*, Mar. 1980, theharvardadvocate.com/article/619/interview-gabriel-garcia-marquez-1980/. Accessed 9 June 2019.
Bell-Villada, Gene H. *Gabriel García Márquez: The Man and His Work.* U of North Carolina P, 2010.
Bell-Villada, Gene H., ed. *Gabriel García Márquez in Retrospect: A Collection.* Lexington, 2016.
García Márquez, Gabriel. *Living to Tell the Tale.* Translated by Edith Grossman, Vintage, 2004.
García Márquez, Gabriel. *Memories of My Melancholy Whores.* Translated by Edith Grossman, Knopf, 2005.
García Márquez, Gabriel. *News of a Kidnapping.* Translated by Edith Grossman. Knopf, 1997.
García Márquez, Gabriel. *The Scandal of the Century.* Translated by Anne McLean, Knopf, 2019.
García Márquez, Gabriel. *Strange Pilgrims.* Translated by Edith Grossman, Vintage, 2014.
MacAdam, Alfred. "Alvaro Mutis, Bolívar and García Márquez." *Review: Literature and Arts of the Americas*, vol. 24, no. 43, 1990, pp. 6465, doi:10.1080/08905769008604607.
Manguel, Alberto. "A Sad Affair." *The Guardian*, 11 Nov. 2005, www.theguardian.com/books/2005/nov/12/featuresreviews.guardianreview15. Accessed 9 June 2019.
Martin, Gerald. *Gabriel García Márquez: A Life.* Knopf, 2009.
McEvoy, Kathleen. "'I Preferred Her Asleep': Gabriel García Márquez Reimagines Briar Rose." *Journal of Modern Literature*, vol. 42, no. 1, Fall 2018, pp. 95–105.
Moretti, Franco. *Atlas of the European Novel, 1800–1900.* Verso, 1998.
Ortega, Julio, ed. *Gabriel García Márquez and the Powers of Fiction.* U of Texas P, 2014.
Palencia-Roth, Michael. "La religión de la estética en Gabriel García Márquez." *Revista Anthropos: Huellas del Conocimiento*, no. 187, Nov.–Dec. 1999, pp. 89–93.
Siskind, Mariano. *Cosmopolitan Desires: Global Modernity and World Literature in Latin America.* Northwestern UP, 2014.
Stone, Peter. "Gabriel García Márquez: The Art of Fiction, Number 69." *The Paris Review*, vol. 62, Dec. 1981, www.theparisreview.org/interviews/3196/gabriel-garcia-marquez-the-art-of-fiction-no-69-gabriel-garcia-marquez. Accessed 9 June 2019.
Williams, Raymond L. *The Colombian Novel: 1844–1987.* U of Texas P, 1991.
Wood, Michael. "After the End, Bolivar in the Labyrinth of History." *Gabriel García Márquez in Retrospect: A Collection*, edited by Gene H. Bell-Villada, Lexington, 2016, pp. 117–27.

CHAPTER 31

THE THREEFOLD SELVES IN GARCÍA MÁRQUEZ'S WRITING

ROBERT SIMS

In Gerald Martin's biography, *Gabriel García Márquez: A Life*, he quotes and comments on a revealing sentence by García Márquez about his life:

> "Everyone has three lives: a public life, a private life and a secret life." Naturally, the public life was there for all to see, I just had to do the work; I would be given occasional access and insight into the private life and was evidently expected to work out the rest; as for the secret life, "No, never." If it was anywhere, he intimated, it was in his books. I could start with them. "And anyway, don't worry. I will be whatever you say I am." (198–99)

The public life corresponds to the autobiographical self; the private self corresponds to his family life and to his hybrid, interview/transcribed/rewrite testimonial self. His secret life is his writerly self, which can only be found in his works. Eli Park Sorensen characterizes García Márquez's threefold selves in the following manner:

> Although García Márquez's fictive works are characterized by explicitly metafictional, anti-mimetic strategies of representation, they have always included an abundance of biographical and historical material; García Márquez's novels and short stories are all unmistakably inscribed as well as circumscribed in a specifically personal, geographical, and historical context. It is this specific and unique representational problematic in the fictive oeuvre of García Márquez which raises a number of interesting aspects in relation to the ways in which he approaches the genre of autobiography, that is, *Vivir para contarla* from 2002. (190)

The key to his threefold selves lies in his secret life/writerly self, which is only accessible in his books and overshadows the public and private lives. For García Márquez, the end is in the beginning and the beginning is in the end, which is another way of saying that his journalism is always in his literary works and vice versa. Hassan El Baz Iguider characterizes the problem this way:

> Now, throughout this work we have seen how the author's memoirs are constructed by various fragments taken from the novels, and in which he tends not to make many changes either of content or of style, which leads us to think that at his age, García Márquez opts for the easiest way to write his past, besides being a way to guarantee that infinite nexus that he wants to make well established between his novels, narratives, and his life. *However, taking fragments directly from the novels leads us to conclude that in García Márquez's memoirs there is little effort and autobiographical rigor. He is content to collect what he had already written in his fictions under the title of memoirs.* Based on our conclusions we must point out that the author, when confronted with the writing of the account of his life, does not propose to reveal truths never known, nor to uncover situations of scandalous character, nor secrets that concern him in his most intimate areas. The result is the final text that we have avoids any reference to his secret life. His image as a writer has not been left at the end of the text polemicized by some revelation that readers do not know beforehand. (414; translation and emphasis mine)[1]

García Márquez remains one of the most popular writers in the world with readers and critics, due in no small measure to the incredible and enduring success of *Cien años de soledad* (*One Hundred Years of Solitude*). His response to this overwhelming success and the danger of being solely identified with this novel would be to rely on the journalistic *refrito* or follow-up story format and vary his bricolage writing method as defined by Claude Lévi-Strauss:

> The "bricoleur" is adept at performing a large number of diverse tasks; but, unlike the engineer, he does not subordinate each of them to the availability of raw materials and tools conceived and procured for the purpose of the project. His universe of instruments is closed and the rules of his game are always to make do with "whatever is at hand," that is to say with a set of tools and materials which is always finite and is also heterogeneous because what it contains bears no relation to the current project, or indeed to any particular project, but is the contingent result of all the occasions there have been to renew or enrich the stock or to maintain it with the remains of previous constructions or destructions. (*The Savage Mind* 11)[2]

The crucial step in the development of his writing occurred when he worked for *El Espectador* in Bogotá in 1954–1955. He wrote a series of follow-up articles in which he used a "reconstruction and balance" method. This format enabled him to maintain his anonymity and avoid revealing anything personal about himself. The bricolage approach to his writing allowed him to continuously rearrange and reorder the heterogeneous elements at his disposal. We see that the magical realist elements steadily decrease after the publication of *One Hundred Years of Solitude*. *Vivir para contarla* (*Living to Tell the Tale*) represents the triumph of the refrito/bricolage combination because he uses assorted fragments from his writing and journalism and stops in 1957. In other words, his memoir is just the latest step in the combinatory process of the two elements.

His narrators show different degrees of transparency and opacity. They seem to fit Flaubert's conception of the ideal narrator: "An author in his book must be like God in the universe, present everywhere and visible nowhere."[3] García Márquez's public/autobiographical self has been ubiquitous and highly visible over the years. By contrast, his private/testimonial self has been at the very least semiopaque and indirect. His secret/writerly self has been completely opaque. His answer to Gerald Martin that if his writerly self were anywhere, it was in his books, is a perfectly bricolage answer because each work constitutes the latest version of this process.

Autobiographical Self/Writerly Self

García Márquez provides an interesting comment on writing and the role of autobiography in his writing:

> All books resemble their authors. In one way or another every book is autobiographical. And every fictional character is an alter-ego or a collage made from this or that aspect of the author, his memories and his knowledge. It seems to me that a writer's work develops as a result of digging down inside oneself to see what is there, for the key to what one is looking for and the mystery of death. We know that the mystery of life will never be deciphered. (Elnadi 1996)[4]

The constant theme of his autobiographical self in interviews and *Living to Tell the Tale* is his desire to become a writer from childhood onward. In one interview he touches upon one of these early moments:

> Around 1950 or '51 another event happened that influenced my literary tendencies. My mother asked me to accompany her to Aracataca, where I was born, and to sell the house where I spent my first years. When I got there it was at first quite shocking because I was now twenty-two and hadn't been there since the age of eight. Nothing had really changed, but I felt that I wasn't really looking at the village, but I was *experiencing* it as if I were reading it. It was as if everything I saw had already been written, and all I had to do was to sit down and copy what was already there and what I was just reading. For all practical purposes everything had evolved into literature: the houses, the people, and the memories. (Stone)[5]

In his memoir, *Living to Tell the Tale*, García Márquez makes it clear that the writerly self is at the center and mediates between the other two:

> Neither my mother nor I, of course, could even have imagined that this simple two-day trip would be so decisive that the longest and most diligent of lives would not be

enough for me to finish recounting it. Now, with more than seventy-five years behind me, I know it was the most important of all the decisions I had to make in my career as a writer. That is to say, in my entire life. (*Living* 5)[6]

What interests García Márquez is the topopoetic configuration of Aracataca and his childhood house:

> Using a kind of lingua-topo-analysis as he terms it, Moslund reads literature as geography, looking at the *lang*scaping of the novel or reading the novel's *land*guage to signal the integral connection in literature between land, earth, place and language. *Langscaping* the novel discloses how places and landscapes are *presenced* in literature—that is, how they are brought before our senses so that we may actually experience the spatial setting of the novel. (Tally 3)

García Márquez infuses his autobiographical and fictional/writerly self with the place in which he grew up: "Before adolescence, memory is more interested in the future than the past, and so my recollections of the town were not yet idealized by nostalgia. I remembered it as it was: a good place to live where everybody knew everybody else, located on the banks of a river of transparent water that raced over a bed of polished stones as huge and white as prehistoric eggs" (*Living* 5).[7] What García Márquez seeks is an all-encompassing polysensorial and physicality of place through memory that will enable him to tell the tale.

García Márquez's autobiographical self in the first chapter of *Living to Tell the Tale* constitutes a placial experience inscribed by the house and circumscribed by the town of Aracataca. Instead of making a nostalgic return to Aracataca, to his origins, he does not express any profound personal desire to do so. As he says in his epigraph, he is not interested in the life he lived (he considers his public life available to everyone; his private life remains semiopaque and requires more investigation), but in what one remembers and how one remembers in order to recount it. Whatever Gerald Martin says in his biography of García Márquez never involves any scandalous, deeply personal revelations that might affect his writerly self. Of course, this self cannot be controlled by him after he dies, but he makes sure that the information provided is guided by the three techniques of paralepsis (provide an overabundance of information, much of which turns out to be of limited value), paralipsis (lateral or selective partial omissions of information, like what he and Fidel Castro discussed in reality), and ellipsis (total elimination of information, such as a detailed explanation of his politics). What he does do in the first chapter of his memoir is to present his placial experience of his childhood and avoid the necessity of meaning culture.

William Faulkner accompanies him, so that the fictional world of Yoknapatawpha county will coincide with his return to Aracataca and he will experience a double placial experience: "I began to smoke the way I did in those days, using the butt end of one cigarette to light the next, as I reread *Light in August*: at the time, William Faulkner was the most faithful of my tutelary demons" (*Living* 7).[8] One by one the childhood memories start to accumulate, even some he never experienced: "It was there, my mother told me that day, where in 1928 the army had killed an undetermined number of banana workers. I knew the event as if I had lived it, having heard it recounted and repeated a thousand times by my grandfather from the time I had a memory" (*Living* 16).[9] When García Márquez "sank into the lethargy of *Light in August*" (*Living* 17)[10] on the train to Macondo, he really found himself in a fictional equivalent of the placial experience he would experience once he got to Aracataca. He says that "nostalgia, as always, had wiped away bad memories and magnified the good ones. No one was safe from its onslaught" (*Living* 19).[11]

García Márquez and his mother are traveling in a ghost train; he liked the name of the banana plantation Macondo for its "poetic resonances" (*Living* 21),[12] and as he travels in the train he is collecting the heterogeneous elements of his childhood in addition to the sights, sounds, smells, touch, and taste associated with each element. As Paul Rodaway states:

> A sensuous geography may therefore lay some claim to reasserting a return of geographical study to the fullness of a living world or everyday life as a multisensual and multidimensional situatedness in space and in relationship to places. Its primary aim is to excite interest in the immediate sensuous experience of the world and to investigate the role of the senses—touch, smell, hearing and sight—in geographical experience. Nevertheless, the senses are not merely passive receptors of particular kinds of environmental stimuli but are actively involved in the structuring of that information and are significant in the overall sense of a world achieved by the sentient. In this way, sense and reality are related. (4)

García Márquez is again accessing the senses of his childhood:

> That vision pursued me for many years, like a single dream that the entire town watched through its windows as it passed, until I managed to exorcise it in a story. But the truth is that I did not become aware of the drama of the woman and the girl, or their imperturbable dignity, until the day I went with my mother to sell the house and surprised myself walking down the same deserted street at the same lethal hour. (*Living* 26)[13]

When García Márquez and his mother get off the train in Aracataca, the sensuousness and physicality of the place reach him immediately: "On the other side of the train tracks the private paradise of the banana company, stripped now of its electrified wire fence, was a vast thicket with no palm trees, ruined houses among the poppies, and the rubble of the hospital destroyed by fire. There was not a single door, a crack in a wall, a human trace that did not find a supernatural resonance in me" (*Living* 24).[14] His memory activates spontaneously as he walks through Aracataca; all his memories come flowing back and collapse the autobiographical I and the fictional I into this centripetal narrator.

When García Márquez and his mother finally arrive at the right house, the lines between fiction and reality disappear. As soon as he enters his childhood home he realizes its importance to him as a writer: "The rooms were simple and did not differ from one another, but a single glance was enough for me to know that in each of their countless details lay a crucial moment of my life" (*Living* 36).[15] When he sees the room in which he was born, he is immediately reminded of an experience in which he soiled his underwear and relates it to his writing: "That is, it was not a question of hygienic prejudice but esthetic concern, and because of the manner in which it persists in my memory, I believe it was my first experience as a writer" (*Living* 38).[16]

They share a meal with some friends and the bodily sensorium comes alive: "From the moment I tasted the soup I had the sensation that an entire sleeping world was waking in my memory. Tastes that had been mine in childhood and that I had lost when I left the town reappeared intact with each spoonful, and they gripped my heart" (*Living* 31).[17] No doubt a variation on the Proustian madeleine, but it opens the door to polysensoriality, to stratigraphic vision, in which the topos is understood to comprise multiple layers of meaning (Tally, *Spatiality* 142), and to a topopoetic reading that involves a panperceptual appreciation of the work: "We read the work's geography with our entire body and all odorous, haptic, auditory and visual evocations of place combine as the presencing of a great synesthetic experience or event of place. Smells, tastes, hardness, softness, temperatures, sounds, and sights hit us all 'at one stroke'" (Tally, *Geocritical Explorations* 34-5)

Aracataca/Macondo establishes itself through a bodily sensorium associated with the landscape that enables his memory to collect these elements. It is clear that the answers to the questions "who speaks?" and "who sees?" come from an autobiographical "I" speaking and perceiving as an adult because he wants a clear path between his memories and how he is going to narrate.: As Moslund states, "Rodaway notes the in-gathering power of the senses in this connection: especially taste, touch, smell and sound are sensations of closeness which create participatory geographies: they cause us to be transported into the being of a place as its properties enter our bodies through the senses in a rich, unfocused and unstructured way—like the boundaryless and structureless ambience of a sound which cannot be reduced to meaning"Moslund, *The Presence of Place in Literature* 5). His journey back to Aracataca enables him to consolidate the inside and outside of his house, the town, "to" set fluid boundaries through a participatory sensorial and physical process and thus convert this place into the interstitial epicenter between his autobiographical and writerly selves.

The word "writer" appears 103 times in his memoir. As early as four years old he became aware that his destiny was to become a writer: "But when my grandfather gave me the dictionary, it roused so much curiosity in me about words that I read it as if it were a novel, in alphabetical order, with little understanding. That was my first contact with what would be the fundamental book in my destiny as a writer" (*Living* 99–100).[18] Everything about him becoming a writer is a self-revelation and/or confirmed by others: "It was tattered and incomplete, but it involved me in so intense a way that Sara's fiancé had a terrifying premonition as he walked by: 'Damn! This kid's going to be a writer.' Said by someone who earned his living as a writer, it made a huge impression on me" (*Living* 105).[19]

So fixated is he that he becomes a *voyeur voyant* who watches himself become a writer from the moment he is born: "Today it seems clear: something of mine had died with him. But I also believe, beyond any doubt, that at that moment I was already an elementary-school writer who needed only to learn how to write" (*Living* 107).[20] The retrospective certitude and inevitability of his destiny borders on narcissism: "The individual can no longer simply look upon his or her own reflection in the pool as a means of narcissistic self-affirmation but rather must look outward to the Other in order to be able to see the Self. This type of narcissism, that comes to the fore in the novels that I discuss, can be termed voyeuristic narcissism, looking from the perspective of reader/narrator Self to the protagonist Other" (Reagan 22). In other words, García Márquez utilizes voyeuristic narcissism to map out his destiny in order to become a writer. He reveals a tendency common to his writing, which is to occupy the center of power in which the narrator is a protagonist disguised as the writerly self of García Márquez.

Numerous other statements in his memoir demonstrate this defining characteristic. Nothing can prevent him from becoming a writer: "In other words: the years were flying by and I did not have the slightest idea what I was going to do with my life, for much more time would still have to go by before I realized that even that state of defeat was propitious, because there is nothing in this world or the next that is not useful to a writer" (*Living* 242).[21] He chronicles the meticulous process of becoming a writer: "Above all because of the affinities of all kinds that I found between the cultures of the Deep South and the Caribbean, with which I have an absolute, essential, and irreplaceable identification in my formation as a human being and as a writer. After I became aware of this, I began to read like a real working novelist, not only for pleasure but out of an insatiable curiosity to discover how books by wise people were written" (*Living* 404).[22] From beginning to end, García Márquez's memoir chronicles his development as a writer through a centripetal collapsed narrator who manipulates his different selves to enshrine his writerly self.

The (Interview/Transcription/ Rewrite) Testimonial Self

While the chalk circle around Colonel Aureliano Buendía in *One Hundred Years of Solitude* marks his solitude, the same circle might, narratively speaking, also serve as a mise en abyme of the center of power where García Márquez likes to place himself. He has made several comments on power that indicate his fascination with it:

> The more power you have, the harder it is to know who is lying to you and who is not. When you reach absolute power, there is no contact with reality, and that's the worst kind of solitude there can be. A very powerful person, a dictator, is surrounded by interests and people whose final aim is to isolate him from reality; everything is in concert to isolate him. (Stone)[23]

As Geovanny Vicente Romero says: "The world-famous Gabriel García Márquez pointed out that 'absolute power is the highest and most complete realization of every human being and therefore sums up all his greatness and all his misery.' That power that our Gabo defined, Henry Kissinger, the master of American diplomacy, was already telling us that 'power is the strongest aphrodisiac" (n.p.).[24]

In narrative terms, this creates a problem for the testimonial "I" who, on the one hand, struggles against direct and indirect forms of power that oppress the freedom of the people. On the other hand, while this" I" cannot exercise power except in writing, which still places him on the margins of power, he can interview, transcribe, and rewrite himself into his journalistic/literary accounts of power. The primary way to accomplish this is to use a follow-up format. The journalistic *refrito* is made up of the odds and ends of a previous story, and the journalist-bricoleur can reassemble the finite components at his disposal.

From the beginning of García Márquez's journalism career, he worked in a bricolage space that was not constrained by strict standards or a predetermined outcome. He was assigned a daily column in which he could experiment with his writing and reorganize the finite elements in whichever order he wished:

> It is not easy to detect the different basic structures of a newspaper column which, like "Another Story" in Cartagena and "La Jirafa" in Barranquilla, allowed the inclusion of absolutely everything that the journalist wanted to write in it, from a formal point of view, without, it seems, a chief editor calling his attention to any style sheet. The fact that the journalist in question lacked any formal training and that, presumably, he only knew that the column had to be well written, do not help explain the situation. (Sorela 51; my translation)[25]

He could mix factual and fictional material that he had on hand every day. As a consequence, he started to develop his bricolage writing style and crisscross generic boundaries from the start. Each day was new *refrito*.

García Márquez's journalistic work for *El Espectador* in Bogota in 1954–1955 featured several longer articles as a result of his investigative reporting. All these articles were *refritos* in which he simultaneously respects the facts and transcends them. He was able to hone his bigeneric writing in this stricter journalistic space. Pedro Sorela describes the crucial moment when he is sent to Medellin, Colombia, to follow up on the tragic story of a mudslide:

> The paper sent García Márquez on his first assignment to undertake the thankless task of reporting on something that, in principle, had already been fully covered. Upon arriving in Medellín, the journalist was just about ready to return and forget his assignment. His story would have been different. He did not do it and quite the contrary he returned with his article whose principal characteristics were already announced in the title—*evaluation and reconstruction*—and which would capture the attention of the newspaper's editors. (Sorela 51; my translation)[26]

This first follow-up story opened up the space of the news stories since he did not have to narrate the story as either an eyewitness or I witness. This approach allowed him to establish his collapsed first-person perspective, which he characterized thus: "García Márquez used to say that the journalist should be like a mosquito, which is there to irritate those in power, buzzing incessantly" (Juanita León).[27] His voyeuristic narcissism enables García Márquez simultaneously to observe the displeasure of the Rojas Pinilla dictatorship, position himself at the center of power, and subvert the official version of the mudslide in Medellín. The title of his article, "Evaluation and Reconstruction of the Catastrophe in Antioquia," published in serialized form on August 2, 3, and 4, 1954, allowed him to restrategize and modify his narrative position. Evaluation and reconstruction define his initial narrative technique, perfected in the spaces of his daily columns, his feature articles, and his concomitant experimental and imitative literary efforts. The exact source of his preference relates to the desire to maintain his writerly self untarnished from the outset. His approach to journalism and fiction is a modified form of omniscience:

> This new type of omniscient narrator is "a trope, a figure of speech denoting a particular type of narratorial performance, and not, or not only, a quality of narratorial knowledge" (Dawson, 148). We need not take the notion of an "allknowing" narrator literally. The second mode, which I will call the literary historian, relies upon the authority of the historical record and the possibilities of imaginatively recovering private or occluded moments in history opened up by postmodern theory. Unlike historiographic metafiction—a form which Linda Hutcheon claims the term postmodern fiction should be reserved for—this mode displays a faith in the literary imagination to supplement the historical record, rather than undermine the narrative "truth" of history. (Dawson, 153)

García Marquez's testimonial self seldom assumes the role of a first-person narrator who speaks for the community and who can be replaced by another voice; rather, it is a collective phenomenon in which the I-narrator does not occupy a privileged position. García Márquez's collapsed I-narrator is "all-knowing," but the degree of omniscience is always influenced by his narratorial performance. Since it is voyeuristic and slightly narcissistic, he must co-opt the first-person account and cohabit the same space. He is like a narratorial second responder to a disaster whose task is not to present the simple facts of the disaster because, actually, it has already happened. His task is to follow up on the disaster and present a first-person account of the disaster from the "human perspective," or "imaginatively recovering private or occluded moments" of the event. The performance aspect of his narrative stance is chronotopic and bifocal, one lens for close-up and another for distance, alternating between a past-present and a present-past perspective.

One of the most revealing places to look for the changing configurations of the testimonial self in the guise of a collapsed centripetal I-narrator are the prologues to three of his longer nonfiction works. In the prologue of *Relato de un naufragio* (*The Story of a*

Shipwrecked Sailor, 1986) entitled "The Story of This Story," he conducts an intensive interview with Luis Alejandro Velasco, during which his transcribed "I" comes to the fore:

> In twenty daily sessions, each lasting six hours, during which I took notes and sprang trick questions on him to expose contradictions, we put together an accurate and concise account of his ten days at sea. It was so detailed and so exciting that my only concern was finding readers who would believe it. Not solely for that reason but also because it seemed fitting, we agreed that the story would be written in the first person and signed by him. This is the first time my name has appeared in connection with the text. *(The Story* vii)[28]

The balance and reconstruction of the story belong to the interview/transcribed self, which will become the testimonial self. As Antonio Vera León says, "Like the 'bricoleur' the transcriber operates halfway between the scriptural subject that is the original source of stories, and the subject of the referential writing" (189; my translation).[29] The fact that they agreed to write it in the first person and have him sign it authenticates the I-narrator protagonist and the testimonial/observer "I" who observes and titillates power. García Márquez, ensconced in the center of power which he dealt with on a daily basis, is also a voyeur voyant who watches his own bricolage writing unfold, as in the following comment: "As we boarded that morning, Ortega was on the bridge, talking about his wife and children, which was no coincidence, because he never talked of anything else. He had a refrigerator, an automatic washer, a radio, and a stove for them. Twelve hours later, Ortega would be stretched out in his bunk, dying of seasickness. And twenty-four hours later, he would be dead at the bottom of the sea" (*The Story* 7)[30]

All the sailors have permeable minds that the omniscient narrator can penetrate. The use of prolepsis is very common with this new omniscient narrator: "The most interesting aspect of contemporary historical fiction is the way it employs the proleptic voice of history to exploit the narrating instance and establish a temporal gap between modern narrator and historical story; meaning that the narrator's omniscient authority is simultaneously heightened and problematized by their distance from the events of the story" (Dawson 153). The extensive use of prolepsis means that eye/I witness/I Luis Alejandro Velasco passes through the interview/transcribed/process, which enables García Márquez to reconstruct the story so that his voyeur/voyant testimonial self can observe/narrate/manifest itself. This seer-seeing position can satisfy his narcissistic impulse to observe/titillate/criticize the Rojas Pinilla dictatorship.

When García Márquez interviews and transcribes, he creates a palimpsest in which his testimonial self can assume an observer/eye/I witness. The palimpsest consists of the first-person account of Luis Alejandro Velasco "in his own words" and the other first-person narrator linked to the previous text, which is the interview. We must not forget that this work first appeared in fourteen serialized segments in *El Espectador*. The text is a merging of the two palimpsestic textual layers in which the two first-person narrators occupy one mind. In the preface to *La aventura de Miguel Littín clandestino en Chile*

(*Clandestine in Chile: The Adventures of Miguel Littín*, 2010), García Márquez not only creates a centripetal first-person narrator but also undergoes an identity transformation so that Miguel Littín can travel around Chile secretly filming the dictatorship:

> Early in 1986 in Madrid, when Miguel Littín told me what he had done and how he had done it, I realized that behind his film there was another film that would probably never be made. And so he agreed to a grueling interrogation, the tape of which ran some eighteen hours. It encompassed the full human adventure in all its professional and political implications, which I have condensed into ten chapters. Some of the names have been changed and many of the circumstances altered to protect those involved who are still in Chile. *I preferred to keep Littín's story in the first person, to preserve its personal-and sometimes confidential-tone, without any dramatic additions or historical pretentiousness on my part. The manner of the final text is, of course, my own, since a writer's voice is not interchangeable, particularly when he has to condense almost 600 pages into less than 200.* (*Clandestine* xxix; emphasis added)[31]

The most important segment appears in italics because the preservation of the first-person narrative is essential to maintaining the opacity/visibility of the centripetal I-narrator and the palimpsestic two-layered structure.

The other fascinating aspect of this work is that Miguel Littín must undergo a physical and psychological transformation to carry out his mission: "I had to become unrecognizable even to my friends. Two psychologists and a movie makeup expert, under the direction of a specialist in clandestine operations sent from Chile, brought off the miracle in a little less than three weeks, relentlessly resisting my instinctive determination to go on being me" (*Clandestine* 4).[32] At the end of the preface, García Márquez remarks that this *refrito* is fundamentally different:

> Yet it is something more: the emotional reconstruction of an adventure the finality of which was unquestionably much more visceral and moving than the original—and effectively realized—intention of making a film that made fun of the dangers of military power. Littín himself said, "This may not have been the most heroic action of my life, but it is the most worthwhile." It is, and I believe that therein lies its greatness. (*Clandestine* xxx)[33]

When Miguel Littín undergoes his transformation, he becomes a physical voyeur voyant and García Márquez a voyeur-voyant narrator. Together they will travel to the center of power, where the testimonial self will assume an observer role, watching someone else experience the exhilaration of penetrating the center of power. García Márquez's voyeuristic narcissism reveals itself much more strongly because there is no break in Littín's first-person account. Garcia Márquez's fascination with power comes to the fore in this work as Miguel Littín and his crew wend their way toward the Moneda Palace:

> At about eleven o'clock on our second day in the Moneda Palace we suddenly heard the quick steps of martial boots and the ratting of metal. Our chaperone officer

quickly changed his demeanor, brusquely ordering us, with a brutal gesture, to turn off the lights and stop the cameras. Two plainclothes bodyguards planted themselves in front of us with the obvious purpose of preventing any attempt at filming. We had no idea what this was all about until we saw General Augusto Pinochet himself, his face puffy and greenish, on the way to his office, accompanied by one military and two civilian aides. (*Clandestine* 105)[34]

The switch to the first-person plural includes García Márquez as voyeur voyant, and his testimonial self observes but does not even obliquely express opposition to Pinochet. Indeed, García Márquez relinquishes the power of protest to the cinematic version.

In *Noticia de un secuestro* (*News of a Kidnapping*, 1997), García Márquez finds himself in the same position, but he must now resort to third-person omniscience because he discovers that ten people were involved in this meticulously planned event:

This belated realization obliged us to begin again with a different structure and spirit so that all the protagonists would have their well-defined identities, their own realities. It was a technical solution to a labyrinthine narrative that in its original form would have been confused and interminable. But this meant that what had been foreseen as a year's work extended into almost three, even with the constant, meticulous assistance and collaboration of Maruja and Alberto, whose personal stories are the central axis, the unifying thread, of this book. (*News* i)[35]

He interviewed as many participants as he could, and his cousin Margarita Márquez Caballero assumed responsibility for "the transcription, verification, and confidentiality of the intricate raw material that we often thought would overwhelm us" (*News* ii).[36] Again we have the substratum transcription of the interviews by another person. This time we have a narratorial "I-as-uninvolved-eyewitness" in the reconstruction of this complex, multivoiced, and layered event. García Márquez will modulate and vacillate between an omniscient third-person narrator who is omnipresent and omni-absent, a voyeuristic narcissism and a more active testimonial self.

The Writerly Self

The follow-up story holds the key to García Márquez's writerly self because it has enabled him to maintain it intact and manifest itself obliquely in his bricolage-constructed works. When *Crónica de una muerte anunciada* (*Chronicle of a Death Foretold*) was published in 1981, he defined bigeneric writing:

For the first time I achieved a perfect balance between journalism and literature and that's why the book is called *Chronicle of a Death Foretold*. That supposedly bad influence that journalism has on literature isn't true. First of all, because I don't think anything destroys the writer, not even hunger. Secondly, because journalism helps you stay in touch with reality, which is essential to for working with literature. And vice versa, because literature teaches you how to write, which is also essential for journalism. In my case, journalism was the springboard to literature, and I learned to write journalism by writing good literature. (De Martínez 72; my translation)[37]

García Márquez's journalism and literary career are intertwined and indispensable components of his writerly self: "Many talented journalists are marred by literary ambitions; but there are narrators who owe a substantial part of their art to the training of journalism. García Márquez is one of them. It is this complex alliance that will strengthen the marriage well with the poetics of the triumphant author" (Franco 194; my translation).[38]

The hybridized generic status of García Márquez's writing; the bricolage narrative structuring of his works; his voyeur-voyant, voyeuristic narcissism; the refusal to write a personal, firsthand account of an event; his *costeño* humor; his ample use of parody and metaparody; and his dazzling reconfiguration of traditional generic forms—all combine to produce a body of original work. The following quotation from *Chronicle of a Death Foretold* shows how García Márquez positions himself in the reconstruction of a tragic event he never witnessed and had to wait thirty years to write:

> For years we couldn't talk about anything else. Our daily conduct, dominated then by so many linear habits, had suddenly begun to spin around a single common anxiety. The cocks of dawn would catch us trying to give order to the chain of many chance events that had made absurdity possible, and it was obvious that we weren't doing it from an urge to clear up mysteries but because none of us could go on living without an exact knowledge of the place and the mission assigned to us by fate. But most of those who could have done something to prevent the crime and did not consoled themselves with the pretext that affairs of honor are sacred monopolies, giving access only to those who are part of the drama. (*Chronicle* 96–97)[39]

First of all, the centripetal, bifocal I-narrator collapses into one and situates himself in a "we" perplexed-omniscience group. He never delves deeply into the minds of the other characters, much less his own. There is a strong urge to observe the crime as a voyeur voyant's vicarious experience more than there is to solve it. His testimonial stance is rather weak, remaining much more observational than proactive:

> In point of fact, the narrator's authority is just as lacking as the other authorities of the novel. The narrator admits himself to be one of the few people not present the morning of the murder, which automatically detracts from his own testimony. He claims to have been with María Alejandrina Cervantes and his account merely summarizes other's accounts. In other words, his eyewitness account is absent the most important hours of the events. In this way, the narrator's role is more journalistic, although he presents the events as a witness, and the external sources he does use are compiled in a way that seems haphazard. (Reagan 207)

In *Living to Tell the Tale* the epigraph represents a definition of his writerly self. Indeed, *Living to Tell the Tale* constitutes a bricolage mosaic of the moments leading to the creation of his writerly self. He radically insists on the sacrosanct idea that Marcel Proust established in his work *Contre Sainte-Beuve*, a critic who had explained literary works strictly by the author's biography. Proust considered this approach a trivialization of a literary work and insisted that the life that one leads has nothing to do with the person who writes. This idea has become a controversial issue in certain quarters because some artists who have committed serious crimes are condemned and their work is judged unworthy of acceptance. If in *Chronicle of a Death Foretold* he was able to display all three selves at different moments, *Living to Tell the Tale* focuses solely on his writerly self to the exclusion of almost everything else. What García Márquez undertakes in this memoir is characterized by Eli Park Sorenson:

> The instability of borderlines is one that is strongly felt in García Márquez's memoir *Vivir para contarla*, which constitutes the first part of what is planned to be an autobiographical trilogy. As the inaugurating work on the author's life, *Vivir para contarla* mainly recounts the time of the author's childhood, and the first literary successes as a young writer in a historically turbulent Colombia. As such, it is also a meditation on beginnings, origins, sources, roots, and aetiologies in general; and in particular a reflection on the genesis of García Márquez's distinct mode of writing, whose intricate trace he has elaborately explored in his fictive works, works that have "made" his name, so to speak, that is, the proper name "Gabriel García Márquez" identifying the Nobel-prize winning author. Together with García Márquez, we remember countless episodes, anecdotes, quotations, gestures, voices, characters, and a lot of other things that we know from his fiction, and which are imperceptibly and seamlessly weaved into the autobiography's text. To the reader, the autobiography's many echoes of García Márquez's novels seem to activate a fictive memory, like an uncanny déjà-vu, which makes the text unfamiliarly familiar. (191–92)

His memoir is pure voyeur voyant where he watches his real/fictive double experience these crucial events, leading him to become a writer. He intends his memoir to serve as a foundational text of the process of becoming a writer. Although the book ends in 1957, he has laid the groundwork for his writerly self, which will continue to evolve. In a sense, García Márquez relinquished the surrogate role of writing his (auto)biography to Gerald Martin so that he could dispense with revealing anything personal and concentrate his efforts on writing a memoir on his writerly self. So, once again, the palimpsest emerges with the first text—his biography and the underlying one—his bricolage mosaic of how he became a writer.

In a final twist to complete his writerly self, he resorts to parody and metaparody in *Memoria de mis putas tristes* (*Memories of My Melancholy Whores*, 2004). There is a remarkable contrast between the cover of *Living to Tell the Tale*, with the photograph of a one-year-old García Márquez, and the Spanish-language edition of *Memories of My Melancholy Whores*, which has a photograph of an old man dressed all in white shuffling away, possibly offstage, perhaps into the great beyond: as if turning his back on life for the last time (though the novel itself defies such an interpretation). The picture also looks eerily like that same García Márquez. Nothing would be more Garciamarquian than providing a parodic double of his writerly self in a *refrito* work of fiction, *Memories of My Melancholy Whores*, and then proceeding to metaparody himself:

> I don't have to say so because people can see it from leagues away: I'm ugly, shy, and anachronistic. But by dint of not wanting to be those things I have pretended to be just the opposite. Until today, when I have resolved to tell of my own free will just what I'm like, if only to ease my conscience. I have begun with my unusual call to Rosa Cabarcas because, seen from the vantage point of today, that was the beginning of a new life at an age when most mortals have already died. (4–5)[40]

Like his memoir, this novel is composed of odds and ends relating to García Márquez's life and fiction dispersed throughout, even a parody of the first sentence of *One Hundred Years of Solitude*:

> At one time I thought these bed-inspired accounts would serve as a good foundation for a narration of the miseries of my misguided life, and the title came to me out of the blue: *Memories of My Melancholy Whores*. My public life, on the other hand, was lacking in interest: both parents dead, a bachelor without a future, a mediocre journalist who had been a finalist four times in the Poetic Competition, the Juegos Florales, *of Cartagena de Indias, and a favorite of caricaturists because of my exemplary ugliness. In short, a wasted life off to a bad start beginning on the afternoon my mother led me by the hand when I was nineteen years old to see if El Diario de La Paz would publish a chronicle of school life that I had written in my Spanish and rhetoric class*. It was published on Sunday with an encouraging introduction by the editor. Years later, when I learned that my mother had paid for its publication and for the seven that followed, it was too late for me to be embarrassed, because my weekly column was flying on its own wings and I was a cable editor and music critic as well. (*Memories* 19–20; emphasis added)[41]

At the end of the novel he parodies *One Hundred Years of Solitude*: "It was, at last, real life, with my heart safe and condemned to die of happy love in the joyful agony of any day after my hundredth birthday" (*Memories* 181)[42]

García Márquez succeeds in maintaining his secret life/writerly self intact, constantly reinventing himself in his fictional and nonfictional works and affording his readers, critics, and biographers access only through his works. The personal part of his secret self has been elliptically eliminated, and so to all of us he says: "Don't worry. I will be whatever you say I am." This is exactly what has transpired over the years. Even though his papers have been sold to the University of Texas and *One Hundred Years of Solitude* will become a miniseries on Netflix Español, his writerly self remains virtually untouched. While it is true that he was beginning to have symptoms of dementia and suffered from other ailments that contributed to his decision to stop writing, it is also possible that he decided to do this so he would not have to discuss Fidel, *One Hundred Years of Solitude*, and other personal matters. As he says in his last interview concerning his second volume of memoirs:

I don't think I'll write it. I have some notes written, but I don't want it to just be a professional operation. I've realized that if I publish a second volume, I'm going to have to say things I don't want to say, because of some personal relationships that are not so good anymore. The first volume, *Living to Tell the Tale*, is exactly what I wanted it to be. In the second, I met a number of people that just had to come along and that— caramba, I don't want them showing up in my memoirs. It would be dishonest to leave them out, because they were important in my life, but they didn't end up being very kind to me. (Streitfeld 94)[43]

Notes

1. "Ahora bien, a lo largo de este trabajo hemos visto como las memorias del autor son construidas por diversos fragmentos sacados de las novelas, y en los cuales tiende a no hacer muchos cambios ni de contenido ni de estilo, lo que nos lleva a pensar que a su edad, García Márquez opta por la forma más fácil para escribir su pasado, además de ser una manera de garantizar ese infinito nexo que quiere dejar bien establecido entre sus novelas y narraciones, y su vida. Sin embargo, el hecho de coger fragmentos directamente de las novelas nos hace concluir que en las memorias de García Márquez hay poco esfuerzo y rigor autobio-gráfico. Se conforma con recopilar lo que ya había escrito en sus ficciones bajo el título de memorias. De nuestras conclusiones debemos señalar que el autor, al afrontar la escritura del relato de su vida, no plantea revelar verdades nunca sabidas, ni destapar situaciones de carácter escandaloso, ni secretos que lo atañen en su profunda intimidad. El resultado es el texto final que tenemos entre manos, que elude referencia alguna a su vida secreta. Su imagen de escritor no ha quedado al final del texto polemizada por alguna revelación que los lectores no sepamos con anterioridad" (El Baz Iguider 414).
2. "Le bricoleur est apte à exécuter un grand nombre de tâches diversifiées; mais, à la différence de l'ingénieur, il ne subordonne pas chacune d'elles à l'obtention de matières premières et d'outils, conçus et procurés à la mesure de son projet: son univers instrumental est clos, et la règle de son jeu est de toujours s'arranger avec les 'moyens du bord', c'est-à-dire un ensemble à chaque instant fini d'outils et de matériaux, hétéroclites au surplus, parce que la composition de l'ensemble n'est pas en rapport avec le projet du moment, ni d'ailleurs avec aucun projet particulier, mais est le résultat contingent de toutes les occasions qui se sont présentées de renouveler ou d'enrichir le stock, ou de l'entretenir avec les résidus de constructions et de destructions antérieures " (Lévi-Strauss, La Pensée Sauvage 29).
3. "L'auteur dans son oeuvre doit être comme Dieu dans l'univers, présent partout et visible nulle part" (Flaubert, *Correspondance* 204).
4. "Todos los libros se parecen a sus autores. De una manera u otra cada libro es autobiográfico. Y cada personaje de ficción es un alter ego o un collage hecho de este o aquel aspecto del autor, sus recuerdos y su conocimiento. Me parece que el trabajo de un escritor se desarrolla como resultado de cavar dentro de uno mismo para ver lo que hay, para la clave de lo que uno está buscando y el misterio de la muerte. Sabemos que el misterio de la vida nunca será descifrado" (Elnadi et al.).
5. "Alrededor de 1950 o 51 sucedió otro evento que influenció mis tendencias literarias. Mi madre me pidió que la acompañara a Aracataca, donde nací, y que vendiera la casa donde pasé mis primeros años. Cuando llegué allí era al principio bastante chocante porque

ahora tenía veintidós años y no había estado allí desde la edad de ocho. Nada había cambiado realmente, pero sentí que realmente no estaba mirando el pueblo, sino que lo estaba experimentando como si lo estuviera leyendo. Era como si todo lo que veía ya hubiera sido escrito, y todo lo que tenía que hacer era sentarme y copiar lo que ya estaba allí y lo que estaba leyendo. Para todos los propósitos prácticos todo había evolucionado en literatura: las casas, la gente, y los recuerdos" (Stone).

6. "Ni mi madre ni yo, por supuesto, hubiéramos podido imaginar siquiera que aquel cándido paseo de sólo dos días iba a ser tan determinante para mí, que la más larga y diligente de las vidas no me alcanzaría para acabar de contarlo. Ahora, con más de setenta y cinco años bien medidos, sé que fue la decisión más importante de cuantas tuve que tomar en mi carrera de escritor. Es decir: en toda mi vida" (*Vivir para contarla*, 5).

7. "Hasta la adolescencia, la memoria tiene más interés en el futuro que en el pasado, así que mis recuerdos del pueblo no estaban todavía idealizados por la nostalgia. Lo recordaba como era: un lugar bueno para vivir, donde se conocía todo el mundo, a la orilla de un río de aguas diáfanas que se precipitaban por un lecho de piedras pulidas, blancas y enormes como huevos prehistóricos" (*Vivir para contarla* 5–6).

8. "Empecé a fumar a mi manera de entonces, encendiendo uno con la colilla del otro, mientras releía *Luz de agosto*, de William Faulkner, que era entonces el más fiel de mis demonios tutelares" (*Vivir para contarla* 7).

9. "Fue allí, según me precisó mi madre aquel día, donde el ejército había matado en 1928 un número nunca establecido de jornaleros del banano. Yo conocía el episodio como si lo hubiera vivido, después de haberlo oído contado y mil veces repetido por mi abuelo desde que tuve memoria" (*Vivir para contarla* 17).

10. "Me sumergí en el sopor de *Luz de agosto*" (*Vivir para contarla* 19).

11. "La nostalgia, como siempre, había borrado los malos recuerdos y magnificado los buenos. Nadie se salvaba de sus estragos" (*Vivir para contarla* 21).

12. "Resonancia poética" (*Vivir para contarla* 23).

13. "Aquella visión me persiguió durante muchos años, como un sueño unánime que todo el pueblo vio pasar por las ventanas, hasta que conseguí exorcizarla en un cuento. Pero la verdad es que no tomé conciencia del drama de la mujer y la niña, ni de su dignidad imperturbable, hasta el día en que fui con mi madre a vender la casa y me sorprendí a mí mismo caminando por la misma calle solitaria y a la misma hora mortal" (*Vivir para contarla* 28).

14. "No había una puerta, una grieta de un muro, un rastro humano que no tuviera dentro de mí una resonancia sobrenatural" (*Vivir para contarla* 26).

15. "Los cuartos eran simples y no se distinguían entre sí, pero me bastó con una mirada para darme cuenta de que en cada uno de sus incontables detalles había un instante crucial de mi vida" (*Vivir para contarla* 40).

16. "Es decir, que no se trataba de un prejuicio de higiene sino de una contrariedad estética, y por la forma como perdura en mi memoria creo que fue mi primera vivencia de escritor" (*Vivir para contarla* 42).

17. "Desde que probé la sopa tuve la sensación de que todo un mundo adormecido despertaba en mi memoria. Sabores que habían sido míos en la niñez y que había perdido desde que me fui del pueblo reaparecían intactos con cada cucharada y me apretaban el corazón" (*Vivir para contarla* 34).

18. "Sin embargo, cuando el abuelo me regaló el diccionario me despertó tal curiosidad por las palabras que lo leía como una novela, en orden alfabético y sin entenderlo apenas. Así

fue mi primer contacto con el que habría de ser el libro fundamental en mi destino de escritor" (*Vivir Para Contarla* 109).

19. "Estaba descosido e incompleto, pero me absorbió de un modo tan intenso que el novio de Sara soltó al pasar una premonición aterradora: '¡Carajo!, este niño va a ser escritor'" (*Vivir para contarla* 115-16).

20. "Hoy lo veo claro: algo mío había muerto con él. Pero también creo, sin duda alguna, que en ese momento era ya un escritor de escuela primaria al que sólo le faltaba aprender a escribir" (*Vivir para contarla* 118).

21. "Mejor dicho: los años volaban y no tenía ni la mínima idea de lo que iba a hacer de mi vida, pues había de pasar todavía mucho tiempo antes de darme cuenta de que aun ese estado de derrota era propicio, porque no hay nada de este mundo ni del otro que no sea útil para un escritor" (*Vivir para contarla* 266).

22. "Sobre todo por las afinidades de toda índole que encontraba entre las culturas del sur profundo y la del Caribe, con la que tengo una identificación absoluta, esencial e insustituible en mi formación de ser humano y escritor. Desde esta toma de conciencia empecé a leer como un auténtico novelista artesanal, no sólo por placer, sino por la curiosidad insaciable de descubrir cómo estaban escritos los libros de los sabios" (*Vivir para contarla* 442-43).

23. "Cuanto más poder tienes, más difícil es saber quién te miente y quién no. Cuando alcanzas el poder absoluto, no hay contacto con la realidad, y esa es la peor clase de soledad que puede haber. Una persona muy poderosa, un dictador, está rodeada de intereses y personas cuyo objetivo final es aislarlo de la realidad; todo está en concierto para aislarlo" (Stone).

24. "El inmenso Gabriel García Márquez señaló que 'el poder absoluto es la realización más alta y más completa de todo ser humano y por eso resume a la vez toda su grandeza toda su miseria'. Ese poder que nuestro Gabo definía, ya el maestro de la diplomacia americana Henry Kissinger, nos decía que "el poder es el afrodisiaco más fuerte" (Vicente Romero)

25. "No es fácil detectar las diferentes estructuras básicas de un espacio periodístico que, como *Punto y aparte,* en Cartagena y *La jirafa* de Barranquilla, admitía absolutamente todo lo que el periodista quisiera escribir en él, desde un punto de vista formal, sin que, al parecer, ningún redactor jefe le llamara la atención sobre un libro de estilo, inexistente. Tampoco ayuda el hecho de que el periodista en cuestión careciera de toda formación periodística teórica, y que, también presumiblemente, no supiera de la columna más que debía estar bien escrita" (Sorela 51).

26. "El 31 de julio de1954, *El Espectador* 'llamaba en primera' para un reportaje de su enviado especial García Márquez sobre el *Balance y reconstrucción de* la *catástrofe de Antioquia*. Era lo que en la jerga profesional española se conoce por el nombre de 'refrito': un tema más o menos periódico en la prensa colombiana, un derrumbe con víctimas, del que los periódicos habían hablado hasta hartarse durante los días anteriores. A García Márquez el periódico lo envió en su primera misión de reportero para cubrir la difícil papeleta de contar algo que, en principio, ya estaba contado. Al llegar a Medellín, el periodista—afirma—estuvo a punto de volverse y dejar la misión. Otra hubiera sido su historia. No lo hizo, y por el contrario regresó con un reportaje cuyas principales características están ya anunciadas en el título—*Balance y reconstrucción*—y que haría a los directores de su periódico fijarse en el para futuros grandes reportajes" (Sorela 51).

27. "García Márquez solía decir que el periodista debería ser como un mosquito, que está ahí para irritar a los que están en el poder, zumbando incesantemente" (León et al.).

28. "En veinte sesiones de seis horas diarias, durante las cuales yo tomaba notas y soltaba preguntas tramposas para detectar sus contradicciones, logramos reconstruir el relato compacto y verídico de sus diez días en el mar. Era tan minucioso y apasionante, que mi único problema literario sería conseguir que el lector lo creyera. No fue sólo por eso, sino también porque nos pareció justo, que acordamos escribirlo en primera persona y firmado por él. Ésta es, en realidad, la primera vez que mi nombre aparece vinculado a este texto" (*Relato de un náufrago* 12).
29. "Como el 'bricoleur', el transcriptor opera a mitad de camino entre el sujeto escritural que es fuente original de relatos, y el sujeto de la escritura referencial" (León et al. 189).
30. "Esa madrugada, cuando nos embarcamos, el cabo Miguel Ortega estaba en el puente, precisamente hablando de su esposa y sus hijos, lo cual no era una casualidad, porque nunca hablaba de otra cosa. Traía una nevera, una lavadora automática, y una radio y una estufa. Doce horas después el cabo Miguel Ortega estaría tumbado en su litera, muriéndose del mareo. Y setenta y dos horas después estaría muerto en el fondo del mar" (*Relato de un náufrago* 22–23).
31. "Hace unos seis meses, cuando Miguel Littín me contó en Madrid lo que había hecho, y cómo lo había hecho, pensé que detrás de su película había otra película sin hacer que corría el riesgo de quedarse inédita. Fue así como aceptó someterse a un interrogatorio agotador de casi una semana, cuya versión magnetofónica duraba dieciocho horas. Allí quedó la aventura humana, con todas sus implicaciones profesionales y políticas, que yo he vuelto a contar condensada en una serie de diez capítulos. Algunos nombres han sido cambiados y muchas circunstancias alteradas para proteger a los protagonistas que siguen viviendo dentro dc Chile. He preferido conservar el relato en primera persona, tal como Littín me lo contó, tratando de preservar en esa forma su tono personal—y a veces confidencial—, sin dramatismos fáciles ni pretensiones históricas. El estilo del texto final es mío, desde luego, pues la voz de un escritor no es intercambiable, y menos cuando ha tenido que comprimir casi seiscientas páginas en menos de ciento cincuenta" (*La aventura de Miguel Littín* 7–8).
32. "Tenía que resignarme a dejar de ser el hombre que había sido siempre y convertirme en otro, insospechable para la misma policía que me había forzado a abandonar mi país, e irreconocible para mis propios amigos. Dos psicólogos y una maquillista de cine, bajo la dirección de un experto en operaciones especiales clandestinas, destacado desde el interior de Chile, lograron el milagro en poco menos de tres semanas, luchando sin reposo contra mi determinación instintiva de seguir siendo quien era" (*La aventura de Miguel Littín* 16).
33. "Pero es más: la reconstitución emocional de una aventura cuya finalidad última era, sin duda, mucho más entrañable y conmovedora que el propósito original y bien logrado de hacer una película burlando los riesgos del poder militar. El propio Littín lo ha dicho: 'Este no es el acto más heroico de mi vida, sino el más digno.' Así es, y creo que ésa es una grandeza" (*La aventura de Miguel Littín* 9).
34. "El segundo día en La Moneda, como a las once de la mañana, percibimos de pronto una agitación invisible en el aire y sentimos ruidos apresurados de botas y fierros marciales. El oficial que nos acompañaba sufrió un cambio súbito del humor y nos ordenó con un gesto brutal apagar las luces y parar las cámaras. Dos escoltas de civil se plantaron sin disimulos frente a nosotros dispuestos a impedir que intentáramos seguir filmando. No supimos qué sucedía, hasta que vimos pasar al general Augusto Pinochet en persona, verdoso y abotagado, caminando hacia su despacho con un ayudante militar y dos civiles" (*La aventura de Miguel Littín* 175).

35. "Esta comprobación tardía nos obligó a empezar otra vez con una estructura y un aliento diferentes para que todos los protagonistas tuvieran su identidad bien definida y su ámbito propio. Fue una solución técnica para una narración laberíntica que en el primer formato hubiera sido fragorosa e interminable. De este modo, sin embargo, el trabajo previsto para un año se prolongó por casi tres, siempre con la colaboración cuidadosa y oportuna de Maruja y Alberto, cuyos relatos personales son el eje central y el hilo conductor de este libro (*Noticia de un secuestro* 5).
36. "La transcripción, el orden, la verificación y el secreto del intrincado material de base en el que varias veces nos sentimos a punto de naufragar" (*Noticia de un secuestro* 6).
37. "Por primera vez conseguí una confluencia perfecta entre el periodismo y la literatura, por eso se llama *Crónica de una muerte anunciada*. Ese supuesto mal que le hace el periodismo a la literatura no es cierto. Primero, porque considero que al escritor no lo mata nada, ni el hambre. Segundo, porque el periodismo ayuda a mantener el contacto con la realidad, lo que es esencial para trabajar en literatura. Y viceversa, la literatura te enseña a escribir, lo que también es esencial para el periodismo. En mi caso, el periodismo fue el trampolín para la literatura y aprendí a hacer periodismo haciendo buena literatura" (De Martínez 72).
38. "A muchos periodistas de talento los estropean las ambiciones literarias; pero hay narradores que deben parte substancial de su arte al adiestramiento del periodismo. García Márquez es uno de ellos. Es esta compleja alianza la que fortalecerá el casaba bien con la poética del triunfante autor" (Franco 194).
39. "Durante años no pudimos hablar de otra cosa. Nuestra conducta diaria, dominada hasta entonces por tantos hábitos lineales, había empezado a girar de golpe en torno de una misma ansiedad común. Nos sorprendían los gallos del amanecer tratando de ordenar las numerosas casualidades encadenadas que habían hecho posible el absurdo, y era evidente que no lo hacíamos por un anhelo de esclarecer misterios, sino porque ninguno de nosotros podía seguir viviendo sin saber con exactitud cuál era el sitio y la misión que le había asignado la fatalidad. Pero la mayoría de quienes pudieron hacer algo por impedir el crimen y sin embargo no lo hicieron, se consolaron con el pretexto de que los asuntos de honor son estancos sagrados a los cuales sólo tienen acceso los dueños del drama" (*Crónica de una muerte anunciada* 94).
40. "No tengo que decirlo, porque se me distingue a leguas: soy feo, tímido y anacrónico. Pero a fuerza de no querer serlo he venido a simular todo lo contrario. Hasta el sol de hoy, en que resuelvo contarme como soy por mi propia y libre voluntad, aunque sólo sea para alivio de mi conciencia. He empezado con la llamada insólita a Rosa Cabarcas, porque visto desde hoy, aquél fue el principio de una nueva vida a una edad en que la mayoría de los mortales están muertos" (*Memoria de mis putas tristes* 10).
41. "Alguna vez pensé que aquellas cuentas de camas serían un buen sustento para una relación de las miserias de mi vida extraviada, y el título me cayó del cielo: Memoria de mis putas tristes. Mi vida pública, en cambio, carecía de interés: huérfano de padre y madre, soltero sin porvenir, periodista mediocre cuatro veces finalista en los Juegos Florales de Cartagena de Indias y favorito de los caricaturistas por mi fealdad ejemplar. Es decir: una vida perdida que había empezado mal desde la tarde en que mi madre me llevó de la mano a los diecinueve años para ver si lograba publicar en El Diario de La Paz una crónica de la vida escolar que yo había escrito en la clase de castellano y retórica. Se publicó el domingo con un exordio esperanzado del director. Pasados los años, cuando supe que mi madre había pagado la publicación y las siete siguientes, ya era tarde para avergonzarme,

pues mi columna semanal volaba con alas propias, y era tarde para avergonzarme, pues mi columna semanal volaba con alas propias, y era además inflador de cables y crítico de música" (*Memoria de mis putas tristes* 17–18).

42. "Era por fin la vida real, con mi corazón a salvo, y condenado a morir de buen amor en la agonía feliz de cualquier día después de mis cien años" (*Memoria de mis putas tristes* 109).
43. "No creo que lo escriba. Tengo algunas notas escritas, pero no quiero que sea una operación profesional. Me he dado cuenta de que si publico un segundo volumen, voy a tener que decir cosas que no quiero decir, debido a algunas relaciones personales que ya no son tan buenas. El primer volumen, *Living to Tell the Tale*, es exactamente lo que quería que fuera. En el segundo, conocí a un número de personas que sólo tenía que venir y que—Caramba, no quiero que aparezcan en mis memorias. Sería deshonesto dejarlos fuera, porque eran importantes en mi vida, pero no terminaron siendo muy amables conmigo" (Streitfeld 94).

Works Cited

Dawson, Paul. "The Return of Omniscience in Contemporary Fiction." *Narrative*, vol. 17, no. 2, May 2009, pp. 143–61.

De Martínez, Adelaida López. Review of *Crónica de una muerte anunciada* by Gabriel García Márquez. *Chasqui: Revista de literatura latinoamericana*, vol. 10, nos. 2/3, 1981, pp. 70–72.

El Baz Iguider, Hassan. *Realidad y ficción en "Vivir para contarla," memorias de Gabriel García Márquez*. 2015. Universidad de Málaga, PhD thesis.

Elnadi, Bahgat, et al. "Gabriel García Márquez: The Writer's Craft." *UNESCO Courier*, Feb. 1996, en.unesco.org/courier/febrero-1996/gabriel-garcia-marquez-writers-craft-interview. Accessed 12 June 2019.

Flaubert, Gustave. *Correspondance*, vol. II (July 1851–Dec. 1858), edited by Jean Bruneau, Pléiade, 1980.

Flaubert, Gustave. *The Letters of Gustave Flaubert: 1830–1857*. Edited and translated by Francis Steegmuller, hup.harvard.edu/catalog.php?isbn=9780674526365. Accessed 31 May 2019.

Franco, Sergio R. *In (ter)venciones del yo: Escritura y sujeto autobiográfico en la literatura hispanoamericana (1974-2002)*. Iberoamericana, 2012.

García Márquez, Gabriel. *La aventura de Miguel Littín clandestino en Chile*. Random House Mondadori, 1998.

García Márquez, Gabriel. *Chronicle of a Death Foretold*. Translated by Gregory Rabassa, Vintage International, 1982.

García Márquez, Gabriel. *Clandestine in Chile: The Adventures of Miguel Littín*. Translated by Asa Zatz, NYRB Classics, 2010.

García Márquez, Gabriel. *Crónica de una muerte anunciada*. Vintage Español, 1981.

García Márquez, Gabriel. *Living to Tell the Tale*. Translated by Edith I. Grossman, Vintage International, 2004

García Márquez, Gabriel. *Memoria de mis putas tristes*. Vintage Español, 2004.

García Márquez, Gabriel. *Memories of My Melancholy Whores*. Translated by Edith Grossman, Vintage International, 2005.

García Márquez, Gabriel. *News of a Kidnapping*. Translated by Edith Grossman, Vintage International, 1997.

García Márquez, Gabriel. *Noticia de un secuestro*. Penguin Books, 1996.

García Márquez, Gabriel. *Relato de un náufrago*. Vintage Español, 2014.
García Márquez, Gabriel. *The Story of a Shipwrecked Sailor*. Translated by Randolph Hogan, Knopf, 1986.
García Márquez, Gabriel. *Vivir para contarla*. Vintage Español, 2002.
León, Antonio Vera. "Hacer hablar: La transcripción testimonial." *Revista De Crítica Literaria Latinoamericana*, vol. 18, no. 36, 1992, pp. 185–203. *La Voz Del Otro: Testimonio, Subalternidad y Verdad Narrativa*.
León, Juanita, et al. "Gabriel Garcia Marquez: Chronicle of a Journalism Untold." *The Listening Post*, www.youtube.com/watch?v=lNJGocOv5X8. Accessed 7 June 2019.
Lévi-Strauss, Claude. *La Pensée Sauvage*. Plon, 1963.
Lévi-Strauss, Claude. *The Savage Mind*. Translated by George Weidenfeld and Nicolson Ltd., U of Chicago P, 1966.
Martin, Gerald. *Gabriel García Márquez. A Life*. Knopf, 2009.
Moslund, Sten Pultz. *Literature's Sensuous Geographies: Postcolonial Matters of Place*. Palgrave Macmillan, 2015.
Moslund, Sten Pultz. *The Presence of Place in Literature—with a Few Examples from Virginia Woolf*. www.sdu.dk/-/media/files/om_sdu/institutter/ilkm/.../placeinliterature.pdf. Accessed 12 June 2019.
Reagan, Patricia Elaine. *The Other "I": The New Narcissism of Postmodernism First Person Non-Protagonist Narrators in Novels by José Donoso, Elena Garro, Gabriel García Márquez and Mario Vargas Llosa*. 2009. University of Virginia, PhD dissertation.
Rodaway, Paul. *Sensuous Geographies: Body, Sense and Place*. Routledge, 2002.
Sorela, Pedro. *El otro García Márquez: Los años difíciles*. Mondadori, 1975.
Sorensen, Eli Park. "Between Autobiography and Fiction: Narrating the Self in Gabriel García Márquez's *Vivir para contarla*." *Stories and Portraits of the Self*, edited by Helena Carvalhão Buescu and João Ferreira Duarte, Rodopi, 2007, pp. 189–201.
Stone, Peter H. "Gabriel García Márquez, the Art of Fiction." *Paris Review*, no. 82, Winter 1981, www.theparisreview.org/interviews/3196/gabriel-garcia-marquez-the-art-of-fiction-no-69-gabriel-garcia-marquez. Accessed 15 June 2019.
Streitfeld, David. *Gabriel García Márquez: The Last Interview and Other Conversations*. Translated by Theo Ellin Ballew et al., Melville House, 2015.
Tally, Robert T, editor. *Geocritical Explorations: Space, Place, and Mapping in Literary and Cultural Studies*. Palgrave Macmillan, 2011.
Tally, Robert T. *Spatiality*. Routledge, 2012.
Vicente Romero, Giovanny. "El Poder, ¿para Usarlo O Abusarlo?—Eurasia Hoy". n.d., https://eurasiahoy.com/23042018-el-poder-para-usarlo-o-abusarlo/. Accessed 21 Feb. 2020.

CHAPTER 32

THE FILMIC LITERARY WORKS OF GABRIEL GARCÍA MÁRQUEZ

ALESSANDRO ROCCO

Like many other twentieth-century writers, Gabriel García Márquez not only had a passion for the movies but also an active interest in them, initially as a critic, commenting on and reviewing international cinema for Colombian audiences in the early 1950s, and then, above all, in a long involvement as a screenwriter. This is why a not insignificant part of his literary production is made up of *filmic* writings, both stories and screenplays, many of which then became films, thanks to the work of various directors, while others remained only on paper. We thus have on the one hand a García Márquez *filmic-literary production*, consisting of texts written for cinema, often in collaboration with other authors, and which have remained largely unpublished aside from some gathered in book form and in literary magazines, and on the other hand, a García Márquez *filmography*, consisting of films made by various directors using his film stories and/or screenplays (excluding those based on his novels or stories but made without his direct participation). They are two separate, albeit connected, textual entities. The former are works for reading, classifiable under the literary genre of film writing, analogous to that of drama. The latter are films which, thanks to the creative interpretations of various directors, have brought stories invented and/or developed for cinema by García Márquez to the screen. Bearing this distinction in mind, in this article I attempt to outline the aesthetic characteristics and narrative developments of this production.

The prelude to this history is the experimental film *La langosta azul* (*The Blue Lobster*), made in Colombia in 1954 by a group of intellectuals known as El grupo de Barranquilla, and in particular by the writer Álvaro Cepeda Samudio, to whom García Márquez has often attributed his discovery of the artistic value of cinema (*Living* 436). Little is known about García Márquez's involvement in this film, but his work in cinema had definitely begun by the time he was in Mexico in the early 1960s. Here, he was engaged in two very ambitious film projects by the producer Barbachano Ponce: the adaptation of two texts by eminent author and literary figure Juan Rulfo. The first of these was *El gallo de oro*, written expressly for the screen by Rulfo and directed by Roberto Gavaldón, and the second was the famous novel *Pedro Páramo*, working together on the adaptation with writer Carlos Fuentes and the director of the film, Carlos Velo. Both ventures were described some years later by García Márquez as highly frustrating experiences and as examples of the difficulties of expression encountered by writers in catering to the demands of the film industry. Both films, he recalled, ended up as very different from what he originally intended in his adaptations (Torres, "El novelista" 47; Torres, "Entrevista" 44). The recent discovery in Mexico of the first draft of the "El gallo de oro" screenplay, written by García Márquez and Fuentes in December 1963 (Pérez), makes it possible for us to appreciate the literary qualities of the filmic writing of the Colombian Nobel laureate, involved in this case in a creative dialogue with one of his most beloved authors (García Márquez, "El gallo"). It was also in Mexico, after an initial 1963 story called "El charro" ("The Cowboy"), that he wrote his first screenplay of note, "Tiempo de morir", published in a literary magazine in 1965, the same year the film was produced, directed by Arturo Ripstein. In this work García Márquez manages to give an accomplished filmic form to his literary imagination, creating the memorable character of the old *charro* (Mexican cowboy), modeled on the elderly colonel in the novel *El coronel no tiene quien le escriba* (*No One Writes to the Colonel*), whose determination and dignity are inspired also by the character Umberto D. in the film of the same name by Vittorio de Sica and Cesare Zavattini, about which García Márquez had written a passionate review a few years earlier (García Márquez and Gilard, *Entre cachacos* 320-21). The aim of the narrative structure of "Tiempo de morir" is, as the title suggests, to create the effect of surprise with the fulfilment of a foretold destiny, that is, a death threat made to the main character at the beginning of the story by the sons of a man killed in a duel many years before, in a way not much unlike the novel *Crónica de una muerte anunciada* (*Chronicle of a Death Foretold*). But what makes the screenplay even more interesting is its time structure, in which the threat, based on past guilt, comes to mean the actual return of ghosts from the past, revealing to readers and to the more astute viewers that, under the guise of a Western-style *charros* film, there is an interpretation of one of García Márquez's most beloved classics, Sophocles's *Oedipus Rex*.

The sophisticated narrative structure of "Tiempo de morir" makes it clear that, in these years, García Márquez intended screenwriting to be entirely and organically within his literary sphere. This is further confirmed by a highly significant although now little-known work entitled "Dios y yo" ("God and I"), a film story written in 1965 together with screenwriter and director Luis Alcoriza, centering on the figure of a South American dictator (Rocco, *Gabriel García Márquez* 19-25). One of the actions narrated in this scenario—to be used again in the novel *El otoño del patriarca* (*The Autumn of the Patriarch*)–is the kidnapping of a large group of children, their concealment for an extended time in one of the wildest and most remote regions of the country, and their subsequent secret drowning in the sea. Apart from this episode, however, what makes this filmic text important is the embryonic presence of a number of aesthetic principles that were to be fully matured in the writing of the later novel. In particular, there are glimpses of a shift from realistic stories to representations verging on the unusual and the extraordinary, with hints of mythological characterization in the portrayal of the dictator (Mendoza 110). Moreover, the subjectivity of the dictator in the film story is significant in that it constitutes a form of empathy--albeit controlled by ironic detachment--that anticipates the complex identification of the author with the character in the novel itself (Canfield 967). This shows, again, how working on film scripts was, for García Márquez, a literary activity closely and productively related to the imagining and development of his novels and stories. We see this again in the screenplay entitled "La increíble y triste historia de la cándida Eréndira y de su abuela desalmada" ("The Incredible and Sad Tale of Innocent Eréndira and Her Heartless Grandmother"), written by García Márquez in 1968 and published in part in 1970 in two literary magazines. Two years later, following the abandonment of the film project, the script was published as a novella, an act described by the author as a *"literaturalización"* ("literaturization") of the screenplay (Ríos and García Videla 8). The changes, apart from the omission of some of the episodes, mainly had to do with the prose style of the text, which remains, basically, a film story. This brings to mind other previous works by García Márquez–in particular *No One Writes to the Colonel, La mala hora (In Evil Hour)*, and some of the stories in the collection *Los funerales de la Mamá Grande (Big Mama's Funeral)*–in which the tendency to write in such a way as to conjure up an imaginary film in the mind of the reader is evident, even in works not intended for cinema (Durán 31). A clear example of this, without doubt, is the story "En este pueblo no hay ladrones" ("No Thieves in This Town"), which the author proposed to director Jorge Isaac as a virtually ready-made screenplay for the film of the same name, made in Mexico in 1964 (García Riera, *Historia documental* 185). "Innocent Eréndira", however, has an important place in the filmic-literary aesthetic of García Márquez in that its narrative register mixes reality and fantasy in new and unexpected ways, following the extraordinary results achieved by the author in *Cien años de soledad*. As Vargas Llosa notes, in the screenplay there is an expansion of the imaginary and all-embracing world of the novel with, most notably, the constant presence of the circus and fairgrounds seeming to saturate the depiction of reality (627-28). The film, though, was not made immediately and only came out at last in 1983, directed by Ruy Guerra, and this was not the only cinematic project of García Márquez to take many years to come to fruition. An important case in point is *Presagio (Portent)*, a scenario made ready for Luis Alcoriza's co-screenwriting and directing already in 1965 but not completed until 1974 (García Riera, *Historia documental* 216). The essence of the story, as outlined in a talk given by García Márquez at a conference in Caracas in 1967 that was subsequently published in a literary magazine ("Esto lo contó García Márquez"), can be summarized as follows: a premonition, initially of little consequence, eventually leads to the catastrophic evacuation of an entire town. The narrative development of this idea moves in two directions: on the one hand there is the collective nature of the story, in which different events, held together by the fact that they occur in the same place and are related in some way to the omen, are interwoven; on the other hand, there is the ambiguous interplay between the portrayal of fantastical and mysterious happenings and the way they are explained as being the result of superstition and conflicts between the characters. This structure reminds us in a way of the novel *In Evil Hour*, in which there is a passage that could well lie at the origin of the screenplay: the priest, Father Angel, meets an old blind woman who exclaims "The world is coming to an end this year . . . burning ashes will rain down on her head" (*In Evil Hour* 148), the very same words as in "Presagio" (47). We know, however, that García Márquez wanted to accentuate the mysterious aspects of the omen in order to give a particular mood to the story, mixing supernatural, paradoxical moments with distinctly realistic ones (Herrera 356). In this sense, both the final version of the screenplay and the film directed by Alcoriza are clear examples of how the evolution of García Márquez's narrative aesthetic, with its novel and surprising ways of combining reality and fantasy, is expressed also in his filmic writing. This should come as no surprise, in that the inspiration for this literary poetic, often associated with the concept of magical realism, also had an important cinematic source, namely, the 1951 De Sica and Zavattini film *Miracolo a Milano* (*Miracle in Milan*). Such an inference is borne out not only by the splendid review written by García Márquez in 1954 (García Márquez and Gilard, *Entre cachacos* 120–22), but also by the provocative question posed by the author several years later: "Has no one ever suspected that *Miracolo a Milano* is the most likely source for magical realism in the Latin American novel?" (Eligio García Márquez 232). However, it is important to remember that the aesthetic evolution of the author toward certain narrative registers far removed from traditional realism is in constant tension with a political interest that reaches its peak in the 1970s (Martin 420–51). Hence, in his films too, García Márquez explores and tests new ways of articulating political themes by means of a broader and fuller concept of the representation of the real, which excludes neither the fantastical imagination—the mythical and the marvelous—nor its darker side, the nightmarish and the absurd. Two works from the early years of the decade appear to be particularly significant in this sense: an original story, unpublished and never filmed, called "Para Elisa," written by García Márquez probably in 1973, and the film adaptation of the short story "Blacamán el bueno, vendedor de milagros" ("Blacamán the Good, Vendor of Miracles"), written by García Márquez together with an Italian co-screenwriter, this too unpublished and never filmed.

"Para Elisa" is a story that clearly evokes the reality of Colombia, torn apart by an atavistic civil war, with evident reference also to the historical episode that marked both the high point and the origin of the violence in the country: the assassination of Liberal politician Jorge Eliécer Gaitán on April 9, 1948, which sparked an explosion of mass rage in the city of Bogotá. These events are represented in the story as the culmination of a decidedly surreal venture: the transporting, across the impervious South American terrain, of a luxurious European grand piano, which becomes the symbol of an increasingly violent and absurd quarrel. When the piano reaches the capital, there erupts around it "a genuine popular revolution, with shops looted, churches set on fire, murders in cold blood, etc." (3). The effect of the contrast between the riot scene and the value and function of the piano as an object is incomparable, expressing and summarizing in a visually perfect way the tragic absurdity of the Colombian situation: "advancing like a sinister coach," the piano succeeds in getting through that "raging sea of humans," and the little girl it was meant for is able, "without any particular surprise," to play "a trivial little tune" (3). This short story, "Para Elisa," gives us the idea for a film in which the poetics of the unusual and the extraordinary and García Márquez's profound historical concern for his country's destiny are combined in an exemplary way.

"Blacamán, venditore di miracoli" is a film story based on the short story "Blacamán the Good...," whose relationship with the novel *The Autumn of the Patriarch* has been stressed many times by García Márquez himself ("Todo cuento es un cuento chino"). This filmic text, written in June of the year he finished the novel, 1974 (Martin 418), gives us a closer look at the link between the figure of the dictator and the two magicians in the story, especially in terms of their relationship with the idea of power, illusion, and death. Both the novel and the story encourage the reader to reflect on the power of illusion and the illusion of power, to the extreme point of overcoming death. The tale ends, in fact, with one Blacamán living an eternal life of grandeur and the other condemned to die and be resurrected perpetually, enclosed in his mausoleum. In the filmic version, Blacamán is a character who, over the centuries since the colonial era, has had the job of embalming the viceroys so that they can go on ruling after death, in a transparent metaphor of power as death and illusion. The conflict between the two magicians is also directly linked to the military occupation of a Caribbean country by the US Marines, with one of the magicians, dazzled by the marvels of modernity, allying himself with the occupiers and even becoming the perfect candidate for the US presidential elections—the supreme instance of power as illusionism and manipulation. The film scenario thus makes the political backcloth to the story more explicit, laying the basis for a movie—unfortunately never to be made—that could be characterized as magical-political.

"Magical-political" could also be used to define the first film from this period that was actually made, *El año de la peste* (1978; *The Year of the Plague*), directed by Felipe Cazals, about a modern-day plague epidemic in Mexico City. It was inspired by a work much loved by García Márquez because of its literary-chronicle style: *A Journal of the Plague Year* (1722), by the English writer Daniel Defoe (Eligio García Márquez 305). The interesting thing about this screenplay is the meaning García Márquez attributes to the pestilence, which on the one hand refers to a metaphysical dimension, and on the other hand manifests itself as a social catastrophe (Vargas Llosa 195–96). Thus, the account of the epidemic's devastating impact on the metropolis is not only tinged with fatalism and mystery but also packed with heightened political symbolism. In particular, the screenplay insists on portraying the authorities and the means of communication as working together to deny the reality of the disease against all evidence, always ready to label the sick and their would-be helpers as "subversives" to be eliminated and hidden away, in an evident metaphor for the brutal and systematic violations of human rights not only in South American dictatorships but also in formally democratic states like Mexico, in a period that ideally connects the Mexican student massacre of 1968 to the Chilean, Uruguayan, and Argentinian dictatorships of the 1970s (Cazals, "Re: 2as consideraciones").

Another film from this period is *María de mi corazón* (*María of My Heart*), shot by Mexican director Jaime Humberto Hermosillo in 1979, with a theme reworked by García

Márquez first of all in the form of a press note (García Márquez, *Notas de prensa* 98–100), and then as a short story called "Sólo vine a hablar por teléfono" ("I Only Came to Use the Phone"), published in the collection *Doce cuentos peregrinos* (*Strange Pilgrims*). In this film, too, the narrative tends to bring together techniques that elicit mystery and generate uncertainty, in a register oriented more toward a political critique of social reality, its discourses, and its institutions. The screenplay centers initially on the relationship—odd, complicated, and yet joyful and free—between a couple, which is altered drastically by the intrusion of an authoritarian, repressive institution: the mental hospital. The main character is actually admitted to hospital completely by chance, and from then on it becomes impossible for her to prove she is not a patient. Clearly, this makes it possible to play on the unusual and out-of-the-ordinary aspects of what happens, accentuating the disturbing sense of precariousness surrounding all certainties. But at the same time, the film continues to highlight the violent, coercive treatment that the character undergoes in the hospital, and the inhuman conditions that patients are subject to, reduced to beings with neither identity nor dignity (García Riera, "Conversación" 30). Hospitals are thus associated with prisons, with the conditions of the patients-inmates also reflecting the female condition in society in general (Hermosillo). The film's condemnatory message is further strengthened by its dysphoric dramatic structure, which subverts any potential expectation of a happy ending, intensifying the sense of frustration to the point that the heroine finally becomes a "real madwoman" and completely negating the role of the boyfriend hero as savior.

This series of the most overtly political of García Márquez films culminates with a text of an explicitly celebratory character about the Sandinista Revolution in Nicaragua. The origin of this screenplay is best explained by referring to a famous newspaper report by García Márquez, published in Colombia in 1978, in which he describes the spectacular seizure of the National Palace in Managua ("El golpe sandinista"). Twice in the report, García Márquez mentions a similar action a few years earlier, "the famous invasion of a Somoza family party in 1974," when a detachment of guerrillas burst into the Nicaraguan oligarchy's family villa and demanded the release of political prisoners and the broadcast of their proclamation on the radio (207). The author narrates this event in a screenplay that, while never made into a film, was published from 1982 onward in various editions and under various titles, such as *¡Viva Sandino!*, *El secuestro*, and *El asalto* (*Long Live Sandino!*, *The Kidnapping*, and *The Attack*). The choice to narrate a specific action and not the entire history of the Sandinista Revolution clearly demonstrates García Márquez's profound knowledge of the mechanisms of film writing, in that it functions at the same time as both a dramatically effective unit of action and a model for condensing historical and political information about Sandinismo. The objective is to explicitly pay tribute to the ethical and political values of the Sandinista Front, as well as to give a decidedly epic tone to the action. Not by chance, the story begins and ends with the Sandinista battle cry: ¡Viva Sandino!

This text is the only exclusively historical-political—almost documentary—film narrative by García Márquez known to us, and it was published shortly before the making of two major films of a markedly magical realist character: *Eréndira*, directed by Ruy

Guerra, in 1983, and *Un señor muy viejo con unas alas enormes* (*A Very Old Man with Enormous Wings*), directed by Fernando Birri, in 1988. These two films, taken together, express a particular creative vein of the author, linked to fairy tales, magic, enchanted beings, and fantastical happenings, but also with a more sinister side often hinted at in these kinds of stories. As mentioned earlier, the first version of the screenplay "Eréndira" was written in 1968, but a new version had to be scripted for the film, based mostly on the novella published in 1972 (Ciment 17). Also written in 1968 was the short story "Un señor muy viejo," and Birri worked for several years on the script together with García Márquez in order to complete the preparatory work for the film (Birri, *Fernando Birri* 38). In both projects, the author's inclination to accentuate and highlight the fanciful and extraordinary aspects of the stories can be noted, with explicitly social and political interpretations being avoided, unless filtered through a certain kind of poetic and symbolic lens. They concentrate, rather, on the mixture of styles, the hybridization of narrative genres, and the possibility of incorporating different forms of artistic expression into cinematic language.

Two narrative motifs contribute to the composition of the story of *Eréndira*: the journey of the characters and their amazing entourage from the desert toward the sea, and the dialectic of the young Eréndira's subjugation and liberation from the family slavery she is subjected to by her heartless grandmother. When making the film, Ruy Guerra takes pains to emphasize the mythical and fantastical aspects of García Márquez's tale with the use of cinematic techniques, such as framing and scenography, by which he is able to construct a system of narrative and poetic symbols. Right from the very first sequences, the characters are rendered dreamlike and surreal by the setting, with its conspicuously symbolic elements such as the clocks on the walls in the grandmother's house, the red and blue colors denoting the spaces occupied by the characters, the candle flames that anticipate the burning of the house, and above all, the multicolored fish floating in the air during the violent scene that marks the beginning of the girl's sexual slavery. In the final sequences, the grandmother's monstrous, fantastical nature provides the cue to a series of references to the narrative codes of theater, opera, and even cartoon. The first attempt by the young Ulises to save Eréndira by killing the grandmother with a poisoned cake brings out a series of deluded, surreal monologues from the old woman, after which she loses her hair and starts laughing madly, as if in a farcical burlesque. In the second attempt, the effects upon the grandmother's body of a dynamite explosion in the piano are cartoon-like, and in the ensuing hand-to-hand struggle to finish her off, the action is operatically exaggerated and stylized (Philippon 47). In the end, the girl's final escape and the abandonment of her savior, exhausted after slaying the monster, is an obvious parody reversal of the fairy-tale model.

The heart of Ferando Birri's film is the carnivalesque fair that, in García Márquez's story, takes shape around the figure of the mysterious old man with wings discovered by chance in a Caribbean village: an exuberant and colorful staging of the syncretism so typical of Latin American society and culture, seen through the prism of a grand theatrical spectacle that mixes the sacred and the profane, the religious and the circus-like, and the ancient and the modern, as if at a huge, spontaneous, and popular cultural crossroads. The character of the winged old man takes on the physiognomy of the artist's alter ego, with the almost magical power of being able to imagine and create a new reality which, in this work, molds itself into and through language, or rather, through a plurality of languages (Birri, Interview). According to the director, creation in cinema is always a collective process, involving the orchestration or synthesis of different languages and techniques, with all members of the team becoming coauthors (Birri, *Cómo se filma un film* 223). The film *A Very Old Man* thus presents itself as a device capable of incorporating and harmonizing artistic expressions such as design, graphics, video art, music, and theater dance, cinematically portraying the mixture of styles and narrative registers of García Márquez's story and denoting the two authors' joint search for a space untrammeled by overly rigid and ineffective customs and expressive codes, a space defined by Birri as *magical-critical realism* (De Pascale 44–45).

By the time this film was being shot, García Márquez's "film career" had already shifted its axis from Mexico City to Havana. As Gerald Martin writes, since 1983 Fidel Castro and García Márquez had been thinking about starting a school of Latin American cinema, based in Havana (515). Also, as early as 1960, García Márquez is known to have drawn up very detailed plans for a film school in Barranquilla, Colombia, to be launched together with Álvaro Cepeda Samudio (Gilard). Moreover, calls and attempts by many Latin American filmmakers to create and champion a militant and innovative cinema, referred to mostly as Nuevo cine latinoamericano, had come from far and wide—since at least 1967, when, in Viña del Mar in Chile, more than sixty filmmakers formed a mutual aid committee to support the production of socially and politically committed films (Mahieu 171). Thus, in 1985 the Fundación Nuevo Cine Latinoamericano was founded in Cuba, presided over by García Márquez—"an institution for . . . recuperating and consolidating Latin America and Caribbean cultural identity" ("Acta de creación")—to be followed a year later by the San Antonio de los Baños School of Cinema and Television, this also in Cuba, which was to bring about a qualitative leap in the expressive and narrative capacity of Latin American film (Birri, *Fernando Birri* 34). García Márquez not only connected it ideally to the inspiration and teachings of neorealist Italian cinema, "the most low-budget and human cinema ever," but also announced a large-scale production project to support the activities of the school with the making of a series of six full-length feature films ("Palabras de García Márquez"). An important aspect of this project to be emphasized is that, while the six films were made by six different directors, the only author to be involved in all the stories and screenplays was García Márquez himself. At the very core of these productions, therefore, was García Márquez the screenwriter, who became the mind and pulsating heart of the entire series. The significance of this to the history of his involvement in cinema is clear and almost has the air of a deliverance from those years when he himself used to define the role of the screenwriter as that of a writer always destined, aside from rare exceptions, to remain in the shadows of creation (García Márquez, "La penumbra").

Thus was born the series known as *Amores difíciles* (rendered into English as *Dangerous Loves*), with its six independent stories, all by García Márquez, made into films in collaboration with the different directors and co-screenwriters. Two of the stories were taken from *El amor en los tiempos del cólera* (*Love in the Time of Cholera*); two from themes which then also became stories, published in the collection *Strange Pilgrims*; and two were original screenplays. The common thread that runs tenuously through the entire series is that of difficult, unusual, and complicated relationships becoming resolved in surprising ways. The thematic range is varied: filial love, friendly or passionate relationships, and a few deviant kinds of relationships. What the episodes all share is a more or less unusual starting point and a narrative development based on elements of surprise and a tendency to play on audience expectations, always with a certain degree of unpredictability and estrangement, but with the dramatic tension and impact being weakened by television broadcasting.

As mentioned earlier, two of the films in the series were based on film stories that had also been made into short fictions: *El verano de la señora Forbes* (*The Summer of Miss Forbes*), by Mexican director Jaime Humberto Hermosillo, and *Milagro en Roma* (*Miracle in Rome*), by Colombian director Lisandro Duque Naranjo, also published as a press note (García Márquez, *Notas de prensa* 159–61). This, in a very similar way to the earlier film *María de mi corazón*, further demonstrates how interlinked and intercommunicating the author's creative processes were in his favorite narrative genres: story, screenplay, novel, and journalistic reporting. But even more significant is the fact that the two screenplays are based on literary models that act as identification devices: for the former, the drama *Penthesileia*, by German playwright Henrich von Kleist, expressly suggested by the actress Hanna Schygulla (Hermosillo), and for *Miracle.*, the work and figure of the writer and filmmaker Cesare Zavattini. By means of these two models, García Márquez and the two directors explore not only the depths and contradictions of the human soul, but also—between the outstanding and the everyday, and between dreams, desire, and reality—the limits of verisimilitude.

The plot of *The Summer of Miss Forbes* hinges on the dual personality of the main character, a German governess as rigid by day as she is dissolute by night, who torments the two boys under her care (with the children devising and activating a plot to murder her) while at the same time burning with desire for a young man (Aquiles), who spurns her. In her passion, she identifies herself with the character Penthesilea in von Kleist's drama. To begin and end the film, by express wish of the authors, there are two dreamlike, symbolic sequences in underwater settings (Hermosillo). In the first one, Aquiles fights a shark, conjuring up the death instincts that permeate the entire narrative. In the second, Aquiles stabs the woman, in an underwater scene that represents the final passage to the obscure, passionate side of Miss Forbes's personality. By identifying with the story of the Amazon Penthesilea, the woman lives and dreams her own death as an erotic act, reciting to Aquiles the verses from the deathly conclusion to von Kleist's play—upon which, with the roles of executioner and victim reversed, the film ends: "'Penthesilea, my spouse, what are you doing? Is this the promised feast of the roses?' Achilles asked, as the woman and her dogs sank their teeth into his chest and devoured him" (García Márquez and Hermosillo, *El verano de la señora Forbes*).

The film *Miracle in Rome* is based on an extraordinary and remarkable case which, not without significant changes, was also to inspire the novel *Del amor y otros demonios*

(*Of Love and Other Demons*): the incorruptibility of a girl's body years after her death. The protagonist is the father, a Colombian called Margarito, who, after discovering the miracle, goes to Rome, apparently to convince the Vatican to acknowledge the holiness of his daughter. The Roman setting alone, used for most of the film, tells us that with this story García Márquez is recalling his time spent in the Città Eterna as a young man; more precisely, the title tells us that what we really have here is an homage to his intense and moving intellectual encounter with the world of neorealist cinema, which he so admired, and in which Cesare Zavattini emerges as a real literary legend. The reference to the famous film *Miracle in Milan* is not by chance, in fact, and it helps us see more clearly that *Miracle in Rome* is one of the most Garciamarquezian films he ever wrote, especially because of the way he uses his characteristic writing techniques of miraculous or fantastical elements peacefully coexisting amid normal, almost domestic everyday life, enriched with a subtle hint of humor. After the discovery of the child's incorrupt body, the sequence passes almost seamlessly from an initial sacred, quasi-sublime register, with the father displaying his daughter to the crowd amid clouds of smoke, wind, prayers, and acclamations, to a comically grotesque situation in which the priest claims that the miracle is evidence of the Lord's approval of the plan for a new, modern cemetery. This is even truer in the closing sequence when the father resurrects the child, proving himself to be in possession of extraordinary spiritual powers, in a scene in which the emotional charge and sublime tone are immediately brought down to earth, back to the familiar everyday life of a girl who, risen again after many years, wishes for no more than to get to the ice cream cart down below in the street. It comes as no surprise, therefore, that in García Márquez's short story "La Santa" ("The Saint"), it is Zavattini himself who suggests that Margarito should try reawakening his daughter. In this way, by attributing the key idea of the film *Milagro en Roma* to Zavattini, García Márquez pays homage to the maestro in an extraordinary way, recalling the times when a tale of his was enough to make the portentous miracle of cinema and literature appear, understood then and there, as one and the same thing.

The reference to literature comes out even more clearly in the two films based on themes from the novel *Love in the Time of Cholera*, these being *Cartas del parque* (*Letters from the Park*) and *Fábula de la bella palomera* (*Fable of the Beautiful Pigeon Fancier*), made by Cuban director Tomás Gutiérrez Alea and Ruy Guerra respectively, representing the Cuba of the early 1900s and the Brazil of the late 1800s. Here, poetry and literary creation are part of the everyday world, and literature assumes the role of an aesthetic language utilized in an interesting play on the identities of the characters and their relationships. In the first of these films, an exchange of letters between two lovers—written by the same scribe—entails its direct quotation, in the form of fragments of poems, stories, and philosophical and literary thoughts. Reading becomes a recital-listening process and part of the film's soundtrack, incorporating the voice of poetry into cinema in a unique way. In the second one, the social hierarchies that enable a rich merchant to obtain sexual favors from a humble pigeon fancier are both disguised and laid bare in a complex ritual of play-acting and poetic and theatrical recital, this too featured in the film. In *Letters from the Park*, in the course of the story each character establishes an authentic and personal relationship with writing which, for the scribe, translates into an actual epistolary work that accentuates and emphasizes the uniquely literary tone of the film. In *Fable*, on the other hand, the characters seem to use poetry and theatrics in order to idealize and mystify their identities and relationships, but without finding an authentic way forward, or rather, remaining trapped in their own play-acting, to the extent that the only sincere gesture is that of the man revealing his desire for possession by writing on the woman's body to endorse his appropriation of it.

Finally, there are the two films in the series based on original screenplays: *Un domingo feliz* (*A Happy Sunday*), by Venezuelan director Olegario Barrero, and *Yo soy el que tú buscas* (*I'm the One You're Looking for*), by the Spaniard Jaime Chávarri. In both stories, one set in Caracas and the other in Barcelona, the characters leave their everyday environment and go through a series of exceptional experiences that lead to a final death scene. In the first one a child from a rich family fakes his own kidnapping to escape the solitude of his home and has a day of happiness with a young musician who, in the end, is mistaken for the kidnapper by the police. The second film focuses on the obsession of a woman who, after being raped, sets out to hunt for the rapist and comes into contact with a sort of underworld—half sordid and half surreal—that ends up being swept away by a fire caused by a character who literally burns with love for her. As explained previously, the films in the series are not linked in terms of narrative but have a common format and model of production that places the stories chosen by García Márquez at their very center. In some cases, these stories were developed together with students from the screenwriting courses at the Cuban school, as can be seen in the books containing transcripts of the discussions: *Cómo se cuenta un cuento* (*How One Tells a Story*) and *La bendita manía de contar* (*The Blessed Story-telling Mania*). This same model is also to be found in some slightly later productions, such as the three medium-length films made in Mexico in 1991, entitled *Con el amor no se juega* (*One Does Not Play with Love*), and the six-episode TV series *Me alquilo para soñar* (*I Rent My Dreams*), shot by Ruy Guerra in Cuba in 1992, this too discussed at the San Antonio school. It could be argued that the narrative ideas and themes in these productions, as well as being varied, are also somewhat eccentric, and quite marginal to García Márquez's main literary corpus. His last film project, however, takes him back to a central and perhaps even primary theme on his cultural horizon: the retelling of Sophocles's *Oedipus Rex*, associated with the representation of the violence in Colombia.

The film in question, *Edipo Alcalde* (*Oedipus the Mayor*), is, in more than one way, the ideal ending to García Márquez's story as a screenwriter, both because it returns to a work that lies at the very origins of his literary growth and development and because its theme, the inevitability of destiny, had already been partially explored in his first film, *Tiempo de morir*. Also, the director of *Edipo Alcalde*, Jorge Alí Triana, had directed the Colombian remake of that very film in 1985 and, above all, was the ideal person to get García Márquez's attention back to Colombia, after finally abandoning the idea of filming the "Para Elisa" screenplay. Thus, this final film project confirms the importance that García Márquez attributed to his cinema work and how he saw it as an integral part of his general literary activity.

The key to this adaptation of *Oedipus Rex* to the Colombia of the 1990s lies in identifying the plague with the civil war that had been devastating the country for decades. Vargas Llosa had already explained this clearly: at least since the famous Bogotazo revolt of April 9, 1948, political violence in Colombia had been ongoing on such a scale that, in the eyes of García Márquez, it appeared to be as devastating, supernatural, and out-of-control a force as the plague in the works of Sophocles or, as mentioned earlier, in that of Defoe (194). Starting from this link, the *Edipo Alcalde* screenplay weaves together two narrative threads: one about the dynamics of the conflict between the guerrillas and the powerful landowner class that largely sees itself as—and controls—the state, and the other a retelling of the Oedipus story. These two interwoven threads, however, cannot correspond entirely to the structure of the ancient tragedy, inasmuch as in the tragedy, the guilt of Oedipus and the ongoing plague appear to be actually interdependent (Serra 37), whereas in the screenplay the Colombian armed conflict and the vicissitudes of the Sophoclean character clearly exist in different spheres. In other words, the mayor (the Oedipus of the screenplay) has no possibility of resolving the conflict, but can only decide to proceed with an investigation that not only will reveal his incestuous, parricidal story but also will produce a hypothesis about the origin of the evils that afflict the village. In this sense, we feel there is a profound link with the novel *The Autumn of the Patriarch* and its reflections on the theme of power. In fact, in one of the last sequences of *Edipo Alcalde*, the mayor goes to Creon to tell him that the power he finally succeeded in conquering is, in truth, nothing but a retribution: "We have come full circle. Now you are master of the power that is omnipotent. You have Laius's killer. You have his faults purified by your blood and mine, and by those of the numberless dead of this land of ill-fortune. You have the keys that open and close all the doors, the doors of war as well as the doors of peace. This is your retribution" (García Márquez, "Edipo Alcalde" 124). Basically, what this Oedipus seems to be saying in his speech to Creon is that the desire for power is the real root of evil and that power itself, without justice, is an illusion, a punishment, pure vanity.

Edipo Alcalde, then, can be seen as an authentic concluding summary of García Márquez's filmic work, showing yet again how in this corpus of over thirty years of writing for cinema, the characteristic obsessions, thoughts, and images of the rest of his literary art reappear, relocated in a constant productive process of intertextual interchange and circulation. The fascination with premonition and destiny and their historical and narrative implications; the obsession with the apocalyptic aspects of political violence and their association with catastrophes and epidemics; the profound reflections on the nature of power; the representation of a carnivalesque and circus-like world; the desire to discover and recount a sphere of reality permeated with myth, dream, and fantastical elements; the interest in bringing the prodigious, the unusual, and the absurd to the surface between the cracks in everyday life; the passion for literary models and the mixing and hybridization of genres, codes, and languages—all these are some of the indisputably Garciamarquezian traits that have been identified and highlighted in the corpus reviewed in these pages. Naturally these aspects reappear here in the context of a specific composition and narrative configuration, modeled on the characteristics and prerogatives of cinematic language. This may seem obvious when discussing films that have been made, that is, actual audiovisual texts, but we should always remember that what lies at the basis of their narrative structure are stories and screenplays by García Márquez. Essentially, this means acknowledging the existence of a literary genre, or rather a filmic-literary genre, in which the film writings of our author can be located— also in order better to understand some of their general characteristics, such as, for example, the relevance of dramatic structure, the peculiarities of spatial and temporal configuration, the attention given to the symbolic value of visual and concrete elements, and the need to find ways of synthesizing and condensing narrative action (Rocco, "El guion publicado"). Thus we can appreciate the profound knowledge developed by García Márquez of the mechanisms and techniques of filmic narration in years of intense and undying passion for cinema. And we can also understand how the fruits of his production in this context are not just a minor reflection of his work in general, but original creations in which his creative vein finds a new and unique form, enriching in no small way his already extraordinary literary universe.

Works Cited

"Acta de creación de la FNCL." Fundación Nuevo Cine Latinoamericano, Apr. 1985, cinelatinoamericano.org/fnclhistoria.aspx?mnu=2&cod=21#up. Accessed 7 May 2021.

Birri, Fernando. *Cómo se filma un film: Taller de dirección de Fernando Birri*. Córdoba-La Habana, Diputación de Córdoba-Fundación del Nuevo Cine Latinoamericano, 2007.

Birri, Fernando. *Fernando Birri: Por un nuevo nuevo cine latinoamericano (1956-1991)*. Cátedra/Filmoteca Española, 1996.

Birri, Fernando. Interview with author. 7 Dec. 2011.

Canfield, Martha. "Dos enfoques de *Pedro Páramo*." *Revista Iberoamericana*, vol. LV, nos. 148–49, July–Dec. 1989, pp. 965–88.

Cazals, Felipe. "Re: 2as consideraciones." Received by Alessandro Rocco, 19 Jan. 2016.

Ciment, Michel. "Entretien avec Ruy Guerra." *Positif*, no. 268, 1983, pp. 17–22.

De Pascale, Goffredo. *Fernando Birri, l'altramerica*. Le Pleiadi, 1994.

Durán, Armando. "Conversaciones con Gabriel García Márquez." *García Márquez habla de García Márquez*. edited by Alfonso Rentería Mantilla, Rentería, 1979, pp. 29–35.

En este pueblo no hay ladrones. Directed by Alberto Isaac. Grupo Claudio, 1964.

García Márquez, Eligio. *Tras las claves de Melquiades*. Mondadori, 2003.

García Márquez, Gabriel. *El asalto: Operativo con que el Fsln se lanzó al mundo*. Nueva Nicaragua, 1983.

García Márquez, Gabriel. *La bendita manía de contar*. Escuela Internacional de Cine y Televisión—Ollero & Ramos, 1998.

García Márquez, Gabriel. "El charro." Typescript, 1963.

García Márquez, Gabriel. *Cómo se cuenta un cuento*. Escuela Internacional de Cine y Televisión—Ollero & Ramos, 1996.

García Márquez, Gabriel . "Edipo Alcalde." Typescript, 1992.

García Márquez, Gabriel. "Esto lo contó García Márquez." *Imagen: Quincenario de arte, literatura e información cultural*, no. 6, 1967, pp. 5–6.

García Márquez, Gabriel. "El golpe sandinista: Crónica del asalto a la casa de los chanchos." *Por la libre: Obra periodística 4 (1974–1995)*, Mondadori, 1999, pp. 205–20.

García Márquez, Gabriel. *In Evil Hour* (1962). Avon, 1979.

García Márquez, Gabriel. "La increíble y triste historia de la cándida Eréndira y de su abuela desalmada." *Papeles*, no. 11, June 1970, pp. 7–25.

García Márquez, Gabriel. "La increíble y triste historia de la cándida Eréndira y de su abuela desalmada." *Siempre*, no. 456, Nov. 1970, pp. I–VII.

García Márquez, Gabriel. *Living to Tell the Tale* (2002). Penguin, 2008.

García Márquez, Gabriel. *Me alquilo para soñar*. Escuela Internacional de Cine y Televisión—Ollero & Ramos, 1997.

García Márquez, Gabriel. *Notas de prensa: 1980–1984*. 2nd ed. Mondadori, 1991.

García Márquez, Gabriel. "Palabras de García Márquez." Fundación Nuevo Cine Latinoamericano, 4 Dec. 1986, cinelatinoamericano.org/fnclhistoria.aspx?mnu=2&cod=28#up. Accessed 7 May 2021.

García Márquez, Gabriel. "Para Elisa." Typescript, 1973.

García Márquez, Gabriel. "La penumbra del escritor de cine." García Aguilar, Eduardo. *La tentación cinematográfica de G. García Márquez*, UNAM/Filmoteca UNAM, 1984, pp. 99–105.

García Márquez, Gabriel. *El secuestro*. Nueva Nicaragua-Lóguez, 1983.

García Márquez, Gabriel, screenwriter. *Tiempo de morir*. Directed by Jorge Alí Triana, Focine, Icaic, 1985

García Márquez, Gabriel. "Tiempo de morir." *Revista de Bellas Artes*, no. 9, May–Jun. 1966, pp. 21–59.

García Márquez, Gabriel. "Todo cuento es un cuento chino." *El País*, 5 Nov. 2000, elpais.com/diario/2000/11/05/opinion/973378808_850215.html. Accessed 7 May 2021.

García Márquez, Gabriel. *¡Viva Sandino!*. Nueva Nicaragua, 1982.

García Márquez, Gabriel, et al., screenwriters. *El año de la peste*. Directed by Felipe Cazals, Conacite II, 1978.

García Márquez, Gabriel, et al., screenwriters. *Cartas del parque*. Directed by Tomás Gutiérrez Alea, Televisión Española S.A., International Networg Group S.A., 1988.

García Márquez, Gabriel, et al., screenwriters. *Con el amor no se juega*, Directed by Carlos García Agraz (*El espejo de dos lunas*), José Luis García Agraz (*Ladrón de sábado*) and Tomás Gutiérres Alea (*Contigo en la distancia*), Producciones Amaranta, 1991.

García Márquez, Gabriel, et al., screenwriters. *Un domingo feliz*. Directed by Olegario Barrera, Televisión Española S.A., International Networg Group S.A., 1988.

García Márquez, Gabriel, et al., screenwriters. *Edipo Alcalde*. Directed by Jorge Alí Triana, Producciones Amaranta, 1996.

García Márquez, Gabriel, et al., screenwriters. *El gallo de oro*. Directed by Roberto Gavaldón, Manuel Barbachano Ponce, 1964.

García Márquez, Gabriel, et al., screenwriters. *La langosta azul*. Directed by Alvaro Cepeda Samudio et al., Nueve-Seis-Tres, 1954.

García Márquez, Gabriel, et al., screenwriters. *Me alquilo para soñar*. Directed by Ruy Guerra, Televisión Española S.A., International Networg Group S.A., 1992.

García Márquez, Gabriel, et al., screenwriters. *Yo soy el que tú buscas*. Directed by Jaime Chávarri, Televisión Española S.A., International Networg Group S.A., 1988.

García Márquez, Gabriel, and Luis Alcoriza. "Dios y yo." Typescript, 1965.

García Márquez, Gabriel, and Luis Alcoriza. "Presagio." Typescript.

García Márquez, Gabriel, and Luis Alcoriza, screenwriters. *Presagio*. Directed by Luis Alcoriza, Producciones Escorpión S.A., 1974.

García Márquez, Gabriel, and Fernando Birri, screenwriters. *Un señor muy viejo con unas alas enormes*. Directed by Fernando Birri, Laboratorio de Poéticas Cinematográficas de Fernando Birri s.r.l., 1988.

García Márquez, Gabriel, and Giancarlo Del Re. "Blacamán, venditore di miracoli." Typescript, 1974.

García Márquez, Gabriel, and Carlos Fuentes, "El gallo de oro: El guion (Versión preliminar, diciembre de 1963)." *Juan Rulfo en el cine: Los guiones* de Pedro Páramo y El gallo de oro, edited by Douglas J. Weatherford, Editorial RM—Fundación Juan Rulfo, 2020, pp. 237–312.

García Márquez, Gabriel, and Carlos Fuentes, screenwriters. *Tiempo de morir*. Directed by Arturo Ripstein, Alameda Films, 1965.

García Márquez, Gabriel, and Jacques Gilard. *Entre cachacos I: Obra periodística*, vol. 2, 2nd ed. Bruguera, 1982.

García Márquez, Gabriel and Ruy Guerra, screenwriters. *Eréndira*. Directed by Ruy Guerra, Les Films du Triangle, 1983.

García Márquez, Gabriel, and Ruy Guerra, screenwriters. *Fábula de la bella palomera*. Directed by Ruy Guerra, Televisión Española S.A., International Networg Group S.A., 1988.

García Márquez, Gabriel, and Jaime Humberto Hermosillo, screenwriters. *María de mi corazón*. Directed by Jaime Humberto Hermosillo, Universidad Veracruzana y Asociados, 1979.

García Márquez, Gabriel and Jaime Humberto Hermosillo. Screenwriters. *El verano de la señora Forbes*. Directed by Jaime Humberto Hermosillo, Televisión Española S.A., International Networg Group S.A., 1988.

García Márquez, Gabriel, and Lisandro Duque Naranjo, screenwriters. *Milagro en Roma*. Directed by Lisandro Duque Naranjo, Televisión Española S.A., International Networg Group S.A., 1988.

García Riera, Emilio. "Conversación con Jaime Humberto Hermosillo." *Primer Plano: Revista de la Cineteca Nacional*, no. 1, Nov.–Dec. 1981, pp. 3–30.

García Riera, Emilio. *Historia documental del cine mexicano*, vol. IX. Era, 1969–1978.

Gilard, Jacques. "García Márquez: Un projet d'école de cinéma (1960)." *Cinémas d'Amérique Latine*, no. 3, 1995, pp. 24–38.

Hermosillo, Jaime Humberto. Interview with author, 25 Oct. 2011.

Herrera, Javier. "Gabriel García Márquez y el cine: Dos proyectos con Luis Alcoriza a través de una correspondencia inédita." *Cuadernos para Investigación de la Literatura Hispánica*, no. 37, 2012, pp. 351–69.

Mahieu, José Agustín. "Los ojos del 2000: Del Festival de Cine Latinoamericano de La Habana, la Escuela y otras cosas." *Cuadernos Hispanoamericanos*, no. 458, Aug. 1988, pp. 167–76.

Martin, Gerald. *Gabriel García Márquez: Una vida*. Random House Mondadori, 2009.

Mendoza, Plinio Apuleyo. *La llama y el hielo*. Planeta, 1984.

Pedro Páramo. Directed by Carlos Velo. Producciones Barbachano Ponce, 1966.

Pérez, David Marcial. "Ve la luz el primer guion escrito por Gabo." *El País*, 2 Feb. 2020, elpais.com/cultura/2020/02/02/actualidad/1580658258_261904.html. Accessed 2 Apr. 2020.

Philippon, Alain. "Poésie en Contrabande." *Cahiers du cinéma*, no. 354, 1983, pp. 46–48.

Ríos, Humberto, and Adolfo García Videla. "Gabriel García Márquez: El origen de mis historias es la imagen." *Plural*, no. 142, 1983, pp. 7–10.

Rocco, Alessandro. *Gabriel García Márquez and the Cinema: Life and Works*. Tamesis-Boydell & Brewer, 2014.

Rocco, Alessandro. "El guion publicado: Un nuevo género narrativo." *Cine/Literatura: Nuevas aproximaciones a viejas polémicas*, edited by Giovanna Pollarolo, Pontificia Universidad Católica de Lima, 2019, pp. 83–94.

Serra, Giuseppe. *Edipo e la peste: Politica e tragedia nell'Edipo Re*. Marsilio, 1994.

Torres, Augusto M. "Entrevista con Gabriel García Márquez." *Cuadernos para el diálogo*, no. 66, 1969, pp. 44–45.

Torres, Miguel. "El novelista que quiso hacer cine." *García Márquez habla de García Márquez*, edited by Alfonso Rentería Mantilla. Rentería, 1979, pp. 45–48.

Vargas Llosa, Mario. *García Márquez: historia de un deicidio*. Barral, 1971.

Index

Figures are indicated by *f* following the page number

Abad Faciolince, Héctor, 560
Abe, Kōbō, 283–84
Abranches, Henrique, 211–12
Absalom, Absalom! (Faulkner), 114, 117
Achebe, Chinua, 209, 215, 216–18
Adichie, Chimamanda Ngozi, 217–18
Advani, Rukun, 267–68
Afro-Caribbeans
  African religion and, 151–52, 158–59, 549–50
  The Autumn of the Patriarch
    and, 148–51, 160
  Chronicle of a Death Foretold and, 152
  In Evil Hour and, 146–47
  The General in His Labyrinth and, 148,
    155–57, 160
  Of Love and Other Demons and, 6, 157–60,
    539–40, 547, 549–50
  Love in the Time of Cholera and, 148–49,
    152–55, 160
  miscegenation and, 145, 147, 151–52, 156,
    159–60
  One Hundred Years of Solitude and, 2, 147–48,
    155–56
  sex and sensuality among, 6, 145, 146–50,
    151–55, 157, 160
  slavery and, 145, 148, 151, 152, 157–59
  Strange Pilgrims and, 151–52
After That (Òkédìjí), 218
Agamben, Giorgio, 365
Agualusa, José Eduardo, 211–12, 213–14
Ah Cheng, 253–54, 257–58
Ahmad, Aijaz, 264–65
alchemy
  Blake and, 397–98
  chemistry and, 394
  coniunctio and, 403–5, 406

homo duplex and, 326
magnets and, 399
One Hundred Years of Solitude and, 7–8, 326,
  383, 391–407
self-realization, 404, 405–7
transmutation and, 394
unity and resolution in, 326, 391, 403
Alcoriza, Luis, 294–95, 597–99
Alexander, Jacqui, 192
Algeria
  elections (2016) in, 243
  García Márquez's arrest in, 55, 233, 240, 243
  National Liberation Front and
    independence movement in, 55–56, 233
Allende, Isabel, 40, 105, 130
Allende, Salvador, 56–57, 210, 242, 445, 570
Alonso, Alonso, 280–81
Alonso, Carlos, 514, 527–28
Alonso, Dámaso, 293
Alrefai, Talib, 233
Álvarez, Federico, 294
Álvarez, Julia, 97–98
Amado, Jorge, 213, 223, 328
Amin Dada, Idi, 210–11, 222–23
Amorós, Andrés, 298, 302
Anaya, Rudolfo, 103–4
Anderson, Jon Lee, 543–44
Angola
  Afro-Caribbean culture and, 146
  civil war in, 57, 212, 213–14
  Cuba and, 57–59, 209, 210–11, 212, 308
  international extractive industries and,
    58–59
  literacy rate in, 209–10, 211
  Operation Carlota and, 19, 57–59, 63, 210–12,
    213–14

Angola (*cont.*)
  Portuguese colonization of, 58
  poverty in, 58
  religious traditions in, 214
  US military intervention in, 57
Angola a Year Later (García Márquez), 210–12
anime, 7, 277, 281–82, 285–86
Antaki, Ikram, 240
Anthropocene Age, 375–76, 383, 387n.3
Anzoátegui, Ignacio B., 295
Aquinas, Thomas, 132, 500, 551–52
the Arab Other, 235–40, 242–43
Aracataca (Colombia)
  García Márquez's childhood in, 15–20, 24–25, 112, 147, 170–73, 172f, 175–76, 458, 486–87n.6, 494–95, 497, 506, 577, 578–79
  immigrant populations in, 54–55
  Leaf Storm and, 146
  Living to Tell the Tale account of García Márquez's return to, 494–95, 497, 506, 565–66, 576–79
  map of, 174f
  One Hundred Years of Solitude and, 1, 17–18
  superstition in, 20
  Wayúu Indians in, 171–73, 174–75
Arafa, Amr, 232–33
Arguedas, José María, 326–27, 449–50
Aristotle, 110, 405, 473–74
"Artificial Roses" (García Márquez), 247–48
As I Lay Dying (Faulkner), 121
Aslam, Nadeem, 267–68
Asociación China del Estudio de la Literatura Española, Portuguesa y Latinoamericana, 248
Asturias, Miguel Ángel, 1, 31, 249–50, 477, 568–69
Atuma, Uche, 215
Aub, Max, 294
Auschwitz concentration camp (Poland), 355, 358, 364–66
The Autumn of the Patriarch (García Márquez)
  African literary cultures and, 209, 218–19, 221
  Afro-Caribbean characters and culture in, 148–51, 160
  Arab literary culture and, 243
  baroque literature and, 117

  "Blacamán the Good, Vendor of Miracles" and, 600
  Chinese literary culture and, 247–48, 249–50
  colonialism and, 3, 150
  communal narrators in, 121
  deterioration and death of the patriarch in, 62, 525–27
  dictatorship and power in, 3, 8–9, 61–62, 64–65, 150, 196, 447, 524–27, 528–33, 607
  Global South and, 59–60, 61, 65
  international debt in, 59–60, 61
  international extractive industries and, 5–6
  Japanese literary culture and, 286–88
  kidnapping in, 597–99
  love and, 129–30, 131
  music and musical allusions in, 414, 416–20
  panoptic view of Caribbean in, 151
  Rabassa's translation of, 150
  sex and, 150, 151, 195–96, 526–27, 528–29
  slavery and, 151
  Spain's literary culture and, 301–2
  subdued voices in, 346–47
  women characters in, 189–90, 195–96

Bâ, Mariama, 217, 220–21
Baah, Robert Nana, 386–87n.2
Bach, Johann Sebastian, 429
Backsheider, Paula R., 15–17
Bada, Ricardo, 17
Badosa, Enrique, 300
Bakhtin, Mikhail, 336, 474, 483–84, 524, 534
Balcells, Carmen, 133, 294–95
Baldwin, James, 220–21
Balzac, Honoré de, 216–17, 341
Bandung Conference (1955), 52–53, 265–66
Bangladesh, 269–71
Baquero, Gastón, 295
Barbier, Jules, 422–23
Barcha, Mercedes, 16, 516, 566–67
Barea, Arturo, 100–1
baroque literature
  coincidence of opposites in, 117–18
  culteranismo and *conceptismo* branches in, 115
  Don Quixote and, 117
  drama and, 117
  Faulkner and, 114–15

García Márquez's appreciation and
adaptation of, 110–11, 114–18, 121–22
Of Love and Other Demons and, 547–49,
550–52
New World Baroque and, 548
poetry and, 116, 118
unreality of perception and, 117
Barranquilla Group, 54–55, 100–1, 293, 462–63,
470n.16, 596–97
Barrero, Olegario, 606
Barriteau, Eudine, 194–95
Barth, John, 31–32
Barthes, Roland, 126, 132, 348, 478–79
Bartók, Bela, 414
Baum, Samuel Lisman, 357–58
Beckman, Ericka, 58–61
Bécquer, Gustavo Adolfo, 293
Begin, Menachem, 240–41
Bell, Michael, 518–20
Bell-Villada, Gene H., 31–32, 324, 374, 448
"The Beloved though Distant Homeland"
(García Márquez), 442
Beltrán Almería, Luis, 324–25, 332
Benet, Juan, 102, 297–99
Bengelstorff, Anja, 224
Benítez-Rojo, Antonio, 149
Benjamin, Jessica, 193–94, 198
Benjamin, Walter, 356–57
Betancur, Belisario, 304
Beti, Mongo, 209, 215–16, 220, 223, 224
Bhabha, Homi, 31, 64–65, 97, 264–65
Bhuiyan, Shahabuddin, 273
Biava, Pedro, 430
The Bible
    Faulkner and, 114
    miracles and, 42–43, 113–14
    One Hundred Years of Solitude and, 114, 325,
    332, 475–76
"Big Mama's Funeral" (García Márquez)
    African literary cultures and, 219
    belief and unbelief in, 345
    Chinese literary culture and, 247–48
    competing notions of history and story in,
    342–43
    Cuban Revolution and, 22–23
    death of despotic order in, 85
    Marquesita of La Sierpe and, 214

monstrous innocence and vulnerable
    outsiders in, 492, 493–94, 496–97
older narrative traditions and, 341
the pope in, 62–63
sex and, 197–98
Spain's literary culture and, 296
women characters in, 196–98
Binyavanga Wainaina, Kenneth, 217
Birri, Fernando, 22–24, 601–3
"Blacamán the Good, Vendor of Miracles"
    (García Márquez), 62–63, 506, 597–600
Blacks. *See* Afro-Caribbeans
Blake, William, 397–98, 399–400, 401–2
Blanco Amor, José, 301–2
Blanco Vila, Luis, 302
Bloom, Harold, 5, 111
The Blue Lobster (Baranquilla Group), 596–97
Boehme, Jacob, 395, 406
Bofill, Rosario, 297–98
Bogotá (Colombia), 566
Bolaño, Roberto, 105, 561
bolero music
    The Autumn of the Patriarch and, 417–18
    García Márquez's admiration of, 107n.12
    Love in the Time of Cholera and, 348–50
    Love Story and, 331–32
    Memories of Melancholy Whores and,
    429–30
    One Hundred Years of Solitude and, 348
Bolívar, Simón. *See The General in His
    Labyrinth* (García Márquez)
"Bon Voyage, Mr. President" (García
    Márquez), 151–52, 159–60, 503–4, 562
Borges, Jorge Luis
    Arab literary culture and, 232
    Chinese literary culture and, 246–47
    cyclical time in the work of, 479–80
    Europolitanism and, 482
    García Márquez and, 4, 100–1, 300, 564–65
    Kafka's *Metamorphosis* and, 119
    on literary predecessors, 110–12, 121
    magical realism and, 31, 249–50
    on memory and literature, 175–76
    The Orient and, 234–35
    Pinochet regime in Chile and, 564–65
    short stories of, 100–1
    South Asian literary cultures and, 266

Boubaker, Messaouda, 232–33
Bousoño, Carlos, 328
Bouteflika, Abdelaziz, 243
Bowers, Maggie, 447
Brant, Sebastian, 484–85
Breytenbach, Breyten, 220–21
Bronfen, Elizabeth, 138
Bruant, Aristide, 423
Bruckner, Anton, 417, 429
Bryce Echenique, Alfredo, 130
Buchenwald concentration camp (Poland), 355, 364
Buehrer, David, 373–74, 386n.1
Buñuel, Luis, 223, 293–94, 307
Buschmann, Friedrich, 415

Caballero Bonald, José Manuel, 294–95
Cabello Pino, Manuel, 386–87n.2
Cabeza de Vaca, Álvar Núñez, 442–43
Cabrera Infante, Guillermo, 23–24, 130, 213, 217
Cai Xiang, 255–56
Calderón de la Barca, Pedro, 110–11, 117–18, 293
Calomarde, Joaquín, 302
Camus, Albert, 560–61
Cano, Guillermo, 359
Cano, María, 89
Cano Pérez, Mercedes, 565
Capitalocene Era, 7–8, 375–76, 382–83, 384–85
Cardenal, Ernesto, 333
Cardoza Aragón, Luis, 116–17, 326–27
Carey, Peter, 104
The Caribbean
    Afro-Caribbean population and culture in, 2, 214
    Catholic Church and, 81–82
    contemporary gender relations in, 194–95
    cultural understanding of the supernatural in, 80
    economic instability in, 77
    García Márquez's journalistic coverage of Colombian areas of, 78, 145–46
    Global South and, 53–54
    international extractive industries and, 83–84
    maroon societies in, 81–82
    matrifocal societies in, 196–97
    modernization and socioeconomic disruption in, 77, 82, 83–84, 86, 87–88, 90–91
    Panama Canal and, 84
    settlement of Colombian regions of, 81–82
    sex and sexuality in, 191–92
Carpentier, Alejo
    Haiti and, 209
    historical referentiality in the work of, 542
    The Kingdom of This World and, 209, 476–77, 542–43
    on "Latin American Boom," 252
    magical realism and, 1, 39, 249–50, 284–85, 355–56, 476–77
    neo-baroque style of, 129–30
    radio production and, 413
Cartagena de Indias (Colombia), 539, 542–46
Caruso, Enrico, 424, 431
Casals, Don Pablo, 429
Casanova, Pascale, 102–4, 358
A Case of Exploding Manges (Hanif), 64–65
Castelo Branco, Camilo, 213
Castillo, Alvaro, 25–26
Castillo, Ana, 40
Castro, Fidel
    ascent to power (1959) of, 22–23
    Chronicle of a Death Foretold and, 23–24
    Fundación Nuevo Cine Latinoamericano and, 603
    García Márquez and, 5, 16–17, 19, 22–25, 56–58, 309, 368n.13, 445, 565, 570, 603
    González case and, 23–24
    Non-Aligned Movement and, 265–66
Catelli, Nora, 303
Catholic Church
    The Caribbean and, 81–82
    Chronicle of a Death Foretold and, 517–18
    Colombia and, 113–14
    coloniality and, 444
    confession and, 381
    John Paul II's papacy and, 564
    Living To Tell The Tale and, 113
    Of Love and Other Demons and, 158–60, 547, 549–51
    Love in the Time of Cholera and, 381
    magical realism, 113
    Memories of My Melancholy Whores and, 138
    miracles and, 42–43
    One Hundred Years of Solitude and, 42–43, 85, 128–29

romantic love and, 126
"The Saint" and, 564
Spain and, 113–14
"A Very Old Man with Enormous Wings" and, 500
Virgin Mary cult and, 128–29
Cazals, Felipe, 600
Cela, Camilo José, 273, 279–80
Cepeda Samudio, Álvaro, 99, 100–1, 571, 596–97, 603
Cervantes, Francisco, 298–99
Cervantes, Miguel de. *See Don Quixote* (Cervantes)
Cervera Salinas, Vicente, 374
Chakrabarty, Dipesh, 443–44
Chandran, Mini, 272
Chandran, Subash, 271
Chang Cheng, 251–52
Chaudhuri, Supriya, 269
Chávarri, Jaime, 606
Cheney-Coker, Syl, 209–10, 216, 220–22
Cheng, Vincent, 99
Chen Guangfu, 247–48, 249–50
Chen Zhongyi, 252
Chile
  Allende assassination in, 56–57, 210, 445
  Borges and, 564–65
  Clandestine in Chile and, 241–42, 440, 559, 583–85
  Palestinian immigrants in, 241–42
  Pinochet dictatorship in, 23–24, 56–57, 151–52, 242, 448, 520–21, 564–65, 583–85
China
  avant-garde literature in, 246–47, 250–51, 253–54, 258, 260n.4
  Cold War and, 279–80
  Cultural Revolution in, 6, 246–47
  Flower Mountain writers' group in, 256–57
  Foreign Literature Report in, 247–48
  Four Modernizations policy in, 246
  Hangzhou Meeting and, 255–56
  magical realism and, 6, 246–51, 253–55, 256–57
  May Fourth Movement in, 246, 255–56
  modernism and, 6, 254–55
  One Hundred Years of Solitude and, 247–49, 250–51, 253–54, 255, 258–59

  Root-seeking Literature in, 246–47, 250–51, 253–58, 260n.3
  Soviet Union and, 249–50
Chinweizu, 66
Chiziane, Paulina, 211, 223
Chronicle of a Death Foretold (García Márquez)
  African literary cultures and, 209, 213–14, 219–20
  Afro-Caribbean characters and culture in, 152
  Arab characters in, 236–40
  Arab literary culture and, 6, 238–39
  atavistic tradition in, 87–89, 131
  baroque literature and, 117
  blend between journalism and literature in, 585–86
  A Case of Exploding Mangoes and, 64–65
  Castro and, 23–24
  Catholic Church and, 517–18
  Chinese literary culture and, 248
  communal narrators in, 121
  detective format and, 514–18
  epigraph and, 134
  fate and, 8, 512–14, 517–18, 519–20
  free will and, 8, 519–20
  historical events as basis for, 512–13
  love and, 116, 126, 130–31, 195, 516–18, 519–20
  magistrate's lyrical distractions in, 348
  murder and investigation in, 63–65
  revenge killing in, 237–38, 447, 512–14, 515–19
  setting of, 63
  sex and sexuality in, 152, 189, 195, 237–38, 515–16, 519–20
  slavery and, 152
  South Asian literary cultures and, 266–67, 270, 271
  Spain's literary culture and, 302
  women characters in, 189, 195, 238
Ciénaga plantation strike (Colombia, 1928), 17, 19–22, 24–25, 89, 458, 577–78
Círculo de Lectores book club (Spain), 294–95, 299
Cisneros, Sandra, 103–4
Civantos, Christina, 238–39
Clandestine in Chile (García Márquez), 241–42, 440, 559, 583–85
Clinton, Bill, 565

Cobo Borda, Juan Gustavo, 326–27
Coetzee, J. M., 221–22
Cold War, 52–53, 58–59, 62, 130, 169–70, 247–48, 258–59, 566–67
Colombia
    Arab immigrants in, 239–40
    Catholic Church and, 113–14
    Ciénaga plantation strike (1928) in, 17, 19–22, 24–25, 89, 458, 577–78
    Civil War (1884-85) in, 82–83
    constitution (1863) in, 82–83
    constitution (1991) in, 113–14
    drug-trafficking and paramilitary violence in, 84, 137, 305–6, 607
    Global South and, 103–4
    kidnappings in, 26
    La Violencia and, 77–78, 84, 458–63
    modernization in, 77, 78, 79–80, 82, 83–84
    National Front coalition government (1958) and, 84, 459, 461
    Panama Canal and, 84
    settlement of Caribbean regions of, 81–82
    slavery in, 158–59
    United Fruit Company and, 17, 19, 20–25, 83
    United States and, 99
    War of the Thousand Days (1899-1902) in, 20, 83, 89
    wars of independence and, 81
"Colombian Literature, a Fraud to the Nation" (García Márquez), 459–60, 461–62
coloniality
    Catholic Church and, 444
    "Dreams for the Twenty-First Century" and, 442, 446–47
    Eurocentrism and, 440–44, 445–46
    indigenous resistance tactics and, 444
    "Latin America Exists" and, 442, 445–46
    Latin American regional identity and, 446–47
    modernity and, 440
    Otherizing and, 440–41
    "The Solitude of Latin America" and, 441, 442–44, 445
    United States and, 442, 444, 446
    "Words for a New Millennium" (García Márquez) and, 444–45
Congo, 209, 210, 212–13

Congreso Internacional de la Lengua Española, 310–11
Conservatives (Colombia)
    Catholic Church and, 113–14
    Civil War (1884-85) and, 82–83
    García Márquez's distaste for, 558
    La Violencia and, 458
    National Front coalition government (1958) and, 84
    One Hundred Years of Solitude and, 85, 113–14, 180–81, 378–79, 475–76
Conte, Rafael, 297, 299–300, 304, 306
Cooper, Brenda, 221–22
Cornejo-Parriego, Rosalía, 525–26
Coronil, Fernando, 60–61
Cortázar, Julio
    Arab literary culture and, 232
    Arguedas's debates (1967-69) with, 449–50
    Cuban Revolution and, 4
    García Márquez and, 100–1, 324
    magical realism and, 39, 249–50
    Nobel Prize and, 4
    short stories of, 100–1
    Spain's literary culture and, 302–3
    urban background of, 169
Cortés Vargas, Carlos, 20–21
Cortot, Alfred, 430
cosmopolitanism, 41–42, 54–55
Costa Andrade, Fernado, 211–12
Couto, Mia
    African translation and, 218, 224
    disappearances in the work of, 219–20
    García Márquez and, 96, 98, 103–4, 216
    Macondo Literary Festival and, 224
    magical realism and, 97, 216
    naparama warriors in the work of, 211
Crane, Stephen, 560–61
Cruz, Juan, 304
Cuba
    Angola and, 57–59, 209, 210–11, 212, 308
    "Big Mama's Funeral" and, 22–23
    Congo and, 209, 210
    García Márquez and, 4, 16, 19, 22–25, 56–59, 308–9, 359, 445, 448, 459
    Hemingway and, 100
    Operation Truth and, 22–23
    political prisoners and, 23–24

revolution (1959) in, 4, 22–24, 279–80, 308–9, 359, 445, 448, 459, 558
   US embargo of, 445, 448
Cultural Revolution (China), 6, 246–47
Curiel, Rosario, 375

Dai Jinhua, 257
Dan, Keizuke, 285–86
Dangarembga, Tsitsi, 217–18
Dangerous Loves film series (García Márquez), 603–4
Darío, Rubén, 129–30, 234–35, 295, 416–17
dark ecology
   abuses by centralized governments and, 377–79
   Capitalocene Era and, 7–8, 375–76, 382–83, 384–85
   definition of, 373, 376
   "hauntology" and, 376
   hyperobjects and, 376, 379–80, 382, 384–85
   Love in the Time of Cholera and, 373–74, 376–77, 379, 380–83, 384–86
   multinational corporations and, 377–78, 379–80, 383–85
   One Hundred Years of Solitude and, 373–74, 376–80, 382–86
Dash, Michael, 149–50
Dawson, Paul, 582, 583
Dazai, Osamu, 281
"Death Constant Beyond Love" (García Márquez), 85–86, 90, 115, 129–30, 149
The Death of Alec (Jamarillo Agueldo), 181–82
The Death of Artemio Cruz (Fuentes), 4, 474, 479–80
De Certeau, Michel, 541–42
Deepwater Horizon oil spill (2010), 60–61
Defoe, Daniel, 568, 600, 607
Delibes, Miguel, 297–98
de Oliveira, Margareth, 286
de Rougemont, Denis, 5–6, 126–29, 133, 139
Derrida, Jacques, 376, 407
de Sica, Vittorio, 596–99
de Sousa Santos, Boaventura, 54–55
de Torre, Guillermo, 293, 298–99
Díaz, Antolín, 82
Díaz-Granados, José Luis, 326–27
Díaz-Plaja, Guillermo, 298

Diego, Gerardo, 561
Dissanayake, Daya, 270
Divakaruni, Chitra Banerjee, 267–68
Dohmann, Barbara, 259
Dongala, Emmanuel, 212–13
Donoso, José, 249–50, 251–52, 514–15
Don Quixote (Cervantes)
   as baroque literature's canonical text, 117
   García Márquez's admiration of, 115, 117–18, 293
   Japanese translation of, 277–78
   One Hundred Years of Solitude and, 117, 323–24, 329, 475
   Real Academia de la Lengua edition of, 105
   unreality of perception and, 117
Dos Passos, John, 2–3
dos Santos, José Eduardo, 212
Douaihy, Jabbour, 232–33
"Dreams for the Twenty-First Century" (García Márquez), 442, 446–47
Duan Ruochuan, 249–50
Dumas, Alexander, 568
Duque Naranjo, Lisandro, 604
Durruti, Buenaventura, 562
Dyer, Richard, 147

Echavarría Ferrari, Arturo, 326
Eco, Umberto, 329, 331
ecocriticism, 7–8, 373, 375
EDHASA (publishing house in Spain), 297, 299
Ediciones Era, 294–95
Ediciones Iberoamericanas, 295–96
Editorial Sudamericana, 294–95, 297
Editorial Vergara, 295–96
Edwards, Jorge, 309–10
El Baz Iguider, Hassan, 574–75
Eliade, Mircea, 176, 324–25, 335–36, 482
Elias, Akhtaruzzaman, 269
Eligio García, Gabriel, 15–16, 19
Elío, María Luisa, 294–95
Eliot, T. S., 121–22
ElSherief, Eman, 374
The Embassy in the Building (Arafa), 232–33
Emezi, Akwaeke, 222–23
En agosto nos vemos (García Márquez), 24–25
Endo, Shuzaku, 287
Erdrich, Louise, 40

Eréndira (Guerra), 601–2
Escalona, Rafael, 415
Escobar, Pablo, 137–38, 305–6, 560–61
Escuela Internacional de Cine, Televisión y Video (EICTV), 22–25, 441
Espanca, Florbela, 223
Espresate Xirau, Neus, 294–95
Exemplary Novels (Cervantes), 482–83
"Eyes of a Blue Dog" (García Márquez), 126

Fable of the Beautiful Pigeon Fancier (Guerra), 605–6
Fagunwa, D. O., 215–16
Fals Borda, Orlando, 5, 78–79, 81, 87–88, 169–70
Fanon, Frantz, 146, 221
Fan Ye, 259
Faris, Wendy B., 447
Faulkner, William
   Absalom, Absalom! and, 114, 117
   baroque literature and, 114–15
   The Bible and, 114
   The Caribbean and, 100, 101, 120, 146
   García Márquez and, 2–3, 55–56, 98–100, 101, 102, 108n.13, 108n.14, 110–11, 112, 114–15, 117, 120–21, 146, 221–22, 459, 577–78
   As I Lay Dying and, 121
   modernism and, 102–3
   on the past, 121–22
   racially divided preindustrial cultures and, 103–4
   recurring characters in work of, 341
   as "temporal accelerator," 102–3
   Vargas Llosa and, 101–2, 108n.13
Fauré, Gabriel, 423
The Feast of the Goat (Vargas Llosa), 525–26
Federman, Raymond, 32
Fellini, Federico, 129–30
Fernández-Braso, Miguel, 308
Fernández Retamar, Roberto, 449–50
Ferré, Rosario, 130
Ferreira, Lídia do Carmo, 213–14
Finnegans Wake (Joyce), 399, 402–3
Flaubert, Gustave, 38, 132, 136, 328, 576
Flores, Ángel, 284–85
Flower Mountain writers' group (China), 256–57

Foreign Literature Report (China), 247–48
Foucault, Michel, 200, 355, 394, 403, 562–63
Foundation for a New Ibero-American Journalism, 441
Fragrance of Guava (Mendoza and García Márquez), 146, 148–49, 152, 248
Franco, Francisco, 113–14, 292–93, 296–97, 308, 562
Freely: Journalistic Work (García Márquez), 233–34
Freixas, Laura, 304
Frente Nacional (Colombia), 459, 461
Fuenmayor, Alfonso, 100–1
Fuentes, Carlos
   Arab literary culture and, 232
   Cuban Revolution and, 4, 23–24
   The Death of Artemio Cruz and, 4, 474, 479–80
   film work by, 597–99
   García Márquez and, 64–65, 306, 323–25, 331
   magical realism and, 31–32, 104, 249–50
   Mexican mythology and, 333
   new sentimental narratives and, 130
   Nobel Prize and, 4
   urban background of, 169
Fuguet, Alberto, 104–5, 439
Fundación Nuevo Cine Latinoamericano, 603

Gabriel García Márquez Foundation for New Ibero-American Journalism, 543
Gaitán, Jorge Eliécer, 77–78, 458, 558–59, 599–600
Gallegos, Rómulo, 100–2
Gallo, Marta, 35–36
The Game of Contemporaneity (Ōe), 280–81
Gamis, Lorenzo, 297–98
García, Cristina, 40, 103–4
García Ascot, Jomí, 294–95
García Espinosa, Julio, 22–24
García Lorca, Federico, 279–80, 293, 302, 304
García Márquez, Gonzalo, 16, 26
García Márquez, Jaime, 26
García Márquez, Rodrigo, 16, 26
García Nieto, José, 303
García Posada, Miguel, 304
Garcilaso de la Vega, Inca, 5, 118, 134, 136, 549–50

Gardel, Carlos, 419, 425–26, 428
Garuba, Harry, 221–22
Gavaldón, Roberto, 596–97
Gaviria, César, 560–61
The General in His Labyrinth (García Márquez)
  Afro-Caribbean characters in, 148, 155–57, 160
  Bolívar and, 8–9, 116, 155–57, 160, 304, 447, 525, 527–28, 529, 532–34, 568–70
  Castro and, 570
  Chinese literary culture and, 248
  contest between love and time in, 116
  the general's deterioration and death in, 525–26, 527–28, 569–70
  Japanese literary culture and, 286
  Latin American unification and, 532
  miscegenation and, 156
  older narrative traditions and, 341
  plantations in, 157
  power and, 524–26, 527–30, 531–34
  reviews of, 568–69
  the sea in, 156–57
  sex and, 528–29
  slavery and, 156–57, 529
  Spain's literary culture and, 304
General Report on Chile (Littín), 242
A General Theory of Oblivion (Agualusa), 213
Gentile Chimento, Cayetano, 512–13
Ghosh, Amitav, 267–68
"The Ghosts of August" (García Márquez), 561–62
Giacoman, Helmy, 323–24
Gilard, Jacques, 77–78, 146, 359–61, 362
Gilroy, Paul, 545–46, 549–50
Gimferrer, Pere, 297–98, 301–2
Gironella, José María, 300
Glissant, Édouard, 53–54, 102
Global North, 2, 31, 50–51, 52–53, 439, 441, 444, 450
Global South. *See also* Third World
  Atlantic slave trade and, 60
  cosmopolitanism and, 54–55
  defining elements of, 52–54
  dispossession and exploitation in, 53–54, 63
  Eurocentrism and, 443–44
  Global North and, 52–53
  international debt and, 59–60, 61–62

  international extractive industries and, 58–59, 60–61
  magical realism and, 31, 51–52, 64–65, 97–98, 103–5
  One Hundred Years of Solitude and, 2, 50–52, 54, 59–61, 65, 96, 98, 103–4, 105
"God and I" (Alcoriza and García Márquez), 597–99
Goehr, Lydia, 414
Goethe, Johann Wolfgang von, 135
"The Golden Cockrel" (García Márquez and Fuentes), 596–97
Gómez, Sergio, 99–100, 105
Gómez de la Serna, Ramón, 293, 300–1
Góngora, Luis de, 114–15, 293
Goñi, Javier, 303
González, Aníbal, 324–25, 332
González, Elián, 23–24
González, Felipe, 307, 309
González, Manuel Pedro, 301–2
González, Reinol, 23–24
González Echevarría, Roberto, 324–25, 408n.16, 542–43
Gorbachev, Mikhail, 309
Gordimer, Nadine, 215
Gossaín, Juan, 148–49
Goytisolo, Juan, 23–24, 279–80
Goytisolo, Luis, 298
Grass, Günter, 31–32
Greene, Graham, 215–16, 364
Grenet, Eliseo, 419
Grever, María, 349
Grossman, Edith, 154
Grosso, Alfonso, 300
Guajiro Indians. *See* Wayúu Indians
Gubar, Susan, 138
Guelbenzu, José María, 297–98
Guerra, Ruy, 597–99, 601–2, 605–6
Guevara, Che, 58–59, 210–11, 212–13
Guilbert, Yvette, 423
Guillén, Nicolás, 146, 150–51
Guimarães Rosa, João, 215
Guinote, Ana, 525
Gulliver's Travels (Swift), 211
Gullón, Ricardo, 324, 474
Gutiérrez Alea, Tomás, 22–24, 605–6
Gutiérrez Mouat, Ricardo, 407

Haiti, 209, 476–77, 549–50
"The Handsomest Drowned Man in the World" (García Márquez), 4, 62–63, 86–87, 130, 218, 492, 498, 500–2, 507
Hangzhou Meeting (China), 255–56
Hanif, Mohammed, 64–65, 69n.33, 267–68
Han Shaogong, 253–55, 256–58
Han Yuhai, 257
A Happy Sunday (Barrero), 606
Haq, Kaiser, 270
Haque, Syed Shamsul, 269
Harris, Wilson, 40
Harry Ransom Center (University of Texas), 24–26
Harss, Luis, 259
Hart, Stephen, 492–93
Hassan, Waïl, 235, 238–39
Hawthorne, Nathaniel, 110–11, 561
Head, Bessie, 105, 215
Hegerfeldt, Ann, 32–34
He Guimei, 254
Heisenberg, Werner, 485n.1
Hemingway, Ernest, 2–3, 55, 99–100, 216–17, 459, 560–61
Hermes, 398–99
Hermosillo, Jaime Humberto, 600–1, 604
Hernández, Felisberto, 100–1
Hernández, Miguel, 328
Herrera Soto, Roberto, 20–21
Hirohito (emperor of Japan), 281–82
Hoffman, Alice, 104
Hopscotch (Cortázar), 4, 302–3, 324, 479–80
Hugo, Victor, 212–13
Humboldt, Alexander von, 178–79, 180–81, 356–57, 483–84
Hungarian Revolution (1956), 355, 358, 566–67
Hutcheon, Linda, 534, 582
Hyder, Qurratulain, 268
hyperobjects, 376, 379–80, 382, 384–85

I Am Not Here to Give a Speech (García Márquez), 233–34, 259, 440–41
Iguarán Cotes, Tranquilina, 15–16, 20, 119–20, 474, 478
Ikezawa, Natsuki, 277, 282–83, 286
Imam, Adel, 232–33
I'm the One You're Looking for (Chávarri), 606

The Incredible and Sad Tale of Innocent Eréndira and Her Heartless Grandmother (García Márquez)
　Afro-Caribbean characters and culture in, 149
　as screenplay, 597–99
　sex work in, 63, 149
　Spain's literary culture and, 300–1
　Wayúu characters and culture in, 175
India, 265–66, 269
In Evil Hour (García Márquez)
　Afro-Caribbean characters and culture in, 146–47
　omen in, 597–99
　publication in Spain of, 295–96, 299–300
　racial heterogeneity among characters in, 146–47
　violence and, 84, 457–58, 462, 464–67
Innocent Eréndira and Other Stories (García Márquez), 90, 129–30, 156–57
Inoue, Hisashi, 282
"I Only Came to Use the Phone" (García Márquez), 562–63, 600–1
Irigaray, Luce, 188
Isaac, Alberto, 294, 597–99
Isaacs, Jorge, 177, 572
Isegawa, Moses, 216, 222–23
"I Sell My Dreams" (García Márquez), 564–65
Ishii, Yuka, 7, 288
Izquierdo, Luis, 298

Jacinto, António, 211–12
Jackson, Mahalia, 426–27
Jahan, Nasreen, 270
Jakobson, Roman, 329
Japan
　Christian Century (1549–1650) in, 277–78
　emigration to Latin America from, 278
　fantastic literature in, 281–82
　Hiroshima and Nagasaki atomic bombings in, 281–82
　imperial family in, 280–81
　magical realism and, 277, 281, 284–86, 288
　Meiji era (1868–1912) in, 281
　naturalism in, 281
　Okinawa and, 279–80

One Hundred Years of Solitude and, 277–81, 283–88
   Shintoism and, 285–86
Jaramillo Agudelo, Darío, 181–82
Javed, Khalid, 266–67
Jia Pingwa, 257–58
Jiménez, Juan Ramón, 293
Jiménez, Mario, 419
John of Patmos (saint), 114
John of the Cross (saint), 129
John Paul I (pope), 564
John Paul II (pope), 23–24, 564
A Journal of the Plague Year (Defoe), 568, 600, 607
Joya, Abdelaziz al, 234
Joyce, James
   Achebe and, 216–17
   biography genre and, 16–17
   as colonial subject, 99, 101
   Finnegans Wake and, 399, 402–3
   García Márquez's admiration of, 2–3, 55, 98–99, 101, 102, 110–11, 116, 459
   Ulysses and, 395–96
Juan Carlos I (king of Spain), 307, 309
Jung, Carl, 391, 394, 399–400, 403–4

Kádár, Janos, 566–67
Kafka, Franz
   Abe and, 283–84
   Borges on, 110
   García Márquez's admiration of, 55–56, 98–99, 101, 108n.14, 110–11, 119, 459, 474
   The Metamorphosis and, 98–99, 119, 123n.26, 474, 486n.4
   minority literature in majority language and, 99, 101
   on Paradise, 335–36
Kamal, Ajmal, 266–67
Kantor, Roanne, 64–65
Kapuściński, Ryszard, 559
Kawabata, Yasunari, 281, 287, 561
Keizuke Dan, 285–86
Kempadoo, Kemala, 191–92
Kerala (India), 7, 266, 268–69, 271
Khalifah, Khaled, 232–33
Khomeini, Ayatollah, 267–68
Khosa, Ungulani Ba Ka, 223

Khoury, Elias, 6, 64–65, 69n.33, 238–40
Kierkegaard, Søren, 110
Kimani, Peter, 216
Kimura, Eiichi, 286
The Kingdom of This World (Carpentier), 209, 476–77, 542–43
Kinsella, William Patrick, 104
Kissinger, Henry, 210, 581
Kleist, Henrich von, 604
Kourouma, Ahmadou, 62, 216, 221, 222–23, 224
Kroetsch, Robert, 40
Kureishi, Hanif, 267–68
Kurosawa, Akira, 287–88

Laforet, Carmen, 297–98
Lago Graña, Josefa, 374
Laing, Kojo, 219–22
Lara, Agustín, 107n.12, 326–27, 428
The Last Harmattan of Alusine Dunbar (Cheney-Coker), 220
"Latin America Exists" (García Márquez), 442, 445–46
The Laughing Cry (Lopes), 212, 221
La Violencia (Colombia), 77–78, 84, 458–63
Lavoe, Héctor, 414
Laye, Camara, 212–13, 216
Lázaro Carreter, Fernando, 88–89, 305
Leaf Storm (García Márquez)
   criollo perspective in, 146
   as García Márquez's first novel, 1, 15–16, 98, 357–58
   interface of family life and major historical events in, 81
   international extractive industries and, 462–64
   modernity and socioeconomic disruption in, 77, 82, 84, 91
   popularity in Colombia of, 462
   publishers' initial rejection of, 293, 295–96, 326–27, 462–63
   Spain's literary culture and, 295, 299–300
   violence and, 82, 457–58, 459–60
   Wayúu Indians in, 173
León, Juanita, 582
Leonard, John, 568–69
León-Portilla, Miguel, 333–34
LePera, Alfredo, 419

624   INDEX

Letters from the Park (Gutiérrez Alea), 605–6
Levi, Primo, 365
Lévi-Strauss, Claude, 324–26, 330–31, 476, 575
Lezama Lima, José, 129–30
Liberals (Colombia)
    Arab immigrant communities and, 237–38
    Catholic Church and, 113–14
    Civil War (1884-85) and, 82–83
    La Violencia and, 77–78, 458
    modernization and, 77
    National Front coalition government (1958) and, 84
    One Hundred Years of Solitude and, 83, 85, 113–14, 147, 180–81, 378–79, 475–76
    War of the Thousand Days (1899–1902) and, 83
    women's emancipation and, 89
Li Deming, 248
Life and a Half (Sony), 218–19, 221
"Light Is Like Water" (García Márquez), 561, 564
Li Hangyu, 253–54
Li Jiefei, 247, 257–58
Lin Yi'an, 247–48, 249–50
Littín, Miguel, 241–42, 583–85
Li Tuo, 246–47, 254–55, 259
Liu Zhenyun, 256–57
Living to Tell the Tale (García Márquez)
    Catholic Church and, 113
    Ciénaga plantation strike (1928) and, 577–78
    Colombian politics discussed in, 558
    epigraph of, 19
    on García Márquez's grandparents, 113
    on García Márquez's time as border at a bordello, 139
    illegitimate children of García Márquez's grandfather discussed in, 18, 147
    Japanese literary culture and, 286
    journey to Aracataca described in, 494–95, 497, 506, 565–66, 576–79
    love between parents of García Márquez described in, 19
    Love in the Time of Cholera and, 19
    One Hundred Years of Solitude and, 17–18, 566–67
    personal literary evolution of García Márquez described in, 98–101, 110–11, 112, 115, 116, 117–18, 560–61, 565–67, 574–75, 576–77, 579–80, 586–87
    planned sequel to, 19, 567, 588–89
    poetry and, 326–27
    reviews of, 17
    Spain's literary culture and, 306
    Story of a Shipwrecked Sailor and, 572
    The Thousand and One Nights and, 559
    "Tuesday Siesta" and, 18, 494–95
    on women's powers to sustain, 326
Lleras Camargo, Alberto, 359, 558
Llorca, Carmen, 298
Lobo-Antunes, António, 102
Lope de Vega, 131, 293, 473–74
Lopès, Henri, 65, 212, 219–20, 221
López, Alfred, 52–53
López-Baralt, Luce, 324
López Llausàs, Antonio, 294–95
López Mejía, Adelaida, 529–31
López Pumarejo, Alfonso, 82
Love in the Time of Cholera (García Márquez)
    Afro-Caribbean characters and culture in, 148–49, 152–55, 160
    apocalypse and, 373–74
    Arab literary culture and, 232–33
    bolero music and, 348–50
    Catholic Church and, 381
    Chinese literary culture and, 259
    cholera in, 135–36, 154
    civil wars in, 133
    communal narrators in, 121
    ecological awareness and, 7–8, 133, 373–74, 376–77, 379, 380–83, 384–86
    film adaptations based on, 603–4, 605–6
    Japanese literary culture and, 286
    Living To Tell the Tale and, 19
    love in, 3–4, 19, 115–16, 126, 130–33, 193–94, 198–200, 373–74
    Midnight Mass scene in, 19
    music and musical allusions in, 414, 420–27
    Oprah's Book Club and, 25–26
    Pentecost and, 131–32, 381
    racism in, 155
    sex and sexuality in, 24–25, 152–55, 189, 192–93, 195, 199–200
    South Asian literary cultures and, 266–67, 270
    Spain's literary culture and, 303, 306
    violence in, 192–93
    women characters in, 189, 193–94, 195, 198–99

Love in the Western World (de Rougemont),
  5–6, 126–29, 133, 139
Lovesey, Oliver, 221
Love Story (bolero song), 331–32
Ludmer, Josefina, 326
Lyotard, Jean-François, 534

Mabanckou, Alain, 209–10, 212–13, 222–23
MacBride Commission, 56–57
Macondo Literary Festival (Nairobi), 6, 51–52,
  66, 224–25
Madhavan, N. S., 268–69, 272
Madrigal, Luis Íñigo, 301
magical realism
  African literary cultures and, 209, 220–22
  anime and, 7, 277, 281–82, 285–86
  Catholic Church and, 113
  Chinese literary culture and, 6, 246–51, 253–
    55, 256–57
  defining features of, 1, 32–38, 97
  faith-based forms of, 42–43
  fate and, 517–18
  Global South and, 31, 51–52, 64–65, 97–98,
    103–5
  Japanese literary culture and, 277, 281,
    284–86, 288
  McOndo literary movement and, 104–5
  One Hundred Years of Solitude and, 1, 15–16,
    31–44, 51–52, 64, 103–4, 117, 129, 209, 281,
    298, 507, 571–72
  petro-magical realism and, 60–61
  postcolonialism and, 447
  pseudo-magical realism and, 2
  "remystification" of narrative and, 43
  South Asian literary cultures and, 264–69, 271
  Spain's literary culture, 298
  Third World–First World polarity in, 17–18,
    478–79
Mahfouz, Naguib, 6, 232, 234, 243
Mahler, Anne Garland, 52–53, 57–58
Maisterra, Pascual, 298
Makumbi, Jennifer Nansubuga, 65, 217–18
Malraux, André, 482
Mañach, Jorge, 331
Manguel, Alberto, 571
Manrique, Jorge, 116–17, 326–27
Manzoorul Islam, Syed, 270–71
Marco, Joaquín, 297, 300–2

Marechera, Dambudzo, 217
"María dos Prazeres" (García Márquez), 503–4,
  562
María of My Heart (Hermosillo), 600–1, 604
Márquez Caballero, Margarita, 585
Márquez Iguarán, Luisa Santiaga, 15–16, 19, 494
Márquez Mejía, Nicolás, 15–16, 17, 19–20,
  24–25, 113, 495
Martí, José, 475–76, 540–41
Martin, Gerald, 15, 24–25, 56, 59–60, 170, 240–41,
  342–43, 346, 374, 566–67, 570, 574, 577, 587
Martínez, Tomás Eloy, 306
Martínez García, Melissa, 26
Martínez Ruiz, Florentino, 302
Martín Gaite, Carmen, 301
Masoliver Ródenas, Juan Antonio, 300, 306
Mason, Michael A., 158
Masuda, Yoshio, 277–78
Matamoros, Miguel, 418, 429–30
Maugham, Somerset, 16, 19
Mauthausen concentration camp (Poland),
  355, 364
May Fourth Movement (China), 246, 255–56
McEvoy, Kathleen, 561
McHale, Brian, 43–44
McLaren, Joseph, 221
McOndo literary movement, 2, 51, 104–5, 224,
  439, 566–67
Mda, Zakes, 215, 218
Memon, Muhammad Umar, 271–72
Memories of My Melancholy Whores (García
  Márquez)
  Catholic Church and, 138
  as García Márquez's final novel, 15–16
  Japanese literary culture and, 286–87
  love in, 3–4, 116, 136–37, 138–39, 567–68, 571
  music and musical allusions in, 414, 420,
    427–31
  old age and, 9
  parody and, 587–88
  reviews of, 138, 571
  sex in, 195, 287
  South Asian literary cultures and, 271–72
  Spain's literary culture and, 306
  Thousand Days' War and, 558
  women characters in, 138, 195
Mendoza, Plinio Apuleyo, 24–25, 80, 89, 146,
  324–25, 357–59, 360–61

Mendoza, Soledad, 358, 360–62
Meng Fanhua, 256–57
Mercury, 398–99
The Metamorphosis (Kafka), 98–99, 119, 123n.26, 474, 486n.4
Mignolo, Walter, 41–43, 440–42
Millington, Mark, 519–21
Miracle Feliú, Carmen, 294
Miracle in Milan (De Sica and Zavattini), 597–99, 604–5
Miracle in Rome (Duque Naranjo), 604–5
miscegenation, 145, 147, 151–52, 156, 159–60, 546
Mishima, Yukio, 281
"Miss Forbes's Summer of Happiness" (García Márquez), 505–6, 563–64, 604
Mistral, Gabriela, 4
Mitterrand, François, 309
Miyazaki, Hayao, 285–86
modernism
    Chinese literary culture and, 6, 254–55
    cosmopolitanism and, 54–55
    Faulkner and, 102–3
    García Márquez influenced by, 98–100, 102
modernization theory, 78–79
Mohamed, Nadifa, 217
Mohen Hart, Patricia, 525–26
Molina, Lucía, 236–37
Molina Fernández, Carolina, 362
Moliner, María, 178–79
Momsen, Janet, 196–97
"Monologue of Isabel Watching It Rain in Macondo" (García Márquez), 173
Monsiváis, Carlos, 303
Moore, Jason, 375–76, 382–83
Moravia, Alberto, 211–12
Moretti, Franco, 566
Morrison, Toni, 2, 31, 40, 103–4, 105, 147–48, 216–18, 222–23
Morton, Timothy, 376
Moslund, Sten Pultz, 579
Movimiento al Socialismo (Venezuela), 441
Mo Yan, 17–18, 103–5, 256–58
Mozambique, 6, 216
Múnera, Alfonso, 539, 545, 549
Murakami, Haruki, 7, 17–18, 31, 39, 277, 284–85
Mutis, Álvaro, 294, 324–25, 568–69

"My Personal Hemingway" (García Márquez), 99–100

"Nabo, the Black Man Who Made the Angels Wait" (García Márquez), 146
Nagarkar, Kiran, 267–68
Naipaul, V. S., 559
Nair, M. T. Vasudevan, 266
Nan Fan, 257–58
Napier, Susan J., 280–82
National Liberation Front (NLF, Algeria), 55–56, 233
National Union for the Total Independence of Angola (UNITA), 57, 210–11
Navagattegkama, Simon, 270
The Navidad Incident (Ikezawa), 282–83
Neerlandia Treaty, 83, 558
Neoplatonism, 135–36, 139, 397–98
Neruda, Pablo, 4, 107n.11, 216, 234–35, 326–27, 564–65, 570
Neto, Agostinho, 57, 210–12, 213–14
News of a Kidnapping (García Márquez)
    abductee perspective in, 5–6, 560–61
    drug cartels and, 9, 137, 560
    love in, 126, 136–38
    narrative structure of, 581
    Spain's literary culture and, 305–6
Ngugi, James, 215
Ngũgĩ wa Thiong'o, 54–55, 62, 66, 209, 210–12, 215, 216–18, 219–20, 221, 222–23, 224
Nicaragua, 601
Nichols, John, 40
"The Night of the Eclipse" (García Márquez), 307
Ni Luo, 253
Non-Aligned Movement, 52–53, 265–66, 363–64
No One Writes to the Colonel (García Márquez)
    African literary cultures and, 213–14
    Black attorney character in, 146
    Chinese literary culture and, 248
    colonel's pension in, 63, 89, 467–69
    Quintana as model for female character in, 294
    resurrection of murdered son in, 520–21
    South Asian literary cultures and, 266–67
    Spain's literary culture and, 296, 306, 308
    violence and, 84–86, 457–58, 462

"No Thieves in This Town" (García Márquez), 146, 247–48, 294, 597–99
Noya, Fumiaki, 280–81, 282–83, 286
Numancia (Cervantes), 301
Nyerere, Julius, 210–11

Oakes, Penelope, 530–32
The Odyssey (Homer), 31–32, 129–30, 137–38
Ōe, Kenzaburō, 2, 277, 280–82
Oedipus the Mayor (Triana), 606–8
Offenbach, Jacques, 422–23
Of Love and Other Demons (García Márquez)
　African literary cultures and, 213–14
　Afro-Caribbean characters and culture in, 6, 157–60, 539–40, 547, 549–50
　The Atlantic and, 156–57
　baroque aesthetic and, 547–49, 550–52
　Cartagena de Indias as setting of, 539, 542, 544–46
　Catholic Church and, 158–60, 547, 549–51
　chronicle genre and, 540–41, 544–45
　fate and, 550–51
　Garcilaso de la Vega's poetry and, 118, 136
　humor and, 2
　hybridity and, 539, 550
　Japanese literary culture and, 286
　love in, 3–4, 116, 126, 130–31, 133–36
　Miracle in Rome and, 604–5
　miscegenation and, 159–60, 546
　modernity and, 540–42, 551–52
　music and dance in, 158
　pseudo-magical realism and, 2
　rabies in, 135–36, 159, 195, 538–39, 549–50
　sex and, 157, 159–60, 189, 538
　slavery in, 157–60, 175, 447, 545–46, 549–50
　Spain's literary culture and, 305
　temporal framework in, 542
　unearthing of crypt in, 543–44
　women characters in, 189–90, 195, 196–97
Òkédìjí, Oládèjo, 218
Okinawa, 279–80
Okri, Ben, 17–18, 40, 103–5, 214, 216–17, 221–23
Olsen, Margaret, 541
Ondaatje, Michael, 7, 266
"One Day after Saturday" (García Márquez), 492, 496–97, 499, 503–4, 506–7
One Hundred Years of Mud (Ishii), 7, 288

One Hundred Years of Solitude (García Márquez)
　African literary cultures and, 209, 213–14, 216–19, 220, 223–25
　Afro-Caribbean characters and culture in, 2, 147–48, 155–56
　alchemy and, 7–8, 326, 383, 391–407
　apocalypse and, 331
　Arab characters in, 235–37
　Arab literary culture and, 233–34, 236–37
　The Bible and, 114, 325, 332, 475–76
　bolero music and, 348
　Catholic Church and, 42–43, 85, 128–29
　Chinese literary culture and, 247–49, 250–51, 253–54, 255, 258–59
　Colombian national history and, 169–70, 439–40
　colonialism and decolonization in, 41–43, 51, 181
　communal imperative in, 40–41
　Conservative faction in Colombia and, 85, 113–14, 180–81, 378–79, 475–76
　criollo perspective in, 179–80
　cyclical time in, 323, 332, 401–3, 479–80, 481–82, 484–85
　Don Quixote and, 117, 323–24, 329, 475
　ecological awareness and, 7–8, 373–75, 376–80, 382–86
　fate and, 517
　Global North critics and, 104
　Global South and, 2, 50–52, 54, 59–61, 65, 96, 98, 103–4, 105
　gypsies in, 383–85, 398–99, 401, 475–76, 484
　hope and, 331–32
　humor and, 331, 392
　hyperbolic style in, 37
　illegitimate sons of Colonel Buendía in, 18
　insomnia plague in, 40–41
　interface of family life and major historical events in, 81
　international extractive industries and, 5, 17, 23–24, 39–40, 51, 58–59, 60–61, 84, 377–78, 379–80, 383–85, 447, 475–76, 484, 558
　Japanese literary culture and, 277–81, 283–88
　land dispossession in, 83, 85
　Liberal faction in Colombia and, 83, 85, 113–14, 147, 180–81, 378–79, 475–76

One Hundred Years of Solitude (García Márquez) (*cont.*)
  Living To Tell the Tale and, 17–18, 566–67
  love in, 126, 128–29, 180, 188
  as magical realism, 1, 15–16, 31–44, 51–52, 64, 103–4, 117, 129, 209, 281, 298, 507, 571–72
  modernization and disruption in, 86, 91
  monstrous innocence and vulnerable outsiders in, 497–98
  music and musical allusions in, 414–16
  mystical symbolism in, 394–400
  myth and, 7, 324–26, 332–36
  naming system in, 374, 391
  narrative viewpoints in, 473–85
  Netflix adaptation of, 26, 323–24, 588
  "One Day after Saturday" and, 496
  Operation Carlota and, 58–59
  Oprah's Book Club and, 25–26
  plantation strike in, 20–22, 35–36, 59–60, 89, 447
  poetry and, 326–29, 336
  polyvalent narrator and multilayered perspectivism of, 8
  prophecy in, 325–26
  Rabassa translation (1970) of, 1, 272
  repetition in, 35–36, 392–93
  sex and sexuality in, 188–89, 191–93, 195, 200, 201, 280–81, 325–26, 330–32, 395, 498
  South Asian literary cultures and, 266, 268–69, 271, 273–74
  Soviet literary culture and, 249
  Spain's literary culture and, 294–95, 296–303, 304, 306, 308, 310–11
  spatial fluidity in, 36–37, 40
  surprise in, 344–45
  syncretism of cultures and, 40
  temporal fluidity and, 35–37, 40
  travel in, 354–57
  War of the Thousand Days and, 83
  Wayúu Indian characters and culture in, 2, 6, 39–40, 173–75, 177–78, 180–81, 184n.12
  women characters in, 89–90, 189–95, 200–1
"One of These Days" (García Márquez), 4, 493–94
Operation Carlota (García Márquez), 19, 57–59, 63, 210–14
orientalism, 234–35, 236–37, 242–43

Orlando (Woolf), 474, 485
Ortega, Julio, 540–42, 549–50, 561
Osorio, Manuel, 146
Otero Silva, Miguel, 561
"The Other Side of Death" (García Márquez), 20
Ouologuem, Yambo, 214, 215–16
Ousmane, Sembène, 223–24
Overbeck, Jennifer, 524–25
Ovid, 324–25, 329
Owuor, Yvonne Adhiambo, 224

Pacavira, Manuel, 211–12
Pacheco, Medardo, 17, 27n.4
Pachón, Maruja, 137, 560–61
Padilla, Heberto, 23–24
Palestinians
  García Márquez's support for nationalist cause of, 6, 210–11, 240–41
  migration to Latin America by, 239–40, 241–42
  Sabra and Chatila massacres (1982) and, 240–41
Panama Canal, 84
Panguana, Marcelo, 223
Papini, Giovanni, 445–47
Paracelsus, 399–400
"Para Elisa" (García Márquez), 597–600, 606
Parkes, Nii, 209, 216–17
Parkinson Zamora, Lois, 40–41, 447, 548
Patterson, Orlando, 156
Paz, Octavio, 23–24, 238–39, 252, 310, 333–34, 335–36
Pedro Páramo (Rulfo), 477–78, 597–99
Pelayo, Rubén, 499–500, 502–3
People's Movement for the Liberation of Angola (MPLA), 57, 210–11, 213–14
Pepetela (Artur Carlos Pestana dos Santos), 212, 223–24
Perés, Ramón D., 299
Pérez Minik, Domingo, 298
Perón, Juan Domingo, 363–64
Perrin, Michel, 176–77
Peru, 102
Pestana dos Santos, Artur Carlos (Pepetela), 212, 223–24
Piamba Tulcán, Diva Marcela, 375
Pigafetta, Antonio, 354–55, 442–43, 484–85, 565

Pillai, Meena T., 272–74
Pinochet, Augusto, 23–24, 56–57, 242, 520–21, 584–85
Pinto de Andrade, Mário, 213–14
Plato, 133–36, 404–7
Points of View (Eliot), 121
Poland, 564
polyphonic novel, 474
Ponce, Barbachano, 418, 596–97
Pope, Alexander, 16–17
Porrúa, Francisco, 294–95
Portent (Alcoriza and García Márquez), 597–99
Prakash, Uday, 271
Prashad, Vijay, 52–53
"¿Problemas de la novela?" (García Márquez), 101
Propp, Vladimir, 324–26
Proust, Marcel, 101, 131–32, 326, 579, 586–87
Puccini, Giacomo, 424–25, 428
Puig, Manuel, 130, 514–15
Pu Songling, 256–57

Quetzalcóatl myth, 332–35
Quevedo, Francisco de, 110–11, 115–17, 118, 550–51
Quijano, Aníbal, 150, 269–70, 440, 546
Quiñonero, Juan Pedro, 301
Quintana, Tachia, 294
Qu Yuan, 256–57

Rabassa, Gregory, 1, 150, 272, 419–20
Rabelais, François, 55–56, 417
Rainy Season (Agalusa), 213–14
Rama, Angel, 542–43, 545, 547, 550
Ramakrishnan, E. V., 268
Ramos, Julio, 359
Ranjan, Prabhat, 266–67
Reagan, Patricia Elaine, 586
Real Academia de la Lengua, 105, 299
Reed, Carol, 364
"Rented Wives" (García Márquez), 210–11
Restrepo, Indira, 171
Revolutionary Armed Forces of Colombia (FARC), 84
Reyes, Rubiella, 20
Richards, Tim, 525–26

Richardson, Lance, 26
Ripstein, Arturo, 597
Rita de Casia (saint), 113
Rivera, Diego, 280
Rivera, José Eustasio, 177
Roa Bastos, Augusto, 221, 249–50, 534
Roberto, Holden, 210
Rocha, Glauber, 129–30
Rodaway, Paul, 578, 579
Rodó, José Enrique, 446
Rodríguez de Francia, José Gaspar, 534
Rodriguez Juliá, Edgardo, 541–43
Roetker, Susana, 541–43
Roh, Franz, 43
Rojas, Fernando de, 473–74
Rojas Pinilla, Gustavo, 84, 357–58, 359, 459, 582, 583
Rojo, Vicente, 294–95
Romero, Francisco, 295
Romero Castañeda, Rafael, 20–21
Root-Seeking literature (China), 246–47, 250–51, 253–58, 260n.3
Roy, Arundhati, 104
Royal Spanish Academy, 310
Ruiz, Raúl, 213
Rulfo, Juan
  Chinese literary culture and, 246–47, 249–50, 256–57
  Faulkner and, 477–78
  films based on the work of, 597–99
  García Márquez and, 4
  magical realism and, 31, 249–50
  Okri and, 222
  Pedro Páramo and, 477–78, 597–99
  South Asian literary cultures and, 266
Rushdie, Salman
  García Márquez and, 7, 64–65, 96, 98, 103–4, 216–17, 264, 268
  Khomeini's condemnation of, 267–68
  magical realism and, 17–18, 39, 97–98, 104, 267–68
  syncretism of cultures in work of, 40
Ryahi, Kamal, 232, 234

Sabato, Ernesto, 323
Sabra and Chatila massacres (Lebanon, 1982), 240–41

Sacred River (Cheney-Coker), 220–21
Sadat, Anwar, 241
Sáenz, Manuela, 569
Saer, Juan José, 516
"The Saint" (García Márquez), 564, 604–5
Saldívar, Dasso, 170, 304
San Antonio de los Baños School of Cinema and Television, 603, 606
Sánchez, Luis Rafael, 326–27, 331
Sánchez Prado, Ignacio, 64
Sancholuz, Carolina, 541
Sandinista Revolution (Nicaragua), 601
Sangari, Kumkum, 63, 264–65
Santería, 151–52, 158–59, 549–50
Santos, Dámaso, 298–99
Sanz Villanueva, Santos, 303
Saramago, José, 219–20
Sartre, Jean-Paul, 23–24, 102, 482
Satanic Verses (Rushdie), 267–68
Sauvy, Alfred, 363–64
Savimbi, Jonas, 210, 212
The Scandal of the Century and Other Writings (García Márquez), 440, 448–50, 566–67
Schiller, Friedrich, 563
Schroeder, Shannin, 407n.1, 408n.17
Schwartz-Bart, André, 40, 215–16
Schygulla, Hanna, 604
Sealy, I. Allan, 267–68
"The Sea of Lost Time" (García Márquez), 87
Senapati, Fakir Mohan, 268
Senghor, Léopold Sédar, 209
Serpell, Namwali, 65, 217–18
Serrano, Eduardo, 419
Serrat, Joan Manuel, 299–300
The Seven Solitudes of Lorsa Lopez (Sony), 219–20
"Seventeen Poisoned Englishmen" (García Márquez), 503, 507, 562
"Shadowy Months: Che in the Congo" (García Márquez), 210–11
Shahid, Mohammed Hameed, 271–72
Shameful State (Sony), 219, 221
Sharon, Ariel, 240–41
Shih, Shu-mei, 53–54
Shimazaki, Toson, 287
Shintoism, 285–86
Sierra Leone, 220

Silko, Leslie Marmon, 105
Simon, Bernd, 530–32
Siraj, Syed Mustafa, 269
"Sleeping Beauty and the Airplane" (García Márquez), 287, 427, 561
Solano López, Francisco, 534
"The Solitude of Latin America" (García Márquez)
  on colonialism and loneliness, 330
  coloniality and, 441, 442–44, 445
  on fiction and utopia, 400
  on Latin America's condition of dispossession, 63
  Pigafetta and, 354–55, 442–43, 484–85, 565
  on poetry and quotidian life, 80
  solidarity with dreams and, 406
  United States criticized in, 570
  on violence and inequity, 392–93
Sommer, Doris, 40–41
Sontag, Susan, 527–28
Sony Labou Tansi, 209–10, 212–13, 217–20, 221
Sophocles, 463–64, 516, 596–97, 606–7
Sorela, Pedro, 581
Sorensen, Eli Park, 574, 586–87
South Asia
  colonialism in, 264
  English translations as source for vernacular language translations in, 272
  magical realism and, 264–69, 271
  One Hundred Years of Solitude and, 266, 268–69, 271, 273–74
  vernacular language literature in, 266, 268–72
Soviet Union
  China and, 249–50
  Cold War and, 279–80
  collapse of, 62, 130
  de-Stalinization in, 359, 362
  García Márquez's travel writings from, 355, 359, 362–63
  One Hundred Years of Solitude and, 249
  Sixth World Youth Conference (1957) and, 358
Soyinka, Wole, 209, 214–15, 216–17, 220–21, 224
Spain
  Catholic Church and, 113–14

Círculo de Lectores book club in, 294–95, 299
civil war in, 292–93
European Union, 309–10
Franco dictatorship in, 113–14, 292–93, 296–97, 308, 562
García Márquez influenced by the culture of, 292–94, 307
magical realism and, 298
One Hundred Years of Solitude and, 294–95, 296–303, 304, 306, 308, 310–11
Speratti-Piñero, Emma, 500
Spivak, Gayatri, 264–65
Stalin, Joseph, 355, 362–63
Stars of the New Curfew (Okri), 222
Stone, Peter, 576, 580
Story of a Shipwrecked Sailor (García Márquez), 7, 300, 306, 462, 512–13, 559, 572, 582–83
Strange Pilgrims (García Márquez). *See also specific stories*
  Afro-Caribbean characters and culture in, 151–52
  European setting for stories in, 561
  film adaptations based on, 603–4
  Global North and, 2
  as global travel writing, 7
  monstrous innocence and vulnerable outsiders in, 502–7
  Spain's literary culture and, 305
Strauss, Johann, 422
Strecher, Matthew C., 284–85
Studio Ghibli, 7, 285–86
Sucre (Colombia), 146, 152, 239–40, 512–13
Suñen, Luis, 302–3

Takahata, Isao, 98–99
Talib, Jamal Eldin, 243
Tanizaki, Jun'ichirō, 281
Tanzania, 210–11
Tashi Dawa, 256–57
Tchivéla, Tchichellé, 66
Terayama, Shūji, 287–88
Tharoor, Shashi, 267–68
Theresa of Avila (saint), 129
Thibault, Jacques, 430
"The Third Resignation" (García Márquez), 177

Third World. *See also* Global South
  Cold War and, 52–53
  magical realism and, 17–18, 264–65
  Non-Aligned Movement and, 52–53, 265–66, 363–64
  Perón and, 363–64
Thoth, 398–99
The Thousand and One Nights, 55–56, 232–33, 482, 559, 571
Tilaksena, Ajith, 270
The Time of the Hero (Vargas Llosa), 4
"Time to Die" (García Márquez), 596–99, 606
Torrente Ballester, Gonzalo, 301–2
Torres, Daniel, 326–27
Torres Giraldo, Ignacio, 89
Torrijos, Omar, 56–57, 570
"The Trail of Your Blood in the Snow" (García Márquez), 562–63
"Tramontana" (García Márquez), 562
travel writing from Eastern Europe by García Márquez
  "90 Days Behind the Iron Curtain" and, 360–61, 365–66
  Holocaust sites and, 364–66
  Hungarian Revolution (1956) and, 355, 358, 566–67
  Latin Americanist aesthetico-political identity and, 355, 362–63
  Mendozas as basis for fictionalized characters in, 357–59, 360–62
  Soviet Union and, 355, 359, 362–63
  Travel across Socialist Countries and, 357
  West Berlin and, 363
Triana, Jorge Alí, 606
Tricontinental Conference (1966), 52–53
Tristran and Isolde, 139
Tshuma, Novuyo Rosa, 65, 217
Tsuzumi, Tadashi, 277–79, 288
"Tubal-Cain Forges a Star" (García Márquez), 20
"Tuesday Siesta" (García Márquez), 4, 18, 24–25, 247–48, 492, 493–96
Turner, Victor, 334
Tusquets Editores, 300
Tutuola, Amos, 209, 214–15, 216, 220, 222
"Two or Three Things about the Novels of La Violencia" (García Márquez), 459–62
Tyutina, Svetlana, 234–35, 242–43

Ulysses (Joyce), 395–96
Unigwe, Chika, 216–17
United Fruit Company (UFC), 5, 17, 19, 20–25, 59–61, 83, 147–48, 191, 458, 475–76, 494
Updike, John, 126
Uspensky, Boris, 473, 475

Valenzuela, Luisa, 514–15
Vallejo, César, 216
Vallejo, Fernando, 138
vallenato, 107n.12, 180–81, 414–15
Valls, Fernando, 304
Varèse, Edgard, 431
Vargas, Germán, 100–1, 568
Vargas, Jennifer, 268
Vargas Llosa, Mario
  Chinese literary culture and, 246–47
  Cuban Revolution and, 4, 23–24, 306
  Faulkner and, 101–2, 108n.13
  The Feast of the Goat and, 525–26
  García Márquez and, 16, 23–24, 173, 309, 323–24, 326–27, 329, 336, 597–99
  magical realism and, 104
  new sentimental narratives and, 130
  Nobel Prize and, 4, 565
  Ōe and, 280–81
  Peru and, 102
  South Asian literary cultures and, 266
  Spain's literary culture and, 296–97, 309
Vásquez, Juan Gabriel, 439–40, 560
Velasco, Luis Alejandro, 357–58, 582–84
Velo, Carlos, 596–97
Venuti, Lawrence, 272
Vera León, Antonio, 583
Vergara, Isabel, 527
Vernet Mateu, José, 299
"A Very Old Man with Enormous Wings" (García Márquez)
  canonical status of, 4
  Caribbean popular culture and, 500
  Catholic Church and, 500
  communal imperative and, 40–41
  film version of, 601–3
  love and, 130
  monstrous innocence and vulnerable outsiders in, 492, 498–500, 503, 507
  narrative experimentation in, 482–83
  spectacle and confusion in, 86–87
Vescio, Theresa K., 525, 528
Vicens, Lluís, 293
Vicente, Gil, 131, 134, 517
Vicente Romero, Geovanny, 581
Vieira, Luandino, 211–13, 215, 223–24
Vijayan, O. V., 268–69
Villamizar, Beatriz, 137, 560–61
Vinyes, Ramón, 100–1, 293–94
Viyangoda, Gamini, 270, 272
Vodou, 476–77
von Köchel, Ludwig Ritter, 417

Wainaina, Binyavanga, 217
Waiting for the Vote of Wild Animals (Kourouma), 62
Walesa, Lech, 564
Waliullah, Syed, 269
Wang Yangle, 249, 251–52
Wang Zengqi, 257–58
War of National Liberation (Bangladesh), 269
War of the Thousand Days (Colombia, 1899–1902), 20, 83, 89
Warsaw Ghetto (Poland), 355, 364–65
Wayúu Indians
  ancestral languages of, 171–72, 174–76
  The Incredible and Sad Tale of Innocent Eréndira and Her Heartless Grandmother and, 175
  One Hundred Years of Solitude and, 2, 6, 39–40, 173–75, 177–78, 180–81, 184n.12
  as servants in García Márquez's childhood home, 2, 6, 173–74, 175–76
  shamanic logic and the supernatural among, 175–78
We'll See Each Other in August (García Márquez), 24–25, 307
Wenzel, Jennifer, 60–61
White, Hayden, 533–34
Whitehead, Colson, 216
Whitman, Walt, 336
Wilde, Oscar, 16–17
Wilder, Thornton, 571
Williams, Raymond L., 375, 566
Wizard of the Crow (Ngũgĩ wa Thiong'o), 62, 210–11, 219–20, 221

"The Woman of the Dunes" (Abe), 284
women characters in García Márquez's fiction
   "Big Mama's Funeral" and, 196–98
   Chronicle of a Death Foretold and, 189, 195, 238
   love and, 187–88, 190–92, 194–95, 202
   Of Love and Other Demons and, 189–90, 195, 196–97
   Love in the Time of Cholera and, 189, 193–94, 195, 198–99
   as matriarchs, 89–90, 189–90, 191, 192, 196–98, 238
   Memories of My Melancholy Whores and, 138, 195
   One Hundred Years of Solitude and, 89–90, 189–95, 200–1
   patriarchal gender hierarchies and, 187–88, 190, 191, 192–94, 195, 196–97, 200, 201–2
   power and, 188–90, 191, 196–202
   sexuality and, 188–90, 191–93, 194–96, 197–98, 199–200, 201
   violence against, 188, 192–95, 201
Wood, Michael, 569
Wood, Tony, 448
Woolf, Virginia
   García Márquez's admiration of, 2–3, 55, 99, 101, 108n.14, 110–11, 459
   Orlando and, 474, 485
"Words for a New Millenium" (García Márquez), 444–45

Yacine, Kateb, 102
The Year of the Plague (Cazals), 600
Yeats, William Butler, 175–76
Ye Weilin, 256–57
Yin Changlong, 254
Yunnan People's Publishing House, 256–57

Zahir, Shaheedul, 270
Zambrano, Gregory, 286
Zapata Olivella, Manuel, 358
Zavattini, Césare, 358, 596–99, 604–5
Zheng Wanlong, 253–54
Zheng Yi, 253–54
Zingarelli, Nicola, 428–29